The Ultimate Windows Server 2003 System Administrator's Guide

The Ultimate Windows Server 2003 System Administrator's Guide

Robert Williams

Mark Walla

Addison-Wesley

Boston • San Francisco • New York • Toronto • Montreal
London • Munich • Paris • Madrid
Capetown • Sydney • Tokyo • Singapore • Mexico City

The publisher offers discounts on this book when ordered in quantity for bulk purchases and special sales. For more information, please contact:
U.S. Corporate and Government Sales
(800) 382-3419
corpsales@pearsontechgroup.com

For sales outside of the U.S., please contact:
International Sales
(317) 581-3793
international@pearsontechgroup.com

Visit Addison-Wesley on the Web: *www.awprofessional.com*

Library of Congress Cataloging-in-Publication Data
Williams, G. Robert
The Ultimate Windows Server 2003 system administrator's guide / Robert Williams, Mark Walla.
p. cm.
ISBN 0-201-79106-4 (alk. paper)
1. Microsoft Windows server. 2. Operating systems (Computers) 3. Microsoft framework. 4. Client/server computing. I. Walla, Mark. II. Title.
QA76.76.O63 W554675 2002
005.4'4769—dc21 2002021545

Text printed on recycled and acid-free paper.

ISBN 0201791064

4 5 6 7 8 9 CRS 07 06 05 04

4th Printing September 2004

Contents

Foreword

When I'm not managing the Windows engineering team, I like to play hockey. This helps me understand the mentality of IT managers and systems administrators because, like you, I play defense. As a matter of fact, I'm a goaltender, which means I'm the last one standing when my defensive line fails. If we're down a few goals at the end of a period, you'll find me ranting and raging in the locker room, "Where's my defense?" You know how this feels. It's often you defending your system against hackers, you resetting the client machines after an application or configuration "accident," you dealing with a bogged-down network, you trying to stay one step ahead of threats that change speed and direction and seem to shoot toward you at 100 miles per hour. And if the "opponent" scores, it shows up on your record.

Wouldn't it be great if you weren't the last line of defense? Wouldn't you rather be the offense, focusing on adding value for your users, making them more productive, making the tools they need easier to access, getting crucial data to them faster—basically getting (and keeping) them connected to everything they need to do their jobs well? With Windows Server 2003, we've worked to build something as fast, solid, and smooth as the ice on a hockey rink.

We've made file server and web server performance at least twice as fast as Windows 2000; file system performance is 140 percent better; and Active Directory searches are more than four times faster. A range of new and improved features, including memory mirroring, Hot Add Memory, and health detection in Internet Information Services (IIS) 6.0, enhances reliability. Clustering for up to 8 nodes and network load balancing is built in, and, as with Windows 2000, several major OEMs will guarantee 99.9 to 100 percent availability. Configuration wizards install and set up services automatically based on the server roles you choose; settings are securely locked down by default.

During this product cycle, we stopped the development machine to dedicate every Windows employee to an intense security review of every line of Windows Server 2003 code to identify and eliminate possible fail points and exploitable weaknesses so that your Windows server won't go down unless you turn it off.

Windows Server 2003 will help you get more done faster. The .NET Framework is fully integrated and saves developers from writing "plumbing" code so that they can focus their efforts immediately on writing code. Group Policy Management Console (GPMC) has a new user interface that dramatically simplifies policy administration. The addition of Resultant Set of Policy reporting and scripting means that now you're able to model settings in a test domain before copying the policy objects to production domains in your enterprise. With the new volume shadow copy service, users can retrieve previous versions of files from servers instantly, without requiring you to dig through backup tapes. We've greatly enhanced the command-line functionality in the Windows Server 2003 family and added "headless server" capabilities that allow IT administrators to install and manage a computer without a monitor, VGA display adaptor, keyboard, or mouse. And we ship it with ready-to-use scripts. Software Update Services collects new updates from Microsoft as they are released and automatically deploys the ones you approve to clients and servers. And this is just a sample of what Windows Server 2003 offers to clear the way for you to add more value for users.

Deploying Windows Server 2003 is like drafting the right players, suiting them up with the right equipment, and giving them the home rink advantage. Now all you need to maintain a winning style is a great coach and playbook to guide you through using the tools and resources in the right combination at the right times. In *The Ultimate Windows Server 2003 System Administrator's Guide,* coaches Williams and Walla describe best practices for designing and deploying the Active Directory, sharing and securing network resources, getting users connected no matter where they are, and managing and maintaining Windows Server 2003 servers in your enterprise. This book will be a supportive resource to help you know how to use the tools and features Microsoft shipped, but even better, it guides you through enough of the product internals to approach administration more strategically. A good coach tells you what to do to win; a great coach helps you develop the skills to win on your own. Enjoy this great book.

Brian Valentine
Senior Vice President
Microsoft Windows Division

Preface

Windows Server 2003 is more an update of Windows 2000 than a new operating system. This latest version of the base Windows NT technology now expands to support Microsoft's .NET Framework and new security initiatives. This book reflects these changes by expanding our previous book, *The Ultimate Windows 2000 System Administrator's Guide*. Mindful that Windows 2000 will continue to be deployed, this book not only reflects the new features of Windows Server 2003 but also provides continued support for Windows 2000 administrators.

Windows 2000 and Windows Server 2003 are complex, feature-rich operating systems whose deployment in an enterprise requires highly skilled individuals to support its installation, maintenance, and optimization. These individuals are aided by the abundance of tools and wizards for effective operating-system management that Microsoft has provided. Indeed, many of the enhanced tools should shift the traditional role of administrator to that of proactive manager of computing environments. Thus, the depth of function, flexibility, and granularity of Windows 2000 and Windows Server 2003 ultimately represents both opportunity and challenge for system administration.

This book is written to help you succeed in the administration of the Windows Server 2003 and Windows 2000 Server family. Much of the information it provides is also applicable to the desktop Professional versions of the software. Although the use and management of client software is incorporated, the server side is clearly our primary focus. In this preface we provide a framework for the primary topics covered, define the target audience, and describe how to use this book.

THE ROLE OF THE ADMINISTRATOR

Windows Server 2003 will not eliminate the system administrator. To the contrary, features such as the Active Directory and the Microsoft Management Console (MMC) will vastly broaden this role. Rather than spend time on mundane tasks and the management of dozens of disjointed tools, the consolidated approach provided by Windows Server 2003 will free the administrator to concentrate on more mission-critical activities.

The functions of the Windows Server 2003 system administrator are generally those that support the user population and those that support the system. The following list summarizes the most common responsibilities:

USER-ORIENTED TASKS

- Addition and removal of users
- Group management
- User application support
- End-user customer service, education, and communication
- Management of basic services such as mail and printing

SYSTEM-ORIENTED TASKS

- Booting, shutdown, and everything in between
- Backups and restoration
- Hardware maintenance, additions, and removal
- System accounting and monitoring
- System administration logs
- System security and password aging
- Network support
- General troubleshooting

Obviously, this list only scratches the surface of system administration and IT management. However, as a means of setting the reader's expectations, it does underscore the types of activities for which this book can be a guide.

BASIS OF OUR RESEARCH

In preparing this book, we used three primary sources of information. First, we relied heavily on our combined professional experience in application development, system administration, and IT management. Unlike many books written on theory by technical writers, our recommendations did not emerge from a vacuum but are based on reality and experiences. We hope the knowledge and experience we bring to this book will assist our fellow IT professionals to manage an enterprise as effectively as possible.

Second, we used observations from system administrators in the field to provide "reality checks" to our conclusions. Theoretical understanding of Windows Server 2003 is a nice beginning, but it is no substitute for the actual experience of system administrators. Because Windows Server 2003 is a new product, one of our primary sources was Microsoft's Beta Program and the participants' experiences with final beta and final release versions of the operating system.

Finally, we performed numerous tests and simulated real-world environments in an extensive laboratory environment. The tests centered primarily on the Standard Edition and Enterprise Edition server versions; however, Windows Server 2003, Web Edition, and Windows XP Professional were also tested, and we refer to them periodically as client software within the broader enterprise framework. Windows Server 2003, Datacenter Edition, was not available for testing at the time this book was written, so references to it are based on published Microsoft specifications. Where differences exist in the version levels, we call attention to them.

AUDIENCE

The Ultimate Windows Server 2003 System Administrator's Guide was written for system administrators and other IT professionals who manage a Windows environment. Administrators coming from other operating-system environments, such as UNIX, will find numerous familiar technologies as well as many significant conceptual differences. Seasoned Windows 2000 and NT administrators will find many familiar aspects, but many significant differences as well, that will require a general updating of their technical skills. The addition of the Active Directory, a new domain model, advanced authentication technologies, and the enhanced MMC are just a few examples of entirely new or expanded operating-system features.

Our aim was to produce an intermediate reference guide for administrators, leaving out specialized architectural and programming topics. Thus, this book should be used to gain an understanding of key concepts and for common "how-to" walk-through support. Experienced professionals should find the discussions of operating-system migration and the use of the new enhanced tools valuable. Those with moderate system administration experience can also benefit, but we assume these readers already have hands-on operating-system experience. Novices will need to learn network and operating-system fundamentals.

Attempting to provide useful information to an audience of system administrators was a challenge. Inevitably, some of this book's material may appear either overly basic or too advanced, and depending on a reader's level of experience, some discussions will be more helpful than others. To accommodate this wide variance in knowledge, we cover each major topic first from a conceptual basis and then expand this foundation with discussions on applying specific, advanced Windows Server 2003 functions.

System administrators coming from UNIX might find our sister publication, *Windows NT and UNIX: Administration, Coexistence, Integration, and Migration* (Addison-Wesley, 1998), very helpful. For Windows 2000 administrators, look at *The Ultimate Windows 2000 System Administrator's Guide* (Addison-Wesley, 2000).

ORGANIZATION

The book is organized into three sections and an appendix:

- The first four chapters focus on Windows Server 2003 concepts, deployment, and installation. They cover the role of the system administrator, Windows Server 2003 features, operating-system structure, and deployment and installation. Chapter 4 discusses getting started with tools such as the Microsoft Management Console.
- The heart of the book, Chapters 5 through 14, is a discussion of fundamental administration topics. In a series of very technical chapters, we cover the Active Directory, user management, group policies, security, printer and file services, networking, and other topics essential to Windows Server 2003 system administration.
- The last section of the book covers advanced tools and concepts (Chapters 15 through 17). It examines the Internet Information Service (IIS) and optional components—Terminal Services, System Management Server (SMS), Indexing Services, Message Queuing Services (MQS), Cluster Services—and other topics applicable to enterprise-level system administration.
- The appendix, "Windows Server 2003 Commands and Utilities," is a quick reference for the most significant commands in the operating system and in the Windows Resource Kit.

A glossary of common terms is also provided.

OTHER REFERENCES

There is a wealth of information that should be used by system administrators to supplement this book. The Windows Server 2003 operating system provides extensive online help, which is available from the **Start** → **Help** facility. Microsoft also regularly posts white papers on its Web site, which should be checked regularly for updated information. An administrator should also check the Microsoft TechNet postings for updates.

Acknowledgments

This book is a result of the efforts of many individuals whose support the authors would like to acknowledge.

The special effort of contributors and technical editors:

- Ellen Beck Gardner, a technical author and senior consultant, deserves our thanks for her extra efforts in the development of this book and in the preparation of the appendix and other segments.
- James Edelen, MVP for SharePoint Server who resides in Philadelphia, is an acknowledged expert in Microsoft networking and Internet technologies.
- James Morris, a systems engineer with the University of Washington, focuses on designing and managing large-scale computing systems based primarily on Microsoft Windows 2000/XP and on developing tools to automate much of a system administrator's tasks.
- Rick Kingslan, a consultant and technical trainer in Omaha, Nebraska, is a Microsoft MVP.

A very special thank-you is due to Addison-Wesley editor Stephane Thomas for her support and enthusiasm. We also thank the entire Addison-Wesley team, including Curt Johnson, Michael Mullen, Marilyn Rash, Patrick Cash-Peterson, and John Fuller. The day-to-day production details were managed by Diane Freed during the early and late evolution of this book as well as our previous book. Finally, but certainly not the least, copy editor extraordinaire Joan Flaherty stayed with this project for months and did a superior job on every level.

Microsoft was extremely cooperative in the development of the book. Brian Valentine provided an excellent foreword. Other friends at Microsoft who deserve a nod include Liz Brackett, Ryan Calafato, David Derwin, Bill Forsyth, Joel Greenberg, Meredith Guarraci, Eric Leseberg, Doug Miller, Charles Pritcher, Michael Sandoval, Jan Shanahan, and so many others. In addition to these individuals, we want to acknowledge the support of the Windows Division, Solutions Offering Unit, and the Security Practices Unit.

A special acknowledgment also to our associates at Secure Logistix Corporation, including Anthony Noblett, Chris McClenaghan, and David Parkhill.

Bob Williams has these special personal and professional acknowledgments. Thanks to family members Flora Williams, Sue and Mike Montgomery, and Pete Froman. Great appreciation for years of support to friends Bill Kuehl, Deb Murray, Ed Nichols, Ellen and Kevin Gardner, Ivory Curtis, Jim Fry, Dr. James and Wanda Riviere, Karen Bircher, Mark and Toni Sehnert, Martha McGavin, Mike and Mary Glynn, Roger Ayan, Roger Caauwe, Scott Woodland, Tony and Cathe Noblett, John and Linda Ford, Diane Rowihab, Michael and Heather Sandoval, and Jim Kazaroff. Finally, here's to my goddaughter, Emily, and her brother, Alex.

Mark Walla expresses personal thanks to a number of people who have provided support and encouragement. Special thanks to his parents Gary Walla and Sandy Minter and their respective spouses Kay and Jules, and to brother Tom and Brittany Walla. Professional and personal thanks also to Carl Castillo, Joseph Chen, Daniel Chinen, Todd Cramer, Jim Fitzgerald, Bryan Keil, Dave Kovsky, John LaPorte, Kevin Lichwalla, Troy Love, Dave and Anne Peterson, Dem Pilafian, Darrel Ritchie, Peter Shen, Frank Smith, Kent Tang, and Jim Welch.

About the Authors

G. Robert Williams, Ph.D., is President of Secure Logistix Corporation. Due to his security expertise, he is actively involved in U.S. government antiterrorism activities and has received federal commendations for his efforts. His experience includes positions as founder of e-learning Enterprise Certified Corporation; president of the professional services for PDS Advanced Technologies; president and founder of the UNIX applications developer Decathlon Data Systems; senior executive at UNISYS/System Development Corporation; and dean of research at both the University of California, Los Angeles, and California State Polytechnic University. He regularly consults for Fortune 1000 companies and governmental agencies. Dr. Williams has been the featured speaker at international road shows sponsored by Microsoft, Hewlett-Packard, Compaq, and Tech Data. He is in high demand as a speaker for industry conferences such as Windows Decisions Expo, Microsoft Fusion, LinuxWorld, and ASPWorld. Williams is the coauthor of *Windows NT and UNIX: Administration, Coexistence, Integration, and Migration* (Addison-Wesley, 1998), *The Ultimate Windows 2000 System Administrator's Guide* (Addison-Wesley, 2000), the forthcoming *The Ultimate .NET Enterprise Server Guide* (Addison-Wesley, 2004), and other books. He contributes regularly to several trade magazines, including *Computer World, InformIT.com, ITWorld.com, WindowsAdvantage.com, LinuxWorld.com,* and *Windows NT/2000*.

Mark Walla is President of Enterprise Certified Corporation. He previously served as chief technology officer at PDS Advanced Technologies. He has consulted for Microsoft Corporation and Hewlett-Packard, where he helped develop integration strategy and materials for the national tour Integration 97/98. While consulting for US West, he evaluated network management tools, and at Bay Networks he was the technical lead for sustaining released software and customers' hot site issues. He was also a software engineer at Motorola with software design and testing responsibilities and an embedded software engineer at Storage Technology. Walla has written a number of technical articles for *Computer World, Platform Decisions,* and *Windows NT/2000* magazines and was a contributor to and technical editor of the book *Windows NT and UNIX: Administration, Coexistence, Integration, and Migration* (Addison-Wesley, 1998), as well as the coauthor of *The Ultimate Windows 2000 System Administrator's Guide* (Addison-Wesley, 2000).

CONTRIBUTOR

Ellen Beck Gardner is an authority and consultant on UNIX and Windows NT/2000 operating systems. Her UNIX experience began at NCR Corporation, where she managed technical support services for field locations throughout the United States. She refined her UNIX expertise as a senior vice president at Decathlon Data Systems, Inc., a pioneer in UNIX office automation and groupware applications. Ms. Gardner is the coauthor of *Windows NT and UNIX: Administration, Coexistence, Integration, and Migration* (Addison-Wesley, 1998) and has written a number of articles with others. In 1997 she contributed to the *Microsoft BackOffice Bible.*

Chapter 1

Administrative Overview

Windows Server 2003 is an impressive evolutionary step forward rather than a revolutionary leap into the future of operating system nirvana. The role of the administrator remains central to its successful deployment and maintenance. It builds on the Windows NT and Windows 2000 foundation with significant expansion to support the brave new world of Web-based services. From an administrative perspective, these changes represent both challenges and opportunities. In this book we seek to familiarize you with the many refinements afforded by the Windows Server 2003 product line. If you are moving from a Windows 2000 environment, the changes should be welcome and easy to embrace. If your orientation is still Windows NT-centric, then the learning curve might be substantial but not overwhelming. In this case, the same basic mindset that was required for Windows 2000 migration applies to Windows Server 2003. However, if you are an administrator unfamiliar with the Windows server platform, a serious shift in your approach will be necessary. For example, UNIX administrators with skills in developing character-based scripts in order to facilitate operating system (OS) management may find the graphical approach very different. For those of you in this category, take heart . . . Windows Server 2003 makes a number of positive accommodations that will permit both standard graphical and character-based, script-oriented management.

This chapter is an overview of the Windows Server 2003 components from an administrative perspective. The pure breadth and depth of Windows Server 2003 suggests that a concise view from 30,000 feet will be valuable to those with little knowledge of the operating system. For those with a baseline knowledge of Windows 2000 or Windows Server 2003, subsequent chapters will have greater value. This chapter explores several topics:

- Windows Server 2003 from a historical perspective
- The Windows Server 2003 product family
- The implications of key features to system administration

WINDOWS SERVER 2003: A HISTORICAL PERSPECTIVE

The fundamental differences between Windows Server 2003 and its predecessor, Windows 2000, reside in its embrace of the Microsoft .NET Framework, tightened security features, improved scalability, and enhanced administrative tools. While explored later, the .NET Framework deserves special mention here since it propels the Windows environment into a transparent Internet-services-based operating system. Yes, Windows Server 2003 includes hundreds of other operating system enrichments . . . but it is the .NET Framework enhancements that shift the paradigm from a classic client/server environment to an Internet services orientation. Microsoft has carefully crafted a computing environment that borrows heavily from earlier operating systems while adding an enhanced front-end, advanced features, and numerous administrative tools. The operating system incorporates some of the best functional elements of UNIX, NetWare, VMS, DOS, and OS/2 while providing a uniquely Microsoft interface. To a very large extent, Microsoft has succeeded in producing a robust environment that captures the best of older technologies while leveraging the new way of Internet services.

The history of Windows Server 2003 is short, but its lineage can be traced back over two decades. Windows Server 2003 is built on Windows NT technology and its formal history began in 1993. At that time, Microsoft had recently parted company with IBM on OS/2 and decided to change directions. The first released version of Windows NT was widely viewed as a curious little network operating system (NOS) designed as an alternative to IBM's OS/2 LAN Manager. However, Microsoft had bigger plans than what was perceived by early industry naysayers. The first upgrade came a year later as version 3.5 and offered many significant improvements in performance and functionality. Microsoft then upstaged itself with the release of Windows 95, and Windows NT was relegated to the back burner. The 1995 release of Windows NT 3.51 added to the networking functionality and offered a greatly enhanced suite of server products known as BackOffice. With this release, Microsoft became a serious threat to NOS vendors like Novell.

Since its release in late 1996, Windows NT 4.0 has experienced significant market acceptance. The most important advancement made with the release of Windows NT 4.0 is the incorporation of the Windows 95 user interface (UI). In fact, Microsoft internally referred to NT 4.0 as the Shell Update Release (SUR), referring to the Windows 95 front end. (By contrast, Windows Server 2003 might be considered the Internet services update to Windows 2000.) In addition to a UI, Windows

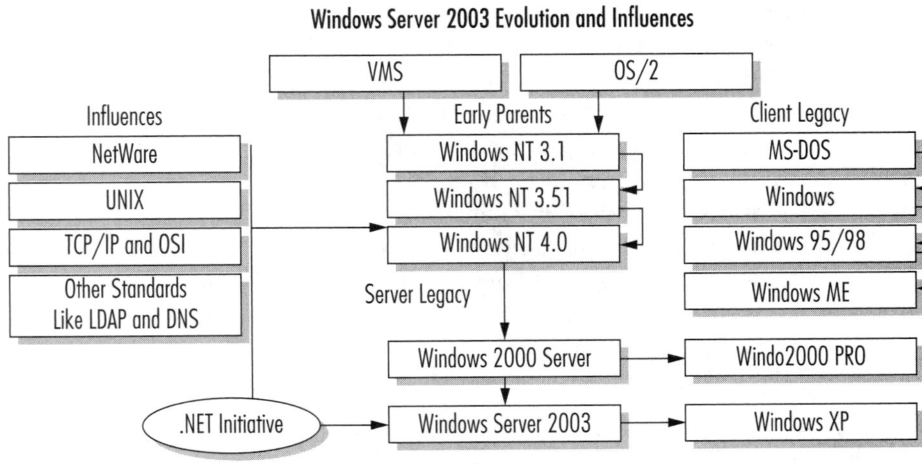

FIGURE 1.1 Historic Perspective

NT 4.0 added the Distributed Common Object Model (DCOM) and enhanced Domain Name Server (DNS) support for its TCP/IP transport. Moreover, a great number of components—in particular, the Exchange Server—were added to the optional BackOffice suite.

Despite its many enhancements and solid sales, Windows NT 4.0 was criticized for a number of real and perceived shortfalls, especially within larger enterprise environments. Windows 2000 was designed to overcome these shortfalls with a product family to meet the needs of environments ranging from workgroups to the largest enterprises. Windows Server 2003 expands on this targeted market.

Windows 2000 was more than a renaming of the next version of Windows NT. Significant changes revolved around the new server domain architecture, inclusion of Active Directory, and vastly enhanced networking and security features. Although Windows 2000 was originally slated to be released as Windows NT 5.0 to mark a significant OS upgrade, Windows XP and Windows Server 2003 might be regarded as something closer to Windows NT 5.5. Although many enhancements and new features are available in Windows Server 2003, it remains faithful to the basic Windows 2000 design and architecture. Windows 2000 system administrators will find adopting Windows Server 2003 relatively easy.

Figure 1.1 shows the history of and influences on Windows Server 2003.

THE WINDOWS SERVER 2003 FAMILY: WHAT'S IN A NAME?

What's in a name? Apparently Microsoft believes there is much to be gained from shifting the name of its flagship operating system from Windows NT to Windows

2000 and then to Windows Server 2003. Since NT stood for "new technology," the 2000 moniker seemed to herald a new millennium of computing. Windows Server 2003 is designed to take on the brave new world of Internet services. In development, the client and server versions were code named Whistler. By the time of release and despite common architectural structure, Microsoft decided to launch the client and server product lines with different names. The client versions inherited the Windows XP name to underscore what Microsoft hoped would equate to a new user eXPerience. The Windows Server 2003 line's designation underscores its Internet readiness. In renaming Windows XP and Windows .NET, the company has created a family of OS products that addresses the entire market from desktop to the largest enterprise. Table 1.1 compares the Windows NT and Windows Server 2003 product lines.

Windows XP Home and Professional Editions

Until the release of Windows XP, Microsoft's client software was divided into two radically different architectures. Windows 3.x and Windows 9x operating systems were based on MS-DOS with a graphical front end. The last iteration of the MS-DOS operating system was the marginally successful Windows Millennium Edition. While Windows ME had a short shelf life, a few new design features, such as expanded device support, found their way into Windows XP. With Windows XP, support for MS-DOS ends. By contrast, Windows NT and Windows 2000 Professional were the first client operating systems based on the Windows NT kernel. Windows XP exploits Windows 2000 Professional with two editions . . . one designed for home use and one for business and small workgroup environments. Microsoft's promotion of Windows XP has centered on the cleaner user interface, which reduces clutter and expands usability. In addition, Windows XP makes significant leaps in interconnectivity, multimedia support, security, general system stability, and Help functions. Although this book focuses on the server versions, Windows XP's enhanced features are noted as they relate to administration. For a list of Windows XP's specific features, see Microsoft's Web site.

TABLE 1.1 Comparison of Windows NT and Windows Server 2003 Products

Windows Server 2003	Windows 2000	Windows NT Equivalent
Windows XP	Windows 2000 Professional	Windows NT Workstation
Windows Server 2003, Web Edition	No equivalent	No equivalent
Windows Server 2003, Standard Edition	Windows 2000 Server	Windows NT Server
Windows Server 2003, Enterprise Edition	Windows 2000 Advanced Server	Windows NT Server EE
Windows Server 2003, Datacenter Edition	Windows 2000 Datacenter Server	No equivalent

Windows Server 2003, Web Edition

The new addition to the Windows operating system server family is Windows Server 2003, Web Edition. Given Microsoft's commitment to Internet readiness, this is a functionally focused Web server, as the name implies. It does not include many of the common features, like Active Directory, that other Windows Server 2003 servers provide. However, it is specifically optimized as a platform for Web services and hosting. With .NET Framework components like the innovative ASP.NET feature, the sharing of application services in a Web environment becomes possible. The Windows Server 2003, Web Edition facilitates the development and deployment of XML-based services and applications.

Windows Server 2003, Standard Edition

Windows Server 2003, Standard Edition refocuses the previous Windows 2000 Server version to address everyday organizational needs such as sharing files and printers and secured Internet connectivity. Like its predecessor, this version is designed for smaller client/server environments, but can manage a moderately complex organization. In system administrator terms, this server is best for an extended LAN and small WAN infrastructure, such as an enterprise that comprises a central office of modest size and several remote branch offices. Windows Server 2003, Standard Edition supports two-way symmetric multiprocessing (SMP) and up to 4 GB of memory.

Windows Server 2003, Enterprise Edition

Windows Server 2003, Enterprise Edition expands the core of networking and Internet functionality for medium and large enterprises. It is the default general business server operating system. Specifically designed for multidepartment use, it is equally well suited as an applications server and for e-commerce transactions. Windows Server 2003, Enterprise Edition supports up to 32 GB of main memory—a significant advance over the 8-GB limitation of Windows 2000. It also supports eight-way SMP and four-node clustering with enhanced load-balancing applications. Windows Server 2003, Enterprise Edition ships in either 32-bit or 64-bit versions.

Windows Server 2003, Datacenter Edition

Windows 2000 Datacenter was Microsoft's first entry designed to seriously compete in the heavy iron marketplace of the enterprise. Windows Server 2003, Datacenter Edition provides yet greater availability, especially for mission-critical solutions. The crown jewel of Microsoft's server line, it supports 32 SMP and eight-node clustering. This product is also available in 32-bit and 64-bit versions. Table 1.2 offers a comparison of features available with Windows Server 2003.

Table 1.3 provides a quick reference for system requirements for each of the Windows Server 2003 platforms. In practical terms, the minimum requirements are

TABLE 1.2 Comparison of Windows Server 2003 Features

Feature	Web Edition	Standard Edition	Enterprise Edition	Datacenter Edition
.NET Framework	Yes	Yes	Yes	Yes
Internet Information Services (IIS) 6.0	Yes	Yes	Yes	Yes
ASP .NET	Yes	Yes	Yes	Yes
UDDI Services	No	Yes	Yes	Yes
Clustering Load Balancing	Yes	Yes	Yes	Yes
Cluster Services	No	No	Yes	Yes
VPN Support	Partial	Yes	Yes	Yes
Session Initiation Protocol Service (SIP)	No	Yes	Yes	Yes
IAS Internet Authentication Service	No	Yes	Yes	Yes
Network Bridge	No	Yes	Yes	No
Internet Connection Share	No	Yes	Yes	No
Active Directory	No	Yes	Yes	Yes
Metadirectory Services	No	No	Yes	No
Distributed File System	Yes	Yes	Yes	Yes
Shadow Copy Restore	No	Yes	Yes	Yes
SharePoint Team Services	No	Yes	Yes	Yes
Removable/Remote Storage	No	Yes	Yes	Yes
Fax Services	No	Yes	Yes	Yes
Services for Macintosh	No	No	Yes	Yes
IntelliMirror	No	Yes	Yes	Yes
Resultant Set Policy	No	Yes	Yes	Yes
WMI Command Line	No	Yes	Yes	Yes

TABLE 1.2 Continued

Feature	Web Edition	Standard Edition	Enterprise Edition	Datacenter Edition
Remote OS	No	Yes	Yes	Yes
Remote Install Services	No	Yes	Yes	Yes
Internet Connection Firewall	No	Yes	Yes	No
PKI Services & Smart Card Services	No	Yes	Yes	Yes
Remote Desktop Administration	Yes	Yes	Yes	Yes
Terminal Server	No	Yes	Yes	Yes
Terminal Server Session Directory	No	No	Yes	Yes
64-Bit Itanium Support	No	No	Yes	Yes
Hot Add Memory	No	No	Yes	Yes
Non-uniform Memory Access (NUMA)	No	No	Yes	Yes

TABLE 1.3 Comparison of Server System Requirements

Requirement	Web Edition	Standard Edition	Enterprise Edition	Datacenter Edition
Minimum CPU Speed	133 MHz	133 MHz	133 MHz × 86 733 MHz 64-bit	133 MHz × 86 733 MHz 64-bit
Recommended CPU	550 MHz	550 MHz	733 MHz	733 MHz
Minimum RAM	128 MB	128 MB	128 MB	512 MB
Recommended Minimum RAM	256 MB	256 MB	256 MB	1 GB
Maximum RAM	2 GB	4 GB	32 GB × 86 64 GB 64-bit	128 GB × 86 512 GB 64-bit
Multiprocessor Support	1 or 2	1 or 2	Up to 8	Minimum 8 Maximum 64
Disk Space for Setup	1.5 GB	1.5 GB	1.5 GB × 86 2.0 GB 64-bit	1.5 GB × 86 2.0 GB 64-bit

woefully inadequate. The recommended levels should be regarded as a practical target.

UNDERSTANDING THE .NET FRAMEWORK

The .NET Framework attempts to transform applications to online services that can be used over the Internet or in intranet environments. The underlying goal is to provide customized and comprehensive solutions to users regardless of a user's location or computer system. To achieve this goal, the server-centric approach to computing that currently defines the Internet must change. Another challenge is to break away from the concept of localized client-based applications. Looking into the future, a user should be able to log on to any system and get access to its data, applications, and even familiar settings. To realize this ability requires looking at applications and systems not as standalone entities but as services that are called on demand by the user. These application services could replace packaged software and be rented or leased over the Internet. Packaged software will probably not disappear, but Microsoft officials believe that this new model will radically affect the way businesses and consumers obtain up-to-date products and conduct business. Individual and corporate users conceptually will be able to get applications on demand through either a subscription or a rental arrangement. A prime example of how this could work is the automatic operating system update facilities provided by Windows XP and Windows Server 2003. When patches need to be applied, updates over the Internet can be applied automatically or interactively.

Foundation Technologies

The concepts underlying .NET are industry-standard technologies that should enhance its acceptance and interoperability. Microsoft believes that this approach is founded on the basic principles of common description, connection, communication, and discovery.

The eXtensible Markup Language (XML) is the centerpiece of the .NET strategy. This open standard is managed by the World Wide Web Consortium (W3C). Stated simply, XML changes the way in which applications talk to one another. It is designed to enable the development of applications that permit the easy exchange of data between any enabled computing devices. XML separates the underlying data from how the data is displayed. This schema effectively "unlocks" the data so that it can be reorganized, edited, and exchanged with any Web site, device, or enabled application.

In addition to XML, the .NET Framework utilizes other rapidly emerging standards:

- The Simple Object Access Protocol (SOAP) was developed by Microsoft but turned over to the W3C for open standards management. SOAP enables communications and makes service requests.
- The Web Service Description Language (WSDL) is a standard format that publishes function names, required parameters, and returned results from an XML Web service.
- Discovery services are provided by the Universal Description, Discovery, and Integration (UDDI) standard. In theory, it makes it easy to locate XML services and facilitates. UDDI is the "yellow pages" of XML Web services.

Components of .NET and Product Layers

The .NET Framework consists of three primary layers. The universal run-time engine handles the lowest level of services, which includes thread management. Conceptually similar to Sun Microsystems's Java Virtual Machine, this engine manages environmental matters. A common class library rests on the universal run-time engine. The code objects can communicate with applications written in any programming language. This facility makes it possible to use large amounts of legacy code for .NET-enabled environments. Active Server Pages Plus is the highest layer and serves to separate scripts from Web-based code.

The .NET initiative was initially a vision exposed by Microsoft Chairman and Chief Software Architect Bill Gates. Unlike so many industry "visions" of the future, the concepts were soon transformed in a Framework with a wide range of Windows 2000-centric products. Products such as Microsoft Exchange 2000 and Microsoft SQL Server 2000 are the first component products to be released with .NET-enabling technology. As the following list shows, the complete suite of .NET products provides an impressive solution set. In addition to server back-end products, flagship customer products like Microsoft Office are emerging as .NET-enabled.

BACK-END APPLICATIONS AND TOOLS

- *BizTalk Server 2000/2002*. This product uses XML to integrate Web services with business application logic and data.
- *Host Integration Server 2000*. This product is designed to communicate with legacy networks, applications, and data.
- *SQL Server 2000*. This advanced database provides more analytical support and data warehousing capacity than previous versions.
- *Visual Studio.NET and C#*. This is the next iteration of the Visual Studio suite and it encompasses the C# language, XML support, and other features. Probably more than any other offering by Microsoft, the Visual Studio .NET suite should ensure the viability of the .NET Framework and the success of the Windows Server 2003 family.

MID-TIER SUITES

- *Application Center 2000*. This server product provides the management, scaling, and deployment of applications.
- *Commerce Server 2000/2002*. This server is designed for greater Web site design including enhanced user tracking.
- *Content Management Server 2001*. As the name implies, this manages Internet-based content delivery.
- *SharePoint Portal Server*. This server is used to find, share, and publish information easily by employing a flexible portal solution model.
- *Exchange Server 2000*. This version expands its integration with Active Directory and provides more Web-enabled collaborative work and messaging.
- *Mobile Information Server*. Mobile Information Server enables secure access to data on Exchange and Enterprise servers for mobile users.

FRONT-END TIER

- *Internet Security and Acceleration Server 2000*. This server provides caching of Web data together with firewall protection.

The development of applications that take full advantage of .NET is critical to its ultimate success. Microsoft released Visual Studio.NET in early 2002.

The release of new versions of .NET Servers together with completely new products is anticipated to continue at fever pace. Don't be surprised if the names of the products just mentioned undergo change. As more .NET components are added, the ability of these products to take full advantage of underlying Windows Server 2003 functionality should be enhanced.

NOTE At the time of this book's publication, Microsoft was making considerable noise about .NET My Services (formerly code named "hailstorm"). This is a rapidly evolving technology that should be commercially available soon.

.NET My Services is a family of user-centric Web services. The purpose of the technology is to enable businesses to build deeper customer relationships and improve operational efficiency. Another stated objective is to make applications and devices easier for consumers to use. One portion of the technology is .NET Alerts, which includes communication tools that permit direct interaction between businesses and clients.

Use of .NET My Services is activated and controlled by the user optionally. For example, a .NET Alerts provider can send an XML message to the .NET Alerts service. The service routes the message to a user's desktop, cellular phone, mobile device, or e-mail address. The user determines where the message is delivered. As an administrator, you should keep an eye on how this technology evolves.

BackOffice Suite Moves Forward as Renamed .NET Products

The much ballyhooed BackOffice suite that supplemented Windows NT and Windows 2000 has quietly slipped to the very back of the office. Although the BackOffice bundle is no longer marketed, the individual components are available. Several of these products have been renamed, as have other server products, including:

- The Commercial Internet System is now Commerce Server.
- The Exchange Server retains its name but with a new extension.
- The Proxy Server is now the vastly enhanced Internet Security Acceleration Server 2000.
- The Site Server can still be used as an intranet deployment tool primarily but is largely replaced by Commerce Server 2000.
- The System Management Server, version 2.0, is still one of the primary management tools and is widely used for software administration.
- The SNA Server is now Host Integration Server.
- The SQL Server retains its name but with new extensions and vastly expanded functions.

Microsoft Operations Manager

Microsoft provides three options in server products designed to assist administrators: (1) Application Center, (2) System Management Server (SMS), and (3) the new Microsoft Operations Manager (MOM). We provide an overview of these three optional administrative server products in Chapter 17; here we offer an overview of MOM to underscore the potential importance of this tool set for administration. Stated simply, MOM extends the management tool set of Microsoft operating system servers and .NET Enterprise Server products. Through third-party extensions from vendors like NetIQ, other platforms can also be consistently managed. The following are some major features of MOM:

- *Event management*. MOM provides event management for Windows 2000 Server, Active Directory, Internet Information Services (IIS), some .NET Enterprise Servers and Windows NT Server 4.0. This includes an enterprise event log that collects and reports on problems and information.

- *Proactive monitoring and alert messaging.* MOM's distributed capabilities track and monitor information. Based on levels of urgency, the MOM will issue alerts to pagers, through e-mail, or by other external means.
- *Reporting and trend analysis.* MOM provides reporting and trend analysis features that examine problems across time and generate detailed reports.
- *Specialized management packs.* In order to focus domain-specific operations better, detailed management packs for different Microsoft technologies and products are available. Packs are available for Windows NT Server 4.0, Windows 2000 Server, Active Directory, IIS, Terminal Services, Microsoft Distributed Transaction Coordinator (MDTC), Windows Internet Naming Service (WINS), Dynamic Host Configuration Protocol (DHCP), Domain Name Service (DNS), Routing and Remote Access Service, Microsoft Transaction Service (MTS), Microsoft Message Queuing (MSMQ), Exchange Server, Microsoft SQL Server, Proxy Server, Systems Management Server, Commerce Server, and Host Integration Server.
- *Scalable management.* MOM provides a sophisticated, load-balancing, multitier architecture designed to manage IT environments with thousands of Windows-based servers and applications.
- *An agile solution to meet the changing needs of business.* MOM 2000 provides business flexibility via management rules. It is shipped with default rules that allow you to benefit quickly from the product. The rules can be customized to meet the changing needs.
- *Interoperation with other management systems.* MOM 2000 integrates with other enterprise management systems by using Simple Network Management Protocol (SNMP) and Windows Management Instrumentation (WMI), which is based on the Common Information Model (CIM) supported by the Desktop Management Taskforce (DMTF).

WINDOWS SERVER 2003 ADMINISTRATIVE ROLES

Windows Server 2003 defines a universe of system administration responsibilities. Yet only a few system administrators have the broad enterprise-level view. Instead, they have specialized responsibility for planning and deployment of such things as domain controller servers, domain models, the Active Directory, sites, security policies, and network infrastructures.

Because the majority of administrators perform these more specialized functions, Windows Server 2003 allows the assignment and delegation of both broad

FIGURE 1.2 Roles of System Administrators

and function-specific roles (Figure 1.2). An administrator could have all or a portion of these management responsibilities:

- *Operating system maintenance*—the health of the operating system's processes and services. The monitoring and logging tools help tune individual computers, domain controllers, and specialized server performance. In this work, many administrators find both standard tools and custom scripts handy.

- *User and group management*—adding, modifying, and deleting user accounts and group policies. Windows Server 2003 security groups are used to establish the rights and privileges of individuals and groups of users. Underlying group policies are the establishment and enforcement of security and user behavior. The Active Directory services manage the distribution of group policies. This includes such activities as logon and password management, and granting or restricting permissions and access.
- *Hardware and device management*—the health of the physical network devices, computers, and peripherals. Microsoft provides a Hardware Compatibility List (HCL) to assess the viability of a given item of hardware in a Windows environment. This also permits the system administrator to ensure that the most recent device drivers for the hardware components are being used. This involves not only traditional network hardwired connections but also such items as wireless devices and assessment of Internet and intranet bandwidth.

Scope of Responsibility

Windows Server 2003 provides for levels of administrative authority, for which there exists a relative hierarchy. An administrator gains authority by becoming a member of one or more built-in or default security groups, inheriting the rights, privileges, and restrictions associated with each (Figure 1.3). In Chapter 7 we explore group policies in depth. However, for the sake of this discussion of administrative roles, we note that responsibilities are assigned through the accumulation of group memberships.

Another important concept is specialized function versus broad responsibility. Members of different groups have broad-based authority to manage domain activities. These include Administrators, Domain Admins, and Enterprise Admins. The scope of authority can be granted to other users with specialized functions—for example, printer support or backup operations. The specialized security groups are Account Operators, Backup Operators, Printer Operators, Replicators, and System Operators. Membership in these groups can be assigned individually or in any combination.

The final major concept is granularity. The organizational unit (OU) is a structural mechanism (also viewed as a container object) by which domains can be divided into smaller elements such as a sales department. In turn, this OU can be divided into other units that involve users, devices such as printers, and network components. Each parent and child OU can then be assigned specific system administrators to manage the allotted functions.

WINDOWS SERVER 2003 FEATURES AND ADMINISTRATIVE IMPLICATIONS

Windows Server 2003 enhances Windows NT and Windows 2000 features and adds many functions, each of which has a direct impact on system administration. Rather

FIGURE 1.3 Levels of Administrative Responsibility

than merely outline the major new features and enhancements, we will look at them from the administrator's perspective.

.NET Framework

The greatest single implication of the .NET Framework for administrators is the requirement to look at the network as a global entity. The enterprise is no longer just a group of users that must get access to clients and servers. Traditional views of static applications must give way to the concept of computing services. This global view forces the administrator's job to expand greatly in scope and complexity. Therefore, in order for an operating system like Windows Server 2003 to be successful, it must enhance the flexibility and power of the system administrators.

Make no mistake about this brave new world . . . for every functional advancement, there will be additional challenges. Clearly, any time productivity depends on the exchange of communication outside the enterprise, security takes center stage. With each opportunity to perform management functions remotely, the potential for unwanted intrusion can raise its ugly head.

Despite these issues, the role of the system administrator should be augmented greatly by Windows Server 2003. Mundane responsibilities such as applying an endless number of software patches will be reduced. In the same instant, your ability to improve the user experience is also possible. By providing the ability to gain access to real-time services that are managed safely by the system administrator, the universe of computing will be greatly enhanced. As you begin to understand and use Windows 2003 Servers and the .NET Enterprise Server applications, understand that you must move cautiously but deliberately toward an Internet services paradigm.

The Active Directory

In Windows Server 2003, everything is treated as an object, including users, computers, files, and network elements. A core innovation of Windows 2000 and Windows Server 2003 is the Active Directory, which manages all domain objects in a hierarchical and replicated structure, thus allowing a significant difference in the way an administrator can conduct business. From a central location, administrators with appropriate permissions can add, delete, modify, and view objects and services anywhere in the domain, domain tree, or forest.

Some highlights of the Active Directory, detailed in Chapters 5 and 6, are:

- *Advanced data query functions.* The Active Directory's Global Catalog of objects on the network makes it easy for the system administrator and authorized users to drill down to the object attribute level.
- *Directory replication.* The Windows NT structure of a primary and a backup domain controller is replaced by a multimaster arrangement in which directory replication occurs across peer domain controllers. This provides greater redundant operations and higher data availability.
- *Adherence to standards.* System name resolution in the Active Directory depends on the Domain Name System (DNS) over TCP/IP. System administrators with network knowledge of TCP/IP and DNS will have an advantage when managing the directory.
- *Extensible schema.* The Active Directory can be dynamically altered to include new objects and even to modify attributes of existing objects. This means that the administrator can dynamically change the object definitions and associated attributes to meet enterprise requirements. Windows Server 2003 specifically improves the manageability of the schema by permitting the deactivation of attributes and classes.
- *Interoperability.* Working with different operating systems and directory services is a constant challenge. The goal of the Active Directory is greater interoperability. Consequently, for example, the directory allows integration with the Lightweight Directory Access Protocol (LDAP v3) to resolve objects in Windows Server 2003 and heterogeneous environments. With Windows Server 2003, LDAP binds are now supported. The Name Service Provider Interface

(NSPI) provides directory services interplay with Microsoft's Exchange Server. The Windows Server 2003 enhancement that allows the removal of RDN restrictions that are not X.500-compliant should also enhance interoperability.

- *Greater flexibility*. Windows Server 2003 specifically expands the flexibility of Active Directory in many directions including an expanded ability to handle objects and reconfigure trees and domains.

The Interface

The interface to the operating system involves much more than how windows are displayed and the pull-down menus function. Yes, a clean and familiar user interface makes user training and support easier. With regard to system management, it also dictates how easily administrative tasks can be accomplished locally, through a network, or over the Internet. Equally important is the flexibility of the interface to accommodate both standard tools and custom scripts. Chapter 4 focuses on the administrative and user interface improvements provided in Windows XP and Windows Server 2003.

THE USER INTERFACE

The default user interface of Windows XP and Windows Server 2003 is newly enhanced to reduce clutter and improve accessibility. However, if a user prefers the familiar Windows 98 look and feel, the "classic view" can be applied.

Easy navigation through the operating system is basic to overall usability. The Adaptive Start function, for example, tracks the most used features and promotes them on the menu, and hides other items until they are required. This reduces the clutter of older menus. Even so, system administrators can count on receiving calls from users about "missing" functions until the users become familiar with the Adaptive Start feature.

The enhanced search and help features should lighten the system administrator's load. On the client side, users can now seek support online from fellow workers. Working with the Active Directory, users can locate objects anywhere in the domain. All persons and resources are treated as objects with specific attributes. Searches can be conducted based on the name of the object (or a part thereof) or its attributes. In the case of a document, one attribute would be its contents.

Personal settings established by users can be mirrored in a central store that permits easy retrieval. Thus, users can log on to any computer on the network and have their personal preferences reflected in that environment. A comfortable user is generally a happy user.

In global enterprises, internationalization becomes an important end-user support issue for the administrator. The multilingual support of Windows Server 2003 makes it possible to edit in any supported language or combination of languages.

THE ADMINISTRATOR INTERFACE AND TOOLS

Most system administrators seek simplicity but demand power in their interface. For that reason, administrative tools—in particular, those that hide the background process, like Windows wizards—must be rock solid, stable, and reliable. Many administrators coming from character-based environments distrust automated tools they cannot directly control at all stages. Administrators coming from largely character-based environments such as UNIX should alter this view, because much of Windows Server 2003 administration is based on wizards. Fortunately, our testing shows that the stability and reliability of wizards have been largely achieved. For greater interoperability, Microsoft also offers the optional Services for UNIX 3.0 suite that provides a complete POSIX environment and hundreds of UNIX commands within Windows Server 2003.

System administrators also rely on facilities that support character-based command-line interfaces and a wide variety of scripts. The Windows Scripting Host provides a direct interface to VBScript and Jscript facilities. The user can write and execute scripts to these engines in the same way a UNIX user might write a Perl or Korn shell script.

Underlying the management of Windows Server 2003 is Microsoft's Zero Administration Windows (ZAW) initiative. While the term "zero administration" is at best an oxymoron because all operating systems require some level of management, Microsoft's goal was to provide a more intelligent approach to system management. Many of the tools under the ZAW umbrella go a long way toward it. ZAW is divided into several initiative areas that deserve mention here:

- *Central policy administration*. User and group policies can be effectively managed by a centralized system administration function. These policies can be applied by a site, a domain, or an organizational unit. The most common types of centralized policy administration involve security, file use, software publishing/distribution, and scripting.
- *Web-Based Enterprise Management (WBEM)*. Windows Server 2003 embraces Web-Based Enterprise Management using the industry standard Common Information Model (CIM) for application and system management as adopted by the Desktop Management Task Force. WBEM is designed to provide consistency across operations and configuration management. Scripts can be written to interface with it, through the Windows Scripting Host, and to query enterprise systems. The Common Object Model (COM) API is employed with WBEM, ensuring greater extensibility for both system administrators and third-

party software and hardware vendors. As an example, the WBEM initiative resulted from the efforts of Microsoft, BMC Software, Cisco Systems, Compaq Computer, Intel, and many other DMTF member companies to establish management infrastructure standards; it provides a standard way to access information for various hardware and software components. Windows Management Instrumentation (WMI) is a management infrastructure that allows administrators to monitor and control managed objects in the network that emerged from the WBEM initiative.

- *System management tools*. As discussed throughout this book, administrators are provided a wide range of graphical tools for administration of both local systems and domains. For example, with the Computer Management tool a local user can assume an administrative role (providing Administrator rights are granted) to fine-tune the performance of a local machine. For the system administrator, this tool also supports troubleshooting for remote systems on the same network or virtually anywhere. The Task Scheduler allows the user and the system administrator to establish specific parameters for the execution of programs and events at the desired time. Windows Server 2003 system backup is now integrated with the Task Scheduler, giving automatic system backup without direct human intervention to hard drives, tape, recordable CD-ROM, robotic changer tape banks, and the like. The Removable Storage Manager can administer tape or disk mounting at the scheduled time. However, file shares, system sessions, and connections are more effectively managed with the Files Service Manager. The foregoing represents only a small portion of the tools available to the system administrator.
- *Software management*. The software management infrastructure permits the assignment of applications to specific users and computers. Applications can also be "published" to a server and then added, upgraded, or removed as the user requires. The concept of publishing applications to the enterprise reduces traditional system administrator support of common applications installation. Users who must roam among systems can get access to those applications in which they have assignment through the IntelliMirror technology. Finally, as systems are replaced, the need for individualized application installation is greatly reduced.
- *Microsoft Management Console (MMC)*. A common frustration in computer management is attempting to learn and manage a variety of disjointed tools. To alleviate it, Windows Server 2003 permits the consolidation of tools into one or more Microsoft Management Console(s), illustrated in Figure 1.4. Because the MMC is extensible, "snap-in" application tools can be included as Windows Server 2003 evolves and as third-party management software becomes available. Microsoft publishes an API to facilitate the development of

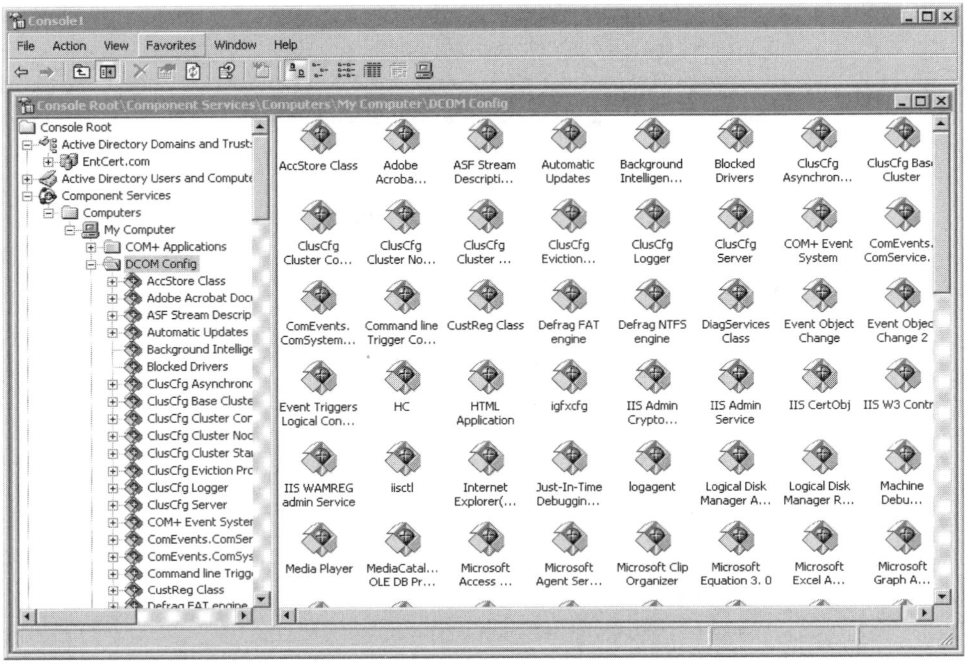

FIGURE 1.4 The Microsoft Management Console

management tools with a common look and feel. Thus, administrators can now go to a single point and use tools that have the same interface. The MMC can be shared with other administrators and used to delegate selected tasks.

Networking and Communications

Network connectivity and other forms of communication are another area of concern to system administrators. Given the central role of Web services for Windows Server 2003, this may be the most significant focus for administrators. Windows Server 2003 has a number of wizards that facilitate connectivity and reduce some of the more mundane system administrator activities. Its tools and support for protocols aid in the management of Internets and intranets.

Windows Server 2003 supports a Network Connections Wizard that walks the end user and system administrator through network, dial-up, virtual private network (VPN), and serial connections. This facility controls configuration setup and management, allowing protocols and services to be set for each connection. From a user's perspective, offline browsing that permits review of a Web page after disconnection and subscription support for automatic Web page updates is a valuable addition.

In addition to the more standard forms of connectivity, Windows Server 2003 provides administrator tools to support advanced communications—for example, the creation, viewing, and management of VPNs. Windows Server 2003 embraces both the Point-to-Point Tunneling Protocol (PPTP) and the Layer 2 Tunneling Protocol (L2TP), and Internet Protocol Security (IPSec) can be employed as an alternative approach. VPNs permit a sales office to connect "virtually" through the Internet to corporate headquarters in a secure tunnel.

The Windows Server 2003 family has added many enhancements in the communications and networking arena. They include:

- Enhanced support for the TCP/IP suite, including a Telnet server and SMTP native support
- Reliance on dynamic Domain Name Services (dynamic DNS)
- Multiple protocol routing through the Routing and Remote Access Service (RRAS) that enables IP, IPX, and AppleTalk routing
- The PPTP and L2TP
- The Routing Information Protocol (RIPv2).
- Asynchronous Transfer Model (ATM) support
- Fibre Channel 1-GB-per-second bus data transfer

Hardware Support

Hardware management can be a nightmare. However, Windows Server 2003 is based solely on Intel-compatible systems, so the requirement to support dozens of proprietary architectures is reduced. Even so, hardware support will continue to be an important administrative task. To confirm hardware compatibility, it is recommended that you refer to the regularly updated Hardware Compatibility List on the Microsoft Web site.

The Win32 Driver Model (WDM) theoretically establishes binary driver compatibility and I/O services with earlier Windows environments and Windows .NET. Windows NT system administrators frequently complained about the lack of support for certain devices supported by Windows 95/98. Windows Server 2003 is working to overcome this limitation, which should greatly reduce administrative headaches caused by hardware incompatibility. However, given the thousands of devices available, the updating process will surely continue for many years.

Windows Server 2003 provides a more robust Plug and Play facility with a significantly larger set of device drives. Support for the universal serial bus (USB) permits the operating system to dynamically detect connected hardware and then the device driver is automatically installed. Printer device improvements are particularly significant. Users can send documents (including those using the Image

Color Management 2.0 API) to printers connected to an intranet or the Internet. The Advanced Configuration and Power Interface streamlines both Plug and Play and power management. Also supported is fibre channel technology for the transmission of data at 1 GB per second. Smart cards (e.g., for secure transmission of online banking) and flash memory can also be used in connection with Windows Server 2003. Finally, Windows Server 2003 supports such graphics and multimedia standards as DirectX 8.0, Direct3D, and DirectSound acceleration technology.

Windows provides an assortment of utilities that make life easier on the desktop. The Hardware Wizard attempts to find and configure attached devices, although we found this to be a mixed blessing because it is difficult to turn off. The Device Manager, however, is a handy application designed to configure devices and resources interactively. Also useful is the Windows Installer service, which manages application installation, and the OnNow applet, which places the system in hibernation when not in use, thereby reducing battery use on portable systems.

File and Storage Systems

Disk management and storage and backup cause many headaches for system administrators. A number of automated tools in Windows Server 2003 greatly reduce these manual burdens while enhancing utilization. They include:

- *Windows 95/98 and Windows NT file system compatibility.* Windows Server 2003 maintains base-level compatibility with earlier Windows environments. Its native file system is NTFS 5, enhancements to which include file encryption using public keys and tracking of distributed links. With respect to Windows 98, Windows Server 2003 fully supports the FAT32 file system; disk defragmentation is supported for FAT, FAT32, and NTFS volumes.
- *Disk quota utility.* The Windows Server 2003 supports disk quotas to limit user storage and to monitor the status of such limits.
- *Universal Disk Format.* This format permits the exchange of data with DVD and compact disk media.
- *Removable Storage Management.* RSM supports tape and disk libraries through a common interface.
- *Remote Storage Service.* RSS intelligently monitors frequently used files and periodically sends the most used items to backup. In conjunction with RSM, RSS sends infrequently used files to the library, where they can be filed until retrieved as needed. All directory information on the files is retained so that retrieval becomes seamless. RSS greatly reduces the need to add local hard disk capacity.

- *Distributed File System (DFS).* With this distributed model, a single directory tree can be created and maintained across several file systems, file servers, or even the entire enterprise. This permits a more global view of resources and data across the network.

Security and Authentication

Windows Server 2003 comes of age as a greatly enhanced security-aware enterprise operating system. As discussed in detail in Chapters 9 through 11, it fully embraces a wide variety of technologies to protect the enterprise. For example, Kerberos security standard is used by the Active Directory for single-point enterprise logons. Public key certification is based on the X.509 standard and is integrated with the Active Directory. To facilitate administration, the Security Configuration Editor permits fine-tuning of security-sensitive registries, files, and system services.

Microsoft has adopted the IPSec model in its IP Security management tools. The Encrypted File System extends the NTFS with the ability to provide public key encryption of disk-based files. Finally, a smart card infrastructure permits secured transmission of sensitive data between systems and in mobile situations.

The enhanced support of new security technologies by Windows Server 2003 represents a real opportunity for system administrators. Through the proper development and deployment of security policies, better protection from unwanted breaches can be achieved. For example, the administrator can monitor potential attacks and close possible security leaks before damage is done. In essence, the administrator becomes a proactive agent for security rather than a reactive defender of the realm.

POSTSCRIPT

Windows Server 2003 is a powerful enterprise operating system, particularly in its management tools and security features. The consolidation of many system administrator activities under the Microsoft Management Console streamlines the administrative burden, and the Web-based interface provides the consistency that was missing in earlier versions of Windows NT. Moreover, the addition of scripting should make life more controllable for system administrators grounded in other operating systems such as UNIX. The addition of tools makes management of Microsoft Windows Server 2003 both easier and more complex. Such is the reality of modern enterprise system administration.

Chapter 2

Windows Server 2003 Structure and Architecture

The underlying operating system structure and the relationship of component parts are fundamental to deploying and managing Windows Server 2003 environments. By understanding the operating system architecture, the system administrator should be in a better position to install, configure, optimize, and troubleshoot Windows Server 2003. This chapter is an architectural overview of Windows Server 2003. After reading it, you should have the following:

- An understanding of the operating system's structural layers, subsystems, and managers, including the executive kernel modes and user modes, subsystems, and managers
- A working knowledge of Windows Server 2003 process management, including multitasking, the interplay of processes and threads, process viewing, and management tools
- A perspective on physical and virtual memory management
- A basic understanding of the boot process
- A working grasp of the registry's function and structure
- An understanding of application dependencies and software compatibility with Windows Server 2003 through the use of its tools

There have been relatively very few underlying architectural changes made from Windows 2000. However, there are a number of enhancements that will have a beneficial impact on administration.

STRUCTURAL MODES, SUBSYSTEMS, AND MANAGERS

A surface view of the Windows Server 2003 structure reveals an eloquently simple arrangement of functions that separates system-related events from user-related events. As you move deeper into the components of Windows Server 2003, you will see that Microsoft has designed a very compartmentalized operating system. In this section we will review:

- The structural layers of the kernel mode, the Hardware Abstraction Layer (HAL), and the user mode
- The role of the Windows Server 2003 executive mode and its managers
- The role of the Windows Server 2003 user mode and its subsystems

Structural Layer Modes

Windows Server 2003 functions in two primary modes: the privileged kernel, or executive, mode and the open nonprivileged user mode (Figure 2.1). Low-level operating system services, system data, and interfaces to hardware are controlled by the kernel mode.

The user mode handles everything else that is subject to user interface or intervention, including the default Win32 subsystem, optional subsystems, and applications. The user mode interacts with system data and hardware through a tightly integrated API.

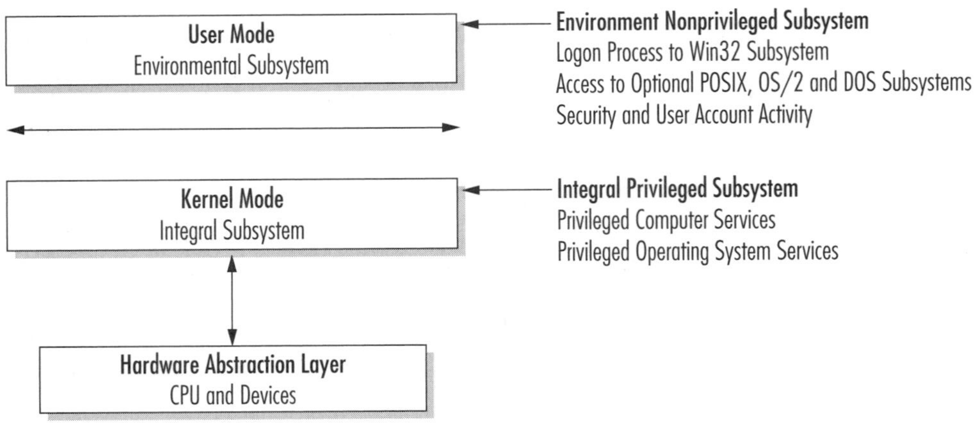

FIGURE 2.1 Relationship of the User and Kernel Modes

The Windows Server 2003 Executive Mode

The Windows Server 2003 Executive (Figure 2.2) is also known as the kernel mode and the privileged executive mode. Windows Server 2003 breaks its operations into five segments that run in the kernel or privileged mode:

- Hardware abstraction layer (HAL)
- Microkernel
- Device drivers
- Executive managers
- Executive services buffer

Collectively, these elements handle the system responsibilities that are hidden from the user. In Windows Server 2003, the Executive controls essential operating system functions. Other functions are pushed into the nonprivileged area or into protected subsystems, as discussed in the next section. The elements of the Executive are discretely independent and exchange data through defined interfaces. In theory, any component can be deleted and replaced with a technologically updated version. Assuming adherence to the interface APIs, the operating system should function without difficulty after swapping Executive components.

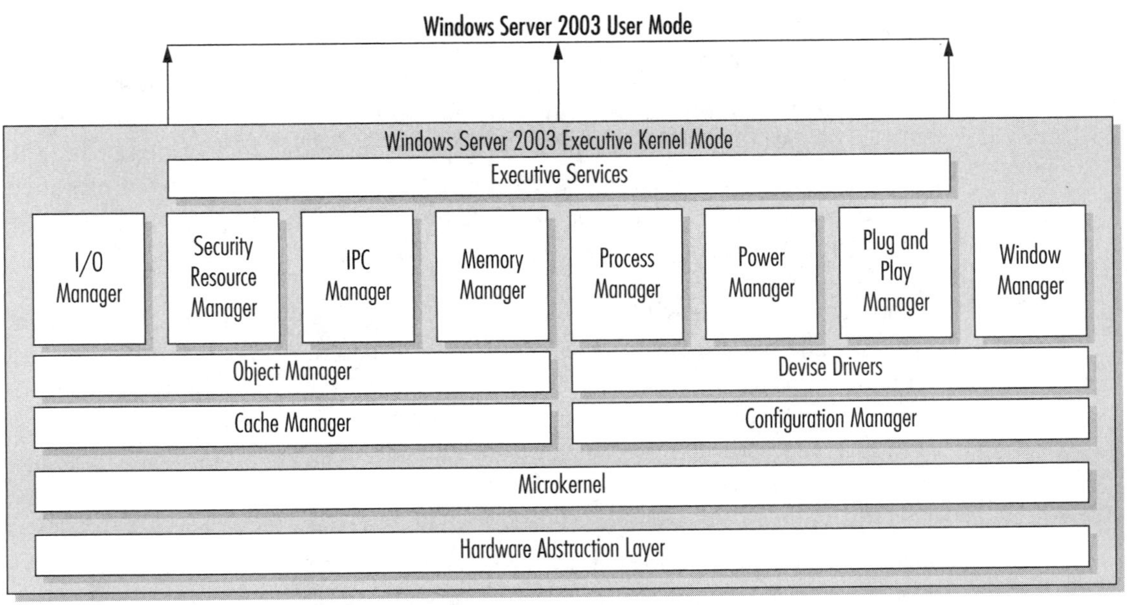

FIGURE 2.2 The Windows Server 2003 Executive Kernel Mode

Each element of the Executive provides two discrete functions. The system services are available in both user-mode and kernel-mode mode operations. By contrast, the internal routines are used only to communicate with other managers or components within the Executive itself.

THE HARDWARE ABSTRACTION LAYER

At the base of the Windows Server 2003 Executive is the Hardware Abstraction Layer. Microsoft originally placed hardware-related interfaces in a discrete segment of code as a means of ensuring greater portability across platforms. Early Windows NT was to be a cross-platform operating system in which HAL provided a layer of code that accounted for system differences. This design criterion has been eliminated. In Windows Server 2003, HAL deals with Intel-compatible CPU and related device-dependent issues.

Concentrating on a single architecture makes the writing of device drivers considerably more straightforward. With a published API, application developers can write instructions for a device that is optimized for Windows Server 2003. Whenever possible, system administrators should use such enhanced device drivers.

In multiprocessor systems, HAL serves an additional function of automatically synchronizing hardware-related threads with the next available CPU. Priorities range from real-time processes (with the highest priority) to variable, or dynamic, processes (lower priority), as discussed in a subsequent section.

THE MICROKERNEL

In operating systems such as Windows Server 2003 and UNIX, the base-level functions in operating system operations are managed by a kernel. In Windows Server 2003 this component takes the form of a nonconfigurable and nonpageable microkernel. By *nonconfigurable,* we mean that the microkernel is never modified and never recompiled; by *nonpageable* we mean that the 4-KB memory pages associated with the microkernel are fixed and not referred to the pagefile.sys file, where dynamic paging activities are retained.

The microkernel dispatches and controls threads. (Where multiprocessors are involved, it also synchronizes that workload.) Dispatcher objects implement and synchronize events, semaphores, timers, threads, and mutants (defined by mutually exclusive resource access). Control objects regulate virtual address processes, system interrupts, thread profiles, and asynchronous procedure calls.

DEVICE DRIVERS

A device driver is a set of instructions that coordinates the operating system with hardware such as printers, storage units, modems, network equipment, fax machines, scanners, and digital cameras. The Windows Device Model (WDM) theoretically allows a common set of device drivers. In theory, the WDM should greatly reduce the system administration's burden of maintaining multiple device driver versions. With the release of Windows Server 2003 and Windows XP, this objective has been largely achieved for the first time.

In the case of streaming media software, the WDM has shifted the processing from the user mode to WDM Kernel Streaming. The objective was to improve overall speed and performance. An application must be specifically written for WDM to take advantage of this architecture. The same principle applies to the new WDM Still Image Architecture for specific support of digital cameras and scanners.

The space available for device drivers and system space has significantly increased. In Windows 2000, device drivers were limited to 220 MB; Windows Server 2003 supports up to 960 MB. Windows 2000 had a total system virtual address space of 660 MB, compared to the 128 GB of Windows Server 2003.

EXECUTIVE MANAGERS

The fourth segment of the Executive is a collection of tightly coupled applications. Known collectively as the Executive managers, they allow the subsystems and user applications to access system resources. Perhaps the biggest change since Windows 2000 is the inclusion of a Cache Manager, which replaces memory storage in paged pools, and the Configuration Manager, which now implements the Registry. The Executive managers are the following:

- *The Object Manager*. This manager is responsible for the creation, deletion, and interim management of object resources: files, directories, threads, processes, ports, semaphores, events, symbolic links, and shared memory.
- *The Virtual Memory Manager (VMM).* The VMM regulates the allocation of 32-bit or 64-bit linear memory. Windows 2003 supports virtual addressable memory—by default, half is allocated to system tasks and half to application workload. (Windows 2003 Enterprise and DataCenter Editions in certain configurations permit the shifting of memory allocation to allow additional dedicated memory for application support. Applications must be coded to use the Very Large Memory (VLM) APIs.) As required, the VMM pages information to disk or physical memory. It also regulates demand paging, which uses the physical hard drive to effectively expand total memory availability.
- *The Process Manager*. Windows Server support for program processes is controlled by threading. A thread is a logical sequence of instructions that is executed to completion or until a higher-priority thread temporarily preempts it. The Process Manager specifically monitors thread and related process objects. Later discussion will clarify the roles of threads and processes.
- *The Interprocess Communication Manager*. This Executive manager regulates both local procedure calls (LPCs) and remote procedure calls (RPCs). The Local Procedure Call Facility manages client and server communications within the

computer. As a local procedure that impacts system resources is launched from the user mode, the server elements in the kernel mode are called. The Remote Procedure Call Facility manages client/server communication across different computers.

- *Security Reference Monitor (SRM).* To create or gain access to an object, a request must first flow through the Security Reference Monitor (Figure 2.3). Unlike some of the other Executive managers, the SRM operates in both kernel and user modes. As discussed later, each Windows Server object has a descriptor known as the access control list (ACL). Each user and group with object rights is provided an individual access control entry (ACE) that contains its security ID (SID). Upon logging on, each user is assigned an access token that operates as a passkey to objects that match his or her entry levels. For greater detail, refer to Chapter 9, "Permissions Security, Folder Sharing, and Dfs."

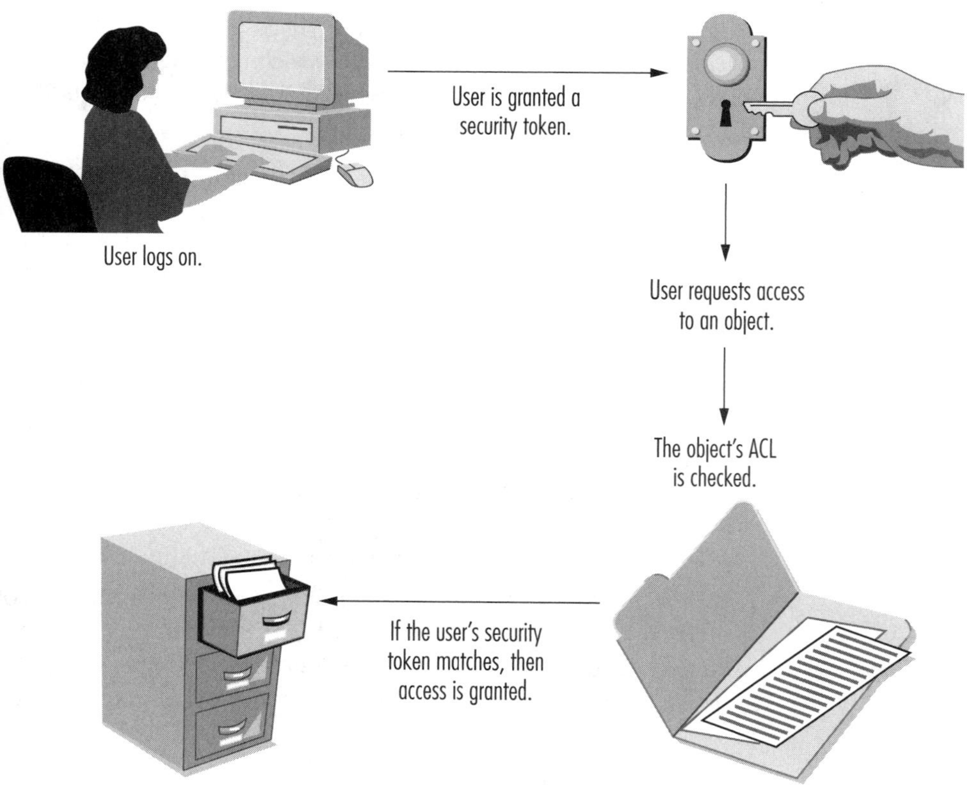

FIGURE 2.3 The Flow of Security Reference Monitoring

- *I/O Manager*. All input and output functions are controlled by the I/O Manager. These activities are broken into several components that regulate the input and output of the system cache, file system, network drivers, and specified devices (Figure 2.4).
- *Windows Manager and Graphics Device Drivers*. The Windows Manager and Graphics Device Drivers (GDDs) were moved from the user mode, where they resided in Windows NT 3.5 and earlier versions, to the kernel mode in Windows Server 2003. Applications can address the Win32K.sys interface; the GDD talks directly to HAL.
- *Plug and Play Manager*. The new Plug and Play Manager reduces the mundane system administration burden of identifying and configuring devices on the network. It activates devices and adds devices via automatic discovery or with the assistance of the Hardware Wizard.
- *Cache Manager*. This manager monitors pages faults that are required for disk reads and data already in memory. The operating system faults data and code into memory from disk in 4-KB page chunks and then releases before demand. The Cache Manager helps to prefetch pages. It also monitors the initial stages of an application startup (up to 10 seconds). The Cache Manager works in conjunction with the Task Scheduler to signal a named event, and it calls the Memory Manager to read data or code.
- *Configuration Manager*. This manager has been recoded to regulate between registry settings with the executive kernel-mode subsystem. It is designed to significantly increase the size of Registry hive (formerly 376 MB) and therefore

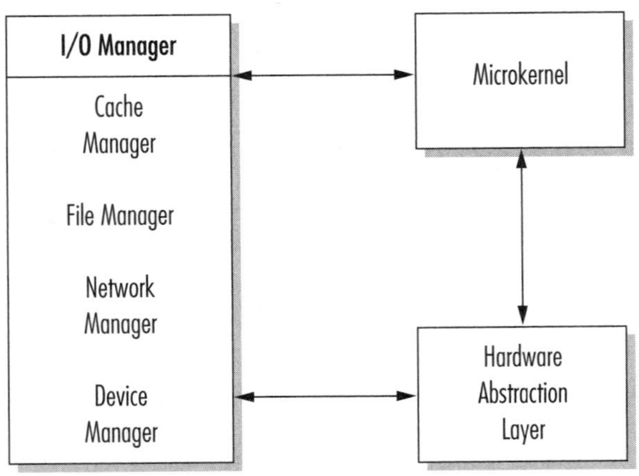

FIGURE 2.4 The I/O Manager

have no hard-coded limitations. This increases performance and adds greater support for Terminal Server systems. The Configuration Manager also plays a security role, maintaining its own cache of security descriptors that may be used by multiple keys.

- *Power Manager*. This manager regulates the power to computers and devices. In systems with power management client interfaces, Windows Server 2003 can automatically and remotely order a system to boot, shut down, or go into temporary hibernation.

THE EXECUTIVE SERVICES BUFFER

The Executive Services buffer consists of a relatively small layer of code that sits on top of the other Executive components. It separates the kernel and user modes and acts as the medium for passing API and system calls.

The Windows Server 2003 User Mode

The user mode comprises components that work together to facilitate user and application integrity. It has two parts:

- *Protected environmental subsystems*. Windows Server 2003 supports user-mode subsystems that maintain specific requirements for native Windows (16/32-bit and legacy MS-DOS), POSIX, and OS/2 applications as well as user-related system calls. An examination of protected subsystems follows.
- *Dynamic integral user intervention*. This part oversees the unprotected actions of individual users. We discuss the impact of this dynamic intervention when we deal with the processes later in this chapter.

THE PROTECTED USER MODE SYSTEM

The subsystem structure can be viewed as a buffer between user applications and the kernel-mode services structure. The term *protected* refers to these subsystems because they are not directly changed or modified by the administrator or the user but merely pass and manage API calls. They are configurable only through APIs and built-in utilities.

Windows Server 2003 supports two protected subsystems:

- The integral subsystem performs underlying operating system tasks—for example, security management.
- The environmental subsystem establishes the foundation for applications and user interfaces.

Integral Subsystems

The integral subsystems overlay and interact with the environmental subsystems. For example, the API that provides access to the network is either the Workstation Services or the Server Services subsystem, depending on the version of Windows Server installed. As another example, the integral Security subsystem acknowledges logon requests, authenticates logons, monitors the use of resources by a user, and manages user rights and permissions.

Environmental Subsystems

The user mode supports three environmental subsystems, as shown in Figure 2.5. The intent behind this was to provide support for applications originally written for other operating systems or to make porting of applications easier. Depending on the environmental subsystem, this "support" ranges from executing shrink-wrapped applications to merely providing programming APIs. With Windows Server 2003, this multiple environment subsystem support has been reduced.

Environmental subsystems may be thought of as operating system "multiple personalities." The Win32 subsystem provides native support for applications written to support Microsoft's 16- and 32-bit APIs. The other subsystems are a set of APIs that emulate other operating system calls.

- *Win32 subsystem.* Win32 is the mother of all subsystems. It supports standard Windows Server input and display output. Specifically, it controls the graphical user interface. All Win32 applications are run directly inside this subsystem. Win32 also takes on a type of arm's-length relationship with the other subsystems by switching personalities when necessary.

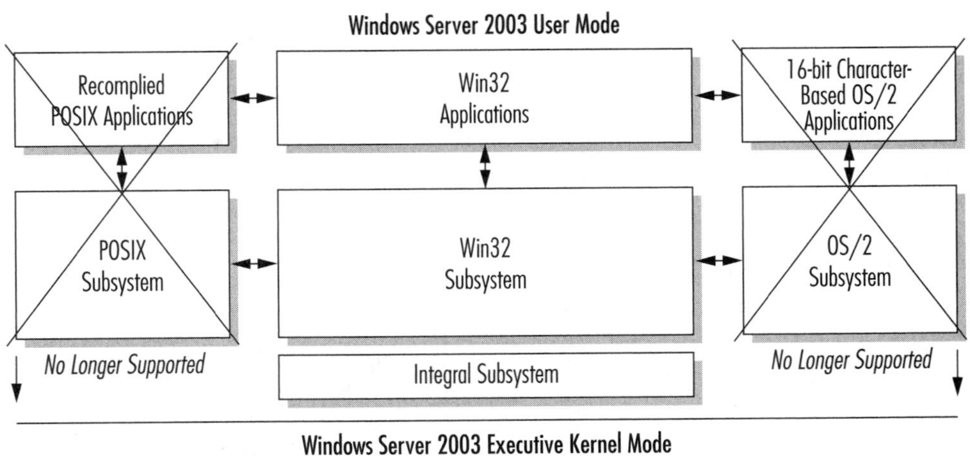

FIGURE 2.5 Windows Server 2003 Subsystem Relationships

MS-DOS and 16-bit applications use both the Virtual DOS Machine (VDM) and the Win32 system. The VDM is created automatically when these programs are launched. The application process technically runs as a VDM process, but its display handling is offloaded to Win32. Because API "stubs" support the old graphical drivers and dynamic-link libraries (DLLs), Win16 applications generally operate without affecting other operating system activities. It should be remembered that Windows Server 2003 is a preemptively multitasking operating system that supports numerous single processes simultaneously. In the case of Win16 applications, WOW, or Windows on Windows, defines the interplay between VDM and Win32.

- *OS/2 subsystem.* The OS/2 subsystem was available in Windows NT and Windows 2000 but is not supported on Windows Server 2003.
- *POSIX subsystem.* The Portable Operating System Interface computing environment subsystem was available in Windows NT and Windows 2000 but is not supported on Windows Server 2003.

For those interested in POSIX and UNIX interoperability, Microsoft has made available its Services for UNIX 3.0. This offers an assortment of third-party UNIX applications and utilities, including Korn and C shell support and NFS. By adding these features, it is possible to use many scripts written in a UNIX environment and move them directly across to Windows Server 2003. This is to be offered as part of an optional service package known as Microsoft Services for UNIX. The Interix code actually replaces Microsoft's POSIX subsystem and overlays a complete UNIX 95 environment within Windows. In this configuration, true operating system interoperability is achieved. It is also possible to migrate existing UNIX applications to Windows Server 2003 with comparative ease. Among the common UNIX features that Interix provides are the following:

- More than 300 UNIX commands and utilities
- Shell support for the Korn shell, Bourne shell, and C shell
- Scripting languages—awk, Perl, sed, Tcl/Tk—with full shell job control
- POSIX.1, POSIX.2, and ANSI C interfaces
- BSD sockets implemented with Winsock
- SVID IPC (message queues, semaphores)
- Shared memory, memory-mapped files
- ODBC and OpenGL application library support
- X11R5 Windowing System clients and libraries
- The X11R6.3 Windowing System display server

- X11R6 fonts and font management
- The OSF/Motif® 1.2.4 Window Manager and libraries
- Execution of Win32 applications from Microsoft Services for UNIX
- Full tty semantics mapped to console windows and pseudoterminal support
- Full integration with the Windows NT security model, administration, file systems, networking, and printers
- Telnetd and rlogind services (multiuser logon support)
- Berkeley r-utilities (servers and clients)

MKS and its DataFocus division's NutCRACKER development product also provide POSIX utilities and application porting directly to the Win32 API.

WINDOWS SERVER 2003 PROCESSES

Windows Server 2003 processes are viewable through a surprisingly simple yet informative set of graphical utilities. Using the Task Manager (with three equally helpful screens), the Event Viewer, the Services Manager, and the Resource-Kit-based Process Viewer, a system administrator can review and govern many of the process-oriented activities of the local server. The Task Manager can also rapidly address many performance issues. These tools effectively manage a robust process-oriented, multitasking, and multithreading operating system.

After reviewing this section, a system administrator should have sufficient baseline information to do the following:

- Understand Windows Server 2003 processes, threads, pipes, and handles.
- Use the Task Manager and Services Manager to identify, start, and kill processes.
- Use the Event Viewer to diagnose process success and failure.
- Employ the Process Viewer to ascertain priorities.
- Schedule processes.

Processes, Threads, and Handles

A Windows Server 2003 process is an executable that flows through a logical sequence of events until the appointed action is complete. Technically, an executable program is composed of the base code and related data, a dedicated memory address space, defined system resources, and at least one thread. A *thread* is the portion of the process being executed. It has a unique identification, its client ID, and a register that defines its microprocessor state. Every thread maintains reserved memory stacks for the execution in the user and kernel modes. It also has storage memory for interaction with other applications, DLLs, run-time libraries, and environmental subsystems.

Processes use threads to invoke an action with a reaction, pipes to connect threads, and semaphores to synchronize activities. Unlike UNIX processes, which involve exec/fork replication and parent/child relationships, Windows Server 2003 utilizes handles. Handles are assigned to threads and identify resources such as a Registry key used for access by a program. (Handles are also applied to events, semaphores, pipes, processes, and communications.)

A Windows Server 2003 process is treated as an object. As such it has a number of characteristics, including a virtual memory address, defined resources, and a security profile. Each process has one or more thread objects associated with its execution. As an object, the thread also has a unique memory stack and system state. The thread is an agent that does the bidding of the process. The Object Manager controls both process and thread objects.

When a new process is created, the CreateProcess() and CreateThread() calls are made. As additional threads are required to support a given process, other CreateThread() calls are invoked. The thread should be thought of as a unit of execution. Between the ends of the thread is a pipe, both ends of which must be open. If either end is broken, the process data is lost.

Windows Server 2003 also uses named pipes to transmit information. These pipes are viewed similarly to file objects and operate within the same security framework. A named pipe retains information in memory and dispenses the data as requested by a process. It acts like a regular data file, except that the information is in resident memory, not physically archived on disk. Figure 2.6 illustrates the hierarchy of processes.

Windows Server 2003 is a multitasking and multithreaded operating system. One of its strengths is its ability to manage and synchronize multiple threads. On a single-processor system, only one thread can execute at a time, but, as a result of context switching, it appears to the user that multiple threads are running. In this scheme (Figure 2.7), a thread executes until it has completed its task, is in-

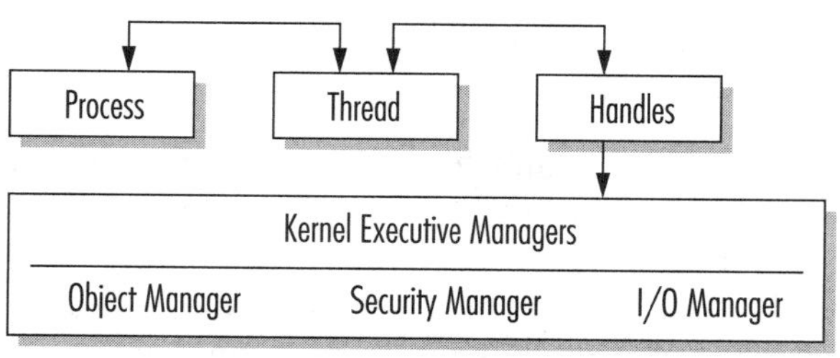

FIGURE 2.6 Process Hierarchy

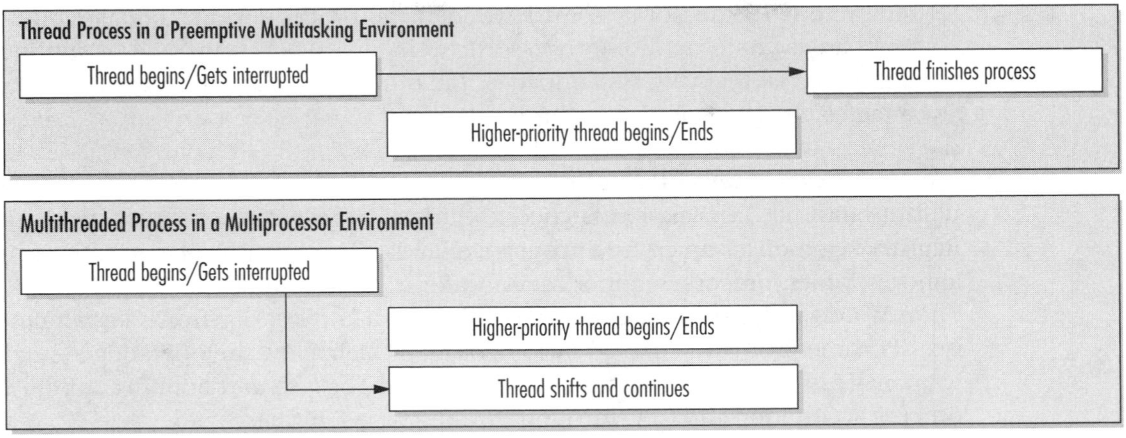

FIGURE 2.7 Single and Multiprocessor Preemptive Multitasking

terrupted by a thread with a higher priority, or waits for system resources. During an interruption, the Windows Server saves the "context" of the thread and reloads it when the CPU is free to continue.

Windows Server 2003 provides a robust process and thread priority facility. The programming API permits the setting of application process priorities, or states, that include idle, normal, high, and real-time; within each of these states two subpriorities can be established. It is important for a programmer to consider the impact of this facility on the entire system. There are 32 priority levels numbered 0 through 31. The first 16 (0–15) are reserved for the user mode, and the remainder are reserved for the kernel mode. After a base priority level is set for a process or a thread, the kernel may dynamically raise it in the event of user interaction. By the same token, the kernel can lower the priority rating for strictly computer-associated operations.

How long a thread is allowed to execute is controlled by a property known as a quantum. A quantum type can be of fixed or variable length. By default, Windows Server 2003 versions give priority to fixed-quanta background services, although Windows XP gives higher priority to applications that generally use variable-length quanta. In theory, these priorities provide greater smoothness to key multitasking functions of the respective environments.

MULTIPROCESSOR SUPPORT

Where processing load is significant, systems with more than one CPU can reduce thread executing wait times. Windows Server 2003 uses symmetric multiprocessing (SMP), which allows user and kernel-mode activities to use any available processor.

Symmetric multiprocessor systems have identical processors and functions. (By contrast, an asymmetric multiprocessor system allocates resources to a specific processor even if that CPU is overloaded and others are relatively free.) The clear advantage is the balancing of the processing load across all resources.

Process Accounting and CPU Throttling

With its Internet Information Services, Windows Server 2003 adds two features that make multiuser environments more efficient. The first is processor accounting, which measures the number of processor cycles consumed by Web requests. The second is CPU throttling, which restricts Web applications from overwhelming CPU time. Both are enabled by job objects, which allow the operating system to manage groups of processes as a single unit. The use and administration of process accounting and CPU throttling are discussed in Chapter 16.

Interprocess Communication

Interprocess communication (IPC) and remote procedure call (RPC) are basic to Windows Server 2003. (At the risk of being overly simplistic, RPC can be regarded as the distributed network version of IPC.) Microsoft claims that its implementation of RPC is compliant with Distributing Computing Environment (DCE).

Windows Server 2003 employs a direct relationship between processes and threads. At any given time, there is a producer and a consumer (similar to BSD socket library calls in UNIX). The objective is to achieve a very scalable operating system that permits easy load balancing of discrete measured threads. Windows Servers also employs a FIFO (first-in, first-out) message model.

Windows Server 2003 Component Services

A Windows Server 2003 service is a special class of process with fixed characteristics. The Component Services Manger is similar to the UNIX daemon in that they perform tasks defined as in either the foreground or the background. They can be managed either locally or remotely (Figure 2.8).

The Windows Server 2003 Component Services Manager provides the list of all defined services, their current status, and their status at startup. These services can be started, stopped, paused, continued, or defined for system startup with a simple mouse click.

To view or change the status of a service, press the **Start** menu → select **Programs** → select **Administrative Tools** → select **Computer Services**. In the left pane, click **Services**. All defined services on the system will appear in the right pane. Double-click a target service to view its properties. You can make changes or simply view the current status via four tabs: General, Logon, Recovery, and Dependencies.

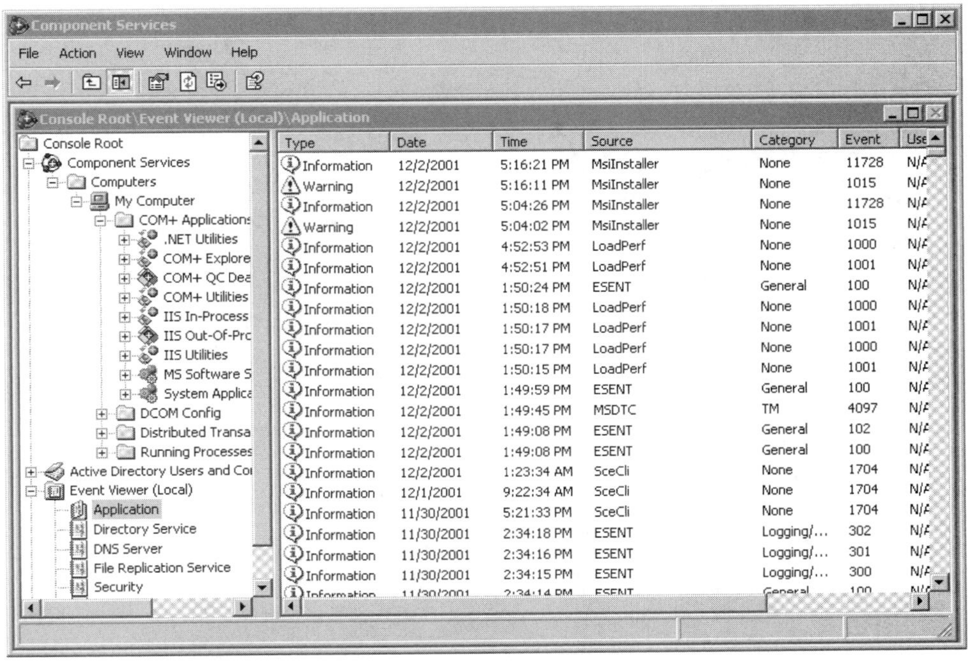

FIGURE 2.8 Windows Server 2003 Component Service Manager

The Task Manager

The Task Manager is a handy system administration tool that provides a snapshot of computer system activity. It is readily available to an administrator at any point during a logon session. The two most common methods of executing the Task Manager are:

1. Click the right mouse button on the **Task** bar and select **Task Manager**.
2. Press CTRL+ALT+DEL and select **Task Manager** from the Windows Server Security window.

The Task Manager provides four window tabs for Windows XP and five tabs for Windows Server 2003 and provides very different views of operating system process activities:

- The Applications window permits the view and control of all user-mode applications. Applications may be responsible for one or more processes (Figure 2.9).

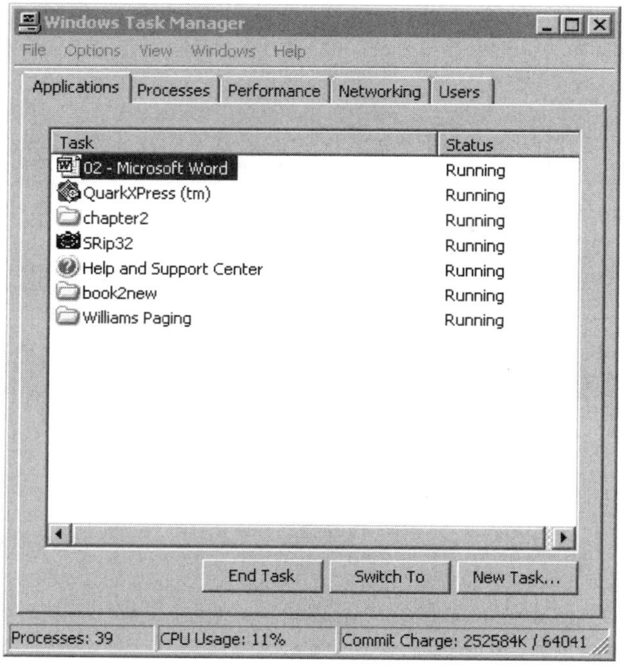

FIGURE 2.9 The Task Manager Applications Window

- The Processes window provides in-depth information about individual processes, including resource utilization.
- The Performance window provides a graphical and numeric view of the system based on the current application and process load.
- The Networking tab identifies the amount of current network activity on the computer.
- The Users tab (Windows Server 2003 only) identifies local users and remote users by name, ID, activity status, and client system name.

A simple dissection of the Applications window shows the application name in the first column followed by the current status. The bottom set of buttons permits the administrator to **End Task**, **Switch to** another task, or invoke a **New Task.** At the bottom of the screen is a system summary status that includes a number of open processes, CPU usage, and memory utilization.

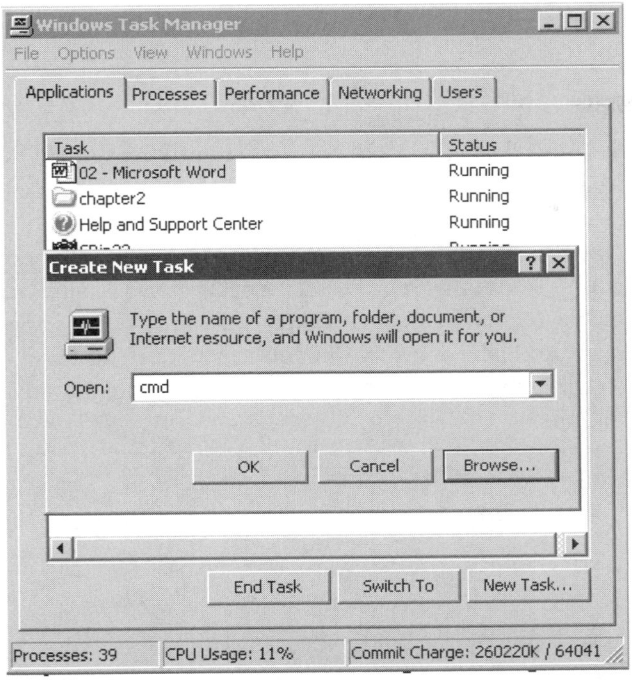

FIGURE 2.10 The New Task Dialog Box

STARTING AND KILLING PROCESSES

Invoking an application from an icon or command-line instruction ordinarily starts processes. As discussed in a later section, processes can also be initiated through scheduling services like the At utility. The Task Manager can start a new task as well if this option is selected at the bottom of the screen. When **New Task** is selected, a new dialog box, such as that shown in Figure 2.10, appears.

Ordinarily, processes are terminated by the graceful exit of the application through its own kill signals. However, from time to time more radical solutions are required. Processes can be easily killed using the Task Manager. In the Applications window, simply highlight the offending process and select **End Task** at the bottom of the screen. In the Processes window, select **End Process**, also at the bottom of the screen. In both cases, a confirming message will appear before termination. At this point, all handles, threads, and pipes are destroyed and data being transmitted is lost.

Figure 2.11 provides a real-time view of network utilization on the local client or server system.

NOTE Administrators coming from the UNIX environment occasionally face a runaway process known as a zombie. Microsoft claims that zombies will not occur in Windows Server 2003 because its processes do not use the parent/child relationship inherent in UNIX. Each Windows Server process is discrete and independent of the presence or health of a parent. While this may be technically true, certainly some processes (generated by either Microsoft or third-party software) begin sapping very large amounts of memory and become very difficult to kill. Use the Task Manager or the Process Viewer to kill such processes. On rare occasions, you may have to invoke the action more than once.

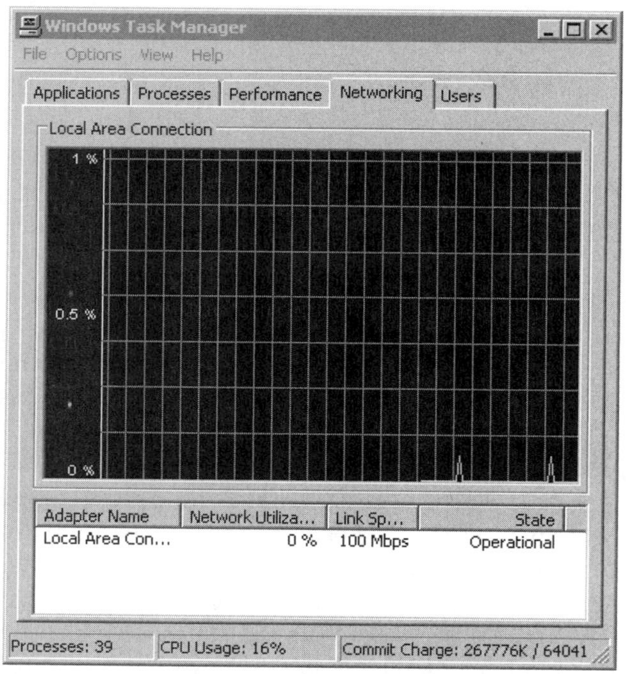

FIGURE 2.11 Task Manager Local Area Connection Monitor

SCHEDULING TASKS

Early versions of Windows NT supported the UNIX-like utility known as the **at** command. This command is still supported, but its functions are greatly enhanced by the Task Scheduler. The Task Scheduler and the **at** command can work together, which is important for older scripts that rely on **at**. When a task is invoked by the **at** command, it appears in the list in the Scheduled Tasks window. The Task Scheduler also can use **at** to run tasks automatically.

The **at** program is invoked from the CMD command line for single-event scheduling. The **at** command schedules commands and programs to run on a computer at a specific time and date. The Schedule service must be running to use the **at** command.

Scheduled Tasks are accessible from Control Panel. The Scheduled Tasks Setup (Figure 2.12) is invoked by double-clicking this icon. Tasks are added by dragging scripts, programs, or documents from Windows Explorer or the desktop to the Scheduled Tasks window. They can also be deleted or modified this way.

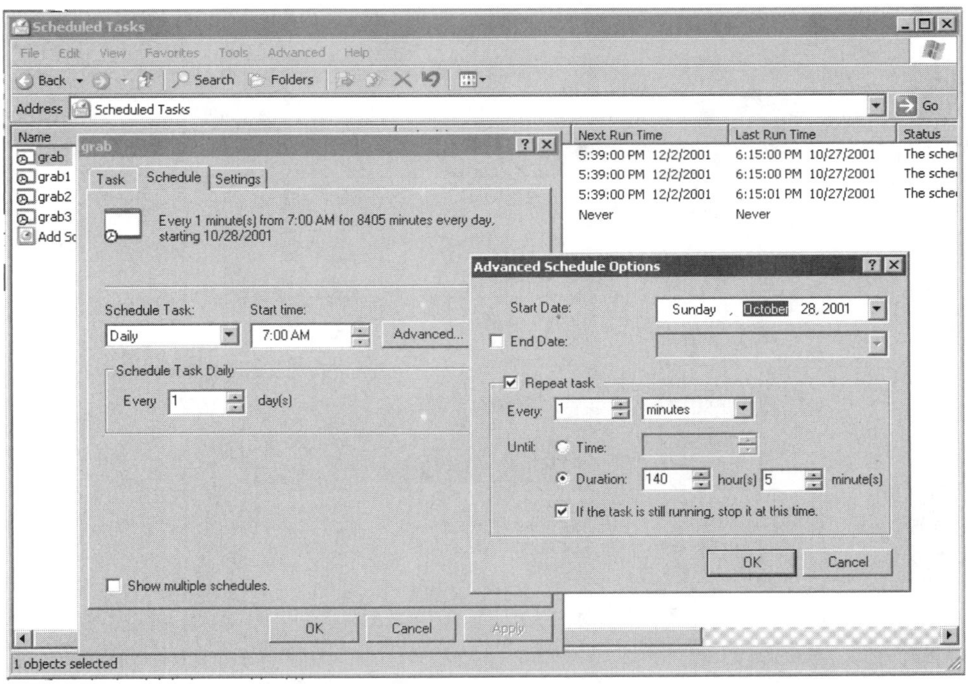

FIGURE 2.12 The Scheduled Tasks Setup Window

VIEWING PROCESSES

The Processes window provides system administrators with a very good snapshot of their system's activity. Its default screen has five process checkpoints: Image Name, User Name, Session ID, CPU, and MEM Usage (Figure 2.13). A total of 22 items may be selected for analysis by changing **Select Columns** in the **View** menu. When the dialog box appears, use the mouse to click the additional reporting parameters. If all options are selected, the system administrator has a reasonably comprehensive view of active processes and their impact on the overall system, as shown in Figure 2.14.

The Task Manager Performance screen (Figure 2.15) displays four graphical representations and four boxes of numeric data for the entire system:

- *CPU Usage* shows current CPU utilization (in this example, the CPU has reached a critical utilization state).
- *CPU Usage History* is a longer-term view generally showing CPU usage over time. Unfortunately, in this window there is no ability to change time intervals or to save or print this information. A tool to refine this view can be accessed by pressing **Start → Programs → Administrative Tools → Performance**.

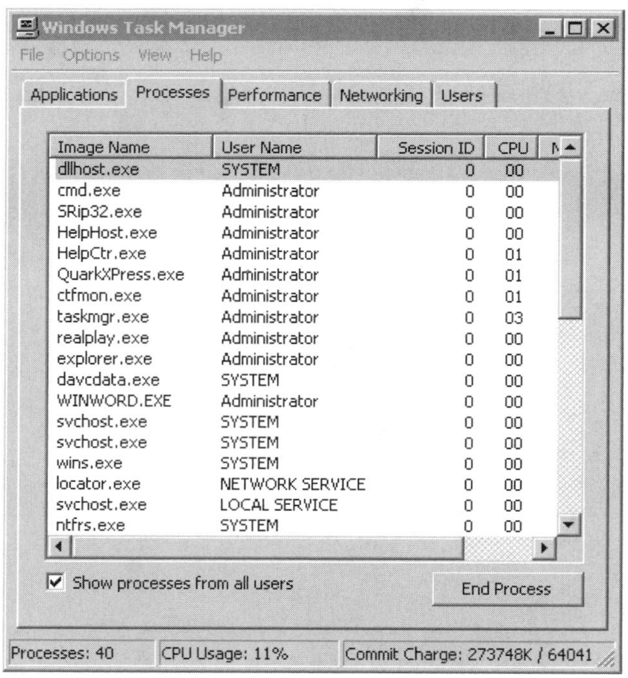

FIGURE 2.13 The Task Manager Process List

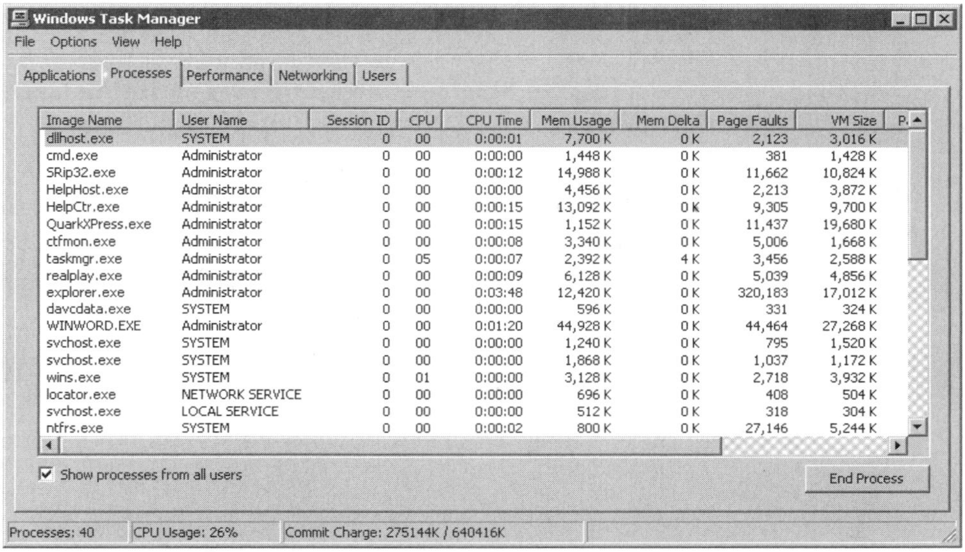

FIGURE 2.14 Expanded View of Process Activities

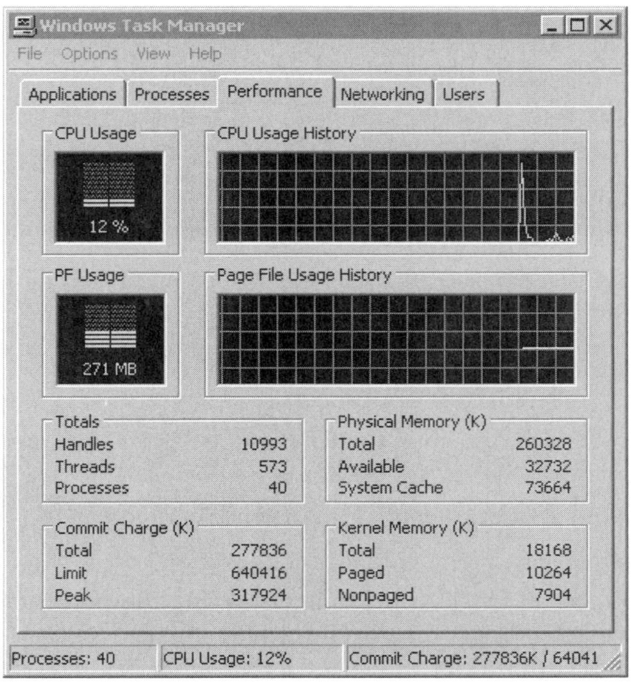

FIGURE 2.15 The Task Manager Performance Window

- *PF Usage* shows utilization based on pagefiles.
- *PF History* shows fluctuation of pagefile usage over time. You can refine this view by pressing **Start** → **Programs** → **Administrative Tools** → **Performance**.
- *Totals* shows the number of open handles, threads, and processes.
- *Physical Memory* summarizes the system memory defined as a total, currently available, and cache available in kilobytes.
- *Commit Charge* shows the total memory allocated to programs, the system limit, and peak memory, including swap memory.
- *Kernel Memory* defines the total memory allocated to kernel-mode activities, broken down by paged and nonpaged events.

New performance tools available with Windows Server 2003 include:

- Disk input and output (I/O)
- Memory management (e.g., working set management, page fault)
- Image load and unload
- Process and thread activities such as process create, thread create, and context switching
- Registry
- Driver delays
- Pool allocations
- Heap allocations
- Central profiling that examines both kernel-mode and user-mode activities

Monitoring processor activity is effectively accomplished by looking at the Process and System object counters. In addition to providing information on utilization, it can pinpoint bottlenecks. The specific items you should examine are:

- Processor\% Processor Time for processor usage
- Optionally, you can also monitor Processor\% User Time and % Privileged Time along with % Processor Time for more detail
- System\Processor Queue Length for bottleneck detection

The Processor\% Processor Time counter is used to gauge the activity of the processor. Look specifically at the counter showing the percentage of elapsed time that a processor is busy executing a non-idle thread.

An examination of processor usage is not straightforward. For example, high processor values could indicate either the efficient handling of a heavy workload or a struggle to keep up. Typically, you will need to understand which applications cause peak processor loads such as software that involves heavy computations. When these applications are churning, anticipate peak loads. If this becomes a problem that impacts other applications, then workload scheduling is appropriate. By contrast, if the processor is peaking because many clients are using the system, then consider adding system resources or offloading some users to another system.

A processor bottleneck simply occurs when too many threads place demands on the processor. A processor queue develops as the threads back up. CPU-bound applications and driver components are notorious for creating bottlenecks. The System\Processor Queue Length counter is used to determine the existence of bottlenecks. A queue of two or more items indicates a bottleneck over time (a snapshot of a number higher than 4 should also be considered a critical bottleneck number.) When this occurs, you have only a couple of options. From a hardware perspective, you can get a faster processor or add a processor. Alternatively, you can restrict application and user activity.

Interrupt activities can also cause a bottleneck. The Processor\Interrupts/sec counter measures the rate of service requests from I/O devices. An increase of the counter value without a corresponding jump in system activity suggests a hardware problem. The Processor\% Interrupt Time is also a modestly good indicator of the interrupt activity of disk drivers, network adapters, and other devices.

NOTE Windows Server 2003 has new Performance security groups. Members of the Performance Monitor Users group can monitor performance counters on the server locally and from remote clients. Members of the Performance Log Users group can manage performance counters, logs, and alerts on the server locally and from remote clients. These features permit the delegation of responsibilities without granting full administrative rights.

Performance Monitoring of Multiple Servers

Windows Server 2003 allows administrators to collect performance counter data for a group of servers. All performance objects, counters, and instances can be utilized.

The select multiple objects in Performance Monitor (PerfMon) permit visualization and analysis of performance data. Specifically, this feature supports log monitoring and alerts services. To invoke this feature: **Start → Control Panel → Performance and Maintenance → Administrative Tools → Performance → System Monitor**.

It is important to note that this feature is not available in SysMon for real-time monitors because there is too much data.

Command-Line Options

Windows Server 2003 adds performance control command-line tools. They include functions that provide management of the control performance counter, event trace log scheduling, and collection and analysis on local and remote computers. These functions are accomplished without the need for the System Monitor (Sysmon) UI. The new tools and the functions they allow managers to perform are:

- *Logman*—Start, stop, query, and schedule performance data and event trace log collection.
- *Relog*—Given specified intervals, sample performance counter logs to extract specific counters and write to a new log file in a different format.
- *Tracerpt*—Report and analyze process kernel, Active Directory, and other transaction-based trace event logs.
- *Typeperf*—Write performance data to the command line every "*n*" samples.

These command-line tools are available by typing the command in the command prompt window.

THE EVENT VIEWER

The Event Viewer provides a defined log for both normal and abnormal system events. It can be one of the most valuable system administrative tools for troubleshooting problems. A regular analysis of these logs should be undertaken if system problems are suspected.

In Windows an *event* is any system occurrence that requires notification. One type of event recorded in the Event Viewer system log is a dysfunctional driver or load failure (Figure 2.16). The Source column identifies the application that initiated the message. The Category classifies the event as being related to security, object access, logon/logoff, detail tracking, system, policy changes, account management, and miscellaneous (none).

The level of importance of an event message is shown as an icon in the extreme left column: Error, Informational, Warning, Success Audit, and Failure Audit. This application can be launched from the Event Viewer for the local system by clicking the **Start** menu → selecting **Run** → typing **eventvwr** → clicking **Enter**. Alternatively, the Event Viewer is available from Administrative Tools.

The Event Viewer has a very flexible set of options that permits long-term tracking of system, security, and application problems. These options are described in Table 2.1.

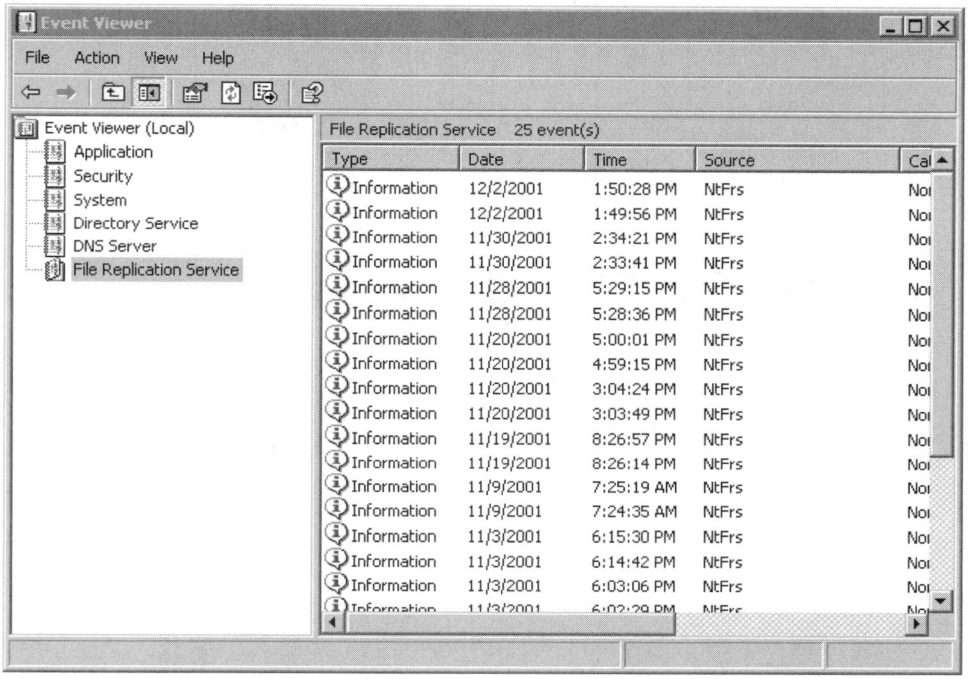

FIGURE 2.16 The Event Viewer Screen

To review details, highlight the item in the right detail panel and double-click. The appropriate event properties window will then be displayed for analysis and action. As seen in Figure 2.17, a significant amount of information is provided to

TABLE 2.1 Event Viewer Options

Option	Description
Logging	Rolls events as needed; removes events after a defined number of days; prohibits overwriting of events (requires manual event removal).
Sorting	Sorts events based on categories, sources, user, or machine.
Archiving	Saves event records in native Event format (*.EVT) or in normal or comma-delimited ASCII text (*.TXT) format.
Details	Provides additional information on the event.
Filtering	Filters desired events or characteristics.
Find	Locates events based on type, category, source, computer, or other criteria.

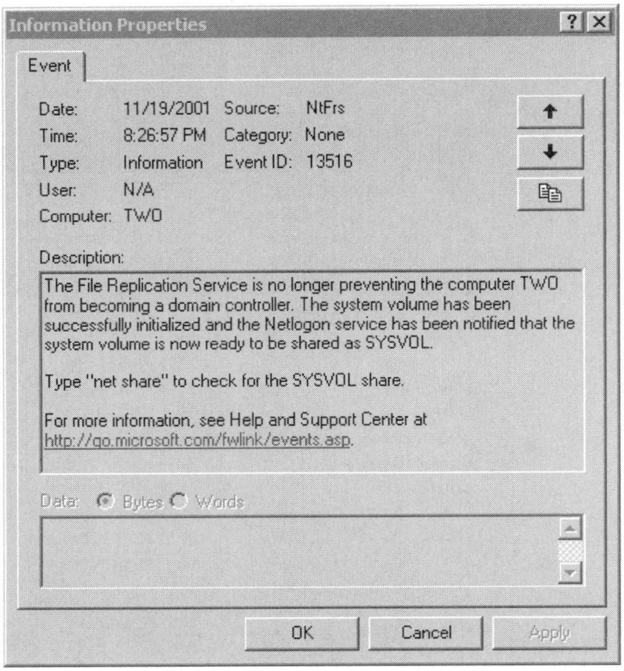

FIGURE 2.17 Event Log Properties

permit zeroing in on the precise location of the event. If a warning or error occurs, appropriate action can then be taken.

NOTE In Windows 2000, the Event Viewer feature was introduced that allowed Event Log error messages to manually add hyperlinks to Web sites by changing .RC and .MC files. Windows Server 2003 automatically adds a standard phrase and a Uniform Resource Locator (URL) to each message with the message properties dialog initialization. In addition, an optional string value can be added to the registry to specify the target URL.

NOTE System logs are essential to system performance analysis. Windows Server 2003 provides the generation of Perf Logs to the size of 1 GB. With a new file format, these logs can be appended to an existing log file.

STORED AND VIRTUAL MEMORY

Stored memory is the storage of data bits on devices such as a hard drive. Its management is predicated on the type of file system being used. The role and dynamics of storage for Windows Servers vary radically among the native NT File System (NTFS), the file allocation table (FAT), and FAT32. In general, stored memory is designated as "storable" and "retrievable archival." All three file system types are supported on x86 computer systems.

Virtual memory is defined as dynamic or temporary. *Physical memory,* known as random access memory (RAM), combines with temporary disk storage. For example, if a process requires more memory than is available from the system's RAM, the hard drive is used to temporarily store process data. It uses a set of temporary registers where information about processes is stored during execution. This is known as *paging*.

Stored Memory and File System Basics

Windows Server 2003 supports three file systems, NTFS, FAT, and FAT32, each of which has unique characteristics. For base-level security we have already established the clear advantage of native NTFS. However, under some circumstances, such as a need to switch between older Windows versions and Windows Server 2003, the FAT file system is necessary. FAT32 is an expanded version of FAT that allows larger disk partitions and is used primarily in the Windows 98 operating system. The relative merits of the three file systems are examined in detail in Chapter 14, but a brief review is appropriate at this stage.

THE FILE ALLOCATION TABLE: FAT AND FAT32

For the sake of this discussion, FAT and FAT32 are viewed as the same system except where specifically noted.

A file allocation table, FAT, is a simple file system that dates back to the days when the 5 1⁄4-inch floppy drive was the default medium and a 10-MB hard drive was an expensive luxury. In many cases, a system administrator may install Windows Server 2003 using FAT because of legacy MS-DOS or Windows 3.x applications that simply have not been updated to take advantage of Win32 functionality. FAT32, introduced to support Windows 98, is simply an extension of FAT with additional 32-bit application support.

A number of limitations, such as reduced security, are inherent in FAT and FAT32. Even so, these file systems are acceptable for legacy environments. One very nice feature Microsoft has included is the ability to convert the file system from FAT to NTFS (but not vice versa) when appropriate. This is accomplished by invoking the **convert** command from the Virtual DOS Machine with the following syntax:

```
CONVERT [drive:] /fs:ntfs [/nametable:filename]
Where filename is the name of file that is created during the
conversion process that contains a name translation table for unusual
filenames.
```

The file allocation table includes the following basic information about a file:

- The name of the file or directory (folder) with a structured maximum 8-character name and a 3-character mandatory extension, known as the 8.3 format
- A pointer to the physical location of the first byte of data associated with the file
- The size of the file in bytes
- The designation of the file's attributes as hidden, read-only, archive, or system-based

In the context of file storage on a disk or partition, the FAT hierarchy is very simple (Figure 2.18). The first sector contains the machine BIOS block followed by the file allocation table and a duplicate image. The root directory is the first set of information visible to a user. Individual files are stored in the root directory or in created subdirectories.

THE NTFS FILE SYSTEM

NTFS was introduced with Windows NT 3.1 as an outgrowth of the original OS/2 High-Performance File System (HPFS). With the introduction of Windows NT Server 4.0, the NTFS file system has taken a giant leap forward in terms of stability

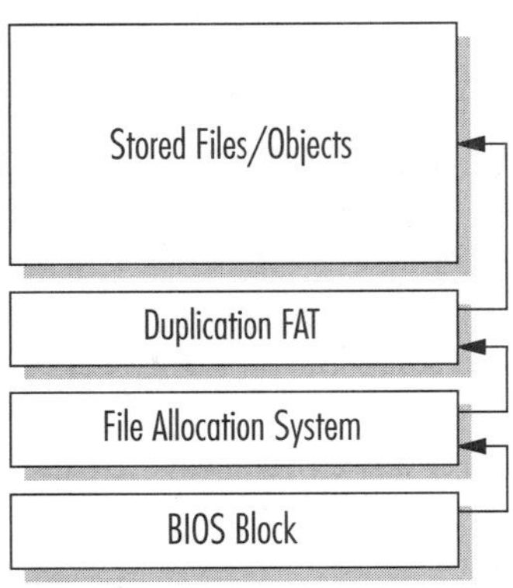

FIGURE 2.18 Disk Structure of the FAT File System

and flexibility. It boasts numerous advantages over the FAT file system, including the following:

- *Superior security* extends to files, processes, and user access protection.
- *Fault tolerance* uses a redundant array of inexpensive disks (RAID 1-5) to create duplicates of all files on servers. If a bad partition is detected, for example, Windows Server 2003 can use these copies to create a new sector.
- *Unicode* supports file names, dedicating 16 bits per character with a maximum of 255 characters. This facilitates internationalization. FAT supports only 8 characters using 7- or 8-bit ASCII and ANSI standards.
- *Master File Table redundancy* ensures recovery of system data in the case of corruption.
- *32-bit virtual memory support* has 2 GB allocated to system requirements and 2 GB to applications.
- *File name length* is 255 characters but also automatically generates the shorter DOS files names for backward compatibility.

NOTE Windows Server 2003 tightens the security of NTFS by providing only the administrator the right to write to the root directory. In previous versions, Everyone has full control in the root directory. The tightened security also prevents anyone other than administrators from modifying files in the root directory that were created by other users.

The NTFS file system maintains a number of key files that should not be removed or unnecessarily modified. Table 2.2 summarizes several of the most important keys.

TABLE 2.2 NTFS Files

File	Description
$	Root directory name
$Bitmap	Bitmap representation used by MFT for tracking volume contents
$Boot	Boot file listing bootable volumes
$Mft	Master File Table (MFT)
$MftMirr	MFT mirror
$Volume	Volume name and version information

NTFS Version 5 Differences

The Windows Server 2003 implementation of NTFS is version 5, which differs in a number of ways from the NTFS used in Windows NT for versions before Service Package 4. It is not backward compatible. Rather, during installation, if NTFS 4.0 is detected on a disk, it is upgraded to version 5.

One of the principal differences between NTFS version 5 and earlier versions is that NTFS 5 can undertake something akin to symbolic linking through the use of reparse points. The *reparse point* is 16 KB of data that takes the form of a tag that identifies the device driver. When a Windows Server 2003 NTFS process sees a reparse point tag, it redirects the action to the defined device driver. A *symbolic link* is a special type of reparse point used to redirect the NTFS process to a specified file or directory.

NTFS 5 has a useful link-tracking facility. Anytime a linked item is moved anywhere within the same domain, the link is tracked and remains intact.

NTFS 5 also supports disk quotas. These quotas are important because they permit regulation of disk usage. The specific management of disk quotas is discussed in Chapter 14.

Another important enhancement with NTFS 5 is support for the Encrypting File System (EFS). When a user wants to encrypt a file, a file encryption key (FEK) is generated. The Windows Server 2003 EFS uses an extended variant of the Data Encryption Standard algorithm (DESX).

NTFS 5 expands support of the CD-ROM File System (CDFS) that was based on a read-only principle. It now supports the Universal Data Format (UDF), which is emerging as the DVD-ROM format.

Finally, NTFS 5 supports FAT32 drives. Windows NT should not interpret FAT32 partitions or drives, nor can it boot from a FAT32 partition. Windows Server 2003 NTFS overcomes both of these limitations.

FILE OBJECTS IN THE NTFS FILE SYSTEM

NTFS boasts a relational database structure that uses B-trees to organize and stream file object management. Microsoft publishes precious little information about the internal structure of this database, known as the Master File Table (MFT), although it is the first line in an NTFS partition. The *MFT* is in a mirrored format for redundancy. Pointers from the boot sector describe the location of the MFT and its mirror.

Think of the MFT as the trunk of the B-tree in which small files and directory data are stored in residence (Figure 2.19). Large files and directories are stored as nonresident in extents (branch extensions) or runs (runners). Nonresident data can cross multiple extents or runs.

File and directory objects are similar in structure and use the same form for defining information sometimes known as metadata; however, their back ends dif-

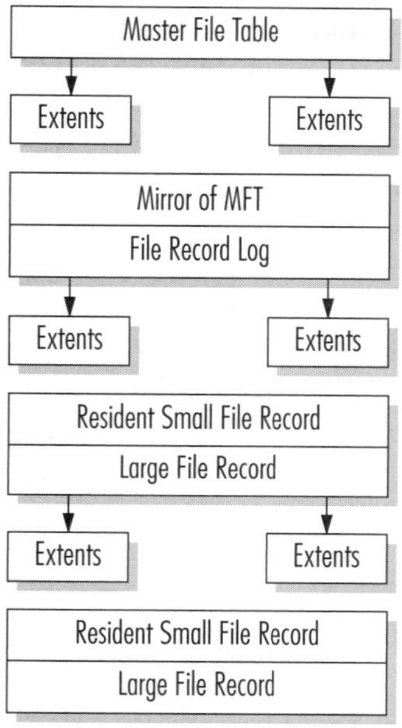

FIGURE 2.19 A Simplified View of the MFT Structure

fer. The NTFS treats directory objects as a special form of file object. Both files and directories contain standard attributes, a file name, and security descriptors (Figure 2.20). Files also include raw data that is otherwise not managed by the operating system. The directory object holds indexes of the relative location and size of the directory, plus a bitmap representation of the directory structure. The term *bitmap* does not refer to the kind of bitmap graphic commonly known to any PC user; here the bitmap is utilized by the database as a kind of road map depiction of the structure.

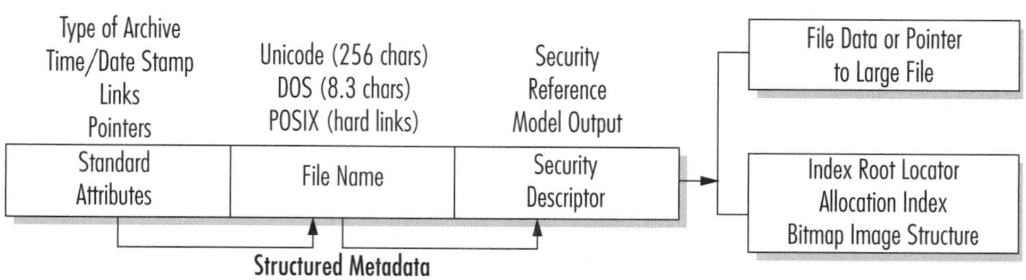

FIGIRE 2.20 The NTFS View of Files and Directories

File names follow a specific convention depending on the file system; FAT has an 8-character maximum with a 3-character extension (8.3) and NTFS has a maximum of 255 characters. Directories are separated in all cases with the backslash (\). Windows NT directories are similar to UNIX directories in that they are a special form of file object that merely maintains information about the files they manage.

The NTFS database structure facilitates system recovery, which is not available with the file allocation table. NTFS's transaction database methodology employs a logging process to initiate disk-writing instructions. Data enters cache memory, where it is then directed to the VMM for background or lazy writing to disk. The VMM sends the data to the fault-tolerant driver (assuming the existence of a RAID structure), which then attempts to physically write to the drive. If it is successful, the transaction in the database is released. If not successful, the record of the logged process is retained in the transaction table until restoration.

The Virtual Memory Manager and Paging

Windows Server 2003 uses a flat 32-bit virtual and linear memory scheme, reserving half of the capacity for system resources and half for applications. It allows tuning of addressable memory for applications, which was unavailable to Windows NT. For information on how this is accomplished for your version of the operating system, examine the Help files. The VMM allocates each process an address space, which is then mapped to physical memory in 4-KB pages (Figure 2.21). As memory is required, the system swaps between physical memory (hardware RAM) and pageable memory stored on the hard drive.

The VMM provides memory mapping through a table that defines virtual addresses. It also regulates the paging process—the movement from physical to disk memory. The area on a disk drive where paging occurs is known as the *pagefile*, the proper sizing of which can be critical to overall system performance. By default, Windows Server 2003 sets up a pagefile equal to the amount of installed RAM plus 12 MB (unless the available disk space is less than that formula). The mini-

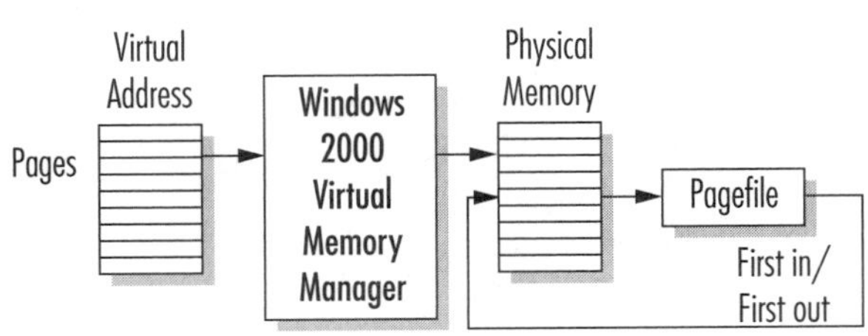

FIGURE 2.21 Virtual Memory and Paging

mum pagefile size is 2 MB. Since hard drive space is relatively inexpensive, we recommend expanding the pagefile if system performance becomes an issue.

Pagefile size is changed in the following steps after you log on as the administrator: Open **Control Panel** → double-click the **System** icon → select **Advanced System Properties** → click **Performance** → click **Change** → if multiple drives are listed in the **Drive** box, select the drive containing the pagefile → in the **Initial Size** box, increase or decrease the amount → click **Set** → click **OK** to close the **Virtual Memory** box → click **OK** on the **Performance Options** box → click **OK** on the **Systems Property** box. The computer must be restarted for the change to take effect.

THE BOOT PROCESS

The Windows Server 2003 booting sequence involves a series of system configuration checks, hardware activation, and application loading. The following lists the boot process:

- *Power on self-test (POST)* checks whether key hardware elements are present, such as sufficient memory, keyboard, video card, and so forth.
- *Startup initialization* checks the hard drive's first sector for the Master Boot Record (MBR) and partition table. If either is missing or corrupted, the process terminates.
- *Memory switch and system driver load.* An operating system load driver, Ntldr, instructs the microprocessor to convert from real mode to protected memory mode used by Windows Server 2003. Appropriate system drivers are then started that are actually built into Ntldr and that identify the type(s) of file system(s) present.
- The *boot loader* permits the selection of the desired environment where there are multiple operating systems on the system. The system looks for Ntldr in the root directory (by reading Boot.ini and invoking Ntdetect.com and Bootsect.dos). A typical boot loader screen (for a dual-boot environment) is shown here. (A single boot screen would show only Windows Server.)

```
Please select the operating system to start:
    Windows Server 2003 (or Standard, Enterprise, DataCenter, Web)
    Windows 2000
Use ≠ and Ø to move the highlight to your choice.
Click Enter to choose.
Seconds until highlighted choice will be started automatically is: 23
```

Boot.ini is divided into two sections: boot loader and operating systems. The boot loader defines the number of seconds before an automatic load of the default operating system (whose path is defined in the next line). The operating system lists the environments available for initiation. In this case, two modes of Windows Server 2003 and Windows 98 are available.

The Boot.ini file is set as read-only, system, and hidden to prevent unwanted editing. To change the Boot.ini timeout and default settings, use the **System** option in **Control Panel** from the **Advanced** tab and select **Startup** (Figure 2.22).

NOTE If Windows 98 rather than Windows Server 2003 is selected at this stage, Ntldr executes Bootsect.dos. This file contains an image of the boot sector as it existed prior to installation of Windows Server. At this stage, the boot processes inherent in Windows 98 take control.

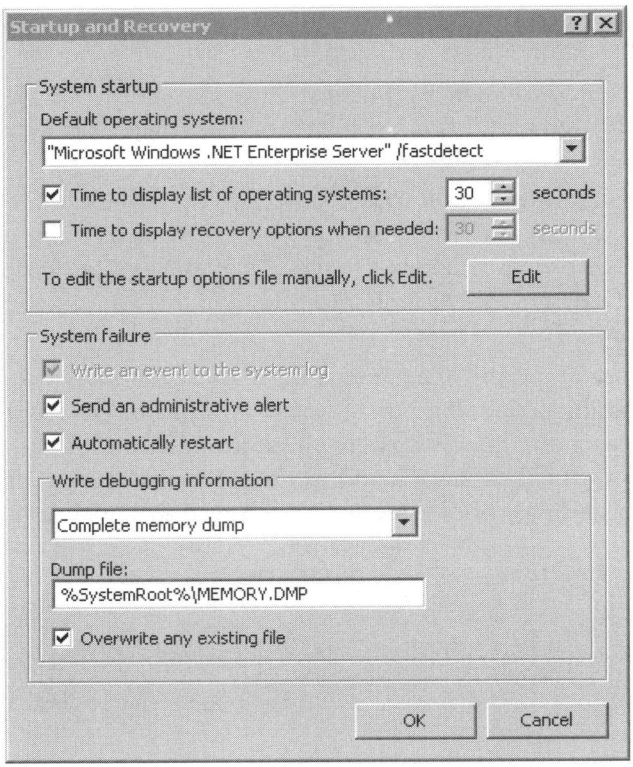

FIGURE 2.22 The System Option Screen to Change Boot.ini Timing and Default

CAUTION Dual booting, although obviously possible, is generally not recommended. A number of security issues arise in a dual-boot environment. The dual boot is generally used only if a legacy application is not supported by Windows Server 2003.

- *The hardware configuration review*. At this stage, information about the system and attached devices is gathered by Ntdetect.com. This information is later included in the Windows Server Registry as HKEY_LOCAL_MACHINE\HARDWARE.
- *Kernel load and preliminary initialization*. As dots are drawn across the computer screen, Windows Server loads the kernel with Ntosknrl.exe and the hardware abstraction layer's Hal.dll. The Windows Server Registry HKEY-LOCAL_MACHINE\SYSTEM is then loaded. Ntldr loads device drivers with a value of 0x0 and is specified in the Registry as HKEY_LOCAL_MACHINE\SYSTEM.
- *Kernel initialization*. The actual initialization of the kernel occurs when the blue screen appears and identifies the Windows Server version and build number and your system configuration. Behind the scenes several activities occur. First, a Registry key for hardware is created from the gathered information as HKEY_LOCAL_MACHINE\HARDWARE. This is where hardware system specs and device interrupts are stored. A clone set of system references is created and remains unchanged within the Registry HKEY_LOCAL_MACHINE\SYSTEM\Select subkey. The kernel initializes devices after scanning the Registry for HKEY_LOCAL_MACHINE\SYSTEM\CurrentControlSet\Services.

NOTE Depending on severity, the boot process may continue or fail if errors are detected in the initialization of devices. There are four levels of error control values. With an ErrorValue of 0x0, the boot process continues uninterrupted. An ErrorValue of 0x1 is not sufficiently critical to halt the boot process, but warning messages are displayed. A severe ErrorValue of 0x3 causes a failure in the boot process. At this stage, the system automatically restarts and uses the LastKnownGood control set, and then continues the boot process. The critical ErrorValue of 0x4 halts the process and attempts to restart, as with 0x3. A 0x4 message will then be displayed if the LastKnownGood control set also is defective.

- *Starting of services*. The Session Manager (smss.exe) launches the subsystems and services that are defined to start immediately.
- *User logon*. The Win32 subsystem starts the Winlogon.exe and then the Local Security Authority (lsass.exe). The Service Controller scans the HKEY_LOCAL_

MACHINE\SYSTEM\Set\Services subkey for all service start entries. Two additional subkeys are scanned: DependOnGroup and DependOnService. The system is ready to use when the Begin Logon box appears with instructions to press CTRL+ALT+DEL to log on. Windows Server 2003 does not consider the startup procedure complete until the first user has logged on.

NOTE During the initial boot phase, it is possible to enter an alternative boot sequence and invoke the Advanced Menu system. When F8 is pressed during the initial sequences, the **Advanced** menu is displayed, which is used strictly for repair and maintenance activities. It permits you to invoke the system in safe mode, Enable Boot Logging, Enable VGA Mode, or Last Known Good configurations. In the "Disaster Management" section of Chapter 14, we discuss how these options are applied. We also discuss other system recovery methods.

THE WINDOWS SERVER 2003 REGISTRY

The Windows Server 2003 Registry is a database that contains operating system, hardware, and software information for the local computer system. It is used by many programs, including the Windows Server kernel, device drivers, setup, and detection executables. One example of the type of information stored in the Registry is a list of all properly installed applications. Therefore, when you double-click a file name with the Windows Server Explorer, its extension is matched with a list of installed applications and launches the appropriate software. Other items stored in the Registry include:

- Hardware configuration data
- Program group and desktop settings for each user
- User profile data
- Local language and time settings
- Network configuration data
- Security information for users and groups
- ActiveX and OLE server data

NOTE The relationship between the Registry and the Active Directory is very close. The Registry maintains information for the local system, and the Active Directory provides object information about the domain network as a whole.

The Registry Structure

The Registry is based on a logical hierarchy of information, beginning with five subtrees known as keys. The concept of keys and subkeys follows the same principle as folders and subfolders within a directory tree. Every key and subkey has at least one entry that contains its name, data type, and configuration value (Table 2.3).

The keys and subkeys are stored in collections known as hives. Hive files are stored in %systemroot%\System32\Config or for user data in \%systemroot%\Profile\username. When changes are made to the Registry data, the data is compared to the logs before it is written. The log file is written first in a type of data streaming mechanism. When it is saved to disk, changes are updated to the hive key components. In this way, hive information is coupled with associated log files in an effort to minimize corruption.

If the Registry is lost or damaged, Windows Server 2003 cannot function. Therefore, its care and feeding is a critical system administrator responsibility. The first rule is to retain an emergency copy of the Registry in case of damage or loss. As stated previously, the Registry information is found in %systemroot%\System32\Config, where %systemroot% is the root directory for a system, such as \winnt. For system recovery, the Windows Server Setup program also creates a %systemroot%\Repair folder that contains the following files:

- *Autoexec.nt*—a copy of %systemroot%\System32\Autoexec.nt used to initialize the MS-DOS environment.
- *Config.nt*—a copy of %systemroot%\System32\Config.nt used to initialize the MS-DOS environment.

TABLE 2.3 Registry Keys

Key	Description
HKEY_LOCAL_MACHINE	Information about the local system such as hardware and operating system data; major keys are hardware, SAM, security, software, and system.
HKEY_CLASSES_ROOT	File allocation and OLE/ActiveX data; includes association of extensions to applications.
HKEY_CURRENT_CONFIG	System startup configuration that permits changes to device settings.
HKEY_CURRENT_USER	Profile for current active user as well as console, Control Panel, environment, printer, and software data.
HKEY_USERS	Profiles for all active users as well as default profile.

- *Default*—the Registry key HKEY_USERS\DEFAULT in compressed format.
- *Ntuser.DA*—A compressed version of %systemroot%\Profiles\DefaultUser\Ntuser.dat. The process uses Ntuser.da_ if this area needs repair.
- *Sam*—The Registry key HKEY_LOCAL_MACHINE\SAM in compressed format.
- *Security*—The Registry key HKEY_LOCAL_MACHINE\SECURITY in compressed format.
- *Setup.log*—The log of installed files with cyclic redundancy check (CRC) data. This file is read-only, system, and hidden by default.
- *Software*—the Registry key HKEY_LOCAL_MACHINE\SOFTWARE in compressed format.
- *System*—the Registry key HKEY_LOCAL_MACHINE\SYSTEM in compressed format.

During system startup, the Windows Server kernel extracts information from the Registry, such as which device drivers to load and their load order. The Ntoskrnl.exe program also passes other information, including its version number, to the registry.

The Registry Editor

System administrators may find it necessary to regularly view and edit the Registry. The Registry Editor tool (regedt32.exe) is located in the \System32 directory. Generally speaking, it is best to use the Windows Server administrative tools to resolve system issues prior to editing the Registry. However, from time to time, it is necessary to go to the source of system data. That is when the Registry Editor (Figure 2.23) comes into play.

NOTE The older style regedit is no longer supported. If regedit is invoked from the command prompt, regedit32 is automatically invoked.

CAUTION The Registry Editor is not a toy. Its improper use can result in fatal system behavior. When viewing and copying the Registry, always turn the Editor to read-only mode. When directly editing, always think twice before entering information. The Registry Editor automatically saves all changes, so once they are entered you must live with the consequences. Changes are reflected automatically.

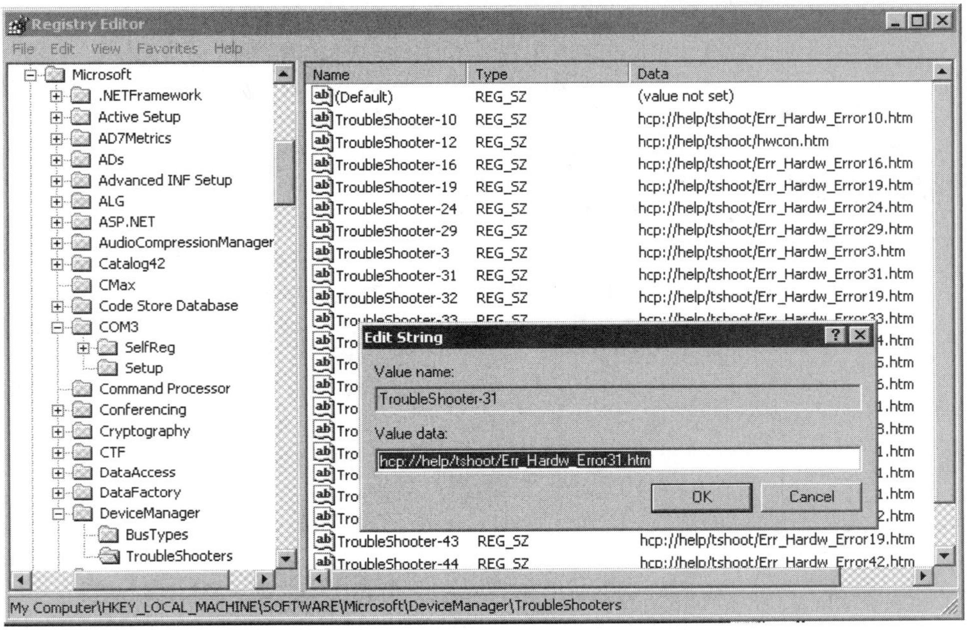

FIGURE 2.23 The Registry Editor

SOFTWARE TRACING

Tracing the activity of software applications can significantly enhance an administrator's ability to fine-tune a system's performance. The software tracing feature supports the use of macros and a preprocessor to scan code, generate message identification numbers, and create file definitions. Software tracing provides the following:

- Drivers, kernel components, services, applications, and other components can define trace events and globally unique identifiers (GUIDs).
- Components are able to use multiple-event class definition.
- Components are independently enabled and disabled.
- Components can be grouped at a higher level.
- Event information is retained in binary form.
- Trace trial activity is postprocessed for later examination.
- A failed in-memory trace is dumped by a debugger extension.

In the event of a system dump, a kernel debugger extension displays the trace elements that remain in memory. Software tracing is invoked by **Start → Control Panel → Performance and Maintenance → Administrative Tools → Performance → Performance Logs and Alerts → Trace Logs**.

VIEWING APPLICATION DEPENDENCIES

Anytime an application fails to execute properly or fails to load, a support tool in the Windows Server 2003 Resource Kit, called the Dependency Walker, can be an excellent analytical utility. It shows the minimum set of files required to run an application or load a DLL, and it shows which functions are exposed by a particular module and which ones are called by other modules. Moreover, it illustrates the full path of all modules being loaded by an application, plus their base addresses. When an application fails, the Dependency Walker provides an error message about the problematic components.

The Dependency Walker operates by recursively scanning all dependent modules required by an application. Missing files are detected first; then corrected or invalid files are identified. For example, a 16-bit version of a DLL might be present when a 32-bit version is required. Circular redundancy problems and CPU mismatches are also detected during the recursive scans.

The Dependency Walker (Figure 2.24) identifies different types of dependencies between modules, which are briefly described in Table 2.4.

To review an application's dependencies, load the Dependency Walker from the **Start** menu → choose **Programs → Windows Server 2003 Support Services → Tools**. From the **Files** menu select **Open** and browse to the desired application or DLL.

The Dependency Walker can also be used for application profiling. This technique permits it to detect dynamically loaded modules in a running application that may not be reported in the static import tables. The profiler is also used to detect that a module has failed to initialize. This activity is initiated once an application is loaded into the Dependency Walker. From the **Profile** menu, select **Start Profiling**. You will then need to select the options from the **Profile Module** dialog box. Continue the process until the desired information is obtained. To terminate the analysis, select the **Profile** menu → **Stop Profiling**.

NOTE The Windows Server 2003 Resource Kit also supplies a command-line method of launching the Dependency Walker through the depend.exe command-line utility.

Figure 2.25 displays the dialog box that permits the selection of the stable operation system for a given application.

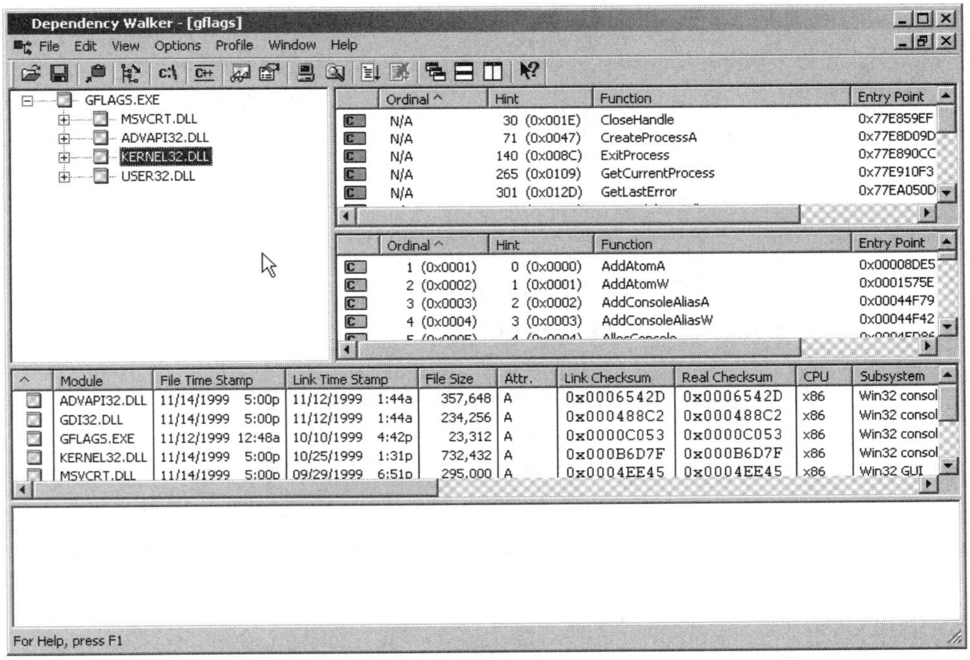

FIGURE 2.24 The Windows Server 2003 Resource Kit's Dependency Walker

TABLE 2.4 Types of Dependency between Modules

Type	Description
Implicit	A load-time dependency in which one module calls functions in another module. Even if no direct calls are made to the second module, that module is still loaded into memory.
Delay-Load	A dynamic dependency in which a module is loaded only when a specific call is made to it by the application.
Forward	A dependency in which an application calls a function in a dependent module that is actually available from another module. The call is forwarded from the second module to the third module.
Explicit	A run-time dependency, that is, a dynamic load of library functions common to OCXs, COM objects, and Visual Basic applications.
System Hook	A dependency that occurs when a specific application action is undertaken; for example, the use of a mouse will result in a new process.

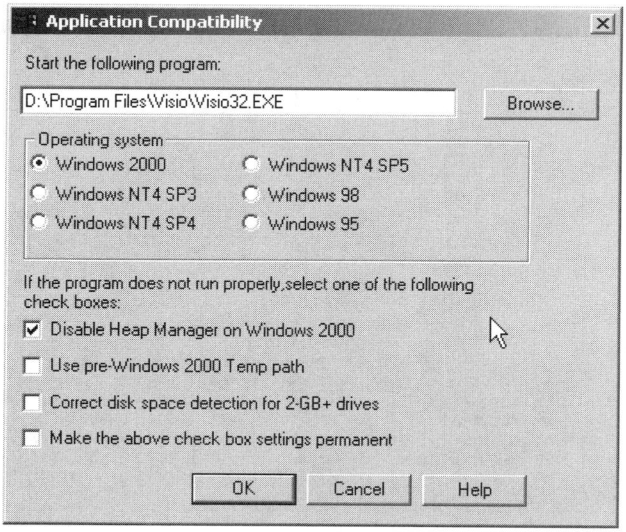

FIGURE 2.25 The Windows Server 2003 Resource Kit's Application Compatibility Tool

APPLICATION COMPATIBILITY

A major administrative headache with Windows 2000 was coping with issues of compatibility with earlier applications. Windows XP and Windows Server 2003 have made a significant leap in assuring backward compatibility. A set of new technologies and support infrastructures isolate OS differences and application bugs. This greatly increases the chances that applications that support Windows 95, Windows 98, Windows Millennium Edition, and Windows 2000 work on Windows Server 2003 and Windows XP. A key new technology called AppFixes solves such problems as the incorrect detection of the operating system by an application. It also addresses the issue of an application's referencing memory after it should have been freed. A database of applications, problems, and fixes drives which AppFixes are enabled. Microsoft maintains an updated database of these fixes as part of the Auto Update feature discussed in Chapter 3. In addition, the end user can enable an applications compatibility mode for custom-built applications.

When an application that ran on an earlier legacy version of Windows cannot be loaded during the setup function or if it later malfunctions, you must run the compatibility mode function. This is accomplished by right-clicking the application or setup program and selecting **Properties** → selecting **Compatibility** → selecting the previously supported operating system.

NOTE A common duty of a system administrator is to manage software versions and builds. This responsibility is extremely time consuming and often accomplished in a less than methodical manner. Software tracing provides a means to minimize the need for checked builds. With this feature, participating components—such as a driver, kernel component, service, or application—can define their own trace events and GUIDs. As such, components can have multiple event classes defined and independently enabled or disabled. Each event retains its binary form. A trace activity can be examined while it is occurring or after the event. If the system fails the in-memory trace, it can be dumped by a debugger extension or reviewed in an appropriate tool. There is also a kernel debugger extension that has the ability to display the trace elements that remain in memory at the time of a break point or a system crash, or from a crash dump. This feature is invoked via **Start → Control Panel → Performance and Maintenance → Administrative Tools → Computer Management**.

Unauthorized Applications

The Windows installer has a group policy configuration that prevents anyone except administrators from installing non-elevated applications. In versions of Windows server products prior to Windows Server 2003, this option was not enabled by default. Windows Server 2003 enables this feature by default in order to ensure greater security out of the box.

INTELLIMIRROR AND OTHER INNOVATIONS

Prior to moving on to installation of Windows Server 2003, several other innovations should be highlighted. Specifically, the manner in which IntelliMirror, Remote OS Installation, and System Management Server interplay may affect the way Windows Server is installed and administered.

IntelliMirror technology should be regarded as a collection of functions rather than a specific application. Microsoft simply calls IntelliMirror the "follow me" function. In an Active Directory environment, system settings, applications, and data will move with the user regardless of which physical computer system the user logs on to. IntelliMirror was built on the original Zero Administration Initiative in order to minimize management costs associated with user frustration in moving between computers or coping with system failures. For example, if a user accidentally removes a critical dynamic-link library (.dll), IntelliMirror can be configured to seek out that component and automatically reinstall it when the application is launched. Yet another example is a user who moves between physical locations, as is common for consulting, sales, and technical support personnel. When such a user logs on to a computer in a different location, IntelliMirror will launch the same desktop environment and data access as would be available in the home office. In the broadest terms, IntelliMirror provides three basic functions:

1. Management of desktop settings including any customizations and restrictions
2. Software maintenance and installation including configuration, repair, and application removal known as the Software Installation and Maintenance Feature
3. User data access and management including policies that define properties and the location of user folders

Remote OS Installation is a set of technologies that supports administration of Windows Server 2003 client installation and configuration. It supports the new Preboot eXecution Environment (PXE) remote boot technology, which requests an installation of Windows XP from a delegated server. (Using Remote OS Installation is not recommended for Windows Server 2003 because of the number of configuration issues involved.) The specific application of these technologies is discussed in the next chapter. Coupled with IntelliMirror, Remote OS Installation facilitates the rollout of the Windows Server 2003 operating system and then automatically creates and maintains end-user applications and settings.

The final ingredient in the scenario is the optional System Management Server (SMS version 2.0 with Service Pack 2 or higher), which is discussed in greater detail in Chapter 17. SMS can be used to perform enterprise-wide inventory and troubleshooting. This includes management of systems other than Windows Server.

Each of these technologies offers the system administrator different advantages. The Remote OS Installation permits automatic installation and repair of Windows XP client systems. IntelliMirror provides a "just-in-time" approach to software installation and user environment management. SMS provides an advanced set of just-in-time applications for application deployment and system management. A system administrator should take a careful look at each of these technologies and apply them to more efficient management of client environments.

POSTSCRIPT

In this chapter we provided a view of Windows Server 2003 basic architecture. The chapter did not attempt to view this OS in a networked or enterprise environment. Instead, we examined the basic operating system internals and provided information about several useful system administration tools. System administrators need this high-level perspective to manage more demanding system issues. Subsequent chapters will expand on the topics reviewed here.

Chapter 3

Planning and Installation

This chapter provides baseline planning guidelines and Windows Server 2003 installation instructions. With very few exceptions, the tasks needed to plan and install this new operating system are fundamentally the same as those needed to install Windows 2000 Server versions. Unless otherwise noted, the installation of Windows Server 2003 and Windows 2000 are treated in the same light. Since there are more significant differences with regard to migrating from Windows NT, we call out these changes specifically.

The first part of the chapter is primarily for system administrators who have more global responsibility for the design and maintenance of the enterprise. However, an administrator with a smaller scope of responsibility, such as the management of an organizational unit, might also find this material helpful because it puts into perspective some of the considerations that go into planning Windows Server installations. Most of these considerations have equal applicability in an enterprise-wide scheme and in an organizational unit deployment scheme. The second part of the chapter walks through the Windows Server 2003 operating system installation process.

This chapter provides information that enables a system administrator to do the following:

- Understand the critical difference between the logical and physical structures inherent in Windows Server 2003.
- Construct a checklist of baseline considerations that must go into the planning of a Windows Server 2003 implementation, by first evaluating the current computing environment and then addressing anticipated changes.
- Use a series of underlying planning tips.

- Prepare a checklist of information that must be gathered in the preinstallation phase of Windows Server 2003 deployment.
- Formulate key decisions about Windows NT and Windows 2000 upgrades.
- Perform a standard Windows Server 2003 installation.
- Design and perform remote Windows Server 2003 installation procedures.
- Design and perform automated or ghost Windows Server 2003 installations.

NOTE The creation of a Windows Server 2003 enterpise is not trivial. Although Microsoft has given the system administrator a number of wizards and other tools, planning based on a solid understanding of Windows Server strengths and potential pitfalls is critical to successful deployment. A misstep during the early stages can be very costly. Therefore, we strongly encourage an early investment in the creation of a planning and deployment team, which should be empowered to consult system administrators and operational managers. They should gather all appropriate information discussed in this chapter as well as data unique to the environment. To translate this information into a working structure, the team must have a credible knowledge of Windows Server 2003 and its underlying technologies. The cost in time and money for a lead team of internal professionals and/or external expert consultants should be factored into a Windows Server deployment budget; Microsoft's much promoted reduction in total cost of ownership (TCO) is predicated on making the correct decisions during the planning phase.

LOGICAL AND PHYSICAL STRUCTURES

Windows Server 2003 is designed to take into account both logical and physical structural parameters. The *logical structure* can be described as the conceptual way an organization breaks down into a hierarchy of units and subunits. These units may be business groups, product lines, geographic locations, and the like. As discussed in Chapters 5 and 6, the Windows Server 2003 enterprise model relies on the concepts of forests, domain trees, domains, and organizational units to formulate the logical structure. These divisions are based on an assortment of criteria, including domain names, security boundaries, resource availability, and administrative authority. Users, computers, devices, applications, and other system objects are grouped into organizational units where function and responsibility are logically assembled. The logical structure of most organizations is very dynamic, and the Windows Server's logical structure can effectively accommodate change.

The *physical structure* is defined in Windows Server 2003 primarily by network connectivity. Windows Server assumes that reliable and cost-effective connectivity achieves optimal performance. A *site* is the Windows Server base unit of the physical structure and is defined by well-connected TCP/IP subnets. The planning process will determine how sites are linked to best facilitate directory service replication, user logons, and data flow.

Independent accounting for both logical and physical structural paradigms adds levels of complexity. However, through careful planning and deployment, administration of the enterprise can be greatly enhanced. The demands of the logical organizational structure coupled with the potential limitations of the physical structure require careful review. When planning a Windows Server 2003 enterprise, both sides of the equation require attention.

In this chapter, we look at the logical and physical structures from a more homogeneous vantage point. That is, we do not distinguish between them at this stage of this discussion for a reason that can be classically defined as the "chicken and the egg" dilemma. To appreciate the distinction between Windows Server's treatment of logical and physical structures, it is necessary to understand the topics covered in the next several chapters (specifically those dealing with the Active Directory and networking). Unfortunately, to get to those topics, it is vital that foundations of information be laid. In the real world, attention must be paid to both the logical and the physical enterprise. While the two can be independently administered, their interplay is vital to effective Windows Server deployment. For this reason, we recommend that you use the information outlined in this chapter after at least a minimal review of the Active Directory (Chapters 5 and 6), user management (Chapter 7), group policies (Chapter 8), and networking (Chapters 12 and 13).

UNDERSTANDING THE CURRENT ENTERPRISE

There is no such thing as a one-size-fits-all computing environment. Thus, the IT infrastructure design for one enterprise will not be appropriate to all other enterprises. Complicating the uniqueness of enterprise infrastructures is the element of change. Organizations are dynamic, with constant shifts in mission, personnel, and technology affecting responsibilities. Enterprises also have inherent limitations, which include the political and the budgetary. Finally, legacy hardware, applications, and data stores influence any migration plan. For all these reasons, the first step in deploying Windows Server 2003 in the enterprise is to take very careful stock of the organization, its strengths and limitations, and its future. With this baseline of data, it is possible to determine the best use of Windows Server 2003 for current and future computing needs.

Taking Stock: First Inventory, Then Document

The first step is to carefully inventory the enterprise and document the results from several perspectives. We understand that nothing is probably less thrilling, but the pain associated with failing to take this important step can be crippling.

The meaning of inventory is much broader than a simple list of all computing equipment. An IT inventory involves a very analytical look at how and where this equipment is used, underscored by the need to ask how Windows Server 2003 will positively affect existing infrastructures. A decision on equipment and network retention begins at this stage.

Throughout this process there is one clear message: You must document, document, and then document some more. Table 3.1 is a partial checklist of IT-specific information that should be minimally inventoried and reduced to quick reference documentation. Note that since some of the items are covered in greater detail in other sections of the book, some cross-referencing may be required.

LEGACY ENTERPRISE ANALYSIS

Reviewing the current configuration of hardware and software will reveal issues that must be addressed as part of the migration. The following issues will influence a successful deployment:

- *Windows NT upgrades*. For existing Windows NT environments, you will need to identify the domain model in use and rethink the current network topology. This topic is explored in the section on upgrading. Existing Windows 2000 installations can use the same domain model or you can modify it easily.

TABLE 3.1 Inventory Checklist of the Enterprise

Document Item	Inventorying Tasks
IT Organization Itself	Understand the number, location, and skills of existing IT talent. Review current available skills and required training at the site or organizational unit level.
Network Operating Systems	Identify the NOS environments currently in place and determine the future configuration. Also determine any protocols that will enhance interoperability with Windows NT/2000. For example, what directory services are in use for existing networks based on Windows NT, UNIX, or Novell? If DNS is employed, what is the level and does it support Dynamic DNS and SRV record (BIND 8.1.2 or better, RFC 2052- and RFC 2136-compliant) functionality? Networking upgrades and operating system interoperability will be predicated on this data.

TABLE 3.1 Continued

Document Item	Inventorying Tasks
Physical Network Structure hubs, and Traffic Patterns	Document the existing network structure, specifically end nodes, switches, and routers. Also determine network traffic patterns, bandwidth availability, and overall reliability, and extrapolate future network requirements. This information will define Windows 2000 sites.
Addressing Scheme	As discussed in Chapter 5, Windows 2000 supports a number of industry-standard naming conventions. The default network protocol is TCP/IP. The Windows 2000 directory services, Active Directory, uses Dynamic DNS, DHCP, and LDAP. Active Directory also embraces a hierarchical domain scheme. In most enterprises, a new naming scheme for nodes and servers may be required. Careful consideration of domain naming must begin prior to installing Windows 2000 and when adding nodes. Computer names must be unique across the forest.
Internal and External Connectivity	Inventory internal LANs, WANs, and Internet connectivity. Also look at phone lines, dial-up networking, fax services, ftp services, and so on.
Software Licensing	Look at current licensing operating system software and determine if it is the most appropriate. Base a licensing decision on this evaluation.
File Storage Policies (especially with operating systems)	If you anticipate using UNIX, Novell, or other environments with Windows 2000, assess how technologies such as NFS, Samba, and SMB are used. Also look at file server connectivity.
Backup and Restoration Policies	Make sure that the backup and restoration routines and scripts in use will be compatible with Windows 2000, including encryption or compression methodologies. Also compare current devices to Microsoft's Hardware Compatibility List (HCL).
Applications Services	The issue of managing applications either in a distributed or centralized fashion will play in the planning process. Review how application servers are currently used.
Network Applications and Management Tools	Although operating system network tools will probably be sufficient for smaller organizations, larger enterprises will probably need to invest in tools that support Simple Network Management Protocol (SNMP) and other protocols. Network equipment vendors typically provide SNMP tools. Third-party products such as Hewlett-Packard's OpenView or Microsoft's System Management Server can prove invaluable in very large networks. The important point is to evaluate your needs early and make appropriate provisions for network management tools.

- *Operating system interoperability*. In many environments, heterogeneous operating systems such as UNIX and NetWare will continue to be used. It is important to understand that Windows Server 2003 needs to simply coexist or be fully integrated. Pay particular attention to network connectivity and directory service interoperability. Mapping the total enterprise and understanding how heterogeneous operating systems will interplay is an important planning step. A number of excellent reference books discuss related topics, including *Windows NT & UNIX: Administration, Coexistence, Integration, & Migration* (Williams and Gardner, Addison-Wesley 2002).
- *Legacy system life cycle*. A life-cycle analysis of legacy systems should be undertaken to determine realistic migration schedules. You must determine how much of the enterprise you are going to migrate. A decision to migrate, coexist, or integrate presents both opportunities and costs. Most organizations do not have the luxury to abandon existing equipment, software, and, most important, staff with older skills.
- *Personnel training*. Evaluating legacy systems is only one aspect of the equation; "retrofitting" staff to use the new operating system must enter into the scheme. Ultimately, technology is only as good as the people using it.

ORGANIZATIONAL STRUCTURE ANALYSIS

Analysis of the organization is a key component in defining the logical structure of a Windows Server 2003 enterprise. As discussed in Chapter 6, Windows Server offers a hierarchical domain structure that accommodates very granular administration. A domain tree comprises a root domain and one or more child domains that share a security boundary and namespace. A domain can be divided easily into components known as organizational units (OUs), the administration of which can be delegated to individuals or groups. At the other end of the spectrum, domain trees can be joined to form a forest. Trust is established between these structures that permits users with permission to access any resource in the OU, domain tree, or forest. The inherent Windows Server design accommodates very complex organizations of virtually any size. It also takes change into account by permitting the movement of OUs as well as their pruning from the tree when they disappear.

With this type of facility in mind, it is obvious that the initial design of the Windows Server 2003 enterprise must take into account the structure of the organization. An organization's structure affects the type of computing environment that should be put into place. The planning process should begin with an understanding of both the formal management structure and the physical sites to be served. In some cases, separate child domains might be created for the sales, engineering, and manufacturing organizations. In other cases, an enterprise may be organized around product lines, and a product line child domain might be in order: OUs would then be formed to separate the internal sales, engineering, and manufacturing resources.

CENTRALIZED VERSUS DECENTRALIZED MODELS

A key question is the administrative model to be used. This will determine Active Directory hierarchies, administrative delegation schemes, and many security parameters. Generally, three classic administrative models are applied in the planning processes:

- *Centralized administrative model*. Under this scenario, all administrative responsibilities are controlled by a central authority. This model works well for relatively small organizations, but can prove unwieldy for very large enterprises.
- *Decentralized administrative model*. In this model, multiple OUs have full responsibility for the management of their IT resources. While it provides extensive grassroots autonomy, decentralization raises the issue of incompatibility and nonstandard policies. It is preferred by many organizations, but can lead to conflict where communication among units is necessary. Fortunately, the Windows Server 2003 domain and OU model can overcome some inherent conflict, especially if careful planning occurs at the outset.
- *Mixed administrative model*. The most common for larger enterprises, the combined centralized/decentralized model delegates authority to organizational units. Responsibilities are defined by the centralized authority. The decentralized authority granted to the OUs may vary significantly, obviously resulting in a new level of complexity. The Windows Server domain model is particularly useful in creating complex mixed models.

ORGANIZATIONAL PROCESSES AND DYNAMICS ANALYSIS

The type of access to network resources required among organizational units, domains, trees, and forests becomes a significant planning issue. Every organization has its own dynamics. The computing requirements for a manufacturer are radically different from those of a finance house. Information can be very structured or completely ad hoc.

Access to resources is typically granted on the basis of need. Process management breaks apart a business's functions, tasks, and responsibilities to determine the relative needs of each. The identification of computing needs is vastly enhanced by an understanding of how data flows through the entire organization. For example, the accounting, marketing, and manufacturing departments need access to customer information, but the human resources department may not. By the same token, human resources departments have many data files that are processed and stored on a confidential basis. Understanding the business relationships of departments and their processes makes it easier to configure and implement the relative group policies. It also provides a road map for managing permissions to avoid unauthorized use of network resources.

CHANGE AND GROWTH

It is not always be possible to predict the future of an organization. Nevertheless, effective planning involves breaking out the crystal ball to make reasonable projections. Windows Server 2003 is designed to facilitate unexpected changes; however, the more that change can be anticipated, the better the deployment. This requires that the planning team engage key executives and operational managers in sometimes very confidential discussions regarding potential growth and downsizing. Since the job of the professional system administrator is to handle sensitive information pertaining to many security issues, this is a good place to gain additional respect within the organization.

Plans should attempt to reflect organizational change for three to five years. The checklist of growth and change items to be integrated into the plan includes the following questions:

- What are the projections for growth and reduction both on an enterprise level and within each organizational unit?
- How are shifts going to be distributed both organizationally and geographically?
- Where are reorganizations most likely to occur and what will be the overall impact?
- What is the impact of mergers, acquisitions, and business unit spinoffs?
- What new or emerging technologies are most likely to affect the plan?

SECURITY REQUIREMENTS ANALYSIS

Windows Server 2003 offers a vastly enhanced set of security technologies and implementation policies. A careful review of current security mechanisms and policies should be undertaken very early. User and group policies and permissions may be the first issue to consider. Thereafter, issues involving Windows Server Kerberos authentication and public key infrastructure, as discussed in Chapter 11, can be examined for their impact on the way business is conducted. Start with a baseline of current policies and how they relate. In a move from a Windows NT environment, these policies should translate rather transparently; however, greater functionality can be added through an early security assessment and plan.

USER PROFILES ANALYSIS

When it comes time to define user and group profiles, an understanding of inherent commonalities and differences will greatly facilitate the deployment and management process.

The size of the user base on an enterprise-wide and organizational-unit basis must be identified. Users' geographical distribution and need for multilingual support should then be assessed, as should likely movement within and among organizational units. In addition, many users may belong to matrix organizations where reporting relationships and responsibility cross boundaries, so there must be plans to apply policies to them.

Mobile or roaming user requirements must also be addressed. For example, will the user need to maintain the same set of data on home and field office computer systems? These requirements, once defined, can be translated into policies that will permit transparent Windows Server 2003 synchronization of files. Issues of remote access connectivity will also be resolved based on this planning data.

PHYSICAL STRUCTURES ANALYSIS

Windows Server 2003 establishes the concept of a site to help the management of physical connectivity to resources. Microsoft defines a site as one or more well-connected TPC/IP subnets. A "well-connected" operating system usually is defined by the administrator, but ideally is based on transmission speeds that do not negatively affect network performance. One of the early tasks is to review the definition of logical sites based on Windows Server criteria. For example, each remote office might be defined as an individual site and intersite communication can then be managed. With such information, it is possible to plan wisely and schedule information flow among sites efficiently.

A physical site structure is often defined as a specific building. However, physical sites can be as small as a couple of adjoining offices or as large as network segments or even entire cities. Again, the key is reliable connectivity. Geography is usually a defining method of establishing sites and domains in a large enterprise. The planning process involves site definition, domain controller and Global Catalog requirements, and Active Directory replication schedules.

The checklist of information that is generally required in the early assessment of the physical structure includes the following:

- The number of physical locations that must be served
- The geographic location of all remote sites, both domestic and international
- The number of buildings, floors, square footage, and other factors that could affect networking for each geographic location

- The business function of each possible site, which determines the level of bandwidth and networking support required

Bandwidth and Network Speeds

An assessment of current network activity provides a baseline for Windows Server 2003 deployment, but you must assume that network activity will increase with Windows Server, especially in connection with Active Directory replication and Global Catalog inquiries. LAN speed requirements within a site can generally be accommodated by the addition of domain controllers to handle the internal target. Intersite traffic, however, is more complex. Two primary areas must be assessed when planning intersite network requirements:

- *Intersite link speeds*. Link speeds are defined by how rapidly packets of data can be transmitted between network segments or geographical locations. Unfortunately, speed and reliability between links can vary radically. Therefore, control of Active Directory replication and other data transmission may be required. It is important to identify the weak links and plan to apply appropriate properties to them.
- *Bandwidth requirements*. Network bandwidth is the space available for the flow of traffic. It is important to assess when the maximum amount of bandwidth is available for transmission and replication, including the conditions that exist during normal, busy, and off-peak hours. Again, this information will be used to set intersite link properties to control reliable communication.

Physical Structure Design

Planning the physical structure includes the early design of site topology, server placement, domain controller requirements, and replication policies. The specific requirements associated with each of these demand an understanding of the Active Directory and networking, so we recommend a review of these technologies first. However, it is important to then return to the planning process in order to clearly define the intersite and intrasite connectivity requirements well before deployment.

Commonsense Planning and Deployment Tips

There are a number of commonsense tips for implementing Windows Server 2003. Here are ten of them:

1. *Make the plan available for review and comment*. The biggest mistake that any IT organization can make is to force change and do so from an ivory tower. Publishing a draft set of policies and procedures can promote an early buy-in by both managers and end users. Everyone should understand that the planning document is dynamic and subject to input; feedback is very healthy during all phases of migration or implementation. Contributions by teams of users or individuals can often prove invaluable and also prevent being blindsided by hidden agendas. User input reflects the true nature of a group and thus greatly helps in the creation of child domains and organizational units.

2. *Think carefully about leveraging current investments*. The conventional wisdom of utilizing current assets whenever possible was true when the cost of personal computers regularly exceeded $2,500 and access to reliable, inexpensive networks was a rarity. However, significant changes have occurred recently. Personal computers priced at less than $500 may become increasingly commonplace even within corporate environments, and DSL (or greater) connectivity between sites is readily available and becoming less expensive. This might mean that current environments may eventually prove more costly than simple replacements. There are times, however, when it is possible to "recycle" the systems in one department to another department as needs change. A valid plan must include buy-versus-retention analysis.

3. *Think early about personnel needs*. Windows Server 2003 is a complex enterprise-level operating system that requires support by senior system administrators. You should conduct a skill survey early in the process and count on providing additional training.

4. *Determine hardware, software, and funding availability*. A plan to migrate or integrate operating systems must be cost justified via a series of subjective questions. Will organizational performance be enhanced? Will productivity be increased? Will lower-cost network connectivity and equipment demonstrably impact cash flow? What is the anticipated cost of system administration? Can legacy mission-critical applications be supported in the new environments? A TCO analysis underscores this part of the planning process.

5. *Use test environments*. Create a test lab, particularly for the introduction of the Windows Server 2003 Active Directory into the environment. Within existing Windows NT enterprises, take a current Backup Domain Controller (BDC) offline to a test environment. By upgrading the BDC and promoting it with the Active Directory as a Windows .NET domain controller, you will retain all security and configuration information. Add other systems and common devices to test the environment, and invite some of your users to play in the test bed to get further feedback. After testing, the promoted domain controller can then serve as the root for the new Windows Server 2003 enterprise. These pilot and test environments will also help with staging the implementation, as discussed in the next tip. Also, please note that best practices suggest that you always start with a fresh installation when going into production rather than move a test machine into production.

6. *Consider deployment staging*. Any deployment must occur with minimal impact on the user and mission-critical business activities. To that end, a number of questions must be resolved in advance. For example, do you unpack the equipment at the user's workstation or preload the software? Because of the time required to upgrade or install Windows Server, we recommend using a staging area if possible to preload and configure. As a part of this strategy, consider the use of remote automated or ghost installations to decrease direct user impact.

7. *Enlist the support of others in the rollout*. The best way to create a supportive environment is to enlist as many users as possible in the process. To gain their confidence, it is equally important that all IT professionals involved be fully equipped to handle common questions. Remember, deployments without some level of crisis are rare. Buffer these crises with knowledgeable people who will offer support despite and beyond temporary shortfalls.

8. *Get operational management early*. An operational management plan, with clear policies and procedures, must be in place. Because Windows Server 2003 permits very granular administration, there may be an increased early burden. If people are being assigned as printer administrators, they must be fully equipped from the beginning to react to system management issues. This is where documentation proves extremely valuable to the management team. Standard operational procedures and policies normally evolve from this type of documentation.

9. *Begin training and support early*. Two primary levels of training are generally required. Clearly, the first in line are system administrators and support personnel, which is where most of the training budget should be focused. However, do not overlook the end user. While Windows Server 2003 should feel comfortable to most users of Windows 95/98 systems, some differences may require explanation. Fortunately, much end-user training can be accomplished with computer-aided training or Web-based tools.

10. *Audit use and perform monitoring*. Determine the nature and level of event auditing and performance monitoring. Establish baselines early and build metrics into your processes to help you identify and correct performance bottlenecks proactively.

Regardless of the relative perfection of your plan, there will always be issues that mar otherwise exceptional performance. As an IT manager or system administrator, you must realize that your profession is often thankless. However, if everything goes well, your reward will be fewer trouble calls, and you can kick back and congratulate yourself for a job well done. Remember, though, that the job is just beginning. A system administrator must always strive to be proactive, not reactive.

PLANNING FOR UPGRADES

The issues discussed in previous sections of this book all apply to planning an upgrade for a Windows NT enterprise. However, a number of additional issues must be taken into account that do not exist when creating a Windows Server 2003 enterprise from scratch.

NOTE This discussion assumes that administrators who are involved with the upgrade from Windows 200/NT have full working knowledge of that operating system. If you do not have administrative knowledge of Windows NT, please seek additional reference information on it. Although it is possible to perform an upgrade from Windows NT to Windows Server 2003 without knowing Windows NT, doing so could result in problems.

Native versus Mixed-Mode Installations

Windows Server 2003 can exist in one of two primary modes (see Figure 3.1). The first is the *native mode.* Here all domain controllers with a domain or forest use Windows Server exclusively, although down-level clients and servers can still run using other versions of Windows 2000 and Windows NT, Windows 3.x, and Windows 9x. The second is the *mixed mode,* in which Windows Server 2003, Windows

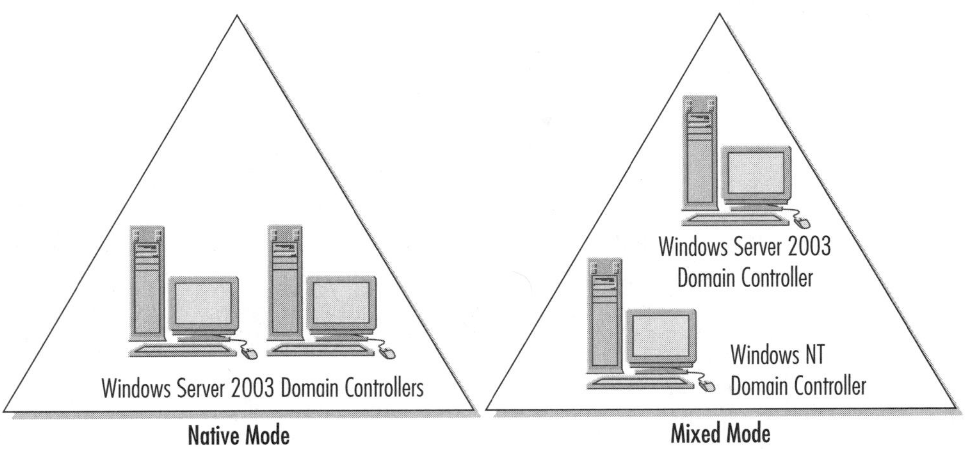

FIGURE 3.1 Native versus Mixed Mode Domains

2000, and Windows NT domain controllers are accommodated. The two modes are compared in Figure 3.1.

Active Directory domain and forest functionality is governed in part by the version levels of the downstream domain controllers. Windows 2000 introduced the concept of native and mixed mode levels of functionality. The Windows Server 2003 family provides four levels of functionality for domains, as shown in Table 3.2. Raising the level of functionality is discussed in Chapter 6.

Table 3.2 Comparison of Active Directory Mode Functionality

Feature	Windows 2000 Mixed (default) Windows NT4.0 Windows 2000 Windows Server 2003	Windows 2000 Native Windows 2000 Windows Server 2003	Windows Server 2003 Interim Windows NT 4.0 Windows Server 2003	Windows Server 2003 Native Windows Server 2003
Domain Controller Rename Tool	Disabled	Disabled	Disabled	Enabled
Update Logon Timestamp	Disabled	Disabled	Disabled	Enabled
User Password on InetOrgPerson Object	Disabled	Disabled	Disabled	Enabled
Universal Groups	Distribution group enabled; security group disabled	Enabled for distribution and security groups	Distribution group enabled; security group disabled	Enabled for distribution and security groups
Group Nesting	Disabled for security groups except domain local groups with global group members	Enabled	Disabled for security groups except domain local groups with global group members	Enabled
Converting Groups	Disabled	Enabled	Disabled	Enabled
SID History	Disabled	Migration between domains for security principals		Migration between domains for security principals

Forest functionality is also influenced by domain controller version levels. The default Windows 2000 mode has a great number of functions disabled in part or in whole, including Global catalog replication improvements, defunct schema objects, certain forest trusts, linked value replication, domain renaming, AD replication algorithm enhancements, dynamic auxiliary classes, and InetOrgPerson object Class changes. These functions are achieved by managing a native Windows Server 2003 environment. However, it is important to note that once the domain controllers are advanced it is not possible to change back to a Windows 2000 mixed environment.

THE PDC EMULATOR IN MIXED ENVIRONMENTS

Since the Windows Server 2003 domain model is based on a multimaster domain scheme in which all domain controllers replicate information as peers, the Windows NT Primary Domain Controller (PDC) and Backup Domain Controller model is replaced. However, in mixed mode, Windows Server must also fill the role of the PDC. Therefore, it includes a PDC Emulator that permits continued interaction with Windows NT BDC and member servers.

A Windows Server domain controller is selected to serve as the PDC Emulator. When requests for changes in the Windows NT Security Account Management (SAM) database occur, the PDC Emulator maintains SAM and replicates that information using NTLM to the BDC. It also supports authentication logon requests for LAN Manager (LANMAN), but this activity is transparent to down-level clients. The PDC Emulator communicates changes to the Active Directory so that normal replication can occur between domain controllers. While all Windows Server 2003 objects are maintained by Active Directory, this data is exposed to down-level clients as a flat Windows NT data store.

NOTE The scalability of the Active Directory in a mixed environment is limited to 40 MB as a result of the size limitation that existed on Windows NT domain controllers. This limitation can be overcome and full scalability provided to the Active Directory only by moving to native mode.

MIXED-MODE SECURITY

Mixed-mode environments involve a number of security-related concerns. They are briefly outlined here.

- *Object security and relative identifiers.* The relative identifier (RID) identifies the domain controller that creates objects and limitations, and is always unique. Every domain controller can create objects and assign a RID in a native environment. However, in Windows NT domains only the PDC assigns identifiers based on sequential numbers. This situation creates an obvious possibility for conflict. Therefore, in a mixed environment every domain assigns a Windows Server domain controller (usually the upgraded PDC) to act as a RID Master. The RID Master creates the security identifiers (SIDs, also known as security principals) for down-level domain controllers. Each domain controller is assigned a set of RIDs within a domain by the RID Master. The domain controllers then use RIDs in conjunction with their unique domain IDs to issue security IDs for new groups, user accounts, and computer accounts.

- *SAM database*. When a PDC is upgraded, all information stored in the Security Account Manager is moved to the Active Directory. In mixed environments, the PDC Emulator communicates down-level changes to the SAM databases in the remaining BDC. Table 3.3 illustrates migration of a SAM database to the Active Directory.
- *System security application*. Windows NT group policies used by clients and servers are processed by Windows Server 2003; however, once an upgrade occurs, only Windows Server 2003 group policies will be recognized. Older Windows NT policies can be used on an upgraded system via an option set to enable them. However, this should be done with great caution. A better approach is to create policies that mimic the desired Windows NT policies and apply them as part of the Windows Server deployment.
- *Trust relationships*. As discussed in Chapter 6, Windows .NET uses two-way transitive trust relationships between domains. These are not automatically supported by Windows NT down-level domain controllers. To permit authentication between domains in a mixed environment, Windows NT domain controllers must establish an explicit trust.

MIXED-MODE VARIATIONS

The mixed-mode environment limits some of the Windows Server 2003 services. A partial list of limitations in mixed-mode environment includes the following:

- *Logon services*. When Windows Server 2003 clients try to log on, they first use the DNS to find a Windows Server domain controller and use Kerberos for authentication. If a Windows Server domain controller cannot be located, the client uses the NTLM protocol and logs on to a Windows NT domain controller. In this case, no Windows Server 2003 group policies and scripts are processed. A minimum of one Windows .NET domain controller per site should be installed to prevent this rollover.

TABLE 3.3 Migration of SAM Database Information to the Active Directory

SAM Database Component	Moved to Active Directory
User Accounts	→ User container
Computer Accounts	→ Computer container
Built-in Local/Global Groups	→ Built-in container
Non–Built-in Groups	→ User container
PDC Computer Account	→ Domain controller organizational unit
NTFS File and Folder Permissions	→ Retained, not changed

- *Replication services.* Windows Server 2003 uses the File Replication Service (FRS). FRS replaces the Windows NT LAN Manager Replication (LMRepl) service, which Windows Server 2003 does not support. Therefore, these services in mixed environments must be bridged. The Windows NT export directory server should be upgraded last and those containing the import directory first. Add the export list on Windows Server by use of the Server Manager. The Windows NT scripts directory should be copied to the Windows Server 2003 domain controller system volume.

Domain Models

Windows Server 2003 is designed under a multimaster replication domain model, which is much less complex than the four models available under Windows NT. The transitive trust relationships between domains in Windows Server 2003 permit flexible configurations that greatly simplify the older models. Note that it may be appropriate to go directly to the Chapter 6 discussion of the Windows Server domain model after reading this section.

In the upgrading of Windows NT domain models, it is important to understand how the current model will be used in Windows Server 2003. The following is a brief summary of how the Windows Server 2003 domain model relates to Windows NT domains.

- *Windows NT single domain model.* The Windows NT single domain model converts directly to the Windows Server 2003 domain model. It provides the added value of being able to break the existing domain into organizational units in which administrative delegation can occur.
- *Windows NT master domain model.* In Windows NT, the master domain model provided a hierarchy in which child domains were used as resource domains. One-way trust relationships went from the resource domains to the master domain. This model can remain in place under Windows Server 2003 with the added value of two-way transitive trusts between domains. The master domain should be upgraded first and will become the root domain for the Windows Server domain tree. Alternatively, the Windows NT resource domains can be included in a single Windows Server domain and treated as administrative organizational units.
- *Multimaster domain model.* The Windows NT multimaster domain model provides two-way trusts between two or more master domains. It was used primarily in large enterprises where decentralized account management was desired. To move this model across, you will need to create a domain tree. The root domain should initially be created and remain empty. The master domains should then be upgraded as child domains in the domain tree.

- *Complete trust domain model*. The complete trust model provided two-way trusts between all the domains. The upgrade can take the form of a single forest with multiple domains or the creation of multiple forests with explicit trust.

Figure 3.2 illustrates how existing Windows NT domains can be adapted to Windows Server 2003. In the cases of existing Windows NT multimaster domain model and the complete trust domain model, two alternative migration paths are illustrated.

Upgrade Steps

Six primary steps should be taken during the upgrading of a Windows NT enterprise to Windows Server 2003. The objective of these steps is to preserve account information and other data from the Windows NT environment.

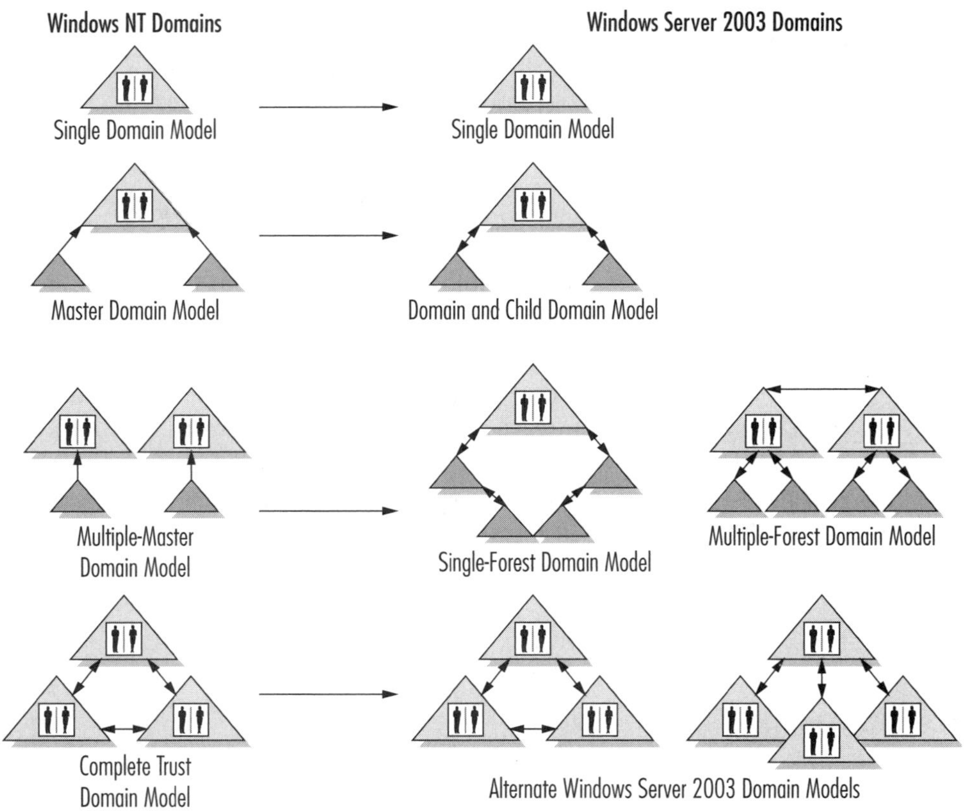

FIGURE 3.2 Changing Domain Models

1. *Review the domain structure and determine the DNS name*. As suggested previously, changes to the domain structure may be required. At this stage you will need to understand the current trust relationships and how they will be implemented under Windows Server 2003, as well as determine the number of domain controllers per domain. Also, you must assign DNS-compliant names during the upgrade process. If you do not have a DNS name, we recommend that you select one and register it through one of the Internet name registration authorities.

2. *Establish a backup and recovery plan*. Guarding against accidents or improper upgrade installations is very important. First, back up all services running on the PDC, and test the backup media prior to continuing. Second, make sure that the PDC and all BDCs are fully synchronized. Third, remove a BDC from the network, promote it as a standalone PDC, and demote it back to BDC status. Make sure that no data corruption occurs and that the system is fully operational. The system should remain apart from the network until the upgrade to Windows Server 2003 has been carried out and fully tested. This BDC is your lifeline if Windows Server 2003 fails and it is necessary to revert to Windows NT. In such a case, the Windows Server 2003 domain controllers would be removed and this system would go back online and be promoted as the PDC.

3. *Upgrade the Primary Domain Controller*. The PDC is always the first domain controller to be upgraded. If the current PDC is older, slower, and lacking sufficient disk and memory, consider replacing it before upgrading. The root Windows Server 2003 domain controller initially serves many functions, including the Schema Master and Global Catalog server functions. To make this upgrade, install a new system as a BDC and then promote it to the PDC. Now Windows Server 2003 can be installed. After the basic installation is completed, install the Active Directory. The Windows NT SAM database security components, including user accounts, local and global groups, and computer accounts, are moved into the Active Directory. If other domains exist, they should be upgraded after the root Windows Server 2003 domain controller with the Active Directory fully operational. (The initial upgrade should be done off-line in a test environment.)

4. *Upgrade the secondary domain controllers*. BDCs should be upgraded as soon as possible to prevent continued use of a mixed mode. When the existing BDCs join the domain, they are automatically promoted to peer-level domain controllers, and should then be added to the replication topology. (Retain a BDC until the Windows Server 2003 installation has been judged to be successful.)

5. *Upgrade workstations and member servers*. Workstations and member servers can be upgraded in any order. We suggest installing the Active Directory client so that organizational units are visible. Systems without Active Directory client software, or down-level systems, view objects as flat stores without information about which organizational unit they reside in.

6. *Verify and test the upgrade*. Verification and testing should take place from both the domain controller and the user client vantage point. From the root domain controller, review the dcpromo.log file. In addition, run two scripts available with the Windows Server 2003 Resource Kit: listdc.vbs to list all the domain controllers, and listdomains.vbs to list domain names within a tree. From the client perspective, attempt several user logons to verify if logon authentication is operational, user and group accounts have been applied, and logon scripts are being run.

NOTE Upgrading cluster environments involves a very precise set of procedures. Microsoft provides more than forty pages of instructions for this specialized installation. These instructions are included in the release notes of Windows Server 2003 products. We strongly advise that you refer to the release notes before initiating any such upgrade.

INSTALLATION

Installing Windows Server 2003 is straightforward, but it requires advance information and caution. As in the installation of Windows NT, a series of blue character-based screens begins a fresh installation of Windows Server 2003. Once the basic configuration is complete and system files have been copied to the server's hard drive, the graphical Windows wizard completes the process.

The wizard leads the administrator through the installation process in a logical fashion, but some very important questions are asked that require knowledge of both Windows Server 2003 and the enterprise. Preparing well for the installation will save both time and frustration. This section helps in that preparation and then goes through the entire process. The discussion assumes that the installation is being conducted for an Intel Pentium–class server.

NOTE The reference to "Intel Pentium–class servers" or "CPU" is generic. In addition to Intel processors, we conducted tests on processors manufactured by Advanced Micro Devices (AMD). Although extensive benchmarking of these processors was outside our scope, we can report that they all fared well in supporting base-level Windows Server 2003 functions.

For specific questions on CPU and other component compatibilities, refer to the latest version of the Hardware Compatibility List available on the Microsoft Web site. You should also check this list with regard to the system's other component equipment.

Preparation

If you are in the installation phase, it is assumed that you have a fundamental plan for deployment. If not, one message cannot be overstated: Windows Server 2003 is a very complex operating system that requires careful consideration and planning. If so, you now must take seven additional steps:

1. Gather critical system information.
2. Have ready answers to the questions that will be asked during installation.
3. Determine when optional components will be installed.
4. Determine the order in which to migrate existing servers.
5. Determine the DNS-compliant names for the domain or workgroup.
6. Create domain computer accounts and administrative passwords.
7. Perform a final review of the installation checklist provided.

NOTE All release notes should be reviewed in advance. In addition, be prepared to download operating system patches from the Microsoft Web site. If Windows NT 4.0 provided any indication of the type of evolution that will occur with Windows Servers, regularly checking Microsoft's site for tips, technical updates, and system patches will be required. As a company, Microsoft corporation is very aggressive in providing this level of technical support. It is an excellent resource and it should be used regularly.

GATHERING CRITICAL SYSTEM INFORMATION

The installation process requires critical data, whether it is a fresh installation or an upgrade. This section provides very helpful information that may prevent aborted installations. Take the time to gather this data and make sure that system requirements are fully available.

System Requirements

Prior to any installation, the system administrator should compare minimum Windows Server 2003 hardware requirements and compatibilities with those available on destination systems. Microsoft freely publishes minimum system requirements that can change over time. Note that there is a major difference between minimum requirements and those for optimal performance. With the declining cost of computer hardware, it may be better to purchase new equipment than to retrofit systems for Windows Server 2003 use. Older systems with at least a 133-MHz CPU can be used with Windows XP; systems with less power can be used as Window 98 clients during the migration phase. Table 3.4 lists system requirements.

TABLE 3.4 System Requirements

Component	Standard Server or Enterprise Server Requirement*
CPU	Intel Pentium class with a minimum clock speed of 133 MHz minimally required. In practical terms, we do not recommend installation on a system with less than 550 MHz. A 733-MHz CPU is required for Itanium systems.
RAM	A minimum 128 MB is required for installation. A member server should have a minimum of 128 MB; a domain controller should have at least 256 MB. Specialized functions (e.g., an applications server) require another 128 MB at minimum.
Hard Disk	A 1.5-GB hard drive partition is the minimum for system files and basic swapping but inadequate for more use. A bare minimum for network use is 4 GB. More is recommended.
Network	Standard network adapter card(s). A second interface card is recommended for domain controllers.
Display	Monitor and adapter with minimum resolution of the VGA (video graphic adapter) standard.
Other	CD-ROM (12X or higher recommended) for installation, keyboard, mouse, or other pointing devices.

*The above system requirements are considered minimums.

GATHERING ADAPTER INFORMATION

The Windows Server 2003 installer attempts to identify the devices and hardware adapters. If a device does not respond in a normal fashion, it may be necessary to supply additional drivers or remove it for installation at a later time. As a backup, the following data should be gathered about a system prior to installation. Not all adapters or settings are applicable to all computer systems.

- Advanced Configuration and Power Interface—settings enabled or disabled
- BIOS—revision level and date
- External/internal modem—COM port connection (i.e., COM1); IRQ and I/O address for the internal modem
- I/O port—IRQ, I/O address, DMA (if used) for each I/O port
- Mouse—type (serial, bus, USB) and port
- Network—IRQ and I/O address, DMA (if used), and bus type
- PC card—Optional PC card information
- SCSI controller—Model or chip set, IRQ, bus type
- Sound adapter—IRQ, I/O address, DMA (if used)

- Universal Serial Bus—devices and hubs attached
- Video—adapter or chip set and number of adapters

Maintain this list for quick reference; it greatly facilitates finding proper device drivers. Check the Microsoft and device manufacturers' Web sites to download the latest device drivers for Windows .NET.

KEY QUESTIONS

During the installation process of Windows Server 2003 versions, the system administrator is prompted for a series of important decisions. An incorrect decision could result in having to start the installation again.

Disk Partitions

Windows Server 2003 must be installed on a single disk partition. You have four choices to make with regard to partition creation or use:

- Create a new partition on a non-partitioned portion of a hard disk.
- Create a new partition on a partitioned hard disk.
- Install Windows Server 2003 on an existing partition.
- Remove an existing partition and create a new one for installation.

Several other partition-related decisions must be made. One is the file system in which to format the partition (as described in the next section). Another involves size. While it is possible to install the operating system in a 600-MB partition, doing so is not practical. The Windows Server 2003 partition should be much larger than 1 GB. As a general rule, we recommend that applications and data files be placed on separate disks to ensure better performance.

When installing a new system, we recommend that you create a multigigabit partition. If additional non-partitioned space remains on the hard drive, the Disk Administration tool can be used after the initial installation to partition the remaining space.

On systems with preexisting partitions, you will have two alternatives. You can delete the current partitions and properly size and format a new one. Or, if the size of the existing partition is adequate, you can install Windows Server 2003 without modification.

File System: FAT, FAT32, or NTFS?

During the installation process, you will need to determine what file system partition will be used for Windows Server 2003. FAT or FAT32 should be selected only in environments where security is not an issue and where legacy applications reside that do not support NTFS. FAT can support up to a 2-GB partition; FAT32 supports partitions greater than 2 GB. In the event that FAT or FAT32 is initially selected for Windows Server installation, it is possible to migrate later to NTFS with the **convert** command.

As a general rule, NTFS should be selected because it supports the full Windows Server suite of security features, file compression, disk quotas, and file encryption. For a server to support the Active Directory as a domain controller, NTFS is a prerequisite.

It is also possible to create a dual-boot environment in which multiple operating systems can be launched—for example, Windows 98 on one partition and Windows Server 2003 on a second one. When booting the computer, the user can select one of the two. We do not recommend a dual-boot system, however, because it might cause a number of security and performance problems.

Licensing Modes

Windows Server 2003 offers two distinct types of licensing. When installing the operating system, you will be required to define the type of license that will be used. Each licensing mode has advantages depending on the nature of the environment (Figure 3.3):

- *Per seat mode* permits an unlimited number of concurrent clients to connect to the server, providing each has a client access license (CAL), which permits the client to connect to any Windows Server 2003 in the domain. This method is very practical for large organizations with multiple Windows Server 2003 or a great number of roaming users.
- *Per server mode* sets the number of concurrent users or clients that can log on to a specific server. It is ordinarily used for organizations with a relatively fixed environment in which extra client utilization can be predicted. In a 24-hour customer service environment, for example, it is possible to predict the maximum number of users using the server at any given time. It is more economical to invoke a per server license than to purchase individual licenses for every client computer system.

NOTE CALs are not required for anonymous or authenticated access to Windows Server 2003 Internet Information Services or other Web server access. Also, Telnet and FTP connections do not require CALs.

Workgroups versus Domains

A decision must be made as to whether the computer will join a workgroup or a domain. A brief explanation of the two environments is appropriate here:

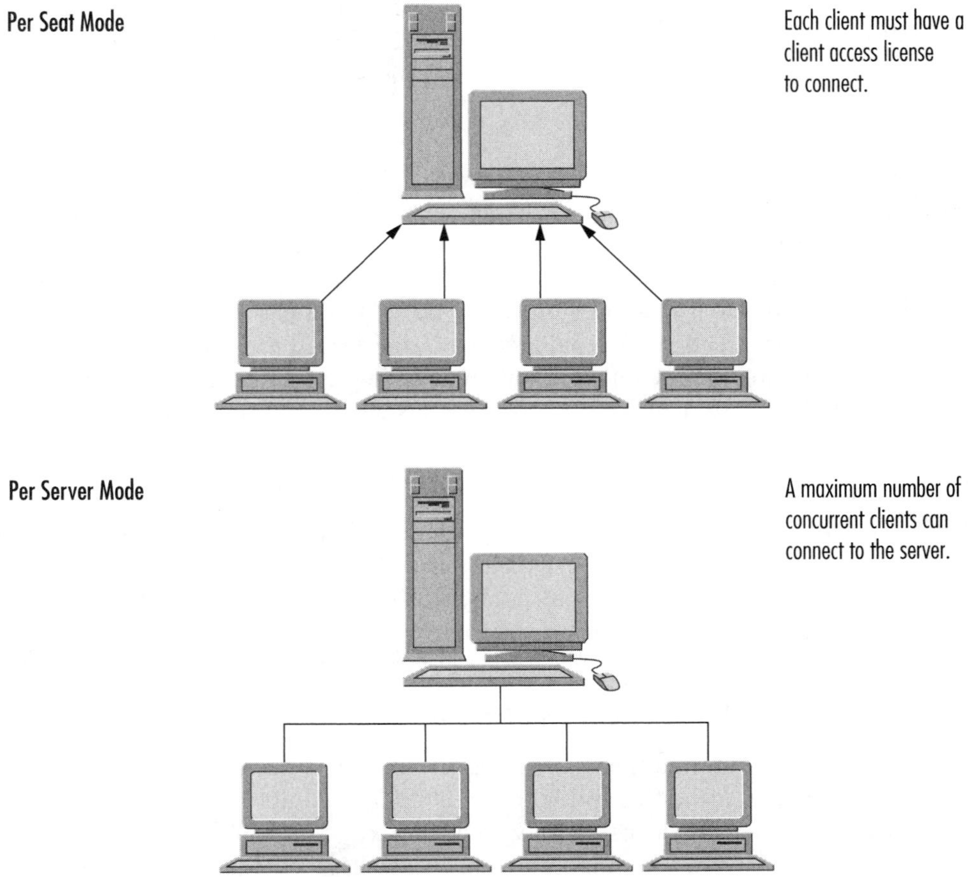

FIGURE 3.3 Per Seat versus Per Server Licensing

- *Windows Server 2003 workgroup*. The workgroup is a logical peer-to-peer connection of computers. The systems do not share a security database. All security databases are stored locally, which means that user accounts must be created on each workstation. This is a decentralized model most commonly used by small organizations. In this type of environment, a workgroup name must be assigned to the computer.
- *Windows Server 2003 domain*. This domain is a group of network resources that share a security database and namespace. (A *namespace* is the domain name used in the DNS naming convention, like EntCert.com.) As described in Chapters 5 and 6, the domain model uses a directory service known as the Active Directory, which is replicated among servers known as domain controllers.

Rather than the Primary and Backup Domain Controller technology used in Windows NT, Windows Server 2003 maintains peer relationships among its Active Directory domain controllers. This model supports a single source for user logon and a central focal point for system administration.

NOTE To join a domain, an existing domain controller must be available for connection. This assumes that the Active Directory and the DNS are fully operational. In our enterprise, we give our users our domain name, EntCert.com. A computer account in the domain must also be created before the client computer can join the domain. If the domain system administrator has not created the computer account, access to the domain may be denied during the installation process, but will be granted later when the basic installation is completed.

NOTE If this is the first Windows Server 2003 installation, it really doesn't matter whether you join a workgroup or a domain. You will automatically be the first domain controller when you promote the server by installing the Active Directory. See Chapters 5 and 6 for related information.

OPTIONAL SERVICES AND COMPONENTS

The system administrator can install a number of optional components, but as a general rule this should be avoided in the initial installation. Don't install options unless it is clear that they are required.

Several optional components, such as Certificate Services, also require technical sophistication. Moreover, Cluster Services and Terminal Services on the same server are mutually exclusive. Since these optional services and components can be installed at a later time, it may be best to do so after the base-level installation and configuration are completed. Once the system administrator becomes familiar with each of the desired service components, the basic procedures can be modified for future installations.

Table 3.5 lists the optional components that can be selected during the initial installation process. Unless otherwise noted, these services are described in later chapters. Specific installation requirements and methods are included in those discussions.

SERVER MIGRATION ORDER

Since each system in a workgroup maintains discrete security databases, the selection of which system to upgrade first is moot. This is not true of a domain model.

TABLE 3.5 Optional Services and Applications

Component	Description
Accessories/Utilities	Includes familiar Windows applications like WordPad, Paint, games, and CD player. Generally safe to install. Click the **Details** button to select individual components.
Certificate Authority	Advanced X.509 digital certificate authentication support for secure e-mail, Web access, dial-up accounts, and smart cards (see Chapter 11).
Cluster Services (Enterprise and DataCenter Servers Only).	Failover of two or more servers that mirror each other. If one fails, the other continues to provide resources (see Chapter 17).
Indexing Services	Indexes documents for user search of document properties. Generally safe to install without prior system knowledge.
Internet Information Services (IIS)	Suite of Web-based applications for site creation and administration, plus FTP, NNTP, and SMTP (see Chapter 16).
Management and Monitoring Tools	Communication monitoring and management tools, including SNMP. Recommended option for network environments.
Message Queuing	Infrastructure for messaging across heterogeneous environments (see Chapter 17).
Microsoft Scripting Debugger	The script development module, valuable to system administrators seeking to customize the environment.
Network Services	An essential suite that includes DNS, COM Internet Service Proxy, DHCP, IAS, TCP/IP, and WINS (see Chapter 12).
Other Network File and Print Services	Used for environments where UNIX printer services or Macintosh file or printer services are required.
Remote Installation	Provides server-based remote installation (see the Network Services Installations section devices.
Terminal Services	Allows client machines to run applications on the server in a "thin" client environment (see Chapter 15).
Terminal Services Licensing	Provides licenses for Terminal Services; must be installed with them (see Chapter 15).
Windows Media	Multimedia Internet extensions for the Advanced Streaming format.

Domain member workstations and servers can be upgraded in any order as well. The biggest consideration comes when promoting a server to a domain controller, since the first domain controller becomes the root of the domain tree. In existing Windows NT environments, the PDC or a reliable BDC is usually selected as the first domain controller to have Windows Server 2003 with the Active Directory installed. Another consideration when dealing with existing domains is the possible conversion of a multidomain model to a single domain with multiple organizational units. Prior to installing the Active Directory and placing a Windows Server 2003 domain controller into service, review Chapters 5 and 6 for specific planning and installation instructions.

Installation Steps

Now it is time to begin the installation, but first review the checklist. With this information available, the Windows Server 2003 installation should go very smoothly. Depending on your system, the installation should take at least two hours.

INSTALLATION CHECKLIST

The checklist for an upgrade installation is slightly different from that for a fresh installation. Use Table 3.6 as a baseline for all installations.

To upgrade existing systems to Windows Server 2003 take these additional steps:

- Back up files as a precaution.
- Disable disk mirroring.
- Uncompress existing volumes.
- Determine whether existing FAT or FAT32 file systems are to be upgraded.
- Disconnect the server from UPS and clustering environments.

TABLE 3.6 Decisions Common to All Domain Installations

System requirements are sufficient.	Yes → Proceed.
Hardware is on Microsoft's HCL.	Yes → Proceed.
Sufficient hard disk partition exists.	Yes → Proceed.
Partition/file system has been selected.	Yes → Proceed.
Licensing method has been determined.	Yes → Proceed.
Domain or workgroup name has been obtained.	Yes → Proceed.
Computer account exists for joining a domain.	Yes → Proceed; No → Proceed and join later.
Optional components have been selected.	Yes → Proceed.
Administrative password has been selected.	Yes → Proceed to completion.

Basic Installation

The first phase in the installation process involves working through a series of blue character-based screens, after which the computer will reboot to the graphical setup wizard. This supports the base-level installation. The network installation process then follows. Finally, optional components are configured. For example, if the system is to become a domain controller, Active Directory installation, as described in Chapter 6, is undertaken after the basic installation is complete.

NOTE You cannot upgrade Windows 2000 domain controllers in a forest without first preparing the forest and domain on the respective Schema Master and Infrastructure Master. Depending on the replication schedule for your organization, the time it takes to propagate preparation data will vary. The Windows 2000 Active Directory forest and domain need to be prepared for Windows Server 2003. The forest and domain are prepared by running Adprep on the respective Schema and Infrastructure Masters. To prepare the Windows 2000 forest and domain, perform the following procedures in the order given.

To prepare a Windows 2000 forest for Windows Server 2003:

1. Click **Finish** to exit Setup.
2. At a **command** prompt, type:

```
adprep /forestprep
```

Once the forest preparation data has replicated throughout the forest, prepare the domain for Windows Server 2003 on the Infrastructure Master. The domain preparation operation must be performed on the Infrastructure Master for each domain in the forest.

To prepare a Windows 2000 domain for Windows Server 2003:

1. At a **command** prompt, type:

```
adprep/domainprep
```

2. Do one of the following:
   - If you are running Adprep on the Infrastructure Master, Adprep will perform the domain preparation operation. In this case, skip steps 3 through 5, and then upgrade the domain controller by running Windows Server 2003 Setup (Winnt32.exe).
   - If you are running Adprep on a computer that is not the Infrastructure Master, Adprep will display the name of the Infrastructure Master for the domain. In this case, continue with step 3.

3. On the Infrastructure Master, open the installation media. At a **command** prompt, change to the directory of Winnt32 on the installation media and type:

```
winnt32.exe /checkupgradeonly
```

This will copy the Adprep files from the installation point to the server.

4. After the compatibility report has run, click **Finish**.
5. At the next **command** prompt, type:

```
adprep /domainprep
```

Once the domain preparation data has replicated throughout the domain, upgrade the domain controller by running Windows Server 2003 Setup (Winnt32.exe).

INSTALLATION OF WINDOWS SERVER 2003 VERSIONS

Since the installation screens are reasonably self-explanatory, we have not listed every option. However, the following steps should be observed to install the Intel Pentium–class version of Windows Server 2003, Standard Edition or Enterprise Edition:

1. Insert the Windows Server 2003 CD:
   - For a system that is currently powered off, turn the power on and press **Enter** when prompted to boot off the CD.
   - For a system that is live and running Windows NT or Windows 95/98, press **Start** → select **Run** → **Browse** to the CD → select **Setup**.
2. The installation loads a minimal version of Windows Server 2003 into memory and starts the setup program.
3. Select the type of installation. For new systems, the only choice is **Clean Install**. If you select **Clean Install** for an upgrade, all files, settings, and applications will be deleted and replaced with a fresh copy of the operating system. For existing systems, the **Upgrade** option preserves system settings and installed applications.
4. You are prompted to read the Windows Server 2003 license. Accept it to continue.
5. You are prompted to make decisions on the disk partition. See the previous discussion on disk partitions for additional information.
6. You are prompted to select the file system on which Windows .Server 2003 will be installed. See the previous discussion on file system selection for additional information.
7. Select the location of the operating system program files. The default location is `%systemroot\%winnt`. If this is a dual-boot environment in which an ear-

lier version of Windows NT exists on the specified partition, you should move the Windows Server 2003 program files to another location like winnt2. Otherwise, it is generally recommended that the default setting be accepted.

8. Files are now loaded on the hard drive. Once complete, the computer will restart with the Windows Server 2003 Setup Wizard.
9. The Windows Server 2003 Setup Wizard goes through a series of screens as follows:
   - ***Regional Settings.*** This provides an opportunity to change the language, locale, and keyboard settings for international or special use.
   - ***Name and Organization.*** Enter the user's name and organization. In most cases, the default Administrator should be the user name.
   - ***Licensing Mode.*** See the previous discussion on the per site and per server license options. This is an important decision because it will determine all Windows Server 2003 licensing for the server.
   - ***Computer Name.*** The computer name can be up to 15 characters to reflect the constraints of NetBIOS naming conventions. It cannot be the same as those for existing network computers, workgroups, or domains. A default name is displayed. It can be accepted or modified.
   - ***Password for Administrator Account.*** Enter the administrative password for the administrator.
   - ***Windows .NET Optional Components.*** See the previous discussion on optional components.
   - ***Display Setting.*** Set and test screen resolution, refresh frequencies, and display colors now, or perform this fine-tuning after the initial installation.
   - ***Time and Date.*** Make adjustments to the time zone, time of day, and date.

The network component phase of the Windows Server 2003 installation is now initiated. The wizard detects system components, permits the selection of network protocols, and allows the choice of joining a workgroup or domain. During this process, you will be asked to interact at several stages:

1. The detected network adapter card must be verified.
2. Selection of network protocols must be confirmed. The default or typical installation will include (1) Client for Microsoft Networks; (2) File and Printer Sharing for Microsoft Networks; and (3) the standard Windows Server 2003 networking environment, TCP/IP. See Chapters 12 and 13 for additional information.
3. The opportunity to join an existing workgroup or domain is presented. See the previous discussion.

The process of confirmation and installation takes 15 to 45 minutes depending on the system. Relax as the installation program copies files, saves configurations, removes temporary files, and restarts the system for use.

INSTALLATION OF WINDOWS SERVER 2003 ACROSS A NETWORK

Rather than run the installation for each machine from individual CD-ROMs, it is possible to store a copy of the operating system on a network server and permit downloading across the network. The first prerequisite is that the target machine must have installed the network client to a point where it can connect to the distribution server. The second prerequisite is that the distribution server must be configured to share out the directory in which the operating system Windows Server 2003 installation files reside. An archive distribution server is created either by sharing out the CD-ROM containing Windows Server 2003 or by copying over the /i386 folder from the CD to a shared folder on the server.

The steps that must be taken to install over a network follow:

1. Boot the target system with the network client.
2. Connect to the archive distribution server and move to the Windows Server 2003 shared folder.
3. Run the Winnt.exe command from the shared folder. Winnt.exe performs a series of functions:
    - Create the four Windows Server 2003 boot disks on Drive A of the target machine (be prepared to swap diskettes).
    - Create a temporary folder on the target machine called Win_nt.~ls.
    - Copy all the Windows Server 2003 files from the archive distribution server's shared folder to the temporary folder on the target system.
4. Disconnect and reboot the target system with Setup diskette 1 in Drive A.
5. Install Windows Server 2003 in the same fashion as described in the previous section.

SYSTEM CONFIGURATION

During the first logon, a screen will prompt you to complete the specific configuration tasks. Most of these specialized installation roles and configurations are covered in other chapters of the book. A server can be configured to provide multiple roles, although some functions may be mutually exclusive. It is recommended for performance and security reasons that a server perform only two to four roles.

To retrieve the wizard at any time, press **Start → Programs → Administrative Tools → Configure Your Server**. Figure 3.4 shows the initial Configure Your Server Wizard window.

The following list outlines the server roles (Figure 3.5) that can be assigned to your system:

DHCP server. Dynamic Host Configuration Protocol servers maintain TCP/IP configuration information that is then provided to clients. The server database

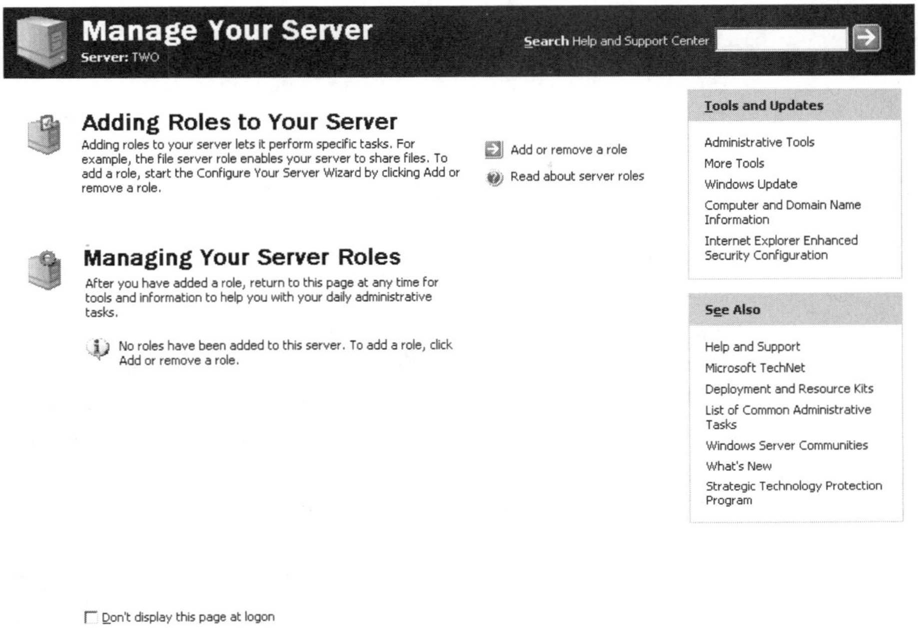

FIGURE 3.4 Configure Your Server Wizard

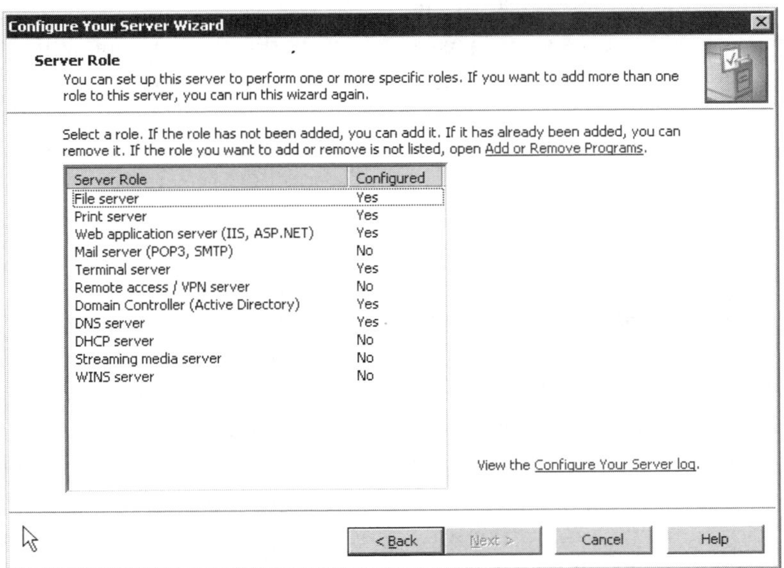

FIGURE 3.5 Server Role Dialog Selection Box

includes valid configuration parameters for all clients on the network, valid IP addresses maintained in a pool for assignment (including reserved addresses), and the duration of a lease (length of time) offered by the server. DHCP server permits DHCP-enabled clients to obtain their IP address and related configuration parameters dynamically.

DNS server. Domain Name System is used for the naming of computers and network services. It is organized into a hierarchy of domains. TCP/IP networks such as the Internet use DNS to locate computers and services through user-friendly names.

Domain Controller (Active Directory). As discussed in Chapters 5 and 6, this form of server is promoted to a domain controller using the Active Directory Installation Wizard. The wizard installs and configures components that provide directory services to network users and computers in a Microsoft Active Directory environment.

File server. In a client/server environment, this is one of the most common specific configurations. The file servers provide and manage access to files.

POP3 server. This permits the configuration of the Post Office Protocol 3 (POP3) service.

Print server. Like the file server, printer servers are commonly used in client/server environments. The special function is simply to administer print jobs across the network.

Real-time communication server. This server manages the authentication and routing of network traffic.

Remote access server. This server calls the Routing and Remote Access services to businesses in local area network (LAN) and wide area network (WAN) environments. It also supports communication over secure virtual private network (VPN) connections using the Internet. Remote access also connects remote or mobile workers to organization networks.

Server cluster node (Windows Server 2003, Enterprise and Datacenter Editions only). As discussed in Chapter 17, a server cluster is a group of independent computer systems (or nodes) that work together as a single system. Their purpose is to ensure that mission-critical applications and resources remain available. Clustering allows users and administrators to access and manage the nodes as a single system rather than as separate computers.

SharePoint Team Services server. This server supports Web publishing and collaboration. It is a superset of FrontPage® Server Extensions 2002. It includes all of the features available with the server extensions.

Streaming media server. Improved for Windows Server 2003, this specialized function manages streaming media over the Internet.

Terminal Services server. As discussed in Chapter 15, Terminal Services provides remote access to a client computer through "thin client" software. This allows the client computer to serve as a terminal emulator. Only the user interface of the program to the client is transmitted and data is stored and executed on the server.

Web server. The Web user interface for server administration allows the administration of your server from a remote computer using a Web browser. The Web UI is tuned for the server role selected.

WINS server. Windows Internet Name Service provides a distributed database for registering and querying dynamic mappings of NetBIOS names for computers and groups on your network.

NOTE New to Windows Server 2003 is the ability to decommission a server's role using the same tool that assigned the task. For example, a server assigned to support DNS can have this role removed using the Configure Your Server tool.

Changing the Basic Setup

When a large number of installations are anticipated that require changes to the default settings, it may be advisable to modify the basic setup installation process. From the **command** or the **run** prompt, it is possible to set switches as described in Table 3.7. For repeated use, modify the autoexe.com file line that contains Winnt.exe on Setup diskette A.

Automated or Unattended Installations

The Setup Manager Wizard, available from the Resource Kit, can be used to create scripts to facilitate unattended installations. The key is to create or modify an answer file that is queried during the installation process. An answer file will bypass the questions that would otherwise be asked interactively of the installer. A sample answer file is shipped on the Windows Server 2003 compact disk.

When the Setup Manager Wizard is invoked, first you need to determine whether to create a new answer file or one based on the current machine's configuration, or to modify an existing answer file. The Setup Manager Wizard can create the following types of answer files:

- Windows XP unattend.txt setup file
- Windows Server 2003 (all levels) unattend.txt setup file

TABLE 3.7 Switch Options for Customizing Setup Winnt.exe

Switch	Description
/a	Turns on accessibility options.
/e	Identifies any additional commands to be run after the wizard setup.
/I[:]infile	Sets the name of the setup information file; the default is DOSNET.INF.
/r	Identifies optional directory/folder to be installed.
/rx	Identifies optional directory/folder to be copied.
/s[:]sourcepath	Identifies the source path of the Windows 2000/.NET installation files.
/t[:]tempdrive	Designated temporary setup file location; overrides default location.
/u	Used for unattended operation or optional script file (also requires /s.)
/copydir:folder	Creates additional folders.
/cmd:command	Executes the specified command prior to the final setup action.
/cmdcons	Installs files for the recovery and repair console.
/debug level:file	Creates a debug log for the level specified.
/syspart:drive	Copies the setup files to a drive that can be moved later.
/tempdrive:drive	Establishes which drive to use for the temporary setup files.
/unattend num:file	Uses the optional answer file to perform unattended installation.

- Remote Installation Services (RIS) remboot.sif file
- System Preparation tool sysprep.inf file (used with disk duplication, discussed in the next section)

The wizard will walk you through other questions that permit the setting of user interaction levels. Simply enter the level you desire.

Automated installation is particularly useful when creating domain controllers. As part of the setup script, the command to complete the basic setup, dcpromo/

```
answer:<answer file>,
```

should be invoked.

Disk Duplication

On systems with identical hardware, the most efficient method for installation is to duplicate hard drives. The master image of Windows Server 2003 can be copied to many disks with comparatively little effort via the System Preparation tool (sysprep.exe). Note that you cannot use sysprep to clone domain controllers.

STEPS FOR SUPPORTING DISK DUPLICATION

Disk duplication involves a series of steps as outlined:

1. Windows Server 2003 should be installed and configured on a master computer.
2. Other installation and application software should also be installed on the master computer.
3. From the **command** prompt → run **sysprep.exe**. Alternately, the Setup Manager Wizard can inactively create a sysprep.inf file. This method creates a Sysprep folder on the root of the drive, which the mini-setup program checks for.
4. Restart the master computer.
5. Use a third-party image-copying tool to create a master image.
6. Use a third-party image-copying tool to make multiple images on destination drives.

Once the destination disks are installed in the computers and booted for the first time, the mini-setup program prompts for computer-specific variables, including the administrator's password and the computer's name. However, if the sysprep.inf file is present, all invention by the user will be bypassed if the settings so designate.

CONFIGURING THE SYSTEM PREPARATION TOOL

The System Preparation tool used for master hard disk duplication primarily deletes SIDs and other user- and system-specific data. The new SID and related information are regenerated when the system reboots from the loaded disk image. The syntax used when running sysprep.exe follows. Sysprep.exe switches are listed in Table 3.8.

```
Sysprep.exe /-option
```

Remote OS Installation

The Remote OS Installation provides the use of the new Preboot eXecution Environment (PXE) remote boot technology. PXE is based on DHCP. PXE combines

TABLE 3.8 System Preparation Tool Switches

Switch	Task
-quiet	Runs the mini-setup without user invention.
-pnp	Forces the detection of Plug and Play devices on the destination system.
-reboot	Invokes the reboot rather than shutdown option.

with server-based distribution software to support client installation of Windows XP. This permits administrators to remotely install Windows Server 2003 and desktop images without onsite support. Once the client operating system is installed, IntelliMirror can be used to manage user desktops, data, settings, and application software.

The Remote OS Installation supports Remote Installation Services in which a server hosts an equivalent to the CD copy of Windows XP. The implementation of a CD-type RIS installation is discussed in the next section. Alternatively, a preconfigured Remote Installation Preparation (RIPrep) can be used to provide a desktop image. In this case, administrators can clone desktop configurations and applications across identical computer systems. Once the first system is properly configured, an image can be created and then replicated using the RIS Wizard.

Client remote boot is initiated either by the computer's BIOS or through use of a remote boot floppy disk–based program. DHCP provides an IP address for the client system when the remote service boot is requested. When connection to the RIS server is made, the user initiates the download by pressing the F12 key. Depending on the level of automation that was established by the RIS administrator, the user may have to input a few configuration settings or none at all. The Active Directory will then determine what installation options and other rights for a particular user are to be used based on those established in Group Policies.

RIS INSTALLATION OF WINDOWS XP

The Remote Installation Services permit the installation of Windows XP clients located anywhere on the network from a central location. RIS can be run from either a domain controller or a member server. DNS, DHCP, and Active Directory services must be fully operational.

The RIS server must be installed on a volume shared over the network. This volume must be of sufficient size to contain both the RIS software and a complete image of Windows XP. Moreover, it must be formatted with NTFS, and it cannot run on the partition that is running Windows Server 2003.

The Remote Installation Services Setup Wizard installs the RIS software and copies Windows XP installation files to the server. It adds a variation of the Unattend.txt file that has a .sif ending. As a final step it sets up the Client Installation Wizard screens that appear during the actual remote installation.

The RIS component is added as follows: Invoke the **Windows Components Wizard** → select **Add/Remove Programs** → select **Start and Run** → type **risetup** → select **OK**. RIS is configured via the Active Directory Users and Computers snap-in tool discussed in Chapter 6.

Troubleshooting the Installation

Countless issues can create problems during the installation process, and it would be impossible to outline every one. However, to provide a basis for troubleshooting, Table 3.9 lists the most common points of failure.

TABLE 3.9 Potential Points of Failure

Failure	Possible Remedy
CD-ROM or Media Error	Contact Microsoft or your computer manufacturer (in the case of OEM versions) for a replacement CD. If the physical CD-ROM is incompatible, it will be necessary to replace it.
Insufficient Memory	Add a minimum of 128 MB.
Insufficient Disk Space	Run the setup program to check the partitioning. It may be necessary to create new partitions and perhaps delete some partitions. Replacement of the hard drive may also be necessary.
Services Fail to Start	Could occur if service dependencies are not met, most commonly with networks. Return to the Network Settings and check what network adapter(s) and protocols are installed. Also, in the case of clients, make sure the computer account is established and unique within the domain forest.
Failure to Connect to the Domain Controller	Verify that the domain controller is running, the DNS service is running, the domain name is correct, and protocol and adapter settings are properly set.
Windows Server 2003 Refuses to Install or Start	Could be a hardware compatibility issue. Make sure that Windows Server 2003 is detecting the hardware and that it is on the Hardware Compatibility List.

DEVICE DRIVER MANAGEMENT

One major drawback of Windows 2000 was its sometimes spotty device drive support. This was in part due to Microsoft's intent to support devices that were most likely to be found in business environments and ignore those common to home users. The driver database for Windows 9.x and Me was different from those of the Windows 2000 product family. Windows XP and Windows Server 2003 consolidate the old and new device driver databases, ensuring greater hardware compatibility. For example, support for digital cameras and scanners has been significantly augmented. The Windows Image Acquisition (WIA) common system dialog boxes provide four dialog boxes as follows.

- *Scanner* common dialog allows the user to preview, crop, scan, and input scan properties such as brightness and contrast.
- *Still camera* common dialog allows the user to view thumbnail images, preview full-sized pictures, view picture information, and delete pictures.
- *Video camera* common dialog supports the viewing of a live or recorded video stream. Captured frames can be retrieved as standard WIA pictures.
- *Device selection* dialog allows the user to select from among multiple installed WIA devices and to set the device property information.
- The *Printer Wizard* supports a significantly larger number of devices (more than 300) and permits shared printer setup.

In addition to the wider range of support device drivers, additional management capability has been added.

Device Driver Rollback

The installation of a new and untested device always represents a potential problem. Much of the "blue screen of death" system termination on Windows NT and Windows 2000 systems can be traced directly back to improperly behaving device drivers. The new Device Drive Rollback facility permits you to remove a bad driver and return to an earlier version when appropriate. In order to invoke this facility, right-click **My Computer** → **System Properties** → **Device Manager** → click a **Device Driver** → **Rollback Driver**.

Device Drive Last Known Good Files

To ensure greater system integrity, a copy of the device driver that existed at the time of system booting is retained even when a new device driver is installed. In the event that the new driver causes system instability, the Last Known Good File can be substituted. This feature is used when the system cannot be rebooted in normal mode. To regain control, the user can boot the computer into safe mode and use the Last Known Good configuration to restore the driver.

NOTE It is now possible to change the transfer rate of a device without having to restart the system, as was required with Windows 2000. Changes in the transfer rate are accomplished through the Device Manager. When changes are made, they are automatically reflected without system interruption.

HARDWARE AUTOPLAY

Plug and Play functionality has become more reliable with the AutoPlay feature. It enables users to connect a new device or insert media and the operating system will recognize it without the need to reboot or reconfigure the computer. When the operating system senses a connection, it determines the content and automatically starts the appropriate application. The supported media types include flash cards, compact disks (CDs), digital video discs (DVDs), Zip disks, removable disk drives, PC cards, and external IEEE 1394 standard hot-plug fixed drives. The supported content types include pictures, music files, video, and mixed content. This feature greatly reduces common installation headaches. The hardware AutoPlay feature is invoked by plugging in a new device or by pressing **Start → Control Panel → Add New Hardware** (for non–Plug and Play devices).

WINDOWS PRODUCT ACTIVATION

In an effort to minimize product piracy, Microsoft has instituted the Windows Product Activation (WPA) scheme on all operating systems and many productivity software products. Activation of the code must occur during a prescribed time period, which varies among products.

Activation is applicable to all retail purchasers of selected Microsoft products such as Office XP, Windows XP, and Windows Server 2003. Users who purchase new machines may or may not be required to activate, depending on whether the hardware OEM has completed the activity at the factory. In most cases, large corporate account users will not be concerned with activation because of the nature of volume account licenses.

From a user's perspective, activation is relatively simple and can be accomplished either over the Internet in a couple of mouse clicks or by telephone. The process does not require the user to give personal information except his or her country. Unlike product registration, the user may elect to provide additional information such as name and e-mail address on a strictly voluntary basis. The product activation verifies that a software program's product key is associated with a particular computer. The actual installation ID includes an encrypted form of the product ID and a hardware hash. Microsoft uses a one-way mathematical algorithm to create the hash. The hardware hash is an 8-byte value that is created by running 10 data pieces from the personal computer through the one-way algorithm. When hashed, a processor's 96-bit serial number becomes 128 bits. The Microsoft hashing scheme uses 6 of those bits that cannot be backward calculated. The activation code includes not only the 6 bits from the processor hash, but also similar information from other pieces of hardware. The product ID (9 bytes) and the hardware hash (8 bytes) form the activation request. The resulting confirmation ID is 42 integers.

Microsoft strongly contends that the process is completely anonymous and confidential. The process does not collect data from the individual (except country of origin) and certainly does not scan hard drives for stored information. It simply surveys the installed hardware to develop a computer ID that can be associated with the software.

Another concern is the ability to change hardware configurations or move the software to another system. Microsoft's activation scheme accommodates both of these situations. If you substantially change the hardware in your computer (e.g., replace the CPU or primary hard drive), the information contained in the hardware hash may no long appear valid. Therefore it will probably be necessary seek new activation. In the case of retiring one computer and moving the software to a new system, activation will also be necessary. In both cases, you will merely need to call Microsoft at the telephone number provided in the activation dialog window.

If you are in a highly secured environment where activation might be viewed as a possible security breach, contact Microsoft directly. Microsoft product managers have assured us that special accommodations can be made to activate your code under these circumstances.

AUTOMATIC PRODUCT UPDATE

The initial installation of any operating system or productivity application is only the beginning. Applying updates and patches is a never ending activity for administrators. The Automatic Update (AU) features available under Windows XP and Windows Server 2003 should significantly lessen this burden. Automatic Updates is a proactive service that enables individuals with administrative privileges to download and install Windows updates on a computer. Updates are downloaded to the user's computer in the background, although the user is notified prior to installation and given the opportunity to postpone it because the installation might require restarting the computer. This feature also includes:

- *Detection:* Automatic Updates uses the Windows Update control to scan the system and decide which updates are applicable to a particular computer.
- *Downloads:* AU uses its innovative bandwidth-throttling technology for downloads. Bandwidth throttling uses only idle bandwidth so that downloads will not interfere with or slow down other network activity, such as Internet browsing.
- *Install:* AU uses the Windows Update control for installing downloaded updates.
- *Security:* The AU service checks user security privileges on each method call. It will process calls coming only from administrator user sessions.
- *Resolving user collisions:* The service will allow the automatic update client to run only for one administrative user at a time.

The AU feature provides the following for clients:

- *User interface:* All dialog boxes, notification balloons, and icons perform in "intuitive" ways, and the user has the choice of the classic or the new view (discussed in Chapter 4).
- *Security:* It will perform security checks so that it can run only in an administrative user session.

The AU features begins when a user with administrative privileges logs on, but it can also be manually launched by invoking **Start → Control Panel → Performance and Maintenance → System → Automatic Updates.**

NOTE Windows Server 2003 has the Dynamic Update feature, which provides application and device compatibility updates, some driver updates, and emergency fixes. This is used for setup operations. Microsoft periodically posts updates on the Internet when Dynamic Update requirements such as security fixes are warranted. When installing or upgrading the operating system from a CD, invoking the Dynamic Update feature during setup will search Microsoft's Web site for the latest and greatest patches. This guarantees that a new installation is current.

FILE TRANSFER WIZARD

When installing a new system, the transfer of files or system states from one computer to another can be a complex and sometimes haphazard activity. The new Files and Settings Transfer Wizard takes the difficulty out of this task. This feature supports the transfer of files and settings (state) from one computer to another by walking the user through the migration process. The Files and Settings Transfer Wizard has two paths that are selected to either engage state collection or state application. The state collection wizard is used on the old system, which is also known as the source. Source computer operating systems include Windows 9.x, Windows NT 4.0, Windows Me, Windows 2000, Windows XP, and Windows Server 2003. The wizard state application is run on the new computer, also known as the destination. Only the Windows XP OS supports destination systems. The actual file transfer is accomplished either by connecting the two systems to a network or through the use of a removable storage device like a floppy disk or CD. The File Transfer Wizard is invoked by pressing **Start → More Programs → Accessories → System Tools → Files and Settings Transfer Wizard**.

SYSTEM RESTORATION

There are times when a system will simply malfunction for any number of reasons. Rather than require countless hours of diagnostic work to hunt down the problem, Windows XP and Windows Server 2003 provide a System Restore feature. This can be particularly useful if a virus has been introduced into the system during a session and disables operating system functions. The system restoration returns the computer to a previous state without losing personal data files.

System Restore actively monitors changes to the activity of the system and some application files. It then automatically creates identifiable references known as *restore points*. These restore points are created either on a daily basis or when a significant system change, such as the installation of a new application, is noted. Optionally, the user can create and name restore points at any time. This is certainly recommended for any administrator engaged in downloading and applying untested applications or operating system patches. There are several methods of accessing the System Restore functions: **Start → More Programs → Accessories → System Tools → Backup Start → Help and Support Services → Tools → System Restore; Start → Control Panel → Performance and Maintenance → System → System Restore; Start → Help and Support Services → Performance and Maintenance → Use System Restore.**

NOTE System Restore monitors only critical operating system files and does not monitor changes to or recover user personal data files. Users are still responsible for backing up personal files.

UNINSTALLING WINDOWS XP OPERATING SYSTEM

If, for whatever reason, you install Windows XP and decide the operating system does not meet your needs, it is possible to revert to Windows 98 or Windows Me. (No other Windows operating systems are supported for this backward uninstall process.) For a system administrator charged with client system maintenance, this feature may periodically be handy especially when an end user becomes uncomfortable with the new operating system. Windows XP Uninstall is achieved as follows: **Start → Control Panel → Add or Remove Programs**.

POSTSCRIPT

Planning is always advised when a system administrator is performing any Windows Server 2003 system task. It is absolutely critical, however, during initial installation and deployment. This chapter provided an overview of planning concepts that should be implemented when deploying a Windows Server 2003 enterprise. It also provided core instructions on installing the basic operating system. Subsequent chapters will explore planning and installation issues relevant to other topics such as the Active Directory.

Chapter 4

Getting Started: The OS Interface

This chapter reviews items that are essential to the use and administration of Windows Server 2003. Some of the discussion will be elementary to those already familiar with Windows environments; however, a number of topics are either new or sufficiently enhanced to warrant review. Having read this chapter, the system administrator should have the following:

- An understanding of the Windows Server user and administrative interfaces
- A working knowledge of the Microsoft Management Console
- The ability to work with other administrative tools
- The ability to use the greatly expanded Help facility
- The skills to find objects with the Search function
- Understanding of the other usability enhancements of Windows Server

INTERFACE BASICS

The Windows Server 2003 provides two alternative user interfaces. The new interface mirrors the more visual approach first introduced in Windows XP. It is recommended that this view be used whenever possible. The second user interface, which we call the "classic view," should be familiar to anyone who has used Windows 98 or Windows NT with Internet Explorer 4.0 or later. Throughout this book, we alternate screen shots to reflect these two user interfaces. In the unlikely event that you have not used these products, this section provides a view of the user interface from 30,000 feet. Even for experienced users, there may be a few tips worthy of brief review. While the options available to an administrator and the typical user are different, the underlying interface is the same.

The Windows Management Services interface is based on the industry initiative Web-Based Enterprise Management (WBEM), which attempts to establish infrastructure management across heterogeneous environments. It identifies the underlying methods for accessing data on a variety of platforms. WBEM is derived from the Common Information Model (CIM) as defined by the Distribution Management Task Force (DMTF).

Microsoft's implementation of WBEM is called the Windows Management Instrumentation (WMI). WMI supports traditional administration that uses scripts that kick off other applications. It also goes further by permitting the use of scripts at the object level. WMI can be thought of as the method in which things get done. The Windows Scripting Host, discussed in Chapter 17, automates the action. Finally, the Microsoft Management Console (MMC) discussed in this chapter determines how the administrative tools are to be presented. The MMC user interface creates linkages to the WMI.

The Windows Server 2003 interface is basically a desktop comprising a customizable toolbar and a group of icons that serve as shortcuts to applications, folders, files, and other objects. As menus or iconic items are opened, Microsoft Explorer windows are launched and objects are displayed with a Web browser look and feel.

In Chapter 8, "Group Policies," we discuss how a system administrator can standardize the desktop to add or restrict the menu and desktop items available to a user or group.

The Toolbar and Cascading Menu System

All Microsoft Windows environments provide a **Start** toolbar and cascading pull-down menus (Figure 4.1). If you have not already played with toolbar and menu setups, take a few moments to get acquainted with them. Also, take the time to customize the **Start** toolbar and menus by clicking **Start** → then select **Settings** → select **Taskbar and Start Menu**. One of the first changes a user will notice when working with Windows XP or Windows Server 2003 is the new look and feel of the **Start** menu. It has been redesigned to reflect important and frequently used tasks better. There is now a **Frequently Used Programs** list that displays the most frequently used programs. The **Start** menu and toolbar can be customized by right-clicking it and selecting **Properties**. Alternatively, the **Start** menu can be modified as follows: **Start** → **Control Panel** → **Appearance and Themes** → **Taskbar and Start Menu** → select **Start Menu** or **Taskbar** tab. At this stage, any item can be added to the **Start** menu or toolbar by clicking it in the dialog box. Other modifications are possible, including changing the location of the **Start** toolbar itself.

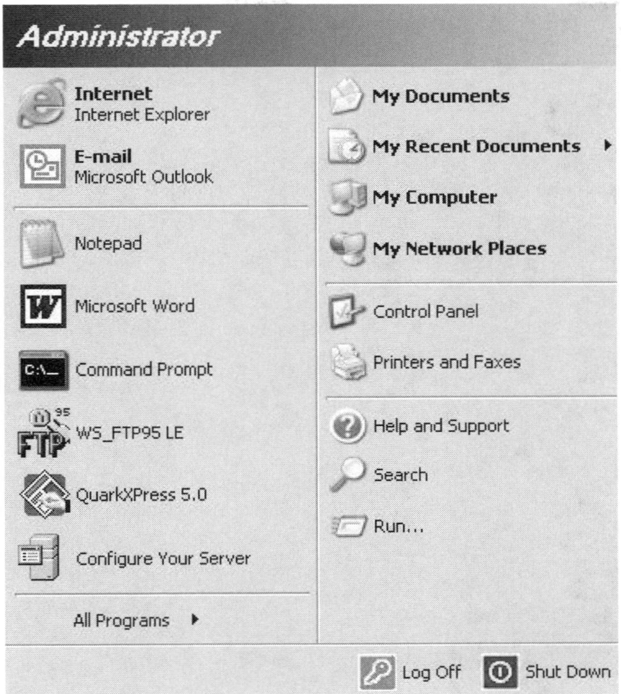

FIGURE 4.1 New Start Menu

(Its default location is at the bottom of the screen, as it appears in Figures 4.1 and 4.2 where the new and classic menu views are shown, respectively.)

Desktop Icons

The desktop displays default icons and others added by the user or system administrator. They are mere representations of the programs, folders, and files. The typical desktop icons include

- ***My Documents***—a shortcut to the user's default directory that displays files and folders resident in the folder. Among the new folders located in each user's My Documents are media folders called **My Pictures** and **My Music**, both of which are designed to organize multimedia files.
- ***My Computer***—a shortcut to resources available on the local computer, including disk drives, CD drives, removable media, and the like.

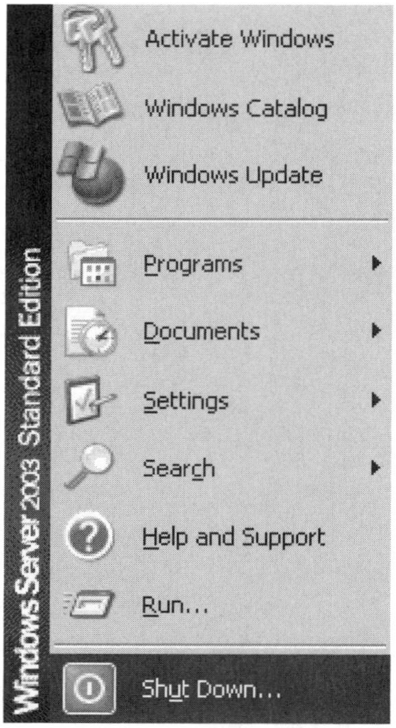

FIGURE 4.2 Classic Start Menu

NOTE Windows XP and Windows Server 2003 provide a Desktop Cleanup Wizard to help users keep desktops free of shortcuts they don't use. The Cleanup Wizard periodically checks the desktop for unused shortcuts and provides a means to remove those shortcuts without harming the installed program. The Desktop Cleanup Wizard runs automatically every 60 days. It can be manually invoked by clicking **Start → More Programs → Accessories → System Tools → Disk Cleanup**.

- ***My Network Places***—a display of connected network resources that provides access to resources the user has permission to use.
- ***Recycle Bin***—a temporary storage area for documents marked for removal. This is basically a safety measure that permits the retrieval of documents deleted by mistake. Users should be instructed to empty the **Recycle Bin** periodically, thereby permanently removing the files and freeing disk space.
- ***Internet Explorer***—access to Microsoft's Web browser. If connected to the Internet, the browser permits surfing to sites on the World Wide Web. It also permits viewing objects on the local system or internal network to which the user has permission.

A number of actions can be taken to manage desktop icons, including the following:

- *Moving icons to the desktop*. When a file, folder, or application is in common use, it should be added to the desktop. You can move it there directly simply by holding the right mouse button down on it and "dragging" it across the screen to where you want it.
- *Creating shortcuts from the desktop*. Another method of gaining access to a commonly used object is to create a pointer, known as a shortcut, to it. This duplicate iconic representation can then be dragged to the desktop. A shortcut is created by selecting the target object → then right-click the object → select **Create Shortcut**.
- *Reorganizing the desktop icons*. Icons can be dragged to any location on the desktop.
- *Adding desktop icons to the Start toolbar*. It is sometimes convenient to list desktop icons on the **Start** toolbar. Selecting the target icon and dragging it to the **Start** toolbar accomplishes this action.
- *Deleting icons from the desktop*. Deleting the actual object deletes the access to the application, folder, or file. However, shortcut icons can be deleted and the actual program, folder, or file remains. The deletion is accomplished by clicking the icon, pressing the **DELETE** key, and confirming by pressing **Yes** when prompted.

THE MY COMPUTER TOOL

Double-clicking the desktop **My Computer** icon provides a view of the resources available on the local computer system. Alternatively, the Microsoft Explorer view provides a default two-panel view: On the right is an icon view of objects and folders, and on the left is the cascading menu view. The Microsoft Explorer view is obtained by a right-clicking **My Computers** → select **Explorer**. To drill down to either panel, simply select the folder and double-click. Alternatively, the cascading menu can be opened or closed by selecting the PLUS SIGN, +, or the MINUS SIGN, –, respectively.

Expanding the View of Folders and Files

Windows Server 2003 presents default files that are generally visible to the user or system administrator. The view can be expanded to include hidden (Figure 4.3) and operating system files. To view such files from the **Tools** menu, select **Folder Options** from the toolbar of the My Computer or other Explorer window, select the **View** tab, and select the items to be modified. (This dialog box is also available from the **Control Panel** under **Folder Options**.)

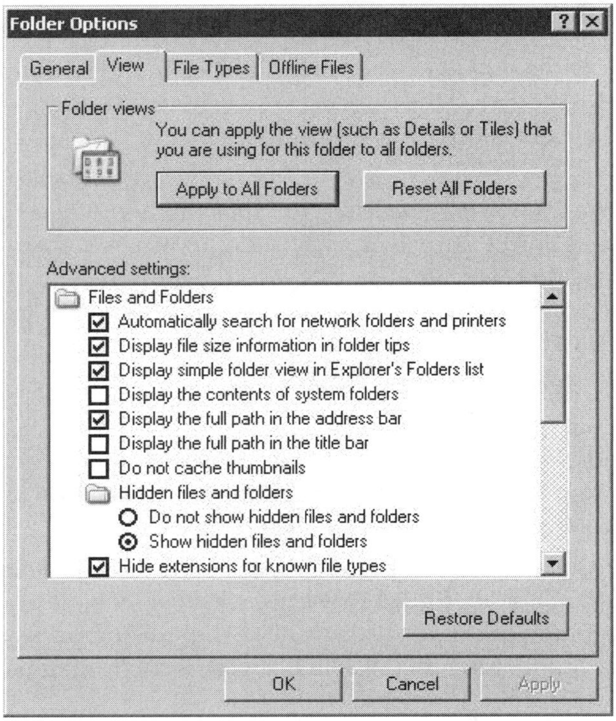

FIGURE 4.3 Viewing Hidden Files

File Association User Interface Improvements

In order for a file to be usable, it must be associated with a specific application in a recognized format. The File Association User Interface feature enhances the control of file associations at installation and the inclusion of certain basic file types (.zip, .pdf, .cab, and .css). It also controls reserved file classes such as Audio CD. When unassociated files are detected, the operating system will suggest possible applications that support the file type. If the user can confirm the association between the file and the suggested application, then that match will be retained the next time a file of that type is discovered. In the event that no suitable applications are found on the system, an Internet-connected computer can search an online database of candidates.

Another use of this feature is to permit the user to designate an alternative application to associate with a particular file type. For example, a user might have a preferred photo editor. When a GIF file is opened, the associated photo editor will be launched.

To invoke the file association feature: **Start → Control Panel → Appearance and Themes → Folder Options → File Types**.

File Management Improvements

The Windows XP and Windows Server 2003 user interface leverages WebView and ListView technologies. Although the classic views familiar to users of earlier Windows versions can still be invoked, Microsoft believes these new views deliver a higher level of usability. This interface exposes common folder and file tasks dynamically in WebView, a technology that uses HTML to display information. The facility also provides new grouping behavior and visuals. For example, files may be displayed graphically. Sorting of files is also improved so that greater refinement is possible. To invoke file management options: **Start → Control Panel → Appearance and Themes → Folder Options**.

My Computer Customization

The **Tools** pull-down menu on the My Computer (Figure 4.4) and any Explorer window permits three important local system views and accessibility:

- ***Map Network Drive***. This option permits the local "mounting" of a remote disk drive. From a user's perspective, the remote drive looks local.

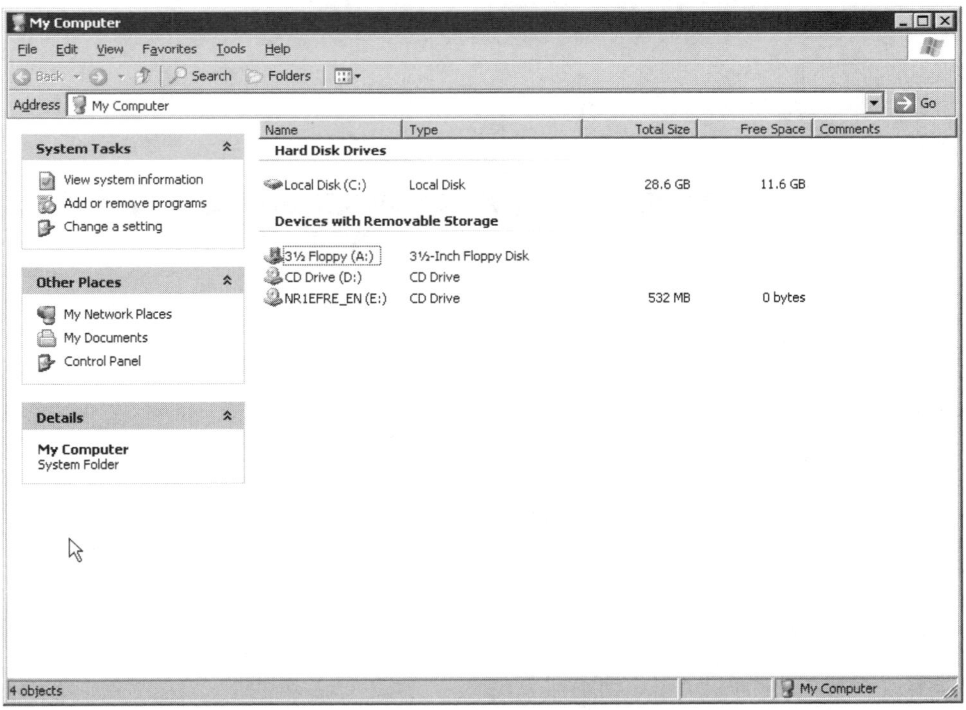

FIGURE 4.4 My Computer

- ***Disconnect Network Drive***. This option disconnects a previously mapped drive.
- ***Synchronize***. This option permits the synchronization of data that was changed while working offline with information on the server. It is possible to define the data to be synchronized and schedule the process.

MY NETWORK PLACES

Known in previous Windows versions as the Network Neighborhood, My Network Places is an improved network interface. When opened, it typically reveals several icons. One of them is **Entire Network**, with which you can drill down to lower levels of the present network. To view resources in the Microsoft Windows Network, double-click that icon. This will display all the connected Microsoft-based workgroups and domains (Figure 4.5).

Network Directory Search

By selecting the **Directory** icon, the system administrator is shown the Domain User and Computers folders (Figure 4.6). You can drill down any of the folders to view and manage associated users, groups, computers, and other objects. As discussed later, this method can be used for some remote administration.

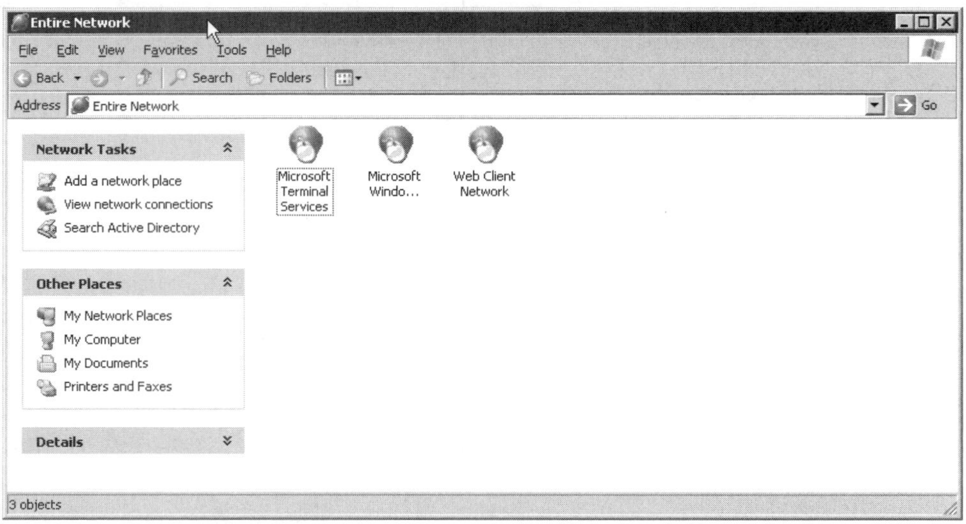

FIGURE 4.5 Entire Network

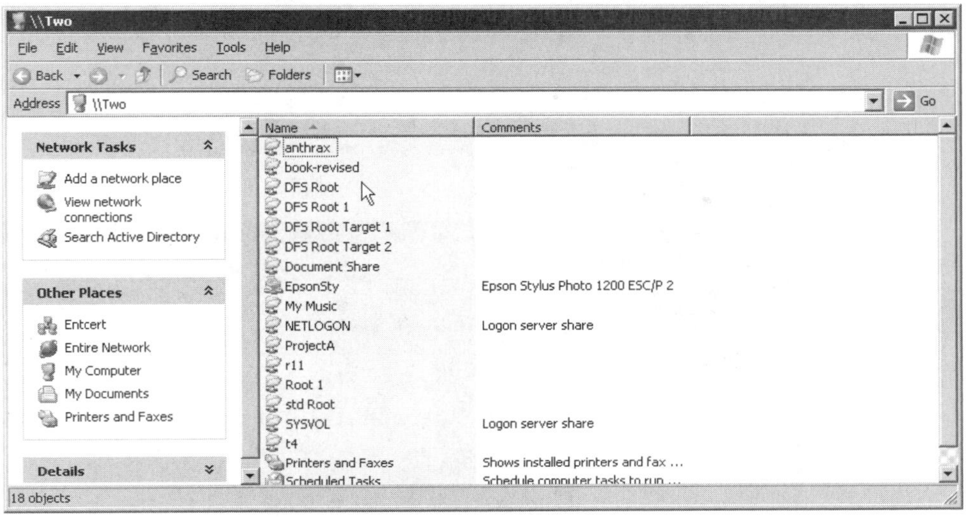

FIGURE 4.6 View of Network Folders and Appliances

The **Directory** icon can also be used to find resources within the domain. For example, to find a printer, follow these steps (see Figure 4.7):

1. Right-click any **Directory** icon (and domain name) → select **Find**.
2. Select **Advanced Tab** from the **Find** dialog box.
3. Select **Printer** from the **Find** pull-down menu → complete whatever data is known in the three tabs.
4. Click **Find Now**.

Another option for finding network resources from the **My Network Places** interface is to use the **Search** button on the toolbar. Complete the information in the left pane and click **Search** (Figure 4.8). The Search Companion will be activated.

DUALVIEW MONITORING FACILITY

The DualView Monitoring Facility extends the multimonitor feature of Windows 2000. This is a hardware-dependent facility that requires high-end display adapters that support two interfaces. In mobile computers, this takes the form of internal display and the external connector for a monitor or other display. DualView enables these two interfaces to display different outputs simultaneously. This feature is activated as follows: **Start → Control Panel → Printers and Other Hardware → Add New Hardware**.

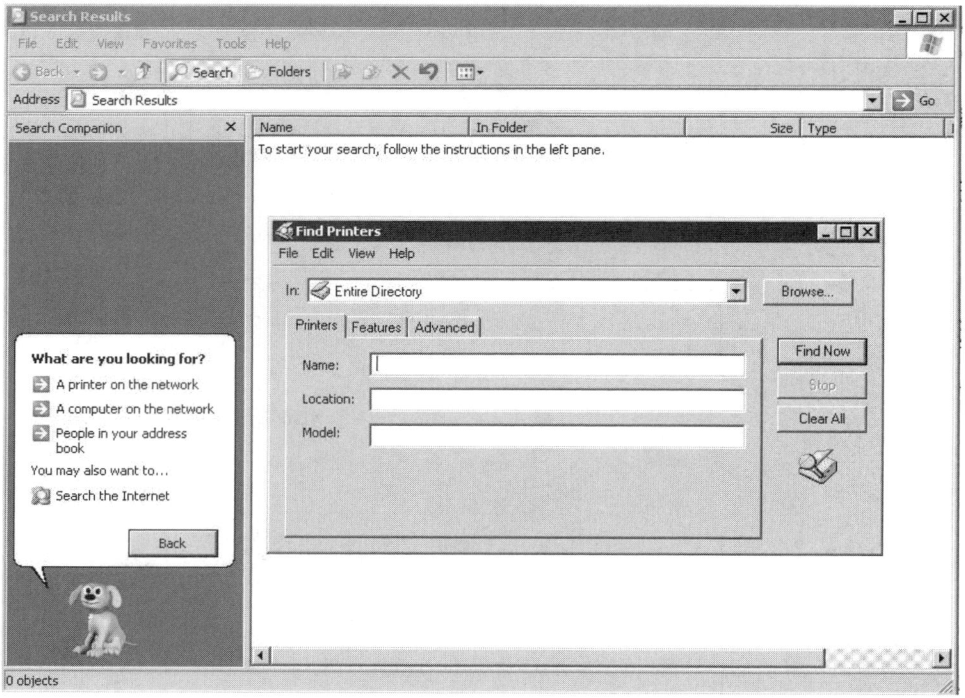

FIGURE 4.7 Finding a Network Printer

Microsoft Management Console

One of the strengths of Windows Server 2003 is its consolidation of many administrative tools into a single interface. The Microsoft Management Console has the familiar look and feel of the Microsoft Explorer. By default, it is divided into two panels: On the left is a list of the tools that have been added to the console; on the right are details for the selected administrative tool.

Administrative tools are called *snap-ins* and are hosted in the MMC framework. All components in an MMC snap-in are organized hierarchically in order to view relationships and provide a logical structure for administration. Each MMC can contain one or more administrative tools. It is also possible to create multiple MMCs and to group similar snap-in functions in a cluster. The decision to add or remove snap-ins is the system administrator's. The snap-ins include both those bundled with Windows Server 2003 and others from third-party vendor applications that adhere to API guidelines.

The MMC also facilitates the delegation of administrative responsibility. As discussed in later chapters, Windows Server 2003 permits the creation of organizational

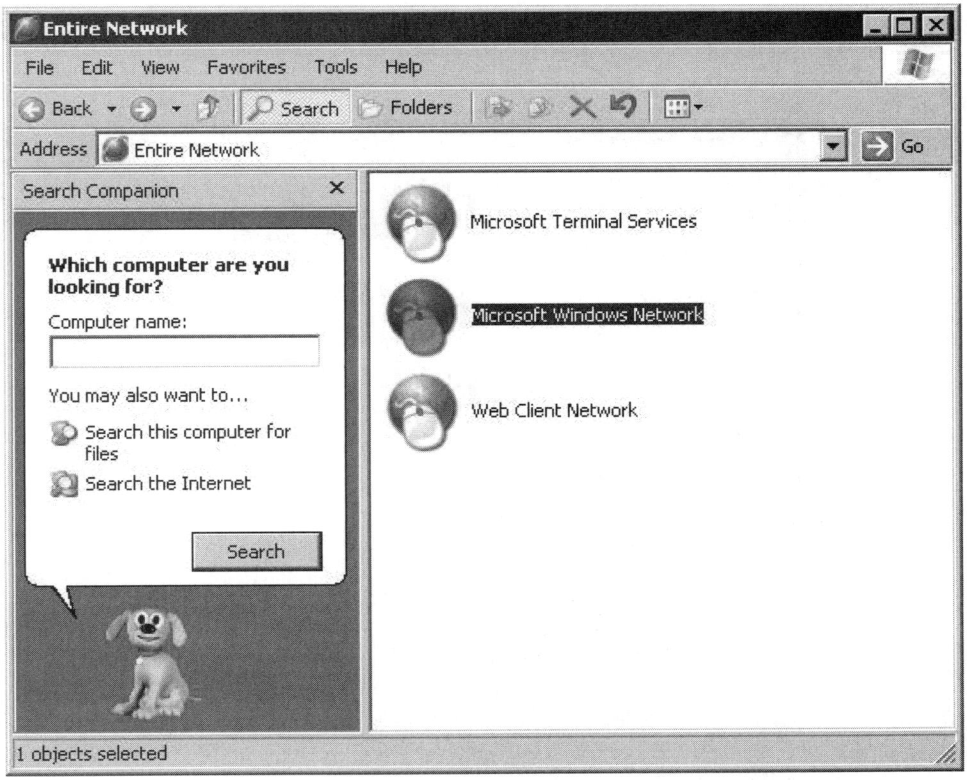

FIGURE 4.8 Network Find Dialog

units, the smaller administrative components in which specific and granular responsibility can be assigned. An MMC can be created for a specific set of responsibilities and provided to the administrator of the OU.

CREATING AND USING MMCS

MMCs provide a consistent and single point of access for administrating Windows 2000/.NET. The initial step is to create the first Microsoft Management Console (Figure 4.9): click **Start** → select **Run** → type **MMC** → click **OK**. This procedure can be used to create additional consoles, or you can create a new MMC from within an existing console.

The MMC permits a number of methods to interact with snap-ins. The toolbar is used to select the following options:

- ***Console***, used in the author mode, primarily adds or removes snap-ins and provides other customizations.

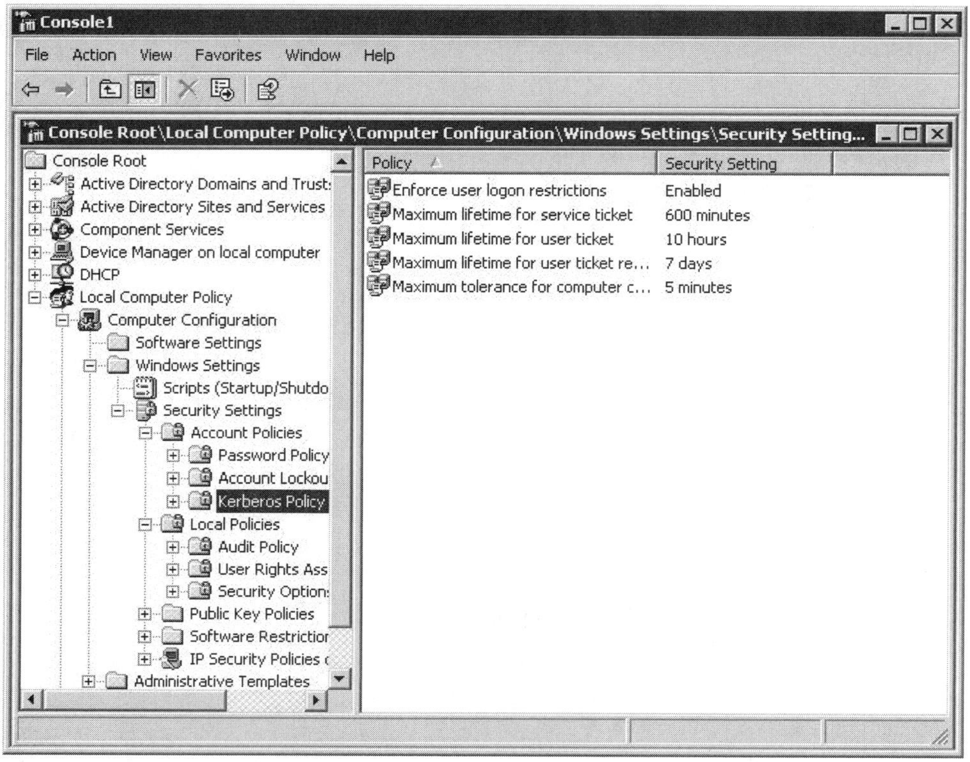

FIGURE 4.9 The Microsoft Management Console

- ***Action*** lists the possible actions that can be taken for each snap-in. The options are different for each one.
- ***View*** provides a list of methods to customize the view of each administrative task. Each snap-in has a different view.
- ***Favorites*** is used in much the same way as Web browser favorite links for rapid maneuvering to snap-in components.

ADDING A SNAP-IN

As shown in Figure 4.10, the MMC snap-ins are added by following these steps:

1. While in the author mode, open a new or existing MMC.
2. Click **Console → select Add/Remove Snap-in**.
3. From the dialog box listing the current snap-ins (Figure 4.11), click **Add**.
4. Select the destination snap-in → click **Add**.

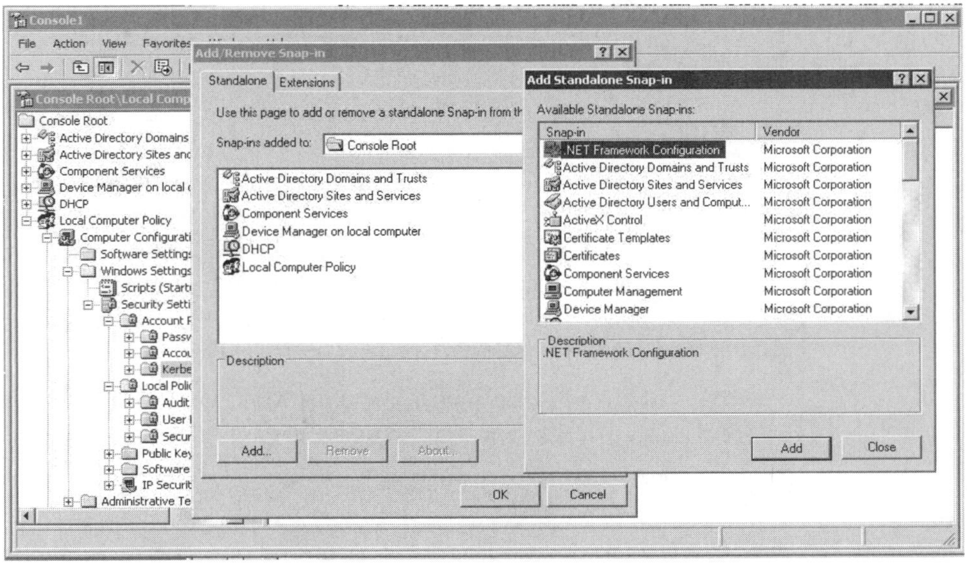

FIGURE 4.10 Adding Snap-Ins

FIGURE 4.11 The Snap-in Dialog

5. Repeat this for all additional snap-ins → click **Close**.
6. Click **OK** to complete the addition of snap-ins.

MMC MODES

The Microsoft Management Console operates in two primary modes. *Author* mode is used for the creation of an MMC and the setting of options, and offers full control over the MMC and all related snap-ins. *User* mode comprises three levels ranging from internal full access to strictly delegated utilization; its purpose is to restrict the addition, removal, and modification of snap-ins. The three levels of the user mode assign the following rights:

- *Full Access*. The user can customize the MMC with the snap-ins provided. The only Console option is to exit, so this user cannot add or remove other snap-ins.
- *Delegated Access*. The Console, **Window** menu, **Help** menu, and main toolbar are not displayed.
- *SDI Delegated Access*. The user is provided one view or window to administrative tasks. SDI has the same restrictions as its non-SDI delegated counterpart; plus, it removes the **Console System** menu controls.

Setting MMC Modes

Modes can be set only by an individual with author mode control. They are set in a very straightforward fashion. Once the MMC is open, select **Options** from the **Files** menu → select the desired level from the **Console mode** drop-down list box (Figure 4.12). The four options for default access to a console:

- Author mode
- User mode—full access
- User mode—limited access, multiple window
- User mode—limited access, single window

SAVING MMC LOCALLY OR TO DELEGATED ADMINISTRATORS

Once the console has been created with the mode set, it can be saved to the system administrator's desktop or to a delegated administrator. If the MMC is to be saved on the author's desktop, **Save** is the only action necessary. To save the MMC to another administrator's desktop, select **Save As** → change the name of the console if desired → select the drive location → select **Documents and Settings** → select the user's folder → select **Desktop** → click **OK**.

When creating an MCC for another user, the use of *task pads* is helpful to provide a restricted or simplified view of a selected number of tasks. In order to cre-

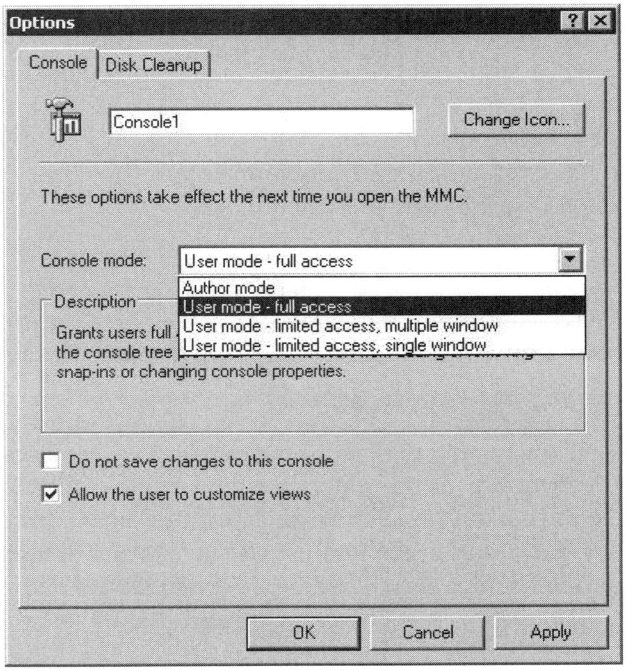

FIGURE 4.12 The Options Dialog to Change the MMC Mode

ate console task pads, the following procedures should be followed using the target tool (in this example, we will use Computer Management):

- Launch the MMC and select the target management tools (in this case, select **Computer Management**).
- From **Computer Management** → open **System Tools** → open **System** → select **Event Viewer** → right-click **System** → select **New Taskpad**.
- Use the wizard to set the properties and other configuration items.

NOTE Many of the MMC Snap-in tools provide data logging functions. Windows Server 2003 provides an expanded log management facility. Full read and write support is now available for log files bigger than 1 GB. A new log file format supports performance data to be appended to an existing log file format. The old format will also be supported with the new format becoming the default binary log file format type. This feature is launched automatically with the operating system.

Working with Individual Administrative Tools

Windows Server 2003 administrative tools can be used as standalone applications or as snap-ins to Microsoft's Management Console. In most cases, they are presented in the same console format as the MMC, which guarantees a consistent and familiar interface. Other administrative tools are also available from Control Panel and through character-based command-line utilities.

CONTROL PANEL

In an attempt to make Windows Server 2003 more administrator "friendly," the selection of **Control Panel** from the **Start** menu now displays a long list of options by default. If preferred, the administrator or server user can change back to a more graphical environment. In Windows Server 2003, Control Panel (Figure 4.13) has a different look and feel from previous Windows versions. As with the **Start** menu, you can return to the older look and feel by selecting **Switch to Class View**. While the control panels are similar for the client and server versions of Windows, the tools available in the Windows XP version are different from those in the Standard and Enterprise Server Editions. For Windows XP, the most important tools are available individually from **Control Panel**. Server versions of

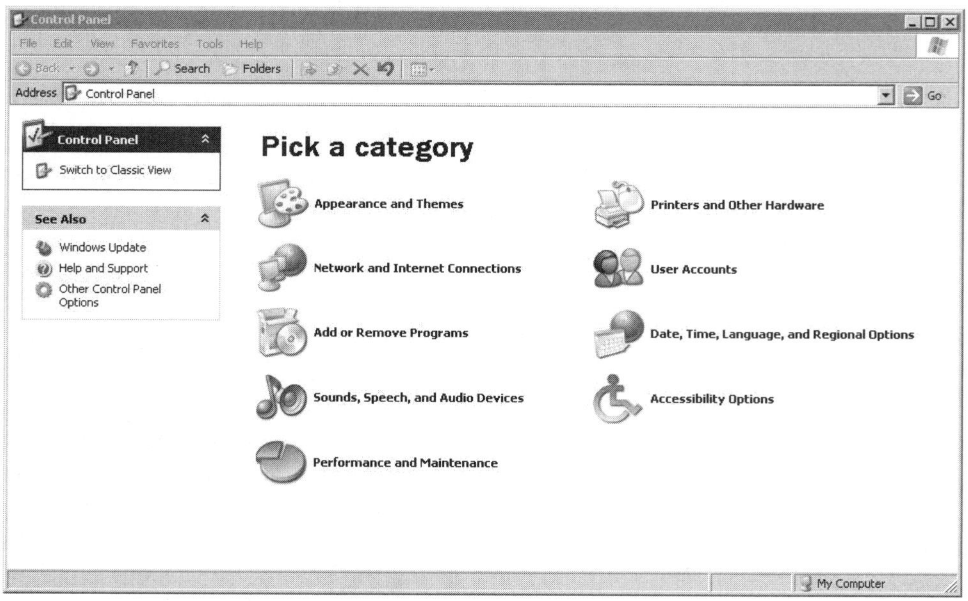

FIGURE 4.13 Windows Control Panel. Switch from Category View to Classic View for Windows 2000 UI.

Windows Server 2003 can access major applications by double-clicking the **Administrative Tools** icon in **Control Panel**.

To gain access, click **Start** → select **Settings** → select **Control Panel**. Then double-click the item you want to open.

NOTE Windows XP and Windows Server 2003 use Microsoft WebView technology to display the contents of Control Panel. WebView is the Hypertext Markup Language (HTML) view of file folders. If you prefer the old look and feel of Control Panel, you can easily revert to it by invoking the following: **Start** → **Control Panel** → **Switch to Classic View** or **Category View**.

Administrative Tools

There are a number of ways for an administrator to access **Administrative Tools**. As discussed, these tools can be launched from the **Start** → **Programs** → **Administrative Tools** menu or as MMC snap-ins. They can also be launched from the command prompt or through **Control Panel** (Figure 4.14). As shown in Figure 4.13, double-clicking the **Administrative Tools** icon will display a secondary window containing the available management applications. (In Windows XP **Control**

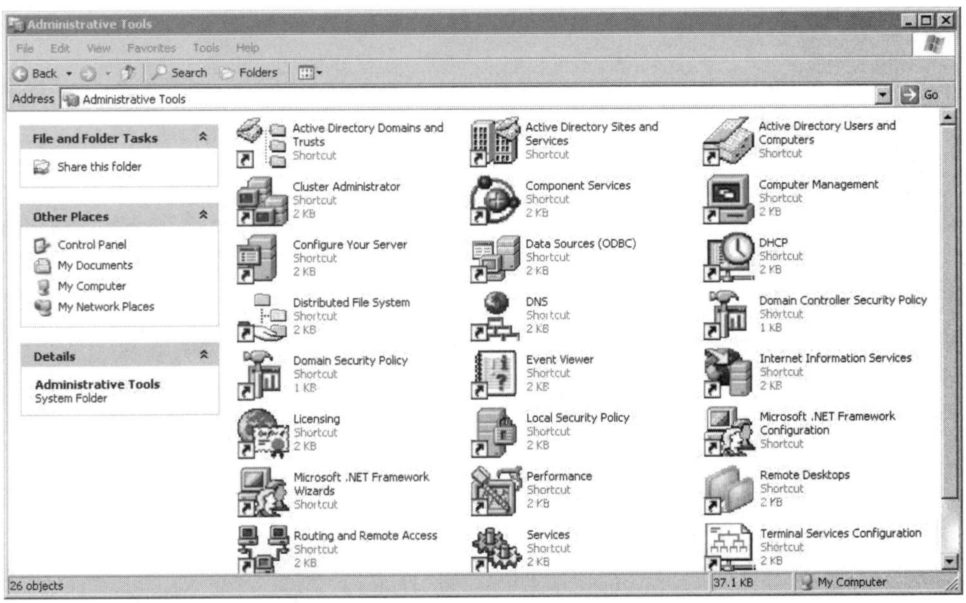

FIGURE 4.14 Administrative Tools Available from the Classic View Control Panel

Panel is the primary method for accessing Administrative Tools.) To launch an administrative tool, simply double-click its icon.

NOTE Control Panel is also used to add, modify, and delete users for the purely client-based Windows XP Home and Professional editions. Where user access should be confined strictly to a local system, then the use of this Control Panel method is appropriate.

Add Hardware Example

A good example of Control Panel tools operation is the Add/Remove Hardware Wizard. One of the first things to notice about this tool is its automatic detection of hardware. With this feature, Windows Server 2003 can determine both the presence and the health of attached system devices and components. Once the detection process is complete, the system administrator can analyze the hardware device or subcomponent. If a new device is found, the wizard will prompt the system administrator to have it automatically added to the found device drivers (Figure 4.15). Alternatively, the administrator can manually select drivers if, say, they are not fully Plug and Play compatible. One of the nice aspects of this wizard is that it always attempts to load the most current drivers for a given device.

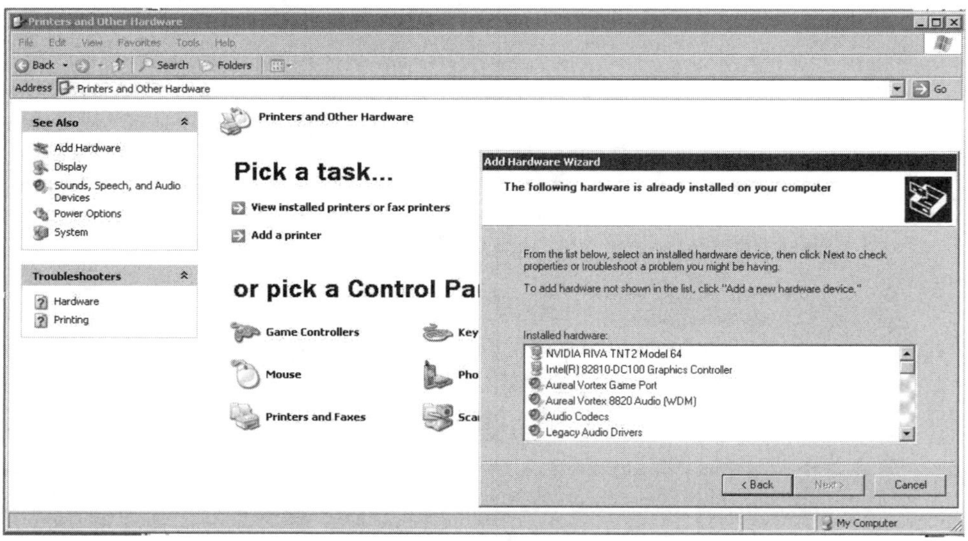

FIGURE 4.15 A Dialog from the Add/Remove Hardware Wizard

Computer Management Example

To illustrate the use of individual administrative tools, we briefly review the Computer Management application, which looks at the health of the local computer or member server and performs appropriate management actions (Figure 4.16). This chapter is designed as an overview, so we will not walk through each of the powerful management options.

CHARACTER-BASED ADMINISTRATIVE INTERFACE

Windows Server 2003 provides a primary graphical user interface, but it is also possible to perform most administrative activities through a character-based interface. For seasoned UNIX system administrators, this will be a much more familiar approach. The text interface is required for some administrative tasks, as illustrated in the appendix, "Windows Server 2003 Commands and Utilities."

The command prompt is the interface to the character-based world (Figure 4.17). It opens an MS-DOS–like window in which commands and flags can be set. The command prompt is available by clicking **Start** → select **Program** → select **Accessories** → select **Command Prompt**.

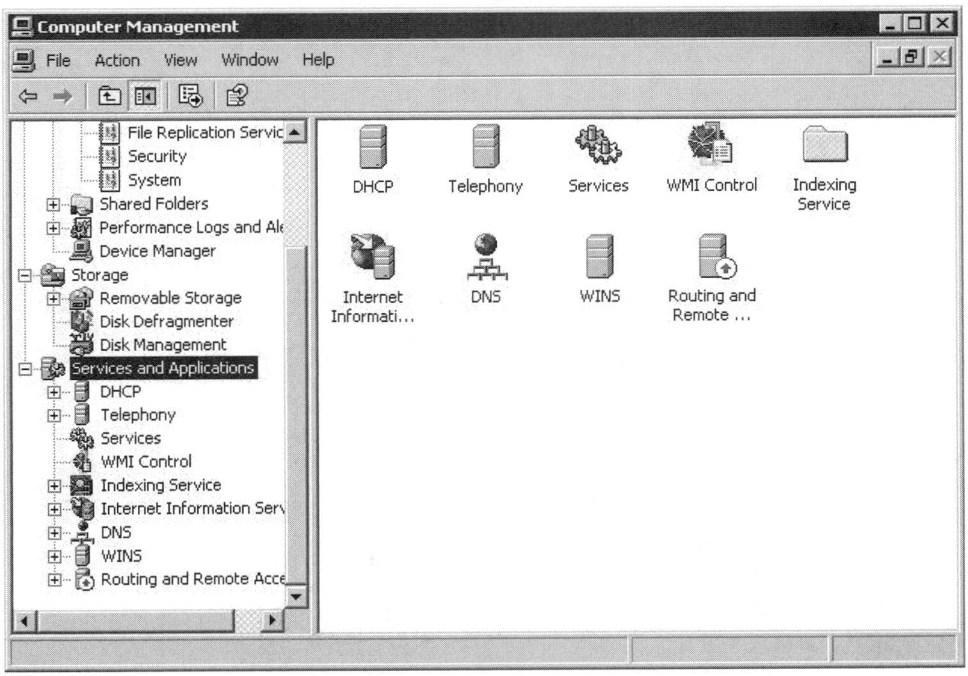

FIGURE 4.16 The Computer Management Console

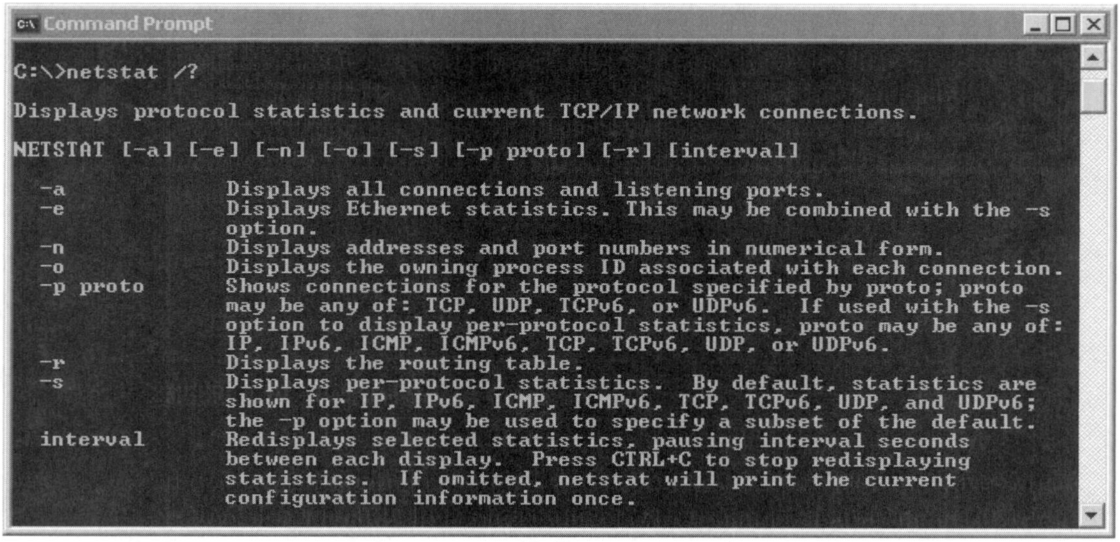

FIGURE 4.17 The Command Prompt Character-Based Interface

The appendix provides a review of the most common graphical and character-based administrative tools. Chapter 17 also reviews aspects of the Windows Scripting Host environment. However, it seems appropriate to list some of the most useful character-based administrative tools here. New command-line tools or utilities are provided in Windows Server 2003 to improve management and administration of computers. These tools are available from **Start → More Programs → Accessories → Command Prompt** or **Start → Run → cmd.exe**. Common command-line tools include:

Bootcfg.exe—View or set the properties of the boot.ini file on a local or remote server (not on 64-bit).

DriverQuery.exe—View the currently loaded device drivers and their memory usage.

bitscli.exe—Manage Background Intelligent Transfer Service (BITS) downloads.

Dsadd—Create an object instance of a specified type to the Active Directory.

Dsmod—Modify select attributes of an existing object in the Active Directory.

Dsrm—Remove an object or the complete subtree under an object in the Active Directory.

Dsmove—Move an object from its current location to a new parent location within the same naming context or to rename an object in the Active Directory.

Dsquery—Find objects in the Active Directory that match search criteria.

Dsget—Get or view select properties of an object in the Active Directory when the location of the object to be viewed is known.

Eventtriggers.exe—Launch a process based on the occurrence of an event written to the event log.

Eventquery.vbs—Specify the type of events to extract from the event log; the selected events can be displayed on the screen or saved to a file.

Eventcreate.exe—Create a user-defined event to any event log.

GPresult.exe—Launch the Resulting Set of Policies (RSoP) and list of policies that are applied to a computer.

IIS scripts—Provide command-line tools to configure, provision, and manage IIS server and Active Server Pages (ASP) applications.

Ipseccmd.exe—View and modify the policies and properties of Internet Protocol (IP) security.

NetDom.exe—Get and set the Machine Name, set the computer name and DNS first label of a machine.

NetSh.exe—Access a configuration tool, which now adds the basic network diagnostic features provided by the older NetDiag.exe tool.

Openfiles.exe—View the list of connected users and files in use per share on a computer.

Pagefileconfig.vbs—Get the current pagefile size or set a new pagefile size.

Print scripts—Manage printer services, drivers, and queues.

Reg.exe—View, set, and edit registry keys.

SC.exe—Start and stop and manage Win32 services.

SchTasks.exe—Get, set, or edit a scheduled task using the existing Win32 scheduling service.

Shutdown.exe—Shut down or restart a computer; allows a restart explanation to be written to the event log.

Systeminfo.exe—View basic properties of a machine (such as CPU and memory).

TaskKill.exe—Kill or stop a running process.

TaskList.exe—View or identify all running processes with PIDs.

Tsecimp.exe—Import Telephony Application Programming Interface (TAPI) user account properties and access rights.

Windows Server 2003 makes standard other command-line tools and utilities that were previously found in the Resource Kit:

Choice.exe—Select batch file execution from a menu.

Clip.exe—Redirect **cmd** line output to the clipboard for copy/paste into GUI applications.

Forfiles.exe—Restrict operations to selected file types.

Freedisk.exe—Permit operation if x% disk space is free.

Gettype.exe—Determine product type.

Inuse.exe—Permit the removal of file loaded into memory on reboot.

PowerCfg.exe—Enable power management.

Setx.exe—Set environment variables with batch files.

Takeown.exe—Administrator takes ownership of orphaned files.

Timeout.exe—Pause a batch file for a specified number of seconds.

Waitfor.exe—Pause batch files until a signal is received.

Whoami.exe—Identify logged-on user.

Where.exe—Locate files.

NOTE Windows Server 2003 adds a very useful command-line facility for any administrator engaged in a mixed operating system environment. The Windows Management Instrumentation Command (WMIC) utility is a command-line interface to the WMI infrastructure. It includes a set of commands and control functions to facilitate Windows management. In addition, it follows standard DOS and UNIX conventions. WMIC interoperates with existing shells and utility command. It can extend by scripts or other administration-based applications. Aliases are used to mediate between the WMI infrastructure and the command-line utility. Aliases can be used to rename classes, rename properties and methods, and arrange properties in named formats that include property values and are formatted in a manner appropriate to some specific presentation strategy or function.

INTERACTIVE MODE

$ wmic <CR> from command line or any shell

wmic:root\cli> <type a command or switch> or /? for help, which is implemented as progressive help disclosure. Examples:

wmic:root\cli> /? —lists the syntax and available aliases

wmic:root\cli> process /? —displays options available for Process Alias

NON-INTERACTIVE MODE

$ wmic /?<CR> for help

Launching Tools from the Run Menu

The **Run** dialog is provided specifically to launch applications, including administrative tools (Figure 4.18). Located from the **Start** menu, it is generally very straightforward and reliable. If you know the location of the application, it is very easy to type from path to executable in the text box and click OK. If you do not know the location, the **Browser** option will permit you to move between locations until you find the executable file.

HELP AND SUPPORT

If you are a system administrator coming from a UNIX environment, the Windows Server 2003 Help facility (Figure 4.19) makes the UNIX manual's pages pale in comparison. Even if you are moving from previous versions of Windows, you should be pleasantly surprised by the number of innovative enhancements. Anytime the end user can easily resolve computer issues, this is good news for system administrators . . . and there is a lot of good news here. As was the case with Windows 2000, related topics are hyperlinked, making it very easy to drill down to a subject or move laterally to related information. Within any Windows Server system console it is possible to jump to the Help and Support Center by clicking **Help**. Alternatively, click **Start** → select **Help**.

The first thing that stands out is the very different interface to the Help function. Windows XP and Windows Server 2003 servers use the concept of "Headlines" to display the most common groups of inquiry topics. Under the "Pick a Topic" heading, you can gain assistance on broad-based topics ranging from networking to security administration. A new innovation is the "Ask for Assistance" topic list. By the default, the user is given the option to request assistance from a friend or to find

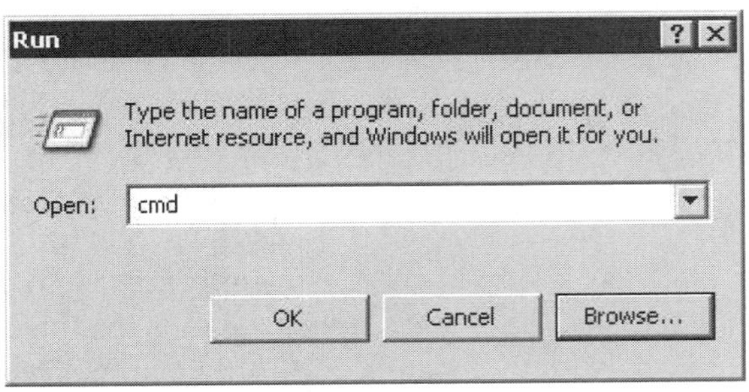

FIGURE 4.18 Run Dialog Box

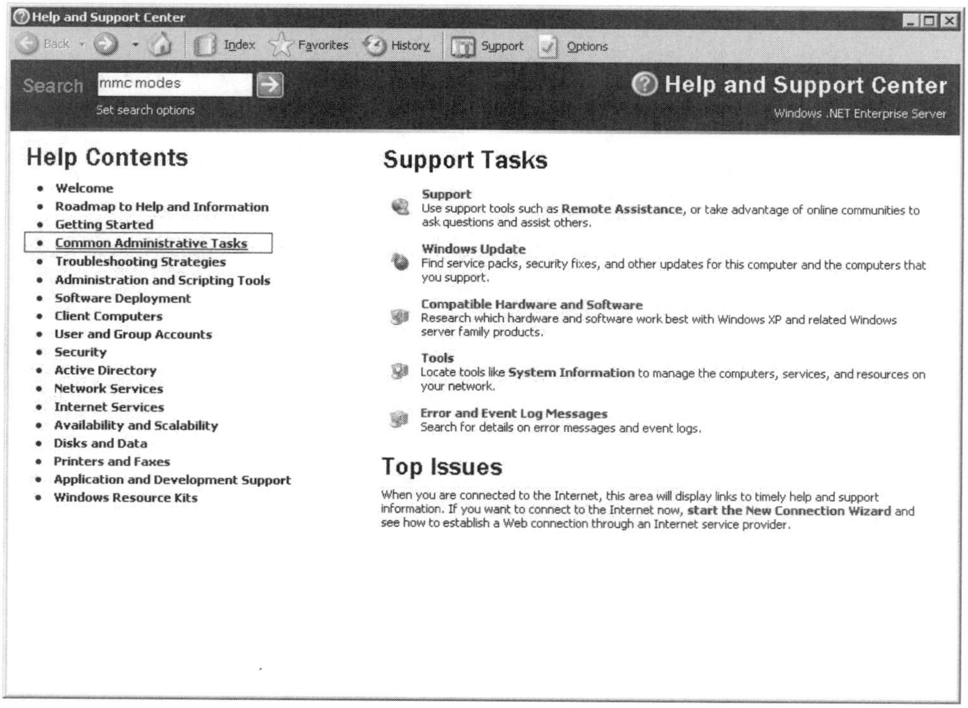

FIGURE 4.19 Help and Support Center

the answer from online sources like user newsgroups. "Pick the Task" organizes actions for which help is often sought. For example, if an issue exists regarding compatibility hardware or software, the user is led to an interactive session so that problem can be solved in real time. Finally, the "Did you know?" group provides tutorials on topics of common interest.

If the Microsoft "Headlines" approach to help does not provide the type of desired outcome, the **Search** dialog box can be used. When a word or phrase is entered, the Windows Help function will display responses broken into several categories including "Suggested Topics" and references from the "Microsoft Knowledge Base."

Selecting **Options** from the Help taskbar provides extensive control over searches. For example, with regard to Full-text Search Matches, you can restrict the action to the words you type or expand the search to look for similar words.

Tables 4.1 and 4.2 contain many of the most important Help advances. The functions are listed in two tables to separate Help functions that involve innovative interactive approaches and those that significantly enhance the Help functions of earlier Windows products.

TABLE 4.1 Innovative Interactive Help Functions

Help Function	Description
Assisted Support—Microsoft Incident Submission and Management	Allows users to submit electronic support incidents to Microsoft, collaborate with support engineers, and manage submitted incidents. Rather than telephone Microsoft for support, the user launches **Help and Support** to submit an electronic incident to Microsoft. Data is collected on the problem and submitted to Microsoft along with the incident description and contact details. **Start → Help and Support → Support → Get Help from Microsoft**.
Compatibility "Support Task"	Provides up-to-date hardware and software compatibility. **Start → Help and Support → Compatible hardware and software**.
Extensible Search Mechanism	Enables a user to search for content across multiple remote and online providers. For example, a single search can secure information from the local system and from the online remote resources. **Start → Help and Support → Search**.
Remote Assistance	Permits users and support professionals to remotely view and control a computer for any support task. Chat and file transfers are also available. With the user's permission, the expert who is helping can get full control of this computer to perform necessary tasks. Two tasks must be complete to invoke this process: **Start → Help and Support → Ask for Assistance → Invite a friend to connect to your computer with Remote Assistance**. Permissions: **Start → Control Panel → Performance and Maintenance → System → Remote → Remote Assistance → Advanced**.
Windows Update Integration	The user can download appropriate updates from within **Help and Support: Start → Help and Support → Windows Updates** or **Start → All Programs → Internet Explorer → Windows Update.**

TABLE 4.2 Enhancements to Earlier Windows Help Functions

Help Function	Description
Device Driver Referral Site (client systems)	Assists users with installation of device drivers that are not included with Windows or on disk with the device; includes linking directly to device manufacturer. **Start** → **Help and Support** → **Compatible hardware and software**.
Full Text Search	Searches the entire Help file base, using Boolean operators, and returns an aggregate list of results. **Start** → **Help and Support** → **Search**.
Multiple Instances	Allows two help sessions to be launched at the same time.
Printing Node	Allows all Help chapters to be output to a printer. **Start** → **Help and Support** → right-click a selected topic → **Print.**
Troubleshooting Diagnostic Tool (client)	Simplifies analysis that might be beyond end users' ability; presents a series of check boxes to apply step-by-step system changes to help the diagnostic work. **Start** → **Help and Support** → **Tools**.

NOTE In an attempt to tighten security, Windows .NET provides remote assistance auditing. In the event that a Remote Assistance ticket and password is stolen, this feature permits administrators to view the history of Remote Assistance local system operations. Administrators can audit the machine to look for possible security problems and monitor the usage of Remote Assistance in the machine. The feature is invoked by selecting **Programs** → **Administrative Tools** → **Computer Management** → **Computer Management (Local)** → **System Tools** → **Event Viewer** → **Application**. The administrator should examine the event source named Remote Assistance.

SEARCH

The extremely powerful search function in Windows Server 2003 is valuable to both the system administrator and the regular user. If you are not sure about the name of the object, general attributes can be supplied to locate the network resource. To launch this function, select **Start** → select **Search** → select the search category.

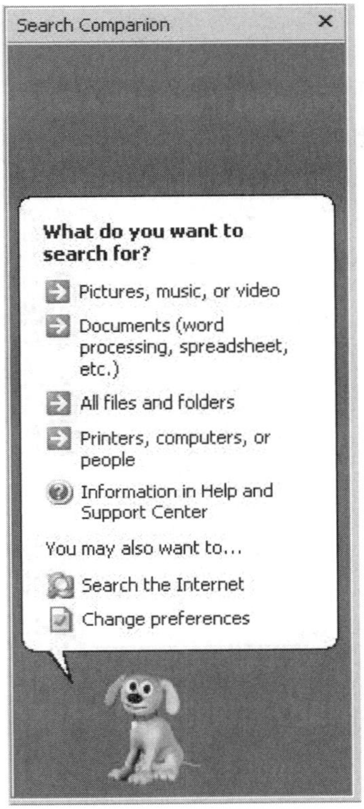

FIGURE 4.20 Search Dialog Box

The **Search** dialog box (Figure 4.20) provides a number of options to fine-tune the action. For example, if you are looking for files or a folder, you can search by name or content to receive a list of results (Figure 4.21). Take the opportunity to use this facility. It is regularly used by both system administrators and users.

Search Companion Integration

The Search Companion is a new brokering feature that analyzes user's queries. It then identifies the task the user is trying to accomplish and restates the query for clarification. It then passes the query to the most appropriate search engines when the information is not readily found on the local system. The new Search Pane uses MSN as the default search engine. The brokers seek other third-party search engines when the Search Companion believes better results can be found elsewhere. The Search Companion is automatically invoked during a search.

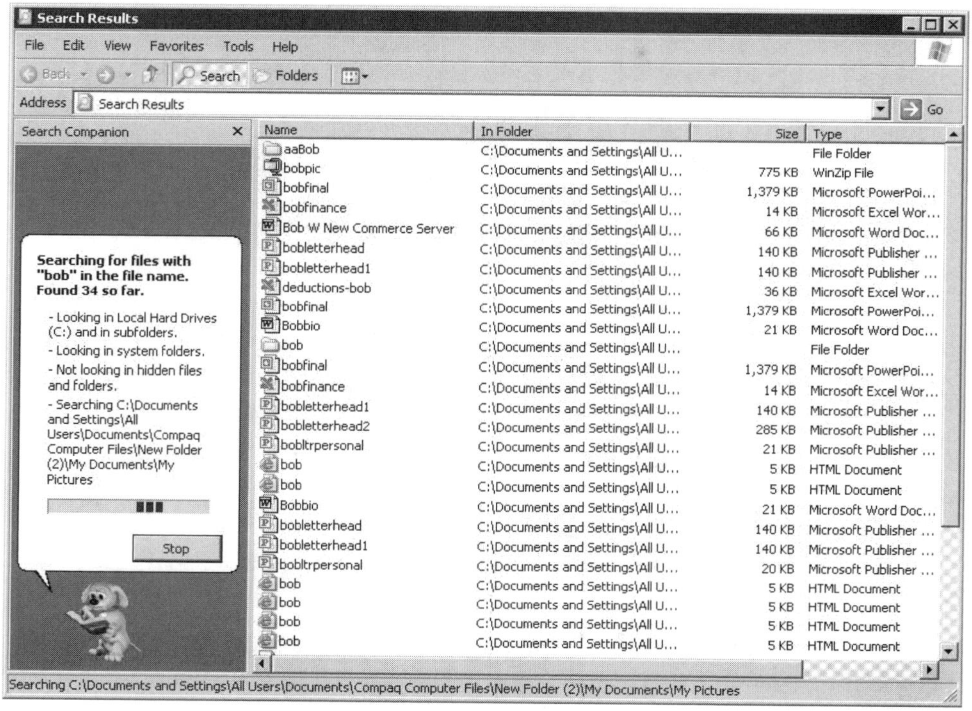

FIGURE 4.21 Search Results

INTERNET CONNECTIVITY AND INTERNET EXPLORER 6.0

The cornerstone of the .NET Framework is enhanced Internet access and functionality. Some of the more visible enhancements affect the way connectivity is provided and with new features to the Internet Explorer Web browser.

Internet Connectivity Enhancements

The Internet connection enhancements provide easier configuration and usability, built-in security, and Web-based sharing capabilities.

NOTE The **Connection Manager Profiles** function provides the ability to turn on log files of client utilization. This is helpful to quickly and accurately troubleshoot connection problems in **Connection Manager**. This facility is turned on or off from the **Connection Manager** options.

NOTE The Connection Manager Administration Kit (CMAK) has enhanced wizard functions. This includes the ability to perform most advanced customization tasks prior to creating user profiles. A number of configurable administrative actions, such as establishment of VPN connections, are supported by the CMAK Wizard.

ALL-USER REMOTE ACCESS SERVICE CREDENTIALS

This feature permits the creation of an Internet connection to all designated users without the requirement of a user name or password. Designed for greater convenience, for example, it allows a home user to establish a connection with an ISP and establish it as an All-User connection. Credentials are saved that permit members of the family to gain Internet access without logging on and using a password. This facility can streamline accessibility but it also comes with obvious risks. This is not a facility we would recommend using in a business environment where access to a connected system may be restricted. However, if you have a very controlled situation and don't want associates or family to be "burdened" with a user name or password, then you can configure the computer: **Start → Control Panel → Network and Internet Connections → Internet Options**.

AUTO-CONFIGURATION FOR MULTIPLE NETWORK CONNECTIVITY

Auto-Configuration for Multiple Network Connectivity provides easy access to network devices and the Internet. This feature can be particularly useful for mobile computer users that regularly connect to office and home networks. Unlike previous operating system versions that required manual reconfiguration of Transmission Control Protocol/Internet Protocol (TCP/IP) settings, this new feature specifies that TCP/IP will use an alternative configuration if a Dynamic Host Configuration Protocol (DHCP) server is not found. In practice, an office environment typically would use a DHCP server; such a network configuration would be rare for home use. When moving between these environments, the operating system automatically recognizes the appropriate network settings. To manage the Auto-Configuration for Multiple Network Connectivity: **Start → Control Panel → Network and Internet Connections → Internet Options**.

CONNECTION-MANAGED FAVORITES

The Communication Manager can now be configured so that settings like dialing rules and access numbers can be stored and easily accessed by the user when moving between physical locations. The Favorites feature for Connection Manager eliminates repetitive configuration of properties when a user is switching between dialing locations. To configure the Connection Manager Favorites: **Start → More**

Programs → Accessories → Communications → Network and Dial-up Connections.

CONNECTION FIREWALL

While firewall technology is discussed in greater detail in later chapters, it is appropriate to highlight here the built-in firewall technology that ships with Windows XP and Windows Server 2003. It is designed primarily as a small business and home firewall that should meet most simplified Internet security packet-blocking needs and port scanning. In an enterprise environment, a more sophisticated approach is recommended. The Internet Connection Firewall provides protection on computers directly connected to the Internet. The environments it supports include LAN or dial-up networking, VPN, and Point-to-Point Protocol over Ethernet (PPPoE) connections. The configuration of Internet Connection Firewall is invoked in one of three ways:

1. **Start → Network Connections → Make New Connection Wizard**.
2. **Start → Programs → Accessories → Communications → Home Networking Wizard**.
3. **Start → Control Panel → Network and Internet Connections → Network Connections**.

INTERNET CONNECTION SHARING

In home or small business environments, dial-up or broadband Internet connectivity may be limited to a single line. Connection sharing permits more than one computer to share a dial-up or broadband Internet connection. Internet Connection Sharing (ICS) provides Network Address Translation (NAT) functionality that allows multiple computers to access the Internet at the same time. ICS also provides DHCP and DNS client services. This feature is invoked in one of two ways:

1. **Start → More Programs → Accessories → Communications → Home Network Wizard**.
2. **Start → Control Panel → Network and Internet Connections → Internet Options → Connections**.

ICS provides simplified connection and disconnection facilities. For example, when a user needs to use the telephone line, the dial-up connection can be terminated from the client PC. Reconnection is just as easy. This service automatically launches as part of ICS.

CONNECTION MANAGER VPN SERVER SELECTION

The Connection Manager Administration Kit supports the creation of a Connection Manager profile that allows users to select a virtual private network server from the corporation's network. The use of VPN networks is covered in Chapter 13, but it is appropriate to note here that the Connection Manager VPN Server selection facility is available from within the Connection Manager Administration Kit.

Internet Explorer 6.0 Enhancements

With each progressive release of Internet Explorer, Microsoft has introduced incremental improvements. Windows Server 2003 shipped with IE6 configured with enhanced security settings, together with other features to reduce administrative headaches. Some global enhancements include:

- Visual refresh and enhanced support for Document Object Model (DOM) Level 1 and Cascading Style Sheet (CSS) Level 1.
- Media Acquisition enhancements that include support for My Videos and My Music folders as defaults for those media types.
- Built-in playback support for Flash and Shockwave files.
- Improved privacy; cookie handling has been enhanced along with Passport and related authentication dialog credential management.

A notable absence is native Java Virtual Machine (JVM), which is not shipped with Internet Explorer 6.0. Some OEM manufacturers have elected to include a JVM with their version of the operating system, but in most cases a JVM must be downloaded to support Java applets and related code. This might be a concern for system administrators. We suggest that system administrators select a designed JVM and include it during Windows XP or Windows NT installations. This will ensure more consistent browser behavior and eliminate users' questions about loading a JVM when attempting to load a Web page that can run Java.

ENHANCED SECURITY CONFIGURATION

The standard configuration for IE6 assumes heightened security settings and thereby reduced threats. A conscious decision must be made to lower predefined settings. The assumption is that access to Internet and intranet sites is achieved on a zone basis by the administrator or the client user adding Trusted sites. You should add the Web page that hosts the application to the Trusted sites zone when you want to run a browser-based client application over the Internet. Running a browser-based client application over a protected and secure local intranet requires adding the Web page that hosts the application to the Local intranet zone. Security Configuration is achieved by launching **Internet Explore** → select **tools** → select the **Security Tab.**

CONTACTS AND INSTANT MESSAGING INTEGRATION

Instant messaging, which has been in common use by Internet providers like Yahoo and AOL, is now available through IE 6.0. Instant messaging permits people to communicate quickly over the Internet. This can be accomplished through MSN Messenger, Outlook Express, and Outlook contacts in a side-pane with the browser. Windows Message is installed by default.

EASY IMAGE ACQUISITION AND AUTOMATIC IMAGE RESIZE

Capturing an image from a Web page was problematic in earlier versions of Windows. It typically required the user to examine the source file and then track down the identified image by name from the Temporary Internet folder. This process is now greatly streamlined. With Internet Explorer 6.0, the user need merely place the cursor on the desired image, right-click, and select **Save** or **Print**.

Another nice feature of IE 6.0 is its intelligent display of large images. Rather than users having to scroll across an image that is simply too large to be displayed with the browser, IE 6.0 automatically resizes the image to fit the screen.

Home Networking Wizard

The Home Networking Wizard is really very poorly named because it is an excellent tool for the establishment of small business LAN environments. When Windows XP Home or Professional Edition is installed in a home or small business network, this wizard will set up connectivity with the Internet and among existing local computers. These local computers use this facility while still running downlevel operating systems like Windows 9.x, Windows Me, and Windows NT. The Home Networking Wizard is not used for networking environments based on Windows Server 2003. To invoke the Home Networking Wizard: **Start** → **More Programs** → **Accessories** → **Communications** → **Home Networking Wizard**; or **Start** → **Control Panel** → **Network and Internet Connections** → **Network Connections**.

Web Publishing

Working in conjunction with the my.NET functions, this feature enables the publication of files to a Web-hosting service. The Passport Signup Wizard is used to sign up users so there is no need to enter a password with the Web site. Web publishing is accomplished in one of three ways:

1. **Start** → **My Documents** → **select files** → **Publish this file to the Web**.
2. **Start** → **More Programs** → **Microsoft Web Publishing** → **Web Publishing Wizard**.
3. Right-click the selected file → **Send To** → **Web Publishing Wizard**.

WINKEY QUICK KEYS

To streamline keyboard interaction, the operating system ships with Winkeys, which minimize the requirement to use the mouse to invoke tasks. Note that keyboards from some computer manufacturers extend the basic list of these quick Winkeys. Refer to the computer manufacturer's documentation on these extended key sets. The Winkey is available on most keyboards and has the image of the Microsoft Windows logo. Following are the common Winkey quick key combinations and the functions they activate:

- Winkey opens or closes the **Start** menu.
- Winkey + BREAK displays the **System Properties** dialog box.
- Winkey + TAB moves the focus to the next application in the taskbar.
- Winkey + SHIFT + TAB moves the focus to the previous application in the taskbar.
- Winkey + B moves the focus to the notification area.
- Winkey + D shows the desktop.
- Winkey + E opens Windows Explorer showing My Computer.
- Winkey + F opens the Search panel.
- Winkey + CTRL + F opens the Search panel with Search for Computers module selected.
- Winkey + F1 opens Help.
- Winkey + M minimizes all.
- Winkey + SHIFT+ M undoes minimization.
- Winkey + R opens **Run** dialog.
- Winkey + U opens the Utility Manager.
- Winkey + L locks the computer.

INTERNATIONALIZATION AND LOCALIZATION

Windows XP and Windows Server 2003 have vastly expanded their support for international languages. In addition to the languages formerly supported by Windows 2000, Windows Xpand .NET can support Galician, Gujarati, Kannada, Kyrgyz, Mongolian (Cyrillic), Punjabi, Divehi, Syriac, and Telugu. This support includes not only standard languages but also sublanguages like Canadian French and UK English. Along with this support, the operating systems reflect regional settings including calendars, keyboards, currency, numbers, and date and time formats.

Localization settings can be modified by following these actions: **Start → Control Panel → Date, Time, Language, and Regional Options → Regional and Language Options → Languages → Details**.

CLEARTYPE MOBILE COMPUTER/ LIQUID CRYSTAL DISPLAY ENHANCEMENTS

Users of mobile computers like laptops can achieve a more readable text display by using Microsoft's ClearType technology. According to Microsoft, ClearType triples the horizontal resolution of text on liquid crystal displays (LCD) and digital interfaces. To obtain this level of resolution: **Start → Control Panel → Appearance and Themes → Display → Appearance → Effects →** click **Use the Following Method to Smooth Fonts →** select **ClearType**.

SHADOW COPIES

A new usability feature is Shadow Copies of Shared Folders, which provides for the remote storage and retrieval of files that may be damaged or lost on a local system. Shadow Copies of Shared Folders allows a user to access shared files and folders as they existed in the past. This affords not only an ability to compare earlier documents, but it also provides an excellent means for file recovery. The client software for Shadow Copies of Shared Folders is located on the server and requires client deployment through the **Disk Properties MMC Snap-in**. The client software for Shadow Copies of Shared Folders is installed on the server in the \\%systemroot%\system32\clients\twclient directory. Group Policy tools are commonly used for deployment. Client views of shadow copies are accessed through the **Previous Versions** tab of the **Properties** dialog box of the shared file or folder. The minimum amount of storage space that can be specified is 100 megabytes (MB). There is a limit of 64 shadow copies that can be stored on a volume.

POSTSCRIPT

This chapter provides a view from 30,000 feet of the Windows Server 2003 user interface and its administrative management tools. Subsequent chapters explore proper use of these tools in the real world.

Chapter

5

The Active Directory

The next two chapters examine the directory services known collectively as the Active Directory. This is one of the new breed of metadirectories, and so it is integral to the Windows Server 2003 operating system's infrastructure, security, and maintenance. First introduced in Windows 2000, Active Directory has been refined for Windows Server 2003. Active Directory is supported only in the Standard, Enterprise, and Datacenter Editions of Windows Server 2003.

Because of the volume of information that must be covered to properly explain the Active Directory technology, our review spans this chapter and Chapter 6, "Active Directory Management and Use." An understanding of the conceptual underpinning of the Active Directory and how it can be managed is fundamental to Windows Server system administration.

After reading this chapter, you should have a working knowledge of the following Active Directory concepts:

- *The role of directory services*—the function of the Active Directory and an identification of some of its important features for system administrators.
- *Active Directory logical structure components*—the role of domains, domain trees, forests, and organizational units.
- *Active Directory physical structure components*—the role of sites and domain controllers.
- *Active Directory schema*—how the Active Directory schema defines object classes and attributes.
- *Open standards support and naming conventions*—the Active Directory's use of open standards like DNS and LDAP together with its employment of the most common naming conventions to ensure interoperability.

- *Migration and application programming interfaces (APIs)*—the support provided for the migration and/or integration of the Active Directory with other directory services such as Novell's NDS and API options available for both third-party application development and administrative scripting.
- *The Global Catalog and replication services*—the new Global Catalog feature and the directory replication services.
- *Security and trust relationships*—the roles of domains, trees, and forests with respect to security and trust relationships.
- *Administrative delegation*—how the Active Directory structure lends itself to very granular resource management and the delegation of system administration authority.

DIRECTORY SERVICES

The Windows Server 2003 Active Directory is Microsoft's consolidation of the major enterprise-wide directory services into a single, replicable data store and administrative interface.

A directory is a listing that helps organize and locate things. The index of this book is one example. The reader becomes the directory service provider that scans the entries, locates the page number(s) for a topic, and turns to the page.

In computing terms, the two components of a directory are the data store and the services that act on that data. In Windows 2000 and Windows Server 2003, a directory is simply a store of objects, within which those objects can be located anywhere in the enterprise and can include applications, databases, printers, users, and other workstations or servers. A directory service performs many functions that act on that store: replication, security rule enforcement, data distribution, and much more.

NOTE An *object* is a representation of real things such as a user, a data file, a printer, and a software application. Every object has named attributes that describe the item. Thus an *attribute* of a printer might be its location, its manufacturer, or its type. A *container* is a special class that has both a namespace and attributes. It does not represent anything real or concrete but instead holds one or more objects. A *tree* is simply a hierarchy of objects and containers. As discussed later, the domain tree is a special form of tree that defines a domain directory hierarchy. The endpoint of any tree branch is an object; the branch is typically viewed as a container for multiple objects. Think of a tree as the relationship of objects and their paths from the root. For example, the user container holds the objects associated with all users on a computer system. Branches hold the objects associated with individual users.

What Is the Active Directory?

Stated very simply, the Active Directory is a network-based object store and service that locates and manages resources, and makes these resources available to authorized users and groups. An underlying principle of the Active Directory is that everything is considered an object—people, servers, workstations, printers, documents, and devices. Each object has certain attributes and its own security access control list (ACL). Objects can be organized within the Active Directory in a special kind of object known as a container, which can be used on a very granular level. Specifically, the Active Directory plays several very important roles in a Windows Server 2003 enterprise, which include but are not limited to the following:

- A store for information about every network object and its attributes
- A security conduit for ACL authentication and domain trusts
- A focal point for system administration
- A mechanism for operating system interoperability
- A means of consolidating divergent directory services
- A system for replication of object data

The Active Directory, as illustrated in Figure 5.1, is a distributed, hierarchical, replicated, and secure directory service designed for Windows Server 2003 that is theoretically capable of interoperability within heterogeneous directory service environments.

The Active Directory catalogs file objects with their attributes in a hierarchical arrangement, fully embracing naming resolution services like DNS. It also organizes users and groups according to their attributes. The Active Directory plays an important role in identification of security policies across the network, integration of e-mail, Internet addressing, and groupware applications. In essence, the Windows Server 2003 Active Directory merges all of these directory services within an extensible system environment.

A user inquiry about an object is passed through the Global Catalog (GC), which, as we will discuss later, is an abstraction of object information contained in the Active Directory data store. The GC resolves the common object inquiries. It is created and refreshed with updated information for the Active Directory. The schema residing in the Active Directory presents object definitions. The Active Directory manages the store of data through an extensible storage engine (ESE). The upper functions of the directory services themselves are separated from the ESE by APIs through the Directory System Agent (DSA) layer. No direct calls are made to the ESE.

Figure 5.2 illustrates the structural relationship of the data store and extensible storage engine to Active Directory's system agent. Queries made by a user are

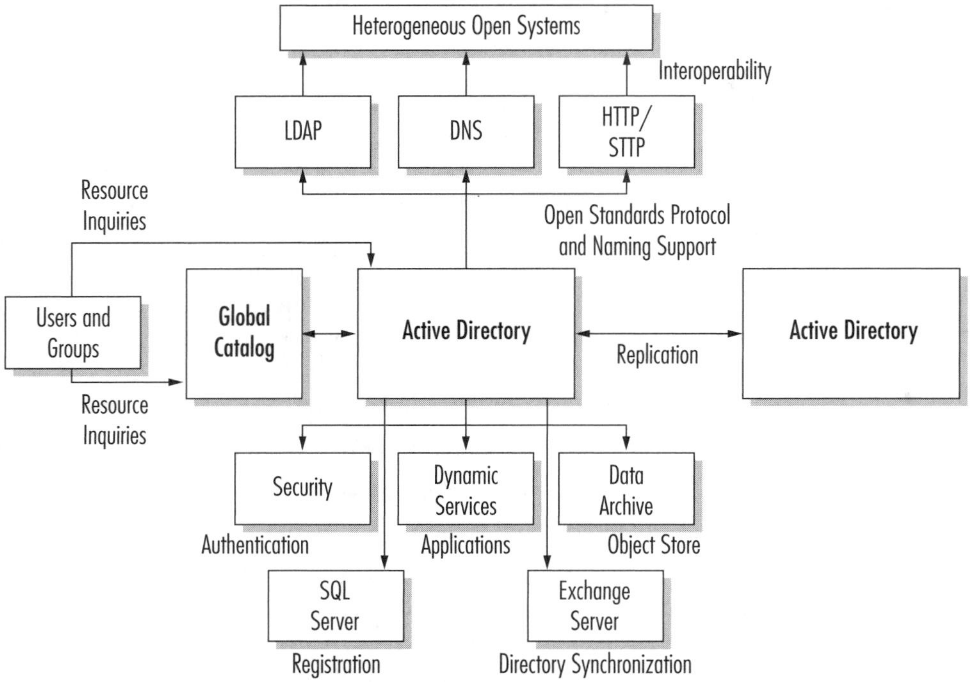

FIGURE 5.1 A View of the Active Directory Relative to Other Elements

passed through the Global Catalog. If the object cannot be resolved by the GC, it is passed to the data store via the ESE database API.

FILE STRUCTURE

The Active Directory stores database and log files. It is important to understand the nature of these files in order to facilitate a backup and restoration policy in the event of system corruption.

The Active Directory database file is Ntds.dit and is stored in the %system%/NTDS folder. Every domain controller has a copy of it. Ntds.dit stores all domain objects and their attribute data organized into several tables. The *schema table* contains the definitions of the objects that can be created. The *object table* organizes a single object per role, with a column provided for every attribute that contains data. Finally, the *link table* contains the relationship data between the object and the object table.

The Active Directory creates and stores four types of log files on the maintenance and management of transactions. These files are stored in %systemroot%/NTDS and include:

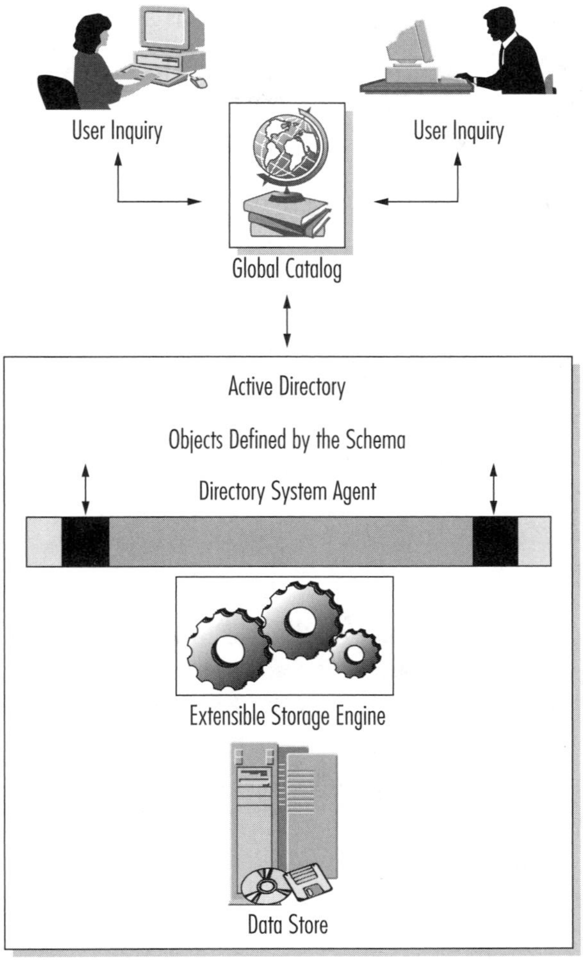

FIGURE 5.2 Structure View of Data Store and Extensible Engine

- *Transaction log files*. The current transaction file is Edb.log, which by default contains information about recent transactions and is limited to 10 MB. When this limit is reached, transaction files are automatically created with the name edbxxxxx.log (*x* is a sequential number). They are retained until the transactions are committed to the Active Directory. Every 12 hours, previous transaction files are purged during a process known as garbage collection. If you do not want continued collection of these transaction files, it is possible to set circular logging, where the current file is overridden when it is filled. This action is not recommended because it could limit your ability to recover recent transactions.

- *Checkpoint files*. The checkpoint file is Edb.chk, and it used to list transactions that have been committed to the Active Directory and those that remain uncommitted. Each time a transaction is committed, it advances to the next entry. If all transactions are not committed at the time of shutdown, the checkpoint file is read when the system is rebooted and all remaining transactions are then committed to the Active Directory.
- *Reserved log files.* The reserved log file can be a number sequence of logs, with a maximum size of 10 MB, named res1.log, res2.log, and so on. These logs are used in place of the transaction log when the creation of a new log file is attempted but insufficient disk space is available. When this occurs, the system will automatically shut down.
- *Patch files*. Patch files (with a .pat suffix) are used during the backup and restore process of the Active Directory. Database entries are sometimes divided during backup into what is known as split transactions. The patch files are used to record these splits and "patch" the transaction back together during restoration.

Data Stores and Partitions

To facilitate information storage and replications, the Active Directory uses three types of data store for directory partitions, each of which is replicated as a separate unit according to its own schedule. The three Active Directory partitions are:

- *Schema data*. Schema information comprises definitions of the objects that are available or can be created in the Active Directory. It also includes the required and optional object attributes.
- *Configuration data*. The logical structure of the domain is reflected in configuration data. Common to all domain trees and forests is a strategy for replicating all three Active Directory partitions between domain controllers. This replication topology is stored in the configuration data partition.
- *Domain data.* All objects in the tree are stored as domain data. This information relates strictly to the objects in the domain and is not replicated to other domains. Instead of total replication of all domain object information, a subset is derived for the Global Catalog. In addition to this subset, the GC server contains the schema and configuration data. It becomes the index for locating data within a domain or across a tree or forest.

An Administrative View of the Active Directory

From a system administrator's perspective, the Active Directory provides many keys for success.

- Since the Active Directory network is organized hierarchically, it is possible to finitely organize the infrastructure for better management.
- The ability to assign and delegate the administration of Windows Server 2003 to manageable elements is one of its major strengths. The Active Directory is responsible for managing the hierarchical structure of the domain, the child domain, and the OUs with logical administrative boundaries.
- The Active Directory provides a consolidated, single point for administration and system replication services.
- The Active Directory includes support for a number of open standards (DNS and LDAP), rich APIs (using C/C++, Java, Visual Basic GUIs, and scripts), extensible schema, and streamlined object lookup and network logon via the new Global Catalog.
- The Active Directory provides easy migration and backward compatibility with earlier Windows NT versions and theoretical interoperability with NetWare and UNIX.

Based on the use of objects and attributes, as shown in Figure 5.3, Active Directory forms associations.

The scope of the Active Directory is scalable and includes every object and container in the domain tree. In essence, the Active Directory can scale from a single server to an extremely large enterprise network. The primary qualities are fast connectivity and security, discussed later.

ACTIVE DIRECTORY STRUCTURAL COMPONENTS

The two primary Active Directory components are its logical and physical structures, which involve the organization and communication of objects, respectively. A third component, known as the schema, defines objects that make up the Active Directory. For the sake of convenience, the discussion of the schema is included in the logical structure section.

Logical Structure

The base logical components of the Active Directory are objects and their associated attributes. *Object classes* are merely definitions of the object types that can be created in the Active Directory. The schema is the Active Directory mechanism for storing object classes. It also permits the addition of object classes and associated attributes.

Active Directory objects are organized around a hierarchical domain model. This model is a design facility that permits the logical arrangement of objects within

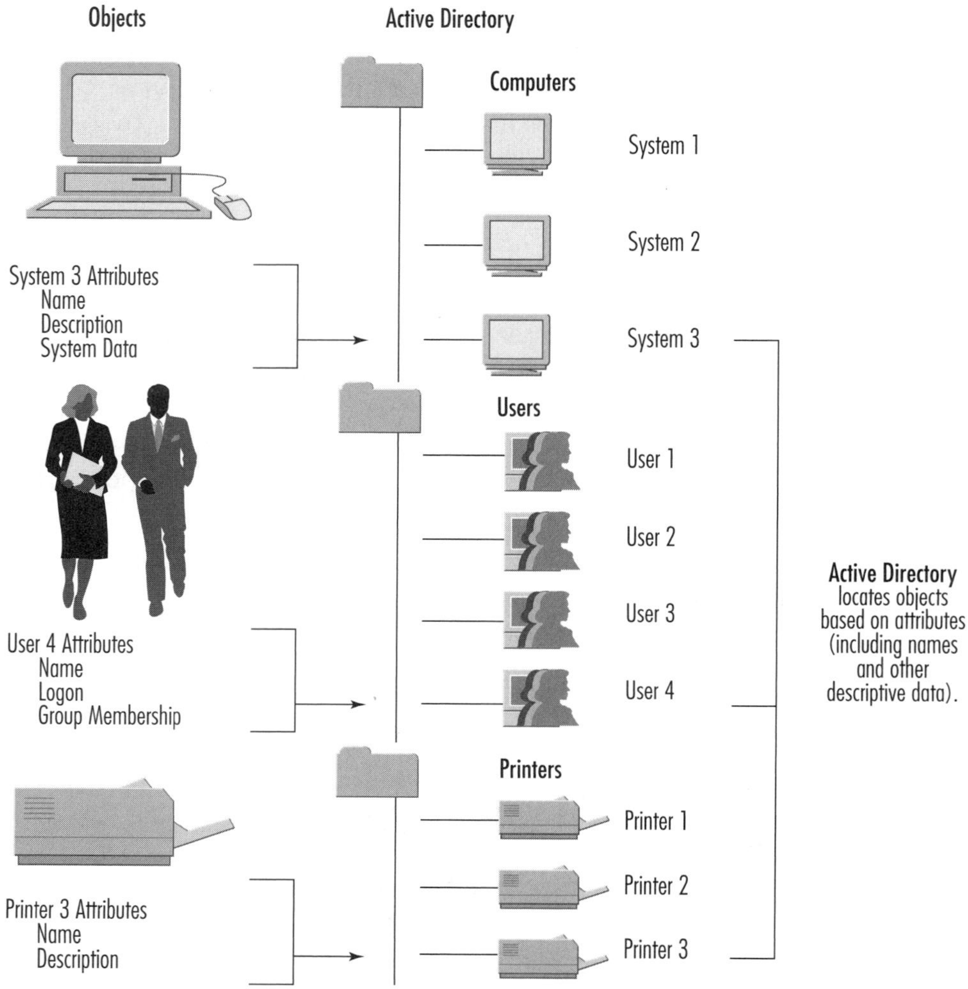

FIGURE 5.3 Locating Objects Using Attributes

administrative, security, and organizational boundaries. Each domain has its own security permissions and unique security relationships with other domains. The Active Directory uses multimaster replication to communicate information and changes among domains.

The following sections provide an overview of domain model building blocks: domains, domain trees, forests, organizational units, and the schema.

DOMAINS

The Active Directory manages a hierarchical infrastructure of networked computers with the domain as the foundation. A domain comprises computer systems and network resources that share a logical security boundary. It can store more than 17 terabytes in the Active Directory database store. Although a domain can cross physical locations, all domains maintain their own security policies and security relationships with other domains. They are sometimes created to define functional boundaries such as those between administrative units (e.g., marketing and engineering). They are also viewed as groupings of resources or servers that use a common domain name, known as a namespace. For example, all servers or resources in the *EntCert.com* namespace belong to a single domain.

In very simple terms, every domain controller has the following information as part of its Active Directory:

- Data on every object and container object within the particular domain
- Metadata about other domains in the tree (or forest) to provide directory service location
- A list of all domains in the tree and forest
- The location of the server with the Global Catalog

DOMAIN TREES

When multiple domains share a schema, security trust relationships, and a Global Catalog, a domain tree is created, defined by a common and contiguous namespace (Figure 5.4). Thus, for example, all domains with the ending namespace of *EntCert.com* belong to the *EntCert* domain tree. A domain tree is formed through the expansion of child domains like *Sales.EntCert.com* and *Research.EntCert.com.* The first created domain is known as the *root domain,* and it contains the configuration and schema data for the tree and (as we shall see) the forest. (In Figure 5.4, the root domain is *EntCert.com.)* A tree structure is formed by adding child domains. There are a number of reasons for creating multiple domains in a tree, some of which follow:

- Discretely managing different organizations or providing unit identities
- Enforcing different security boundaries and password policies
- Requiring a better method of controlling Active Directory replication
- Better handling of a very large number of managed objects
- Decentralizing administration

A single domain contains a complete Active Directory partition for all of its objects. It is also, by definition, a complete domain tree. As child domains are added

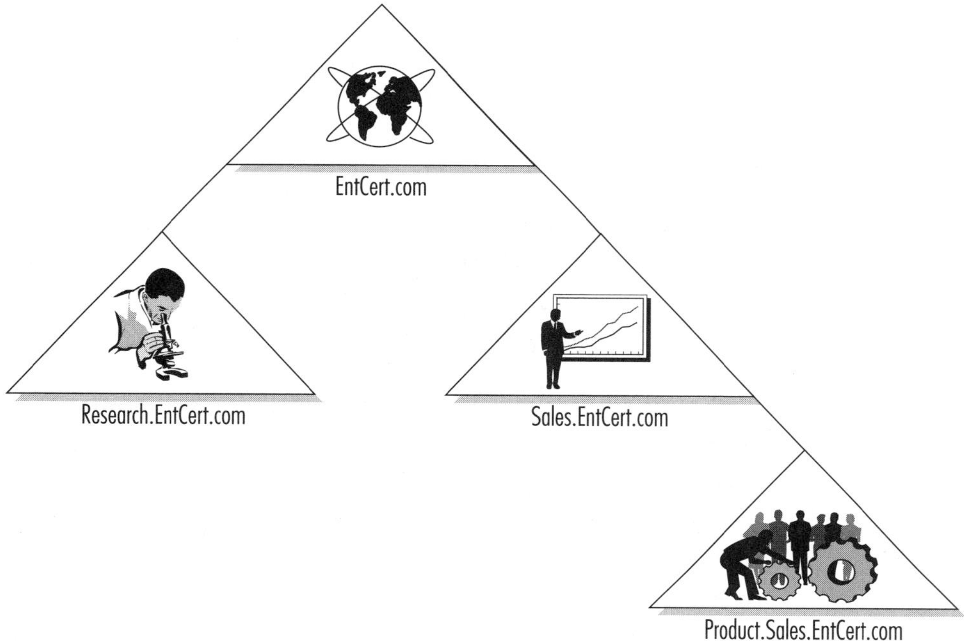

FIGURE 5.4 A Domain Tree Common Namespace

to the domain tree, Active Directory partitions are replicated to one or more domain controllers within each of the domains.

DOMAIN FORESTS

Trust relationships can be formed between domain trees with different namespaces. When this occurs, a domain forest is created, which allows the enterprise to have different domain names, such as "*EntCert.com*" and "*unint.com.*" By default, all Windows Server 2003 forests are set at Windows 2000 functional levels.

All trees in the forest share a number of attributes, including a Global Catalog, configuration, and schema. A forest is simply a reference point between trees and does not have its own name. As discussed later, forests use the Kerberos security technology to create transitive trust relationships between trees. Figure 5.5 illustrates how two domain trees form a forest.

Domains and child domains can be internally divided into administrative substructures known as organizational units (OUs), each of which can compartmentalize over 10 million objects. As container objects, OUs can be nested within other OUs. For example, the marketing division may be defined as an organizational unit and the product groups within this division as suborganizational units. A domain

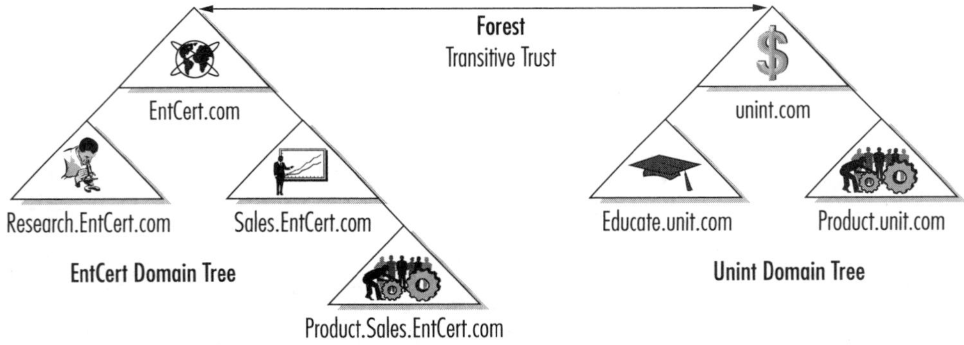

FIGURE 5.5 A Domain Forest's Organizational Units

usually comprises one or more organizational units arranged hierarchically. Objects can be organized within organizational units for administrative purposes. The OU acts as a container that lists the object contents, including users, computer systems, and devices such as printers.

An organizational unit is a logical subset defined by security or administrative parameters. In this administrative arrangement, the specific functions of the system administrator can also be easily segmented or delegated with the organizational unit level. From a system administrator's vantage point, this is very important to understand. It is possible to delegate system management responsibility solely to certain activities within a domain, OU, or child subsidiary OU. For example, a person in an organizational unit could be delegated authority to add, modify, or delete user accounts within that group.

Figure 5.6 illustrates the relationship of an organizational unit to a domain tree. Organizational units are subunits with a domain or child domain.

TREES AND FOREST SCALING AND EXTENSIBILITY

The Active Directory scales across environments ranging from a single server to a domain of one million users or more. The basis of this scaling is the peer-to-peer directory service relationship that is established between domains. Every domain server (known as a domain controller) is provided updated information on Active Directory objects. Consistency across domains is ensured through the automatic replication services. To avoid extremely large and unwieldy directories, the Active Directory creates tree partitions that comprise small portions of the entire enterprise directory. However, every directory tree has sufficient information to locate other objects in the enterprise. In addition to greater efficiency, objects that are used more frequently are placed in the local store for more rapid access. A trust relationship is automatically established between the domains in the same tree, so it is

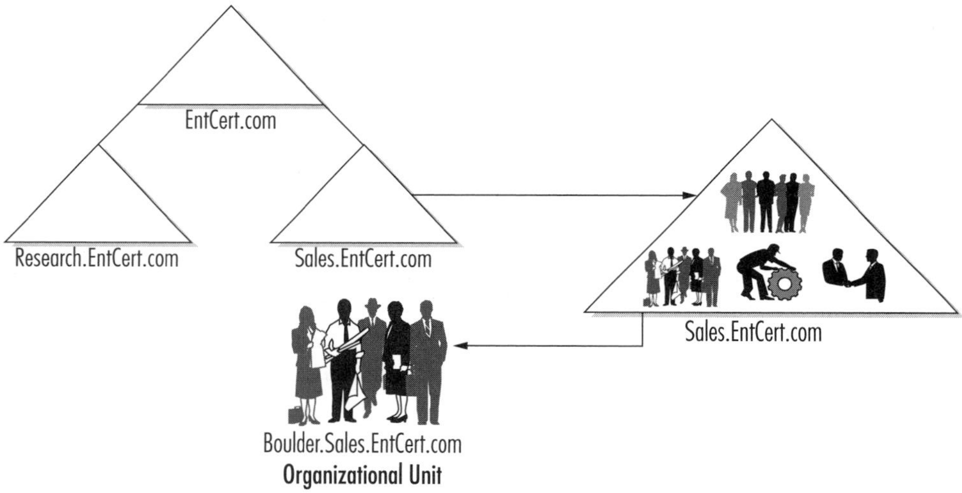

FIGURE 5.6 A Domain Tree and Organizational Units

possible to transparently locate resources anywhere in the tree or forest enterprise where the Active Directory resides.

SCHEMA

The *schema* is simply a framework of definitions that establishes the type of objects available to the Active Directory. These definitions are divided into object classes, and the information that describes the object is known as its attributes. There are two types of attributes: those that must exist and those that may exist. For example, the schema defines a user object class as having the user's name as a required attribute; the user's physical location or job description is optional. Attributes are used to further distinguish one object from another. They include object name, object identifier (OID), syntax, and optional information, as shown in Figure 5.7.

The schema is stored in the Active Directory database file Ntds.dit. Object definitions are stored as individual objects, so the directory can treat schema definitions in the same way it treats other objects. The default schema is created with the first installation of the Active Directory. It contains common objects and properties for such items as users, groups, computers, printers, and network devices. It also establishes the default Active Directory structure that is used internally.

Because schema is an extensible component, new object classes may be dynamically added to the current schema and old object classes can be modified. It was not possible to modify or deactivate system classes and attributes under Windows 2000, but it is now possible with Windows Server 2003.

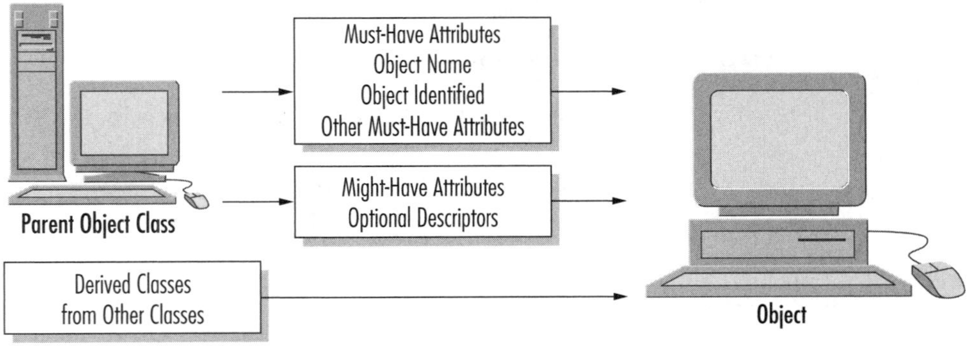

FIGURE 5.7 The Active Directory Schema Object Relationship

NOTE Schema data should not be confused with configuration data, which provides the structural information for the Active Directory. The schema provides information on what objects and attributes are available to the directory. Configuration information maintains the directory structure that represents the relationship between the actual objects and indicates how to replicate this structure between domain controllers.

The schema is accessible only to the Enterprise Administrators and Schema Admins user groups by default. It is managed through the Active Directory Schema snap-in tool. (The Active Directory Schema snap-in becomes available only after the adminpak application is installed from the Windows Server 2003 CD within the I386 folder.) Active Directory schema elements are dynamic and available to applications after the initial startup of the system. Attributes and classes can be added to the schema to provide dynamic extensibility to the Active Directory.

Using the Schema Active Directory Service Interface (SADS) is another method to facilitate the browsing and extending of functions and relationships of a schema object or attribute. The four SADS objects and schema object containers are listed in Table 5.1.

The schema object container attaches definitions to the directory tree. It is typically represented as a child of the directory root. In turn, each instance has a unique individual schema.

The Schema Operations Master domain controller (as discussed in greater detail in Chapter 6) manages the structure and content of the schema. It replicates schema information to the other domain controllers in the forest. Every domain controller loads a copy of the schema in a RAM-based cache, ensuring rapid access

TABLE 5.1 Schema ADSI Objects

Object	Description
Schema	Contains all the information involved in a particular Active Directory schema.
Object Class	Establishes the classification of the object. Examples are computers, users, and groups. Object classes include: • Name • Object identifier (OID) • "May contain" optional attributes • "Must contain" required attributes • Parent object classes • Derived classes from secondary or auxiliary classes
Property	Describes the defined properties (a device type, screen color, etc.). Properties are not subdivided into functional sets as occurs with directory service objects, like a group object.
Syntax	Describes first how the properties are defined, then specific options.

to current object and attribute definitions. If changes occur in the schema, the cache is refreshed.

NOTE With Windows Server 2003, deactivation of attributes and class definitions in the Active Directory schema is now possible. This permits the redefinition of attributes and classes if an error was made in the original definition. In addition, deactivation can be used to supercede the definition of an attribute or class after it has been added to the schema. This is useful if an error was made in setting an immutable property. Deactivation is also a reversible operation so that an administrator can undo an accidental deactivation.

Physical Structure

The second component of the Active Directory is the physical structure, which holds the mechanisms for data communication and replication. This section covers two physical structure topics: the definition of the IP subnet network structural component that constitutes Active Directory sites, and the physical server that stores and replicates Active Directory data known as the domain controller and the related Global Catalog.

SITES

In an ideal world, network communication would always be rapid and reliable. Unfortunately, geographic and other limitations result in the need to create smaller networks, known as *subnets*, to facilitate communication within and between locations. Although rapid and reliable network communication can be achieved within the larger unit, communication between subnets can vary radically. Therefore, to ensure the most effective network communication by Windows 2000 and Windows Server 2003, the Active Directory offers methods of regulating inter-subnet traffic.

The physical network structure of the Active Directory is based on a unit known as a *site*. The role of the administrator is to design sites that ensure the greatest network performance. A site comprises one or more Internet Protocol (IP) subnets that are tied together by high-speed, reliable connections. The speed considered sufficient is really arbitrary. For example, in small networks a 128-Kbps connection could be sufficient, whereas the bandwidth for a large network might need 3 Mbps or more. The administrator must determine the speed that best accomplishes the goal of minimum performance loss due to network traffic and establish sites accordingly. Many subnets can belong to a single site, but a single subnet cannot span multiple sites.

The primary goal of a site is rapid and economical data transmission. An important part of that is efficient directory services replication. The Active Directory physical structure governs when and how replication takes place. This is true of both intersite and intrasite replication. Network site performance also impacts the location of objects and logon authentication. As users log on to the network, they are able to reach the closest domain controller site through the previous assignment of subnet information. This is accomplished through DNS network-matching discovery of the closest domain controllers. The system administrator uses the Active Directory Sites and Services snap-in to manage the topology of replication services. With intrasite replication, the defined high-speed connection normally ensures rapid deployment. With intersite replication, the WAN bandwidth may be considerably slower. The site structure permits the management of Active Directory replication scheduling between sites.

Administrative granularity is significantly enhanced through the concept of the site and its relationship to domain and organizational units. In many cases, sites have the same boundaries as a domain or an organizational unit; thus, delegation of site responsibility might be mirrored in OU or domain administration.

SITES AND DOMAIN RELATIONSHIPS

No formal relationship exists between the boundaries of a site or domain. A site can have multiple domains, as a domain can have a number of sites (Figures 5.8 and 5.9). In addition, sites and domains do not have to maintain the same namespace.

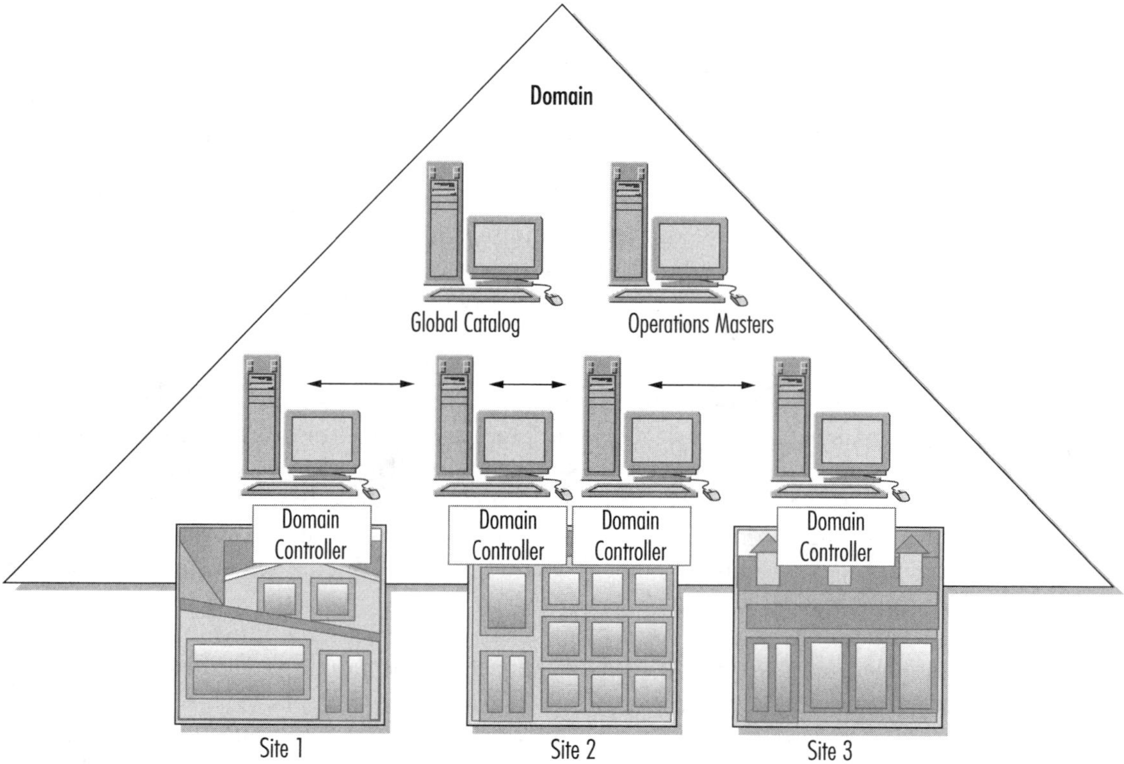

FIGURE 5.8 A View of Multiple Sites in One Domain

DOMAIN CONTROLLER

A *domain controller* is a server that contains a copy of the Active Directory. All domain controllers are peers and maintain replicated versions of the Active Directory for their domains. The domain controller plays an important role in both the logical and physical structures of the Active Directory. It organizes all the domain's object data in a logical and hierarchical data store. It also authenticates users, provides responses to queries about network objects, and replicates directory services. The physical structure provides the means to transmit this data through well-connected sites.

The Active Directory replaces the Windows NT Primary Domain Controller (PDC) and its Backup Domain Controller (BDC) counterparts. Now all domain controllers share a multimaster peer-to-peer relationship that hosts copies of the Active Directory. Another big difference from Windows NT is that all domain controllers in Windows Server 2003 have read and write capability to the Active Directory. In

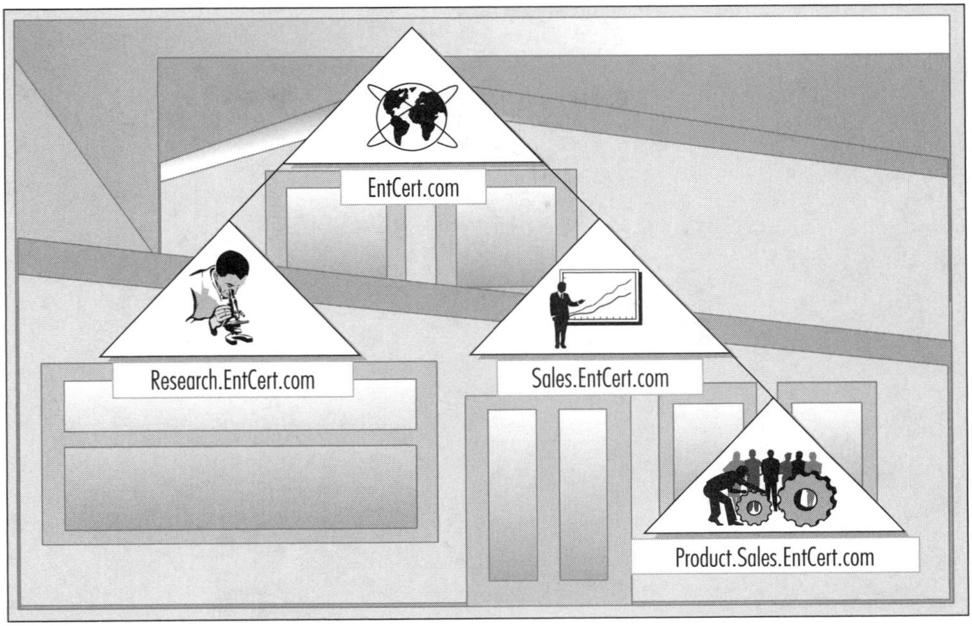

FIGURE 5.9 A View of Multiple Domains in One Site

previous versions only the PDC was read/write capable and initiated replication. Now any Active Directory domain controller can initiate the replication process when data is added.

Figure 5.10 illustrates that multiple domain controllers can exist within each domain or child domain.

Reasons to Create Multiple Domain Controllers

An Active Directory domain may have one or more domain controllers that replicate the directory partition. Among the reasons for having multiple domain controllers in a domain are:

- Better user connectivity
- High-volume user activity
- Greater failover and redundancy of information

When creating multiple domain controllers, the system administrator must take into account the added network load that will result from replication traffic. Still, it is recommended that each domain and each site have more than one domain controller so as to provide logical and physical structure redundancy and fault

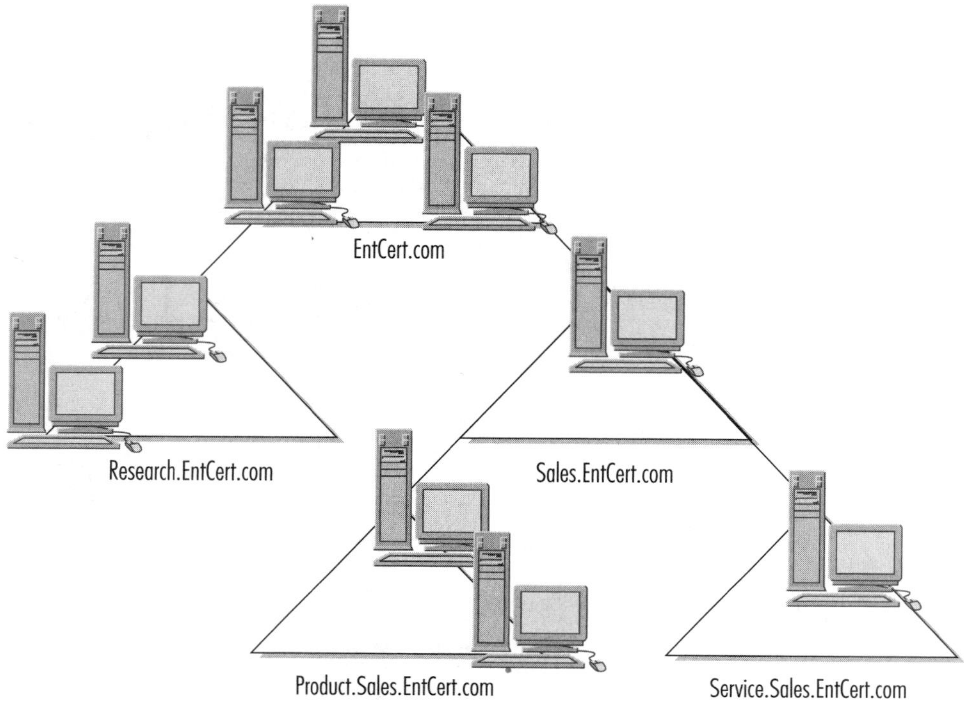

FIGURE 5.10 Domains Have One or More Domain Controllers

tolerance. It is important to protect both key domain information and geographical site connectivity.

NOTE It is probably not overkill to emphasize that in the event of domain controller problems, without this protection users will not be able to log on. In addition, in the event of a total failure, all Active Directory information is lost unless regular backups or replications have been achieved.

Domain Controller Site Membership

A domain controller is assigned to a site during installation of the Active Directory and stays there unless the administrator manually intervenes to relocate it. The site location of a domain controller is part of the Active Directory replication topology and other system requests.

Whereas a domain controller is assigned to a specific site, sites of client systems may change. When a client computer boots and an IP address is assigned by DHCP, site membership may shift to a different subnet.

Replication

Active Directory replication between domain controllers is managed by the system administrator on a site-by-site basis. As domain controllers are added, a replication path must be established. This is done by the Knowledge Consistency Checker (KCC) coupled with Active Directory replication components. The KCC is a dynamic process that runs on all domain controllers to create and modify the replication topology (Figure 5.11). If a domain controller fails, the KCC automatically creates new paths to the remaining domain controllers. Manual intervention with the KCC will also force a new path.

The Active Directory replaces PDCs and BDCs with multimaster replication services. Each domain controller retains a copy of the entire directory for that particular domain. As changes are made in one domain controller, the originator communicates these changes to the peer domain controllers. The directory data itself is stored in the ntds.dit file.

Active Directory replication uses the Remote Procedure Call (RPC) over IP to conduct replication within a site. Replication between sites can use either RPC or the Simple Mail Transfer Protocol (SMTP) for data transmission. The default intersite replication protocol is RPC.

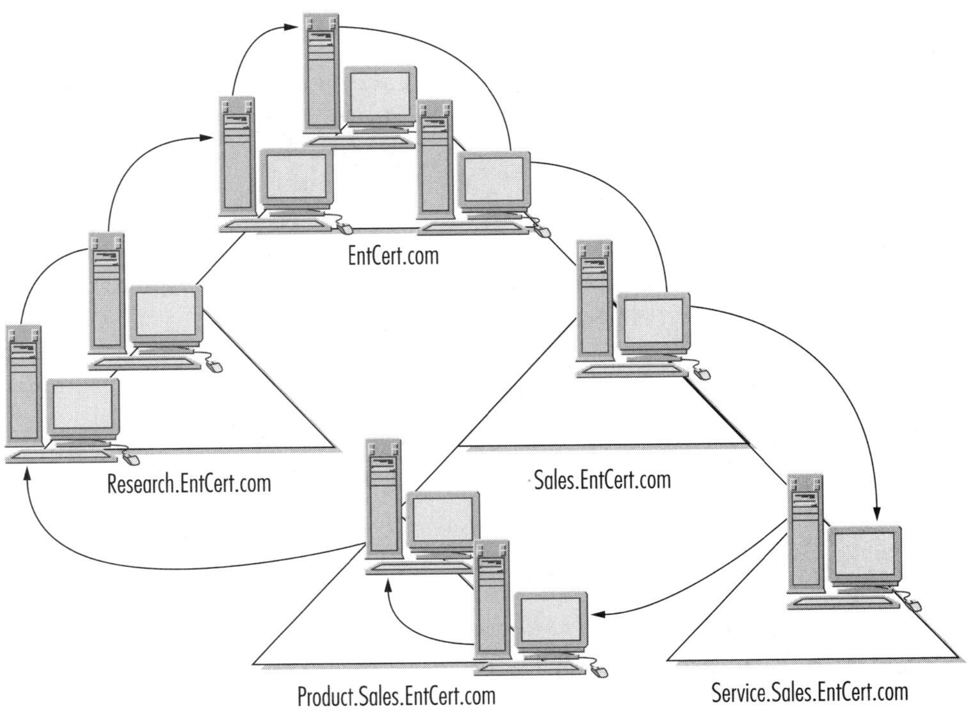

FIGURE 5.11 Active Directory Replication

INTERSITE AND INTRASITE REPLICATION

There are distinct differences in internal and intersite domain controller replication. In theory, the network bandwidth within a site is sufficient to handle all network traffic associated with replication and other Active Directory activities. By the definition of a site, the network must be reliable and fast. A change notification process is initiated when modifications occur on a domain controller. The domain controller waits for a configurable period (by default, 5 minutes) before it forwards a message to its replication partners. During this interval, it continues to accept changes. Upon receiving a message, the partner domain controllers copy the modification from the original domain controller. In the event that no changes were noted during a configurable period (by default, 6 hours), a replication sequence ensures that all possible modifications are communicated. Replication within a site involves the transmission of uncompressed data.

NOTE Security-related modifications are replicated within a site immediately. These changes include account and individual user lockout policies, changes to password policies, changes to computer account passwords, and modifications to the Local Security Authority (LSA).

Replication between sites assumes that there are network connectivity problems, including insufficient bandwidth, reduced reliability, and increased cost. Therefore, the Active Directory permits the system to make decisions on the type, frequency, and timing of intersite replication. All replication objects transmitted between sites are compressed, which may reduce traffic by 10 to 25 percent; however, since this is not sufficient to guarantee proper replication, the system administrator has the responsibility of scheduling intersite replication, as described in Chapter 6.

REPLICATION COMPONENT OBJECTS

Whereas the KCC represents the process elements associated with replication, the following comprise the Active Directory object components:

- *Connection object*. Domain controllers become replication "partners" when linked by a connection object. This is represented by a one-way path between two domain controller server objects. Connection objects are created by the KCC by default. They can also be manually created by the system administrator.
- *NTDS settings object.* The NTDS settings object is a container automatically created by the Active Directory. It contains all of the connection objects and is a child of the server object.

• *Server object*. The Active Directory represents every computer as a computer object. The domain controller is also represented by a computer object, plus a specially created server object. The server object's parent is the site object that defines its IP subnet. However, in the event that the domain controller server object was created prior to site creation, it will be necessary to manually define the IP subnet to properly assign the domain controller a site.

When it is necessary to link multiple sites, two additional objects are created to manage the replication topology: site link and site link bridge.

• *Site link*. The site link object specifies a series of values (cost, interval, and schedule) that define the connection between sites. The KCC uses these values to manage replication and to modify the replication path if it detects a more efficient one. The Active Directory DEFAULTIPSITELINK is used by default until the system administrator intervenes. The cost value, ranging from 1 to 32767, is an arbitrary estimate of the actual cost of data transmission as defined bandwidth. The interval value sets the number of times replication will occur: Fifteen minutes to a maximum of once a week (or 10,080 minutes) is the minimum; 3 hours is the default. The scheduled interval establishes when replication should occur. While replication can be at any time by default, the system administrator may want to schedule it only during off-peak network hours.

• *Site link bridge*. The site link bridge object defines a set of links that communicate via the same protocol. By default, all site links use the same protocol and are transitive. Moreover, they belong to a single site link bridge. No configuration is necessary to the site link bridge if the IP network is fully routed. Otherwise, manual configuration may be necessary.

PREVENTING DATA REPLICATION COLLISION

The Active Directory issues a unique identifier known as the update sequence number (USN), which is given to every change made to an object. This number is incrementally changed whenever the object is modified. Each property of an object is also issued a USN. A source domain regularly communicates USN sequence changes to the peer domain controller. The latest USN is then registered in each domain controller to ensure the freshness of an object's state. The Active Directory uses a timestamp only when changes are made at approximately the same time to the same object. At this point, in order to avoid data collisions, the change with the latest timestamp will be replicated by default. In all other cases, the Active Directory disregards the timestamping process.

Special Domain Controller Roles

Some domain controllers are assigned specific roles to facilitate performance and to reduce conflict. While the principle of multimaster replication of services across all domain controllers is the underpinning of the Active Directory, certain functions are best performed by a single domain controller. Therefore, Windows Server 2003 supports two forms of specialized function: the Global Catalog and operations masters. Forests share a Global Catalog and some operations masters.

THE GLOBAL CATALOG

The GC has two primary functions. First, it acts as a domain controller that stores object data and manages queries about objects and their most common attributes (called the Global Catalog Partial Attribute Set, or PAS). Second, it provides data that permits network logon. In single-domain controller environments, the Active Directory and GC reside on the same server. Where multiple domain controllers exist, as we discuss later, it is often advisable to move the GC to its own dedicated domain controller. All domain trees have a GC and must reside on a domain controller.

NOTE In the absence of a GC, a user can log on only to the local system. However, a member of the Domain Administrators group can log on to the network without a GC.

NOTE In Windows 2000, processing a user logon in native mode required a domain controller (DC) to contact a Global Catalog server in order to expand a user's Universal Group membership. As a result, it was recommended that the GC server be located in a remote site to avoid network-related logon failures. Windows Server 2003 reduces this need through group membership caching. Domain controllers within a site can cache the Universal Group membership so that user logon processing can occur in the absence of a GC. The cache is refreshed periodically when the site-based DC can contact the GC. This feature is turned on by configuring a site to use Global Catalog-less logon in the Active Directory Sites and Services snap-in.

The Global Catalog server stores and replicates an assortment of information, including the domain forest schema data and configuration data. It can also be seen as a data repository and engine for rapid object searches. The GC lists all the objects in a domain tree or forest. However, it differs from the Active Directory in that it is comprised of a partial list of object attributes. A list of the most requested or common object attributes is contained in the GC in an abbreviated format that results from partial replication of domain data. By cataloging domain objects, locating objects can be faster without the need to search the entire source domain. Clearly, the reason for a dedicated GC is to separate the inquiry process from the updating and management processes within a directory service, as shown in Figure 5.12.

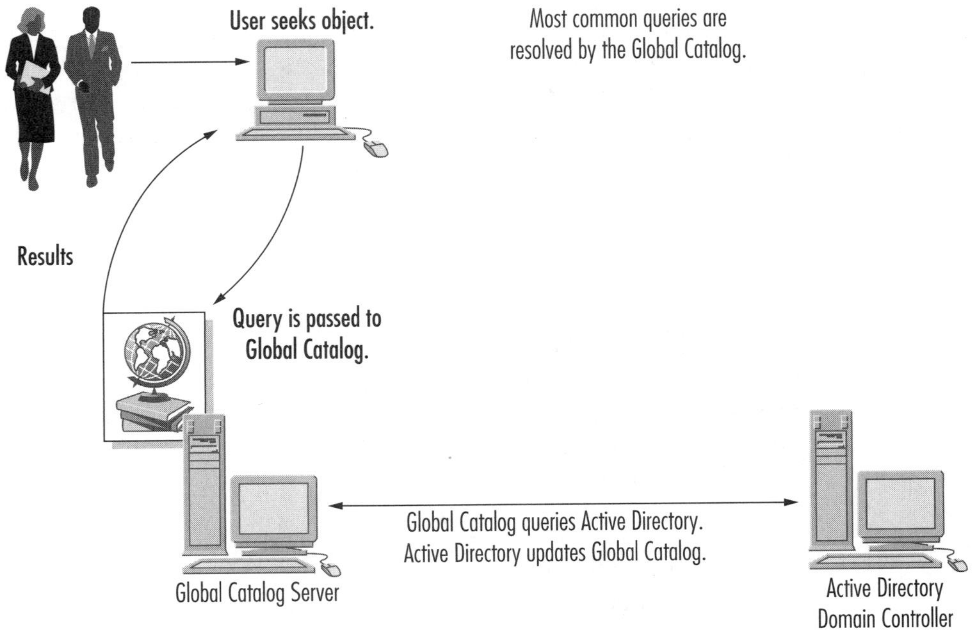

FIGURE 5.12 Global Catalog Relationship

An object's distinguished name typically provides sufficient data to identify the partition that holds it. The GC contains a partial copy of every distinguished namespace on the Active Directory.

The Global Catalog supports a set of default object attributes that are considered the most common or the most frequently queried—for example, a user's first and last names. However, for greater control over the defined attributes for a particular domain, Windows Server 2003 provides a means to modify the default settings. The system administrator can use the Schema Manager snap-in to update the attributes included in the GC replication.

When the first Active Directory is installed, it creates a default Global Catalog. More than one GC server can exist depending on the size of the enterprise, the number of physical sites, and the quality of network connectivity. Global Catalog servers are added through the Sites and Servers Management snap-in of the Microsoft Management Console (MMC). Moving the GC to another domain controller is accomplished by modifying the NTDS Setting Properties in the Sites and Server Management snap-in.

In selecting a system to become the GC server, it is important to consider both capacity and network connectivity. The system should have sufficient storage capability to support the management of a million or more objects. The CPU system speed should be sufficient to permit the processing of a steady flow of queries.

NOTE Global Catalog synchronization has been improved. In Windows 2000, the GC Partial Attribute Set required full synchronization cycle of its read-only (RO) naming context (NC) with propagation of extended PAS (addition of an attribute to the PAS). The purpose was to provide up-to-date attribute-extended replica images on other domain controllers. Windows Server 2003 has a mechanism to preserve the GC synchronization state rather than reset it. This feature is activated through the Active Directory Users and Computers snap-in.

Global Catalogs and Sites

Network connectivity to the GC server must be fast and of high quality, since access to a GC is required for successful network logon. Given that a site is bounded by rapid and reliable network connectivity, at least one GC domain controller per site is recommended.

Master Operation Roles

Multimaster domain replication assumes that all domain controllers eventually receive synchronized Active Directory information. However, there are master domain controller relationships to handle certain Active Directory information within a domain or forest. The master roles are:

- *Domain Naming Master*. This domain controller manages the addition and removal of domains in the forest. A forest can have only one Domain Naming Master, which can be transferred to another domain controller through the Active Directory Domains and Trusts snap-in.
- *Infrastructure Master*. The domain controller is responsible for managing group and user references. Expect a delay in changes when they are made across domains. Updates to other domains are made by the Infrastructure Master domain controller via a process called multimaster replication. This master role can be transferred to another domain controller through the Active Directory Users and Computers snap-in.
- *PDC Emulator*. In a mixed Windows Server 2003 and Windows NT environment, the PDC Emulator supports the BDCs. Thus, it manages user account and password changes and forwards that information to the Windows NT BDC. In a native mode Windows Server 2003 environment, the PDC Emulator receives preference in the replication of user account passwords. Before a logon fails, it is checked for updated information. This master role can be transferred to another domain controller through the Active Directory Users and Computers snap-in.

- *Relative ID Master*. A single Relative ID (RID) Master in each domain of a tree manages the allocation of sequential RIDs to each domain controller. This makes all security IDs (SIDs) created in a domain relative to the domain controller. This master role can be transferred to another domain controller through the Active Directory Users and Computers snap-in.
- *Schema Master*. The Schema Master controls updates to the domain schema data. There is one Schema Master in the entire forest. It can be transferred to another domain controller through the Active Directory Schema Master snap-in.

CAUTION Microsoft issues a word of caution regarding potential conflicts between the Infrastructure Master and the Global Catalog. In environments with more than one domain controller, the GC should not be hosted on a controller that also hosts the Infrastructure Master. Since the Infrastructure Master compares its data with the GC, there may be significant replication impacts and full replication may fail. In particular, outdated information will not be seen. The exception to this rule about separating the GC and the Infrastructure Master is an environment where every domain controller retains a copy of the GC.

NOTE In Windows 2000/Server 2003 Active Directory, the membership of a group is stored and replicated as a single unit. As a result, a change to a group with large membership causes the entire membership to replicate. This could easily consume large amounts of network bandwidth and processor load. In addition, this also results in failed replication conflict resolution. Now, when a forest is advanced in a Windows Server 2003 native mode, group membership is changed to store and replicate values for individual members. Membership is not treated as a single unit. No administrative action is required to activate this improvement since it is integral to Windows Server 2003. This does not apply to Global Catalog systems.

OPEN STANDARDS SUPPORT AND NAMING CONVENTIONS

One of the strengths of the Active Directory is its conformity to several important industry standards and conventions, permitting greater interoperability within a heterogeneous environment. While the interplay of the Active Directory with other directory services is far from seamless, open industry standards do provide the potential for greater information exchange among multiple operating systems. The Active Directory embraces the Domain Name System and supports the Lightweight Directory Access Protocol (LDAP). DNS resolves domain names to IP addresses in the Internet and within intranets. LDAP extends directory service interoperability by providing directory access across heterogeneous networks. One LDAP control called DirSync is used to retrieve changed information from the directory. This feature provides a method to imbue the DirSync control with the ability to perform access checks like those performed on normal LDAP searches. In addition to its support for these protocols, Active Directory uses industry-standard naming conventions, which are listed in Table 5.2.

NOTE Active Directory also supports HTTP, which defines the methods of displaying information on a Web browser. Objects in Active Directory can be displayed as HTTP pages.

TABLE 5.2 Industry Standards Used by Active Directory

Standard	Reference	Description
DNS Dynamic Update	RFCs 2052, 2163	Service location (SRV) and dynamic updates
Dynamic Host Configuration Protocol (DHCP)	RFC 2131	Network IP address management
Kerberos, v5	RFC 1510	Authentication
Lightweight Directory Access Protocol (LDAP) v3	RFC 2251	Directory access
LDAP 'C'	RFC 1823	Directory API
LDAP Schema	RFCs 2247, 2252, 2256	Directory schema
Simple Network Time Protocol (SNTP)	RFC 2030	Distributed time services for networks (formerly 1769)
Simple Mail Transfer Protocol (SMTP)	RFC 2821	Message transfer (formerly 821)
Transfer Control Protocol/ Internet Protocol (TCP/IP)	RFCs 791, 793	Network transport protocols
X.509 v3 certificates	ISO X.509	Authentication

The Active Directory and DNS

The DNS resolves names within a TCP/IP network; it translates a domain name such as *EntCert.com* into an IP address and vice versa. All Active Directory domain names follow the DNS naming convention, allowing easy access to the IP address of Active Directory objects that use DNS names. Windows Server 2003 DNS is a Microsoft-developed implementation and not a port of public domain software, but does follow the RFC and BIND (Berkeley Internet Name Domain) standards.

In spite of its long-time use in UNIX and other operating systems, DNS is a long way from being an automated or self-managed service. Maintenance of DNS is often viewed as a system administration burden. In most legacy environments, the system administrator labors with manual manipulation of flat text files. Most recently, the advent of the Dynamic DNS protocol has emerged to streamline the use and maintenance of this popular name locator. Windows Server 2003 bundles its own version of Dynamic DNS that tests and updates DNS registration across defined intranets and the Internet.

While Microsoft bundles its version of Dynamic DNS, other third-party versions with base-level functionality are also supported by Active Directory. By "base-level functionality," we refer to the requirement for the third-party DNS to support both Dynamic DNS and Service Resource Records (SRV RR) technology as defined by RFCs 2052 and 2136 and BIND 8.1.2. Active Directory with Dynamic DNS installed will check TCP/IP addresses across the network to make data correction and appropriate deletions. Local services are published through the SRV RR in DNS with the following structure: <service>.<protocol>.<domain>. For example, if a commercial version of sendmail were used to support the *EntCert.com* domain, the SRV RR would then look like this: <sendmail>.<tcp>.<EntCert.com>. Since Active Directory can support other third-party DNS programs, the actual infrastructure can take one of three basic forms:

- Microsoft's own Dynamic DNS is installed and used by Active Directory.
- A third-party Dynamic DNS that supports SRV RR is used by Active Directory.
- Microsoft's Dynamic DNS installed as a backend via a delegated zone from the older server, thereby providing new support for SRV RR and Dynamic DNS technology features.

In addition to interoperability with DNS servers in other operating systems, Active Directory's Dynamic DNS reduces other administrative burdens. With the release of Windows NT 4.0, Microsoft integrated DNS with its Windows Internet Naming Service (WINS). In a Windows NT environment, clients may have fixed IP addresses or can be assigned an address at startup that employs the Dynamic Host Configuration Protocol (DHCP).

INTEROPERABILITY ISSUES

In many cases, UNIX-based DNS servers exist within an enterprise. A desire to maintain DNS on UNIX often prevails due to established investment and maintenance of these servers. While Windows Server 2003 supports this approach, Microsoft contends that there are a number of compelling reasons for use of the Windows OS DNS server in heterogeneous environments. The basis of the argument is the support of the latest RFC standards that may not be available with older versions of UNIX. The UNIX system can meet Active Directory DNS requirements by upgrading the BIND DNS server to version 8.1.2 or later. Support for SRV resource records is also required. Dynamic updates are desirable but not compulsory.

Where DNS servers that are not running Windows Server 2003 are to be used for the root zone, Windows DNS services should be employed to support Active Directory registration and updates. This may require modification of the other DNS namespace design. Under one scenario, you can establish a new subdomain to root the first Active Directory domain. For example, if the established root domain name is *EntCert.com,* the Active Directory subdomain might become *win2k.EntCert.com.* Another approach is to create multiple subdomains based on the second-level domain that support Active Directory registration. Both scenarios involve the delegation of the DNS namespace into additional zones.

Namespace and Naming Conventions

The Active Directory's naming conventions serve a number of important purposes. First, all directories are based on the concept of a namespace, that is, a name is used to resolve the location of an object; when name resolution occurs, it converts the namespace locator to the specific object, such as a printer on the third floor. Everything hangs off the Active Directory's using the namespace to identify and locate persons, places, and things in an enterprise.

NAMING CONVENTIONS

In keeping with the namespace concept, the Active Directory uses four name types to recognize every object:

- The *distinguished name (DN)* defines the domain and related container(s) in which an object resides. It matches several defined attributes to the description—the basic attributes are Domain-Component (DC), Organizational-Unit (OU), and Common-Name (CN). For example, a representation of a printer in the *EntCert.com* domain and sales organizational unit, physically located on the third floor, would have the distinguished name *DC=COM, DC=EntCert, OU=sales, CN=printer, CN=3rdFloorPrinter.*

- The *relative distinguished name (RDN)* is really an attribute of the object itself. In the preceding example, *CN=3rdFloorPrinter* is relative to its parent, *CN=printer*. The RDN is compared to the DN in Figure 5.13.
- The *globally unique identifier (GUID)* avoids duplication of objects and ensures uniqueness. It is a 128-bit number assigned to an object at the time of creation and stored with it. This permits applications—for example, a word processor file with embedded graphical objects—to retrieve an updated version of a drawing by use of the GUID that is stored within the document.
- The *user principal name (UPN)* is considered a "friendly" naming convention. It combines the user account name with the DNS domain name where the account exists. The name *bob@EntCert.com* is the UPN for user account bob in the *EntCert.com* domain tree.

ADDITIONAL USE OF INDUSTRY NAMING STANDARDS

Active Directory supports a number of industry standard formats to facilitate interoperability with other directory services. Microsoft's Universal Naming Convention (UNC), which takes the form *\\EntCert.com\Administration\budget.doc,* is the base naming convention. The Active Directory also incorporates RFC 822, which defines the common Internet e-mail naming structure of *user@domainname.com.* It supports the familiar HTTP URL, which takes the form *http://EntCert.com/specific page,* as well. Finally, borrowing from the X.500 communication protocol, the Active Directory incorporates the LDAP URL as defined in the draft of RFC 1779, which breaks the name into very specific subunits that might look like the following:

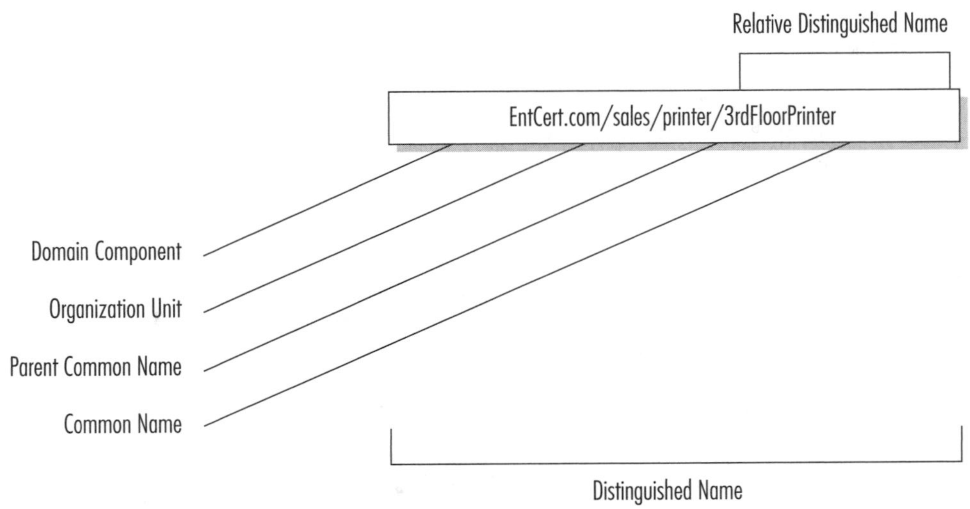

FIGURE 5.13 Distinguished versus Relative Distinguished Names

//EntCert.com/CN=myname, OU=mybranch, OU=myproduct, DN=division-area. The initials provide greater object specification. CN is the user's first and last names. The two hierarchical OUs distinguish the branch of the company and the specific product area. Finally, DN defines the work area, such as engineering or accounting. Under Windows Server 2003, all LDAP traffic between domain controllers and the administrative tools is now signed and encrypted by default.

ACTIVE DIRECTORY USE OF LDAP

The Lightweight Directory Access Protocol, defined by the Internet Engineering Task Force (IETF) RFC 2251, is a simplified version of the X.500 DAP. Microsoft's Windows Server 2003 utilizes LDAP versions 2 and 3. LDAP permits the exchange of directory data between services. For example, since Novell Directory Services data is LDAP compliant, it can be passed to and from the Active Directory.

LDAP is used to access information from compliant directory services such as the Active Directory. LDAP searches the Active Directory for information about stored objects and their attributes. It uses both distinguished names and relative distinguished names to locate the object and works closely with DNS throughout this process (Figure 5.14). DNS provides resolution to locate the appropriate Active Directory domain controller; LDAP resolves the object itself. The process follows these basic steps:

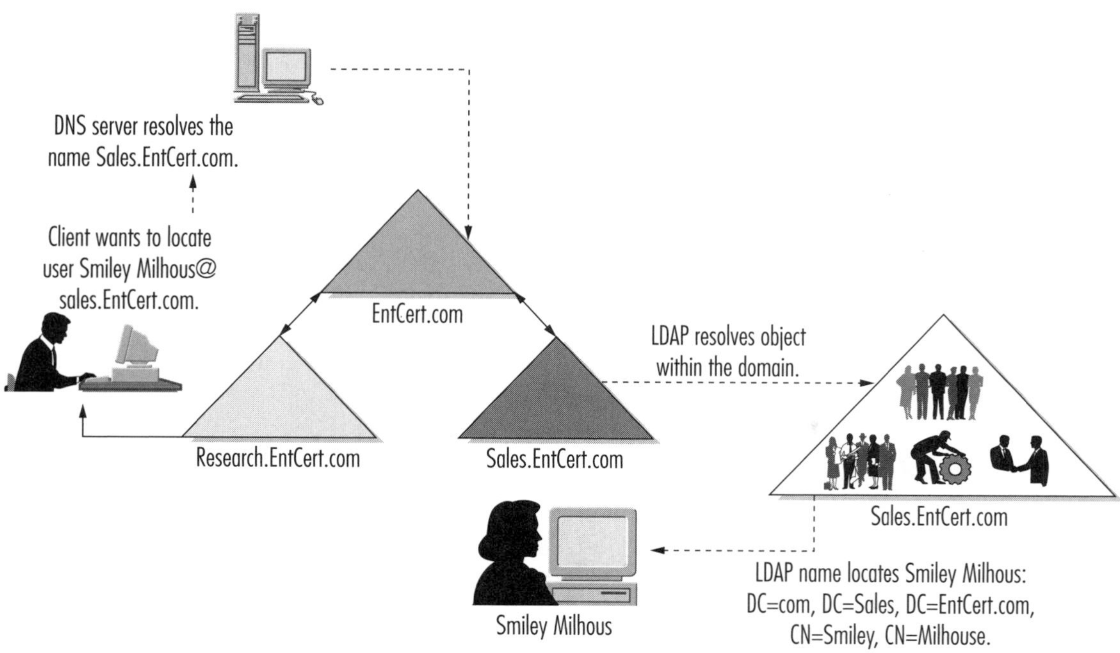

FIGURE 5.14 The Relationship of DNS and LDAP in Locating Objects

1. A client queries DNS for an LDAP server (Active Directory domain controller).
2. The client queries the domain controller for information about the object.
3. If the requested object is not in the domain but the domain controller knows there are child domains or a forest domain, it issues a referral to contact the other domain controllers until object resolution is achieved.
4. The object information is sent to the client.

LDAP's C language API (RFC 1823) permits the development of application enhancements and the building of related applications. Developing interfaces using the LDAP C API is perhaps the easiest way to provide interoperability of LDAP directory-compliant services. Existing LDAP directory service auxiliary applications that migrated to communicate with Windows Server 2003 Active Directory may not need modification. If API code changes are required as well, they are typically for the identification of objects unique to Active Directory.

In addition to the aforementioned conventions introduced in Windows 2000, the Windows Server 2003 Active Directory implementation adds a number of facilities to its LDAP support:

- Active Directory now has support for dynamic store entries as defined by the Internet Engineering Task Force standard protocol RFC 2589. Entries in the directory can additionally be assigned Time-to-Live (TTL) values that determine when the entries will be automatically deleted.
- Transport Layer Security (TLS) connections to Active Directory over LDAP are now protected using the IETF standard TLS security protocol (RFC 2830).
- The Digest Authentication mechanism (DIGEST-MD5 SASL authentication) over an LDAP connection to Active Directory is supported (RFC 2829).
- Virtual List Views (VLV) LDAP extensions as defined by the Working Group of IETF is supported.
- Support for Dynamic Auxiliary classes and instances are supported.

NOTE An extension of LDAP is its replication technology protocol LDUP (LDAP Duplication/Update Protocol), an open standards specification that is not embraced by Active Directory services. LDUP does a complete real-time replication of directory elements that requires that compliant directory services adhere to very specific rules and data structures. Violation of any rules such that a directory entry is not understood can lead to cascading errors throughout the directory. Rather than LDUP, Active Directory uses a synchronization methodology to populate and update directories.

NOTE Microsoft did not include major portions of the X.500 protocol in the Active Directory primarily because of its dependence on an OSI networking layer and a lack of interest. The excluded elements are the Directory Access Protocol, the Directory System Protocol, the Directory Information Shadowing Protocol, and the Directory Operational Binding Management Protocol. LDAP is the most significant element of X.500 incorporated in Windows 2000 and Windows Server 2003.

MIGRATION AND BACKWARD COMPATIBILITY

Many operating system upgrades of the past can best be described as nightmares. Microsoft has provided solid upgrading solutions, especially for those migrating from early versions of Windows NT. Chapter 3 discusses Windows Server 2003 in both mixed mode and native mode environments, but a further review in the context of Active Directory services is appropriate here.

Active Directory services is designed with backward compatibility as its cornerstone. Thus, a layer of code in Windows Server 2003 fully emulates the directory services of Windows NT 3.51 and 4.0. In fact, Active Directory is designed to operate either in a native Windows Server 2003 environment or in a mixed enterprise with Windows NT.

Migration can take one of two forms: a rapid and systematic upgrade of Windows NT to Windows 2000, or coexistence of Windows Server 2003 and Windows NT for an undefined period. In the first instance, the existing Primary Domain Controller should be the first server upgraded as a Windows .NET Active Directory domain controller. User and group accounts are automatically loaded into the Active Directory during the installation process. Backup Domain Controllers are then upgraded to Windows Server 2003 with Active Directory services, and copies of the Active Directory are then automatically promoted as peer domain controllers.

NOTE An improved Active Directory Migration Tool (ADMT 2) is used primarily to migrate from Windows NT4 to Windows 2000/Windows Server 2003 or to restructure Windows 2000/Windows Server 2003 deployments. With ADMT, an administrator moves objects between domains in the same or different forests. ADMT supports common migration tasks including moving users, groups, and computers. Also, a new scripting interface was added. ADMT can now be driven from any language and supports COM interfaces such as Visual Basic Script, Visual Basic, and Visual C++. This facility is available from a download called the Domain Migration Cookbook at *http://www.microsoft.com.*

NOTE When connecting to domain controllers running Windows 2000, precautions must be taken to ensure that signing LDAP traffic guarantees packaged data comes from a known source. By default, Windows 2000 Active Directory does not sign and encrypt all LDAP traffic. We strongly recommend that all Windows 2000 domain controllers be upgraded to Service Pack 3 or later in order to add these security functions. Alternately, although not recommended, signed and encrypted LDAP traffic can be disabled on Windows Server 2003.

NOTE Group information is migrated only from Windows NT domain controllers to Windows 2000 or Windows Server 2003. Group policy, security, and other data that was created in a workgroup environment will remain local and is not migrated. The local security database remains separate from the Active Directory.

Once the first Windows Server 2003 Active Directory domain controller is in place, the enterprise can start taking advantage of greater functionality. This is true even if the Windows NT BDCs are maintained for some protracted period. BDCs and associated Windows NT workstations will operate in the same manner as before. In environments where BDCs exist downstream, the same PDC/BDC relationship will continue to function. The older installations will immediately gain the added value of the Global Catalog to improve object resolution. At the same time, the Active Directory domain controller will still act as a peer with other Windows Server 2003 domain controllers. Over time, the older BDCs may be upgraded as needed and become peer domain controllers.

In either case, client systems can be added easily. The Windows NT Workstation is upgraded simply by installing Windows XP Professional. Windows 95/98 clients can take advantage of Active Directory awareness by installing a downloadable patch from Microsoft's Web site. This will permit downlevel clients to use Kerberos security and to fully support applications that recognize Active Directory.

For organizations with a heavy investment in Exchange Server, it will be good news that this popular groupware suite will also use the Windows Server 2003 Active Directory, eliminating the need to maintain two sets of user accounts and other data.

ADMINISTRATIVE INTERFACE SNAP-INS

The Active Directory offers system administrators consolidated management of all objects in a network. This is through the administrative user interface, which is

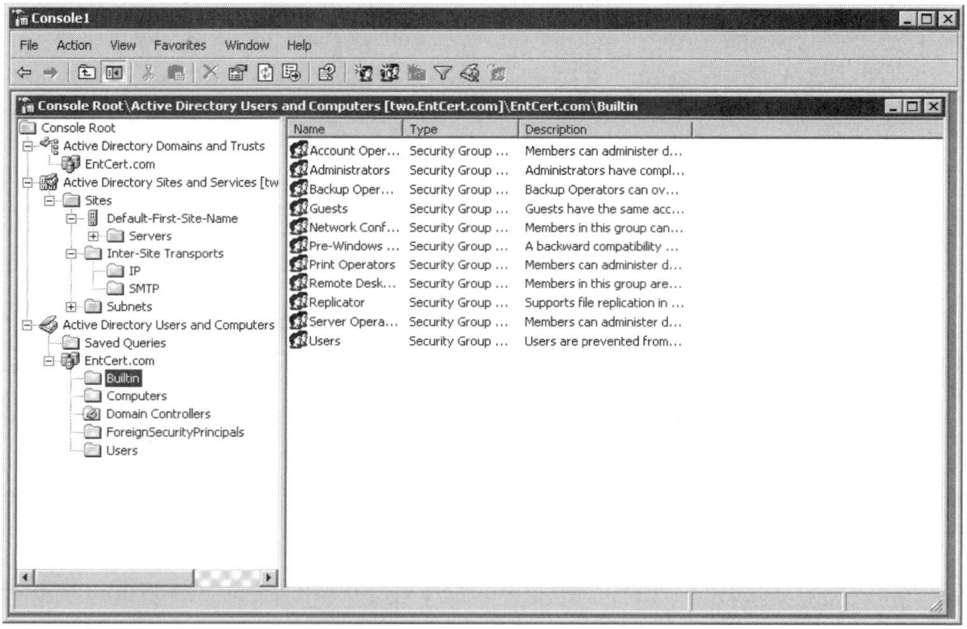

FIGURE 5.15 MMC Active Directory Snap-Ins

based on the Microsoft Management Console and its snap-in applications. The MMC is visible only to system administrators, not to the end user. The four primary MMC snap-ins associated with the Active Directory (Figure 5.15) are:

- Active Directory Domains and Trusts Manager
- Active Directory Sites and Services
- Active Directory Users and Computers
- Active Directory Schema Manager (available from the adminpak on the Windows Server 2003 CD under the I386 folder)

Specific use of these managers is discussed in other chapters of this book.

API OPTIONS

The Active Directory supports development of additional snap-in administrative tools through its Active Directory Services Interface (ADSI) API. The primary purposes of this API are to permit third-party software vendors to develop additional tools, to allow system administrators to write related scripts, and to afford more open interfaces with other directory services.

ADSI Resources

ADSI is perfect for automating administrative tasks such as changing passwords, creating users complete with Exchange mailboxes, working with file shares, and creating computer accounts.

The ADSI is based on the common object model (COM). Since it is a set of COM-based interfaces on the Active Directory, as well as to Win9x and Windows NT, it permits the administrator or software developer to work with the Active Directory without worrying about its internals. As is true with all COM development, a number of programming languages can be used, including C, C++, Java, and Visual Basic. Associated APIs that can be modified within the context of the Active Directory are the LDAP API (RFC 1823 for the C language) and MAPI.

ADSI is part of the Windows Open Services Architecture (WOSA) and the Open Directory Service Interfaces (ODSI). A discussion of these models, architectures, and interfaces is outside the scope of this book, but system administrators who desire additional information can download an assortment of white papers directly from the Microsoft Web site.

The architecture of the Active Directory employs a number of service interfaces that manage the object mode, schema, caching, namespace, navigation, and searching. It is based on an object model consisting of ADSI host objects and dependent objects. The host and dependent object relationship is different from the container/contents relationship that is part of the Active Directory itself, in that it acts as a parent and child relationship only for the directory service objects.

The ADSI provider implements requests made to the host and dependent objects. The objects can be one of two types—container objects and leaf objects. Directory service container objects can hold other ADSI objects. They include Namespace, Country, Locality, Organization, Organizational Unit, Domain, and Computer. Directory service leaf objects cannot be used as containers of other objects. They include User, Group, Alias, Service, Print Queue, Print Device, Print Job, File Job, File Service, File Share, Session, and Resources.

ADSI, which is currently at version 2.5, is available from Microsoft at *http://www.microsoft.com/adsi.* For development work, both the ADSI and ADSI SDK are necessary. The SDK contains a large variety of samples in C++, VB, and J++, as well as a sample ADSI provider and some tools to explore ADSI.

SAMPLE ADSI SCRIPTS

James Morris, a software engineer for the University of Washington, kindly offered the following two example scripts that can be used in connection with ADSI.

SAMPLE 1: VB CODE FOR ADDING FULL NAME AND DESCRIPTION TO A USER

```
Private Sub Form_Load()
' Define the user object
```

```
Dim user As IADsUser
' Set the Domain equal to your domain
domain = "DOMAIN"
'Bind to the user object Administrator using the WinNT provider
Set user = GetObject("WinNT://" & domain & "/Administrator")
' Set the properties
user.FullName = "Jane Doe"
user.Description = "Senior Accountant" & domain
'It's important to commit the changes!
user.SetInfo
End Sub
***
***
```

SAMPLE 2: VBSCRIPT TO ENUMERATE OBJECTS ON A COMPUTER

```
Dim ComputerName
'Set the name of the computer to work with
ComputerName = "computer1"
'Bind to computer object using the WinNT provider
Set compobj = GetObject("WinNT://" & ComputerName & ",computer" )
'Echo the objects to the screen
For each obj in compobj
wscript.echo obj.Name
Next
***
```

The User Interface

Active Directory's UI data is stored in a Display Specifier object, whose attributes define the UI elements. The property pages for the Active Directory can be a COM object or an HTML file. The Display Specifier object stores the URL of the HTML page or the universally unique identifier (UUID) of the COM object.

For system administrators, the properties associated with system management are stored in the Admin-Property-Pages. Those for end users are stored in the Shell-Property-Pages. Menus for end users are different from those for administrators. Thus, the context menu for users is Shell-Context-Menu; for administrators, Admin-Context-Menu.

ADMINISTRATIVE SECURITY AND TRUST RELATIONSHIPS

Domains are fundamental security boundaries, which by default restrict users in one domain from gaining access to objects in another domain. However, "trust" relationships can be created between domains to allow object accessibility across these secure borders.

Since administration can be delegated to domains and OUs, Windows Server 2003 establishes certain administrative defaults. The Domain Administrator group can control activities only in that domain, which means that administrative privileges do not automatically flow down to other domains. Thus, a system administrator for the root domain must be explicitly allowed rights to its child domains.

Administrative rights on another domain can be either limited or full. To be granted full rights in another domain, the user must be specifically added to that domain's Administrator group. For more limited rights, that administrator must grant permissions to certain objects or organizational units.

Remember that domains are organized into trees that share a namespace and are composed of a single domain or a root domain with child domains. All domains in the tree share Active Directory. Active Directory objects are contained on domain controllers in each individual domain.

Users gain access across domains within the tree through trust relationships. The hierarchical structure of the domain tree (extending internally to the organizational units) permits the flow of permissions to an OU. With appropriate group and OU permissions, a user in one domain can use resources or gain access to objects in another domain.

In trust relationships, user logons are honored between trusted domains. When two trees are trusted at the root domain, users in one tree can log on to domains in the other tree. However, specific access to objects is based on specific permissions associated with that user and the object's ACL. The Active Directory supports two trust relationship models:

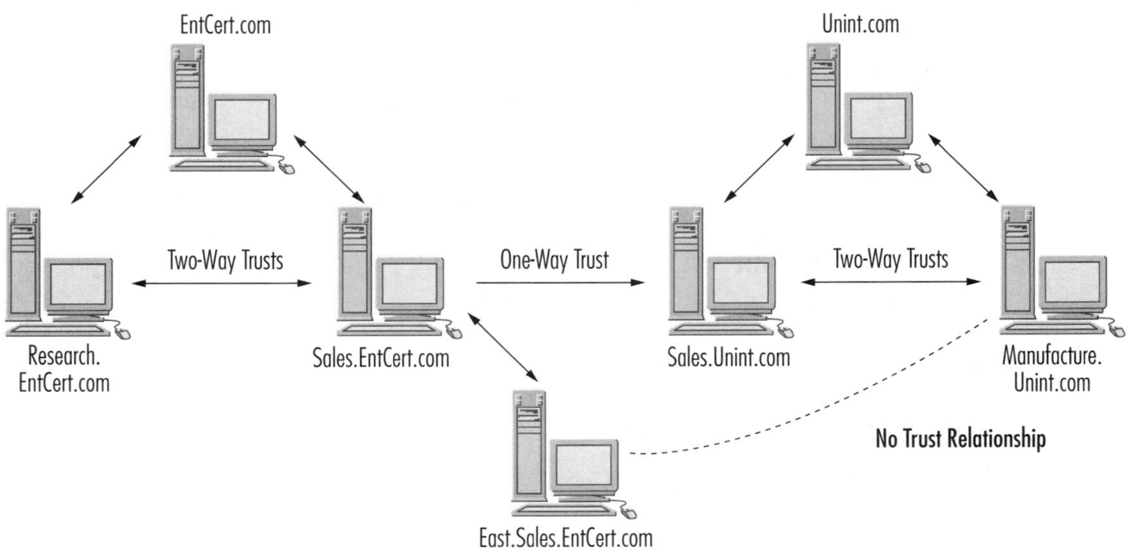

FIGURE 5.16 Trust Relationships

- A two-way transitive trust is automatically achieved between domains in the same tree or it can be established between root domains on different trees.
- Explicit one-way trusts are created between specific domains in different forests and provide one-way, restricted permissions. As shown in Figure 5.16, the domain *Sales.EntCert.com* has granted logon authentication to users in *Sales.unint.com*; however, the relationship is not bidirectional, nor does it flow to any other domain in the tree or forest. (Note that explicit trust can also be established with the same forest to provide shortcuts between domains.)

ADMINISTRATIVE DELEGATION

Each domain or domain tree has security boundaries. The system administrator can grant rights to individuals in organizational units with greater granularity. In fact, certain administrative responsibilities can be granted on an OU basis without endangering system security. As more users become "empowered" to manage aspects of their normal work within their environment, the mundane responsibilities of system administration are reduced.

If a system administrator considers a security boundary as a logical management segment, responsibility for each boundary or segment can be delegated to other administrators. A system administrator in one domain is not automatically the administrator in another domain. Alternatively, an administrator may want to extend his or her control over many domains. Administrative privileges can be delegated by organizational unit, domain, tree, or forest.

Another important aspect of this containerized OU and domain tree strategy is how it copes with organizational change. In many operating systems, changes or deletions usually require many hours of a system administrator's manual labor. The Active Directory permits OU changes to be accommodated by pruning, grafting, and merging branches from one domain tree to another. It also provides simple drag-and-drop functionality. For example, if the widget department in Ohio is to be consolidated with the super-widget department in Michigan, the system administrator need only drag that object to the domain tree of the merged organization.

POSTSCRIPT

In essence, the Active Directory should eliminate much of the drudgery of system administration while providing significantly more control. System administrator interaction and maintenance of the Active Directory are explored in Chapter 6.

Chapter 6

Active Directory Management and Use

The previous chapter defined base-level concepts surrounding the Active Directory core technology. This chapter explores its management and practical utilization.

Having read this chapter, you should be able to perform the following Active Directory system administrative tasks:

- Plan for the Active Directory.
- Install the Active Directory both on a fresh server and as part of a PDC or BDC promotion.
- Use these primary Active Directory Administrative tools to carry out key management tasks:

  —Active Directory Domains and Trusts

  —Active Directory Schema Manager

  —Active Directory Sites and Services

  —Active Directory Users and Computers

  —Active Directory Replicator
- Create a domain and perform basic domain controller management.
- Create organizational units.
- Locate and manage objects.
- Use the Active Directory scripting functions.
- Manage Active Directory object access.
- Delegate Active Directory administration.
- Manage the Global Catalog.

PLANNING FOR THE ACTIVE DIRECTORY

The proper implementation of the Active Directory requires forethought and planning. Chapter 3 outlines many of the basic planning issues involved in the installation or upgrade of Windows Server 2003. Since these issues apply equally to the Active Directory, we strongly advise you to review that chapter in conjunction with the discussions here. In this chapter, you will learn the importance of planning for the creation of namespaces, domains, sites, and organizational units. As discussed in Chapter 4, such planning is based on the system administrator's knowledge of the current IT infrastructure, business computing requirements, anticipated change or growth, and available connectivity and bandwidth.

The DNS Namespace

The Domain Name System (DNS) is an industry standard name-resolution vehicle that the Internet uses to match IP addresses to specific namespaces, like ours, *EntCert.com*. Since domains and domain trees are defined by a common namespace based on DNS, the importance of establishing this strategy early is key. At the least, a baseline understanding of DNS and domain name registration is required prior to the installation of the Active Directory. For additional information on DNS, including its installation, refer to Chapter 12, "Networking Basics and Naming Services."

DNS NAMES FOR CHILD DOMAINS AND FORESTS

Defining namespaces is based on an understanding of the organization's current and projected structure, growth, and relationship with related organizations. In most cases, a single domain name can accommodate even very large organizations. However, it can also be used to create child domain relationships where such division is necessary. The child name is a single, descriptive text string that is added to the front of the domain name and separated from it by a period. Child domains can have children of their own. In this case the child name is added before the parent name, again separated by a period, giving the syntax *child2.child1.domain.com.* A child domain name should be fairly generic. Locations or broad, functional descriptive names are generally good choices. For example, for the domain *EntCert.com,* a location—*asia.EntCert.com*—or a function—*sales.EntCert.com*—is broad enough. The objective is to create child domain names that can survive over time.

Where multiple domain names are required or forced on an administrator because of preexisting names (such as when two companies merge but maintain separate identities), forest relationships need to be established. The forest is created by joining two-way transitive trusts multiple domain trees with different DNS namespaces. Separate identities are maintained while transitive trusts to network resources are provided.

DEBUGGING AND REPORTING INCORRECT DNS CONFIGURATION

New to Windows Server 2003, the DNS feature will not be noticed by the administrator if it is properly configured. However, in the event of a problem, this feature should make debugging and reporting easier. It should also help guide the administrator through a proper configuration setup. When DC promotion occurs with an existing forest, the Active Directory Installation Wizard contacts an existing DC to update the directory and replicate from the DC the required portions of the directory. If the wizard fails to locate a DC, it performs debugging and reports what caused the failure and how to fix the problem. In order to be located on a network, every DC must register in DNS DC locator DNS records. The Active Directory Installation Wizard verifies a proper configuration of the DNS infrastructure. All DNS configuration debugging and reporting activity is done with the Active Directory Installation Wizard.

DOMAIN NAMES FOR INTERNAL AND EXTERNAL USE

Another important namespace issue is whether the domain name will be extended for both internal and external use. In the first case, the goal is a single user logon for all Internet and intranet communications. To achieve this end, the system administrator must create two DNS zones: the first resolves the name for internal resources; the second resolves names for external mail systems, Web services, TCP, news, and Telnet connectivity.

In the second case, an organization may choose different domain names for internal and external use. If so, two namespaces must be reserved and domain trees created to manage the respective resources, and transitive trust relationships must be formed by grouping the trees into a forest. This approach to domain naming increases administrative tasks. However, each user should maintain a single logon name.

RENAMING A DOMAIN

A new feature available with Windows Server 2003 supports changing the DNS and/or NetBIOS names of existing domains in a forest. As organizations change, the ability to rename a domain permits the resulting forest to be "well-formed." A renamed domain retains its underlying domain globally unique identifier (GUID) and its domain security ID (SID). A computer's domain membership does not automatically change as a result of the holding domain's being renamed. It is important to note that although a forest root domain can be renamed, a different domain cannot be designated to become the new forest root.

This feature is primarily used when an organization changes its name or when an organization is merged with another corporation.

Although it is now possible to rename the domain, it comes with a little bit of administrative pain. For example, every member domain controller must be rebooted and every member server must be rebooted twice. This extra procedure is in place so that domains are not renamed casually.

The Physical Structure: Sites and Replication

The underlying objectives of the physical structure are easy Active Directory replication, rapid user logons, and efficient resolution of queries for network objects. When planning the physical structure, and site topology in particular, remember that there is no direct relationship between sites and domains. A site can have multiple domains or portions of multiple domains, and vice versa. It is defined by fast and reliable connectivity, so the most critical issue in site planning is the bandwidth and other network constraints for related traffic. This means that site parameters should be dictated by the creation of subnets that share cheap, fast, and reliable connections.

In some cases, two or more remote locations can still be treated as a single site. However, if they are in different area codes and connectivity is based on more expensive connection technologies, the creation of multiple sites is probably in order. Each site should have at least one domain controller that is configured for each location, with replication services set for times when traffic is minimal and at the lowest rates.

Later in this chapter we will explore specific management of intrasite and multisite network traffic and topology. Before that, however, it is important to understand site requirements and site replication and topology.

NOTE With Windows Server 2003 there is an ability to turn off compression of the replication traffic between domain controllers residing in different sites. This should reduce CPU utilization on the domain controllers and provide greater availability. This feature should be activated when CPU spiking occurs. By not compressing the replication traffic between domain controllers, you should free up CPU cycles.

PREPARING FOR REPLICATION AND SYNCHRONIZATION

To prepare for the creation of sites, it is important to understand data transfer and how it works in the Active Directory. There are two forms of data transfer. First, replication is used when Windows Server 2003 domain controllers communicate changes to each other. All domain controllers in a domain tree share a number of traits, including the same schema and control models. When a modification is recorded by one domain controller, it is automatically "replicated" to all other domain controllers in the domain tree according to prescribed scheduling rules. The transitive trust relationships that exist among all domains ensure that new information is written to all domain controllers. This is transparent and fairly rapid within one site. For intersite replication, the system administrator should determine the time and frequency of these updates based on an analysis of network traffic and cost.

Second, synchronization is used for communication between the Active Directory and other directory services such as Novell Directory Services (NDS). To share information, the two services must use an agent known as a *security principle,* which determines what schema information is common to both and selects the data to be shared. Since the structures of directory services vary, the data must then be mapped. This can be streamlined by directory services that employ LDAP, which provides a common method of resolving object names.

Some large enterprises may have more than a hundred different directory services in place, so planning consideration must be given to both Active Directory replication and heterogeneous synchronization. Clearly, Active Directory does not have the ability to synchronize data with all third-party directory services. However, services that employ both DNS and LDAP v3 are good candidates.

Planning the physical structure requires knowing where replication and synchronization might occur. Where possible, confine synchronization to intrasite topologies where internal traffic is the most reliable. Once the synchronization has taken place between Active Directory and other directories' services within a site, the receiving domain controller can replicate the data to other domain controllers throughout the domain tree.

REPLICATION LATENCY

When updates occur on one domain controller, varying amounts of time can pass before they are replicated to others. This is known as *replication latency,* and within a site it typically resolves within a few minutes (every 5 minutes by default). Depending on how the system administrator has configured replication among sites, latency can take place every few minutes or at intervals up to a week.

A part of intersite planning is determining how long a site can exist with latent data. In branch offices that perform well-defined activities and are not subject to regular change, latency is not much of an issue and replication can be safely set for a daily update. Since there is an acknowledged latency, the remote domain controller is in a state called *loose consistency* of Active Directory information. By the same token, a division headquarters site might demand replication from critical sites every half hour.

NOTE One of the concerns of any administrator should include having an assurance the replication is occurring. A new feature available with Windows Server 2003 is the WMI classes that permit an administrator to view whether replications between domain controllers were successful. At the time this book went to publication, the method for applying these WMI classes was sketchy. However, the Microsoft development team suggested the classes will make it possible for administrators or third-party software developers to develop scripts or applications designed to monitor the health of replication.

REPLICATION TOPOLOGY

The Active Directory's Knowledge Consistency Checker (KCC) automatically establishes the most efficient replication topology. To formulate connection rules, the system administrator must input information that is critical to the calculation of the best connectivity routes. The KCC also dynamically establishes alternative connectivity to other sites in the event that a site has only one domain controller and that system fails.

One-directional connection objects are created by the KCC (or manually by the system administrator). Contained in a domain controller's NTDS settings object, each connection object points in one direction to a replication partner. Two paired connection objects create a bidirectional relationship between the partners. Connection objects replicate the three Active Directory partitions of schema, configuration data, and domain data.

The KCC uses the connection objects to establish a two-directional ring between intrasite domain controllers. It attempts to make connections such that there is a maximum of three hops between intersite domain controllers. When a domain controller receives a change, it notifies its partner domain controllers. Additional partners are then notified after a configurable delay, which is 30 seconds by default. By design, intrasite replication of a change should be passed to all domain controllers within 15 minutes.

Typically, intrasite replication requires minimal intervention by the system administrator. However, he or she must review the intersite topology and make manual changes where appropriate. As we shall illustrate later, topology links can be modified with the Active Directory Sites and Services administrative snap-in, but this requires that the connection objects be manually established. (If the KCC automatically creates the same connection object through its normal analysis of input data, no new manual connection objects are created.) Manual connection objects can never be deleted by the KCC. If they fail, however, the KCC automatically attempts to create a new connection to a domain controller.

The Active Directory Sites and Services administrative snap-in can also be employed to force replications or to execute the KCC manually, as explained later.

While the initial site topology is generally accomplished by the KCC, it is important to know the relative costs of connectivity between sites. It is also critical to define the minimum acceptable frequency of replication; this information is required by the KCC. After Windows Server 2003 is in place, several tools will allow you to analyze those segments that require manual intervention. The typical basis for this review is network traffic. The Network Monitor measures RCP and SMTP traffic between domain controllers, the Performance Monitor measures traffic from a specific server, and the Replication Monitor provides a view of intrasite topology.

APPLICATION DIRECTORY PARTITIONS AND REPLICA PLACEMENT

New to Windows Server 2003, Active Directory can dynamically host data without affecting network performance. This is accomplished by providing control over the scope of replication and placement of replicas. An application partition is a new type of naming context (NC) used with Active Directory services. This new NC can be organized into a hierarchy of any type of object except security principals (users, groups, and computers). It also can be configured to replicate to any set of domain controllers in the forest. No administration is necessary since this feature is now integral to the Active Directory.

Another use of application partitions relates to the range and replication of the DNS zones. Such DNS data stores result in a reduced number of objects stored in the Global Catalog. By default, as discussed in subsequent chapters, DNS-specific application partitions contain only domain controllers running the DNS server. The strength of this feature centers on the fact that replicating occurs only on the subset of domain controllers specified in the application partition. This is done while enabling replication of the DNS zone to DNS servers running on different domains within an Active Directory forest.

PLANNING FOR OPERATIONS MASTER LOCATIONS

As described in Chapter 5 and later in this chapter, each domain tree offloads important activities to selected domain controllers that perform up to five specialized activities. These operations master domain controllers perform the same activities as their peers plus one or more specialized functions.

Since all domain controllers rely on the information processed by the operations masters, it is important to carefully plan the location of the operations master domain controllers. As a general rule, they should be placed in a site with the best primary and secondary connectivity to the rest of the organization.

Logical Structure Planning

Planning for the Active Directory is predicated on an understanding of the organization itself. In centralized frameworks, a single domain may serve all requirements and is obviously the easiest to administer. In larger and decentralized environments, multiple domains are often required. In both cases, it may be most efficient to divide the domain into organizational units to manage user accounts and resources. In planning for the Active Directory, early mapping of domains and organizational units is highly recommended. In so doing, it is also important to determine where administrative authority is to be granted and delegated. Best practices in forming domains and organizational units include the following considerations:

- Providing users with authority to use appropriate network resources while restricting visibility to all other objects
- Ensuring that administrators have rapid visibility to all resources
- Accommodating current operational and business structures while providing for organizational changes
- Organizing resources and accounts into OUs to permit delegation of administrative authority
- Logically dividing OUs into smaller, more manageable units

SINGLE DOMAIN AND ORGANIZATIONAL UNITS

Even though Windows Server 2003 fully supports multiple domains and organizational units, the KISS (keep it simple, stupid) principle still applies. Complexity increases as the number of domains and OUs grows. Always weigh the tradeoffs between administrative granularity and greater complexity. When creating organizational units, try to mirror the functional setup of the business structure; for example, the sales group might logically be a single OU. Likewise, resources can be grouped into organizational units, say, all printers in one domain. In this way, it is possible to delegate one administrator to manage the printer OU and another to manage the sales group user account OU.

A common planning question is when to create a child domain versus an organizational unit. Unfortunately, there is no clear answer, although it is generally determined by scope and complexity. In the next section we list some of the reasons for forming child domains. Here we will say that when control of smaller user groups or resources can be logically delegated, organizational units are more appropriate. Also, where change is anticipated within the organizational structure, OUs can more easily accommodate such shifts.

DOMAIN TREES AND CHILD DOMAINS

While the single domain is the simplest to create and maintain, there are organizational and administrative situations in which multiple domains, trees, and forests must be created. Security, administrative, and connectivity borders separate domains. When planning a domain tree or forest, it is important to understand how these components interact.

When Should Child Domains Be Created?

By default, a domain tree is created when the first domain controller is promoted with its own Windows Server Active Directory. When domains are added, they become child domains to this first, root, domain. In addition to automatic transitive trusts, all domains in the tree share a schema, configuration, and Global Catalog. Beyond this point, however, domain characteristics within a tree can vary. This is important because it is at this level of setting specific characteristics that decisions must be made about child domains. If you answer yes to one or more of the following questions, a child domain could be in order:

- *Is decentralized administration desired?* If it's necessary or desirable to manage assets or specific business activities in several locations, a decentralized model with separate child domains might be beneficial.
- *Does the organization need tight and/or localized administration?* For example, in global organizations it may be appropriate to localize administration within a given domain to account for differences such as language and time zone.
- *Do business activities or relationships dictate separate domains?* Competing business units or joint ventures may require autonomy, including the management of their own domains.
- *Do account policies need to differ?* Since account policies are applied at the domain level, it may be appropriate to logically group users into domains that have distinct policy requirements.
- *Does replication suggest a need for different domains?* While replication can be controlled by site, it can also be controlled based on a logical structure to reduce network traffic—for example, between international offices.

FORESTS

A forest is formed by joining two or more domain trees at the root. Transitive trusts are created by the forest relationship such that network resources become available to any tree in the forest and its associated domains. The resulting hierarchy permits the same Active Directory to resolve inquiries for objects in any of the trees in the forest. Each tree has a DNS namespace, but shares the schema, configuration, and Global Catalog. The forest itself is identified by the DNS name of the first tree created in it.

LDAP inquiries are conducted only within a tree and do not extend to the forest. The Global Catalog is used to resolve queries between trees; by default it is located on the first domain controller created in the forest. Part of the planning effort must be determining whether a dedicated domain controller should be used for Global Catalog activities. In addition, it must be decided if replicated Global Catalog domain controllers will be created to offload heavy intertree query traffic. For these reasons, the placement of the Global Catalog in the network is a key administrative task. Make sure there is fast and reliable connectivity to it.

The creation of a forest involves three primary steps. First, a DNS name must be selected (and registered) for the domain trees. Second, the configuration of each domain tree as described earlier must be laid out. Finally, the new tree must be added to the forest while the first domain controller is promoted through the Active Directory installation process. You will need to select **Create New Domain Tree in an Existing Forest** from the installation wizard.

When Should a Forest Be Created?

Despite the fact that management of a forest is considerably more complex than that of singular trees, situations still arise where distinct namespaces are required. If you answer affirmatively to one or more of the following questions, a forest may be necessary.

- *Are the business activities extremely different?* Organizations that operate on radically different bases may require separate trees with distinct namespaces.
- *Are there reasons for maintaining separate identities?* Unique trade or brand names often give rise to separate DNS identities. This is particularly true when organizations merge or are acquired and naming continuity is desired.
- *Do joint ventures or partnerships exist that require tighter control over network resources?* Organizations often form partnerships and joint ventures. While access to common resources is desired, a separately defined tree can enforce more direct administrative and security restrictions.

MULTIPLE FORESTS

Relationships between forests are not based on transitive trusts. They are generally established to created limited access for one domain in one forest to one domain in another forest. The trust relationship is one-directional and must be explicitly set.

It does not impact any other domains. If it is necessary to create multiforest relationships, plan trust and resource management well in advance. Make sure that access is limited only to those resources required for the life of the relationship.

CROSS-FOREST AUTHENTICATION

Cross-forest authentication provides secure access to resources between forests. Using either Kerberos or Windows NT LAN Manager (NTLM), the feature provides security without sacrificing the single sign-on and administrative benefits. Cross-forest authentication includes:

- *Supported authentication*. Four types of authentication are used across forests: (1) Kerberos and NTLM network logon for remote access to a server in another forest; (2) Kerberos and NTLM interactive logon for physical logon outside the user's home forest; (3) Kerberos delegation to N-tier application in another forest; and (4) user principal name (UPN) credentials are fully supported.
- *Name resolution*. When Kerberos and NTLM cannot resolve a name on the local domain controller, the Global Catalog is used to attempt name resolution. In the event the GC fails, an authentication call is placed to the cross forest. The name-matching function compares the security principal name with trusted namespaces from all trusted forests. A trusted forest name as routing hint is returned if the name is matched on the cross forest.
- *Request routing*. Kerberos and NTLM use routing hints to route authentication requests. This is done along the trust path from the originating domain to the probable destination domain. In the specific case of Kerberos, the Key Distribution Center (discussed in Chapter 12) generates referrals that follow the trust path. NTLM uses a secure channel to chain together the trust path.

Planning for Upgrades to the Active Directory

Upgrades to the Active Directory from Windows NT Server environments are handled slightly differently depending on the domain structure in the current enterprise. Remember, as discussed in Chapter 5, the multimaster replication model of the Active Directory supplants the four types of domain models employed by Windows NT. Consider the following issues when planning an Active Directory promotion:

- *Upgrading the single Windows NT domain model*. When the single Windows NT domain model is upgraded to the Active Directory, it remains a single domain. The primary change is in the added functionality afforded by the Active Directory and the optional use of organizational units.

- *Upgrading the master Windows NT domain model*. The Windows NT master domain model assumes a top-down hierarchy that is mirrored by the Active Directory, but since Windows NT did not support organizational units, additional domains were often formed to separate resources and users into more manageable components. One of the planning decisions when upgrading from a Windows NT master domain model is whether to collapse existing domains into a single Active Directory domain so that previously defined Windows NT domains can become organizational units. However, there is no requirement to convert an existing master domain model infrastructure to a single domain; Active Directory will fully accommodate the existing structure. The primary domain controller must be upgraded first to Windows Server 2003 and the Active Directory. Child domains can then be upgraded to form an Active Directory domain tree. They simply join the existing Windows Server domain during the promotion installation.
- *Upgrading the complete Windows NT trust model.* In this model, Windows NT provided trust between domains. Active Directory provides upgrade options that allow for transitive trust between domain trees and/or forests. It also allows one-way trusts between selected domains in two nonrelated forests. The key issue when upgrading Windows NT from a complete trust model is the level of trust desired.

UPGRADING THE PDC AND THE BDC

Sound planning of an upgrade usually requires a conservative approach to full deployment. Therefore, we recommend that the initial Active Directory installation and domain tree formation be separate from the installation of the production environment. One way to accomplish this and preserve Windows NT domain data is to pull an existing BDC off production and promote it to a PDC in a detached lab environment. At this stage, installation of Windows Server 2003 and the Active Directory can go forward on this domain controller while initial testing and fine-tuning are completed. When satisfactory testing is achieved, the domain controller can be returned to production as the root domain controller.

An alternative and less conservative approach is to install the Windows Server 2003 Active Directory in a production environment, first removing an existing Windows NT BDC from the network and production for safety purposes. In the unlikely event that the Windows Server 2003 deployment fails, you can remove it from production and restore the previous Windows NT environment. The offline BDC is put back in service and promoted to the PDC.

Planning for Domain Controllers

Every domain and child domain must have at least one domain controller. The addition of domain controllers generally improves reliability, speed, and flexibility.

Since a user's network logon is predicated on access to a domain controller, fast and reliable connectivity is required. Therefore, we recommend that there be more than one domain controller for each domain and each site.

It is often wise to establish at least two domain controllers to serve as operations master domain controllers. The PDC Emulator and Relative Identifier Master roles should be assigned to these mirrored domain controllers for redundancy.

The role of the standard domain controller and Global Catalog are also often filled by different domain controller servers. It is always advisable to separate the GC from the domain controller assigned to the Infrastructure Master role.

Sizing the Active Directory

Sizing the minimal requirements for the Active Directory server hardware involves a series of estimates. The process entails creating a sample population of Active Directory objects and then applying size factors to each. This should include a real-world collection of objects including users, computer accounts, groups, printers, and files. Objects that are security principals should be allocated 3,600 bytes each. Nonsecurity principal objects should be allocated 1,100 bytes. For each attribute of 10 or fewer characters, allocate an additional 100 bytes. Attributes that contain binary information should include the size of the data plus a 25 percent buffer.

We recommend a simple spreadsheet be used to calculate the size requirements of the sample population. The sample population's storage requirements are estimated by adding the numbers for the objects and associated attributes, as illustrated in the following example. Make sure to include in the calculation every attribute associated with an object.

The next step is to estimate the number of objects that must be managed by the Active Directory. This estimate should include all users, groups, printers, contacts, and files on the system and should then be doubled. The storage requirements can then be proportionately extrapolated by using the number of objects you estimate for your enterprise. For example, if the sample population represented 1/10 of 1 percent of the Active Directory objects, multiply that amount by 1,000. If the sample population storage estimate were 360,000 KB, then the requirements for the Active Directory size would be 360,000,000 KB, or 360 MB. It is generally recommended that the disk space be two to three times larger than the estimated size of the Active Directory to accommodate possible miscalculation and growth.

Determining Domain Controller Resources

New to Windows Server 2003 is a versioning mechanism that can be used by Active Directory core components to determine what features are available on each domain controller in a forest. This feature can flag domain controller setup and release inconsistencies. Many enterprises have a requirement for the same level of

Windows Server Active Directory. This feature permits a rapid review of all domain controllers to ensure product release management. For example, there are two new features in Active Directory that cannot be activated until all the DCs in a forest are upgraded to Windows Server 2003: (1) Active Directory: Group Membership Replication Improvements and (2) Active Directory Improved Inter-Site Replication Topology Generator.

INSTALLING THE ACTIVE DIRECTORY

The installation of Active Directory services is remarkably straightforward. The Active Directory Installation Wizard leads the system administrator through a series of decision points. Whether you are promoting an existing Windows NT PDC or Windows 2000 domain controller to Windows Server 2003 with the Active Directory or creating a new domain tree, the process is largely the same. Always begin with the server that is the root. Once the first Windows Server 2003 with Active Directory is running, all other domains in the tree are treated as its children.

NOTE When upgrading a domain from Windows NT 4.0 or Windows 2000, it is necessary to update the schema. To do so, update the forest first by invoking the **adprep** command against /forestprep. Then update the domain using **adprep** against /domainprep. During the installation process, you will be prompted to perform these tasks before an upgrade to Windows Server 2003 will be successful.

A major prerequisite is that DNS be installed with Windows Server 2003 or an existing DNS server be designed prior to the completion of the Active Directory installation. Because of this dependence on DNS, this installation section will walk through the following:

- Use of the Active Directory Installation Wizard to create a new domain and in so doing create the first domain tree.
- Installation of Microsoft's DNS to support the Active Directory. A third-party DNS server can also be used, providing it supports service resource records (SRV) and dynamic DNS update functionality.

Other dependencies must also be addressed prior to installation. The computer must have an installed version of Windows Server 2003. The NTFS partition or volume must be sufficiently large to accommodate Active Directory requirements. Correct system date, time, and zones should be set. Finally, TCP/IP should be installed. DNS can be preconfigured or installed with the Active Directory; it is required for the Active Directory to function.

Before installing the Active Directory, it is important to understand the process. Two primary sets of files are created: the directory store and log files, are located in %systemroot\Ntds; and a Shared System Volume, located in %systemroot\Sysvol, which contains scripts and some group policy objects for the enterprise.

NOTE During the Active Directory installation you will be asked if you want to configure the server for an additional specialized function. We recommend that you return to this task after you have created a stable Windows Server Active Directory environment.

Active Directory Installation Wizard

The Active Directory is installed by following the steps outlined below. The wizard provides a series of options from which the system administrator must make educated and informed selections.

If this is the first system to be configured with Windows Server 2003 and the Active Directory, it will become the root domain controller. During installation of Windows 2000/Server 2003, you will have been prompted to determine whether this is a standalone server or part of a network.

If this system is being installed in an existing Windows Server domain or if it is being configured as a child domain, the Active Directory installation process will automatically make the appropriate connections and establish initial default trust relationships. The same process occurs when promoting a Windows NT PDC or BDC to the status of Active Directory domain controllers. Replicas of the Active Directory are then installed on the new domain controller.

ACTIVE DIRECTORY INSTALLATION EXAMPLE

The example of an installation here is based on the first domain controller to be promoted. The creation of child domains and forests is covered in subsequent sections and merely involves a decision to join an existing tree or forest; otherwise, the steps are generally the same.

The following steps should be observed when installing the Active Directory:

1. Launch the Active Directory Installation Wizard (Figure 6.1) by invoking the **command prompt** → **dcpromo.exe** → **ENTER**. (Alternatively, the **Configure Your System** dialog is launched as part of the logon process, or it is available via **Start** → **Administrative Tools** → **Configure Your Server** → move through

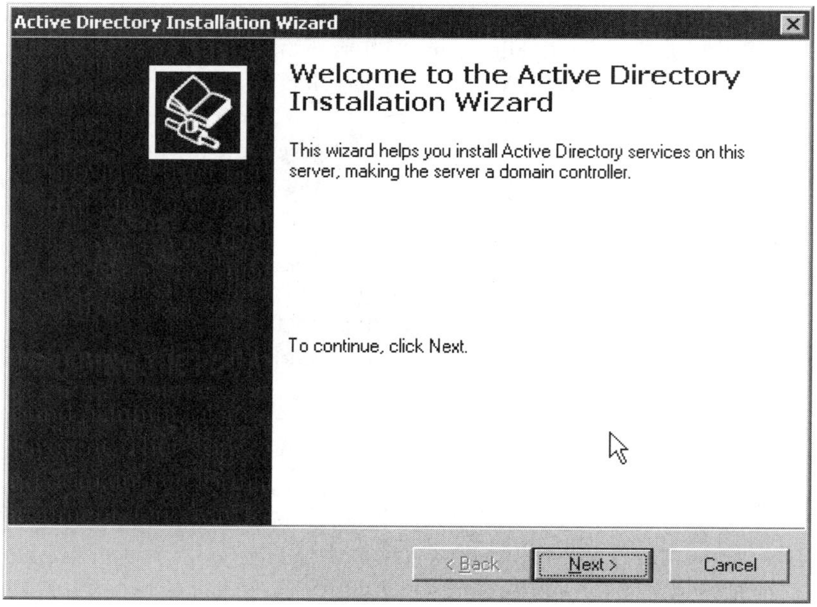

FIGURE 6.1 The Active Directory Installation Wizard

menu until the **Server Role** screen appears → select **Domain Controller (Active Directory)** → **Install**.

The text in the first wizard screen is very explicit, stating that the installation of Active Directory services will make the server a domain controller. While you may repeat this process with other servers, this first domain controller becomes the forest root as well as the root of the first tree in the forest.

Click **Next** to continue.

2. The next dialog box provides the choice of making this a controller for a new domain or adding it to an existing domain (Figure 6.2). Since this example assumes a new domain, select the first option and click **Next**. This option also creates a new child domain or domain tree. The second option is used only to create additional domain controllers in the same domain.

Click **Next** to continue.

3. At this stage you must be able to clearly see the forest for the trees. Therefore, in this example, in the list following **Create a new**, select **Domain in a new forest**, as shown in Figure 6.3. The first domain controller is automatically the root domain, tree, and forest. The second option in this dialog box is selected only if you are creating a new tree that is to have a trust relationship with a preexisting domain forest, and/or providing users in an existing forest access to the new domain. Click **Next** to continue.

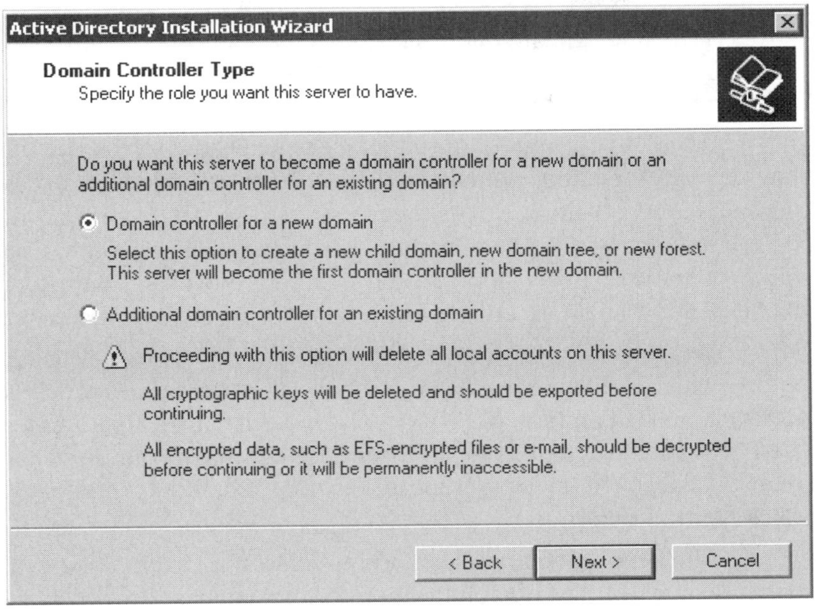

FIGURE 6.2 Defining Domain Controller Type

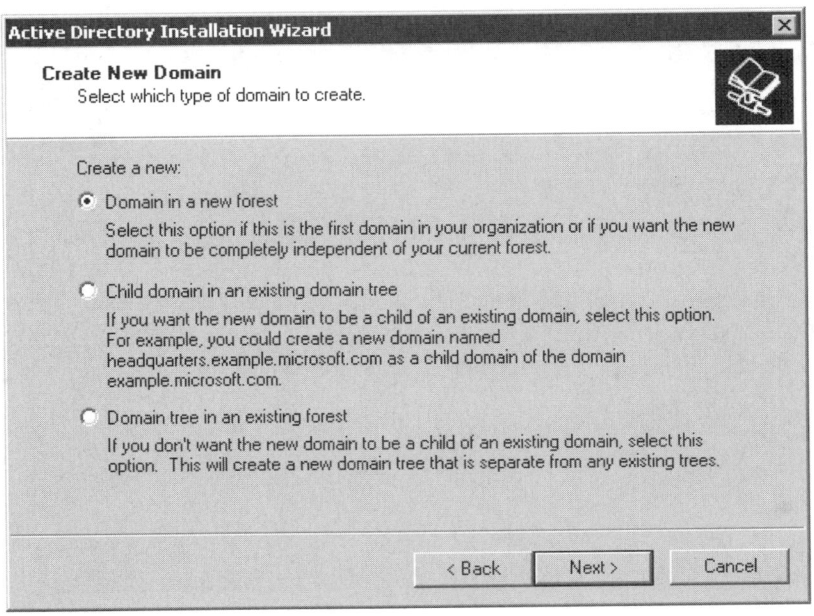

FIGURE 6.3 Joining or Creating a Forest

NOTE If this is the first domain controller for a new forest, the Active Directory Installation Wizard will present another set of simple screens.

4. This is a very important step; the domain name selected at this stage will follow through the entire domain and domain tree. (If you have not yet registered a domain name, obtain one from the registration service in your country. Also, if you do not understand DNS and naming conventions, please refer to Chapters 5 and 14 before completing this step.) In the text box shown in Figure 6.4, type the full name of the domain; in our example, the user typed ***EntCert.com***. Click **Next** to continue.

5. The next dialog box identifies your NetBIOS name, which is used by Windows clients that employ WINS to resolve system names. In this case, the ENTCERT NetBIOS name was automatically inserted. Note that if your domain name is longer than 15 characters, it will be truncated to the maximum length for NetBIOS names. Click **Next** to continue.

6. The next dialog box allows you to select the location of the Active Directory database and log. The default location for the database and log in which Windows Server 2003 is installed in \WINNT is %systemroot%\ \NTDS. Ordinarily, the default location is recommended. Click **Next** to continue.

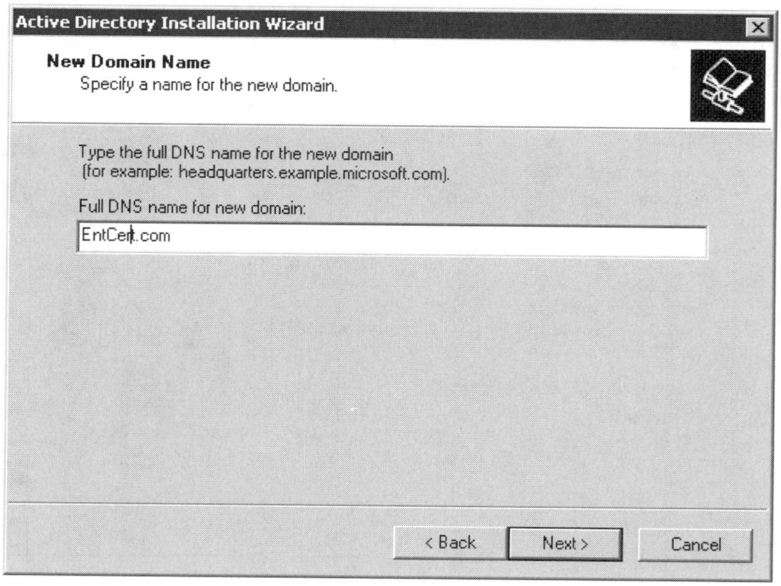

FIGURE 6.4 Designating the Name of the Domains

7. The next dialog box gives you the opportunity to select the location of the Shared System Volume, which stores all the shared information that is replicated between domain controllers. The default is %systemroot% \SYSVOL. If you choose to accept this, click **Next** to continue.

8. The next wizard screen provides a way to change the permissions associated with the RAS Server. Unless you have a specific reason to make changes at this time, click **No**. Click **Next** to continue.

9. You will then be presented a set of wizard screens to set permissions levels and establish administrative passwords. Insert the response appropriate to your installation. The Active Directory Review Setting page should now appear. Take a moment to review this information. If anything is incorrect, use the **Back** button to return to the screen that requires a change and make the appropriate modifications. If everything appears correct, click **Next** to continue.

10. Active Directory is now being configured on your system, which can take a few minutes. The final wizard screen in the basic installation process should then appear. Click **Finish**. You will see the prompt to **Restart** the computer. Select this option now if you have already configured DNS; but if you have not, proceed to DNS installation. The Active Directory cannot be configured without DNS.

The Active Directory Installation Wizard should automatically take you to the Configure DNS screen (Figure 6.5). Click **Yes**, then click **Next** to continue. (If you

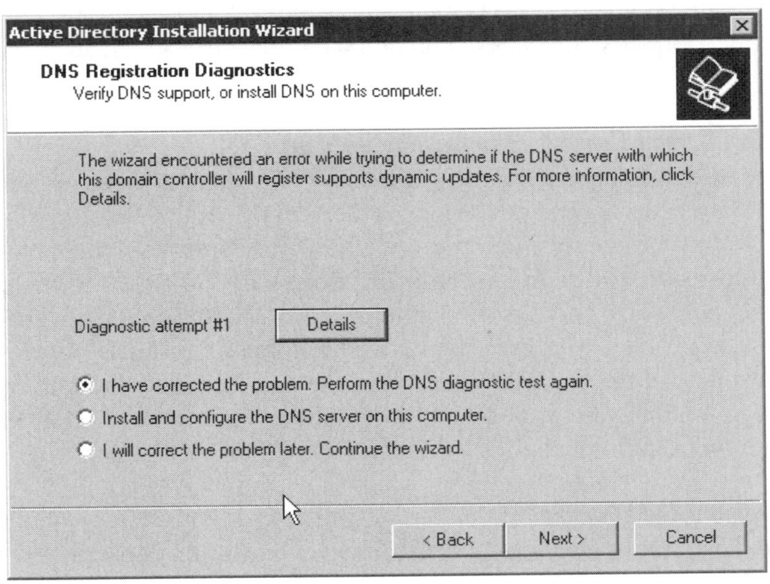

FIGURE 6.5 Configuring DNS

select **N** or if you want to configure DNS prior to installing the Active Directory, select **Start → Administrative Tools → Configure Your Server → Networking → DNS → Install**.)

For complete instructions on configuring the TCP/IP network with DNS, please turn to Chapter 12.

You will then be presented a set of wizard screens to set permissions levels and establish administrative passwords.

NOTE Windows Server 2003 offers an alternative approach to DC promotion. We recommend that this function be used only when the production-level Active Directory is stable and applies to downlevel domain controllers. This feature enables faster creation of replica DCs of a preexisting domain. Instead of replicating a complete copy of the database over the network, an administrator can initially source the new DC with an initial replication from files created when backing up an existing DC or Global Catalog server. To achieve this type of promotion, run the Active Directory Installation Wizard in Advanced Mode or from the command line, type **promo.exe/adv**.

INSTALLATION OF DIFFERENT STRUCTURES

The example just completed assumed that the installation was being carried out on the first domain Active Directory. There are some variations when creating additional domain controllers, child domains, and trees within an existing forest (Figure 6.6). These are described in the following sections.

Adding Domain Controllers to Existing Domains

After the domain is created, domain controllers can be added by running dcpromo.exe from the new Windows Server. The Active Directory Installation Wizard will prompt you to determine the domain controller type. Select **Additional domain controller for an existing domain**. You will need to specify the user name, password, and domain name of a user account that has rights to create domain controllers. The DNS name for the domain must also be provided. Finally, you will need to establish where database and log files, together with the Shared System Volume, are to be located. Generally, the default location will be used. All other installation questions will be the same as in the walk-through example.

Creating a Child Domain

The creation of a child domain also involves executing dcpromo.exe from the new Windows Server 2003 or installing Active Directory directly. The Active Directory Installation Wizard will prompt you to determine the domain controller type. Se-

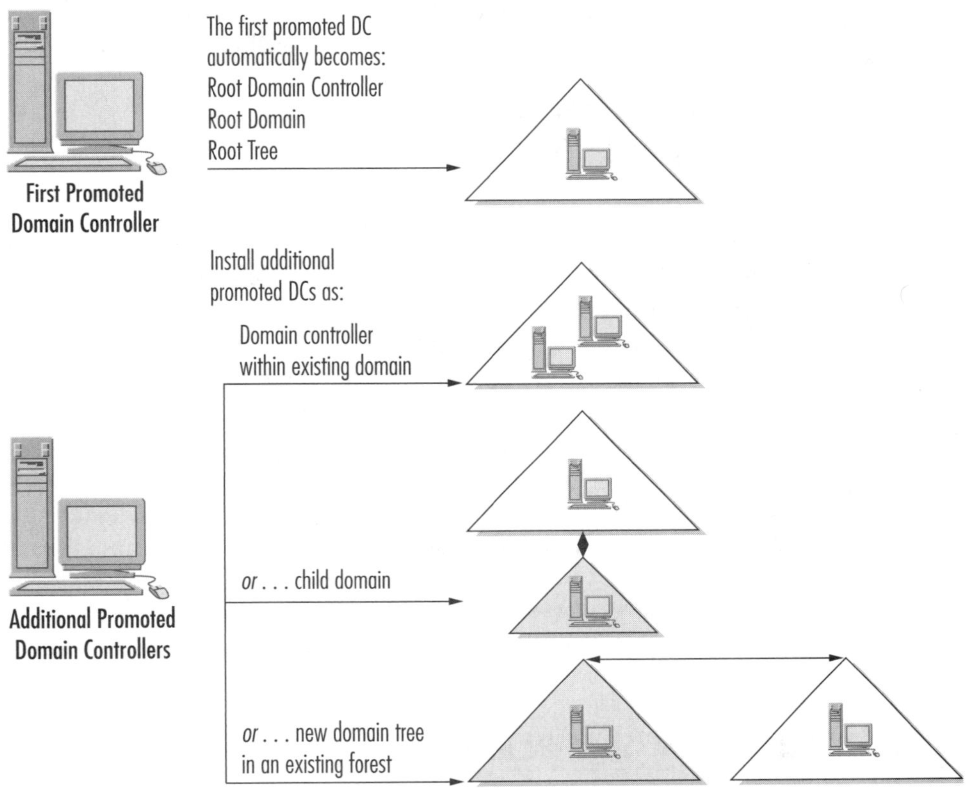

FIGURE 6.6 Optional Domain Controller Installations

lect **Domain controller for a new domain**. In the next screen, which allows you to create trees or child domains, select **Child domain in an existing domain tree**. You will need to specify the user name, password, and domain name of a user account in the Enterprise Admins group that has rights to create domains. You will also need to supply the parent's DNS name and the name of the new child domain. Remember that the child name is added to the front of the parent DNS name, separated by a period. Also specified here is the NetBIOS name for the new domain. After the root domain has been created, child domains can be logically added. As before, you will need to establish where database and log files, together with the Shared System Volume, will reside. Generally, the default location will be used.

Finally, you will need to determine whether to weaken permissions in order to provide Windows NT 4.0 RAS access. This is generally not recommended unless you plan to continue using Windows NT for a substantial period. All other installation questions will be the same as in the walk-through example.

Creating a Tree in an Existing Forest

Once the root domain tree is created, it is possible to add a tree to the forest by running dcpromo.exe from the new Windows Server. The Active Directory Installation Wizard will prompt you to determine the domain controller type. Select **Domain controller for a new domain**. In the next screen, where you can create trees or child domains, select **Create a new domain tree**. From the next screen, select **Place this new domain tree in an existing forest**. You will need to specify the username, password, and domain name of a user account in the Enterprise Admins group that has rights to create domains. You will also need to supply the new tree's DNS name and specify the NetBIOS name for the new domain. After the root domain has been created, child domains can logically be added.

You will need to establish where database and log files, together with the Shared System Volume, are to be located—generally, the default location will be used. Finally, you will need to determine whether to weaken permissions in order to provide Windows NT 4.0 RAS access. This is generally not recommended unless you plan on using Windows NT for a substantial period. All other installation questions will be the same as in the walk-through example.

ACTIVE DIRECTORY MMC SNAP-IN TOOLS

The MMC snap-in tools handle most of the Active Directory management. This section examines how to use these tools to perform the most common Active Directory functions. Excluded is the use of these tools in relation to user, group, and group policy management; that is covered in Chapter 7, "User Accounts and Groups," and Chapter 8, "Group Policies."

Three Active Directory snap-in administrative tools are part of the standard installation; two optional tools are installed separately:

- Active Directory Domains and Trusts Manager
- Active Directory Sites and Services Manager
- Active Directory Users and Group Manager
- Active Directory Replication (optional, available from the Resource Kit)
- Active Directory Schema Manager (optional, available from adminpak)

The standard tools are obtained from the **Start → Administrative Tools** menu and the optional tools are obtained from **Start → Service Tools** (Figure 6.7). They may be added to the MMC by following these steps:

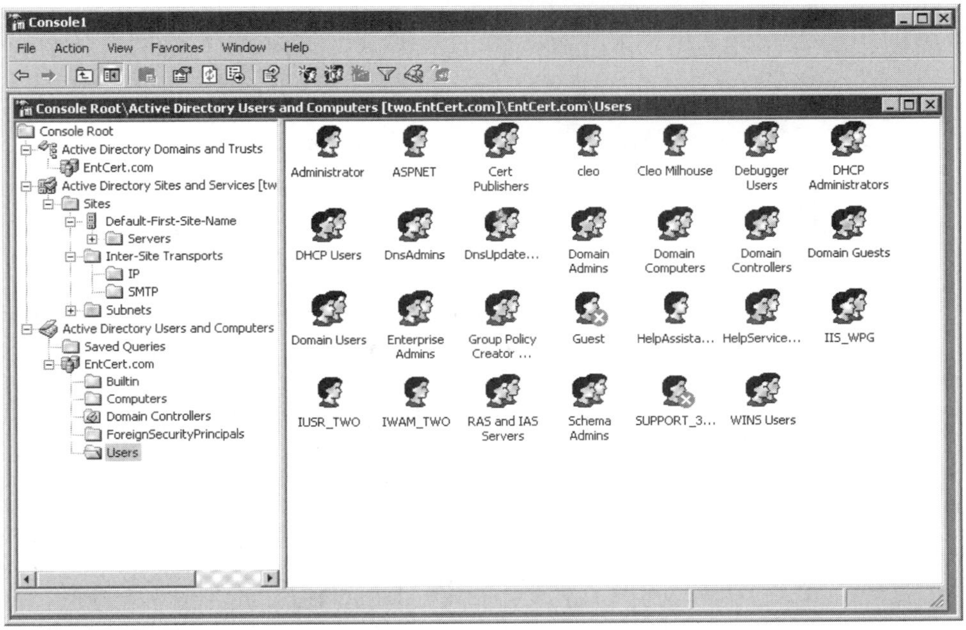

FIGURE 6.7 Active Directory MMC Standard Components

1. Launch Microsoft Management Console.
2. Select the **Console** (you must be in author mode to select this option).
3. Select **Add/Remove Snap-in** → in the **Add/Remove Snap-in** dialog, click **Add** → highlight the **Active Directory** snap-in from the **Add Snap-in** dialog box → click **Add**.
4. Repeat this process for each snap-in.
5. Click **Close** for the **Add Snap-in** dialog box → click **Close** for the **Add/Remove Snap-in** dialog.

These snap-in tools provide support for a wide assortment of Active Directory administrative functions.

The Active Directory Domain and Trust Manager

The Active Directory Domains and Trusts snap-in provides the system administrator support for the management of trust relationships among domains, trees, and forests. It also provides assistance for managing mixed-mode environments involving Windows Server 2003 and earlier Windows NT/Windows 2000 domains. In this section we will review how to use the Active Directory Domains and Trusts snap-in to perform the following tasks:

- Create trust relationships, both transitive two-way and explicit one-way.
- Change from mixed to native Windows Server mode.
- Add UPN suffixes for alternative user logon.
- Assign a Domain Naming Master domain controller.
- Delegate domain controller administration.

Windows Server 2003 enhances the scope of forest trust relationships. Microsoft recognized that independent organizations maintain their own IT infrastructures but may need to share information and resources. The new enhancements simplify cross-forest security administration. They also enable the trusting forest to enforce constraints on what security principal names it trusts other forests to authenticate. There are three forms of trust functionality:

- *Forest trust*. This trust type allows all domains in one forest to transitively trust all domains in another forest. This is accomplished through a single trust link between the two forest root domains. Forest trust is not transitive at the forest level across three or more forests. Forest trusts can be one-way or two-way.
- *Trust management*. A new wizard is provided to create all types of trust links and forest trust. A new property page is available to manage the trusted namespaces associated with forest trusts.
- *Trusted namespaces*. Trusted namespaces are used to route authentication and authorization requests for security principals. The domain, UPN, service principal name (SPN), and security identifier SID namespaces are automatically collected when a forest trust is created, and refreshed by the Active Directory Domains and Trust User Interface. A forest is trusted to be authoritative for the namespaces it publishes. In order to avoid collisions, this data is accepted on a first-come basis. Overlapping trusted namespaces are automatically rejected.

NOTE

When Windows Server 2003 is installed, user-based Group Policy and roaming user profiles (RUPs) are not processed when a user is in a different Active Directory forest. This tightening of security denies user-based Group Policy across a forest boundary and cross-forest RUPs.

In order to facilitate cross-forest policy management, a new setting allows Group Policy and RUPs to be processed in this situation. However, this policy must be explicitly enabled. Also added is new Event Log message to inform the administrator that "loopback" processing took place. See Chapter 7 for more information on group policies.

CREATING TRUST RELATIONSHIPS

The previous chapter describes the types of trust relationship that can exist in a Windows Server 2003 enterprise. The Active Directory Domains and Trusts MMC snap-in tool is the easiest method for managing these relationships.

The default relationship between domains in the same tree or forest is transitive. Users have access to resources in the same tree or forest, assuming they have access permission to a requested object.

Explicit one-way trusts are created only between otherwise nonrelated forests. The trusting domain permits access to resources by a trusted domain in a one-directional interaction. The one-way trust is limited and does not create a permanent link. Nor does it automatically provide access to other domains in the tree. To extend the one-way relationship to other domains, additional explicit relationships are required.

Explicit Transitive Two-Way Domain Trusts

Two-way (shortcut) transitive trusts are established by following these steps:

1. Open the **Active Directory Domains and Trusts** snap-in.
2. Right-click the domain you want to administer → click **Properties** → click the **Trusts** tab.
3. Click the **Domains trusted by this domain,** click **Add**, type in the targeted domain name, and supply the password information; then select the **Domains that trust this domain** and follow the same procedure. (For Windows 2000, the domain name is the DNS name for the domain. For earlier Windows NT domains, type the name of that domain.)
4. If the domain to be added is a Windows Server 2003 domain, type its DNS name. Or, if the domain is running an earlier version of Windows, type the domain name.
5. Gain Administrative logon to the targeted trust domain and repeat steps 1 through 4.

Explicit One-Way Domain Trusts

Explicit one-way domain trusts are created by following these steps (Figure 6.8):

1. Open the **Active Directory Domains and Trusts** snap-in.
2. Right-click the domain you want to administer → click **Properties** → click the **Trusts** tab.
3. Click **Domains trusted by this domain,** click **Add**, and type in the targeted domain name and password information. (For Windows 2000, the domain name is the DNS name for the domain. For earlier Windows NT domains, type the name of that domain.)

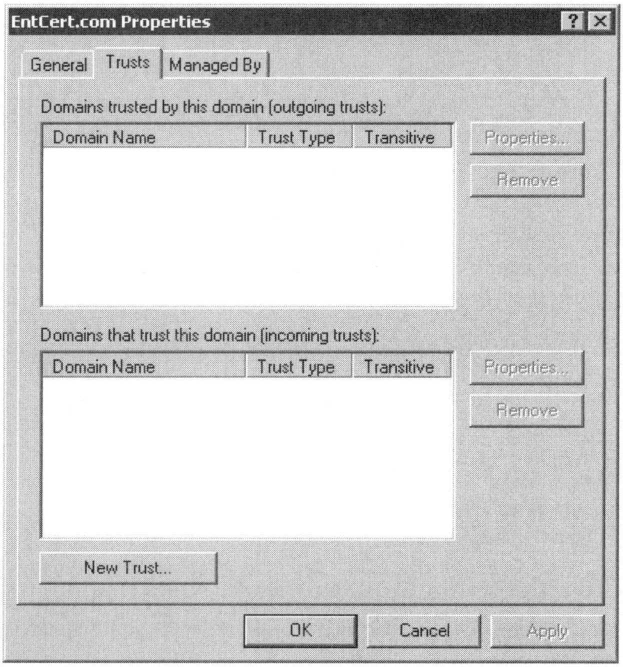

FIGURE 6.8 Creating a One-Way Explicit Trust

Verifying a Trust

Once the process of establishing a trust is completed or during the normal course of auditing a domain, the trust relationship can be verified. To do so, take the following steps:

1. Open the **Active Directory Domains and Trusts** MMC snap-in.
2. Right-click the domain you want to administer → click **Properties** → click the **Trusts** tab.
3. In either the **Domains trusted by this domain** or the **Domains that trust this domain** list, click the trust to be verified, then click **Edit**.
4. Click **Verify/Reset**.

Removing a Trust

As organizational relationships change, trust relationships between domains may need to be removed. To do this, perform the following steps:

1. Open the **Active Directory Domains and Trusts** MMC snap-in.

2. Right-click the domain you want to administer → select **Properties** → click the **Trusts** tab.
3. In either the **Domains trusted by this domain** or the **Domains that trust this domain** list, click the trust to be revoked, then click **Edit**.
4. Click **Remove**.
5. Repeat the process for the corresponding trusted domain.

RAISING THE DOMAIN AND FOREST FUNCTIONAL LEVEL

Many enterprises will initially operate in the default Windows 2000 mixed or Window Server 2003 interim mode (see Chapter 3). In order to achieve full functionality, it is necessary to raise the version level to Windows Server 2003 native mode.

To raise the domain function level open the **Active Directory Domain and Trust** MMC for the node, right-click the domain to be raised, and click on **Raise Domain Functional Level**. Click either **Windows 2000 native** or **Windows Server 2003** for the desired level, and then click **Raise**.

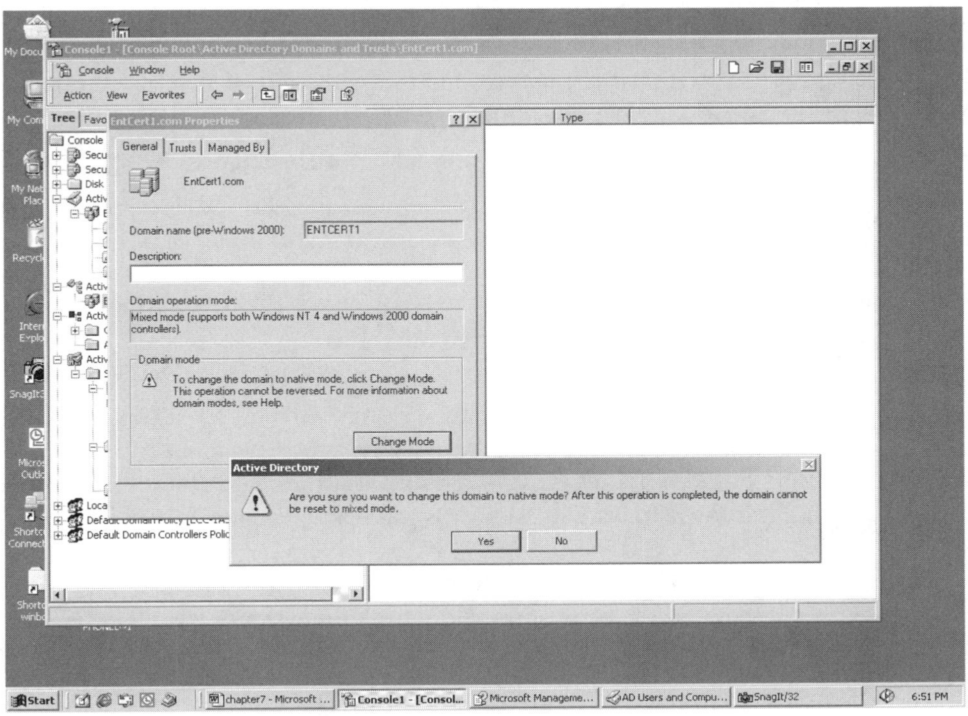

FIGURE 6.9 Changing from Mixed to Native Mode

To raise the forest functional level, right-click on **Active Directory Domain and Trust node,** and click on **Raise Forest Functional Level.** In **Select an available functional level,** click **Windows Server 2003,** then click **Raise.**

CAUTION It is impossible to reverse the upgrading of a domain to native mode. If any Windows NT domain controllers exist in the domain, they must be upgraded to Windows 2000 or Server 2003 and the Active Directory in order to be properly recognized.

ADDING UPN SUFFIXES FOR USER LOGON

Alias domain names can be applied to a user account, perhaps to provide a user account with a different identity by shortening long domain or child domain names. The user principal name suffix is the portion of the DNS name that identifies a user's domain of origin. For example, *@EntCert.com* is the UPN suffix of the e-mail address *bob@EntCert.com.* For administrative and security reasons, alternative UPN suffixes can also be assigned to a user logon name (the UPN prefix).

To add UPN suffixes (Figure 6.10), follow these steps:

1. Open the **Active Directory Domains and Trusts** MMC snap-in.
2. Right-click **Active Directory Domains and Trusts** and then click Properties.
3. From the **UPN Suffixes** tab, type an additional or alternative UPN for the domain and then click **Add**.
4. Repeat the previous step to add more alternative UPN suffixes.

When creating a new user account (as discussed later in this chapter), you can select which of the alternative domain UPN suffixes will be assigned to that user, as shown in Figure 6.11. In this example, three alternatives can be applied to user bob.

ASSIGNING A DOMAIN NAMING MASTER

In a multidomain controller environment, certain operation management tasks should be delegated to particular domain controller servers. The Active Directory Domains and Trusts snap-in permits the system administrator to identify and change the location of the Domain Naming Master domain controller. The original location of the Domain Naming Master is the root domain controller.

Identifying the Domain Naming Master

The current location of the Domain Naming Master is identified by the following steps:

1. Open the **Active Directory Domains and Trusts** MMC snap-in.
2. Right-click **Active Directory Domains and Trusts** → and select **Operations Masters**.

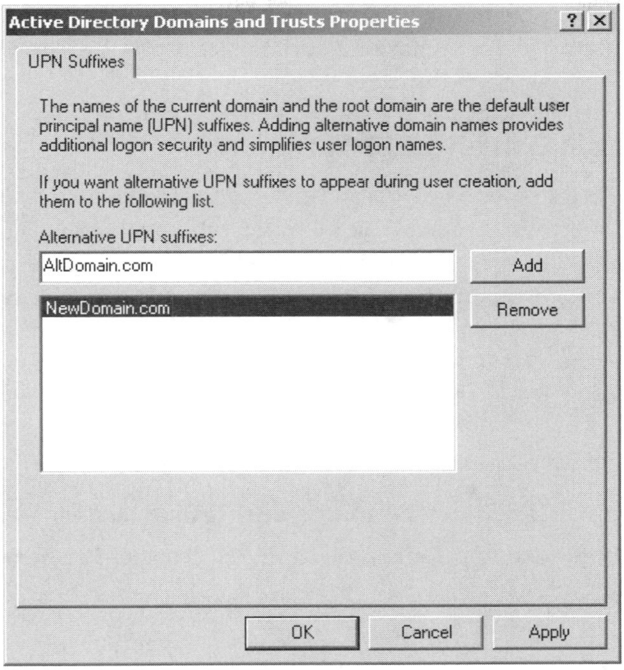

FIGURE 6.10 Adding Alternative Domain Name Aliases

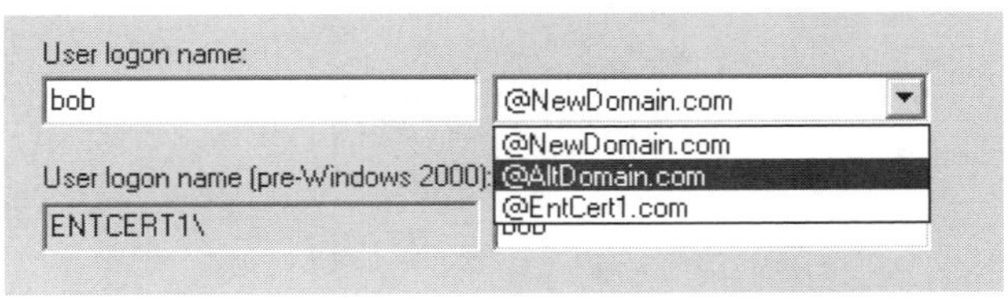

FIGURE 6.11 Selecting Domain Identities When Adding Users

3. The name of the current Domain Naming Master appears in **Domain naming operations master**.

Changing the Domain Naming Master's Location

The location of the Domain Naming Master is changed from one domain controller to another by following these steps:

1. Open the **Active Directory Domains and Trusts** snap-in.
2. Right-click **Active Directory Domains and Trusts**, select the **Connect to Domain Controller,** choose the targeted domain controller, and click **OK**.

3. Right-click **Active Directory Domains and Trusts**, select the **Operations Masters,** and make sure the targeted domain controller is listed in the second dialog text window. Click **Change**.

DELEGATING DOMAIN CONTROLLER ADMINISTRATION

System administrative responsibility can be delegated to specific user groups, but this should be done with great care. Remember, when authority is delegated to a domain controller or the entire domain, the rights to create or demote other domain controllers are vested in other people. Granting such authority might be appropriate when a designated group of IT professionals shares system administration responsibility for the domain. It also makes sense when an administrator needs temporary authority while the primary system administrator is on leave or on vacation.

Authority is delegated to a domain or domain controller (Figure 6.12) as follows:

1. Open the **Active Directory Domains and Trusts** MMC snap-in.
2. Right-click the domain or domain controller and select **Properties**.

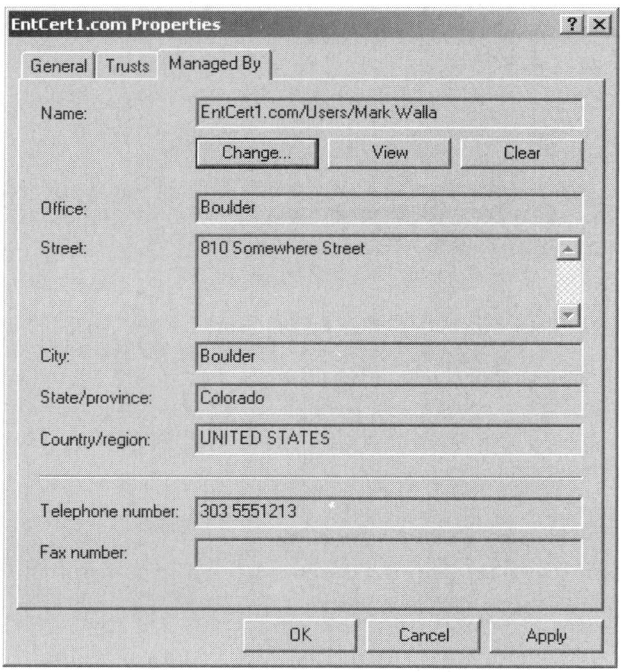

FIGURE 6.12 Displaying Domain Authority

3. On the **Managed By** tab, select the name of the group, click **Change**, and **Add** the desired user or group.
4. Click **OK** to confirm the new setting.

The Active Directory Schema Manager Snap-In

The Active Directory Schema Manager is not loaded as part of the default Active Directory installation. Presumably, Microsoft made it an extra step because schema changes should be treated with great care. If a system administrator who has the knowledge truly needs to make modifications to the schema, he or she must deliberately install this tool. Installation is from the adminpak application suite available on the Windows Server 2003 or higher CD within the I386 folder. The following steps should be followed:

1. Load the adminpak from the Windows Server 2003 installation CD in the I386 folder, double-click **Support**, double-click **adminpak**, select **Setup**, and follow the instructions for **Typical** installation.
2. Launch the **Microsoft Management Console,** select the **Console** menu, click **Add/Remove Snap-in**, and click **Add** from this dialog box. In the **Add Snap-in** dialog box, double-click **Active Directory Schema** and select **Close**. Click **OK**.

Active Directory objects represent resources within the network. The most common domain objects include user accounts, groups, printers, computers, domain controllers, organizational units, and shared folders. The Active Directory schema defines the structure, the classes, and the attributes of allowable objects. These definitions can be viewed as the framework of the Active Directory.

Object classes inherit characteristics of parent objects. This creates a ripple effect in that changes can both positively and negatively affect objects down the line. The schema can be extended dynamically to modify and add to the objects stored by the Active Directory. In addition to the Admin group, the Schema Management group is the default system administrator group with full control to make schema changes. Other groups can be added, but with great caution. If the Active Directory schema were inappropriately changed or damaged, your domain could be brought to its knees.

In this section, we will explore how to use the Active Directory Schema snap-in for the following tasks:

- Identify and modify object classes.
- Identify and change attributes.
- Change the Schema Master domain controller.
- Ensure schema availability and restoration.

CAUTION Changes to the Active Directory schema should be made only after full consideration of their impacts. It should be noted that the Schema Master by default cannot accept modifications. Modifications must be enabled manually by checking that the schema may be modified on this server in the Active Directory Schema snap-in's **Operations Master** dialog. However, while this protects the enterprise from accidental changes, other actions should be taken. If the system administrator makes modifications, the domain controller that functions as the Schema Manager should first be removed from the network. This will allow for recovery if those modifications prove inappropriate or harmful. Alternatively, changes in the schema can be tested in an isolated network environment and moved over for replication only after full testing and troubleshooting are completed.

IDENTIFYING AND MODIFYING OBJECT CLASSES

To view the attributes associated with a schema object class, simply click the targeted class in the **Active Directory Schema** snap-in → **Classes**. As shown in Figure 6.13, the right pane displays the attributes for classSchema. If you look closely, you will note that both optional and mandatory attributes are identified. That is because all object attributes are either "must have" or "may have." Changing the mandatory setting will significantly impact the class's function and integrity.

To view additional information about a class or to make specific changes, right-click the desired object and select **Properties**. The **Properties** dialog box displays four tabs:

- ***General*** *provides the class common name, description, X.500 OID number, and class type*. (Most Active Directory default classes have a structural class type, but a few, like country, are of the class type abstract.) The class category is also shown with an option to change a class to one of the other classes available. An option to display classes of the same type and to deactivate the class is provided as well. Obvious caution should be used in making any changes to the schema's structural classes.
- ***Relationships*** *provides information on how a class fits into the class hierarchy*. For example, the "group" class is identified as a "top"-level parent class. It lists several auxiliary classes, including mailRecipient, so it is logical to assume that a group member also can receive mail. Other auxiliary classes can be associated with the group class by selecting **Add** and choosing among listed classes. This tab also lists classes that have a Possible Superior position, such as organizationalUnit, domainDNS, builtinDomain, and container classes. You can use the **Add** button to select other classes.

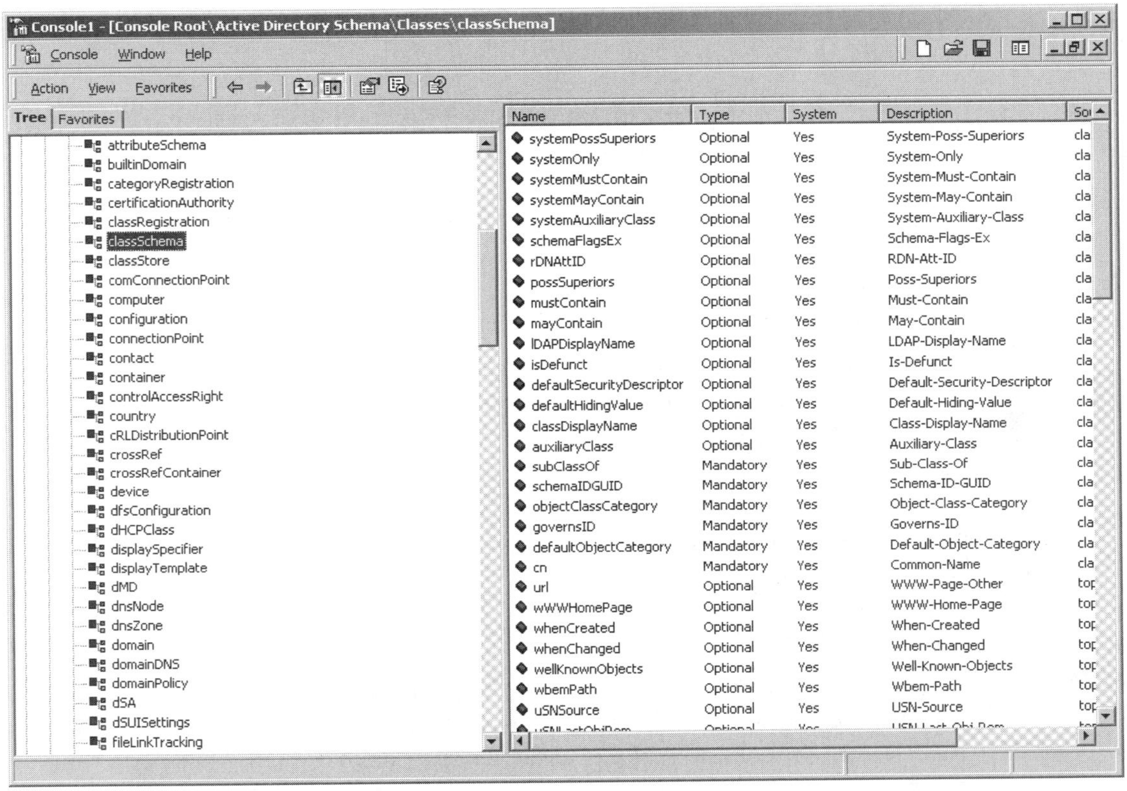

FIGURE 6.13 Classes and Associated Attributes

- ***Attributes*** *provides a list of both mandatory and optional attributes*. While no option can increase or change the mandatory attributes, click **Add** to add optional attributes, which can be deleted by clicking **Remove**.
- ***Security*** *provides the list of permissions granted to different groups for each class*. By default, Authenticated Users have Read permission for most objects. The Domain Administrator Group and the SYSTEM Group generally have Read, Write, and Full Control. These two groups are also authorized to create and delete child classes for some of the classes. Other groups or specific users can be added to the permissions lists.

Class Types

In creating or modifying objects, it is necessary to identify their class type. The full-fledged object will be a member of the structural class. The abstract and auxiliary types are used in the formation of the structural type. The Active Directory schema recognizes four types of object class:

- *Structural class*. The structural class is important to the system administrator in that it is the only type from which new Active Directory objects are created. Structural classes are developed from either the modification of an existing structural type or the use of one or more abstract classes.
- *Abstract class*. Abstract classes are so named because they take the form of templates that actually create other templates (abstracts) and structural and auxiliary classes. Think of abstract classes as frameworks for the defining objects.
- *Auxiliary class*. The auxiliary class is a list of attributes. Rather than apply numerous attributes when creating a structural class, it provides a streamlined alternative by applying a combination of attributes with a single include action.
- *88 class*. The 88 class includes object classes defined prior to 1993, when the 1988 X.500 specification was adopted. This type does not use the structural, abstract, and auxiliary definitions, nor is it in common use for the development of objects in Windows Server 2003 environments.

NOTE Remember that the schema is loaded in the domain controller cache for easy access. To ensure cache consistency, there is a five-minute delay after changes are written to disk until they are moved to the cache. Threads that might have been running prior to the cache rebuild will continue to use the previous definitions. New threads use the definitions associated with the rebuilt cache.

IDENTIFYING AND CHANGING ATTRIBUTES

Attributes are defined only once but may be applied to multiple classes. As discussed, the attributes associated with a specific class can be identified through the **Class Properties** dialog or directly from the Active Directory Schema snap-in.

A list of available attributes is found in the **Active Directory Schema** snap-in → **Attributes**. The right pane of the MMC lists the attributes alphabetically. By right-clicking any attribute, you can select **Properties** to learn more about its features and configuration (Figure 6.14). The information provided includes the description, common name, X.500 OID, syntax (such as integer, octet string, text, etc.), and range. Other options are also provided, such as deactivation and indexing within the Active Directory. It is important to note that attributes can never be deleted once they are created. Their use can be prevented only through deactivation.

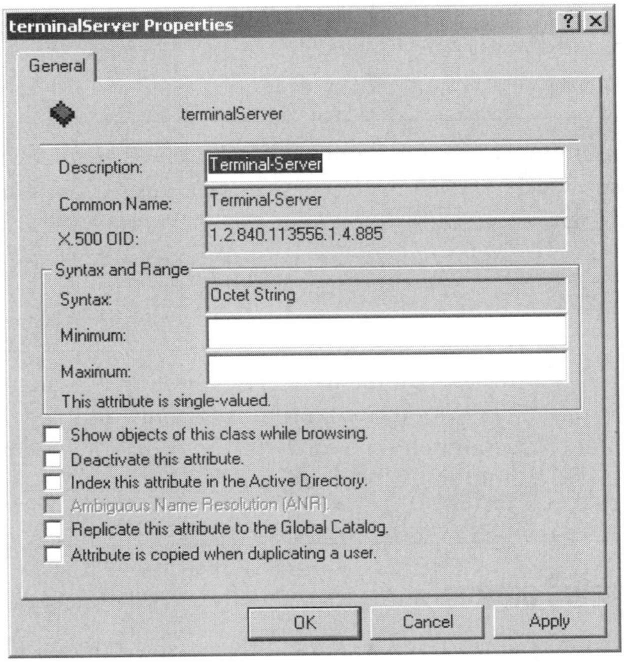

FIGURE 6.14 Attribute Properties

CREATING A NEW OBJECT CLASS OR ATTRIBUTE

When a new object class or attribute is created, it becomes a permanent part of the enterprise. It cannot be removed, only disabled. The following steps create a new object class or attribute:

1. Open the **Active Directory Schema** snap-in.
2. Right-click **Active Directory Schema** → right-click either **Classes** or **Attributes** → select **New** → select **Class** or **Attribute**.
3. In the message box, click **Continue** (or **Cancel** to discontinue).
4. In the supplied dialog box, enter a **Common Name**, the **LDAP Display Name,** and a valid **OID** number, and identify the **Parent Class** and the **Class type** → click **Next**.
5. In the next dialog box, click **Add** to include **Mandatory and Optional** attributes.
6. Click **Finish** to complete the process.

For the creation of attributes, the process eliminates the need to set the parent class with syntax and appropriate ranges.

NOTE One of the requirements in creating a new object class or attribute is the use of a valid OID number, which, like DNS numbers and IP addresses, is assigned on a national basis. For example, in the United States an OID number can be requested from the ANSI Web site at *http://www.web.ansi.org/public/services/reg_org.html.*

NOTE Whenever possible, adding an attribute to a class is generally cleaner than creating a new class. Remember, classes cannot be removed, only disabled. However, if it is necessary to create a class, much time can be saved by starting with a parent class that provides generic definitions. Attributes can then be added and the new class inherits the characteristics of its parent.

REMOVING LINGERING OBJECTS

Objects that serve no ongoing purpose should be removed. Windows Server 2003 provides a command called **Repadmin** that provides the ability to delete lingering objects in the Active Directory. Lingering objects may exist in the Active Directory due to a long unavailability of a domain controller. During this period objects can become "tombstoned" because their lifetimes have expired. By invoking the **Repadmin** command, inconsistency among replicas of the Active Directory is reduced. In turn, this reduces the growth of the Active Directory database and thereby improves performance.

CHANGING THE DOMAIN SCHEMA MASTER

In a multidomain controller environment, certain operation management tasks should be delegated to different domain controller servers. From the Active Directory Schema snap-in, it is possible to identify and change the location only of the Schema Master manager. The Active Directory Schema snap-in separates the definitions of classes and attributes.

Identifying the Schema Master

The Schema Master domain controller can be identified by following these steps:

1. Open the **Active Directory Schema** MMC snap-in.
2. Right-click **Active Directory Schema** and select **Operations Masters**.

3. The name of the current Schema Master appears in **Domain Schema operations master**.

Changing the Schema Master's Location

The Schema Master can be moved to another domain controller by the following steps:

1. Open the **Active Directory Schema** MMC snap-in.
2. Right-click **Active Directory Schema**, select **Connect to Domain Controller,** choose the targeted domain controller, and click **OK**.
3. Right-click **Active Directory Schema**, select **Operations Masters,** and make sure the targeted domain controller is listed in the second dialog text window. Click **Change**.

ENSURING SCHEMA AVAILABILITY AND RESTORATION

The Schema Master domain controller must be available to perform modifications or extensions. The Active Directory will not cease functioning if the Schema Master is not available, however, it will remain static until connectivity is achieved. When this occurs, the first action of a system administrator is to check the network and the system health of the domain controller that is serving as the Schema Master. It may be necessary to resize the resources on the Schema Master domain controller to accommodate increases in the number of objects, classes, and attributes being stored. If it becomes necessary to pull the Schema Master domain controller offline, it is highly recommended that its function be transferred to another domain controller.

In the event that the Schema becomes damaged or otherwise corrupted, the restoration of a default schema or a backup version will become necessary. The process of simply reloading the schema from backup is done by opening the **Active Directory Schema** snap-in → right-click **Active Directory Schema** → select **Reload Schema**.

The Active Directory Sites and Services Snap-In

The Active Directory Sites and Services snap-in tool ensures efficient user logon authentication, the locating of directory services and objects, and more effective control of Active Directory replication. Specifically, it is used to create sites and subnets, move servers between sites, and formulate site links and bridges.

As discussed previously, three Active Directory partitions must be replicated within and between sites. The schema data and configuration data partitions are replicated to all domain controllers in the tree or forest; the domain data partition is replicated solely to domain controllers in the domain. Replication within a site is based on a bidirectional circular topology created automatically by the KCC service. Replication of all three partitions can use the same topology ring if the site supports a single domain. In the event that two or more domains share the site, a topology ring for the schema and configuration partitions is established and separate domain topology rings are created for each domain using the site. The system administrator manually defines intersite replication. Figure 6.15 illustrates the relationship between intrasite and intersite replication.

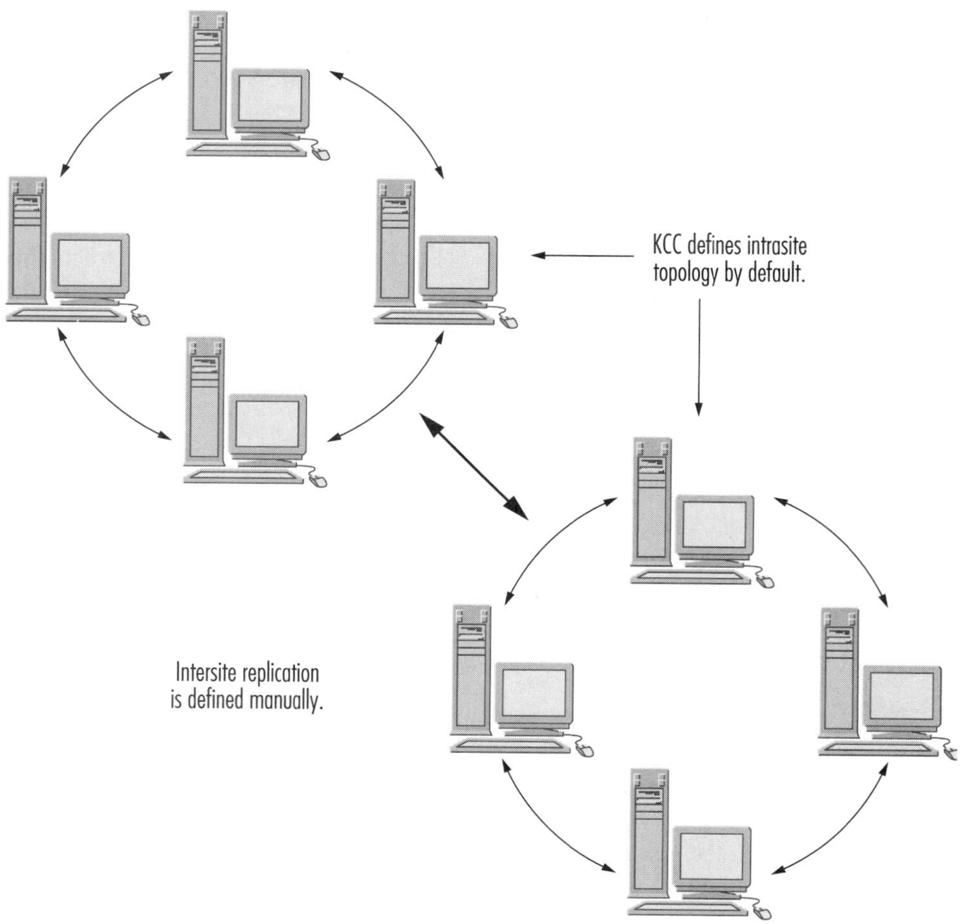

FIGURE 6.15 Intrasite and Intersite Replication Topology

NOTE In Windows 2000, the process that automatically created replication connections between domain controllers in different sites was limited. It could not be used when a forest contained a large number of sites. As a result, administrators had to create and maintain manual intersite replication topologies. With Windows Server 2003, the Inter-Site Topology Generator (ISTG) has been updated. An improved algorithm is used to scale forest support. The major trick is that all domain controllers in the forest that run the ISTG role must agree on the intersite replication topology. This new algorithm is not activated until the forest has advanced to a native Windows Server 2003 Active Directory forest functionality level. Once in Windows Server Active Directory native mode, no administrative action is necessary to activate this feature.

The physical structure is created by the KCC based on information provided by using the Active Directory Sites and Services snap-in. Active Directory uses this information to determine how to replicate directory information and handle service requests. As an administrator, you can manually override the topology created by the KCC of the Active Directory. This is particularly true with respect to intersite communication and replication. The basis of intersite communication is the use of site links, which comprise four components.

- *Cost*. The cost is a representation of a path's relative priority. The higher its cost, the lower a path will be regarded in the utilization of a link.
- *Replication frequency*. Where latency is an issue, the interval between replications should be fairly short.
- *Transport mechanism*. Intersite links can use either RPC over TCP/IP or send replicated data as e-mail using SMTP.
- *Scheduling*. When the frequency of replication can be deferred, the administrator can determine off-peak times when replication should be scheduled.

The Active Directory Sites and Services snap-in manages the replication of Active Directory information both within and among sites. The system administrator can balance the timing of Active Directory data synchronization against the availability of network bandwidth and costs associated with remote connectivity. This balance is accomplished by customizing the site link connectivity properties.

When a user logs on or makes an inquiry of the Active Directory, an attempt is first made to contact the domain controllers in that defined site. In most cases, the authentication is resolved by a domain controller on the local site. The local workstation, as part of a subnet, will seek out authentication in that subnet (which is typically a local site). By not having to transmit information to a remote domain controller, network traffic is reduced, so domain controller placement must also be taken into consideration.

This section examines how to use the Active Directory Sites and Services snap-in to perform the following tasks:

- Create new sites.
- Create site subnets.
- Create intersite links.
- Establish an intersite replication schedule.
- Select an application-licensing server.
- Move domain controllers between sites.
- Repair a domain controller.
- Remove a domain controller from a site.

NOTE Windows Server 2003 provides the ability to delegate to a group the responsibility to monitor Active Directory replication without the need to provide other administrative rights. Users assigned to this group will not be able to write or read other Active Directory information unless these rights are explicitly added.

NOTE Site links are required before a domain controller can replicate information outside its own site. They are not automatic but require an explicit action by the system administrator to exchange Active Directory data. As new sites are created, the domain controllers are assigned to the specified site. This is accomplished when a domain controller is assigned a subnet address associated with a specific site. Links must then be established among sites in order to guarantee domain controller replication throughout the domain.

NOTE When creating links among sites where replication activity is high, consider dedicating a single domain controller to the intersite synchronization. Known as *bridgehead servers,* these domain controllers accept changes made to the Active Directory in one site and transmit them to other sites. Once this information is posted, internal domain controller synchronization can occur with reduced impact on remote network connections.

CREATING SITES

The topology of intersite replication spans the entire tree or forest. When all sites can find a replication route, the topology is considered functional. As the system administrator, you can create site links from any domain controller in any site to any other domain controller in any site throughout the enterprise.

The process for creating a new site is very straightforward. Launch the **Active Directory Sites and Services** snap-in, right-click **Sites,** and select **New Site**. In the upper text box, enter the name of the new site and highlight the site container. Click **OK**. You will receive a confirmation message that the site has been created along with a list of the following tasks that should be carried out:

- Make sure that the new site is appropriately linked to other sites.
- Add the subnet addresses to the subnet container listed in the snap-in.
- Install one or more domain controllers within the site.
- Select a licensing server for the site.

CREATING SITE SUBNETS

Site subnets are created from within the Active Directory Sites and Services snap-in by right-clicking the **Subnet** menu and then selecting **New Subnet**. The **Subnet** dialog box appears, as shown in Figure 6.16. Each site typically gets its own subnet and mask. First highlight the targeted site name from the list provided in the **Select a site object for this subnet** list box; then insert the network address and subnet mask. Click **OK**.

CREATING INTERSITE LINKS AND TRANSPORTS

By default, the Active Directory Sites and Services snap-in provides transport link options for Internet Protocol and Simple Mail Transport Protocol. To create site links for either or both, right-click either **IP** or **SMTP** from within the Active Directory Sites and Services snap-in and select **New Site Link**. The **New Object—New Site Link** dialog box appears. To link the sites, simply highlight the site(s) in the first column entitled **Sites Not in This Site Link,** click **Add**, and click **OK**. Repeat this procedure for all sites in which links are desired.

THE INTERSITE REPLICATION SCHEDULE

The Active Directory Sites and Services snap-in provides a nice graphical interface to schedule directory data synchronization among sites. From the **Active Directory Sites and Services** snap-in → select the folder of the intersite transport that requires a schedule adjustment → right-click the targeted site shown in the details

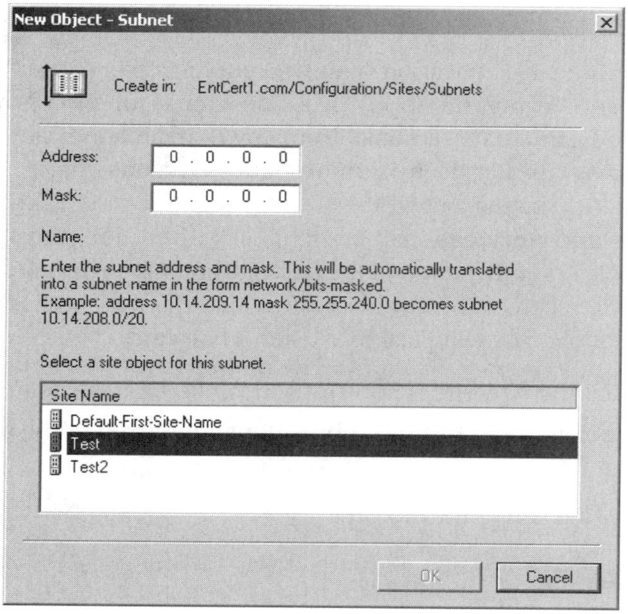

FIGURE 6.16 Creating Subnets

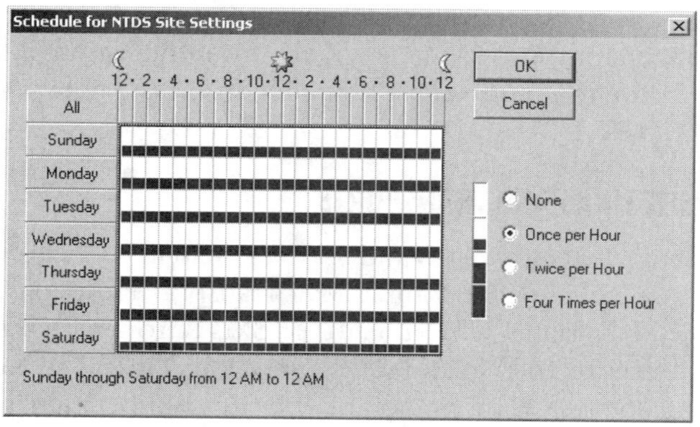

FIGURE 6.17 Scheduling Intersite Active Directory Replication

pane and select **Properties** → click **Change Schedule** → in the **Schedule for NTDS Sites Settings** dialog box (shown in Figure 6.17), make the appropriate schedule changes.

SELECTING AN APPLICATION LICENSING SERVER

When it is created, the Active Directory creates services for application licensing. For every site, there should be an application-licensing server installed. Unlike many other important services, the licensing server does not have to be a domain controller. However, it must have installed a copy of Windows Server 2003. To move or select the licensing server, follow these steps:

1. Open the **Active Directory Sites and Services** snap-in.
2. Open **Sites** and select the targeted site.
3. From the right pane, click **Licensing Site Setting** to open the **Licensing Site Settings Properties** dialog box.
4. Select **Change** and then choose the server to be the licensing server.

MOVING DOMAIN CONTROLLERS BETWEEN SITES

The movement of domain controllers provides more effective load balancing and accommodates change or redundancy in a site. Rather than install additional domain controllers, it is easy to move a domain controller from a site with fewer Active Directory demands. The following procedure should be followed:

1. Open the **Active Directory Sites and Services** snap-in.
2. Open the **Sites** folder, then domain controller sites, then **Servers**.
3. Right-click the destination domain controller and select **Move**.
4. Select the new site from the dialog box and click **OK**.

DOMAIN CONTROLLER BACKUP AND RESTORATION

Periodic backup of Active Directory services (discussed in Chapter 14) should be a regular part of system administration. Of particular interest when backing up a domain controller is System State data, which constitutes the Active Directory, the Sysvol, and the Registry. There are several forms of restoration:

- *Nonauthoritative*. The entire replica of the Active Directory is transferred under a nonauthoritative restore. Assuming that other domain controllers exist, once the replica is installed, the normal replication services will update the system with changes since the last backup. To perform this type of restoration, the server must be restarted in safe mode (press F8 during the reboot to initialize the safe mode). After the files have been restored, a flag is set in the Registry indicating that the Active Directory must be reindexed at the next reboot. When the system is rebooted, it communicates with the Active Directory and is updated with changes.
- *Authoritative*. The authoritative restore permits the tagging of certain database information to prevent its being overwritten during a restoration. This will avoid its inadvertent destruction. When a restoration occurs, the tagged information will not be touched. It will, however, become part of the normal Active

Directory database when the system is brought back online. This can apply to a single object, an OU, or an entire domain. To conduct an authoritative restore, the system must be restarted in safe mode. From the command prompt, run the Ntdsutil.exe and type **restore subtree OU=name of unit, DC=domain, DC=.com**. Insert the appropriate information in the italicized portion of the command. Restart the system once the Ntdsutil has confirmed its completion. The USN must be modified to ensure that it is authoritative. The authoritative information is then replicated to the other domain controllers.

The Ntdsutil command-line utility can be run from the command prompt. Help for the Ntdsutil utility can also be found at the command prompt by typing **ntdsutil/?**.

FORCED REPLICATION CHECK

Repairing an Active Directory domain controller can be accomplished by forcing a check of the replication.

NOTE The need to repair a domain controller is not a normal event. Repair should be undertaken only when it is obvious that fundamental Active Directory databases or functions are corrupted.

The domain controller replication check is accomplished by these steps:

1. Open the **Active Directory Sites and Services** snap-in.
2. Open the **Sites** folder → select the folder of the targeted domain controller.
3. Right-click **NTDS Setting** → select **All Tasks** → select **Replication Check**.
4. Select the specific items to be repaired → click **OK**.

REMOVING A DOMAIN CONTROLLER SERVER FROM A SITE

A domain controller may need to be removed from a given site periodically for a variety of reasons. This can be done by following these steps:

1. Open the **Active Directory Sites and Services** snap-in.
2. Open the **Sites** folder → select the folder of the site of the targeted domain controller.
3. Open the **Server** folder → right-click the targeted domain controller.
4. Move to the **Action** menu → click **Delete**, and confirm with **OK**.

NOTE If this is the only domain controller in the domain, be sure to promote another member server prior to removing the Active Directory. If this is not done, all information will be lost and users will not be able to log on to the network.

The Active Directory Users and Computers Snap-In

The Active Directory Users and Computers snap-in is possibly the most important and most used system administrative tool. It supports the ability to add, modify, delete, and organize users, computer accounts, security groups, distribution groups, and resource publications. Because of the importance of user administration and group policies, we have broken their treatment into other chapters: Chapter 7, "Users and Groups"; Chapter 8, "Group Policies"; and Chapter 9, "Files and Objects Permissions."

This section examines how to use the Active Directory Users and Computers snap-in to perform the following administrative tasks:

- Computer Account Management
  - Add computer accounts
  - Remove computer accounts
  - Locate computer accounts
  - Move computer accounts
    - — Save queries
    - — Edit multiple user objects
- Management of local computer accounts
- RID, PDC, and Infrastructure Master management

COMPUTER ACCOUNT MANAGEMENT

The Active Directory Users and Computers snap-in facilitates the addition, removal, location, movement, and management of computers in the domain and the tree. Remember that a computer account must be created in the Active Directory before a new computer can join the domain. This is generally before Windows Server 2003 is installed.

Computer systems are treated as objects within the Active Directory, much like user accounts. To identify a computer account or change components, use the **Active Directory Users and Computers** snap-in → select **Computers** → highlight the desired computer → right-click **Properties**. From this dialog box, you can navigate to find the identification of the computer's general attributes such as names and role, installed operating system, group and domain membership, physical location, and system management data (Figure 6.18). As the next section suggests, the Active Directory can track even those computer accounts that are not based on the Windows Server 2003 operating system.

Adding Computer Accounts

Adding a computer account to the Active Directory is required before member computers and servers can join the domain. This is an easy and straightforward process, as follows:

1. Open the **Active Directory Users and Computers** snap-in.
2. Open the targeted **domain** → **Computers** (or OU folder).
3. Right-click Computers → select **New** → **Computers**.
4. Enter the computer's name, (optionally) change user groups authorized to use this computer account, check the box if computers running systems earlier than Windows Server 2003 are to use this account → click **OK**.

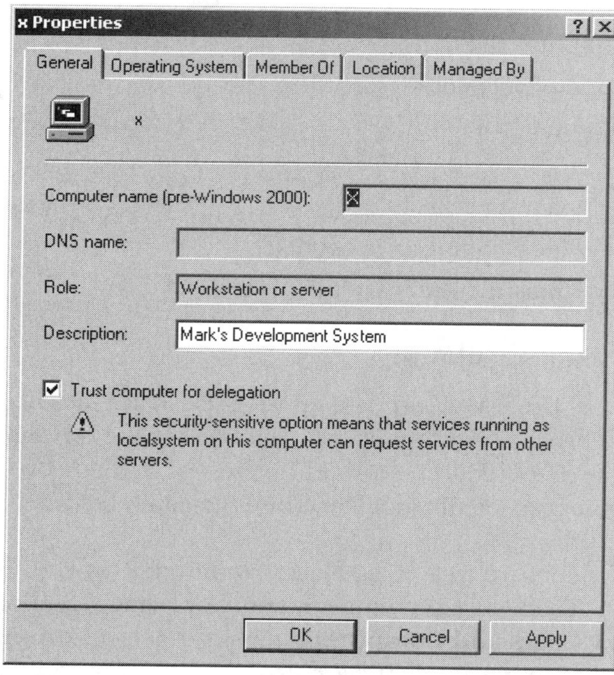

FIGURE 6.18 Computer Account Properties

Removing Computer Accounts

When systems are taken out of service, they should be removed from the Active Directory. Consider this merely a housekeeping activity. To remove computer accounts, follow these steps:

1. Open the **Active Directory Users and Computers** snap-in.
2. Open the targeted **Domain** → **Computers** (or OU folder).
3. From the right pane, right-click the targeted **Computer** → select **Delete**.
4. Confirm **Yes** to remove this object.

Locating Computer Accounts

To perform any function on a computer account, the account must first be located. Manual identification within a very large enterprise can be time consuming, but an alternative method is as follows:

1. Open the **Active Directory Users and Computers** snap-in.
2. Right-click the Domain → select **Find**.
3. Enter the appropriate information in the dialog box.
4. Click **Find Now**.

Moving Computer Accounts

As organizations change or IT requirements shift, the computer account should be transferred to the appropriate domain or organizational unit as follows:

1. Open the **Active Directory Users and Computers** snap-in.
2. Open the targeted **Domain** → **Computers** (or OU folder).
3. From the right pane, right-click the targeted **Comput**er and select **Move**.
4. In the **Move** dialog box, highlight the targeted container → click **Enter**.

Managing Local Computer Accounts

From within the Active Directory Users and Computers snap-in, it is possible to launch the Computer Management MMC applications for the listed computer systems (Figure 6.19). The method is outlined as follows:

1. Open the **Active Directory Users and Computers** snap-in.
2. Open the targeted **Domain** → **Computers** (or OU folder).
3. From the right panel, right-click the targeted **Computer** → select **Manage**.
4. The **Computer Management MMC** appears.

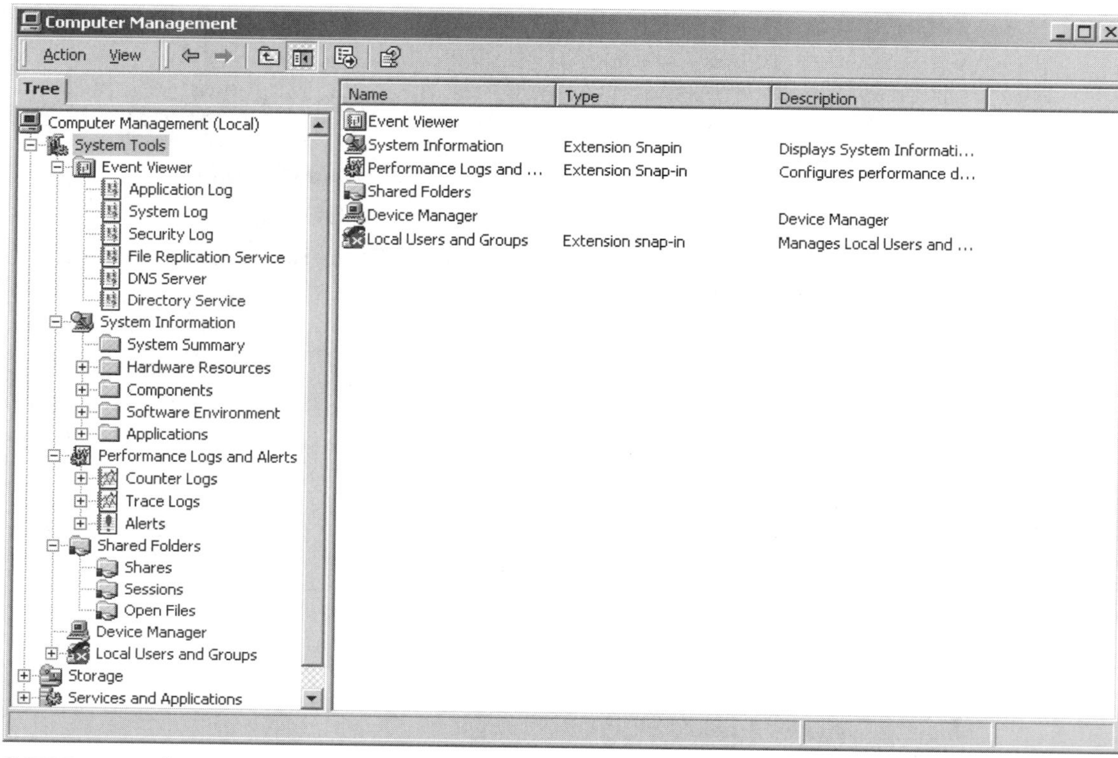

FIGURE 6.19 The Computer Management MMC

Saving Queries

A query is a search against a data set (the directory) for items that match particular criteria. A feature new to Windows Server 2003 allows queries to be saved, reopened, refreshed, and e-mailed. Query objects and results can be viewed and manipulated in the user interface. Administrators can retrieve and reuse these queries. This feature is available by opening the Active Directory Users and Computers snap-in. When prompted whether you wish to save the query, click **Yes**.

Editing Multiple User Objects

With Windows Server 2003, editing user objects is greatly streamlined. This feature allows selection of multiple user objects. The administrator can then bring up a set of property sheets and clear or set object attributes across all the selected objects. Although only specific property sheets and attributes will be available for editing multiple objects this way, it should reduce the sometimes painful task of user account management. This feature is available by opening the Active Directory Users and Computers snap-in, where you can choose **Edit Multiple Objects.**

RID, PDC, OR INFRASTRUCTURE MASTERS

Three of the domain operations masters are managed from the Active Directory User and Computers snap-in. The RID Master establishes object IDs with numbers relative to a specific domain; the PDC operations master manages the PDC Emulator functions; and the Infrastructure Master manages group and user references. From the Active Directory Users and Computers snap-in, it is possible to identify and change the location of the RID, PDC, and Infrastructure Master managers. Their original location is the root domain controller.

Identifying the RID, PDC, and Infrastructure Masters

In larger enterprises with many domain controllers, it may not be obvious which one is serving as the RID, PDC, or Infrastructure Master. To find this out, use the steps that follow:

1. Open the **Active Directory Users and Computers** MMC snap-in.
2. Right-click **Active Users and Computers,** then select **Operations Masters**.
3. The name of the master appears in the respective **Domain Master** tab.

Changing the RID, PDC, and Infrastructure Masters

When an operations manager is taken offline, another domain controller must be promoted to perform this function. The promotion must be accomplished *before* the older domain controller is taken offline. Promotion of a domain controller to a RID, PDC, or Infrastructure Master is accomplished as follows:

1. Open the **Active Directory Users and Computers** MMC snap-in.
2. Right-click **Active Users and Computers**, select the **Connect to Domain Controller**, and choose the targeted domain controller. Click **OK**.
3. Right-click **Active Users and Computers,** select **Operations Masters**, and make sure the targeted domain controller is listed in the second dialog text window → click **Change**.

The Active Directory Replication Monitor

The Active Directory Replication Monitor is not loaded as part of the default installation but as part of the Windows Server 2003 Resource Kit located on the Windows Server 2003 or higher CD in the /support/tools folder. This tool does exactly what its name implies—monitor Active Directory replication—and can be very useful. It is used specifically to view replication topologies, identify replication partners, and map transitive replication partners.

CREATING ORGANIZATIONAL UNITS

The organizational unit provides both flexibility and greater control. It is really an administrative container in which a logical grouping of network resources can be collected and their management delegated. Its form is hierarchical; that is, parent and child relationships exist between top- and lower-level OUs. The objects that constitute an OU are strictly up to the domain administrator. For example, the third floor of a large building can be defined as an OU; since the sales staff occupies the third floor, each of these users can be regarded as an OU as well. An organizational unit can contain other OUs. Thus, the printer OU can be placed inside the sales staff OU and the administration printer support can be delegated to an individual on the third floor.

Creating, Deleting, Modifying, an Moving an Organizational Unit

The creation, deletion, modification, and moving of organizational units is a simple process. However, the ease of these activities belies the importance of proper planning.

CREATING AN ORGANIZATIONAL UNIT

The following steps should be followed to create an organizational unit within a domain or child domain:

1. Open the **Active Directory Users and Computers** MMC snap-in.
2. Right-click **Domain** → click **New** → select **Organizational Unit**.
3. In the OU dialog box, enter the **Name** for the organizational unit. Click **OK**.

DELETING AN ORGANIZATIONAL UNIT

An organizational unit can be deleted as easily as it was created. However, great caution should be used in such deletion since objects in the OU will also be removed (Figure 6.20). For example, deleting the sales OU deletes all its users and resources. The following steps are invoked to delete an OU:

1. Open the **Active Directory Users and Computers** MMC snap-in.
2. Right-click **Organizational Unit** → select **Delete**.
3. Confirm the deletion by clicking **Yes**.

MODIFYING ORGANIZATIONAL UNIT PROPERTIES

The properties of an OU are modified like any other Active Directory object. A discussion of standard object modification appears earlier in this chapter. Follow these steps to modify OU properties:

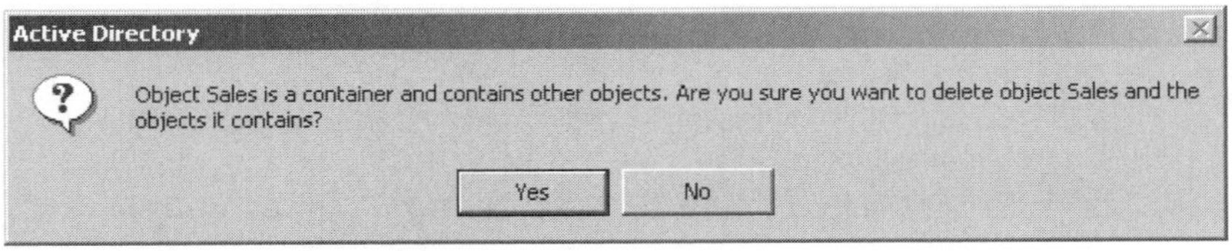

FIGURE 6.20 Deleting an OU and Its Objects

1. Open the **Active Directory Users and Computers** MMC snap-in.
2. Right-click the targeted **OU** → select **Properties**.
3. Make changes within the **General, Managed By**, and/or **Group Policy** tabs.
4. Click **OK**.

MOVING ORGANIZATIONAL UNITS

One of the major innovations of Windows Server 2003 is the ability to easily move or relocate an OU to another domain or child domain to reflect the changes that regularly occur in an enterprise. The steps are as follows:

1. Open the **Active Directory Users and Computers** snap-in.
2. Expand the targeted **Domain** or **OU** → right-click the **OU** → click **Move**.
3. Highlight the new location of the **OU** in the **Move** dialog box → Click **OK**.

RENAMING ORGANIZATIONAL UNITS

To accommodate shifts in names or functions, the OU renaming function is handy. It requires the following steps:

1. Open the **Active Directory Users and Computers** MMC snap-in.
2. Expand the targeted **Domain** or **OU** → right-click the **OU** → click **Rename**.
3. Enter the new name → Click **OK**.

LOCATING OBJECTS

Finding Active Directory objects in an enterprise is accomplished through the Microsoft Management Console. If **Find** is invoked from within a specific snap-in, as shown in Figure 6.21, the items managed by the snap-in will appear in the Find window and searches will center on that branch of the Active Directory. If it is not clear where the object is located, you can use the Directory Management snap-in. The interface for finding an object is straightforward and requires no further explanation.

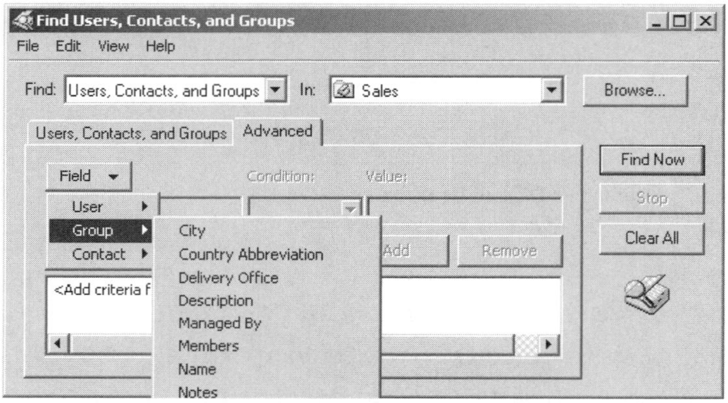

FIGURE 6.21 Finding an Object with Advanced Definitions

Active Directory Object Access

The security model of the Active Directory mirrors to a large extent Windows Server 2003 NTFS. A security descriptor defines which users and groups are assigned permissions to an object. Every object has an access control list (ACL) that contains information about who has access to it and what they can do with it. For every user or group, specific levels of permission can be assigned. As a general rule, at least one user will have full control over an object, but full control for all users is seldom recommended. Where no permission is granted, that object becomes unavailable to the user or group. Also, when permission is specifically denied, all other rights are overridden. For example, a user can belong to a group that has permission to use a network resource, but if that user is specifically denied permission, any rights to that resource granted to him as a group member are canceled.

By default, an object inherits the permission rights of its parent. One use of the organizational unit is to group objects with the same permissions.

Access control lists are discussed in greater depth in Chapter 7. The ACL is managed through a user interface that permits simplified component creations and editing. Windows Server 2003 provides enhancements to the standard access control list editor user interface (ACLUI), including:

- Reset permissions to a default.
- Show effective permissions for a selected security principal.
- Indicate the parent from which permission was inherited.
- Check box to indicate the existence of additional permissions

Editing is accomplished by selecting the **Properties** tab of any file, Registry key, and Active Directory object. Select the **Security** tab and make appropriate changes.

Object Picker UI Enhancements

New to Windows Server 2003, Object Picker is a user-interface component that allows the selection of one or more users, computers, groups, or contacts from Active Directory services. The new components include administrator workflow optimization, which facilitates rapid location of objects. This feature should reduce impact of the directory service network in terms of both speed (time) and overall utilization (space). The Object Picker provides the ability to scope a search down to a specific OU using a more flexible query function. This new function is available from the Active Directory Users and Computer Snap-in.

STANDARD AND SPECIAL PERMISSIONS

The Active Directory supports two types of permission: standard and special. The five standard permissions, which may be applied in any combination to a user or group, are:

- *Read.* The user can see the object and attributes, can identify its owner, and has other permissions where applicable.
- *Write.* The user can change the object's attributes.
- *Create Child Objects.* The user can create child objects in an OU.
- *Delete Child Objects.* The user can remove child objects.
- *Full Control.* The user can perform any action on the object, including taking full control.

Special permissions are extensions to the standard permissions and vary for each object.

Setting and Viewing Object Permissions

The security permission settings can be viewed for every object from its **Properties** dialog. The properties for all objects can be retrieved from the Active Directory Schema snap-in. To retrieve and set object permissions, the following steps should be taken (Figure 6.22):

1. Open the **Active Directory Schema** snap-in.
2. Open the **Classes** folder.
3. Right-click the targeted object class.
4. In the **Properties** dialog box, select the user or group for which permissions are to be set, **Add** or **Remove** a user or group to provide new permissions.

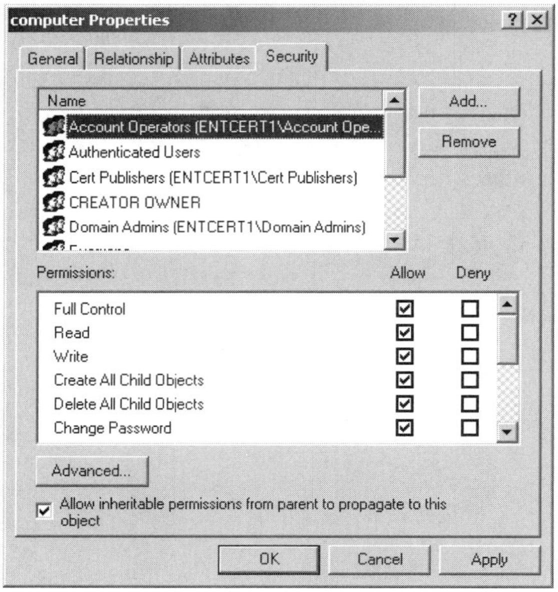

FIGURE 6.22 Setting Object Permissions

5. Click the desired **Permission**.
6. Repeat these steps for each user or group for which permissions are to be modified.
7. Click **OK** to complete.

To simply view the special permissions assigned to an object, click **Advanced** and double-click **Permissions** (Figure 6.23). Changes in this list can then be applied by clicking or clearing the boxes to designate special permission.

Permission Inheritance and Preventing Inheritance

By default, permissions are inherited from parent objects, which means that rather than have to set all permissions for every object, the system administrator can rely on the fact that permissions set on a parent object will filter down the object tree. Sometimes this facility needs to be short-circuited, accomplished as follows:

1. Open the **Active Directory Schema** snap-in.
2. Right-click **Active Directory Schema** and click **Permissions**.
3. On the **Security** tab, click the group whose permissions you want to change.
4. In **Permissions,** select **Allow** or **Deny** for the permissions you want to change.
5. Alternatively, remove the check mark at the bottom of the **Permissions** dialog that states, **Allow inheritance permissions from the parent to propagate to this object**.

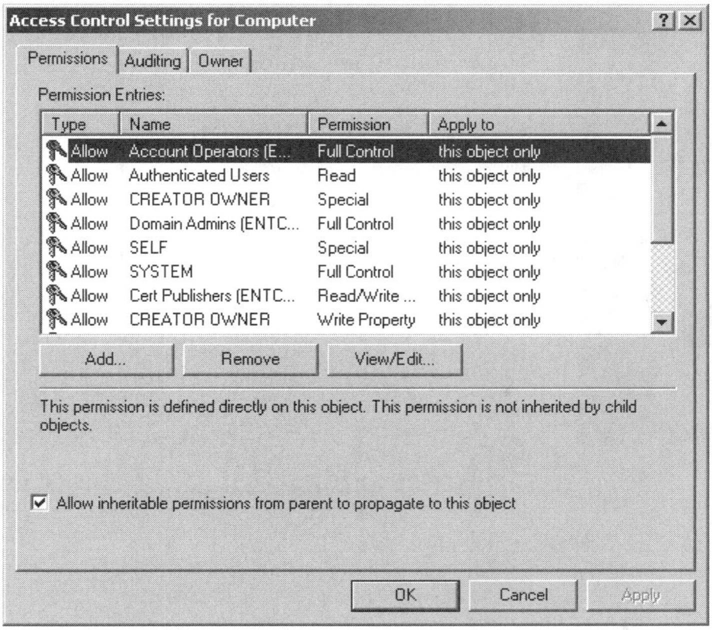

FIGURE 6.23 Reviewing Permission Settings

ACTIVE DIRECTORY ADMINISTRATIVE DELEGATION

The ability to delegate administrative responsibility is a major strength of Windows 2000/Server 2003. This delegation can be set at the domain, organizational unit, or object level and involves the assignment of appropriate permissions ranging from Read-Only to Full Control. As a general rule, objects should be placed in OUs prior to delegation. For example, by placing all printers in an OU, it is possible to provide permissions to a group of users to manage these devices. All users in the Sales department might be in another organizational unit. A trusted administrator can then be delegated to manage the user accounts. Obviously, responsibility must be delegated with care.

The Delegation of Control Wizard

Two best practices should be used when delegating authority: Delegate at the organizational unit level whenever possible for ease of permission tracking; and use the Delegation of Control Wizard as follows:

1. Open the **Active Directory Users and Computers** snap-in.
2. Right-click the predefined organizational unit → select **Delegate Control** (Figure 6.24).

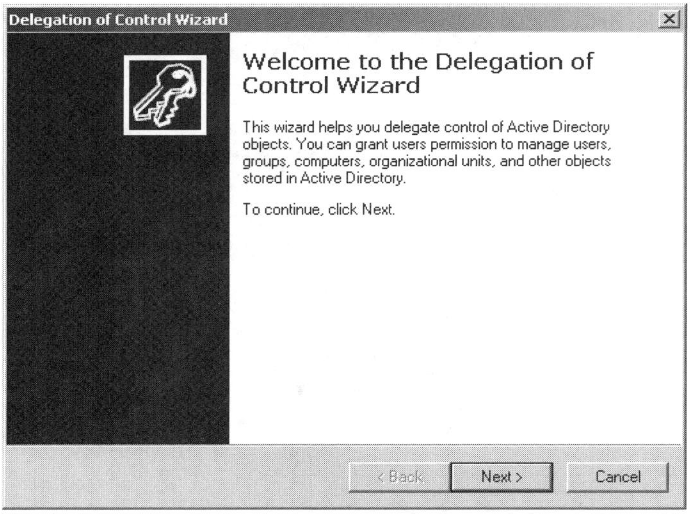

FIGURE 6.24 The Delegation of Control Wizard

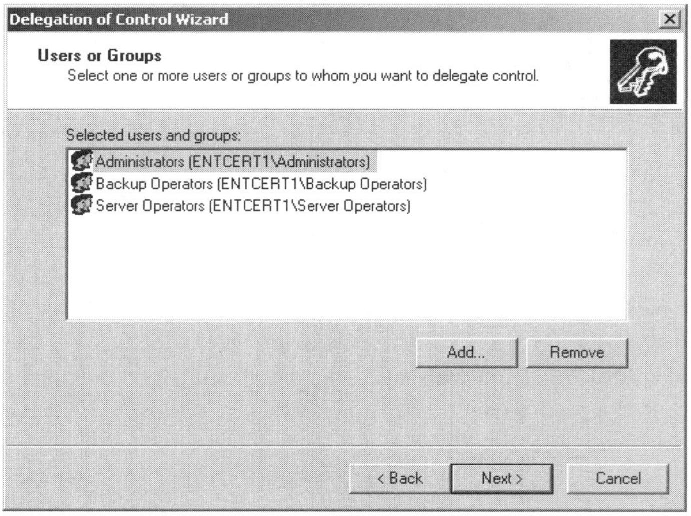

FIGURE 6.25 Selecting Users and Groups

3. Select the user(s) or group(s) to whom authority is to be delegated (Figure 6.25).
4. For common tasks, select from the items listed; for expanded and specialized authority, click **Create a custom task to delegate** (Figure 6.26).

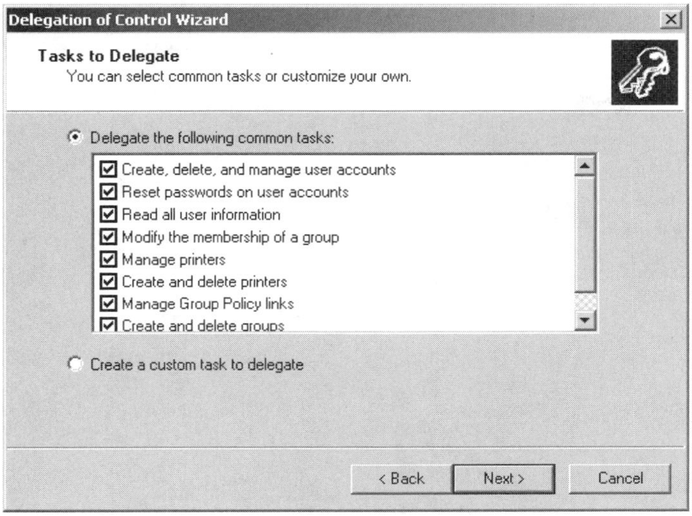

FIGURE 6.26 Delegating Common Tasks

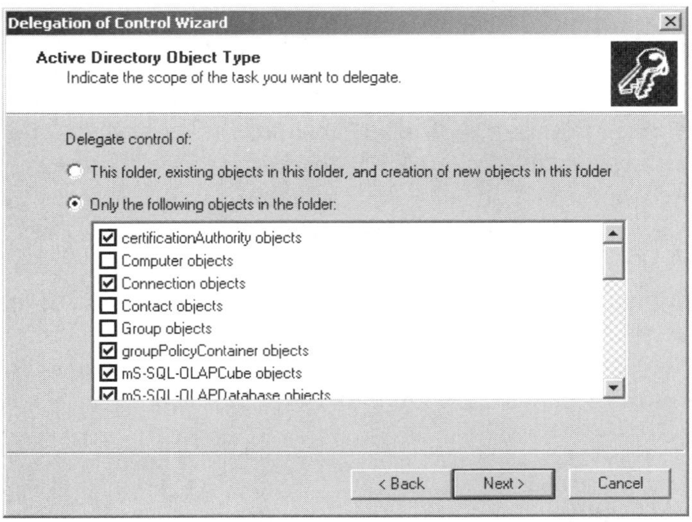

FIGURE 6.27 Delegating Custom Tasks

5. If **Custom Tasks** was selected, mark those items to which delegated authority is to be granted (Figure 6.27).
6. Select the permission level that is to be delegated (Figure 6.28).

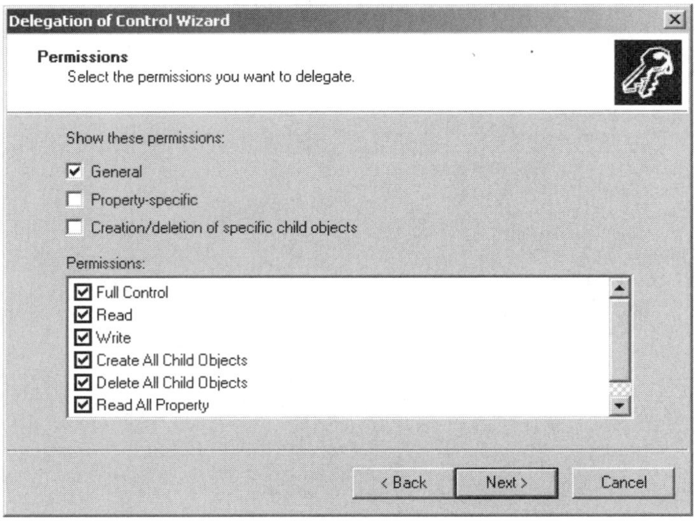

FIGURE 6.28 Selecting Level of Permissions

REFINING THE GLOBAL CATALOG

The Global Catalog authenticates network user logons and fields inquiries about objects across a forest or tree. Every domain has at least one GC that is hosted on a domain controller. In Windows 2000, there was typically one GC on every site in order to prevent user logon failures across the network. The establishment of site-based GCs is less critical with Windows Server 2003 since the site DC can be configured to cache the user's Universal Group membership. This feature is turned on by configuring a site to use logon without Global Catalog in the Active Directory Sites and Services snap-in.

Although Active Directory creates the initial GC during initial installation, a system administrator may invoke a number of additional interactions that improve performance.

Enabling a Global Catalog

A domain controller must be taken offline or out of service sometimes. If this domain controller is also the sole GC for the domain, it is critical that another GC domain controller be placed into service first. Remember, with the exception of the Domain Administrator group, no user can log on to the network without an operative GC. Therefore, prior to running dcpromo.exe to demote the GC domain controller, enable a new GC by following these steps:

1. Create at least a second domain controller.
2. Open the **Active Directory Sites and Services** snap-in.
3. Open the **Site** → **Server** → targeted the domain controller.
4. Right-click **NTDS Settings** → select **Properties** → at the bottom of the **General** tab, click **Global Catalog**.

NOTE On rare occasions, it may be necessary to force the demotion of a domain controller when it exhibits a massive error state and cannot be demoted due to a replication error. This feature removes the Active Directory and returns the computer to member server state. Generally, applications and data are not affected. This feature is invoked by running dcpromo.exe /forcedremoval from the command prompt.

Moving, Removing, and Duplicating the Global Catalog

In larger enterprises, it is recommended that the GC be moved to a separate domain controller. As noted in Chapter 5, this new location should not be the Infrastructure Master domain controller. Moving the GC is accomplished by following these steps:

1. Create at least a second domain controller.
2. Open the **Active Directory Sites and Services** snap-in.
3. Open the **Site** → **Server** → targeted the domain controller.
4. Right-click **NTDS Settings** → select **Properties** → at the bottom of the **General** tab, click **Global Catalog**.
5. To remove the original GC: repeat steps 1 and 2; in step 3, return to the domain controller that originally contained the GC; and in step 4, at the bottom of the **General** tab, remove the check mark next to **Global Catalog**.

To create multiple copies of the GC, simply follow steps 1 through 4 on several domain controllers.

Indexing and Adding Attributes to the Global Catalog

The Global Catalog is used to rapidly locate domain objects. In some cases, users query more common attributes to locate network resources. So that the GC recognizes these attributes, the system administrator can force it to both add and index them. To force the addition and/or indexing of an attribute, follow these steps:

1. Open the **Active Directory Schema** snap-in.
2. Open the **Attributes** folder.

3. In the right pane, right-click the targeted attribute that should be added or indexed to the Global Catalog → then click **Properties**.
4. Click **Index this attribute in the Active Directory**.
5. Click **Replicate this attribute to the Global Catalog**.
6. Click **OK**.

THE ACTIVE DIRECTORY CONNECTOR

The Active Directory connector technology helps to synchronize information with other directory services. As an example, this section discusses synchronization with Microsoft Exchange Server's directory services. Connectors to other directory services will be made available through Windows Server 2003 Service Packs and third-party vendors.

The Active Directory Connector (ADC) is not installed as part of the standard Active Directory setup process. Instead, ADC setup is available on the Windows Server 2003 CD in the \Valueadd\MSFT\MGMT\ADC folder, and the only decisions it requires are where to store the installed software and what to name the service account and password for the group authorized for Connector use. The Exchange Server must be available to complete the configuration.

ADC uses LDAP v3 to resolve information about objects to be synchronized. Connection agreements synchronize information among directory services. Synchronization is achieved when the services' respective databases have equivalent, but not necessarily identical, information. Connection agreements must identify servers, targeted objects, selected containers, and the schedule for data transfer.

NOTE A fairly significant improvement of Windows Server 2003 is the ability to perform multiple LDAP binds on one connection for the purpose of authenticating users. Application developers can use this feature to bind multiple LDAP directories. The feature is designed to allow users to gain rapid authentication and to improve system performance.

Configuring Connection Agreements

The ADC must be configured to ensure proper synchronization. The Active Directory Connector snap-in is used to define the configuration properties, via the primary configuration tabs described here:

- ***General*** establishes the direction of synchronization as two-way directions or one-way from/to the Active Directory or Exchange Server.

- ***Connections*** establishes the method of authentication for both the Active Directory and the Exchange Server for bridgehead servers.
- ***Schedule*** sets the time in which changes are to be synchronized (by default the systems are polled every 5 seconds for modifications during this scheduled period).
- ***From Windows*** and ***From Exchange*** define which containers are polled, which changes are to be written, and the type of objects for synchronization.
- ***Deletion*** defines where deleted objects from one directory service are stored in the corresponding directory. By default, deleted objects are not removed. However, if you select deletion, it occurs on both sides.
- ***Advanced Settings*** establishes the number of entries per page of synchronization, known as paged results. It also defines the connector as primary.

POSTSCRIPT

This chapter and the last one provide a framework for Active Directory use. The chapters dealing with users (Chapter 7), group policies (Chapter 8), and security (Chapter 9) provide additional information on use of Active Directory services.

Chapter 7

User Accounts and Groups

User accounts and group management are core system administration responsibilities. Indeed, it is impossible to introduce the concept of user account management without a discussion of groups. All users belong to one or more groups. Rights and privileges are assigned to default "built-in" or customized groups, and the user receives rights by becoming a group member.

Administrators with Windows 2000 experience should find the user and group account management very familiar. The primary differences reside in refined functionality. Windows NT administrators should also find the transition relatively straightforward, although a number of key interfaces, tools, and functions have been substantially advanced.

This chapter explores the nature of user accounts and groups and provides related management information. Upon completing it, you should be able to:

- Understand the concepts underlying Windows Server 2003 user accounts and groups
- Add, modify, and remove local and domain user accounts
- Add, modify, and remove local and domain groups
- Apply group membership to user accounts

USER ACCOUNTS

In order to gain access to Windows Server 2003, a user must have a valid user account. A user account determines three important factors: when a user may log on; where within the domain or workgroup the user can log on; and the privilege level he or she is assigned. Primary user account elements are logon name, password, group membership, and allowable logon hours.

Privilege level and access permissions are assigned to a user account with security credentials. When an account is created, it is given a unique access number known as a security identifier (SID). Every group to which the user belongs has an associated SID. The user and related group SIDs together form the user account's security token, which determines access levels to objects throughout the system and network. SIDs from the security token are mapped to the access control list (ACL) of any object the user attempts to access. (The ACL is discussed in Chapter 9.) The user is granted rights to the object based on the permissions or lack of permissions the ACL indicates are assigned to him and his groups (Figure 7.1).

NOTE The *security identifier* is a unique number generated when a user account or group is created. If you delete a user account and attempt to recreate it with the same user name and password, the SID will be different. This means that all objects that use the old SID to assign permissions are useless to the new user. Permissions must be reassigned to the new user account SID. The same principle applies to groups: Deleting a group and recreating a group with the same name will not generate the same group SID.

Any object trying to access a resource must do so through a user account. In this case, an object can be a computer user or an application. For instance, the Internet Information Services Web server creates the IUSR_systemname user account to provide anonymous Web users access to the local system.

Windows Server 2003 allows two types of user account: local and domain. Local accounts are supported on all Windows Server 2003 systems except domain controllers. They are maintained on the local system and are not distributed to other systems. The local security database manages the user account information. The domain user account permits access throughout a domain and provides centralized user account administration using Active Directory components. Let's take a closer look at these accounts.

Local User Accounts

Local user accounts are supported on member servers participating in domains and on standalone systems participating in workgroups. The local user account authenticates the user for local machine access only. This authentication is handled through a local security database (Figure 7.2). Local accounts do not support access

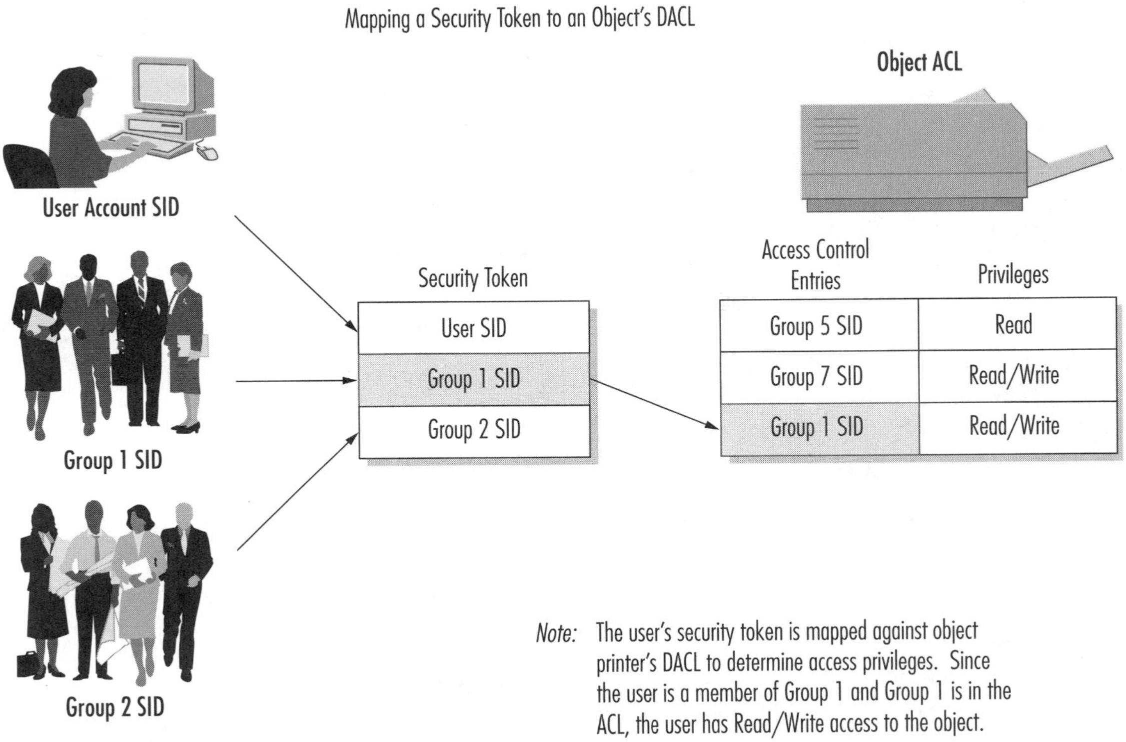

FIGURE 7.1 Relationship of User and Group SIDs to Object ACLs

to resources on other computers and they require separate logons to access remote systems.

NOTE It is best not to create local user accounts on member servers; they cannot be centrally administered and create added administrative headaches. However, they are useful when isolating applications from the rest of the domain. Local accounts on member servers or standalone servers can be added at any time.

NOTE The new Credential Management feature of Windows Server 2003 provides a consistent single sign-on experience for users. This can be useful for roaming users who move between computer systems. The Credential Management feature provides a secure store of user credentials that includes passwords and X.509 certificates.

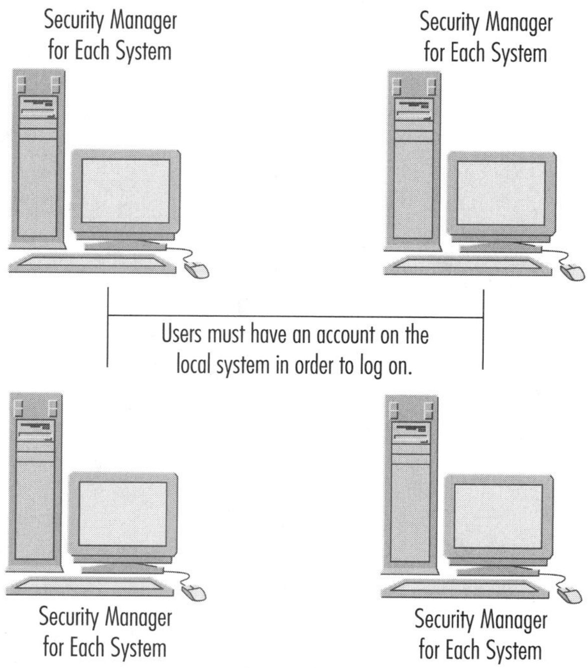

FIGURE 7.2 Local Computers with Separate Security Managers

The Credential Management feature provides access to authorized applications. When the user first attempts to access a targeted application, the authentication mechanism prompts the user to supply a credential. After the credential is presented, it will be associated with the requesting application. The saved credential is reused without prompting the user when access to the application on the company network is requested. To activate this feature, action must occur on both client and server sides. Action by the client: **Start → Control Panel → User Accounts**; action by the server (using the Windows Server 2003 or Window XP Control Panel View): **Start → Control Panel → Other Control Panel Options → Windows Keyring**. The Credential Manager is disabled through the Group Policies snap-in.

At a minimum, the Administrator and Guest accounts will already exist as local accounts. These are built in to the operating system. The Administrator account permits user account management, group management, and policies for the local systems. The Guest account is designed for temporary users who require limited system access.

CREATING A LOCAL USER ACCOUNT

User accounts comprise two mandatory pieces of information: user name and password. Other personal information is optionally tracked. Following are some restrictions and suggestions on the creation of user names and passwords.

- User and logon names are interchangeable. Domain account names must be unique in the domain, although the same logon name can be used on several systems with local logon configurations. Logon names are not case-sensitive, must not contain more then 20 characters, and must not contain the following characters: +, *, ?, <, >, /, \, [,], :, and ;.
- Passwords should not contain such items as full words, family names, pop culture references, pets, and locations. They should contain both numeric and alphanumeric characters and should not be the same as the user name. The maximum number of characters is 128 and the minimum is determined by group policy. Password filtering is discussed in Chapter 11, "Additional Security Issues and Solutions."

Local User Accounts on Windows Server 2003

Creating a local user account involves the steps that follow. As noted, local user accounts are available only on member servers and workstations. Domain controllers have no local accounts and creating them on member servers is not recommended. However, if there is a reason to provide temporary restricted user accounts, here is how:

1. Create a new user account on a workgroup server by selecting **Start → Programs → Administrative Tools → Computer Management** (Figure 7.3).
2. From the **Computer Management** snap-in, click System **Tools → Local Users and Groups**. Right-click **Users**, then select **New Users**. The **New User** dialog box should appear (Figure 7.4).

NOTE Windows Server 2003 permits administrators to add computer accounts to security groups from the Local Users and Groups snap-in. This is useful for determining which computer accounts are admitted into the Session Directory Computers Group when administering Terminal Services.

The **User name** field will contain the user's logon name. The password properties are the same as those for the domain user discussed in the next section. User accounts are viewed in the details window of the Computer Management tool under the **Users** node.

3. Enter the user's user name, full name, and description. Click **Create**.

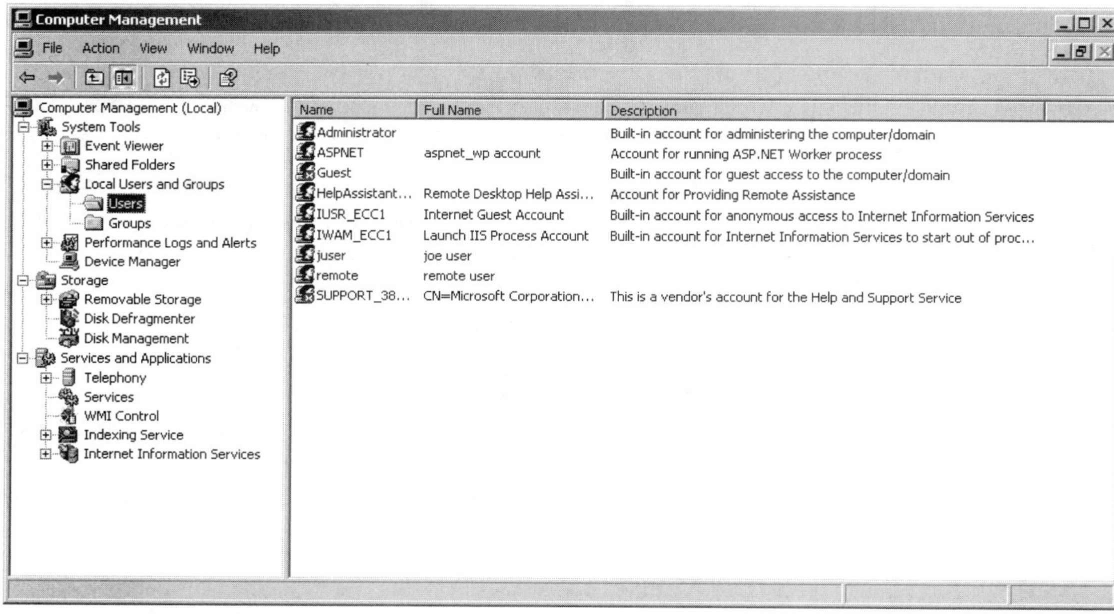

FIGURE 7.3 Local Users and Groups

Local User Accounts on Windows 2000 Professional and Windows XP

Windows 2000 Professional and Windows XP are designed either as a client system in a network environment or as a standalone workgroup computer. In this example, we illustrate the client setup for Windows 2000 Professional because it is a more complex process than setting up Windows XP. Setting up Windows XP user accounts is also achieved through the Control Panel, but it leads the user or administrator through a simplified set of wizard-based dialog boxes. Domain and local accounts that already exist may be assigned access to the local system using the following steps:

1. To permit existing user accounts access to the local system, select **Start** → **Settings** → **Control Panel** (Figure 7.5). From **Control Panel,** double-click the **Users and Passwords** icon. The **Users and Passwords** dialog box should now display all user accounts on the system (Figure 7.6).
2. To give another user access to the local system, click **Add**.
3. Choose a domain name and or local user account name and type it into the **Domain** box (Figure 7.7). If the account is a local one, enter the name of the local system. Click **Next** to continue.

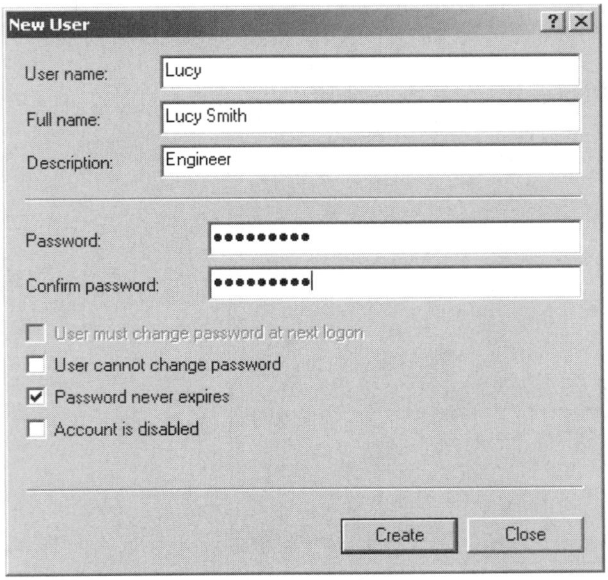

FIGURE 7.4 The New User Dialog Box

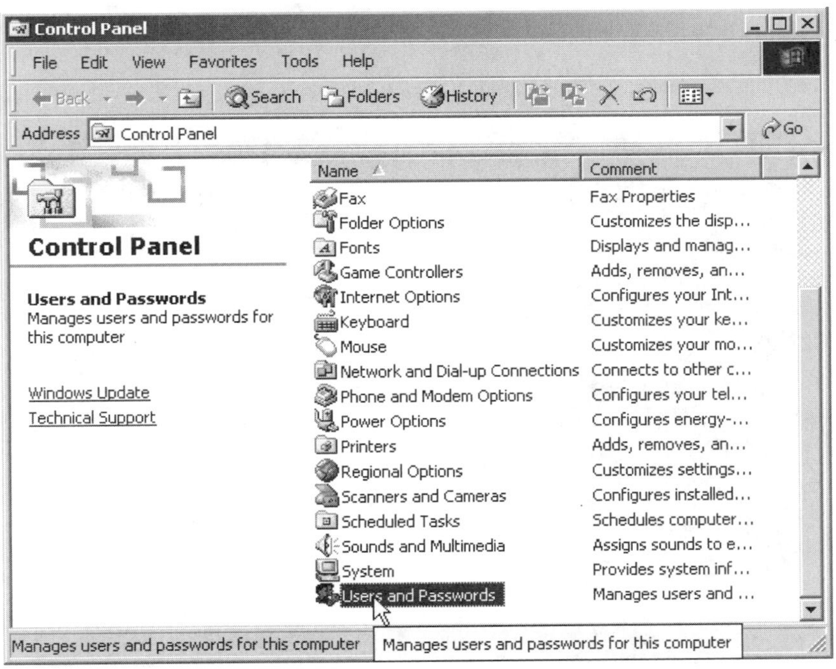

FIGURE 7.5 Users and Passwords

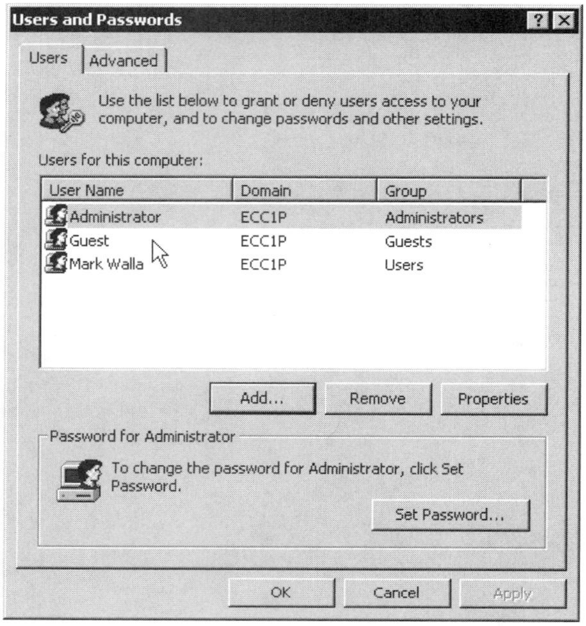

FIGURE 7.6 The Users and Passwords Dialog Box

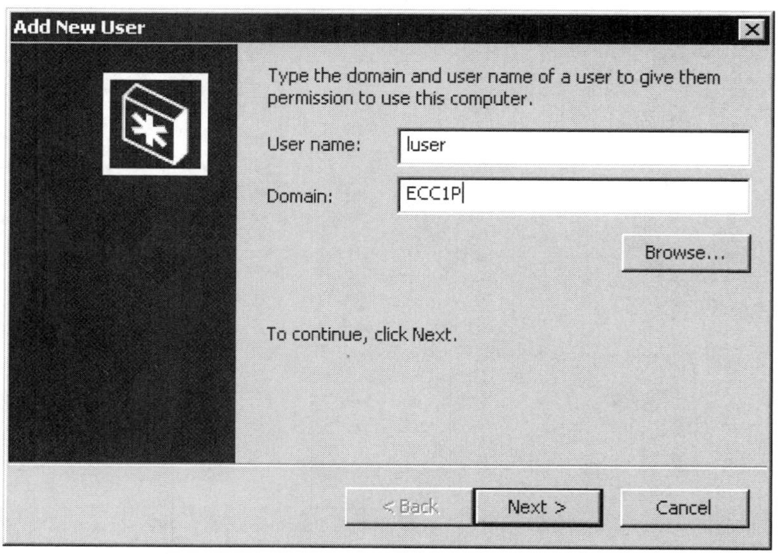

FIGURE 7.7 Assigning Permissions to a New User

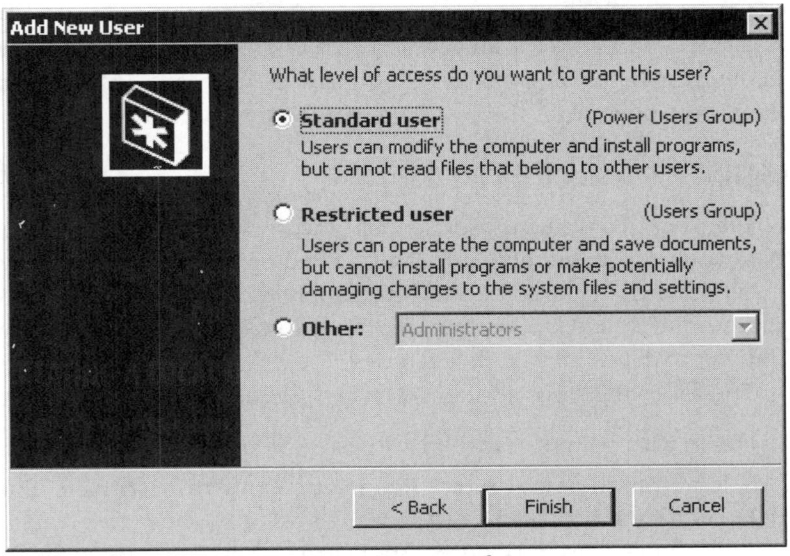

FIGURE 7.8 Setting the User's Permissions Level

4. On the next screen, enter a valid password for the user. Enter it also in the **Confirm password** box.
5. The next screen determines the permissions level for the user (Figure 7.8). There the option assigns the user to the Power Users group; the **Restricted user** selection assigns the user to the Users group. The user may become a member of any other security group using the **Other** option. These initial membership settings may be easily modified later.
6. Click **Finish**.

The account will have the access rights you have just assigned. Denying a user account access to the local system is accomplished by clicking **Remove** in the **Users and Passwords** dialog box (Figure 7.6).

Domain User Accounts

A domain user account allows access to resources in a domain or domain tree. This account is created in a domain container in the Active Directory database and then propagated to all other domain controllers in the domain, permitting the user to log on to any of the domain's systems or resources. The domain model centralizes user account administration from all domain controllers or member servers in the domain.

Once the user has been authenticated against the Active Directory database using the Global Catalog, an access token is obtained. All resources in the domain will determine permissions based on the user's access token and ACL. The access token is dropped from the system when the user logs off.

CREATING A DOMAIN USER ACCOUNT

The creation of a domain user account involves the assignment of a logon name, a password, group membership, and several optional steps. Windows Server 2003 default settings dictate that only a member of the Administrators group (like Domain Admins or Enterprise Admins) can add users to a domain; however, administrative privileges may be delegated.

The following steps should be taken to add a domain user account:

1. Log in with administrative privileges.
2. Select from the **Start** menu **Programs** → **Administrative Tools** → **Active Directory Users and Computers** to bring up the Active Directory Users and Computers snap-in (Figure 7.9). Select the appropriate Active Directory container to house the new user account. This may be a domain or an OU.
3. Next, click **New User** to create the new user account. This will bring up the **New Object—User** window (Figure 7.10).
4. Enter the user's first and last names in the **First name** and **Last name** boxes, respectively. Windows Server 2003 automatically enters the **Full Name**. Enter a user name in the box under **User logon name**. This name, along with the user's domain name (such as *jengineer@Entcert2.com*), uniquely identifies a

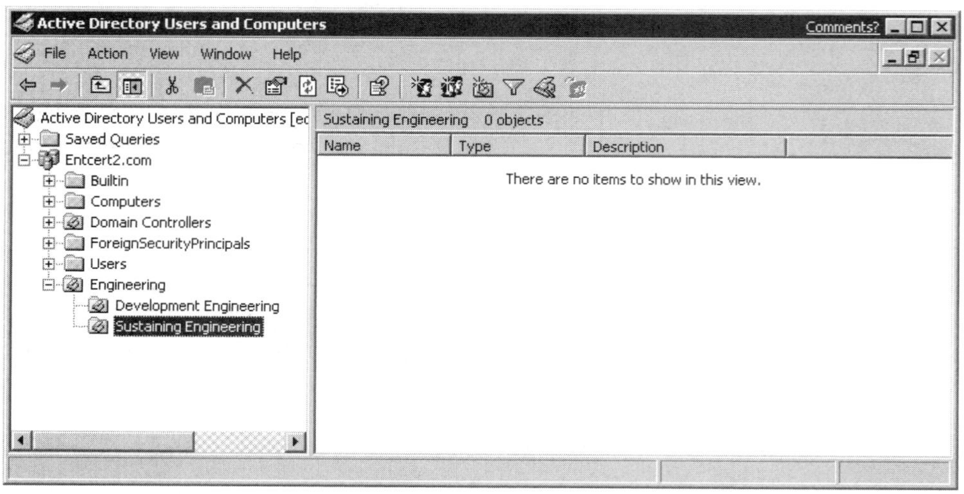

FIGURE 7.9 Active Directory Users and Computers

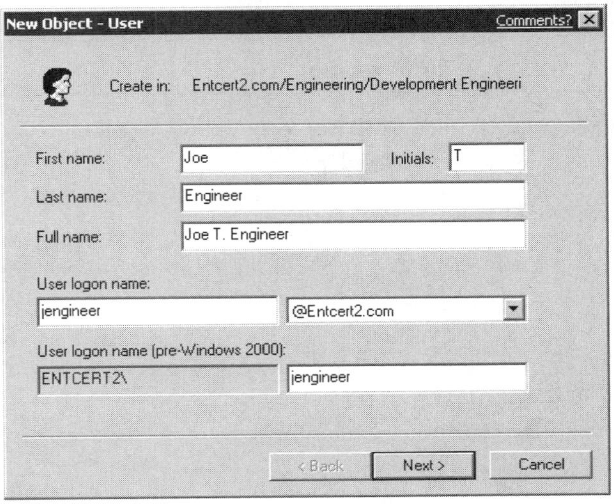

FIGURE 7.10 Creating a New User

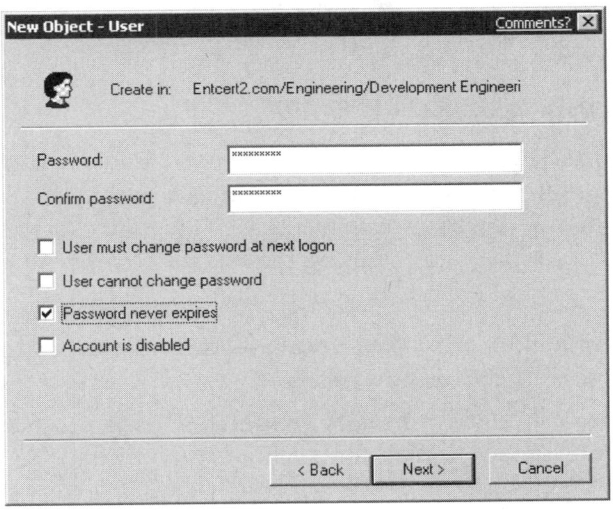

FIGURE 7.11 Password Properties

user in a domain, tree, or forest. This is not to be confused with an external Internet DNS domain name. To access the domain from a client server that is not running Windows Server 2003, use the downlevel (e.g., Windows NT 4.0 and 3.51) logon name as the user account name. Click **Next**.

5. Enter a password for the user in the **Password** box (Figure 7.11). Retype the password in the **Confirm password** box. Check the appropriate boxes for the password options, as shown in Table 7.1.

TABLE 7.1 Password Properties Options

Property	Description
User must change password at next logon	Password just assigned will be changed the first time the new user logs on.
User cannot change password	Account's password can be changed only with Administrator privileges.
Password never expires	User is not required to change his or her password periodically.
Account is disabled	Deactivate an account when user does not need it; may be useful for extended leaves or when planning future accounts.

6. Click **Next** to bring up the user account confirmation screen (Figure 7.12). This verifies the restrictions and the account name assigned to the new domain user account. Click **Finish** to finalize the new account and view the new user within her Active Directory container from the Active Directory Users and Computers snap-in.

UNDERSTANDING USER ACCOUNT PROPERTIES

As with all Windows Server 2003 objects, the user account has a number of associated properties or attributes. Once the domain user account has been created, these properties may be modified from the Active Directory Users and Computers snap-in. Set the appropriate tabs by using the following steps. An explanation of each tab setting is provided in subsequent sections.

1. From the **Start** menu, select → **Programs** → **Administrative Tools** → **Active Directory Users and Computers** snap-in.
2. Right-click the desired user → select **Properties**. Table 7.2 shows the default tabs in the basic Windows Server installation (with Terminal Server).

User Account Properties General Tab

The General tab (Figure 7.13) contains the domain user's first and last names, description (usually a job title that will appear on the management console), office location, telephone number(s), e-mail address, and home page(s).

User Account Properties Address Tab

The Address tab (Figure 7.14) should contain a post office mailing address. It's helpful to have this information when you want to mail software upgrades, manuals, and other packages.

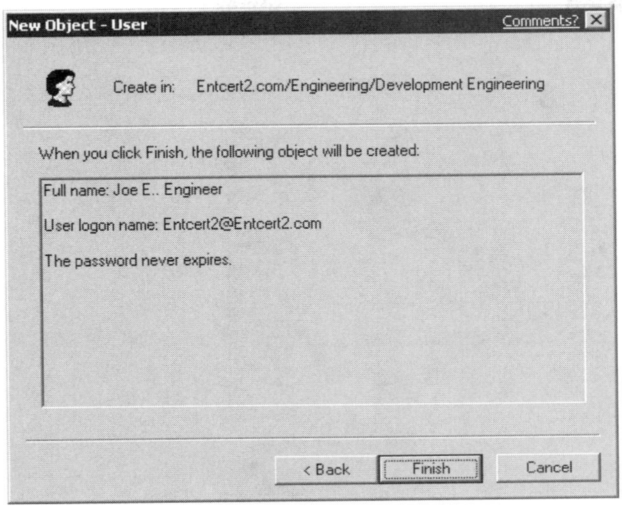

FIGURE 7.12 Finalizing a User Account

TABLE 7.2 User Account Properties Tabs

Tabs	Description
Member Of	The user's defined group membership
Dial-in	Remote access and callback options
General	User's first name, last name, display name description, office location, telephone, e-mail, and Web pages
Address	User's post office mailing address
Account	Logon name, domain, logon hours, logon to server name, account options, and account expiration date
Profile	User profile path, profile script, home directory path and server, and shared document folder location
Telephones/Notes	Home, pager, and mobile phone numbers and comments on where to contact user
Organization	Job title, company, department, manager, and people who report to user Environment Applications to run from Terminal server client
Sessions	Timeouts for Terminal Services
Remote Control	Permissions for monitoring Terminal Service sessions
Terminal Service Profile	Location for Terminal Service home directory

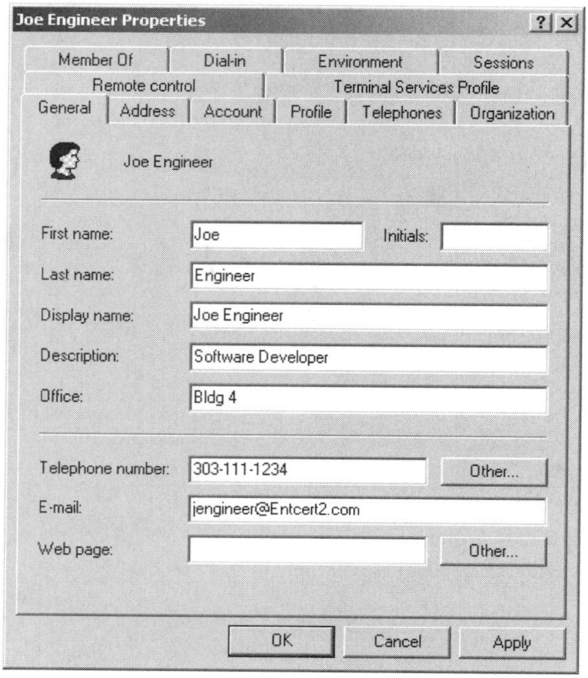

FIGURE 7.13 The User Properties General Tab

User Properties Account Tab

The Account tab (Figure 7.15) looks very similar to the screen used to create the domain user account. However, there are two new options here, listed in Table 7.3.

Clicking **Logon Hours** displays the days and times of the week that the domain user is permitted to log on to the domain (Figure 7.16), which is useful for preventing employees from logging on while backups are being performed. To prevent sharing violations, current user sessions with backup targets must be terminated before backups begin. Logon hour selections are made in two ways:

- Select day and hour cells and click **Logon Permitted** to indicate the time "zone" during which a user is permitted to log on.
- Select day and hour cells and click **Logon Denied** to create a time zone during which a user is not permitted to log on.

NOTE Changes to the user account will not affect a user who is logged on to the system. The restrictions will apply during the next attempted connection.

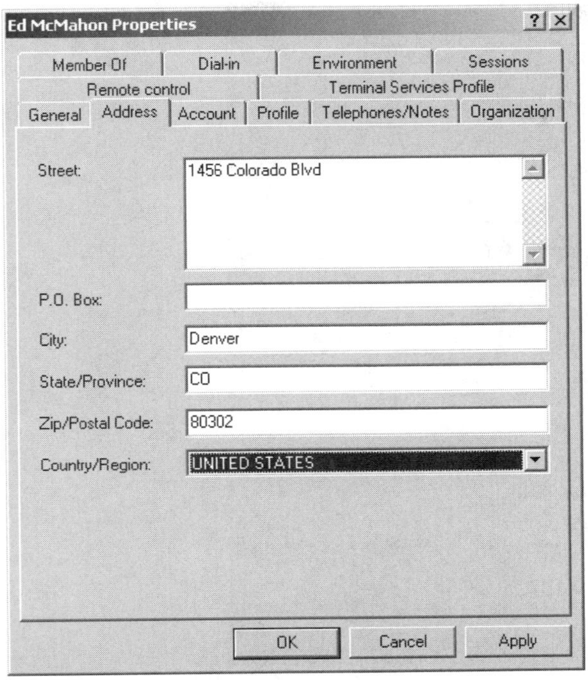

FIGURE 7.14 The User Properties Address Tab

TABLE 7.3 User Properties Account Tab Options

Definition	Description
Save password as encrypted clear text	Must be selected on Macintosh computers, which store passwords only in encrypted clear text.
Account expires	Takes precedence over the **Password never expires selection**. The **Account expires** date must be advanced to reenable the user account.

Clicking **Log On To** from the **Account properties** tab displays the **Logon Workstations** window (Figure 7.17). This facility allows the administrator to restrict user from logging on to certain computers in the domain. The main issue here is that the computer name must be the NetBIOS name. Also, the NetBIOS protocol must be installed on all machines that use this account policy. Remember that a machine's NetBIOS name must be fewer than 16 characters.

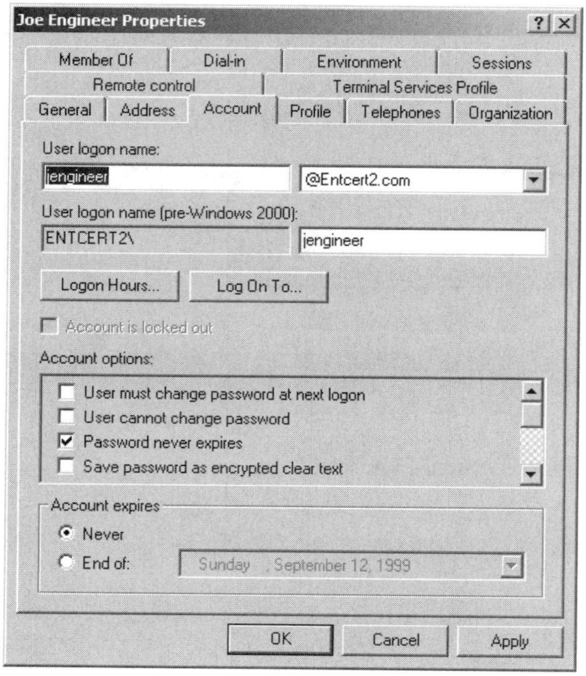

FIGURE 7.15 The User Properties Account Tab

User Account Properties Telephones Tab

The Telephones tab allows the storage of home, pager, mobile, fax, and IP phone numbers for quick reference (Figure 7.18). Entering information into the boxes of this tab is optional. Clicking **Other** allows you to enter alternative numbers. The **Comments** section provides room to track the user's schedule and availability at these numbers.

User Account Properties Member Of Tab

Member Of (Figure 7.19) is perhaps one of the most important user account properties tabs. Each domain user belongs by default to the domain users' group. To add the user to other security groups, click **Add** and choose a group from the directory. Group selection can be made from the current domain and trusted domains. As discussed in subsequent sections, the user inherits the appropriate permissions and rights associated with that group.

User Account Properties Dial-in

A user can be granted access to the domain through a telephone dial-in or virtual private network (VPN) connection only if **Allow access** is selected on the **Dial-in** tab (Figure 7.20). When the domain is switched to native mode, the **Control Access through Remote Access Policy** option is displayed instead.

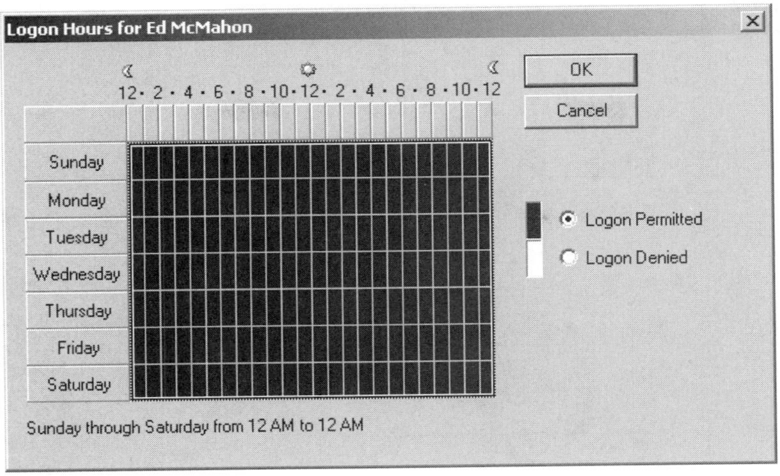

FIGURE 7.16 The Logon Hours Dialog Box

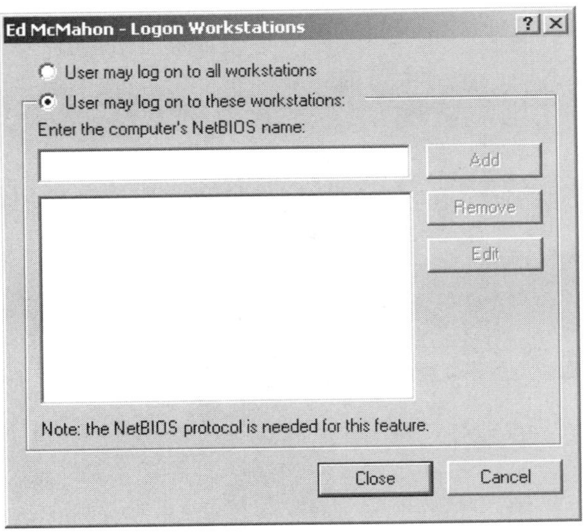

FIGURE 7.17 The Logon Workstations Window

There are three options for the treatment of dial-in authority. The default is to permit no callbacks; the user can dial directly into the domain through a Remote Access Service (RAS) server to gain access to the network. The second option permits a defined callback; the user can specify a callback telephone number that the RAS server will recognize in order to establish a remote session. This is good for traveling professionals and prevents large long-distance telephone bills. It also provides phone records of people who log on to the server. Finally, a single predefined number can be established for dial-in security. The RAS server will call back only the

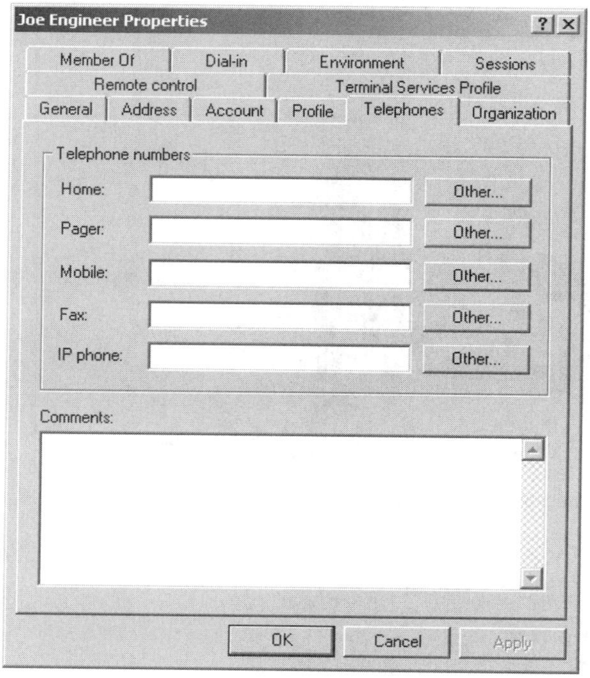

FIGURE 7.18 The Telephones Tab

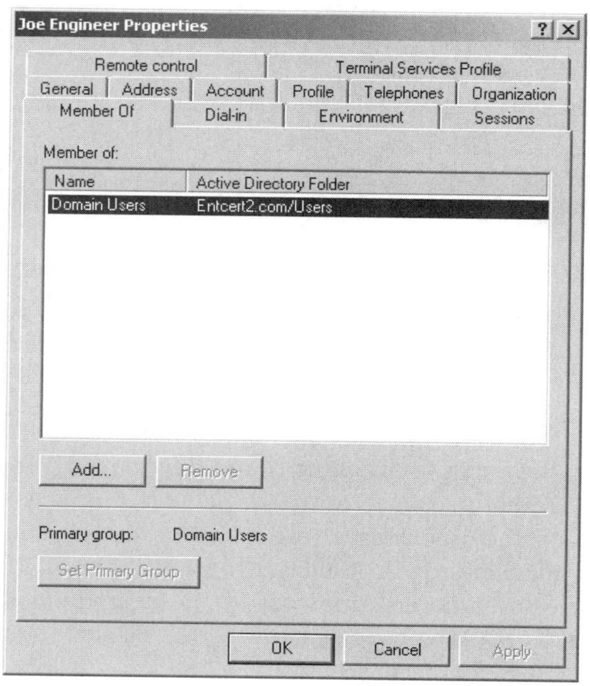

FIGURE 7.19 The Member Of Tab

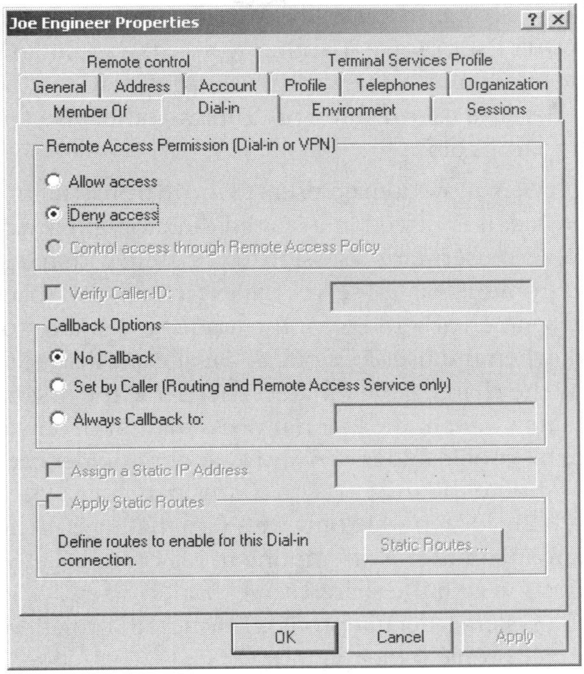

FIGURE 7.20 The Dial-in Tab

number designated in the **Always Callback to** field, so only someone at that telephone number can establish a RAS session.

User Profiles

A user's profile determines the desktop environment. This includes such items as the display type, applications available from the **Start** menu, shortcuts on the desktop, and desktop arrangement. Connections to remote computers are remembered and reestablished from the last logon session. Profiles offer consistent desktop settings and document management regardless of which system in the domain the user logs on to.

USER PROFILE TYPES

Every user has a profile that defines how, when, and where a logon is possible. The three types of user profile in Windows Server 2003 are:

- *Local user profiles* are maintained on each system the user logs on to in the user's profile directory. If the user logs on to another system in the domain, the local profile does not apply. The first time the user logs on to a system, a profile is created if one does not already exist. It is copied from the \Document and Settings\Default User profile. In other words, the Default User folder is a template for the creation of the new local user profile, which is created in the Document and Settings*userid* directory (unless otherwise specified in the user account Properties tab).

- *Roaming user profiles* allow domain users to move from system to system and maintain one profile. It is placed in a shared directory on a server in the domain, and whenever a user starts a session on a system within that domain, the profile is copied from the shared server folder to local disk space. All the documents and environmental settings for the roaming user are stored locally on the system, and, when the user logs off, all changes to the locally stored profile are copied to the shared server folder. Therefore, the first time a roaming user logs on to a new system the logon process may take some time, depending on how large his profile folder is. A My Documents folder can be very large. However, the next time the user logs on to this particular system, the profile server will update the local profile only with files that have changed since the last session. If a roaming user is attempting to log on to a system that cannot establish a connection with the shared server folder, a new local profile is created based on the system's default profile. This new information is not copied to the shared server profile folder.

NOTE Windows Server 2003 has added policies to govern roaming user behavior including the ability to disable roaming profiles and to prevent propagation of profiles made to the local system to the users shared profile folder.

- *Mandatory user profiles* are read-only and cannot be changed. Modifications to the desktop are not saved to the user's profile once she logs off, so mandatory profiles are used when users must see the same desktop consistently. A user's profile is made mandatory by changing the file extension on the NTUSER.dat file to NTUSER.man.

User Profile Directory Structure

Regardless of whether the user's profile is roaming or local, the profile directory has a common folder structure. Table 7.4 describes the standard Windows Server 2003 profile folders.

There are also some hidden profile directories (Table 7.5 and Figure 7.21) that can be viewed by selecting **Tools** → **Folder Options** from Windows Explorer, clicking the **View** tab, and then selecting **Show hidden files** from the **View** tab's advanced settings.

TABLE 7.4 Basic Contents of the Profile Directory

Sub-Profile Directory	Description
Cookies	Personalized data files stored on your system by Web sites that you visit; must be disabled/enabled at the browser level
Desktop	Shortcuts and files that comprise the user's desktop
Favorites	Files and folders used as Favorite pull-down options from My Computer, My Computer in Explorer mode, and Internet Explorer
My Documents	Default location for file storage of Microsoft Office products
Start Menu	All applications the user will have access to from the Start menu

TABLE 7.5 Profile Files Hidden by Default

File	Description
Application Data	Application-specific data such as preferences and licensing.
Local Settings	Contains a history of Web sites visited through the browser and all documents, applications, and Help pages accessed from My Computer, classified into today's, yesterday's, last week's, and two weeks' ago time frames. Application data, such as Outlook Express Inbox, is also stored here.
NetHood	Domains and file structures accessed from My Network Places. This is the system's current network neighborhood.
PrintHood	Printer data information and shortcuts.
My Recent Documents	Recently accessed files and folders.
SendTo	Shortcuts to common file storage areas.
Templates	Templates for Microsoft Office applications.

ALL USER AND INDIVIDUAL USER PROFILE SETTINGS

Besides understanding the contents of folders in a user's profile, it is important to understand the \Document and Settings\All User profiles. Two program groups are supported under Windows Server 2003 (Figure 7.22): common and personal. The most effective profile is the individual user's profile combined with the All Users profile

Common program groups are applied to all users who log on to a system. Their profile is located in the \Document and Settings\All User folder and includes

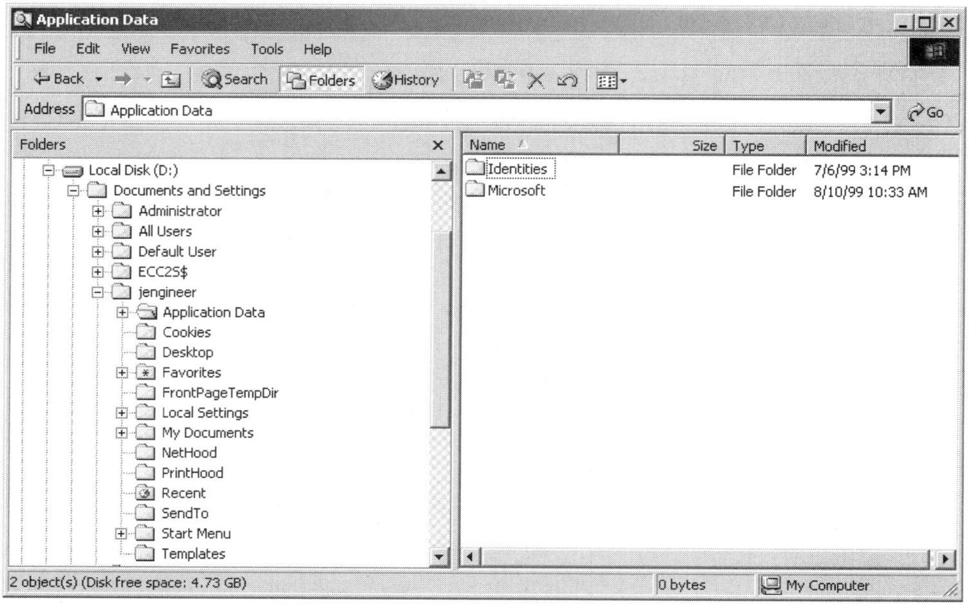

FIGURE 7.21 User Profile Directories

a subset of the folder structure previously discussed. For instance, the **Start** menu folder in the \Document and Settings\All User directory dictates program availability from the **Start** menu for all users who log on to the system. Each user's personal profile, locally located in \Document and Settings*username* (user name varies), is then overlaid on this common profile to provide additional Start menu application access and custom desktop setups. The user's personal profile, with the information in Table 7.5, can be either locally stored on each system in the domain or defined as roaming.

NOTE The \Document and Settings\All Users folder contains profile information that applies to all users. For example, say you wanted to restrict access to Microsoft Excel from the Start menu. The \Document and Settings\All Users\Start Menu\Program folder would contain the Microsoft Excel shortcut if it was installed for general access. To restrict some users from access to it from the **Start → Program** menu, remove the shortcut from the All Users folder and place it in selected personal user profiles. Of course, the Microsoft Excel executable should be restricted to users intended to run the application. Distributing applications to specific users could also be handled using the assign and publish methods, which are discussed in Chapter 8.

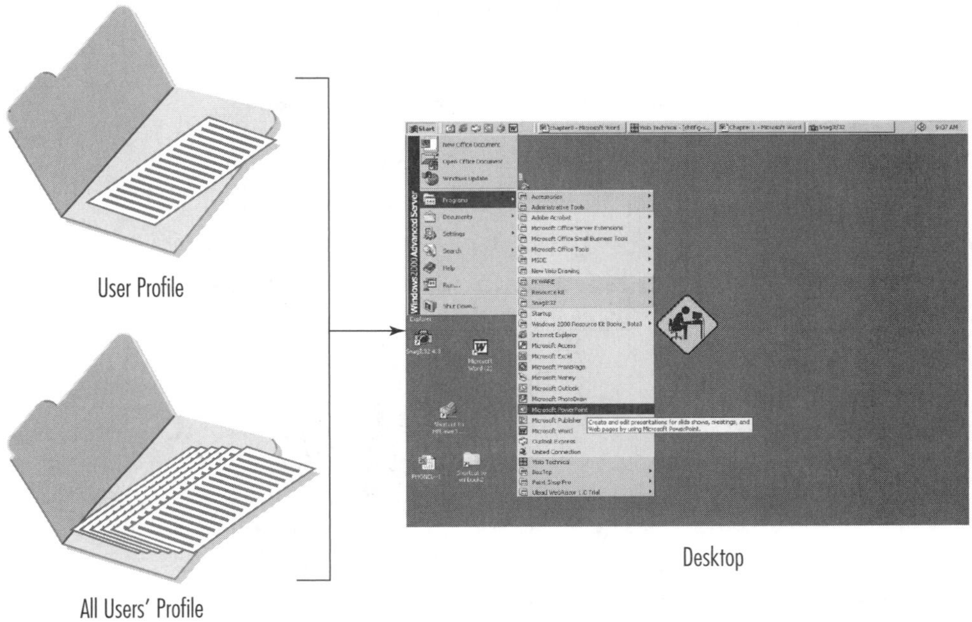

FIGURE 7.22 Combining All Users and User Profiles

CREATING USER PROFILES

Now that you have some background, we can apply the user profile to individual user accounts. The Profile tab (Figure 7.23) displays several fields in relation to a user's profile:

- **Profile path** dictates where a user's profile will be stored. If no directory is entered, the default location is \Documents and Settings*username*.
- **Logon script** contains the path to an optional executable or batch file. Users who are logged on to Windows Server 2003 systems may take advantage of JavaScript (.js) and Visual Basic Scripting (.vbs) in addition to the traditional MS-DOS command scripts (.bat, .com, and .exe). Stick with the MS-DOS scripts for downlevel operating systems that may not support the Windows Scripting Host (WSH).

The home directory is specified on the local machine in the form Drive label:\ directory path or targeted on a shared folder accessible through the network. The network connection requires a network drive letter (available from the pull-down menu), which identifies how the remote connection will be referenced from the

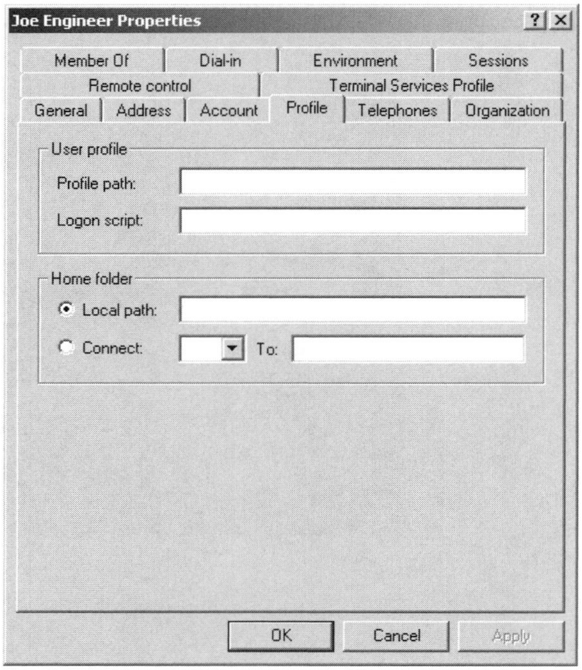

FIGURE 7.23 Profile

local machine, a machine name, and a directory path. The **To** field should be in the form \\system name\directory path. The remote directory will be displayed from My Computer and will be the default directory within the command prompt. This is a good way to centralize your documents on a networked server for backup convenience and version control.

NOTE The command prompt defaults to the home directory. However, if most administrative shell scripts, for example, are located in a directory called d:\scripts, you may want to make that directory your default instead. The home directory is also the default file storage directory for some applications such as Notepad. These applications will default to the home directory if it contains other files that match the application's type. Most Microsoft Office applications, however, default to the My Documents directory and ignore the home directory setting.

Local User Profile Setup Example

The following example illustrates how to set up a user profile. For example, create a new user account with the user ID 1user.

1. View existing user profiles by clicking **Start** → **Settings** → **Control Panel**. Double-click **System**. Click **Advanced** and click **Settings** (Figure 7.24).
2. Notice that **Profiles stored on this computer** does not list luser, because a profile for 1user has not been created yet.
3. Log off your system and log back on under the new account, luser. The profile for luser has now been created by copying \Document and Settings\Default User to \Document and Settings\luser.

NOTE You may have to configure local system group policies to permit local log on. From a policy setting snap-in (see Chapter 8), add the luser to the policy setting list by invoking **Computer Configuration** → **Windows Settings** → **Security Settings** → **Local Policies** → **User Rights Assignment** → **Log on locally**.

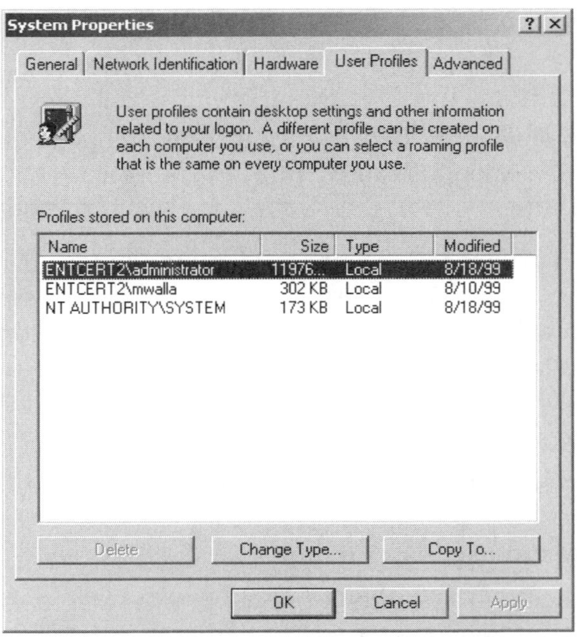

FIGURE 7.24 User Profiles

4. Right-click the desktop and select **Properties**. Choose a new theme from the **Theme** pull-down menu. Log off and log back on as Administrator.
5. Repeat step 1 and view the current user profiles. The account luser should now exist as a local profile.
6. Log off and log back on as luser. Notice that the user's screen background is preserved.

Roaming User Profile Setup Example

The roaming user profile is set up by the following steps:

1. Log on as Administrator and run **mmc** from the **command prompt**. Add the **Active Directory Users and Computers** snap-in and create a new domain user account named ruser.
2. Create a new share with Full Control permissions to the Everyone group on a network server called *profiles*. This will later be referenced as \\servername\profiles.
3. From the **Active Directory Users and Computers** snap-in for the domain, right-click **ruser** and select **Properties**. Select **Profile** and type the name of the roaming user folder in the **Profile path** box (Figure 7.25). Use the form \\servername\profiles\ruser to ensure that the correct network server path is accessed.

NOTE When setting up a roaming user profile, it is extremely important to follow these steps precisely. Any deviation will cause permission problems.

---

4. Before we log on to the new account, a profile must be copied to the roaming profiles directory (\\servername\profiles\ruser) so that the roaming profile folder is used and a local one is not created. Open **Control Panel** and double-click the **Systems** icon. Click the **Advanced** tab and click **User Profiles Settings**.
5. Select the **luser** account created earlier and click **Copy To**.
6. Enter the roaming profile folder directory in the form \\servername\Profiles\ruser (Figure 7.26).
7. Under **Permitted to use,** click **Change**.
8. Type **ruser** in the **Enter the object name to select** field (Figure 7.27).
9. Click **OK** to create the new directory \\servername\profiles\ruser, copy the luser profile to the new location, and permit the new remote user, ruser, access to the directory and child directories.

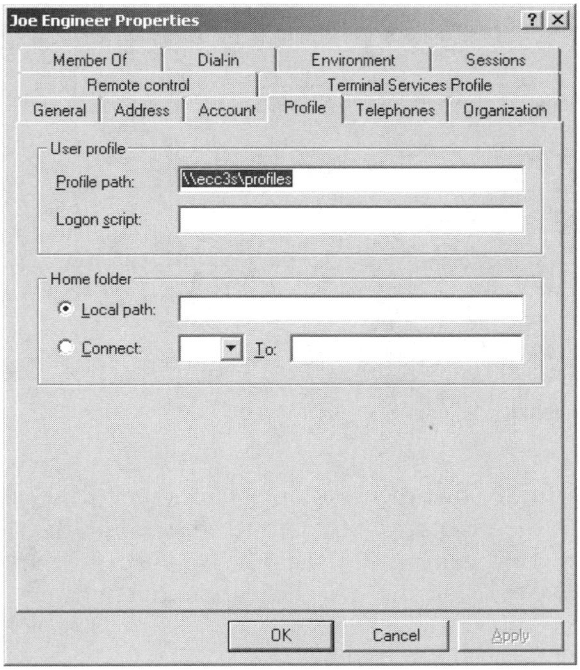

FIGURE 7.25 Roaming User's Profile Path

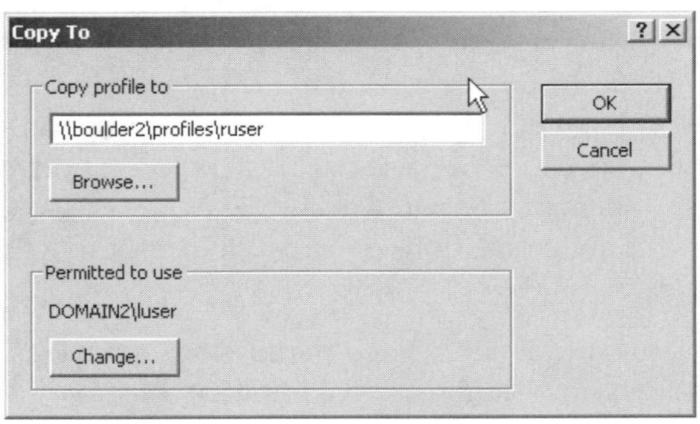

FIGURE 7.26 The Copy To Window

10. Click **OK** on the **Copy To** dialog box.
11. Click **OK** on the **User Profiles** box. Click **OK** on the **Systems Properties** dialog box.
12. Permit local logon if system is a domain controller (see earlier note).
13. Close all applications and log off.

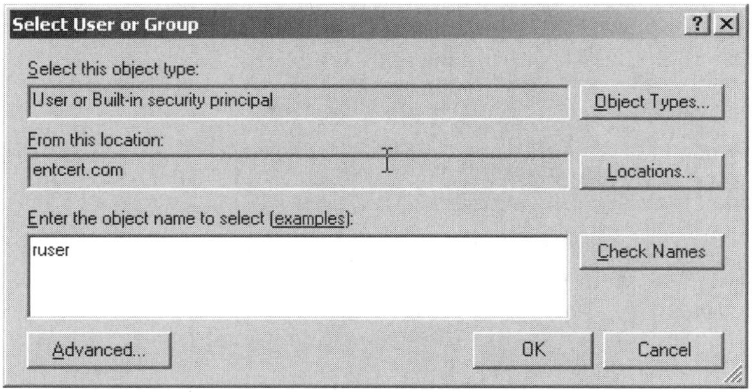

FIGURE 7.27 Choosing the User

14. Log in as **ruser**. Notice that the desktop environment is initially the same as luser. Changes to the ruser environment will be saved on the shared \\server\profiles directory. Try logging on from another server in the same domain. The ruser's profile should follow the user throughout the domain.

GROUPS

A *group* is a collection of users, computers, and other entities. It can be a Windows Server 2003 built-in group or one created by the system administrator to conform to required attributes. Windows Server uses standard groups to reflect common attributes and tasks. These groups are built in to the OS so that common tasks can be assigned to users with a defined set of specifications and permissions. For instance, members of the Backup group will have access to tape drives, backup applications, and server folders that require backup.

Groups enforce security permissions or carry out distribution functions. They perform three main tasks:

1. Security groups primarily assign limited permissions to groups that need access to certain folders, applications, and computers.
2. Security groups also filter out the effect of group policies assigned to their members through a Group Policy Object (GPO). (See Chapter 8, "Group Policies.")
3. Distribution groups facilitate e-mail and contact information.

NOTE Security groups determine how a GPO will be applied to an Active Directory container. Security groups do not add members to the container. They only restrict or enable current members to apply the GPO.

Group-to-Group and Group-to-User Relationships

Rights and privileges are assigned at the group level. They represent an accumulation of the rights and privileges of all the groups to which a user belongs. Typically a user belongs to more than one group and therefore is granted or denied rights on that basis. To complicate this relationship, groups can be nested, overlapped, or completely independent. Say, for example, that three groups exist for an organizational unit, and that Group 3 members have been nested as automatic members of Group 1, while Group 2 is independent. Thus, User 1 has been assigned to Group 1 and Group 2. Since Group 3 is also a member of Group 1, User 2 inherits the rights of Group 1. On the other hand, User 2 is assigned to Group 2 and Group 3. The relationship between Groups 1 and 3 flows only one way. Therefore, User 1 does not become a member of Group 3 and so does not inherit any of that group's rights (Figure 7.28).

Let's take a look at the relationship from a slightly different perspective. A single user, computer, or group can belong to many groups. As shown in Figure 7.29, User 4 belongs to both Group 2 and Group 3. Because Group 1 is a member of Group 2, User 2 and User 5 have all rights associated with Groups 1 and 2. However, User 3, User 4, and Computer 2 do not receive Group 1 access rights.

A user's rights and privileges are cumulative. If a user is a member of two groups, one having Read and Write privileges and the other having Modify privileges, then the user has Read/Write/Modify rights on an object. By the same token, if any of the groups is denied rights to that object, the user will inherit that denial. The Deny access permission has priority over Allow access permissions. Any member of a group that has been denied permission to an object may not

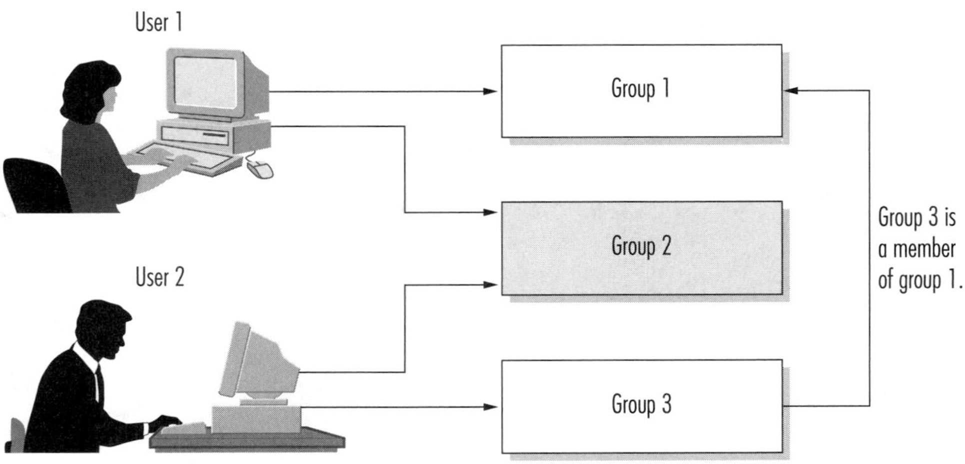

FIGURE 7.28 Relationships of Groups and Users. User 2 becomes a member of Group 1 via inheritance.

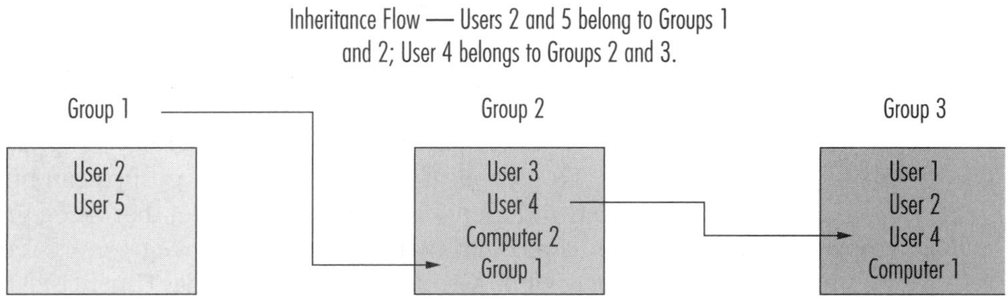

FIGURE 7.29 An Alternative View of Group Relationships

reinstate or counteract rights with membership to another group. (For greater detail, see Chapter 9, "Permissions Security, Folder Sharing, and Dfs.")

NOTE It is good practice to keep group nesting to a minimum. The reason is visibility—a complicated group membership and permission structure makes it difficult to determine a user's rights. The Deny access permission should also be used sparingly. Overriding permissions that another group has established complicates the user's privilege level. Never use the Deny access permission with the Everyone or the Authenticated Users groups.

Group Scope

Proper planning of group structure affects maintainability, especially in an enterprise environment where multiple domains are involved. Windows Server 2003 groups are classified into one of three group scopes. Each deserves careful examination. Group membership is predicated on a group's intended scope. Underscoring this entire discussion are the assumptions that trust relationships exist between domains and that access is determined by the ACL of the network resource. The three group scopes follow:

- *Domain local groups* assign access permissions to global domain groups for local domain resources.
- *Global groups* provide access to resources in other trusted domains.
- *Universal groups* grant access to resources in all trusted domains.

NOTE Participating domain member servers can view all directory groups. However, group scope is not visible from them. Determining whether a security group is domain local or global must be done at a domain controller. It can be made easier by choosing a group name that identifies the group's scope. For example, instead of calling a group *Engineering*, call it *Global Engineering* or *Local Engineering*. This may prove troublesome, however, to users.

DOMAIN LOCAL GROUPS

Members of domain local groups can be from any domain, although group permissions are assigned only to resources in the local domain. These groups may contain users, computers, or groups from any domain in the enterprise (Figure 7.30), and they also may contain individual users from their own domain.

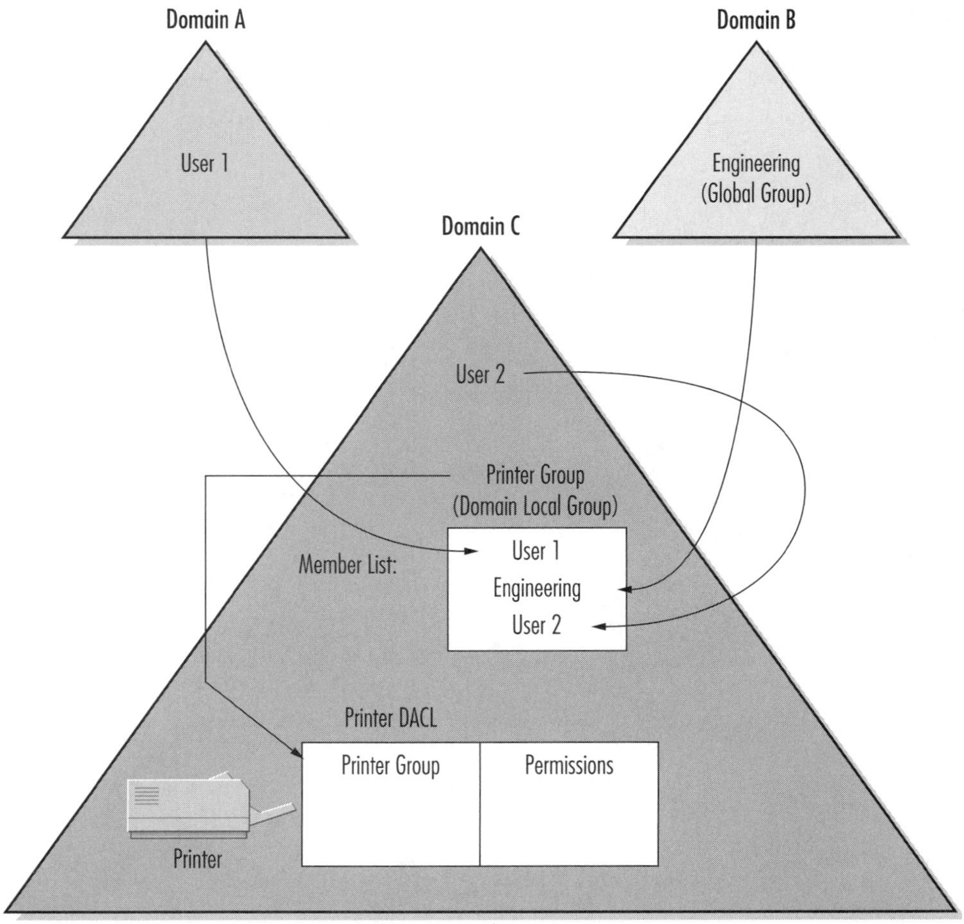

FIGURE 7.30 A Domain Local Group

The domain local group may be assigned permissions to any object in its domain. For example, in Figure 7.30 the Printer Group is the domain local group in Domain C and is assigned access rights to a printer in that domain only. The Printer Group may not be assigned permissions to objects outside its own domain. When implementing domain local groups, some additional guidelines should be followed. First, let's define *global group.*

NOTE Although individual users may be assigned permissions to resources, this is not recommended.

GLOBAL GROUPS

Global group members may come only from the local domain, but they can be assigned permissions to resources in any trusted domain. They may also join any group in a trusted domain (Figure 7.31). For example, User 1 and Group 1, created

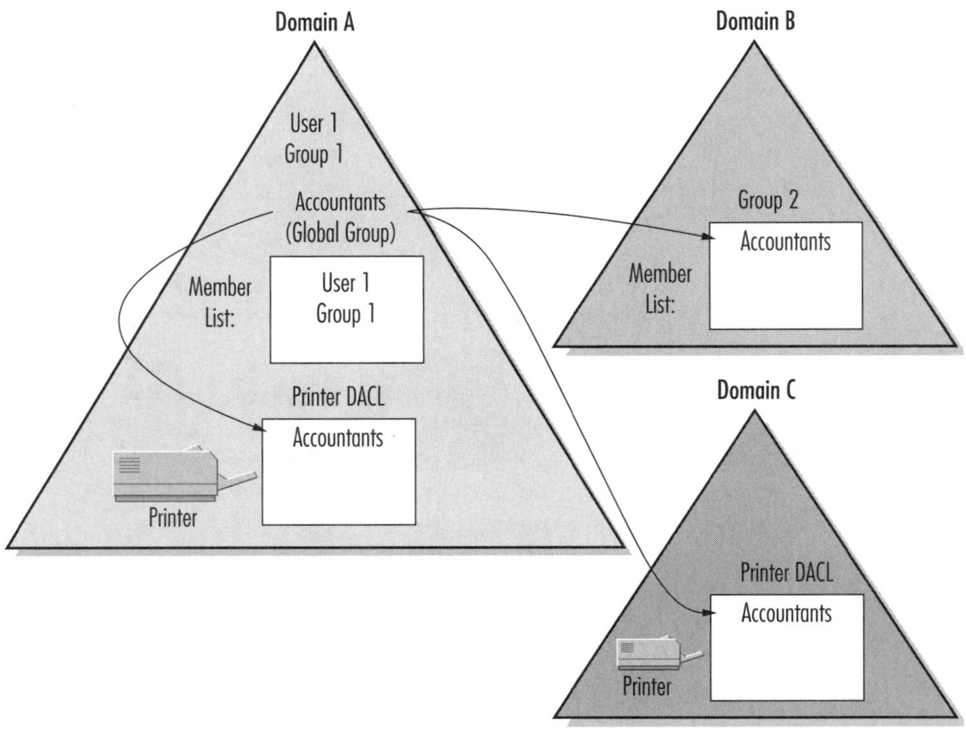

FIGURE 7.31 A Global Group

in Domain A, are members of the global Accountants group, which is then assigned membership to Group 2 as well as permissions to a printer in Domain C and to a printer in its own Domain A. Again, this only demonstrates global group capabilities and does not reflect how they should be implemented.

NOTE Although the Accountants' global domain group may be assigned permissions to resources, this is not recommended.

UNIVERSAL GROUPS

Universal group members are from any domain and may be assigned permissions to any resource in any trusted domain. The universal group has no restrictions on its member list and can be assigned to any object throughout the enterprise.

NOTE Universal groups are allowed only in native-mode Windows Server 2003 environments. Native mode requires that all domain controllers be promoted to Windows Server 2003 Active Directory.

Group Types

In addition to proper group scope, the group type must be determined. The two group types are

- *Security (security principals)*. These groups may be assigned to discretionary access control lists (DACLs) with associated permissions. They may also be used for e-mail distribution.
- *Distribution (not security principals)*. These groups cannot be assigned permissions through DACLs. They are intended only for e-mail distribution.

Since both security and distribution groups can be used for e-mail distribution, why do distribution groups exist? Optimization. When a user logs on to the domain, a security token is created that consists of the user's account SID and his group SIDs. Creating the token adds time to the logon process. Additionally, the security token is presented to any system a user accesses throughout the enterprise; and if it is large, it creates more network traffic. Distribution groups do not participate with security credentials and are not included in the user's security token. Adding a user to multiple distribution groups will not increase the size of the user's security token. Security groups may be converted to distribution groups and vice versa as long as the domain is operating in native mode. A mixed-mode environment does not support such conversions.

Using Groups

There is no such thing as a perfect world when defining groups in a heterogeneous computing environment. Windows Server 2003 supports several group scopes, and the system administrator must understand how to use them.

The Windows Server 2003 group scopes may seem confusing at first. Group management might be less complex if universal groups could always be implemented. However, universal scope has some practical drawbacks, chiefly that it works only in native mode. Most enterprise networks require downlevel compatibility. Because of the heterogeneity of a mixed Windows Server 2003 and Windows NT environment, the administrator must deal with global and domain local groups. Another consideration is that universal groups tax the network by passing group membership information between trusted domains and forests.

The Global Catalog stores domain local and global domain group names, and replicates changes made to group names to all GC servers. It maintains universal group membership on all GC servers as well. Whenever a member is added or removed from a universal group, the change is replicated throughout the trusted domain structure.

The recommended implementation for global and domain local groups involves further restrictions on group use. In general, object permissions should be assigned to domain local groups, whereas users and computer accounts should be placed in global groups. The global groups are then nested in domain local groups to gain access to network resources. To illustrate, we will look in depth at group implementation using default Windows Server 2003 groups.

DEFAULT USER ACCOUNT MEMBERSHIP

Consider the case of a user named Joe Engineer with a logon name of jengineer. Joe's user account is created in a Windows Server 2003 domain and added to the global group Domain Users by default (Figure 7.32). The Domain Users group is a member of the domain local group Users, and the Users group is used to assign permissions to local objects within a system or domain.

The Administrator account behaves in a similar fashion. The Administrator is a member of the Domain Admins global group by default. The Domain Admins group is a member of the domain local group Administrators, and the Administrators group is included in ACLs for objects throughout the system.

Remember that these are default conditions and can be modified with the necessary authority. New security groups should be implemented the same way.

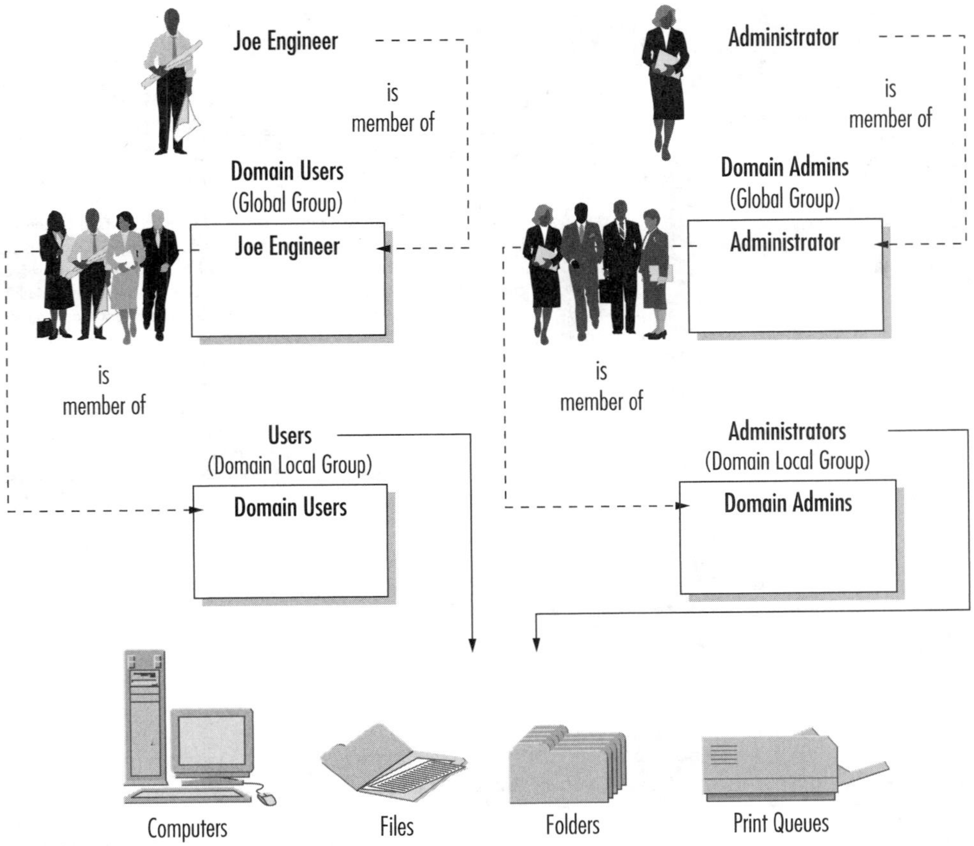

FIGURE 7.32 A Sample Domain Membership

Built-in Local Groups

The Built-in folder contains predefined groups that reflect common functions. Figure 7.33 lists default domain local groups from the perspective of the Active Directory Users and Computers administrative snap-in tool. Although the membership and permissions associated with these groups (Table 7.6) can be modified, they cannot be deleted or removed from the system.

Common Global Groups

The Users folder (Figure 7.34) contains the default global domain groups (Table 7.7), which grant domain-wide privileges through domain local group memberships. Default domain local group membership grants global domain groups sweeping access rights throughout the network.

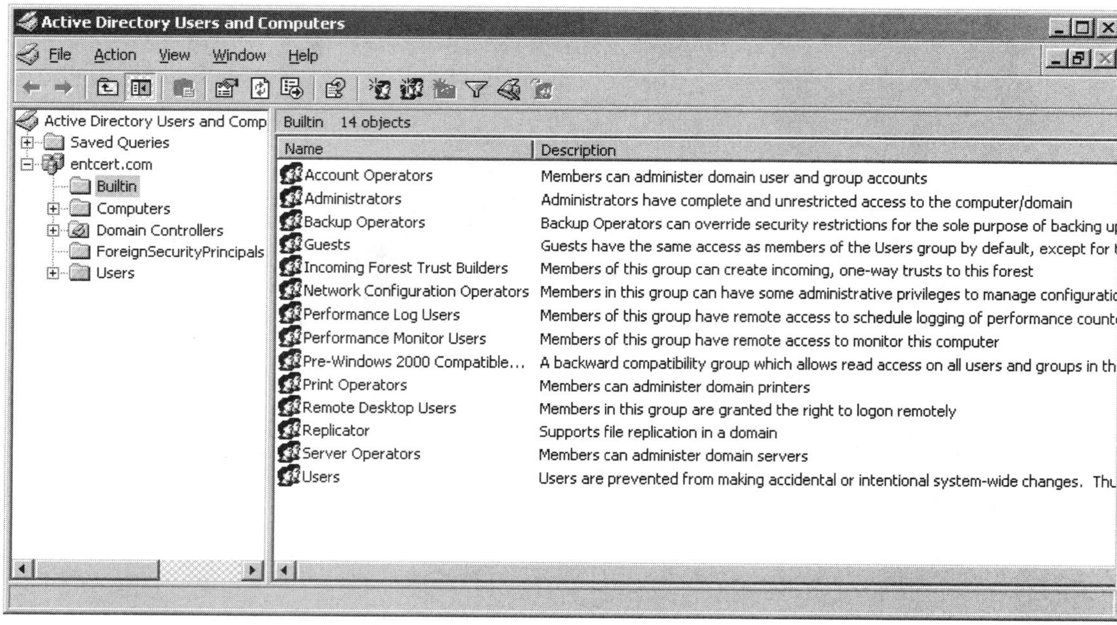

FIGURE 7.33 Default Domain Local Groups

TABLE 7.6 Domain Local Group Members

Group	Permissions/Access Level
Administrators	Full control over the local computer system with all rights and capabilities; default members include the Domain Admins, Enterprise Admins, and Administrator accounts.
Account Operators	Administration of Domain Users.
Backup Operators	Back up and restore files on the local system regardless of permissions; also log on and shut down on the system. Group policies can restrict these permissions.
Guests	Limited logon/shutdown on the local system.
Print Operators	Administration of the local printers.
Replicator	Allows Active Directory replication functions; only persons supporting Replicator services should have membership.
Server Operators	Administration of the local system.
Users	Application execution, printer access, logon/shutdown/locking, and local group creation and modification; domain users are members by default.

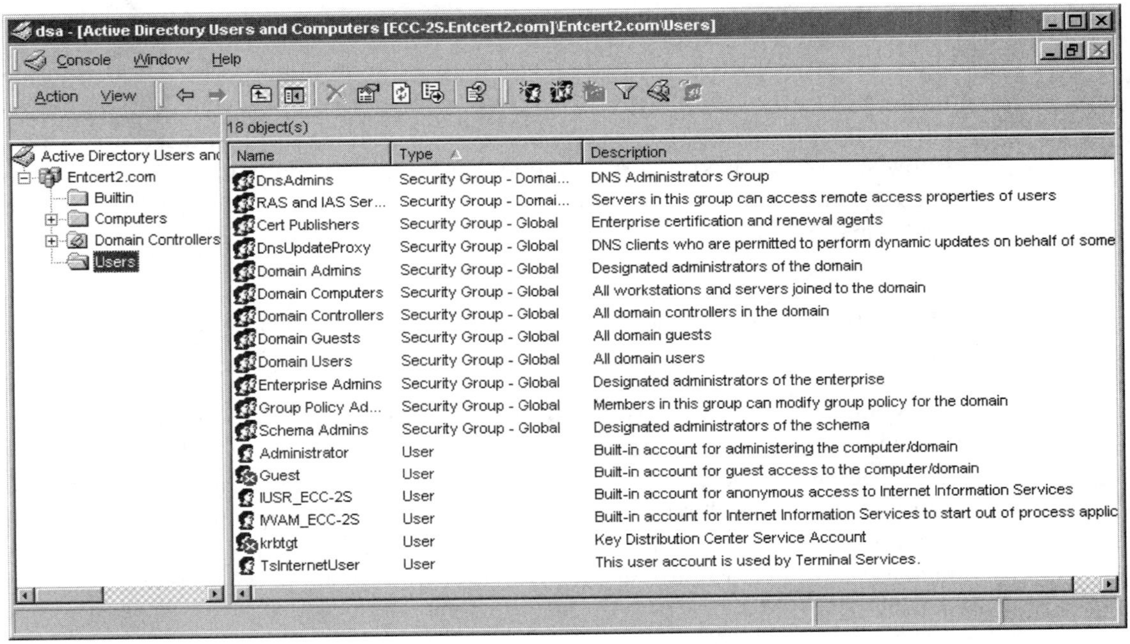

FIGURE 7.34 Global Groups

TABLE 7.7 Global Group Members

Group	Permissions/Access Level
Domain Admins	Sweeping administrative privileges on all systems throughout the domain
Domain Computers	All domain computers
Domain Controllers	All domain controllers
Domain Guests	Membership to the Guests domain local group
Domain Users	Membership to the Users domain local group
Enterprise Admins	Membership to the Domain Admins group for each domain, granting forest-level privileges and rights
Group Policy Creators Owners	Members allowed to modify group policy
Schema Admins	Members permitted to modify the Active Directory schema

ASSIGNING GROUPS

Three group scopes imply three implementation strategies. Thus, a system administrator must decide the type of group a situation requires. Think about the resources the group needs to access. If you are assigning permission, a domain local group should be used. Users inside and outside your domain should be put in global groups and added to domain local groups to provide access within your local domain.

Another way to choose a group type is to ask two questions:

- Is the purpose of the group to collect resources for user access?
- Is the purpose of the group to collect users for resource access?

When collecting resources for user access, assign the same domain local group to each resource. Permissions are then assigned to an object by adding the domain local group to the object's ACL. When collecting users for resource access, put the common users in a global group, which is then given membership to the domain local group with access permissions. As a general rule, add permissions only to domain local groups or universal groups. This can be illustrated best by the example that follows.

GROUP SCOPE AND MEMBERSHIP EXAMPLE

A company maintaining two domains (Figure 7.35), called *Entcert1.com* and *Entcert2.com,* is trying to permit engineers from both domains access to some folders and software configuration applications, all of which reside in the *Entcert2.com* domain. (This example assumes that a trust relationship exists between the two forests permitting *Entcert1.com* access to resources in *Entcert2.com*. If you only have one domain, simply drop the *Entcert1.com* domain and Entcert1 Engineers group from the example.) Two global groups must first be created to manage users in *Entcert1.com* and *Entcert2.com.* Membership in these groups should be based on common resource needs.

Create Global Groups

To create the two global groups, take the following steps:

1. Open the **Active Directory Users and Computers** snap-in.
2. Right-click the targeted domain or, in this example, ***Entcert2.com***. Select **New** → **Group**. (You can also select the targeted domain and click **New Group** instead.)

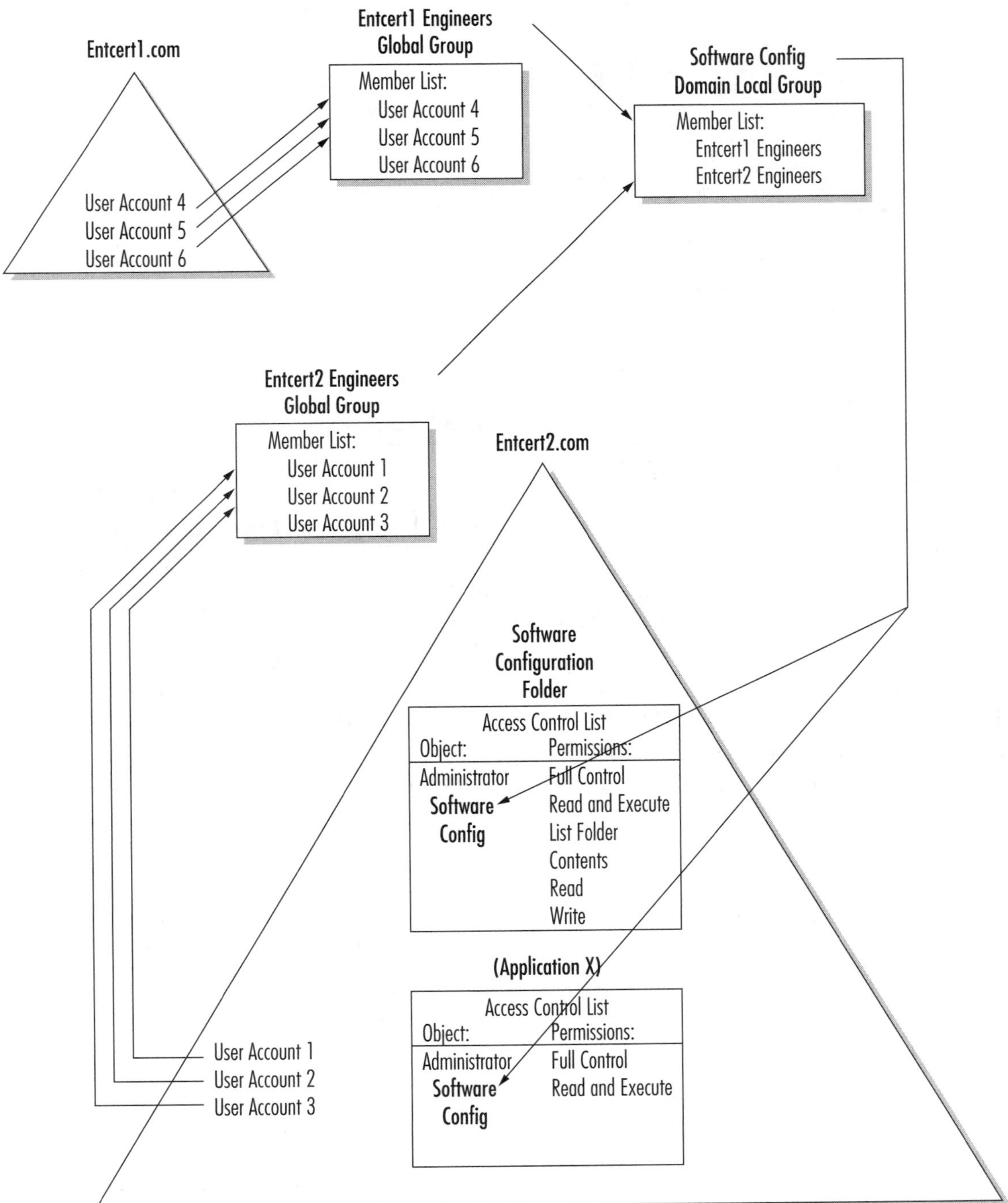

FIGURE 7.35 An Example of Domain Local and Global Domain Group Usage

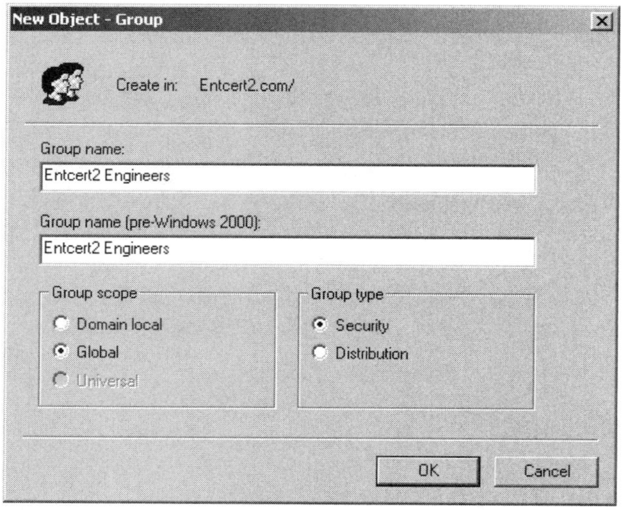

FIGURE 7.36 Creating a Group

3. Enter a name for the new group—in this example, **Entcert2 Engineers** (Figure 7.36).
   - Set the **Group scope** to **Global**.
   - Set the **Group type** to **Security**.
   - Click **OK**.
4. In the details pane, right-click the **Entcert2 Engineers** node and select **Properties**. Select the **Member** tab and click **Add** (Figure 7.37).
5. Find an available user account by entering part of a user's name in the box **Enter the object names to select**. Click **Check Names** and select an appropriate user account from the search result. Click **OK** to add the group member (Figure 7.38). Put all engineers who need access to the same resource in this group.
6. Create a new global group for engineers in the ***Entcert1.com*** domain, following the same procedure, and call it Entcert1 Engineers. (This is optional.)

Two global groups have now been created. They can be used to assign administrative responsibilities, allocate resources, and deny resources.

Create New Domain Local Group

The Software Config domain local group will now be created and given permission to access the Software Configuration folder and a file, Application X.

1. From the **Active Directory Users and Computers** tool, right-click your domain node or, in this example, ***Entcert2.com***. Select **New** → **Group**. (You

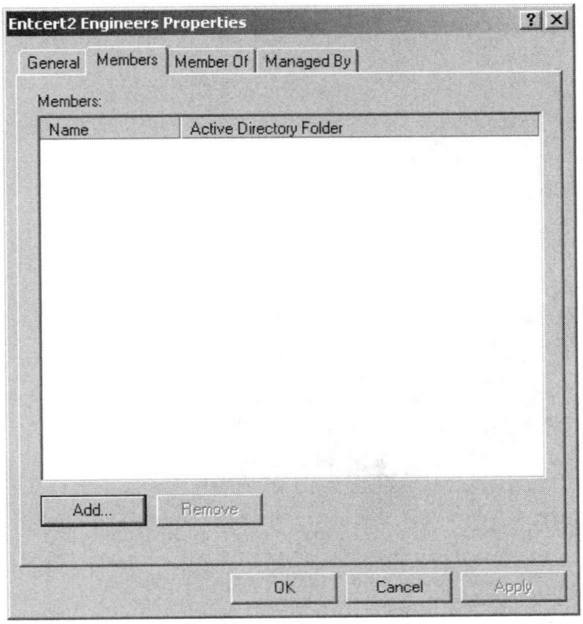

FIGURE 7.37 Group Membership in Entcert2

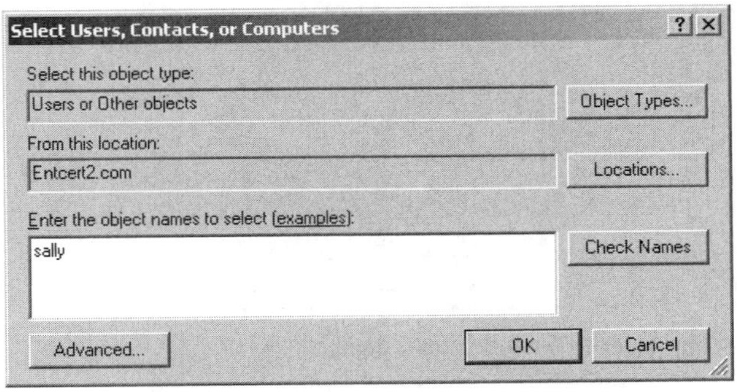

FIGURE 7.38 Adding a User to a Group

can also select the domain node (***Entcert2***) and then click on **New Group** instead.)

2. For the group name, type **Software Config,** for **Group scope,** select **Domain local,** and for **Group type**, select **Security** (Figure 7.39). Click **OK**.
3. Double-click the new group from the **Active Directory Users and Computers** snap-in and select the **Members** tab. Click **Add**. The **Select Users, Contacts, Computers**, **or Groups** dialog box appears (Figure 7.40).

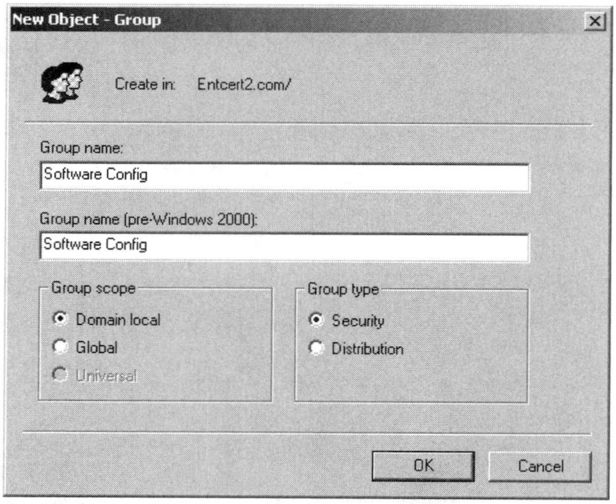

FIGURE 7.39 Creating a Group

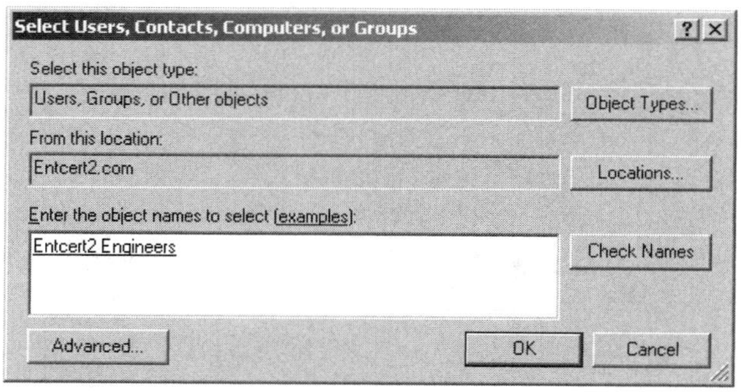

FIGURE 7.40 Selecting Security Groups from a Domain

4. Type **Entcert** as search criteria in the **Enter the object names to select** box and click **Check Names**. Select **Entcert2 Engineers** group from the available domain groups and users. Click **OK**.

You have successfully added one global group to a domain local group (optionally two). The member list for the domain local group Software Config should look like the one in Figure 7.41.

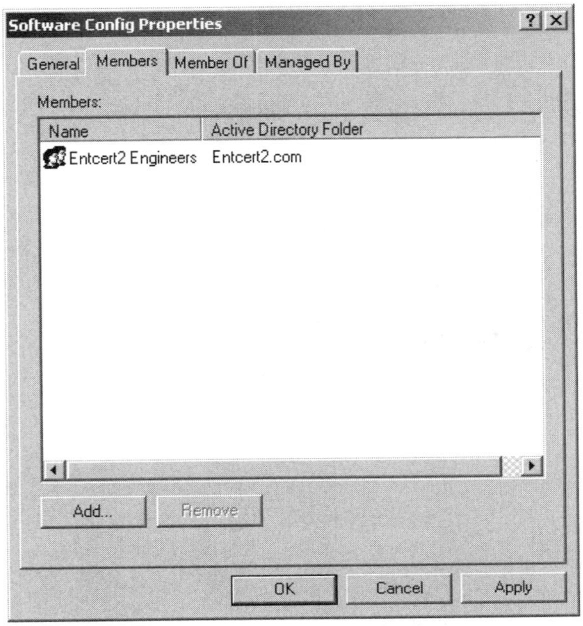

FIGURE 7.41 Software Config Properties

Assign Permissions to Domain Local Group

To create folders on your server to simulate the folders and applications to which engineers from *Entcert1.com* and *Entcert2.com* require access, use the procedure that follows:

1. Right-click **My Computer** and select **Explorer**. On an NTFS volume, create a folder called *Software Configuration* by selecting **File → New → Folder**.
2. Right-click **Properties** on the Software Configuration folder. Select the **Sharing** tab and click **Share this folder**.
3. Choose the **Security** tab and click **Add**. Choose the **Software Config** group and click **OK**.
4. Modify the **Permissions for Software Config** to allow and deny the appropriate permissions. In Figure 7.42, the engineers have been granted Full Control.
5. The Software Config group could also be added to an application object and permissions could be set to allow **Read & Execute** privileges for the Engineers group.

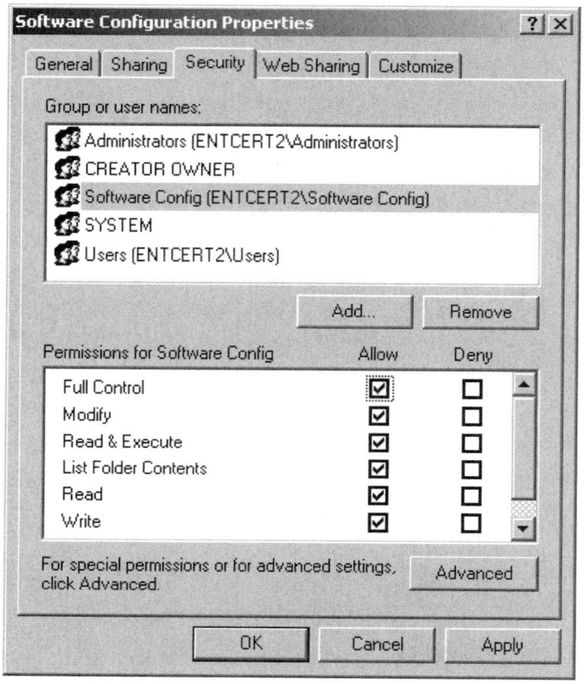

FIGURE 7.42 Software Config Security

POSTSCRIPT

This chapter addresses some of the basic issues and considerations in dealing with user accounts and Windows Server 2003 groups. Proper planning of domain user accounts and profiles can lead to effective centralized management and a familiar desktop for the user. The complexities involved with domain local and global domain security groups are also presented. Correctly implementing security groups can lead to a maintainable access control design that will grow and change with your network.

Chapter 8

Group Policies

Windows Server 2003 offers extensive control over system configuration and user environments through a feature called Group Policy. Group Policy settings may be applied to domain, site, and organizational unit (OU) Active Directory containers, giving the administrator more granular control over system configurations and user settings. The OS adds refinements to the group policies functions but does not substantially change the administrative interface or their basic nature in Windows 2000. More than 160 new policy settings are now available in Windows Server 2003. Among the affected functionality are settings for Control Panel, error reporting, Terminal Server, Remote Assistance, networking and dial-up connections, Domain Name System (DNS), network logon, Group Policy, and roaming profiles.

This chapter is divided into three main sections. The first reviews the concept of group policies; the second provides a number of implementation examples; and the third explores the underlying concepts of Microsoft's IntelliMirror. Upon completing this chapter, you should have the following:

- A working knowledge of group policies
- The ability to establish and modify group policy properties.
- The ability to apply group policies to user accounts
- An understanding of IntelliMirror technology and the ability to employ it

UNDERSTANDING GROUP POLICIES

Since group policies are designed to apply to a great number of users, they have the potential to reduce system administration support. Once a Group Policy setting is established on a user account, it is automatically applied to the desired administrative unit. This facility is especially helpful when applying security policies, but it is also widely used to establish consistency in user environments. For example, through the use of group policies, an administrator can control the options available on users' desktops and the delivery of applications.

Group Policy also implements the bulk of the Microsoft IntelliMirror technology. This strategy capitalizes on the centralized management of client/server systems while maintaining the flexibility and convenience of the distributed computing model. For example, users can log on from anywhere in the network and preserve user profiles, application data, security requirements, application access, and backup offline files. Microsoft's IntelliMirror, as discussed in this chapter, provides more examples and details for this technology.

Group policies can be extended by third-party application vendors as well to manage desktop settings for their applications.

NOTE A user planning to modify group policies must have administrative privileges for the Active Directory and associated containers.

Group Policy Management and Active Directory

Group Policy management is accomplished by assigning Group Policy Objects (GPOs) to specific machines, sites, domains, and OUs from the Active Directory. Applying Group Policy involves determining which users and computers require policy settings so that selected Active Directory containers can group users and computers accordingly. GPOs are then applied to the desired Active Directory containers and are inherited by child containers. Windows Server 2003 follows the LSDOU model in which inheritance flows in this order: **local computer (L) → site (S) → domain (D) → organizational unit (OU).**

The LSDOU inheritance model may seem unnatural at first (Figure 8.1). Local computer GPOs are the first applied to any user who logs on to that particular system. They can be overridden by the GPOs assigned to the user's site, which are overridden by domain GPOs, which are overridden by relevant OU GPOs. This order gives the local administrator the first chance to set the computer's policies.

When GPO policies are enforced, any child GPO settings applied to a system are disabled. The local computer GPOs may not enforce policies. They are the first to be set, but may be nullified by further policy inheritance.

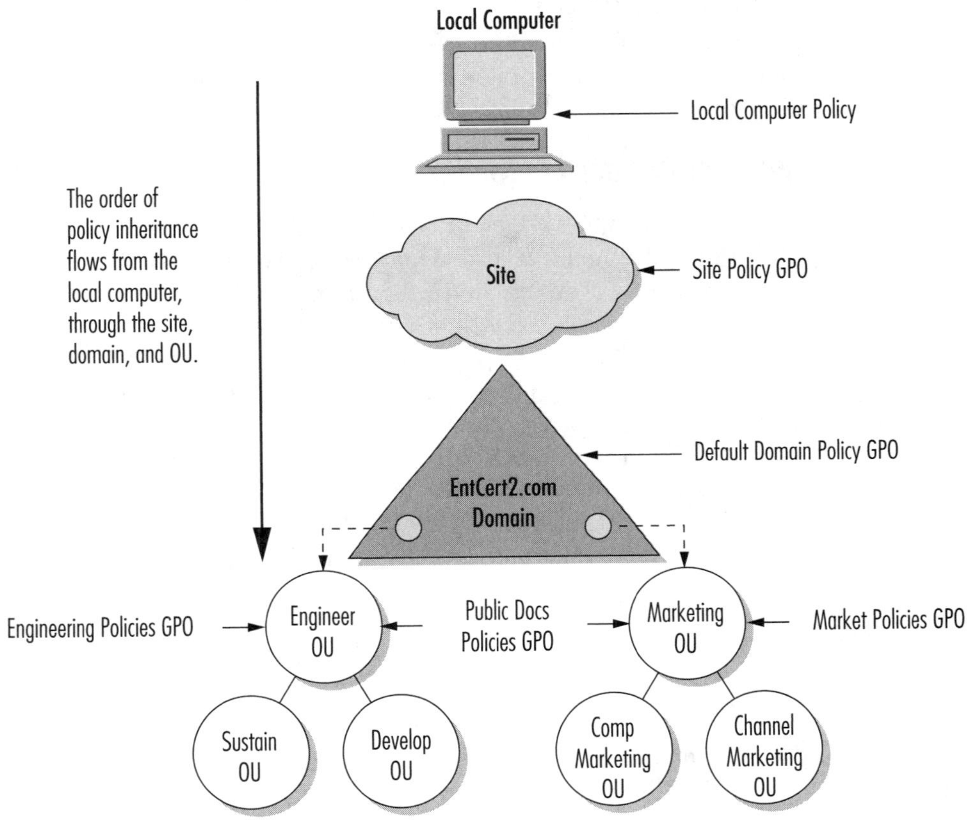

FIGURE 8.1 The Order of Policy Inheritance

NOTE The exception to the LSDOU model comes into play when using Windows NT 4.0 policies that are set with the Policy System Editor. These are applied before the local GPOs. In other words, if the NTConfig.pol file exists, it will be used first to apply policies. These policies may be overwritten by GPOs applied to the domain, site, and OU containers.

The LSDOU model provides a reference point for determining the users and computers a GPO affects. A GPO can be applied to any of three container types: site, domain, and OU. In Figure 8.1, the Default Domain Policy GPO has been assigned to the *Entcert2.com* domain, so the users and computers in that domain as well as all OUs within it will receive these policy settings. The same GPO may also be applied to more than one Active Directory container. In the figure, the Public Docs Policies GPO is applied to both the Engineering OU and the Marketing OU. This is referred to as *linking*.

GROUP POLICY OBJECT STORAGE

Before introducing the Group Policy feature set, it is important to understand, on the local and domain levels, Group Policy storage. Local computer policies are stored on the local system in the %SystemRoot%System32\GroupPolicy directory. They are not replicated to other systems, nor do they cover the complete range of policies accessible to enterprise-wide GPOs applied to Active Directory containers.

Active Directory GPO storage is a little more complicated. These policies are stored in the Group Policy container (GPC) and the Group Policy template (GPT). The GPC includes version, status, and extensions for the GPO. As discussed earlier, it may be a site, domain, or OU Active Directory object, and is synchronized with other domain controllers on its own update schedule. Small amounts of information that are modified infrequently are stored in the GPC, which is assigned a globally unique identifier (GUID), such as {31B2F340-016D-11D2-945F-00C04FB984F9}, which corresponds to a GPT. Data stored in the GPC is used to determine whether the GPO is enabled and to ensure that the correct GPT version is applied to user and computer accounts in the container.

The GPT is stored on domain controllers in the %SystemRoot%\SYSVOL\sysvol\domainname\Policies\GUID folder for domain-wide replication and access. Standard folders in this directory are Adm, USER, and MACHINE. All user and computer policy settings for the GPO are stored in the GPT and synchronized on a different schedule from that of its sister GPC information. The GPT contains the raw policy settings, including security settings and software installation information. It can be thought of as the folder structure you can see when modifying a Group Policy object from an MMC snap-in, such as is shown later in Figure 8.6.

REFINING GROUP POLICY INHERITANCE

In addition to inheritance order, several other rules control which users and computers are assigned group policies. These rules allow the administrator to refine policy application:

- Policy inheritance
- Blocking policy inheritance
- Enforcing policy inheritance
- Using security groups to filter group policies

Policy Inheritance

The LSDOU model discussed earlier generally describes how Group Policy inheritance is implemented in Windows Server 2003. A clear example may shed light on how it works. In Figure 8.1 the Engineering Policies GPO applied to the Engineering OU is also inherited by the Sustaining and Development OUs. This shows that whereas child Active Directory containers inherit group policies, Group Policy inheritance does not flow upward to parent containers.

Let's dissect the example in Figure 8.2 to illustrate this flow in greater detail. Policies inherited by the Marketing OU from its parents are applied to members of the Channel Marketing OU. Users and computers in the Channel Marketing OU also apply the Marketing Policies GPO and Public Docs GPO to their systems upon bootup and logon. The Distribution Centers GPO is applied last and may override group

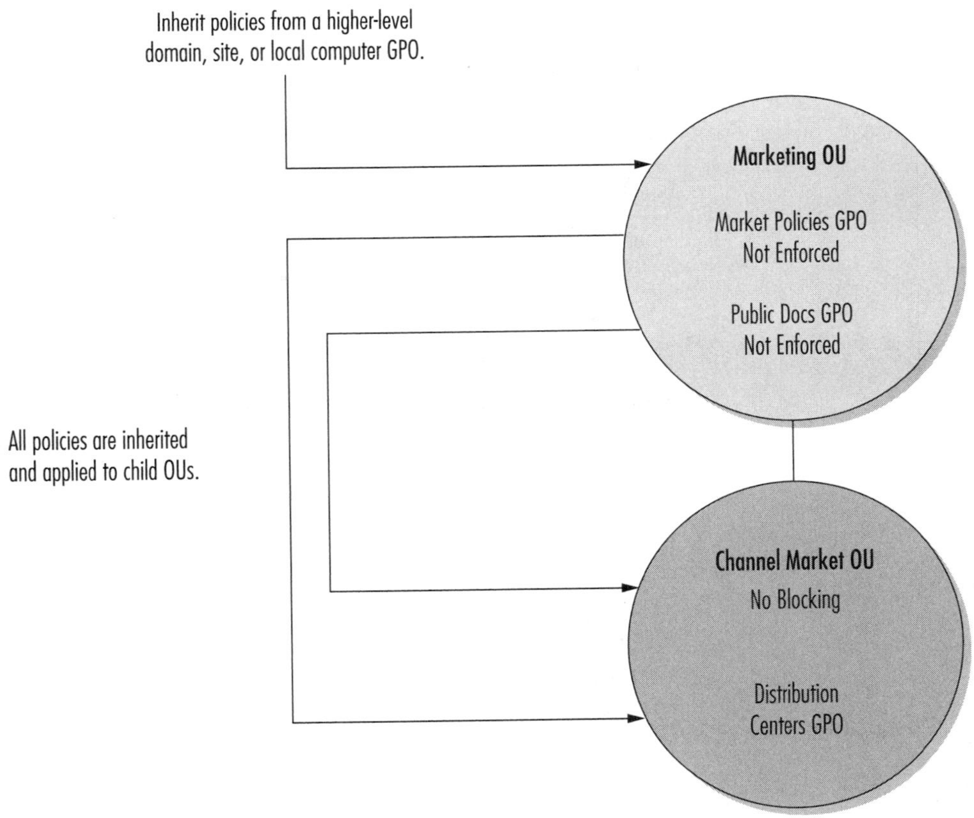

FIGURE 8.2 An Example of Policy Inheritance

policies previously applied to the Channel Marketing OU. Thus, the lowest-level Active Directory container has the last opportunity to override inherited policies.

NOTE As levels are added to the Active Directory hierarchy, more GPOs are applied to a user account when a user logs on to the network. A vertical domain container structure generally results in additional policies applied to the user, so it will take slightly longer to log on. Also, more GPOs make it more complex to determine which policies apply to a user. A very horizontal Active Directory structure may eliminate some of this complexity and logon delay, illustrated in Figure 8.3.

Blocking Policy Inheritance and Enforcement

The inheritance hierarchy can be modified by use of the Override or Enforce function, which blocks inherited features associated with parent GPOs. The Engineering OU (Figure 8.4) has enforced the Design Access GPO policies and not the Engineering GPO policies. The Sustaining OU has elected to block inheritance, so it does not inherit the Engineering GPO policies since they are not enforced. However, the Design Access GPO policies are enforced at the Engineering OU level and

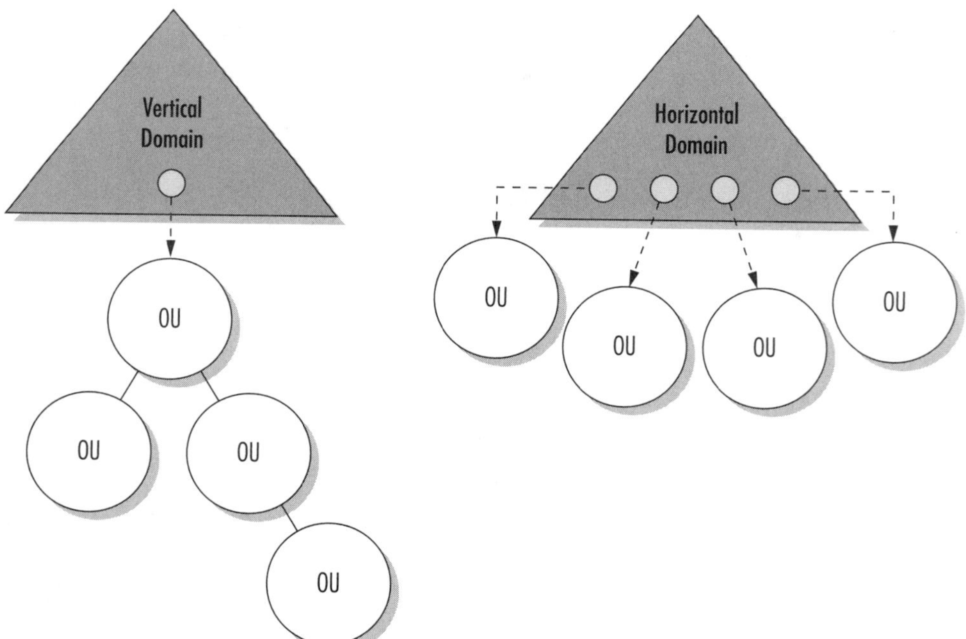

FIGURE 8.3 Horizontal and Vertical Domain Structures

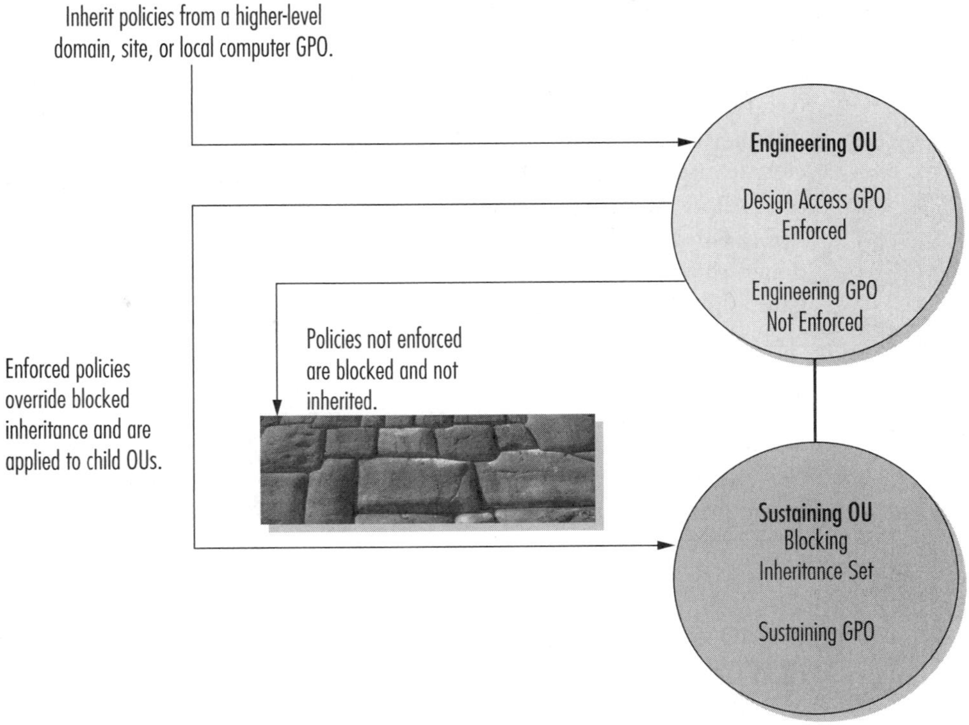

FIGURE 8.4 An Example of Blocking Policy Inheritance

thus override the Sustaining OU's desire to block inheritance. In other words, the enforcement of parent group policies takes precedence over policy blocking on child containers.

NOTE Both policy blocking and policy enforcement should be kept to a minimum. This capability makes it difficult to track policies that affect the user.

Security Group Filtering

As with files and other objects in Windows Server 2003, the discretionary access control list (DACL) determines permission levels for users and computers that access a GPO. Each GPO has its own security settings determined by a DACL and associated permissions. Access control entries (ACEs) usually take the form of security groups, rather than individual users, and assign sweeping privileges to many users at once. Each ACE can be assigned Allow and Deny permissions through the GPO security settings (Figure 8.5).

The Authenticated Users group is one of the default security groups assigned to a new GPO. Read and Apply Group Policy permissions are set to Allow, which means that all newly authenticated users mapped to this GPO will apply its policies. Consistent with other Windows Server permissions, Deny takes precedence over Allow. Members of a security group may "filter" group policies by denying the Apply Group Policy permission. A filtered security group will not accumulate logon delays due to the GPO. Group Policy access permissions can also be used to delegate administrative authority to security groups and users. A user must have Read and Write access to make GPO changes.

CAUTION Security group filtering should be used sparingly because determining which policies affect a user may become quite complex. As with all security permissions, use of the Deny setting to override Allow should be used with caution.

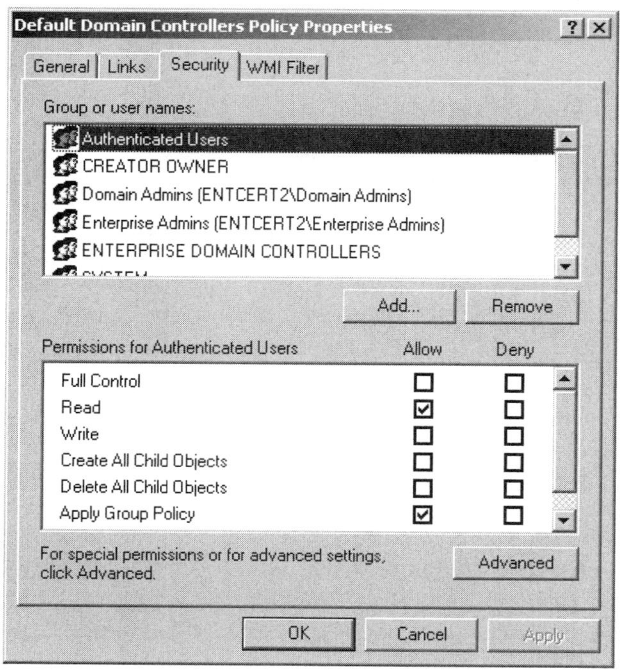

FIGURE 8.5 GPO Security Properties

Group Policy Settings

Group policies are broken into five areas, each of which is discussed in the following sections. Example implementations are provided at the end of the chapter. Keep in mind that individual policies affect all aspects of a system's operation.

Following are the five policy categories defined in the Group Policy snap-in.

- *Administrative templates (Registry-based)* policies primarily affect the user interface and available tools and desktop settings.
- *Security settings* limit user access to systems and user account policies.
- *Software installation* policies allow the publishing and assignment of available software.
- *Scripts* configure scripts for logon, logoff, startup, and shutdown.
- *Folder redirection* settings permit the relocation of user profile folders (e.g., My Documents, Application Data, Start menu) to other system network shares.

NOTE Windows Server 2003 adds a Web view for the Group Policy snap-in. This Group Policy feature is available in the Administrative Template extension snap-in. This information is also available on the **Explain** tab of the **Property** page of each setting.

USER AND COMPUTER POLICIES

A GPO divides policies into two major sections, Computer Configuration and User Configuration (Figure 8.6). Policies within Computer Configuration are applied during the boot sequence and affect all sessions that follow on that system. User Configuration policies are applied when the user first logs on. Computer policies apply to the system; user policies follow the user.

Either the Computer Configuration or the User Configuration portion of a GPO may be disabled to save time and processing. For instance, if a GPO does not enable any computer policy settings, the Computer Configuration portion of the GPO should be disabled. This is demonstrated in the following sections.

ADMINISTRATIVE TEMPLATES

Both user-related and computer-related Administrative Template nodes are used to modify Registry settings. The related Registry database settings are located in the HKEY_CURRENT_USER (HKCU) and HKEY_LOCAL_MACHINE (HKLM) Registry keys. Whenever policy changes are made to the Administrative Template portion of the GPO, the Registry keys HKCU and HKLM are also updated. If there is a conflict between computer and user settings, the computer settings take priority. A

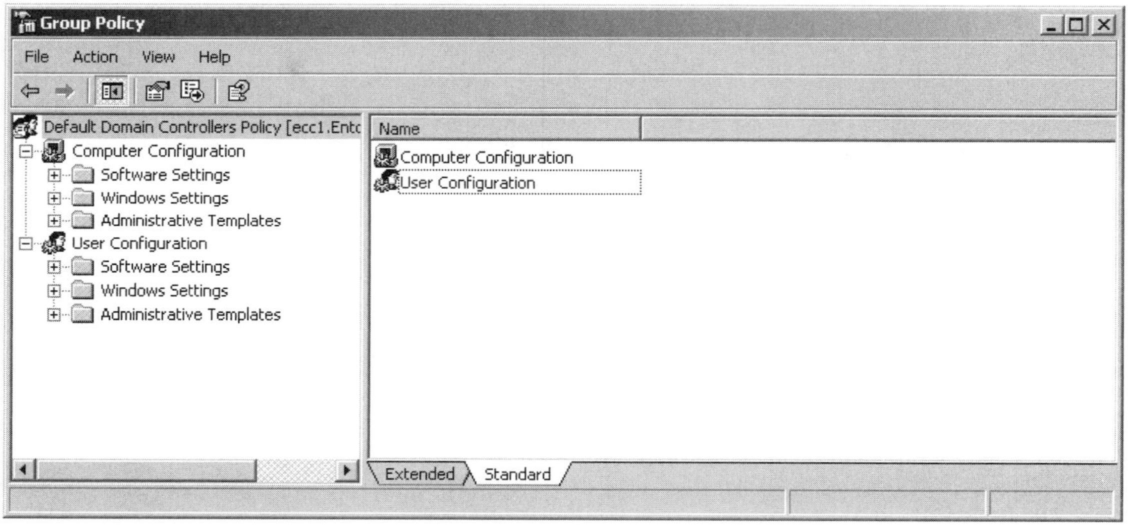

FIGURE 8.6 Computer and User Policies

Registry.pol file in the %systemroot%\SYSVOL\sysvol\domainname\Policies\GUID\MACHINE and USER directories maintains group policy changes to the Registry. Any changes made through administrative template policies are made in the Registry.pol file and then mapped onto the Registry.

The policies available under the Administrative Templates node take the form of the ASCII files such as system.adm and inetres.adm by default (Figure 8.7). The default Windows Server 2003 installation includes other administrative templates that may be loaded in order to modify policies for specific applications or network architectures (Table 8.1).

In addition to these templates, located physically in the %systemroot%\inf directory, custom .adm files may be created for specific application needs. Guidelines for doing this can be found in the Windows .NET Help tool under Creating Custom .adm Files. Application developers can also customize group policies by creating an MMC extension snap-in.

NOTE In enterprises that implement the Windows Server 2003 Remote Installation Services, several group policies can be used to govern what installation options are available to the client. For instance, the administrator may choose to restrict which users may install an Active Directory domain controller. The policy to control this setting, located via **gponame → User Configuration → Windows Settings → Remote Installation Services → Choice Options**, can dictate an automatic installation setup that prevents user control over installation options.

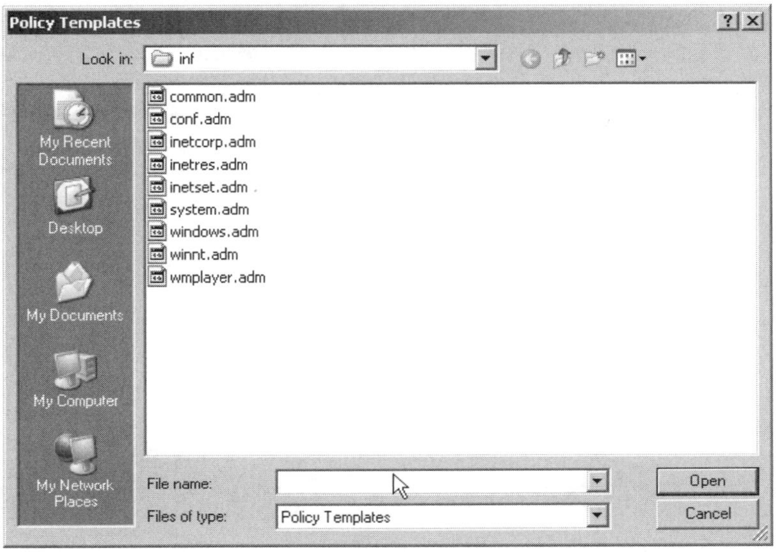

FIGURE 8.7 Policy Templates

SECURITY SETTINGS

Group security policies apply to nine different areas in the Windows Server 2003 Group Policy Editor. The Security Configuration Editor can be used to compare the system's security policy settings with suggested settings. Security templates located in the %systemroot%\Security\Templates directory can be modified using

TABLE 8.1 Administrative Template Options

Template	Purpose
common.adm	Windows NT 4.0, 98, and 95 policies
conf.adm	Microsoft NetMeeting policies
inetcorp.adm	Language, Dial-up, and Temporary Internet File policies
inetres.adm	Internet policies
inetset.adm	Internet restriction policies
system.adm	Default template with policies specific to Windows Server 2003
windows.adm	Windows 98 and 95 policies
winnt.adm	Windows NT 4.0 policies
wmplayer.adm	Windows Media Player policies

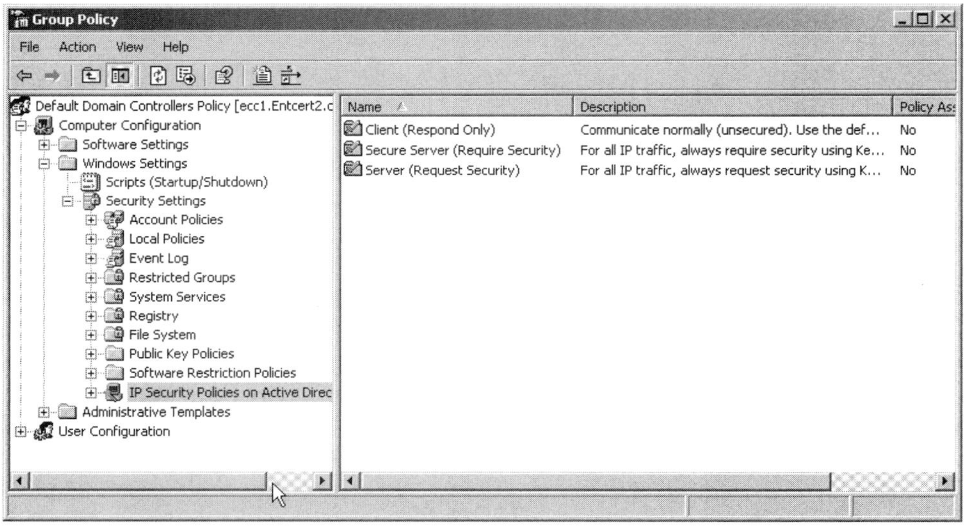

FIGURE 8.8 Group Policy Security Settings

the Security Templates snap-in tool. They can then be imported to the Security Settings portion of the Group Policy tree. The security group policy settings, illustrated in Figure 8.8, include those listed in Table 8.2.

An understanding of security policies would not be complete without a review of Restricted Groups, Registry, and Files System settings.

Restricted Groups

When the Restricted Groups settings are applied to a system, the current group memberships are modified to match them. Only groups listed in the Details window of the Restricted Groups node are affected. Any group added to Restricted Groups has its own member and "Member of" lists. These lists are then enforced on the local system, overwriting group membership assigned by the Active Directory.

To add a restricted group:

1. Right-click the **Restricted Group** policy node and select **Add Group**.
2. Click **Browse** and select a group from your directory (Figure 8.9).
3. Click **OK** and right-click the new group. Select **Security**.
4. Add **Members of this Group** and **This group is a member of** entries as desired (Figure 8.10).

If you were to add the **Power Users** group to the **Restricted Groups** setting and not include any users in the **Members of this group** list, the policy would remove current users from the Power Users group. Oddly enough, if the **This**

TABLE 8.2 Group Policy Settings

Security Setting Node	Description
Account Policies	Password policies—uniqueness, maximum age, minimum length. Account lockout—invalid logon attempt. Kerberos policy—ticket lifetime, synchronization.
Local Policies	Audit policy—user rights, local machine security such as shutdown privileges and autodisconnect.
Event Log	Size and time limits for event logs.
Restricted Groups	Designates some security groups to allow only designated members to participate in the group for any length of time; if a nondesignated member is added to the group, the user will be removed.
System Services	System service startup mode (Automatic, Manual, Disabled) modification for the next system boot.
Registry	Security access permissions on portions of the Registry; permissions for the CLASSES_ROOT, MACHINE, and USERS Registry keys may be assigned using security groups or user IDs.
File System	Security permissions for files and folders set and applied when user logs on to the system.
Public Key Policies	Designate trusted root certificate authorities and recovery agents for file encryption.
Software Restriction Policies	Limit applications that can run on a system.
IP Security Policies on Active Directory	IP security level for the system; set software Authenticode, user authentication, and encrypted communication methods.

FIGURE 8.9 Adding a Group

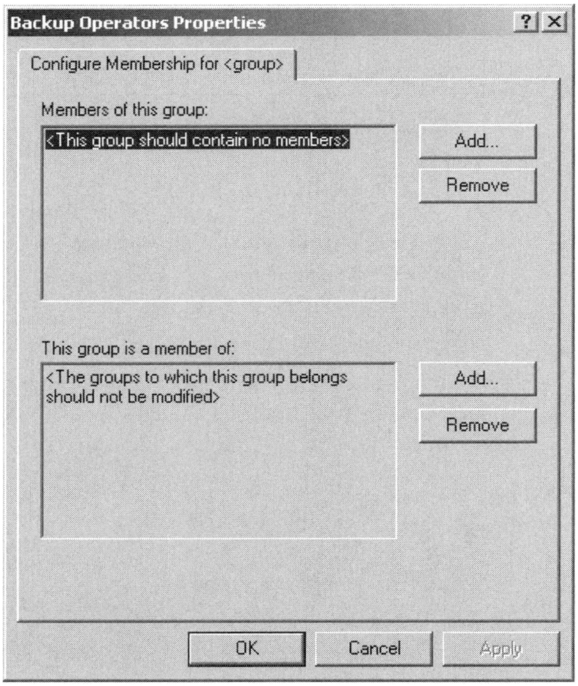

FIGURE 8.10 Group Membership

group is a member of list is empty, no modifications are made to other group memberships. In other words, it is additive only. The restricted group will be added to the groups listed in the **This group is a member of** field. This policy setting is good for limiting membership to select groups, but it should be used sparingly.

File System and Registry Policy

Group Policy can be used to set permissions on files and Registry keys. The File System and Registry settings allow the administrator to configure the ACLs on a per file/folder/Registry directory basis.

NOTE When applied at the domain level, these settings can lock down all system Registries, protecting against meddling users and ensuring uniform permissions settings throughout an OU or a domain.

Right-click the **GPO → Computer → Windows Settings → Security Settings → Registry** node and select **Add Key**. This produces the **Select Registry**

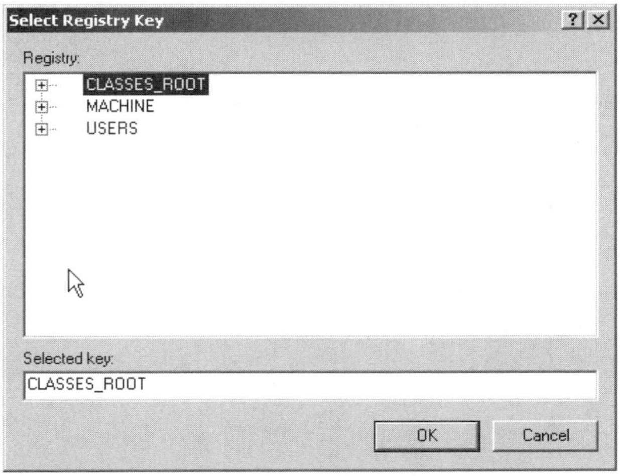

FIGURE 8.11 Setting Registry Security Policies

Key dialog box (Figure 8.11). Three Registry keys can be explored, and permissions may be selectively applied to the key structure.

Right-click the **GPO** → **Computer** → **Windows Settings** → **Security Settings** → **File System** node and select **Add File**. This produces the **Add a file or folder** dialog box (Figure 8.12). The entire directory structure can be explored and selectively assigned permissions.

After an item is selected, security permission (Figure 8.13) can be assigned, as covered in Chapter 10, "Kerberos and the Public Key Infrastructure."

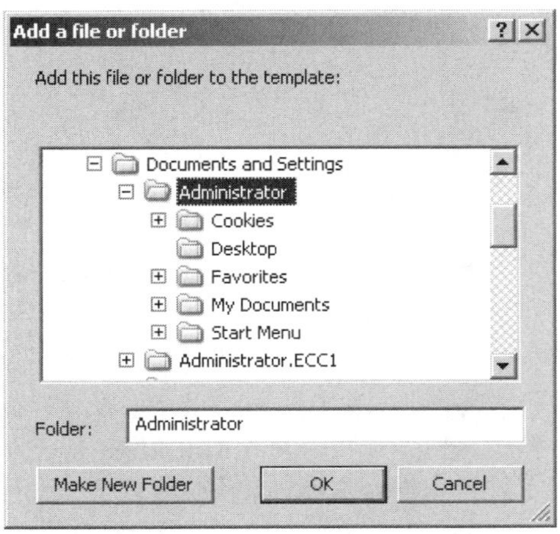

FIGURE 8.12 Setting File Security Policies

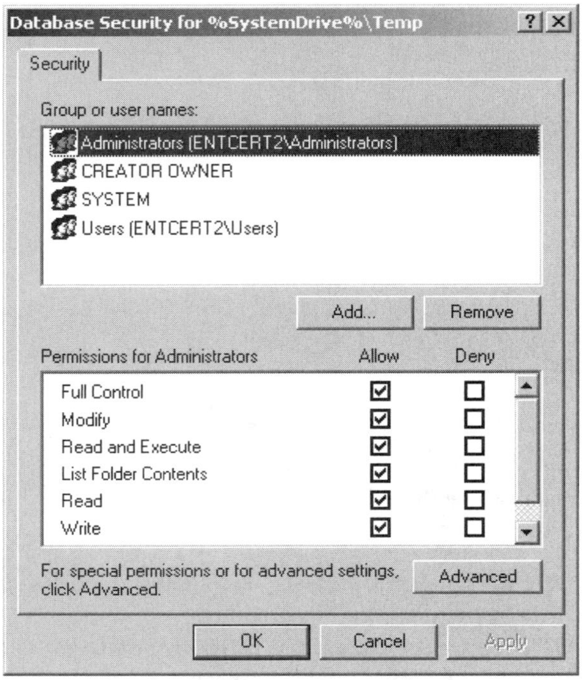

FIGURE 8.13 Assigning Registry and File Permissions

Once permissions have been assigned, inheritance properties are requested. Selecting the **Configure** option applies the permissions according to these subchoices, shown in Figure 8.14:

- ***Propagate inheritable permissions to all subfolders and files.*** This option applies the permissions set to the current object and all child folders and files. Any specific or explicit user or group that has been added to a child file or subfolder is not overwritten. In other words, all permissions that were inherited are replaced with the new permissions, but Joe Engineer, who was given Read privileges on a specific subfolder, still maintains his user right.
- ***Replace existing permissions on all subfolders and files with inheritable permissions.*** This option applies the new policy settings to all child folders and files, overwriting all existing permissions.

If **Do not allow permissions on this file or folder to be replaced** is selected, the current file or folder and its child file and folders are immune to permissions assigned in this GPO. This policy is needed only if a parent to this file or folder has been assigned new permissions within this GPO and you want this branch to keep its permissions and ignore the new settings.

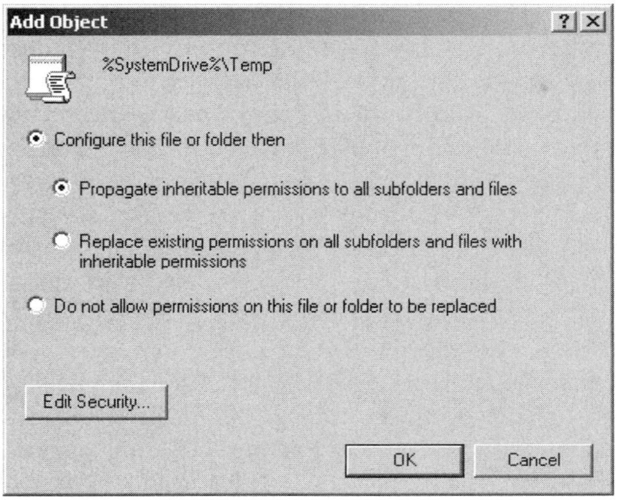

FIGURE 8.14 Requesting Permissions Inheritance

SOFTWARE INSTALLATION: ASSIGNING AND PUBLISHING

The Software Installation and Management feature provides two strategies for distributing software applications throughout the network to the groups in Group Policy. The *assign* method places a shortcut to the application on the **Start** menu and loads the application advertisement into the Registry. Applications may be assigned with user or computer settings. Applications assigned via user settings are installed on the local system the first time the application is executed. In this way they maintain consistent application availability for a set of users, who benefit from enhanced desktop usability since their **Start** menu will always appear the same regardless of where they log on. If the needed application is not already installed on the system the user is using, application installation can be invoked by selecting the application from the **Start** menu or by opening a file of the application's type. Applications assigned with computer settings will be installed on those systems when booted. Application availability is based on the computer system, not the user.

NOTE The discussion of application installations involves elements of Microsoft's IntelliMirror that are discussed at the end of this chapter. The ability to set policies on applications that can be intelligently mirrored across the enterprise is one of the primary functions of IntelliMirror technology.

The second method for distributing software is to *publish* the application. A published application leaves the software installation up to the user without the aid of shortcuts and local Registry modifications. The user may install a published application by clicking the **Add/Remove Programs** icon from **Control Panel** or by opening a file that matches the published application type. An application must be published with user settings so that its availability will follow the user, regardless of which system is used. Software cannot be published using computer settings. Published software does not have the resilient quality of assigned software. If a library or file associated with the application is deleted, the software will not be repaired.

The ability to assign or publish software for group policies relies on the Windows Installer to manage application installation. A software package with an .msi file name contains information necessary to install the application on different platforms, and to deal with previous versions and different configurations. The resiliency of the Windows Installer is a key new feature that rolls back application versions or repairs missing libraries when necessary. Assigned applications modify the Registry and persist on the system even when the user deletes an application or associated libraries. They will be reinstalled or repaired the next time the program is invoked.

Packaging Applications

For a software application to be assigned or published, a package for the software must be obtained in a couple of ways:

- Use a Microsoft Installer (MSI) package from the software vendor or repackaging software to generate an .msi file.
- Use a .zap file to guide software installation.

The MSI package and associated files are fairly straightforward. However, when an MSI package is not available, a .zap text file can be used to add applications using the Software Installer, rather than the Windows Installer, to publish (not assign) them. This of course means that the application will not be resilient or repair itself when damaged. The user instigating the Software Installer must also have access permissions to write to the required installation directories, because, unlike the Windows Installer, the Software Installer is not granted sweeping privileges to make system modifications. The installation procedure will also probably involve user intervention and therefore lead to more handholding and user guidance.

A .zap file requires an application section, designated by line 1, and two required tags on lines 2 and 3. The **Friendly Name** tag indicates the application name that will appear in the **Control Panel** → **Add/Remove Programs** utility, and the **Setup** command is the executable to instigate the application's installation. The following tags are optional and relate to parameters that are displayed in the **Add/Remove Programs** utility. The **Ext** marker on line 8 indicates the optional extension section. File extensions specified here will be stored in the Active Directory and linked to the newly installed application. The extension is listed without the period.

```
line 1: [Application]
line 2: FriendlyName = ECC W2K Starter
line 3: SetupCommand = setup.exe
line 4: DisplayVersion = 1.0
line 5: Publisher = Enterprise Certified
line 6: URL = http://www.EntCert.com/Software
line 7:
line 8: [Ext]
line 9: CUR=
```

Software Installation Example

The software installation component of the IntelliMirror technology allows the publishing or assigning of software applications to users and computers. As previously discussed, assigning software applications puts the software's icon on the **Start** menu. The application is then installed when invoked by the user and will "follow" the user wherever he goes within the network. Obviously, software application installation takes time and network resources. If the application is assigned to a computer, the software is installed at the system's leisure, which usually means that installation will occur when the system is booted. Publishing software requires the user to invoke the **Add/Remove Programs** tool from **Control Panel**. Software components, published to the user or computer, are listed under the **Add New Programs** menu. They are then installed at the user's request.

In order to publish or assign software, an MSI package must be obtained for the application from the software vendor. In this example, the Microsoft Office 2000 package is used to assign software to domain users. For more information on the MSI/MST formats, see the Help pages.

NOTE Repackaging tools, such as VERITAS WinINSTALL LE, are included on the Windows Server 2003 CDs. These tools examine the system before and after application installation, record system changes, and package the final system state. The resulting MSI package enables resilient application publish and assign capabilities.

---

1. Find an MSI software package and copy it to a network share named Network Docs and Settings.
2. Open the **Default Domain Policy** (or other GPO) and right-click **User Configuration → Software Settings → Software Installation** and select

New → **Package** (Figure 8.15). Find the software package from the **Find File** window. BE SURE TO ENTER THE NETWORK PATH to the network share and software package. If it is on the local drive, reference the packet in \\servername\Network Docs and Settings. Clients must be able to access the package from the network using the full file name given here. Click **OK**.

3. Select whether the application is to be **Published** or **Assigned** (Figure 8.16). Click **OK**.
4. Once the application has been added to **Software Installation,** policy properties can be viewed. Right-click the newly added package and select **Properties** (Figure 8.17). Configurable items (discussed further in the coming sections) include
   - ***General***—name and product and support information.
   - ***Deployment***—deployment type, options, and the allowed user interface during installation.
   - ***Upgrades***—packages that upgrade this package and those that this package upgrades.

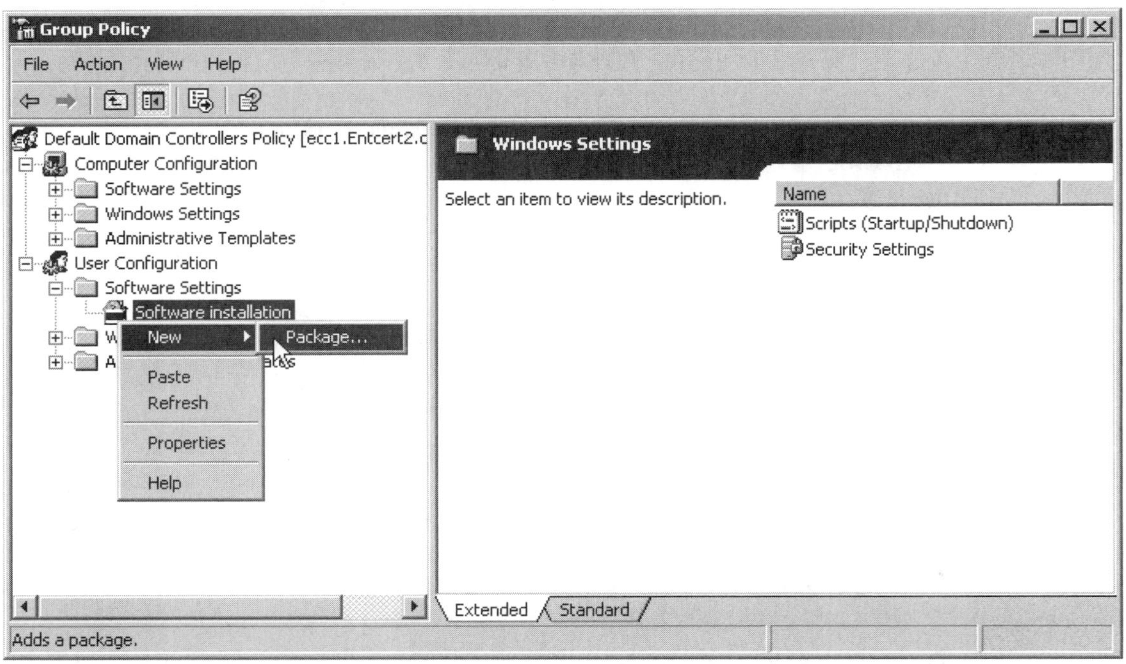

FIGURE 8.15 Adding a Software Package

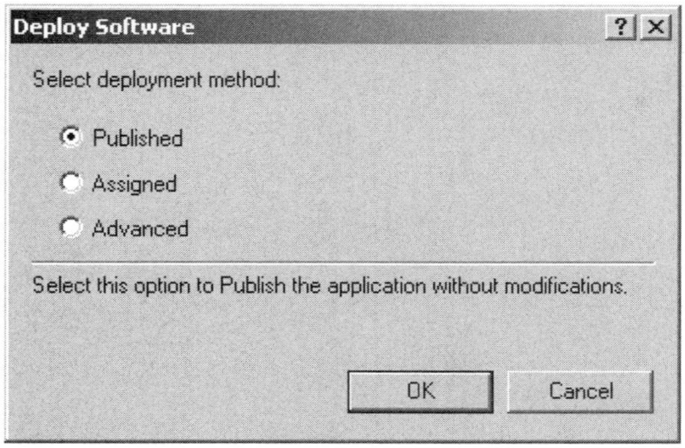

FIGURE 8.16 Selecting the Deployment Method

- ***Categories***—categories in which this application will be listed. New categories can be created to group software types. A category called Accounting might contain several accounting packages.
- ***Modifications***—.mst files or transforms to customize software installations.
- ***Security***—users and groups with access to modify this package's GPO setting.

Once the user logs on again, on any machine, the software will be installed once activated from the **Start** menu or accessed by double-clicking a file of the application type from **My Computer**.

Modifying the Deployment Method

Once the package has been installed on a network share and added to a GPO, its deployment configuration may be further modified. Right-clicking the **Software installation** node for the GPO that contains the new software package and selecting **Properties** presents several configuration tabs. The **General** tab (Figure 8.17) presents product and support information for the application.

The **Deployment** tab (Figure 8.18) allows configuration of the deployment type, the deployment options, and the user interaction. Under **Deployment type,** you can change the deployment method, **Published** or **Assigned**. The **Deployment** options include the following configurations:

- ***Auto-install this application by file extension activation.*** This option applies only to published applications. It allows you to prevent or allow installation of an application when a user double-clicks a file name with an extension that matches the published application.
- ***Uninstall this application when it falls out of the scope of management.*** This option determines whether the application is uninstalled from a

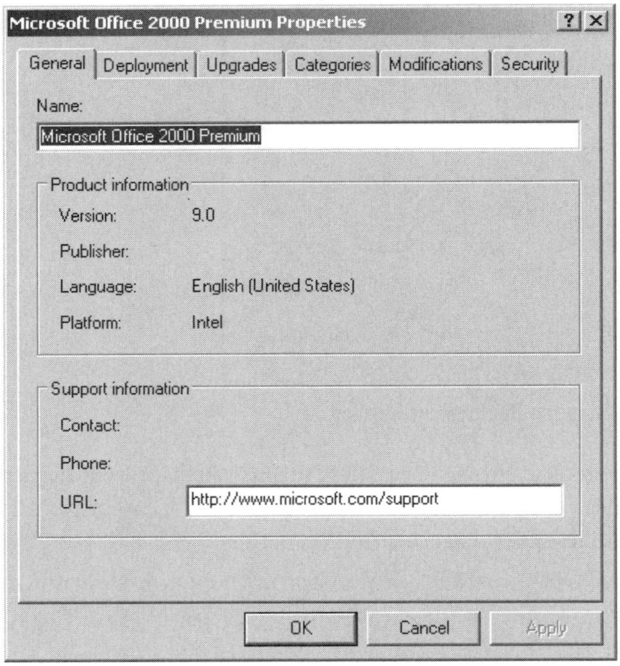

FIGURE 8.17 The Application Properties General Tab

user or computer when leaving the scope of the current GPO. If a user no longer falls under the jurisdiction (scope) of this GPO, the application will be removed if this option is checked.

- ***Do not display this package in the Add/Remove Programs control panel.*** If this option is checked, the user will not be able to browse for the application and install it from Control Panel. If the user invokes or double-clicks a file name with the application's extension, the application will be installed.

The user interface options determine that the application will be installed using default values (**Basic**), or they prompt the user for installation configuration information (**Maximum**).

The **Advanced** button allows removal of previous installations not governed by group policies. An option also exists to disregard language configuration during the installation.

Upgrades

There are two ways to distribute software upgrades. A mandatory upgrade involves a check mark in the box next to **Required upgrade for existing packages** (Fig-

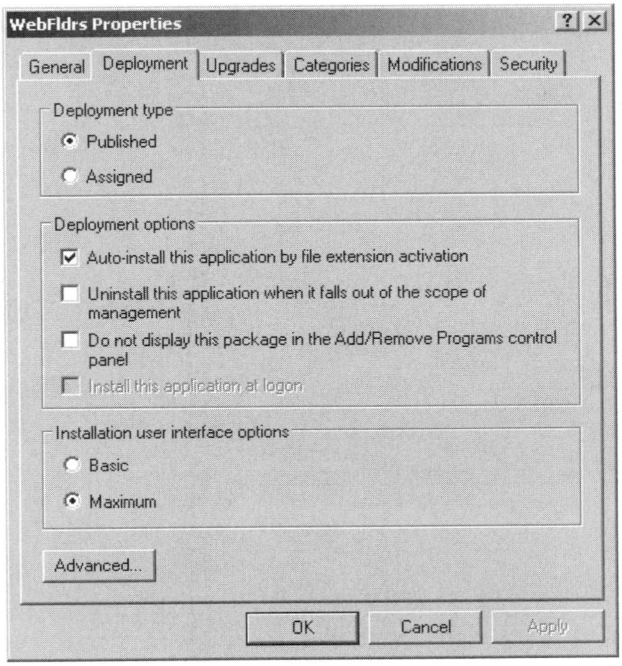

FIGURE 8.18 The Deployment Tab

ure 8.19). This option requires the user to upgrade her current version of the application with the new package. The optional upgrade (clearing check box) allows the user to install the new application version or to continue using the current one. It also permits her to install the new version in addition to her current version and access both through old and new shortcuts.

To add an upgrade package, go to the **Upgrades** tab (Figure 8.19), click **Add**, and find the upgrade package in the current GPO (Figure 8.20) or browse the directory by selecting the **A specific GPO** and clicking **Browse**. Once the correct GPO is located, select the application package to upgrade from among those associated with that GPO. Then you can **Uninstall the existing package**, **then Install the upgrade package,** or select **Package can upgrade over the existing package**. The Uninstall option is used to replace an existing application with a new one; the Upgrade option is used to upgrade a package with the same product.

Redeploying Software Patches

Once you obtain the new MSI package containing a software fix, replace the old MSI package and associated files with the new package and files on the network share. Select the **Software Installation** node from the GPO that originally

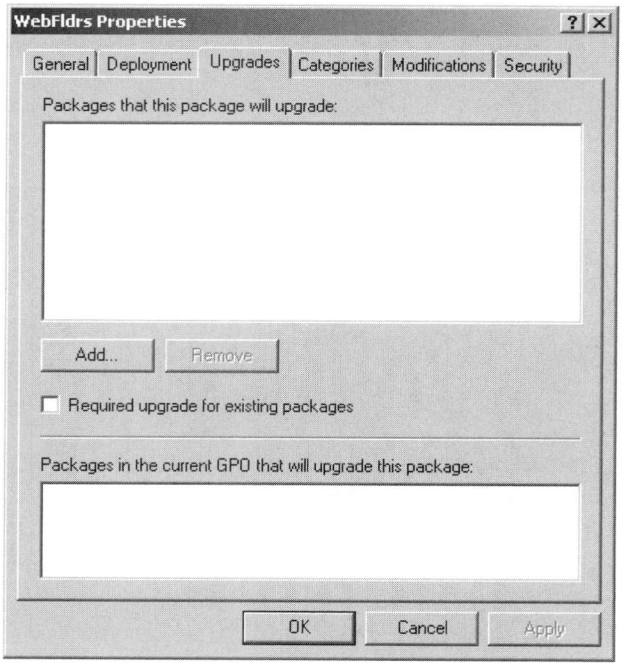

FIGURE 8.19 The Upgrade Tab

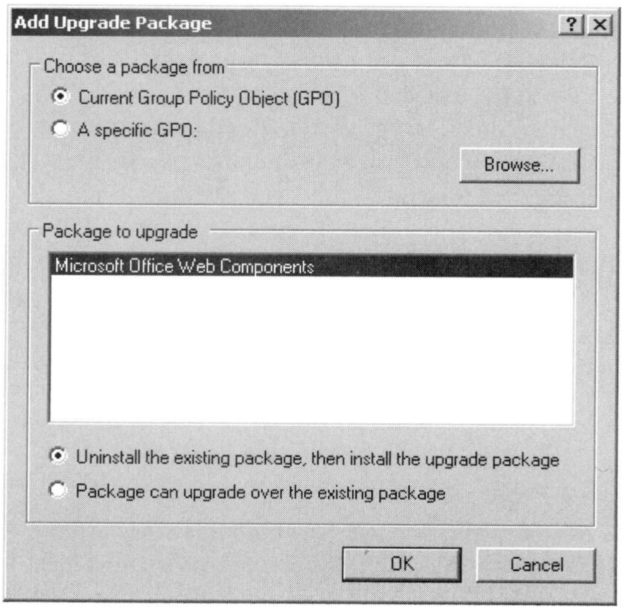

FIGURE 8.20 Adding an Upgrade Package

deployed the software and right-click the software package in the Details window. Select **All Tasks → Redeploy application** and click **Yes** to redeploy the software fix. Regardless of whether the application was published or assigned, the patch will be installed the first time it is started.

Software Removal

Software may undergo either a forced or an optional removal. A forced removal will delete software installed through computer settings the next time the system is booted. The optional removal permits the current application installations to persist but will not allow new installations for the package.

To remove software, select the **Software installation** node from the corresponding GPO. In the Details window, right-click the desired software package and select **All Tasks → Remove**. The **Remove software** dialog appears and presents two software removal methods (Figure 8.21). These options correspond to the forced and optional removal strategies, respectively. After you have selected the method, click **OK** .

File Extensions and Installation

Invoking application installation when a user selects a file of the application's file type is convenient. However, some organizations may have several applications associated with a given file extension. Suppose both Microsoft Office 2000 Premium and Microsoft Office 2000 Standard are deployed using group policies. Right-click the **Software installation** node for a given GPO and select **Properties**. From the **Extensions** tab, access the list by pressing the arrow next to the drop-down box, select an extension, and then assign application priority (Figure 8.22). The application at the top of the list for a selected extension will be installed first. In Figure 8.22, only one office product package has been added to group policies, so no priority decision need be made.

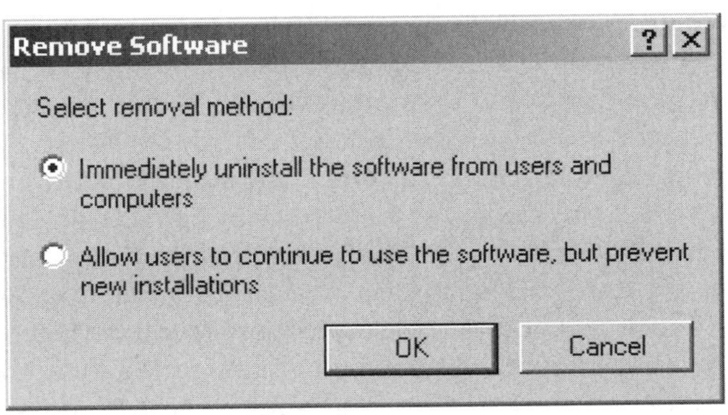

FIGURE 8.21 Software Removal Options

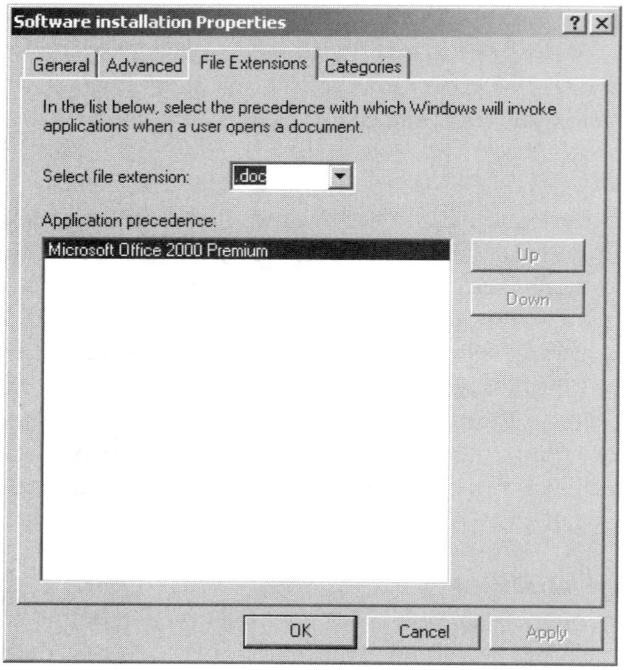

FIGURE 8.22 Associating File Extensions with Applications

Categories

When the user accesses the **Control Panel** to **Add/Remove Programs**, available applications will be listed. Categories can be used to create a hierarchy of application folders to order the software more effectively. Three new categories, *Draw Tools*, *Email Clients,* and *Word Processors*, can classify available applications (see Figure 8.23).

To add categories, right-click the **Software installation** node for a given GPO and select **Properties**. On the **Categories** tab, click **Add** and type in a new category name. Click **Apply** and then press **OK**. The new category will be added to the Active Directory and become available from any GPO in it.

Once the new category name has been made available, software applications may be added to the new category. Add a package by right-clicking a software package in the Details window of the GPO **Software installation** node and selecting **Properties**. On the **Categories** tab, choose a category from the **Available categories** pane and click **Select** to add the current package to it (Figure 8.24). In this example, the Microsoft Office 2000 Premium package would be available under the *Word Processors* category via **Control Panel → Add/Remove Programs**.

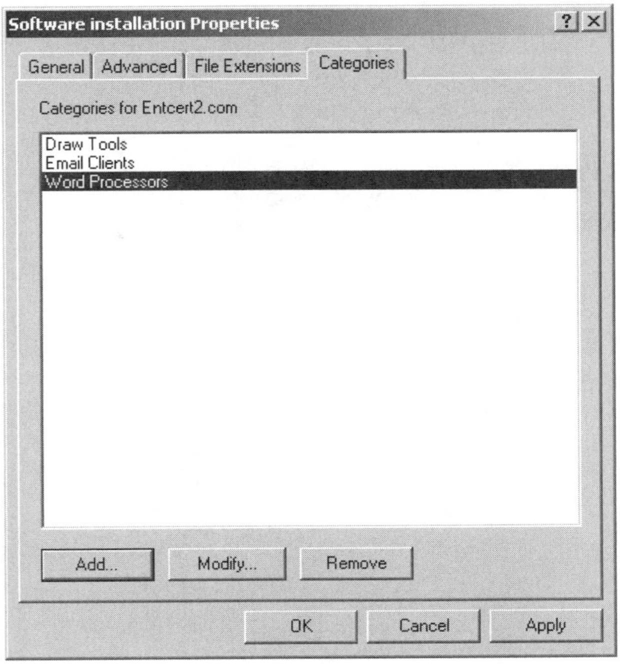

FIGURE 8.23 Adding New Software Categories

Application Modifications

Modifications may be made to customize a software application installation. Different GPOs may apply their own modifications to suit users who require additional features. A transform file or an .mst file is created to indicate application customizations. On the **Modifications** tab (Figure 8.25), click **Add** and browse for the desired .mst file.

In order for modifications to be added, the application must be installed using the **Advanced published or assigned** option from the **Deploy Software** dialog (Figure 8.16 on page 313). Once an application has been deployed, modifications cannot be added or removed.

NOTE The Application Deployment Editor in Windows .NET will contain a new option that allows a user-assigned application to be installed completely at logon. In previous versions, this was accomplished on demand. This could be useful when an administrator is planning to deploy an application to a group of mobile computer users. The application is immediately installed in full at logon. When the application is used offline, all features will then be available. The prompting to install

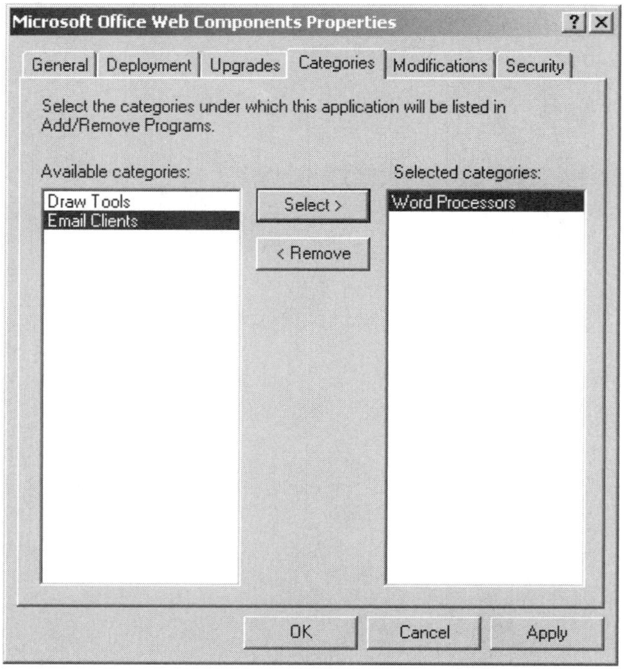

FIGURE 8.24 The Categories Tab

on-demand features is eliminated. This function is set using **Group Policy snap-in → Software Installation → Deployment Properties**. Another enhancement to Windows Server 2003 includes the ability to install 32-bit applications on 64-bit systems; from the Application Deployment Editor, select **Make 32-bit x 86 Windows Installer Application Available to IA64 machines.** Each application may be assigned a URL that is visible when a user clicks **Add/Remove Programs**. Help tips for installing and using the application can be posted at this Web address to minimize Help desk interaction.

NOTE With Windows Server 2003, the administrator can remove links to the Windows Update Web site from the user's desktop. This prevents users from adding software to their systems independent of company standards. Access this policy from the **Local Computer Policy node → User Configuration → Administrative Templates → Windows Components → Windows Update → Remove access to use all Windows Updates features;** for DataCenter Server, invoke **User Configuration → Administrative Templates → Start menu and Taskbar → Remove links and access to Windows Update**.

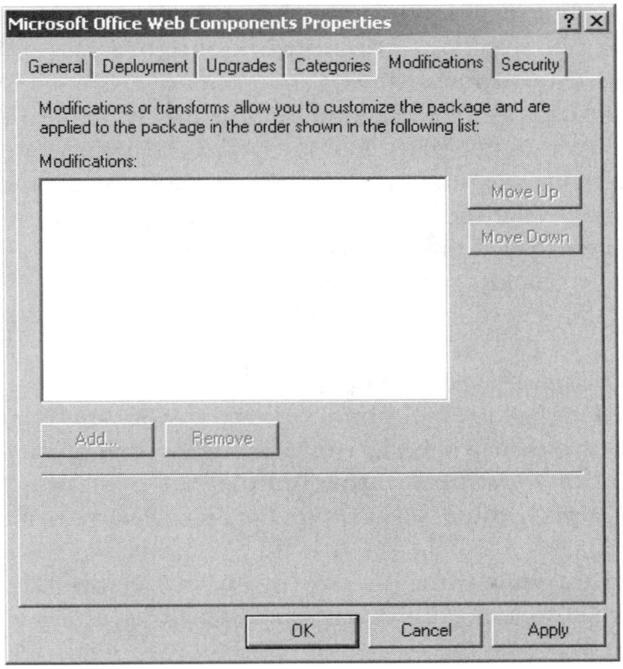

FIGURE 8.25 The Modifications Tab

Scripts

Group Policy enables assigning scripts to entire domains or OUs rather than modifying each user account and tediously mapping logon scripts to it. The Group Policy scripts execute as follows:

- User Configuration
  - Logon scripts, executed when the user logs on to a system.
  - Logoff scripts, executed when the user logs off the system.
- Computer Configuration
  - Startup scripts, executed when the system boots.
  - Shutdown scripts, executed when the system is shut down.

NOTE During the shutdown process, logoff scripts are executed before shutdown scripts. This allows gathering of log data, for example, to be written before the system terminates services and operations.

Scripting group policies for Windows Server 2003 can be found by highlighting the GPO and then selecting → **Computer Configuration** → **Windows Settings** → **Scripts (Startup\Shutdown)** and **gponame** → **User Configuration** → **Windows Settings** → **Scripts (Startup\Shutdown)** (Figure 8.26).

Windows Server 2003 comes equipped with the Windows Scripting Host (WSH) 1.0, which currently supports Javascript (.js) and Visual Basic Scripting Edition (.vbs) in addition to the MS-DOS command scripts (.bat, .com, .exe). The WSH may also be installed on Windows NT 4.0, 95, and 98 to support modern scripting languages on older systems. Scripts are accessed throughout the network by storing them in the server replication directory %systemroot%\SYSVOL\sysvol\domainname\scripts. (WSH 2.0 is discussed in Chapter 17.)

Additional policies that affect script performance can be found under Administrative Templates (Figures 8.27 and 8.28). If the WSH is not installed on the legacy systems, scripts may need to run in the DOS prompt window. Selecting **User Configuration** → **Administrative Templates** → **System** → **Logon** → **Run legacy logon scripts hidden** will minimize the script window or hide scripts from view.

The **Maximum wait time for Group Policy scripts** (Figure 8.28) and asynchronous/synchronous settings are also helpful for centrally managing script behavior.

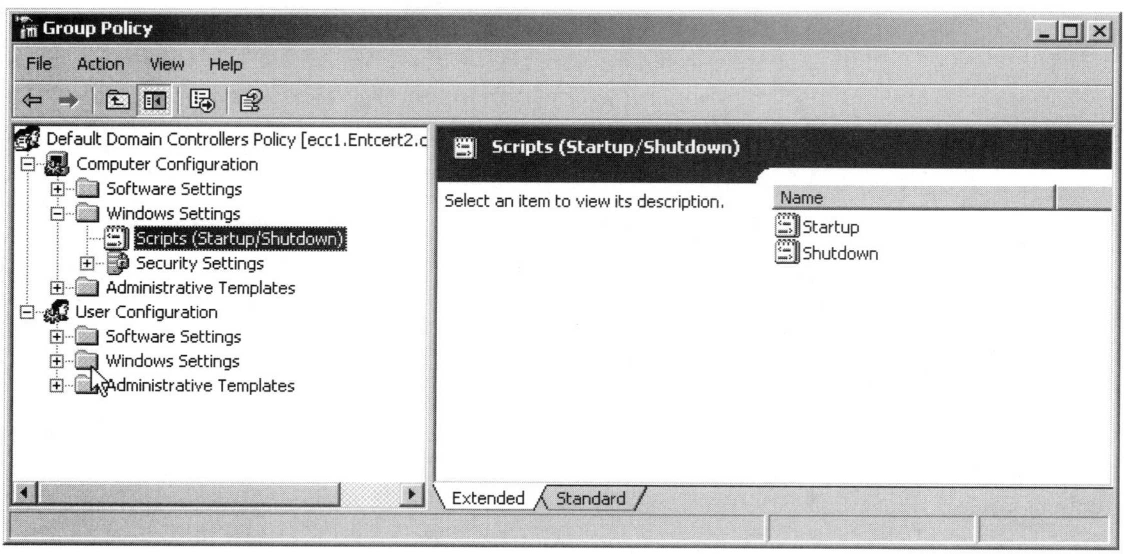

FIGURE 8.26 Shutdown

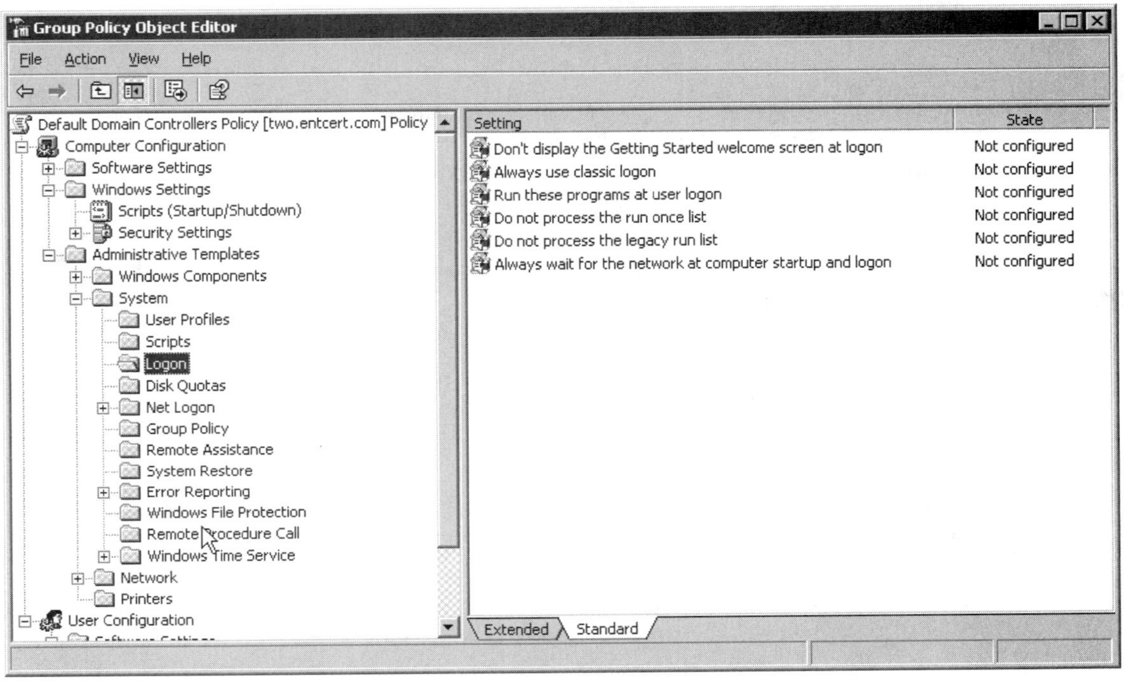

FIGURE 8.27 User Script Properties

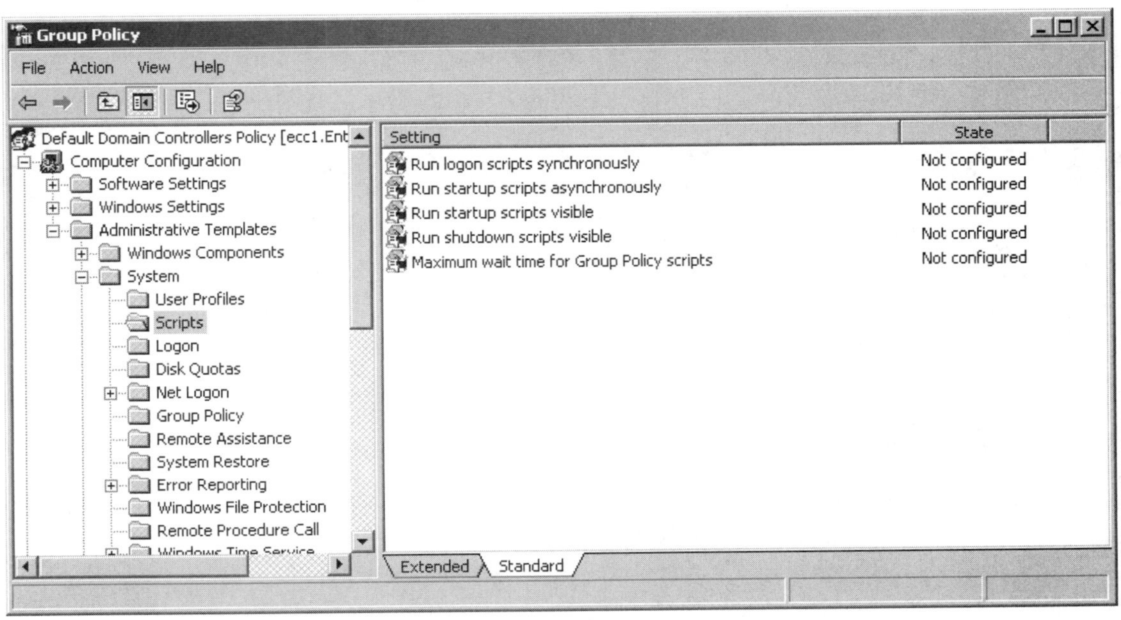

FIGURE 8.28 Computer Script Policies

FOLDER REDIRECTION

The Folder Redirection policies allow the administrator to relocate several directories in the user's profile (Figure 8.29). Even with roaming user profiles, the profile directories are copied to the local system (%SystemRoot%\Documents and Settings*username*) when the user logs on. This can be time consuming and can impact the network, especially for large My Documents folders.

NOTE The discussion of redirection involves elements of Microsoft's IntelliMirror, which is discussed at the end of this chapter. As stated earlier, the ability to set policies on folder direction that can be **intelli**gently **mirror**ed across the enterprise is one of the primary features of IntelliMirror technology.

Redirection policies can relocate four user profile directories to a centrally managed network share so that they are not copied to the local system.

The Offline Folder or Cache settings may be set on the network share to allow local system access to these network profile folders when the user's system cannot access the network. The profile information is cached locally and then updated on the network share when the user has access to the share at a later date.

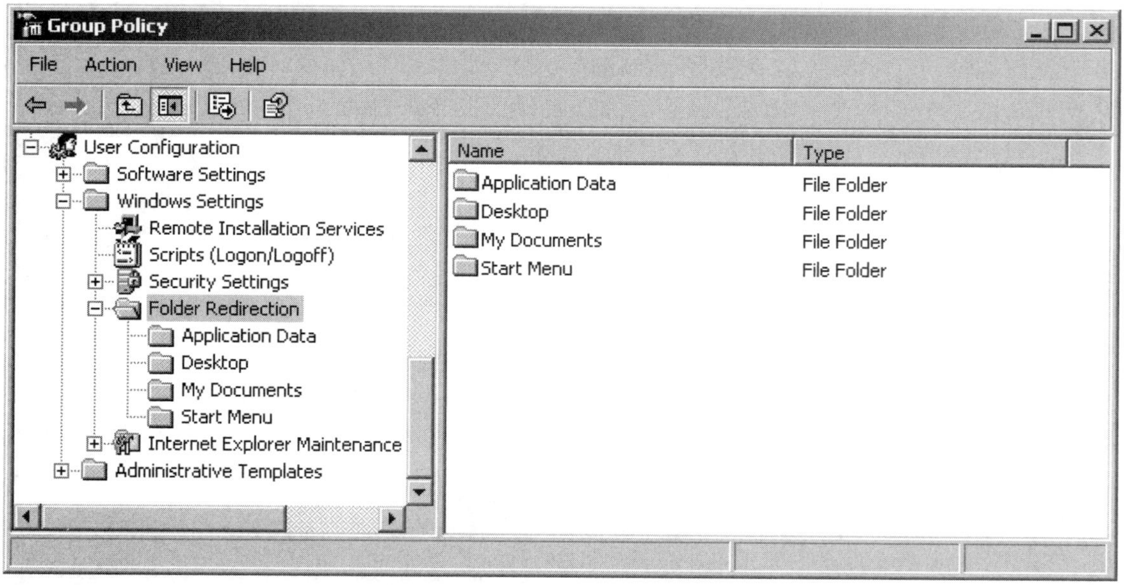

FIGURE 8.29 Folder Redirection Policies

NOTE An administrator can use this feature to transition users from a legacy deployment of home directories to the My Documents model. This will ensure compatibility with the existing home directory environment.

NOTE Group Policy in Windows Server 2003 determines a users right to modify network and dial-up TCP/IP properties. Users may be selectively restricted from modifying their IP address and other network configuration parameters.

GPO IMPLEMENTATION

The previous sections of this chapter provide some understanding of Group Policy application and usage. Before we discuss actually implementing GPO, there are a few systemic issues to address regarding Group Policy behavior.

Refreshing Policy Settings

Understanding the basic Group Policy refresh schedule is helpful when changing group policies on your local system. Once a group policy has been changed on a domain controller, the group policies on the local system must be refreshed in order to take effect. Client computers that are not domain controllers receive policy refreshes every 90 minutes plus or minus a random time interval. The random interval helps distribute client requests evenly so that they do not all come in at the same time. To change the interval in a GPO, select **Computer Configuration → Administrative Templates → System → Group Policy → Group Policy refresh interval for computers** (Figure 8.30).

Domain controllers refresh group policies more frequently. The default Group Policy setting for DCs, via **Computer Configuration → Administrative Templates → System → Group Policy → Group Policy refresh interval for domain controllers,** sets the refresh interval for every 5 minutes (Figure 8.31). This is why successive examples should be executed on a domain controller.

NOTE Security policy refresh can be instigated from the command line. The **gpudate** command has replaced **secedit** utility. Use **secedit** for Windows 2000 servers and **gpupdate** for Windows 2003 servers. These commands are discussed in the appendix; its basic forms are:

```
secedit /refreshpolicy machine_policy /enforce (for Windows 2000
   computer settings)
secedit /refreshpolicy machine_policy /enforce (for Windows 2000 user
   settings)
gpupdate /enforce (Windows Server 2003)
```

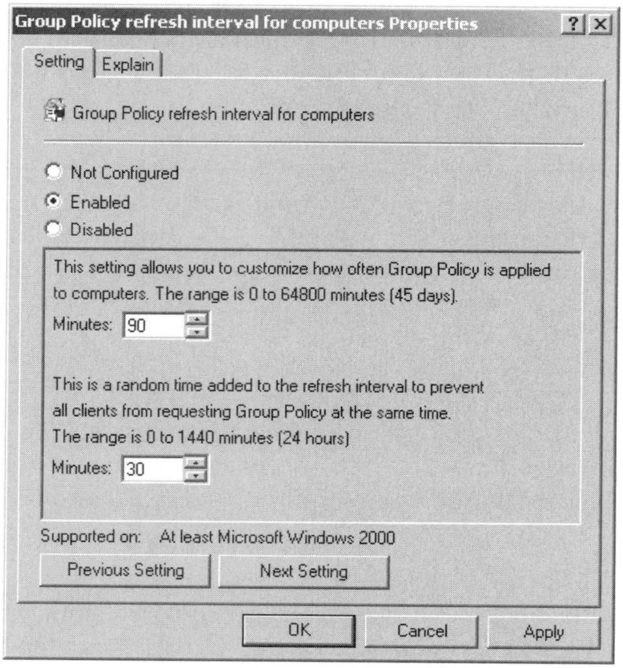

FIGURE 8.30 Setting Client Group Policy Refresh Intervals

Group policies are also refreshed when the system is started. Obviously, shutting down and booting a system could prove troublesome when simply trying to refresh policy settings.

PDC Operations Manager

In addition to performing the functions of the primary domain controller (PDC Emulator), the PDC Operations Manager is the default domain controller that handles Group Policy modifications. When the PDC Operations Manager is not available, an error message is displayed and the administrator may select another domain controller to handle changes. When you do this, be sure that all previous Group Policy changes have propagated throughout the domain and that no other administrator is currently making modifications.

IMPLEMENTING GROUP POLICY

This section provides a number of examples of implementing group policies. These examples are representative of the type of Group Policy management available to the system administrator.

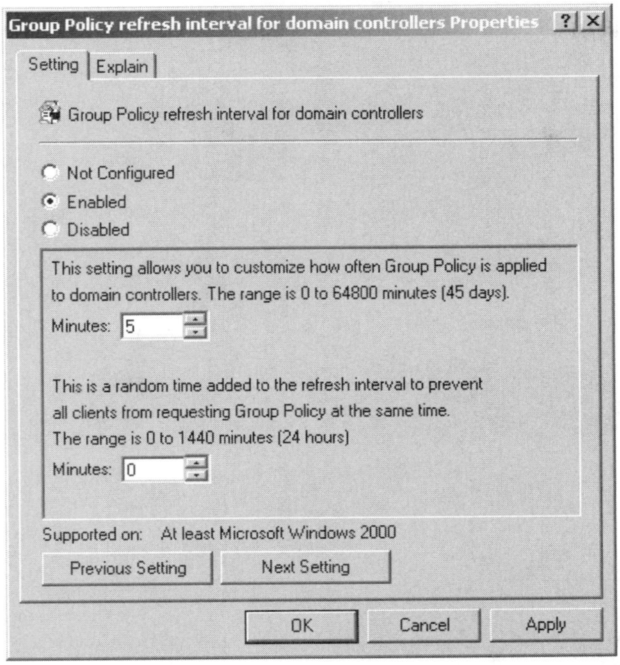

FIGURE 8.31 Setting Domain Controller Group Policy Refresh Intervals

Local Computer Policy

The example that follows shows how to implement the Local Computer Policy snap-in and employ it to manage local GPOs. This is the easiest way to access this GPO; other GPOs can be reached through the Active Directory containers. Local computer policies are centrally managed on remote systems by adding the remote computer policies to the administrator's console. This example loads the local policies for the system the administrator is logged on to.

1. Log on as **Administrator**.
2. Go to **Start** → **Programs** → **Accessories** → **command prompt** or **Start** → **Run,** type **MMC,** and then **Enter**.
3. A **Console** window appears. Click the **File** pull-down menu.
4. Select **Add/Remove** snap-in.
5. The **Add/Remove Snap-in** dialog should appear (Figure 8.32).
6. Click **Add**. The **Add Standalone Snap-in** dialog should appear.
7. Select **Active Directory Users and Computers**.
8. Click **Add**.

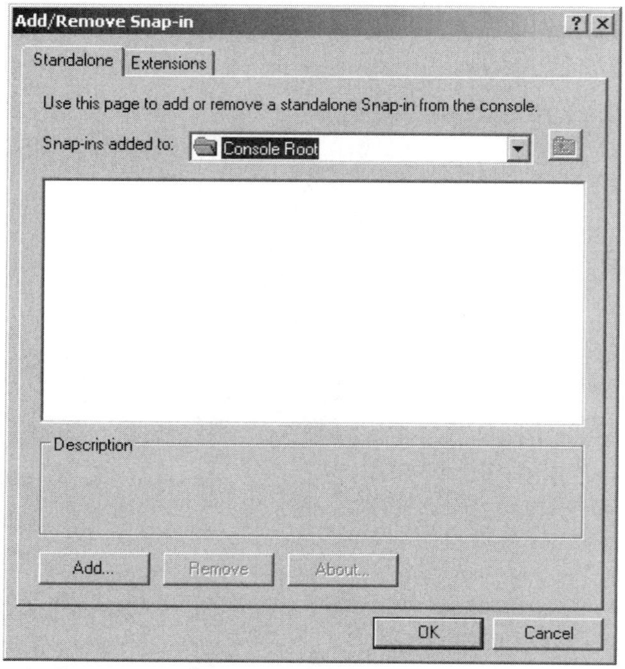

FIGURE 8.32 The Snap-in List

9. From the list of **Available Standalone snap-ins,** select **Group Policy** (Figure 8.33).
10. Click **Add**. The **Group Policy Object** should be LocalComputer (Figure 8.34).
11. Click **Browse**. The **Browse for a Group Policy Object** dialog appears (Figure 8.35).
12. There are four tabs associated with this dialog:
    - The **Domains/OUs** tab displays GPOs for the domain and OU containers.
    - The **Sites** tab displays current sites and their associated GPOs (Figure 8.36).
    - The **Computers** tab allows you to select the local GPO assigned to the current computer or to select another computer from Active Directory. This provides remote administration of local computer policies (Figure 8.37).
    - The **All** tab displays all GPOs for the domain except the local computer policy object (Figure 8.38).
13. For this example, click **Cancel,** and select **Local Computer** as the **Group Policy Object**.
14. Click **Finish**, then **Close,** then **OK**.

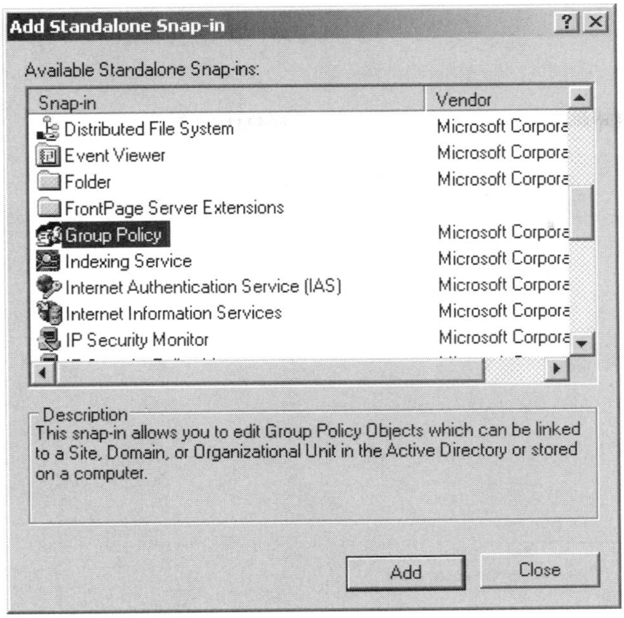

FIGURE 8.33 Adding a Standalone Snap-In

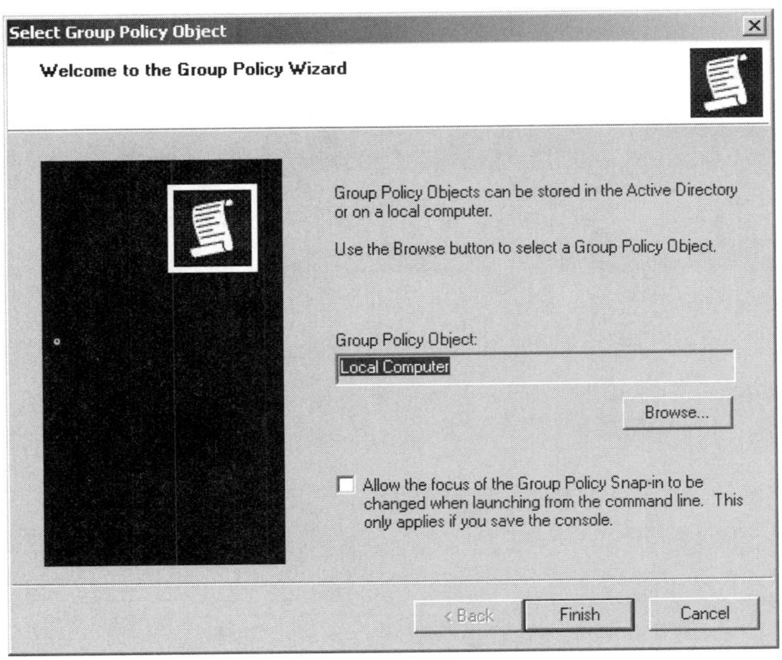

FIGURE 8.34 Selecting a Group Policy Object

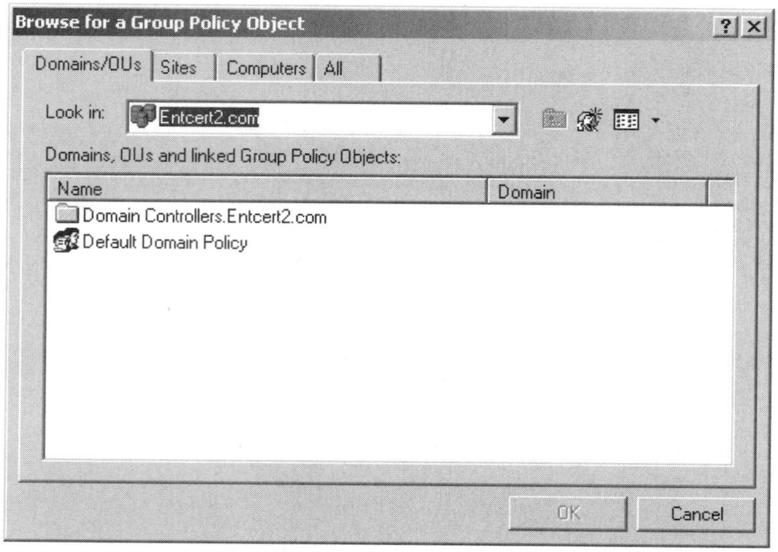

FIGURE 8.35 GPOs Available for a Domain

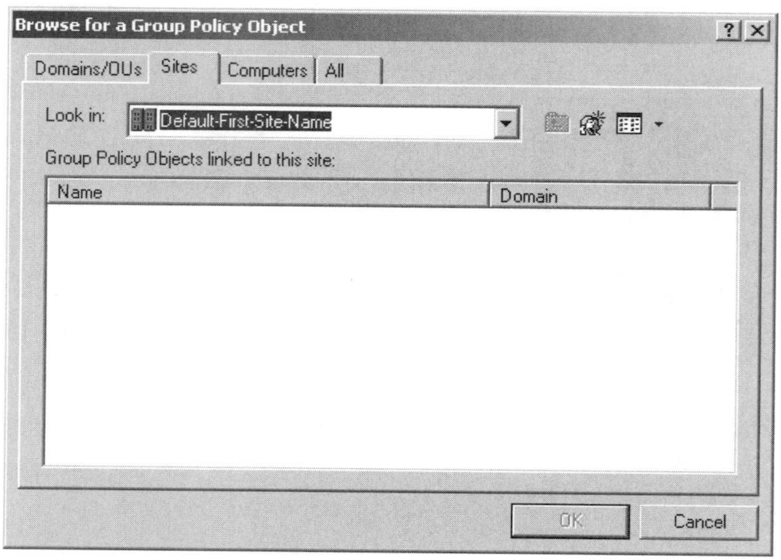

FIGURE 8.36 GPOs Linked to Sites

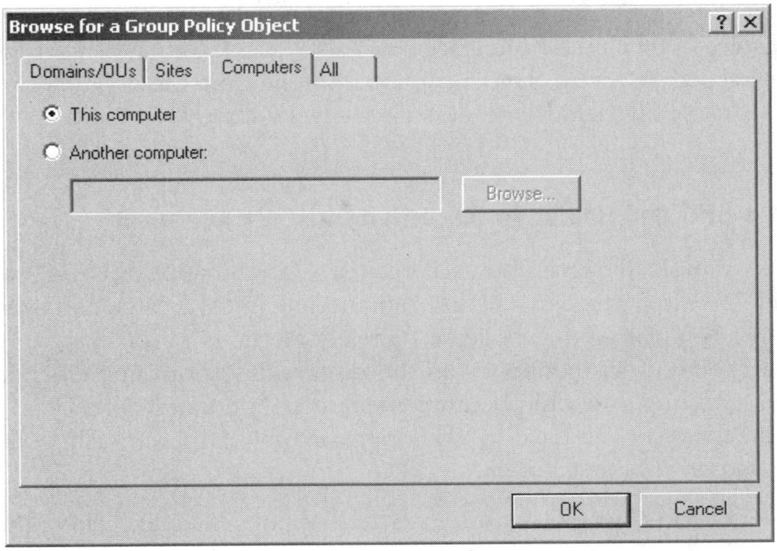

FIGURE 8.37 A Computer GPO

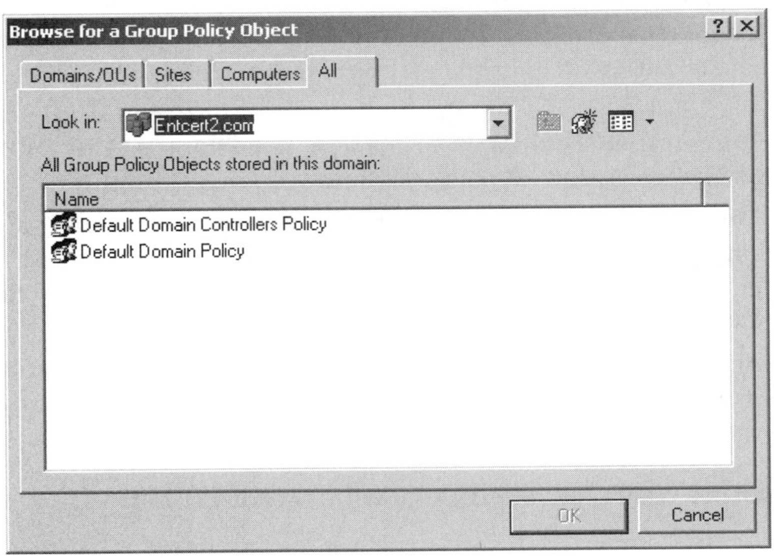

FIGURE 8.38 All GPOs in a Domain

The Local Computer Policy snap-in has now been added to your newly created console. Opening the **Policy** node reveals available local policy settings. When you are finished, select the **Save As** option from the **Console** pull-down menu and save the console on the desktop or in a specific folder.

Creating a GPO and Linking to the Active Directory Container

This example illustrates how to create a GPO and apply it to an Active Directory container. In particular, a new organizational unit is created and then an Administrative Template group policy is enabled. Methods for blocking inheritances are also explored. As mentioned in the discussions about implementation, the following examples should be implemented on a domain controller. Doing so will mean that you will have to wait approximately 5 minutes for policies to be refreshed on your test system.

1. Start the **Custom** console created earlier by double-clicking the console file from **My Computer** or the desktop.
2. Click the plus sign in front of **Active Directory Users and Computers**. Right-click ***Your domain*.com (Entcert2.com)** and select **New → Organizational Unit**. Create a new OU called **Engineering** and add a user.
3. Create an OU within **Engineering** called **Sustaining** and add a user (Figure 8.39).
4. Right-click the **Engineering** OU and select **Properties**. The **Engineering Properties** dialog box appears (Figure 8.40). Select the **Group Policy** tab and click **New**. Name the new object **Engineering GPO** (Table 8.3).
5. Click **Edit** and select the plus sign in front of **User Configuration → Administrative Templates → System → CTRL + ALT + DEL Options**. In the Policy window, double-click **Remove Lock Computer**.
6. The **Remove Lock Computer Properties** dialog window appears. Select **Enabled**. Notice that the **Previous Setting** and **Next Setting** buttons allow you to browse up and down the Policy window. Click **OK**. The **Remove Lock Computer** policy has been enabled at the Engineering OU level (Figure 8.41).
7. Allow Group Policy to refresh and log on as an Engineering user. Press **CTRL + ALT + DEL** and notice that **Lock Computer** appears dimmed. Log on again as the Administrator.

DISABLING COMPUTER AND USER CONFIGURATION SETTINGS

As discussed earlier, it is helpful to disable the portions of a GPO that are not being used to save processing time when applying group policies. User and computer settings can be disabled if no policies are enabled below the node in the policy

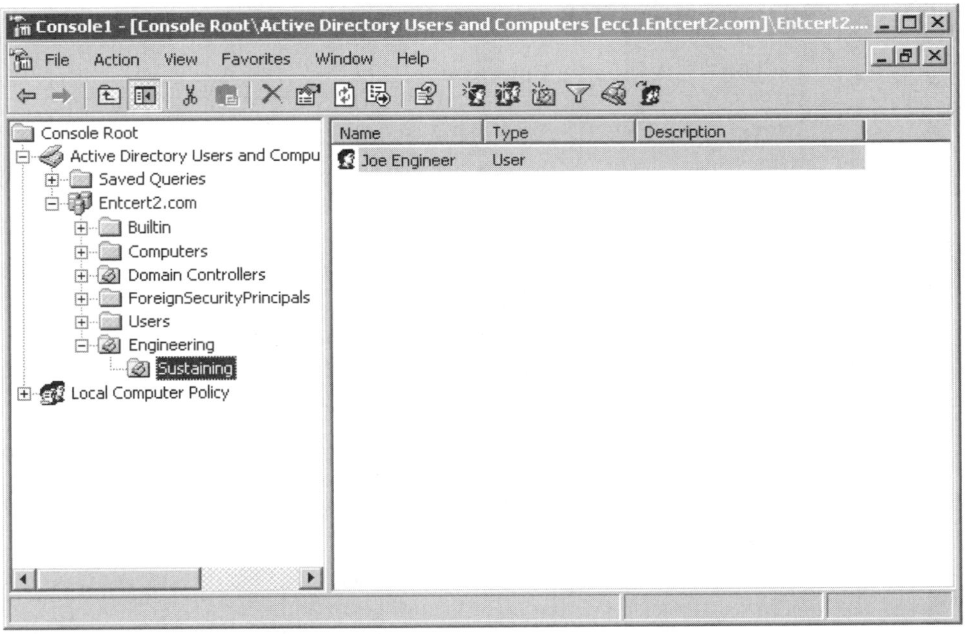

FIGURE 8.39 Creating New OUs

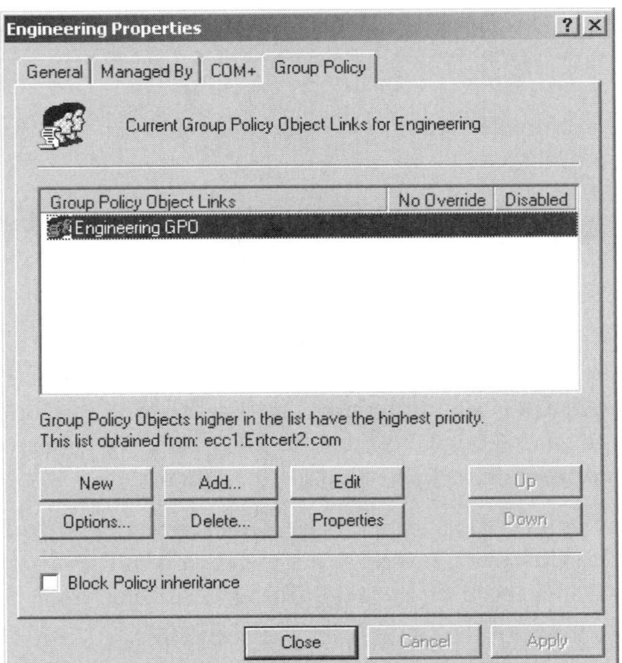

FIGURE 8.40 Create an Engineering GPO

TABLE 8.3 Group Policy Tab Buttons and Functions

Button	Function
New	Creates a new GPO and adds it to the Active Directory container.
Add	Selects from a list of existing GPOs or creates a new GPO to add to the current container.
Edit	Displays the Group Policy tree for the selected GPO and allows policy modification.
Options	Allows user to enforce this GPO on this container and child containers below it or to prevent this policy from acting on the container.
Delete	Removes the selected GPO from the container Group Policy list.
Properties	Allows the administrator to disable the user or computer portion of the GPO to enhance boot-up or user logon speed. Permits this GPO to be linked by other domains and allows access to security settings for the selected GPO.
Up	Promotes the selected GPO in the current GPO list. GPOs are applied from the top of the list to the bottom.
Down	Demotes the selected GPO in the current GPO list. GPOs are applied from the top of the list to the bottom.
Block inheritance	Blocks policy inheritance from a parent container.

hierarchy. In this example, we have set a user policy and can therefore disable the computer portion of the GPO.

1. Right-click the Engineering OU and select **Properties**. Select the **Group Policy** tab. Click **Edit**.
2. Right-click the Engineering GPO root node and select **Properties**. On the **General** tab, select **Disable Computer Configuration settings** (Figure 8.42).

Users in the Engineering OU and its child OUs will also inherit this policy. For a child OU to disable a policy inherited from its parents, it must counteract the policy setting using another GPO. Let's create a GPO at a lower level to override the **Remove Lock Computer** policy setting.

1. Click the plus sign in front of the **Active Directory Users and Computers** selection in the **Custom** console. Open your *domain name* node, the **Engineering** OU node, and then the **Sustaining** OU node.
2. Right-click the **Sustaining** OU and select **Properties**. The **Sustaining Properties** dialog appears. Click the **Group Policy** tab.

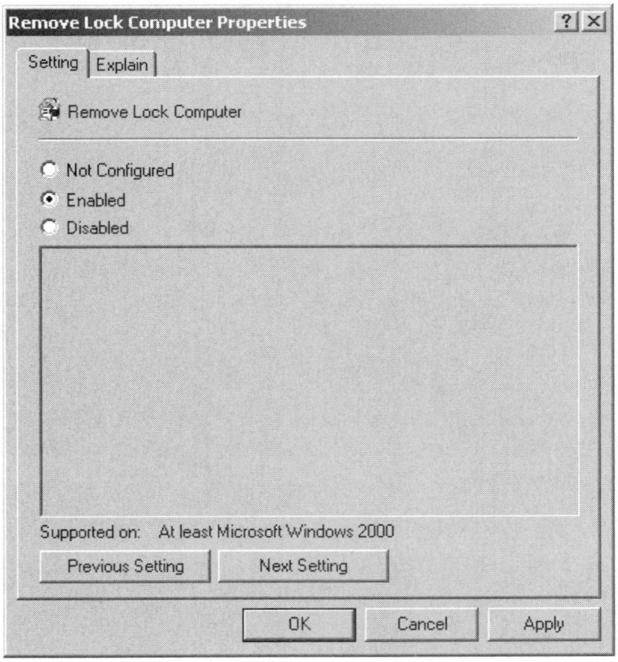

FIGURE 8.41 Policy Details

3. Click **New**. Name the new object **Sustaining GPO.**
4. Highlight the new GPO and click **Edit**.
5. Click the plus sign in front of **User Configuration,** then select **Administrative Templates → System → CTRL + ALT + DEL Options**. In the Policy window, double-click the **Remove Lock Computer** policy. Select **Disabled**. Click **OK**.
6. The **Remove Lock Computer** policy should be disabled at the Sustaining OU level.
7. Log off the system and log on again as a Sustaining user. Notice that the **Lock Workstation** button no longer appears dimmed.

By disabling the Remove Lock Computer policy in the Sustaining GPO, users in the Sustaining OU will be able to lock their systems. Rather than directly override an inherited policy, try using the Block Policy Inheritance feature as follows:

- From the **Custom** console, open the **Sustaining** OU and right-click **Properties**. Select the **Group Policy** tab and select the **Sustaining** GPO. Click **Edit**. Proceed to **Remove Lock Computer** policy → **User Configuration** →

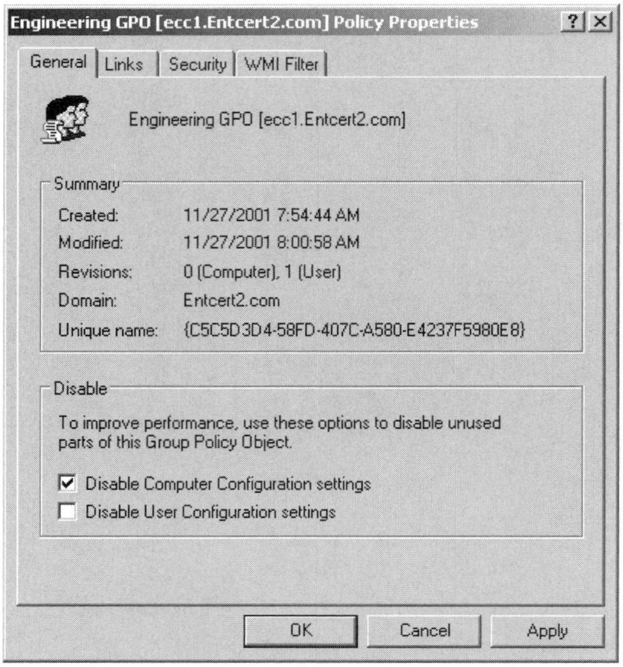

FIGURE 8.42 Disabling Computer Configuration Settings

Administrative Templates → System → CTRL + ALT + DEL Options. In the Policy window, double-click **Remove Lock Computer**. Select **Not Configured**. Click **OK**.

Now the **Remove Lock Computer** policy will again be inherited by the Sustaining OU.

Block policy inheritance from the Engineering OU as follows:

- Close the **Group Policy** window. In the **Sustaining Properties** dialog box, check the **Block Policy inheritance** box (Figure 8.43). Close the **Custom** console, log off, and log on as a Sustaining user. Notice that the **Lock Workstation** box is still accessible. Blocking policy inheritance prevents the Engineering GPO from being applied to the Sustaining OU.

Enforcing a GPO from the Engineering OU takes precedence over both the block policy inheritance and the policy override settings.

1. Open the **Custom** console, right-click the **Engineering** OU, and select **Properties**.

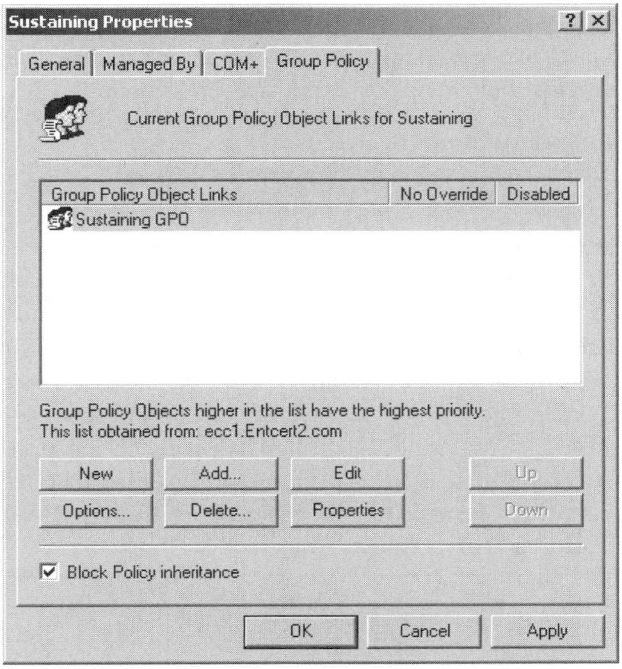

FIGURE 8.43 Blocking Policy Inheritance at the Sustaining OU

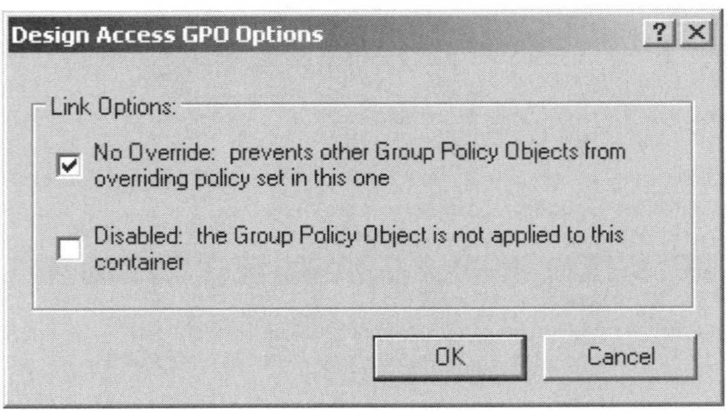

FIGURE 8.44 The No Override Group Policy Object Setting

2. Select the **Group Policy** tab and click **New**. Name the new **GPO Design Access GPO**. Press **Options** and check the **No Override** check box (Figure 8.44). Click **OK**. Notice that the **No Override** column is now checked. This feature can also be enabled/disabled by going to the **Engineering Properties** dialog box and double-clicking in the **No Override** column.

3. The Design Access GPO is now enforced at the Engineering OU level.
4. Exit **Custom** console, log off, and log on as a Sustaining user. Notice that the **Lock Workstation** button appears dimmed once again.

The Sustaining group cannot override an enforced policy from a parent. The Block Inheritance feature is also unable to prevent enforced policy inheritance.

NOTE One of the tasks an administrator should undertake is preventing users from "tattooing" the Registry. From the Administrative Templates node, the user can view user preferences in addition to policy settings. The user can view and modify user preferences that are not stored in maintained portions of the Registry. If the group policy is removed or changed, the user preference will persist in the Registry. This is known as "tattooing," a prominent problem in earlier group policy implementations. Avoid letting users modify user preferences by going to **User Configuration → Administrative Templates → System → Group Policy** → enable **Enforce Show Policies Only** (Figure 8.45).

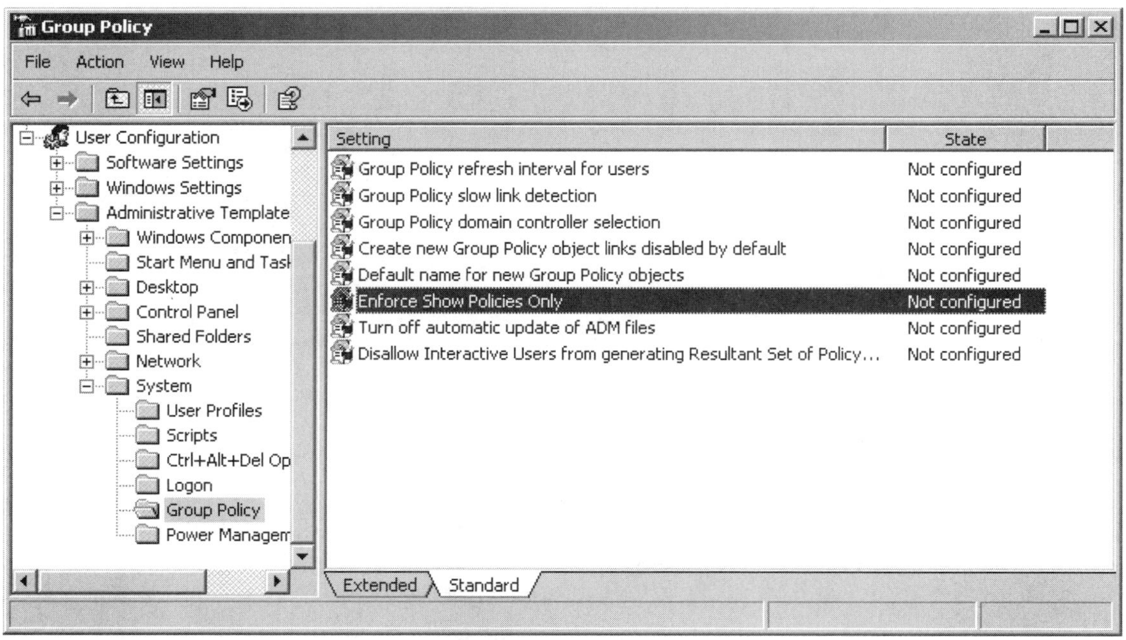

FIGURE 8.45 Limiting Registry Tattooing by Enabling a Policy

Security Group Filtering

GPOs that are linked to a given Active Directory container (site, domain, or OU) apply to all authenticated users in the container by default. However, Security permissions associated with a GPO also govern which users the GPO will apply to. A security group may deny the GPO policy, thereby making all users who are members of that group immune to it. Let's look at an example.

1. Create a domain local security group called **Software Config** and add an **Engineering** OU user to it.
2. Go to the **Engineering** OU, right-click **Properties**, and view the **Group Policy** tab. Select the **Engineering** GPO and click **Properties**.
3. Click the **Securities** tab (Figure 8.46) and click **Add**. Add the **Software Config** security group to the Engineering GPO's access control list.
4. Select the **Software Config** group and check the **Deny** box on the **Apply Group Policy** permissions line.
5. Click **OK** and answer **Yes** to the **Warning** dialog box.

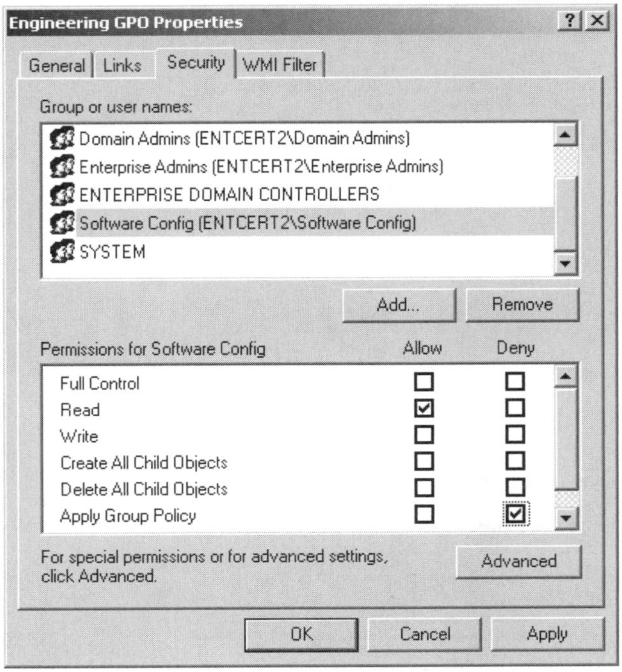

FIGURE 8.46 GPO Security for Software Config

6. Log off and log on as the Engineering OU user previously added to the Software Config security group. The **Lock Workstation** button should be accessible.

This new member of the Software Config group has filtered out the Engineering GPO by denying the Apply Group Policy permission. Even though the user is also a member of the Engineering OU, the Deny permission from the Software Config group takes priority over all other security groups that may allow Apply Group Policy. In the following steps, the Engineering GPO will be rendered useless if neither the Allow box nor the Deny box is marked for the Apply Group Policy permission for all security groups associated with it.

1. Go to the Engineering GPO **Properties** dialog box. Remove all security groups except Enterprise Admins and Software Config. Select the **Software Config** group and ensure that the **Apply Group Policy** box is not checked under **Allow** or **Deny** for either group (Figure 8.47). You may have to press the **Advanced** button and clear the **Inherit from parent the permission entries that apply to child objects** option.

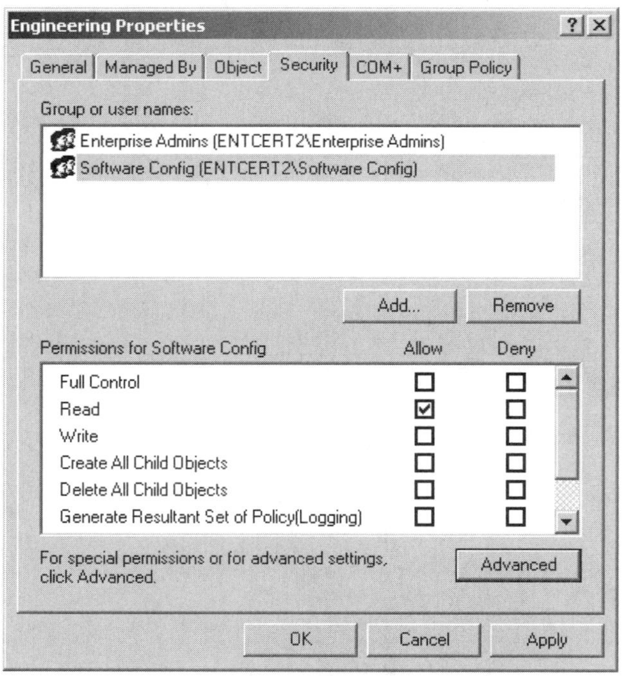

FIGURE 8.47 The Domain Users Security Group

2. The Enterprise Admins group should allow **Read/Write/Create All Child Objects/Delete All Child Objects** so that administrative functions can still be performed on the GPO.
3. Log off and log on as the Engineering user. The **Lock Workstation** button should be accessible. The GPO is not applied to the Software Config group of which the user is a member.

If the Domain Users group allowed Apply Group Policy, then the user would have the group policy applied. A user must be a member of a security group that applies the group policy in order to use the GPO. The default security settings for GPOs apply policies to the Authenticated Users group. This covers most users with interactive logon capability.

Scripts

In a previous section, we discussed the conceptual basis of scripts. For system administration, scripts can be used for numerous activities. A script can be executed in one of four time periods: startup, shutdown, logon, or logoff.

This example runs a test script when the user logs on to a system:

1. Create a very simple test Java script to run on logon. Open **Notepad** and enter the following line:

```
Wscript.echo("You have run the logon script!");
```

2. Save the file as testscript.js on the local hard drive.
3. Open the **Custom** console and find the **Engineering** OU. Open the group policies linked to this OU and edit the **Engineering** GPO.
4. Follow the **User Configuration** → **Windows Settings** → **Scripts** path and double-click the **Logon Properties** (Figure 8.48).
5. Click **Add** to expose the **Add a Script** dialog box (Figure 8.49). Click **Browse** and find the file named testscript.js. Click **OK**.

The script should be available to the user at logon.

Scripts execute from top to bottom and may be rearranged by clicking the **Up** and **Down** buttons. The **Edit** button allows script path modification, name changing, and parameter editing. Scripts are removed by clicking the **Remove** button.

The **Show Files** button displays the scripts stored in the default directory for this GPO. The startup and shutdown script policies may found in **Computer Configuration** → **Windows Settings** → **Scripts**.

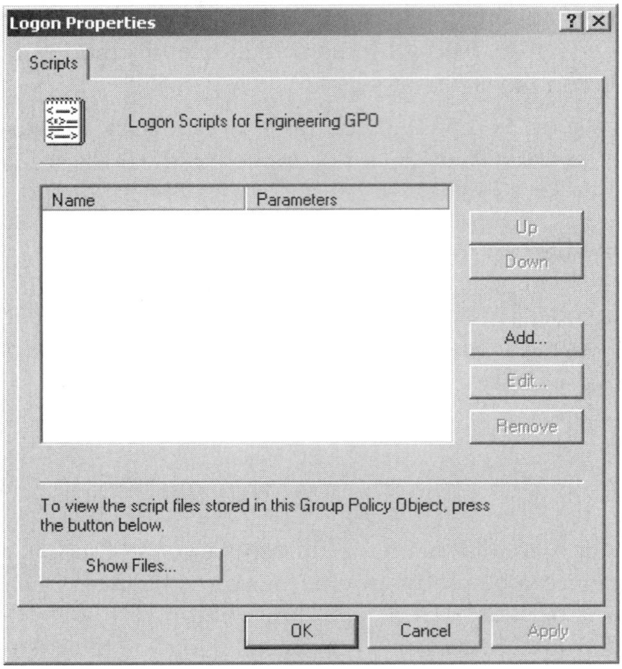

FIGURE 8.48 Logon Scripts

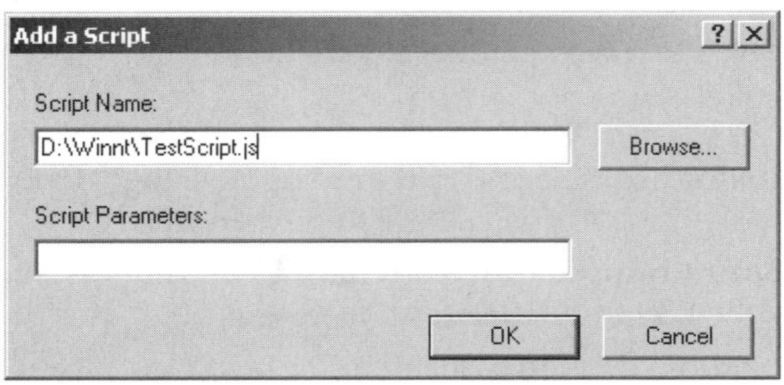

FIGURE 8.49 Adding a Script

Folder Redirection

This example will illustrate how to implement folder redirection. To redirect all My Document folders for the Engineering OU to one common server, follow these steps:

1. Edit the **Engineering** GPO applied to the Engineering OU. Go to **User Configuration → Windows Settings → Folder Redirection → My Docu-**

ments. Right-click **My Documents** and select **Properties**. The **My Document Properties** window appears. From the **Setting** pull-down menu, select **Basic—Redirect everyone's folder to the same location**.

2. Click **Browse** and find a shared server folder for all Engineering users.
3. Click **OK**.

See the later section "IntelliMirror" for examples of folder redirection.

RESULTANT SET OF POLICY

With Windows Server 2003 administrators can determine the actual resulting set of policy for a given user or computer. They can also play what-if scenarios. These features are reflected in two new modes. The *logging mode* allows examination of what was processed on a given computer. The *planning mode* permits performance of "what-if" analysis for a specified location in the directory, security group membership, and WMI filtering properties.

The Resultant Set of Policy (RSoP) wizard guides an administrator through the steps necessary to this process. This tool can determine the state of a target and run scenarios. As the user manipulates the way in which Group Policy might be applied, the impacts can then be analyzed. This allows quick inspection of differences under new criteria. This feature is available in the Resultant Set of Policy Snap-in or the Active Directory Users and Computers Snap-in; right-click a container, user, or computer.

GROUP POLICY WMI FILTERING

The Windows Management Instrumentation (WMI) filtering is an addition to the Group Policy infrastructure of Windows Server 2003. It is designed to enable the administrator to specify a WMI-based query to filter the affect of a Group Policy Object. This is an addition to the GPO Properties page as a new tab. A filter can be specified, created, and edited. Support is also included to allow RSoP to display existing WMI filters. Conceptually, this is similar to how Windows 2000 handled the Security group filtering. The advantage of this feature is to allow an administrator to dynamically determine whether to apply a GPO based on any properties available via WMI especially for exception management. This function is available by invoking **Group Policy Properties** page → **WMI Filter** tab.

INTELLIMIRROR

One of the more widely promoted aspects of Windows Server 2003, IntelliMirror simply brings together other Windows Server technologies to provide more intelligent user interfacing. In particular, it helps to reconcile desktop settings, applications, and stored files for users, particularly those who move between workstations or those who must periodically work offline. This section provides a highlight of IntelliMirror functionality.

Roaming Documents and Preferences

Together folder redirection and offline folders provide centralized management and storage of user documents. Additionally, the user is permitted to access and update documents when not connected to the network. This design is ideally suited to laptop users. Maintaining an offline folder on the network allows the administrator to perform backups on a scheduled basis without direct concern for backing up the laptop system.

REDIRECTING MY DOCUMENT FOLDERS

In this example the user's My Documents folder is redirected to a directory in his name under a shared network folder using group policies. The My Documents folder is designated as offline. A security group is used to determine which users and groups the folder redirection policy will affect.

1. Create a network share called **\Network Docs and Settings.**
2. Create a global security group called **Engineers** and a new user account called **Joe Engineer**.
3. Add **Joe Engineer** to the **Engineers** group.

Redirect Joe Engineer's **My Documents** folder to the network share folder using the Default Domain Policy.

1. From the **Default Domain Policy,** right-click the **User Configuration → Windows Settings → Folder Redirection → My Documents** and select **Properties** (Figure 8.50).
2. Select the **Target** tab and select **Advanced–Specify locations for various user groups**. Click **Add** to reveal the **Specify Group and Location** dialog (see Figure 8.51) and browse for the Engineers group. Click **Add**, then click **OK**.
3. Under **Target Folder Location**, click **Browse** and search for the \Network Docs and Settings folder on the appropriate server. Complete the path name using the \\servername\Network Docs and Settings\%username%. The %username% environmental variable will be used to create a separate directory for each user. Click **OK**.

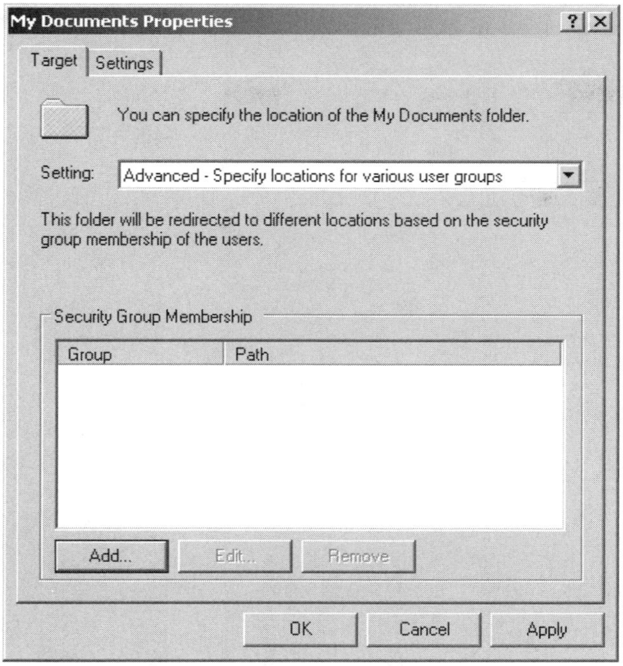

FIGURE 8.50 Folder Redirection

4. On the **Settings** tab, make appropriate choices for policy removal and permissions. The default settings are fine for this example. Click **OK**.

Now all users in the Engineers security group will have their folders redirected to the new network share and have their own My Documents subdirectory below their personal folder. Let's use offline folders to allow the engineering users access to their documents when they are offline.

1. Go to Joe Engineer's laptop and right-click **My Computer** and select **Explore**. From the **Tools** pull-down menu, select **Folder Options**. Select the **Offline Files** tab and enable the **Enable Offline Files** option.
2. From **My Computer**, right-click the **My Documents** folder and select **Make Available Offline**. The **Offline Files Wizard** starts. Click **Next**.
3. Select the **Automatically synchronize the Offline Files when I log on and log off my computer** option to instruct the Synchronization Manager to handle file updates between the remote system and the network share. Click **Next**.

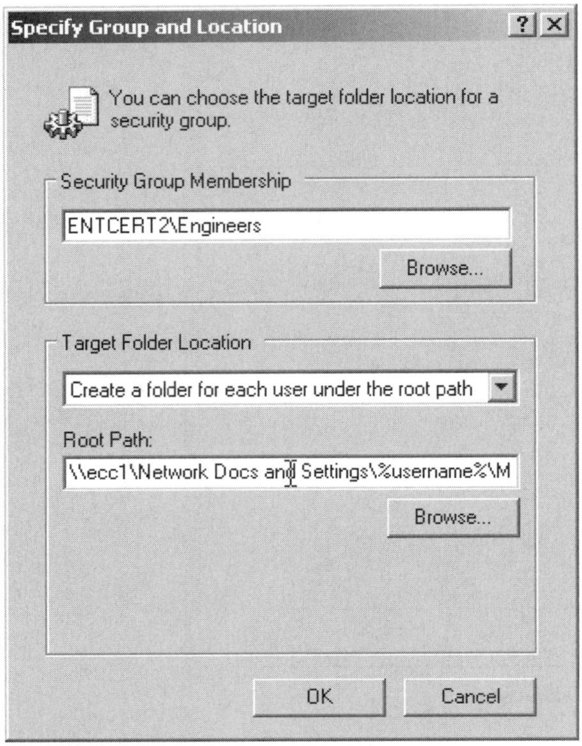

FIGURE 8.51 Redirect Security Group to Target Folder

4. Select the **Create shortcut** option. Click **Next**.
5. Select **Yes, make this folder and all its subfolders available offline**. Click **OK**.

Now when Joe Engineer logs on to his laptop when not connected to the network, an offline dialog warns that the system is offline. An icon on the taskbar appears. Right-clicking the icon gives the user four options:

- ***Status*** indicates whether the folder is offline or online.
- ***Synchronize*** allows manual synchronization of the offline files.
- ***View Files*** displays all files that are available offline.
- ***Settings*** sets reminders, synchronization, and offline availability (see Figure 8.52).

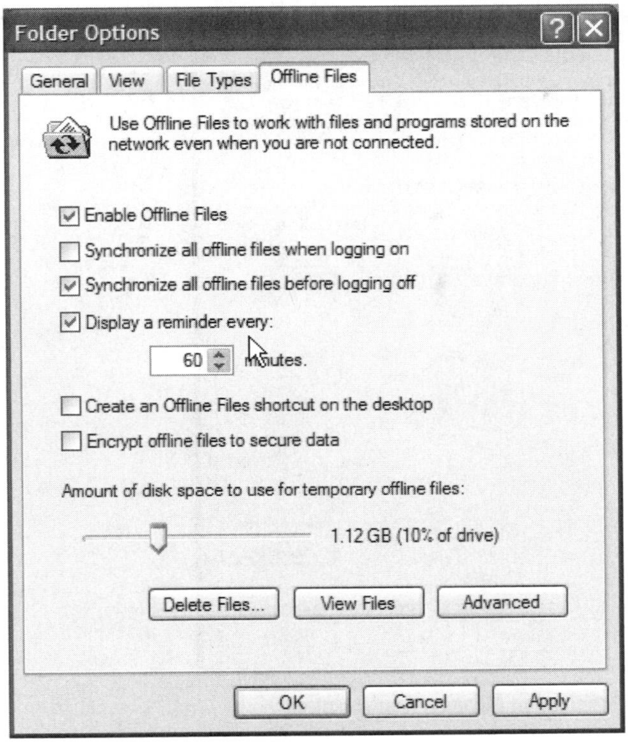

FIGURE 8.52 Offline Settings

The Synchronization Manager may be manually started from either the **My Computer** or **My Network Places** desktop tools. From the **Tools** pull-down, select **Synchronize.** Manual synchronization can be started by selecting the desired directories and pressing the **Synchronize** button. Clicking **Setup** allows configuration via three tabs (Figure 8.53):

- ***Logon/Logoff***—logon, logoff, and prompting before synchronization configuration
- ***On Idle***—idle time before synchronization configuration
- ***Scheduled***—times and directories to synchronize

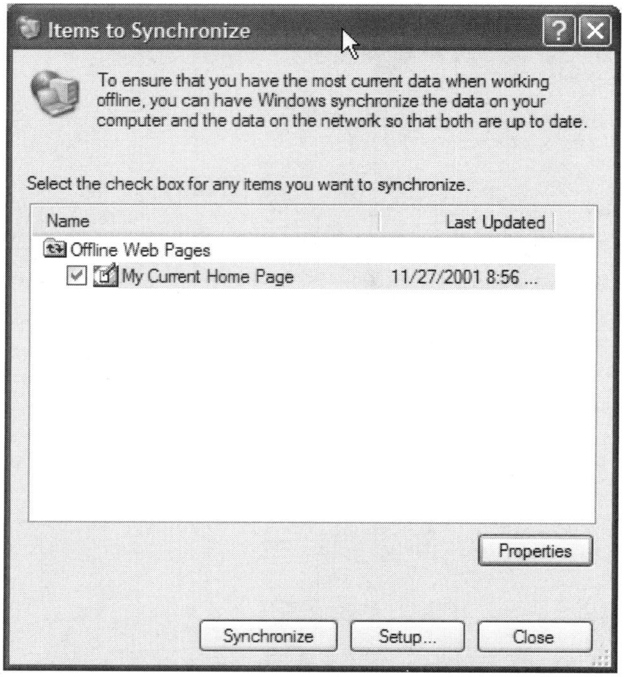

FIGURE 8.53 Synchronization Manager Configuration

POSTSCRIPT

Group Policy is obviously a very powerful system administration tool. When applied cautiously, a GPO can streamline repetitive tasks such as individually setting the rights of every user in an OU. It can also be used to assign and publish common applications. Despite many strengths, group policies can also cause real user and system problems. If a GPO is improperly constructed or assigned, it could have a ripple effect through all child objects and user accounts.

Our advice is to experiment with group policies in a very narrowly defined arena. Once you understand the impact of the GPO on your test environment, you can expand as required. Again, caution is important when using group policies.

Chapter 9

Permissions Security, Folder Sharing, and Dfs

Permissions and remote folder sharing are mainstays of Windows Server 2003 security. NTFS-based permissions allow and deny access to files and folders both locally and across the network. By contrast, folder sharing provides or denies access to objects on a remote computer. The two can be combined to provide granular access and proper control.

FAT/FAT32 and NTFS exhibit different permission functionality. FAT and FAT32 provide no security over locally logged-on users. Only native NTFS provides extensive permission control on both remote and local files. All three file systems do support shared folder permissions that apply to remote users. However, to take advantage of Windows Server 2003 advanced security, NTFS volumes must be used.

This chapter provides both theoretical and hands-on examination of Windows Server 2003 NTFS permissions security and folder sharing. We also examine the use of the Microsoft distributed file system (Dfs) as another means of facilitating access to objects across the network. After completing this chapter, a system administrator should be able to

- Apply permissions on objects.
- Utilize a working knowledge of ownership and how it can be changed.
- Implement shared folders.
- Manage Dfs.

REVIEWING NTFS PERMISSIONS

To protect data from users in a Windows Server 2003 enterprise, the administrator should understand how NTFS employs permissions. NTFS permissions are divided into folder and file categories. Folder permissions control what files and subfolders a user or group may view and which folders a user may open. They also restrict what users and groups may create, delete, and change permissions on the contents of a folder.

Every file, folder, or other object has an owner. For example, every user owns his My Documents home directory, as well as all files he creates and saves in the My Documents folder. As the owner, the user has full control over his objects and can assign permissions for other users to access them. As we shall discuss later, this control ranges from total denial of access to granting ownership of a file or folder to another.

NOTE As an administrator, you also have full control of a user's files and folders. This is particularly useful when the user requests intervention or leaves the organization. However, this privilege should not be abused. Direct administrative modification of a user's file and folder permissions is ordinarily on an "as needed" basis.

Windows Server 2003 uses access control lists (ACLs) to track an object's permissions. All objects have ACLs, which control what users and groups can do with them. The specific user or group is an access control entry (ACE).

The ACL is composed of a system access control list (SACL) and a discretionary access control is (DACL). The SACL configures auditing permissions and determines which file and folder operations will be written to the audit logs; the DACL contains security settings and permissions granted to specific users and groups. Each of the ACL's access control entries (ACEs) has security settings and audit settings (Tables 9.1 and 9.2).

Standard and Special Permissions

Windows Server 2003 supports two overlapping categories of permissions: *special* and *standard*. Standard permissions are generally applied to objects; special per-

TABLE 9.1 DACL Elements

Type	Description
Access Allowed	Identifies users and groups that have explicit permission to use the object.
Access Denied	Identifies the permission denied expressly to a user or group.

TABLE 9.2 SACL Elements

Type	Description
Audit Successful File/ Folder operation	Users and groups logged when attempts to access and modify file/folder attributes and contents are successful.
Audit Failed File/ Folder operation	Users and groups logged when attempts to access and modify file/folder attributes and contents fail.

missions provide finer granularity to file- or folder-based security. The majority of this discussion centers on standard permissions. We will apply their use by example after we review the basic concepts.

PERMISSIONS LEVELS

Six types of permissions can be combined for different results: Read, Write, Execute, List Folder Contents, Modify, and Full Control. They are described in Table 9.3.

The Full Control permission level obviously is automatically provided to the object's creator/owner and to the Administrators group.

TABLE 9.3 Permissions

Abbreviation	Type	Description
R	Read	Provides the designated user or group the ability to read the file or the contents of the folder.
W	Write	Provides the designated user or group the ability to create or write files and folders.
RX	Read & Execute	Provides the designated user or group the ability to read file and folder attributes, view folder contents, and read files within the folder. If this permission is applied to a folder, files with inheritance set will inherit it (see the inheritance discussion).
L	List Folder Contents	Same as Read & Execute, but not inherited by files within a folder. However, newly created subfolders will inherit this permission.
M	Modify	Provides the ability to delete, write, read, and execute.
F	Full Control	Provides the ability to perform any action, including taking ownership and changing permissions. When applied to a folder, the user or group may delete subfolders and files within a folder.

Working with Folder Permissions

Users may overwrite, delete, read, execute, and own NTFS files. It is important to understand that file permissions take precedence over folder permissions. If a user has permission to execute a file she may do so even if she does not have permissions to read and execute the file's folder.

NOTE It is possible for a user to navigate to a file for which he does not have folder permission. This involves simply knowing the path of the file object. Even if the user can't drill down the file/folder tree using **My Computer**, he can still gain access to the file using the Universal Naming Convention (UNC). In this example, the user does not have permissions to do anything in the folder called Book. However, he does have full control over the file called Chapter10.doc that resides in the Book folder. If the user attempted to user Explorer to see the contents of the Book folder, it would not be displayed. However, if the user wanted to execute the file within Notepad, he could do so by using either the **Start → Run** dialog or the **Start → Accessories → command prompt**, and provide the full path to the object:

```
Notepad C:\Book\Chapter10.doc
```

The user must know the file's full path and name, but it is still possible to override the folder permissions.

SETTING PERMISSIONS

Permissions apply differently to files and folders. In addition, NTFS permissions to other objects like applications are accessed and managed in the same way. Setting permissions is accomplished by following these steps:

1. Right-click **My Computer** and select **Explore**.
2. Find a folder on an NTFS volume and right-click **Properties**.
3. The **Program Files Properties** dialog box appears. Select the **Security Tab**.
4. Make changes by selecting **Allow** or **Deny** at each permissions category.

Permissions Properties

Folder permissions are listed with **Allow** and **Deny** check box columns. They are displayed for a user or group selected in the **Group or user names** window, also known as the ACL. The example in Figure 9.1 includes ACEs for Administrators, CREATOR OWNER, Software Config, SYSTEM, and Users.

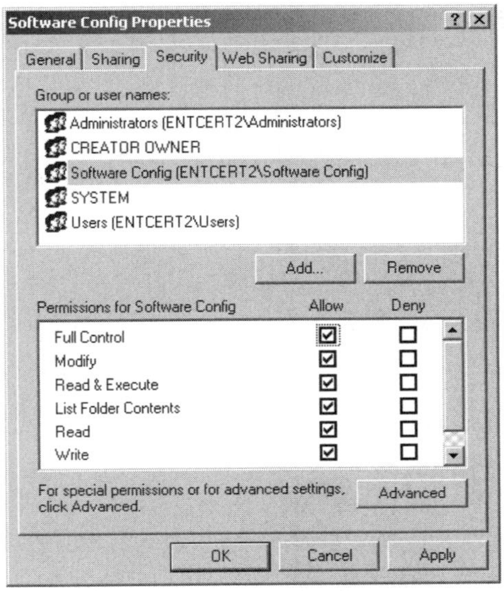

FIGURE 9.1 Software Configuration Properties

Permissions are cumulative. If a user belongs to more than one ACE (multiple group memberships), her permissions are an accumulation of those of each group.

To illustrate how permissions are applied, let's provide and deny permissions to a specific user. Joe Engineer is once again our user.

Allow Permissions Example

Joe Engineer is assigned Read privileges, and he also belongs to the Software Config group, which is assigned Write privileges. The ACE permissions for both Joe Engineer and Software Config are shown in Figures 9.2 and 9.3, respectively. Joe Engineer will have the effective rights of both ACEs, including Read and Write.

Deny Permissions Example

The Allow permissions are cumulative, but the Deny permissions behave quite differently. Deny overrides Allow. For instance, Joe Engineer has been allowed to read specifically the Software Config folder. However, when he joins a new group called Engineers, he loses the previous permissions since this group has been denied access to the SOFTCONF folder.

Let's review how this is accomplished.

1. The new group is added to the ACL by clicking **Add** and choosing the Engineers group from the **Select Users, Computers, or Groups** dialog box (Figure 9.4).

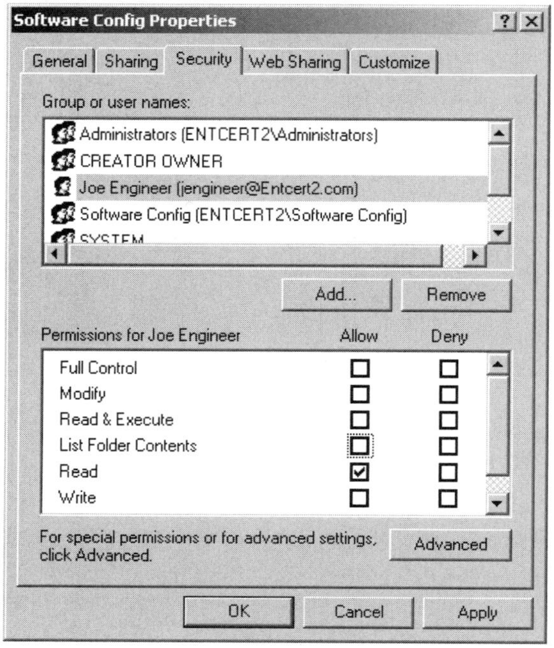

FIGURE 9.2 Joe Engineer Security Settings

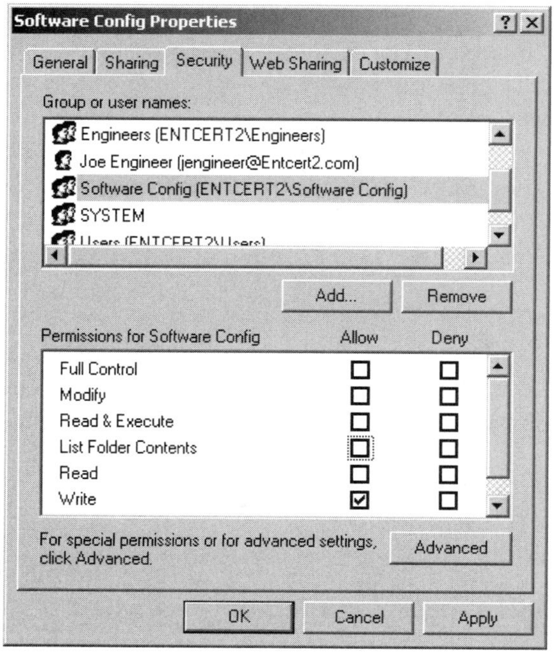

FIGURE 9.3 The Software Config Group Security Settings

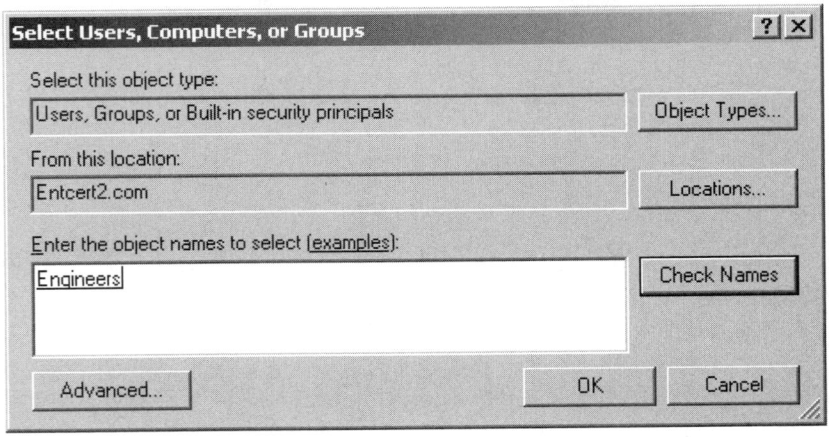

FIGURE 9.4 Select Users, Computers, or Groups

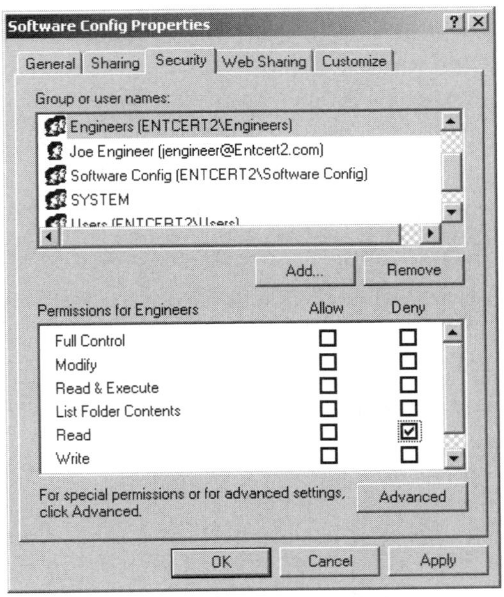

FIGURE 9.5 Software Config Properties

2. From the **Software Config Properties** box (Figure 9.5), select the **Engineers** group and check **Deny** in the **Read** permission row.
3. Click **Apply** to apply the new permission and display a warning (Figure 9.6).
4. Answer **Yes** to the warning. **Engineers** now denies all members Read access to the Software Config folder.

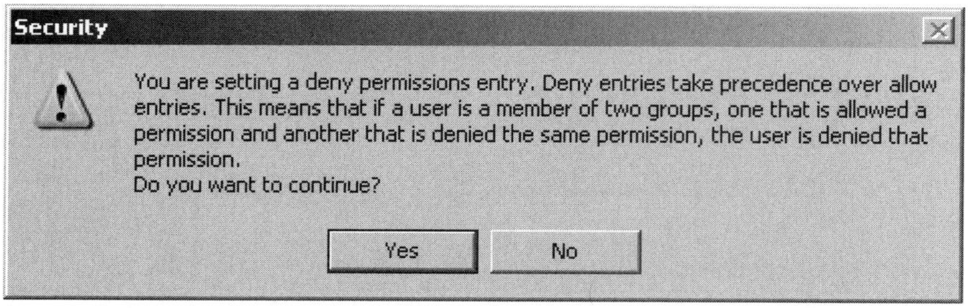

FIGURE 9.6 A Security Warning

No matter what group has granted Joe Engineer permission to read the folder, the Deny permission assigned to the Engineers group takes precedence.

SPECIAL PERMISSIONS

The standard NTFS permissions just discussed provide general control over user and group access. However, on some occasions where greater granularity may be needed, the NTFS special permissions come into play. There are 14 special permissions. They are mapped to the standard permissions, as shown in Table 9.4.

Let's apply special permissions to our example of Joe Engineer:

1. Select **Joe Engineer** from the **Software Config Properties** dialog.
2. Assign **Write** permissions to the user by checking the **Allow** check box.
3. Click **Advanced**. The **Advanced Security Settings for Software Config** dialog appears (Figure 9.7).
4. Select **Joe Engineer** and click **Edit**. The **Permission Entry for Software Config** dialog box appears (Figure 9.8).

   Notice that the allowed permissions, **Create Files, Create Folders, Write Attributes,** and **Write Extended Attributes,** correspond to the **Write** column of the previous table (Table 9.4). They are associated with the standard Write NTFS permission. Each of the six standard permissions is mapped to a subset of the 14 special permissions. In fact, as you add special permissions, the standard permission level changes to include them.
5. Check the **Allow** boxes next to the following four special permissions: **List Folder/Read Data, Read Attributes, Read Extended Attributes,** and **Read Permissions** (Figure 9.9).
6. Click **OK**. Click the next **OK**.
7. The **Software Config Properties** dialog should now show the standard **Read** and **Write** permissions as allowed (Figure 9.10).

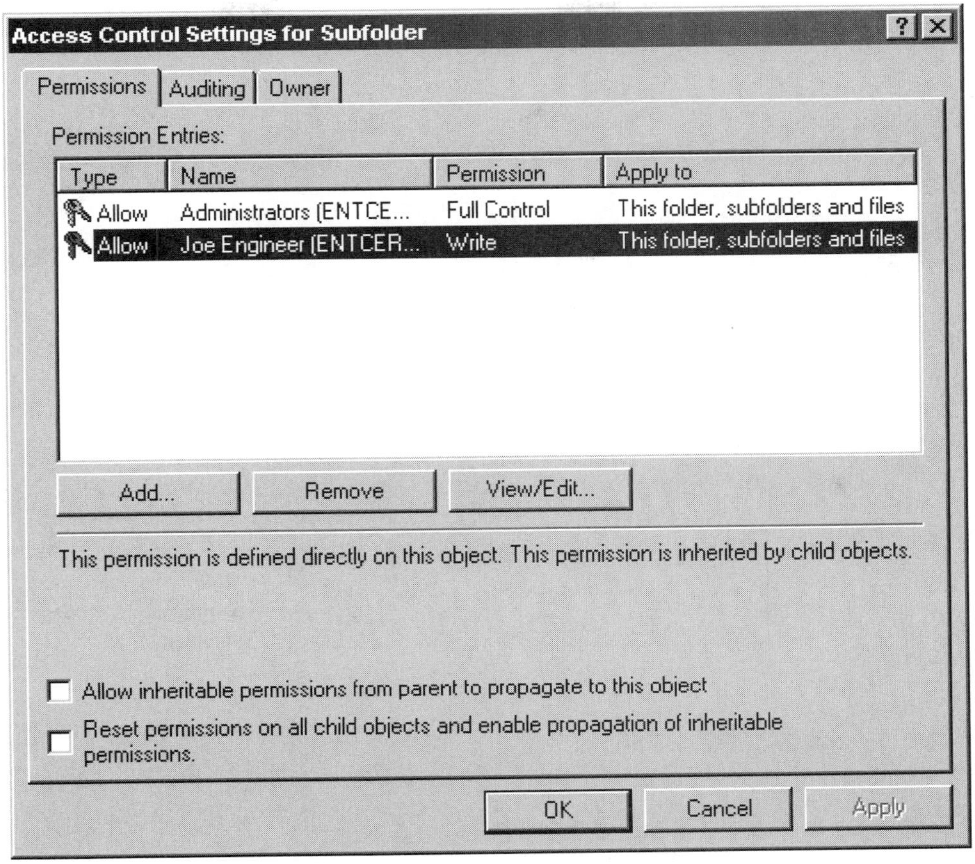

FIGURE 9.7 Access Control Settings

Permission Inheritance

All folders and subfolders inherit permissions from their parent folder by default. This is true of files in a folder as well. In other words, a folder with Read and Write permissions for the Users group will pass these characteristics to subfolders and files unless otherwise changed.

Inheriting NTFS permissions can be prevented at the child folder or file level by clearing the **Inherit from parent the permissions entries that apply to child objects** option. Once permission inheritance has been stopped, permissions may be assigned to the object by copying them from its parents or by clearing all permissions currently assigned. All children of the object will inherit its permissions

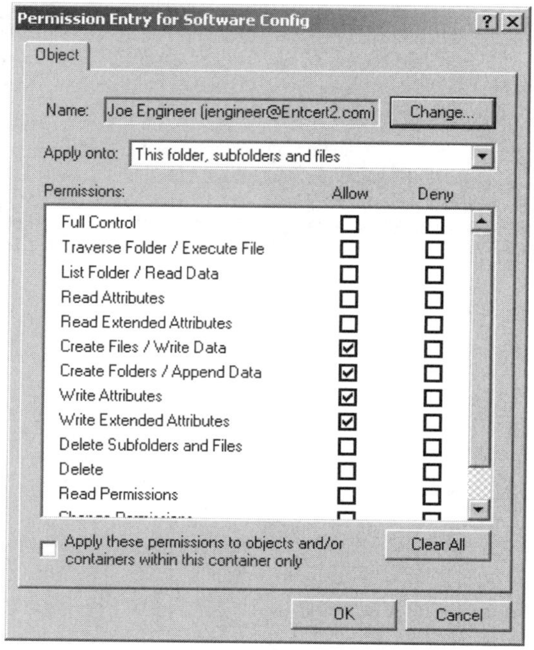

FIGURE 9.8 Permissions Entry for Subfolder

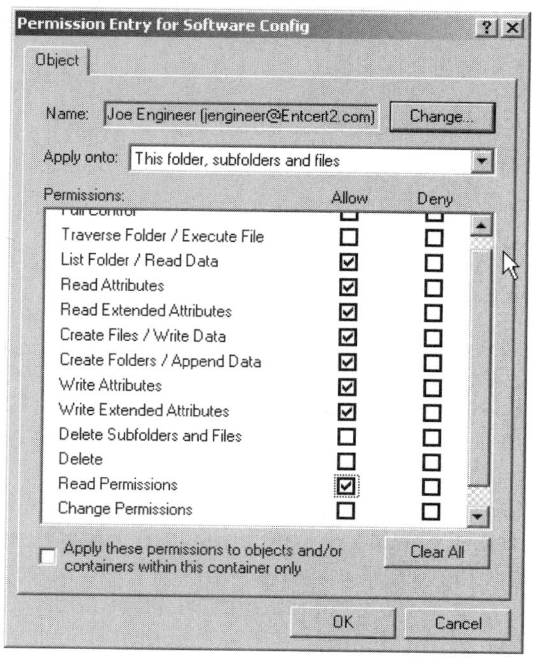

FIGURE 9.9 A Permissions Entry

TABLE 9.4 Mapping Standard Permissions to Special Permissions

Types	Full Control	Modify	Read & Execute	List Folder Contents	Read	Write
Traverse Folder/ Execute File	X	X	X	X		
List Folder/ Read Data	X	X	X	X	X	
Read Attributes	X	X	X	X	X	
Read Extended Attributes	X	X	X	X	X	
Create Files/ Write Data	X	X				X
Create Folders/ Append Data	X	X				X
Write Attributes	X	X				X
Write Extended Attributes	X	X				X
Delete Subfolders and Files	X					
Delete	X	X				
Read Permissions	X	X	X	X	X	
Change Permissions	X					
Take Ownership	X					

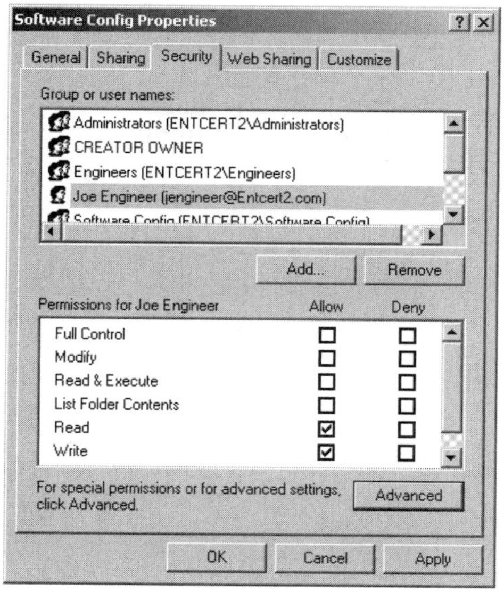

FIGURE 9.10 Special Permissions Update Standard Permissions

rather than those of its grandparents. This point is illustrated with the following example:

1. Create a subfolder within the Software Config folder called ProjectA.
2. Right-click the new folder and select **Properties**. The **ProjectA Properties** dialog appears. Select the **Security** tab and click **Advanced**. Clear the **Inherit from parent the permission entries that apply to child objects** check box (Figure 9.11).
3. The **Security** dialog box (Figure 9.12) appears, presenting three options:
   - Copy parent permissions to the new object.
   - Remove all permissions on the new object.
   - Cancel (abort) the block inheritance operation.

   Selecting either **Copy** or **Remove** will block the inheritance of parent NTFS permissions and allow this branch of the directory tree to propagate its own set of permissions.
4. Click **Remove** and notice that all permissions have been eliminated from ProjectA subfolder.
5. New groups and users can be added by clicking **Add**, and their associated permissions can be assigned.

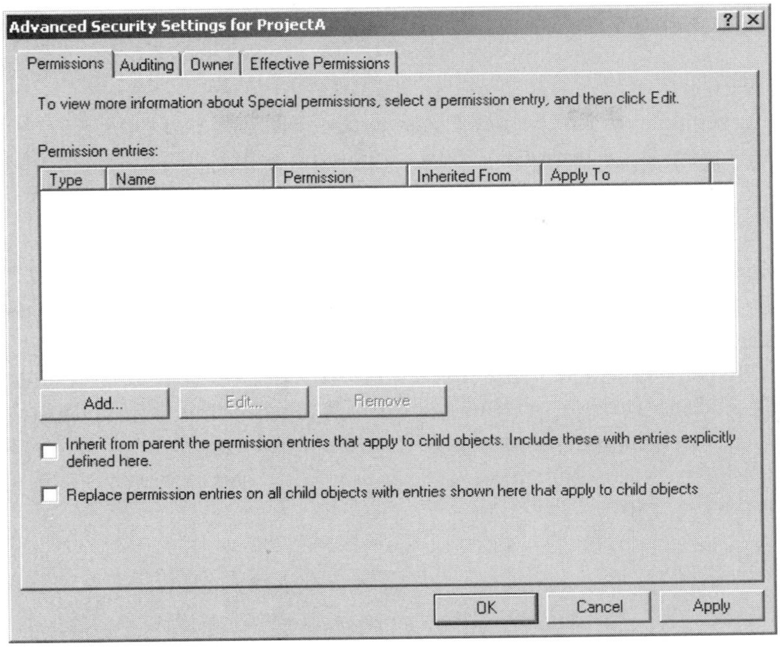

FIGURE 9.11 ProjectA Advanced Security Settings

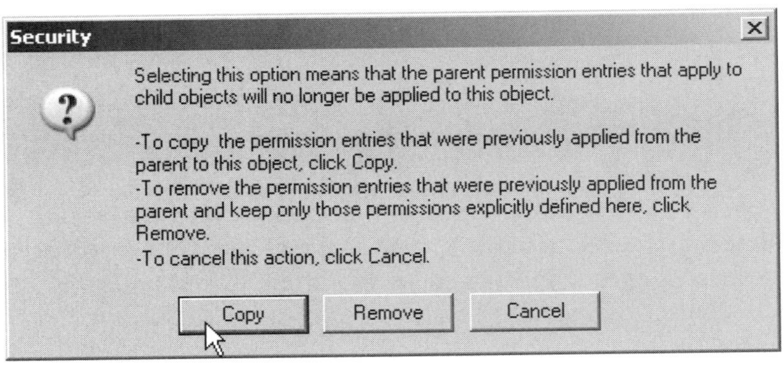

FIGURE 9.12 Permission Inheritance Options

New files and folders created in the ProjectA subfolder will receive the permissions assigned to ProjectA rather than those assigned to the Software Config folder.

MOVING AND COPYING FILE AND FOLDER PERMISSIONS

Moving and copying files can affect their permissions, so it is important to understand the basic rules associated with these actions.

Copying Files and Folders

The copy procedure simply duplicates an existing file or folder to another location. To copy, the user must have at least Read permission for the source file or folder and Write permission for the destination parent folder. Once the new file or folder has been created, it inherits its permission settings from the new parent folder. Permissions are not retained since this is a new object.

Moving Files and Folders

The process of moving a file or folder simply involves removing it from its current location and placing it in a new location. To do this, the user must have Read/ Modify permission on the object and Write permission for the new parent folder. A file or folder moved within the same NTFS volume is not considered a new object and thus retains its permissions once in the new parent folder. However, a file or folder moved to another NTFS volume inherits permissions from the destination parent folder.

NOTE Regardless of whether an object is copied or moved, a file or folder transferred from an NTFS volume to a FAT volume loses all permissions. Remember, FAT/FAT32 does not support permission assignment.

Ownership

Every file and folder has permissions along with an owner. The owner has full control over the object regardless of what other permissions are assigned to that object. Anyone with Full Control can assign the special NTFS permission Take Ownership to someone else. Note, however, that having Take Ownership privilege does not make a user or group the owner. Users with the Take Ownership permission must make themselves owner to obtain full control over a file or folder.

DENYING RIGHTS TO A SUBFOLDER

In the following example, we will test the principle of ownership and folder access. The first step is to deny Joe Engineer Read permission.

1. Deny Joe Engineer the right to read the **ProjectA** subfolder (Figure 9.13).
2. Verify the **Deny** entry by clicking **Advanced** and viewing the ACL settings (Figure 9.14).
3. Select the **Allow** entry for Joe Engineer and click **Edit**.

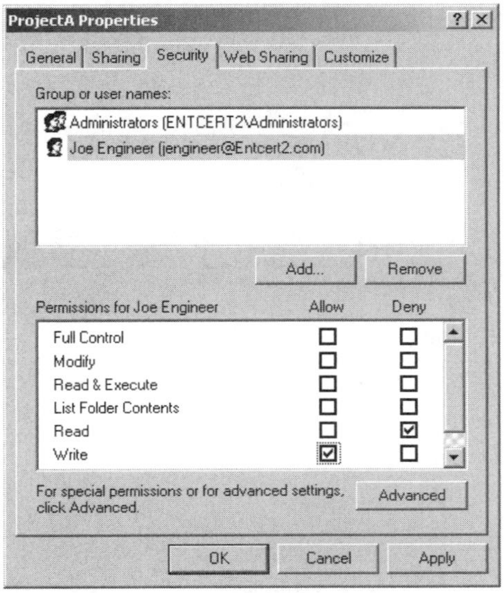

FIGURE 9.13 ProjectA Permissions

TRANSFERRING OWNERSHIP

Transferring ownership involves two primary steps. The first is allowing another user to take ownership. The second is the other user's accepting ownership. The following example walks through the steps required to allow Joe Engineer to take ownership. Once he accepts it, he can change permissions to view and edit ProjectA's contents. This example depends on settings from the preceding examples.

4. Set the allow **Take ownership** special permission (Figure 9.15).
5. Click **OK**. Notice that the modified **Permission** entry for **Joe Engineer** is now **Special** in the **Permission** column (Figure 9.16). Click **OK** again and log off the system.
6. Log back on as Joe Engineer.
7. Try to access **ProjectA** as Joe Engineer. Notice that it is not accessible.
8. Right-click **ProjectA Properties** and select the **Security** tab. No properties are visible. The **Read attributes** permission has been denied Joe Engineer, and security permissions are no longer readable.
9. From the **ProjectA Properties** window, select the **Security** tab.
10. Click **Advanced**.
11. Select the **Owner** tab from the **Advanced Security Settings for ProjectA** window.

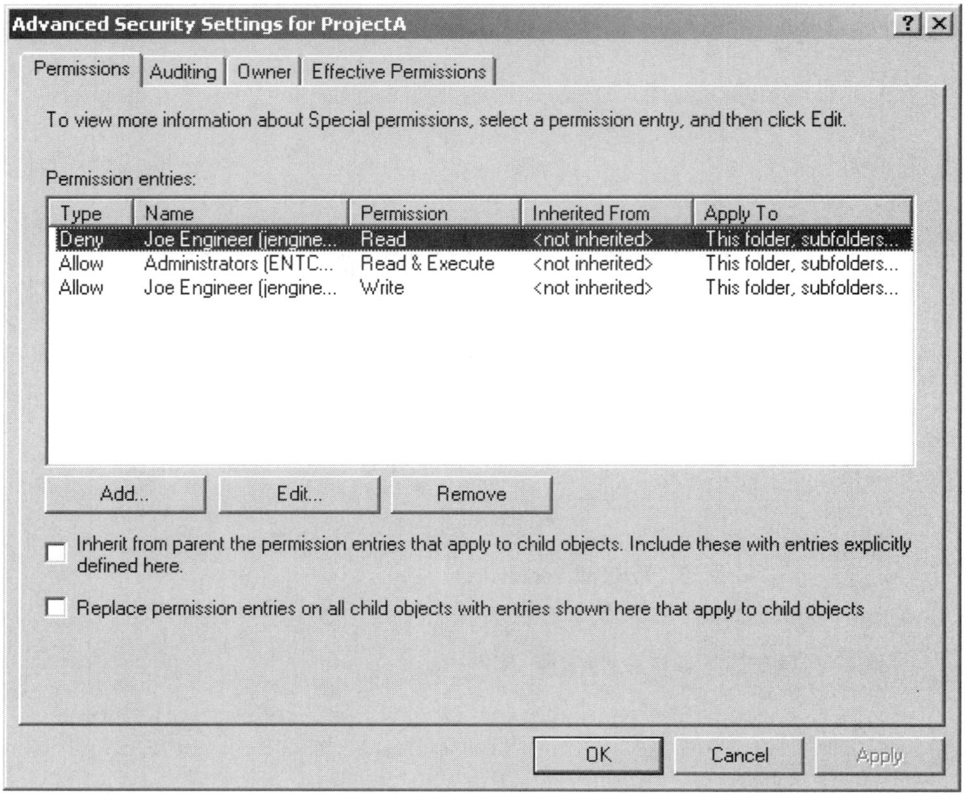

FIGURE 9.14 Access Control Settings

12. Select **Joe Engineer** and click **Apply** (Figure 9.17).
13. Click **OK**. Click **OK** again.
14. Reopen the **ProjectA Properties** window and select the **Security** tab. Joe Engineer can now view and change permissions (Figure 9.18).

OWNER SETS PERMISSIONS

At this stage Joe Engineer has taken ownership of the ProjectA folder. He must now assign himself the permissions to access it.

1. In the **Deny** column, clear the **Read** permission and in the **Allow** column, check **Full Control** (see Figure 9.19).
2. Click **OK**.
3. Try to access **ProjectA**. Joe Engineer now has full control over the folder.

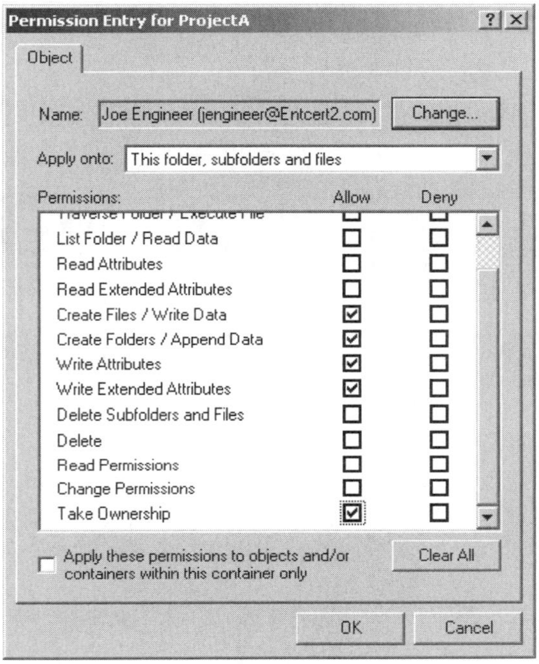

FIGURE 9.15 A Special Permission Entry

IMPLICIT GROUPS AND PERMISSIONS

Users, security groups, and implicit groups are assigned varying levels of permissions for files and folders. Implicit groups are local to all Windows Server 2003 systems but not available through Active Directory or local account databases. They are accessible only when assigning file/folder permissions and reflect how the user accesses the resource. Membership in an implicit group is determined by the operating system, and group SIDs are not passed with Kerberos authorization information.

Implicit groups can be used to assign permissions to folders and files. They are defined as shown in Table 9.5 on page 369.

NOTE With Windows Server 2003, the ACL editing functions have been increased. Enhancements to the standard ACLeditor user interface (ACLUI) include the ability to reset permissions to a default, show effective permissions for a selected security principal, indicate the parent from which permission was inherited, and indicate the existence of additional permissions. The ACL Editor is available from the **Active Directory Users and Computers Snap-in → Security**.

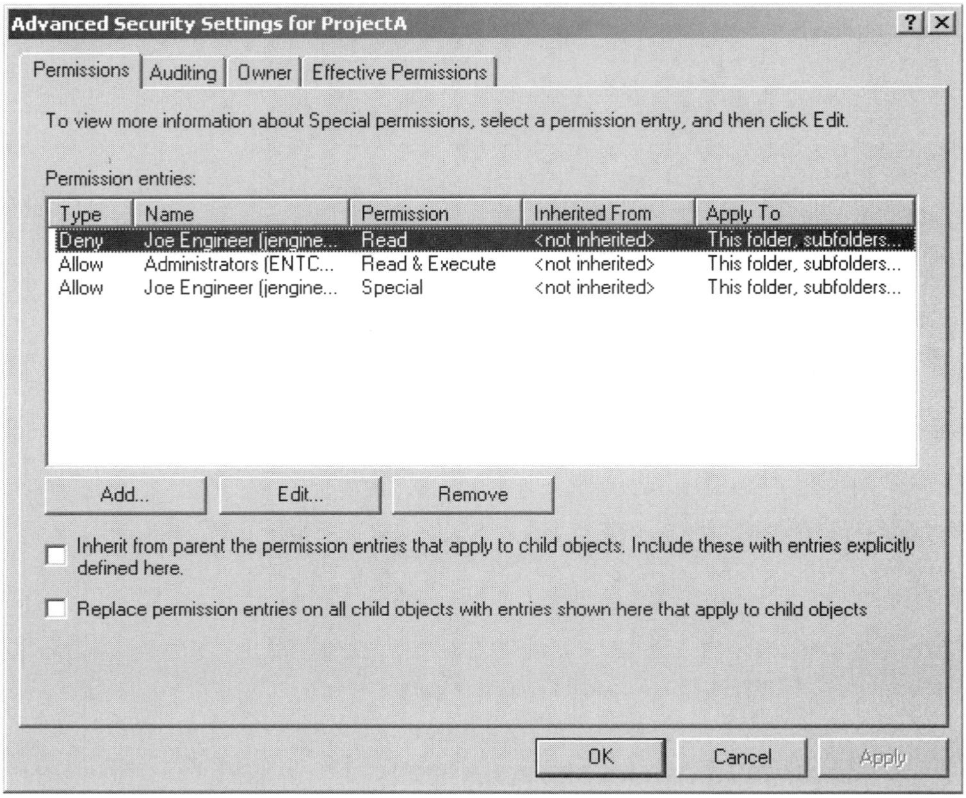

FIGURE 9.16 Access Control Settings

FOLDER SHARING

Folder sharing is used whenever one computer user needs access to a file on another computer's file system. Once a folder is shared, all files and subfolders receive the same shared permissions. Shared permissions apply to the entire folder and not to specific files. Both NTFS and FAT volumes require that shared folder permissions be set for network users to gain access. FAT volumes have no local user authentication, but shared permissions provide security for remote users. Only NTFS volumes can apply file permissions to the objects in a shared folder.

Several additional user rules govern the use of shared folders:

- The effective permission is an accumulation of the user's individual and group membership rights.

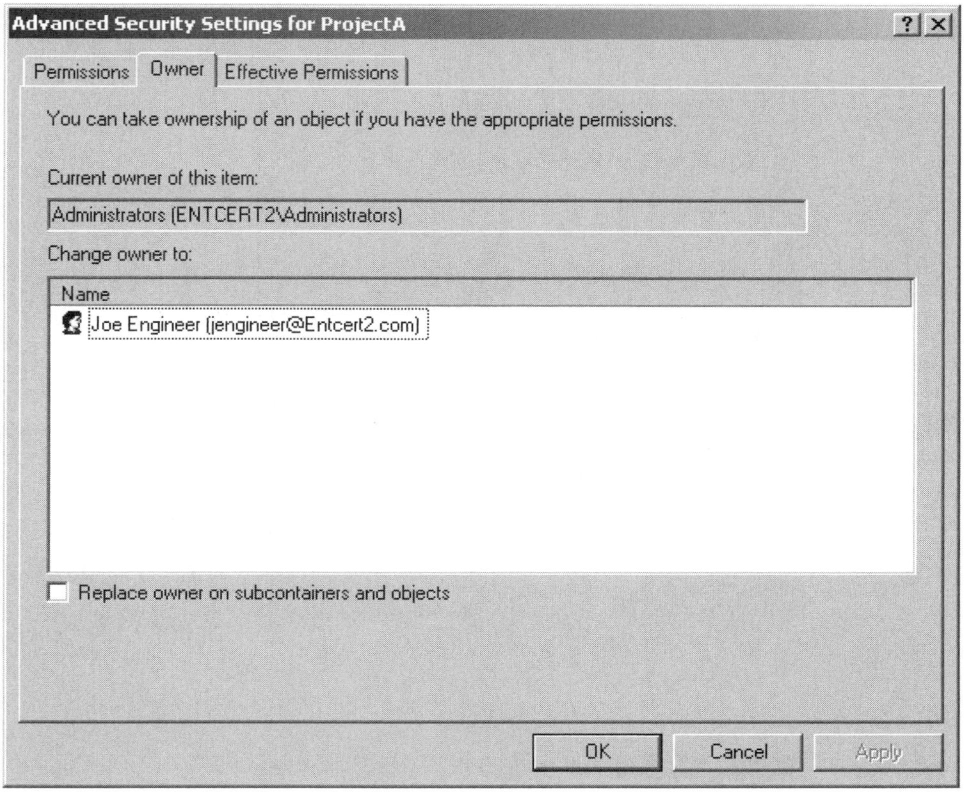

FIGURE 9.17 Ownership

- Deny permissions always cancel corresponding Allow permissions.
- A copy of a shared folder does not retain the "shared" status.
- Shared folder status is discarded when a folder is moved.

Creating Shared Folders

Shared folders work in the same manner for Windows Server 2003 domains and workgroups. The only measurable difference is in who can create them. In a Windows Server 2003 domain environment, the built-in Administrators and Server Operators groups can establish shared folders throughout the domain. In the workgroup, the Administrators and Power Users groups have authority to share folders on the individual server. These two groups can also share folders on standalone servers and on Windows 2000 Professional and Windows XP installations.

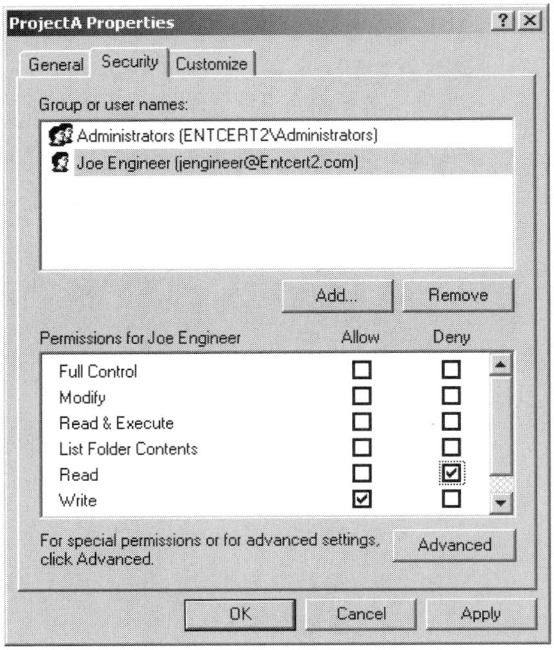

FIGURE 9.18 Security

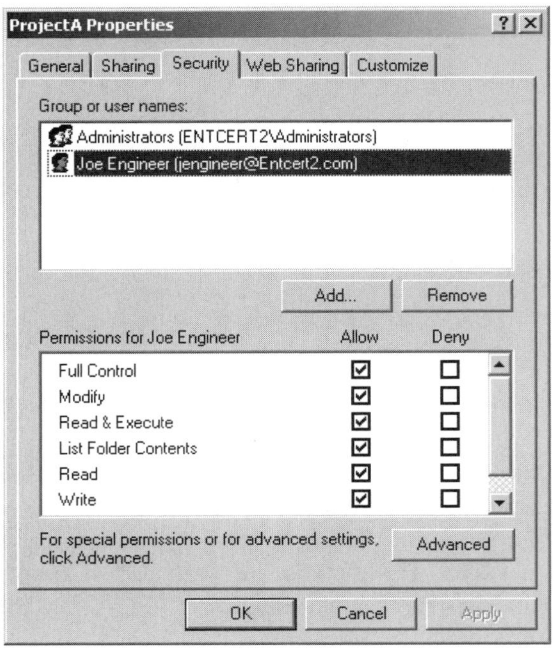

FIGURE 9.19 Subfolder Properties

TABLE 9.5 Implicit Groups

Group	Description
Anonymous Logon	User without system identifier (SID)
Authenticated Users	Same as Everyone but does not contain guests or anonymous users
Batch	Batch program (*.cmd and *.bat) rights
Creator	Creator of the file/folder/print job
Creator Owner	Creator and owner of the file/folder/print job
Dial-up	User accessing the system via the Remote Access Service (RAS)
Enterprise Domain Controllers	Enterprise domain controllers remotely accessing the system
Everyone	Local and remotely logged-on users
Interactive	Locally logged-on user
Network	User logged on to the system through the network
Restricted	Users cannot install programs or make changes to the file system settings
System	Operating system, otherwise known as the local system
Terminal Server User	Terminal server client

SHARING FOLDERS

The creation of a shared folder is similar to application of permissions to a file or folder. The following steps set shared permissions:

1. Log on with administrative privileges.
2. Open **Explorer** and right-click **Properties** on a folder you want to share.
3. Select the **Sharing** tab and click **Share this folder**, as shown in Figure 9.20.
4. Click **Permissions**. The **Permissions for Software Config** dialog box appears, as shown in Figure 9.21.

Three levels of available permissions are presented for each of the named users or groups. Select the **Allow** permission(s) that apply. While you can also **Deny** a specific right, it is generally advisable to use an affirmative approach.

- **Read** allows a user to open files and see subfolder names.
- **Change** allows all privileges offered by Read permissions and allows users to change file contents and delete and create files and subfolders.

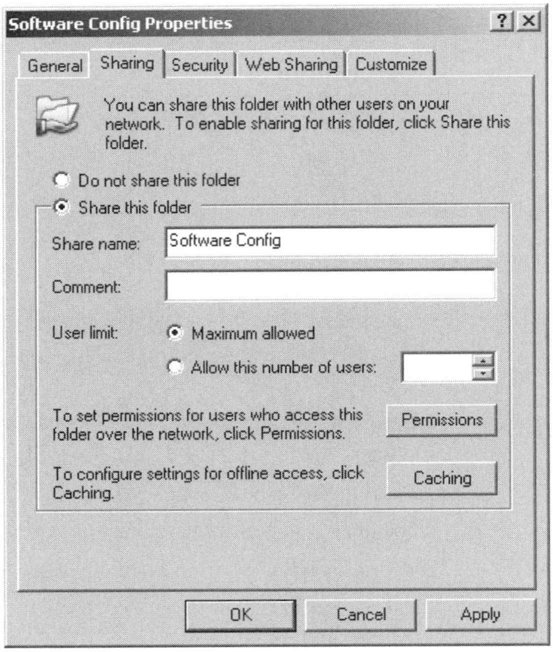

FIGURE 9.20 Share Properties

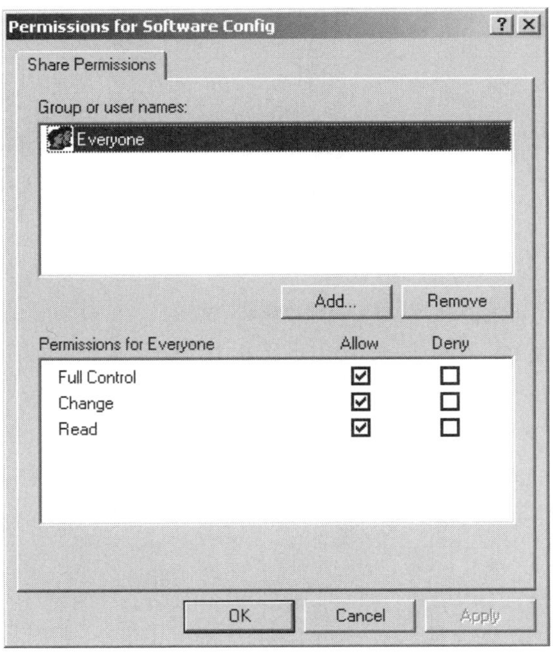

FIGURE 9.21 The Share Permissions Tab

- **Full Control** allows all privileges offered by **Change** and adds the ability to take ownership and modify permissions.

Adding and Deleting Groups and Users

The default share permissions give full control to Everyone. If you want to ensure folder security only to users and groups you add, remove the Everyone group by selecting **Everyone** and clicking **Remove**. To add users or groups,

1. Click **Add** (Figure 9.21).
2. The **Select Users, Computers, or Groups** dialog appears.

NOTE The **From this location** menu displays your domain and other trusted domains. You may add users or groups and then assign shared permissions. Note that a user account in a trusted domain must be selected from its domain, not the local domain.

---

3. Using the **Locations** dialog box (Figure 9.22), select the domain where the user or group resides.
4. Type the name of a desired group or user in the **Enter the Object names to select** box and click **Check Names**. Select an object and click **Add**.
5. Click **OK**.

NOTE In connecting to shared folders, there are three common scenarios:

1. The user is accessing a shared folder in your domain. In this case, she can use her user name and password in the standard form.
2. The user is accessing a shared folder from another untrusted domain. She must use a user name and account for the domain in which the share resides.
3. The user is accessing a shared folder from another trusted domain. *Important:* She must use a user name and password from her home domain. The user name should be in the form *domainname\username.*

Facilitating Shared Access

Once a share has been created, clients may connect to the folder using one of three methods: (1) map a network drive; (2) use **My Network Places**; and (3) use the **Start → Run** menu option.

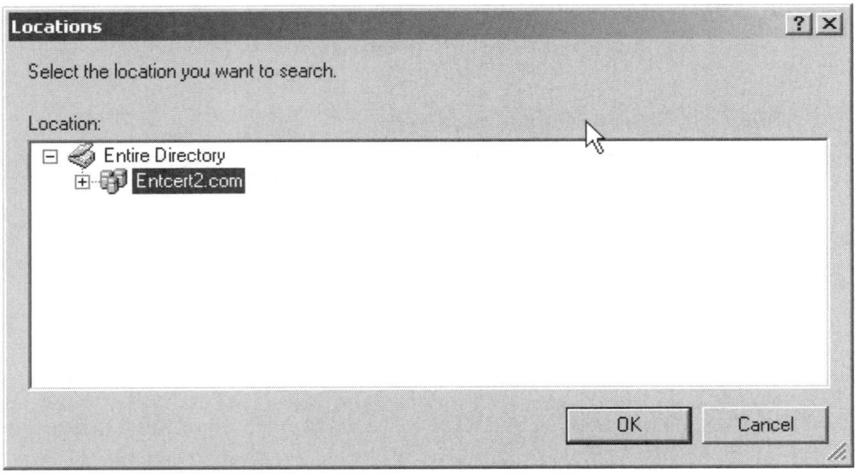

FIGURE 9.22 Select Users, Computers, and Groups

MAPPING A NETWORK DRIVE TO A SHARED FOLDER

Mapping a network drive makes a remote shared folder available to the local machine via **Explorer** or **My Computer**. From all appearances, the remote shared folder looks local. Mapping follows these steps:

1. From **My Computer,** select **Tools** → select **Map Network Drive**.
2. Select the drive letter to be associated with the remote share from the **Drive** drop-down list (Figure 9.23).
3. Click **Browse,** then search for the desired network share. Ensure that the share is addressed in the form *servername**sharedfolder*.
4. From this dialog, you may also log on to the share with another user name. (This is required for access to a share in a trusted domain.)
5. The new folder share will be accessible from **My Computer** as the **Drive** letter.

THE MY NETWORK PLACES LINK TO A SHARED FOLDER

My Network Places can also facilitate access to a shared folder. To use it, follow these steps:

1. From **My Network Places**, find the computer containing the share. If you have trouble connecting to the desired computer, click **Search**, enter the computer name, and click **Search Now**.
2. Open the desired shared folder. If required, enter the appropriate user name according to the preceding note.

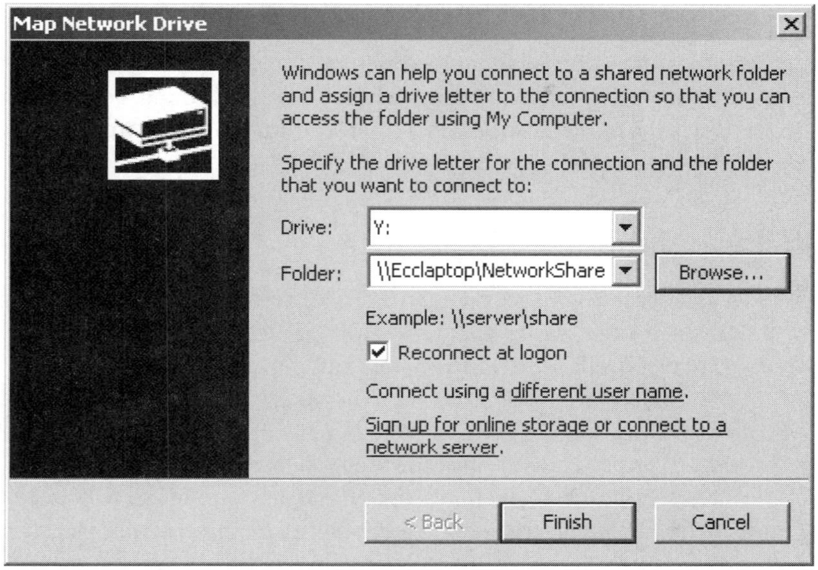

FIGURE 9.23 The Map Network Drive Wizard

USING THE RUN COMMAND TO ACCESS SHARED FOLDERS

Another approach to gaining access to a shared folder is the **Run** command. To use the this option:

1. **Start** → select **Run**. The **Run** window appears as shown in Figure 9.24.
2. Enter the name of the server with the path to the desired share in the form *servername**sharefolder*.
3. Click **OK**.

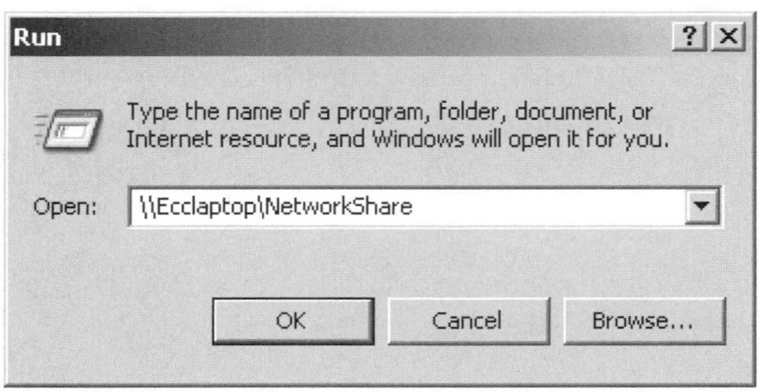

FIGURE 9.24 The Run Dialog Box

ACCESSING A SHARE FROM INTERNET EXPLORER

A share may be accessed from Internet Explorer using the share's Uniform Naming Convention (UNC) name. From the URL address field, enter the share name in the form *servername**sharefolder*. A shared folder address may be added to the Favorites list for convenient access.

Special Hidden Shares

Windows Server 2003 special shares are system root folders accessible to the network but not necessarily visible to normal users. There are several types of administrative share folder, as shown in Table 9.6.

Additional shares may be added for different services. For instance, the Certificate Authority adds its own share when installed. The Shared Folders snap-in may be added to any management console to display all shared folders (Figure 9.25).

The Sessions node displays users and systems currently accessing network shares. The administrator can selectively terminate connections or terminate all sessions at once (Figure 9.26).

The Open Files node displays the files currently being accessed from shares. Individual files may be closed or all files may be closed at once (Figure 9.27).

TABLE 9.6 Special Hidden Shares

Share Name	Description
Admin$	The root system folder is by default C:\Winnt, but may have been placed in a different volume or under a different name during installation. The Administrator group is granted full control and is the only group with any access to this shared folder for remote administration.
Drive$	Each volume is associated with a disk drive designation. A$ and B$ are reserved for floppy disk volumes. C$ through Z$ are designations for hard disks, CD-ROMs, and removable media. The Administrator group has full control over these volumes.
IPC$	Shared memory space for interprocess communication when accessing remote shares and remotely administering a computer.
NETLOGON	Space used by the Net Logon service during logon. Startup/logon scripts are accessed here.
print$	Used for shared printers and contains the device drivers. Administrators, Server Operators, and Print Operator group members have full control over this shared folder.
SYSVOL	Used by the Net Logon service and provides access to Active Directory information.

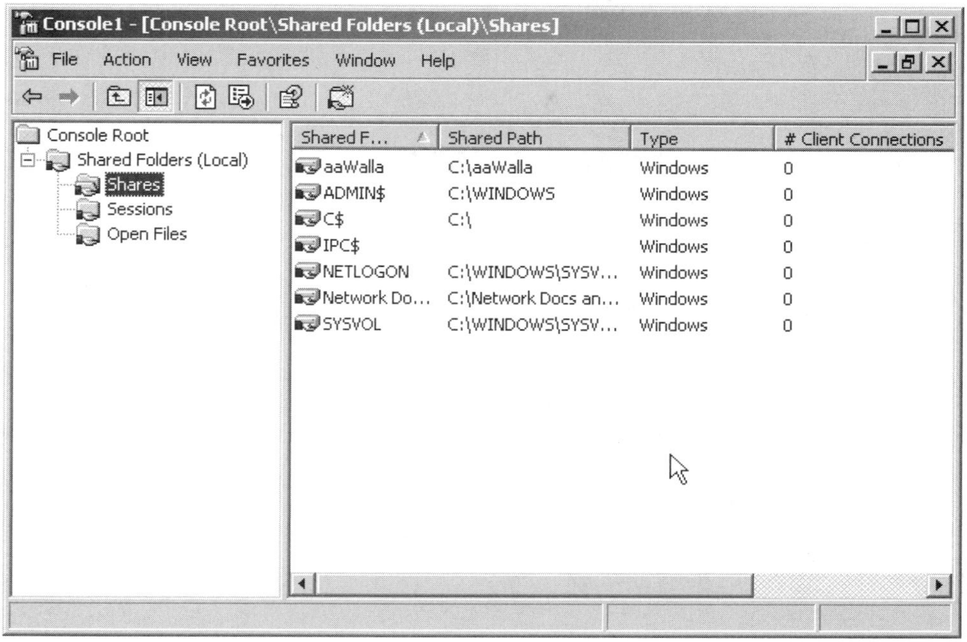

FIGURE 9.25 The Shared Folders Snap-In

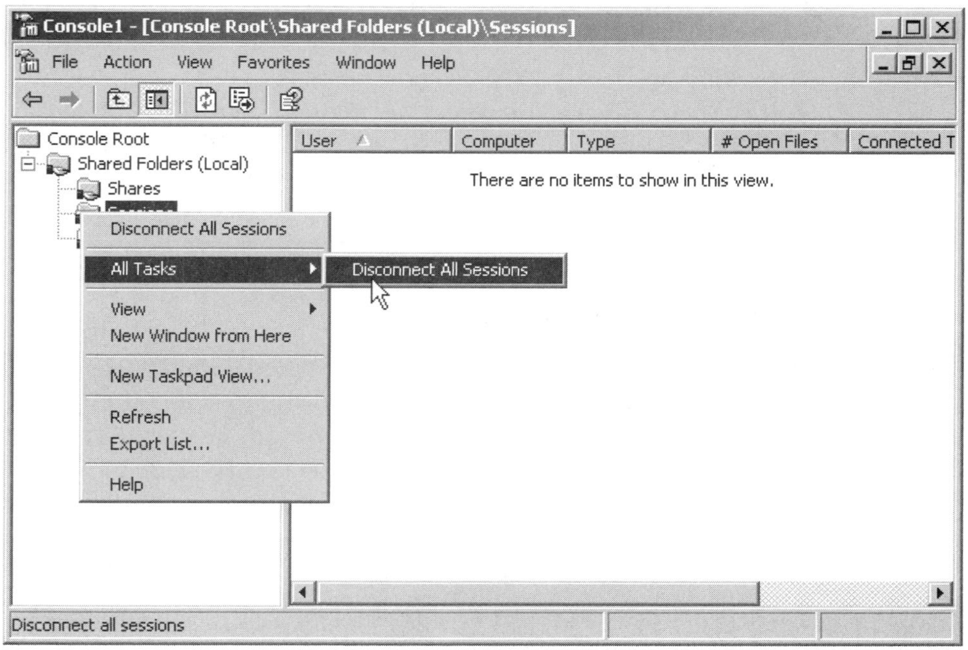

FIGURE 9.26 Current Share Sessions

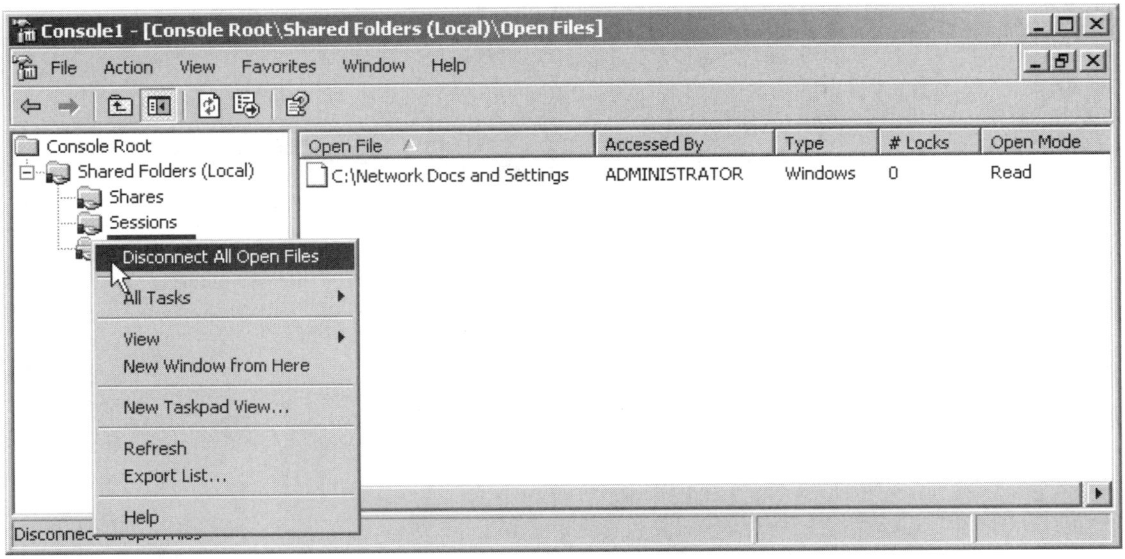

FIGURE 9.27 Open Files Being Accessed

NOTE With Windows Server 2003, it is now possible to use Group Policy to set up Netlogon properties. This simplifies the steps to configure domain members when adjusting Netlogon settings. To use this feature go to the **Active Directory Snap-in → Group Policy**. This can be applied to the properties of any domain, organizational unit, or site object.

Using NTFS Permissions and Shared Folders

While the permissions associated with a shared folder are automatically inherited by the files and subfolders, it is possible to apply additional permissions to individual files on an NTFS volume. Doing so provides greater security for the contents of a shared folder. Both the NTFS permissions and shared folder permissions are applied to objects. Remember that the most restricted set of permissions is used. For example, if the shared folder permits a user only Read permissions, Read will be the overriding permission level even if an individual file delegates the user Full Control NTFS permissions.

Publishing Files and Folders to the Active Directory

Like users, computers, and printers, files and folders may be published to the Active Directory. The Active Directory provides a way to locate published files and folders and secures permissions on the resources. To publish a file or folder, share out the folder and complete the following:

1. Open the **Active Directory Users and Computers** snap-in.
2. Right-click the desired domain node or Active Directory container and select **New → Share Folder**.
3. Enter a name for the share to publish in the **Shared Folder Name** field.
4. Enter a path to the network share in the **Network Path** field in the form *\\servername\sharedfolder*. Click **OK**.

The shared file or folder should now appear in the Active Directory and be available for lookup from the Global Catalog.

DISTRIBUTED FILE SYSTEM SHARING

The distributed file system (Dfs) allows several shared file systems to be mounted from one location. The shares may exist on separate machines, but users can reach them through one folder. This folder is called the root node and is accessible from the Dfs root server. Shared folders on other systems are linked to the root node (Figure 9.28).

Users maintain one connection to the root node on their desktop environment and connect to resources throughout the network without having to establish a connection with each server and folder. The Dfs root node contains link nodes that point to these shared folders and mimic the directory's tree structure. The tree structure can be customized according to users' needs.

Dfs centrally manages shared folders and maintains network permissions. Share and NTFS permissions still apply to individual users—creating the root Dfs share does not compromise previously assigned security permissions.

Standalone versus Fault-Tolerant Dfs

Root nodes can be configured as standalone or fault-tolerant (or domain-based). The standalone server stores the Dfs directory tree structure or topology locally. Thus, if a shared folder is inaccessible or if the Dfs root server is down, users are left with no link to the shared resources. A fault-tolerant root node stores the Dfs topology in the Active Directory, which is replicated to other domain controllers.

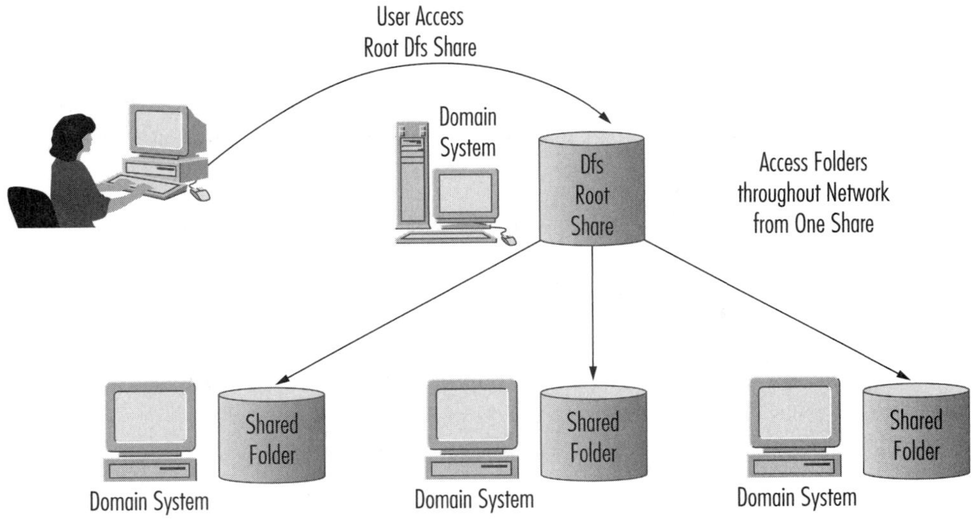

FIGURE 9.28 The Distributed File System

Thus, redundant root nodes may include multiple connections to the same data residing in different shared folders.

A fault-tolerant link node can point to two or more shared folders on different servers that contain the same files. This serves two purposes:

1. The network user requesting access from the fault-tolerant link node will receive address information for each redundant folder. The client then picks the folder closest to it, thereby saving network traffic and time.
2. Redundant shared folders can replicate automatically, providing data redundancy.

NOTE Version control may be an issue depending on how users access the folders. A user may overwrite changes another user made to a file. In this case, automatic replication should be disabled and handled by a person or configuration management tool. It should be noted that replica folders must reside on NTFS v5 volumes running Windows Server 2003. It should also be noted that client Dfs software is required to access Dfs shares. Windows Server 2003, Windows 2000, Windows NT 4.0, and Windows 98 come preconfigured with such software. Client software must be downloaded and installed on systems running Windows 95. Currently, only Windows Server 2003 and Windows 2000 Dfs clients may access fault-tolerant Dfs root shares using the directory location services. Clients may still access fault-tolerant Dfs roots using the full UNC root path.

Creating Dfs

The Dfs is created using the Distributed File System snap-in. It primarily involves the creation of two components: the Dfs root and the Dfs child link.

THE DFS ROOT

As previously discussed, the Dfs root may be created either as standalone or domain based. It collects in one central place all links to folders throughout the network. A domain-based root can have multiple Dfs links and supports Dfs shares below the root folder. Thus, Dfs subfolder shares may be created in the Dfs root folder and be accessible to Dfs clients. The domain-based Dfs root stores topology information in the Active Directory, but if the server hosting the root Dfs folder is shut down, access to all child links is interrupted. A replica for the domain-based root share may be created on a separate server to support a redundant failover point (Figure 9.29). All child links are duplicated on the root replica and effectively function as an alternative for the original Dfs root. Standalone Dfs roots do not support replicas at either the root level or the child level.

NOTE Under Windows Server 2003, support is provided for multiple Dfs roots on a single server. Administrators use this feature to host multiple Dfs roots on a single server. This should reduce the administrative and hardware costs of managing multiple namespaces and multiple replicated namespaces. The feature can be configured using the Configure Your Server Wizard.

Example of Dfs Root Change Replication

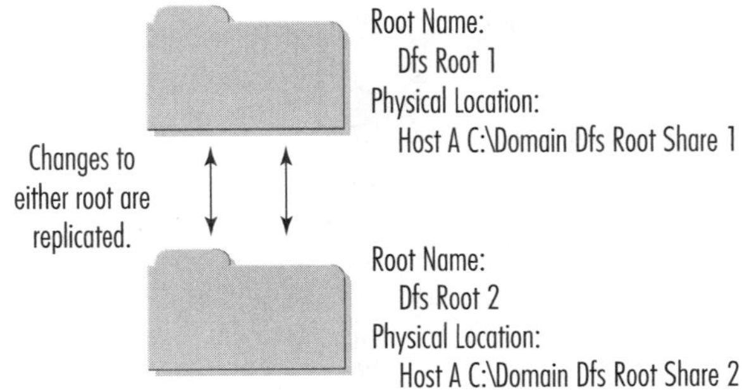

FIGURE 9.29 Root Dfs Replication and Redundancy

THE DFS LINK

Dfs links maintain a mapping or a junction point between the root and individual shared folders throughout the network. When the user accesses a link, the link name resolves the destination shared folder path. The link name simply displays the subfolder within the Dfs root folder; the link is responsible for pointing to the folder's physical location using a full UNC path. A standalone Dfs root can support up to 10,000 links and a domain-based Dfs root can support up to 5,000 links (Figure 9.30).

Each link has a name and owns a replica set with at least one corresponding shared physical folder identified by a fully qualified UNC path name. The replica set may be associated with up to 32 shared folders. The folders in the replica set are meant to contain identical information. To accomplish this, they may be maintained manually or automatically using the Folder Replication Service (FRS).

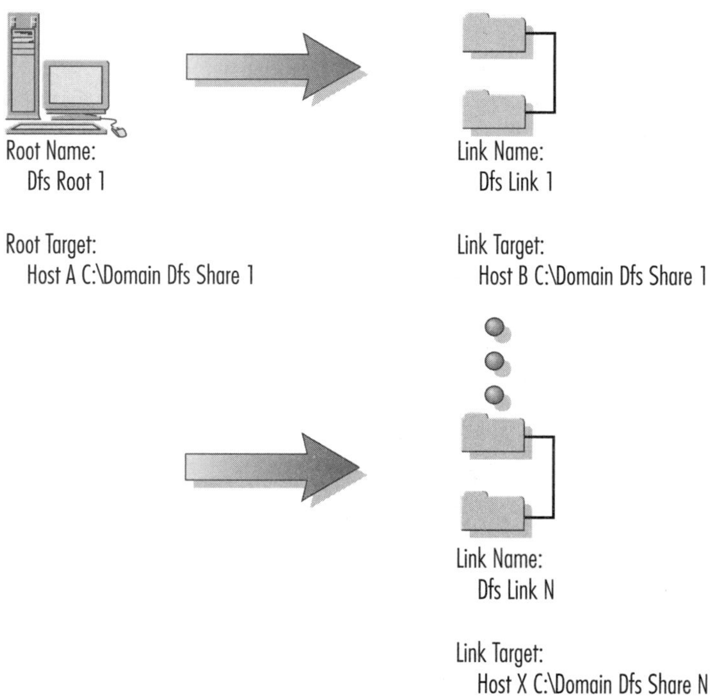

FIGURE 9.30 Dfs Links

NOTE Windows .NET provides a number of enhancements for the Folder Replication Service. This feature exposes more functionality including:

- Removal of replication filtering
- Display of all types of FRS configurations
- Ability to change non-SYSVOL types of FRS configurations
- Definition of FRS replica set
- Topology creation of such elements as full mesh, star, and hub
- Schedule on individual connections

NOTE To host a domain-based Dfs root or fault-tolerant Dfs link replica folder, the host must be running the Distributed File System service for Windows Server 2003 (and be located on an NTFS volume). Windows 2000 Professional does not come with this service preinstalled and therefore cannot be used to host Dfs roots or target folders. Windows NT 4.0 running with Service Pack 3 may host standalone root and target folders.

DFS TOPOLOGY

Dfs maps logical share volumes to physical disk space throughout the network. The main difference between standalone and fault-tolerant, or domain-based, Dfs roots is that domain-based Dfs roots store topology information in the Active Directory in the Partition Knowledge Table (PKT) object, which is distributed to all domain controllers throughout the domain. A standalone Dfs root does not store PKT information in the Active Directory and so relies solely on the Dfs root host to maintain topology information. Additionally, standalone Dfs servers do not support replica sets. A clustering strategy must be implemented to enable fault tolerance with standalone Dfs roots.

Dfs Client and Share Access

Since a domain-based Dfs root automatically publishes information to the Active Directory, a Dfs client running Dfs v5.0 client software (Windows Server 2003) can access a Dfs share in a couple of ways. The first method involves the domain name and the root share name:

```
\\domain name\fault tolerant root name\link name\path\file name
```

The second method involves accessing the fault-tolerant root share name:

```
\\fault tolerant root name\link name\file name
```

The standalone Dfs share is accessed by Dfs v5.0 in the following UNC form. This form is also used by clients running Dfs 4.x accessing either domain-based roots or standalone Dfs shares.

```
\\root host server name\root name\link name\path\file name
```

NOTE As of the writing of this book, both Dfs v4.x and v5.0 are available for Windows 95, Windows 98, and Windows NT 4.0.

Files in the replicas in Figure 9.30 are referenced from a Windows Server 2003 client system using

```
\\domain name\Dfs ROOT 1\Dfs LINK 1\subfolder name\file name
Dfs ROOT 1\Dfs LINK 1\subfolder name\file name
```

or

```
\\HOST A\Dfs ROOT 1\Dfs LINK 1\subfolder name\file name
```

More Dfs Advantages

In addition to the obvious advantages offered by Dfs sharing files, several others need to be highlighted.

BROWSE AND SEARCH DIRECTORIES

Dfs affords naming transparency that allows users to browse and search the network without concern for physical file location. Dfs share names can more accurately reflect logical meaning for data storage and can be limited to the file system naming structure, which is restricted only by a 260-character path name. File search tools available from the **Start → Search** menu may be used to search the logical Dfs structure. This more effectively limits extensive document searches to logical volumes rather than entire physical volumes, which are time consuming.

BRINGING SERVERS OFFLINE WITHOUT USER INTERRUPTION

The logical Dfs namespace allows network resource substitutions to be made without users or client system reconfiguration. A logical share can be redirected to another physical location without affecting the logical Dfs path to file resources. Additional disk space can be added in the form of new subdirectories under an existing Dfs share. Shortcuts and drive mappings on the user's desktop no longer need to be reconfigured as physical hardware changes occur.

EASE OF WEB SERVER MAINTENANCE

Internet Information Server runs on the Windows Server 2003 operating system and acknowledges the Dfs logical drive structure. Web page links in HTML documents do not require update when server names change, or when the underlying physical storage is reorganized, if Dfs logical share references are used.

Concerns Regarding Dfs Use

Although load balancing and high availability can be viewed as positive Dfs attributes, there are some basic concerns. First, since the Dfs client arbitrarily selects a Dfs share path, user access should be distributed evenly among fault-tolerant shares. However, if file and application access is not restricted to Read-Only, multiple versions of a file will be created on replica shares. Even though folder replicas distribute permission, folder, and file changes, file-locking attributes are not replicated. Thus, there is nothing to keep two users from opening the same file on separate Dfs link target folders, which can lead to lost data as a result of overwriting.

Pointing all Dfs clients to a primary share and directing them to an alternative share upon failure of the primary share should alleviate most problems. One share will function as the primary resource, relying on the other one for backup. This can be configured using the Active Directory sites container. Put all computers in the same site as the target host for one of the Dfs link folders. When the Dfs client resolves the link target folder UNC location, it will first attempt connection to the resource within its own site. If this server is down, the client will attempt to connect with the remaining target hosts. In this way, the host in the site container will be the first choice, with the backup being accessed only when the first host is down. This will help eliminate file duplication and data overwrites. Obviously, load balancing will no longer occur, but data loss will be kept to a minimum.

Setting Up a Standalone Dfs Share

Creating a Dfs share involves the following procedure:

1. Log on with administrative privileges.
2. Click **Start** → select **Programs** → choose **Administrative Tools** → select **Distributed File System**.
3. Select the **Action** pull-down window → select **New Root,** as shown in Figure 9.31.
4. The **New Root Wizard** appears. Click **Next** (Figure 9.32).
5. Select **Stand-alone root**.

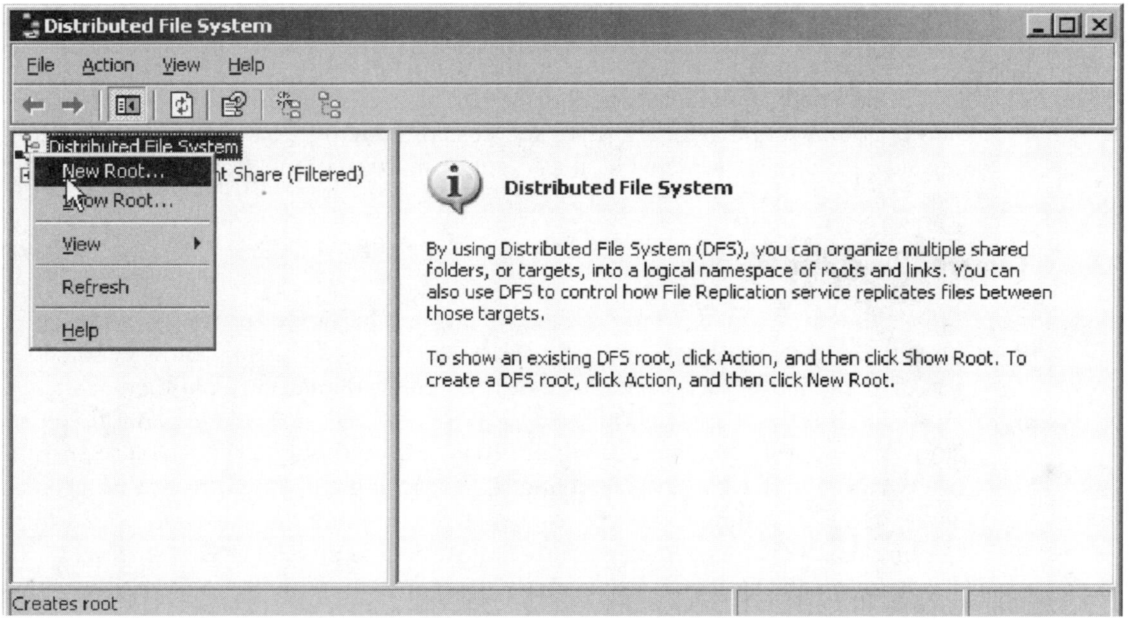

FIGURE 9.31 The Microsoft Distributed File System

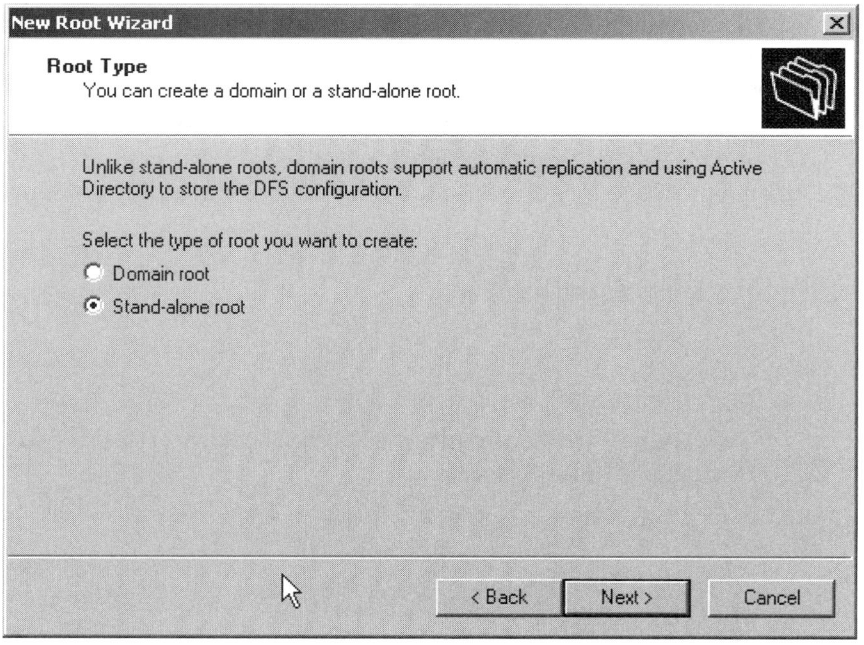

FIGURE 9.32 Creating a Shared Dfs

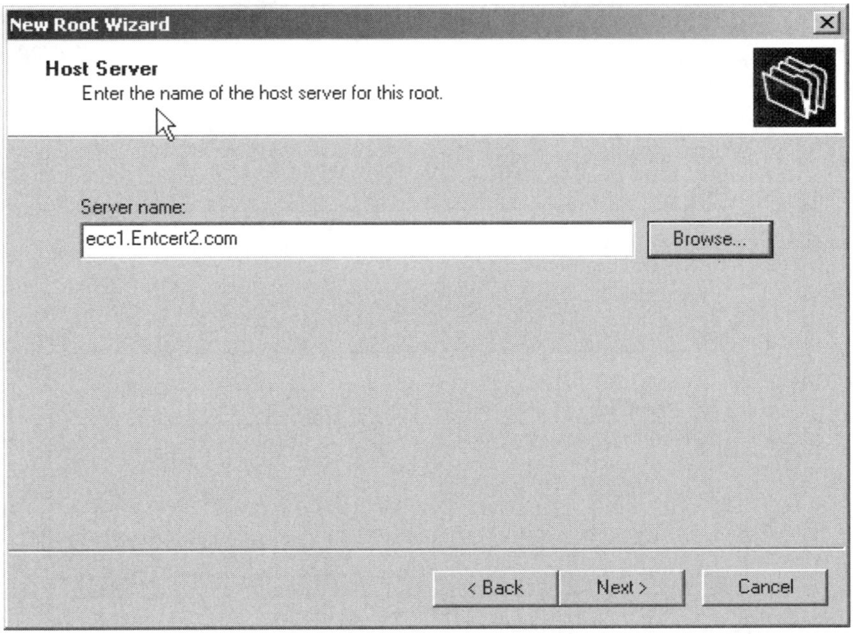

FIGURE 9.33 Naming a Dfs Share

6. Enter the server name on which the Dfs root will reside (Figure 9.33). Click **Next**.
7. Enter a name for the new root in the **Root name** text box (Figure 9.34). Click **Next**.
8. Browse for the folder to share and click **Next** (Figure 9.35).
9. The new Dfs root settings are displayed. Click **Finish**. The new Dfs has been created. Its status may be checked from the Dfs console by right-clicking the share and choosing **Show Status** (Figure 9.36). A green check mark should appear. This can also be used to test child nodes throughout the Dfs structure.

   Create a new Dfs link by following this procedure:

1. Right-click the Dfs Root and select **New Link**.
2. In the **New Link** dialog window, enter a name for the link the **Link name** text box, which will be seen by users (Figure 9.37). Enter the network path for the folder to be referenced from the Dfs root in the **Path to target (shared folder)** text box. Click **OK**.

The **Amount of time clients cache this referral** option defines the period during which the client may use the referral before needing to contact the Dfs root for renewal. However, the Windows Server 2003 Dfs client software will refresh its cache's Time to Live for the client cache after every successful share access.

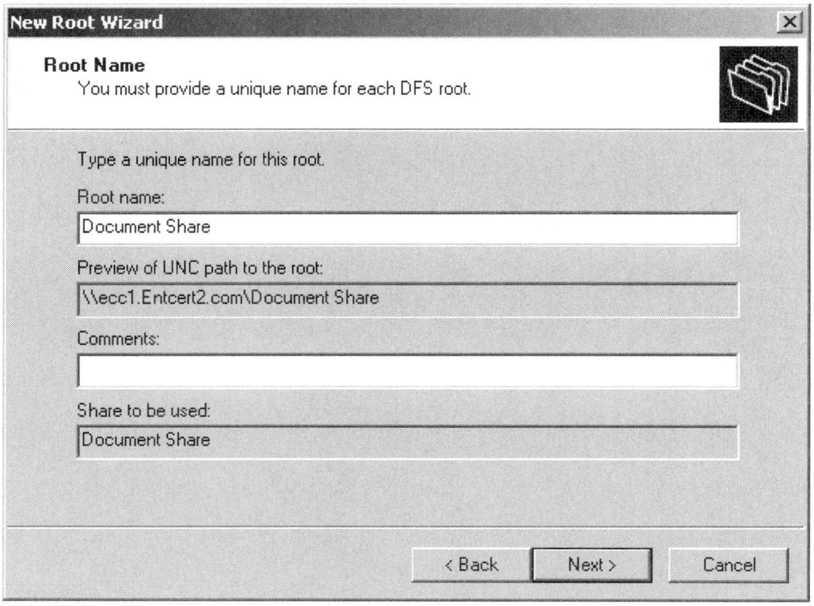

FIGURE 9.34 A Root Volume Share

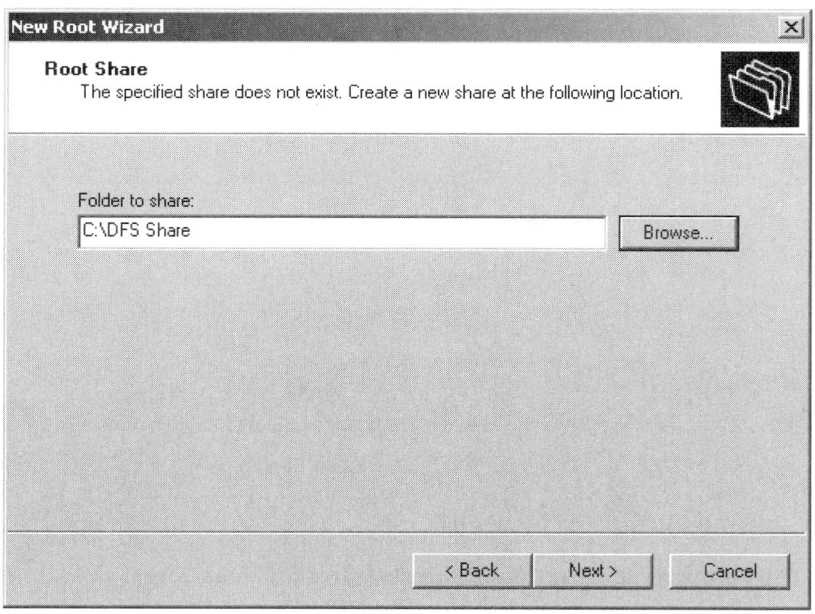

FIGURE 9.35 A Root Name

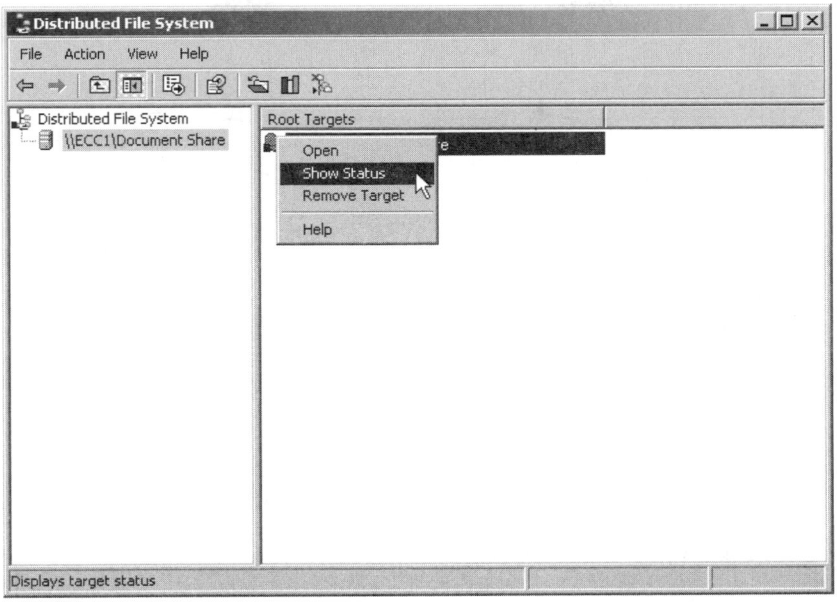

FIGURE 9.36 MCC Action

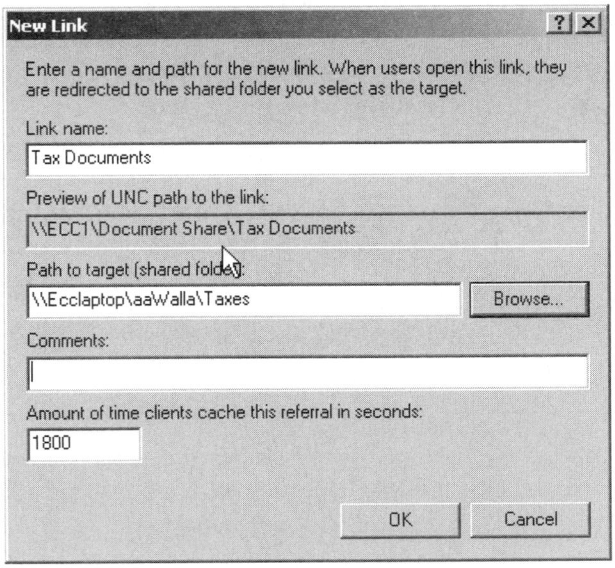

FIGURE 9.37 Create a New Dfs Link

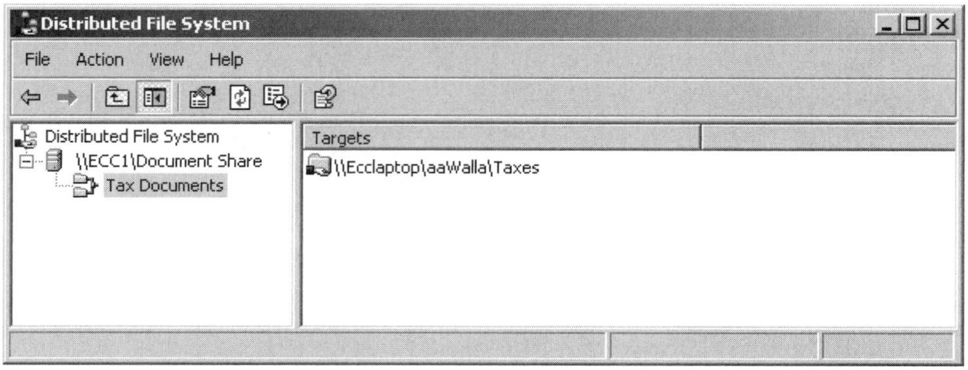

FIGURE 9.38 A New Child Node

The new link should now be visible from the Dfs console (Figure 9.38). The Dfs share has been created and the link connects to a remote machine. It is important to understand that the Dfs root share is now seen as a local folder on the system with the Dfs root. Notice that the link folders are not accessible from the local drive but through **My Network Places**. Find the system with the root share and you will see the folder named after the "share name" configured earlier.

DELETING A DFS SHARE

Deleting a Dfs share is a straightforward process. Log on with administrative privileges. From the **Start menu** → select **Programs** → select **Administrative Tools** → select **Distributed File System.** First remove the targeted share from the Dfs console. Then delete the shared folder from the local drive.

NOTE Currently, only standalone Dfs roots can be used on systems running Microsoft Cluster Server. However, a domain-based Dfs root cannot be used with the cluster product.

POSTSCRIPT

This chapter examines how to apply permissions to files and folders, and how to share folders and use the Distributed File System (Dfs). These facilities provide the baseline Windows Server 2003 security at the file and folder level. In the next two chapters, we examine authentication, public key infrastructure, basic security lockdown, and related topics.

Chapter 10

Kerberos and the Public Key Infrastructure

Authenticating the identity of users during logon is the first step in gaining system access. For local machines not actively participating in a domain, Windows NT LAN Manager (NTLM) protocol is still used to verify a user's name and password. However, in domain environments Microsoft has coupled Active Directory services very closely with the emerging industry standard for authentication from MIT known as Kerberos. Once access is granted, keys are exchanged that permit specific access to other system resources in the domain. This combines underlying Kerberos technology with the Public Key Infrastructure (PKI).

Concepts surrounding both Kerberos and PKI are relatively new in Microsoft environments, and they are important technologies for system administrators to understand. This chapter provides both theoretical and hands-on examination of their implementation on systems running Windows Server 2003.

KERBEROS AUTHENTICATION

Underlying Windows OS security is user authentication. The centralized account management supported by Active Directory Services requires a corresponding authentication protocol for network logon. Based on RFC 1510, Kerberos version 5 provides enhanced authentication for the distributed computing environment and standardization to interoperate with other operating systems. However, while Kerberos is the centerpiece of Active Directory domain authentication, other schemes exist in a Windows Server environment to verify user logons. For example, NTLM protocol is still supported for down-level systems and provides nondomain, local logon capability. In addition, secure channels are used to join domains, make password modifications, and access nontrusted domain resources. Finally, Windows

Server 2003 supports methods of user authentication that depend on whether the connection is dial-up, over the Internet, or within the local network. The Kerberos protocol is the preferred method and first choice for authenticating users and services in a local intranet.

NOTE Authentication verifies the user's identity to the Local Security Authority (LSA). User authentication merely ensures that the user name and password are verified against a highly secure database. As discussed in Chapter 9, the user's eventual ability to use network resources is determined by access permissions assigned to the resource. These permissions are checked after the authentication process completes.

NOTE The NTLM authentication protocol is used in Windows NT and Windows Server 2003 workgroup environments. It is also employed in mixed Windows Server 2003 Active Directory domain environments that must authenticate Windows NT systems. When Windows Server 2003 is converted to native mode, where no down-level Windows NT domain controllers exist, NTLM is disabled. Kerberos then becomes the default for the enterprise.

NOTE New to Windows Server 2003 is support for an Internet Engineering Task Force (IETF RFC 2617) standard Digest Access Authentication for Internet applications. Digest Access Authentication is intended as a more secure method of authentication with Basic authentication. It is fully integrated with the Windows Active Directory and uses the Active Directory as the credentials store. The Windows Digest Security Support Provider (SSP) provides an interface to using Digest Authentication. It is a Simple Authentication and Security Layer (SASL) mechanism. Digest/SASL is used by the Windows LDAP server. The feature can be accessed through the **Platform SDK → The Digest Access Protocol**.

Understanding Kerberos Concepts

Kerberos version 5 is standard on all versions of Windows Server 2003 and ensures the highest level of security for network resources. Its name comes from the three-headed dog of Greek mythology. Its three heads are the Key Distribution Center (KDC), the client user, and the server with the desired service. The KDC is installed as part of the domain controller and performs two services: authentication and ticket-granting. As exemplified in Figure 10.1, three services, or exchanges, are involved when the client initially accesses a server resource:

- Authentication Service (AS) Exchange
- Ticket-Granting Service (TGS) Exchange
- Client/Server (CS) Exchange

THE AUTHENTICATION SERVICE EXCHANGE

When initially logging on to a network, the user must negotiate access by providing a logon name and password that is verified by the AS portion of a KDC within his domain. The KDC has access to Active Directory user account information. Once successfully authenticated, the user is granted a Ticket-granting ticket (TGT) that is valid for the local domain. The TGT has a default lifetime of 10 hours and can be renewed throughout the user's logon session without the user having to reenter his password. It is cached on the local machine in volatile memory space and used to request sessions with services throughout the network.

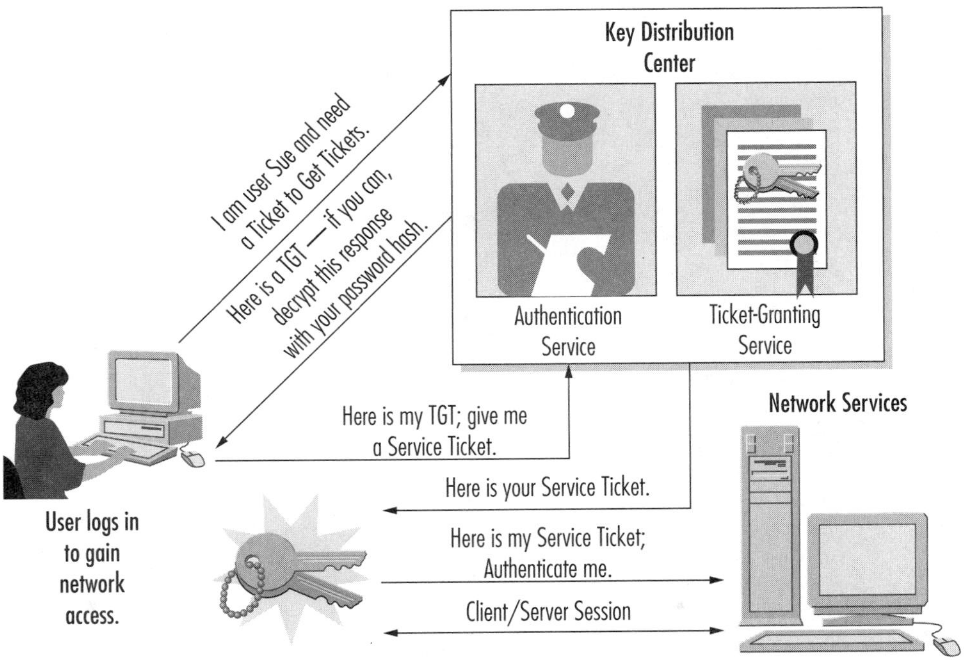

FIGURE 10.1 Kerberos Ticket Exchange

Authentication Service Exchange Details

The AS request identifies the client to the KDC in plain text. If preauthentication is enabled, a timestamp will be encrypted using the user's password hash as an encryption key. If the KDC reads a valid time when using the hash (stored in the Active Directory) to decrypt the timestamp, it knows that the request is not a replay of a previous one. This feature can be disabled for specific users in applications that do not support preauthentication. Access the user account from the **Active Directory Users and Computers** snap-in and select the **Account** tab. In the **Account options** list, select **Do not require Kerberos preauthentication** (Figure 10.2). Table 10.1 outlines the basic elements in the client's AS request to the KDC.

The TGT can be issued with many characteristics identified in the client's request, specified through flag settings. These settings enable various authentication requirements discussed later in the chapter. Table 10.2 defines the TGT flag types.

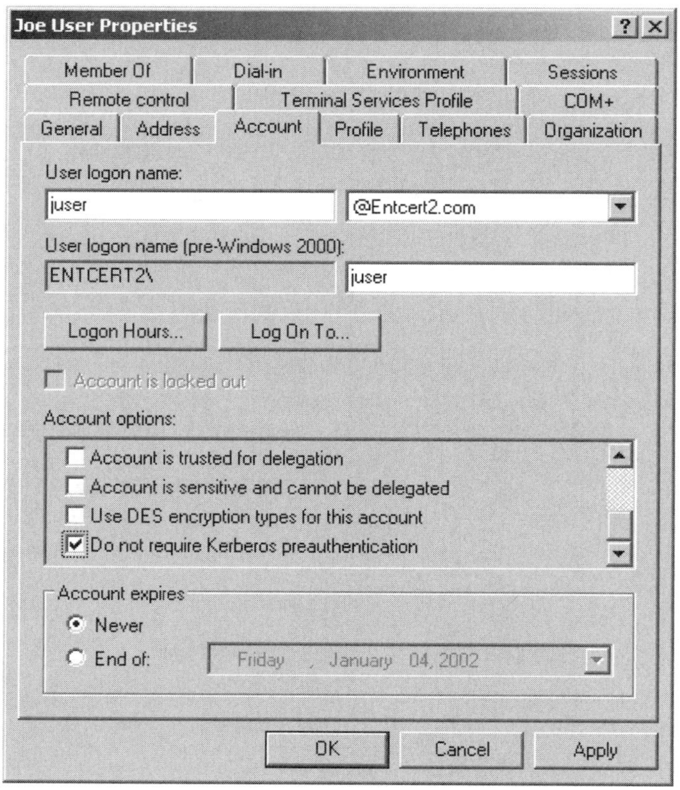

FIGURE 10.2 Disabling Kerberos Preauthentication

TABLE 10.1 Authentication Service Request (Client Request for a TGT from the KDC)

Field	Description
Client ID	Client user ID
Desired Flag Settings for the TGT	Flag settings specified below
Domain Name	Name of the Kerberos realm or Windows Server 2003 domain where client resides
TGS ID	Request for access to the TGS via a TGT
Expiration and TTL Times	Specified ticket expiration and renewal expiration
Timestamp	Timestamp encrypted with user's password hash to prevent replays of this request

If the KDC approves the client's request for a TGT, the reply (referred to as the AS reply) will include two sections: a TGT encrypted with a key that only the KDC Ticket-Granting Service can decrypt and a session key encrypted with the user's password hash to handle future communications with the KDC. Since the client system cannot read the TGT, it must blindly present it to the TGS for Service Tickets. The TGT includes Time to Live parameters, authorization data, a session key to use when communicating with the client, and the client's name. The AS reply is composed of data identified in Table 10.3.

TABLE 10.2 TGT Flag Types

Flag	Purpose
INITIAL	Identifies a TGT-type ticket.
FORWARDABLE	Front-end server is permitted to use the TGT.
FORWARDED	Server is using TGT on behalf of client.
PROXIABLE	Service Ticket may be issued with an address different from the TGT.
PROXY	Service Ticket represents a client with a different address.
RENEWABLE	Ticket's Time to Live (TTL) may be updated.
PRE-AUTHENT	KDC authorized client before issuing ticket.
HW-AUTHENT	Specific hardware is required for authentication.
MAY POSTDATE	TGS may postdate the Service Ticket.
POSTDATED	Ticket will be used on a future date.
INVALID	Ticket is invalid.

TABLE 10.3 Authentication Service Reply—KDC to Client

Field	Description
Section 1: Plain Text	
Client ID	Client identifier
Domain Name	Client's domain
Section 2: TGT Encrypted Portion (KDC Readable Only)	
Flags	Flag setting as identified in TGT Flag (Table 10.2)
TGS Session Key	Session key to be used when communicating with the TGS
Domain Name	Client's domain name
Client ID	Client identifier
Start Time/End Time	Ticket TTL parameters
Authorization Data	User SID and group membership SID info
Section 3: Encrypted Using Password Hash (Readable by Client)	
TGS Session Key	Session key to be used when communicating with the TGS
Start Time/End Time	Ticket TTL parameters
TGS Domain	Domain in which the TGS resides
TGS ID	TGS identifier
Timestamp	Timestamp encrypted with user's password hash

THE TICKET-GRANTING SERVICE EXCHANGE

The user presents the TGT to the TGS for access to a server service. The TGS authenticates the user's TGT and creates a ticket and session key for both the client and the remote servers. This information, known as the Service Ticket, is then cached locally on the client machine.

The client sends its TGT and desired Service Ticket settings to the TGS, which reads it using its own key. If the TGS approves the client's request (Table 10.4), a Service Ticket is generated for the client and the target server. The client reads its portion using the TGS session key retrieved earlier from the AS reply (Table 10.3). It presents the server portion (Table 10.5, Section 2) of the TGS reply to the target server in the CS Exchange, coming next.

THE CLIENT/SERVER EXCHANGE

Once the client server has the Client Server Service Ticket, it can establish the session with the server service. Using its own long-term key with the KDC, the server

TABLE 10.4 Ticket-Granting Service Request

Field	Description
Server ID	Server client wishes to access
Desired Flag Settings for Service Ticket	TGT flag (Table 10.2)
TGT Ticket	TGT encrypted (readable by KDC only)
Expiration and TTL Times	Specified ticket expiration and renewal expiration
Timestamp	Prevents replays of this request

TABLE 10.5 Ticket-Granting Reply—TGS Reply to Client

Field	Description
Section 1: Plain Text	
Client ID	Client identifier
Domain Name	Client's domain
Section 2: Service Ticket Portion Encrypted Using Key Known Only to Target Server and KDC	
Flags	Flag setting as identified in TGT (Table 10.2)
Client/Server Session Key	Session key to be used when communicating between client and server with resource
Domain Name	Client's domain name
Client ID	Client identifier
Start Time/End Time	Ticket TTL parameters
Authorization Data	User SID and group membership SID info
Section 3: Encrypted Using TGS Session Key	
Client/Server Session Key	Session key to be used when communicating between client and server with resource
Start Time/End Time	Ticket TTL parameters
Server's Domain	Domain in which resource resides
Server ID	Server identifier
Nonce B/Timestamp	Prevent replay

TABLE 10.6 Client/Server Exchange Request

Field	Description
Desired Flag Settings for the TGT	TGT flags (Table 10.2)
Service Ticket Encrypted with Key Known Only to Server and KDC	

TABLE 10.7 Client/Server Exchange Reply

Field	Description
Timestamp	Mutually authenticates client and server.
Sequence Numbers	Maintains session through number sequence.

can decrypt the information coming indirectly from the TGS. It can then use the Service Ticket to authenticate the client and establish a service session with it. When the ticket's lifetime is exceeded, it must be renewed to use the service.

Client/Server Exchange Detail

The client blindly passes the server portion of the Service Ticket to the server in the CS request to establish a client/server session (Table 10.6). If mutual authentication is enabled, the target server returns a timestamp encrypted by the Service Ticket session key (Table 10.7). If the timestamp decrypts correctly, not only has the client authenticated itself to the server, but the server has authenticated itself to the client.

NOTE The target server and the KDC never have to communicate directly. This reduces downtime and pressure on the KDC.

FURTHER CLARIFICATION OF THE LOGON PROCESS

A TGT and a Service Ticket are needed to access services on remote computers, but they are also required to successfully log on to a local system. When the logon window appears, password encryption using a one-way hash algorithm occurs immediately, and negotiations commence with the KDC for a valid TGT and Service Ticket. The process is the same as that for accessing a remote service. An access token is created for the user; the token contains all security groups to which he belongs. It is attached to the user's logon session and subsequently inherited by any process or application the user starts.

REFERRAL TICKETS

The Authentication Service and Ticket-Granting Service functions are separate within the KDC. This permits the TGT obtained from an AS in one domain to be used to obtain Service Tickets from a TGS in other domains. This is accomplished through referral tickets.

Once a trust has been established between two domains, referral tickets can be granted to clients who request authorization for services in both. An interdomain key based on the trust password becomes available for authenticating KDC functions. As illustrated in Figure 10.3, a user client in *Entcert1.com* requests authority for a server in *Entcert2.com* using referral tickets. The numbers in Figure 10.3 correspond to the following explanations:

1. The client uses a TGT to contact its domain KDC TGS. The KDC recognizes a request for a session with a foreign domain server and responds by returning a referral ticket for the foreign domain KDC.
2. The client contacts the foreign trusted domain KDC with the referral ticket. This ticket is encrypted with the interdomain key. If the decryption works, the TGS for the foreign domain returns a Service Ticket for the server service in *Entcert2.com*.
3. The client performs the CS exchange with the server and begins the user session with the service.

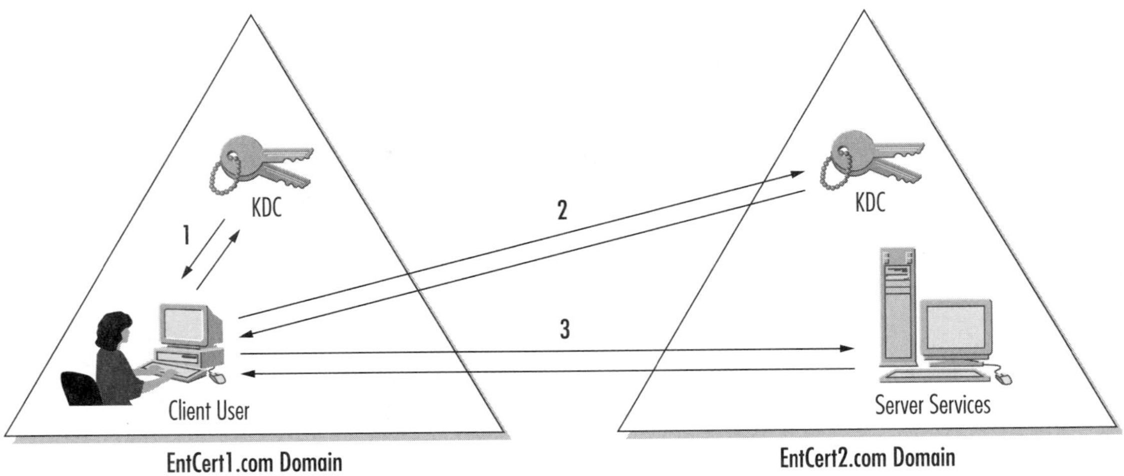

FIGURE 10.3 Key Referral between Trusted Domains

When more domains are involved, the referral process extends and involves the transitive properties between Windows Server 2003 domains. Maintaining many two-way trusts between Windows NT domains was an administrative nightmare, but Kerberos transitive domains cut down on interdomain administration. This can best be explained as illustrated in Figure 10.4, where *Entcert1.com* has a trust relationship with *Entcert2.com*, which has a trust relationship with *Entcert3.com*. Since there is no trust between *Entcert1.com* and *Entcert3.com*, an *Entcert1.com* client accessing a service on a server in *Entcert3.com* would obtain

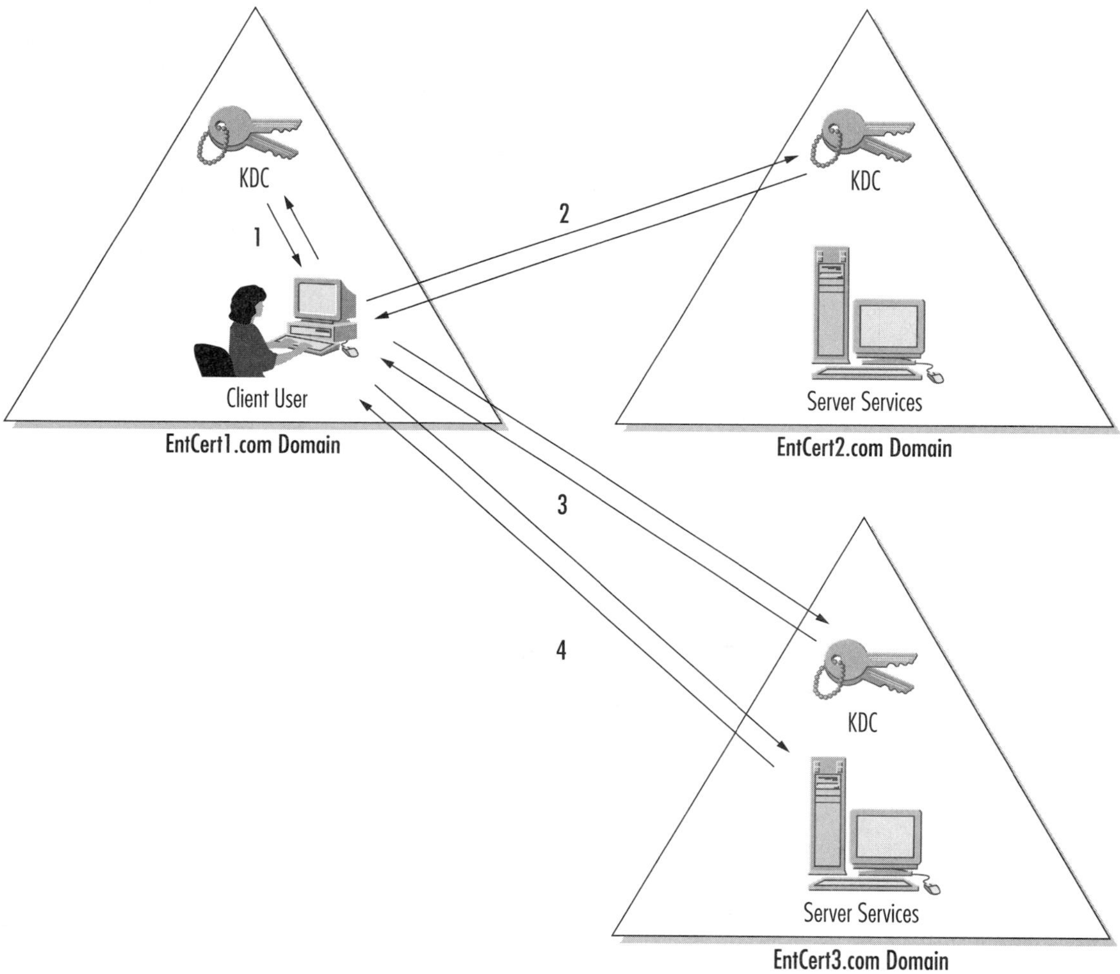

FIGURE 10.4 Key Referrals Enable Transitive Trusts

a Service Ticket through the following steps, numbered to correspond with those appearing in the figure.

1. Use the TGS in *Entcert1.com* to obtain a referral ticket for a KDC in *Entcert2.com*.
2. Use the referral ticket with the TGS on the KDC in *Entcert2.com* and obtain a referral for *Entcert3.com*.
3. Use the second referral ticket with the TGS on the KDC for *Entcert3.com* and obtain a Service Ticket for the server in that domain.
4. Perform the client/server exchange to open a session with the service in *Entcert3.com*.

DELEGATION WITH FORWARDING AND PROXY

Some server services require access to a second server, such as backend database. In order to establish a session with the second server, the primary server must be authenticated on behalf of the client's user account and authority level. This is common in a three-tier client/server model (Figure 10.5) and is usually accomplished with proxy or forwarding authentication.

Proxy Authentication

Proxy authentication requires the client to obtain a Service Ticket for the primary server to use with the secondary server on the client's behalf (Figure 10.6). The client must have the proxy policy enabled when its initial TGT is issued. Then the PROXIABLE flag will be set in the client's TGT. When the primary server requests access to the second server, the client must obtain the second server's name and request a Service Ticket using the proxy-enabled TGT. The KDC then issues a Service Ticket with the PROXY flag set, which the client returns to the primary server. The first server uses the new Service Ticket to establish a session with the desired service on the second server. This new session is based on the client's user ID and address.

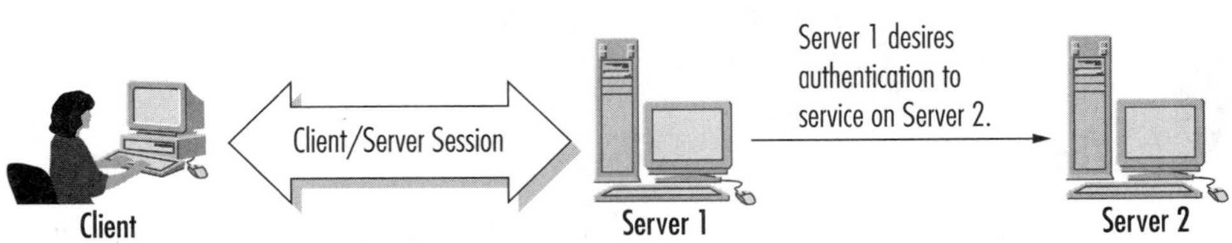

FIGURE 10.5 Proxy and Forwarding Authentication

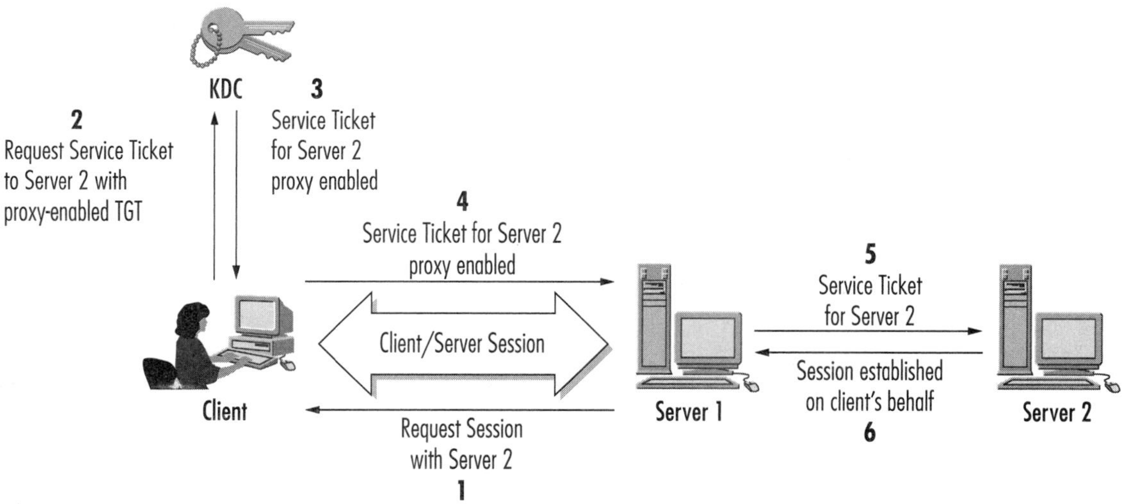

FIGURE 10.6 Proxy Authentication

NOTE The client must learn the name and address of the secondary server. The client is acting on behalf of the primary server and is burdened with retrieving secondary server credentials.

FORWARDING AUTHENTICATION

Forwarding allows the primary server to access the secondary server without requiring the client to participate when establishing a session (Figure 10.7). If the forwarding policy is enabled on the KDC, the client may request a forwarding TGT. When it retrieves the TGT, it must reveal the forwarding server's address (the server will soon act on the client's behalf) during the AS exchange. The FORWARDABLE flag is set on the client's TGT. The client then sends the TGT directly to the server requiring access to a second server. The primary server requests Service Tickets on the client's behalf using the forward-enabled TGT given by the client. New Service Tickets requested by the first server from the KDC also have the FORWARDED flag set and allow the first server to use the Service Ticket with the second server. Unlike in the proxy delegation method, this forwarding doesn't require the client to know the second server's name.

The Kerberos Process

The previous sections discussed ticket exchanges required for user authorization. We now take a look at how these exchanges are handled without compromising user information or causing security breaches.

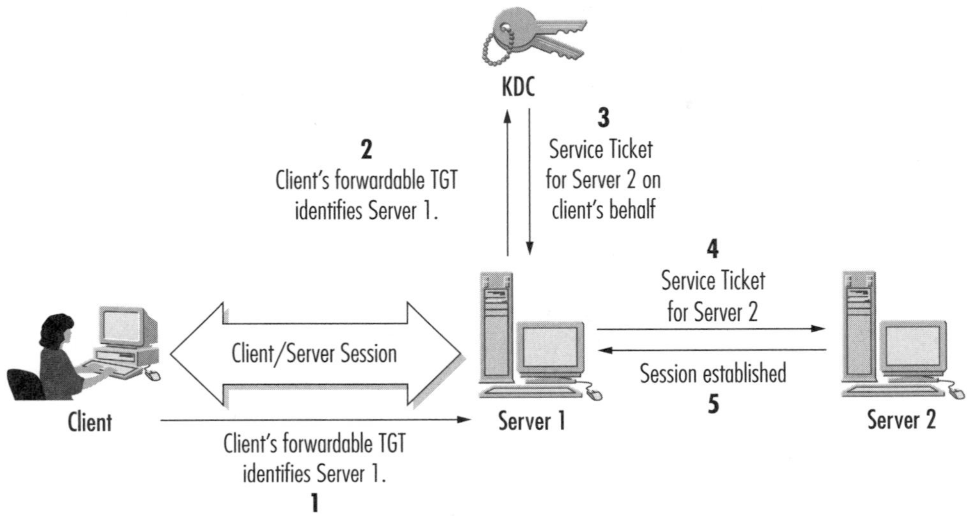

FIGURE 10.7 Forwarding Authentication

SYMMETRICAL ENCRYPTION AND SHARED KEYS

The basis for Kerberos communication and authentication is symmetrical encryption algorithms using shared secret keys. These keys depend on fast and comparatively simple encryption, and their implementation does not require a public/private key infrastructure. Figure 10.8 demonstrates symmetrical encryption and how shared keys work.

Data is encrypted using a standard encryption algorithm such as Data Encryption Standard (DES) (discussed in Chapter 13). The algorithm takes in readable data and a key for producing encrypted data. Depending on the algorithm, this encrypted data is very difficult to decrypt without the corresponding decryption algorithm and key. Two parties can share a secret key using an out-of-band method

FIGURE 10.8 Encryption for Large Amounts of Data or for Continuous Connections

and communicate with a strong degree of confidentiality. For example, they might transfer the secret key through a telephone call or "snail" mail; assuming the sender is the only one with the matching secret key, the receiver has some degree of authentication. This assumes that decrypted data is readable and meaningful to the receiver. There is the possibility that someone is replaying a previously sent message, a scenario addressed in the next section.

SHARED SECRET KEYS

In Kerberos, the shared secret key is generated from the user's password using a one-way hash function that is a combination of the Data Encryption Standard, Cipher Block Chaining (CBC), and Message Digest 5. All Kerberos version 5 implementations must minimally implement this hash function for interoperability. A hash function generally inputs the password text string and generates a 128-bit string that would appear meaningless to anyone without the original password—it is very difficult to obtain the original password string from the generated hash. For further explanation of this hash function, please see William Stallings's excellent book *Cryptography and Network Security: Principles and Practice*, 3rd ed. (Prentice-Hall, 2002). The KDC and all clients are aware of the hash function and can produce the hash, given the user's password. When the user logs on to the client, the password is put through the hash function to produce a hash that is used as a shared secret key to communicate with the KDC.

Preventing the Replay of Previous Communications

One security concern is that someone will intercept a communication and attempt to pass it off as his own and thereby gain authorization. To avoid this, a timestamp is used to prevent someone from replaying a previous communication. Say a client desires to establish a session with a server. The client and the server share knowledge of a common key, based on the user's password. The client sends a request to log on containing its user ID and the current date/time encrypted using the symmetric key. The server reads the requesting user ID and retrieves the correct key for that user, whereupon the date/time is decrypted. If the date/time value is tolerably close to the server's local clock, the time must have been encrypted using the user's password hash and so the client's identity is verified. Since the date/time is constantly changing, an intruder cannot simply resend the same data to the server. The server also saves all logon attempts from that user for the last several minutes and tests each logon to make sure it is later than the previous one. This obviously requires domainwide clock synchronization within the tolerable settings.

Another option to prevent replay is using a *nonce,* which is a number randomly generated by the client and sent to the server. The server encrypts the nonce and sends it back to the client with the reply. It keeps track of previously sent nonces and rejects repeats for a given time period. The client can verify that the server has the shared key if it correctly encrypts the original nonce in the reply.

NOTE In addition to the client's being authenticated to the server, the server is also authenticated to the client. When the client receives a correctly encrypted timestamp from the server, it is certain that the server is who it claims to be. This is known as mutual authentication, another benefit of Kerberos.

NOTE Encryption and session keys function differently. Rather than repeatedly using the user's password hash as the encryption key, a session key can be distributed using the password hash for further communication. The session key is a randomly generated key that is valid only for the length of the communication session.

NOTE A new feature in Windows Server 2003 is Kerberos extended errors facility. This makes more information available for diagnostic and troubleshooting of authentication errors in a domain-based environment. This feature is integral to the operating system and does not require administrative intervention.

Kerberos Policies

The system administrator manages Kerberos through **Group Policy** settings. Kerberos policies are found under the **Security Settings** → **Account Policies** → **Kerberos Policy** node under all Group Policy Objects. Figure 10.9 displays the default settings for the Default Domain Policy GPO.

To modify the current settings, double-click the target policy and make the appropriate changes in the dialog box that appears. The **Enforce user logon restrictions** policy may be disabled to cut down on the number of user right verifications Kerberos must perform. The default lifetimes for the TGT (user ticket) and CS Service Tickets can be increased to lengthen the time between ticket renewals. All systems participating in a Kerberos realm must implement some sort of clock synchronization so that the timestamps are relatively accurate. The clock tolerance interval field can be increased from the default of 5 minutes to provide more time lag between systems.

The standard Kerberos policies that are manageable by system administrators are further explored in Table 10.8.

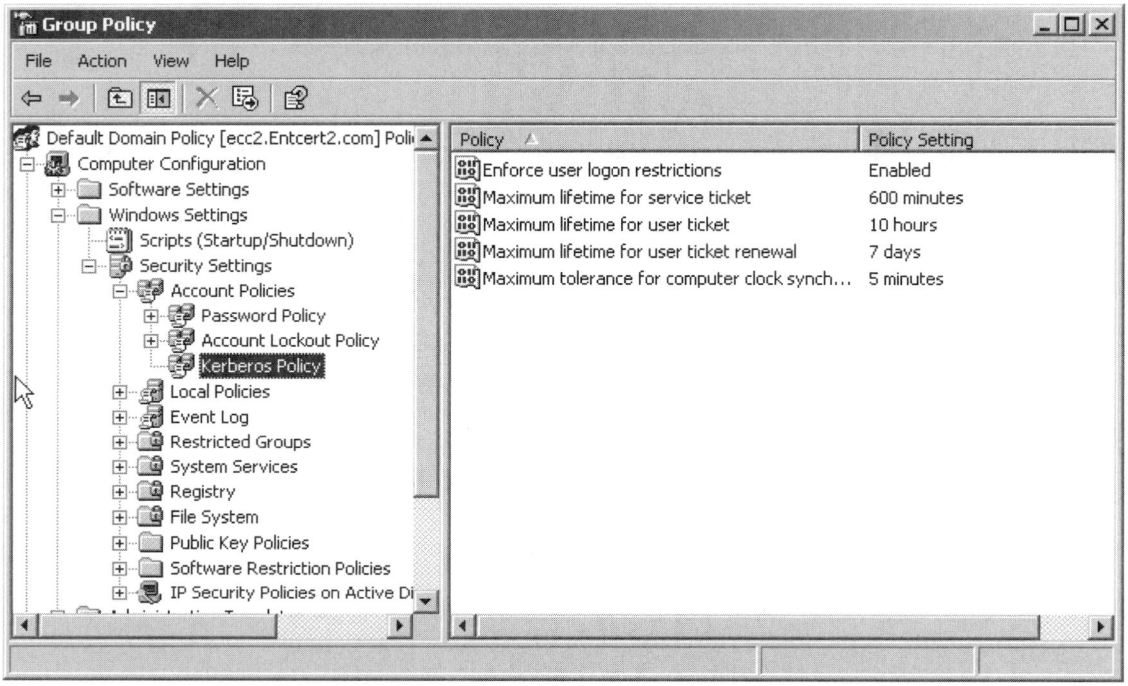

FIGURE 10.9 Kerberos Policies

TABLE 10.8 Standard Kerberos Policy Options

Policy	Purpose
Enforce User Logon Restrictions	If this policy is enabled, users requesting Service Tickets for the local machine must have the right to log on locally, or users requesting Service Tickets for remote machines must have the right to access this computer from the network.
Max Lifetime for Service Ticket	Maximum time until the CS Service Ticket expires.
Max Lifetime for User Ticket	Maximum time until the TGT expires without renewal (user ticket = TGT).
Max Lifetime for User Ticket Renewal	Maximum time until the TGT expires, even when client renews the ticket with KDC.
Max Tolerance for Comp Clock Sync	Maximum time skew between system clocks when verifying timestamps during Kerberos exchanges.

NOTE The **Log on locally** policy and the **Access this computer from the network** policy are modified from a group policy snap-in in the **Computer Configuration → Windows Settings → Security Settings → Local Policies → User Rights Assignment** node.

Cross-Forest Authentication

Multiple forests are sometimes required for security, administrative, or budgetary reasons. New to Windows Server 2003, cross-forest authorization grants access to local resources for users and groups from other forests while using the native names of those external security principals. An administrator can select users and groups from trusted forests for inclusion in local groups or access control lists. This feature maintains the integrity of the forest security boundary. It enables the trusting forest to enforce constraints on the security identifiers it will accept.

When using the cross-forest authentication, group membership, and ACL, rules must be enforced. For example, names must be typed in completely and wild card searches are not supported. The Object Picker and ACL Editor use system application programming interfaces (APIs) to store SIDs in group member and ACL entries. Name-SID translation APIs are enhanced to use cross-forest routing hints. NTLMs are leveraged to secure channels between domain controllers along the trust path to resolve security principal names or SIDs from trusted forests. SIDs are filtered when authorization data passes from the root domain of the trusted forest to the root domain of the trusting forest. The trusting forest will only accept SIDs that are relative to domains it trusts the other forest to manage. SID filtering is automatically enforced for Kerberos and Windows NTLM authentication.

The Global Catalog is called when Kerberos and NTLM cannot resolve a principal name on the local domain controller. In cases where the GC cannot resolve the name, the new cross-forest name-matching function is used. The way this function works is that the name matching compares the security principal name with trusted namespaces from all trusted forests. The trusted forest returns a routing hint when a match is found. Kerberos and NTLM use routing hints to route authentication requests along the trust path. The Kerberos Key Distribution Centers (KDC) generate referrals that follow the trust path. The client then seeks them out in standard Kerberos fashion. For NTLM, DCs chain the request across secure channels. This chain follows the trust path, using pass-through authentication. User principal name (UPN) credentials are fully supported.

NEW TRUST WIZARD

New to Windows Server 2003 is an improved Trust Wizard designed to create both sides of a trust link in one operation. This works where proper credentials are supplied for both sides of the trust. This wizard applies to both Windows 2000 and Windows Server 2003 involved with external or forest trust links. A new Trust API is also provided to support delegation required to deploy resource forests. The function includes matching required credentials to type of trust. With this domain, administrators can create inbound forest trust and enforce quotas on user-created trust links. The new wizard is activated via **Active Directory Domains and Trusts** snap-in → **Domain Properties** → **Trusts** → **New Trust**.

THE PUBLIC KEY INFRASTRUCTURE

The Windows .NET Kerberos version 5 implementation affords a secure, centralized, and efficient solution to domainwide authentication. However, the need to communicate with the Internet represents additional security problems. Most companies today offer extranet and Internet access to a large number of clients beyond their own user database maintained with the Active Directory. This is when the Public Key Infrastructure becomes necessary.

Maintaining passwords for the numbers of end users who communicate via e-mail or access an enterprise's Web server is a daunting task. In addition to authentication, users require confidentiality and integrity in Internet traffic, which is exposed to the world and can be read or monitored with common network sniffing tools available to any personal computer. External users need secure private connections to your network that ensure their identity and limit data tampering and snooping, but they should not have to remember myriad passwords or buy expensive smart card hardware. The PKI provided by Windows .NET limits these problems through a couple of strategies. The first is digital signatures, which overcomes a number of potential problems, including the following:

- *Impersonation*—sending an e-mail message to someone pretending to be someone else or logging on to a Web server or other system under a false identity; also pretending to be the intended message recipient or Web server for a client.
- *Message replay*—replaying messages sent by another party in an attempt to gain access to resources authorized for her use.
- *Message data modification*.
- *Repudiation*.

  —Let the receiver ensure that the sender sent a particular message.

  —Let the sender prove that the receiver received message.

The second strategy used in Windows .NET with respect to the Public Key Infrastructure is the use of *data encryption*. This provides confidentiality by trans-

FIGURE 10.10 Encryption for Confidentiality

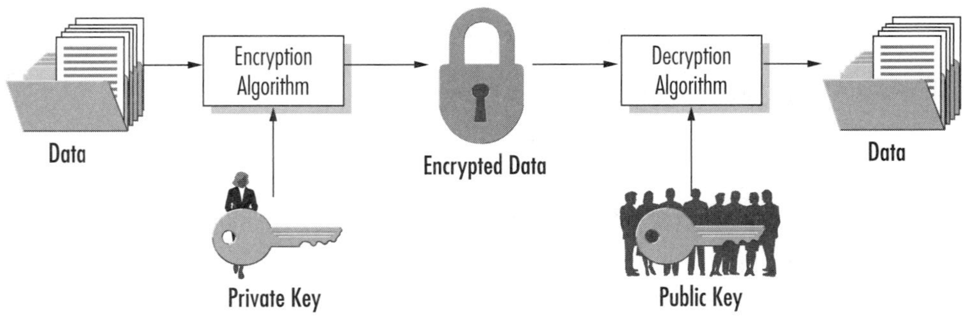

FIGURE 10.11 Digital Signatures for Authentication and Integrity

forming data into an unreadable form that is not reasonably possible to decipher without the corresponding key.

PKI Background

The PKI uses public and private keys to implement digital signatures and data encryption. It provides the basic components and foundation for implementing cryptographic techniques for secure network communications and authentication. Public keys are distributed via the X.509 version 3 certificate standard.

Any entity on the network that wants to secure communication maintains a public key/private key combination. Both keys can be used for encryption but require the other key for decryption (Figures 10.10 and 10.11). Each key is considered *asymmetrical* and can produce encrypted data using an encryption algorithm. The asymmetrical matching key for the public/private key pair is required to decrypt the encrypted data and make it readable. By contrast, *symmetrical keys*, discussed in the Kerberos section, require only one key for both encryption and decryption (Figure 10.8).

DATA ENCRYPTION

Each encryption client is responsible for securing a private key and preventing its exposure to the network. In contrast, the public key is given to all parties with whom the entity wishes to communicate. For example, a Web server client wanting to retrieve information securely from a Web server sends the server its public key, which the server uses to encrypt sensitive data or a secret key and sends it back. The client then uses its private key to decrypt the message data or secret key.

The public/private model allows the two parties to set up a secure channel (Schannel) through the shared secret key using the industry standard Secure Sockets Layer (SSL) or Transport Layer Security (TLS) protocol. The PKI provides authentication and key exchange for small amounts of data. The public/private key encryption process is processor intensive and is best used to set up secret symmetrical encryption keys to handle bulk transfers.

THE DIGITAL SIGNATURE

A very useful aspect of PKI is the digital signature. Suppose a Web server needs to verify that a client is the owner of a public key. The client uses a hash algorithm on the entire message to generate a message hash, which will always be the same value as long as the message data remains unchanged. This hash value is then encrypted using the client's private key, producing a digital signature for the message.

NOTE Some common hashing algorithms are RSA Data Security's Message Digest 5 (MD5), which produces a 128-bit hash, and the Secure Hash Algorithm 1 (SHA-1), which produces a 160-bit hash.

The message data may remain unencrypted and is sent along with the digital signature to the Web server (Figure 10.12). There the client's public key is used to decrypt the message hash from the digital signature. The server recomputes the message hash from the message data using the same hash algorithm as the client and compares the sent hash to the newly computed one. If they are the same, it can be concluded that the digital signature must have been encrypted using the private key that corresponds to the public key. It can also be concluded that the message content did not change en route to the server unless someone else had access to the private key. In this way the digital signature provides message authentication (i.e., it verifies who the data is from) and provides integrity (if the message content had been modified, the computed hash would not match the hash in the digital signature).

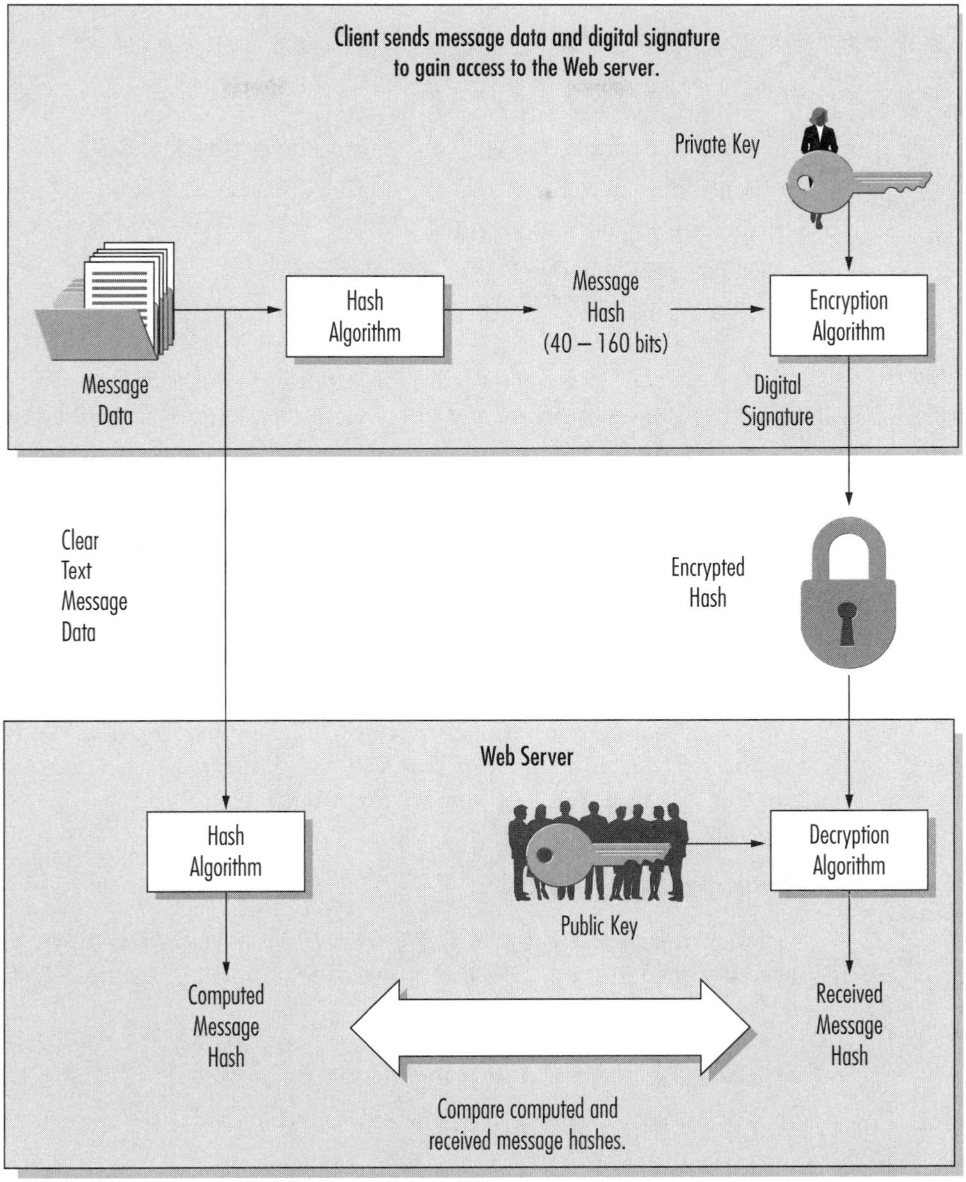

FIGURE 10.12 Using a Digital Signature

Understanding basic public/private key mechanics enables a grasp of the Windows Server 2003 PKI components. Let's examine these key components:

- Certification authority (CA)
- Secure channel (SSL/TLS/server gated cryptography (SGC))
- Authenticode
- Encrypted File System (EFS)
- Microsoft Exchange Server Key Management Server
- IP security (see Chapter 13 regarding networking)

The next sections mainly address Certification Authority concepts and examples. The other PKI components are discussed after a lengthy introduction to the CA.

Certification Authority

The certificate authority server issues certificates to clients (also known as subjects) and assigns certificate policies based on the client. It also verifies the owner of previously issued certificates using a database that maps user identities to their public keys. It is possible to contact the CA and verify the owner of a public key. However, the digitally signed certificate eliminates the need to do this if the client trusts the CA. The digital signature validates the certificate, thus proving that the true owner has the corresponding private key and is the only one who can decrypt information that has been encrypted with the public key.

CERTIFICATE COMPONENTS

Certificates supported by Windows Server 2003 follow the X.509 version 3 standard established by the IETF. Among other things, a certificate contains the following information:

- The subject's public key value
- The subject's name (X.500 distinguished name (DN)) or certificate holder
- Serial number
- Valid from date/time to date/time
- CA that issued this certificate (X.500 DN)
- Digital signature and associated algorithm (protects the contents of the ticket with a hash code and includes the hash algorithm used to sign the certificate)

NOTE The digital signature contains a hash of the entire certificate, which is then encrypted with the issuing CA's private key. Someone can read the certificate, decrypt the hash using the CA's public key, generate his own hash using the specified hash algorithm, and compare the two. This validates the certificate contents and that the certificate was created using the CA's private key. If this is a trusted authority, the user can assume that the contents are correct. This is the standard method for interpreting X.509 certificates.

The certificate authority binds the public key to the subject, which usually takes the form of a person or computer. The subject must have a corresponding private key to validate the certificate for authentication and encryption. A CA is responsible for issuing the certificates to subjects who request them, managing issued certificates, and mapping public keys to their corresponding owners.

An enterprise CA also manages policies or the intended uses for certificates. In this the Microsoft Certificate Management Services follows the guidelines established by the IETF Public Key Infrastructure X.509 (PKIX). Table 10.9 lists some uses for certificates issued by the Windows Server 2003 CA.

TABLE 10.9 Intended Uses for Certificates

Certificate Purposes	Intended Uses
Code Signing	Ensures software came from software publisher and protects software from tampering after publication.
Microsoft Trust List Signing	Signs for the root CA list or certificate trust list (CTL) that domain administrator finds trustworthy for users.
Encrypting File System	Allows data on disk to be encrypted.
Secure E-mail	Ensures that the content of e-mail cannot be viewed by others; protects e-mail from tampering; and ensures that e-mail came from the sender.
Client Authentication	Guarantees the client's identity to a server.
Server Authentication	Guarantees the identity of a server.
Certificate Request Agent	Allows an enrollment agent to request certificates on behalf of the client for smart card programming.
File Recovery	Allows trusted recovery agents to decrypt the EFS when an owner loses his key.

TRUSTED AUTHORITIES AND CERTIFICATE STORES

Now that we have some understanding of certificate components and their possible uses with Windows Server 2003, we can review the CA architecture. The first step is to establish a common trusted certificate authority for all users that intend to communicate with each other.

Clients establish an implicit trust with a certificate authority by retrieving a copy of the CA's certificate and storing it in their local trusted store (Figure 10.13). The user now has the CA's public key and can use it to verify signatures created by it. Windows Server 2003 allows a domain controller to import a CA certificate into Public Key Policies and distribute it to all domain members. An example of this is covered later in the "Certificate Authority Administration" section.

Once a user has established a trusted CA, she may generate her own public/private key pairs and request a certificate by presenting the CA with her public key and identity. The CA uses its private key to encrypt her public key, thus authenticating the certificate. Once the CA issues the certificate, the user stores it in her personal store. She can then exchange certificates with all others who desire secure communication and authentication.

Once users exchange certificates signed by commonly trusted authorities, they may set up services such as secure e-mail, IPSec, secure channels, and so forth (Figure 10.14). Certificates may be issued to users, computers, and services and are kept in several defined stores within Windows Server 2003.

The Certificates snap-in can be used to view the contents of the local system's certificate stores. This is demonstrated in the "Certificate Authority Administration" section. Certificates can be viewed by store or by purpose (Table 10.10).

Certificates are imported and exported, in a variety of formats (to be discussed later), from the Certificates snap-in. This tool is designed to manage personal cer-

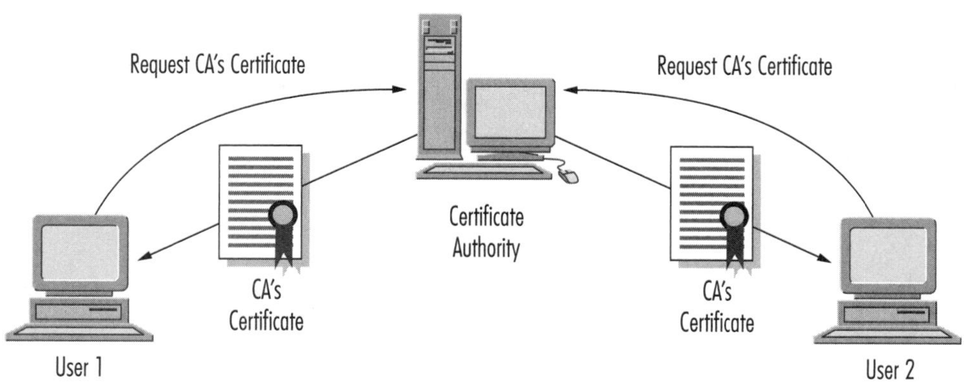

FIGURE 10.13 Storing a CA's Certificate in a Local Trusted Store

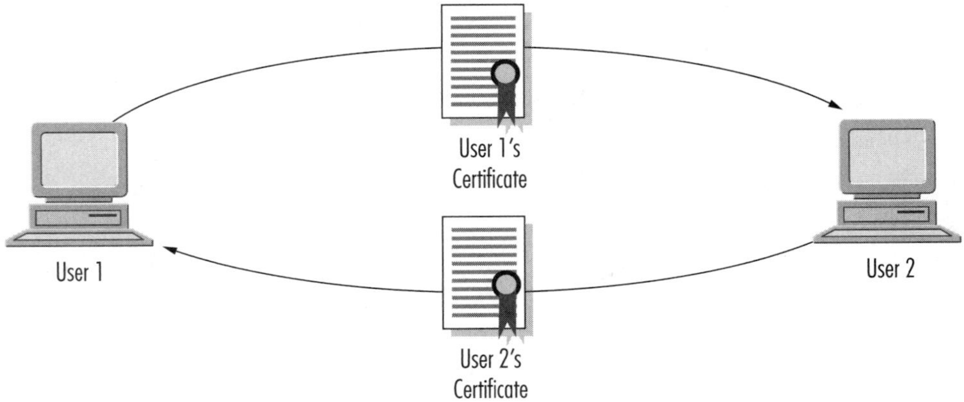

FIGURE 10.14 Certificate Exchange between Users

tificates, certificates for the operating system's service account, and computer certificates (Figure 10.15). Provided that a private key is available for export, the user may back up certificates for later retrieval.

When the Certificate snap-in has been added, certificate stores for the user, computer, or service account may be perused. It can be used to view stores on any computer in the domain (Figure 10.16).

As discussed earlier, a trusted CA may be used to verify a user's identification based on his certificate and corresponding digital signature. Verification of the

TABLE 10.10 Purpose of Certificates Stores

Store	Purpose
Personal	Certificates with associated private keys, used to authenticate a user to other entities and secure inbound communications.
Trusted Root Certification	A certificate from a root CA in this store designates a trust between the user/computer account and the root CA. The user/computer account can then validate certificates issued by the CA.
Enterprise Trust	Store for Certificate Trust Lists. A CTL may set policies for certificates and limit how a certificate may be used.
Intermediate Certification Authorities	Contains certificates belonging to intermediate CAs that verify other CAs through a chain.
Request	Pending certificate request.
Active Directory User Object	Store for user accounts published using the Active Directory.

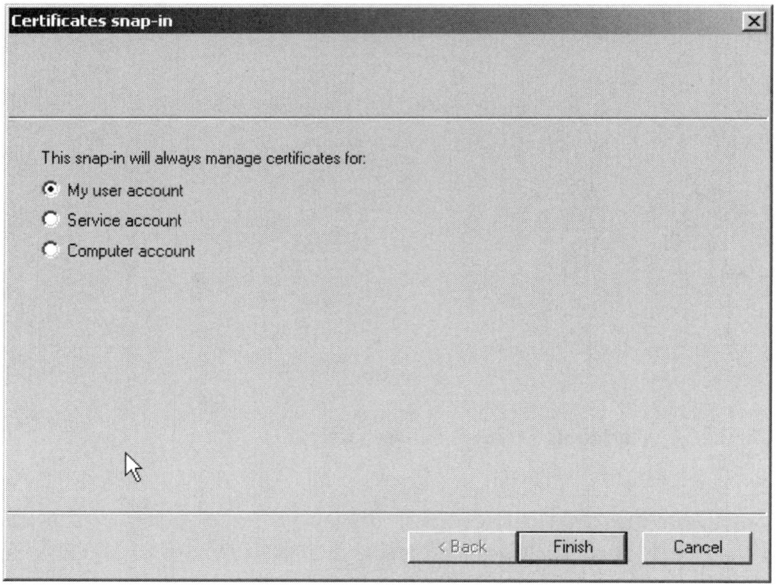

FIGURE 10.15 Account Types for the Certificate Snap-In

trusted CA's signature on the certificate with its public key usually provides enough proof that the certificate is valid. Once this is established, the user must prove that he has the corresponding private key for the certificate, which confirms his identity (Figure 10.17). For example, the Web server can establish secure communication with Joe User once it possesses a copy of his certificate. It uses the public key in the certificate to send information that can be decrypted only with Joe's private key. This enables the Web server to share a temporary secret with Joe and secure future session communications.

Certificate exchange is relatively simple when both users trust the same certificate authority. However, any time users communicate with someone or some service outside of their Windows Server 2003 domain, a trusted CA must be established. This requires an extensible and universal strategy for certificate verification throughout the Internet.

Certificate Authority Hierarchies

Microsoft has adopted the hierarchical model for its simplicity, wide acceptance, and scalability. A CA hierarchy is composed of one or more CAs to form a treelike structure. The parent CA is known as the *root* CA and connects to subordinate *intermediate* and *issuing* CAs. An issuing CA handles user requests for certificates and issues them accordingly. An intermediate CA basically maintains a link in the

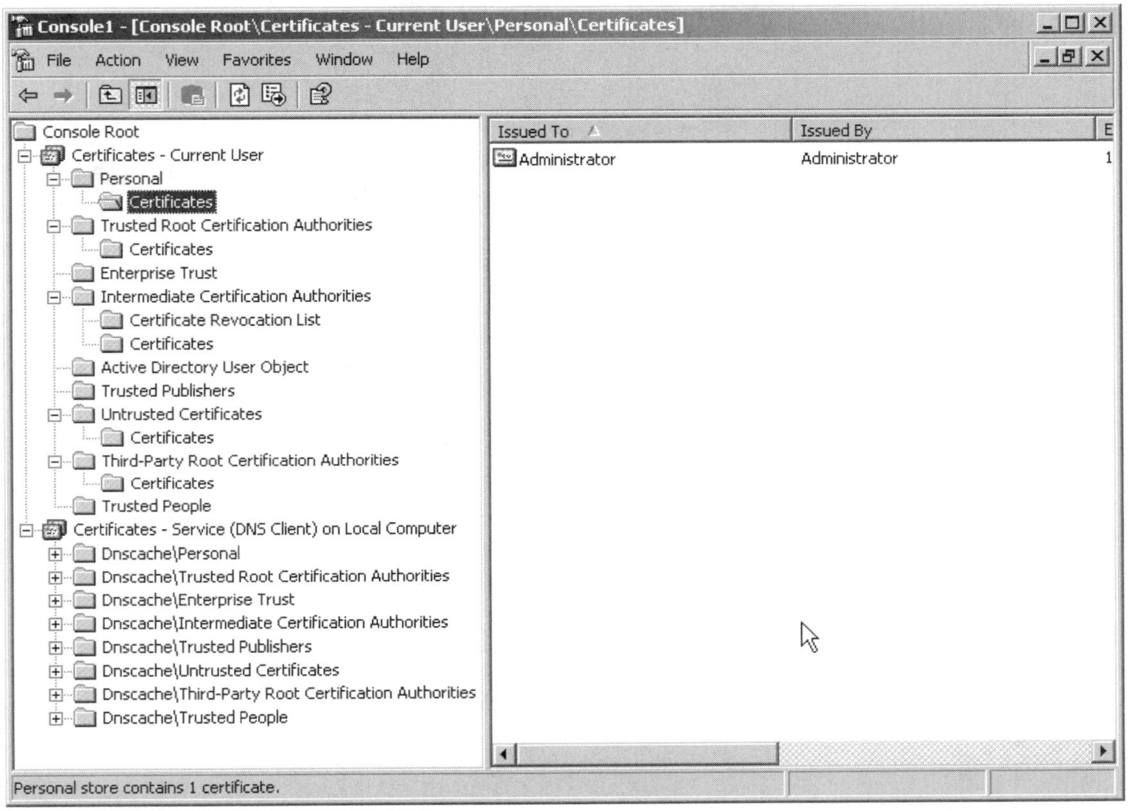

FIGURE 10.16 Local Stores

chain to validate other CAs. The relationship between CAs is established by exchanging their certificates. The root CA gives an issuing CA its certificate and vice versa.

Each CA stores the other's certificate in its Trusted Root Authority store. The certificate authority hierarchy is then built on these mutual trusts (Figure 10.18). It is important not to confuse CA trusts with Kerberos domain trusts. The Active Directory conveniently distributes certificates within the Windows Server 2003 domain, but many hierarchies involve CAs outside the corporate domain and must be manually established. Also, CA hierarchies are not modeled after the DNS hierarchy, which forms one large tree consisting of one root. Rather, they involve an unlimited number of separate and unconnected hierarchies.

With the hierarchy in place, users import and store certificates from a CA that is conveniently accessible. A chaining process is used for validation when a user receives a certificate that has been signed by a CA not in the user's Trusted Root

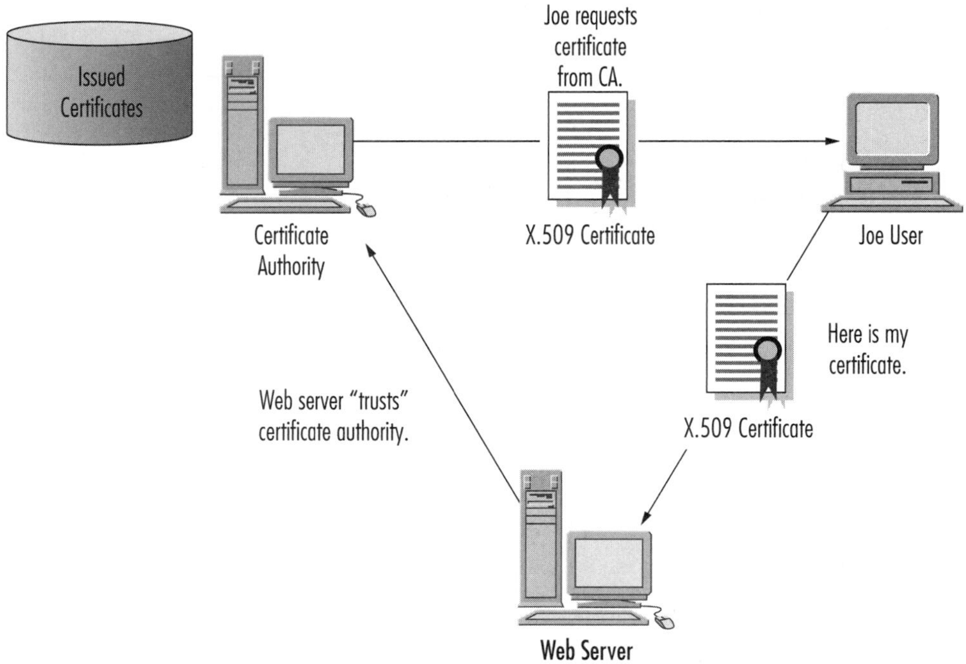

FIGURE 10.17 Verifying Identity by the CA's Signature

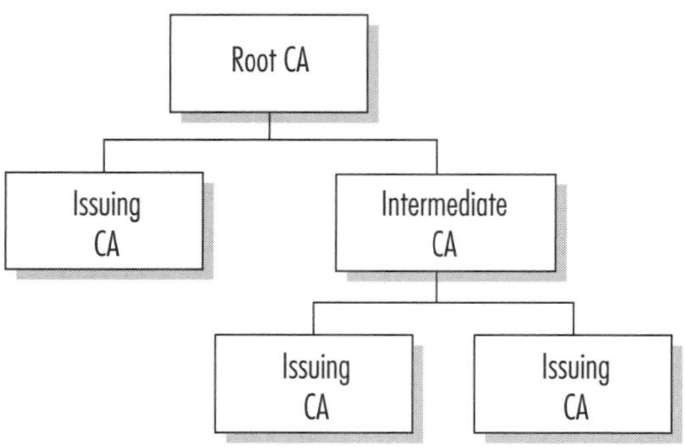

FIGURE 10.18 Certificate Authority Hierarchies Vary

Authority store. If a certificate is validated by a CA in one of the user's trusted hierarchies, the user may contact the point of trust and work her way to the CA that validated the certificate.

Let's look at this process through the example illustrated in Figure 10.19. User 1 has received a certificate from User 2. CA 5 issued that certificate, and to verify it,

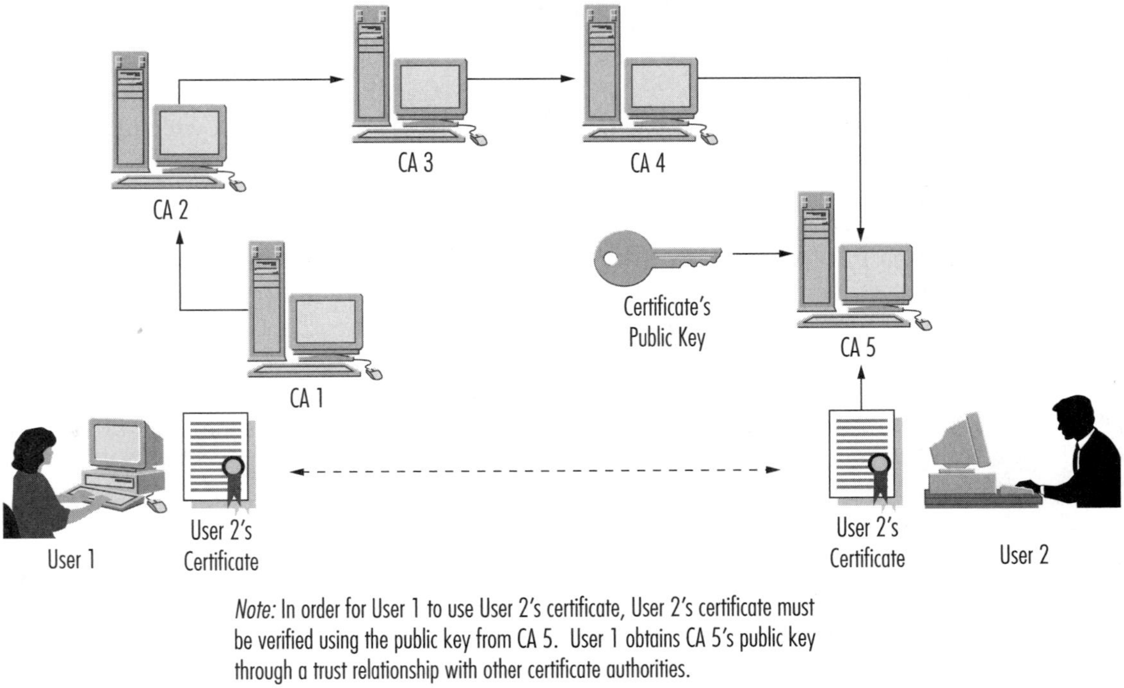

FIGURE 10.19 Chaining within a CA Hierarchy to Validate a Certificate

User 1 must have a public key for CA 5's signature. A certification path is made between User 1's trusted authority, CA 1, and User 2's trusted certificate authority, CA 5. As shown by the hierarchy, we know that CA 1 has a certificate for CA 2, which has a certificate for CA 3. CA 3 owns a certificate for CA 4, who possesses a certificate for CA 5. From this chain of certificates, User 1's system can eventually unravel a public key for User 2's signed certificate.

At first glance, multiple issuing certificate authorities may seem unduly complex. However, they have some advantages, including the following:

- Good network connectivity to an issuing CA relieves the burden on a slow connection to the root CA.
- Certificate policies can be set differently for each issuing CA. OUs and domains may require different intended uses for their certificates as well.
- Parts of a CA hierarchy can be turned off without affecting the rest of the tree.
- Portions of the hierarchy can have shorter validation periods and require more frequent updates for higher security.
- Different cryptography can be chosen for each issuing CA.

THIRD-PARTY CERTIFICATE AUTHORITIES

In previous examples we demonstrated the extensibility of the certification hierarchy model. It is important to remember that the intention of PKI is not only to authenticate users and resources within the domain (this could be handled by Kerberos and Active Directory), but also to authenticate users throughout the Internet. For that reason, PKI is designed for broad Internet and extranet authentication situations. Two people in separate companies trying to authenticate and encrypt communications must both have an established trust with the same CA hierarchy. The two companies can trust a third-party certificate authority—for example, GTE CyberTrust, KeyWitness, and Verisign, Inc.—which can generally be relied on to maintain the CA root. In this case, the third party becomes responsible for performing initial authentication when issuing certificates and then maintaining the CA. Now the two companies share a CA hierarchy trust and can use the PKI to establish secure communication.

NOTE Windows Server 2003 uses the industry standard PKCS-10 certificate request and PKCS-7 certificate response to exchange CA certificates with third-party certificate authorities.

OTHER PKI FEATURES

The Windows Server 2003 PKI implementation has a number of other features that we should note before moving to the next section:

- *Roaming*. Users logging on to a Windows Server 2003 domain can take advantage of roaming user profiles and access their installed personal certificates wherever they log on. Personal certificates are kept in the /Documents and Settings/Username/Application Data/Microsoft/Crypto profile directory. The default location for private keys is in the /Documents and Settings/Username/-Application Data/Microsoft/Protect/UserSid directory. When third-party Certificate Service Providers (CSP) are employed, the certificate and associated private keys cannot roam with the user because they are stored elsewhere.
- *Recovery*. The Windows Server 2003 CA supports the ability to back up and restore its certificate log. This is important for recovering all public/private key pairs and their associated user names.

Microsoft Certificate Authorities

The Microsoft Certificate Authority can be installed as an *enterprise CA* or as a *standalone CA*. The main difference is that the standalone CA does not interact with Active Directory and is intended for use with extranets and the Internet. Both types of

CA support certificates for secure Web services, secure e-mail, digital signatures, and so forth, but the enterprise CA supports logon with a smart card to a Windows Server 2003 domain. Also, both can publish and distribute user certificates and Certification Revocation Lists (CRLs) using the Active Directory. The Exit Module discussed in the "Certification Authority Administration" section demonstrates how this is done.

THE STANDALONE CERTIFICATE AUTHORITY

The standalone CA does not have access to user account information. To authenticate themselves, users must enter more information, specifically the type of certificate they need since certificate templates (discussed later) are not supported by this CA type. A standalone CA should follow the default request action and be set to "pending" so that certificate requests are not automatically fulfilled without the CA administrator's approval. If the request action is not set to "pending," users may request and receive a certificate without identity verification. Since Active Directory user account information is not accessible to the standalone server, the user's identity must be verified from the certificate request form, which involves verifying an address or social security number. Even this may not be enough for verification, and human interaction may be required.

A standalone authority will not issue certificates for smart cards, and the certificate must be distributed either manually to domain users or via the group policies, which is discussed in the "Public Key Policies" section.

THE ENTERPRISE CERTIFICATE AUTHORITY

The enterprise CA automatically publishes certificates and CRLs to the Active Directory for domain users and computers (Figure 10.20). Once installed, its certificate is also placed in all Trusted Root Certification Authority stores for all domain users and computers. The enterprise CA has more features and is more closely coupled with the Active Directory. However, it does not support users who are not a part of the Windows Server 2003 domain. Another consideration when installing an enterprise CA is the difficulty in changing its name because of its tie to Active Directory and previously issued certificates. The enterprise CA uses certificate templates to control which users may retrieve a given certificate type.

Certificate Templates

Certificate templates are used with the Windows Server 2003 enterprise CA to help users choose the type of certificate to request. The administrator assigns certificate purposes to a template and the user simply chooses the template that matches his needs. The templates shown in Figure 10.21 are installed by default.

For example, a feature new to Windows Server 2003 that is created using a certificate template is certificate enrollment. An administrator can create a certificate

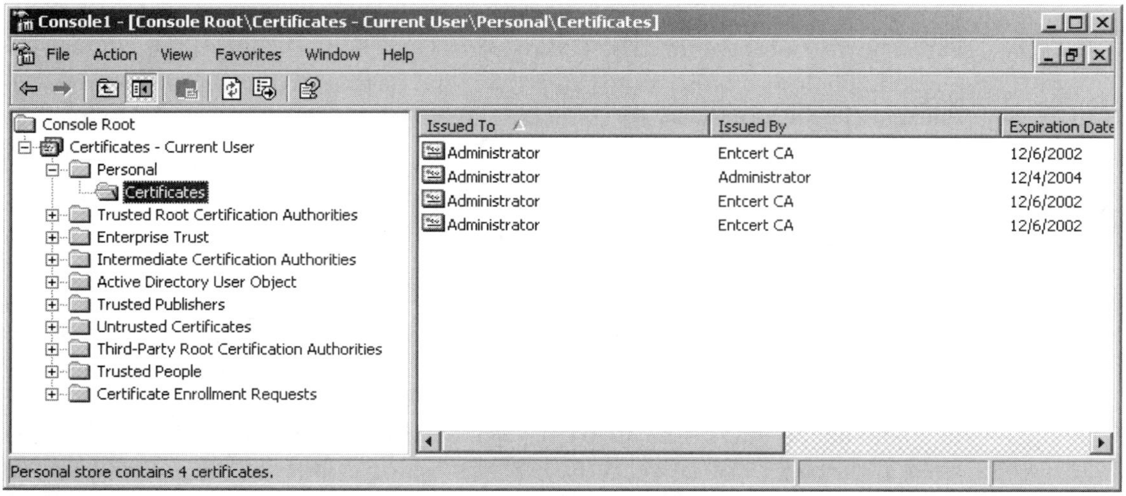

FIGURE 10.20 Publishing Certificate Using the Active Directory

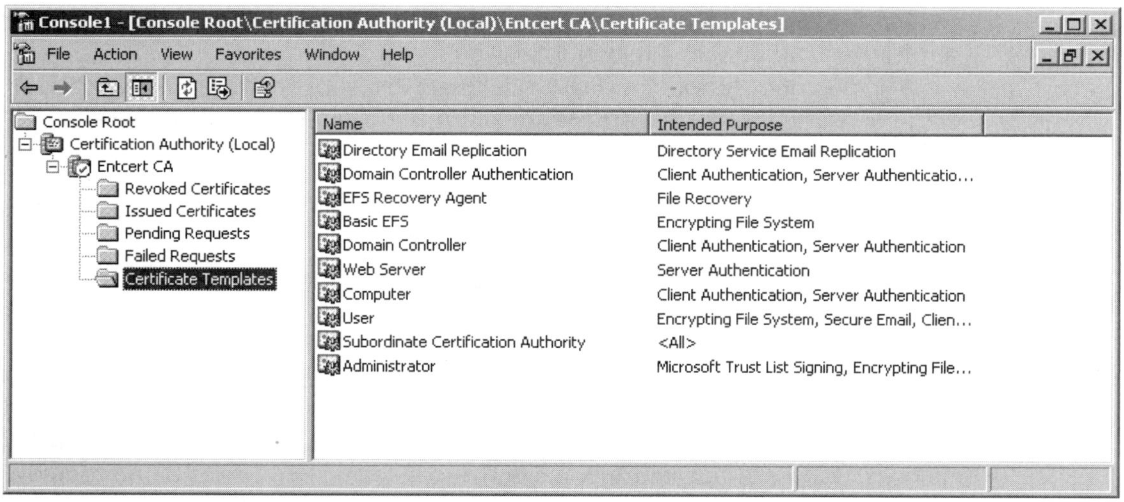

FIGURE 10.21 Default Certificate Templates

template to specify the requirement for additional signatures on the request of specific policies. For instance, a user with a smart card might be required to use it to get access to a particular application. The concept is to enable applications to expect the existence of certificates. Alternative enrollment processes are therefore not required. In theory, users should find coping with certificates easier. The administrator can configure this feature for user autoenrollment, user autorenewal, delegated enrollment, and manual certificate requests.

The Microsoft Windows Server 2003 Help pages have complete information on templates.

Public Key Policies

The Group Policy snap-in provides a means to distribute public key policies throughout an Active Directory site, domain, or OU. Enterprise CAs may not find all of these policies useful because they distribute and publish certificates directly through the Active Directory.

Group policy settings apply to standalone, enterprise, and external certificate authorities. Four main policy areas are set under the Public Key Policies node (Figure 10.22):

- *Encrypting File System*. These specify data recovery agents for EFS, which is discussed in more depth in the "Encrypted File System" section.

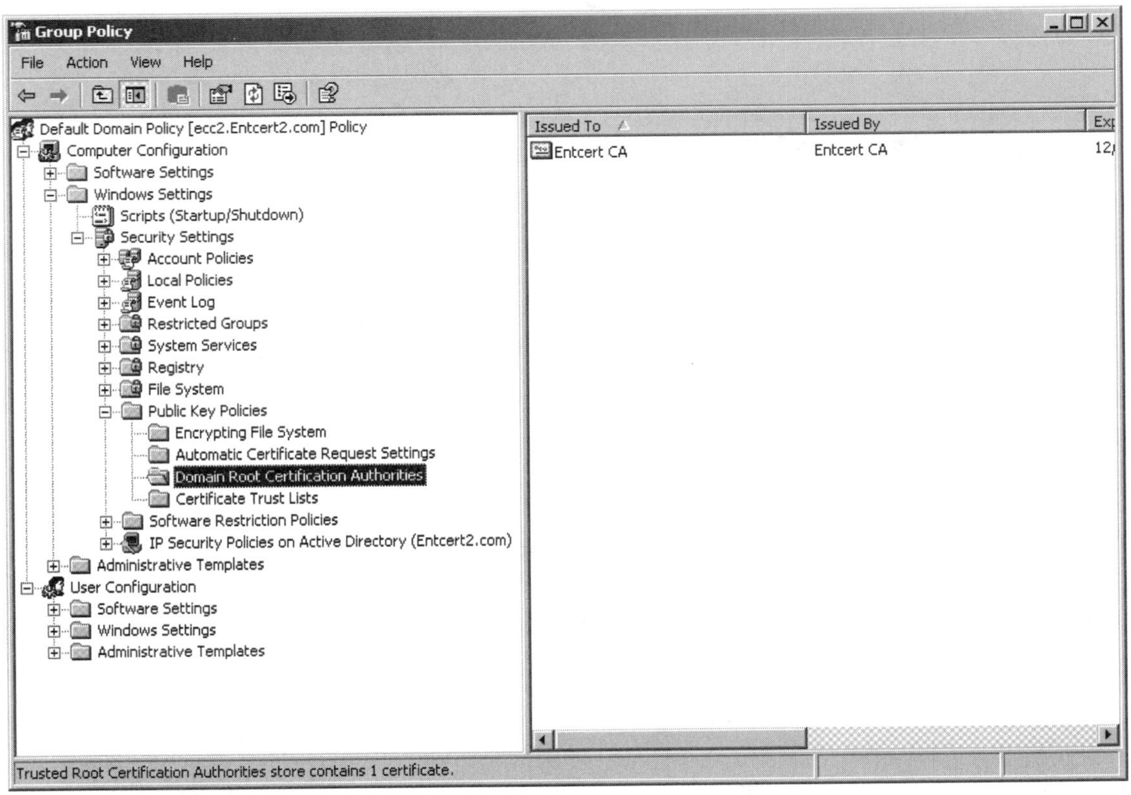

FIGURE 10.22 Public Key Policies

- *Automatic Certificate Request Settings*. These allow certificates to be automatically requested and distributed to computer accounts when systems boot. The certificate type may be selected from the certificate template list. This policy helps ensure that all systems have a certificate to implement IP security.
- *Domain Root Certification Authorities*. This policy is useful for establishing common root trusts throughout the domain or OU to which the policy applies. Certificates for standalone CAs or external CAs imported into this policy are distributed to policy participants. Enterprise CAs do not require this policy; all domain users and computers trust the CA through the Active Directory.
- *Certificate Trust Lists*. These allow the administrator to create trust lists with a designated purpose and lifetime. Each trust list is composed of one or more CA certificates signed by the administrator. In this way, the individual CAs may be limited in the type of certificate they issue to domain users. Since the group policy may be assigned to any Active Directory container, different users can have restrictions on the type of certificate they can obtain.

PKI and Other Components and Applications

Once certificates are made available, users may take advantage of services using PKI technology. In this section, we examine some components and applications that interface with PKI, including:

- Web security
- E-mail
- Encrypted File System
- Smart cards
- Authenticode
- IP security (see Chapter 13)

WEB SECURITY

A number of technologies are commonly applied to Web security. The most common are the Secure Sockets Layer, Transport Layer Security, and Secure channel protocols. In this section, we summarize how these technologies interact with PKI.

Schannel generates a security token for users regardless of whether they are authenticated through PKI or Kerberos. Users can then access objects according to access control lists. Integration of the Schannel and Active Directory permit this type of user authorization.

The CA is used with issued certificates, digital signatures, and SSL/TLS to authenticate and establish a secure channel between an Internet Web client and a server. For simplicity, assume that both the Web client and the Web server have deemed this particular CA a trusted root authority, as exemplified in the following (Figure 10.23):

1. The Web client and Web server have both requested and received a certificate from the CA. They put the certificate into their trusted root authority store, which enables them to trust the CA. All information issued or verified through a trusted root authority is assumed to be accurate and sound.
2. The Web client requests a user certificate from the CA, which is usually valid for about a year but is configurable. The certificate is stored in the Web client's personal store and will be used to authenticate the client to all Web servers, e-mail clients, and entities with whom it wants to communicate.

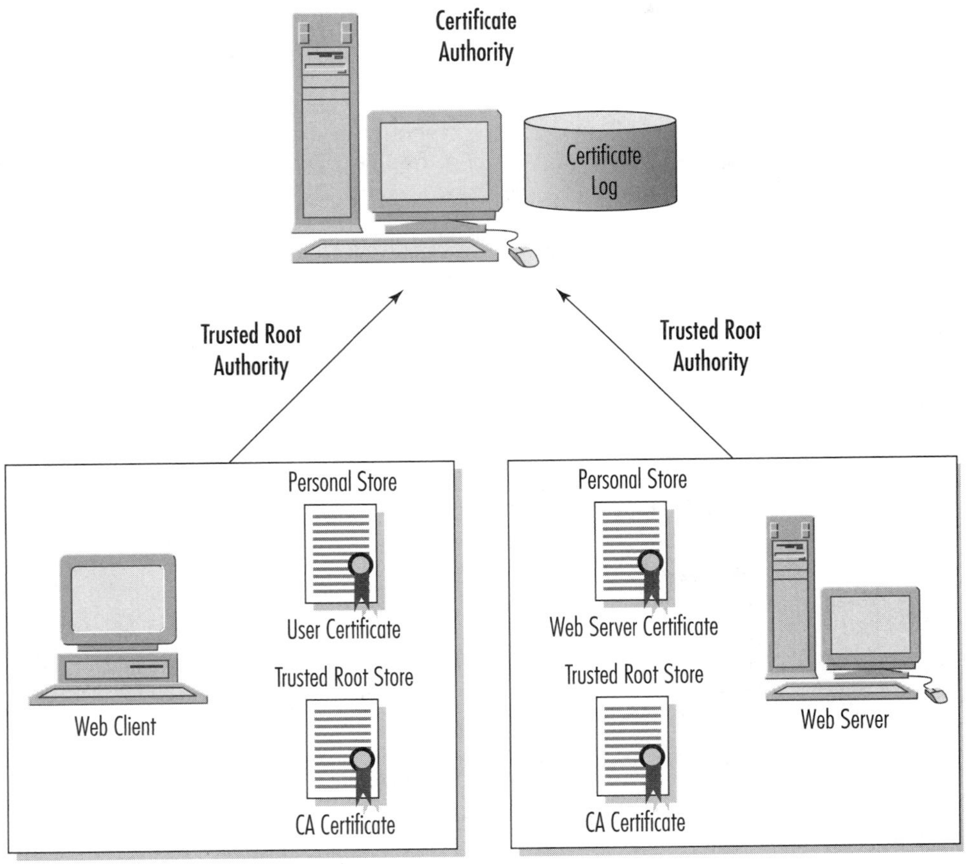

FIGURE 10.23 Relationship of Certificate Authorities

3. The Web server requests a Web server certificate when coming online. It uses this single certificate to authenticate itself to all future Web clients.
4. The basic PKI is now in place.

NOTE Certificates may remain valid for years, so to revoke certificates, the CA distributes a certificate revocation list (CRL), which is retrieved by clients. Revoking a certificate may be necessary if a user's private key is discovered or if the user is no longer employed by an organization. The revocation process is demonstrated in examples at the end of this chapter.

Web clients and servers use certificates to authenticate and confidentially share a symmetrical encryption key. The SSL and TLS protocols use the public key structure to implement a fast and secure channel.

As illustrated in Figure 10.24, the following steps outline how the SSL establishes a connection:

1. The Web client requests a secure connection with the Web server. The server authenticates itself by sending its Web server certificate to the Web client.
2. The Web client decrypts the digital signature with the CA's public key to recover the message hash. The client then generates its own message hash using

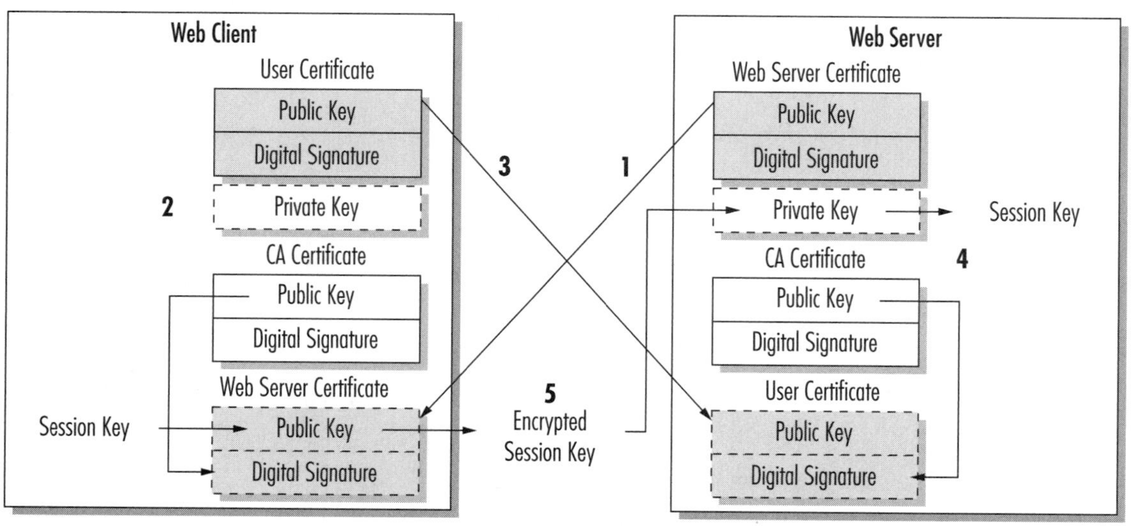

FIGURE 10.24 Public Key Exchange

the same hash algorithm and compares the two. If they are the same, the signature must belong to the trusted CA. The Web client trusts the CA and believes that the Web server is the subject named in its certificate.

3. The Web client sends its user certificate to the Web server.
4. The Web server performs the same signature verification using the CA's public key on the client's certificate. It has now identified the Web client. User ID and password authentication may be used for additional user authentication.
5. The Web client generates a random symmetrical key for this session, encrypted using the Web server public key obtained from the Web server's certificate.
6. The Web server decrypts the symmetrical session key using its private key. The session key is then used for communication throughout the rest of the secure Web connection.

ELECTRONIC MAIL

Most e-mail clients support the two message formats of HTML and plain text. The Multipurpose Internet Mail Extensions (MIME), for example, supports HTML formatting, which allows transmission of graphics, hyperlinks, color, and text settings within e-mail text between mail clients that support it. More advanced systems now implement an extended secure version known as S/MIME.

Some applications that support S/MIME version 3 use PKI to implement any combination of digital signatures and encryption desired by the sender. Certificates are easily exchanged between users employing digital signatures to set up secure communication.

Mail client settings such as **Add sender's certificates to my address book** and **Include my digital ID when sending signed messages** (Figure 10.25) permit the initial exchange of user certificates. Once certificates are obtained for all desired correspondents, the user may send encrypted messages. Microsoft Outlook 98 and Microsoft Outlook Express both support S/MIME version 3 and maintain certificates in the address book associated with each contact. Outlook Express uses only the SHA–1 hashing algorithm for digital signatures and the encryption algorithms shown in Table 10.11.

AUTHENTICODE

Authenticode uses digital signatures to verify software ownership and integrity upon retrieval. ActiveX, .dll, Java applets, .exe, and .cab files can all have the Authenticode digital signature applied and verified before they are executed in the user's system environment. Trusted publishers are referenced from Internet Explorer 6.0 via **Tools → Internet Options → Content → Trusted Publishers** (Figure 10.26).

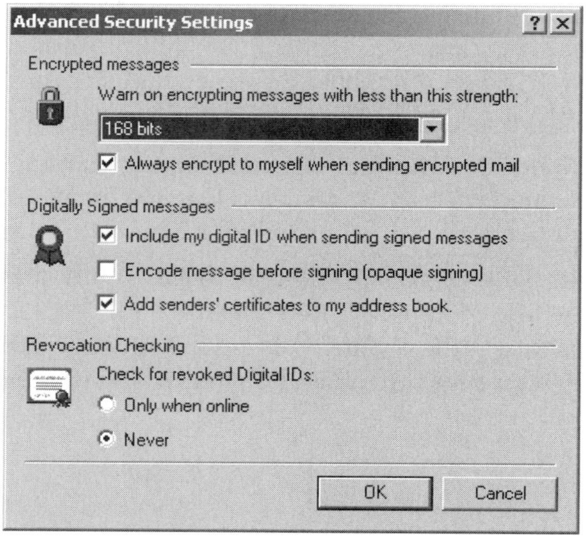

FIGURE 10.25 E-mail Settings for Certificate Exchange

TABLE 10.11 Outlook Express 6.0 Encryption Support

United States/Canada	Export Versions
RC2 40-bit and 128-bit	RC2 40-bit
DES (56-bit)	DES (56-bit)
3DES (168-bit)	Not allowed for export
Decrypt RC2 (64-bit) But Not Encrypt	Decrypt RC2 (64-bit) But Not Encrypt

The user simply retrieves Authenticode certificates from CAs that support them such as Verisign (*www.verisign.com*) and Thawte (*www.thawte.com*).

The Encrypted File System

Windows Server 2003 NTFS supports the Encrypted File System. The EFS process is transparent to the user and file handling requires no special treatment. An encrypted file can be opened and read just like any other file; however, other users will not be able to read, copy, rename, or move it.

A recommended method for maintaining encrypted files is to create an encryption folder to hold them. It is good practice to encrypt the entire folder to

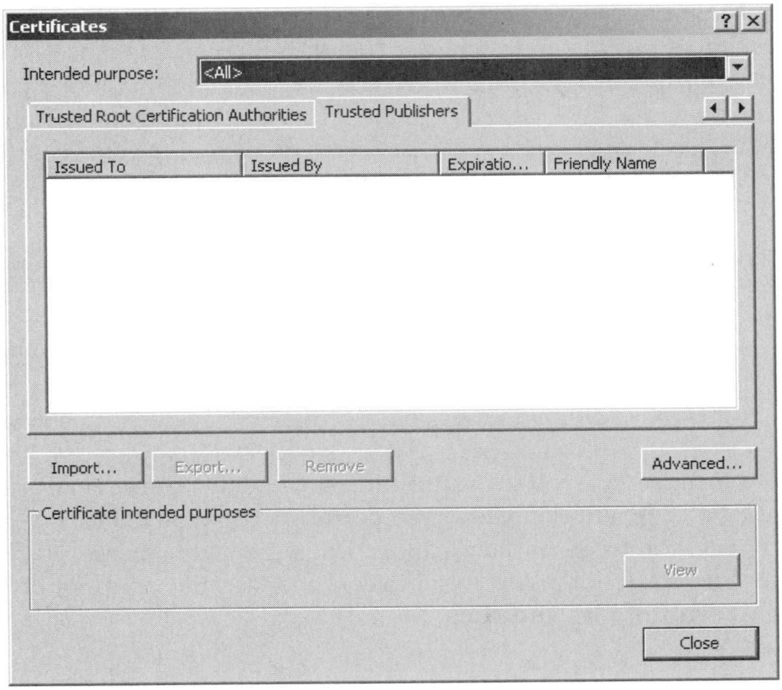

FIGURE 10.26 Trusted Component Publishers

ensure that its files stay encrypted. Encrypting the My Documents folder will secure most personal user documents without the need to change the encryption on individual files. It is also a good idea to encrypt the temp directory so that the files you are editing or opening from your mail client are encrypted as well. Note that an encrypted file will become decrypted if it is moved to a folder with the drag-and-drop method. Instead, use the **Cut** and **Paste** options from the **Edit** pull-down menu.

System and compressed files may not be encrypted, and users with correct permissions may delete an encrypted file.

THE EFS PROCESS

The Microsoft Cryptographic Provider randomly produces a 128-bit (56-bit for the exported versions of Windows Server 2003) symmetrical File Encryption Key (FEK) to encrypt a file. EFS encrypts the FEK with the user's public key from an issued certificate and stores it in the file's Data Decryption Field (DDF). The user's private key is used to decrypt the FEK when accessing the file in the future; the FEK is then used to decrypt the file.

The user may lose her public/private key pair, so Windows Server 2003 designates the domain administrator as the default recovery agent. For each recovery agent, in addition to the Data Decryption Field stored with the encrypted file, a Data Recovery Field (DRF) is maintained. The FEK is encrypted using the recovery agent's certificate. In the event that users lose their encryption certificate, they can e-mail the folder/file to the recovery agent, who can decrypt the object and return it in a readable form.

NOTE See the **cipher** command for encryption at the command prompt.

Although the behind-the-scenes activities may be somewhat complex, encryption from the user interface is quite simple. Simply right-click the file or folder you want to encrypt and select **Properties**. Under the **General** tab, click **Advanced** (Figure 10.27), and check **Encrypt contents to secure data**.

When you are encrypting a folder, a dialog appears (Figure 10.28) asking if encryption should be applied to subfolders and files. Select **Apply changes to this folder, subfolders and files**.

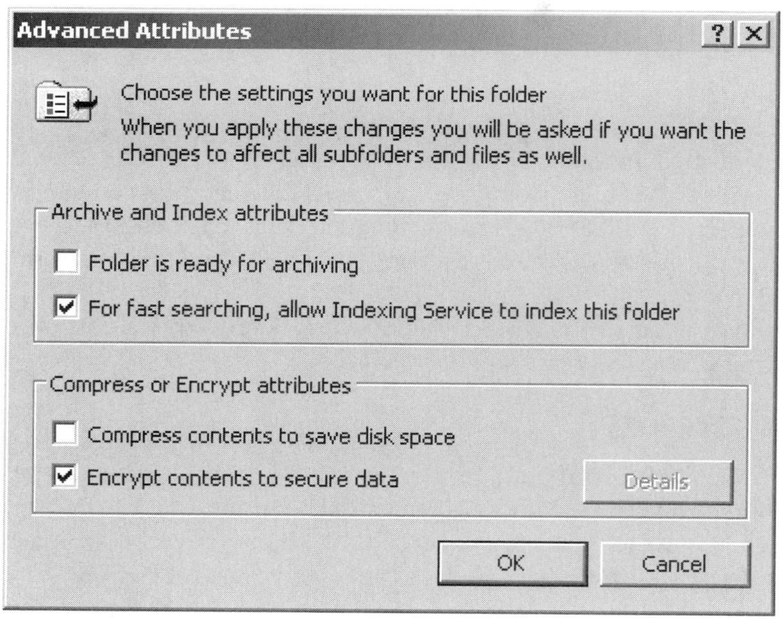

FIGURE 10.27 Encrypting a File

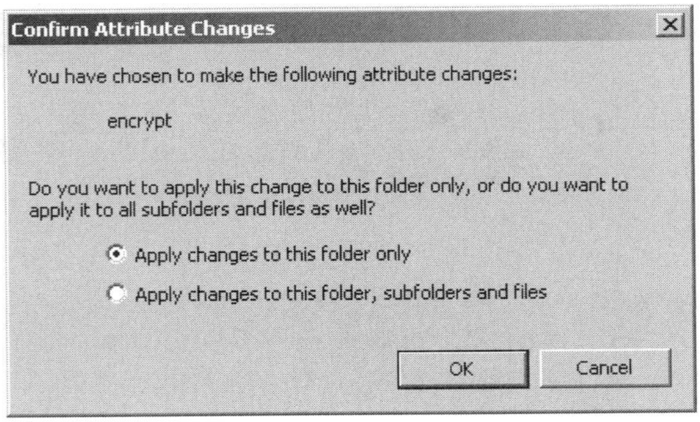

FIGURE 10.28 Encryption Inheritance

EFS ISSUES

A number of best practices apply when using EFS. Here are some of them:

- Both the user and the recovery agent should export certificates and make backups of them. These certificates can be restored later so that encrypted files can be recovered.

NOTE Backing up a certificate with its corresponding private key has some obvious risks. If the backup file were compromised, the certificate would be as well.

- The first time a file/folder is encrypted, the group policy for Encrypted Data Recovery Agents appoints recovery agent responsibility to the administrator. This may be modified with the Group Policy snap-in (Figure 10.29) by right-clicking **Encrypting File System** and selecting **Add Data Recovery Agent**.
- The Add Data Recovery Agent Wizard starts up and allows new user agent designation. If certificates are published to Active Directory (as in the enterprise CA), users can be added without importing certificates. Otherwise, new recovery agents must import new encryption certificates before they become recovery agents.
- Regardless of his decryption ability, a user with Delete permission on a file/folder may delete the object.
- Only files created on NTFS can be encrypted. Using the Backup utility on an encrypted file/folder and then moving that file to a FAT file system or tape backup will preserve encryption, but moving it directly to a FAT file system will not.

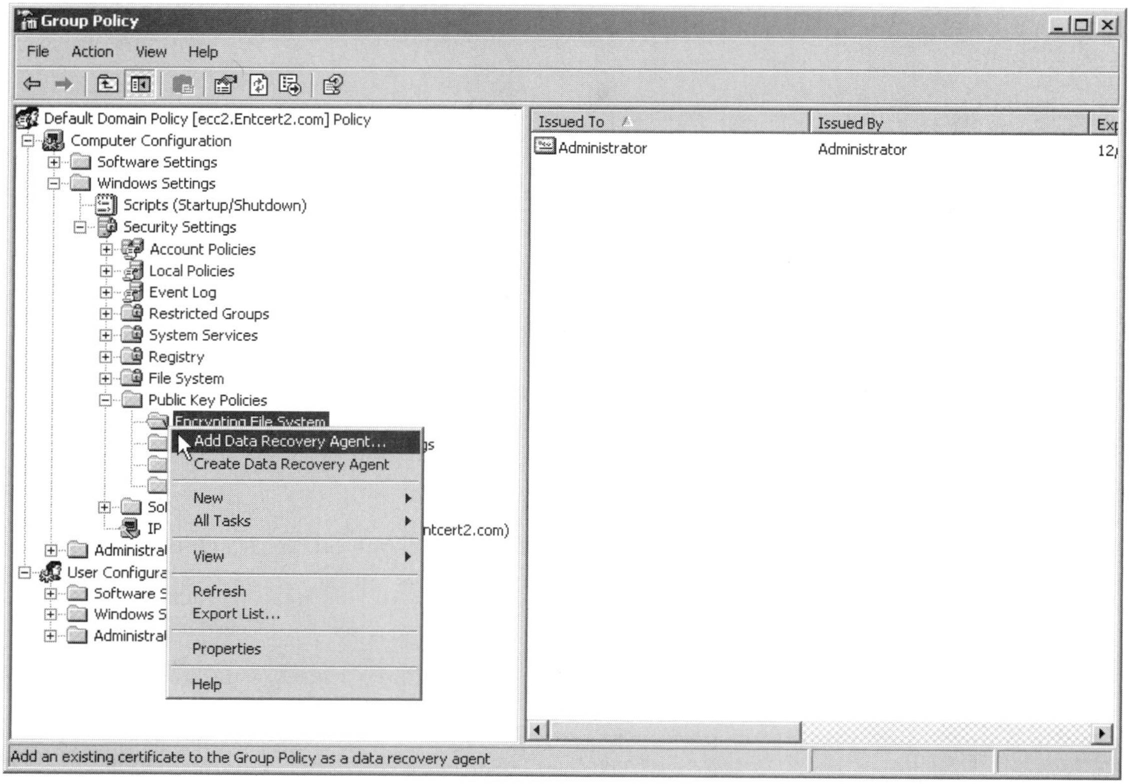

FIGURE 10.29 A Recovery Agent

- Encrypted files may not be shared to the network. However, they may be stored to a remote server. This computer account must have the **Trust computer for delegation** check box selected from the Active Directory before it is permitted to move the files (Figure 10.30). The delegation property is modified by right-clicking the destination Windows Server from the Active Directory and selecting **Properties**. Note that the files are not encrypted while in transit to the destination server. IP security and SSL should be used for secure file transfers.
- Files must be manipulated using **Cut, Copy**, and **Paste** instead of drag and drop.
- Compressed and system files cannot be encrypted.

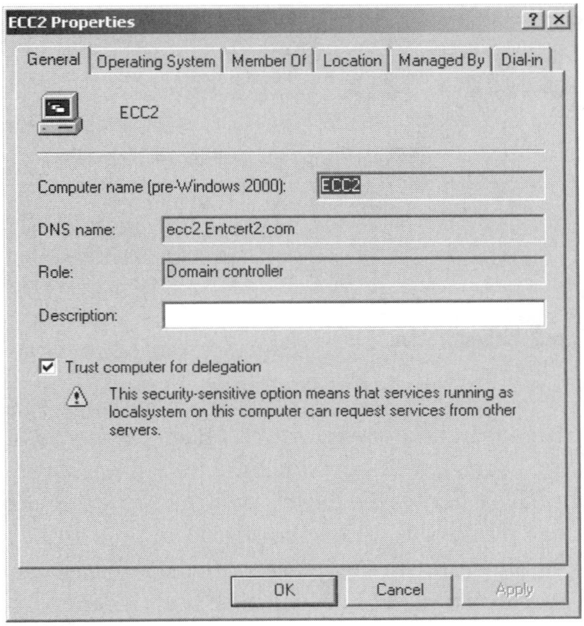

FIGURE 10.30 Properties

NOTE Windows Server 2003 includes delegation model improvements such as the ability to allow any Internet protocol to be used between the client and Web server. The feature then allows the use of Kerberos between the Web server and the back-end data servers. Windows Server 2003 also includes a new model for Kerberos-based delegation that does not require forwardable TGTs. It enforces constraints on delegation. This allows a particular account to delegate only to specific services configured at the domain policy level. This feature is configured by invoking **Active Directory Users and Computers MMC Snap-in → Properties → Delegation → Trust this computer for delegation to specified services only → Add**.

Smart Cards

Smart cards are small storage devices that store the user's public and private keys. They can be used only by systems that support a card reader. Smart cards modify Kerberos authentication, specifically the AS Exchange between a client trying to log on to the network and the KDC. (See the Kerberos section for elaboration on

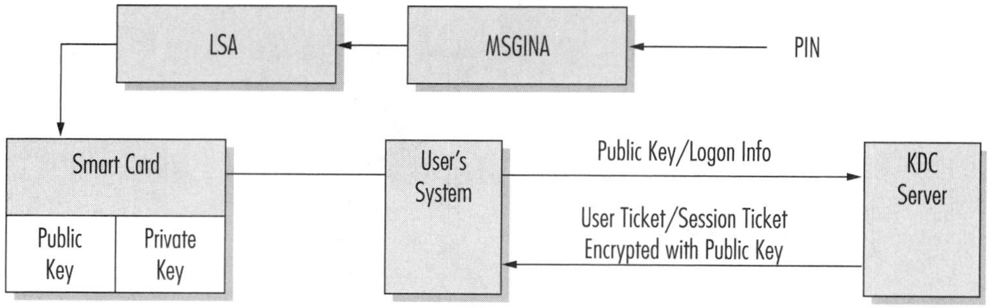

FIGURE 10.31 Smart Card Authentication

the AS Exchange.) Instead of the user's password hash as a key to encrypt the AS reply, the KDC uses the user's public key, obtained from the smart card, to encrypt portions of the reply. This offers stronger encryption and eliminates the need to remember complicated passwords. The smart card requires a PKI CA to obtain a certificate and load a public/private key pair. A certificate must be issued from a trusted CA so that a user may roam the domain and use his card to log on throughout the network.

When a user logs on to a system using a smart card, the **Microsoft Graphical Identification and Authentication (MSGINA)** dialog box starts and requests the usual logon information (Figure 10.31). However, the user needs to enter only his smart card PIN (personal identification number). The Local Security Authority (LSA) will access the smart card with the PIN and retrieve the X.509 v3 certificate for Kerberos authentication. The KDC authenticates the user based on the certificate and returns an encrypted TGT and session key for further communication.

Certificate Authority Administration

The following sections offer basic information on the installation and management of certificate authority. Several examples are provided.

INSTALLATION

Both the standalone and the enterprise CAs may reside on a domain controller or member server within the domain. The enterprise CA requires the domain to have Windows Server 2003 DNS and Active Directory services. The standalone CA may also be installed on a workstation and does not require these services, but does require administrative privileges on the server on which it will be installed. The following actions occur with all enterprise and standalone CA installations when the person installing it is a member of the Domain Administrators group:

- A copy of the CA's certificate is stored in every user and computer's Trusted Domain Root Authority store.
- The CA becomes a member of the Cert Publishers global group, enabling it to publish to the Active Directory. The CA must be manually added to this group in other domains that desire this functionality.

NOTE A standalone CA is used for Internet and extranet user access and for security reasons will probably be placed outside the firewall. It must be installed using Administrative authority and probably should not be installed with Domain Administrative authority. A workstation should be used for deployment.

NOTE Be sure that IIS is installed prior to installing Certificate Services. Terminal Server may not be installed concurrently with Certificate Services on the same server.

NOTE If you install Certificate Services before IIS, the *CertServ* Web pages will not be available. To remedy the problem, remove Certificate Services, install IIS, and then reinstall Certificate Services. To remove it from the **Configure Your Computer** menu, clear the check mark from the component and continue. To install a component, check the box next to the component and continue.

The following steps should be taken to install certificate authority:

1. Open **Control Panel** and double-click **Add or Remove Programs**. Select **Add/Remove Windows Components**. The **Windows Components Wizard** should start (Figure 10.32). Select **Certificate Services**. Click **Next**.
2. Select the type of certificate authority you want to install (Figure 10.33).
3. Click **Next**.
4. Enter the CA identifying information (Figure 10.34). Click **Next**.
5. Confirm where the certificate's database will be stored (Figure 10.35). Remember, all issued and revoked certificate information will be stored here.

Management

Once Windows Server 2003 Certificate Authority is installed, the challenge becomes managing it. The first administrative issue is setting certificate group policies.

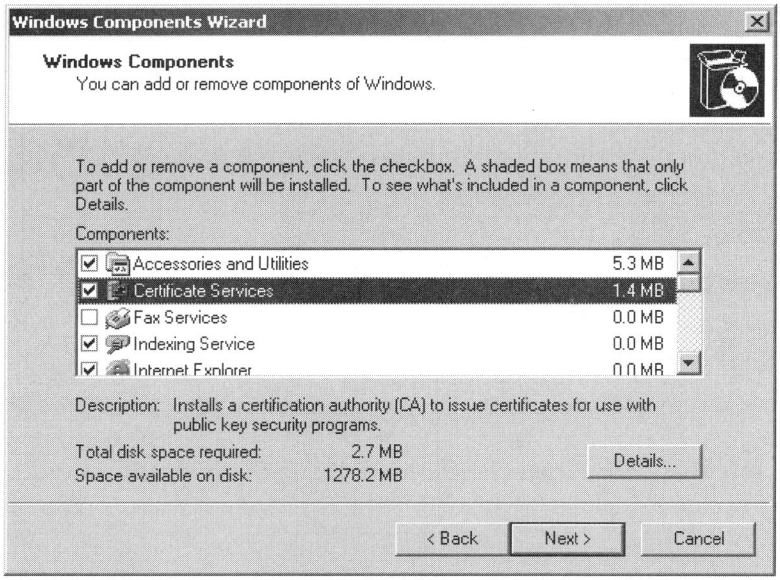

FIGURE 10.32 Selecting Certificate Services from the Windows Component Wizard

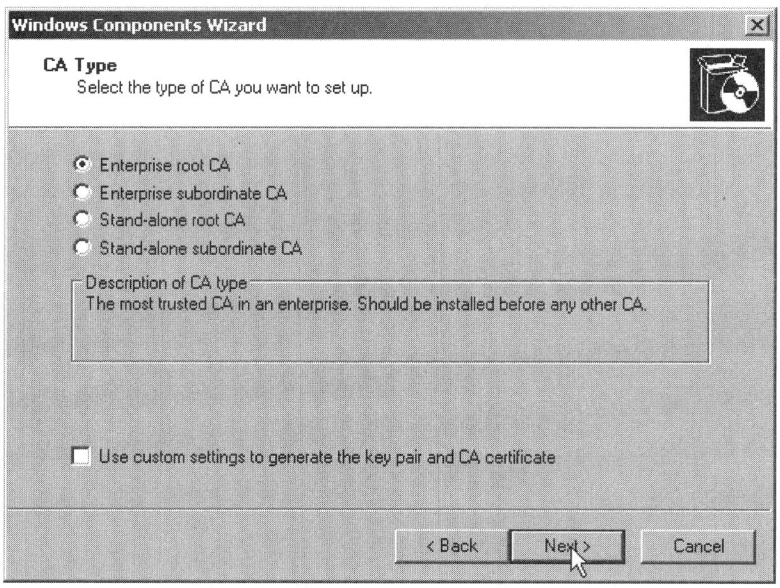

FIGURE 10.33 Selecting Certification Authority Type

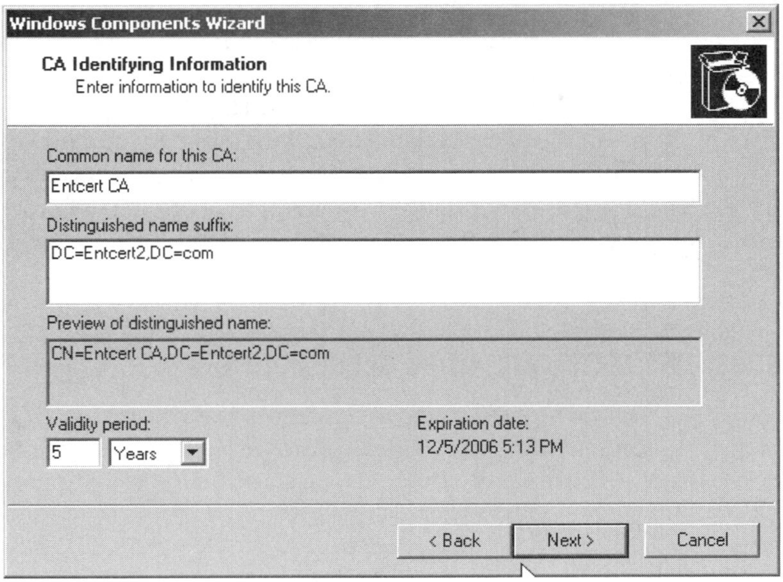

FIGURE 10.34 CA Identifying Information

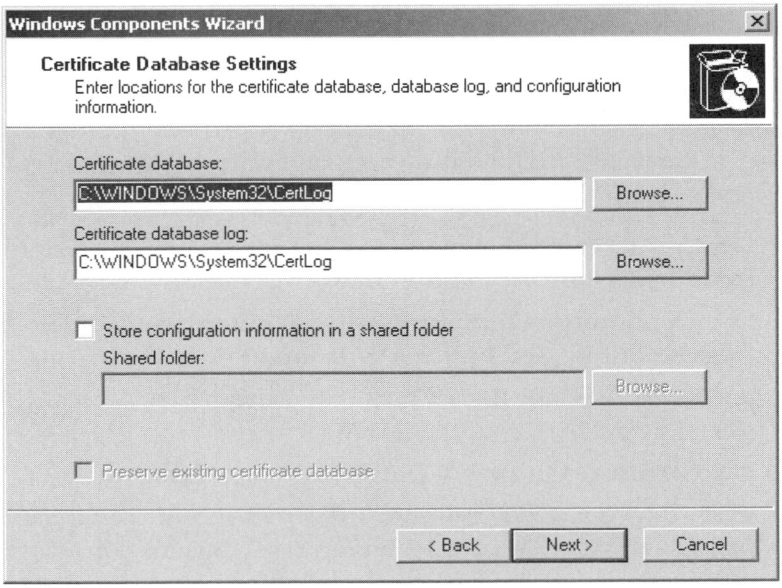

FIGURE 10.35 Certificate Data Storage

NOTE Windows Server 2003 supports certificate mapping based on intermediate certificate authorities. Active Directory Issuer-only (Many-to-One) Client Certificate mapping is accomplished through LEAVE SSL/TLS based on any subordinate Certificate Authority in the certificate chain. In Windows 2000 and previous versions of Windows, it used Many-to-One mapping based on the direct issuer of the end certificates. This feature is configured by invoking **Active Directory Users and Computers** → **Advanced Features** → **Name Mappings** → select exported certificate file of **Subordinate Certificate Authority**.

DISTRIBUTING CERTIFICATES USING GROUP POLICIES

Group Policy is used to distribute certificates throughout a domain. The four group policy nodes under **Computer Configuration** → **Windows Settings** → **Security Settings** → **Public Key Policies**, discussed earlier, that pertain here are:

- Encrypting file system
- Automatic Certificate Request Settings
- Trusted Root Certification Authorities
- Certificate Trusts Lists

The following examples demonstrate how these group policies are used.

Establishing Trusted Root Authorities

The first example demonstrates how to establish a trust with an external CA or standalone CA that cannot publish to Active Directory upon installation. The CA's certificate needs to be placed in the local Trusted Root Certification Authorities store. A domain controller will import it and place it in the Default Domain Policy GPO to establish trust for all domain members.

1. Open a **Microsoft Management Console** and add the **Group Policy** snap-in for the **Default Domain Policy** object.
2. Open **Computer Configuration** → **Windows Settings** → **Security Settings** → **Public Key Policies** → **Domain Root Certificate Authorities**.
3. Right-click **Domain Root Certificate Authorities**. Select **All Tasks** → **Import**. (Figure 10.36).
4. The **Certificate Import Wizard** starts. Click **Next**.
5. When the standalone CA is installed, a root security certificate is put into the \WINDOWS\system32\certsrv\CertEnroll\systemname.domainname file. Import this certificate unless you have a third-party certificate you want to load onto your root CA (Figure 10.37). Like the Windows Server 2003 CA Web interface, a

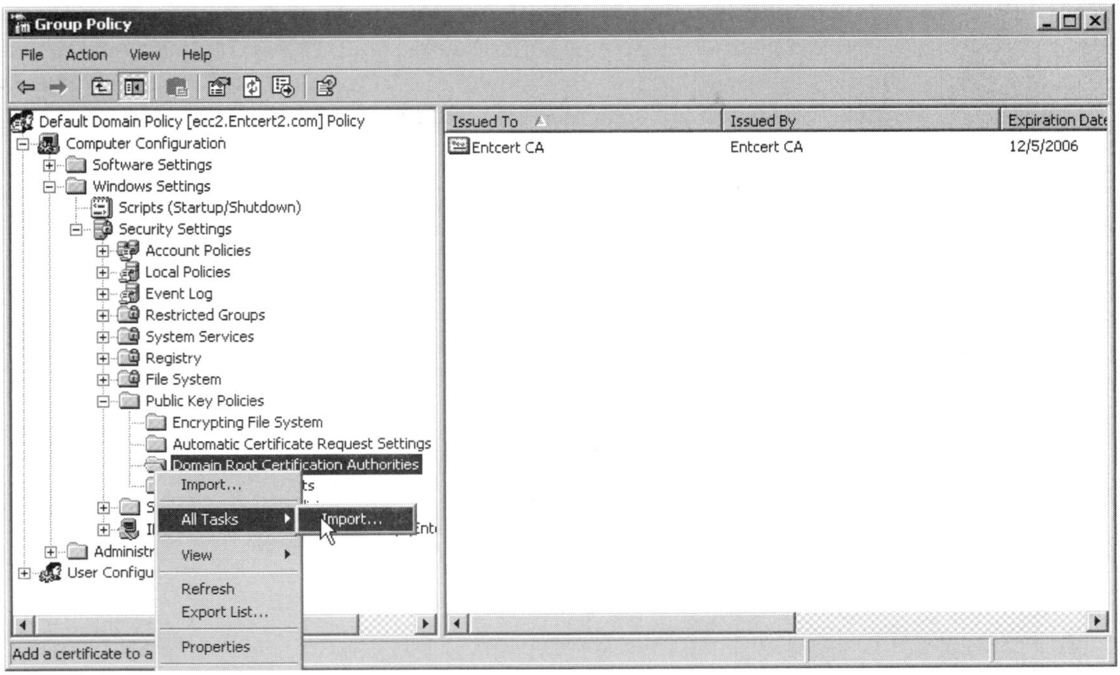

FIGURE 10.36 Group Policy

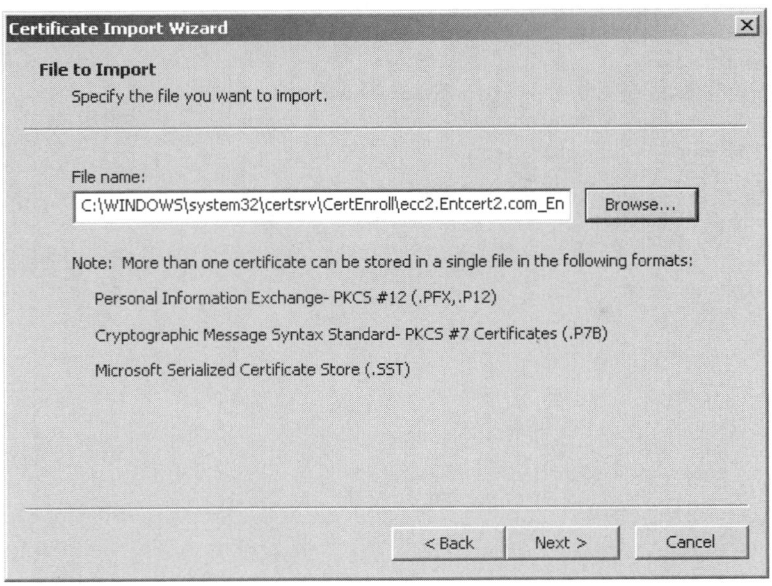

FIGURE 10.37 Import Selection

third-party CA certificate is usually retrieved using a Web browser and then stored locally to disk. Go to the third-party's Web site and request such a certificate. (If you want to use the Web interface to retrieve the CA certificate from either an enterprise or standalone CA, see the "Retrieving Certificates" section.) Click **Next**.

6. Store the CA certificate in the certificate store **Trusted Root Certificate Authorities** (Figure 10.38). Click **Next**.
7. Click **Finish** to complete the import process (Figure 10.39).
8. Click **OK** to acknowledge a successful import.
9. View local **Trusted Root Certification Authorities** stores throughout the domain to verify the domain CA trust. (Refer to the "Viewing Local Certificate Stores" section for directions.)

The Default Domain Policy GPO assigned your newly installed Certificate Authority as the trusted certificate root authority for the domain. To do this, a domain controller imported a certificate from the CA into the policy **Domain Root Certificate Authorities**.

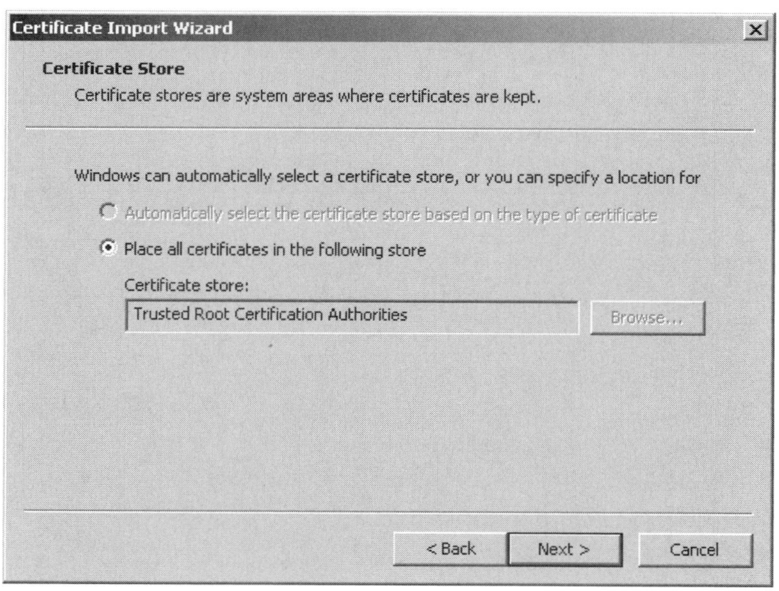

FIGURE 10.38 A Certification Store

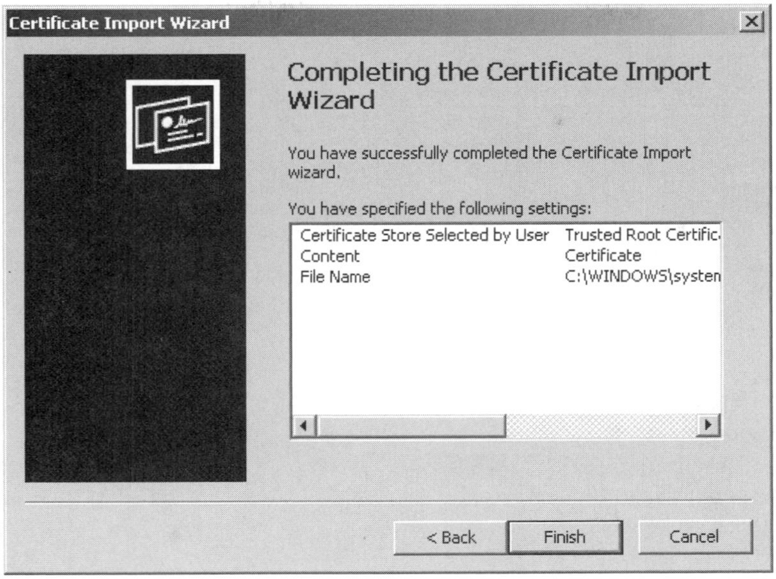

FIGURE 10.39 The Certificate Manager Import Wizard

Automatic Certificate Requests

Automatic certificate requests are generated whenever a user logs on or a computer boots. The group policy node reached via **Computer Configuration → Windows Settings → Security Settings → Public Key Policies → Automatic Certificate Request Settings** specifies the type of certificate to be requested and the CA server to field the certificate request. The following steps demonstrate addition of an automatic certificate request to the Default Domain Policy:

1. Right-click **Automatic Certificates Request Settings** and select **New → Automatic Certificate Request** (Figure 10.40).
2. The **Automatic Certificate Request** dialog box appears. Click **Next**.
3. Select the certificate type to request from **Certificate templates.** Click **Next**.
4. Verify the certificate template selection (Figure 10.41). Click **Next**.
5. Click **Finish** (Figure 10.42). The policy must be allowed to propagate to other domain controllers and clients.

Viewing Local Certificate Stores

Local certificate stores can be viewed through the Certificates MMC snap-in or through a variety of applications such as Outlook Express and Internet Explorer. Here is an introduction to viewing certificate stores using these tools.

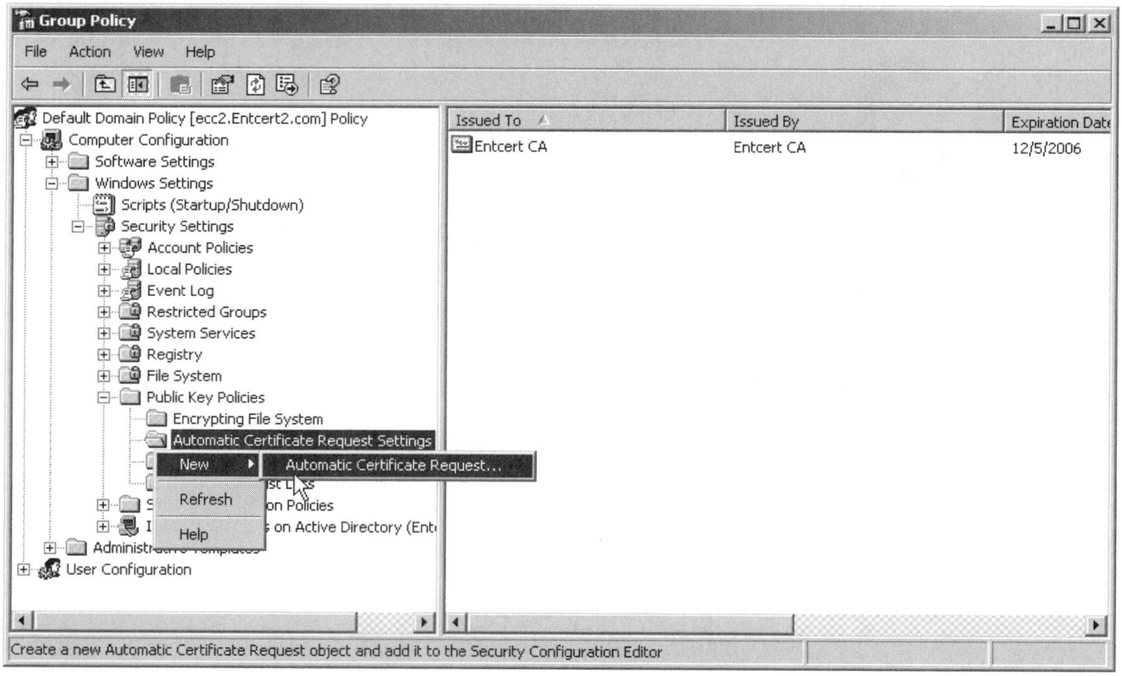

FIGURE 10.40 Automatic Certificate Request

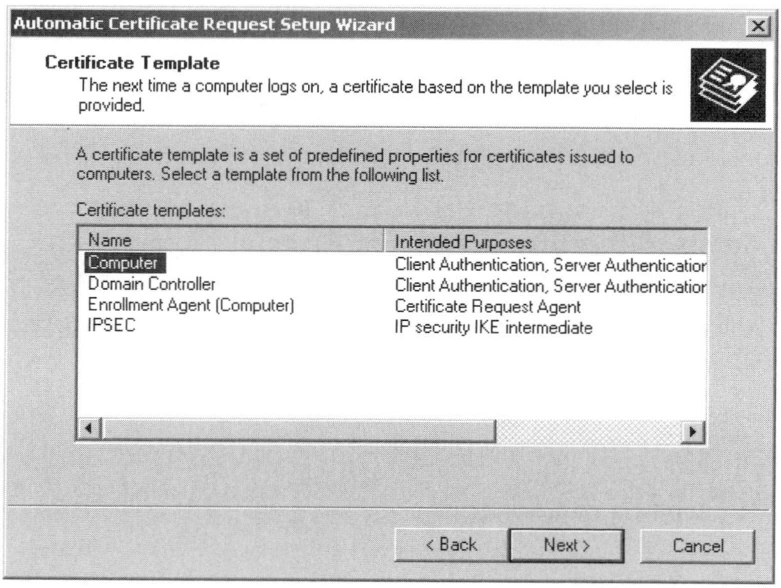

FIGURE 10.41 Certificate Templates

FIGURE 10.42 Certificate Request Completion

Using the Certificate Snap-In

To view local certificate stores with the **Certificates** snap-in, use the following procedure:

1. Open a command window and type **MMC** to start a management console.
2. From the **Console** pull-down menu, select **Add/Remove Snap-in**.
3. Select the **Certificates** snap-in and click **Add**.
4. Select **Computer account** (Figure 10.43). Click **Next**.

At this point you will notice that the Certificate snap-in can be installed to manage one of three types of accounts: user, service, or computer. A different local store will be engaged for each selection. The user account is self-explanatory; the service account deals with how the operating system interacts with the local computer; and the computer account deals with how the computer interacts with the rest of the domain. To participate with IPSec, the computer account must be assigned a certificate. This is addressed in Chapter 13.

5. Select **Local computer** and click **Finish** (Figure 10.44).
6. The **Certificates (Local Computer)** snap-in should be added to your console.

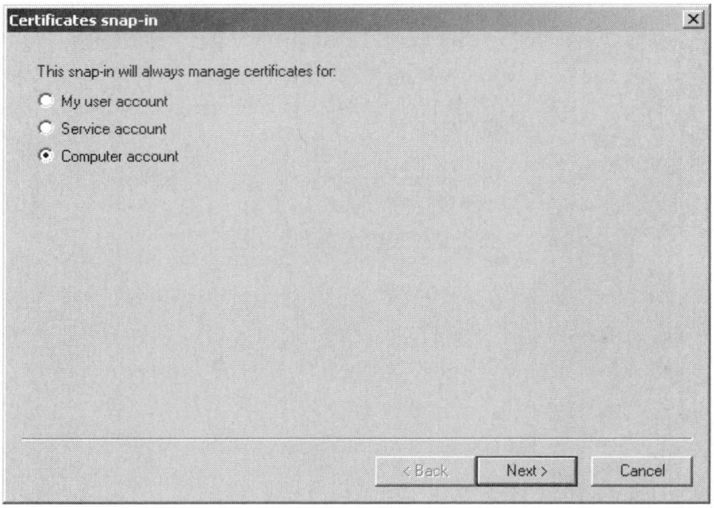

FIGURE 10.43 Choosing a Certificate Store

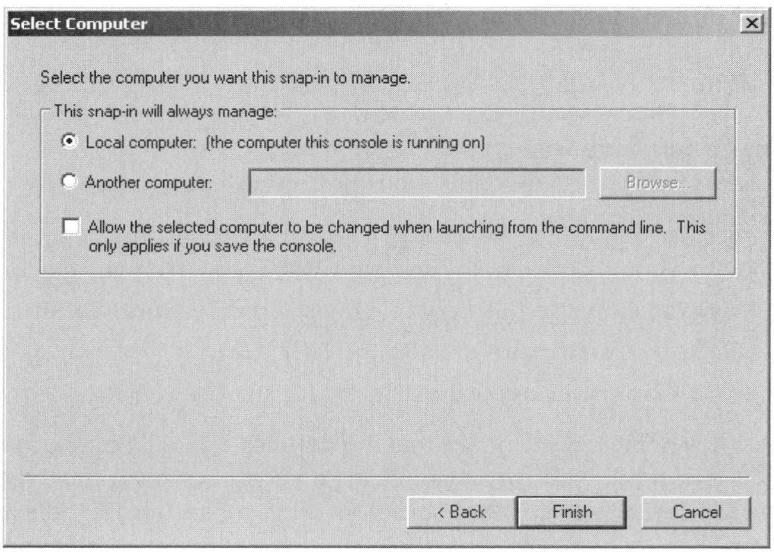

FIGURE 10.44 Selecting the Local Computer

7. From **Console,** open **Certificates → Trusted Root Certification Authority → Certificate**.
8. Find a certificate and double-click. The **General** tab lists the intended uses for the certificate, the valid dates, and who issued it to whom (Figure 10.45).

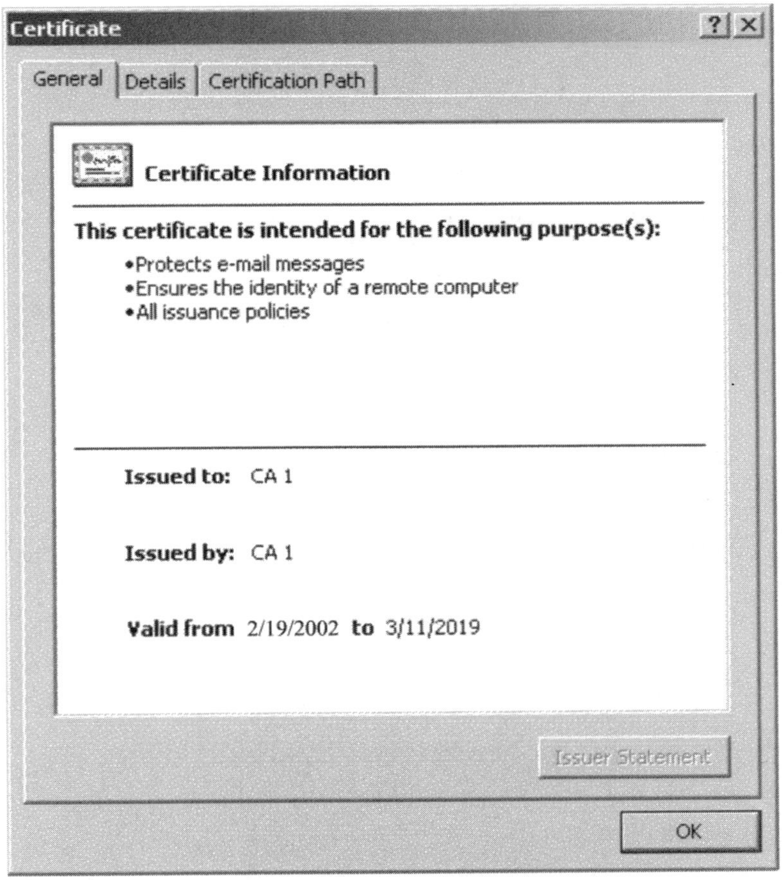

FIGURE 10.45 Certificate Information

9. The **Details** tab displays all the certificate's characteristics (Figure 10.46).
10. The **Certification Path** tab displays the root authority that granted the certificate.

Using Internet Explorer 6.0

To view local certificate stores from Internet Explorer 6.0:

1. From the Web browser you are using, find the **Internet Options** menu (**Tools → Internet Options**).
2. If you are using Internet Explorer 6.0, select the **Content** tab and click **Certificates** (Figure 10.47).

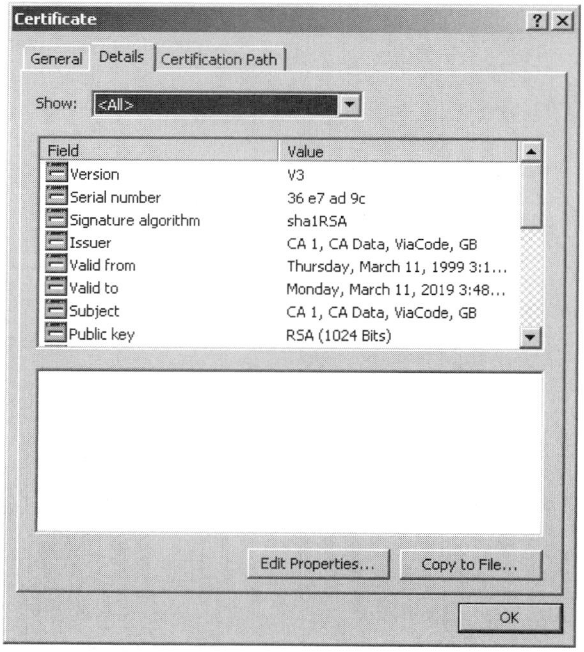

FIGURE 10.46 Certificate Details

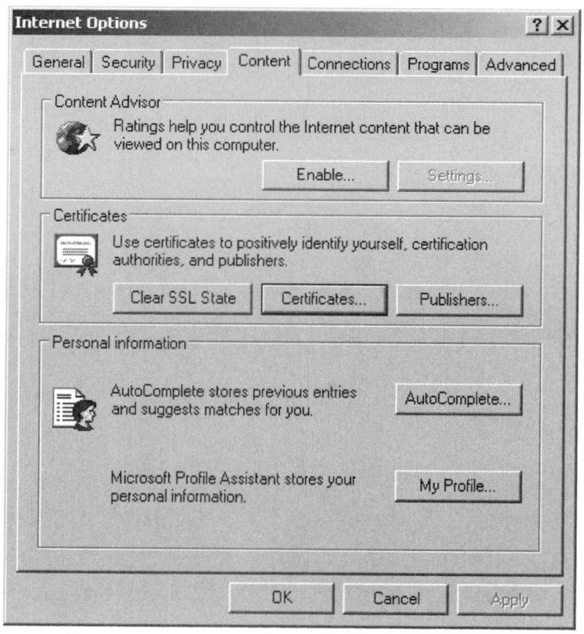

FIGURE 10.47 Internet Options

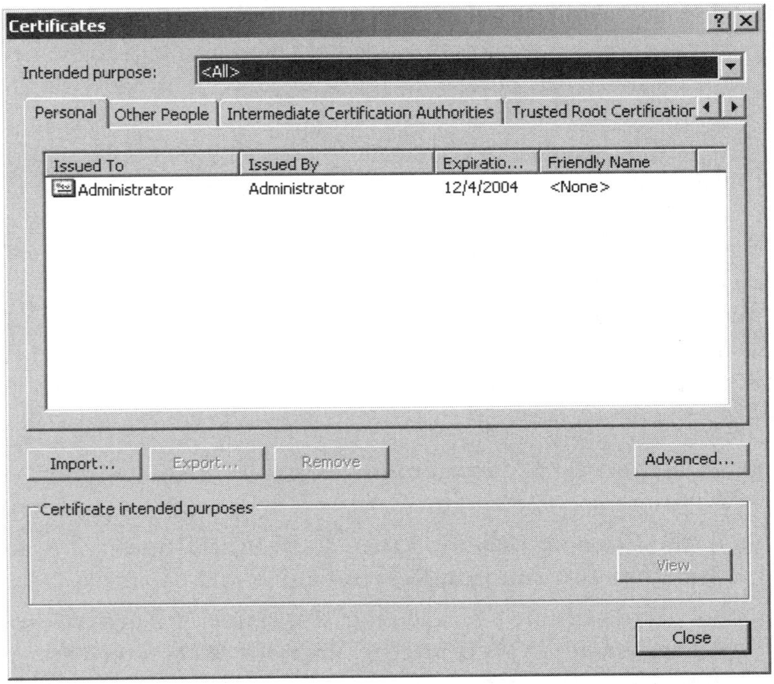

FIGURE 10.48 A Personal Certificate Store

3. Local stores are displayed in tab form (Figure 10.48). Double-click a certificate to view its properties.

A similar procedure enables local certificate store viewing from Outlook Express 6.0.

RETRIEVING CERTIFICATES

There are two basic methods to retrieve certificates from a Windows Server 2003 enterprise CA. One is with the Certificate Request Wizard using the Certificates snap-in; the other is with the Windows Server 2003 Certificate Services Web pages. The standalone CA requires the Web page retrieval method. Once a user retrieves a certificate, she may use it for secure e-mail, IPSec, secure Web transactions, and other services previously discussed.

Windows Server 2003 Certificate Services Web Pages

At this stage of the example, the Web server installed on the CA will be used to populate other systems in the domain with certificates. The Certificate Services Web page offers a few advantages over the Certificate Request Wizard in carrying this out. First, the Web page allows certificates to make their private keys exportable, which means that a certificate and its private key can be backed up. This is important since the private key is not part of the certificate and, unless it is exported concurrently with its associated certificate (containing the public key) during routine backups, it will probably not be saved when a system fails. Second, the user may select the desired hash algorithm, key length, PKCS #7 request standard, and PKCS #10 reply standard when requesting certificates from the Certificate Services Web page.

An optional but recommended action is to review and confirm the installation. To ensure that the CertSrv directory and Web pages are installed and that Windows authentication security is in place for a standalone server on your CA, take these steps:

1. Open a **Microsoft Management Console** or create a new one by typing **MMC** from the command prompt.
2. From the **Console** pull-down menu, select **Add-Remove Snap-in** and add the **Internet Information Server** snap-in to the console.
3. Open the snap-in by selecting **Internet Information Server → *CAservername* → Web Sites → Default Web Site**. Verify that the CertSrv directory exists so that Web-based certificate services are available (Figure 10.49).
4. Right-click **Administration Web Site** and select **Properties**. Select the **Directory Security** tab and click **Anonymous access and authentication control Edit**.
5. Be sure to select only the **Windows Integrated authentication** check box (Figure 10.50 on page 448) to ensure Windows authentication. Click **OK** and exit.

Retrieving a Root CA Certificate

The following steps outline basic certificate retrieval from Windows Server 2003 Certificate Services Web pages. The basic retrieval options are shown in Figure 10.51 on page 449.

1. Go to a system that requires a CA certificate and start a Web browser using the URL *http://caservername/CertSrv*.
2. Select the **Download a CA certificate**, **certificate chain**, **or CRL** link.
3. Select the **Download CA Certificate** link (Figure 10.52 on page 450).
4. In the **File Download** dialog box, click **Open** (Figure 10.53 on page 450).

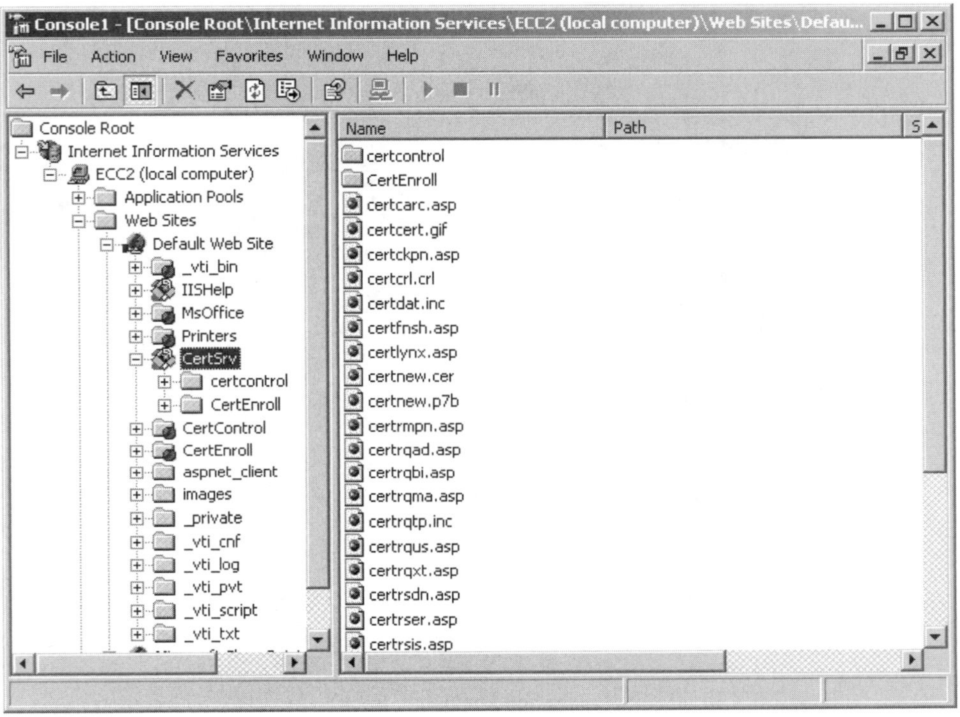

FIGURE 10.49 The Console

5. Click **Install Certificate** (Figure 10.54 on page 451) and start the **Certificate Import Wizard**. Click **Next**.
6. Select **Automatically select certificate store based on the type of certificate** and click **Next** (Figure 10.55 on page 452). This will put the trusted root certificates in the trusted store. Click **Finish**.
7. Import should be successful (Figure 10.56 on page 452).
8. Click **OK** to complete the installation.

The revocation list can be retrieved similarly.

New to Windows Server 2003 is the ability to specify the CRL Distribution Points (CDP). This means that it is possible to change the location of the file where the CRL is published. The possible publication alternatives include Lightweight Directory Access Protocol (LDAP), Hyper Text Transfer Protocol (HTTP), File Transfer Protocol (FTP), and Server Message Block (SMB) Uniform Resource Locators (URLs). This feature is available through the Certificate Authority snap-in.

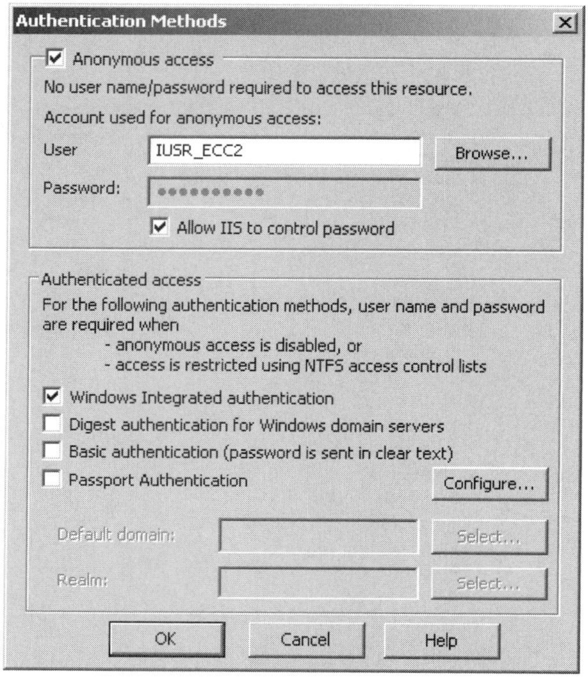

FIGURE 10.50 Authentication Methods

NOTE Also new to Windows Server 2003 is the Update Root Certificates feature. This enables a user to keep up-to-date with the latest list of trusted certificate authorities through Windows Update.

Retrieving a User Certificate

Now let's retrieve a certificate from the CA for uses other than establishing a root CA. By retrieving a user certificate from the Web server, we can access the Web server and communicate securely with other services.

1. Go to the CA certificate Web retrieval site (*http://caservername/CertServ*) and select the **Request a certificate** link (Figure 10.57 on page 453).
2. Select the **User Certificate** link to access resources as a client (Figure 10.58 on page 454).
3. A standalone CA will require you to enter the User Certificate information if you haven't already done so. You may select another Cryptographic Service Provider for the certificate exchange, but sticking with the Microsoft Base

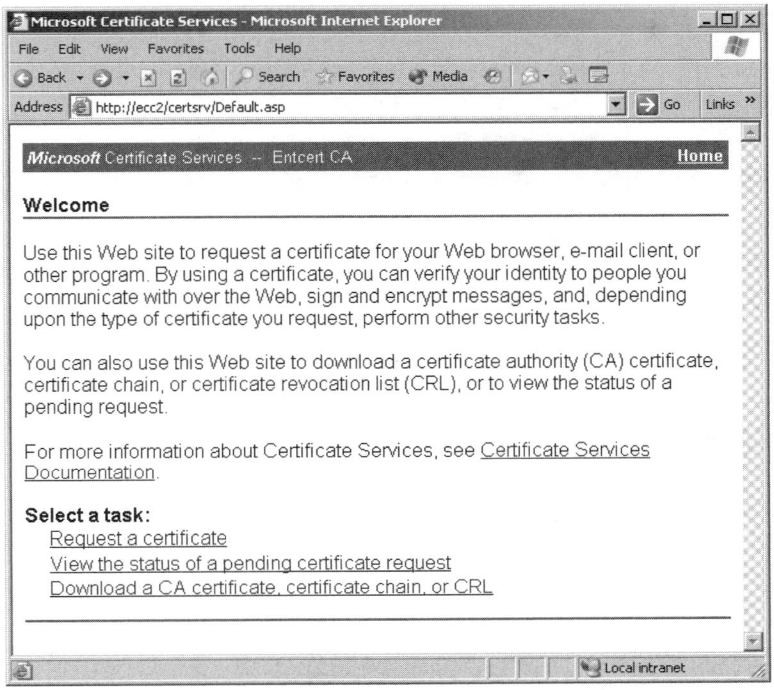

FIGURE 10.51 The Main CA Server Menu

Cryptographic Provider v.1.0 is recommended (Figure 10.59 on page 454). Click **Submit**.

4. Select the **Install this certificate** link.

You have installed the certificate (Figure 10.60 on page 455). However, it may not take effect until some time in the future. The timestamp is checked along with the date stamp. Sometimes certificates are issued to become valid an hour or so after they are issued.

Checking Pending Certificates

As mentioned earlier, standalone CAs should implement the "pending" policy since they cannot authenticate users with the Active Directory.

1. Check on impending certificate requests by selecting the **View the status of a pending certificate request** link from the starting Web page (*http://caservername/CertSrv*).
2. There may be no pending certificate requests (Figure 10.61 on page 455).

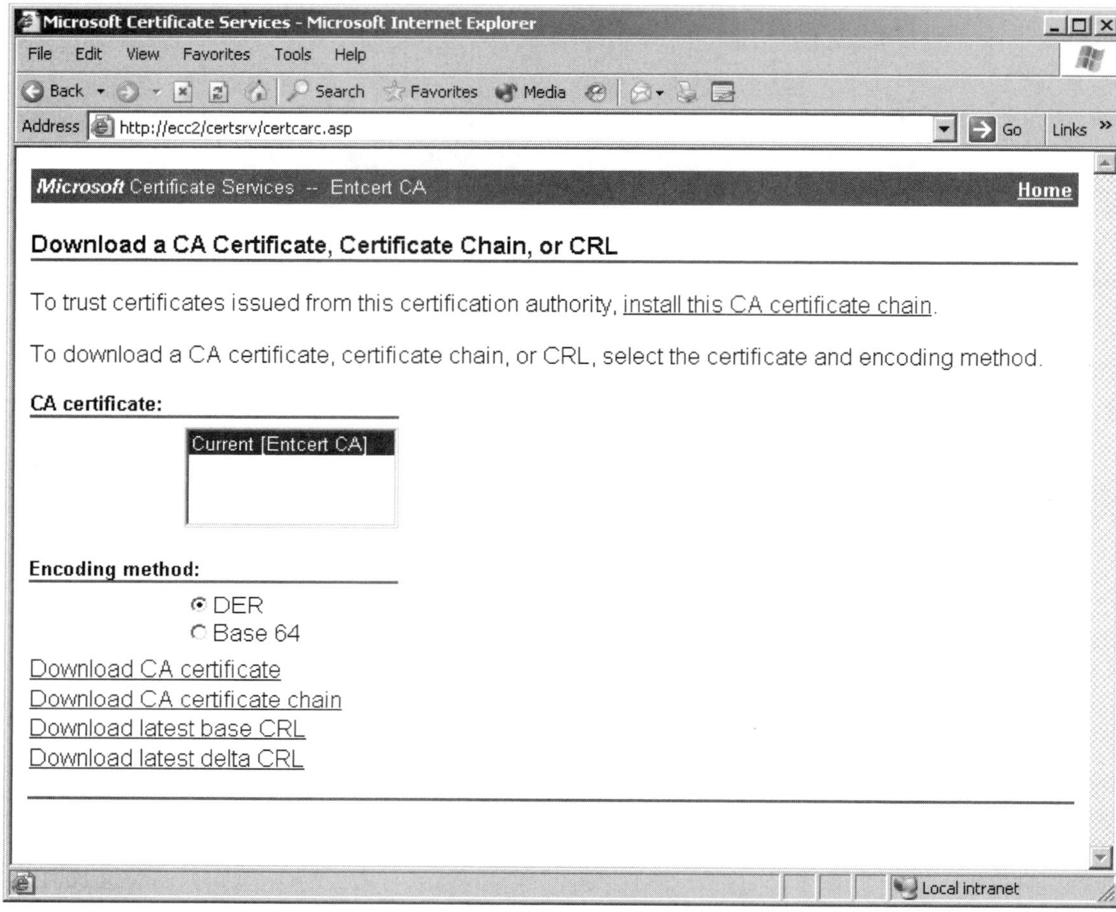

FIGURE 10.52 Retrieving a Certificate

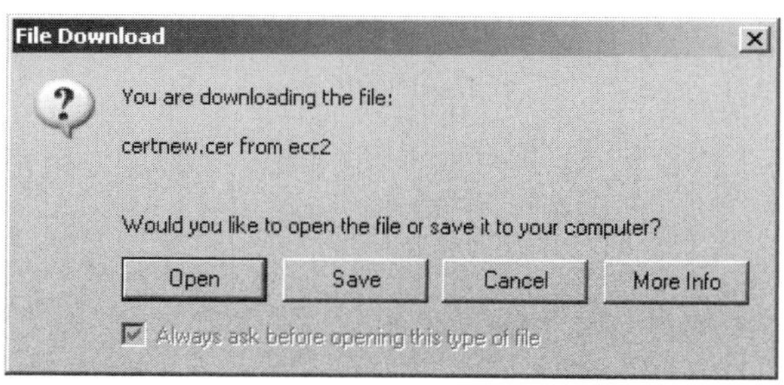

FIGURE 10.53 A Certificate Download

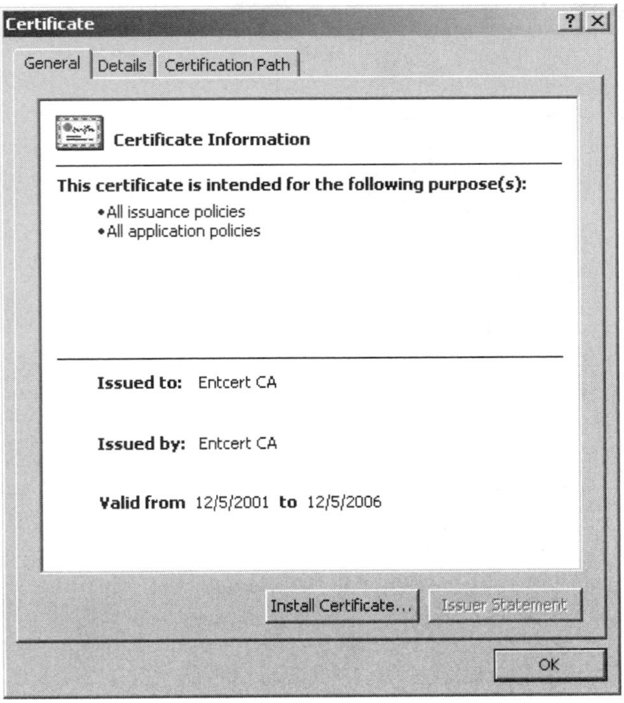

FIGURE 10.54 Certificate Information

Advanced Certificate Requests

An Advanced certificate request allows more options to be selected. Follow these steps to initiate Advanced certificate requests.

1. Go to the original Web site (*http://servername/CertServ*) and select the **Request a certificate** link.
2. Request a user certificate and select the **advanced certificate request** link (Figure 10.62 on page 456).
3. The **advanced certificate request** allows three types of request: submit request, PKCS #10 and #7 file, and certificate for smart card enrollment station. Select the **Create and submit a request to this CA** link (Figure 10.63 on page 457).
4. **Certificate Templates**, discussed earlier this chapter, defines the available certificate types. Pick a template that corresponds to the intended use for the certificate (Figure 10.64 on page 458).

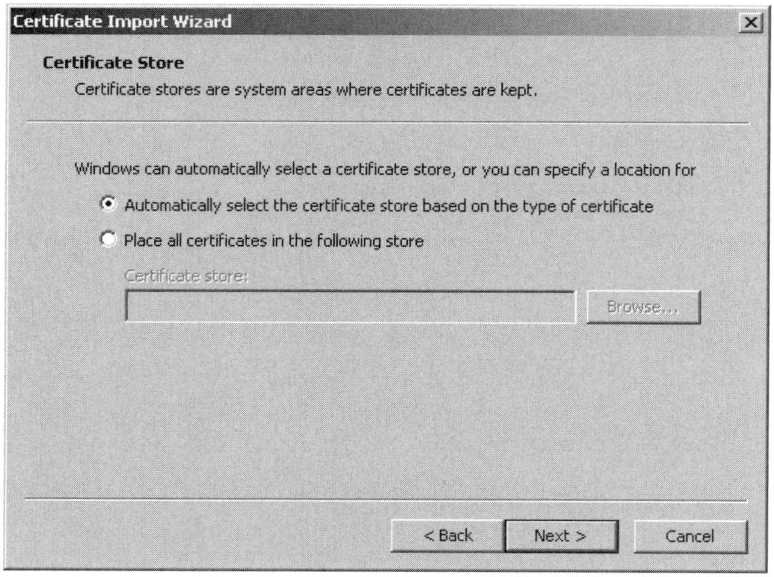

FIGURE 10.55 Selecting a Certificate Store

FIGURE 10.56 Confirmation of Certificate Import

5. Select the type of **Base Cryptographic Provider** to be used for generating the local public/private key pair (Figure 10.65 on page 459).
6. The hash algorithm, key size, key usage, and, most important, the **Mark Keys as exportable** options are all available from the Advanced Certificate Request form.
7. Install the certificate.

Active Directory Certificate Retrieval

Enterprise CAs support the Certificates snap-in with the Certificate Request Wizard. Certificates for EFS and EFS recovery agents may have their private keys marked for export. Follow the steps on the next page to allow Active Directory certificate retrieval.

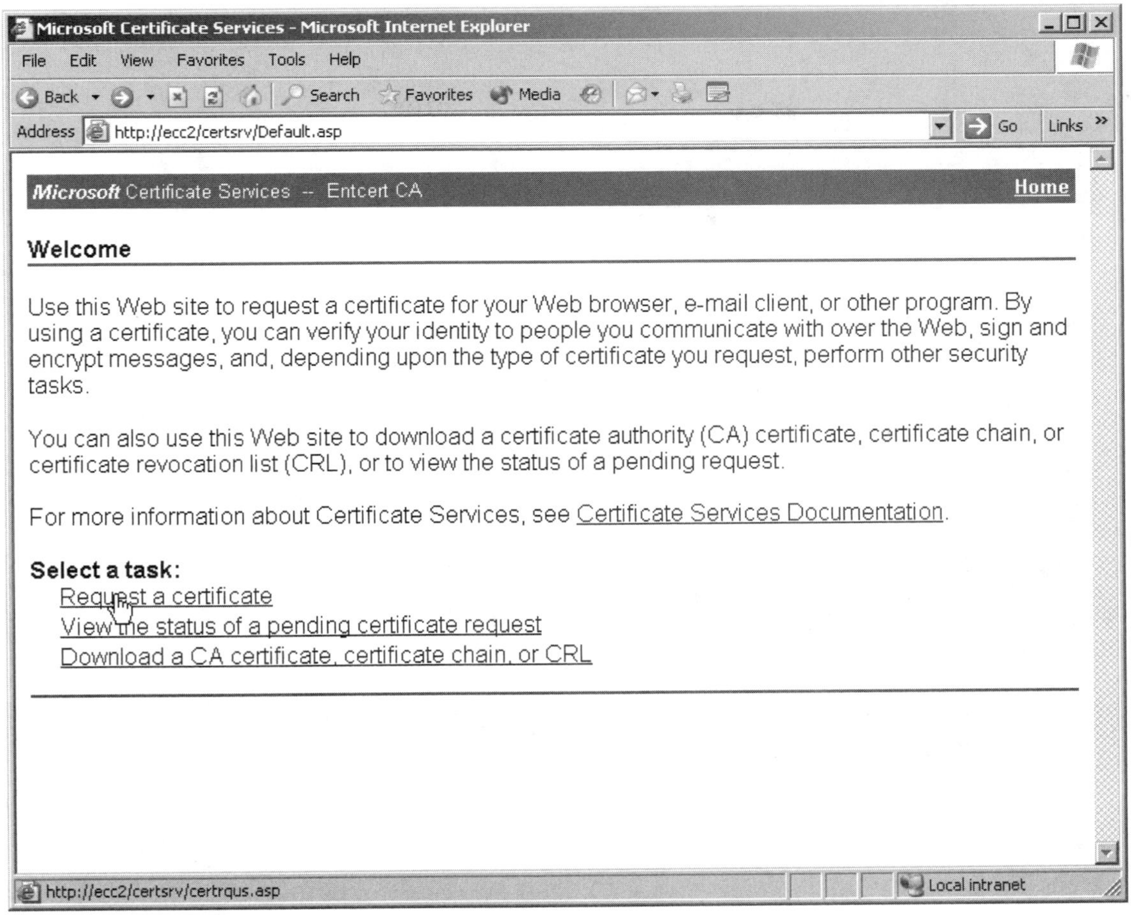

FIGURE 10.57 The Certificate Retrieval Main Menu

1. Add the **Certificates** snap-in for a user account into a **Microsoft Management Console**.
2. Right-click a certificate store and select **All Tasks → Request New Certificate** (Figure 10.66 on page 460).
3. The **Certificate Request Wizard** starts. Click **Next**.
4. Select a certificate type from the available certificate templates. Clicking **Advanced** allows selection of a Cryptographic Service Provider (CSP) (Figure 10.67 on page 460). Click **Next**.

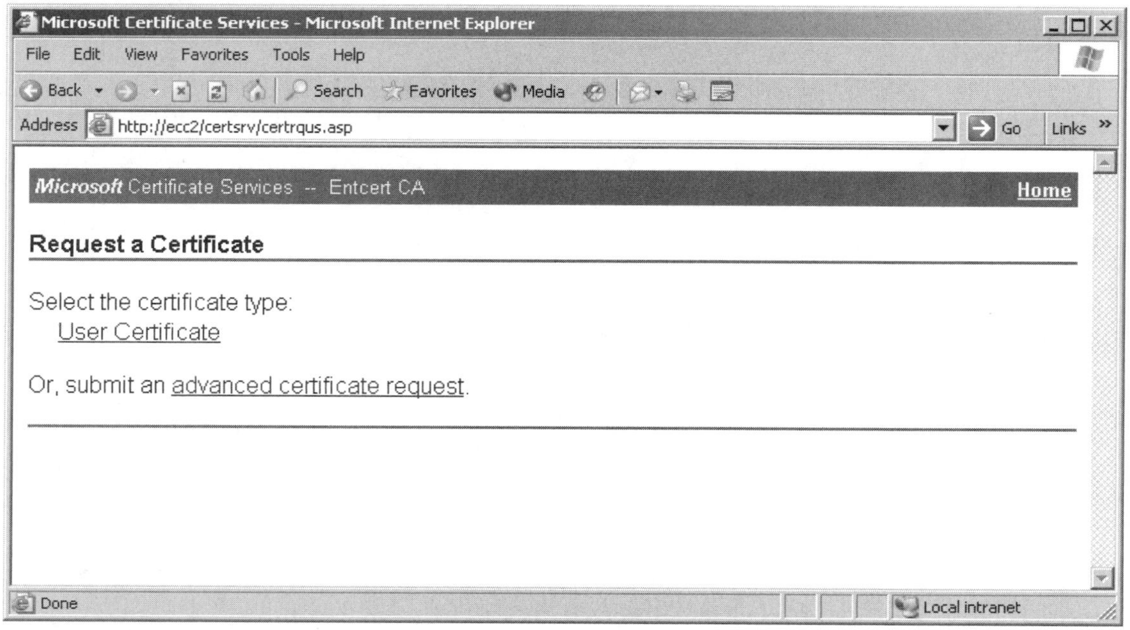

FIGURE 10.58 Choosing Certificate Request Type

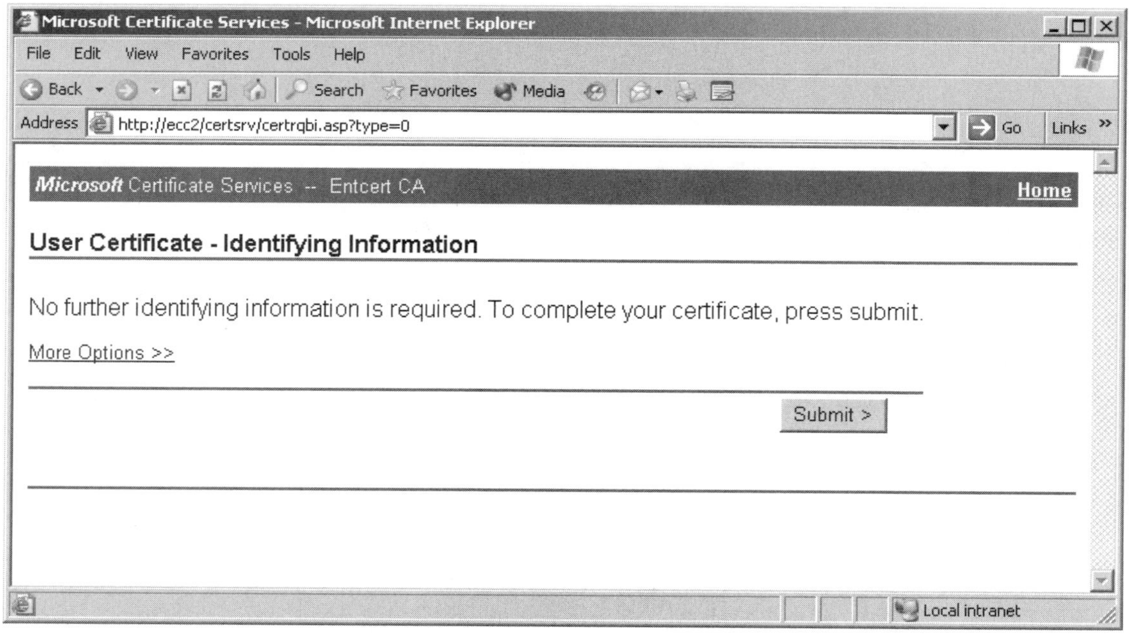

FIGURE 10.59 User Identifying Information

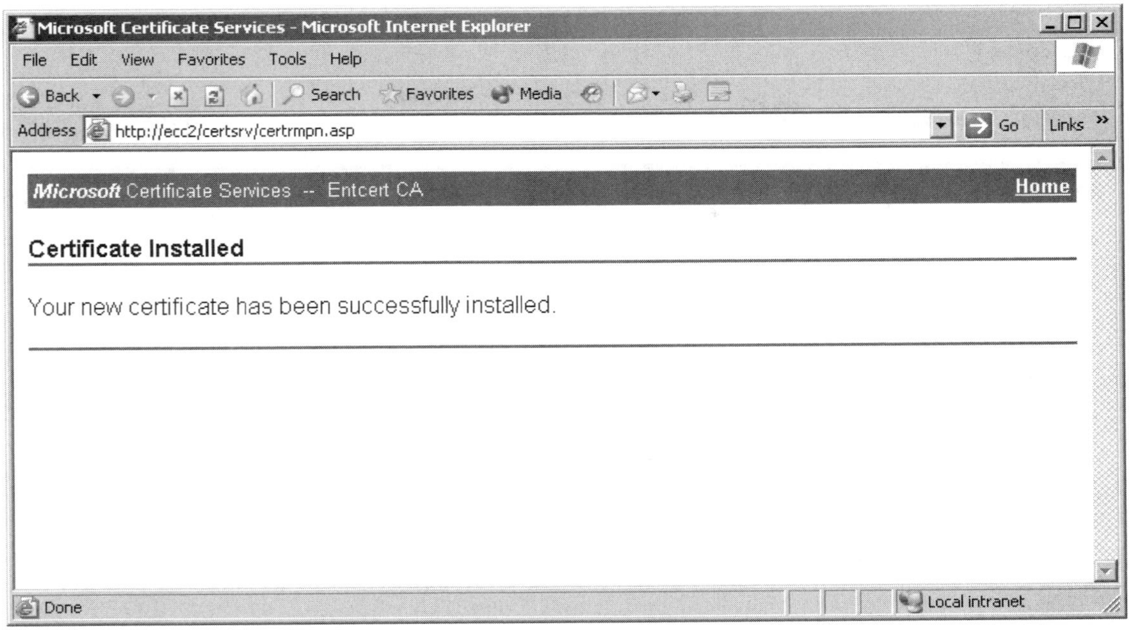

FIGURE 10.60 Installation Confirmation

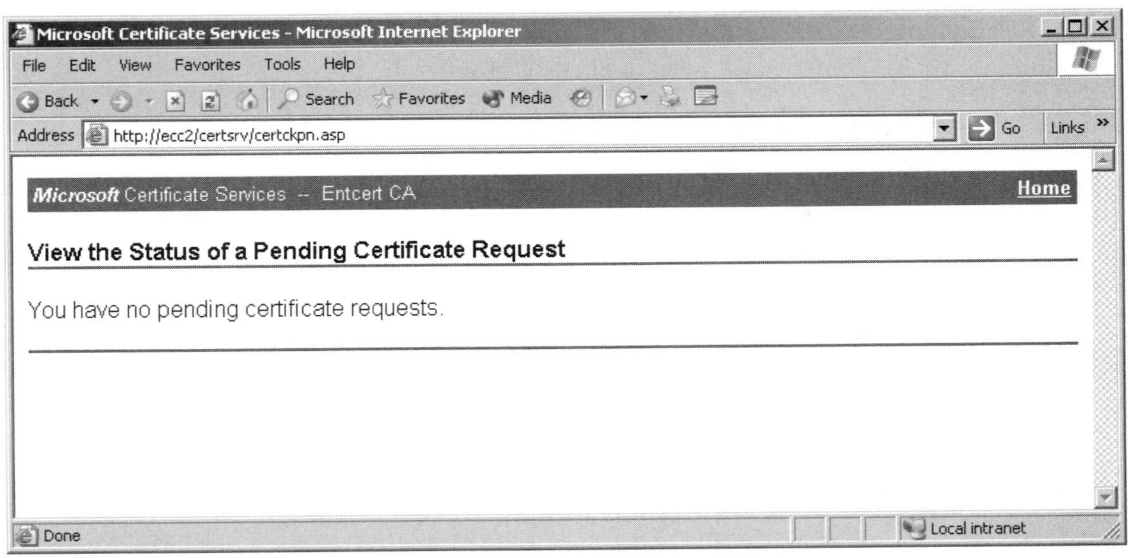

FIGURE 10.61 Pending Status

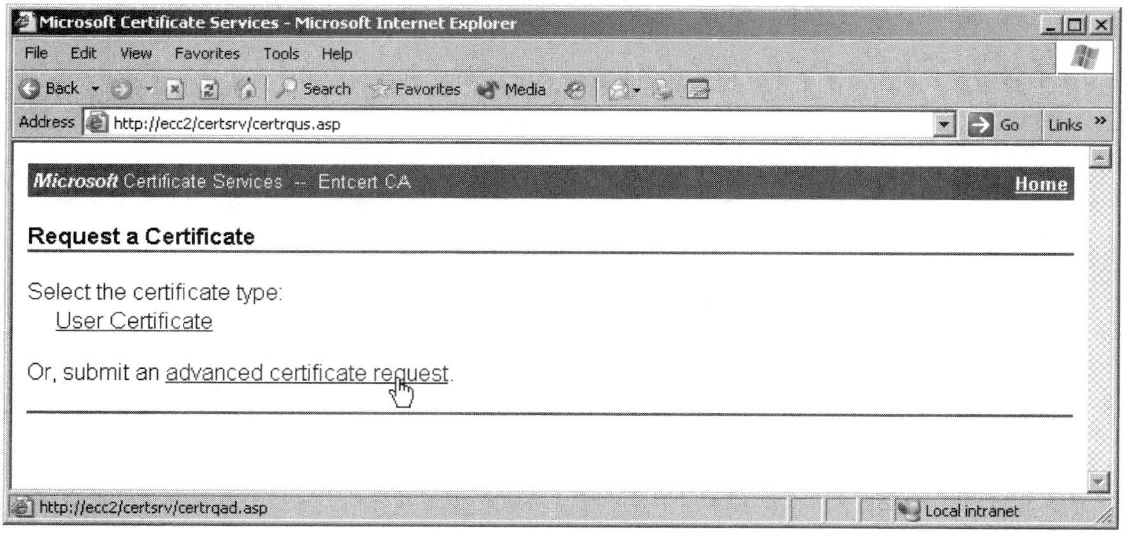

FIGURE 10.62 Request Type Selection

5. Select the cryptographic service provider and mark it as exportable.
6. Choose the enterprise CA to send the certificate request (Figure 10.68 on page 461). Click **Next**.
7. Type a name for the certificate. Click **Next** (Figure 10.69 on page 461).
8. Complete the request by clicking **Finish**.

EXPORTING CERTIFICATES AND BACKUP

A certificate can be exported for backup purposes or simply for transport. It can be exported with its associated private key if it has been marked appropriately. Export is accomplished through the Certificate Export Wizard, which can be invoked from several locations.

1. Open the **Certificates** snap-in.
2. Right-click the certificate to export and select **All Tasks → Export** (Figure 10.70 on page 462).

   To accomplish exporting from within Internet Explorer 6.x, follow these steps:

1. Select **Tools → Internet Options**. Select the **Content** tab and click **Certificates**. Select a certificate from one of the local stores and click **Export** (Figure 10.71 on page 463).

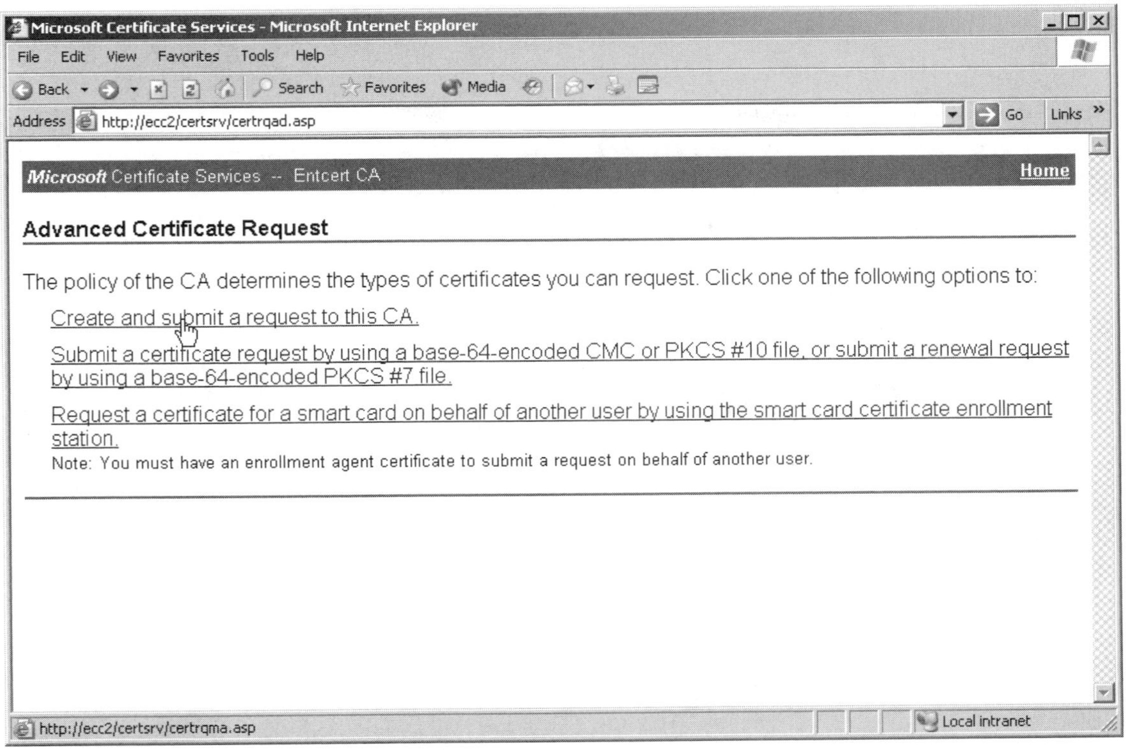

FIGURE 10.63 Advanced Request Options

2. Once the **Certificate Export Wizard** appears, click **Next**.
3. If the certificate is marked for export, you may choose whether it will be accompanied by its associated private key (Figure 10.72 on page 463).
4. If the certificate is exported without the private key, three file formats are available, as listed in Figure 10.73 on page 464. For export with the private key, only the PKCS #12 file format is available. A password must be entered to protect the file only when exporting the private key.
5. Enter the destination directory and file name (Figure 10.74 on page 464) and click **Next**.
6. Click **Finish** to complete the export.

NOTE Certificate exports with the private key are represented by icons that show a key and an envelope (Figure 10.75 on page 465).

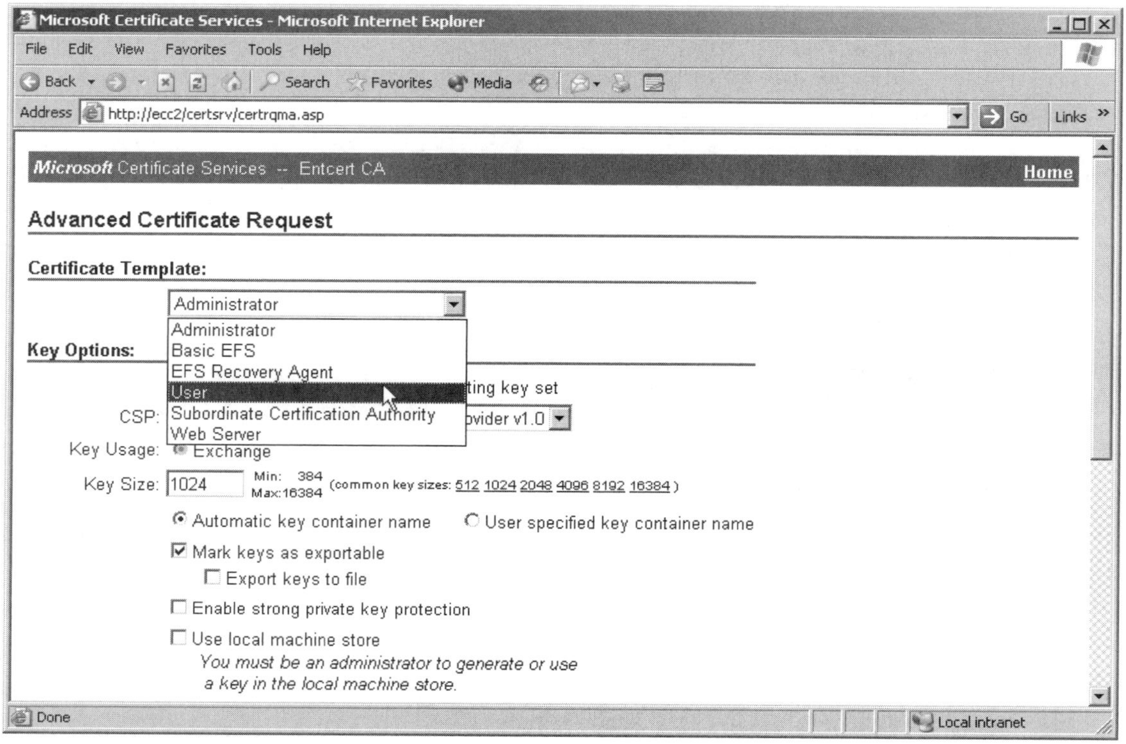

FIGURE 10.64 A Certificate Template

Importing Certificates

The import process is implemented from the Certificate Import Wizard in much the same way that the Certificate Export Wizard is used.

CERTIFICATE AUTHORITY SERVICE MANAGEMENT

The Certificate Authority service management tool provides a number of functions, including administrative logs. Like all Windows Server 2003 logs, CA logs can be a valuable administrative tool.

Certificate Authority Logs

To manage a CA server, the certificate authority has five useful logs, listed in Table 10.12 (page 466). A number of column and filtering options are available to manage the certificates in the viewing window (Figure 10.76 on page 465).

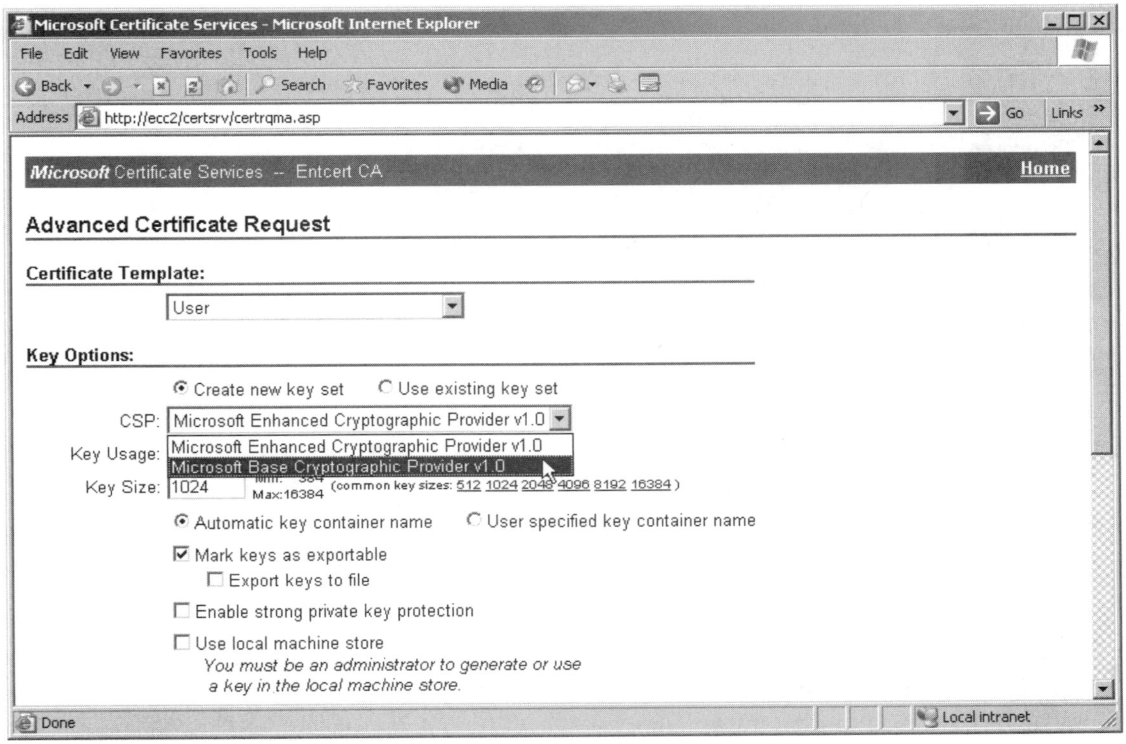

FIGURE 10.65 Cryptographic Provider Options

1. Right-click a certificate log and select **View** → **Add/Remove Columns** to allow control over the columns displayed (Figure 10.77 on page 465).
2. Right-click a certificate log and select **View** → **Filter** to allow the administrator to apply display restrictions or filters that determine what certificates are shown (Figure 10.78 on page 466).
3. Add the **Certificate Authority** snap-in to a **Microsoft Management Console** and open the CA server's node. Right-click a certificate in the **Issued Certificates** log and select **All Tasks** → **Revoke Certificate**.
4. Specify a reason code for revoking the certificate (Figure 10.79 on page 466) and click **Yes**.

   To add a certificate to a Revoked Certificates List:

5. Follow the preceding steps. Check the **Revoked Certificates** log and verify the new certificate status (Figure 10.80 on page 467).

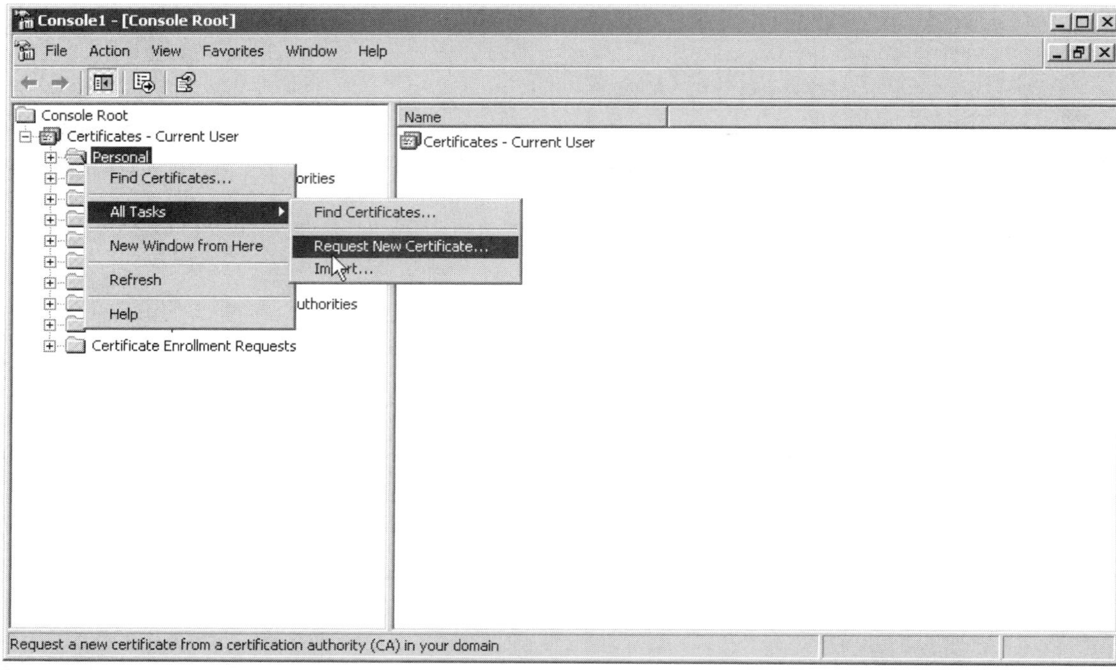

FIGURE 10.66 Starting the Certificate Request Wizard

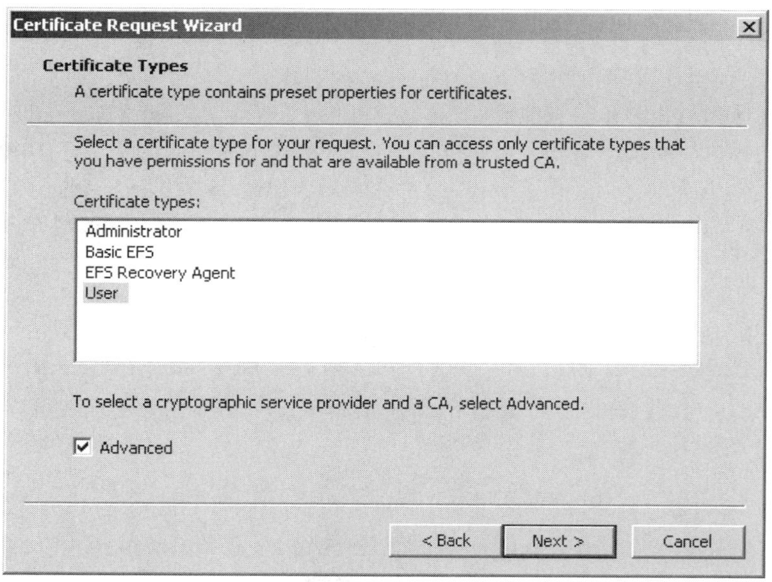

FIGURE 10.67 Selecting a Certificate Type

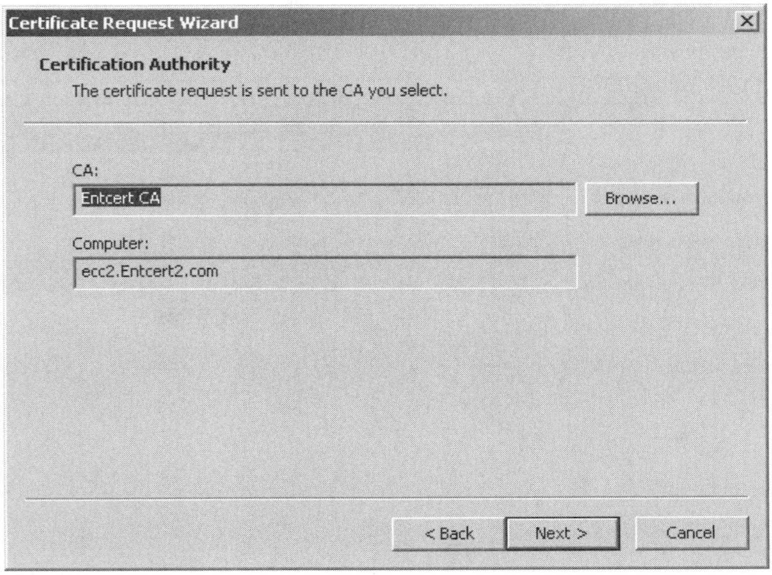

FIGURE 10.68 Enterprise CA Selection

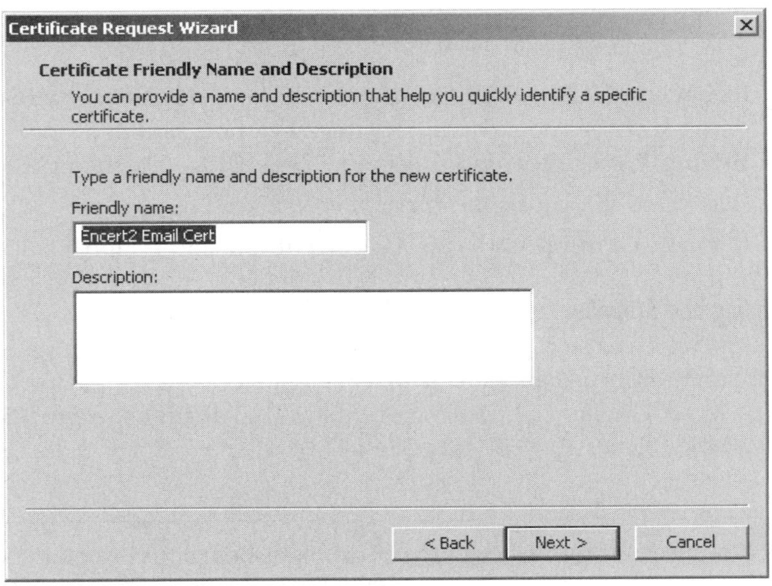

FIGURE 10.69 Entering a Certificate Name

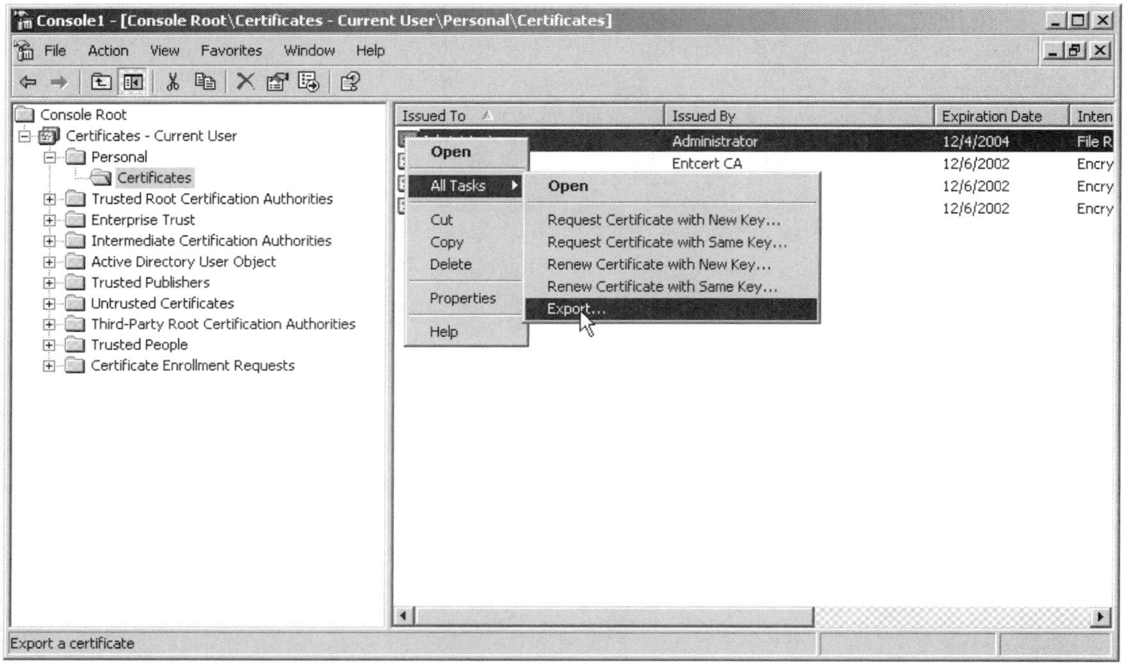

FIGURE 10.70 Exporting from the Certificate Snap-In

To display a CRL and properties:

1. Right-click the **Revoked Certificates** log and select **Properties** (Figure 10.81 on page 467). The publication interval can be modified from the **CRL Publishing Parameters** tab. Select the **View CRLs** tab, then click **View CRL**.
2. Certificate revocation information is displayed.
3. Click the **General** tab to display current CRL info (Figure 10.82 on page 468).

Starting and Stopping the Certificate Service

You can start and stop the Certificate service from the Certification Authority snap-in. Open the **Certification Authority** snap-in tool. Right-click the CA server node and select **All Tasks**. If the server is running, the **All Tasks → Stop Service** option is available (Figure 10.83 on page 468). Otherwise, you might select **Start Service**.

NOTE The Certificate Authority snap-in tool distinguishes status by color codes and icons. A green check mark is visible next to the CA server icon when the CA service is running and a red dot is visible when the service is stopped.

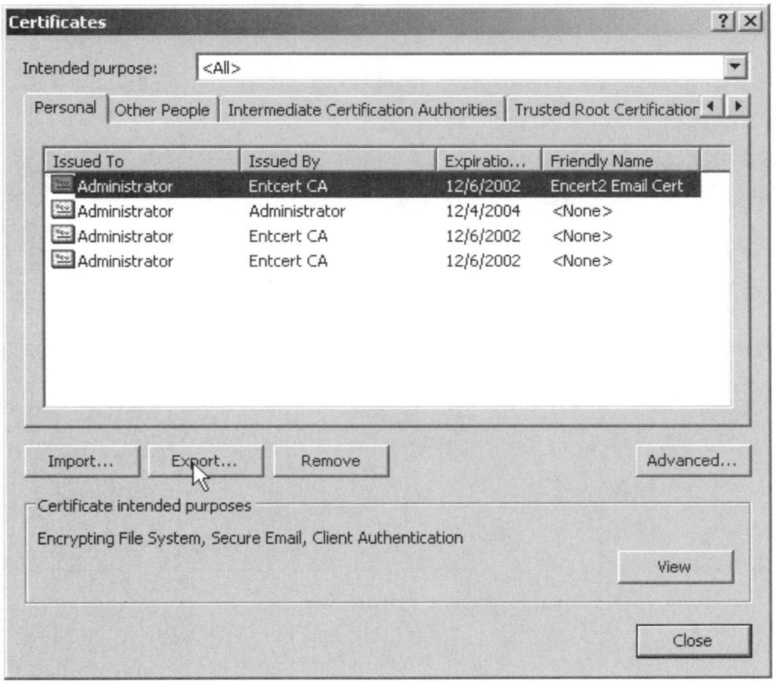

FIGURE 10.71 Exporting from IE 6.0

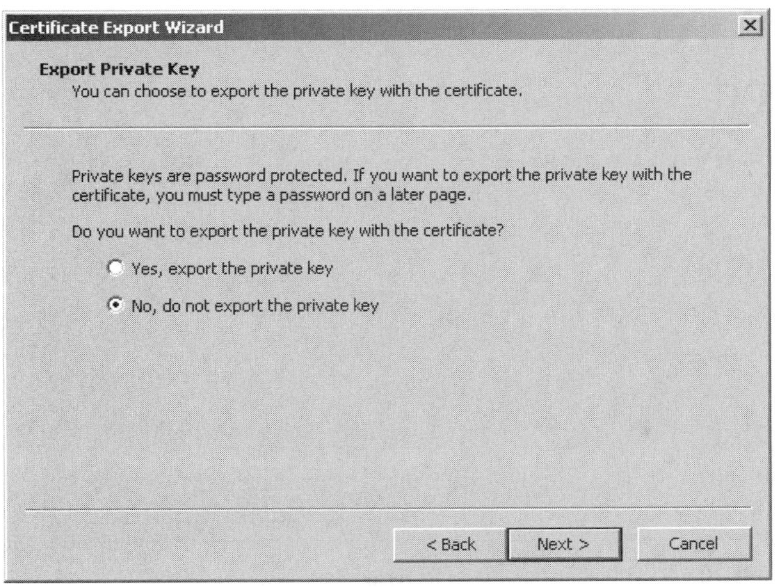

FIGURE 10.72 The Export Private Key Option

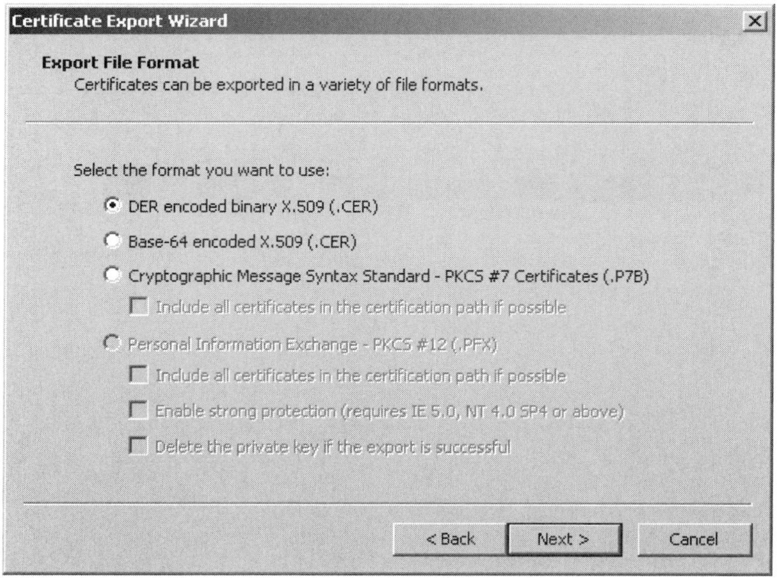

FIGURE 10.73 File Formats without a Private Key

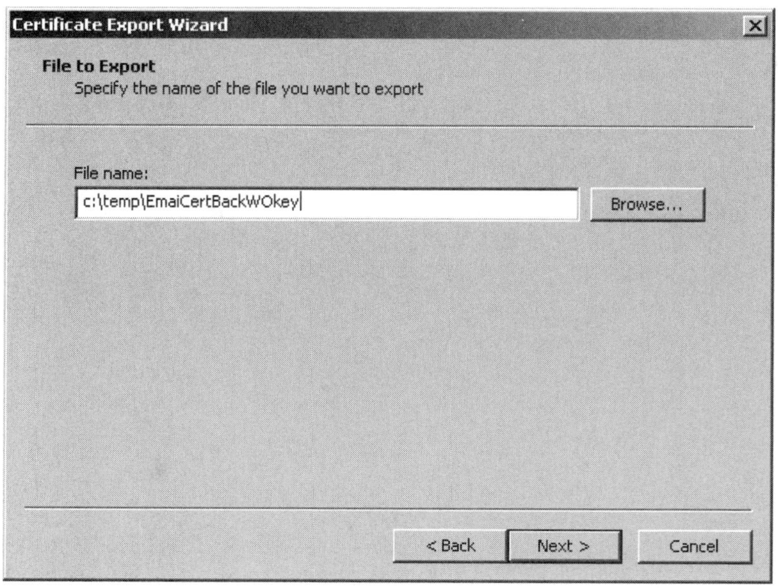

FIGURE 10.74 A Destination for an Exported Key

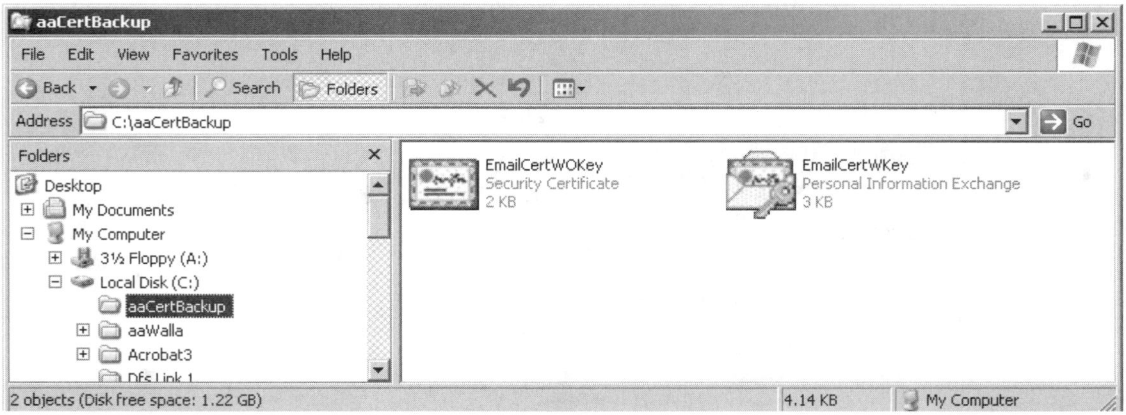

FIGURE 10.75 The Icon for Certificates with and without a Private Key

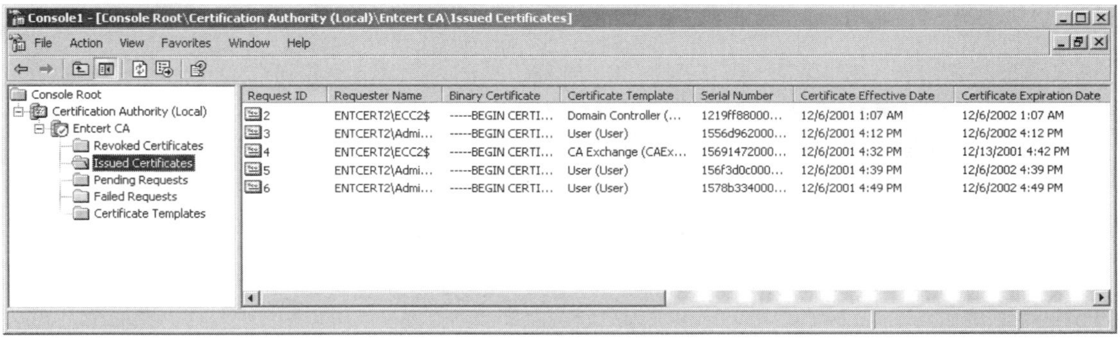

FIGURE 10.76 Certificate Authority Logs

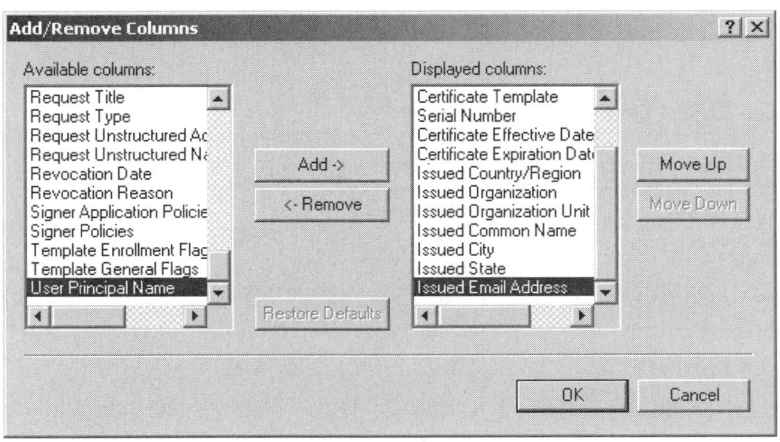

FIGURE 10.77 Columns Displayed

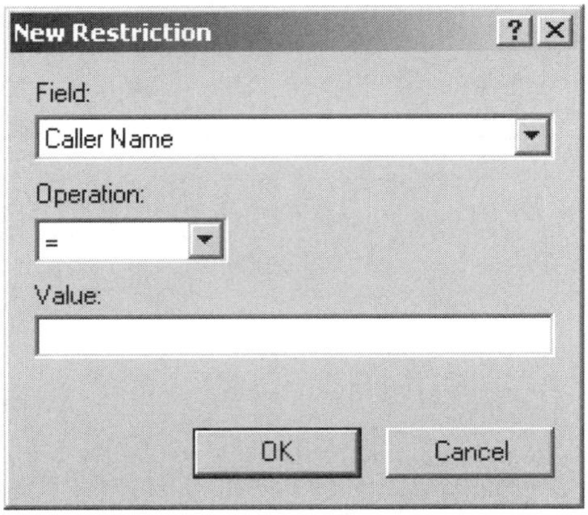

FIGURE 10.78 Displaying Restrictions

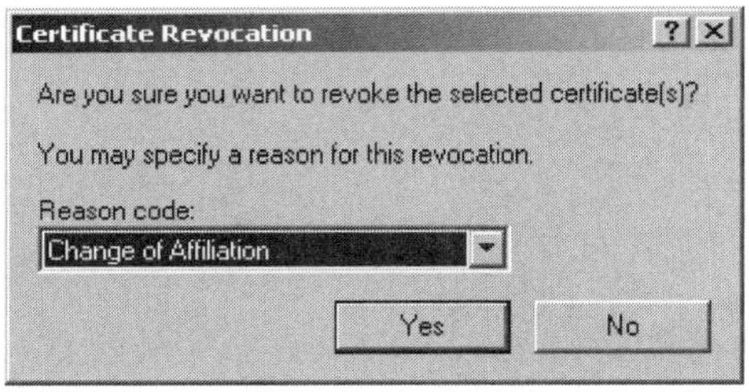

FIGURE 10.79 A Revocation Reason Code

TABLE 10.12 Certificate Authority Logs

Certificate Store	Description
Revoked Certificates	Certificates issued by this CA that are invalid and members of the current CRL
Issued Certificates	Certificates issued by this CA server
Pending Requests	Certificate requests awaiting issue or rejection
Failed Requests	Rejected certificate requests
Policy Settings	Certificate types available for issue based on the Certificate Templates snap-in

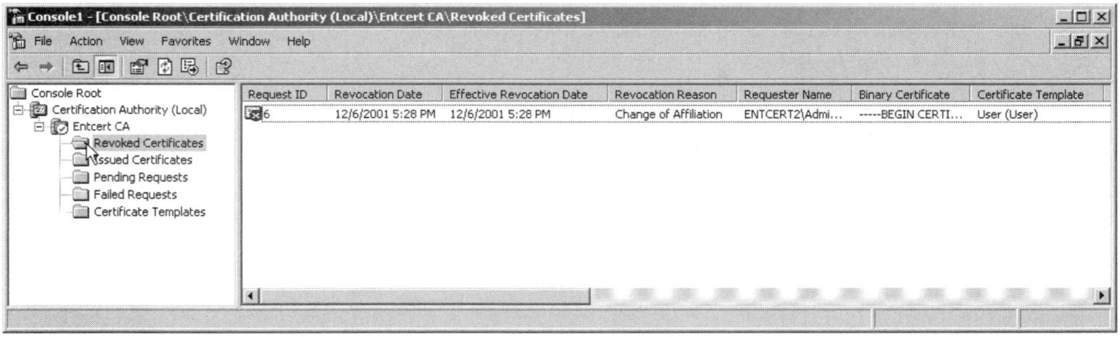

FIGURE 10.80 A CA Revocation List

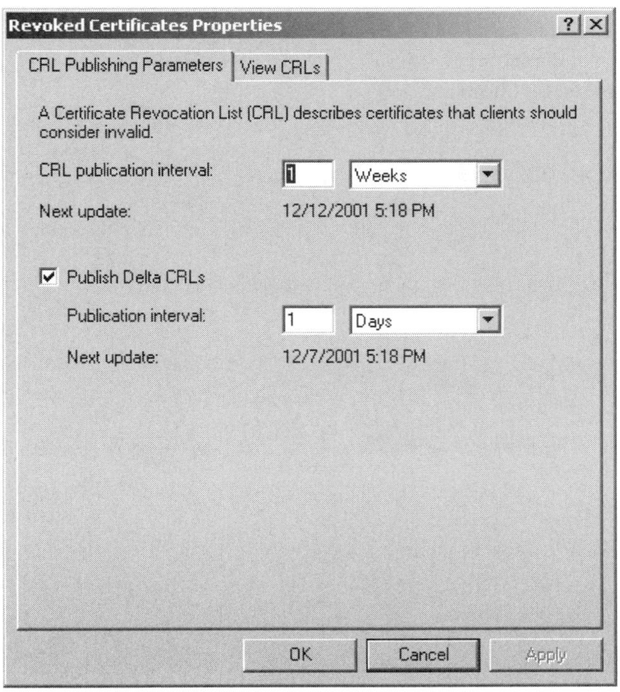

FIGURE 10.81 CRL Publishing Parameters

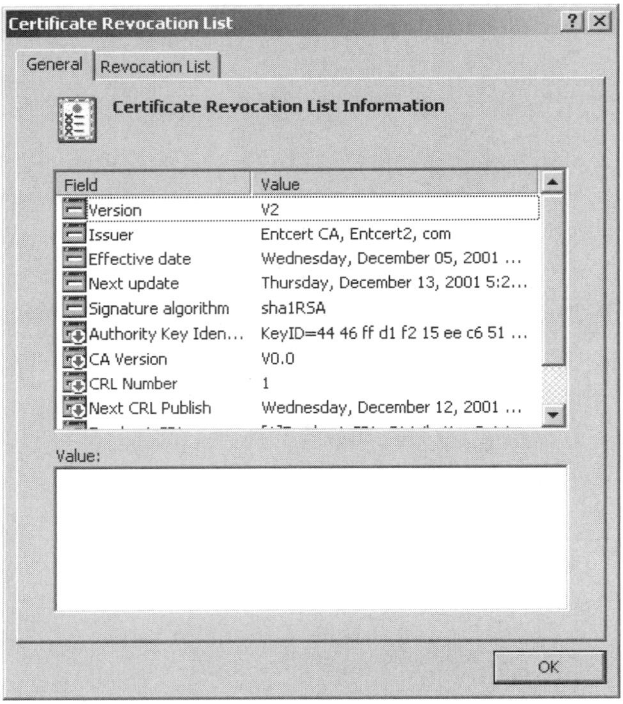

FIGURE 10.82 Revoked Certificates

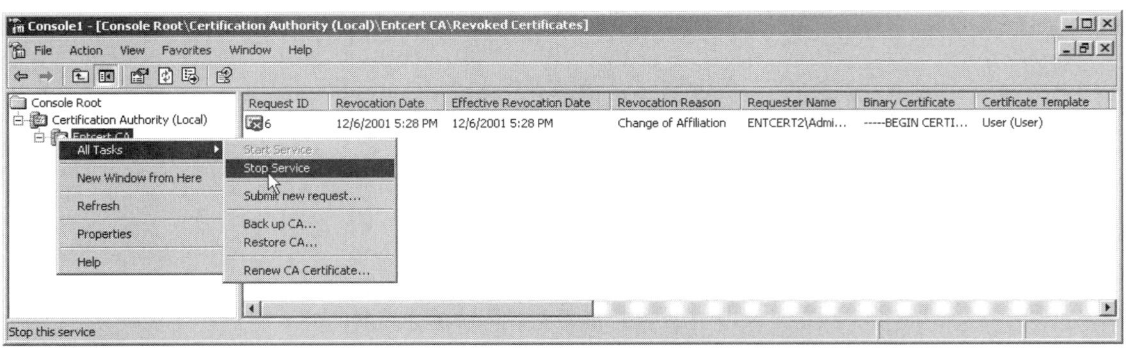

FIGURE 10.83 Starting and Stopping a CA

CERTIFICATE AUTHORITY PROPERTIES

CA properties are viewed from the Certification Authority MMC snap-in as well. Right-click the CA service node and select **Properties**. The **General** tab displays the CA name and description entered during creation or modification. It also displays the CSP and hash algorithm used with the CA certificate. Clicking **View Certificate** will display the CA's certificate via the **Certificate** dialog box, as discussed earlier. The following sections describe some of the remaining tabs.

The Policy Module Tab

The Policy Module tab (Figure 10.84) displays default policy settings for certificates issued by the CA. It sets default CRL distribution points, authority information access points, and the default actions the CA will take when it receives certificate requests. Requests can be denied, accepted, and queued for later authorization.

Policy Module also displays information about the current active policy (name, version, and copyright). Pressing its **Select** button allows the administrator to choose the active policy module from the list of those installed (Figure 10.85). Put

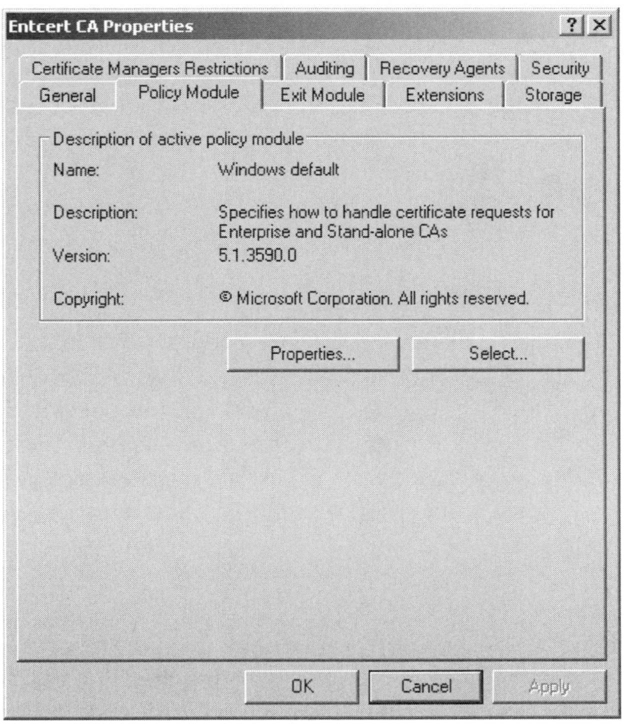

FIGURE 10.84 The Policy Module Tab

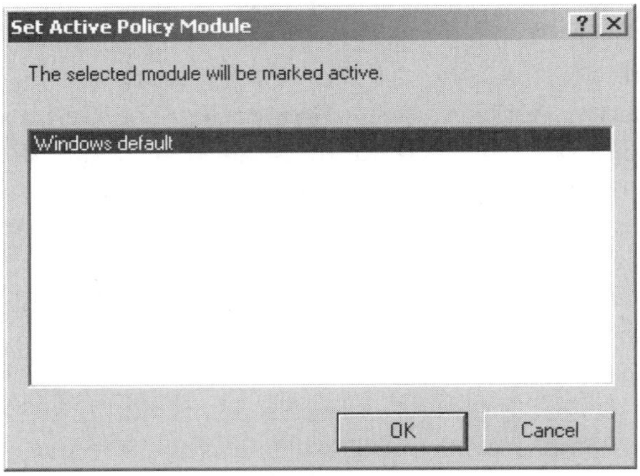

FIGURE 10.85 The Active Policy Module

new modules in the %SystemRoot%\system32 directory and then use the rgsrv32 ***modulename.dll*** command to register new policies.

Clicking **Properties** on the **Policy Module** tab displays the **Request Handling** tab. Only standalone CA servers have policy options here; enterprise CA servers will immediately issue or deny a certificate request based on user information retrieved from the Active Directory. Standalone CA servers usually hold off on issuing certificates until the administrator permits them to do so by selecting the "pending" option from the **Request Handling** tab (Figure 10.86). The administrator must make an informed decision about the type of certificate a user may be issued.

The Extensions Tab

Pressing the Extensions tab displays two more configuration items. CRL Distribution Points (HTTP, FTP, LDAP, and file addresses) are inserted by default into every issued certificate (Figure 10.87). These are URLs that can check for current CRLs to validate the certificate. The Authority Information Access list of URLs specifies where a certificate can be obtained for the CA that issued it. Someone verifying a certificate issued with this policy could search this list and retrieve a CA certificate to verify the certificate.

The Exit Module Tab

Exit modules perform tasks and control actions taken after the certificate has been issued. This is in contrast to policy modules, which determine certificate content. These actions determine if the certificate can be published in the Active Directory and file system. They also determine where the Certificate Revocation List is pub-

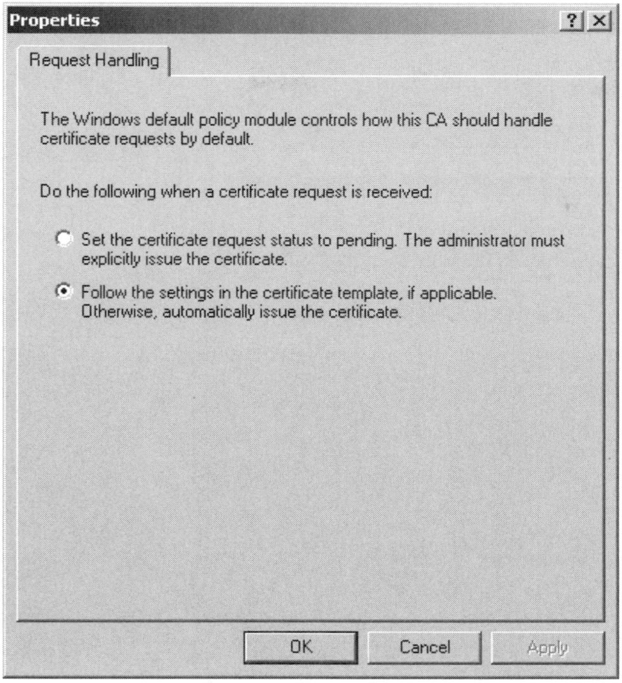

FIGURE 10.86 A Default Action

lished. The Exit Module tab (Figure 10.88) displays exit module details and allows the administrator to add, remove, or select the active exit module.

Clicking **Properties** displays the **Publication Settings** tab (Figure 10.89 on page 474) and determines if the CA server will allow publication to the Active Directory and file system. If publication is permitted, the client being issued the certificate must provide the location in the request. When an Active Directory is present, the default setting is to allow publication to it and restrict publication to a file system. The opposite is the case when an Active Directory is absent.

Storage and Security Tabs

The Storage tab specifies where the certification log is stored. This location is not modifiable on an enterprise CA server. The Security tab allows the assigning of permissions regarding the Certificate Authority snap-in.

CERTIFICATION AUTHORITY BACKUP

Without a current log of the issued and revoked certificates, it is difficult to manage previously issued certificates. This means that the CA should be backed up

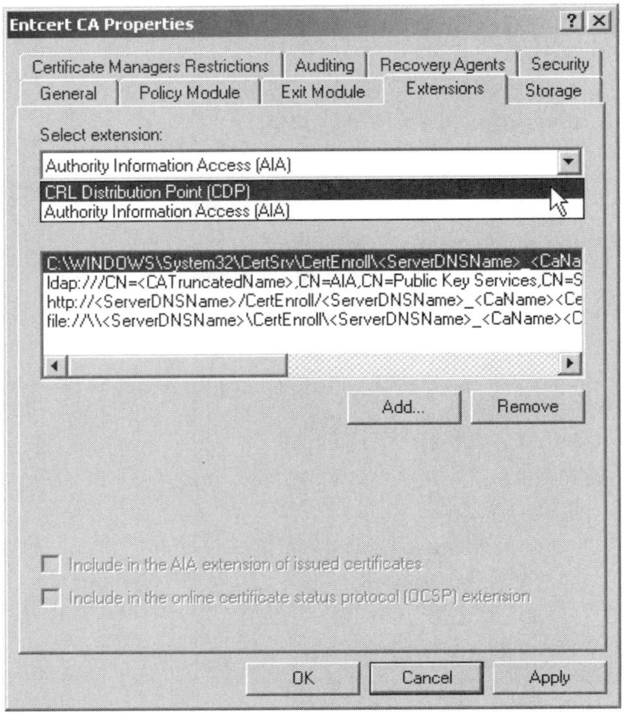

FIGURE 10.87 Extensions

regularly. The created backup file should be placed in a directory that will then be backed up by whatever backup system is in place.

NOTE If you are using Windows Backup, be sure to complete the CA backup and stop the CA service beforehand. Windows Backup may not function properly if the CA service is running.

---

1. Start the **Certificate Authority Backup Wizard** by selecting the CA server from the **Certification Authority** snap-in and right-clicking **All Tasks → Backup CA** to start the wizard (Figure 10.90).
2. Follow the wizard's instructions, but pay close attention to what data types are backed up and where the log is stored (Figure 10.91).

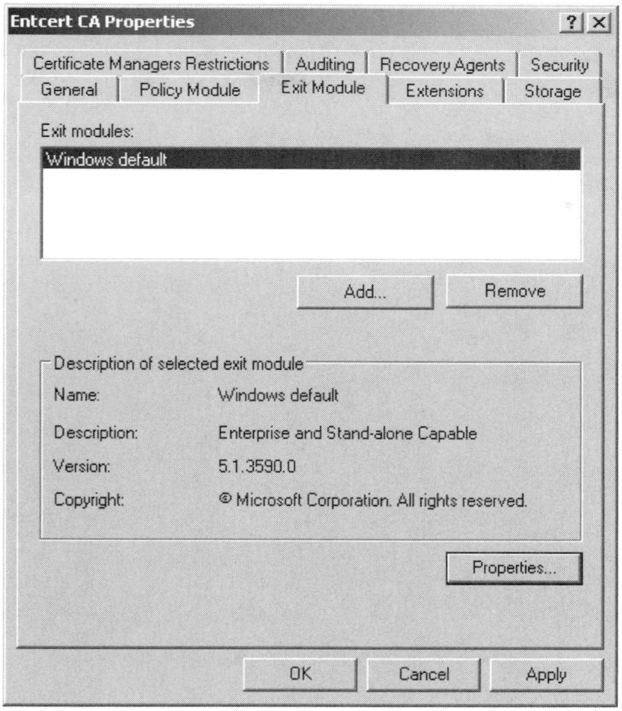

FIGURE 10.88 The Exit Module Tab

3. Use a password to protect the backup file and the CA's private key.

Restoration of the backup is similarly started; however, the CA service must be stopped first.

1. Start the **Certificate Authority Backup Wizard** by selecting the CA server from the **Certification Authority** snap-in and right-clicking **All Tasks → Restore CA**.
2. Follow the wizard's instructions and reenter the password for the selected backup retrieval file.

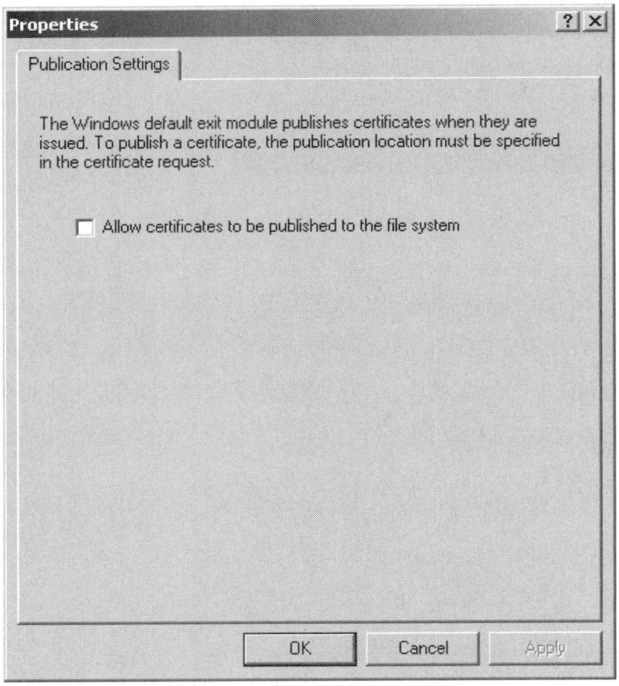

FIGURE 10.89 Publication Settings

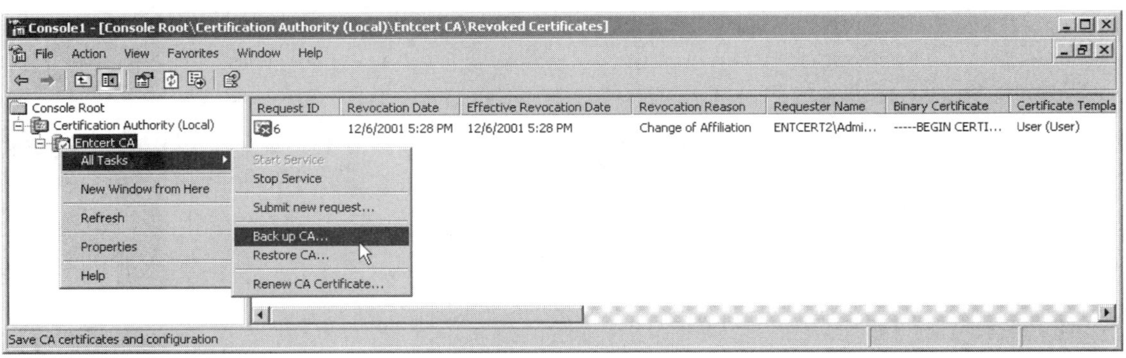

FIGURE 10.90 Backup CA

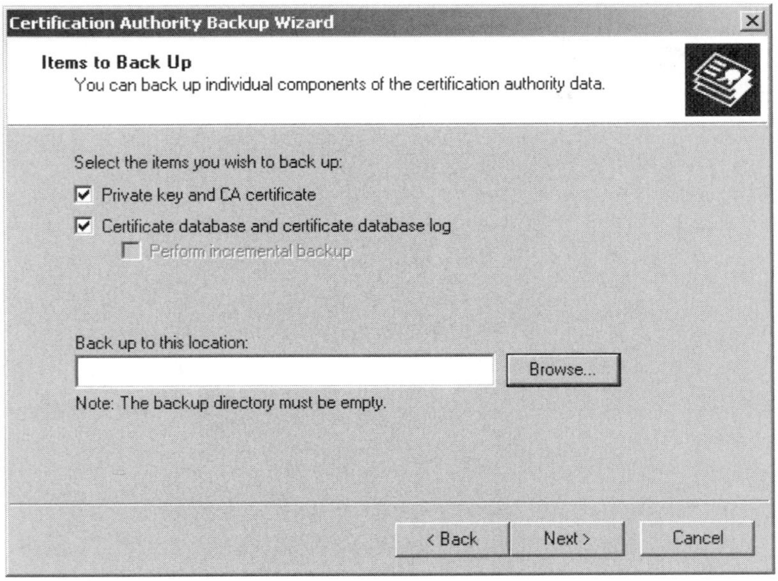

FIGURE 10.91 Data Types

POSTSCRIPT

Both Kerberos and the Public Key Infrastructure are integral parts of the Windows Server 2003 operating system. Kerberos provides domainwide authentication to any service throughout the Windows Server 2003 domain and offers compatibility with many other operating systems. PKI enables secure communication, data storage, and universal authentication throughout Internet and extranet environments. These technologies lay the groundwork for IPSec, VPNs, secure Web transactions, e-mail communications, and centralized user account management.

Chapter 11

Additional Security Issues and Solutions

The previous two chapters examined permissions, the Public Key Infrastructure, and user authentication as aspects of securing a Windows Server 2003 system or domain. Although these are the cornerstones of Windows Server security, a variety of other security issues and solutions must be discussed.

This chapter rounds out the discussion of Windows Server security. First we examine the snap-in tools for security management. Then we look at how to secure the computer systems primarily against internal abuses. Finally we turn our attention to securing the Windows Server 2003 environment against external intrusions over the network.

Security breaches compromise protocols, services, permission settings, readable network data, downloadable components, and e-mail messages. Practically every feature on the operating system can be used against it, which is why it must be secured against outside "crackers," or criminal hackers.

Protecting against malicious outside attack is only one aspect of a totally secure program. Authorized users are also the cause of purposeful or inadvertent data destruction or even system crashes. A proper framework must include control over hardware and file system access, data archiving and restoration, and data transmission.

Security vulnerabilities can result in a number of crippling results. The user is denied service when a system is crashed, damaged, or taxed so that it cannot perform intended duties. Data corruption can cost both time and money. The invasion of privacy through improper sniffing or other forms of intrusion can result in the loss of confidential information. A common hacker practice known as spoofing permits an unauthorized user to pretend to be another person or service. Finally, physical security breaches can result in the theft of equipment or sensitive data. In this chapter, we identify these issues in greater detail and suggest both commonsense and specific Windows Server 2003 solutions.

SECURITY POLICY

A security policy is an important element of the overall security of the computer or network being protected. In general, the more security that is applied to a system or network, the more inconvenient the system will be for users.

A security policy, as well as security procedures, helps to define what you are trying to protect and how to protect it. Because of different goals, each type of industry or organization has different security needs. An e-commerce site needs a different security policy from that of an accounting firm or government agency. Before you begin securing your site, it is wise to see if a security policy has been established. If not, develop one.

Most technology decisions should be based on policy. To develop a security policy, take the following guidelines into consideration:

- In preparing a risk analysis, ask yourself, what am I trying to protect and from whom?
- Determine the probability of risk with a cost/benefit analysis of resource(s) protection.
- Determine who is responsible for protecting the resources.
- Define how you will respond during a breach of security.

Security policies should not be made in a vacuum, but should be approved and supported by people with authority. To be effective, they should not be too difficult to implement. Once the security policy is in place, procedures and guidelines should be established to ensure that it can be monitored and enforced. The security policy snap-ins discussed later should be configured to meet the security goals and policy of the organizational unit, site, and domain structure; the corresponding procedures that are implemented will affect how users do their work. Larger companies may have compartmentalized security that responds to different needs of various sites, divisions, and departments.

There are some general considerations that will determine how security will be implemented and enforced. This list is by no means all-inclusive but is here to give examples of the questions that should be asked.

- Is there an Internet connection, and how can the users use it?
- How are disks and information shared?
- Is data backed up? If so, which data and how often?

- Do the users know their responsibilities?
- What are the remote access requirements?
- How will you know if security has been compromised?
- Is there a firewall in place, and if so, what is permitted to go through it?

Once these questions have been answered, it is necessary to apply them to categories of effort. These questions can be broken down into the following general areas:

- *Confidentiality*. How will you protect information from being read by unauthorized sources? This includes consideration of technologies such as encryption, file permissions, and network sniffing.
- *Integrity*. How will you ensure that your data will not be deleted or modified, and, if it is, that you know the source? You must decide how to deal with file permissions, digital signatures, viruses, and programs that are not secure.
- *Availability*. How will you ensure that your systems remain available? The plan must involve issues like denial of service, acceptable system use, and employment of redundant systems.
- *Recoverability*. How will you recover if your system has been compromised? You will need to determine the best ways to use data backups, hard copies, and remote data stores.
- *Audit*. Will you be able to tell if a security breach has happened? Use of log files, system auditing, event monitors, and alarms to guard against abuse must be factored into the plan.

Implementing security can be a full-time job, and monitoring it and maintaining it can require an even larger time commitment. When designing security policies and procedures, it is important to consider the resources that will be necessary to implement, monitor, and enforce them.

Security Policy Snap-Ins

The security tools for Windows Server 2003 do not introduce new conceptual or technological advancements to PKI, group policies, or the Active Directory, but instead offer a convenient and uniform way to distribute these features. The Security Configuration and Analysis and Security Template snap-ins are the two main components of the Microsoft Security Configuration Tool Set. They configure, analyze, and distribute a subset of the Security Settings portion of the Group Policy tree. These settings include:

- *Account Policies* include passwords, system lockouts, and Kerberos policy settings.

- *Local Policies* include user rights and security events.
- *Event Log* permits review of events that could show a compromise of security.
- *Restricted Groups* provide added security for default Windows Server 2003 groups with predefined functions, such as the Administrators group.
- *System Services* manage local system services security.
- *Registry* sets local Registry key data permissions.
- *File System* sets local file system permissions.

NOTE The Security Template snap-in does not provide a direct means for viewing and modifying public key policies and IP security policies. Rather, these policies must be set or imported from the **Default Domain** snap-in → **Windows Settings** → **Security Settings** → **IP Securities Policies on Active Directory** or **IP Security Policies**, respectively.

It's also important to remember that the Local/Remote Computer Policy snap-in includes only the Account Policies and the Local Policies from the above list.

In addition to distributing consistent security configurations, the tools can analyze security settings and graphically display differences between current and intended settings.

USING SECURITY TEMPLATE SNAP-INS

Group policies are used to apply security templates to designated user and computer accounts. Local Computer Policies can also apply security templates, but only local settings and account policies are affected by them. Security templates make the system administrator's job easier by allowing her to create templates that may then be distributed using group policies across a site, domain, organization unit, user group, or even individual users. They are ASCII files whose names have .inf extensions that can be modified with a text editor. All security templates can be found in the %SystemRoot%security\templates*.inf directory.

CAUTION It is possible to copy, paste, and otherwise modify the .inf files directly as text files within a tool such as Notepad. However, this is not recommended. The Security Template snap-in should be used to create and modify Windows Server 2003 security templates. Copying part of a template within the Security Templates snap-in and pasting it into another template is less risky. Again, use extreme caution.

The Security Templates snap-in, as seen in Figure 11.1, comes with nine predefined templates. These are divided into a *default* template and *incremental* templates.

The default template, **setup security.inf**, is designed to establish a baseline configuration for the system's **Security Settings**. When Windows Server 2003 is initially installed on a clean NTFS partition, the local computer policy should be similar to the setup security*.inf template. If the system is upgraded from Windows NT 4.0, no security settings are applied; the security settings from the previous environment are not overwritten. The default or setup security*.inf template can be used to set a baseline for the upgraded system or for existing installations to match the suggested settings.

The incremental templates (Table 11.1) are meant to overlay or "apply on top of" the current settings to provide the additional security measures implied by their names.

NOTE These templates modify Registry values in addition to setting permissions on the local Registry. There is nothing to stop someone with Read/Write permission from modifying the ASCII .inf templates using an editor and changing Registry parameters outside the scope of Security Settings. That is why the templates must be protected from abuse.

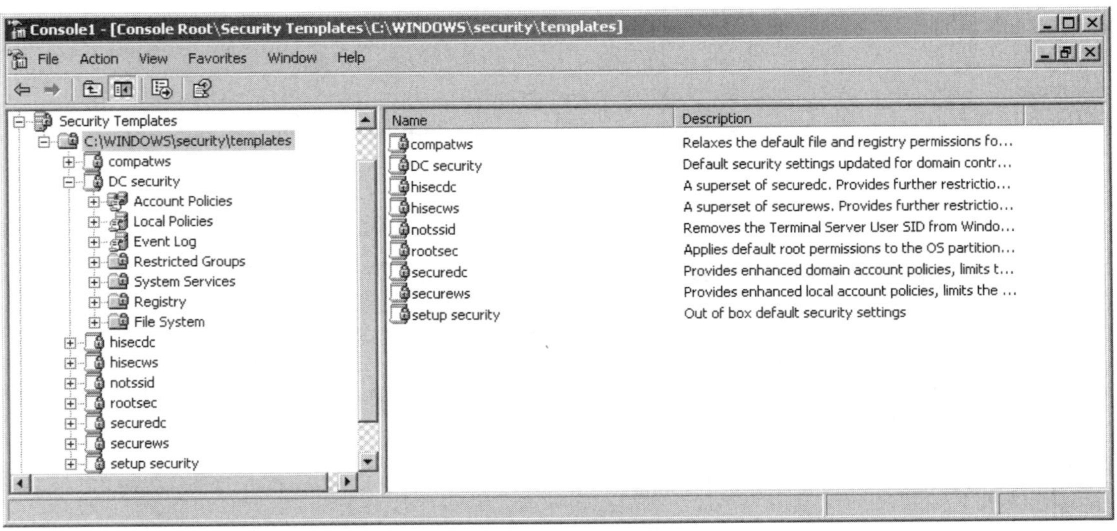

FIGURE 11.1 Building a Custom Template

TABLE 11.1 Incremental Security Templates

Incremental Template	Description
Compatws.inf	Contains the Power Users group without members, which removes all users from that group. The Users group is granted more file system and Registry privileges so that Windows NT 4.0 and other users of earlier systems may run applications on the server.
DC security	Additional security settings applied when a system is promoted to a domain controller.
Rootsec.inf	Sets permissions on the root file system defined by Windows XP. If permissions on the root directory are changed, reapply this template.
Notssid.inf	Removes Terminal Server user SIDs.
Securedc.inf	Imposes stricter Account Policies, Local Policies, and Event Log settings than the default settings. Digital signing and secure channels are requested when possible. Down-level communication with Windows 9x/NT 4.0 Service Pack 4 or higher is possible.
Securews.inf	Same as Securedc.inf except that all users are removed from the Power Users group with the Restricted Groups settings.
Hisecdc.inf	Enables secure channel and digital signing for all communications. Disables NTLM and LM authentication (allows only Kerberos authentication) and all drivers must be signed. All communication is encrypted and authenticated at the highest level possible. Systems configured with this template will not be able to communicate with systems that do not run Windows Server 2003 (Windows 9x/NT 4.0).
Hisecws.inf	Same as Hisecdc.inf except that all users are removed from the Power Users group with the Restricted Groups settings.
Setup security.inf	Saves the original machine configuration after installation.

BUILDING A CUSTOM TEMPLATE

The Security Templates snap-in is handy for viewing template settings, but its *true* purpose is to create custom templates. There are two methods for building a custom template: An existing template can be selected, modified, and then saved as another template; or a completely new template can be created.

Modifying an Existing Template

Creating a new template by using an existing one involves modifying the existing one and saving it under a different name. To do this, follow these steps:

1. Open the MMC **Security Templates** snap-in.
2. Right-click the desired template and select **Save As** from the menu.
3. Enter a new template name and **Save**.
4. Open the new template node and modify settings as needed.
5. Right-click the template node and select **Save** unless it is dimmed. In this case, it is already saved.

Building a New Template

To create a new security template, take the following steps:

1. Open the MMC **Security Templates** snap-in.
2. Open **Security Templates** and right-click the templates directory icon.
3. Select **New Template** from the menu.
4. Enter the file name for the template and **Open** it.
5. Modify the template settings just as the Security Settings for Group Policy Objects (GPOs) are modified.
6. Right-click the template node and select **Save** unless it is dimmed. In this case, it is already saved.

The Security Configuration and Analysis Tool

Analysis of security is a fundamental responsibility of the system administrator. The Security Configuration and Analysis (SCA) snap-in tool is designed to assist in this. Fine-tuning of security is accomplished through regular analysis.

The Security Configuration and Analysis snap-in tool is primarily used to analyze or compare the current computer settings to a personal database and thus view potential discrepancies in the security landscape. It can also be used to configure the local system to match the personal database security settings and to layer templates and produce custom templates for later distribution. All of this is done preferably through a GPO.

Custom security templates are built by layering template upon template to produce security settings. For example, to configure a highly secure domain controller, the basicdc, securedc, and the hisecdc templates would all be applied to the server. Templates can be applied using GPOs, as we saw in the discussion of the Security Settings Extension; or they can be applied with a personal settings database via the Security Configuration and Analysis tool. Importing security templates into GPOs is discussed in Chapter 8, "Group Policies." Note that when GPOs import a template into Security Settings, the enabled settings overwrite previous configurations.

Security templates may be layered to configure high security status, for example, using the Security Configuration and Analysis tool to build a custom template that accumulates all settings from three separate templates. Using GPOs to layer templates and distribute security settings is the method of choice whenever the Active Directory is implemented, but for standalone systems the SCA should be used. The Local Computer Policy snap-in does not allow configuration of the Event Log, Restricted Groups, System Services, Registry, or File System policies.

USING THE SECURITY CONFIGURATION AND ANALYSIS SNAP-IN

There are distinct uses for the SCA snap-in, as its name implies: configuration and analysis. A quick examination of how to use each is appropriate.

Using SCA to Configure Security

Let's demonstrate how the SCA tool can be used to build a highly secure custom template for a domain controller. First, the custom template is created, and then the SCA tool is used to analyze or compare current computer settings with the template settings. Finally, the custom template is used to manually configure the current computer settings. Again, *this last step is necessary only on systems without Active Directory support*. The following specific steps are invoked:

1. Add the **Security Configuration and Analysis (SCA)** tool to a custom console.
2. Right-click the **SCA** snap-in and select **Open database** (Figure 11.2).

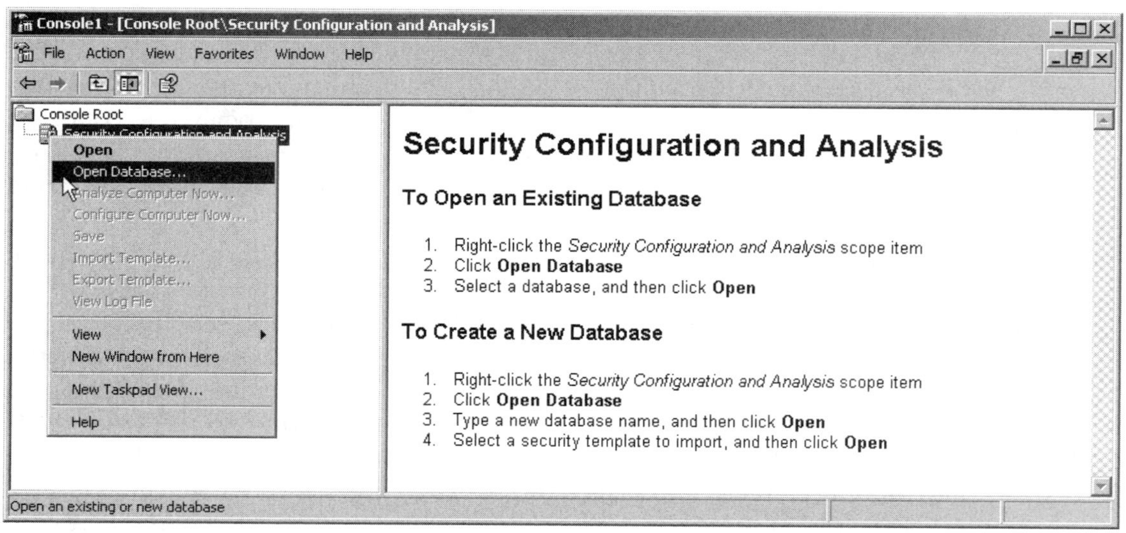

FIGURE 11.2 The Security Template Database

3. Enter the name **Custom High Sec DC.dbd** for the database and click **Open**.
4. Select the **setup security.inf** template from the **Import Template** dialog.
5. Check the Clear this database before importing and click Open. (Figure 11.3).

Repeat steps 1 through 4 for the securedc.inf and hisecdc.inf templates. At this point you have successfully laid three templates on top of each other in an incremental fashion in the Custom High Sec DC database. As a precaution, you must run an analysis on the database before you can export the new template.

1. Right-click the **SCA** snap-in and select **Analyze Computer Now**.
2. Click **OK** to the **Error log file path** dialog box.
3. Wait as the tool compares the current computer settings with the newly created ones.
4. Verify the output of the log to make sure that everything is correct.
5. Right-click the **SCA** snap-in and select **Export Template**.
6. Enter the name **Custom High Sec DC.inf** for the template name and click **Save**.
7. Right-click the **%SystemRoot%\Security\Templates** node below the **Security Templates** snap-in and select **Refresh**. The new template should be displayed among the standard templates.

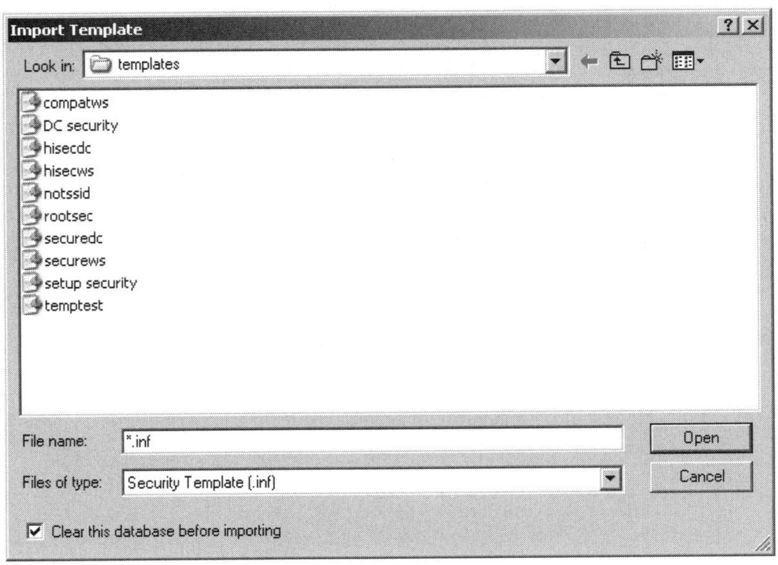

FIGURE 11.3 Import Templates

Under the Security Configuration and Analysis snap-in the **Security Settings** nodes are displayed. Select the **Local Policies → Security Options** node. In the details pane, the **Database Settings** are compared to the **Computer Settings**, as shown in Figure 11.4. Common policy settings are denoted with a green check mark, and conflicting policy settings are denoted with a red X. If either the database policy or the computer setting is not defined, the policy is not marked.

To map the current database settings onto the local system:

1. Right-click the **SCA** snap-in and select **Configure Computer Now**.
2. Click **OK** to the **Error log file path** dialog box.
3. Wait as the tool updates the current computer settings with the database settings.

The local system is now configured with the high security settings. To put the system in its original state, reload the Setup Security template into a database and configure the system with the new database.

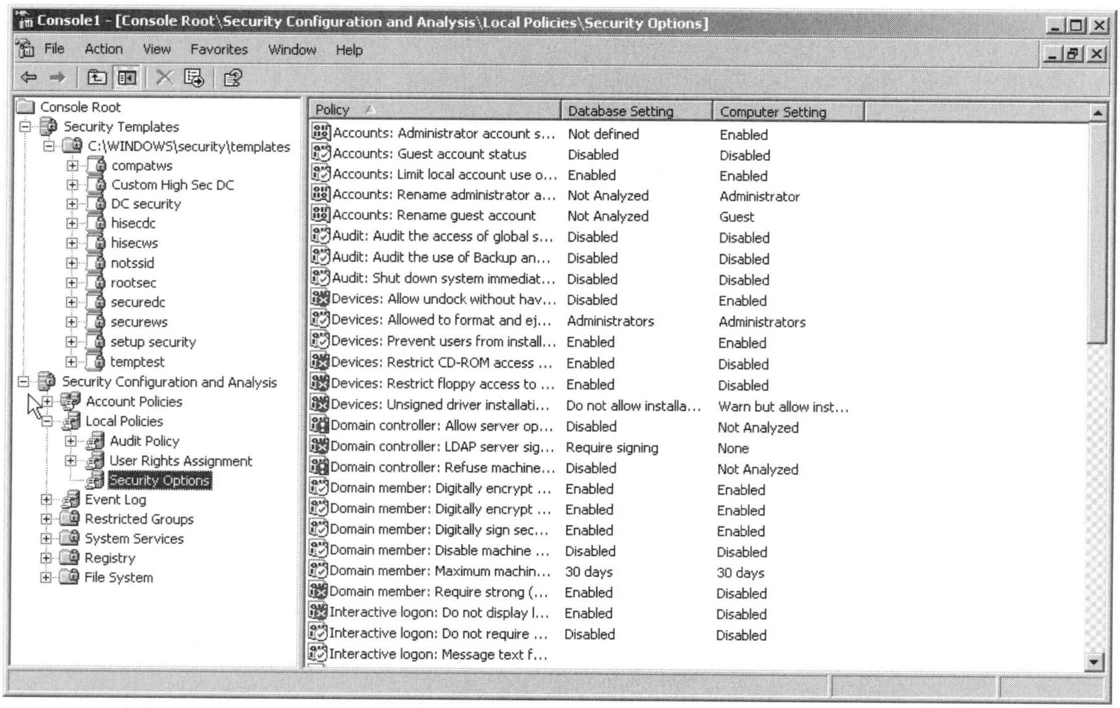

FIGURE 11.4 Security Options from the SCA Snap-In

Analyzing Security

Security analysis involves several steps. The following should be invoked to conduct analysis:

1. Open the **Security Configuration and Analysis** snap-in.
2. Right-click **Security Configuration and Analysis** → click **Open database**.
3. Select an existing database, or create a new personal database by typing in a new file name → click **Open**.
4. Import one or more security templates by right-clicking **Security Configuration and Analysis** → **Open** the working database.
5. Select **Import Template**.
6. Select a template file and click **Open**.
7. Repeat the last step for every template that is to be merged into the database.
8. Perform a security analysis by right-clicking **Security Configuration and Analysis** → click **Analyze System Now**.
9. Click **OK** to use the default analysis log.
10. Review analysis results by right-clicking **Security Configuration and Analysis** → select the security **Lockout Policy** or **Password Policy**.
11. The right pane provides a number of columns, including **Attribute** for the analysis results, **Database Setting** for the security value, and **Analyzed System Setting** for the current security level. If a red X is displayed, inconsistencies exist between the current settings and the base configuration. A green check mark indicates consistency. If no icon appears, that attribute was not set and therefore was not analyzed.
12. Resolve any discrepancies revealed by analysis by accepting or changing some or all of the values flagged → select **Configure System Now**.
13. Repeat the import process and load multiple templates.
14. Once the templates are imported, select **Configure System Now**.

NOTE The **secedit** command can be run from scripts to apply security settings to many computers. It can also be used to force the policy refresh throughout the domain.

NOTE Security policies are applied with the same inheritance precedence as for any other policy. Windows Server 2003 follows the LSDOU model, in which inheritance order flows as follows: **Local Computer (L)** → **Site (S)** → **Domain (D)** → **Organizational Unit (OU)**.

SECURITY AUTHORIZATION MANAGER

Windows Server 2003 includes a roles-based model for authorization designed to simplify administration and development of business process applications. These new functions are available from a MMC snap-in called Authorization Manager. To make the assignment of security more user-friendly and logical, the Authorization Manager permits the definition of common tasks and assignment of tasks to a user's real-life role. For example, managers at certain levels will be authorized according to their positions. The rules can also be associated with scope of responsibility. Access policy is specified, adjusted, and queried within a scope. This should eliminate the need to look at each object in order to ascertain the policy. This feature complements the access control list.

WINDOWS SERVER 2003 SYSTEM LOCKDOWN

Securing the Windows Server 2003 system involves concentrating on a number of possible problem areas. These issues, which are internal to the enterprise and well within the scope of the system administrator's responsibility, include the following:

- User account security
- Proper password management
- Registry and file system lockdown
- Protection of network shares
- Trojan horses and virus control
- Environmental settings
- Removal of services that are not required
- RAS security
- Backup and restoration
- Physical security lockdown
- Dual-booting of multiple operating systems

User Account Security

A hacker's primary method of gaining unauthorized access is through user accounts. The system administrator is directly responsible for maintaining user account accountability and securing the enterprise against improper account usage. The three user accounts that might be the most vulnerable are Administrator, Backup Operators, and Guest.

THE ADMINISTRATOR ACCOUNT

Providing an unauthorized user access to the Administrator account is comparable to giving away the keys to the castle. The Administrator account cannot be removed or locked out. Moreover, it permits an unlimited number of logon attempts so that multiple logons cannot be used to automatically deny the administrator access. Last, it allows a cracker plenty of opportunities to figure out the administrator's password. A number of precautions that can be implemented as a minimum safeguard against assaults are described in the following paragraphs.

The Administrator account should always be associated with a cryptic password that is generally too complicated to be remembered easily. This password should not be confused with the one used by the system administrator who belongs to the Administrators group. The use of the primary Administrator account logon should be limited to extreme situations. System administrators should always log on under their own accounts. As members of respective Administrators groups, they will be able to conduct appropriate support activity under that logon. In theory, a hacker knows that there is always an Administrator account, but he or she is less likely to know the logon names of individual members of the Administrators group.

Alternatively, create a new account and add it to the Domain Admins global group. Only highly trusted system administrators should know its name and password. This account should be used for administrative duties. If each highly trusted administrator has her own account, a rogue administrator account can lock out the other accounts. However, an audit trail will more easily track individual patterns.

What makes a good password? It is easier to define a bad one. That would be your name or anyone's name, any word in the dictionary, your license plate, your phone number, or your social security number, all of which can be guessed by social engineering or can be quickly discovered via a cracking program. An example of a good password is a nonsense phrase—for example, "I like to sip soda in my sneakers." Use the first character of each word, mix some letters with numbers, and add punctuation. It now becomes Il2ss!mS, which is not too hard to remember and very difficult to guess or crack. Of course, this particular password is now bad, since it has been published.

The Domain Administrator account password should be written down and physically protected in a safe place, under lock and key. Again, it should be employed for emergency system restoration, not daily use. This password will be replicated to all domain controllers. It can also be retrieved if the administrator is unavailable or incapacitated for some reason.

The same strategy should be implemented for all local Administrator accounts as well. A different cryptic password should be assigned to each local Administrator account for a site and written down and stored in a safe place. If the physical security of one workstation is compromised, there is a chance the Local Administrator password can be recovered from the file system. The Domain Administrator account should remain protected.

NOTE The suggestion to write down the Administrator account password and store it in a safe place is contrary to what a system administrator should tell a normal user. It is based on the assumption that the administrator will exercise extreme caution in securing it. However, a user should never write down his password, because it is simply too easy for someone to "eye" it in a normal work environment. Instead, since it will be used on a regular basis, the user should be required to retain it mentally. If for some reason the password is forgotten, the system administrator can reset it with little effort. As an added precaution, place the Administrator password in a sealed envelope. If the seal is broken, immediately change the password and reseal the envelope.

NOTE Passwords are used to generate a cryptographic key known as a hash. Even though only the hash of an account's password is stored in the KDC or SAM database, earlier hash algorithms are well known. This is particularly true for the down-level Windows NT 4.0 NTLMv1 hash algorithm. There are crack applications available to determine the account password through brute force. However, Kerberos and NTLMv2, supported on Windows NT 4.0 Service Pack 4 or greater, have much stronger hash-generating algorithms. In addition, disabling the Windows Server Store password by using reversible encryption for all users in domain password policy will make reading the hash very difficult. This can be accomplished by opening the **Default Domain Policy** snap-in → select **Windows Settings → Security Settings → Account Policies → Password Policies**. Double-click **Store password using reversible encryption** from the right panel. In the dialog box, select **Enable** or **Disable** and click **OK**. *One-way encryption is generally stronger. Therefore, we recommend that you disable this feature.* With Windows Server 2003, an administrator can also increase the password security level through the Registry editor using the following key:

```
HKEY_LOCAL_MACHINE\SYSTEM\CurrentControlSet\Control\Lsa, add NoLmHash
value
```

NOTE New to Windows Server 2003 is support for the new NIST Hash Algorithms (FIPS 180-2 and PKCS #1). This feature supports the new National Institute of Standards and Technology (NIST) hashing algorithms, which are part of the latest drafts of

Federal Information Processing Standard (FIPS 180-2) and PKCS 1. The new hashes are included in the Advanced Encryption Standard (AES) RSA Full Cryptographic Service Provider. Public Key Cryptography Standards (PKCS) 1 recommends use of these new hash algorithms for newly developed applications. This feature is integral to the operating system and requires no administrative intervention.

NOTE Another new feature of Windows Server 2003 is support for the FIPS Kernel-Mode Crypto Module that is integral to the operating system. It runs as a driver in kernel mode and implements the cryptographic algorithms approved by FIPS. The kernel driver will go through testing so it can be on the list of FIPS 140-1 Level 1 certified cryptographic modules. The supported algorithms include Secure Hash Algorithm-1 (SHA-1), Digital Encryption Standard (DES), 3DES, and an approved random number generator. It is designed specifically to enable government sectors to deploy Internet Protocol Security that is compliant with FIPS 140-1.

BACKUP OPERATORS

The Default Domain Controllers Policy GPO gives both the Administrators and Backup Operators groups the right to *back up and restore files and directories* by default. This means that the Backup Operators can overwrite the file system regardless of assigned permissions. Two actions can be taken to minimize this problem:

- Use the Backup Operators group sparingly and assign only the most trusted persons to it.
- Remove these user right policies on all systems that do not require domain-level backup privileges.

GUEST ACCOUNT

The Guest account has significantly changed from Windows NT to Windows Server 2003. In Windows NT, it was a convenience to support Web servers and other applications that must run without user authentication. Thus, it had access to all objects with permissions assigned to the Everyone group, and as a result directories like %SystemRoot%System32 were wide open to destruction from it. Windows Server 2003 has a new built-in local group known as Authenticated Users, which is responsible for assigning permissions to users who previously belonged to Everyone. The Everyone group is specifically assigned to most objects with no permissions whatsoever. This has the effect of restricting Guest account privileges. To avoid the problems inherent in the Windows NT Guest account, use the Everyone group, which is disabled by default, very sparingly.

Password Policies

As previously underscored, passwords represent one of the basic areas of security vulnerability. Since password policies can minimize abuses, we highly recommend establishing them.

DOMAIN PASSWORD POLICIES

Password lockdown is accomplished differently when working with domains and local system accounts. Password and account lockout policies should reflect the settings within the securews.inf (for secure workstations) and securedc.inf (for domain controllers) templates. Security templates are used to establish a standard set of policies that can be used repeatedly. For a quick visual inspection, the Security Template snap-in and Default Domain Policy snap-in can be used to rapidly compare template settings against those currently in use. An in-depth comparison can be achieved with the Security Configuration and Analysis snap-in. Refer to Chapter 8, "Group Policies," for information about using and applying policies.

Table 11.3 outlines the password policies that apply to both domain and local computer passwords. To change or view domain password policies, open the MMC **Default Domain Policy** snap-in → select **Computer Configuration → Windows Settings → Account Policy**. Double-click **Password Policy**. Select each listed policy and make the appropriate changes.

TABLE 11.3 Password Policy Options for Domains and Local Computers

Policy	Computer Setting	Description
Enforce Password History Remembered	6 passwords	User's previous six passwords are remembered to prevent reuse.
Maximum Password Age	42 days	Password must be changed by the maximum age.
Minimum Password Length	8 characters	
Passwords Must Meet Password Filter Requirements	Enabled	Microsoft, third-party, or self-created password filter may be used.
Store Password Using Reversible Encryption for All Users in Domain	Disabled	
User Must Log On to Change the Password	Disabled	

PASSWORD LOCKOUT POLICIES

Password lockout policies minimize a hacker's ability to discover a logon name and password. The policies should be liberal enough to permit a user with "sloppy" typing skills to make several attempts at a successful logon but sufficiently tight to frustrate an attacker.

There are three lockout policies (Table 11.4):

- *Account Lockout Counter* establishes the number of unsuccessful logon attempts that will be permitted prior to a lockout. Although there will always be an authorized user who will repeatedly fail, five attempts is a reasonable number.
- *Account Lockout Duration* establishes the period of time in which the lockout will be enforced, after which the system is unlocked and new logon attempts will be recognized. A reasonable time is 30 minutes.
- *Reset Lockout Counter* resets the lockout attempt counter in the period designated. Again, 30 minutes is reasonable.

These policies are available from the MMC **Default Domain** snap-in → select **Computer Configuration** → select **Windows Settings** → select **Security Settings** → **Account Policies** → double-click **Account Lockout Policy**. To modify the displayed settings, double-click the targeted policy and make changes in the dialog box that appears.

LOCAL PASSWORD SETTINGS

If local user accounts are established, strict policies for local passwords should be set. The options available for local passwords mirror those of the domain password settings. They can be viewed and set from the **Security Configuration and Analysis** snap-in → select **Account Policies** → double-click **Password Policy**. They may also be viewed from the **Local Computer Policy** snap-in. Select from the listed policies and make the appropriate changes.

TABLE 11.4 Lockout Policy Options

Account Policy	Computer Setting
Account Lockout Counter	5 invalid logon attempts
Account Lockout Duration	30 minutes
Reset Account Lockout Counter after 30 Minutes	30 minutes

DETERMINING WHO SETS A PASSWORD

Windows Server 2003 configuration allows passwords to be established by the end user or the system administrator. The system administrator typically selects the password when it is likely that the user will choose a weak one or the end user is not very sophisticated. The biggest problem with this scenario is that the administrator is likely to create a password that is very difficult to remember, inclining the end user to write it down for easy reference. Although the intent is to strengthen security, the moment a password is written down, security is compromised.

The alternative approach is to have the end user set the password and enforce rules that make password creation unique. Additionally, the user should be forced to change the password periodically.

PASSWORD FILTERING

One method of ensuring that the created password meets the desired level of complexity is password filters. A password may be filtered as suggested, but it must meet the complexity requirements policy.

The password filter installed with Windows Server 2003 may be used or a custom filter may be applied. Installation is accomplished by modifying the HKEY_LOCAL_MACHINE\SYSTEM\CurrentControlSet\Control\Lsa Registry key and adding the file name with .dll extension to the string list. The *.dll filter should be placed in the %SystemRoot%\system32 folder.

OTHER USER ACCOUNT SECURITY OPTIONS

Windows Server 2003 provides many additional security restriction options for both domain and local users. Describing each of them would require dozens of pages of text, so, since they are fairly obvious, we will point you to them instead. To view and modify these options, open the **Default Domain** snap-in → select **Windows Settings** → select **Security Settings** → select **Local Policies** → select **Security Options**. Double-click the targeted policy and make appropriate changes in the dialog box that is displayed.

Registry and File System Lockdown

Registry and file system permissions are crucial to Windows Server 2003 security. Default security permissions can be viewed from the Security Templates snap-in. The basicdc.inf, basicsv.inf, and basicwk.inf templates are the only ones that modify File System and Registry group policy security settings. A GPO should be used to enforce these default templates and ensure that all users and services are covered by the secure file and Registry settings. These templates also reflect the default file and Registry permissions for all Windows Server installations and are considered secure. The other default templates in the Security Template snap-in are designed to cover other security policy areas.

In addition to manipulating the security templates to reflect the appropriate lockdown levels, administrators should apply these four rules:

- Use NTFS and take advantage of Windows Server 2003 file/folder permissions, auditing, and file encryption.
- Do not place sensitive information or system files on a FAT partition. There are no file/folder permissions for local access on a FAT file system.
- Remember that the file owner always maintains full control over the object. Even if the administrator denies the owner all permissions, the owner can still view and modify security settings.
- When auditing file systems, never neglect the file owner.

NOTE Windows Server 2003 prevents file thumbnails from being placed in exposed directories when a user modifies ACLs or encrypts the file.

Trojan Horses and Viruses

One of the biggest security threats to your network is unauthorized scripts, applications, DLLs, applets, ActiveX, and any other code component that can run on the operating system. These components perform processes that can destroy system operation and data. The concept of the Trojan horse derives from the ancient tale of the battle of Troy, when Greek soldiers passed the Trojan barriers by hiding inside a giant wooden horse that they offered as a gift to Troy. That event created the saying "Beware of Greeks bearing gifts," but it might be better stated today as "Beware of geeks bearing unknown code." What might appear harmless could create significant losses.

Software components constructed by hostile individuals are generally imported through e-mail, FTP, or Web services, or are internally created and distributed within your network. Once a hostile component is strategically placed on a system, the "Trojan horse" waits to be executed by the user. All processes started during a user's session will run with that user's security token. Thus, when a user inadvertently runs a hostile component, that hostile component assumes all of his rights and privileges. Additionally, the process will assign the user's default discretionary ACL to newly created objects, enabling the hostile component to create new elements with permission settings equal to the rightful user's.

If a hostile individual is able to place the component on the user's machine in the first place, she obviously has some level of access (or the user downloaded the component from the Web). This security threat is also probably looking for a way to improve its current access rights, and the administrator's account is its most promising target.

There are a number of defensive practices you can employ against Trojan horses and viruses, including the following:

- Never run applications under the Administrator account.
- Use auditing and scripts to search for components in suspect directories.
- Ensure that environmental parameters are set correctly, as discussed in the next section.
- Don't run software from unknown sources, and use up-to-date antivirus software.

Environmental Path Settings

Path security is all too often overlooked. Most applications started from the command window and from the desktop use environmental parameters to determine common directory locations and system information. The PATH variable determines a logical search path direction through directories (or folders) to find a given component. If a hacker knows the exact location of a component, he can gain access to an object even without permission to the folder. This may take skill, but Chapter 8 discusses how to use absolute paths to override folder permissions. The system administrator should ensure that only the intended directories are included in the PATH variable. These variables can be viewed from **Control Panel → System → Advanced tab → Environmental Variables**. They can also be viewed by typing **path** at the command prompt.

Environmental variables (illustrated in Figure 11.5) are applied in order from the following sources:

- *Autoexec.bat* (tightly restrict access)—first modifies environmental parameters.
- *System environment*—only administrators modify further parameters.
- *User environment*—final modification to environmental parameters can be done by the user.

CURRENT WORKING DIRECTORY SECURITY RESOURCE

A misguided user could be the source of real problems stemming from within his or her current working directory. The default working directory is defined in the user's account properties and is otherwise known as the home directory. If a cracker has somehow broken into a user's account, some level of risk exists. The current working directory is searched in addition to the directories specified in the PATH

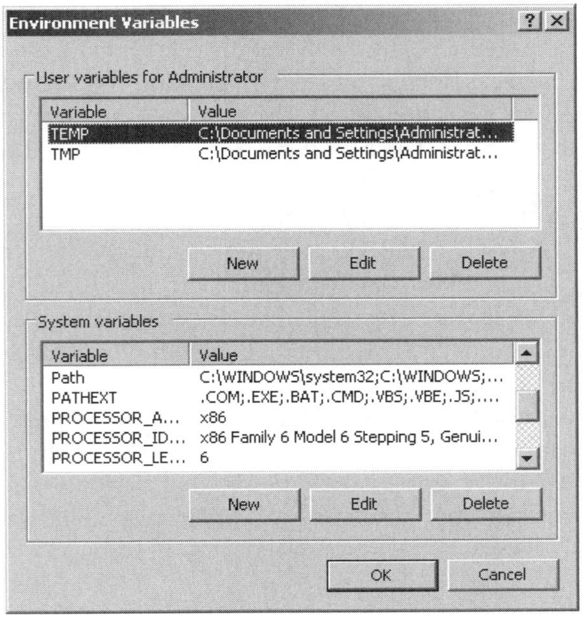

FIGURE 11.5 Environmental Variables

variable. A cracker may place executables in the working directory that replace the intended system calls. Thus, if an application is run from a directory other than the system or program directory, a rewritten .dll impostor may be executed rather than the intended one. This .dll may perform the same tasks as the intended code in addition to providing the cracker access to the system at the user's privilege level. If this happens from an ordinary user's account, the resulting problems will ordinarily be restricted to that account. However, if it happens from an administrator's account, the entire system and perhaps the domain could be damaged. Obviously, this can lead to problems when users, and especially administrators, execute applications from directories that are not secure. To prevent working directory mishaps, the following commonsense steps should be enforced:

- Designate application directories and tightly configure permissions.
- Regularly search the system for .dll files that are not located in the %SystemRoot%, Program Files, or other designated application directories.
- Look for any type of executable created by unauthorized users.

EXTENSION MAPPING TO DISGUISE A FILE TYPE

Windows Server 2003 associates a file name extension with a particular application. When a file from **Explorer** or **My Computer** is opened, it is graphically displayed with the associated application's icon. Changing this mapping is very simple and can render the file nonexecutable. It is achieved by selecting it from the **Explorer** or **My Computer** window, selecting a file, right-clicking the **Properties** option, and clicking **Change**. This does not change the format of the file, but simply alters the **Open With** application list. The best defense is to encourage users to restrict their use of this facility.

A more serious problem can occur if the Registry is somehow violated. The HKEY_LOCAL_MACHINE\SOFTWARE\Classes key stores specific information on the application that is launched with each file extension. With Regedit or Regedit32, it is possible to remap a plain text file (.txt) extension, for example, to any application available in the system. Let's assume that someone has loaded a malignant program that removes all files in the current working directory. Further, through access to the Administrator account, the Registry had been changed so that all .txt extension files are mapped to this damaging program. The obvious effect is that the next time anyone launches a text file, all files in that current working directory will be lost. This is just another reason to guard against unauthorized Registry modification.

SPOOFING SHORTCUTS

Desktop shortcuts are used to streamline access to an application or file. If access is somehow granted to the shortcuts on a user's desktop, it is possible to change the properties and direct the shortcut to another file or application. In the case of a system administrator, a malicious internal user or hacker could direct a shortcut to a damaging virus or Trojan horse. While the administrator believes that he or she is executing a normal application, the shortcut is spoofing the reality of its redirection. This possibility again underscores the need for users not to leave their desktops unprotected.

Extraneous Services as a Security Threat

Common sense dictates that the more services on a server, the greater the opportunities for attack. Thus, a minimalist approach to system administration can be a positive security action. Remove unneeded services and applications from all systems. For instance, some unused subsystems may not have known security holes as yet but without careful monitoring may leave the system vulnerable.

In most environments, for example, the POSIX and OS/2 subsystems serve little or no value. (This statement does not apply if the Interix UNIX 95 environment is used in place of the standard POSIX subsystem.) However, because they communicate with the Windows Server 2003 executive mode, they can create a program or command that does significant damage. Therefore, unless a clear requirement exists, remove the POSIX and OS/2 subsystems by using the Registry Editor to remove the strings "OS/2" and "POSIX" from the Registry key. The modification should be made on the Registry tree level HKEY_LOCAL_MACHINE\System\CurrentControlSet\Control\Session Manager\Subsystems \Optional.

Backups and Restoration Security

Data integrity is not commonly viewed as a security issue, but maintaining system and data backup is fundamental. Securing valuable information through regular backups is the best defense against a disaster, a runaway virus, or a hack job. In Chapter 13 we elaborate on backup and restoration methods in Windows Server 2003

When implementing a backup policy, don't forget to also secure the backup media. For example, if you regularly back up critical data files and then tuck media away in an unsecured desk drawer, you are inviting theft. At a minimum, store backup media in a secure environment. We also recommend that a second set of backup media be periodically archived in a secure remote location.

Physical Security

The importance of physical security cannot be understated; it ranges from issues of outright theft of a system or key storage component to intervention with the boot drive during startup. Let's consider several common scenarios that threaten physical security.

THEFT OF SYSTEMS OR STORAGE MEDIA

At a minimum, efforts must be taken to physically lock down domain controllers and member servers. As powerful systems come in lighter and more portable packages, the ability to take important services out the door without detection becomes increasingly easy.

Theft of critical media is just as easy. If unmonitored access is provided to a critical system like a domain controller, it is really no effort to open the cover and pull a hard drive. Your physical data can be out the door and in the hands of a hacker in just a few minutes.

PHYSICAL ACCESS TO THE BOOT CD-ROM AND FLOPPY DRIVES

Let's consider another hardware-based scenario. Physical access to a floppy drive or CD-ROM on a domain controller or member server during the booting process invites intrusion. For the malicious, it is possible to use boot disks to erase all data or to get system access. With FAT-based Windows Server installations, the boot can also be used to gain direct access to files on the drive. All the invader has to do is abort the install process and revert to a DOS prompt. Even easier is simply booting directly from MS-DOS. Although native-mode NTFS was designed to prevent intrusion, the same type of utilities that plagued Windows NT, such as ntdos.exe, will undoubtedly surface for Windows Server 2003.

General Physical Security Solutions

To prevent this type of serious damage, it is recommended that domain controllers and member servers be physically locked in a server room or, minimally, fitted with locking devices. Also, use passwords to protect BIOS settings, which eliminate floppy disk and CD booting. If the BIOS password is not supplied, settings cannot be modified and thus attempts to boot floppies or CD-ROMs can be denied.

NOTE Many CD-ROMs come with an autorun function, which allows a virus to be executed or copied onto a hard drive without visibility. Turning off this feature is recommended. Using the Registry Editor, move to the HKEY_LOCAL_MACHINE\SYSTEM\CurrentControllerSet\Services\CDROM key. Right-click **Autorun REG_Word** and select **Modify**. Set the value to **0**.

Another commonsense security action is placing critical systems and media in an environment that is not likely to experience water damage. For example, if a pipe breaks over the weekend and results in even a few inches of water, a floor-standing server as well as its data could be damaged.

Dual-Boot Environments

Installing more than one bootable operating system on a machine can breach security. Even NTFS partitions are vulnerable to the Administrator account's being accessed through a secondary operating system. If another operating system is booted, permissions set from the original are useless.

Auditing as a Line of Defense

The Windows Server 2003 audit trail is invaluable. For example, it can determine how a system crashed, how security was compromised, or how much disk space a user is consuming. The OS provides highly granular control over the logged events and the objects and services allowed to record events.

USING SECURITY AUDITING

The Windows Server 2003 auditing properties are viewed and modified through GPOs. The Audit policies found in the Default Domain snap-in via **Computer**

Configuration → Windows Settings → Security Settings → Local Policies → Audit Policy determine what events are recorded in the Security Log. Standard events are shown is Figure 11.6.

The group policies found in the Default Domain snap-in via **Computer Configuration → Windows Settings → Security Settings → Event Log** (Figure 11.7) provide control over a number of properties. This control includes how much disk space is dedicated to the logs, who can access them, how long they are retained, and the method for retaining them.

Event Log Retention

The retention method for a security log configures how the log is updated once it is full. If an overwrite option is not selected, the system will halt when the log is full, whereupon the administrator must take the following steps to enable the system:

1. From the **Start** menu, select **Programs → Administrative Tools → Event Viewer** and save the current logs (if desired). **Clear All Events** from each.
2. Change the Registry key HKEY_LOCAL_MACHINE\SYSTEM\CurrentControlSet\Control\Lsa\crashonauditfail to 1.
3. Restart the system.

OFFLINE AUDITING POLICIES

Reviewing audit reports while offline may prove convenient in some administrative circumstances. Auditing policies for offline folders can be found in the Default Domain snap-in via **User Configuration → Administrative Templates → Network → Offline Files**. See Figure 11.8 for a list of options.

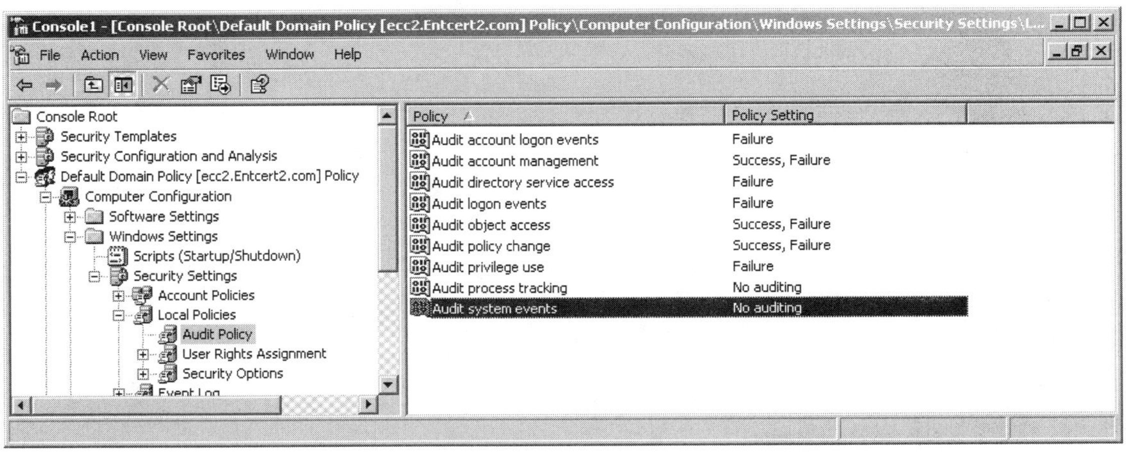

FIGURE 11.6 Possible Logged Events

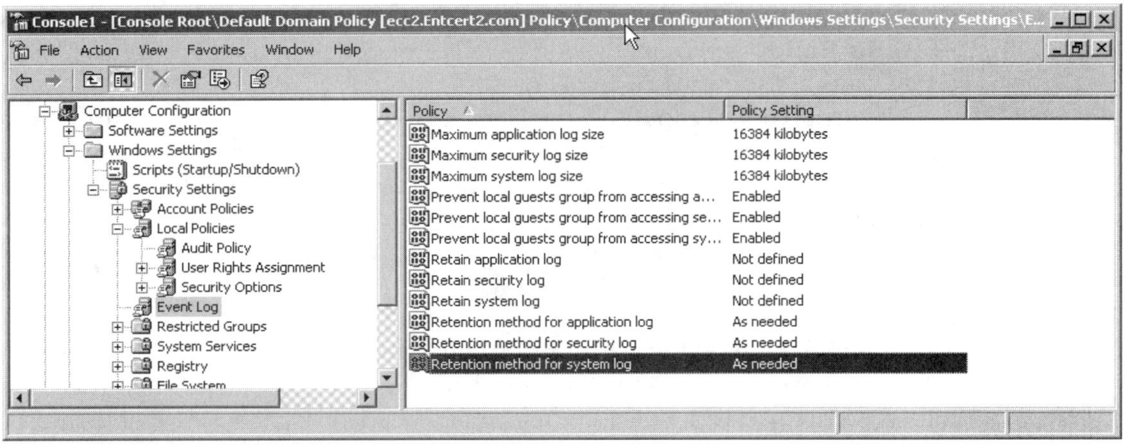

FIGURE 11.7 Settings for Event Logs

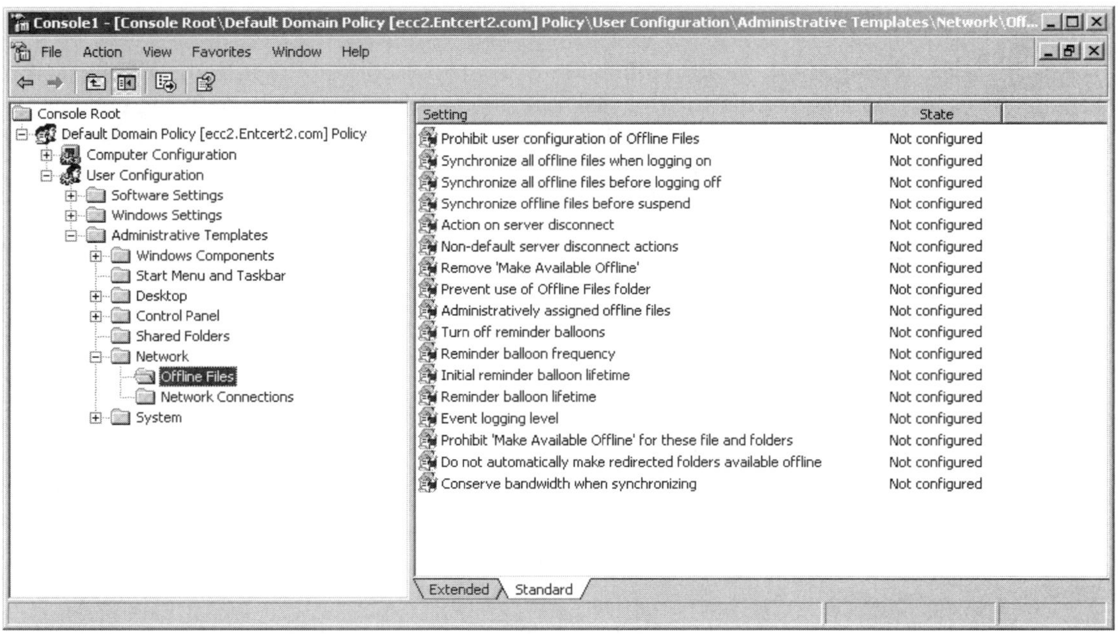

FIGURE 11.8 Offline Auditing Options

EVENT VIEWER USE

The Event Viewer gives the administrator access to six event logs. The Security Log displays successes and failures and classifies them into Object Access, Account Logon, Policy Change, Privilege Use, Directory Service Access, and Account Management categories (Figure 11.9).

The other logs have three types of record—Error, Information, and Warning (Figure 11.10). The Application Log contains events logged from programs running on the system, including all exceptions raised. The System Log records events raised by the Windows Server 2003 operating system (Figure 11.11 on page 505). All users can view the System and Application Logs but only administrators can view the Security Log.

File, folder, printer, Active Directory, group policy, and other system objects have associated access control lists (ACLs). Each ACL is composed of a discretionary access control list (DACL) and a system access control list (SACL). The DACL details user and group access rights to an object (Figure 11.12 on page 506); the SACL determines the users and groups that will be audited when attempting or performing access rights on the object (Figure 11.13 on page 507).

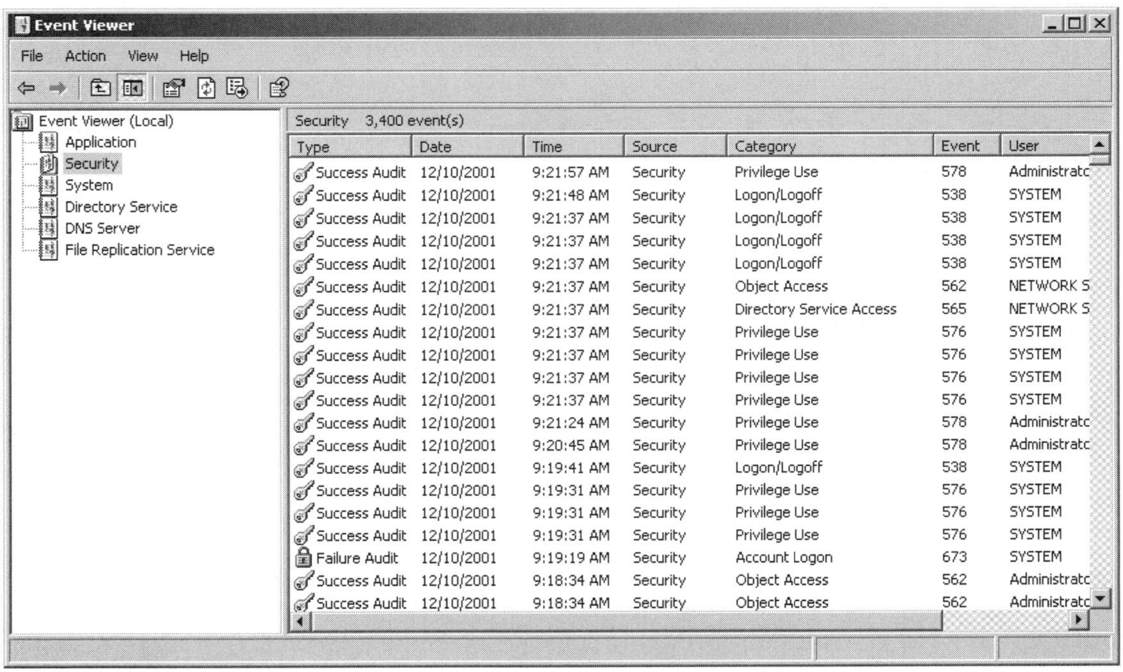

FIGURE 11.9 The Event Viewer Snap-In

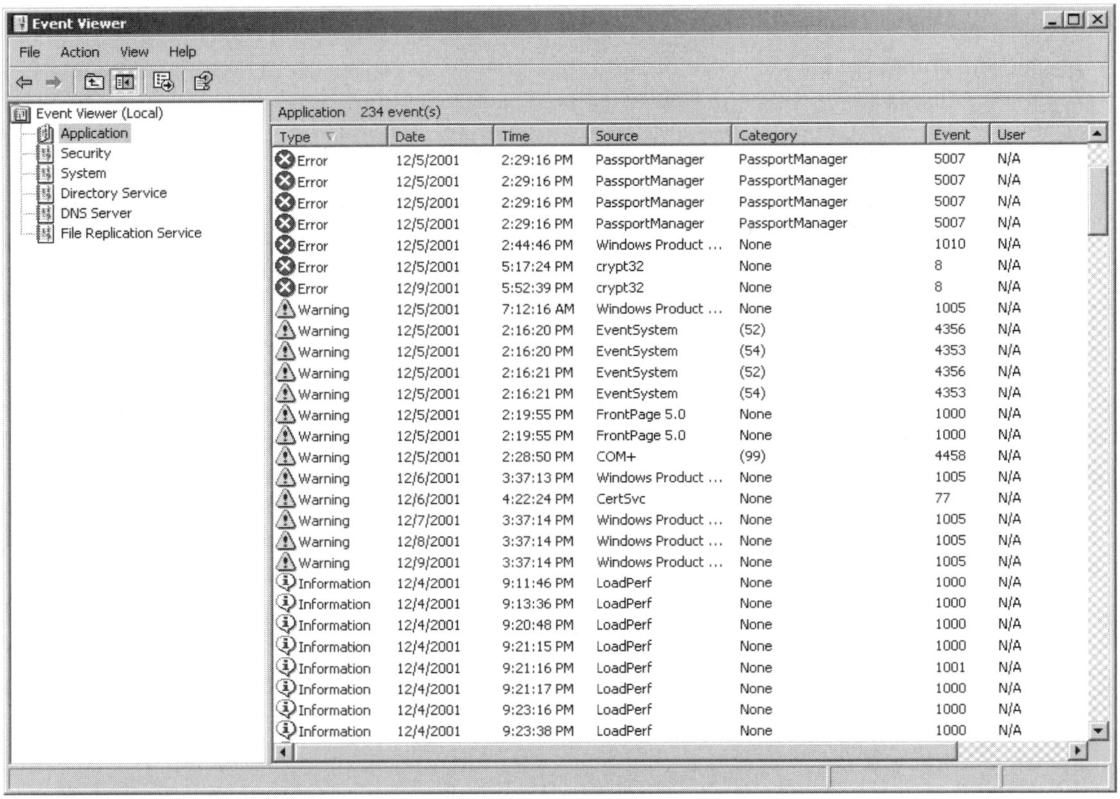

FIGURE 11.10 Log Entry types

GENERAL AUDITING PROCEDURES

The following steps should be observed when using Windows auditing:

1. Set the SACL on objects of interest to identify the group and user access events to monitor.
2. Set auditing policies to record the desired events.
3. Periodically view the logs and clear them out.

NOTE As you establish your auditing strategy, remember that only NTFS files and folders can be audited.

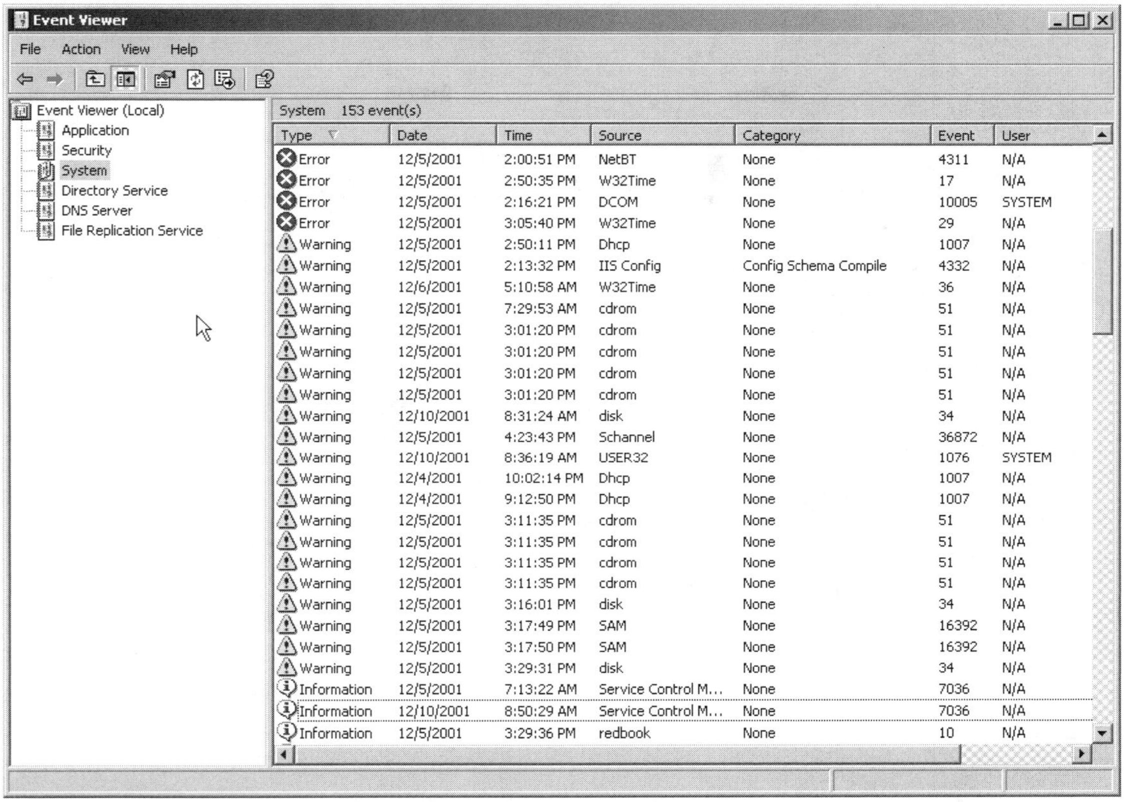

FIGURE 11.11 System Log

AUDIT EVENTS THAT NEED THE MOST CAREFUL REVIEW

No system administrator can track and review all event items, but must restrict her attention to those of greatest importance. As a general rule, audits of the following events are particularly helpful when tracking security threats:

- *Logon/Logoff* provides information on logon failures and may indicate if a certain user account is under attack.
- *Account Management* provides information on users who have sought rights to use administrative tools.
- *Startup/Shutdown* shows who has attempted to invoke a shutdown command and also lists services that were not properly initiated during startup.

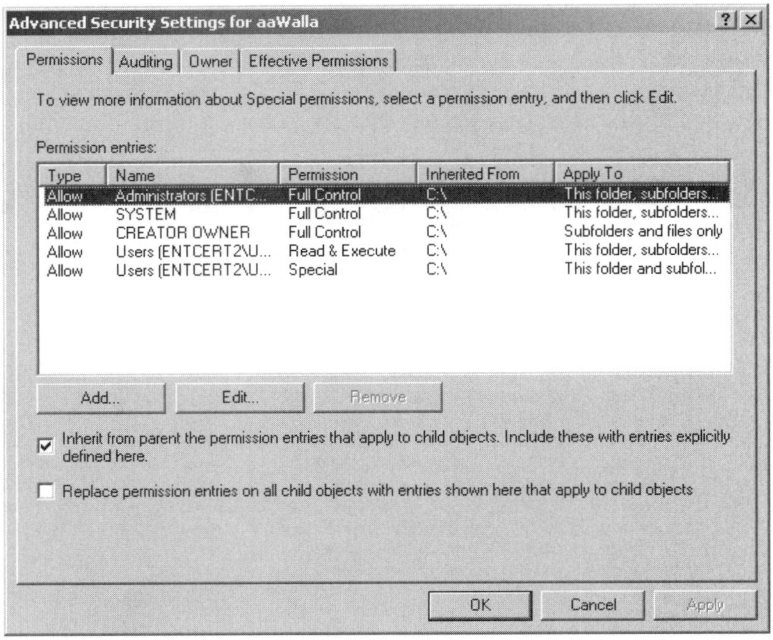

FIGURE 11.12 The Discretionary Access Control List

- *Policy Changes* indicates what policy changes were attempted.
- *Privilege Use* lists attempts to change permissions to objects.

NOTE If a cracker breaks into the system, he will most certainly try to cover his tracks and erase the logs. To guard against this action and retain logs, provide remote logging of the above events to a secure log server that is in a safe place with only local logons, and have critical events printed out to a printer. This will keep the log files intact and help trace security problems.

SECURE NETWORK SERVICES AND ARCHITECTURE

Securing your domain internally is but one aspect of security. The system administrator must also be aware of network security issues. In this section, we explore the need to protect network shares, use firewalls, restrict RAS services, invoke IP security, and use other TCP/IP–based applications safely.

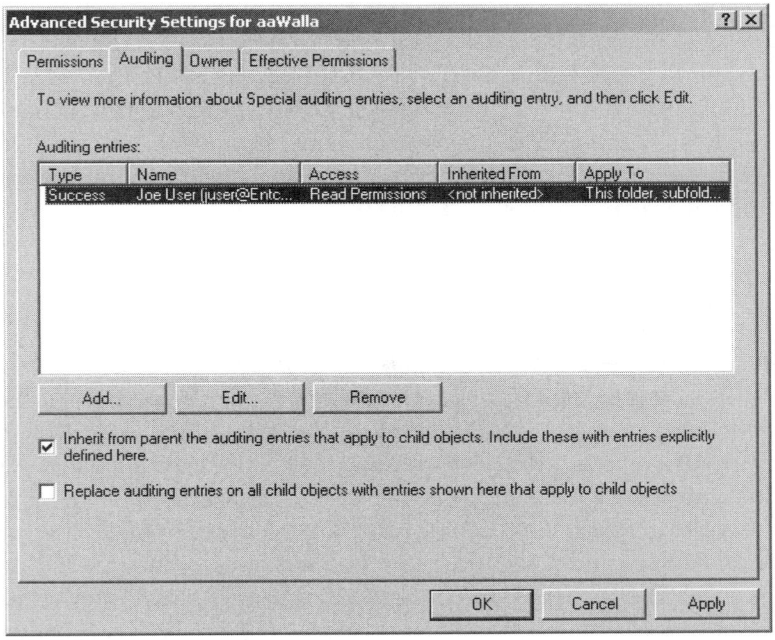

FIGURE 11.13 An Auditing Entry

Protecting Network Shares

Network shares are an important part of the distributed computing environment because they greatly enhance accessibility. However, they also represent a potential security weakness. To minimize problems associated with network shares, keep these administrative concepts in mind:

- The root share determines share permissions for all subdirectories. Subdirectories of a root share cannot be further restricted with share permissions, so NTFS permissions should be used for finer granular control.
- Share permissions restrict only network users, not local users.
- Share names are visible to all users and should not reveal sensitive information or invite an attack.
- Hidden shares can be displayed using the net share command from the command prompt. They should be removed if not in use.

NOTE One way to minimize the risk to hidden administrative shares is to remove them. Using the Registry Editor, set the Registry key HKEY_LOCAL_MACHINE\System\CurrentControlSet\Services\LanManServer\Parameters to 0, which will disable hidden shares C$ and D$ (administrative shares).

However, if you are backing up files using these administrative shares, the 0 setting will prevent you from doing so.

Firewalls

In Internet communications, firewalls are normally established to buffer the intranet from outside attacks. Firewall functions are implemented on packet-forwarding devices, which usually, but not always, have at least two interfaces. They can take the form of a dual-homed host with two interface cards or a piece of network gear known as a router.

A typical firewall configuration (Figure 11.14) consists of an external packet-filtering firewall and a secondary firewall supporting the needed proxy services. The packet-filtering rules are configured to allow external Internet users access to HTTP and FTP services on the company's Web and FTP servers or whatever ports you decide to leave open, including SMTP and RealAudio. Network and transport protocol packets that do not match the packet-filtering rules are dropped. Additional rule sets must be implemented to allow services such as DNS and SMTP to pass from the internal intranet through the packet-filtering firewall to servers on the Internet. Servers located in the zone between the two firewalls, sometimes referred to as the Demilitarized Zone (DMZ), are given dedicated Ethernet segments.

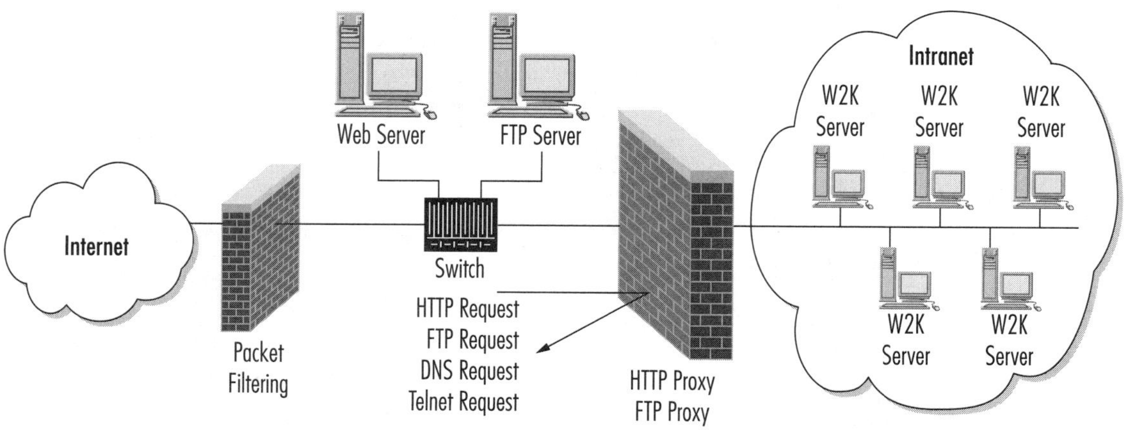

FIGURE 11.14 The Relationship of Firewalls to Intranets and the Internet

If one of them is compromised, a remotely installed network sniffer is prevented from monitoring traffic to the internal network. (This is really dependent on the firewall implementation.) The second firewall proxies Web and FTP services initiated by internal users to the Internet.

The firewall routes packets between interfaces performing packet filtering, stateful inspection, and proxy services. A review of each of these items is appropriate.

PACKET FILTERING

A packet filter is designed to restrict external connections to a limited set of services, protecting the internal network from the Internet. The firewall enforces rules for packet filtering. These rules typically filter protocols, source ports, source addresses, destination ports and destination addresses. Packet rules define connection types that are accepted and those that are rejected. For simplicity and security, it is probably best to establish rules for packets that will be accepted. Everything else is dropped and not forwarded.

Packet filtering occurs mostly at the network and transport protocol levels. If the NetBIOS service ports are not specifically enabled, traffic targeting the NetBIOS services will be blocked from Internet attacks. Attacks using IP source routing can also be stopped by packet filtering.

Packet Filtering Example

The rule set configuration in Table 11.5 allows external clients to access the internal Web server through the packet-filtering router. The rule set allows inbound requests and outbound responses with IP addresses and TCP port settings, as shown in rows A and B in the table. It also allows internal intranet users to connect with external Web servers on the Internet. Packets with destination TCP port = 80 and return TCP port = random number above 1023 are considered inbound HTTP requests from Internet users (row A). In order for the internal Web server to respond to this client connection, the outbound destination TCP port = Random > 1023 and source TCP port = 80 (row B) must be permitted. However, an Internet user who attempts to connect to the intranet using an internal source IP address will not be permitted. Internal IP addresses are forwarded only from the internal to the external interface on the packet filter route.

NOTE The foregoing is a general rule and is by no means absolute. Additionally, a filter may be applied to the incoming or outgoing interface and the ACK bits may be set. Since a cracker can make a request come from any port she wants, you must check the ACK bit in the header to make sure that incoming requests either are to a specific IP address or were already established.

TABLE 11.5 Filtering Example

Line	Source IP Address	Destination IP Address	Source TCP Port Number	Destination TCP Port Number	Description
A	Internet	Intranet	Random > 1023	80	Inbound request
B	Intranet	Internet	80	Random > 1023	Outbound response
C	Internet	Intranet	Random > 1023	80	Outbound request
D	Intranet	Internet	80	Random > 1023	Inbound response

TABLE 11.6 Other Windows Server 2003 Services for Implementing a Packet Filter

UDP Port Number	Description	TCP Port Number	Description
53	Domain Name Service (DNS)	20	FTP Server—data channel
69	Trivial File Transfer Protocol (TFTP)	21	FTP Server—control channel
137	NetBIOS Name Service	23	Telnet Server
138	NetBIOS Datagram Service	53	DNS Transfers
161	SNMP	80	Web Server—HTTP
		139	NetBIOS Session Service
		25	Simple Mail Transfer Protocol (SMTP)

A rule set similar to this example must be implemented for every network service that intends to communicate through the packet filter. Table 11.6 lists common network services and protocols that could take advantage of packet filtering.

We do not recommend allowing TFTP, SNMP, or any of the NetBIOS services in from the Internet. Of course, such a decision must be based on policy, but these services are relatively insecure.

PROXY SERVICES

A proxy server is a popular way to give internal users access to the Internet without compromising external access. The proxy software runs on a host routing between the internal network and the Internet. The main idea is to allow internally initiated connections with the Internet while preventing externally initiated connections. For example, after installing and configuring Microsoft Proxy Server 2.0 for HTTP, the internal users designate the HTTP proxy server in their Web browser. All external Web site requests are directed to it. The proxy receives HTTP URL requests and establishes its own connections with the destination Web sites. It then retrieves the data and relays it to the correct internal client. This translation between internal Web client and external Web server can be transparent to the user. A proxy firewall requires client proxy and server proxy software specifically designed for each proxy service implemented to provide this transparency.

Both Netscape and Internet Explorer provide client proxy software for HTTP. Noncaching proxies degrade network performance but provide a secure firewall. We specifically mention noncaching because a caching server may actually respond much quicker if the answer is in the cache. The Microsoft Proxy Server also has an added caching feature. Commonly visited sites are stored on the proxy's local hard disk, preventing the need for Internet retrieval. Clients receive the pages faster and reduce the required Internet bandwidth. The proxy can also retrieve and refresh popular Web sites automatically without client requests.

STATEFUL INSPECTION

Stateful inspection offers an alternative way to provide internal users with connectivity to Internet resources while preventing external users from initiating inbound connections. As a user makes an outbound request to an external server, the stateful inspection firewall records details about it. The information tracked includes the source address, destination address, protocol, port number, and so forth, and it is evaluated for a certain period of time. When the destination service responds to the internal user, the packet is permitted to return through the firewall.

The firewall performs intelligent packet filtering without requiring the server and client software to support each network service. However, although stateful inspection offers better performance than the proxy model, it reveals internal IP addresses to the Internet. Several stateful inspection products hide internal IP addresses through address translation.

Web Security

When implementing a Web server, you should follow certain basic guidelines to protect against security breaches. A Web server allows users to download designated files and run CGI scripts, Active Server Pages, and server-side applets that are accessible to it. For this reason, the server should not be able to access sensitive files that contain proprietary company information or files pertinent to system security.

Limit the Web server to a specific directory subtree and dedicate a system to Web server duties (Windows Server 2003 uses %SystemRoot%Inetpub\wwwroot).

Also, make sure that Web sites with password security do not place the password security file in a directory the server can read. The Web server should run as a very underprivileged user to limit its own access, with just enough privilege to perform required functions. It should have a firewall between it and the internal network, and no internal host should trust it through Windows Server 2003 domain trust relationships.

RESTRICTING SCRIPTS FROM EXTERNAL SOURCES

Since the Web server is permitted to run local components, all scripts, applets, and active components should be analyzed for unintended uses. Remember, these scripts can be run with freely chosen parameters from the outside, so any service that allows users to download scripts to the server should be carefully scrutinized. FTP users should not be able to download to the Web server's file system area. In fact, almost all services, except HTTP, should be disabled on the Web server.

HTTP SECURITY

HTTP is an unencrypted protocol and will not prevent users from snooping or spoofing your Web server. The Secure HTTP protocol addresses these issues, but your Web clients must be familiar with your server to gain access. The Public Key Infrastructure discussed in Chapter 10 outlines how to use and configure the X.509 certificates and Certificate Authority.

IP Security

The Internet Protocol (IP) is the message delivery portion of the TCP/IP suite. It provides addresses and delivery of data packets. This is a "best-effort" delivery system that does not guarantee arrival of packets or that the information is properly sequenced. Thus, IP packets can be intercepted en route, reviewed, and even modified. The potential misuse is obvious. Let's examine some IP security issues.

IP spoofing can be a major threat. The IP address is ordinarily shown as plain text. The hacker can then direct the packet to the destination with altered information. The use of cryptographic technologies is the best defense against IP sniffing and spoofing.

Internet Browser Security

Downloadable objects accessible from the Internet open a gaping hole in network security because untrusted components can be downloaded right through a firewall. The user must be educated and browsers must be configured to match your network's tolerance for active components and Java applets.

Any browser user can configure his browser to handle untrusted and trusted components. The Microsoft Internet Explorer v6 configures these options through the **Tools → Internet Options** menu selection. Select the **Security** tab and click **Custom Level** for the **Internet** zone. For the purpose of providing an example, we will examine both Java and ActiveX permissions.

RESTRICTING ACTIVEX COMPONENTS

The ActiveX attributes require a Prompt, Enable, or Disable value for each security setting. ActiveX controls do not have the option of running within the sandbox and they have full control over the Win32 API. Therefore, you do not want users to run unsigned ActiveX controls. Period.

Find the **ActiveX permissions** and select **Custom**. Then click **ActiveX Custom Settings**. The attributes that can be modified are shown in Table 11.7. Again, browser permissions should be set at the same relative levels as those of the local server.

NOTE The browser settings just discussed can be automatically assigned to users through a GPO. They are set from the Default Domain snap-in via **User Configuration → Windows Settings → Internet Explorer Maintenance → Security → Security Zones and Content Ratings**.

INTERNET CERTIFICATE MANAGEMENT

From the **Tools → Internet Options → Content** tab, press the **Certificates** button to display currently installed certificates for signing and encryption. See Chapter 10, "Kerberos and the Public Key Infrastructure," for more information on local certificate stores.

TABLE 11.7 ActiveX Permission Settings

ActiveX Attribute	Option
Download Signed ActiveX Controls	Prompt/Enable/Disable
Download Unsigned ActiveX Controls	Prompt/Enable/Disable
Initialize and Script ActiveX Controls Not Marked Safe	Prompt/Enable/Disable
Run ActiveX Controls and Plug-Ins	Administrator approved /Prompt/Enable/Disable
Script ActiveX Controls Marked Safe for Scripting	Prompt/Enable/Disable

Securing RAS Servers

The Remote Access Service (RAS) allows a connection across a phone dial-up so that a user can use resources like a printer in a remote location. Since these connections are made through unsecured telephone lines, many potential security breaches exist. This is particularly true if the RAS is provided a server that is not otherwise protected. A number of actions can be taken to protect the domain from RAS abuses, including these:

- RAS connections should allow dial-in accounts to access only the RAS server.
- The RAS server should have its own domain and maintain separate user accounts.
- There should be a one-way trust between the rest of the network and the RAS server. (Users can put data on the RAS server for remote access, but the server is buffered from the rest of the network.)
- Strong passwords to RAS accounts should be enforced.

Securing Electronic Mail

Electronic mail is the lifeblood of modern organizational communication. The ability to send and receive e-mail messages from external sources is a common requirement. As is the case with any information from external sources, e-mail presents a host of security problems, including:

- *Flooding*. The e-mail server is hammered with a large number of messages, which can result in denial of service and system crash.
- *Spoofing*. The e-mail message has an incorrect sender name or address.
- *Viruses*. Application attachments may contain hostile macros (for example, the ActiveX-based Melissa).
- *Nonrepudiation*. The receiver needs to verify that the sender actually sent the message and the sender needs to verify that the receiver got the message.

PREVENTING E-MAIL SECURITY ABUSES

Packet-filtering messages from sources that are known to flood is effective but reactionary; the mail buffers and disk space can be monitored for excessive use. Spoofing and nonrepudiation are effectively combated with digital signatures.

Digital signatures are easily implemented from Outlook Express 6.0 via the **Tools → Options** selection under the **Security** tab, where encryption and digital signing can be configured for outgoing messages (Figures 11.15 and 11.16). The user and recipient must have a common certificate authority. For additional information see Chapter 10, "Kerberos and the Public Key Infrastructure."

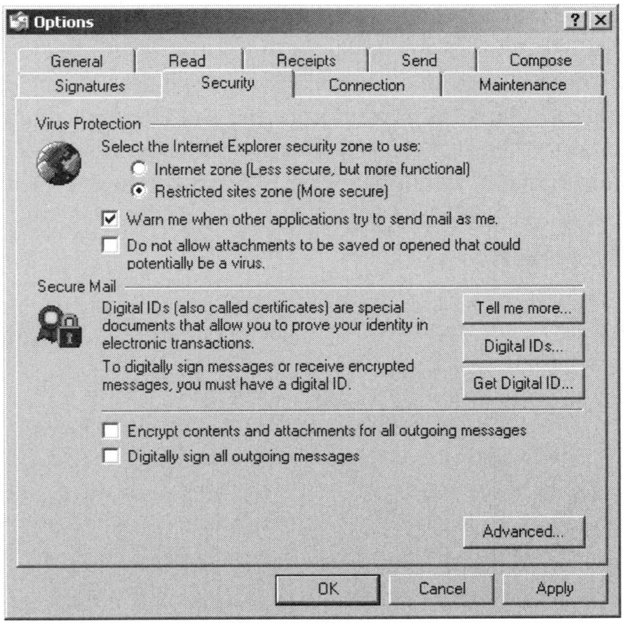

FIGURE 11.15 The Security Tab

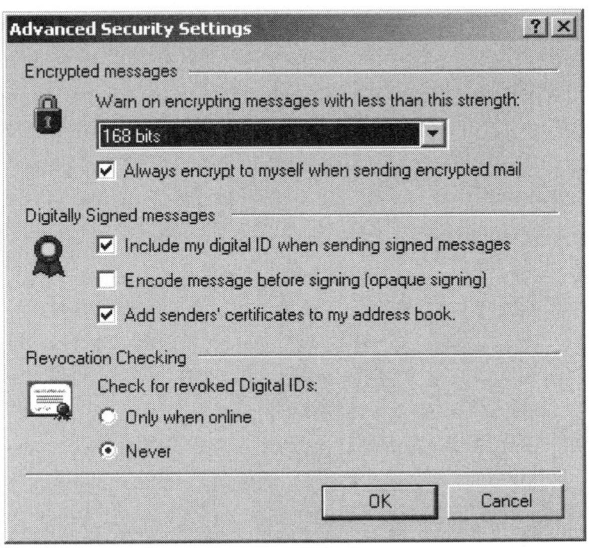

FIGURE 11.16 Advanced Security Settings

Virus attacks are difficult to filter out, especially when e-mail encryption is involved. Several virus scanners are available but are of limited effectiveness. If the scanner has an error and starts dropping all e-mail messages, regardless of viral content, the network and company can end up in a worse predicament than dealing with the virus. Denial of service is a serious downside to these tools, which means that careful monitoring and reaction time are key to successful implementation.

Other TCP/IP Security Issues

The TCP/IP networking suite provides a host of common services and protocols. The following issues could impact Windows Server 2003 environments using the following TCP/IP suite applications:

- *FTP*. The File Transfer Protocol is often used by anonymous user accounts that do not require password protection, which permits access to a system by virtually any user. Once inside, hackers can try to work their magic. To guard against this, set permissions to Read-Only and restrict directory access. (Or do not set up anonymous accounts at all unless you really need them.)
- *TFTP*. The Trivial File Transport Protocol is a relaxed version of FTP, in which generally any files can be transferred without a password—conceivably even system files such as the Windows Server 2003 Registry. We strongly recommend that TFTP be disabled by removing the tftpd file. In Windows Server 2003, make sure that the service is not enabled.
- *Finger*. This utility outputs information about users on the system. Once a hacker has a list of user names, systematically discovering passwords becomes the game. This facility should also be disabled unless absolutely required.
- *DNS*. The Domain Naming Server includes vital network information. Protect yourself by segregating it. For example, two servers can be used with a firewall separating external Internet-required data from inside user account information. You may also want to set filters to allow DNS queries to go to only one specific DNS machine on the DMZ, and allow zone transfers to and from only your parent servers.
- *Telnet*. Telnet data is transmitted in plain text along with the user name and password. This makes Telnet a valuable tool in an internal environment, especially when attempting to view data on heterogeneous UNIX and Windows systems. However, outside a secured environment, the user must be aware that security breaches can occur with this open transmission.

THE END USER'S RESPONSIBILITY

Users have to take a certain amount of responsibility for the security of the computing environment, so it is reasonable for IT professionals to articulate what is expected of users. When these expectations are not met, denial of privilege or restricted use can be invoked. This list represents some practices that system administrators should expect of end users:

- The selection of nonobvious passwords is the first line of defense. The user also should be forced to change her password periodically.
- The password must never be written down or revealed to associates.
- When leaving the work area, the user should be instructed to invoke a password-controlled screen saver or to log off. Logoff must be enforced at the end of each work period.
- The user should be made aware of basic file and folder permissions parameters. This is particularly true if she moves or copies files. Additionally, the user should be aware of the implication of allowing another user to take ownership of a file.
- No user should import applications that are not approved by the system administrator. This is one of the easiest ways to introduce viruses or Trojan horses.

POSTSCRIPT

There will always be a compromise between ease of use and network security. All operating systems and applications have a number of known vulnerabilities whose exploitation is only a mouse click away even for novice users. To reduce vulnerability:

- Act on an aggressive security plan for network and system security.
- Plug security holes with the most current version of the operating system and service patches.
- Apply the same principle to all network services and client applications.
- Back up all system data and be able to reinstall operating components and applications quickly.
- Outline and prioritize the resources needed to maintain a secure network.

Two additional sources should be tapped when administrating Windows Server security. First, keep abreast of regularly posted security update white papers and bulletins on Microsoft's Web site at *http://www.microsoft.com/security*. Also, check the Web site for security patches. As the hacker community goes forward, Microsoft will regularly post protective patches to prevent attacks.

NOTE Install hot fixes to the operating system, IIS, Web servers, and so on. Subscribe to the Microsoft Security Alert mailing list.

Chapter 12

Networking Basics and Naming Services

This chapter is divided into two sections. The first section provides an overview of networking basics from 30,000 feet. It is written as a primer for readers who are not familiar with TCP/IP and related technologies; those experienced with networking may use it as a quick reference. The second section examines naming services, including DNS and DHCP. It provides both theoretical and hands-on information that is vital to all Windows Server 2003 enterprises.

NETWORKING BASICS

Communication among network devices like computers assumes the existence of mutually understood protocols that comprise a set of rules and structural components. Computers must use a common protocol in order to communicate. Underlying communication in Windows Server 2003 enterprise is the default Transmission Control Protocol and Internet Protocol, otherwise known as TCP/IP.

Network Architecture

The Open Systems Interconnect (OSI) model defines network communication in a sequential and hierarchical fashion. As shown in Figure 12.1, it consists of seven layers, a brief explanation of which should provide a better understanding of its conceptual underpinnings. Protocols like TCP/IP embrace only a portion of the total conceptual model.

- *Physical layer*. The physical layer loosely refers to just about any characteristic of the hardware, such as signal voltages and cable and connector specifications.

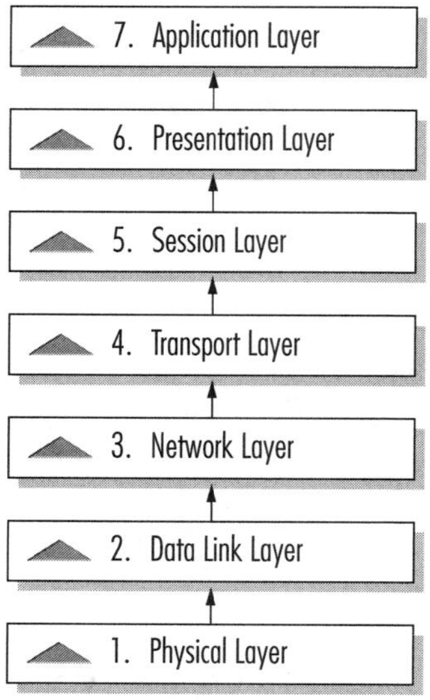

FIGURE 12.1 The OSI Model

It transmits and receives data in the raw bit form of 1s and 0s. Standards such as Ethernet 802.3, RS232C, and X.25 dictate the requirements of this layer.

- *Data link layer*. The data link layer changes the raw bit stream presented by the physical layer into data frames or blocks. TCP/IP typically assumes the use of other standards to specify the data link layer's characteristics.
- *Network layer*. The network layer is the first level in which TCP/IP directly relates to the OSI model. It is where the Internet Protocol manages communication between the application layer and the lower-level physical and data link layers. IP provides the Internet addressing scheme that defines a common structure or format for datagrams. These are packets of data that include information such as destination, type, source, and size. The Internet protocol defines how the datagrams are interpreted, as well as how data is routed between Internet networks and addresses, especially on segmented or subdivided networks.
- *Transport layer*. The transport layer communicates with the application layer. When errors are detected, it may request the retransmission of bad or lost packets. IP traffic typically uses either the Transmission Control Protocol (TCP) or the User Datagram Protocol (UDP). Each transport connection is identified by a port number.

- *Session layer*. The session layer refers to the connectivity and management of network applications. TCP/IP does not directly map this OSI layer.
- *Presentation layer*. The presentation layer establishes the data format prior to passing it along to the network application's interface. TCP/IP networks perform this task at the application layer.
- *Application layer*. The application layer processes data received or sent through the network.

A MODIFIED NETWORK MODEL

There is some debate as to how well TCP/IP maps to the OSI conceptual model. However, for the sake of a simple overview, it may be said that it does conceptually correspond (although not identically) to the OSI model with a four-layer hybrid model having an application layer, a transport layer, a network layer, and a physical/data link layer (Figure 12.2).

IP Addressing

The IP address identifies and addresses the network and devices or nodes such as servers, desktop computers, and routing devices. It consists of a 32-bit value that is separated into four octets. When data segments pass from the transport layer to the network layer, the IP appends its own header information and the new grouping becomes an IP datagram (Figure 12.3). The most important fields in this datagram are the destination and the source addresses.

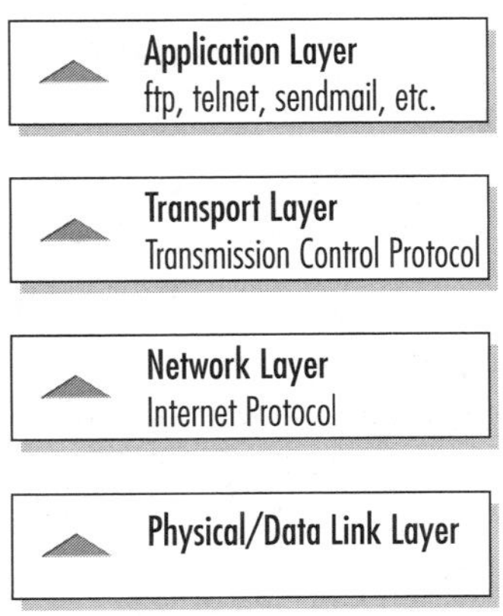

FIGURE 12.2 Layers Used by the TCP/IP Model

FIGURE 12.3 The IP Datagram

NOTE Windows Server 2003 adds optional support for Internet Protocol Version 6 (IPv6), billed as the next generation of the TCP/IP. In its initial implementation it is designed for application developers. The functions that are supported include Developer Edition of the IPv6 protocol driver and utilities, Application Programming Interface (API) set and IPv6-enabled key system components such as Internet Explorer, Telnet, File Transfer Protocol (FTP), Remote Procedure Call (RPC), and others. To enable or disable IPv6, run ipv6.exe from the command prompt.

DISSECTING IP ADDRESSING

There are three classes of IP address. An address class is determined by the following rules:

- *Class A.* In a Class A address, the first number is in the range of 0 through127, with the 0 value reserved for the default route and the 127 value reserved for identifying the local host. This means that only 126 (1–126) networks can be defined as Class A; the other bits in the address are used to assign specific node IP addresses. Although the number of Class A networks is limited, and they are difficult to obtain, the number of nodes they can support is extensive. (x represents a fictitious decimal digit in the following tables.)

Class A Address Example

8-bit Network Address	24-bit Host Address

- *Class B.* A Class B address uses the first value range from 128 through 191 in the first byte. It also uses the second octal byte set for defining the network. The result is that there can be many more networks defined by Class B addresses. The remaining octal sets are used to assign specific node addresses.

Class B Address Example

16-bit Network Address	16-bit Host Address
129.1xx.	111.111

- *Class C*. Class C addresses use the value range of 192 through 223 in the first byte, and the next two octal sets are used to define the network as well. With three octal sets defining networks, many more networks can be established and identified. However, since only one octal set is available to define the IP address of a specific node, the network is smaller, with a potential to provide up to 254 hosts or node addresses (the 0 value identifies the network and the 255 value is reserved for broadcasting).

Class C Address Example

24-bit Network Address	8-bit Host Address
192.1xx.111.	111

SUBNET MASKS

A subnet mask permits the division of a single IP address into multiple subnetworks. A subnet mask defines how the address space is divided among networks and hosts. It is a 32-bit binary number that designates which bits of the IP address are intended for the network and which determine the host. The network portion is identified by 1s, and the host by 0s. Thus, for the previously discussed Class A, B, and C addresses, the subnet masks in the following table would be used.

Class	Network Mask (Decimal)	Network Mask (Binary)
A	255.0.0.0	11111111 00000000 00000000 00000000
B	255.255.0.0	11111111 11111111 00000000 00000000
C	255.255.255.0	11111111 11111111 11111111 00000000

A Class C address could designate the first 24 bits as network space and the last 8 bits as host space on the network. Addressing at the data link layer is handled with Media Access Control (MAC) addresses. Discussing address frame delivery at the data link layer is beyond the scope of this book. However, once a packet is forwarded to the segment with the destination node, the data link media is responsible for frame delivery. In order for this to be accomplished, a node must map the destination IP address to the destination MAC address.

THE ADDRESS RESOLUTION PROTOCOL

A computer system or printer may establish connectivity via a serial port, phone line, interface card, or other device. However, most connectivity strategies for local area networks involve an interface card to one of the more popular media types, such as Ethernet, Token Ring, or FDDI, which implement elements from both the physical and data link layers of the OSI model. The interface card uses these hardware definitions and data link protocols to encapsulate network-level packets into media frames that are then delivered to a destination—another interface card.

Media Access Control addresses identify and address the interface cards. Most consist of six hexadecimal numbers separated by colons (e.g., 00:53:45:00:00:00). The encapsulated network-level IP packet has its own addressing scheme, which must then be mapped onto the MAC address in order to communicate with systems via their interface cards. The Address Resolution Protocol (ARP) maps between MAC and IP addresses on the local network segment.

NOTE Windows Server 2003 has improved device driver support for network cards and equipment. This feature adds network device drivers that are common in home networking and removes earlier device drivers. The feature is accessible from **Start → Control Panel → Performance and Maintenance → System → Hardware → Device Manager**. It also includes improving the quality of networking drivers. Driver categories include:

- *Local Area Network (LAN) Drivers* including 10/100 Network Interface Cards (NICs), IEEE 802.11, and Home Phoneline Networking Alliance (HomePNA).
- *Broadband* including cable modems, Asynchronous Digital Subscriber Line (ADSL), and Integrated Services Digital Network (ISDN).
- *Modems* including driver-based and 56 kbps V.90 modems.
- *Infrared Modems*. IrCOMM Modem is a driver that exposes the IrDA stack to cellular telephones. This feature permits support for older cellular telephones that have IrCOMM virtual serial ports.

For example, if Node A desires to communicate with Node B, it must first map Node B's IP address with its physical MAC address. Once the destination MAC address is resolved, the data link layer is responsible for delivering the frame. Node A broadcasts an ARP request, which contains the destination IP address, to every node on the physical segment (Figure 12.4). Each node reads the request and checks to see if the destination IP address matches its own. Only Node B, owner of the destination IP address, returns an ARP reply to the source MAC address. Node A retrieves the source's MAC address from the ARP reply data link frame and stores the IP-MAC address mapping in its ARP cache. This entry will remain valid in the local volatile ARP cache for a predetermined period of time, usually about 10 minutes. If the address mapping is validated with continued communication, the entry will be refreshed. Once Node A has Node B's IP address and corresponding MAC

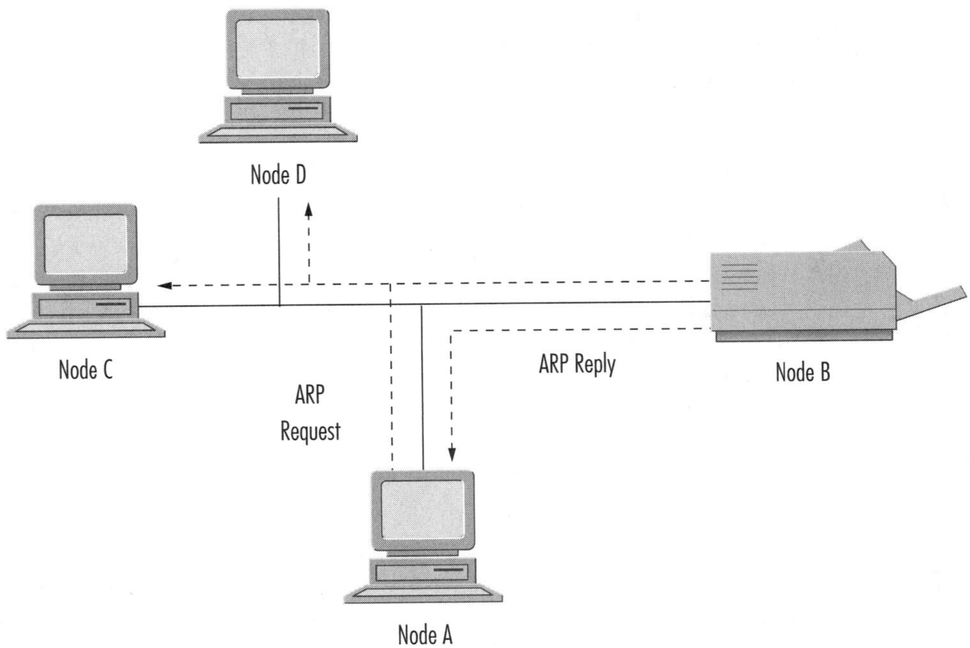

FIGURE 12.4 ARP Resolution

address, communication may be initiated with direct unicast data link frames between the two.

NOTE The contents of a system's ARP cache may be displayed by typing `arp` at the command line. The `ipconfig/?` command is very helpful for displaying and configuring all aspects of the IP implementation on a system. See the appendix to this book or Help pages for further information.

IP Routing

IP packets are forwarded between networks using specialized network equipment known as *routers* or by *multihomed hosts* (i.e., systems with multiple network adapters) with routing software. Upon receiving a packet, the routing device determines which interface produces the quickest route to the destination IP address. The packet is then repackaged and sent out on the correct interface, which the router determines based on its routing table. This table is constructed with manually configured routes, or static routes, and routes obtained via communication with other routers.

NOTE A new feature in Windows Server 2003 is a network bridge that offers the ability to interconnect network segments. A multisegment network system can have multiple adapters such as a wireless adapter, a telephone line adapter, and an Ethernet adapter. By bridging these adapters, computers and devices on each network segment use the bridge to communicate with each other. The New Connection Wizard is used to set up and administer a multisegment home network as follows: **Start → Control Panel → Network and Internet Connections → Network Connections → Create a new connection**.

NOTE Media Bridge support has also been added in Windows Server 2003. The Network Media Bridge is a Layer 2 bridge that simplifies setup and administration. Typically, a multiple-segment IP network includes assigning each network segment a subnetwork number plus configuring hosts on each subnetwork and packet forwarding between the subnetworks. It provides a single IP subnetwork with no configuration necessary on the part of the user. This feature is available from: **Start → Control Panel → Network and Internet Connections → Network Connections → Create a new connection**. Only one bridge is allowed. The Network Media Bridge also supports IEEE 1394 and IEEE 802.11 devices.

Routers communicate these dynamically changing routes through the Routing Information Protocol (RIP), the Open Shortest Path First (OSPF) protocol, and others. Static routes are configured through the command line using the `route` command or through the Routing and Remote Access snap-in.

CLIENT-SIDE ROUTING CONFIGURATION

Three parameters are of particular interest when configuring a host for communication on a network. Double-click an interface from **Start → Settings → Network and Dial-up Connections**. Select the **Internet Protocol (TCP/IP)** and click **Properties** to see them (Figure 12.5):

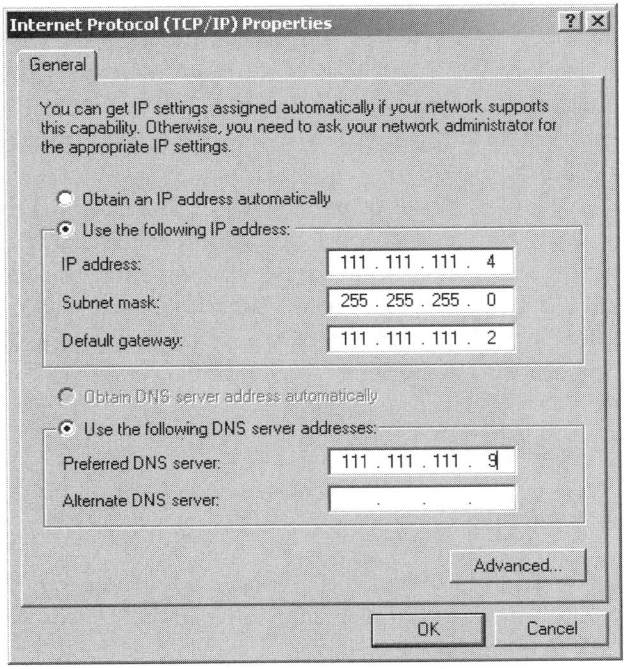

FIGURE 12.5 Internet Protocol Client Configuration

- ***IP address***—unique IP address assigned to the interface.
- ***Subnet mask***—determines network and host portions of the IP address.
- ***Default gateway***—IP address of network's router interface.

A client's IP address may be manually configured with a static IP address or assigned automatically via the Dynamic Host Configuration Protocol (DHCP), discussed later in the chapter. The subnet mask identifies the portion of the IP address that pertains to the network and host addresses, and is mapped against an outbound packet's destination IP address. If the packet is not bound for the local network segment, the client sends it to the default gateway. The gateway forwards the packet onto the destination network using routing tables, as discussed earlier.

NOTE The following command can be used to return TCP/IP settings to default values with Windows Server 2003:

```
Netsh int ip reset logfile
```

NOTE An integral feature of Windows Server 2003 is that the TCP receiving window size is determined by the local NIC. This is important because the window size determines the maximum number of bytes that can be unacknowledged but sent at any time. This can be critical on a slower dial-up network connection where the window size is generally equal to the queue depth on the Remote Access Service server. When the queue is filled with packets from one Transmission Control Protocol connection, a new TCP connection cannot be established until all these packets are sent out. Window size adjustments to make the connection speed are now made to improve the Quality of Service (QoS) Packet Scheduler on a system with Internet Connection Sharing (ICS). This reduces the queue depth at the RAS server. It also enables new connections to work better. ICS must be used with this new feature.

NAMING SERVICES AND IP ASSIGNMENTS

Network naming services were developed to correlate numeric addresses best understood by computers and natural language names that are provided to the same network device. Windows Server 2003 embraces several of them. The DNS is an integral part of Windows .NET and, especially, Active Directory implementations. It has evolved as the primary naming service for the UNIX OS and the Internet. Because of Microsoft's decision to make Windows Server 2003 Internet compatible, DNS has replaced the Windows Internet Name Service (WINS) as the default name-resolution technology.

NOTE A vulnerability of early implementations of DNS centered on security. With Windows Server 2003, the DNS server provides basic compliance with the IETF standard DNS Security Extensions protocol as defined in RFC 2535. The DNS server may now store the record types (KEY, SIG, and NXT) defined in the IETF standard. These records respond to the queries according to RFC 2535. The server does not provide full compliance and does not perform the cryptographic operations specified in RFC 2535. The feature is activated through the DNS snap-in.

This section examines DNS and other naming services and related technologies, including DHCP and the Microsoft WINS. DHCP dynamically assigns IP addresses. While technically not a naming service, it resembles one when deploying networks.

Domain Name System Conventions

The role of DNS is to match a Fully Qualified Domain Name (FQDN) with its IP address. FQDNs are organized in a top-down fashion, forming a hierarchy from general to specific (Figure 12.6). This hierarchy is read from right to left and identifies a specific host in a subdomain. For example, the fully qualified host name *host.EntCert.com* identifies *host* in the *EntCert* subdomain. The root domain, indicated by the period on the far right, is usually omitted from the FQDN for normal use, but is required for DNS configuration files. The *com* portion is, in this example, the highest subdomain under the root domain, indicating a commercially assigned name.

NOTE A new Windows Server 2003 feature helps to identify DNS problems. When a new system attempts to join an Active Directory domain but fails to locate a domain controller (DC) because the DNS was incorrectly configured, the problem is recorded. The administrator receives a report explaining what caused the failure and how to fix the problem. This function is activated from the **System Properties → Computer ID** tab.

In our example (Figure 12.6), we have a real company name and the registered domain name of *EntCert.com*. Enterprise Certified is a private corporation that requested allocation of this subdomain name from the Network Information Center. The host portion is a host within the *EntCert* subdomain that is assigned an IP address for one of its network interfaces. This fully qualified host name can be used to reference this IP address by accessing a domain name server.

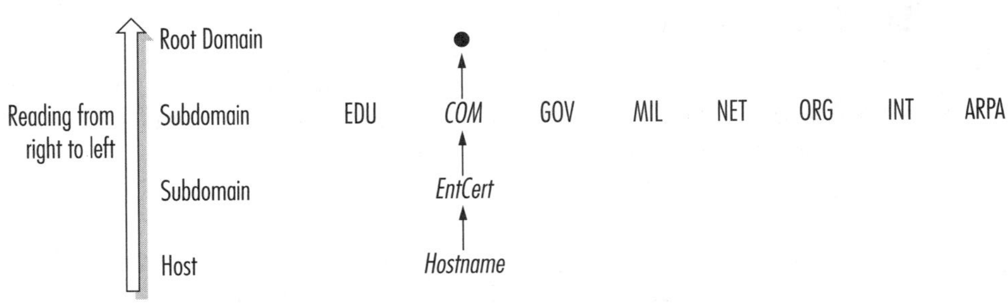

FIGURE 12.6 The DNS Hierarchy

Understanding DNS

The DNS system is composed of clients and servers. DNS servers maintain forward and reverse records for their zones. The forward lookup zone is used to find the IP address of a host using an FQDN; the reverse lookup zone does just the opposite and uses an IP address to locate the subject's FQDN. A configured DNS client maintains the IP address of the DNS server for its zone. When the client attempts to resolve a fully qualified name, it checks three sources:

- *Local cache* obtained from previous queries. These entries are valid for the Time-to-Live (TTL) period defined in the query response.
- *Lmhosts*, or host files that contain host-name-to-address mappings that remain on the hard disk when the client is shut down.
- DNS server.

Once the client has attempted to find a locally valid IP address for the sought-after host name, it will query its DNS server. The server attempts to resolve the client's query using several strategies:

- If the query result is found in the local DNS zone, the server is supporting the host and can respond with an authoritative answer.
- If the result is not found in the local zone, the server references its local cache for a recent query containing the desired name mapping.
- If the local resources fail to provide the needed mapping, depending on its configuration, the DNS server will resolve the client's query in one of three ways:
  —perform a recursive search for client's query
  —forward the query to another DNS server to perform a recursive search
  —refer another DNS server to client's query and let the client perform a recursive search

DNS Recursion

A recursively configured DNS server accepts queries from a client and follows referrals, using the DNS hierarchy, to resolve the client's request. It does so by sending an iterative request to the root "." DNS server. (An iterative request instructs a server to provide a best guess or referral to another server when the query is not known.) The root server then refers the local DNS server to the next authoritative name server in the query's namespace. For example, in order to resolve the FQDN name *host.Entcert.com* from the "clientcompanydomain.com", the client company's local DNS server will query the "." root DNS server and be referred to the ".com". DNS server (Figure 12.7). Since a record exists for the ".com" server in the "." (root)

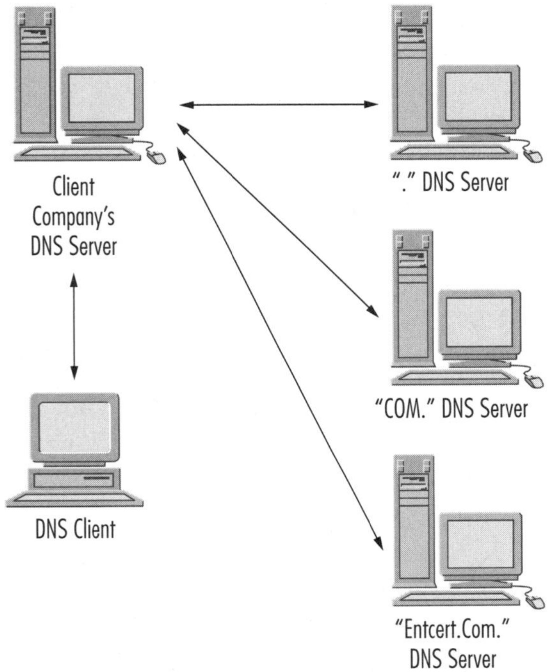

FIGURE 12.7 DNS Name Resolution

server's database, its response is considered authoritative. The local DNS server queries the "com". DNS server and is referred to the "EntCert.com". DNS server. This server offers an authoritative query response and returns the *host.EntCert.com* name-to-IP-address mapping to the local DNS server. The client company's DNS server then returns the response to the client. The client uses the IP address to establish a connection with the remote server.

STANDARD VERSUS DIRECTORY INTEGRATED ZONES

The Windows Server 2003 DNS server may store zone information in two distinct formats: Active Directory integrated and standard zone format as a text file. Active Directory integrated is available when you install the DNS server along with the Active Directory. When this option is installed on a domain controller, the DNS information is updated on other DNS servers on domain controllers using the Active Directory's multimaster update techniques. Secondary zones (used with the standard zone format to back up DNS information and offload client queries) are supported but not required with Active Directory–integrated DNS server zones. Additional domain controllers installed with the Active Directory–integrated DNS server also act as a primary source for the zone.

In order to back up or offload client requests to one Active Directory–integrated server, simply install an Active Directory–integrated DNS server on another domain controller. Active Directory replication will ensure that the two servers have equivalent DNS records, so clients may contact any of the domain controllers and receive up-to-date DNS information. Additionally, the Active Directory–integrated zones support ACLs to restrict access to the zone container so that a particular client can be prevented from performing dynamic updates. For more information on dynamic updates, see the DHCP section.

The standard zone format does not support ACLs and requires secondary zones to offload client queries and back up the DNS database. Secondary zones support their own replication strategy, as discussed in the coming sections. The standard zone is stored in a text file in the %SystemRoot%\system32\dns folder.

INSTALLATION WITH THE ACTIVE DIRECTORY

Active Directory installation, demonstrated in Chapter 7, requires DNS installation. The Active Directory may be fully installed without DNS on the server by referencing another DNS server in the domain. DNS may be installed later on such a domain controller using the Configure Your Server tool.

1. Open the **Configure Your Server** tool by selecting **Start → Programs → Administrative Tools → Configure Your Server**. Once the wizard appears, click **Next**. Click **Next** again to the **Preliminary Steps** window.
2. Select **DNS server** from the **Server Role** window and click **Next**. Click **Finish**.
3. The **Configure a DNS Server Wizard** should appear. Click **Next**.
4. In the **Select Configuration Action** window, select **Create forward and reverse lookup zones**, then click **Next**. (Figure 12.8).
5. Select **Yes, create a forward lookup zone now,** then click **Next**.
6. Select **Primary zone** (Figure 12.9). Ensure that the **Store the zone in Active Directory** box is checked, then click **Next**. This will make the DNS server integrated with Active Directory.
7. Replicate to all domain controllers by selecting **All domain controllers in the Entcert2.com Active Directory domain**.
8. Enter the full DNS name for the new DNS zone and click **Next**. (Figure 12.10).
9. Select **Allow only secure dynamic updates** and click **Next**.
10. Select **Yes, create the reverse lookup zone now** and click **Next**.
11. Select **Primary zone** selection. Ensure that the **Store the zone in Active Directory** box is checked, then click **Next**.

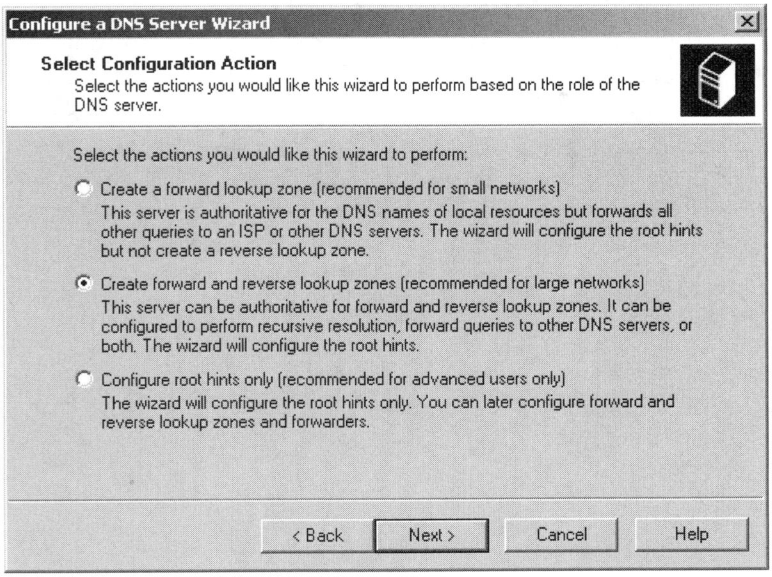

FIGURE 12.8 Create Forward and Reverse Lookup Zones

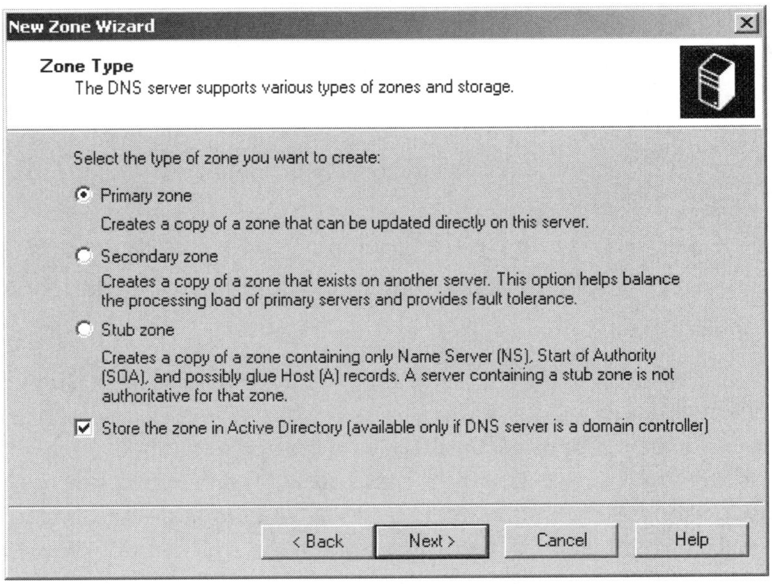

FIGURE 12.9 Primary Active Directory Integrated DNS Zone

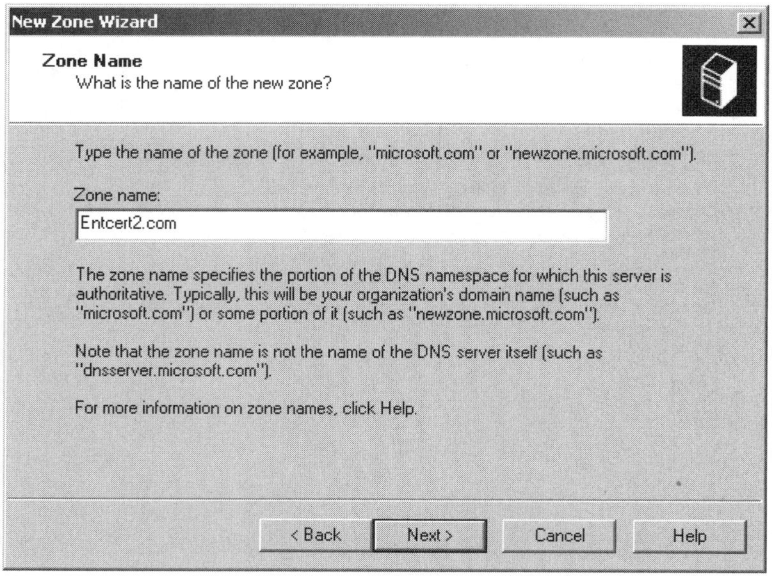

FIGURE 12.10 Creating DNS Zones

12. Select **All Domain Contollers** selection and click **Next**.
13. Enter the network address of the zone for reverse lookup, then click **Next**. (Figure 12.11)
14. Select the **Dynamic Update** preference and click **Next**.
15. Do not permit query forwarding for this example and click **Next**.
16. Click **Finish**.

The new reverse lookup zone should be configured with the new DNS server as the only member. Add new members to both the forward and reverse zones by right-clicking the **Forward Lookup Zone** domain folder and selecting **New Host (A)**. Check the **Create associated pointer (PTR) record** box to simultaneously create the reverse lookup entry (Figure 12.12). Or, add reverse lookup entries individually by right-clicking the reverse zone node and selecting **New Pointer (PTR)** (Figure 12.13). Once the host has been added to the DNS database, the host's DNS client must be configured to the new DNS server.

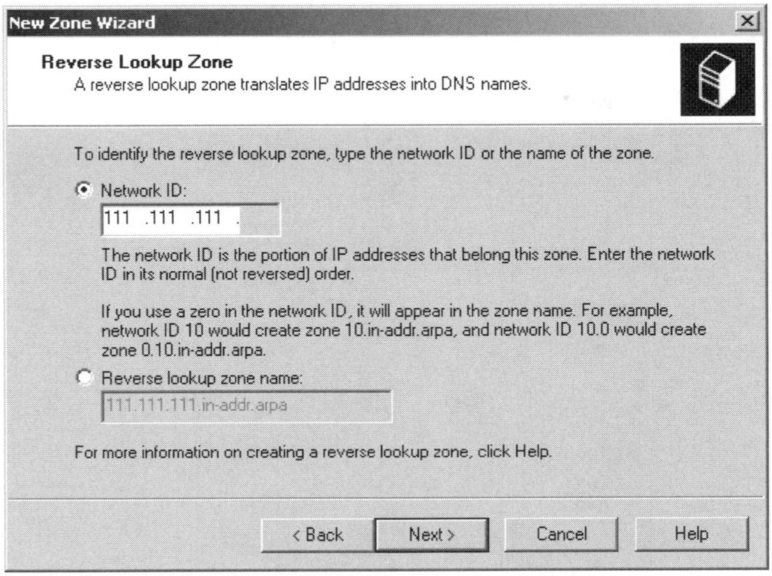

FIGURE 12.11 Network Address for Reverse Lookup Zone

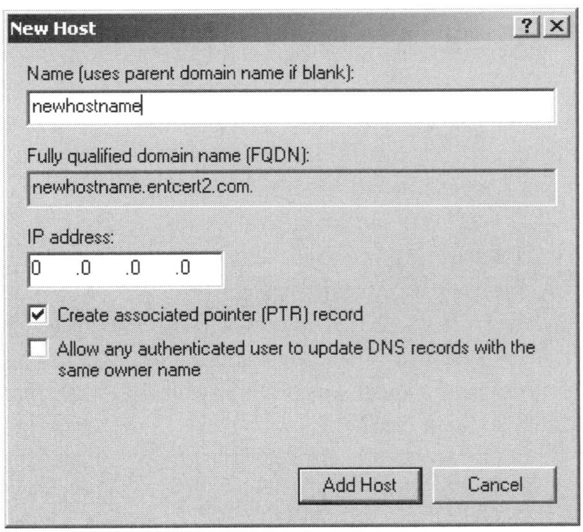

FIGURE 12.12 New Host Record

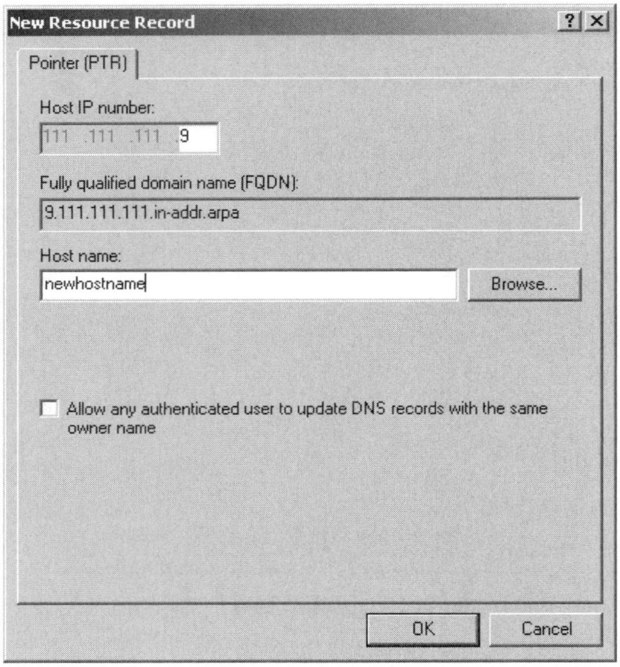

FIGURE 12.13 The Pointer (PTR) Tab of a New Resource Record

NOTE Windows Server 2003 DNS supports *stub zones* and *conditional forwarding.* By contrast, Windows 2000 can be configured to forward DNS queries to only one set of DNS servers. Stub zones involve two DNS server features that provide the ability to control the routing of DNS traffic on a network. A stub zone allows a DNS server to be aware of the names and addresses of servers that are authoritative for the full copy of a zone. This is done without the server having to hold a complete copy. The conditional forwarding feature in Windows Server 2003 allows greater granularity and supports name-dependent forwarding. A DNS server can now be configured to simultaneously forward queries for names ending in *entcert.com*, forward queries for names ending in *entcert.net* to a second set of DNS servers, and forward all other queries to a third set of DNS servers. These features are configured through the DNS snap-in tool.

CLIENT CONFIGURATION

1. From the new client host, select **Start → Settings → Network Connections** and double-click the network interface to handle DNS requests.

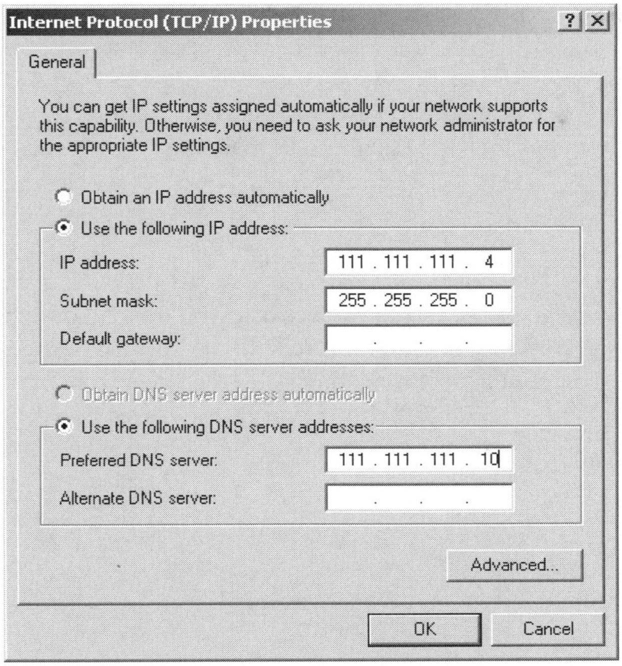

FIGURE 12.14 Choosing the DNS Server's IP Address

2. Click **Properties**. Select **Internet Protocol (TCP/IP)** and click **Properties**. Enter the new DNS server's IP address in the **Preferred DNS server** field (Figure 12.14).
3. Test the reverse DNS lookup feature by going to the **command** prompt and type the ***nslookup host name***.

The following should appear:

```
Server: servername.domainname
Address: xxx.xxx.xxx.xxx
Name: hostname.domainname
Address: xxx.xxx.xxx.xxx
```

DNS ZONES AND FAULT TOLERANCE

When the first DNS server is installed to manage a namespace, it is configured as the primary DNS server for the domain. The namespace it maintains defines the server's responsibility. As subdomain names are added, new zones may be created to maintain them. These new zones may be configured with new DNS servers to maintain each one's name-to-IP-address mapping information. For example, if the

Enterprise Certified Corporation were to extend its namespace with new branches such as Engineering and Marketing, administration of the new branches could be delegated to new zones and respective servers. The *Engineering.EntCert.com* and *Marketing.EntCert.com* domain names could be used to define the two new zones, each of which would have its own database to maintain IP addresses mapped in its namespace (Figure 12.15).

Replication

Each zone may set up secondary servers to back up the primary server in the event of failure. The secondary server synchronizes its own DNS database by sending update requests to its master server, which may be the primary DNS server for the domain or another secondary server (Figure 12.16). The secondary server update request may be for either an incremental or an all-zones transfer. A brand-new secondary server will request an all-zones transfer to completely update its database.

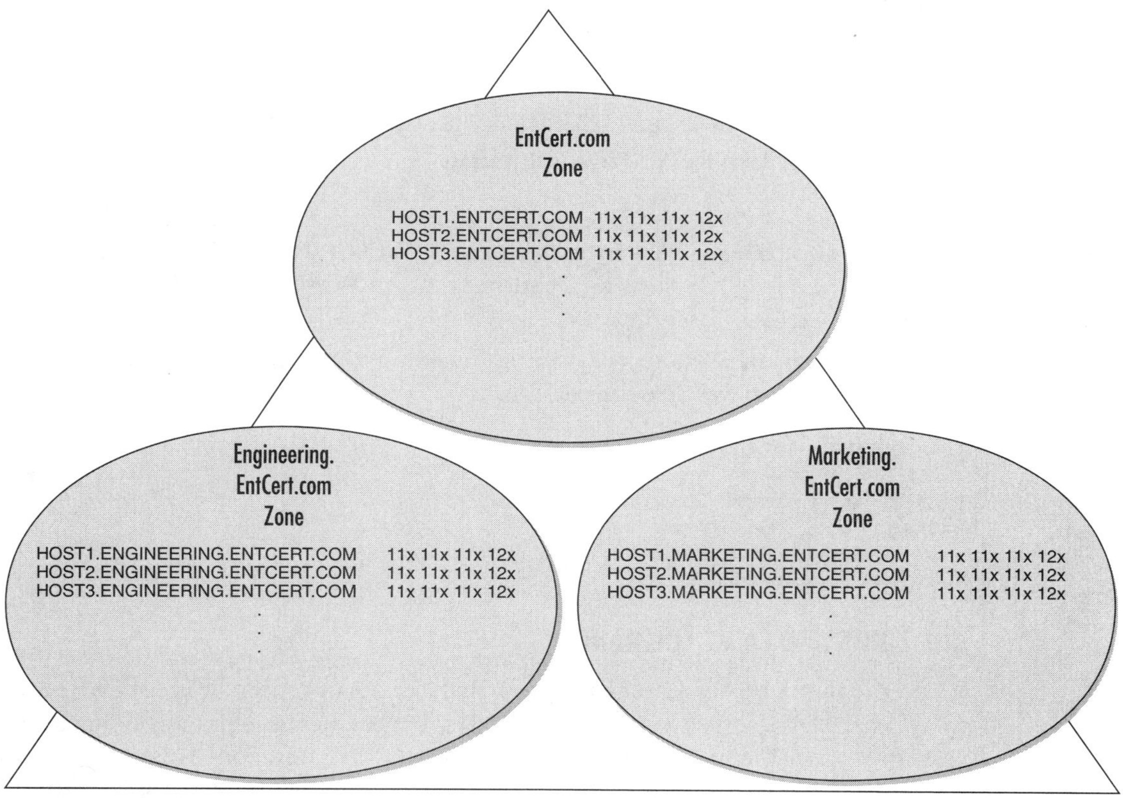

FIGURE 12.15 Individual DNS Zone Databases

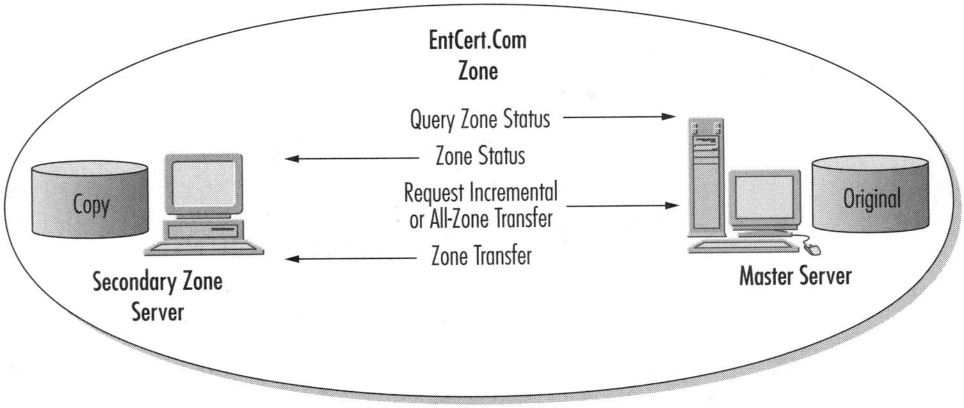

FIGURE 12.16 Replication within Zones

After initialization, the secondary server initiates only incremental transfers, which convey only zone changes to the database, cutting down on network traffic and system resource use.

NOTE Replication within zones is required only when implementing standard zone DNS servers. Active Directory–integrated zones are backed up when more than one DNS server exists in a zone. Multimaster replication among the DNS servers that are running Active Directory services automatically supports updates among domain controllers and supports fault tolerance.

A zone transfer is initiated for several reasons:

1. The secondary server's refresh timer expires (default 1 hour).
2. The master server notifies members of a zone change.
3. The secondary DNS service is started (during either bootup or installation).
4. A zone transfer is manually initiated from a DNS snap-in for a secondary server.

Secondary DNS Server Management

The secondary DNS server installation is similar to the primary installation. Here are the steps required:

1. Install the Windows Server 2003 DNS server from the **Start → Programs → Administrative Tools → Configure Your Server** tool. You can also install it

from **Control Panel → Add or Remove Programs**. Start the **Windows Components Wizard** and select **Networking Services**. Click **Details** to bring up subcomponents for networking services. Select the **Domain Name System (DNS)** and click **OK**.

2. Once the Windows Server 2003 DNS server components have been installed, open the **DNS** snap-in tool from the new DNS server. Any other DNS server can be managed from one system's DNS snap-in by right-clicking the DNS node and selecting **Connect to DNS Server**. Enter the name of the desired server to administer and click **OK**. The new server should appear as a new node under the **DNS** node.
3. Right-click the **Forward Lookup Zones** node and select **New Zone**. Click **Next** to start the **New Zone Wizard**.
4. Select **Secondary zone** and click **Next** (Figure 12.17).
5. Enter the name of the DNS zone the secondary server is supporting and click **Next**.
6. Enter the IP address of the new secondary DNS server's master. A full DNS database transfer will be performed from the master server (Figure 12.18). Click **Add** and click **Next**. Click **Finish** to complete the secondary zone creation.

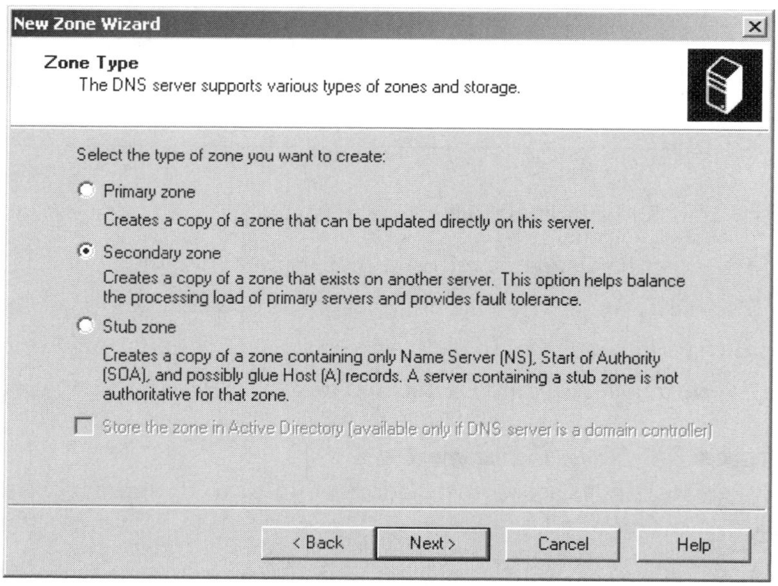

FIGURE 12.17 Selecting a New Secondary Server Zone

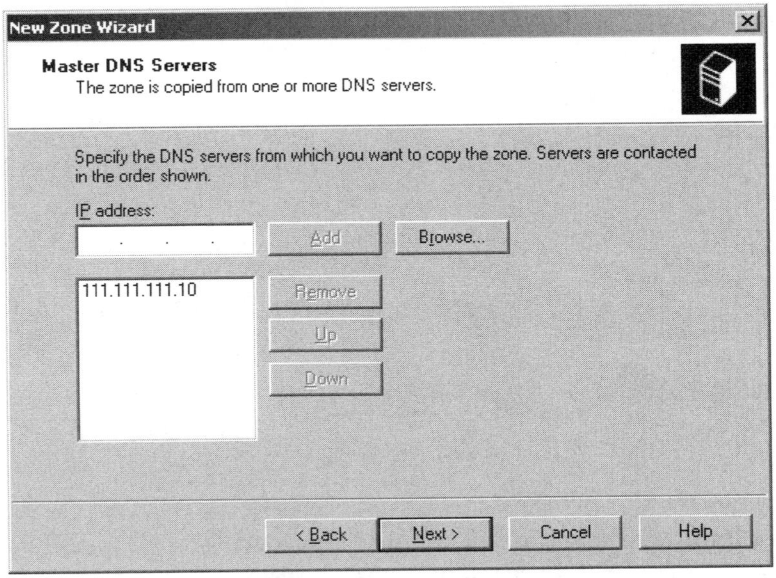

FIGURE 12.18 Configuring Master DNS Server(s) for a Secondary DNS Server

The finished forward lookup zones defined on the master DNS server should be replicated on the secondary DNS server. The easiest visual way to identify the newly created secondary zone is to right-click the new zone and select **Properties**. On the **General** tab, the **Type** field should read **Secondary** (Figure 12.19).

Notification

Secondary DNS servers must initiate the replication sequence to maintain current record sets. DNS notification, as defined by RFC 1996, allows master DNS servers to inform secondary servers that updates have been made to the DNS database. Once the secondary servers receive this notification, they may request zone transfers. Notification is available to primary DNS servers and may be configured as follows:

1. Right-click a primary zone and select **Properties**.
2. Select the **Zone Transfers** tab and click **Notify**.
3. Ensure that **Automatically notify** is checked.
4. Configure a notification list in either of the following ways (Figure 12.20):

   —Select **Servers listed on the Name Servers tab** and add servers that require notification to the **Name Servers** tab.

   —Select **The following servers** option and add IP addresses to this local list.

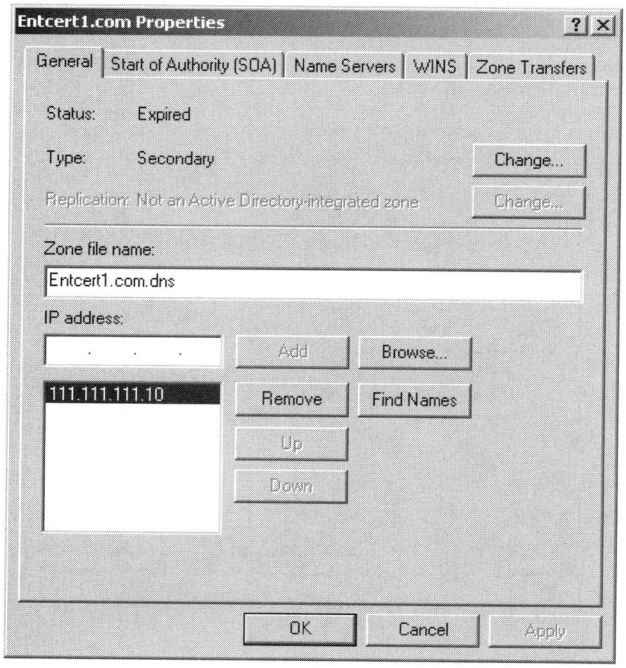

FIGURE 12.19 Forward Lookup Zone Properties

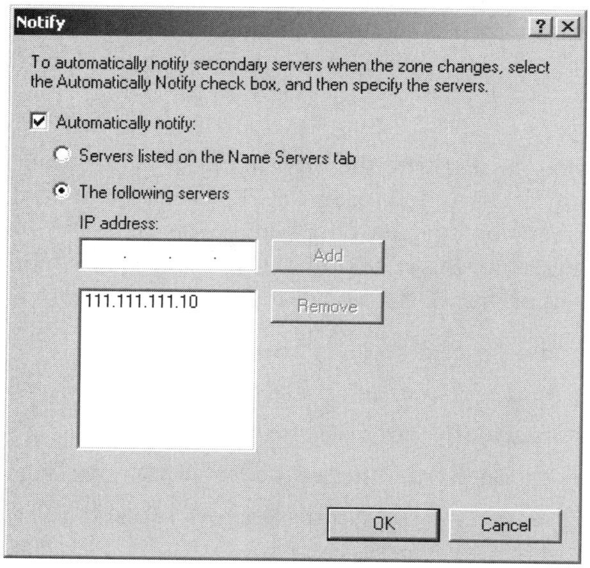

FIGURE 12.20 A Name Servers Notification List

NOTE Active Directory–integrated zones do not require notification. However, with Windows Server 2003 Active Directory can now be integrated with DNS zones stored in application partitions. Storage and replication of the DNS zones stored in the Active Directory can be part of the application partition. The application partition storage reduces the number of objects stored in the Global Catalog. When the DNS zone data is stored in an application partition, it is replicated to only that subset. DNS-specific application partitions contain only those domain controllers that run the DNS server by default. Application partition storage also enables replication of the DNS zone to the DNS servers running on the domain controllers in different domains of an Active Directory forest. This feature is activated through the **DNS Console MMC** snap-in or **Start** → **Accessories** → **command prompt** → **dnscmd**.

Both methods allow notifications to be designated to specific servers. The **Zone Transfers** tab (Figure 12.21) also permits restrictions to zone transfer to limit which DNS servers may be allowed to request zone transfers. Not only will the specified

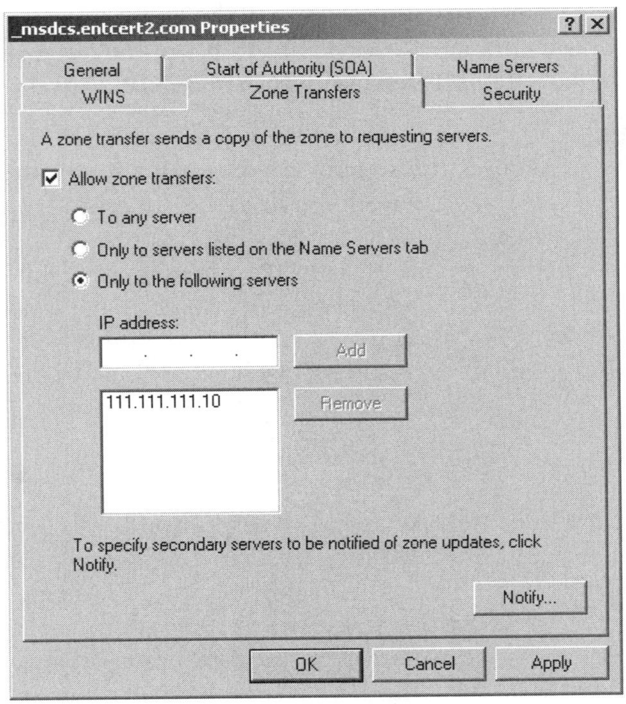

FIGURE 12.21 Restricting DNS Zone Transfers

servers receive notification of record updates, but they also can be set as the only servers permitted to make transfer requests.

NOTE To instigate a manual zone transfer at the secondary server, right-click the zone to transfer from the DNS snap-in and select **Transfer from master**.

FORWARDING

Because the recursive search creates network traffic and consumes system resources, forwarding allows one DNS server to forward name queries to another DNS server. Thus, a network may offload name resolution responsibility to a particular server or set of servers with high bandwidth to the Internet, limiting intensive searches over slow or expensive connections. When requests are forwarded to one server, the system's cache becomes more extensive, enhancing its ability to resolve name queries locally. Ideally a company's ISP can provide a target for the network's forwarding DNS server and offload name query resolution to the Internet.

To forward a DNS server's name queries to another server, follow these steps:

1. Right-click the DNS server node from the **DNS** snap-in and select **Properties**.
2. Select the **Forwarders** tab. Type the IP address of the designated forwarder in the box under **Selected domain's forwarder IP address list** and click **Add** (Figure 12.22).

The **Number of seconds before forward queries time out** specifies how long the DNS server will wait for a response from the designated forwarder. If this forwarder does not respond, the server will try the next one on the list. For a forwarder to be attempted more than once, its IP address must be entered in the list multiple times. Once this list has been depleted, with no resolution, the server will attempt to resolve the query using recursion. To prevent this, select the **Do not use recursion field**. The server returns a failed name query when the forwarder list is depleted.

SCAVENGING

The Windows Server 2003 DNS server can scavenge zones and remove outdated DNS records. By default this feature is disabled and may involve careful planning to ensure that valid resource records are not removed. Scavenging can eliminate incorrect resource records, save disk space, and increase performance. It may be initiated manually or configured to run automatically. Statically configured resource records are configured by default to have a refresh time of zero, which removes them from the scavenging process. Dynamically configured resource records, es-

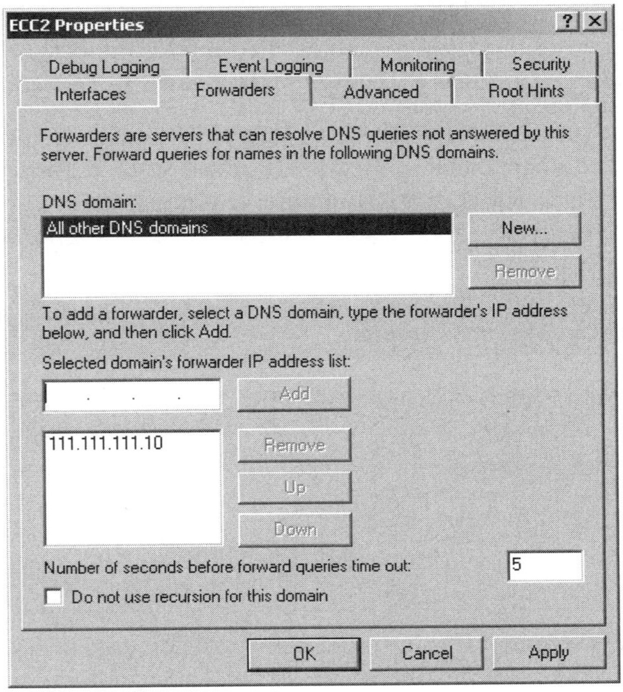

FIGURE 12.22 DNS Forwarder Properties

tablished through DHCP, are configured with a non-zero timestamp, which exposes them to scavenging.

NOTE Configuring scavenging can be complex, so see the Help pages for further explanation before enabling it.

Initiating Manual Scavenging

Manually initiate scavenging by right-clicking the DNS server from the DNS snap-in and selecting the **Scavenge stale resource records** option.

Initiating Automatic Scavenging

Configure automatic scavenging by following these steps:

1. Right-click the DNS server from the **DNS** snap-in and select **Properties**. Choose the **Advanced** tab and check the **Enable automatic scavenging of stale records** box.

2. Scavenging must be enabled at the zone node in addition to the server node. Right-click the desired zone and select **Properties**. Select the **General** tab and click **Aging**. Check the **Scavenge stale resource records** box.

A DNS server is required for all Active Directory implementations. The mapping between FQDNs and their respective IP addresses can be in constant flux. Windows Server 2003 offers two DNS implementations, the Active Directory–-integrated and the standard zone DNS server, which both support dynamic DNS updates.

The Dynamic Host Configuration Protocol

The Dynamic Host Configuration Protocol (DHCP) provides a convenient and centralized method to configure and assign IP addresses on systems throughout the network. Once that is done, the entire network may be configured to retrieve and renew these addresses whenever they boot to ensure correct IP configuration for the current network. This is especially useful for mobile users and dial-in clients.

NOTE Windows Server 2003 provides several DHCP enhancements that were not available in previous versions of the operating system. These enhancements include:

- *Classless Static Route Option*. DHCP clients can request this option to be supplied with a list of routes to add to their routing table. This allows Remote Access Service and virtual private network clients, as discussed in the next chapter, to perform split-tunneling when connecting to remote networks. This feature is integral to the operating system.
- *Classless Source Routing*. This feature allows DHCP to configure a client with multiple classless routes with the use of a subnetwork mask. This feature is configured from the MMC DHCP snap-in tool.
- *DHCP Database Backups*. This feature enables backups of a DHCP database while the service is running. The API takes a directory location on local disk excluding remote paths and the service will back up the current state of the database onto the specified location. If a directory does not exist, it will then create one. This feature is configured from the MMC DHCP snap-in tool under Backup and Restore.
- *DHCP Database NetShell Migrations*. This feature is a great advancement for administrators who use it for migration of a DHCP database from one server to another when it is imported into NetShell (NETSH). This eliminates most manual configurations including editing the Registry and recreating scopes.

The command-line tool, NETSH, is used to locally configure remote access servers and routers. This feature is available from **Start → All Programs → Accessories → command prompt** → type **NETSH.**

- *Enhanced logging for DNS updates performed by DHCP servers.* This feature can help track down DDNS attacks.

SERVER-SIDE DHCP CONFIGURATIONS

To install the DHCP server, follow these steps:

1. Ensure that the DHCP server system is configured with a static IP address. Clients must be configured with a DHCP server address to obtain an IP address (and other information) when booting.
2. From the **Start** menu → **Administrative Tools → Configure Your Server** tool. Click **Next** twice and select **DHCP server**. Click **Next**. Click **Finish**.
3. The **New Scope Wizard** appears. Click **Cancel**.
4. Bring up the DHCP tool by selecting **Start → Program → Administrative Tools → DHCP** (Figure 12.23).

DHCP Authorization

DHCP servers can be installed on domain controllers, member servers, or standalone servers. However, the first DHCP server must participate in the Active Directory and it must be a member server or domain controller. The Active Directory maintains a list of authorized DHCP servers, which a DHCP server participating in the domain can query. If the server finds itself on the list, it will provide DHCP services. If it does not, it will not initialize or provide services. A standalone server

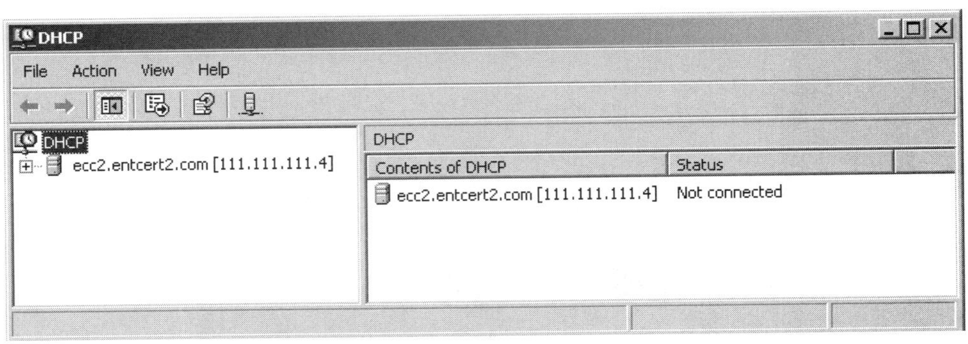

FIGURE 12.23 The DHCP Snap-In

does not participate with the directory service and depends on the limited broadcast DHCP informational message on the local network to invoke responses from functional DHCP servers. These DHCP responses will contain the enterprise root for each DHCP server, which the standalone server queries to obtain the DHCP authorization list for the directory. If it finds its IP address in each list, it will proceed with initialization. Otherwise, the service is stopped.

To authorize a DHCP server for the Active Directory, follow these steps:

1. Open the DHCP tool by adding the snap-in or select **Start → Programs → Administrative Tools → DHCP**.
2. Right-click the **DHCP** node and select **Manage authorized servers**.
3. The **Manage Authorized Servers** dialog appears (Figure 12.24). Click **Authorize** and enter the DHCP server's DNS name or an IP address. Preferably enter the FQDN or the **Name** box will remain empty. Click **OK**.

Scopes and Classes

Once the DHCP server has been authorized for the domain, scopes must be created to define IP addresses and lease durations for its clients. The scope will be applied to all clients who request dynamically assigned IP addresses within its subnet; it will also determine several other client properties:

- Address range
- Address exclusion ranges
- Lease duration
- DHCP options
- Reservations
- Classes

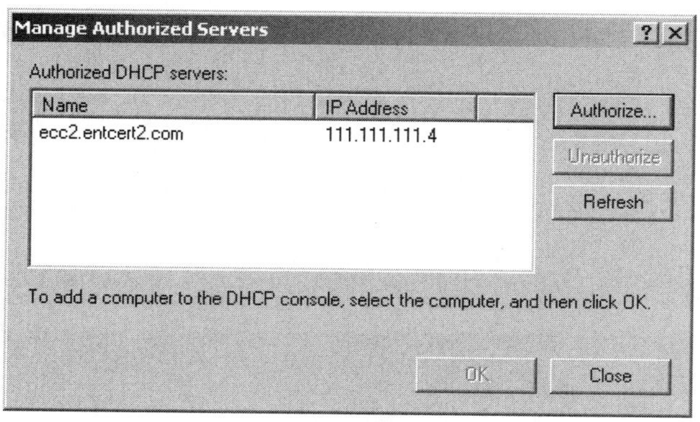

FIGURE 12.24 Authorizing a DHCP Server

Let's look at these properties as we create a scope for the new DHCP server:

1. Right-click the DHCP server in the **DHCP** snap-in and select **New Scope.** The **New Scope Wizard** appears. Click **Next** to start scope creation.
2. Enter a name and description for the new scope and click **Next**.
3. Enter a contiguous address range for the new scope by entering a **Start IP address** and an **End IP address** (Figure 12.25). This address range defines the pool of IP addresses available for DHCP clients who request them. Always assign the entire range of IP addresses to be used for the subnet and then use exclusion ranges to remove addresses from the pool.
4. The subnet mask identifies which bits of the IP address identify the network or subnet address. If the subnet mask bits are contiguous, you can indicate in the **Length** box how many bits there are from left to right. Click **Next**.
5. Add exclusion ranges to remove IP addresses from the available pool to lease DHCP clients. All IP addresses that have been statically configured for network interfaces should be excluded from the scope address range. Obviously, router addresses and the DHCP server's statically configured IP address should be excluded as well. To create an exclusion range, enter beginning and ending addresses, then click **Add** (Figure 12.26). When finished click **Next**.

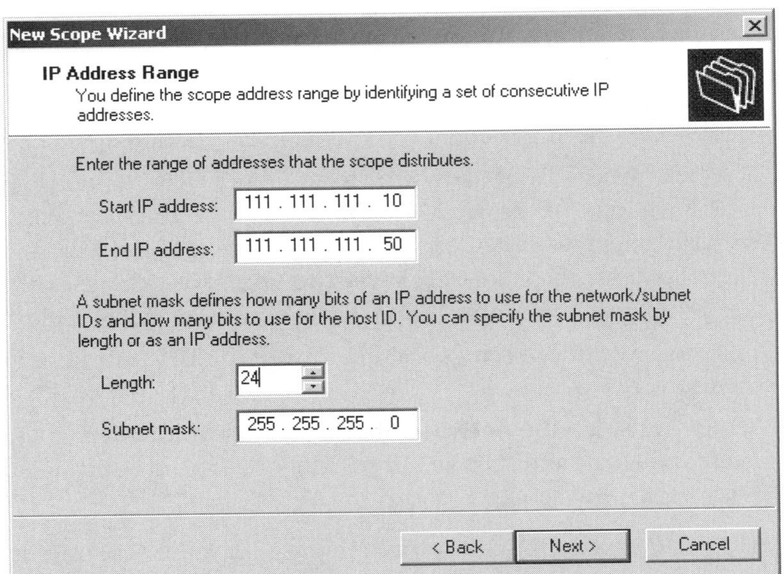

FIGURE 12.25 Scope Range

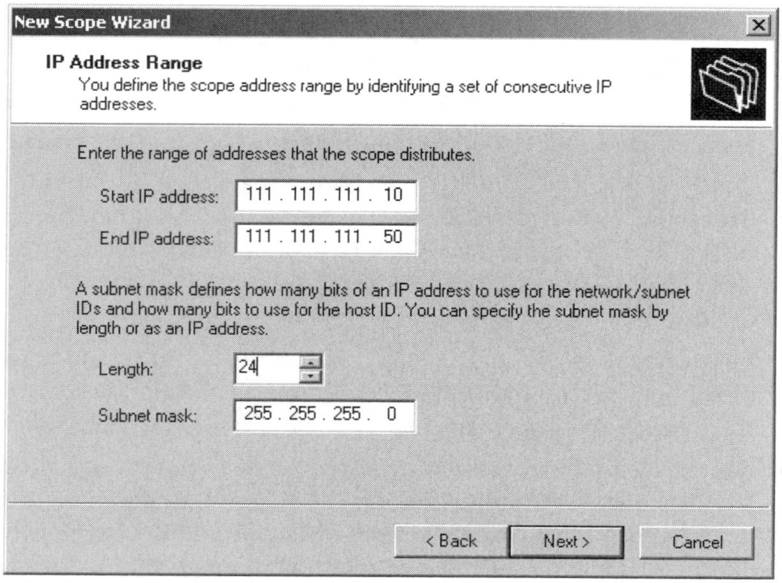

FIGURE 12.26 An Excluded Address Range

6. Enter a time interval for the duration of a DHCP client's lease of the IP address before it expires. Laptop and remote clients that regularly move networks should be assigned shorter lease periods to free up addresses sooner. More stable networks may benefit from longer lease periods (Figure 12.27).
7. The next wizard dialog allows you to configure DHCP options. Although many DHCP options are provided by the DHCP server and detailed in the DHCP standards document RFC 2132, five are supported by all Windows and MS-DOS client systems. Selecting **Yes, I want to configure these options now** (Figure 12.28) permits configuration of the options listed in Table 12.1.
8. Follow the next four screens and configure the DHCP options for clients leasing in the new scope
9. When you reach the **Activate Scope** dialog windows, you may choose to activate the scope and start DHCP service for it. In the last dialog box, click **Finish** to complete scope creation.

The DHCP tool should display the newly activated scope under the server's node (Figure 12.29). The previously configured parameters can be viewed and modified from here. Table 12.2 details the containers within a scope's node.

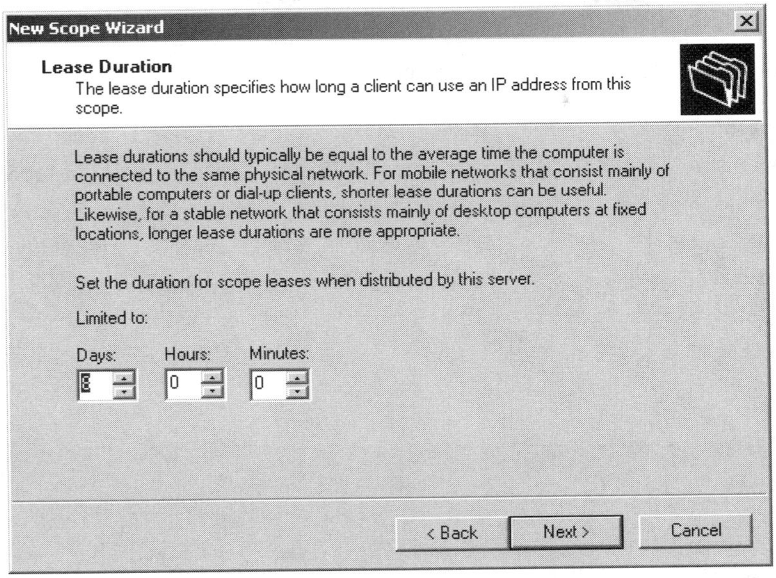

FIGURE 12.27 Lease Duration

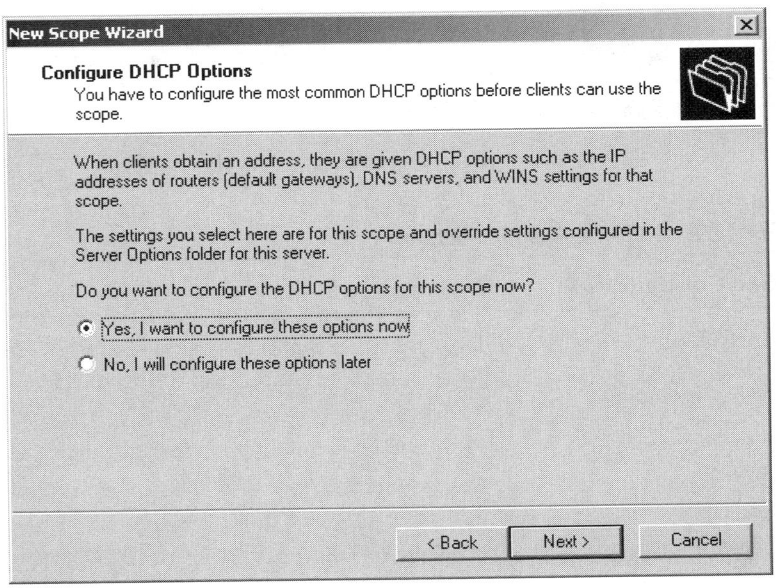

FIGURE 12.28 Activate Scope

TABLE 12.1 DHCP Options

Option	Description
Router	List of available routers in order of preference
DNS Server	List of available DNS servers in order of preference
DNS Domain Name	Parent domain for client name resolution
WINS Server	List of available WINS servers in order of preference
NetBIOS Node Type	Mechanism for NetBIOS name resolution

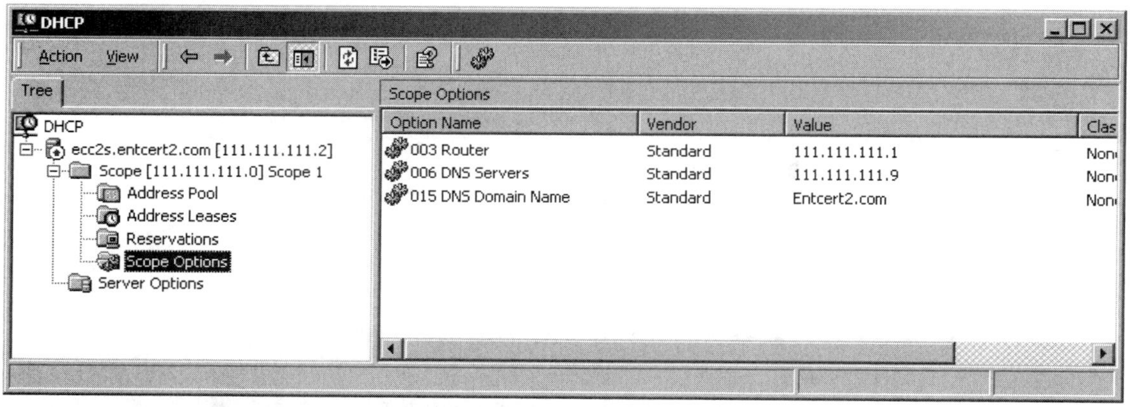

FIGURE 12.29 Scope Configuration from the DHCP Snap-in Tool

TABLE 12.2 DHCP Configuration Options

Scope Configuration	Description
Address Pool	Displays address and exclusion ranges for the scope. Exclusion ranges may be added to and deleted from the scope.
Address Leases	Displays leases currently in use and their expiration dates.
Reservations	Reserves IP addresses for clients that require the same IP address every time they boot.
Scope Options	Displays and modifies DHCP options.

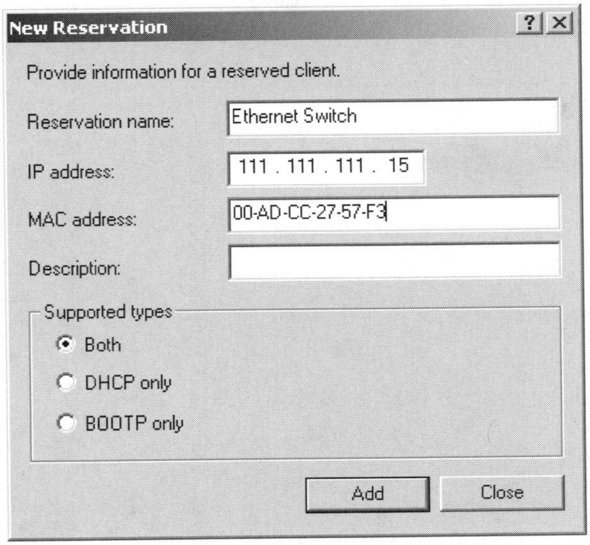

FIGURE 12.30 A Reserved IP Address

Each subcategory in the DHCP scope can be modified by right-clicking the desired node and selecting an action. For example, the exclusion ranges are added to the address pool by right-clicking the **Address Pool** node and selecting **New Exclusion Range**.

Reservations for clients are made by right-clicking **Reservations** and selecting **New Reservation**. The **New Reservation** dialog appears and requests a reservation name, IP address, and MAC address (Figure 12.30). The DHCP server may also selectively reserve IP addresses for DHCP, BOOTP, or both. When it receives a DHCP request message from a client with a source MAC address that matches a reservation, it assigns the reserved IP address to the client's lease.

The DHCP options can be modified by right-clicking the **Scope Options** node and selecting **Configure Options**. In the **General** tab of the **Scope Options** dialog box, options with a check mark will be sent to DHCP clients and may be configured by modifying their **Data entry** fields. The **Advanced** tab of the **Scope Options** dialog box presents several more opportunities to configure options for DHCP server clients (Figure 12.31).

VENDOR AND USER CLASSES

Vendor and user classes allow different DHCP options to be applied to different systems and users. The DHCP server will map the client's vendor class ID from the

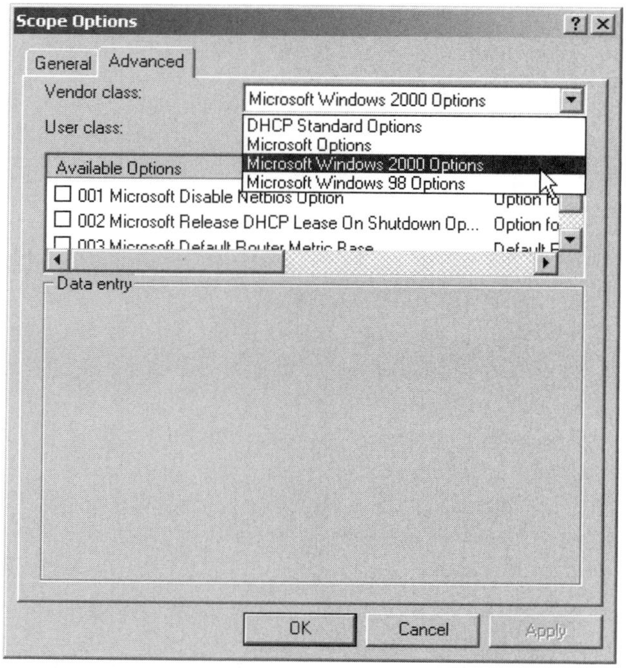

FIGURE 12.31 Advanced DHCP Option Configuration

DHCP request message to the configured vendor class list. The administrator can customize DHCP options for each vendor class. The vendor ID is configured internally only in the DHCP client software and set by the software manufacturer. For example, the Microsoft Windows 98 vendor class is set on Windows 98 clients and cannot be modified. The administrator may point all Windows 98 clients to a certain DNS server, using the vendor class to set the DNS server option.

NOTE The Windows Server 2003 vendor class offers the following additional DHCP options to configure clients:

- Disable NetBIOS on a Windows Server 2003 client.
- Configure the system to release a DHCP lease upon shutdown.
- Define a default router metric for establishing the quickest and most reliable routes.

User classes, on the other hand, can be configured on the client using the **ipconfig** line command. From the command prompt on the client system, type

```
C:\>ipconfig /setclassid "Local Area Connection" "Second Floor Users"
```

The following should be displayed:

```
Windows Server 2003 IP Configuration
DHCP ClassId successfully modified for adapter "Local Area Connection"
```

When the client sends the DHCP request message to the DHCP server, the server looks for a user class identified by the "Second Floor Users" ASCII string.

To create the corresponding user class on the DHCP server:

1. Right-click the corresponding DHCP server name from the **DHCP** snap-in. Select **Define User Classes**.
2. The current user classes are displayed in the **DHCP User Classes** dialog box. Click **Add** to reveal the **New Class** dialog box (Figure 12.32).
3. Enter a name and description for the new user class. Enter the user class ID as either a text string in the ASCII box or a hexadecimal number in the **binary** box. Click **OK**.

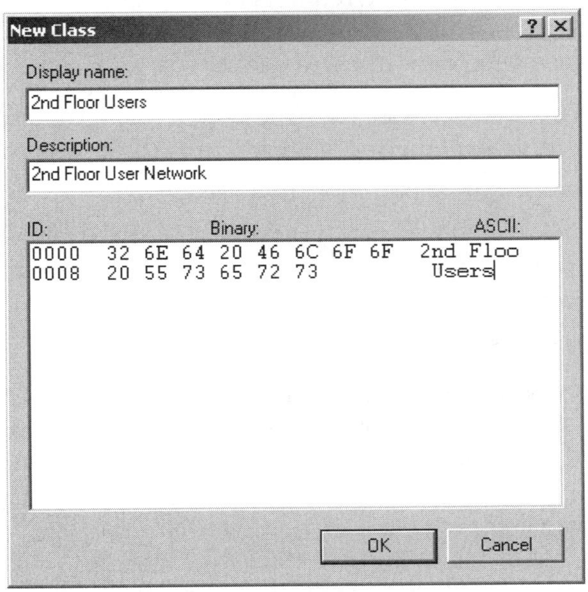

FIGURE 12.32 Creating a New User Class

4. The new user class has been created. Right-click the **Scope Options** node on the server with the new user class and select **Configure Options**.
5. Select the **Advanced** tab and click the pull-down arrow for the **User Class** field.
6. Select the new user class and check DHCP options under the **Available Options** field and configure them using the **Data entry** field.

All clients who request DHCP leases from this DHCP server, configured with the "Second Floor Users" class ID, will receive only DHCP options assigned to this user class.

SUPERSCOPES

The DHCP server must be configured and scoped with IP addresses for all subnets it intends to support. If a server receives a request from a subnet other than its pool of addresses, it cannot lease a meaningful IP address to the client. A DHCP server can be configured to support multiple logical IP networks within one physical subnet. In order to support multiple IP network ranges on the same Ethernet segment, a scope must be created for each network and then all scopes must be grouped under one superscope. The superscope allows one or more scopes to be applied to the local network. Also, when DHCP relays or BOOTP relays are supported, their corresponding requests will be forwarded through IP layer switches and routers. Because the DHCP server will receive requests from other networks, superscopes must be configured.

To create a superscope, follow these steps:

1. Right-click the DHCP server node from the **DHCP** snap-in and select **New Superscope**. The **New Superscope Wizard** starts. Click **Next**.
2. Enter a name for the new superscope, then click **Next**.
3. Select the scopes to include in the new superscope from the **Available Scopes** field. To select more than one scope, hold down the **SHIFT** key and click multiple scopes. Click **Next**.
4. Click **Finish** to complete the wizard.

The new superscope, Super Scope 1, contains Scope 1and Scope 2 and can now service clients requesting addresses for both networks 111.111.111 and 111.111.112 (Figure 12.33). See the Help pages for further superscope configurations.

DHCP AND BOOTP RELAY AGENTS

Both DHCP and BOOTP clients use broadcast addressing to initiate contact with their corresponding server. Routers do not normally permit this broadcast traffic

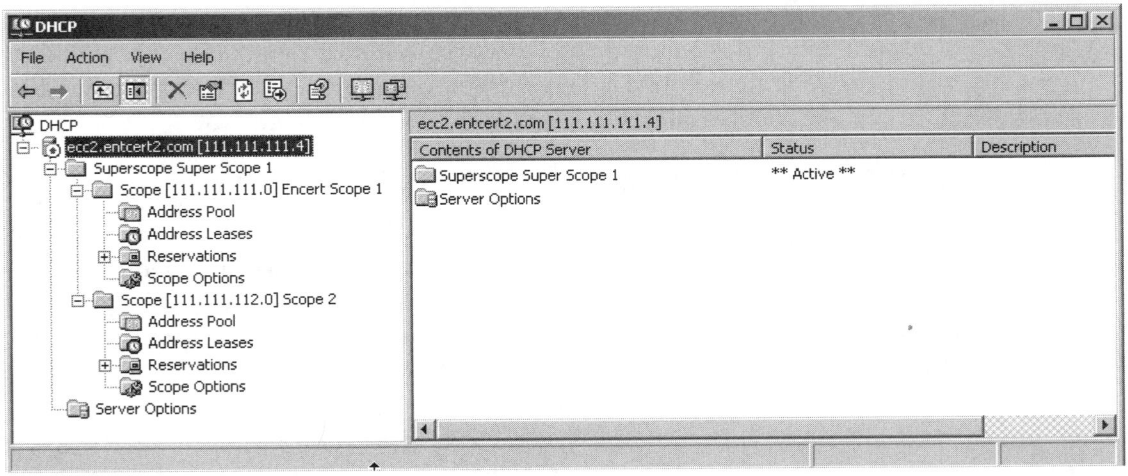

FIGURE 12.33 The Superscope Viewed from the DHCP Snap-In (Supporting Two Networks)

to traverse networks by default, which means that a DHCP/BOOTP server must be allocated for every network in the enterprise, unless routers are configured as DHCP/BOOTP relay agents. Most routers can be configured in accordance with RFC 1542 and forward DHCP and BOOTP packets between network interfaces. Another option is to configure a dual-homed Windows Server with the DHCP relay agent. This server will then forward DHCP and BOOTP requests between the two networks. The DHCP relay agent must also be configured for dial-in/remote access clients. See the Remote Access section in Chapter 13 for details.

THE 80/20 RULE FOR FAULT TOLERANCE

Fault tolerance is most effectively handled by configuring two DHCP servers to lease IP addresses on a given network. One server is configured with 20 percent of the address range; the other is configured with the remaining 80 percent. For instance, to service the 111.111.111.0 network with two DHCP servers, the first server would be scoped with 80 percent of the address range:

```
Scope range: 111.111.111.5 - 111.111.111.254
Excluding: 111.111.111.204 - 111.111.111.254
```

The second server would be scoped with 20 percent of the address range:

```
Scope range: 111.111.111.5 - 111.111.111.254
Excluding: 111.111.111.5 - 111.111.111.203
```

If one of the servers were to fail, the other could renew and issue leases for the network.

Another option is to configure a second, standby server the same way that you have configured the active server. The scopes on the secondary server would remain inactive until the primary server failed. Then they could be activated manually to handle client requests.

CLIENT-SIDE CONFIGURATIONS

Configure DHCP on the Windows Server 2003 client system for a network or dial-up connection by selecting **Start** → **Settings** → **Network and Dial-up Connections** → ***connection name*** → click **Properties**. Select **Internet Protocol (TCP/IP)** and click **Properties**. Select **Obtain an IP address automatically** and **Obtain DNS server address automatically** (Figure 12.34).

NOTE With Windows Server 2003 it is possible to configure network and dial-up connections using Group Policy. An administrator can make a user a member of the Network Configuration Operators Group. This will give the user access to the TCP/IP properties for a local a LAN connection and the ability to set her own IP address. This functionality is granted through the Group Policies snap-in.

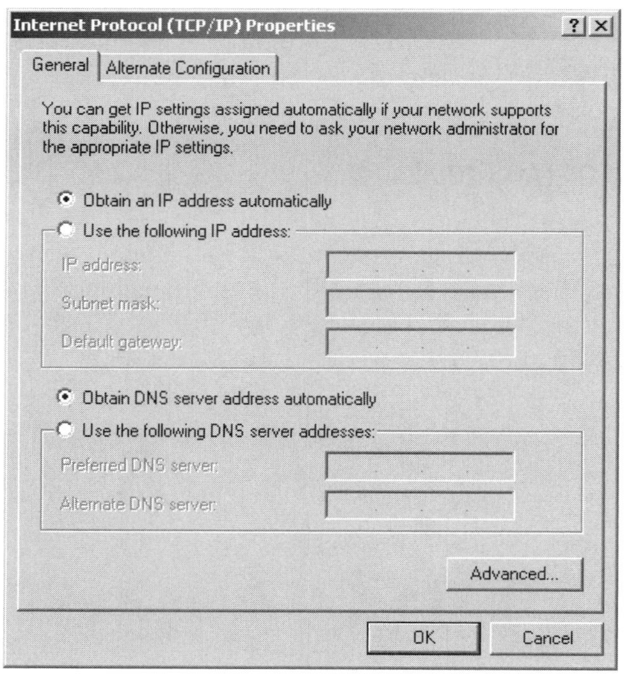

FIGURE 12.34 Configuring a Client for DHCP

Automatic Client Configuration

Windows Server 2003 DHCP clients automatically configure network interfaces when a DHCP server is unavailable. When a client boots up and cannot obtain a response from a DHCP server, it will be configured to boot with an IP address from the Microsoft Class B range 169.254.0.0 with the subnet 255.255.0.0. Automatic client configuration works well for small business and home networks. An ARP request will be used to test if another client on the network is using the selected IP address. If so, the client will continue to search for an available DHCP server every 5 minutes. When one is found, a new IP address is leased, with which the client silently reconfigures the interface. Automatic client configuration also comes into play when the client owns a validly leased IP address and cannot communicate with the DHCP server. The client will ping the default gateway assigned in the original lease. If the router responds, the client assumes it is on the same IP network, has not been moved, and continues to use the previously leased IP address. If no router responds to the request, the client assumes it has been moved off the network and chooses an IP address from the autoconfiguration network range (169.254.0.0).

Client/Server Communication

To understand how DHCP works, it's important to discuss the basic message exchange between client and server. The client approaches the DHCP server according to two scenarios: (1) it is new to a network or its leased IP address has expired, or (2) it is renewing a leased IP address.

- In the first scenario (Figure 12.35), the client broadcasts a DHCP discovery message on the local segment/ring for a DHCP server. If the DHCP server responds with a DHCP offer message, the client obtains a new lease. If not, the client can autoconfigure (configure itself) or continue to send DHCP server requests every 5 minutes. Eventually the client will receive the DHCP offer message and choose to accept the lease by returning a DHCP request to the server. The server sends the client a DHCP acknowledgment message to confirm the lease along with DHCP option configuration information.

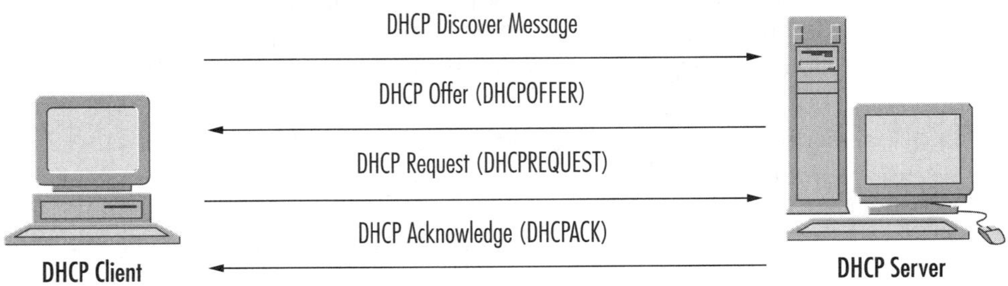

FIGURE 12.35 The DHCP Client/Server Exchange

- The second scenario involves DHCP renewal. The client usually waits until the IP address lease's lifetime is 50 percent spent. Then it attempts to renew the lease by sending a DHCP request to the server who issued the lease. If the client does not obtain a DHCP acknowledgment from the server, it waits until the lease time reaches the rebinding state. Once this occurs, the client will attempt to renew its lease with any DHCP server on the network. Unless another server renews the lease, the client terminates the current IP address and then resorts to the first scenario and attempts to locate a DHCP server with the discovery message.

DNS with DHCP

Domain DNS servers can be updated with dynamically leased IP addresses to support current name/IP address mapping. DHCP servers and clients have several strategies for implementing these DNS entry updates. Configuration on the DHCP client and server determines which one is used.

The Windows Server 2003 DHCP client supports the client Fully Qualified Domain Name (FQDN) option when communicating with the DHCP server. This allows it to instruct the DHCP on how to handle dynamic DNS updates. The **Register this connection's address in DNS** option is the default for Windows Server 2003 clients. It is set through the **Local Area Connection Status → Properties → TCP/IP → Properties → Advanced → DNS** tab (Figure 12.36) and instructs the client to send a DNS update request to the primary domain DNS server. This update will contain only the client's forward lookup record ("A" record—hostname-to-IP mapping) update.

DHCP SERVER CONFIGURATION FOR DNS

The DHCP server is capable of updating both forward and reverse lookup zones on the DNS server for DHCP clients. Several DHCP server configuration options are accessible from the DHCP tool. To reach them, right-click the DHCP server node and select **Properties**. Then select the **DNS** tab to display dynamic DNS update properties (Figure 12.37).

To prevent the DHCP server from updating any DNS information, clear the **Automatically update DHCP client information in DNS** box. Otherwise, a choice must be made between two options: If **Update DNS only if DHCP client requests** is selected, the DHCP will attempt to configure the DNS server according to the client's suggestion; selecting **Always update DNS** will configure the DHCP server to always update both the forward and reverse lookup zones on behalf of the client.

Clients that do not support the client FQDN option (DHCP clients that do not use Windows Server 2003) will not update the forward lookup zone and must rely

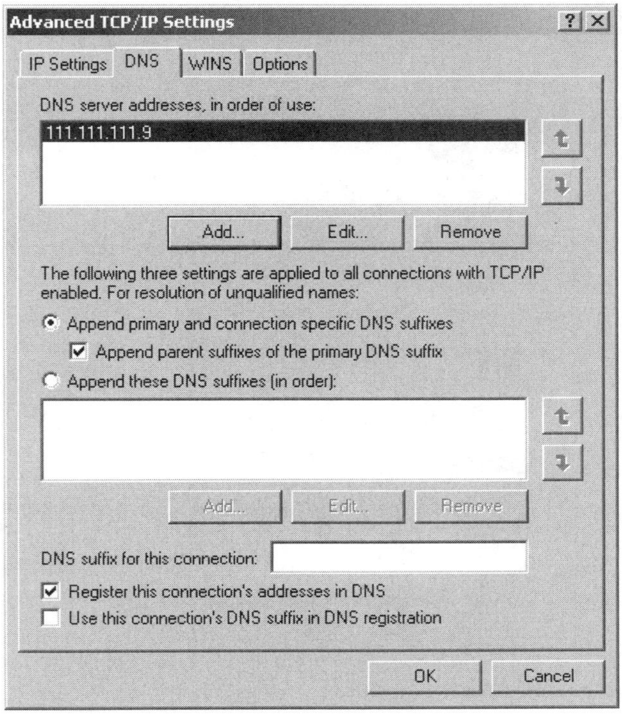

FIGURE 12.36 DHCP Client Update DNS Configuration Options

on the DHCP server to handle the DNS update request. Selecting **Enable updates for DNS clients that do not support dynamic updates** will configure the DHCP server to do this. Selecting **Discard forward (name-to-address) lookups when lease expires** instructs the DHCP server not to send updates for the forward (A) record when leases expire. As long as automatic DHCP updates are permitted, however, the server will still update the reverse lookup zone.

NOTE DHCP servers must be added to the DnsUpdateProxy security group to enable dynamic DNS update. This occurs when the DHCP server is authorized (see the "DHCP Authorization" section).

THE BACKUP AND RESTORE OPTIONS

If the active DHCP server were to crash, many IP addresses would still be leased out to network clients. DHCP server backup is paramount to smooth operation and

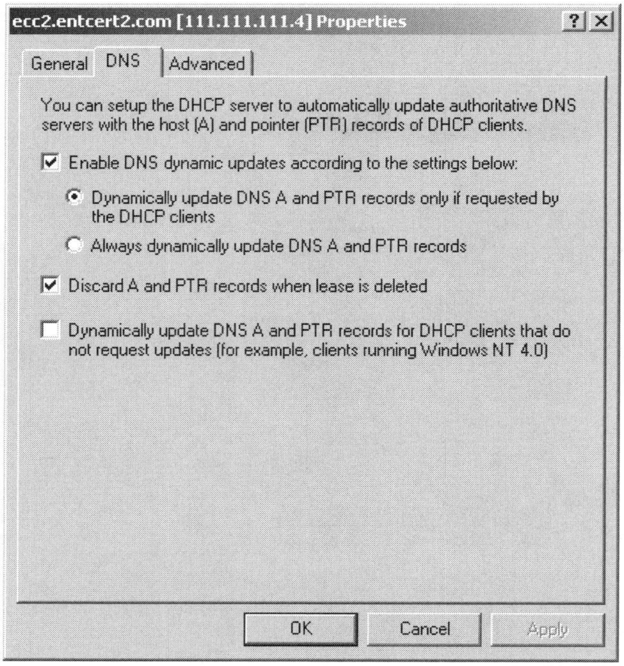

FIGURE 12.37 Dynamic DNS Update Properties

will help prevent duplicate address leases. Use Windows Server 2003 Backup and Restore options or use the NETSH set DATABASERESTORE flag to load a copy of the DHCP dbs from the default backup directory. Use logs to determine if the database is corrupt, indicated by JET errors. Initially try using the Jetpack.exe to repair the database. If this doesn't work, resort to backups. See the Help pages for moving a DHCP server database to another system.

BOOTP

The BOOTP protocol allows diskless clients to obtain IP addresses and boot image (executable code) locations to download software for operation. The image is then retrieved using the Trivial File Transfer Protocol (TFTP). The BOOTP sequence is performed only when the client is rebooted. Dynamic BOOTP address assignment is supported under Windows Server 2003. To enable this feature, right-click a previously created scope node and select **Properties**. Select the **Advanced** tab and then either **BOOTP only** or **Both** to enable dynamic IP address assignment for both protocols (Figure 12.38). A separate lease period available for BOOTP clients is configurable under **Lease duration for BOOTP clients**. The same DHCP options discussed earlier are sent to the BOOTP clients.

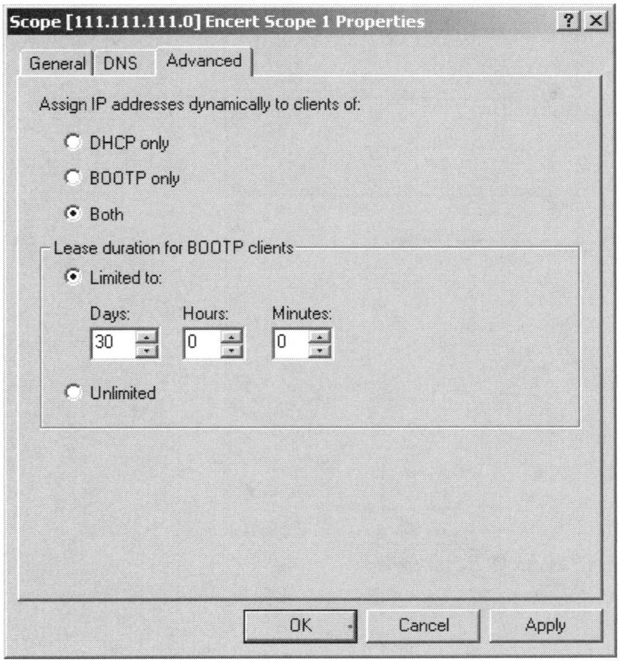

FIGURE 12.38 Scope Properties

In addition to address assignment, BOOTP clients may request file information. This is accomplished in two steps. First, a reservation is established for a BOOTP client, tying the client's MAC address to a single IP address in the same way that DHCP clients reserve IP addresses. Right-click the **Reservations** node on the appropriate scope and select **New Reservation**. Assign an IP address, a name, and a MAC address, and be sure to select either **Both** or **BOOTP only** (Figure 12.39).

Second, an entry is defined in the BOOTP table from the DHCP snap-in. Right-click the DHCP server node and select **Properties**. Check **Show the BOOTP table folder**. Right-click the **BOOTP Table** node and select **New Boot Image**. Enter the image name, directory path, and DNS server name or IP address for the TFTP that hosts the client's boot image (Figure 12.40).

The BOOTP client communicates to the file server using the Trivial File Transfer Protocol to retrieve code and continue booting. Current client images can easily be distributed throughout the network using BOOTP.

WINS

The Microsoft implementation for the Windows Internet Name Service (WINS) provides services similar to those of the DNS server discussed earlier. The WINS server

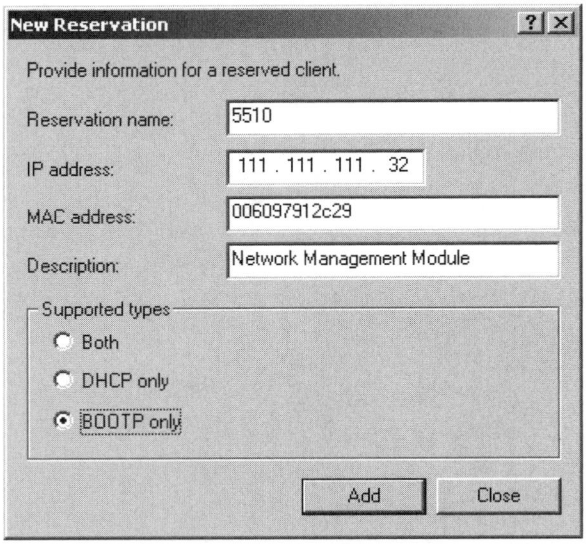

FIGURE 12.39 BOOTP Client IP Reservation

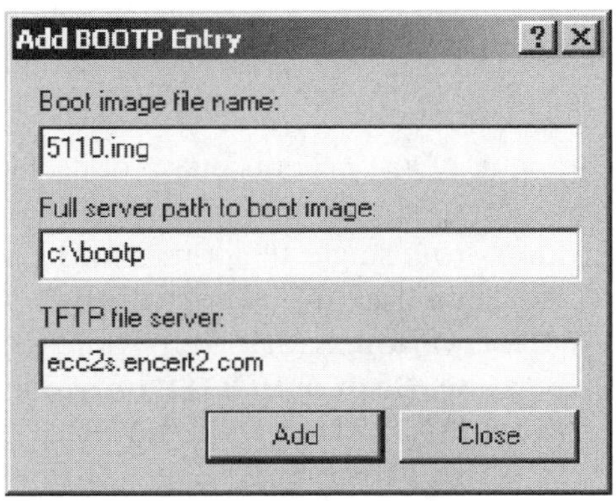

FIGURE 12.40 A BOOTP Table Entry

maps NetBIOS names to IP addresses. This is required for older systems that do not support the DNS FQDN format. The new WINS server supports dynamic updates for IP addresses assigned via the DHCP server. Also, it has no need for troublesome IP broadcasts for internetwork updates. WINS is not the preferred name server; DNS integration with the Active Directory is the primary name-resolution model.

NOTE A new feature in Windows Server 2003 that is integral to the operating system is TCP/IP name resolution without WINS or DNS. This feature provides a NetBIOS over TCP/IP (NBT) gateway. This enables Remote Access Service clients to resolve TCP/IP names on a LAN. Either a DNS or WINS server needs to be in place. This is particularly useful for small home and office networks where DNS might be considered overkill. They do not have DHCP, DNS, or WINS on this LAN. The feature enables all the remote computers to access LAN computers by name.

REAL-TIME COMMUNICATIONS

New to Windows Server 2003 is the Real-Time Communications (RTC) architecture. It is based on the Session Initiation Protocol, which is standardized under IETF's RFC 2543. This protocol was adopted by the telecommunications industry for session management, call control, presence, and instant messaging.

SIP provides the ability to create and manage any type of session. It also provides the ability to separate the physical devices such as telephones. In turn, users and the service logic are removed from centralized control.

SIP provides the ability to locate and communicate with any entity represented by a Uniform Resource Identifier (URI). This addressing schema allows SIP to use any combination of Internet technologies.

TAPI STREAMING SUPPORT

Windows Server 2003 improves the streaming quality for IP-based audio conferencing. This includes support for additional new codecs to improve quality and interoperability, DirectSound to reduce latency and improved mixing, Acoustic Echo Cancellation (AEC), Acoustic Gain Control (AGC) and ambient noise, and jitter buffer control and silence suppression algorithms to reduce latency and improve quality. The audio streaming adjustments are available via **Start → Control Panel → Printers and Other Hardware → Phone and Modem Options → Advanced**. From this point, you can add, remove, and configure the service.

Windows Server 2003 improves the streaming and management aspects of Telephony Application Programming Interface (TAPI) version 3 multicast and H.323 service providers. Support for dynamic stream topology and format changing is now provided, as are controls to enable applications to restrict bandwidth and central processor unit (CPU) usage. The wizard for audio/video device configuration and diagnostic tool is available from **Start → Control Panel → Printers and**

Other Hardware → Phone and Modem Options → Advanced. From this point, you can add, remove, and configure the service.

The OS's video streaming enhancements include improved quality for IP-based video conferencing. It includes new codecs to improve quality and interoperability. Support is also given for some new cameras and support for DirectDraw to improve video performance. Video and voice synchronization permits greater support for lip-synchronization. This feature is available from **Start → Control Panel → Printers and Other Hardware → Phone and Modem Options → Advanced**. From this point, you can add, remove, and configure the service.

DNS CONFIGURATION THROUGH GROUP POLICY

An alternative approach to DNS client configuration can be accomplished under Windows Server 2003 using Group Policy. As discussed in Chapter 7, the great benefit of group Policy is that it enables the administrator to set parameters for a number of users through one policy definition. For example, this new feature can be applied when adjusting DNS client settings such as enabling/disabling dynamic registration of the DNS records. It also applies when using name-resolution of the primary DNS suffix and when populating DNS suffix search lists.

This facility can be accessed from the Active Directory 's Group Policy Snap-in. Look at the properties of any domain, organizational unit, or site object.

NOTE Group Policy support for the DNS suffix search list last parameter will be required in a transition to environments that are not compatible with NetBIOS.

SUPPORT FOR BROADBAND PPPOE CONNECTIONS

Windows Server 2003 adds support for broadband Point-to-Point Protocol over Ethernet (PPPoE) connections. This allows remote access clients with support to use PPPoE for faster broadband connections. In theory, an administrator can make access to the internal LAN more secure by using PPPoE to authenticate LAN access from public areas. In some cases, users have a broadband connection at home that requires a PPPoE logon to connect to the Internet. Windows Server 2003 now accommodates this requirement. To configure this feature, invoke **Start → All Programs → Accessories → Communications → Internet Connection Wizard**.

POSTSCRIPT

The first part of this chapter provides a view of networking protocols and models from a very high level. We hope this conceptual view gives new system administrators a construct from which to work. The second part provides hands-on guides primarily for the installation, configuration, and management of DNS and DHCP. DNS and the Active Directory are closely connected; thus, the two should be viewed collectively in administering a Windows Server 2003 domain.

Chapter 13

Virtual Private Networks and IP Security

Virtual private networks (VPNs) are rapidly becoming the method by which organizations with remote offices use the Internet with relatively secure communications. IP Security (IPSec) secures intranets and is the primary method of securing L2TP tunnels. It can also interoperate with tunneling devices that support only its tunneling standard.

Many of the technologies that underlie VPN and IPSec are covered in other chapters, and so we will not begin with a heavy dose of theory. Instead, most of this chapter provides a hands-on description of how these technologies are deployed.

In this chapter you will learn the concepts relating to VPN authentication, encryption, and tunneling. Examples are also provided for creating a virtual private network. IPSec is then explored as both a complementary and alternative technology to VPN.

VIRTUAL PRIVATE NETWORKS

A virtual private network is a connection between two communication endpoints that ensures privacy and authentication. A tunnel coupled with encryption creates a "virtual private network" between an organization's central network and its branch offices or dial-in users. Thus, these offices and dial-in users may interconnect through the Internet's infrastructure without being subject to unauthorized snooping and impersonation. VPN technology establishes a wide area network (WAN) between sites that allows a user to log on to the network from one location and access company resources throughout the "virtual network." Connecting directly to the Internet through an ISP's point of presence (POP) is cheaper than leasing expensive dedicated circuits or making long-distance telephone calls, which is the reason for the VPN's increasing popularity.

The VPN connections discussed in this chapter are composed of three elements. A connection is considered a VPN when all three are correctly functioning.

- Authentication
- Encryption
- Tunneling

Authentication

Let's first introduce some basic strategies for authenticating users and computers when establishing VPNs. Not all tunneling protocols support every authentication protocol, but a general awareness will allow you to compare technologies for the best VPN solution.

Authentication protocols are designed to guarantee the identity of users and servers, as discussed in Chapter 10, "Kerberos and the Public Key Infrastructure." The password is the basis for most implementations, but X.509 certificates are also used when establishing secure channels and IP Security. There is a difference between user authentication (both passwords and certificates) and machine authentication (usually certificates). Table 13.1 lists the authentication protocols supported by Windows Server 2003.

Role of Encryption

Encryption provides data confidentiality and forms the "black pipe" between tunnel endpoints. Once the tunnel has been formed, packets are encrypted and encapsulated in the tunnel protocol. Usually hidden in the encrypted portions of these packets is the original IP header information, which prevents eavesdroppers not only from reading the encrypted data but also from reading the packet's destination. The destination tunnel endpoint IP address and other IP header information are the only pieces of information required to route a packet from one end of the tunnel to the other. Although there are many implementations and levels of encryption, primarily IPSec and MPPE are used to encrypt tunnels with Windows Server 2003. (See Table 13.2.)

Tunnels

The tunnel is defined by two endpoints that communicate through a tunneling protocol. One end of the tunnel encapsulates incoming traffic and routes it to the

TABLE 13.1 Windows Server 2003 Authentication Protocols

Protocol	Description
Password Authentication Protocol (PAP)	A "last choice" authentication protocol used to authenticate older VPN clients. PAP sends the password in clear text and is not secure.
Shiva Password Authentication	Sends an encrypted password between Shiva LAN Rover and a Windows Server 2003 or Shiva client and Windows Server 2003. Although more secure than PAP, it resends the same encryption for a given password and is therefore susceptible to replay attack.
Challenge Handshake Authentication Protocol (CHAP)	Uses the MD-5 hash algorithm. Although not the same as MS-CHAP, Windows Server 2003 supports CHAP to interoperate with many other remote access vendors and OS.
Microsoft Challenge Handshake Authentication Protocol (MS-CHAP)	One-way (*not* mutual) authentication between client and server using RSA's MD-4/DES encryption. The single session key is generated based on the user's password and thus is the same for every session.
MS-CHAP Version 2	Provides mutual authentication between client and server using two session keys (one for transmitting and one for receiving) based on the user's password and a random string. Each authentication session uses different keys.
IEEE 802.1X Support	Windows 2003 adds support for wireless and Ethernet LANs
Extensible Authentication Protocol (EAP)	EAP-MD-5 CHAP—uses the Message Digest 5 similar to the CHAP protocol but only in EAP format. It uses user name password data and is not for smart card support but good for testing EAP authenticating systems; EAP-Transport Level Security (TLS)—used with smart cards and X.509 v3 certificates for mutual authentication between server and client.

other end. This encapsulation process can occur at either the second or third protocol layer as defined by the Open Systems Interconnections (OSI) model. Layer 2 protocols encapsulate at the data link layer and retain MAC-level addresses and frame information for different media types. Layer 3 protocols encapsulate packets from the network layer up. The Point-to-Point Tunneling Protocol (PPTP) and the Layer 2 Tunneling Protocol (L2TP) are layer 2 tunneling protocols, whereas IP Security implemented in tunnel mode is in layer 3. Windows Server 2003 supports all three, but L2TP is the preferred implementation for Microsoft products.

The following discussion outlines these mutually exclusive protocols in relationship to VPN.

TABLE 13.2 Windows Server 2003 Encryption Method

Method	Description
Encapsulated Security Payload (ESP)	Supports 40-bit DES, 56-bit DES, and 128-bit 3DES encryption standards. Authentication is also provided with either the MD-5 or SHA-1 integrity standards.
Advanced Encryption Standard	New to Windows Server 2003, the Advanced Encryption Standard candidate (Rijndael) was announced by the U.S. National Institute of Standards and Technology (NIST) in October 2000 as the candidate to replace Data Encryption Standard.
Microsoft Point-to-Point Encryption (MPPE)	Requires authentication with MS-CHAP or EAP and supports 40-bit encryption for international use and 128-bit encryption within the United States and Canada.

POINT-TO-POINT TUNNELING PROTOCOL

The Point-to-Point Tunneling Protocol is one way to create a VPN. PPTP relies on the Point-to-Point Protocol (PPP) to initially encapsulate an IP packet coming from a source at one end of the tunnel (Figure 13.1). Microsoft Point-to-Point Encryption (MPPE) can be used to encrypt the PPP payload information. MPPE is set up with keys passed using the MS-CHAP or EAP-TLS authentication methods.

The PPP header and payload are encapsulated into a Generic Routing Encapsulation (GRE) header and an IP header. The source IP address in the IP header corresponds to the tunnel server at the start of the tunnel, and the destination IP address corresponds to the tunnel server at the end (Figure 13.2).

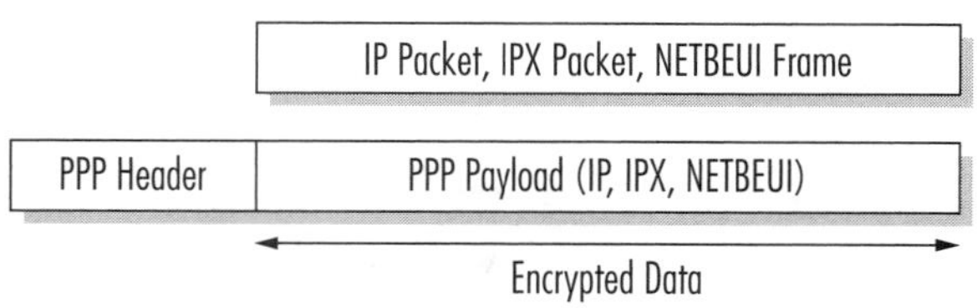

FIGURE 13.1 PPP Encapsulation

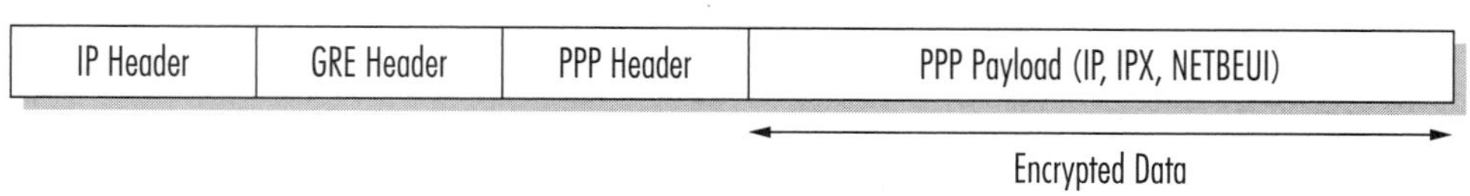

FIGURE 13.2 PPTP Encapsulation

LAYER 2 TUNNELING PROTOCOL

The Layer 2 Tunneling Protocol is the preferred method of establishing a VPN in a Windows Server 2003 environment and also relies on the prepackaged PPP frame (Figure 13.3). L2TP encapsulates the PPP frame with an L2TP header and User Diagram Protocol (UDP) header.

L2TP over IPSec, as illustrated in Table 13.3, is the preferred method of encryption for the L2TP tunnel. An IPSec Encapsulating Security Payload (ESP) header and trailer encapsulate the L2TP payload for encryption and authentication (Figure 13.4). IPSec negotiates the transport level connection using computer certificates and the Internet Key Exchange (IKE) protocol; once this is complete, L2TP tunnel settings are used to establish the tunnel and authenticate the user. The IP header contains the tunnel endpoints for the source and destination IP addresses. The packet's true source and final destination are not visible to the Internet when encryption is enabled. L2TP over IPSec also offers data integrity and authentication without encryption through the use of digital signatures supported in Authentication Headers (AH).

NOTE The current Windows Server 2003 implementation of L2TP does not support connections over X.25, Frame Relay, or ATM networks.

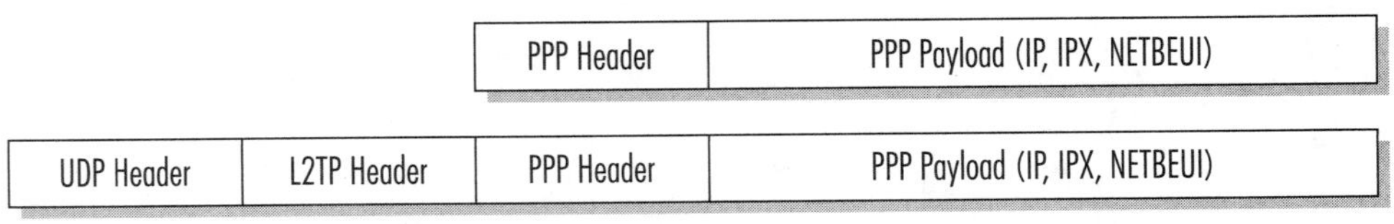

FIGURE 13.3 L2TP Encapsulation

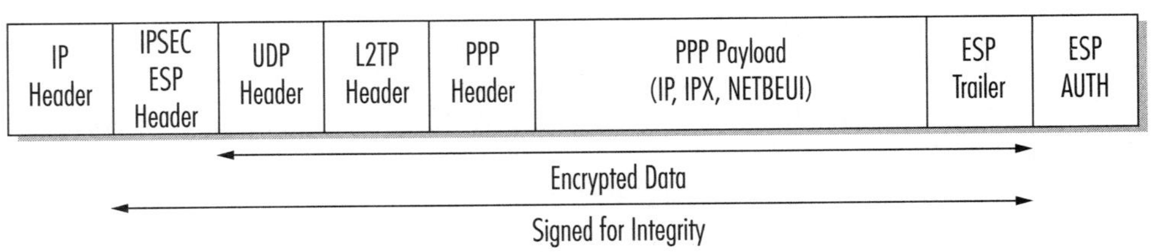

FIGURE 13.4 IPSec Encapsulation and Encryption

TABLE 13.3 Tunneling Protocol Comparison

Capability	PPTP	L2TP/IPSEC	IPSEC Tunnel
Compression		X	
Tunnel Authentication		X	X
Encryption Method	MPPE	IPSec Transport	IPSec Transport
Transit Media Type Support between Tunnel Endpoints	IP	IP, X.25, Frame Relay, or ATM	IP
Datagram/Frame Types Supported between Client Endpoints	IP, IPX, or NetBEUI	IP, IPX, or NetBEUI	IP

NOTE Windows Server 2003 adds support for Network Address Translation (NAT) for both L2TP and IPSec VPN clients. TCP and UDP traffic may now flow through a NAT device without losing encryption protection. Additionally, IPSec can be used to secure L2TP tunneling in accordance with RFC 3193.

NOTE Windows Server 2003 IPSec has added the stronger 128-bit equivalency IKE key. This provides a 2048-bit Diffie-Hellman key generation. This is based on support of the IETF draft (draft-ietf-ipsec-ike-modp-groups-02.txt).

IPSEC TUNNELING

The IPSec tunnel operates at layer 3 and incorporates the IP packet and its contents. When L2TP and PPTP are not available on VPN servers or clients, it may be used for interoperability. IPSec provides two general modes of operation: tunnel and transport. Tunnel mode is discussed first; transport mode is discussed in the next section.

Tunnel mode involves two configurations: Encapsulating Security Payload (Figure 13.5) and Authentication Headers (Figure 13.6). ESP encapsulates IP packets for encryption and integrity. AH signs packets for integrity only. Both append an IP header to the packet that contains routing information between tunnel endpoints.

Comparison of Tunneling Methods

Some implementations of the three tunneling protocols might vary on different operating systems. As Table 13.3 shows, L2TP and IPSec offer the most favorable

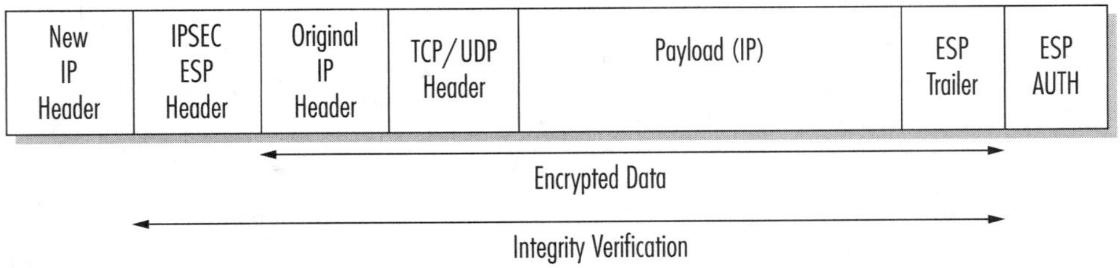

FIGURE 13.5 ESP Tunnel Mode

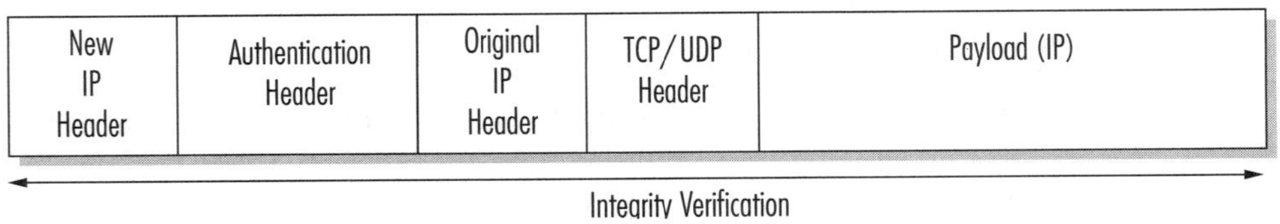

FIGURE 13.6 AH Tunnel Mode

solution, thanks to features inherited from both PPP encapsulation and the IPSec transport.

VPN Configurations

When designing a virtual private network, it is important to understand that there are two general VPN configurations:

- *Router-to-router*—Example: A branch office router is connected to a corporate intranet.
- *Remote access*—Example: One dial-in client establishes a connection at the time of the call.

These configurations are examined in the following sections.

ROUTER-TO-ROUTER

Branch office connections through a router-to-router VPN (Figure 13.7) can be configured to meet a wide range of organizational and physical requirements. For example, they may be *persistent* 24 hours a day or they may be established *on demand.* The nonpersistent router-to-router VPN may cut down on expensive long-distance phone or data connections, and establishing it is transparent to the user. Many users on both networks use a VPN connection concurrently.

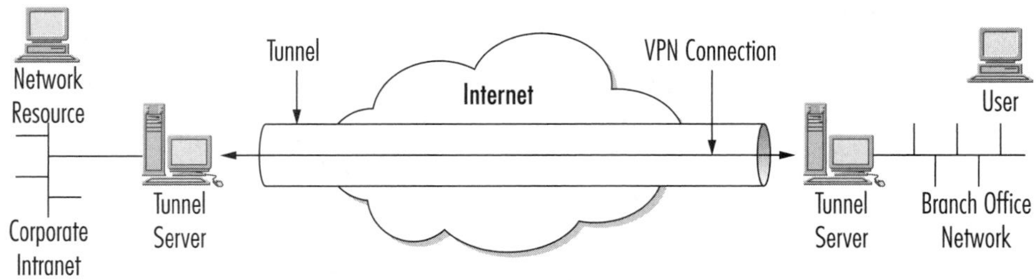

FIGURE 13.7 A Router-to-Router VPN Connection

REMOTE ACCESS

The remote access VPN configuration is established when a single client dials in to either an ISP or a corporate Remote Access Server. The connection is then established between the client and the tunnel server, but not before mutual authentication between them is established. Once the user is identified, remote access policies determine the conditions for the VPN connection setup. If the client dials in to an ISP, the VPN connection remains with the corporate tunnel server and is transparent to the ISP (Figure 13.8).

VOLUNTARY AND COMPULSORY TUNNELS

The two methods for establishing a tunnel between the client and the corporate intranet are voluntary and compulsory. Remote access policy for individual users determines which method will be used. The voluntary tunnel is initiated by the individual VPN client workstation when it accesses the corporate network. The compulsory tunnel is initiated by a VPN client server at the ISP when the user attempts to log on to the corporate network. Policies set on the corporate VPN server force users to set up this mandatory tunnel and may exist on the corporate VPN server or corporate Internet authentication server (IAS), to be discussed in a later section.

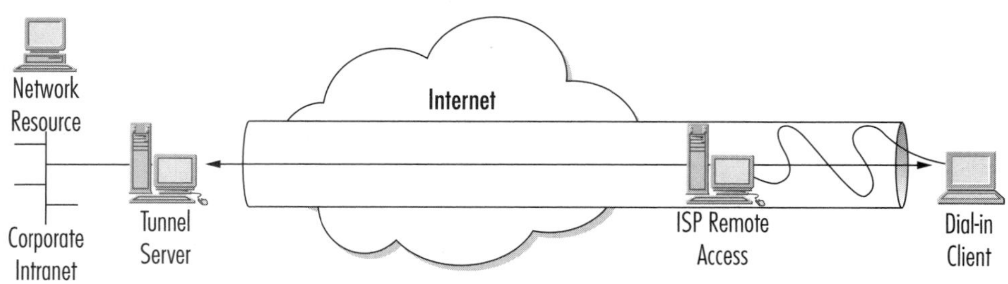

FIGURE 13.8 A VPN Connection Directly between a Client and the VPN Server

VPN Architecture and Configuration

With a conceptual understanding of VPN, we can now turn our attention to the details of implementations associated with the previously discussed VPN configurations. The three common VPN configurations are router-to-router persistent, router-to-router on demand, and remote access over the Internet. Here are the basic steps to implement them:

- Internet/intranet connection interface configuration
- Routing and remote access setup
- Certificates supporting IPSec
- Static routes
- Tunnel port configuration
- Tunnel filter configuration
- Remote access policy
- VPN client configuration

REMOTE ACCESS OVER THE INTERNET

To provide a better understanding of VPN implementation, the following example demonstrates how to configure a RAS server for VPN connections with individual clients. In this scenario, the client establishes a remote connection over an intranet or the Internet using a tunneling protocol and encryption mechanism, as in Figure 13.4. She dials in to her ISP and establishes Internet connectivity. Remote access policies prevent a client connection unless a tunnel is established. The tunnel is therefore mandatory before intranet connectivity is permitted. The RAS will be configured to authenticate clients using L2TP over IPSec encryption. Once a client has been authenticated, and a VPN connection has been established, the RAS will forward data between the client and the intranet behind the server. This is known as configuring a RAS server for VPN.

NOTE Windows Server 2003 has added a few features to accommodate small businesses with servers performing many network functions. These include:

- The ability to install and run RAS, NAT, Active Directory, and Firewall functions on a single system connecting a small company with the Internet.
- A server configured to handle dial-in access and NAT functions may now permit RAS clients access to the Internet.

Setting Up Internet and Intranet Interfaces on the VPN Server

The following provides a step-by-step review of VPN setup using sample IP addresses. (These should *not* be used in a real or test environment. Secure and use your own IP addresses when simulating this example.) For this example, assign 111.111.111.2 and subnet mask 255.255.255.0 to the intranet interface. Then, assign IP address 111.111.112.2 with 255.255.255.0 subnet mask to the Internet interface (Figure 13.9).

1. Select **Start** → **Settings** → **Network Connections** and double-click the intranet interface. Click **Properties**.
2. Select the **Internet Protocol (TCP/IP)** option and click **Properties**. Type the IP address and subnet mask for the intranet interface.
3. Repeat this process for the Internet interface.

Setting Up Routing and Remote Access

To route between the Internet and the intranet, the Routing and Remote Access Service must be installed.

1. Select **Start** → **Programs** → **Administrative Tools** → **Routing and Remote Access**. Right-click the VPN server node and select **Configure and Enable Routing and Remote Access**. The **Routing and Remote Access Server Setup Wizard** starts. Click **Next**.
2. Select **Virtual private network (VPN) access and NAT** and click **Next** (Figure 13.10).
3. Select the interface that is attached to the Internet. This is the network from which the client is communicating (Figure 13.11). In this case that interface is 111.111.112.2. Click **Next**.

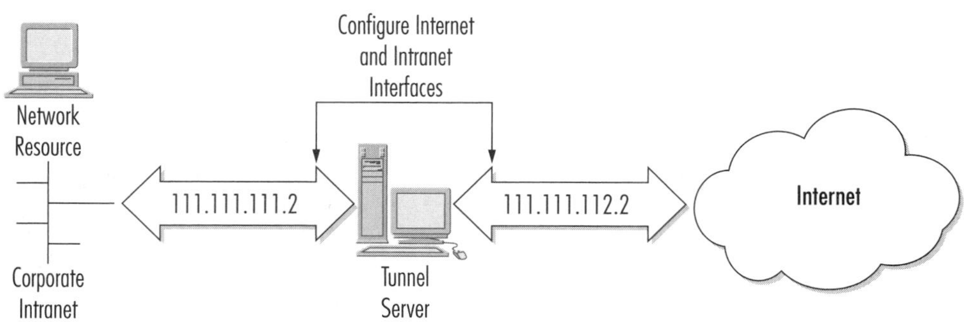

FIGURE 13.9 Configuring Interfaces

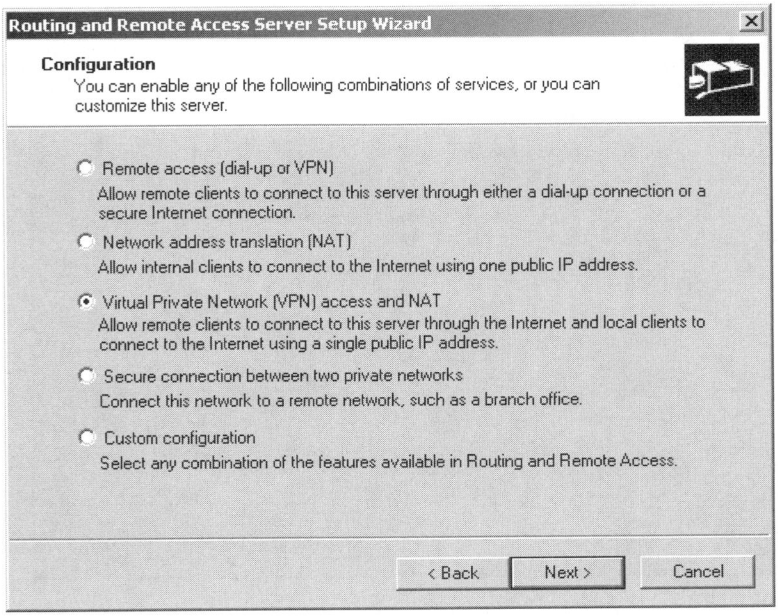

FIGURE 13.10 Common Configuration Options

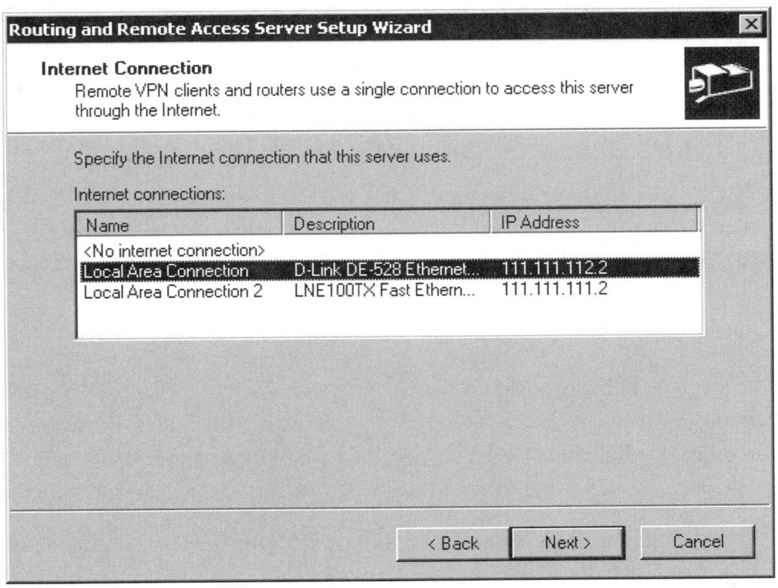

FIGURE 13.11 Network Selection

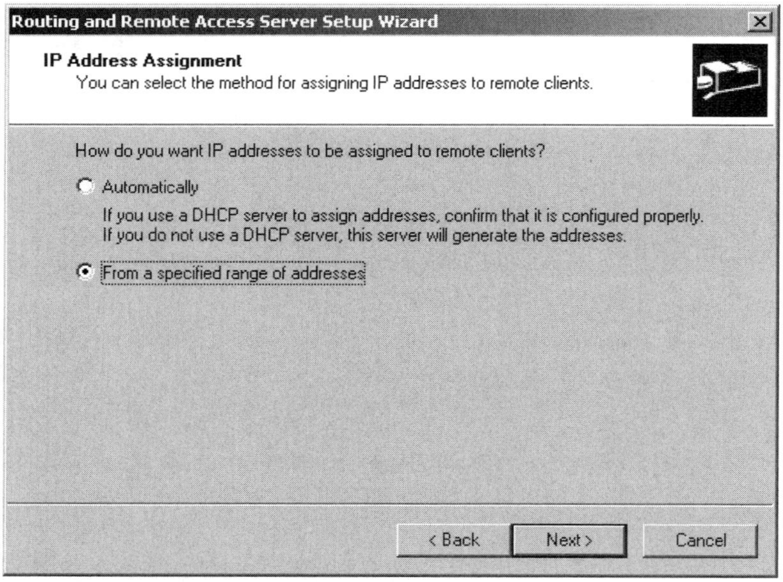

FIGURE 13.12 IP Address Assignment

4. DHCP can be used to assign IP addresses to VPN clients by selecting **Automatically**. For this example, configure a pool of addresses for the RAS server to assign to clients by selecting **From a specified range of addresses** (Figure 13.12). Click **Next**.
5. Create a range of IP addresses to assign VPN clients by clicking **New** (Figure 13.13). Type the **Start IP address** and **End IP address** to designate the new IP address range. Click **OK**. Click **Next**.
6. The next dialog box involves the RADIUS service, which is discussed in another example. Here select **No, I don't want to set up this server to use RADIUS now** (Figure 13.14). Click **Next**.
7. Click **Finish**. The wizard may bring up some suggestions for your RAS installation.

Once the Routing and Remote Access server is up and running, a green dot should be visible on the new server from the Routing and Remote Access snap-in. If you plan to dial directly in to the RAS (as well as access the server over the Internet through a LAN interface), make sure that the following options are enabled.

8. Right-click the new server and select **Properties**. From the **General** tab, ensure that the **Remote access server** option is checked and that **LAN and demand-dial routing** is selected.

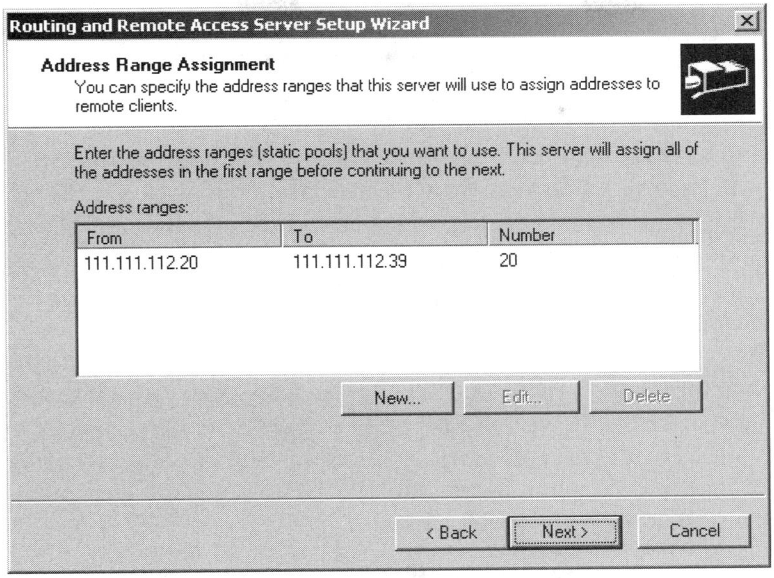

FIGURE 13.13 Address Range Assignment

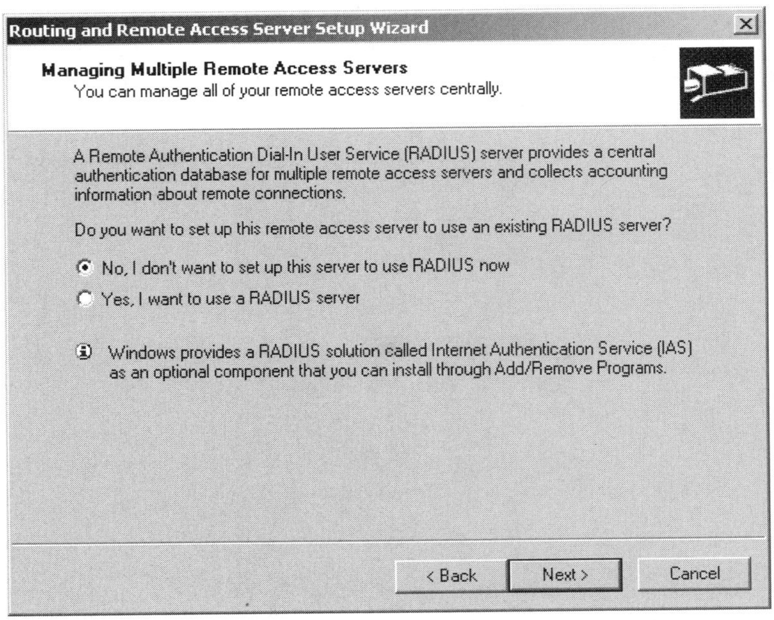

FIGURE 13.14 Managing Multiple Remote Access Services

Applying Certificates for IPSec

IP Security requires an X.509 version 3 certificate to be installed on all participating systems. Install an IPSec machine certificate from a trusted certificate authority. (See Chapter 11 for additional information.) We recommend using the Certificate snap-in to request an IPSec certificate. Right-click the **Personal** store node and select **All Tasks → Request New Certificate**. Follow the Certificate Request Wizard's instructions. If the client is offsite, use the Web server Certificate Request Web pages to request a certificate from the certificate authority. (Again, see Chapter 11.)

Configuring Static Routes

The RAS/VPN server may be configured with either routing protocols—such as the Routing Information Protocol (RIP) and Open Shortest Path First protocol (OSPF)—or static routes to direct traffic between the VPN client and the destination internal networks. For the sake of simplicity, we will examine how to configure RAS/VPN using static routes. All networks the VPN client wishes to communicate with must have a configured route in the table.

1. From the **Routing and Remote Access** snap-in, right-click the **Routing and Remote Access** node → ***servername*** node → **IP Routing → Static Routes** and select **New Static Route**.

To forward external traffic destined for an internal network other than the 111.111.111.0 network (or your intranet network):

2. Select the intranet interface from the **Interface** drop-down list box (Figure 13.15).

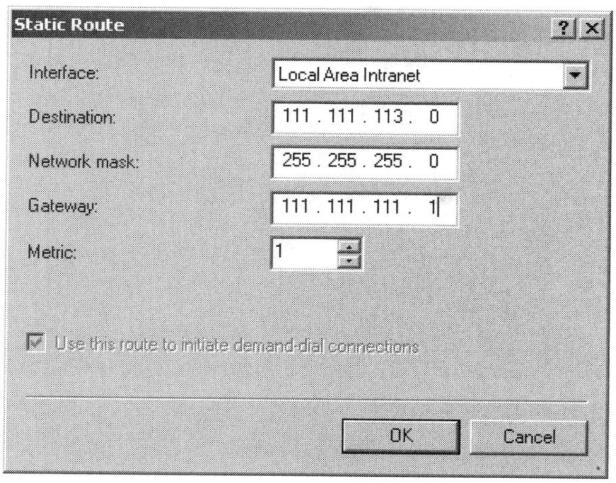

FIGURE 13.15 Adding a Static Route

3. Type the destination network and subnet mask. All IP packets destined for this network will now follow this new route.
4. Type the router interface address responsible for forwarding the packet to the destination network in the **Gateway** box. In this example, a router has an interface on the 111.111.111.0 internal network. It is also capable of routing to the 111.111.113.0 network.
5. A low metric number gives high preference to this route when multiple options for a destination network exist.

For instance, to route incoming packets from the 111.111.112.2 interface onto the 111.111.113.0 network, the entries shown in Figure 13.15 would be made. The Intranet interface address is 111.111.111.2.

To verify the newly created route, display the routes for the VPN server using the route print command from the command prompt (Figure 13.16).

NOTE If there is only one network at the corporate intranet or branch office, no static routes are required. RAS will forward packets between the two interfaces if all packets are destined for addresses on the local VPN network.

The routing table can also be displayed from the **Routing and Remote Access** snap-in by right-clicking the **Routing and Remote Access** node → ***servername*** node → **IP Routing** node → **Static Routes** node and selecting **Show IP**

```
Command Prompt
Interface List
0x1 ........................... MS TCP Loopback interface
0x2 ...00 80 c8 fe a0 67 ...... D-Link DE-528 Ethernet PCI Adapter
0x10004 ...00 80 c8 fe 86 26 ...... D-Link DE-528 Ethernet PCI Adapter #2
===========================================================================
===========================================================================
Active Routes:
Network Destination        Netmask          Gateway       Interface  Metric
      111.111.111.0    255.255.255.0    111.111.111.2   111.111.111.2     30
      111.111.111.2  255.255.255.255        127.0.0.1       127.0.0.1     30
      111.111.112.0    255.255.255.0    111.111.112.2   111.111.112.2     30
      111.111.112.2  255.255.255.255        127.0.0.1       127.0.0.1     30
      111.111.113.0    255.255.255.0    111.111.111.1   111.111.111.2     1
    111.255.255.255  255.255.255.255    111.111.111.2   111.111.111.2     30
    111.255.255.255  255.255.255.255    111.111.112.2   111.111.112.2     30
          127.0.0.0        255.0.0.0        127.0.0.1       127.0.0.1     1
          224.0.0.0        240.0.0.0    111.111.111.2   111.111.111.2     30
          224.0.0.0        240.0.0.0    111.111.112.2   111.111.112.2     30
    255.255.255.255  255.255.255.255    111.111.111.2   111.111.111.2     1
    255.255.255.255  255.255.255.255    111.111.112.2   111.111.112.2     1
===========================================================================
Persistent Routes:
  None

C:\>_
```

FIGURE 13.16 Display of a Routing Table

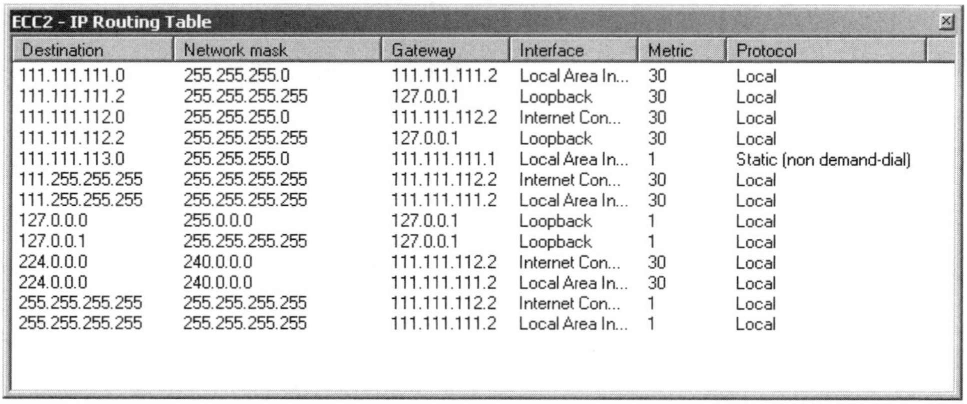

ECC2 - IP Routing Table

Destination	Network mask	Gateway	Interface	Metric	Protocol
111.111.111.0	255.255.255.0	111.111.111.2	Local Area In...	30	Local
111.111.111.2	255.255.255.255	127.0.0.1	Loopback	30	Local
111.111.112.0	255.255.255.0	111.111.112.2	Internet Con...	30	Local
111.111.112.2	255.255.255.255	127.0.0.1	Loopback	30	Local
111.111.113.0	255.255.255.0	111.111.111.1	Local Area In...	1	Static (non demand-dial)
111.255.255.255	255.255.255.255	111.111.112.2	Internet Con...	30	Local
111.255.255.255	255.255.255.255	111.111.111.2	Local Area In...	30	Local
127.0.0.0	255.0.0.0	127.0.0.1	Loopback	1	Local
127.0.0.1	255.255.255.255	127.0.0.1	Loopback	1	Local
224.0.0.0	240.0.0.0	111.111.112.2	Internet Con...	30	Local
224.0.0.0	240.0.0.0	111.111.111.2	Local Area In...	30	Local
255.255.255.255	255.255.255.255	111.111.112.2	Internet Con...	1	Local
255.255.255.255	255.255.255.255	111.111.111.2	Local Area In...	1	Local

FIGURE 13.17 An IP Static Routing Table

Routing Table. The full table is displayed for the routing and remote access server (Figure 13.17).

Tunnel Ports

By default there are 128 PPTP and 128 L2TP ports defined for the RAS server. If you expect more than this number of concurrent VPN connections using L2TP, take the following steps to increase the number of L2TP ports.

1. Right-click the **Routing and Remote Access** node → ***servername*** node → **Ports** node, then select **Properties**. Select **WAN Miniport (L2TP)** and click **Configure**.
2. Increase the **Maximum ports** by typing or selecting a number in the combo box, and click **OK** (Figure 13.18).

NOTE Microsoft's Windows Server 2003 Connection Manager Administration Kit permits administrators to configure VPN servers to redirect client requests for external sites directly to the Internet. When the external VPN client connects to a VPN server, only requests bound for internal servers are forwarded over the company's network. This limits network traffic on the company's network to requests for internal resources.

L2TP over IPSEC Filters

Tunnel filtering can be used to disable all other connection types. Filtering UDP port numbers and source and destination IP addresses is an effective way to elim-

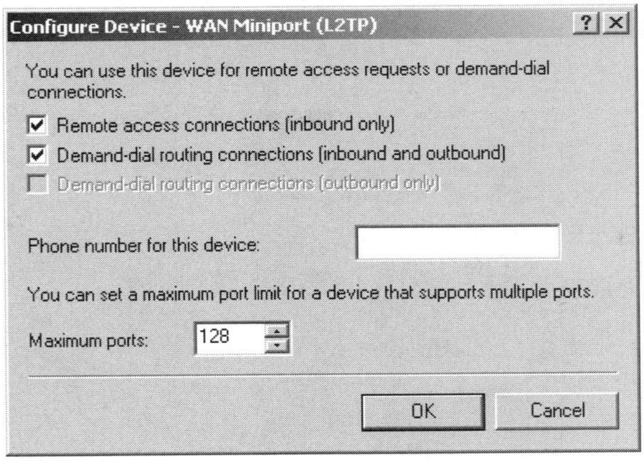

FIGURE 13.18 WAN Miniport Device Configuration

inate connections for other services. Some protection is afforded the VPN server through inbound and outbound packet filtering. To configure L2TP input filters:

1. Open the **Routing and Remote Access** node → ***servername*** node → **IP Routing** node → **General** node, right-click the Internet interface in the details pane and select **Properties**. The **General** tab displays properties for the external adapter.
2. Click **Inbound Filters**. Click **New**.
3. Check the **Destination network** box and type the IP address of the internal interface. Type 255.255.255.255 for the **Subnet mask** (Figure 13.19).
4. Select the **UDP** protocol from the **Protocol** drop-down list.
5. Type **500** for the **Source port** and **500** for the **Destination port** (Figure 13.19). Port 500 is used by the Internet Security Association and Key Management Protocol (ISAKMP) to authenticate keys and negotiate IPSec connections. (ISAKMP is also known as the Internet Key Exchange protocol.)
6. Repeat steps 2 through 5, but make the **Source port** and **Destination port** 1701. Click **OK**. Port 1701 is reserved for L2TP communications.
7. In the **Inbound Filters** dialog box, select **Drop all packets except those that meet the criteria below**. Click **OK**.

At this stage, it is necessary to add appropriate L2TP input and output filtering, as here:

8. In the **Internet adapter's Properties** dialog box, select **Output Filters**.
9. Click **Add** and check the **Source network** box.

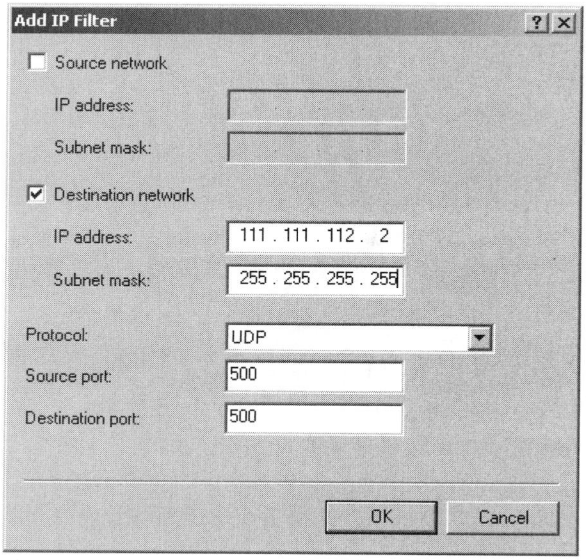

FIGURE 13.19 Add IP Filter

10. Type the IP address of the external interface in the **IP address** box.
11. Type **255.255.255.255** for the **Subnet mask**.
12. Type **500** for the **Source port** and **Destination port**. Click **OK**.
13. Repeat steps 8 through 12, but make the **Source** and **Destination ports** 1701.
14. Select **Drop all packets except those that meet the criteria below**. Click **OK**.

All four filters (two input and two output) should have been applied to the Internet adapter IP address, thereby preventing all other connections from passing through the adapter. The intranet adapter (on the corporate network) will be unaffected by these filter settings, and thus internal systems will still be able to establish any type of connection with the VPN server.

Remote Access Policy

Remote access permissions are granted on a user-by-user basis through the **Dial-in** tab associated with each user account's properties. Right-click a user from the **Active Directory Users and Computers** snap-in and select the **Dial-in** tab. Select **Allow access** or **Deny access** as appropriate to assign VPN or Dial-in permissions (Figure 13.20).

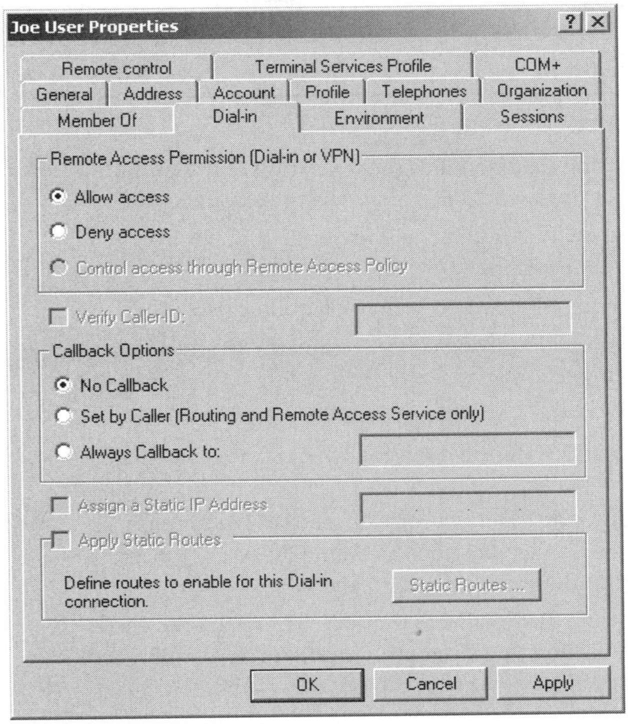

FIGURE 13.20 Dial-in Properties

Remote access policies provide conditions and a profile that clients must meet in order to access the server. To use one, select **Allow access** for each user account. (Native-mode Windows Server 2003 systems have the **Control Access through Remote Access Policy** option instead of **Allow access**.) Once all user accounts have been given remote access capability, additional policies are used to restrict which users and connection types are permitted to access the server. Table 13.4 describes remote access policy attributes. A few examples will be discussed in the next procedural steps.

Setting remote policies is the next step to take to support client use of RAS. To create a remote policy, follow these steps:

1. From the **Routing and Remote Access** snap-in, select the **Routing and Remote Access** node → ***servername*** node → **Remote Access Policies**. Right-click the **Remote Access Policies** node and select **New Remote Access Policy**.
2. Select **Set up a custom policy**. Type something like **VPN Policy** for the policy name. Click **Next**.

TABLE 13.4 Remote Policy Attributes

Attribute	Description	Wildcard (*)
Authentication-Type	Authentication method.	
Called-Station-Id	Text string that identifies the text string of the phone number the user dialed to establish this connection.	
Calling-Station-Id	Text string that represents the phone number from which the client is dialing.	
Client-Friendly-Name	Text string for a RADIUS client computer (IAS only).	X
Client-IP-Address	Text string identifying client computer's IP address (IAS only).	X
Client-Vendor	Vendor of the RADIUS proxy server (IAS only).	X
Day-And-Time-Restrictions	Time periods during the week when user may connect.	
Framed-Protocol	Identifies the framing protocol used. L2TP supports multiple frame types such as Frame Relay, X.25, Serial Line Internet Protocol (SLIP), and PPP.	X
NAS-Identifier	Text string that identifies the NAS with which the client is establishing the "front end" of the tunnel for VPN access (IAS only).	
NAS-IP-Address	Text string that identifies the IP address of the NAS with which the client is establishing the "front end" of the tunnel for VPN access (IAS only).	X
NAS-Port-Type	Media type the caller is using, such as ISDN or phone line.	X
Service-Type	Type of connection the user is attempting to establish (PPP, telnet).	
Tunnel-Type	Tunnel protocols permitted.	
Windows-Group	Windows Server 2003 security group memberships that may be denied or permitted access to the RAS.	

Select several conditions in the following steps:

3. Click **Add**. Select the **Windows-Groups** attribute and click **Add** (Figure 13.21). The **Windows-Groups** condition identifies security group membership required to meet the policy.
4. Click **Add** and select security groups to govern remote access privileges. Click **OK**. Click **OK**. Click **Next**.
5. Select **Grant remote access permission** to allow users who meet this policy's requirements to have remote access privileges. Click **Next**.

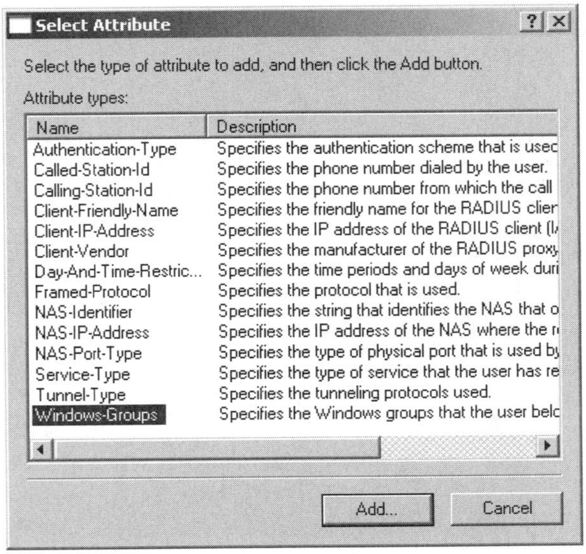

FIGURE 13.21 Remote Policy Attributes

6. Click **Edit Profile** to modify profile settings for VPN Policy. Select the **Authentication** tab. Smart card authentication is configurable from here. Both MS-CHAP v2 and MS-CHAP should be enabled (Figure 13.22).
7. The **Encryption** tab offers the following selections:
   - **Basic**—40-bit DES encryption
   - **Strong**—56-bit DES encryption
   - **Strongest**—3DES encryption (encrypts each data block using from one to three different keys with the DES algorithm—this is only for North American VPN clients)
8. Click **OK**. Click **Next**. Click **Finish**. If other default policies exist, remove them. This will eliminate conflicts with previously established RAS policies.

Remote Access Client Configuration

For the client to dial in to a VPN, specific steps must be taken to configure its remote access. From the client computer, create a local dial-in connection:

1. Start the **Network Connection Wizard** by selecting **Start** → **Settings** → **Network Connections.** Double-click the **New Connection Wizard** icon to start the wizard. Click **Next**.

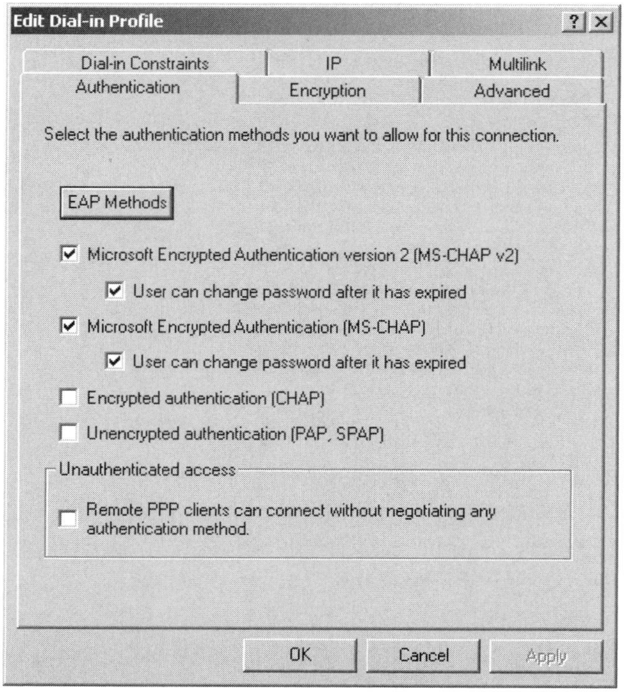

FIGURE 13.22 Profile Properties

2. Select **Connect to the network at my workplace** and click **Next**. Select **Dial-up connection** and click **Next**. This will provide the client Internet connectivity via its local ISP Point of Presence.

The next step involves connecting to the VPN. Create a second connection using the Network Connection Wizard. Make it a VPN connection to be invoked after the dial-in connection is established:

3. Start the **Network Connection Wizard** by double-clicking the **New Connection Wizard** icon. Click **Next**. Select **Connect to the Network at my workplace**. Click **Next**.
4. Select **Virtual Private Network connection** (Figure 13.23). Click **Next**.
5. Type a name for the VPN connection and click **Next**.
6. Select **Automatically dial this initial connection** and select the previously created dial-in connection to invoke the dial-up when this new VPN connection is established. If you plan to access the Internet through a LAN interface, select **Do not dial the initial connection**. You may also select this option and dial up to the Internet manually. Click **Next**.

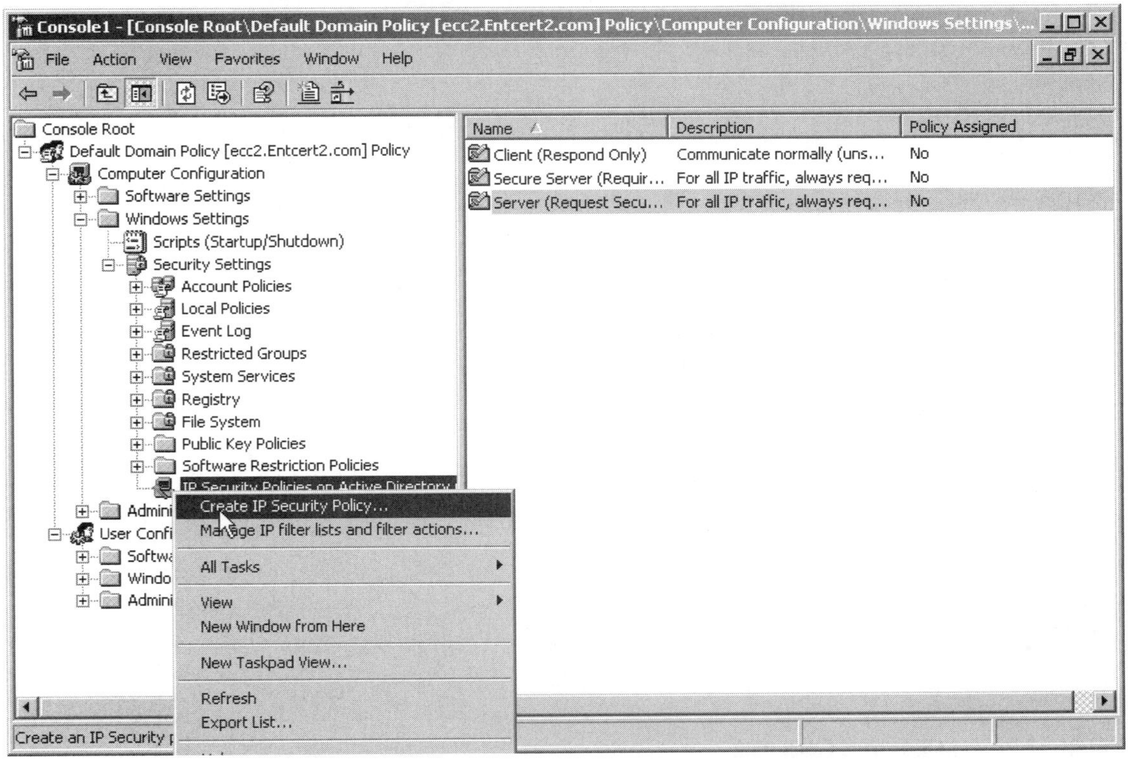

FIGURE 13.23 Setting Up a Client VPN Connection

7. Type the IP address of the VPN server's external interface. Click **Next**.
8. Select whether all users on the system will be able to use the VPN connection. Click **Next**.
9. Click **Finish**.

Once the VPN client's dial-in and VPN network connections are created, the client system is ready to establish a VPN tunnel. The user need only start the dial-in connection first and then the VPN connection. If the VPN connection has been selected to automatically dial the dial-in connection, it alone need be invoked. The same is true if the VPN server is available through a LAN interface (Figure 13.24).

Routing and Remote Access Server Management

The Routing and Remote Access snap-in can perform several functions. To control the server's behavior, right-click the RAS server and select **Start, Stop, Pause, Resume**, or **Restart**.

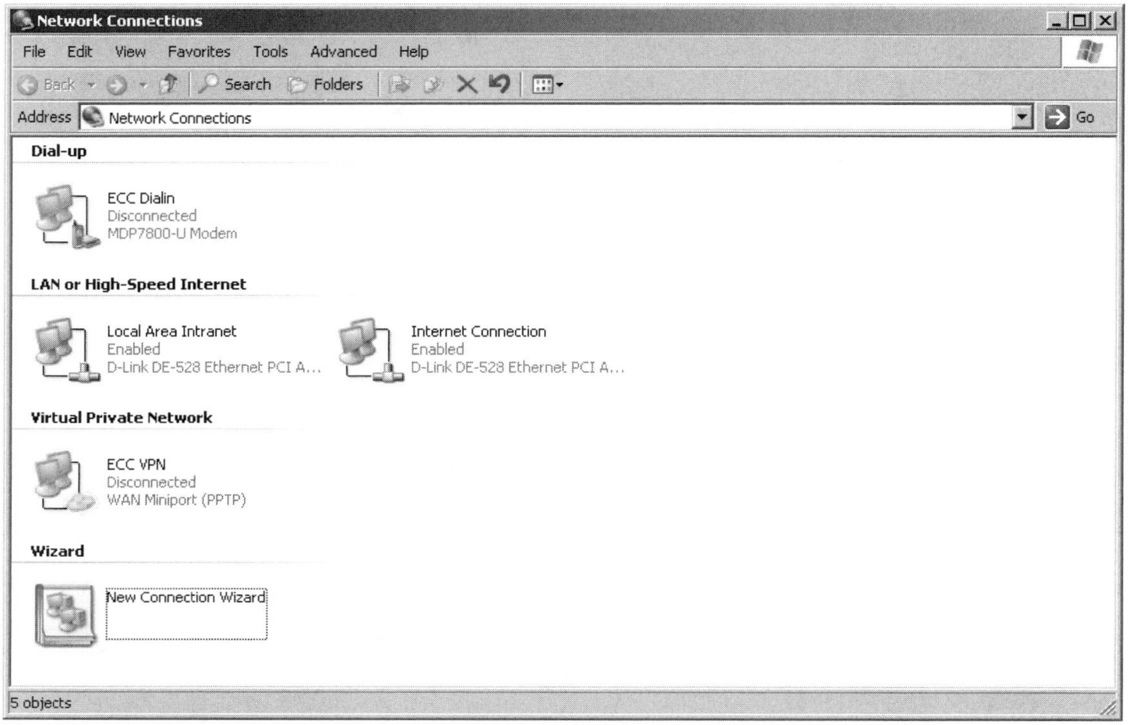

FIGURE 13.24 A Client VPN Connection

VIEWING REMOTE ACCESS CLIENTS

To manage this environment well, a facility for easy viewing of remote access clients is important. Right-click ***servername*** → **Remote Access Clients**, select the desired client from the details pane, and choose

Status to see statistics, errors, and network information (Figure 13.25).

Disconnect to disconnect a client from the VPN server.

Send Message to send a text message to a single client.

Send to All to send text message to all remote clients.

Internet Authentication Service and RADIUS

The Internet Authentication Service (IAS) enables centralized authentication, authorization, and auditing for remote clients. Once the client has been authorized with the centralized account manager, a VPN connection may be established according to the user's account policies. This is accomplished through the Remote Au-

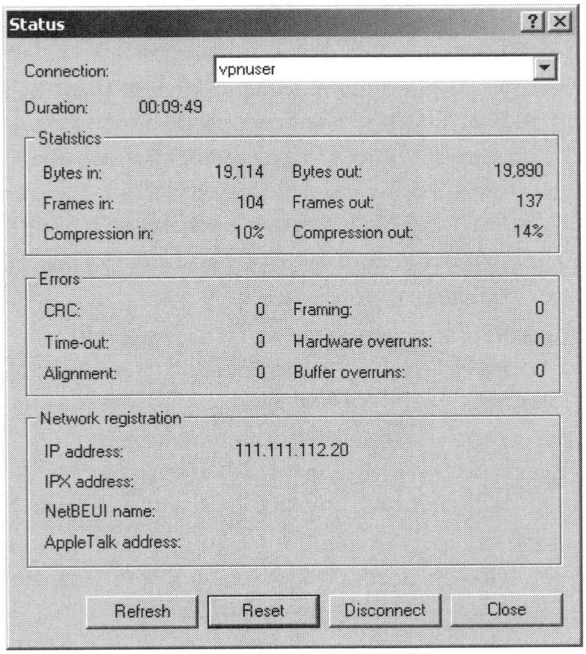

FIGURE 13.25 Remote Access Client Connection Status

thentication Dial-In User Service (RADIUS), which enables the ISP's points of presence (POPs) to authenticate dial-in and VPN clients on one IAS server for the corporation. User account profiles are maintained in one location, not on every VPN server the local network supports. Once the IAS server on the local corporate network has verified the user's credentials, the POP can establish a VPN connection with a local VPN server.

NOTE Windows Server 2003 provides authentication improvements for wireless, remote access, and VPN users in other forests, nontrusted domains, or other RADIUS user databases. A member IAS/RADIUS server provides authentication and authorization for user accounts that are members of the domain or forest. It can authenticate the user account in the other forest where Active Directory forests are in cross-forest mode with two-way trusts. Most of the enhancements to IAS and RADIUS with Windows Server 2003 are:

- IAS Proxy can authenticate users with a RADIUS server outside of a company's network and then authorize the user for local access by assigning the user a locally recognized Active Directory user account.

- IAS can directly map certificates issued by trusted certificate authorities to Active Directory user accounts.
- Systems that reboot while participating in the local Active Directory network using IAS can be reauthorized for network access using their computer account. The system cannot access resources in the local AD framework. Unless the user logs on manually to the AD network with a user account, a subsection of IAS configuration may be replicated between servers using NetShell commands.
- IAS may authenticate users in other forests if a two-way trust has been established between the local and remote forests.
- Access for visiting users and other network devices without authorization can be assigned to local Active Directory using Extensible Authentication Protocol–Transport Layer Security (EAP-TLS).
- Multiple Extensible Authentication Protocol types can be assigned based on network connection type or security group membership. This allows the administrator to assign different EAP types to each access policy.
- Roaming wireless clients can be reauthenticated quickly when moving geographically between wireless access points using the Protect-EAP.
- IAS can negotiate the EAP authentication method with clients.
- In conjunction with Remote Access Server, IAS can quarantine until the client's system configuration has been analyzed and accepted. In this way, administrators can ensure that clients have installed correct antivirus and software patches.
- IAS can require object identifiers (OIDs) on client certificates to enforce the type of certificate required to log on. A user may be forced to log on with a "User" certificate rather than a "Web Server" certificate.
- IAS can be configured to interoperate with Network Access Servers that do not conform to RFCs.
- Wireless devices can be authenticated with user name and passwords in addition to certificate based authentication.
- EAP-TLS authentication event logging has been enhanced to assist troubleshooting.
- RADIUS configuration can be assigned to a range of IP addresses to ease administration.
- A RADIUS Proxy can forward authentication to another RADIUS server. An organization may need this capability for load-balancing reasons or simply to authenticate users from partner sites on its local network.
- Logon hours as assigned in Active Directory user accounts are enforced for RADIUS clients.

The general architecture of IAS has the following components (Figure 13.26):

1. The mobile remote client connects to a nearby ISP's POP using a modem connection and any of the supported authentication methods discussed at the beginning of the "Virtual Private Networks" section. The user's realm name is either provided at the connection logon in the form *username@realm* or provided by the Connection Manager automatically. This name is easier to handle if it corresponds to the corporation's Active Directory user account realm name (discussed later in an example).
2. The ISP dial-in server (soon to be a VPN client with the user's corporate network) forwards the RADIUS request to the RADIUS server configured as a proxy.
3. The proxy sends a RADIUS request to the RADIUS server at the corporate site.
4. The RADIUS server verifies the user's credentials in the Active Directory and checks the user's applicable remote access policies.
5. The RADIUS proxy relays the user's connection request to the VPN client at the ISP. The VPN client at the ISP then initiates a tunnel with the VPN server at the corporate site.

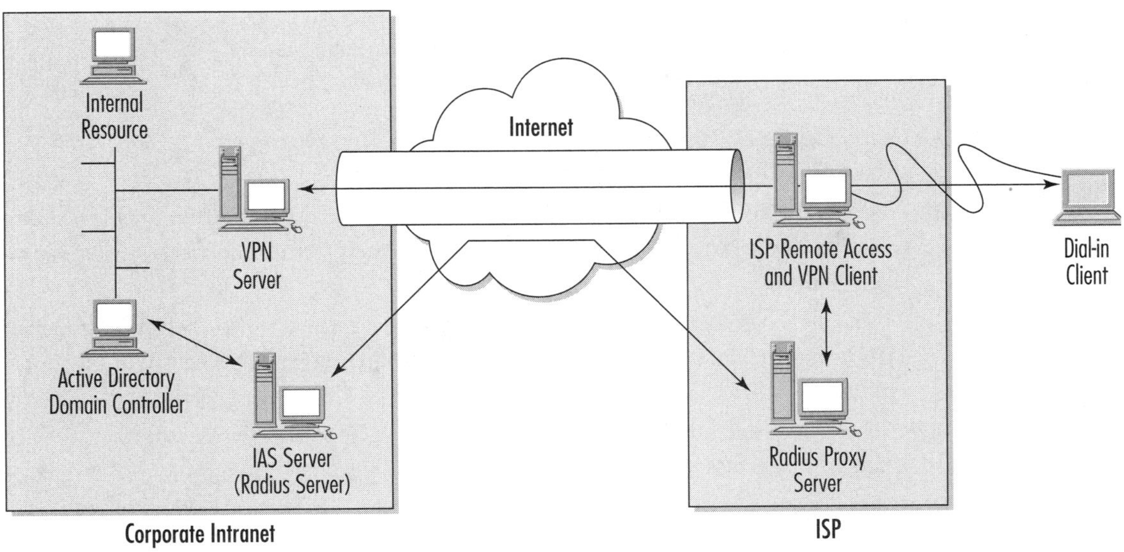

FIGURE 13.26 The IAS Architecture

NOTE The VPN connection is entirely separate from the RADIUS authentication process. The RADIUS server at the corporate site is configured with the Internet Authentication Service snap-in tool. RADIUS clients are added to the RADIUS server's client list, where logging and accounting properties can be configured. Remote access policies and profiles are modified in the same fashion as they are for VPNs. The main difference between the VPN scenarios and the IAS architecture is the method of authentication chosen from the Routing and Remote Access snap-in tool.

Firewalls must be configured to forward RADIUS UDP communications and permit remote connections with the IAS server. This is usually accomplished by putting the IAS server in a demilitarized zone (DMZ) to provide both Internet access and limited intranet exposure.

The RADIUS architecture permits all user requests throughout the Internet to be forwarded to one or more IAS servers maintained and administered from the corporate intranet. In this way, remote access policies can be managed in a central location. ISPs forward requests to the local intranet, which verifies a user's remote access policy. Remote user accounts can be managed from the corporate intranet without the need to constantly update accounts with different ISPs.

IAS INSTALLATION

The IAS installation is not automatic during standard installation. The following steps should be followed to install IAS on a Windows Server 2003:

1. From **Control Panel,** click **Add/Remove Programs** and select **Add/Remove Windows Components**.
2. From **Windows Components,** select **Networking Services** and click **Details**. Choose **Internet Authentication Service** and click **OK**. Click **Next**. Click **Finish**.
3. From the **Internet Authentication Service** snap-in, right-click the **Internet Authentication Service** node and select **Properties**. The following tabs are available (Figure 13.27):
   - The **General** tab configures the logging of accepted or rejected authentication requests.
   - The **Ports** tab identifies UDP ports required for IA to provide authentication and accounting services through a firewall.

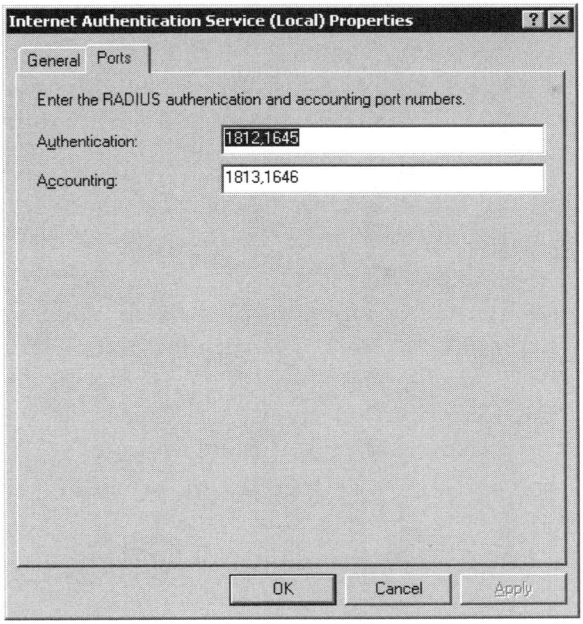

FIGURE 13.27 Authentication and UDP Ports

IAS Remote Access Policy

Remote access policies for IAS must be established. To do so, follow these steps:

1. Right-click the **Remote Access Policy** node and select **New Remote Access Policy**. Click **Next**. Type a name for the new policy, such as **IAS VPN Client Policy**. Click **Next**.
2. Select the **VPN** option. Click **Next**. Grant access to a particular user or group. Click **Next**.
3. Select **Authentication Methods**. Click **Next**.
4. Select **Encryption Levels**. Click **Next**. Click **Finish**.
5. If any other default policies exist, remove them. This will eliminate conflicts with previously established RAS policies.

Registering the IAS Server with the Active Directory

To make IAS available throughout the enterprise, it is necessary to register it with the Active Directory. The following step will do this:

1. Right click the **Internet Authentication Service** snap-in node and select **Register Server in Active Directory**.

Radius Client Configuration

The Network Access Server (NAS) handling the client's dial-in connection also supports the RADIUS client software and configuration. The following example demonstrates configuration of a RADIUS client/RAS server running Windows Server 2003 Routing and Remote Access.

1. From the **Routing and Remote Access** snap-in, right-click the **Routing and Remote Access** node and select ***servername*** node. Select **Properties** and proceed to the **Security** tab.
2. Select **RADIUS Authentication** from the drop-down list under **Authentication provider** (Figure 13.28), then click **Authentication Methods**. Ensure that the MS-CHAP v2 and MS-CHAP authentication protocols are selected (Figure 13.29). Click **OK**. Click **Configure** and type the RADIUS server name or IP address and enter the shared secret by clicking **Change**.
3. Select **RADIUS Accounting** under **Accounting provider** and click **Configure**. Repeat step 2 for RADIUS accounting.
4. Stop and restart the Routing and Remote Access service to make sure the new settings take effect.

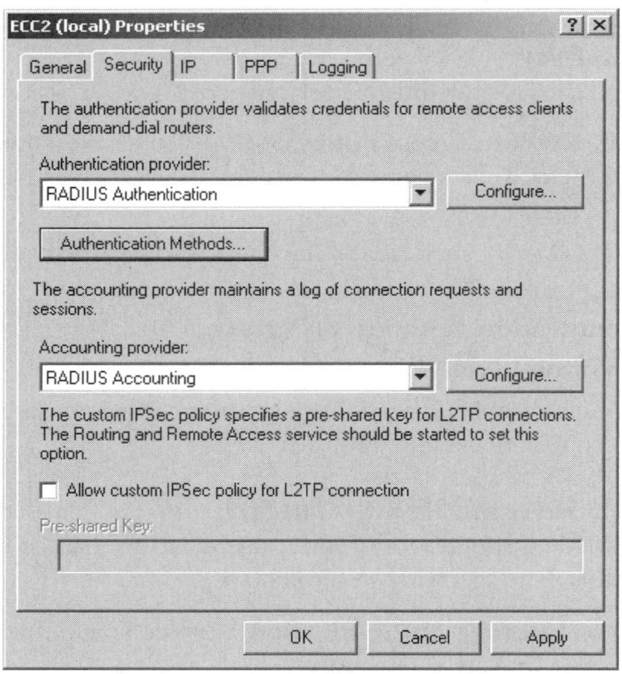

FIGURE 13.28 RADIUS Client Authentication Provider

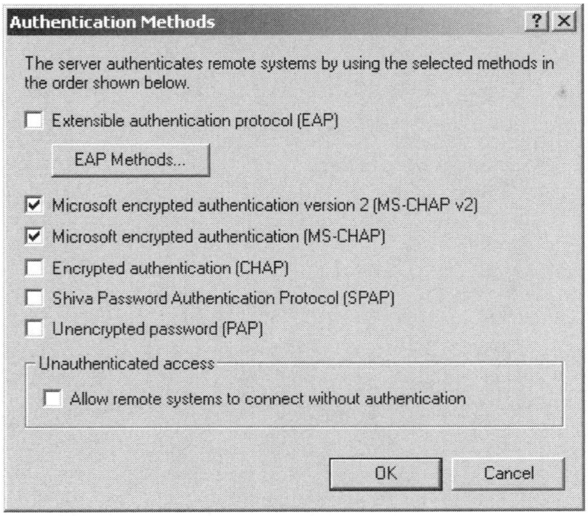

FIGURE 13.29 RADIUS Client Authentication Methods

5. Set up a remote access client by following the steps in the "Remote Access Client Configuration" section and verify client connectivity and RADIUS configuration settings.

RADIUS ACCOUNT LOGGING

RADIUS records authentication and accounting requests made from the RADIUS client. This information can be used to track billing and account activity. To select the types of requests to be logged on to the RADIUS log file:

1. From the **Internet Authentication Service** snap-in tool, select the **Remote Access Logging** node. Right-click the **Local File** and select **Properties**.
2. From the **Settings** tab, three logging characteristics are available (Figure 13.30).

NOTE IAS can be configured to send logging information for accounting requests, authentication requests, and periodic status to a Structured Query Language (SQL) server. This allows IT administrators to use SQL queries to obtain historical and real-time information about connection attempts that use RADIUS for authentication. To configure, obtain properties of the SQL Server™ logging method in the Remote Access Logging folder of the Internet.

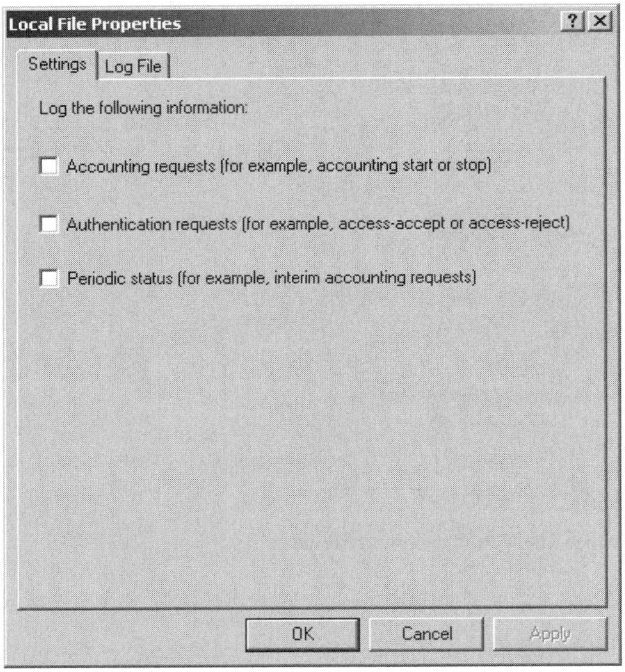

FIGURE 13.30 RADIUS Logging Options

RADIUS PROXY SERVERS

Radius proxy servers are configured at ISPs to forward communications with the desired IAS server. An ISP can configure a proxy server with all necessary IAS server information and can point RAS servers to it. This eliminates the need to configure every RAS server with current RADIUS server information.

RADIUS LOAD BALANCING

Windows Server 2003 provides IAS/RADIUS Proxy load balancing between RADIUS servers. The feature enables greater scalability and geographic failover. The objective is to balance the load of a large volume of authentication traffic. There is little need for administrative intervention since IAS RADIUS proxy dynamically balances the load of connection and accounting requests. Specific RADIUS proxy servers can be designated with higher preference.

IP SECURITY

IP Security was developed by the Internet Engineering Task Force to enable IP authentication, encryption, and data integrity. IPSec services use the Public Key Infrastructure (PKI) to share secret keys over the network and establish secure communication sessions. Once established, the connections are transparent to users and applications. In the section, "Virtual Private Networks," IPSec tunnel mode was discussed and IPSec transport mode was implemented using L2TP over IPSec. Here we will see that when applying IP Security to your internal network, routing and network conditions may alleviate the need for a tunnel, in which case IPSec may be implemented in transport mode. Transport mode has no specified tunnel endpoints, and traffic flows between source and destination hosts without encapsulation or redirection. Group policies applied to Active Directory containers dictate the traffic type that is encrypted and signed either with Encrypted Security Payload or by Authentication Header IPSec drivers. Packets are encrypted on the way out and decrypted on the way in, independent of TCP/IP stack processing (Figure 13.31).

The following are Windows Server 2003 enhancements for IPSec:

- Fail-safe policies are immediately applied to the system during the bootup sequence before Active Directory or local policies are applied to the system. This ensures that the system has persistent IPSec policy settings even if group policies are not successfully applied to the system.

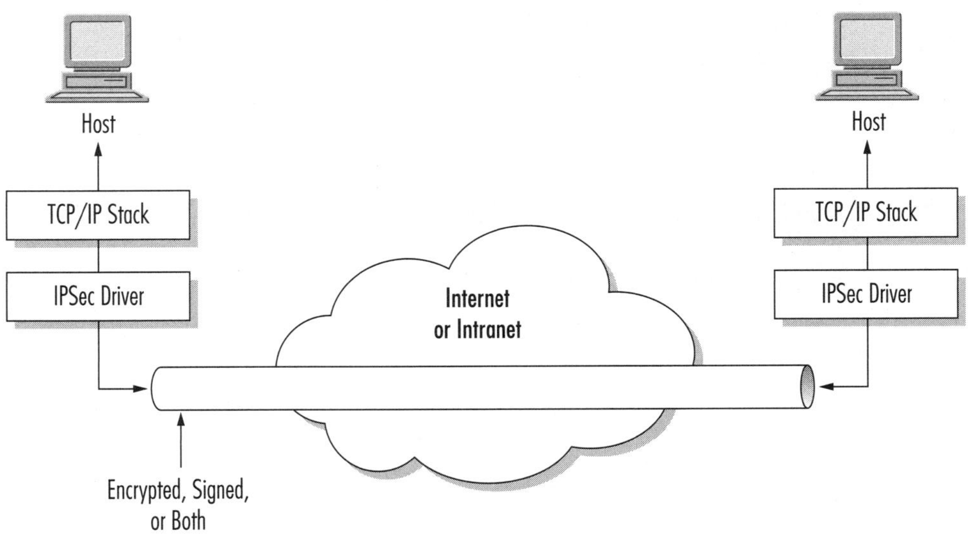

FIGURE 13.31 The IPSec Transport Mode

- When IPSec policies are configured to start automatically, stateful inspection filtering is implemented until IPSec policies are applied. There are a variety of settings for this command using the following command:

```
Netsh ipsec dynamic set config /?
```

- The RSoP snap-in, which is introduced briefly in Chapter 8, can fully analyze IPSec policies on any system in your network.
- The IP Security Monitor snap-in replaces ipsecmon.exe for monitoring current IPSec security states and policies.
- New features available through the IP Security Policy Management and IP Security Monitor snap-ins may be access via scripts using the following command:

```
netsh ipsec <rest of command>
```

Individual IPSec packets use a standard format that involves an Authentication Header and an Encapsulated Security Payload. The AH contains authentication information that uses digital signatures, and the message body is encrypted in the ESP to prevent data snooping. Table 13.5 lists some of the industry standards used with the Windows Server 2003 IPSec implementation.

Understanding IPSec Policies

IP Security policies can be assigned to either local computers or Active Directory containers to determine the security services a system will use when communicating with other systems. Some systems require higher security than others. For this reason, IPSec policies allow the administrator granular control over the security protocols accepted at individual machines.

TABLE 13.5 Windows Server 2003 IPSec Technologies

Technology	Standard Implementations
Shared Secret Keys/Negotiation	Internet Key Exchange (IKE) for Windows Server 2003
Digital Signatures	Hash Message Authentication Code (HMAC)
	Hash Message Authentication Message Digest function 95 (HMAC-MD-5)
	Hash Message Authentication Secure Hash Algorithm (HMAC-SHA)
ESP Encryption	3DES, 56-bit DES, 40-bit DES

SETTING IPSEC POLICIES

IPSec policies are located in the Group Policy tree under **Computer Configuration → Windows Settings → Security Settings → IP Security Policies on Active Directory**. The default policies are defined as follows and may be assigned to any GPO.

- *Secure Server (require security)* accepts initial unsecured communications but requires clients to establish IPSec using a security method acknowledged by it.
- *Server (request security)* accepts unsecured communications but requests that clients establish IPSec using a security method acknowledged by it. This policy allows unsecured communication if the other system does not have IPSec policies.
- *Client (respond only)* should be assigned to computers that are secure within the intranet. When communication is initiated with other computers, IPSec is not presented. However, if the remote computer requests secure communications, this policy is acknowledged.

To assign a security policy to a GPO, right-click the policy and select **Assign**. The **Policy Assigned** column should read **Yes** and all other policies should read **No** (Figure 13.32).

Creating a New IPSec Policy

Creating a new security policy involves right-clicking the **IP Security Policies** from a selected GPO tree and selecting **Create IP Security Policy** (Figure 13.33 on page 605). The IP Security Policy Wizard appears.

The creation process is straightforward, but keep in mind a couple of concepts. First, the default response rule, which is a part of every security policy, can be deactivated by the administrator if so desired (this can be done later). This filter enables the system to establish secure communication when other rules fail. Second, an authentication method must be established (Figure 13.34 on page 606).

AUTHENTICATION METHODS

The system administrator's ability to view security policies is a critical operating system requirement. View policy rules by right-clicking **Properties** for an **IP Security Policy** (Figure 13.35 on page 606), selecting a filter, and clicking **Edit**.

The **Authentication Methods** tab presents the chosen method of authentication (Figure 13.36 on page 607).

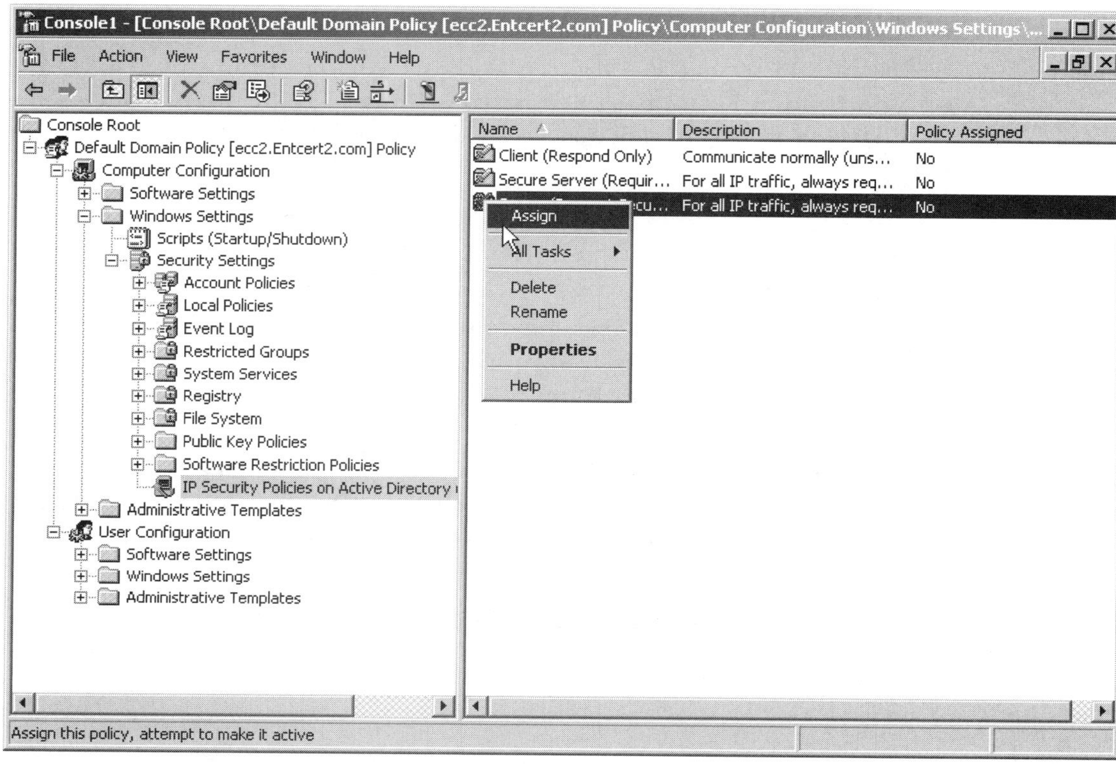

FIGURE 13.32 IP Security Templates

- *Kerberos version 5*—the default authentication method for clients who are part of a trusted Windows Server 2003 domain. The client does not need to be running Windows Server 2003.
- *Public Key Certificate*—used for clients who are not running Kerberos and for extranet and Internet access. The client and server must share a trusted CA to use certificate authentication.
- *Preshared Key*—requires a key to be shared between the client and server using an out-of-band method (telephone, snail mail, etc.) and manually configured on both systems. The shared string is used only for authentication, not for data encryption.

TUNNEL SETTINGS

The **Tunnel Setting** tab allows the administrator to enter the destination or endpoint for an IPSec tunnel. Although we are not discussing tunneling here, this is

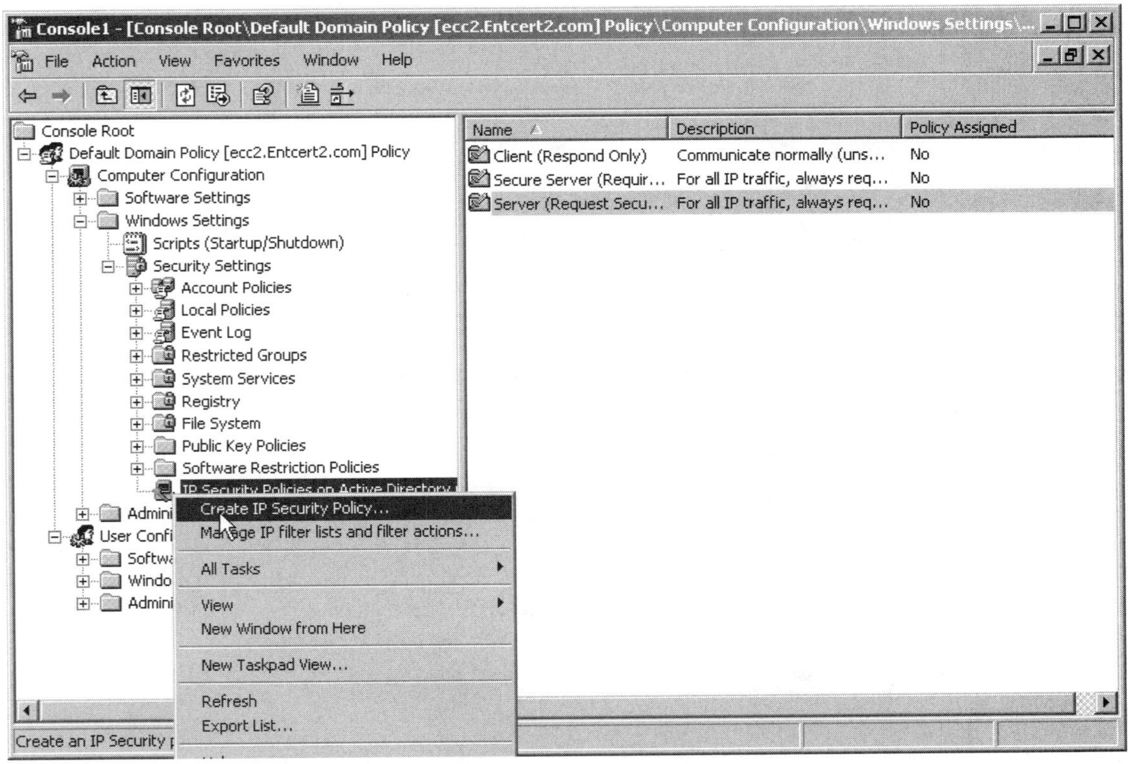

FIGURE 13.33 Creating an IPSec Policy

where IPSec tunneling would be enabled. Windows Server 2003 is equipped with Layer 2 Tunneling Protocol, which is preferred over IPSec as a tunneling implementation. IPSec should be used only for interoperability with systems that do not support PPTP or L2TP. To use L2TP, select the default option **This rule does not specify an IPSec tunnel** (Figure 13.37 on page 608).

CONNECTION TYPE

The **Connection Type** tab enables the user to select the type of connection to be used. The three choices are **All network connections, LAN connections** only, and **Remote access** connections only (Figure 13.38). **Connection Type** allows the security policy to be limited to a couple of network connects. The local area network refers to the local adapter card, and the remote access option applies to both dial-in and VPN connections. When using this policy with tunneling, make sure to enable **Remote access** directly or through the **All network connections** selection.

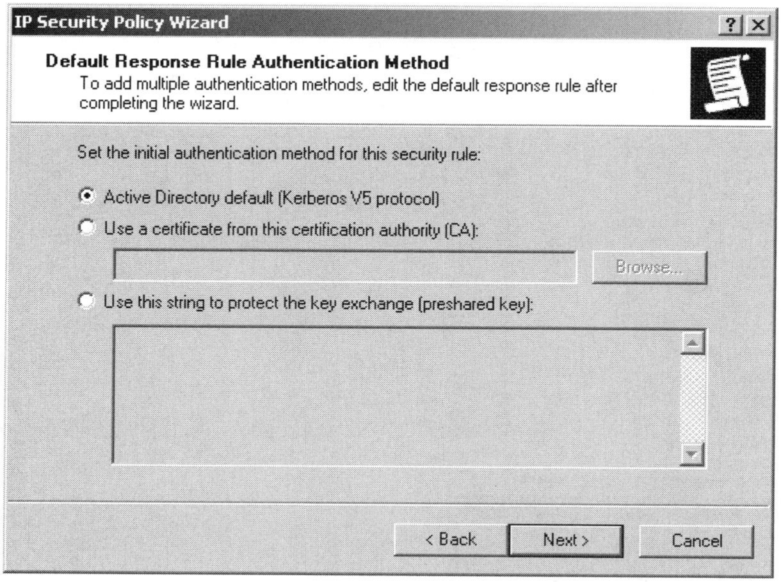

FIGURE 13.34 The Default Response Rule Authentication Method

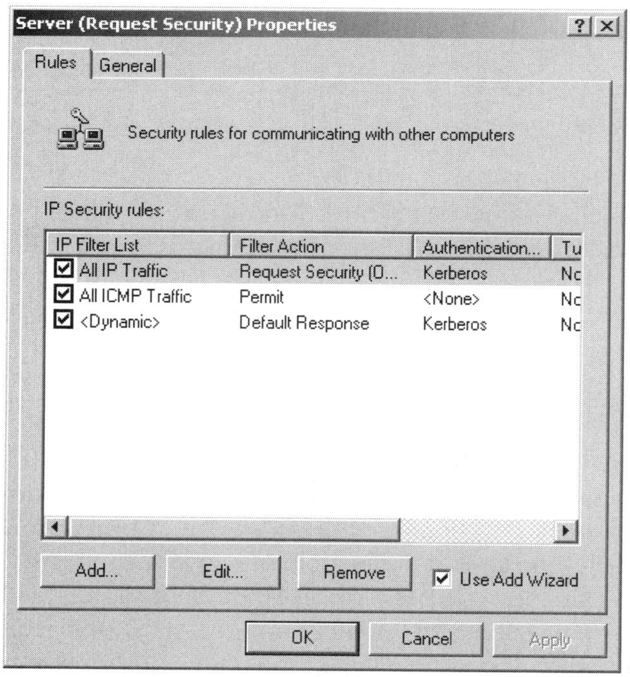

FIGURE 13.35 IP Security Rules

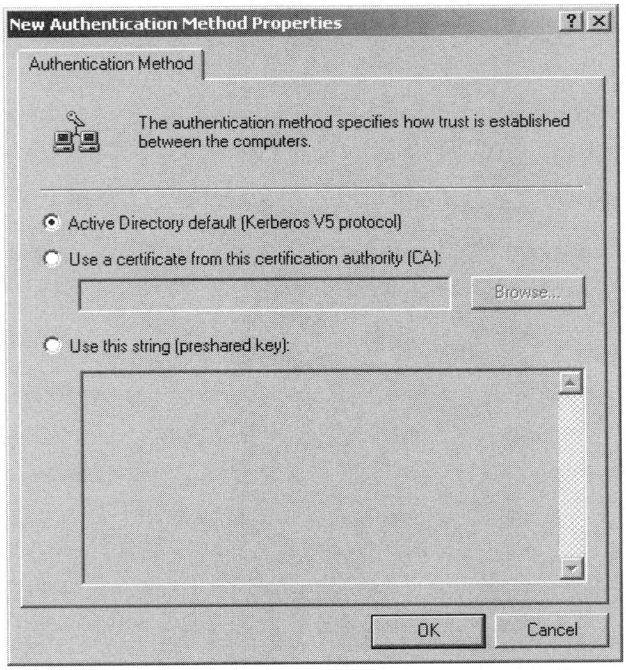

FIGURE 13.36 Authentication Method

IP FILTER LIST

The **IP Filter List** tab enables selection of default filters and addition of filters. These filters define IP addresses and subnets to which the IPSec rule will apply (Figure 13.39 on page 609).

On the **IP Filter List** tab, click **Add** and follow the wizard's instructions to add a filter to the rule. Click **Edit** to modify a filter. Click **Edit** to display filter properties (Figure 13.40 on page 609). On the **Addressing** tab, the drop-down lists under **Source address** and **Destination address** each list five methods for setting filters on the address. Security policies implemented on a successful source/destination address match are determined by the filter actions, to be discussed next.

An IP packet will match the chosen filter if both its source and destination addresses match the filter's source and destination address ranges. From the drop-down lists, you can choose a particular address or a range of addresses.

- **My IP address.** The IP address of the system to which the rule has been applied. If My IP is the filter's source address, the rule is applied to all outgoing IP packets sent to the addresses specified in the filter's destination address. On the other hand, if it is the filter's destination address, the rule is applied to

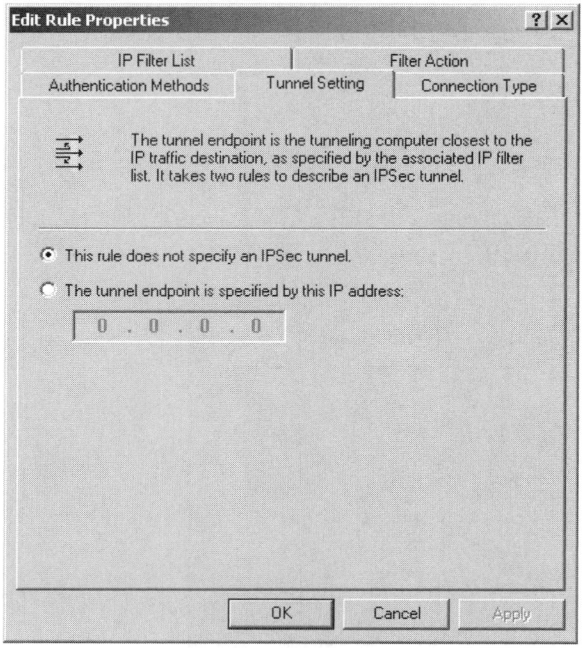

FIGURE 13.37 Editing a Rule Policy for Tunneling

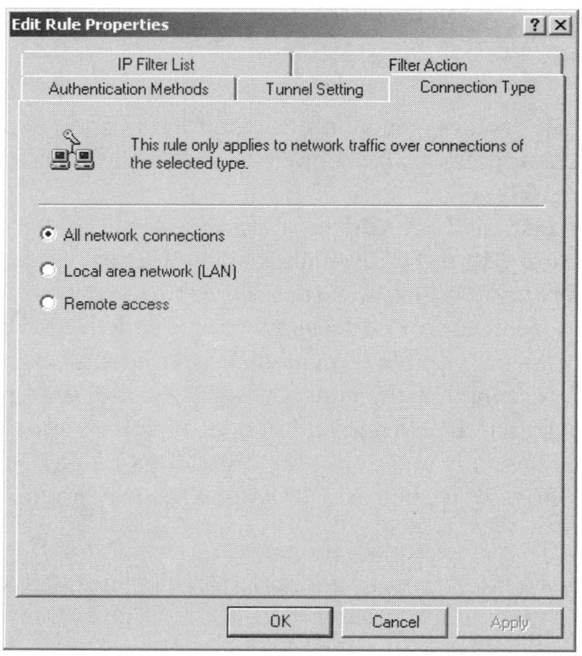

FIGURE 13.38 Connection Types

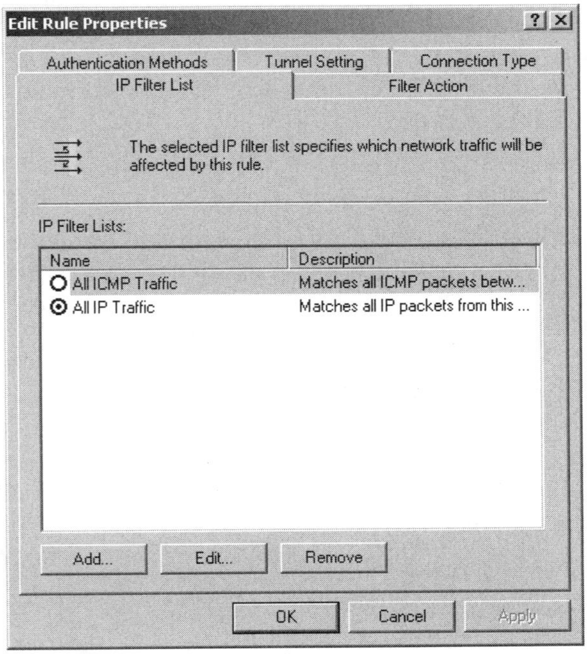

FIGURE 13.39 A Rule Policy for IP Filters

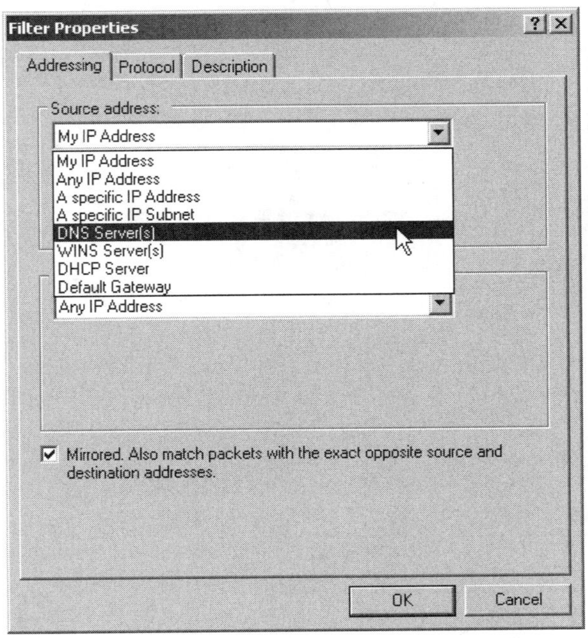

FIGURE 13.40 Filter Properties

all incoming IP packets sent from the addresses specified in the filter's source address.

- **Any IP address.** Any IP value in the source or destination address of the IP packet will match this filter field.
- **A specific IP address.** The entered IP address is compared with the source or destination IP address field in the IP packet.
- **A specific IP subnet.** An IP address range specified by subnet is compared with the source or destination IP address in the IP packet.

Check the **Mirrored** box to create a reverse version of the current filter. This enables the rule to be applied to both inbound and outbound IP packets. **Mirrored** should not be used for IPSec tunneling rules. A tunneling filter specifies the tunnel destination IP address required to set up the IPSec tunnel.

The **Protocol** tab reveals transport layer protocols and port specifications for advanced protocol filtering (Figure 13.41). The **Description** tab allows detailed explanation and filter naming.

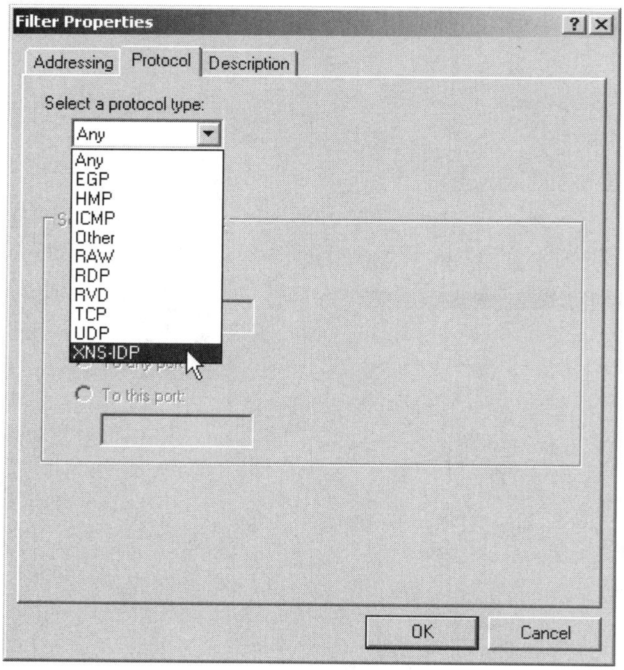

FIGURE 13.41 Filter Property Protocols

IP FILTER ACTIONS

Filter actions determine if and how the rule will negotiate for secure connections and the security methods to be used. On the **Filter Action** tab, click **Add** and follow the wizard's instructions to add a filter action. Select a filter action to modify and click **Edit** (Figure 13.42). This brings up the **Security Methods** tab.

The **Security Methods** tab (Figure 13.43) has several options to configure. The first three work as follows:

- **Permit**. The rule will refuse to negotiate IP security and ignore all incoming secure communications. Only plain-text nonsecured communication will be permitted.
- **Block**. All communications that meet the filter's requirements are blocked. There is no IP secure communication and no plain-text communication.
- **Negotiate security**. Communications that match a rule filter undergo IP security negotiation. Security methods are tried in descending order as listed under **Security method preference order**.

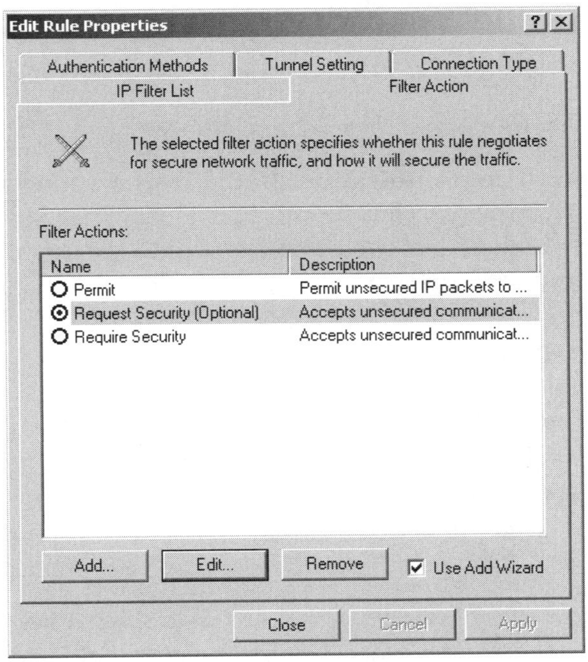

FIGURE 13.42 IP Filter Actions

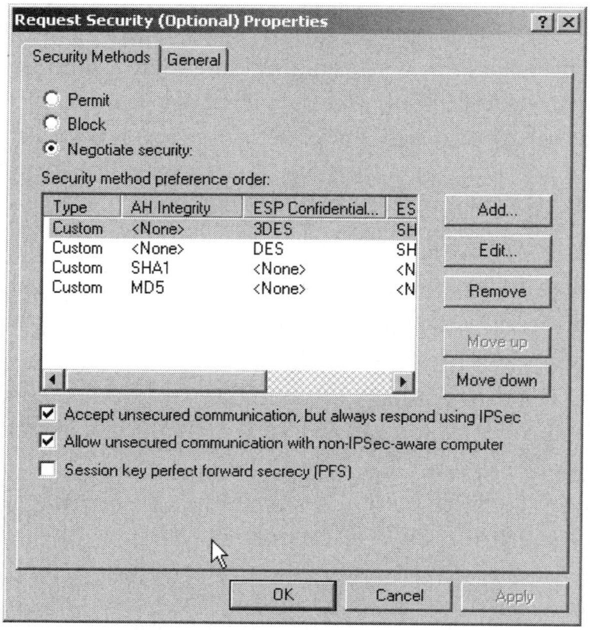

FIGURE 13.43 Security Methods

The security properties options for a connection are

- **Accept unsecured communication, but always respond using IPSec**. This option allows a client to initiate a plain-text communication session but will immediately request that the client agree on a security method. If the client and server cannot establish a secure connection, communication will be terminated.
- **Allow unsecured communication with a non-IPSec-aware computer**. This option will first request negotiation for secure communication, but will disable IP security for clients that do not support IPSec. IPSec security is not required for this rule.
- **Session key perfect forward secrecy**. A new master key will need to be re-generated before a session key is obtained.

Click **Edit** to modify advanced features for security methods (Figure 13.44). To display available custom IP security settings, select **Custom settings** and click **Settings** (Figure 13.45). Specific algorithms for data integrity (AH), encryption (ESP), and session key lifetime are configurable.

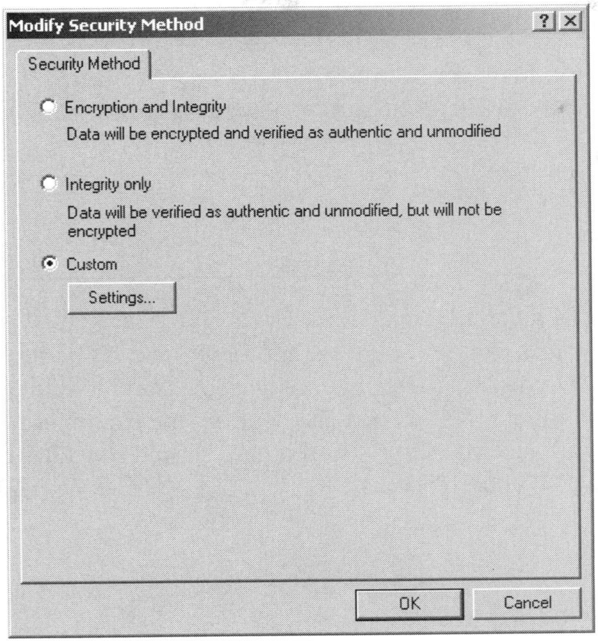

FIGURE 13.44 Modify Security Method

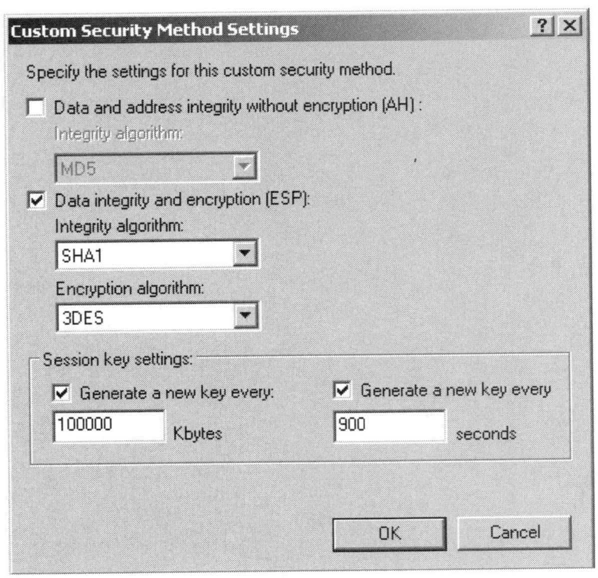

FIGURE 13.45 Custom Security Method Settings

NOTE Shared keys for IPSec may be distributed to users with profiles that were created using the Connection Manager Administration Kit for Windows Server 2003. The user installs the profile when configuring her VPN client to obtain its assigned shared key.

POSTSCRIPT

This chapter provides a practical overview of VPN and IPSec. As the examples illustrate, these technologies can be used together, or IPSec can be configured as a replacement to VPN. We discuss these technologies by example rather than abstract theory. Your environment will likely be different from the examples provided. However, when broadly applied, the steps covered here should provide a reasonable approach to deploying VPN and IPSec.

Chapter 14

Disk Management, Backup and Restoration, and Disaster Recovery

This chapter examines Windows Server 2003 disk management, backup and restore technologies, and disaster recovery, which are all important system administrator functions. Failure to develop and enforce programs that implement them can result in significant damage to an IT organization. This is preventive medicine. Disk management, data restoration, and disaster recovery become important when the unexpected occurs. Unfortunately, this area of administration is often treated as an afterthought, although it should always be regarded as a primary activity.

Upon completion of this chapter, you should have knowledge of the following topics:

- Disk management, management tools, and storage types
- Striped, mirrored, and RAID-5 volumes
- Disk fragmentation
- Storage libraries
- Backup and restore policies and methods
- Disaster recovery

NOTE The most significant Windows Server 2003 enhancement to disk management and storage is the concept of shadow copies. A *volume shadow copy* of a storage volume is a copy of the original entity recorded at some point in time. Although the volume shadow copy appears static, it actually involves a dynamic process that is regularly changing. This feature supports volume shadow copies for Windows NT

File System (NTFS) and file allocation table (FAT) file systems. Key components of the volume shadow copy technology include:

- An API that uses the Common Object Model (COM) infrastructure for registration and configuration
- COM-based "coordinator" service that provides a snapshot process and performs discovery of applications and snapshot providers
- Storage filter driver for volume shadow copy technology using a copy-on-write design
- Interfaces for applications and stores assuring a consistent state

DISK MANAGEMENT

In this section, we examine disk storage types, partitions, and volumes, as well as NTFS disk-related features. The techniques include striping, mirroring, spanning, and RAID-5. We also look at disk quotas, compression, and defragmentation, along with remote storage, libraries, and tape/disk management.

NTFS and FAT/FAT32 Disk Management

NTFS and FAT/FAT32 file systems provide different features and levels of support with respect to disk management. NTFS is the preferred file system because of its expanded functionality. FAT/FAT32 is recommended on a partition only to get access to other Microsoft operating systems such as MS-DOS or Windows 95/98. Otherwise, NTFS should be used because the following features are not available under FAT/FAT32:

- Compression
- Dynamic volume configuration
- Remote storage
- Disk quotas
- Mount points
- Encryption

Disk Management Tools

Windows Server 2003 provides a number of snap-in tools that can be added to the Microsoft Management Console. Some are grouped for convenient system administration. Table 14.1 lists the standard functions in each snap-in.

TABLE 14.1 Disk Management Snap-in Tools

Snap-in and Function Location	Function
Local Computer Policy → Computer Configuration → System → Disk Quota	Sets policies for disk quotas on a local machine.
Default Domain → Computer Configuration → System → Disk Quota	Sets policies for disk quotas on a local machine.
Computer Management → Storage	Accesses Disk Management, Disk Fragmenter, Logical Drives, and Removal Storage tools.
Standalone Disk Management	Primary disk management tool.
Standalone Disk Fragmenter	Disk fragmentation.
Windows Server 2003 Support Tools → Tools → Disk Probe	Optional Resource Kit tools that permit examination and editing of disk sectors.
Standalone Removal Storage	Manages removal storage.
Hardware Wizard (available through Control Panel)	Adds/removes storage media.

NOTE The Diskpart.exe command-line program provides all the functionality of the Disk Manager MMC via the command line. Diskpart also enables storage administrators to expand basic disks, a disk type used by Microsoft Cluster Services.

Disk Storage Types

Windows Server 2003 uses the Disk Management snap-in tool to view, administer, and migrate to disk storage types, partitions, and volumes.

Two disk storage types, basic and dynamic, are supported. The underlying difference between the two is the use of partitions versus volumes for disk management. Both are physical disks, but the basic type contains partitions, extended partitions, logical drivers, and an assortment of static volumes; the dynamic type does not use partitions but dynamically manages volumes and provides advanced storage options, as discussed later.

Partitions are divisions of physical space on the same disk. Volumes can consist of one or more disks or portions of them and must be of the same storage type. Windows Server 2003 initially installs the operating system using a basic disk format. Although the basic format works well, an upgrade to a dynamic disk is required to create spanned, striped, mirrored, or RAID-5 volumes.

UPGRADING A BASIC DISK TO A DYNAMIC DISK

The process of upgrading a disk to dynamic storage is very straightforward. However, several rules can affect this transformation, including the following:

- In cases where a volume crosses multiple disks, all related disks must be upgraded.
- Any operating system other than Windows Server 2003 located on a partition or volume will be rendered inoperable.
- Removable media cannot be upgraded.
- A basic disk with the boot partition cannot be upgraded; instead, it becomes a simple boot volume after the system is restarted.
- When a boot partition is upgraded to a simple volume, it can be used to mirror a volume on another disk for redundancy.

The following steps should be taken to upgrade a disk from basic to dynamic:

- Open the **Disk Management** snap-in from the MMC or from the Computer Management MMC.
- Right-click the targeted basic disk, click **Upgrade to Dynamic Disk**, and follow the remaining steps as prompted.

CAUTION This upgrade cannot be reversed without serious impact. The only way to return to partitions is to delete all dynamic volumes, so make sure you back up all information on the volumes first. Then use the **Revert to Basic Disk** command by repeating the procedure outlined in the previous example.

MANAGING PARTITIONS AND BASIC STORAGE

Basic storage provides backward compatibility with Windows NT 4.0 disk schemes. In an upgrade to Windows 2000 and Windows Server 2003, it is established on the existing partition. Windows NT 4.0 volumes can also be preserved using the Disk Management tool.

NOTE It was possible to create striped and mirrored disk sets under Windows NT Server 4.0, but this is not the case with a Windows Server 2003 basic disk. Existing striped and mirrored volumes will be recognized after a Windows Server 2003 upgrade, but you will be restricted to repairing and deleting them. Creating new fault tolerance is reserved for dynamic disk volumes.

Windows Server 2003 basic disks can consist of up to four partitions on a physical drive, and extended partitions larger than 2 GB can be created, as can logical drives. This is done in the same fashion as on Windows NT Server 4.0, except that restarting the computer system is no longer necessary.

Partition Management

The Disk Management snap-in tool supports four primary basic partition and volume administration actions. The following summarizes how to accomplish the partition management tasks:

- *Formatting a partition*. This is done through the **Disk Management** tool → **All Tasks** → **Format**. Although not recommended, you can use the **Quick** format to format the disk; however, Quick does not scan the disk for bad sectors, and when formatting, all data on the partition is lost.
- *Designating the partition as active*. From the **Disk Management** tool, right-click the targeted partition and select the active (or primary) partition.
- *Assigning drive letters*. Open the **Disk Management** tool, right-click the partition, select **Change Drive Letter or Path**, and make the designation. Up to 26 letters can be assigned, with drives A and B being reserved for floppy disks.
- *Deleting a partition*. From the **Disk Management** tool, right-click the partition to be removed and select **Delete Partition**. Remember, this will destroy all the data on the partition.

MANAGING VOLUMES

Dynamic disk simple volumes cannot include partitions or logical drives. They are used strictly for Windows 2000 and Windows Server 2003, not Windows 95/98/NT or MS-DOS. Despite these restrictions, the dynamic disk system offers many advantages, including the ability to use spanned, striped, and mirrored volumes and RAID-5, as well as support of compression. A brief examination of each of these technologies should underscore dynamic disk volumes' inherent flexibility.

NTFS Compression

Compression of files and folders is an excellent way to use disk space efficiently. Although physical disk costs per storage unit continue to fall, it is still appropriate to use compression, especially for archival information.

NTFS file and folder compression is achieved by right-clicking the object in **Windows Explorer**, selecting **Properties**, and then selecting the **General** tab. As shown in Figure 14.1, the **Advanced Attributes** dialog box permits you to select **Compress contents to save disk space**, and the Confirmation window then permits you to apply the compression only to the current folder or to all subfolders

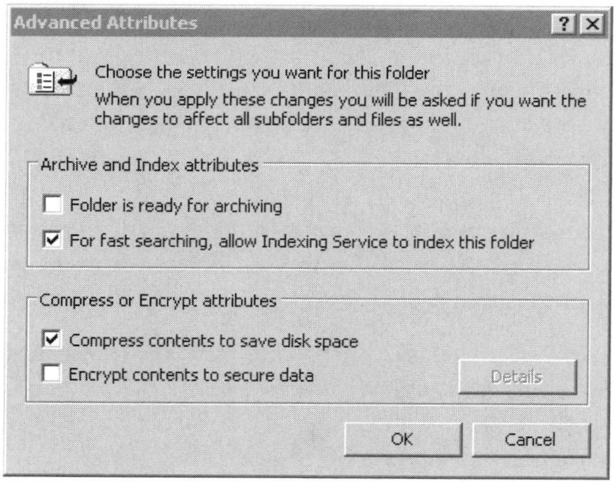

FIGURE 14.1 The Advanced File/Folder Screen

with a check mark as appropriate. A file or folder can be uncompressed by removing the check mark. (You can also assign index attributes and encrypt the connects by selecting the appropriate item in this dialog box.) Compression ratios are generally higher for files such as those created by Word or Excel than for bitmap or graphic files. Applications are usually already optimized for size and generally result in minimal compression.

When moving and copying compressed files or folders within or between NTFS volumes, the compression state remains; however, when copying or moving an NTFS compressed file or folder to a FAT file system, the compression is lost and the file/folder returns to its normal size. Remember, compression is not supported in the FAT file system.

Spanned Volumes

Spanned volume technology is a method of combining free space on 1 to 32 physical disks into a single volume, with each spanned disk containing various amounts of available space. Storage is accomplished by filling the space on one disk and logically moving to each subsequent spanned disk as data storage is added. This involves the concatenation of data from one disk to another (Figure 14.2).

CAUTION Although spanned disks provide greater efficiency, they have two significant downsides. First, fault tolerance is not supported. Second, if one disk in a spanned disk volume fails, the entire volume fails. The only protection for this type of disaster is regular backups.

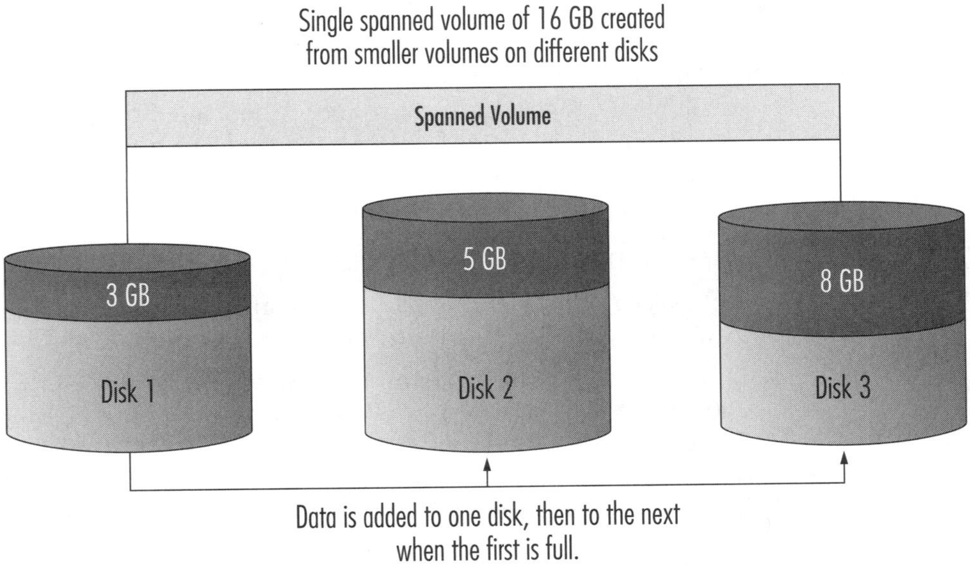

FIGURE 14.2 A Single 16-GB Spanned Volume Created from Smaller Volumes on Different Disks

CREATING A SPANNED VOLUME

Spanned volumes are created from dynamic disks with the Disk Management tool with the following steps:

1. Open the **Disk Management** snap-in tool.
2. Right-click the unallocated volume to be spanned from the dynamic disks, then click **Create Volume** in Windows 2000 or **New Volume** in Windows 2003.
3. In Windows 2000, the **Create Volume** wizard appears; in Windows Server 2003, the **New Volume** wizard appears. Click **Next**, then click **Spanned Volume**, and then follow the remaining instructions.

EXTENDING A SPANNED VOLUME

A spanned volume is extended through the Disk Management snap-in tool. First, the computer system must recognize the space on available disks. To make sure this is properly calculated, select the **Action** pull-down menu and select **Rescan Disks**. To actually expand the volume, right-click the spanned volume, select **Extend Volume**, and then follow the remaining instructions.

Managing Striped Volumes

Striped volumes are similar to spanned volumes in that both permit the use of available space up to 32 disks. However, unlike spanned volumes, which sequentially store data on disks, the striped logical volume distributes the information simultaneously across all its disks. Individual striped volumes are divided into fixed and ordered blocks. Because of this architecture, they have faster I/O.

A failure of a single disk will result in the loss of data on the entire logical striped volume. As discussed later, RAID-5 offers a fault-tolerant version of striped volumes.

A striped volume is created by following these steps:

1. Open the **Disk Management** snap-in.
2. Right-click unallocated space for the dynamic disks, then click **Create Volume** in Windows 2000 or **New Volume** in Windows Server 2003.
3. In Windows 2000, the **Create Volume** wizard appears; in Windows Server 2003, the **New Volume** wizard appears. Click **Next**, click **Striped Volume**, and then follow the remaining instructions.

Managing Mirrored Volumes

A mirrored volume does exactly what its name implies by duplicating data on multiple physical disks. This fault-tolerant technology is highly recommended for mission-critical data stores. If one disk fails, the other disk continues to operate normally without data loss (Figure 14.3).

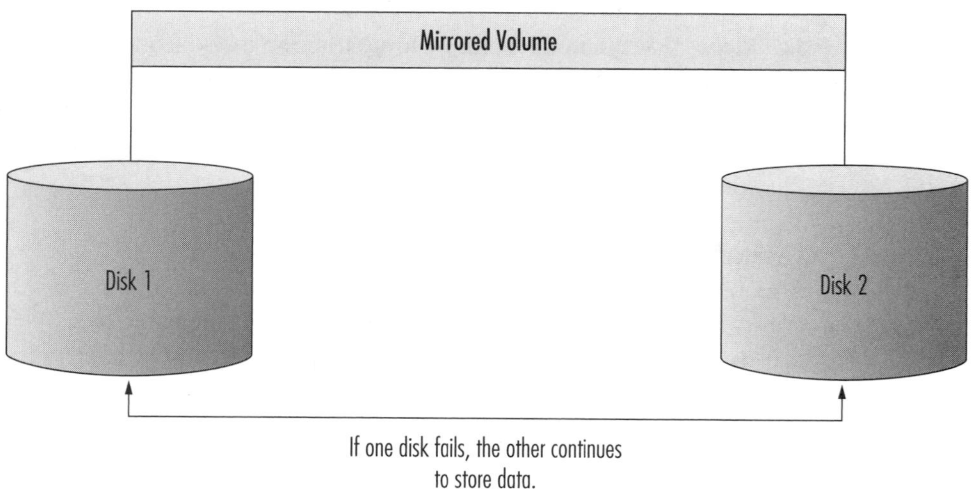

FIGURE 14.3 A Mirrored Volume Containing Duplicate Data

Mirrored volumes generally perform better than RAID-5 (discussed in the next section). Moreover, there is no loss of performance when one volume fails. A disadvantage is that mirrored volumes' use of the physical disk is less efficient. They require a minimum of two disks, whereas RAID-5 requires three. Mirrored volumes are created with the Disk Management tool from dynamic disks by following these steps:

1. Open the **Disk Management** snap-in tool.
2. Right-click the unallocated volume to be mirrored from the dynamic disks, and then click **Create Volume** in Windows 2000 or **New Volume** in Windows Server 2003.
3. In Windows 2000, the **Create Volume** wizard appears; in Windows Server 2003, the **New Volume** wizard appears. Click **Next,** then **Mirrored Volume**, and follow the remaining instructions.

If one of the disks fails and you want to create another mirror, you must manually break the original mirror by using the Disk Management tool. The new mirror is created as in the preceding walk-through.

Managing RAID-5 Volumes

Known as a striped volume with parity under Windows NT, RAID-5 in Windows Server 2003 is a fault-tolerant volume across three or more disks, two of which duplicate the data while the third stores the parity information. If a portion of a disk fails, it can be reconstructed from the data and the parity of the remaining disks. This form of fault tolerance should be considered for environments where disk reading is intense. It is generally a better solution than mirrored volumes, which require a very high redundancy.

RAID-5 can be viewed as a compromise between full redundancy and disk utilization. Remember, mirroring is used for redundancy, striping for greater speed; thus, parity is the middle ground, providing single-bit protection for striped data. Generally, RAID-5 is used when some level of protection is desired but the cost of full mirroring is not justified.

RAID-5 volumes are created with the Disk Management tool from dynamic disks by following these steps:

1. Open the **Disk Management** snap-in tool.
2. Right-click the unallocated volume from the dynamic disks; click **Create Volume** in Windows 2000, **New Volume** in Windows Server 2003
3. In Windows 2000, the **Create Volume** wizard appears; in Windows Server 2003, the **New Volume** wizard appears. Click **Next**, click **RAID-5 Volume**, and then follow the instructions.

The Disk Management Snap-in Tool

In the previous section, the Disk Management snap-in tool was explored as a way to administer spanned, striped, mirrored, and RAID-5 disk configurations, but it has additional functions. For this reason, it is appropriate to step back for a moment and review this tool in more generic terms.

The Disk Management tool can be added as a standalone Microsoft Management Console snap-in. It is also available as part of the Computer Management snap-in or by selecting **Start** → **Programs** → **Administrative tool**. As shown in Figure 14.4, the Disk Management node contains sections that detail various aspects of the system's storage devices. Hard drives, removable disks, CD-ROMs, and other devices are shown with current status and statistics. In the event that the system administrator doubts that this information is current, or if a new device was just added, clicking **Rescan Disks** on the **Action** menu will perform a reevaluation.

In Figure 14.4 the primary partition is a dark blue banner and the logical drive is a lighter blue. Extended partitions (not shown) are green.

Each partition, volume, or logical drive has unique properties. These properties can be viewed or modified by right-clicking the desired partition, volume, or logical drive and selecting **Properties**. The **Local Disk Properties** dialog box is divided into several sections, as shown in Figure 14.5.

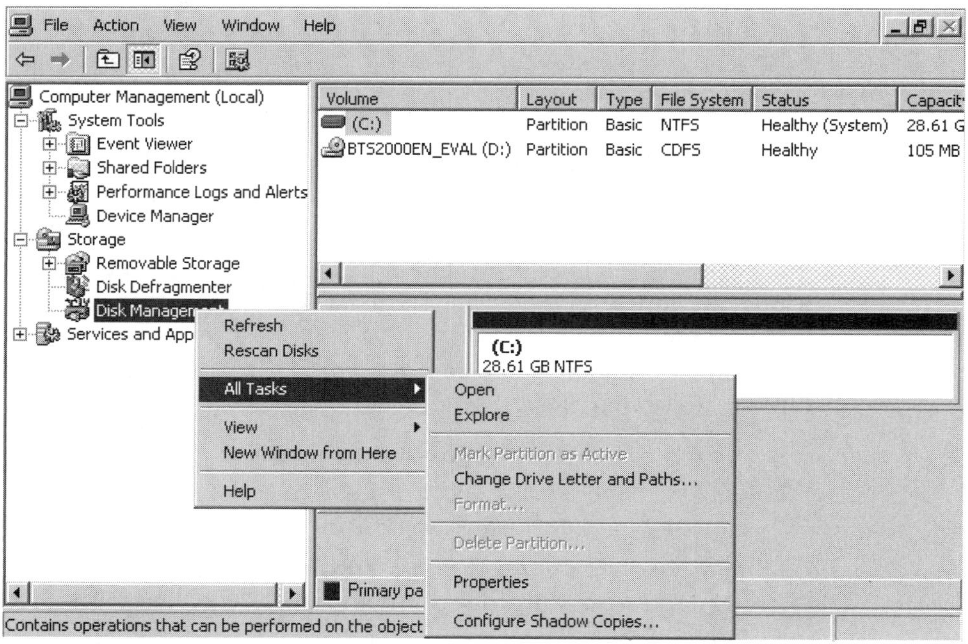

FIGURE 14.4 The Disk Management Snap-in

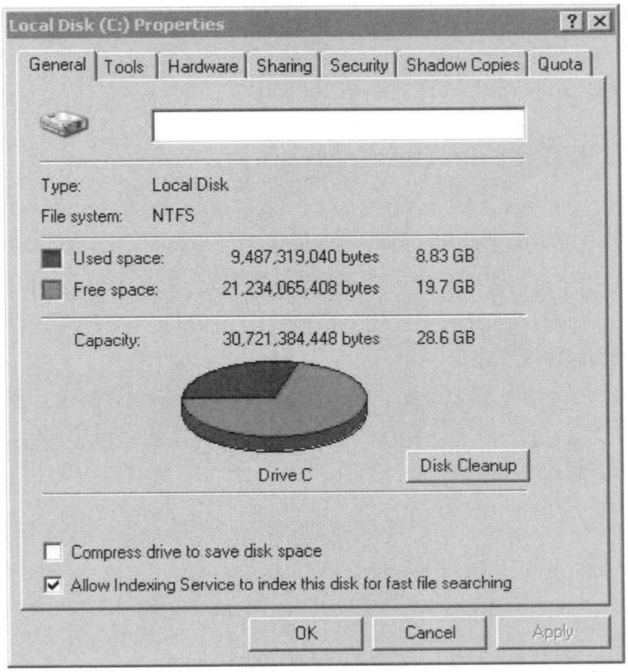

FIGURE 14.5 NTFS Disk Properties Management

DISK PROPERTIES OPTIONS WITH NTFS

The Disk Management tool options are different for NTFS and FAT/FAT32 file systems. Properties tabs for NTFS perform the administrative tasks listed here:

- **General**. In addition to providing basic usage statistics, the administrator can compress the drive, allow the **Indexing Service** to index the disk for fast file searches, and clean up the disk by clicking **Disk Cleanup**.
- **Tools**. These tools support error checking, backup, and disk defragmentation.
- **Hardware**. This tab identifies storage devices. Via the **Properties** tab, new device drivers can be added through the appropriate dialog box.
- **Sharing**. This tab lists the sharing status in addition to permissions and caching. New shares with associated permissions levels can also be created.
- **Shadow Copies**. New to Windows Server 2003, shadow copies allow the viewing of contents in shared folders as contents existed at a previous time.
- **Web Sharing**. This tab establishes whether the disk can be shared on the Web. By default, sharing is not allowed.

- **Quota**. This tab enables quota management, as discussed in a later section.
- **Security**. This tab establishes which users and groups have access to the disk at various permissions levels.

DISK PROPERTIES OPTIONS UNDER FAT/FAT32

The options available for FAT/FAT32 are more limited than those for NTFS. Its **Properties** tabs perform administrative tasks as follows (Figure 14.6):

- **General**. In addition to providing basic usage statistics, the administrator can elect to compress the drive or allow the **Indexing Service** to index the disk for fast file searches.
- **Tools**. These tools support error checking, backup, and disk defragmentation.
- **Hardware**. This tab lists the identified storage devices. The **Properties** tab allows new device drivers to be added through the appropriate dialog box.
- **Sharing**. This tab lists the current sharing status in addition to permissions and caching. New shares with associated permissions levels can also be created.

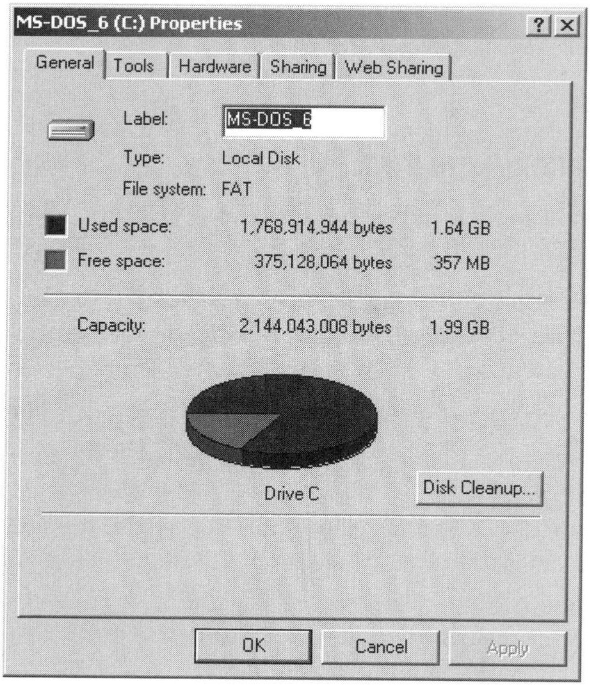

FIGURE 14.6 FAT Disk Properties Management

- **Web Sharing**. This tab establishes whether the disk can be shared on the Web. The default allows no sharing.

DISK QUOTAS

Disk quotas are used to control unbridled storage of data. They can be applied on an individual or a systemwide basis, and permit the system administrator to limit the space allocated for storage of information on a given volume. Quotas are generally recommended. A user is notified when she approaches the maximum allowable disk space, at which point she can delete unwanted files. Alternatively, the user can request additional space for archiving files to backup media. In any case, greater control over disk space is achieved.

Applying Disk Quotas to All Users

Most system administrators initially set the same disk quotas for all system users. As illustrated in the next section, an individual user or group can then receive a unique quota as needed. Applying the same set of disk quotas for all users in a local system is achieved by following these steps:

1. Open **My Computer** and right-click the volume (for example, drive D). Select **Properties.**
2. Select the Quotas tab. Check Enable quota management.
3. Complete the form as appropriate.

The **Quotas** tab (Figure 14.7) requires four decisions: first, whether quota management is to be enforced; second, whether to deny additional space if the quota is exceeded; third, the level at which the quota amount and warning must be set; and finally, the type of event logging required.

NOTE Most system administrators will not expressly deny the use of additional space. To deny a user the ability to save a file can result in hostility and loss of data. As an alternative, the system administrator should use the event-logging facility to determine where abuse might be occurring and then contact the user about disk use. Most users will take appropriate action. If a user continues to abuse privileges, then the more radical step of denial can be taken.

Applying disk quota policies to an entire domain is similar. Open the **Default Domain** snap-in for the target domain, select **Computer Configuration**, select **Administrative Templates**, select **Disk Quotas**, and configure each policy in the right pane.

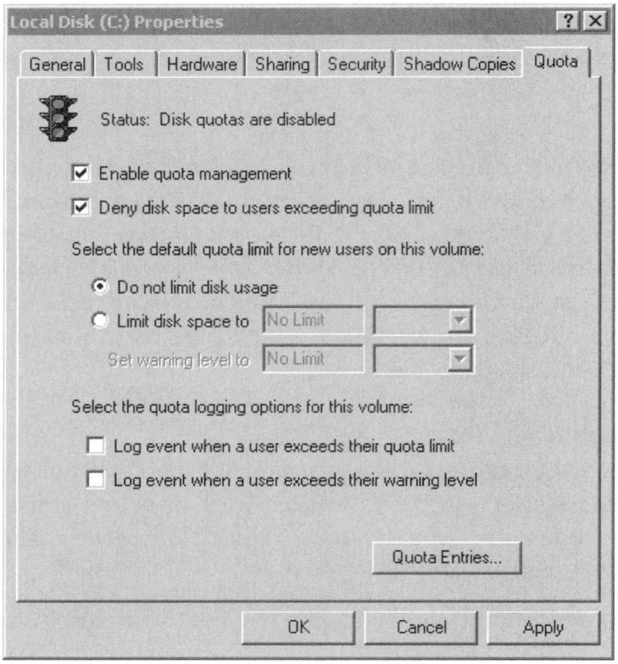

FIGURE 14.7 The Disk Quota Properties Tab

Applying Disk Quotas to Individual Users

As with most things, there are exceptions to disk quotas. Once a global standard is set, it is possible to set limits for individuals or groups. Individual quotas are set by clicking **Quota Entries** in the **Quota** tab. The **Quota Entries for Local Disk** is then displayed, as shown in Figure 14.8. Select the **Quota** pull-down menu and then choose **New Quota**. Add the users and groups to which you want to apply individual quotas. In the dialog box, select the disk quota constraints to be applied.

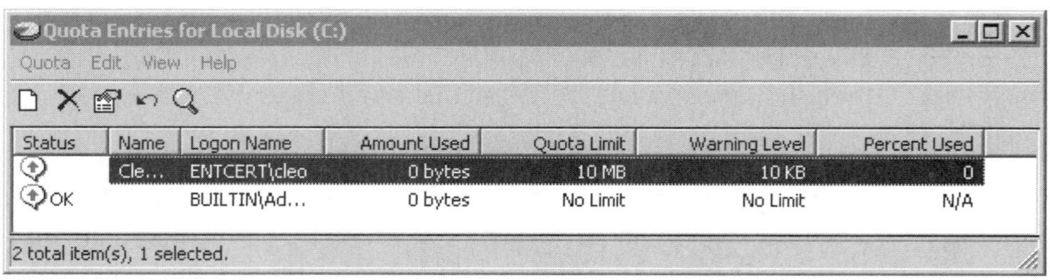

FIGURE 14.8 Quota Entries

DISK FRAGMENTATION MANAGEMENT

Saved data is stored in the first available location on the physical drive. To make a drive its most efficient, a file can be broken up and stored in a number of locations—a process known as "fragmenting." This process ordinarily does not compromise file integrity because the parts are indexed for reassembly. When a large number of files are fragmented, however, indexing can affect performance. In this case, reconstructing a file may require several reads of the hard drive to find all the fragments. To correct fragmentation performance losses, a method known as "defragmentation" is provided to periodically "reorganize" the disk drive to gather the fragments.

Analyzing and Defragmenting a Drive

Defragmentation first collects information about the physical drive and the fragmented files. It then rewrites the disk to rejoin fragmented files in continuous blocks. The analysis and defragmentation of a drive is accomplished with the Disk Defragmenter snap-in tool (Figure 14.9) as follows:

1. Open the **Disk Defragmenter** snap-in tool.
2. Select **Analyze** for the target volume.

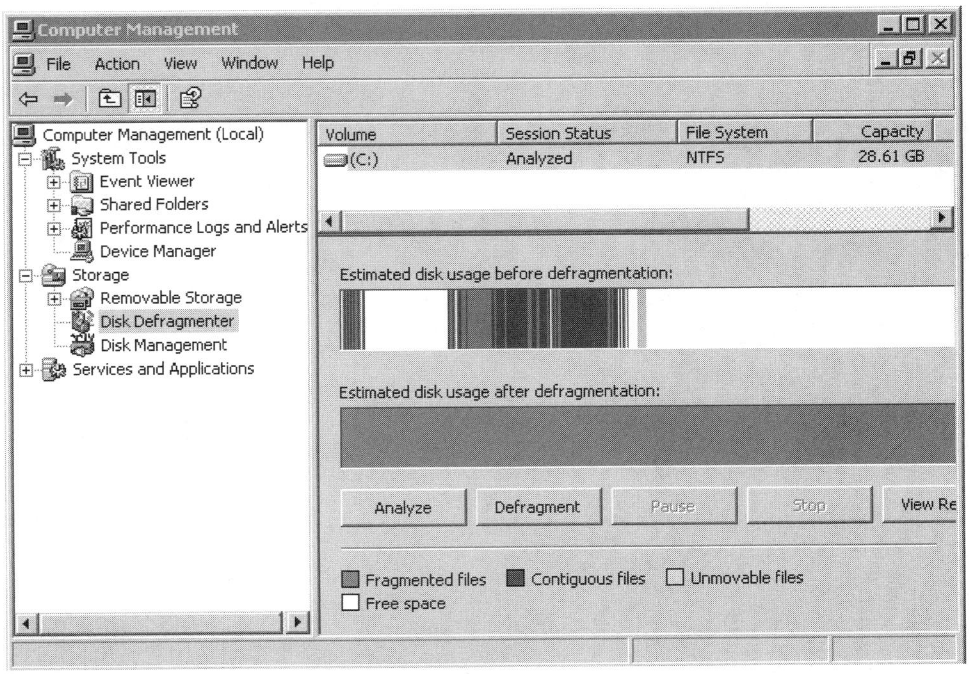

FIGURE 14.9 The Disk Defragmenter Snap-in Tool

3. After the analysis is complete, Windows Server 2003 will prompt you if defragmentation is appropriate. Select **Defragment.**

Removable Media and Library Management

The Removable Media snap-in tool assists in the identification, modification, and management of removable media libraries and devices like ZIP drives, CD-ROMs, and DVDs. As shown in Figure 14.10, removable storage deals with administration of Media, Media Pools, Libraries, Work Queue, and Operator Requests. The tool also permits the insertion and rejection of robotic library media. The Removable Storage tool supports the creation of media inventories, properties viewing, and mounting/dismounting.

WORKING WITH LIBRARIES

In the context of this discussion, a *library* is the combination of storage media and devices that permit the reading and writing of a given removable medium. The type of media can vary widely. For example, in more sophisticated systems, a transport mechanism known as a robotic library (also called a tape or disc changer or jukebox) is used to locate and mount a piece of media into the read or into the

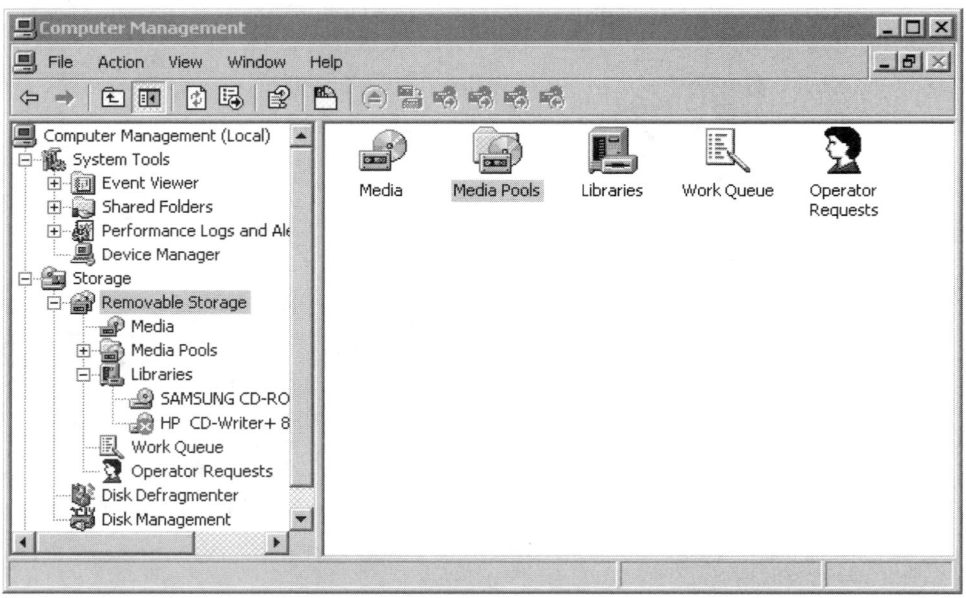

FIGURE 14.10 The Removable Media Snap-in Tool

read/write device. Depending on the robotic library's features, many other items can be managed with the Removable Media tool. The use of such devices is generally manufacturer dependent, so consult the user or administrative manuals for the device.

A much simpler type of library is the single media device that is not automatically loaded or changed, such as a CD-ROM, DVD player, or ZIP drive. The following examples are based on the use of such a simple, standalone library.

Enabling or Disabling a Library

The enabling or disabling of a library involves a few simple steps, as follows:

1. Open the **Removable Storage** snap-in tool.
2. Open the physical device console tree.
3. Right-click the library component and select **Properties**.
4. On the **General** tab, verify that **Enable library** is selected in order to enable this library, or remove the check to disable it (Figure 14.11).

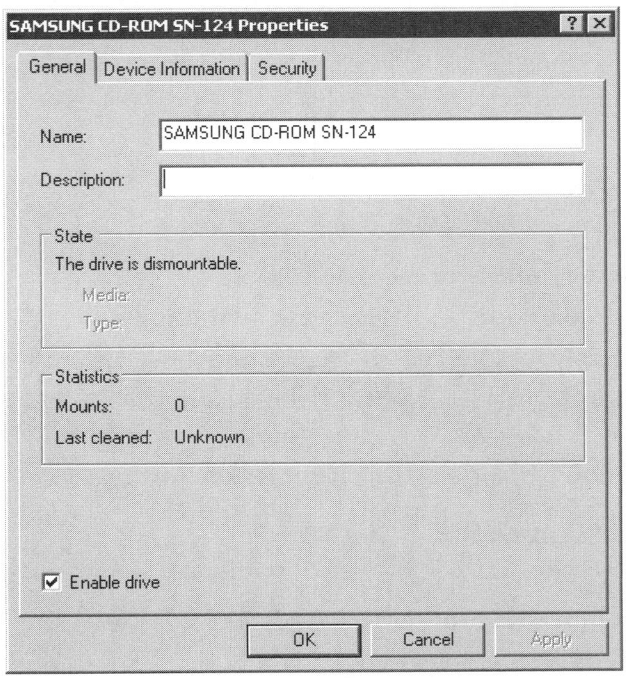

FIGURE 14.11 The Library Properties General Tab with a Library Enabled

Changing the Media Type

Change the media type for a library as follows:

1. Open the **Removable Storage** snap-in tool.
2. Open the physical device console tree.
3. Right-click the library component and select **Properties**.
4. On the **Media** tab, select **Change**.
5. In the **Change Media Types** dialog box, add or remove the media types as desired.

Initiating a Library Inventory

To create an inventory for the library, take the following steps:

1. Open the **Removable Storage** snap-in tool.
2. Open the physical device console tree.
3. Right-click the library component and select **Inventory**.

Working with Media Pools

A *media pool* is any compilation of disks or tapes with the same administrative properties. Multiple media pools can be supported, but they must all be of the same type—disks and tapes cannot be mixed. More than one media pool constitutes a library, which can include media pools of different type and property settings. Since common properties are applied to a media pool, they can also be addressed with multiple libraries (Figure 14.12).

Creating a Media Pool

Media pools are created by following these steps:

1. Open the **Removable Storage** snap-in tool.
2. Right-click **Media Pools** and select **New** → **Media Pool**.
3. On the **General** tab, complete the **Name and Description** text boxes.
4. On the **General** tab, select media from the **Contains media of type** drop-down list.
5. On the **General** tab, set the **Allocation/Deallocation** policy desired.

Deleting an Application Media Pool

Application media pools are deleted by following these steps:

1. Open the **Removable Storage** snap-in tool.
2. Open the **Media Pools** console tree.
3. Click the targeted media pool and select **Delete**.

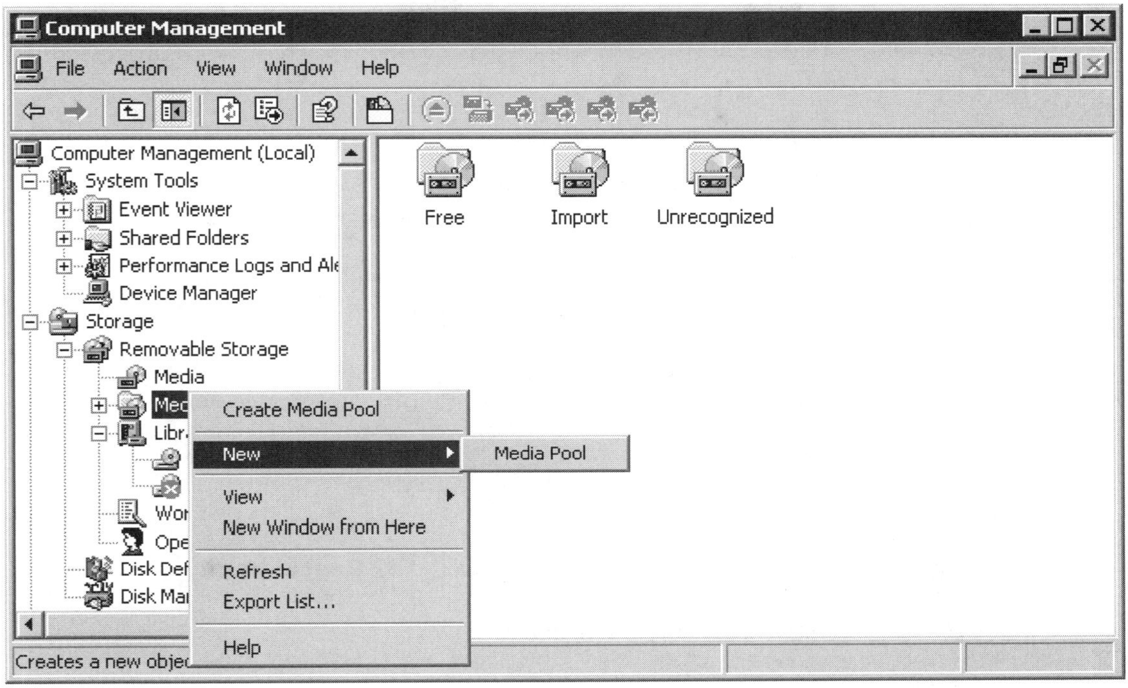

FIGURE 14.12 Creating a Media Pool

Moving Media to Another Media Pool

To move media to another media pool, take the following steps. Remember that the media type and administrative properties of the pool to be moved must be the same as those of the destination media pool.

1. Open the **Removable Storage** snap-in tool.
2. Open the **Media Pools** console tree.
3. Click **Physical Locations** and select the desired application library. Select **Media**.
4. From the right details pane, drag and drop the tape or disk to the destination media pool.

OPERATOR REQUEST MANAGEMENT

The Removal Storage tool permits management of certain operator requests. The options include how to respond to requests, deleting requests from the log, canceling pending operations, and altering the mount order.

Responding to Operator Requests

Operator requests are stored for about an hour after they have been processed. To instruct Windows Server 2003 to respond to them, follow these steps:

1. Open the **Removable Storage** snap-in tool.
2. Open the **Operator Requests** console tree.
3. In the right details pane, right-click the targeted request.
4. To enforce the request, select **Complete**.
5. To disregard the request, select **Refuse**.

Canceling a Pending Operations Request

If a request for a medium is incorrectly made or inappropriately timed, it can be canceled as follows:

1. Open the **Removable Storage** snap-in tool.
2. Open the **Work Queue** console tree.
3. Right-click the request to be canceled and click **Cancel Request** (or **Delete**).

Changing the Mount Order of a Work Queue

Windows Server 2003 makes it easy to change the order in which tapes or disks are mounted. Follow these steps to change the mount order:

1. Open the **Removable Storage** snap-in tool.
2. In the details pane, right-click the mount operation and click **Re-order Mounts**.
3. Through the **Change Mount Order**, select the medium and move it to the beginning, the end, or another location.

SECURING REMOVABLE STORAGE

The Removable Storage snap-in affords ways of determining which users have permission to use removal media and associated devices. The system administrator can add, modify, or delete users and their respective permissions by selecting the **Securities** tab of the media's or device's **Properties**. Refer to Chapter 9 for additional information regarding general permissions settings.

Remote Storage

The Remote Storage facility automatically archives the least used files to another device when space on the local partition or volume becomes tight. Remote storage occurs only when local disk space is required. When the file is needed again, it is retrieved and saved locally.

Remote storage is often maintained on removable storage libraries but always in the same media pool. This means that remotely stored data must all be on one media type with identical administrative properties. Optical disks are not supported for remote storage. Also note that retrieval of remotely stored files is only as fast as the storage device. Thus, if it is necessary to robotically find, mount, and read a tape, for example, the user can anticipate a low to moderate delay.

Remote storage is not automatically installed with the operating system but through the Windows Server 2003 Setup. After installation, it is necessary to verify that a sufficiently large and free media pool exists that is formatted for Windows Server 2003 NTFS.

The administrator establishes the rules and criteria for remote storage, and only those files that meet these specific policies will be eligible for movement. The Remote Storage tool provides a list of default inclusion and exclusion settings for files, which can also be removed or modified. Use the Remote Storage snap-in tool to manage file rules and associated tasks.

BACKUP AND RESTORATION

Backup strategies are based on the effective requirements to restore data. Restoration can range from periodic retrieval of archived information to a full-scale recovery from disaster.

Backup Strategy Basics

A backup strategy requires an understanding of the types of backup available along with their methods and applicable rules. Windows Server 2003 backup should be planned according to these considerations, among others:

- *Frequency of backup*. This varies according to nature of the data. Mission-critical data should be backed up at least daily. Less critical data can be scheduled for backup over the weekend.
- *Archival media*. Depending on the amount of information to be backed up, data can be archived on a variety of media. Capacity of the media must be determined beforehand.
- *Files/folders selection*. The administrator needs a plan for the backup of critical system files (like the Active Directory or the Registry), mission-critical files, and ordinary data files. The files and folders to be backed up must be selected first.

- *Network and local backup*. The plan must include where the backup is to be archived. Obviously, remote backups assume the availability of a fast and reliable network connection. Security over the remote connection is also a consideration.
- *Secure storage of backup media*. The archival plan must include securing media from theft, damage, and unauthorized review.

Available Backup Types

There are four basic Windows Server 2003 backup schemes. Each has its strengths. In most IT environments, all four types are employed at different times, and they can be combined as well. In some backup schemes, when a file changes, a marker is set to flag the change. This marker is known as an *archive attribute*. A backup will clear the marker.

- *Daily.* Selected file and folder backup is performed daily but only of files that were changed during that day. Markers are not reset in daily backups.
- *Incremental.* Only files and folders that have set markers are sent for backup. The marker is then cleared so that future incremental backups do not include them. Incremental backups can be scheduled at any time.
- *Copy.* All selected files and folders are archived without clearing markers.
- *Normal.* All selected files and folders are backed up and their existing markers cleared. Normal backup does not rely on markers but backs up all selected files or folders.

Who Can Back Up

The Administrators, Backup Operators, and Server Operators groups have authority to back up and restore all files of a local computer. Domain Administrator and Domain Backup Operators can perform domainwide backups.

Individual users can back up their own files and folders as well as those in which they have Read, Read & Execute, Modify, or Full Control permissions. File and folder restoration by a user requires Write, Modify, or Full Control permissions.

CAUTION Allowing a normal user with mere Read permission to back up any file or folder creates security risks. For example, such a file could be backed up and spirited out of the organization. It is therefore advised that these rights be restricted. Restrict backup to the owner of the file and the Administrator or Backup Operator. This restriction should be set in the Backup Job Information dialog box.

Managing Backups with Ntbackup

The backup tool, Ntbackup, is invoked from either the **Start → Accessories → System Tools → Backup** menu or the command-line **Ntbackup** utility available through **command prompt** or **Start → Run → Ntbackup**. The Backup and Restore Wizard is shown in Figure 14.13 after selection of **Advanced Mode** from the opening wizard screen.

We recommend the Advanced Mode because it affords greater control. However, if you select to use the base approach, the Backup Wizard walks you through the standard backup decisions, the first of which is presented in the initial dialog box. The first option is to back up everything on the system; the second is to select specific files and folders; and the third is to back up system state data. Selecting any of these options opens up other options.

Let's select the option to back up selected files, drives, or network data, which invokes a dialog box that permits selection of the items to be backed up, as shown in Figure 14.14.

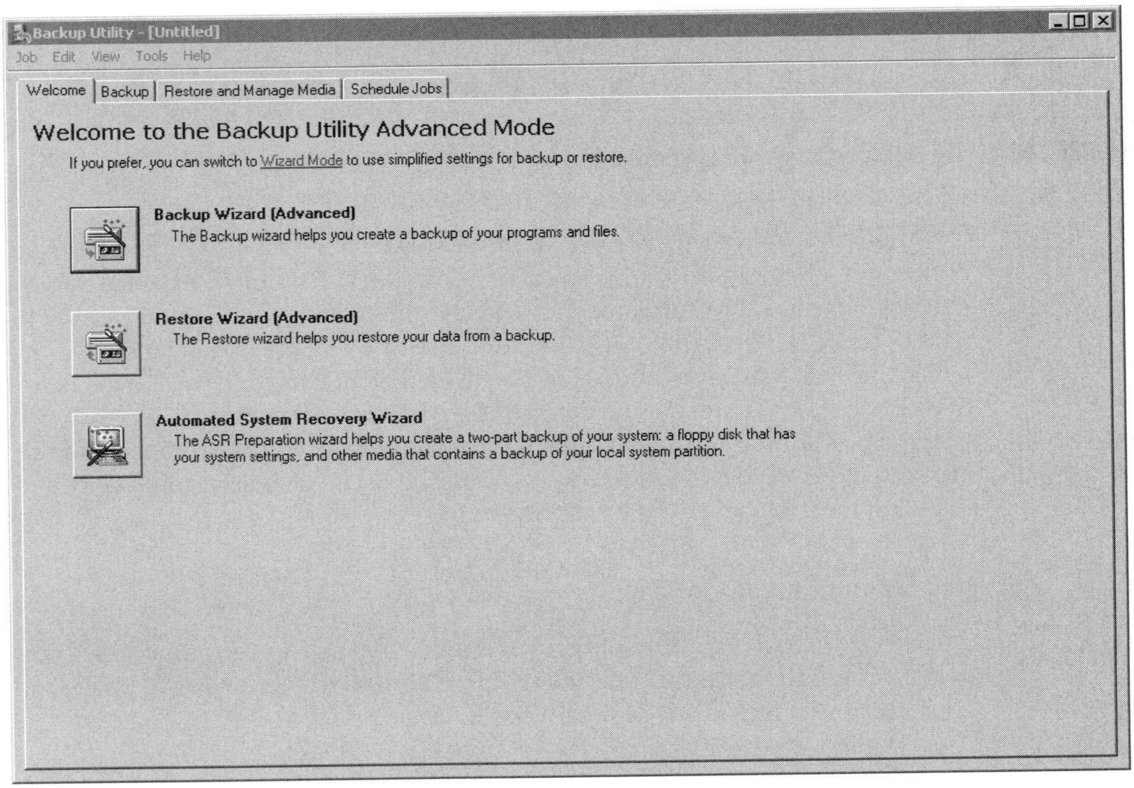

FIGURE 14.13 The Backup and Restore Wizard (Advanced Mode)

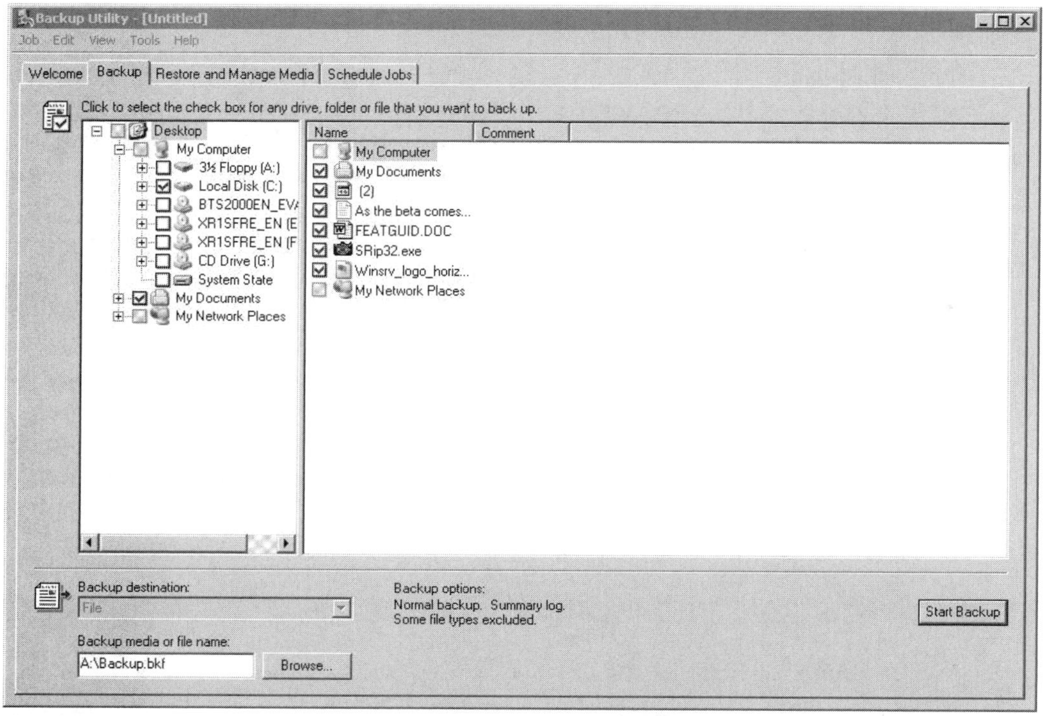

FIGURE 14.14 The Backup Selection Dialog (Advanced)

The next task is to determine where the data will be saved. Use the **Browse** button to navigate to the chosen local or network location and then select **OK** to finish the backup. The **Advanced** button fine-tunes this process. As Figure 14.15 shows, you can select the type of backup, indicate its destination, and enter its name. Subsequent dialog boxes allow you to append information such as the name of the archived volume and the date and time it is to be backed up.

The time for the backup is selected through the **Schedule** tab in the **Advance Mode** (Figure 14.16). Double-click the date. The Backup Wizard is then launched to define the scope and type of backup, as just reviewed.

Changing Default Backup Options

The Ntbackup tool provides a number of options that fit the organization's backup needs. From the Ntbackup application, select **Tools** and then **Options**. Make the appropriate changes in any of the following tabs:

- **General**—General backup rules and reporting methods
- **Restore**—Restore rules

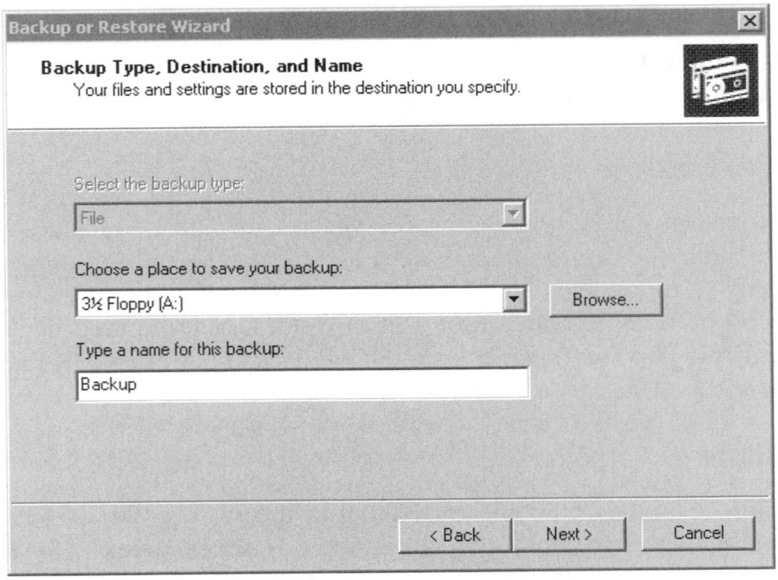

FIGURE 14.15 Selecting the Type of Backup (Basic Backup)

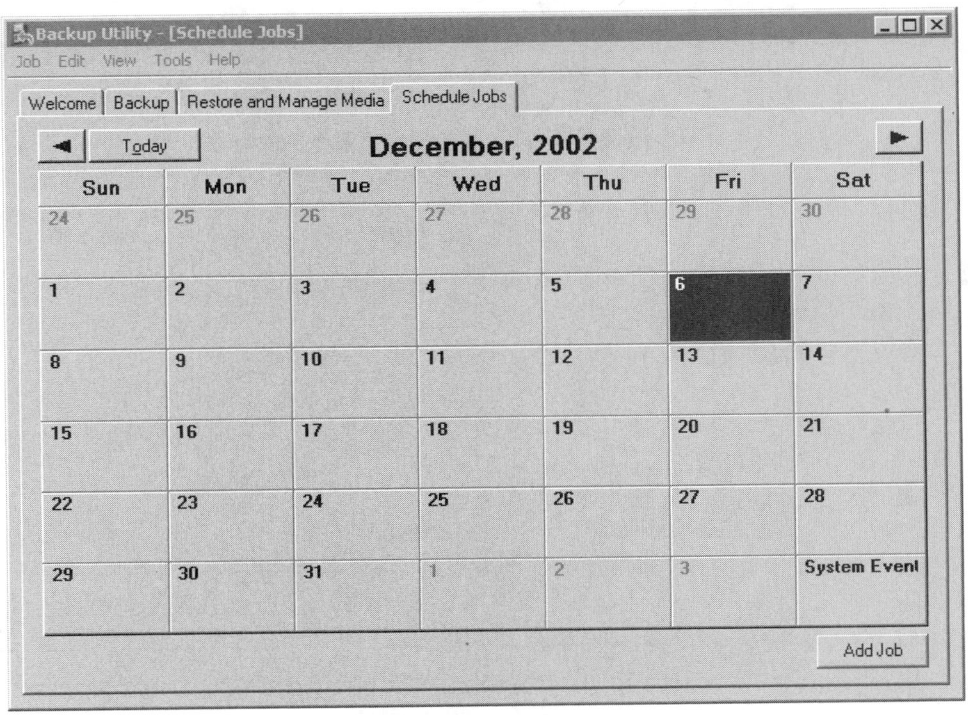

FIGURE 14.16 Backup Scheduling

- **Backup Type**—Default backup types, as discussed previously
- **Backup Log**—Default settings
- **Excluded Files**—Exclusionary rules for backup and restore

Restoration Basics

Restoration is used primarily to recover lost or damaged data. For this reason, maintaining accurate records on backups can save valuable time. With proper records, it is possible to apply only the incremental or daily backup that contains the lost or damaged data. If more radical restoration is required, begin with the last normal backup and then apply incremental backup sequentially until full restoration is achieved.

How to Restore

The process of restoration is carried out by the Restore Wizard, which is available from the Ntbackup application or the **Start → Accessories → System Tools → Backup** menu (Figure 14.17). Again, we recommend use of the **Advance Mode**

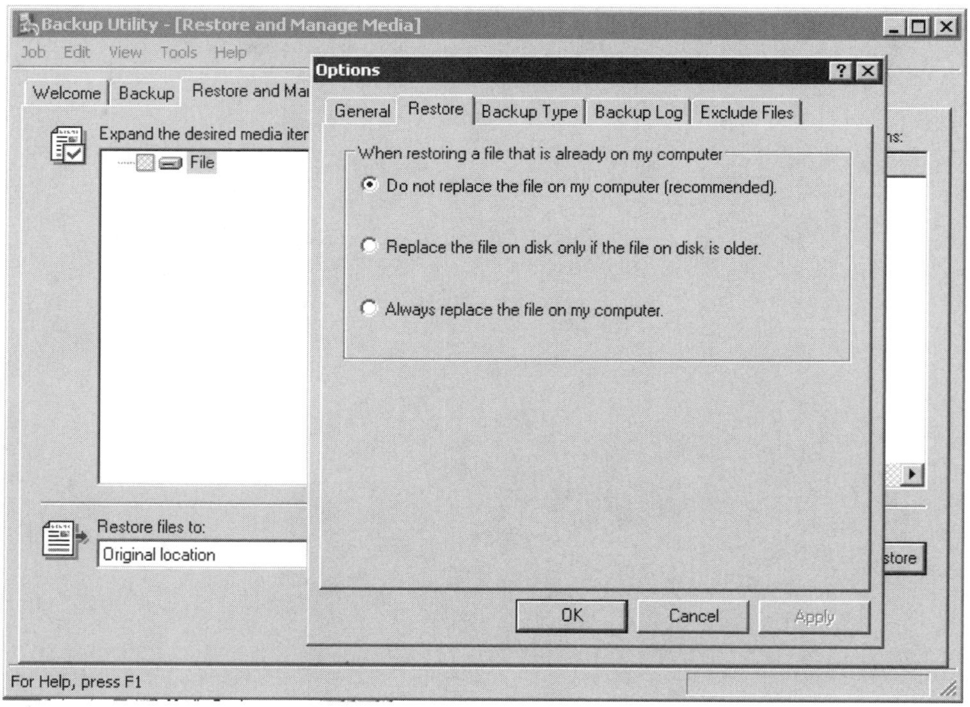

FIGURE 14.17 Backup and Restoration Options

from the initial wizard screen for greater control. This wizard requires you to identify the media and files or folders to be restored according to the following basic procedure:

1. Open the **Ntbackup** application, select **Advance Mode** from the initial wizard screen, select **Restore and Manage Media** tab, double-click the folders or files to be restored (Figure 14.18). Select **Start Restore**.
2. Select the file, folder, or drive to be restored (expand if necessary as you would open subtrees in Explorer). Click **Start Restore**
3. The next prompt allows you to restore the file to the original location, an alternative location, or a single folder (Figure 14.19). Select the location and click **Start Restore**.
4. The next set of options allows you to choose how the restored files will be written. The choices are shown in Figure 14.20. Select the option desired and click **Start Restore**.

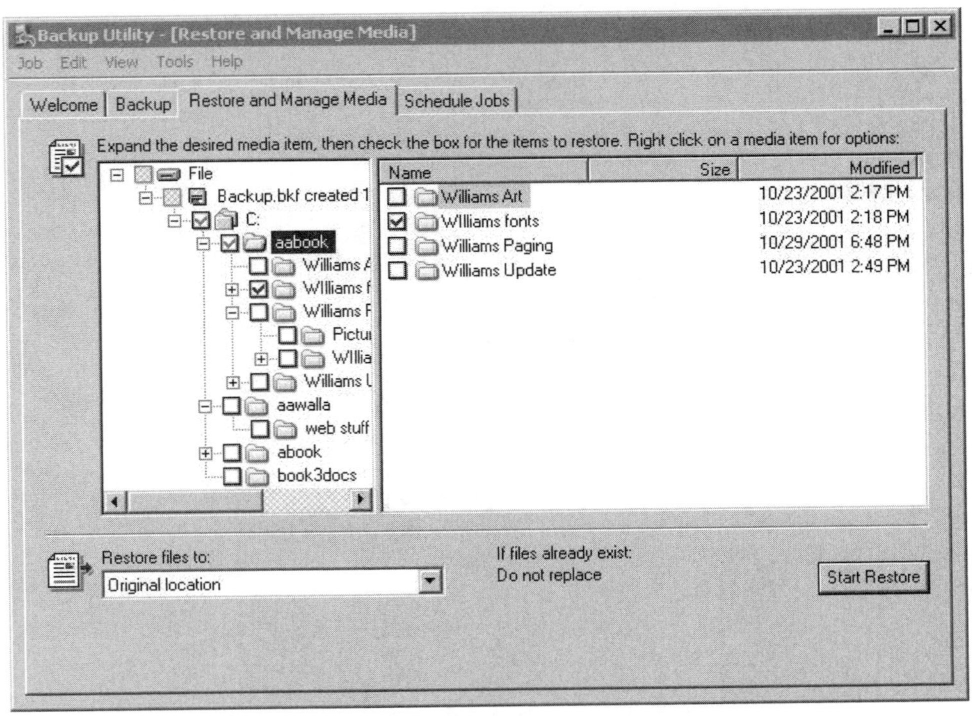

FIGURE 14.18 Selecting Files/Folders for Restoration

FIGURE 14.19 Selecting the Restoration Location (see lower half of screen)

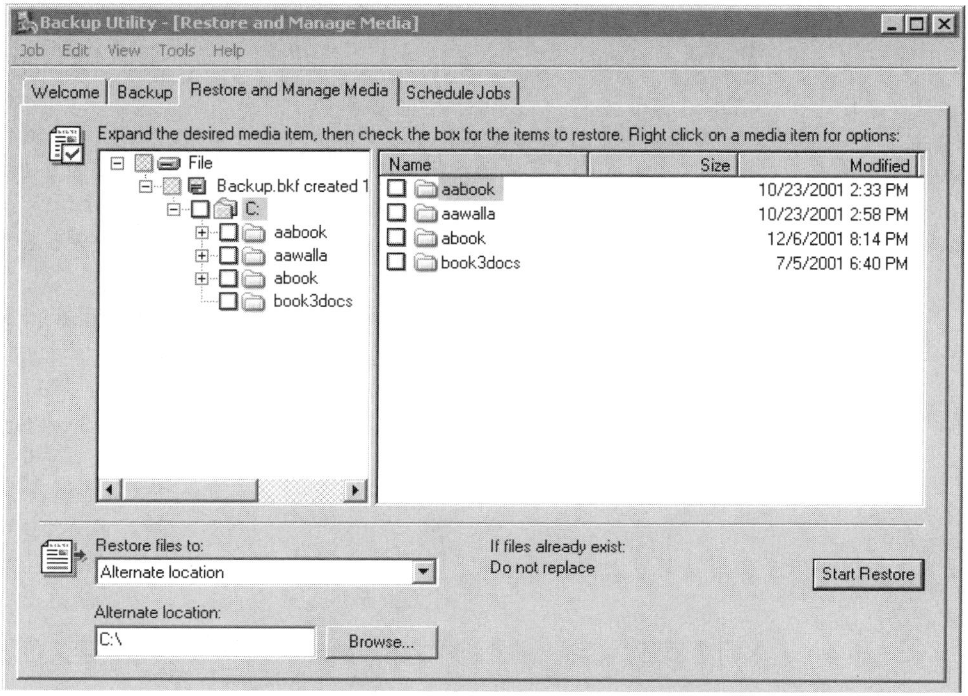

FIGURE 14.20 Writing Restored Files

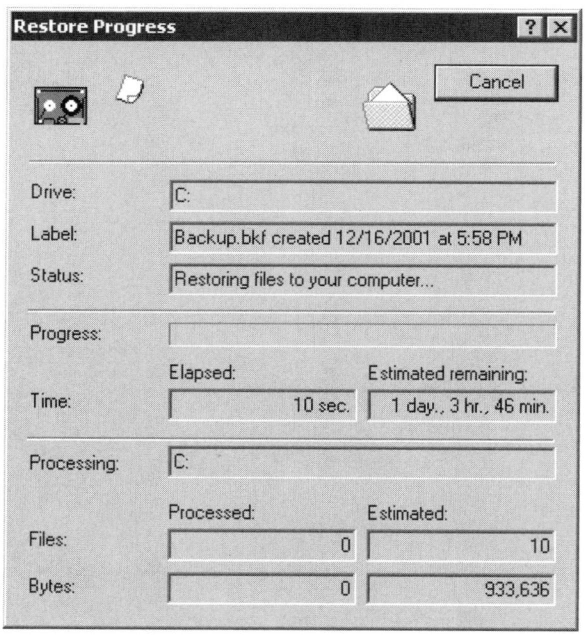

NOTE It is generally advisable to restore files and folders initially in a temporary directory that can be used for testing, which will indicate if the backup data is corrupt or the media are damaged. This kind of testing safeguards against writing corrupted backup data over current data.

Using Batch Restoration

The Ntbackup utility can be employed in a command-line mode to create batch backups, as the following examples illustrate.

Creating a Normal Batch Backup

A normal batch backup is created by typing a command-line statement that is similar to the one that follows from the **Start → Run** menu or from the **command prompt**:

```
ntbackup backup \\ECC-1\c$ /m normal /j " My Current Job 1" /p "Backup"
/n "Command Backup 1" /d " My Command Line Backup Test " /v:yes /r:yes
/l:s /rs:yes /hc:on
```

A brief description of the command line follows:

- `Ntbackup backup` instructs the utility that it is using backup mode.
- `\\ECC-1\c$` identifies a remote share known as ECC-1.
- `/m normal` sets the backup type to normal.
- `/j "My Current Job 1"` is the name of the backup.
- `/p "Backup"` requests that a media pool be used.
- `/n "Command Backup 1"` identifies the name of the tape or disk in the media pool.
- `/d "My Command Line Backup Test"` describes the backup.
- `/v:yes` provides verification when the backup is completed.
- `/r:yes` restricts access to the owner and/or administrator.
- `/l:s` indicates that the log will show a summary statement only.
- `/rs:yes` indicates that remote storage data will also be backed up (not recommended because of the time required).
- `/hc:on` indicates that hardware compression is enabled.

Performing a Batch Copy Backup

A batch copy backup involves a simple command-line statement from the **Start → Run** menu or the **command prompt**:

```
ntbackup backup c:\ /j "Copy Job 1" /a /t "Command Line Example 1" /m
copy
```

A brief description of the command line follows:

- `ntbackup backup` instructs the utility that it is using backup mode.
- `\\ECC-\c$` identifies a remote share known as ECC-1.
- `c:\ /j "Copy Job 1"` identifies the name of the backup for drive `c:`.
- `/t /a "Command Line Example"` appends the backup to a tape named a "Command Line Example."
- `/m copy` sets the type of backup to the copy type.

Authoritative Restoration

Authoritative restoration is useful when system state data such as that associated with Active Directory, domain controllers, or the Registry must be restored. As a default, Windows Server 2003 backup is done in a nonauthoritative mode. Since objects are stored with sequential identification numbers, a nonauthoritative restore will not overwrite an object with a more recent number. Instead, it regards the archived data simply as old. If the Active Directory or Registry has been damaged or corrupted in some fashion, the system state data cannot be restored unless an authoritative override is applied.

The ntdsutil shipped with the Windows Server 2003 permits you to mark objects that need to be authoritatively restored. Update sequence names are changed to a higher level, which allows the substitution of the object. Where multiple domain controllers exist, this new number will be treated as an update and replicated throughout the domain. The ntdsutil must be run after the system state data has been restored and before the system is restarted.

DISASTER MANAGEMENT

IT disasters can come in many forms—floods, fires, earthquakes, tidal waves, and war are some dramatic examples. More common, less dramatic disasters involve the loss of a boot sector, accidental removal of operating system files, power supply interruption, hard drive crashes, and theft of equipment.

Automatic System Recovery

When a system loses its boot sector, critical operating system files, or other data vital to base-level function, the logon processes must be restored. Thus, the first thing automatic system recovery (ASR) does is restore this configuration information as partition structure and file system type. Windows Server 2003 system files are restored with the appropriate hierarchy. The Windows Server 2003 Ntldr and Ntdetect .com files are rebuilt if necessary. Once this is complete, system logon is possible. Then ASR attempts to recover user and auxiliary system files.

CREATING AN ASR SAVESET

To use this important recovery technology, an ASR Saveset must be created as follows:

1. Open the **Backup and Restore Wizard** from the **Start → Accessories → System Tools → Backup** menu or the **Ntbackup** command-line utility. Select **Advanced Mode** from the opening wizard screen.
2. Select the **Automated System Recovery and Preparation** wizard.
3. Select the destination for the ASR Saveset—usually a CD-ROM or diskette set.
4. Click **Finish**.

If you must attempt to repair a nonbootable system, boot from the ASR Saveset diskettes or CD-ROM you created as just discussed. The screens lead you though a logical set of steps. At one stage you must decide to conduct either a fast repair, which automatically attempts to repair items, or a manual repair, which gives you direct control over the process. Unless you are very sophisticated, we recommend the use of the fast repair so that standard approaches are uniformly applied.

Manual Recovery with the Advanced Options Menu

Advanced Options is an alternative boot menu that is invoked by pressing F8 during the initial boot sequence. It provides several alternative approaches to the repair or recovery of a Windows Server 2003 system, as follows:

- *Safe Mode*. The safe mode executes a minimal version of Windows Server 2003 and runs essential services only. You can run it as the default with explorer.exe enabled, with basic networking, or with the command prompt (cmd.exe is loaded instead of explorer.exe). Local applications can be run in safe mode, but the screen resolution will be 640 × 480 and 16 colors by default. Use this mode as it was used in earlier versions of Windows NT and Windows 9x to repair problems manually.

- *Enable Boot Logging*. If this option is selected, it will create a file called ntbtlog.txt that records all boot-related activity. The file is stored at the beginning of the system's root directory and can be reviewed if boot sequence issues, such as bad drivers, occur.
- *Enable VGA Mode*. This was part of the normal boot menu in Windows NT. It is in the **Advanced Options** menu in Windows Server 2003 because it is not something that would be regularly selected. Use this option primarily to correct video display options set during a normal session that somehow render the display output unreadable. Once new sets are in place, you can reboot the system.
- *LastKnownGood Configuration*. Windows Server 2003 stores a new copy of a system's configuration. Copies of previous configurations are numbered sequentially and stored, and the LastKnownGood Configuration is then applied if the current configuration is faulty. Chapter 3 discusses using the Registry Editor to view and modify Registry entries. However, there is no need to use the Registry Editor to apply the LastKnownGood Configuration. When this option is selected from the **Advanced** menu, follow the commands presented and note all warnings. This process will reverse all nonsecurity-related configuration items.

The Command-Line Recovery Console

Another alternative in recovery is the command line–based Recovery Console, which can be used in either normal or safe mode environments. To install the Recovery Console, type the following from the **command prompt** or **Run** menu:

```
<cd designation>:\i386\win32 /cmdcons
```

The Recovery Console is a character-based environment that looks very much like MS-DOS. It permits you to perform a great many command-line tasks, including starting and stopping services. To terminate the Recovery Console type **exit** and press ENTER. Please note that this will also reboot the system.

Because it provides direct control, the Recovery Console is probably the preferred method of experienced system administrators. Commands can be selected as needed by the administrator without the intervention of wizards or other actions that are not visible.

Emergency Repair Disk

The creation of an emergency repair disk (ERD) is a prudent action for any system administrator. Although highly unlikely, it is possible for critical Windows Server 2003 files to be lost or corrupted. The ERD can be used to restart the system so that these files can be restored. The ERD is created through the Backup utility by copying the following hidden system files to a formatted floppy disk:

- Ntldr
- Ntdetect.com
- Ntbootdd.sys
- Boot.ini

Fault Tolerance for Disaster Protection

Fault-tolerant systems are an important first line of defense in protecting data from system failures. As discussed earlier, RAID-5 and mirrored environments are two methods that are well supported by Windows 2000/Windows Server 2003. In Chapter 17 we examine a more expensive but extremely viable fault-tolerant approach known as system clustering. Refer to these sections for additional information on how to apply fault tolerance to your disaster recovery plan.

Uninterrupted Power Supply Management

Power failures happen in any jurisdiction and, along with power spikes and lightning, can destroy sensitive electronic equipment. This is why a relatively small investment can avert disaster. An uninterrupted power supply (UPS) provides sufficient power to permit you to gracefully shut down Windows Server 2003 systems in a power failure and guards against electrical storms and power spikes. The analysis of UPS systems by make and model is outside the scope of this book, but we recommend them. Their configuration is through **Control Panel → Power Options → UPS** tab.

POSTSCRIPT

Disk management, backup, restoration, and disaster recovery are critical system administrator responsibilities. This chapter centers strictly on the maintenance of homogeneous Windows Server 2003 environments; in mixed environments many other considerations exist. For example, if you want to gain access to files on a UNIX system, a number of third-party utilities can be applied to mount such disks. Two are NFS and Samba, which should be investigated by system administrators working in mixed environments. An abundance of information about products that support these technologies is available on the Internet.

Chapter 15

Terminal Services

Terminal Services is Microsoft's answer to thin client technology. In many ways, it mirrors environments that relied on server-based computing and the use of terminals for data input. While a common computer paradigm for many operating systems like UNIX, Terminal Services provides an approach that centers on Microsoft's server. Unlike Microsoft's traditional desktop orientation, where application and data processing occur on the local computer, with Terminal Services these activities are passed to the server. The local system acts merely to display the data and the keyboard/mouse serve as input devices for transmission to the server.

Terminal Services has undergone significant changes with each major Windows NT server family release. In its Windows 2000 incarnation, for example, Terminal Services expanded its reach as not only an applications-serving vehicle but also as a powerful administrative tool. In Windows Server 2003, the advance continues by transforming Terminal Services across the broader Internet while still enhancing functionality and essential services like security management.

NOTE Terminal Services in Windows Server 2003 introduces the Remote Desktop Users group, a new mechanism for granting users remote access to a computer for administration or application sharing. Remote Desktop Users is a built-in group and is administered via policy. Placing a user or group into Remote Desktop Users gives that user the ability to remotely connect to a computer. The user does not also need to be given local logon privileges, as in earlier versions of Terminal Services. The Permissions tab in Terminal Services Configuration can still be used to add users, as it was in Windows 2000. However, users must be granted the Remote Interactive Logon right to be able create a remote Terminal Services connection. This logon right is given to any user or group using the Security policy editor by simply adding that user or group to the Remote Desktop Users group.

NOTE There is an important difference between Windows 2000 and Windows Server 2003 installations. When installing Terminal Services for Windows 2000, you are prompted to select application-server functions or administrative support. Both function sets can be installed sequentially on one server. However, a server can perform only applications or administrative functions at one time. Windows Server 2003 still distinguishes between application and administrative services, but installation and management are now consolidated.

NOTE To prevent Terminal Services being licensed to unauthorized users, Windows Server 2003 adds a new security group. This optional setting restricts the servers to which a Terminal Server License Server will offer licenses or communicate about licensing discovery. To assign a License Server Security Group: **Computer Configuration → Administrative Templates → Windows Components → Terminal Services → Licensing → License Server Security Group**.

CONCEPTUAL REVIEW

Terminal Services is a significant departure from the default Windows Server 2003 environment. In all other discussions in this book we have assumed that the user is operating from a self-contained computer system. Otherwise known as a *fat client,* this system type is responsible for application processing, local storage, and management of the Win32 user interface.

By contrast, Terminal Services uses a *thin client.* Although the local computer might have storage and a resident OS, all processing is remotely performed on the server. The Windows Server 2003 Terminal Services passes the Win32 user interface to the thin client, where it is locally displayed. As keystrokes and mouse clicks are entered, they are sent to the server for interpretation and execution, after which the server refreshes the thin client's local "terminal" screen. The default Windows Server 2003 environment is a decentralized, multiconsole environment, but Terminal Services provides server-based, multiple user capabilities (see Figure 15.1).

The Terminal Server operates with either Windows Server 2003 workgroups or domains (see Figure 15.2). Users of thin-client systems must be authenticated, and as such their privileges are defined by Windows Server 2003 group policies.

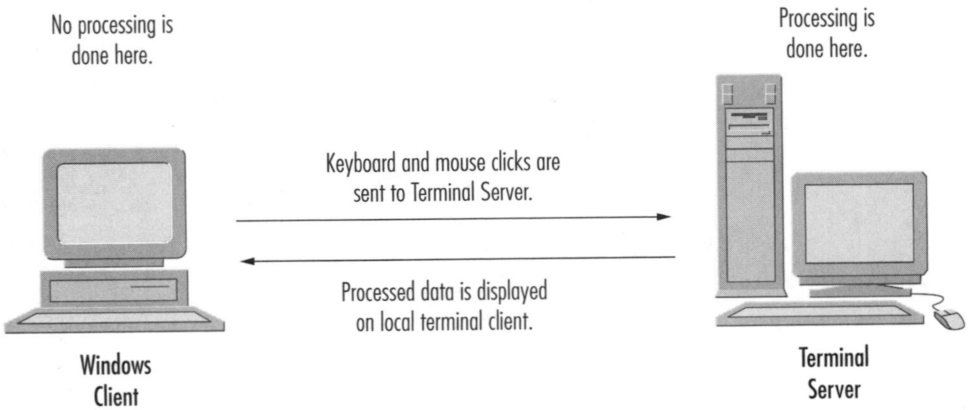

FIGURE 15.1 Terminal Server–Thin Client Relationship

Users of thin-client terminals are like their fat-client counterparts except for some differences in system configuration and hardware availability. Windows Server 2003 Terminal Services supplies terminal clients for Microsoft Windows environments only. Client support for other OSs must be obtained from third-party vendors (Figure 15.2).

INSTALLING TERMINAL SERVICES

Installation of Terminal Services is extremely straightforward but further configuration is required, as discussed later in this chapter. The installation process is:

1. Click **Start** menu → **All Programs** → **Administrative Tools** → **Configure Your Server** → click **Next** until the **Server Role** screen appears, then select **Terminal Services** → click **Next**. (Alternatively, you get to this point from **Control Panel** and add Windows components.)
2. A warning screen appears; it is discussed in the next section. Click **Next**.
3. You will then be asked to set the security levels at **Full Security** or **Relaxed Security,** as shown in Figure 15.3. It is recommended that you select **Full Security** whenever possible. **Relaxed Security** is designed for support of earlier applications. Select the security level and click **Next**.

The installation process gathers information and writes appropriate files locally. When the process is complete, click **Finish** when prompted. Then restart the system so that the installation can take effect.

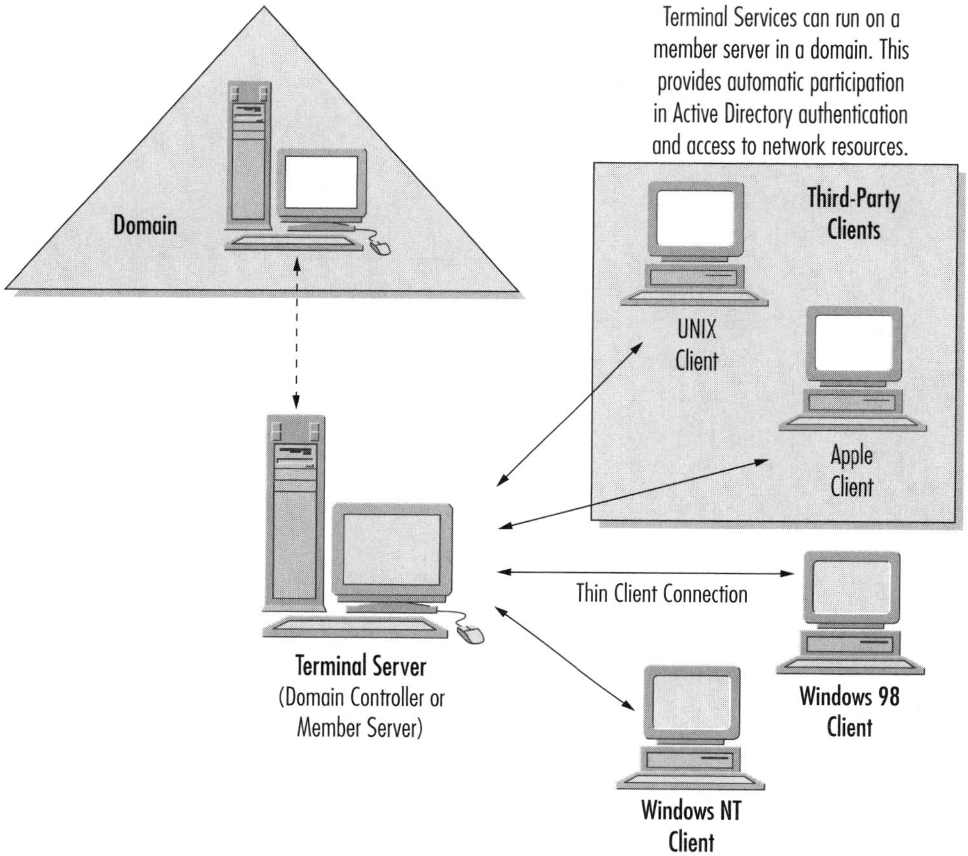

FIGURE 15.2 Terminal Services in a Domain Environment

NOTE If you are supporting older applications that require Relaxed Security, it is recommended that they be moved to a separate server. All other applications should then be run from Full Security servers. This isolation should reduce security breaches.

NOTE Terminal Services provides a 120-day grace period before formal product licensing is required. In order to activate Terminal Services Licensing, select this feature from Add/Remove Application Windows Component wizard, which is available from Control Panel.

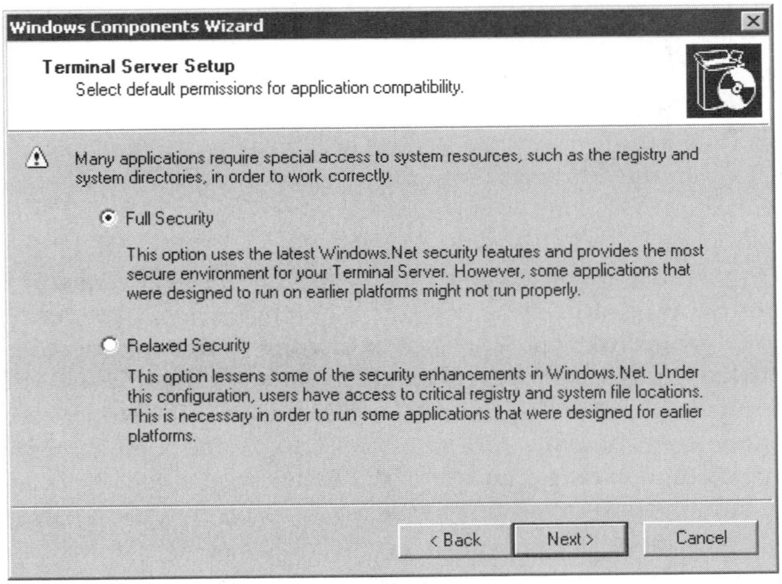

FIGURE 15.3 Terminal Services Security Level Setup

NOTE As noted earlier, Windows 2000 requires Administrative and Application server functions installed in separate actions. The Add/Remove Application Windows Component wizard available from Control Panel for Terminal Services Setup asks you to choose a mode:

- **Remote administration mode** allows an administrator to remotely manage the server.
- **Application server mode** allows users to remotely run applications from the server.

Select the desired setup mode and click **Next**.

NOTE Terminal Services licensing has been streamlined by a new wizard. This includes a new Internet connection method for activating licenses, new error messages, and added support for new types of licenses. This wizard is available from **Administrative Tools → Terminal Server Licensing**.

Installing Applications for Use with Terminal Services

Although Microsoft has tested the compatibility of Terminal Services with many popular commercial software packages, such as its own Office XP, Corel Office, and Lotus SmartSuite, not all applications will run in this environment. When in doubt, check with the third-party software vendor for compatibility and special requirements for installation or configuration.

Applications should be installed after Terminal Server, and they must be set up to work with it. Installation is either through the standard **Control Panel → Add/Remove Programs** wizard or via the command line. When using the **Add/Remove Programs** wizard, select the **Change User Option** and click **All users with common applications settings for universal access** or **Install applications setting for this user only**. To install using the **command prompt**, type **change user /install** and click **Enter**. Then run the application's setup program. Type **change user /execute** and click **Enter** to complete the installation. If available, run the post-installation script, as discussed in the next paragraph.

Applications installed prior to Terminal Services usually need to be reinstalled or properly configured. For example, we installed a popular shareware program before Terminal Services on a member server. When we then attempted to launch the program, the warning message indicated a registry failure. In this case, it became necessary to uninstall the application and to reinstall it. In some cases, it may be necessary to edit the registry manually to remove all references to the application. In other cases, the only changes required are to run a post-installation script located in \Windows\Application Compatibility Scripts\Install. Refer to that directory for compatibility scripts and to the Microsoft Web site for updates.

Figure 15.4 provides an example of the Terminal Services Installation Warning Message.

NOTE To work, an application should store per-user data in the HKEY_CURRENT_USER Registry key. Unfortunately, many applications store information, such as default color or screen size settings, in HKEY_CURRENT_MACHINE key, which means that users cannot customize preferences. However, unless this is hard-coded into the application, the installation script for the specific application can often be modified to correct this problem. Even so, when modifying installation scripts, be sure to test the application prior to deployment.

Sizing Terminal Services Systems

Sizing a system for Terminal Services is not an exact science, given that the applications that will run on the server and the demands placed on the system by indi-

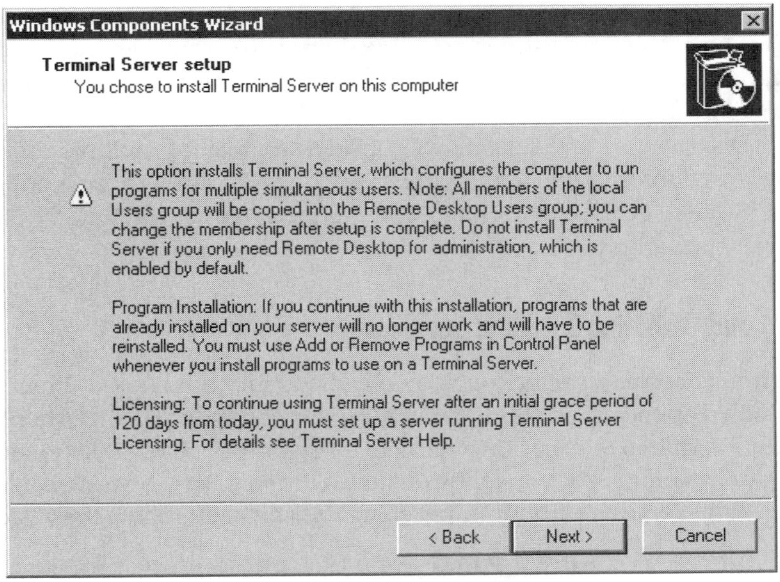

FIGURE 15.4 The Terminal Services Installation Warning Message

vidual users can vary radically. If the typical user maintains a single session and runs a single, medium-level, memory-dependent application, plan on a minimum allocation of 4 to 8 MB of additional RAM per user above the base 64-MB Terminal Services system requirement. (This calculation does not include the base memory required for the operating system.) However, be prepared for the amount of RAM to increase with added demands. A system administrator must monitor the performance of the server and make adjustments to memory, the number of users, and the application types.

The architecture of the applications can also affect performance. Wherever possible, 32-bit software should be used. Windows 16-bit programs that generally date back to the days of Windows 3.11 must be processed through the Windows on Windows (WOW) operating system layer, which translates application processes and therefore requires additional system resources.

NOTE The 64-bit version of Windows Server 2003 limits a number of functions that could affect certain Terminal Services support options. These limitations are listed in the appendix of the book. You should also refer to Microsoft's Web site for changes in 64-bit features.

As for network or asynchronous computer adapters such as an RS323 serial port, use the highest-performance hardware available. Although down-level adapters can generally be employed, interrupts and data flow speed may be significantly impacted.

Disk access is the final major consideration. Since multiple users will be seeking stored information at the same time, speed of throughput is critical. Generally, fast SCSI or SCSI-2 drives are recommended. IDE, ESDI, and ST-506 drives have lower throughput.

Enabling and Disabling Terminal Services

Terminal Services can be toggled off and on, but because of its potential impact on installed applications, this is generally not recommended. Still, there may be times when Terminal Services on a particular server may be necessary, such as for security or system performance. By default, Terminal Services are enabled. To disable Terminal Services without uninstalling the software, follow these steps:

1. Launch the **Control Panel** and select **Add/Remove** programs.
2. Select the **Add/Remove Windows Components**.
3. In the **Windows Components Wizard** dialog box, highlight **Terminal Server**.
4. Select **Details** and remove the check mark from **Terminal Server**.
5. Click **OK**.

Terminal Services can be reenabled by following the preceding steps but adding the check mark in the Terminal Services dialog box.

CONFIGURING TERMINAL SERVICES

The Terminal Services Configuration tool is available from the **Start** menu → **Programs** → **Administrative Tools** or as a Microsoft Management Console (MMC) snap-in. These tools support the administration of Terminal Services Configuration.

Configuring Connections

Terminal Services Connections support the link between the server and client session settings. Its properties are the critical component in determining how and where Terminal Services can be used. The Terminal Services Configuration snap-in tool modifies RDP-TCP properties, including the users and groups allowed to use these services (see Figure 15.5).

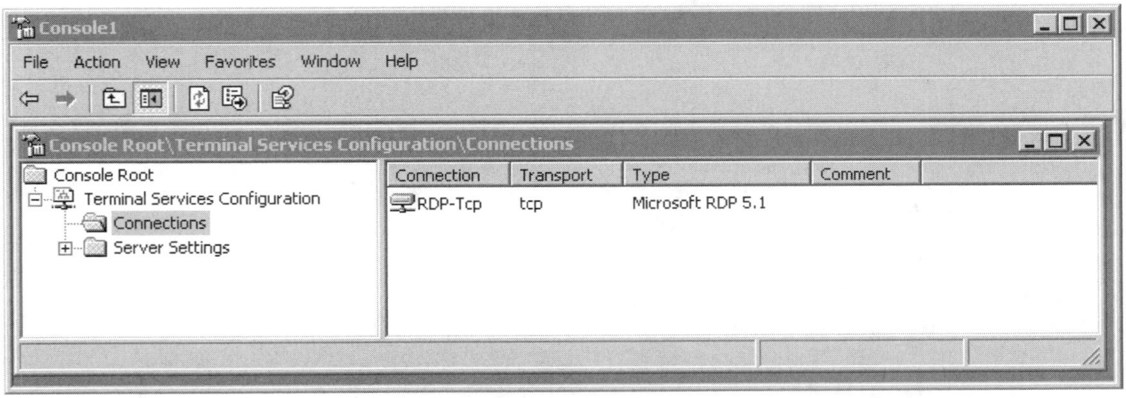

FIGURE 15.5 The Terminal Services Configuration Snap-in Tools

Terminal services use a TCP/IP connection through TCP port 3389 for Microsoft Windows access—specifically, the Remote Desktop Protocol (RDP-TCP) stack.

NOTE Third-party vendor Citrix provides a Terminal Services connection to Apple Macintosh, UNIX, and MS-DOS workstations and terminals. It uses its own ICA protocol on clients to connect through asynchronous communications, IPX/SPX, NetBIOS, and TCP/IP. For information on integrating Citrix's MetaFrame and WinFrame technology, visit the Citrix Web site at *www.citrix.com*.

RDP-TCP configuration is accomplished through a series of Properties tabs, each of which provides options that deserve independent consideration. The **Properties** dialog box is displayed by right-clicking **RDP-Tcp** and selecting **Properties**.

GENERAL SETTINGS

The General tab (Figure 15.6) identifies the Microsoft RDP-version level and the transport used, with TCP as the default. It also allows the system administrator to add comments about this installation.

The most important configuration option on the General tab is the encryption level for data transport. Data encryption is one-directional from the client to the server and must coincide with the server's defined encryption level. Data transmitted from the server is not protected by encryption to the client.

Standard Windows user authentication is confirmed by checking the last option on the General tab screen.

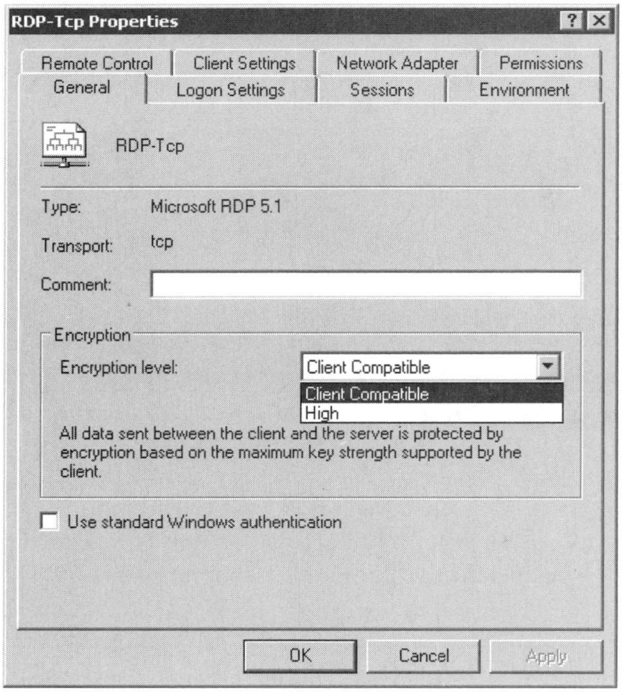

FIGURE 15.6 The General Settings Tab

REMOTE CONTROL OPTIONS

The Remote Control tab (Figure 15.7) establishes how the user can gain access and the level of control to be granted. It is a particularly important setting for a system administrator because it permits control over and observation of a user's session. The Remote Control tab is used to select the level of control desired. The first two options retain the user's default settings on remote control or negate the function; the third option establishes the right to **View the session** and/or **Interact with the session**. If the **Require user's permission** box is checked, the message box will be displayed on the user's desktop when control is attempted so that the user can grant or deny access.

An organizational policy should be considered as to the proper use of this function, since the ability to control and observe a user's session obviously has both positive and negative ramifications. When a user encounters a problem, it is a blessing to the system administrator to be able to view and correct it remotely; however, this also creates concern over eavesdropping and confidentiality.

Remote control is defined differently for domain users and local users. For domain users, follow these steps: From the **Active Directory Users Accounts and**

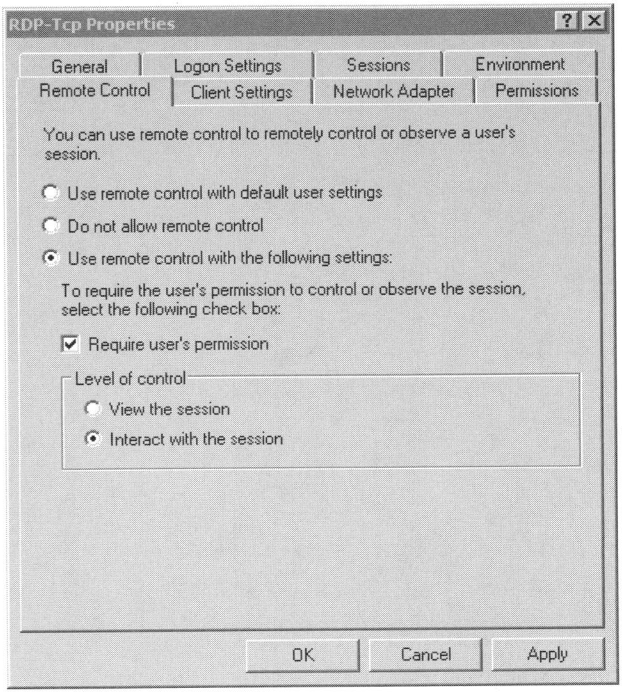

FIGURE 15.7 The Remote Control Tab

Computers snap-in, select the domain, select **Users**, select the targeted user, right-click the user and choose **Properties**, select the **Remote Control** tab, and make the desired changes. For local users, use the **Computer Management (Local)** snap-in, select **System Tools**, select **Local Users and Groups**, right-click the user, select **Properties**, and select the **Remote Control** tab.

CLIENT SETTINGS FOR REMOTE CONTROL

The Client Settings tab enables and disables a number of client-side items. The Connection options (1) connect local drives, (2) connect the local printer, and (3) set the local printer as the default device for applications executed by the user. In essence, these settings direct the respective devices to the terminal user's local environment. As shown in Figure 15.8, each of six mapping options can be disabled by a checking a box next to it.

NETWORK ADAPTER SETTINGS

The Network Adapter tab (Figure 15.9) performs two functions. First, it permits the selection of the adapters that have been found to be compatible for the network,

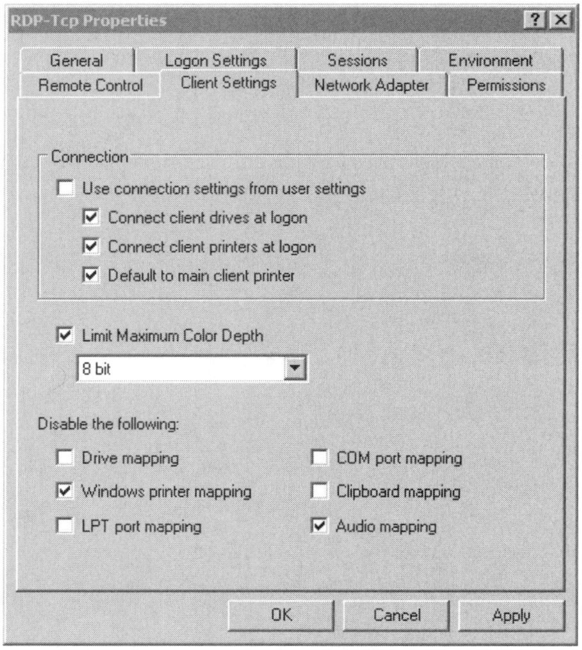

FIGURE 15.8 The Client Settings Tab

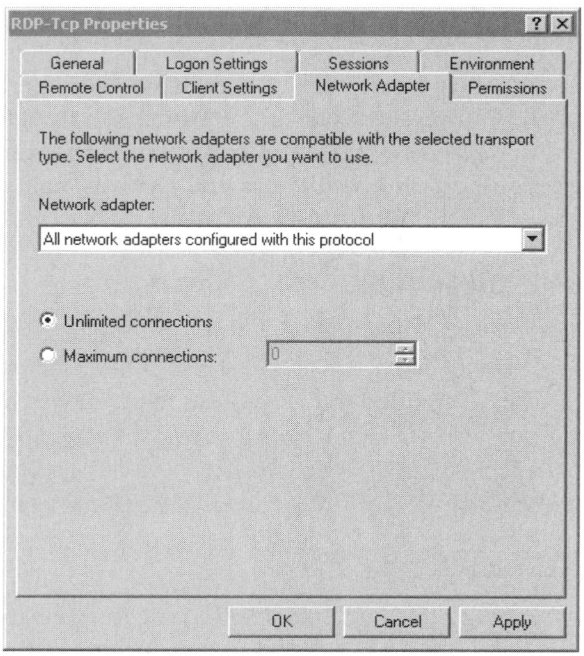

FIGURE 15.9 The Network Adopter Tab

with the default setting **All network adapters configured with this protocol**. Second, it establishes the number of allowable connections. If **Unlimited connections** is selected, there is no limit to the number of connections allowed to the Terminal Server. If **Maximum connections** is selected, a number for the upper limit for concurrent connections must be entered. This option is generally recommended because system performance can be seriously affected by too many connections. Once system capacity is properly sized, setting an upper limit will reduce the possibility of system overload.

PERMISSIONS

The Terminal Services Permissions tab (Figure 15.10) defines which users and groups have rights to assume **Full Control, User Access, and Guest Access**. By default, the Administrator and System groups are allowed all three. This tab is employed to delegate authority to other users or groups for Terminal Server management.

As with other Permissions properties dialog boxes, additional users and groups are included by clicking the **Add** button and deleted with the **Remove** button. The **Advanced** button is used to apply special permissions. (See Chapter 10 for more information about managing this Permissions tab.)

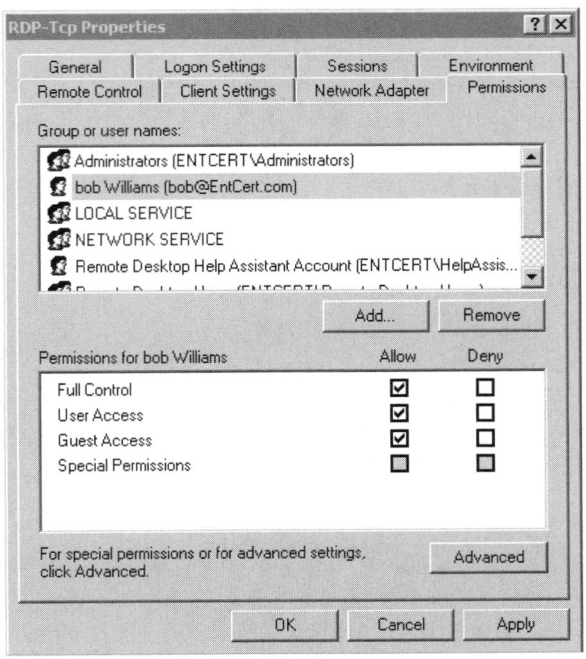

FIGURE 15.10 The Permissions Tab

LOGON SETTINGS

The Logon Settings tab (Figure 15.11) permits the use of either client-provided or administrator-defined logon information. If the latter is selected, complete the text boxes for **User name, Domain, Password,** and **Confirmed password**.

SESSIONS OPTIONS

The Sessions tab (Figure 15.12) establishes parameters around the time a client can remain idle, the maximum length of a session, and whether that client can reconnect. One of the benefits of Terminal Services is that a user can disconnect without terminating the session. Providing that the parameters are set to enable this function and time period, he can reconnect as the same or a different client exactly where he left off.

ENVIRONMENT SETTINGS

The Environment tab (Figure 15.13) permits the user to use an individual profile or overrides these settings with those established in this dialog box. In many environments, only certain applications need be initiated. For example, in a customer service environment, a set of knowledge-based Help applications may be all that is

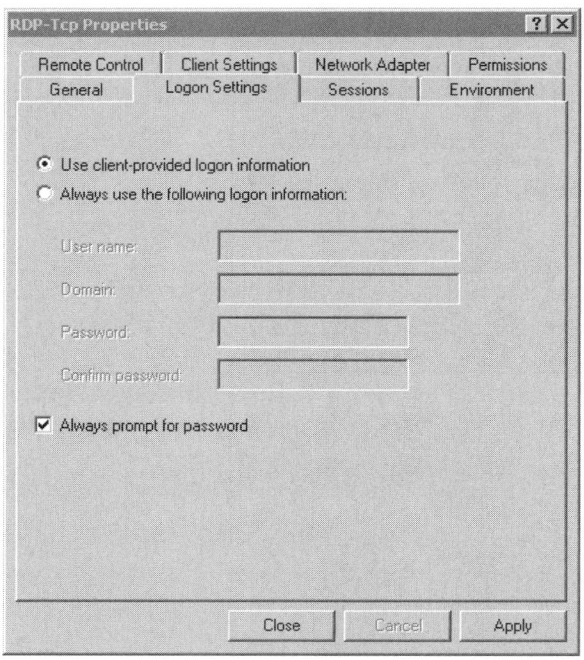

FIGURE 15.11 The Logon Settings Tab

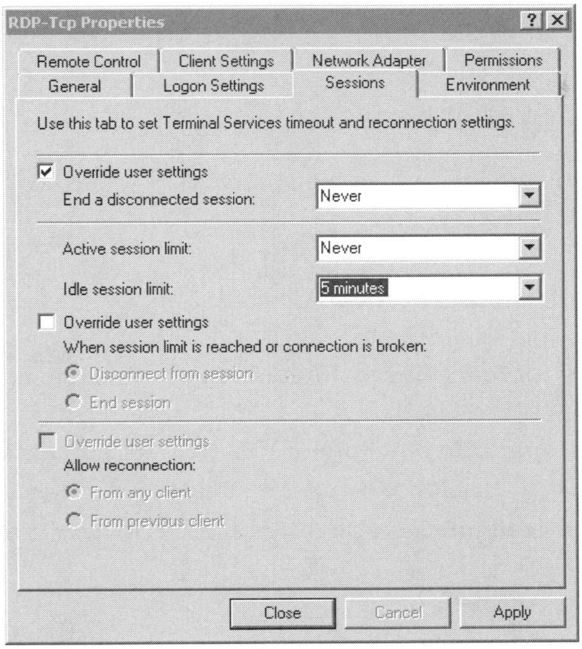

FIGURE 15.12 The Session Tab

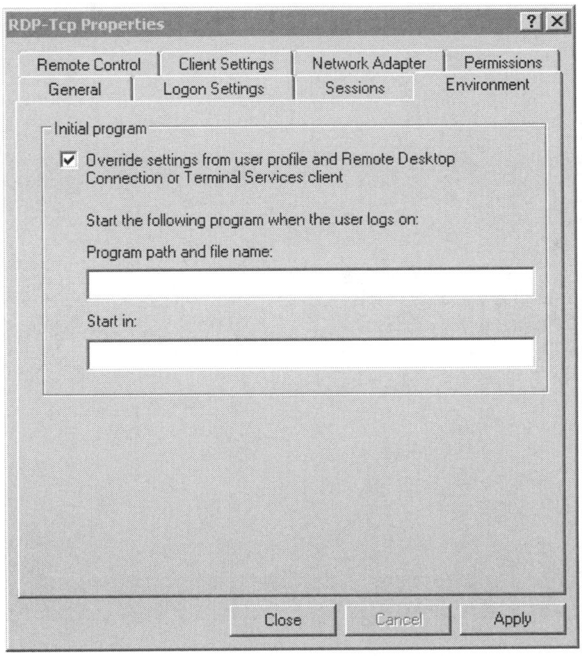

FIGURE 15.13 The Environment Tab

necessary. In such a case, check the **Override** settings and designate the program path and file name.

Terminal Services Server Settings

The Server Settings determine how Terminal Services is applied (with default settings shown in Figure 15.14).

The seven default settings are

- **Delete temporary folders on exit** determines how temporary folders are treated on exit.
- **Use temporary folders per session** determines where temporary folders are created during a session.
- **Permission Compatibility** indicates if security is set **Full** or **Relaxed.**
- **Sessions Directory** enables or disables session directory functions.
- **Restrict each user to one session** places a yes or no restriction on the user sessions.
- **Licensing** defines the basis of the license.
- **Active Desktop** defines whether the Microsoft Active Desktop environment is enabled or disabled.

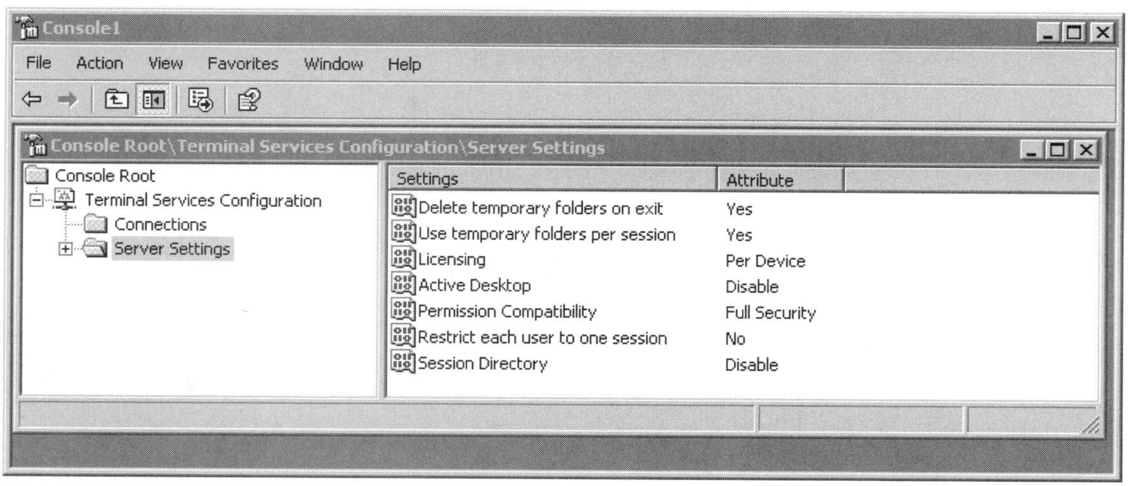

FIGURE 15.14 Server Settings

TERMINAL SERVICES ADMINISTRATION

The Terminal Server allows the administrator to remotely monitor servers, sessions, users, and processes, and supports the centralized deployment of applications, disk management, and device access. It also allows the administrator to manage the applications available to users, logon privileges, and security.

NOTE The Remote Desktop Web Connection includes a downloadable ActiveX control and sample Web pages. These should be used as starting points for running Windows-based programs with Internet Explorer. This is a Windows Server 2003 built-in reversion of the Terminal Services Advanced Client (TSAC). For the latest sample pages, go to the Microsoft Web site.

Administrative Tools

Terminal Services offers a number of system administrative tools. With the exception of the Services Configuration and Connections Manager snap-ins, discussed earlier, the following tools will be explored in this section:

- Terminal Services Manager
- The Active Directory Users and Computers snap-in and the Local Users and Groups snap-in
- Task Manager additions
- Client software generation and installation
- Remote connection
- Common commands

NOTE Up to two such sessions can be created concurrently. However, it is strongly recommended that a single administrator session be used on a given system at one time. Additionally, Windows Server 2003 allows an administrator to connect remotely to the server console. When an administrator logs on remotely, the console is locked at the physical device. To unlock the physical server console, simply terminate the remote console session.

REMOTE DESKTOP MMC ADMINISTRATIVE TOOL

The Remote Desktops MMC snap-in (Figure 15.15) enables administrators to host multiple Terminal Services connections in an easily navigable tree. It is also useful

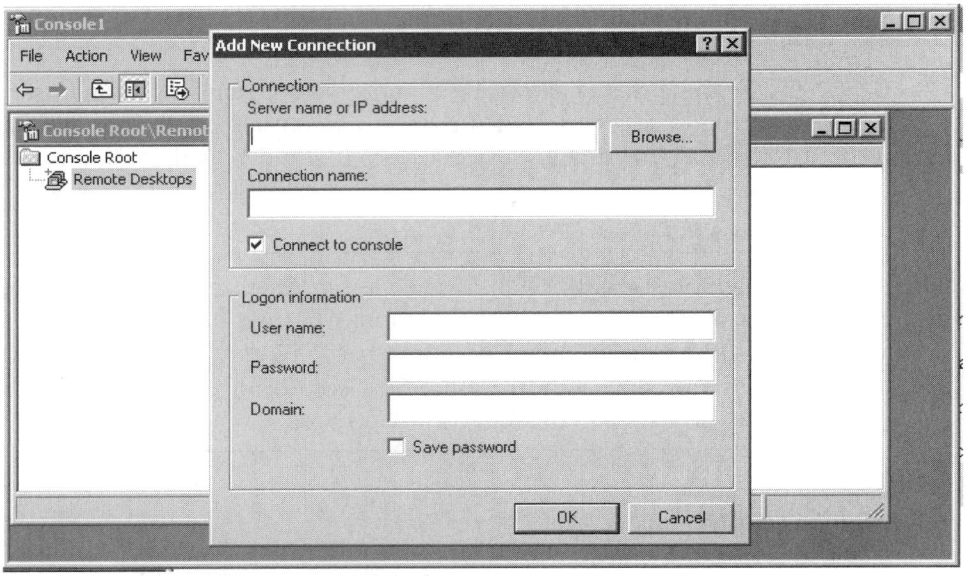

FIGURE 15.15 Remote Desktop MMC Snap-in

for managing many Windows 2003 or Windows 2000 servers. By right-clicking **Remote Desktops,** the administrator can identify the additional servers by selecting **Add New Connection**.

TERMINAL SERVICES MANAGER

Terminal Services Manager (Figure 15.16) is used to view and administer users, active sessions, and processes on terminal servers anywhere on the network. It is available from the **Start** menu → **Administrative Tools** → **Terminal Services Manager**.

The **Actions** menu invokes the ability to connect and disconnect sessions. Users and sessions as well as processes can be displayed by drilling down the administrative tree. Processes can be terminated at this stage.

ACTIVE DIRECTORY USERS AND COMPUTERS SNAP-IN AND THE LOCAL USERS AND GROUPS SNAP-IN

Depending on the environment, the Active Directory Users and Computers snap-in or the Local Users and Groups snap-in establishes Terminal Services settings for individual users. From the respective snap-in, select the local computer or domain, select **Users**, right-click the targeted user, and select **Properties.** Because four of

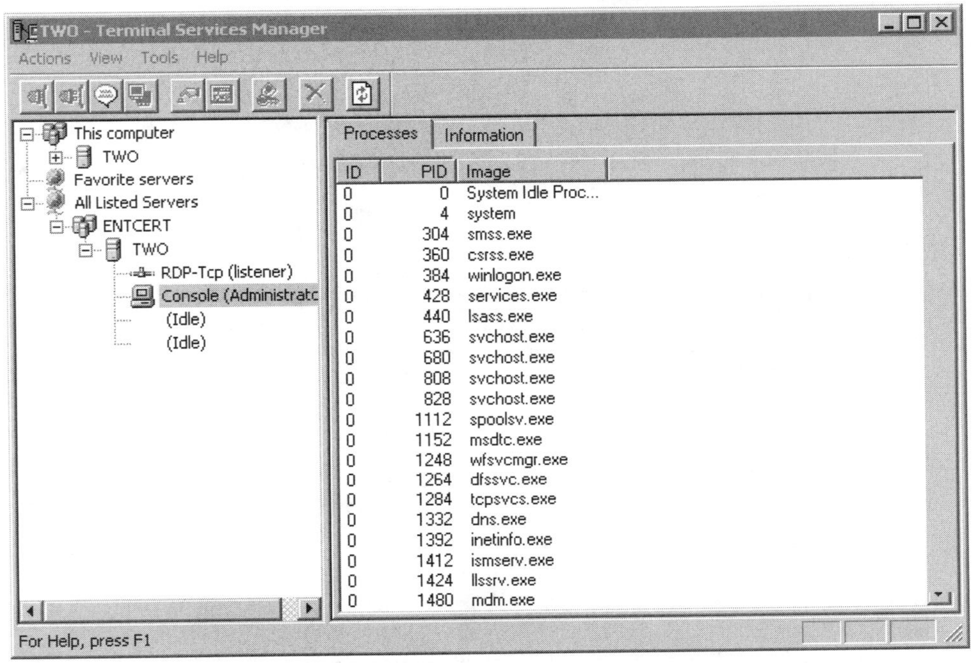

FIGURE 15.16 Terminal Services Manager

the **Properties** tabs are important to Terminal Services, let's briefly examine them:

- **Remote control** establishes the settings for individual user access to Terminal Services. Figure 15.17 shows the **Remote control** options.
- **Terminal Services Profile** establishes the path and file name of Terminal Services profiles for an individual user (see Figure 15.18).
- **Sessions** regulates the flexibility granted to an individual user with regard to session length and reconnection options. Refer to Figure 15.19 for a description of **Sessions** options.
- **Environment** determines which applications are to be launched at logon. The client's local disk drives and printer can be made available under Terminal Services–supported applications.

TASK MANAGER ADDITIONS

The Task Manager also monitors and administers Terminal Services. Two fields have been added to it in Windows 2000 and Windows Server 2003. These are used to

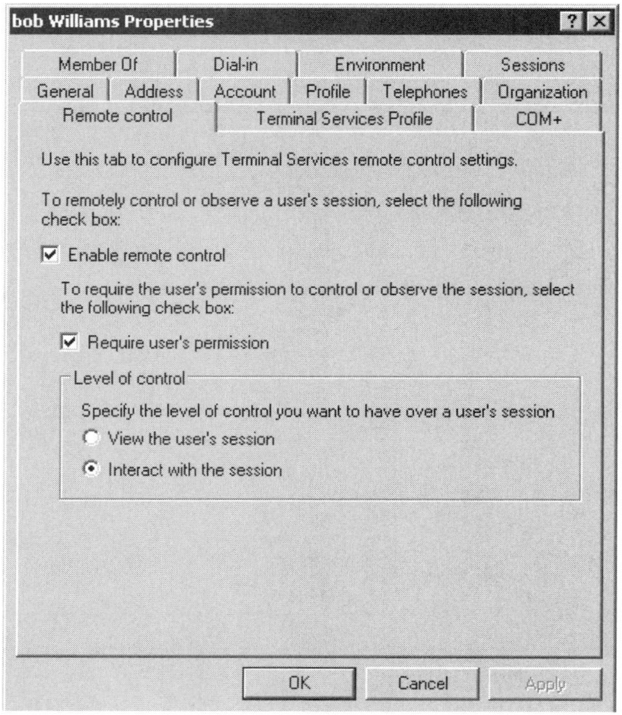

FIGURE 15.17 The Remote Control Tab

view processes and to terminate them as required. The Task Manager is available by pressing **CTRL+ALT+DEL** and selecting **Task Manager**.

Load Management

With Windows Server 2003, load management can be either session-based or server-based.

- The server load management uses Windows Management Instrumentation (WMI) to provide metrics for both network and hardware load balancing. This provides information on server availability and load such as server up/down and the number of supportable server sessions. The load balancer uses this data to control server use.
- Session load management provides a Session Directory facility. This new feature reroutes disconnected users back to their active session. The Session Directory must be started as a service on one computer that is running Terminal Services in a group of servers. Although it can also reside on another server,

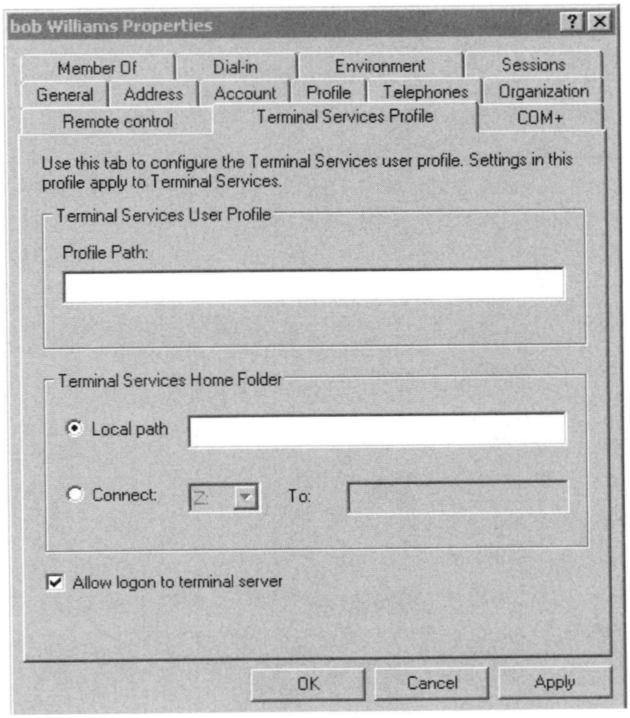

FIGURE 15.18 The Terminal Services Profile Tab

the service must be started through the Computer Management MMC snap-in. Each Terminal Server in the server group must enable the Session Directory access. The name of the server hosting the Session Directory must be identified together with the name of the server group that Terminal Server is joining. This action is accomplished through the Terminal Services Configuration tool under **Server Settings,** or WMI can be used.

Client Software and Installation

The Terminal Services client is now called Remote Desktop Connection. This software is automatically installed as an integral part of Windows XP. For previous versions of Windows operating system clients, the Terminal Services Client software is available at \\Windows\system32\clients\tsclient. Both a 16-bit and 32-bit version are available. The easier way to make the software available for downloading is to share out the tsclient directory. This is achieved by right-clicking **tsclient** → selecting **Properties** → clicking **Share**. Alternatively, the contents of the 16-bit or 32-bit directories can be copied to a diskette or other media like a CD and then

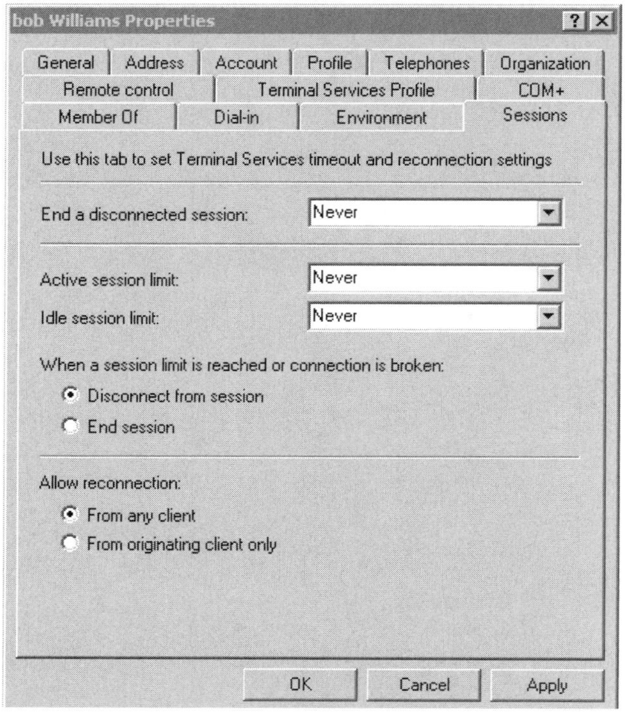

FIGURE 15.19 The Sessions Tab

manually installed on individual systems. In all cases, the installation is accomplished by double-clicking the **Setup** file and following the standard prompt.

Command-Line Programs

Terminal Services provides a number of command-line functions, shown in the following list. They may be executed from the **command prompt** or via the **Run** option on **Start** menu.

- **Change logon** temporarily disables Terminal Service logons.
- **Change port** shifts the COM port mappings required by MS-DOS programs.
- **Change user** executes changes to the .ini policies file mapping for a current user.
- **Cprofile** deletes individual files linked to a user's profiles.
- **Dbgtrace** enables or disables debug traces.

- **Flattemp** enables or disables temporary directories.
- **Logoff** terminates the client session.
- **Msg** sends messages to a user or multiple users.
- **Query process** outputs process information on Terminal Services.
- **Query session** displays Terminal Services session data.
- **Query termserver** outputs a list of network terminal servers.
- **Register** registers an application with execution characteristics.
- **Reset session** deletes a session and reestablishes a connection.
- **Shadow** remotely monitors and controls a user's session.
- **Tscon** connects to other Terminal Server sessions.
- **Tsdiscon** disconnects a user's Terminal Services session.
- **Tskill** kills a Terminal Services session.
- **Tsprof** copies an existing user's configuration and modifies the profile path.
- **Tsshutdn** shuts down the Terminal Services server.

TERMINAL SERVICES FROM A USER'S PERSPECTIVE

From a user's perspective, Terminal Services should provide the same rich experience as operating on a local system. If it is properly sized and configured, the user should not realize a noticeable degradation in performance.

Windows Server 2003 provides a number of enhancements that improve user accessibility to resources through a technology called *redirection*. Redirection must be enabled on both the server and client. Terminal Services Virtual Channel application programming interfaces (APIs) supports the extension of client resource redirection for custom applications. Using Terminal Services Remote Desktop from a Window XP client or other RDP 5.1–enabled client, many resources are available in the Remote Desktop connection including:

File System. The client file system is accessible through the remote desktop as if they were network shared drives.

Parallel and Serial Port Device Support. Applications have access to the serial and parallel ports on the client, thereby allowing devices like scanners and bar code readers to be used locally and reflected on the server.

Printer. The default local or network printer on the client is the default printing device for the remote desktop.

Clipboard. The remote desktop and client computers share a clipboard, therefore assuring greater data interchanged.

The Microsoft implementation of Terminal Services provides application server support on even minimally configured Windows-based personal computers (e.g., old 8086-class machines running Windows 3.1). Using add-on software from third-party vendors, Windows .NET applications can also be displayed and used from UNIX, Apple Macintosh, Java, and MS-DOS platforms. This ability to run applications such as Office 2000/XP using existing hardware equipment, and thus preserve previous hardware investments through the purchase of Terminal Server licenses, can be very attractive.

With Terminal Services, the users of thin clients can immediately run Windows Server 2003 applications while maintaining their current, familiar environment. If the server is properly sized, the response time between a keystroke or mouse click and a displayed result should be transparent to them. This response time is predicated on persistent caching.

A user can roam among thin clients with Terminal Services and not have to log off. Instead, she need only disconnect the session and then, when she returns to the terminal or to another thin-client system, merely log back on to the same session. The user can also maintain multiple concurrent sessions from one or more clients and run several tasks at the same time. Moreover, she can easily cut and paste between terminal sessions. The cut-and-paste facilities are also supported between the local computer and the Terminal Server session.

Finally, printers that are currently operational on the local client can be recognized through Windows Server 2003 Terminal Services.

User Launching

The client software that supports Windows Server 2003 access is newly renamed Remote Desktop Connection. It comes integrated with Windows XP and is available via **Start → All Programs → Accessories → Communications**. When the client software is installed on earlier versions of Windows, the software will be accessible from **Start → Programs → Accessories → Communications**.

Although not recommended, earlier versions of the Terminal Services Client software can also access Windows Server 2003. The reliability, stability, and security of the connection, however, are not as robust. Users of Windows 3.11 launch Terminal Services from **Control Panel** and double-click **TSClient**. For all other Windows versions, use the **Start** menu → select **Programs** → and select **Terminal Services Client**.

TERMINAL SERVICES CLIENT

To disconnect the Terminal Services Client without ending the session, press the X on the terminal services identification notation on the top of the screen. You will then receive a warning that confirms that you are terminating the session but the ap-

TABLE 15.1 Terminal Server Shortcut Keys

Shortcut Keys	Description
ALT+PAGE UP	Switches between programs going right to left.
ALT+PAGE DOWN	Switches between programs going left to right.
ALT+INSERT	Moves though programs in the order they were launched.
ALT+HOME	Displays the Start menu.
CTRL+ALT+BREAK	Switches the client between a full screen and an active window.
ALT+DELETE	Displays the Windows pop-up menu.

plications on the server will continue to run. The user can then reconnect where he left off. Administrators should discourage users from using this approach unless they intend to return to the session in a relatively short period of time. If applications are left running, server resources will be unnecessarily used.

To end the session, select the **Start** menu and click **Shut Down**. From the **Shut Down Windows** dialog box, select **Log Off** and confirm with **OK.**

A number of shortcuts can be used during a Terminal Services session to streamline operations. These are listed in Table 15.1.

NOTE To enhance the user experience, Windows Server 2003 supports Audio Redirection for RDP. This feature enables sound reproduction on a client computer with any application using wave sound. This includes enabling on-the-fly mixing, minimal performance impact of the audio stream I/O, and no user interaction requirement. Note that this feature could place a heavy load on the network.

POSTSCRIPT

Terminal Services offers a thin-client architecture that permits the retrofitting of less powerful computer systems. For an administrator, it also permits remote management of any server in the network. If only for that reason, Terminal Services should be a very popular add-on. In conjunction with other thin-client technologies, such as a Web- or Java-based implementation, Terminal Services adds a broader dimension to the Windows Server 2003 enterprise.

Chapter 16

Internet Information Services

Internet Information Services (IIS) is a fully integrated Web, SMTP, NNTP, and FTP server. Since IIS is integrated at the operating system level, it is difficult to discuss Windows Server 2003 without major reference to it.

The version of IIS (5.0) shipped with Windows 2000 has been the focus of numerous security attacks. The resulting negative publicity together with customer vulnerability has led Microsoft to refocus its attention to IIS. After all, if the .NET Framework is to be embraced, this underlying Internet-directed server technology must be rock solid. The Windows Server 2003 version, IIS 6.0, includes many functional enhancements and stricter security features. An example is the new Web server Security Lockdown Wizard. Although IIS 6.0 is shipped with default settings, it is important to note that security functionality can be adjusted using this wizard as part of the IIS configuration routines. Of course, it would be naïve to assert that any new release of IIS will be impervious to the determined efforts of hackers and crackers. Nevertheless, breaches of IIS 6.0 will be significantly more difficult. In addition, the ability to rapidly apply patches has been improved.

In an attempt to tighten IIS security, Windows Server 2003 has instituted several global precautionary settings. Several areas of IIS have been secured to improve security by reducing the default functionality of the Web server. Some of the more prominent changes are:

- IIS is not automatically installed by default on Windows Server 2003 and must be explicitly installed by the administrator.
- By default, IIS installs only with the ability to service static pages and the use of Active Server Pages (ASP) and ASP.NET functions must be enabled.
- ISAPI extensions and CGIs are disabled by default and must be explicitly enabled through the Web Service Extensions section in IIS Manager.

- Application pools run under an identity with lowered privileges of the IIS_WPG group.
- The Web server core runs under an identity with lowered privileges.

Despite these standard default restrictions and other enhancements, IIS will probably remain a primary target for the hacker community. Therefore, it is critical that administrators monitor security alerts from Microsoft and apply appropriate patches first to nonproduction machines. Once the stability of the patch can be confirmed in rapid fashion, then the patch should be applied to product IIS Servers.

Many of IIS's technological foundations are covered in other chapters, including key integration with the Active Directory, security, and remote networking. For that reason, this chapter centers on functional aspects of IIS, specifically,

- Concepts and features
- Basic administration
- The Simple Mail Transfer Protocol server
- The Network News Transfer Protocol server
- The File Transfer Protocol server

OVERVIEW

Internet Information Services incorporates some of the most advanced Web technologies in a single integrated set of functions. For the system administrator, IIS offers Web security, data and process reliability, Web-based application development, and management tools. A brief examination of these features should put IIS functionality into perspective.

Administrators of IIS 5.0 will find the Windows Server 2003 upgrades to IIS 6.0 operationally familiar; however, beneath the familiar interface reside significant changes to this product's basic architecture. The design of IIS 6.0 assumes an environment that is in a constant state of change. This means that any hosting software must intelligently deal with the legacy approach and the next generation of Internet applications and services. As such, it must proactively be fault tolerant with the ability to dynamically restart processes as necessary while retaining request queues. All this must be accomplished in a very secure environment.

New Manageability Features

The rapid growth of the Internet has resulted in the need for greater scalability and manageability. Increasingly, Web sites are not confined to a single server. Web farms that cluster multiple servers to perform unique functions are becoming commonplace. This reality has only increased the complexity of management. IIS 6.0 introduces two important management features that should be welcomed by any administrator. First, IIS 6.0 adds an XML-based, storage-layer replacement of the configuration store metabase. Second, Windows Management Instrumentation (WMI) support plus command-line support allow more flexible administration outside the IIS 5.0–based MMC IIS snap-in.

The metabase can be edited with built-in safeguards. Windows Server 2003 file-change notification service receives alerts when the metabase file has been edited. After the detection of an edited metabase, IIS compares this file to the corresponding history file of the same version that resides in the History directory. Differences between the two files are evaluated and IIS uses the most recent edit. IIS formulates an appropriate Admin Base Object (ABO) API commands to apply these changes to the in-memory metabase. IIS saves its in-memory metabase values and creates a new history file. The history file is copied into the History directory. Editing is accomplished by first stopping iisadmin, then setting the EnableEditWhileRunning property in the metabase to "1". Restart iisadmin. Alternatively, the administrator can use the **IIS snap-in → Computer Properties → Enable Direct Metabase Edit.**

XML METABASE

The XML metabase is a hierarchical store of configuration values. The information includes inheritance, data typing, change notification, and security. In versions 4.0 and 5.0, IIS configuration store was a nonreadable and noneditable binary file called Metabase.bin. This is replaced by a plain-text, XML-formatted file that can be edited, imported/exported, and reviewed easily for troubleshooting. The XML format provides compatibility with existing public metabase APIs. IIS 6.0 extends ADSI schema and schema extensibility support. Other specific features include:

- *Automatic version and history.* Changes in the metabase are automatically written to disk in a new file called Metabase.xml. Version numbers are automatically assigned so that rollback or restoration can be applied easily.
- *On-the-fly editing.* Metabase.xml can be edited while IIS is running using a program like Notepad, and no reboot is required after edits are complete.
- *Configuration import and export.* Using the new ABO methods of Export ( ) and Import ( ), configurations from any node can be moved across servers.
- *Server-specific backup.* Backup and restoration can be accomplished independently on an individual server basis.

IIS WMI PROVIDER AND COMMAND-LINE ADMINISTRATION

Building on the functionality introduced in Windows 2000 WMI, IIS 6.0 leverages the programming interface to permit greater customization. Any schema extensions developed through ADSI are automatically reflected in WMI. When changes are made to the ADSI schema, they are pushed to the IIS WMI provider.

IIS 6.0 also affords support of scripts, including those shipped in the Windows\System32 folder. Those VB scripts interface with the WMI provider to retrieve and set configuration data within the metabase. The scripts shipped with IIS 6.0 include:

- iisweb.vsb to create, delete, start, stop, and list Web sites
- iisftp.vsb to create, delete, start, stop, and list FTP sites
- iisdir.vsb to create, delete, start, stop, and display virtual directories
- iisftpdr.vsb to create, delete, start, stop, and display virtual directories under an FTP root
- iiscnfg.vbs to export and import IIS configuration to an XML file

---

NOTE The Web Server version of Windows Server 2003 automatically installs the new Web administration tool set. If you are deploying this version of the operating system, this toolset will provide a primary management source.

IIS Security Features

The IIS application suite relies on and is integrated with Windows Server 2003 security schemes. It also relies on additional standard Internet security features. This section reviews IIS high-level security; for additional information about Windows Server 2003 security and authentication, refer to Chapters 8 through 10.

Because IIS 5.0 took heavy hits on security, it seems appropriate to first underscore the enhancements made to IIS 6.0. The new preventive measures are based on analysis of the patterns displayed by the hacker community. The major improvements designed to lock down a site and apply patches include:

- *IIS Lockdown Wizard.* This wizard is designed to permit administrators to enable/disable IIS features. IIS 6.0 is shipped in locked-down state. This means that only static content such as .htm, .jpg, and .bmp is serviced. To make functions such as Active Server Pages or Front Page Server Extensions available, the system administrator must enable them.
- *Configurable work process identity.* As discussed later, the process architecture now isolates activities into something known as work processes.

- *IIS 6.0 runs as a low-privileged account.* By default, the IIS 6.0 work process is a low-privileged account called NetworkService. Running IIS 6.0 as a low-privileged account greatly reduces a hacker's ability to perform broad-based system attacks.
- *FTP user isolation.* Hackers of any operating system using TCP/IP haven't been able to invade via FTP. IIS 6.0 isolates FTP from other system functions.

IIS SECURITY MECHANISMS

IIS security works in parallel with the Windows Server 2003 operating system security; the range of mechanisms includes access control, authentication, encryption, certificates, and system auditing. These are briefly examined in the following list:

- *Access control.* Access control simply oversees how a user who has been granted access to the IIS server can use resources. NTFS permissions are applied to system resources in the same way as they are with any other Windows Server 2003 activity, but IIS also uses HTTP Web security specifications. In particular, WebDAV (described in greater detail later) permits navigation through files and directories. With WebDAV commands, also known as verbs, authorized users can edit, delete, and add files and directories.
- *Authentication.* IIS 6.0 employs several forms of user name and password authentication.
  - — Anonymous Authentication uses the IUSR_computername user account, to which special permissions should be applied, if appropriate, to avoid any user's gaining access to the public content of the Web site or FTP site. When enabled, IIS always authenticates a user through this account first.
  - — Basic FTP Authentication uses the user name and password associated with a specific Windows Server 2003 user account on the system. Its major downside is that passwords are transmitted without encryption and can be captured, exposing user accounts to security breaches.
  - — Kerberos v5 authentication is ideal for intranets in Windows Server 2003 environments. However, since it does not work in conjunction with HTTP Proxy services, it may have significant limitations on the Internet.
- *Encryption.* Encryption scrambles information at one end of the communication and deciphers it at the verified receiving end. It is commonly used for financial and banking transactions such as transmission of credit card numbers. Encryption is based on the Secure Sockets Layer (SSL 3.0) protocol and its extension, Server-Gated Cryptography. In the United States and Canada, IIS encryption can use a minimum 128-bit session key rather than the 48-bit or 56-bit DES standard used in other parts of the world.

- *Certificates.* Certificates are digital documents used in the authentication process. They are required when encrypted data is sent over an SSL 3.0 connection. A certificate is created through Microsoft's Certificate Authority, discussed in Chapter 11, or obtained from third-party certificate grantors.
- *Services auditing*. Monitoring the IIS services for irregular activities is an important security safeguard. Auditing uses logs to detect activities that violate file and directory policies. Either Windows Server 2003 auditing features or IIS 5.0–configured logs can be employed and are generated through the Audit Policies or Internet Information Services snap-in tool.

IIS INTERNET SECURITY TECHNOLOGIES

In addition to security features employed by the Windows Server 2003 operating system itself, such as Kerberos version 5, IIS's Web-specific security schemes include the following:

- *Basic authentication* is derived from the HTTP 1.0 specification and is the most widely used Web-based method for matching user names and passwords for access purposes. A password is sent in Base64 encoded format, but it is not encrypted, which means that in nonsecured environments, it can be captured by a sniffer. For this reason, Basic Authentication provides only marginal Web security. Its major advantage is that most Web browsers support this HTTP 1.0 standard.
- *Digest authentication* is based on the W3C (World Wide Web Consortium) standards for HTTP 1.1. It extends Basic Authentication by using a one-way hash (or message digest) for password interpretation. The password is not decipherable from the hash, which prevents password capture in a nonsecure environment. Only advanced browsers like Internet Explorer 5.0 or later can receive data using this technology; older browsers are returned an error message.
- *Advanced Digest Authentication* is based on Internet Engineering Task Force (IETF) RFC 2617. It behaves similarly to digest authentication except in the way user credentials are stored on the domain controller (DC). Digest authentication only sends users credentials across the network as an MD5 hash. Advanced Digest Authentication mirrors this routine and also stores user credentials in Active Directory on the DC as an MD5 hash. This hash is known as a *message digest.* Advanced Digest Authentication is available to Web Distributed Authoring and Versioning (WebDAV) directories. It does not replace Digest Authentication.
- *Certificate-based Web transactions that use PKCS #7/PKCS #10 protocols* are also supported by IIS. Used with IIS certification functions, PKCS #7 estab-

lishes encryption formats for datalike digital signatures. PKCS #10 determines the request format for certificates.

- *Fortezza* is a U.S. government cryptographic standard used for authentication, nonrepudiation, access control, and systems security.
- *Secure Sockets Layer (SSL 3.0)* uses certification authorities and is one of the most widely used methods on the Web to ensure authentication and message integrity.
- *Server-Gated Cryptography (SGC)* is used primarily by banking and financial institutions over the Internet.
- *Transport Layer Security (TLS)* extends SSL by providing cryptographic authentication. Its API framework permits the writing of TLS-enabled applications.

Applying these standards in an IIS environment is covered in other sections. IIS also supports three security-related wizards:

- *Certificate* leads the administrator through the creation and establishment of life cycles for a certificate.
- *Certificate Trust Lists (CTL)* constructs a list of trusted certificate authorities for a directory.
- *Permissions* consolidates authentication and NTFS permissions for Web site and FTP access.

IIS Data and Process Reliability

To meet changing requirements of the Internet and the new demands of .NET framework, IIS 6.0 relies on a fundamentally altered architecture. IIS 6.0 introduces a concept known as *work process isolation mode,* which separates active process management into an application isolation environment. This actively managed runtime relies on kernel-level request queuing.

The work process isolation mode runs all applications in an isolated environment. Unlike previous versions, which request process hops to an out-of-process DLL host, user mode work processes are pulled directly from the kernel.

From an administrative perspective, the work process isolation scheme supports different Web applications and Web sites to exist in separate pools, known now as *application pools.* Application pools should be viewed as a set of Web applications that share one or more work processes. Each application pool is discrete. This means that if one application pool malfunctions, other application pools are not affected. Another way to look at an application pool is as a namespace group.

An application pool by default consists of a single work process. However, this default can be overridden so that multiple work processes can exist in the same application pool. Such multiple work process application pools are known as *Web gardens*. Conceptually, a Web garden is a single server–based equivalent to a Web farm. One of the best aspects of the Web garden technology is that in the event of a work process failure, new work processes are available to accept queue requests.

Figure 16.1 illustrates the new architecture of IIS 6.0 that separates kernel-mode and user-mode activities.

PROCESS ARCHITECTURE

When shared resources are used, unstable elements can affect the environment. In IIS 5.0, Web services were run in the inetinfo.exe process space and pooled application requests to DLLHost.exe processes. The disadvantage of pooled processes is that if one application fails, all the others die. The advantage is that even in the event of failure, the IIS server will continue to run unaffected. By contrast, IIS 6.0 is redesigned to support two components using kernel-mode drivers. The larger boxed portion of Figure 16.1 shows the relations of the new components of the Http.sys, Web Administration Service, and Work Processes.

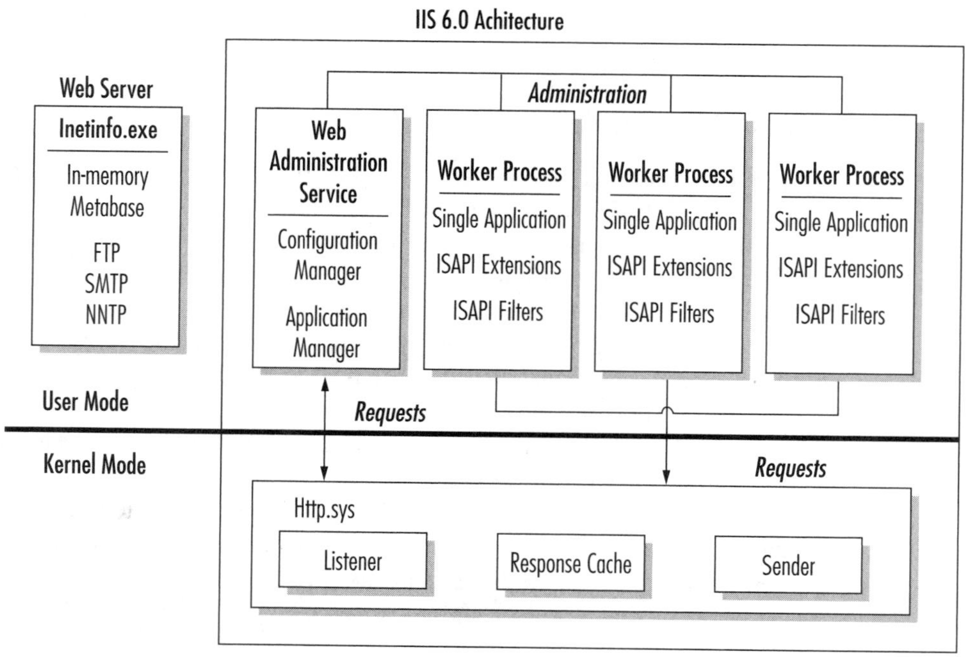

FIGURE 16.1 IIS 6.0 Architecture

- *Http.sys component.* The Http.sys resides in the kernel mode. It is the point of contact for all incoming HTTP requests. It listens for requests and queues them until they are all processed, no more queues are available, or the Web server is shut down. Each request queue is treated as an application pool that is defined as one request queue and one or more work processes. Because this component accepts and processes request queues in the kernel mode, outstanding requests will be restarted even if the user mode Web services crash. Third-party code is never loaded in this isolated component.
- *Web Administration Service (WAS).* Residing in the user mode, WAS is responsible for configuration and process management. The process manager portion reads metabase information and initializes the Http.sys namespace routing table. One entry is entered for each application and includes which application pool requests match the route. A preregistration of applications thereby is established so that the Http.sys can respond to the requests. With every new application or application pool, WAS configures Http.sys to accept the requests for new URLs and other data. WAS is also responsible for controlling work processes that process requests. Therefore, WAS determines when to start a work process or when to restart a process. WAS monitors the health of work processes through a pinging activity. If the ping comes back to indicate that the process is blocked or otherwise nonresponsive, WAS terminates the processes while simultaneously creating a new work process to accept the queued requests.

Several other benefits are associated with this new architecture, including the following:

- *On-demand start.* When the first request is made to the application pool's namespace, the work processes are launched. This eliminates the overhead of supporting nonrequested application pools.
- *Idle timeout.* Application pools can be configured to shut down when a predefined time-out idle time has been reached.
- *Rapid fail protection.* It is possible to configure IIS 6.0 to disable an application pool when WAS detects a predefined number of failures.
- *Orphaning work processes.* By default, WAS terminates an ill work process and starts another. There are times, however, when analysis of the ill work process is required to identify a problem. So, rather than terminate the ill work process, the administrator can have it set aside as an orphan while its work is handed off to a new worker. This course is generally not recommended, however, because orphans can be heavy resource consumers.
- *Recycling work processes.* Rather than having to reboot an entire Web server to account for problems such as memory leaks, IIS 6.0 permits the restarting

of individual work processes. Service interruptions are prevented because a new work process takes on the namespace of the current work process before it completes its last request prior to termination.

- *Persisted ASP template cache.* With IIS 6.0, ASP cache templates are persisted on disk rather than process memory.
- *Large memory support for x86.* IIS 6.0 can support cache of up to 64 GB on an x86 system. Further, the Web garden feature allows scaling of individual application memory requests larger than 2 GB.
- *Win64 support.* IIS 6.0 supports both Win32 and Win64 models.

PROCESS FEATURES COMMON TO IIS 5.0 AND IIS 6.0

With regard to process architecture, IIS 5.0 and IIS 6.0 share a number of underlying features including:

- *Socket pooling.* A socket consists of a default node (computer) address and a port number, such as the server's IP address Internet Web TCP number 80. IIS 5.0 permits the pooling of sockets so that more sites can be bound to the same IP address and use the same port number.
- *Process and bandwidth throttling.* When running multiple sites on the same server, it may be appropriate to limit processes, CPU usage, and bandwidth. This is equally true when multiple applications are running on the IIS server. Process and Bandwidth Throttling allows the system administrator to set these limits, and over time it can be used to obtain maximum system performance. Process accounting should also be employed to measure CPU usage or to determine if an application or script is using a disproportionate amount of resources.
- *Site hosting scalability.* Scalability is achieved by permitting multiple Web sites to share an IP address. Multiple sites can be hosted in IIS by appending port numbers to one IP address or by adding IP addresses to one server. In the first case, the port number is appended to the end of the IP address, such as 111.111.111.111:80 or 111.111.111.111:140. Individuals share the IP address but are connected through different ports. An alternative to ports is to use headers to distinguish sites on an IP address and computer and resolve domain names to that address. Multiple IP addresses are bound to a single network interface card or multiple cards on the same system. Once it arrives at the server, the header determines which site is to be contacted. The simplicity of this alternative can be very attractive because it makes multiple IP addresses or port tables unnecessary. However, it cannot be used in conjunction with SSL and other encryption environments because the header information will not be readable.

- *Clustering for IIS.* For mission-critical Web and FTP environments, clustering (discussed in Chapter 17) should certainly be considered. With clustering, when one node (server) has services or hardware problems, a second system assumes the activities in the failover process. This type of redundancy, although more costly, can provide significantly greater reliability. Also to be considered is the use of a mirrored or RAID-5 disk system, as discussed in Chapter 14.
- *Dfs for Web file systems.* The physical distribution of files across a network has always been a major problem. The distributed file system (Dfs) is easily adaptable to a Web-based environment, allowing the client browser to be used for resource access throughout the network.

IIS 5.0 ISOLATION MODE

With the introduction of work process isolation in IIS 6.0, Microsoft recognized that some earlier applications will simply not operate in that environment. Therefore, Windows Server 2003 provides an IIS 5.0 isolation mode to address applications that demand session-state persistent processes, applications written as read raw file filters, and multiple-instance applications. In this arrangement (Figure 16.2), inetinfo.exe is the master process manager. However, the environment has the added benefit of the Http.sys kernel-mode request queuing and caching.

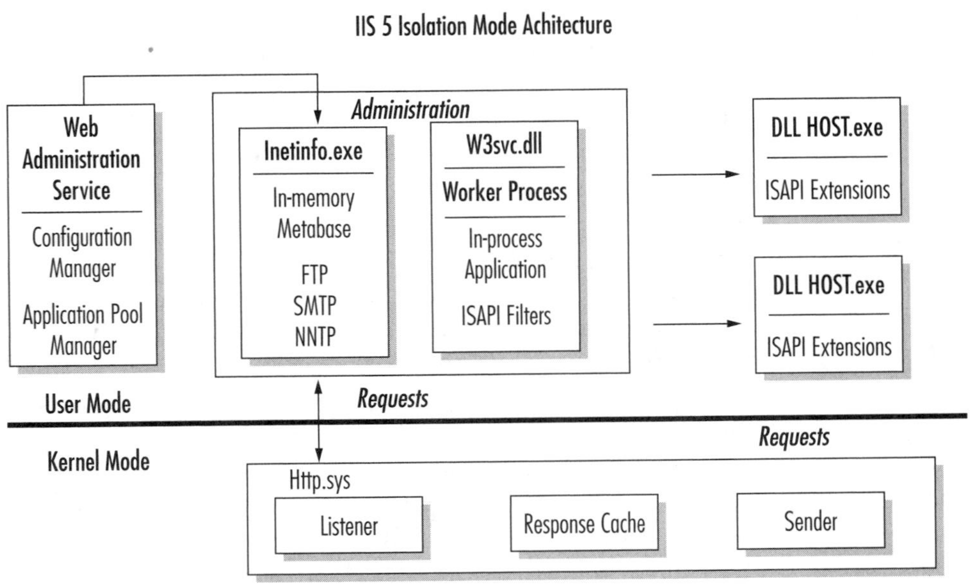

FIGURE 16.2 IIS 5.0 Isolation Mode Architecture

NOTE The isolation modes offered in IIS 6.0 reflect only Web servers. Other services managed by inetinfo including FTP and SMTP work just like they did under IIS 5.0. Only Web services use the Http.sys.

The Web Application Environment

A centerpiece of IIS support for application sharing and development is Web Distributed Authoring and Versioning (WebDAV). This is an extension to the HTTP 1.1 specification that addresses publishing and manipulating Web documents. By setting WebDAV properties and permissions, different Windows Server 2003 clients can have different levels of access such as Read/Write or Read-Only.

Application development for IIS uses Active Server Pages as the preferred Web medium. Although development issues are outside our scope, we note that ASP helps integrate HTML, scripts (including Java and VScript), and COM components.

IIS Management Components

Later in this chapter we will explore how to apply administrative tools to the management of IIS. Here we provide a brief overview of IIS management tools and techniques that are common to IIS 5.0 and 6.0.

- *Command-line script administration*. Much traditional Web administration is UNIX-based and by definition heavily reliant on command-line utilities and scripts. Acknowledging this, Microsoft has made at least a partial effort to permit UNIX-type administrative interaction. For example, the **Cscript.exe** command can invoke Visual Basic scripts. Other commands allow the use of CGI, Perl, and other scripts.
- *Internet Information Services snap-in centralized administration*. A replacement for the older Internet Services Manager, the Internet Information Services snap-in is an integrated tool for creating, modifying, and managing IIS components and properties, which is explored later in the chapter. Its Remote administration is made possible through Terminal Services.
- *Delegation to Web site operators*. One strength of Windows Server 2003 is the ability to delegate certain administrative responsibilities. Web Site Operators is an administrative group with authority over IIS functions. Its responsibility can be extensive or site specific, which can be valuable in environments with multiple sites on one server. A Web site operator for a specific site can be granted full control over it but have no authority over other sites.
- *Custom error messaging*. The system administrator's burden can be reduced greatly through the use of instructive error messages. IIS employs the HTTP

1.1 error-messaging scheme to handle standardized problems. Use of this facility and the errors it handles are dealt with later.

UNDERSTANDING THE IIS WEB SERVER

IIS includes a robust Web server designed to host both internal intranets and public Internet sites. It works closely with many development tools such as Microsoft's FrontPage. Specific IIS components such as FTP and SMPT are not automatically installed and must be selected through the Windows Components Wizard.

Administering IIS Web Services

In this section we explore the major administrative aspects associated with host Web services under IIS. One of the best methods of illustrating the ease of IIS operation is to create and configure a Web site.

CREATING A WEB SITE USING IIS

Here we assume that Web pages have been created with a product such as FrontPage and are ready to be loaded on the Web server for intranet or Internet exposure. Follow these steps to create the site itself:

1. Open the **Internet Information Services** snap-in.
2. Right-click **Default Web Server**, select **New**, and then **Site**. The initial **Web Site Creation Wizard** screen is displayed (Figure 16.3).

FIGURE 16.3 The Web Site Creation Wizard

3. In the **Web Site Description Dialog** box, type a description of the site.
4. In the **IP Address and Port Settings** dialog box (Figure 16.4), enter the **IP address to use**, the **TCP port**, the **Host Header for this site**, and the **SSL port**. The header is a Web site description. An ISP that is hosting a number of Web sites on one server, for example, might make the header the name of each organization.
5. In the **Web Site Directory Location** dialog box, enter the path or click **Browse** to locate the directory that contains the Web pages.
6. In the **Web Site Access Permissions** dialog box (Figure 16.5), check the types of access to be allowed, including **Read**, **Run Scripts**, **Execute**, **Write**, and **Browse**.
7. Click **Finish** to complete the creation process.

BASIC WEB SITE ADMINISTRATION

Basic Web site administration can be illustrated by a walk-through of some activities available from the Internet Information Services snap-in.

Opening or Exploring Components and Browse

To view the component parts of a Web site, use either of the methods described in these steps:

1. Open the **Internet Information Services** snap-in.
2. Right-click the desired Web site and select **Open** or **Explore**.

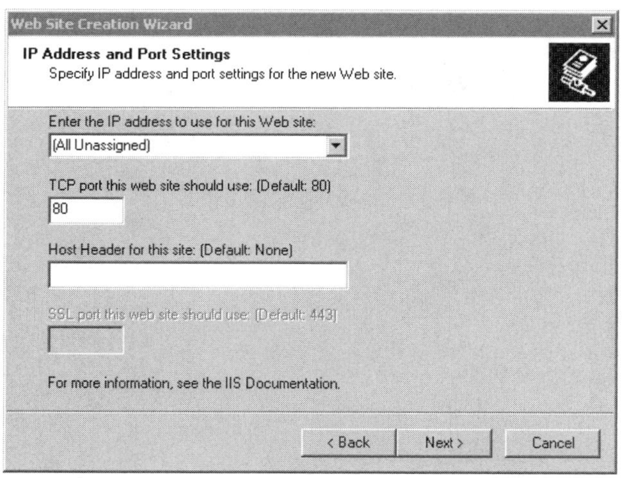

FIGURE 16.4 The IP Address and Port Settings Dialog Box

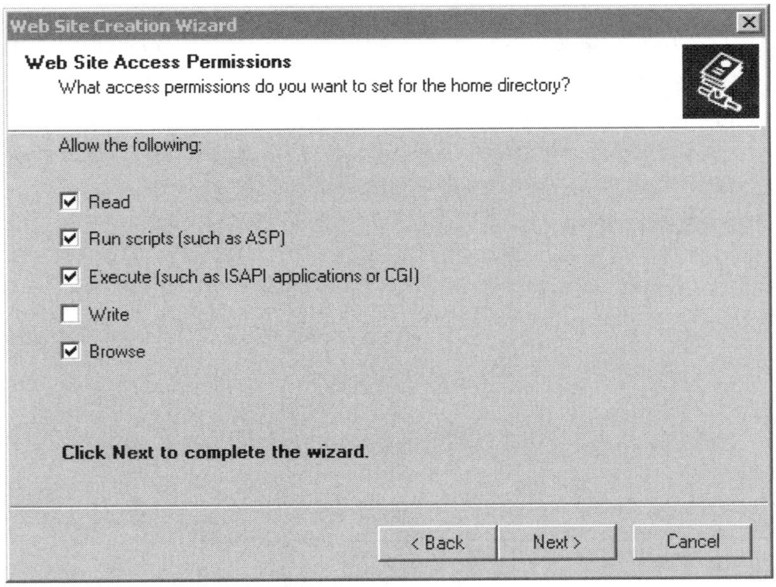

FIGURE 16.5 Web Site Access Permissions

3. Either the **My Computer** view or the **Explorer** view of the contents will be displayed. To browse a Web site from the **Internet Information Services** snap-in, follow steps 1 and 2. Then, in **My Computer** or **Explore**r, select **Browse**.

Using the Web Site Permissions Wizard

Permissions for a site are set with the Permissions Wizard as follows:

1. Open the **Internet Information Services** snap-in.
2. Right-click the desired Web site, select **All Tasks**, and select **Permissions Wizard**.
3. In the first dialog box, select either that the permissions should be inherited from a parent Web site or virtual directory or that new permissions be established. If you select the default inherited permissions, a confirmation box (Figure 16.6) lists the settings. If this is satisfactory, select **Next**, and then **Finish** to complete the task. If you need to set other permissions that are not represented by that parent Web site or virtual directory, select **Cancel** and repeat the process.

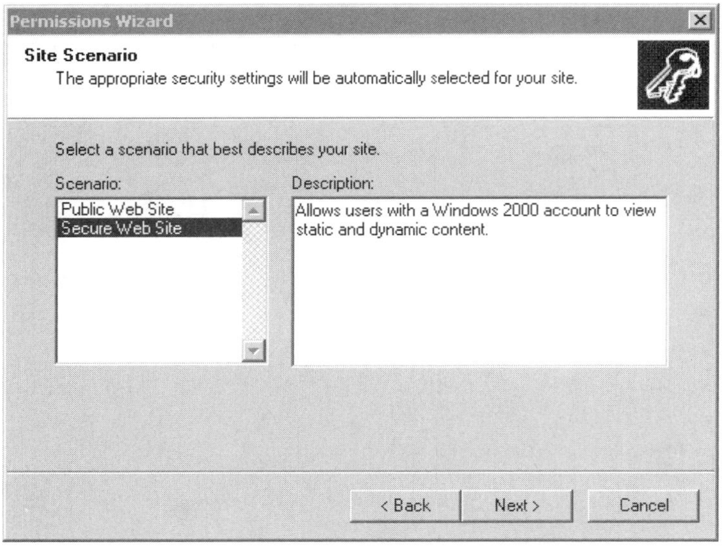

FIGURE 16.6 The Default Inherited Permissions Information Box

4. If new or different permissions are required, select **New permission from a template**. Two standard templates are available. The **Public Web Site** option allows all users to browse static and dynamic content. The **Secure Web Site** option allows only users with a Windows Server 2003 account to do so. If this is satisfactory, select **Next** and then **Finish** (see Figure 16.7).

CONFIGURING WEB SITE PROPERTIES

Web site properties can be set on the site and individual page/directory level. Most are configured through the **Properties** tabs, which are explored in this section. Open the **Internet Information Services** snap-in, right-click the desired Web site, and select **Properties**.

Setting Web Site Properties

The **Web Site** tab (Figure 16.8) provides text boxes for inputting the site **Description**, desired **IP Address**, and designated **TCP Port**. Connections can also be set to unlimited or to a specific limit on this tab. Selecting the **Advanced** button allows an extensive set of logging configurations to be established.

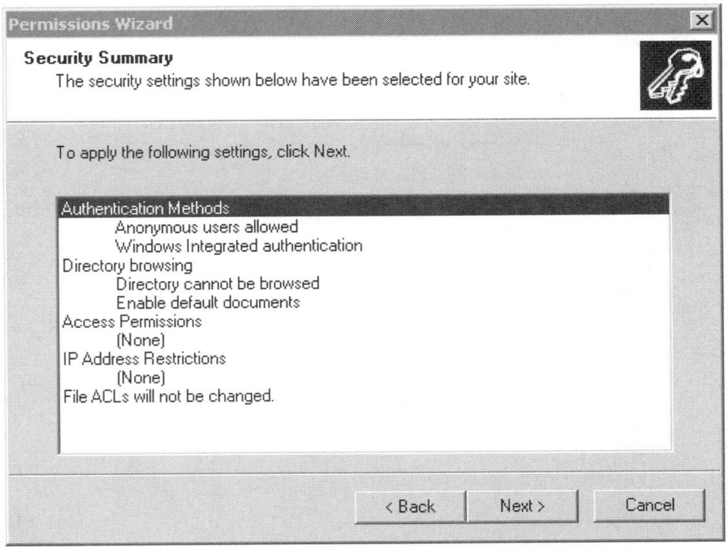

FIGURE 16.7 Secure Site Default Permissions

Setting IIS Operators

The **Operators** tab (Figure 16.9) allows you to delegate authority over a Web site to specific users and user groups. The **Add** button adds users and groups; the **Remove** button deletes them.

Setting IIS Performance Properties

The **Properties Performance** tab (Figure 16.10) is used to set process and bandwidth throttling. In the appropriate box, set the throttling level to establish appropriate limits. Process throttling is based on kilobytes per second. CPU throttling is based on the maximum allowable percentage of CPU resources. The number of anticipated hits measures overall performance based on expected activities.

Setting Execution Filters

Internet Services API ISAPI filters can be applied to expand or limit functions and resources (Figure 16.11). Use the **Add**, **Remove**, and **Disable** buttons as appropriate on filters.

Managing the IIS Home Directory

The IIS home directory can be on a local computer, at a shared location on a remote computer, or on a redirected URL system. This is determined by the **Home**

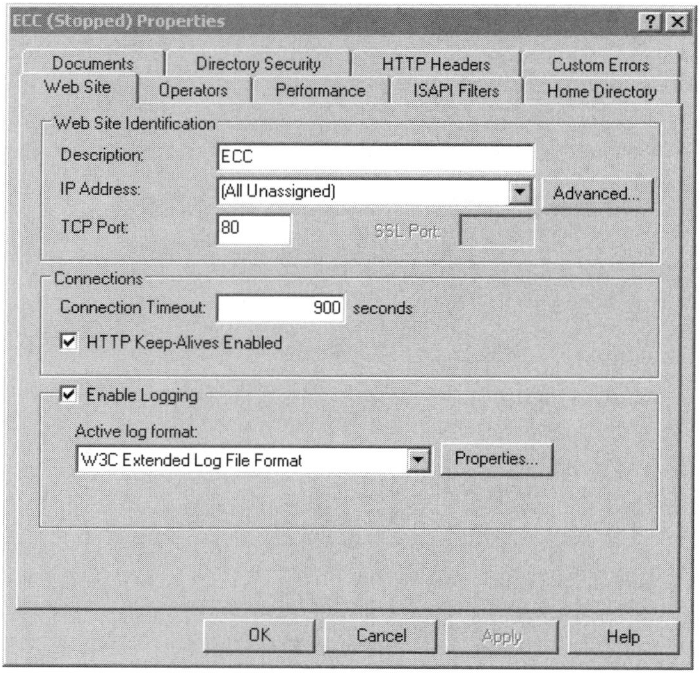

FIGURE 16.8 General Web Site Properties

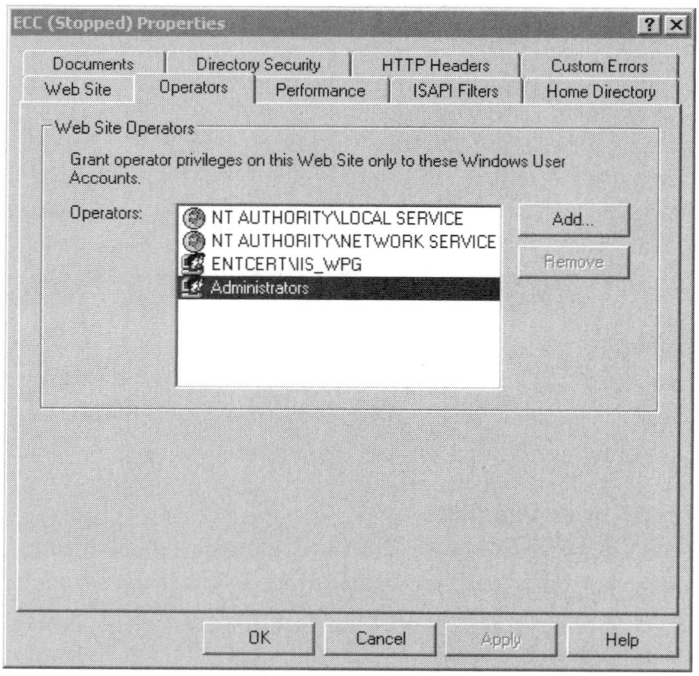

FIGURE 16.9 Web Site Operator Privileges

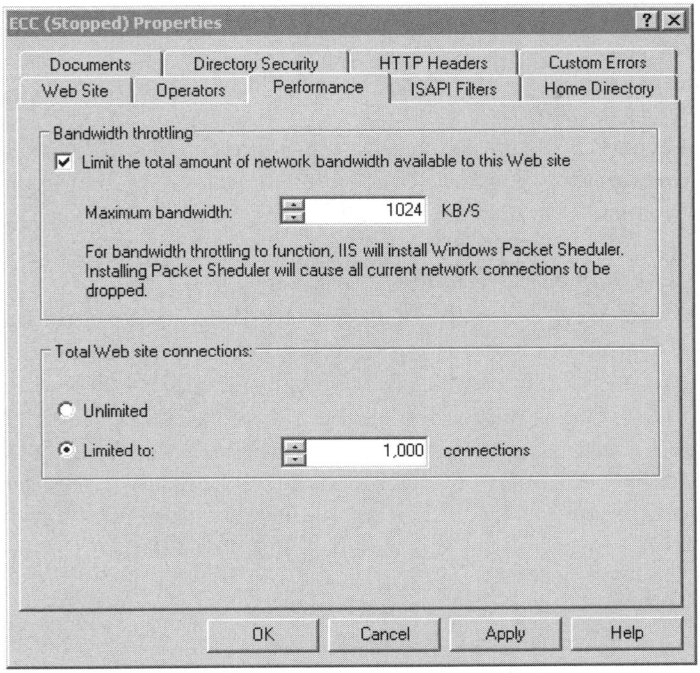

FIGURE 16.10 Performance Settings Including Throttling

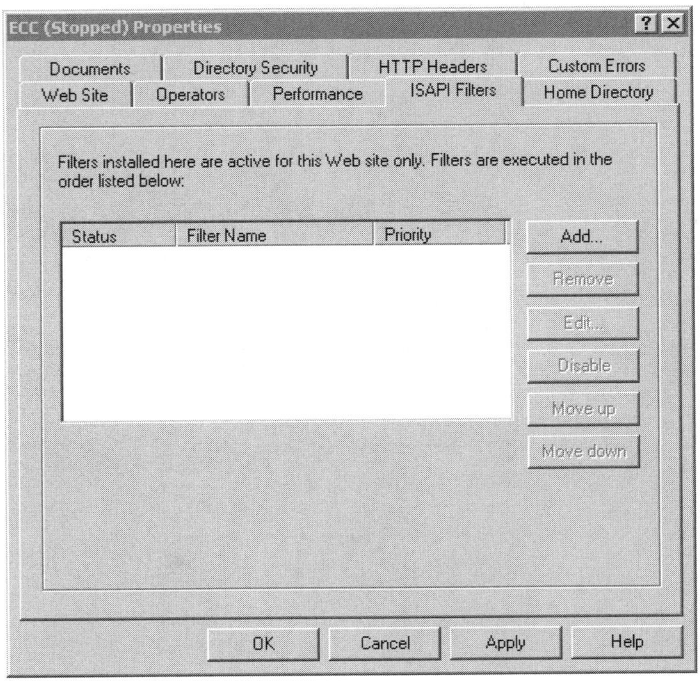

FIGURE 16.11 An ISAPI Filters List

Directory tab (Figure 16.12), which also establishes series of permissions and other properties.

Enabling Default Documents

Access to a Web site's home page is based on the establishment of a default page. The **Documents** tab (Figure 16.13) defines the acceptable name of default pages as well as footer information for the entire Web site.

Setting the Directory or File Security

Directory Security (Figure 16.14) is perhaps the most important tab because it permits the editing of anonymous account access and authentication and defines the IP address and domain restrictions. Through the **Edit** button, access is granted or denied. Secure communication configuration can be set through the **Certificate Wizard**, which is launched by clicking **Server Certificate.**

Permission for anonymous access and authenticated access deserves special examination; anytime access to a server is permitted without a password, a system administrator should take heed. When the **Edit** button is selected, the

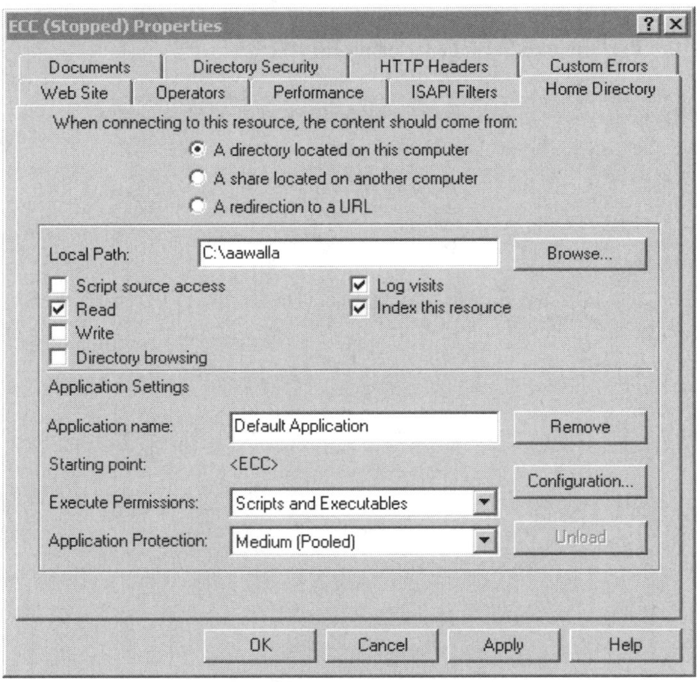

FIGURE 16.12 Home Directory Properties

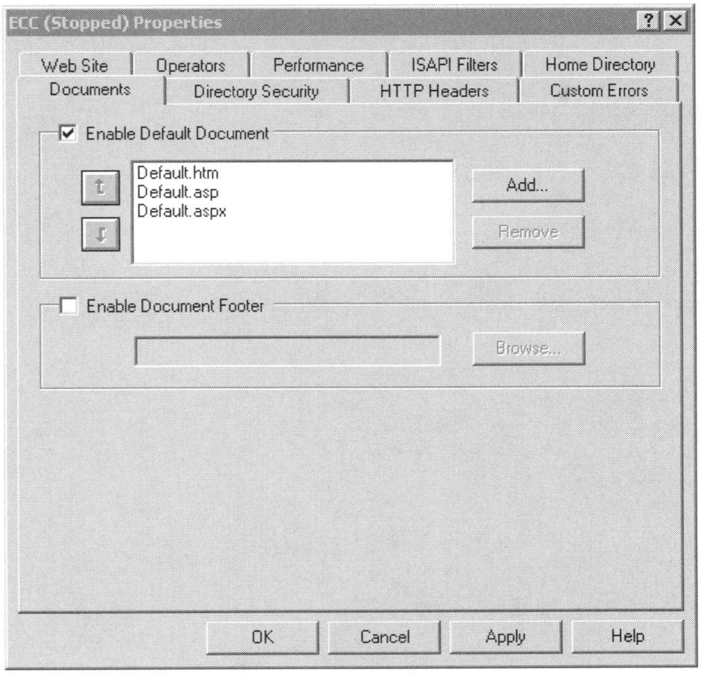

FIGURE 16.13 A Default Documents List

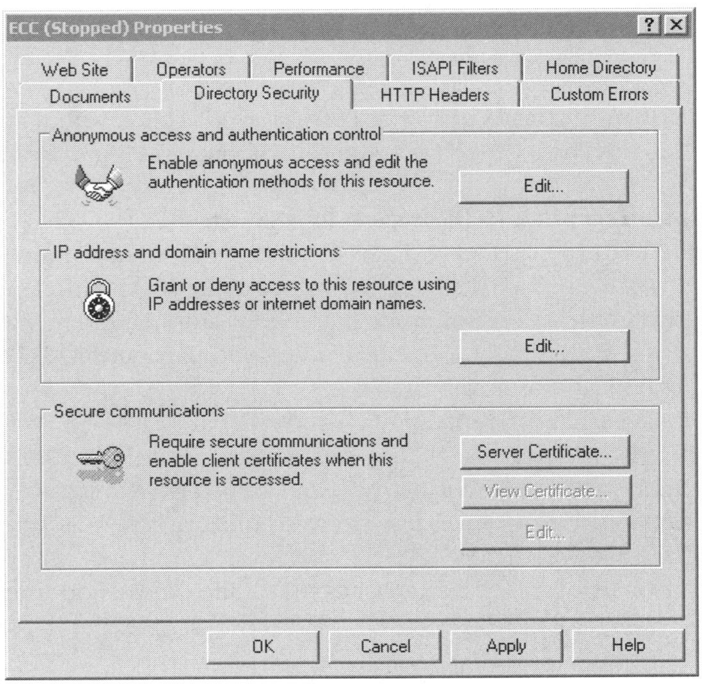

FIGURE 16.14 Web Directory Security Properties

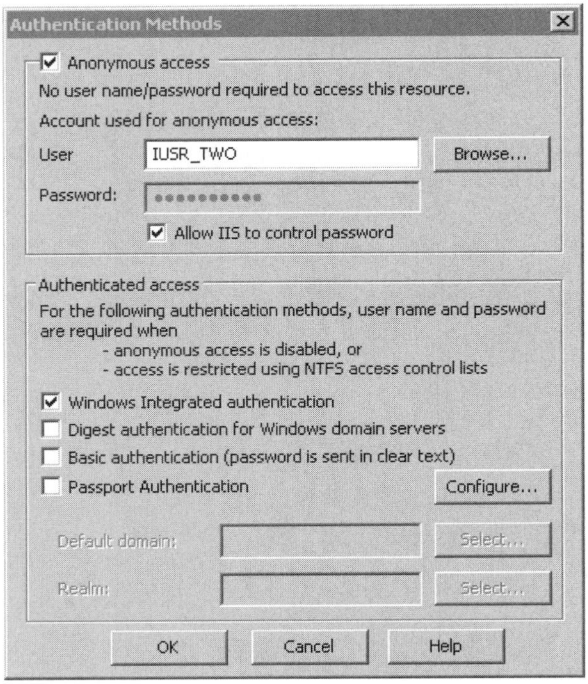

FIGURE 16.15 Authentication Subtab Options

Authentication Methods dialog box is displayed. This is where anonymous account security can be defined and edited, as shown in Figure 16.15.

Setting Content Expiration, HTTP Headers, Ratings, and MIME

The **HTTP Headers** tab (Figure 16.16) permits configuration of a number of important Web site features. The first part enables content expiration. If it is checked, information posted to the site can be marked for automatic removal, which obviously ensures a more timely Web site. The second part permits HTTP headers to be added, edited, and removed.

Headers are used on multisite Web servers that share one IP address to distinguish one site from another. They can be used with the self-regulating rating system of the Recreational Software Advisor Council (RSAC) to rate sites that contain, for example, adult material, and to warn underage visitors prior to entering the sites.

The third part of this tab establishes MIME file types supported by the Web server.

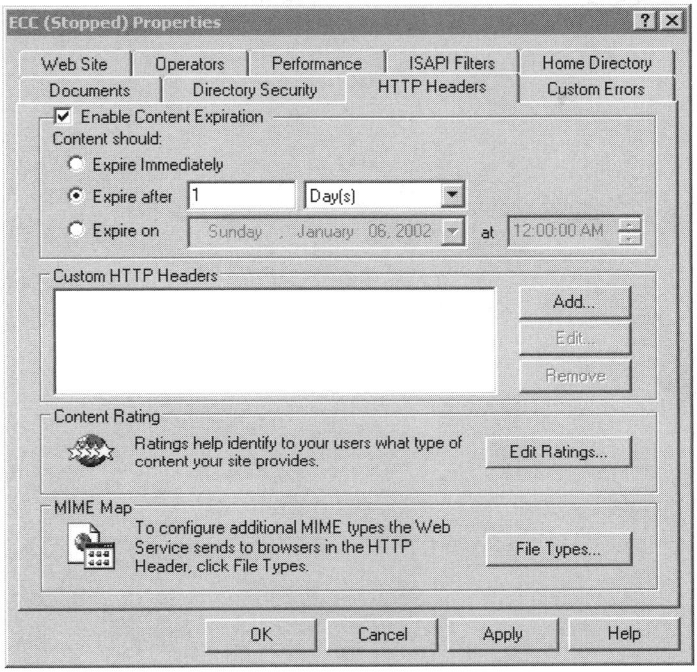

FIGURE 16.16 Web Headers, Rating, and the MIME Map

Customizing Error Messages

The **Custom Errors** tab (Figure 16.17) lists the default set of error messages established by HTTP 1.1 specifications. The **Edit Properties** button permits these messages to be redefined. Each message is directed to a specific HTML file. If further clarification is required, these files should be modified.

Configuring Server Extensions

The **Server Extensions** tab (Figure 16.18) permits the viewing of installed add-ons such as FrontPage Server Extensions. The FrontPage snap-in is used to edit and manipulate those specific extensions. FrontPage Extensions is not automatically installed with the core IIS. It must be added through **Control Panel** → **Add Software** → **Windows Components** → **Internet Information Services** → **Details** → **FrontPage Extensions**. The tab is displayed only when FrontPage Extensions is installed.

Setting Individual Web Page and Directory Properties

Properties for individual Web pages can be set by right-clicking the targeted document and selecting **Properties**. This will display four tabs, as shown in Figure 16.19.

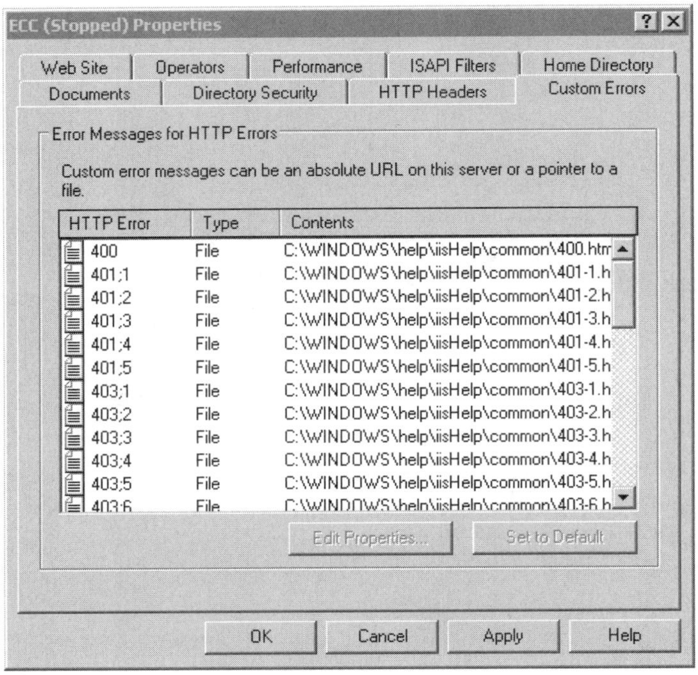

FIGURE 16.17 The Error Message Catalog

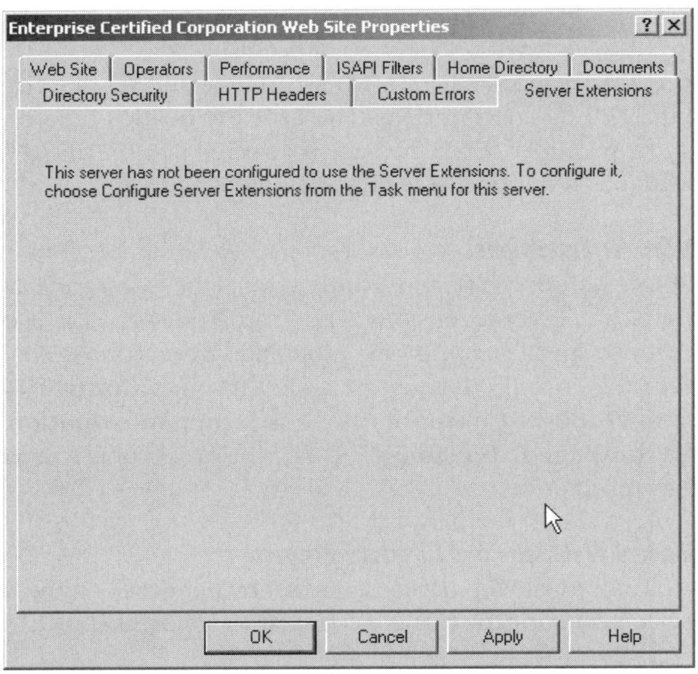

FIGURE 16.18 The Web Server Extensions Tab

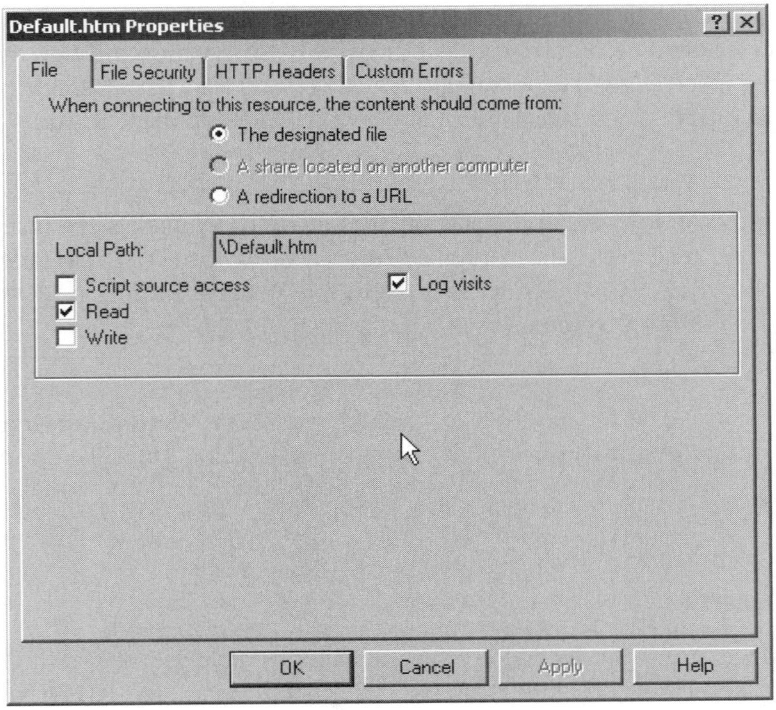

FIGURE 16.19 Directory Properties

The **File Security, HTTP Headers,** and **Custom Errors** tabs are largely the same as previously described. The **File** tab designates the file or the source for redirection, the local path, and basic permissions.

WORKING WITH THE SMTP SERVER

The Simple Mail Transfer Protocol (SMTP) has become the standard Internet protocol for electronic mail. The specifications are established in RFCs 821 and 822. Commonly used on UNIX and Linux environments, SMTP is now integrally connected to mail products like Microsoft Exchange. SMTP Services in IIS provides administrative options for setting routing and message delivery and for governing mail security. It can support hundreds of client mail connections. The SMTP Server is not automatically installed as a default component of IIS. It must be selected from the **Configure Your Server Wizard** from the list provided with the **Add and Remove Programs** option. Select **Web Server Applications** from the list

→ click **Details** → select **Internet Information Services** → click **Detail** → select **SMTP Services,** and then follow the wizard's instruction through the completion of the installation. It is possible to select **FTP** and **NNTP** for installation at the same time as **SMTP** Services are installed by also selecting these features.

NOTE New to Windows Server 2003 is a POP3 service that must also be installed as a separate function using the Configure Your Server Wizard. To do so, select it from the list provided with the **Add and Remove Programs** option. POP3 is available under **E-Mail Services**.

Start SMTP Services by right-clicking the **SMTP Virtual Service** from the **Internet Information Services** snap-in and selecting **Start**. Temporarily suspend and terminate it by selecting **Pause** or **Stop**. Multiple SMTP virtual servers can be established using IIS.

SMTP Properties

SMTP is primarily configured through a series of properties settings. To gain access to the six configuration tabs, right-click the targeted **SMTP virtual server** and select **Properties**.

In environments that use Microsoft Exchange Server, the documentation on specific procedures for that environment explains how to connect SMTP services. Once connected, products like sendmail, which is widely used in UNIX and other operating system environments, can flow transparently.

GENERAL SMTP SETTINGS

The **General** tab (Figure 16.20) permits the setting of the **SMTP virtual server** name, **IP address** (through the **Connection** button), and logging administration.

SETTING SMTP AUTHENTICATION, SECURITY, AND PERMISSIONS

The **Access** tab (Figure 16.21), which deserves a system administrator's special consideration, has four important settings. First, the level of anonymous access (incoming and outgoing message size) is set through the **Authentication** button. Second, under the **Secure communication** section, the **Certificate** button launches the **Certification Wizard** and the **Communication** button defines how the certificate is to be used. The **Connection control** section grants or de-

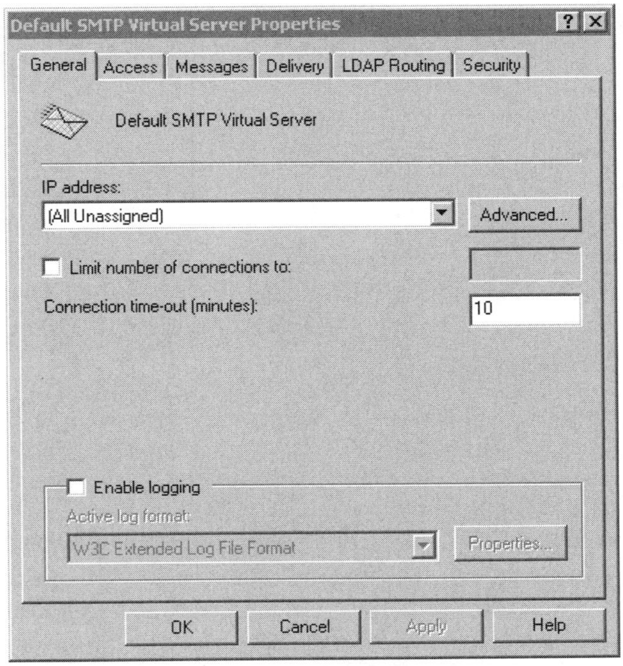

FIGURE 16.20 The SMTP Virtual Server Properties General Tab

nies access depending on IP addresses or domain names. Finally, the **Relay** button establishes permission to relay e-mail through the SMTP virtual service.

REGULATING SMTP DELIVERY

Delivery options are established with the **Delivery** tab for both outbound and local messages (Figure 16.22). For outbound messages, the system administrator can set the number of retries and intervals for them. For local messages, notification and expiration time periods can be established. The **Outbound Security** button defines the type of authentication to be required. The **Advanced** button permits configuration of such communication-specific settings as the maximum number of hops allowable to deliver the mail.

CONFIGURING SMTP LDAP ROUTING

The **LDAP Routing** tab (Figure 16.23) specifies the identity and properties of the directory services server. This is where mail client data and mailboxes are stored.

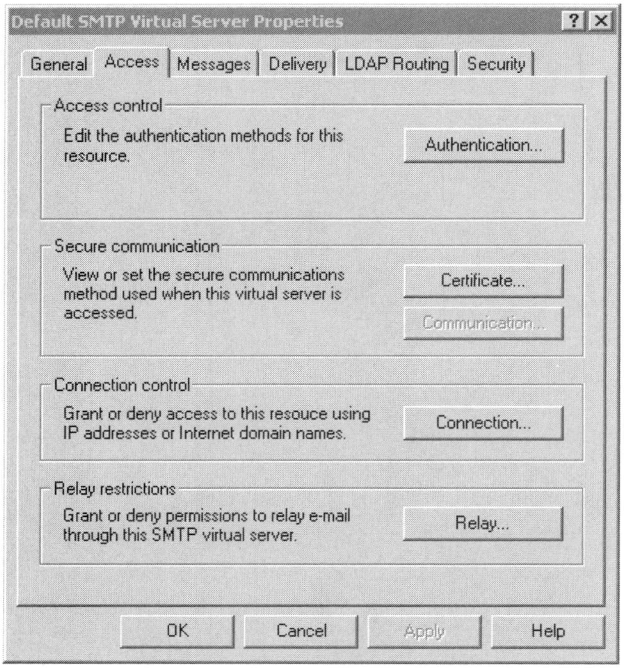

FIGURE 16.21 The SMTP Access Tab

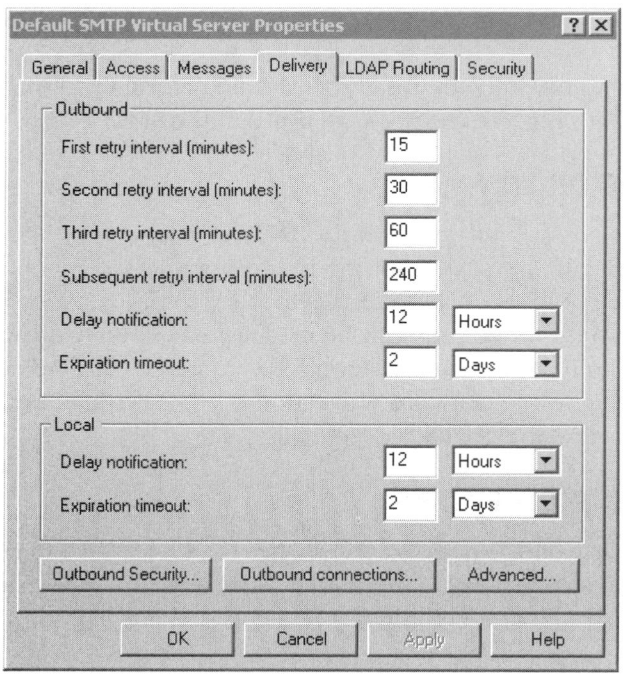

FIGURE 16.22 The SMTP Delivery Tab

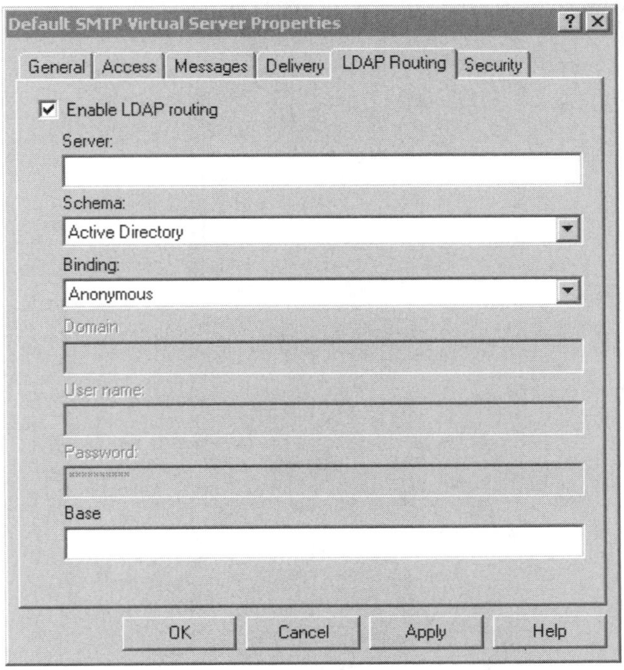

FIGURE 16.23 The SMTP LDAP Tab

Just like the Windows Server 2003 Active Directory, the SMTP virtual server uses the LDAP to communicate with directory services. SMTP "consults" an LDAP server to resolve senders and recipients. Once the **Enable LDAP routing** option is checked, specific LDAP-related configuration can be set for the server, schema, domain, network bindings, user name, and password.

SETTING SMTP OPERATOR SECURITY

The **Security** tab (Figure 16.24) works like any other Windows Server 2003 security operations property setting. Use the **Add** button to increase the users or groups that have permission to administer the SMTP virtual server and the **Remove** button to delete them.

SETTING SMTP MESSAGE LIMITS

The **Messages** tab (Figure 16.25) is used to set limits on file size, length of the mail session, number of messages per connection, number of recipients, and path to where undeliverable mail should be delivered.

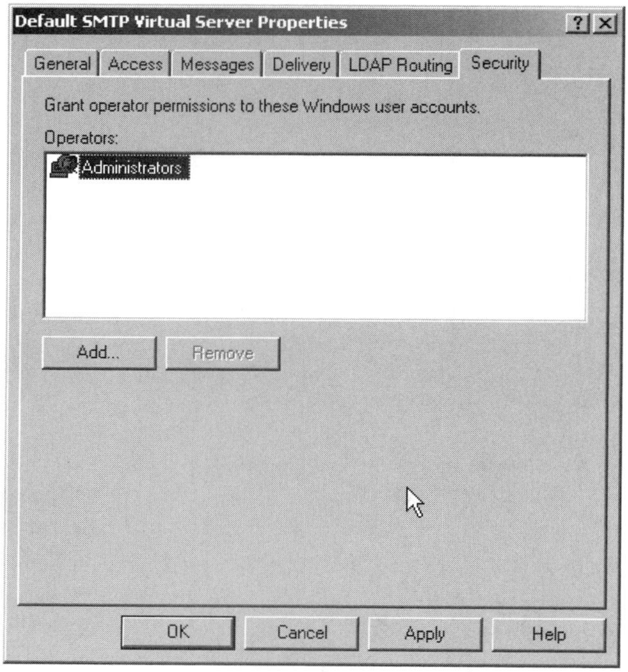

FIGURE 16.24 The SMTP Security Tab

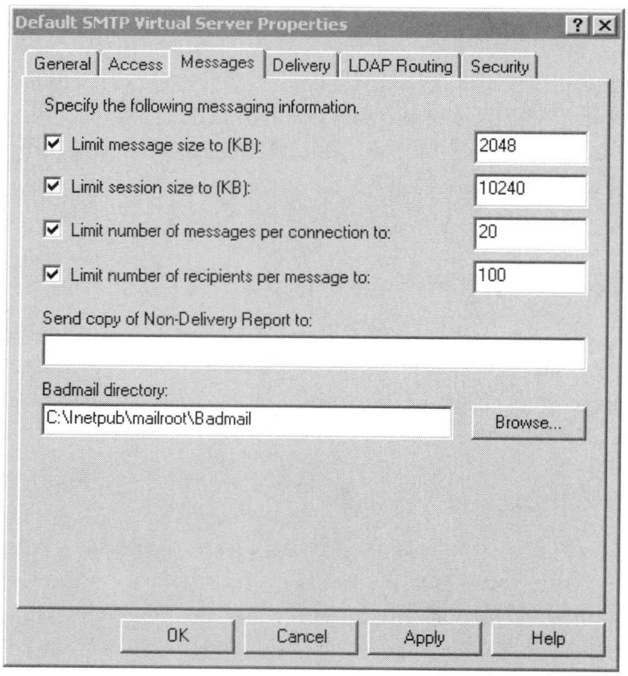

FIGURE 16.25 The SMTP Messages Tab

UNDERSTANDING THE NNTP SERVER

The ability to post and receive messages on a bulletin board is becoming increasingly important in communications. IIS facilitates this through its Network News Transfer Protocol (NNTP). The NNTP Server is not automatically installed as a default component of IIS. It must be selected from the **Configure Your Server Wizard** from the list provided with the **Add and Remove Programs** option. Select **Web Server Applications** from the list → click **Details** → select **Internet Information Services** → click **Detail** → select **NNTP Services**, and then follow the wizard's instruction through the completion of the installation. It is possible to select **FTP** and **SMTP** for installation at the same time as **NNTP Services** are installed by also selecting these features.

Newsgroup communication can be established and administered through the Internet Information Services snap-in. The system administrator can **Start**, **Stop**, or **Pause** it by right-clicking the targeted **NNTP** server and selecting the desired option. Additional NNTP virtual servers are created by right-clicking **NNTP**, selecting **New**, selecting **Virtual Server**, and entering the appropriate data in the associated dialog boxes (see Figure 16.26).

Under the NNTP console tree, policies can be set for newsgroups, expiration, virtual directories, and current sessions. NNTP virtual server configuration is carried out by right-clicking the desired NNTP server, selecting **Properties**, and then sequentially configuring from the four available tabs.

The NNTP **General** tab (Figure 16.27) is used to establish the virtual server's name, IP-assigned addresses, connection options, and enabled logging. The other

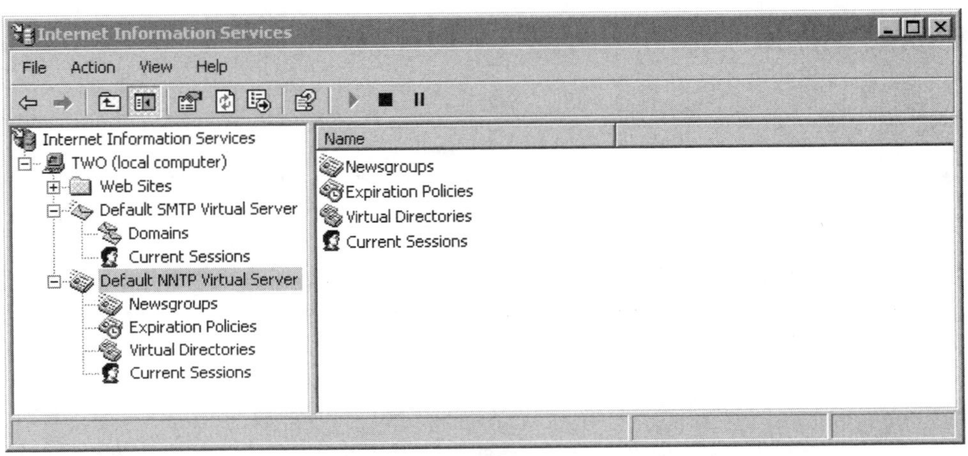

FIGURE 16.26 The IIS Snap-in Tool with Default Administration Tree Options

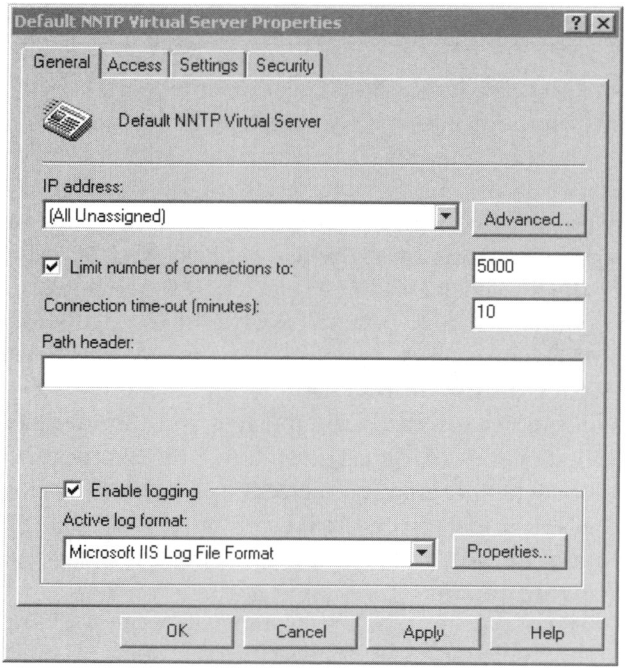

FIGURE 16.27 The NNTP General Tab

three tabs are essentially the same as those for SMTP, which were discussed in the previous sections. They are illustrated in Figures 16.28 through 16.30.

UNDERSTANDING THE FTP SERVER

The file transfer protocol (FTP), one of the mainstays of the TCP/IP application suite, is a way to move files in UNIX environments. The FTP server is not automatically installed as a default component of IIS. It must be selected from the **Configure Your Server Wizard** from the list provided with the **Add and Remove Programs** option. Select **Web Server Applications** from the list → click **Details** → select **Internet Information Services** → click **Detail** → select **FTP Services,** and then follow the wizard's instruction through the completion of the installation. It is possible to select **SMTP** and **NNTP** for installation at the same time as **FTP Services** are installed by also selecting these features.

The FTP Service offered by IIS provides standard industry document-transfer facilities, with which the system administrator can **Start**, **Stop**, or **Pause** FTP services by right-clicking the targeted FTP server and selecting the desired option.

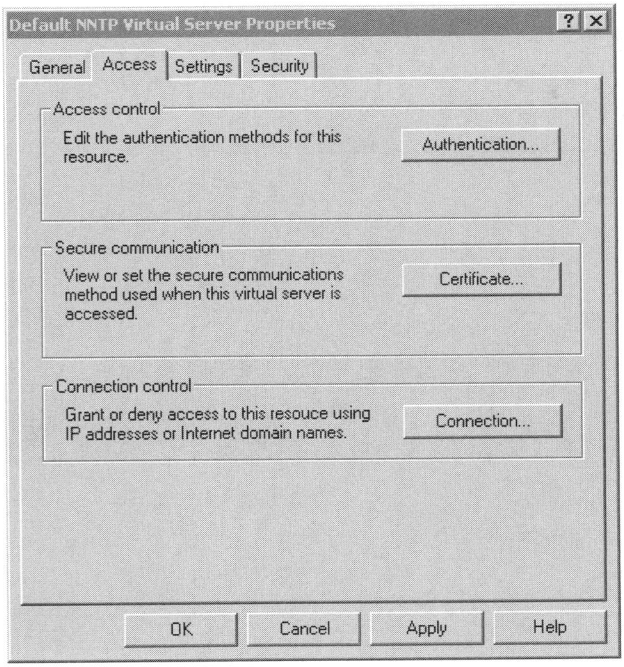

Figure 16.28 The NNTP Access Tab

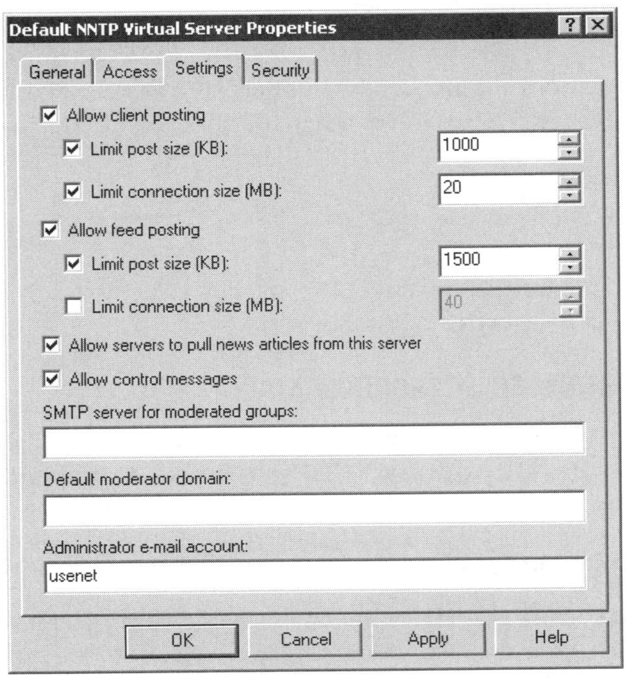

FIGURE 16.29 The NNTP Settings Tab

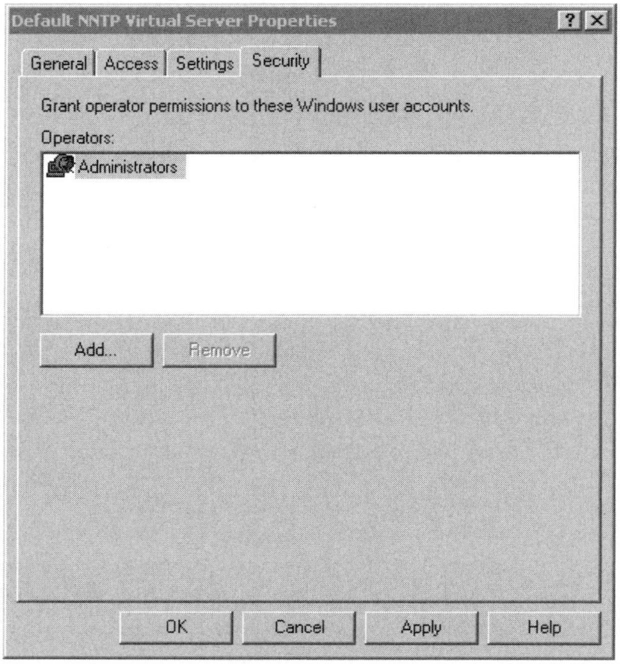

FIGURE 16.30 The NNTP Security Tab

Additional FTP Services are invoked by right-clicking **FTP**, selecting **New**, selecting **Virtual Directory** or **Site**, and entering the appropriate data in the associated dialog boxes.

FTP Properties

To configure FTP, right-click the target FTP site and select **Properties**. A brief description of the six **Properties** tabs follows.

ESTABLISHING GENERAL FTP SITE CONFIGURATION

The **FTP Site** tab (Figure 16.31) is used to configure general specifications such as **Description**, assigned **IP Address**, **TCP Port** number, **Connection** limitations, and **Enabled Logging** format.

ESTABLISHING BASIC FTP SECURITY

The **Security Accounts** tab (Figure 16.32) resolves two important security issues. First, it is used to determine whether anonymous accounts will be allowed. If so,

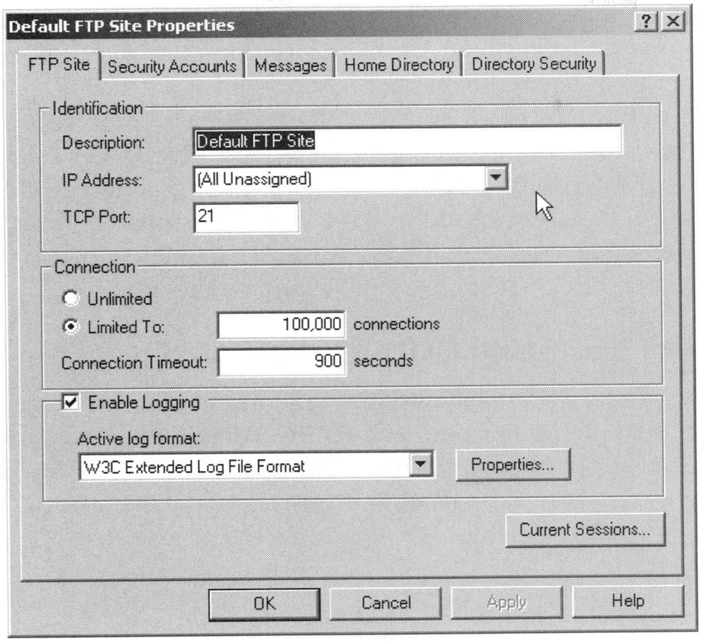

FIGURE 16.31 The FTP Site General Tab

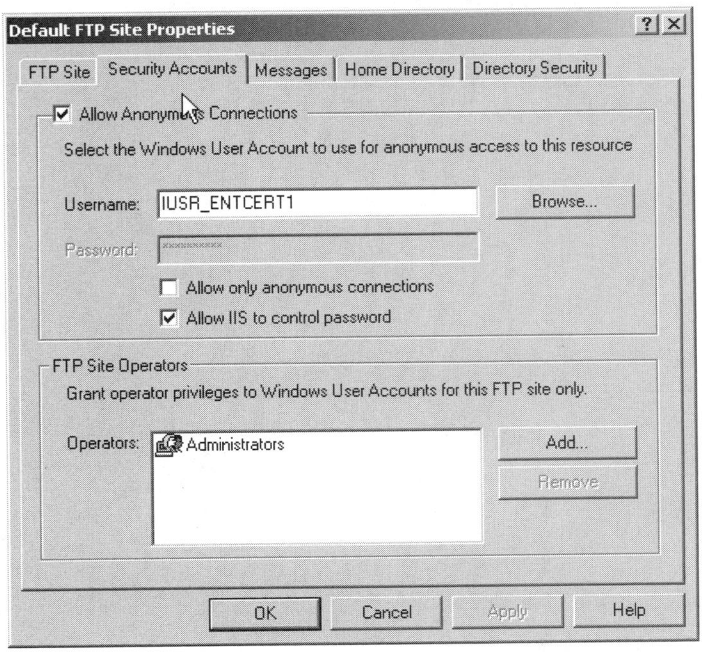

FIGURE 16.32 FTP Security Accounts Tab

the user account name for anonymous logons must be specified, which by default is IUSR_*computername*. If the **Allow Anonymous Connections** box is checked, users will not be required to submit passwords to gain access to the FTP site. If **Allow IIS to control password** is selected, password protection is applied.

The second function of this tab is to establish which users or groups have administrative privileges. By default, the Administrator group has Full Control. Other groups can be added or deleted with the **Add** or **Remove** button.

The **Messages** tab (Figure 16.33) provides a user-friendly face to the FTP site. An introductory or exit greeting can be added via this tab.

ESTABLISHING THE FTP HOME DIRECTORY AND SECURITY

Figures 16.34 and 16.35 illustrate how FTP home directory properties and directory security are established. The **Home Directory** properties tab provides both location information and UNIX or MS-DOS directory style. The **Directory Security** tab designates the IP address subnet masks that are granted or denied access.

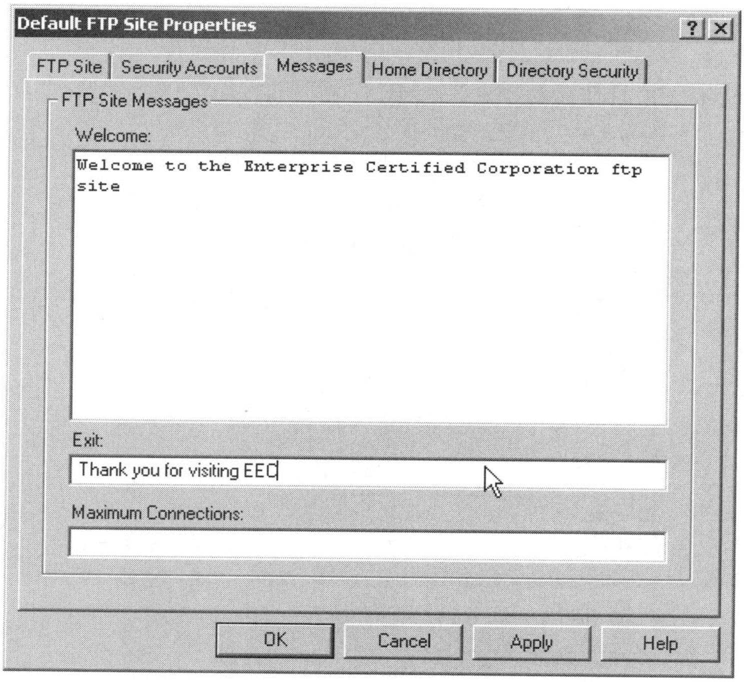

FIGURE 16.33 FTP Messages Tab

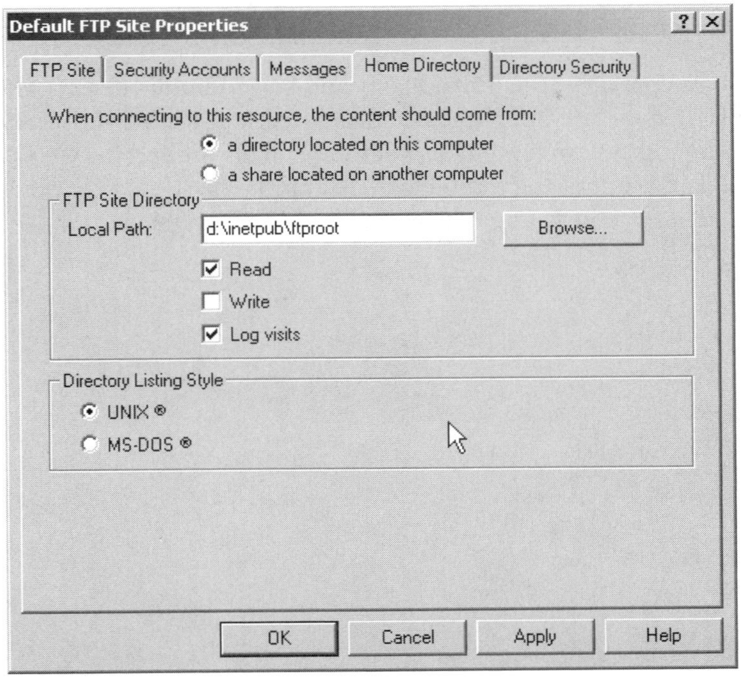

FIGRURE 16.34 The FTP Home Directory Tab

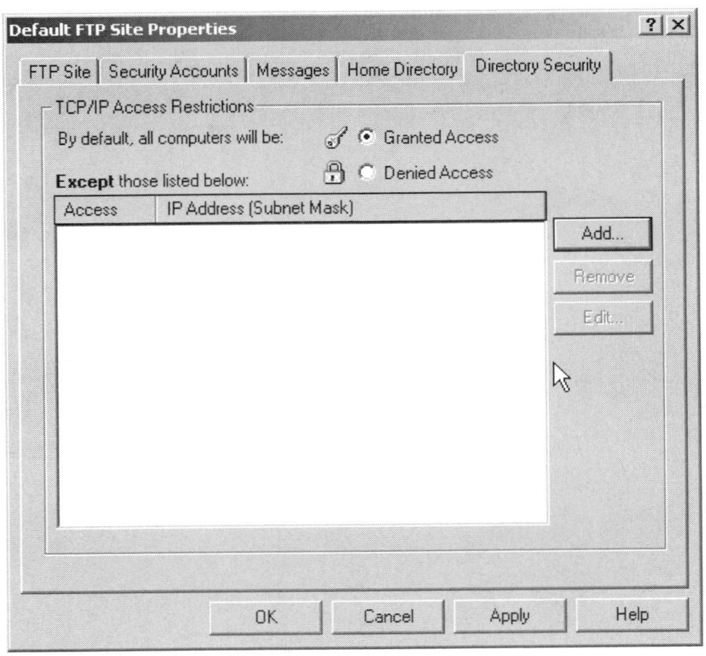

FIGURE 16.35 The FTP Directory Security Tab

POSTSCRIPT

This chapter reviews the functionality and basic administration of Microsoft Internet Information Services. IIS 6.0 is fully integrated with Windows Server 2003 on the operating-system level. It also embraces many important Web standards. With consolidated central and remote administration, IIS should be widely embraced by Web operators and Windows Server 2003 system administrators.

Chapter 17

Cluster, Indexing, Message Queuing, SMS, MOM, and WSH

This chapter examines several advanced features, each of which plays an important role in a Windows Server 2003 enterprise.

- *Clustering* provides high availability for critical services and applications by maintaining two joined servers (or nodes); if one node or subcomponent fails, the other assumes functional responsibility. This chapter provides a conceptual view of Windows Server 2003 clustering technology and base-level administrative information.
- Windows Server 2003 *Indexing Service* builds local and remote disk drive index catalogs.
- *Microsoft Message Queuing Service* (MSMQ) is an interapplication communication system and development tool. It is analogous to electronic mail except that it involves communication between system queues rather than between users.
- *System Management Server 2.0* (SMS) is part of the BackOffice product family and not a core Windows Server 2003 operating system component. Nevertheless, the tools available via SMS can significantly improve system administration, especially in large enterprises.
- *Microsoft Operations Manager* (MOM) is the most recent supplemental system management tool available to the Windows 2000 and Windows Server 2003 product family. SMS and MOM are complementary optional management tools.
- *Windows Scripting Host (WSH 2.0).*

UNDERSTANDING CLUSTER SERVICES

Clustering involves linking two servers (known as nodes) that share a disk drive(s) and configured clustering software. All configuration and resource data is stored on the shared storage devices, and the nodes are networked through independent interconnects that ensure reliable communication. They are grouped under one name. Since all nodes are aware of what is being processed locally and on sister nodes, a single group name is used to manage the cluster as a whole.

In the Windows Server 2003 clustering implementation, there are two forms of software. Clustering software manages intercommunications between the nodes; Microsoft Cluster Services (MSCS) manages internode activities. The Resource Monitor checks on the viability of cluster communications and the health of the nodes. The Cluster Administrator views, configures, and modifies cluster operations and is invoked through **Start** menu → **Administrative Tools** → **Cluster Administrator** or by invoking **cluster** from the **command prompt**.

As a node goes online, it searches for other nodes to join by polling the designated internal network. In this way, all nodes are notified of the new node's existence. If other nodes cannot be found on a preexisting cluster, the new node takes control of the quorum resources residing on the shared disk that contains state and configuration data. It will theoretically receive current information, since Cluster Services maintains the latest copy of the quorum resource database. The quorum-capable resource selected to maintain the configuration data is necessary for the cluster's recovery because this data contains all of the changes applied to the cluster database. The quorum resource is generally accessible to other cluster resources so that all cluster nodes have access to database changes. If the node is the first to be placed in the cluster, it will automatically create the quorum resources database, which can be shared as other nodes come online.

Failover and Failback

Every node is aware of when another node goes offline or returns to service. When one of the clustered servers fails, its processes are transferred to another member node. This process is known as *failover*. When the failed node comes back online, the workload is transferred back to it in a process known as *failback* (see Figure 17.1).

While every node is aware of the activities of all the others, each performs specialized functions while online to balance processing loads. The administrator collects cluster resources into groups and assigns group activities to particular nodes. If a node fails, the affected group functions are transferred to an operational node until the failed node can be brought back online. Every group contains a priority list of which node should execute its functions. Group functions can be owned by

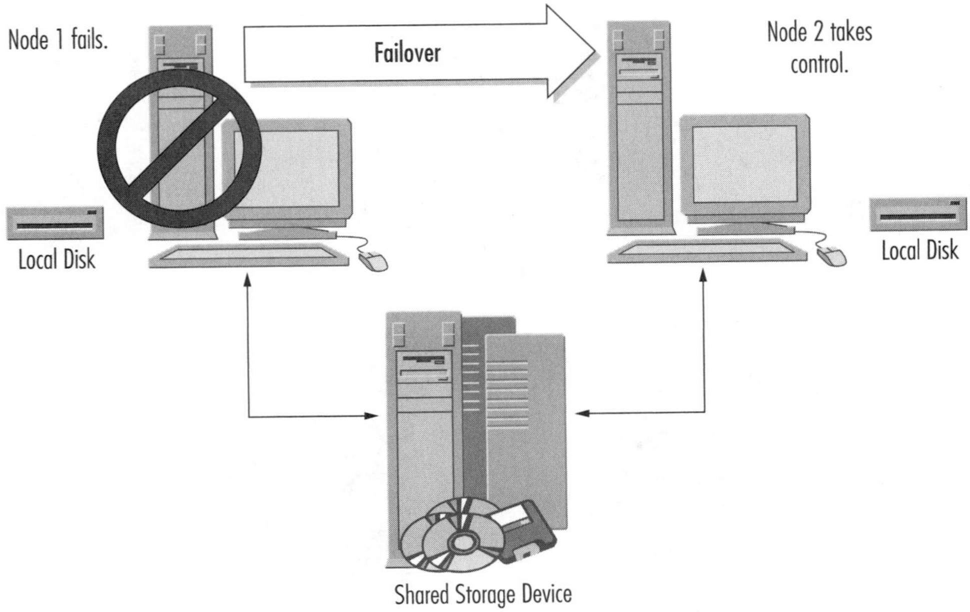

FIGURE 17.1 Basic Cluster Failover

only one server at a time. Although they ordinarily comprise related objects, this is not a requirement. However, resources that depend on one another must reside in the same group.

Clusters can perform a number of general or special functions, but are most often established as file, print, application, and Web servers. These can take the form of physical or virtual servers. A *virtual server* is a special group type that acts ordinarily as a server. However, its functions will failover just like those of any other cluster group. Although like any physical server, virtual servers have a network name and an IP address, failover capabilities make its resources available even when the system fails. Clusters are also commonly created as high-availability file servers, printer servers, Web servers, and application servers (Figure 17.2).

Cluster Network Concerns

Clusters depend on the ability to communicate reliably between nodes. Therefore, they will use any privately available network to locate and communicate with their nodes. For reasons of security and reliability, clusters do not use networks that are configured for public use.

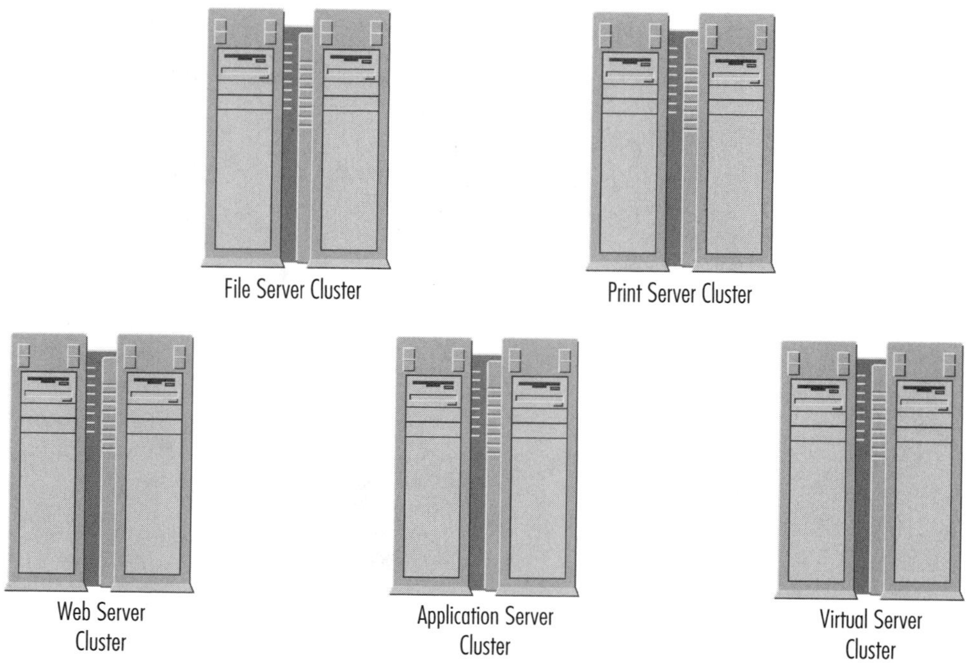

FIGURE 17.2 Common Generic and Specific Cluster Uses

Nodes that are unable to communicate are said to be partitioned. When this occurs, Cluster Services shuts down all but one node in order to ensure data consistency.

A problem can arise if each node has only one network adapter. If an adapter on one of the nodes fails, that node will be unable to communicate with the others, and thus all nodes will automatically attempt to take control of quorum resources. Should the node with the failed adapter take control, all cluster resources will be out of reach by clients that depend on them. For that reason there should be more than one network adapter to provide added redundancy.

Traffic is another clear issue that arises when only one network adapter is available on cluster nodes. The single adapter must handle node-to-node traffic and also cluster-to-client systems traffic. Thus, a multihomed environment is recommended so that all traffic can be appropriately routed.

The Cluster Database

The cluster database is maintained on every node and housed in the Windows Server 2003 Registry. To ensure consistent data, all updates are globally distributed to all nodes in the cluster through periodic checks. As discussed earlier, the quorum resource database creates a recovery log so that configuration and state data can be used in case of massive failures.

In addition to configuration information, the cluster database contains data about cluster objects and properties. A cluster object can be a group of functions that have been gathered to run on a designated node, for example. Cluster objects also include internal network data, network adapters and interfaces, node resources, and cluster resources such as shared storage devices.

Basic Cluster Planning

A number of commonsense steps should be taken during the cluster-planning phase. Since the primary purpose of a cluster is to provide redundancy, risk assessment is one of the steps. The system administrator must minimize any area of potential failure while ensuring that a redundant system will perform in the event of a node failure. The following sections describe key planning issues that should be resolved prior to deployment of Windows Server 2003 clusters.

APPLICATION SELECTION

The selection of applications to be hosted on a cluster represents one aspect of planning. This selection requires that a number of criteria be met by an application before it can be used in a cluster environment, since not all applications have been written to the API and so are not cluster-aware. Nevertheless, many applications that are not cluster-aware can function in a cluster if they meet the following basic requirements:

- Storage of the application data is flexible and configurable. That is, in order to ensure failover of data, it is necessary to direct storage to the shared cluster disks.
- The application is able to retry and recover connection in the event of temporary network disconnections.
- The application uses TCP/IP. Applications that are aware of DCOM, named pipes, or RPC in concert with TCP/IP will have greater reliability.

NOTE Applications written solely to support NetBEUI or IPX are not candidates for Windows Server 2003 clusters.

GROUPING AND CAPACITY

Cluster capacity is often determined by how applications and functions are grouped and assigned to nodes. All cluster-qualified applications must be examined in terms of resource requirements and dependencies, and all those with mutual dependencies should be grouped together. Groups of applications should then be assigned to nodes to achieve a relative workload balance. All nodes must have sufficient disk space for the applications and sufficiently fast CPU capacity and memory. Remember, all nodes in one group must be identically configured in terms of hardware capacity.

Nodes must belong to the same domain as either domain controllers or member servers. Cluster nodes that are also domain controllers require additional system capacity, since they can be heavily burdened by authentication and replication services in large networked environments.

NETWORKS

Clusters are connected through one or more independent physical networks, also known as *interconnects*. It is strongly recommended that there be at least two PCI bus-based interfaces, and that prior to the cluster software installation, the nodes be interconnected using TCP/IP for all interfaces. No routers can be used to connect nodes; they must be directly connected and assigned IP addresses on the same network. DHCP can be used to lease IP addresses, but if a lease expires and the DHCP is unavailable, connectivity can be interrupted or an automatic failover can occur. If DHCP is to be used, obtain a permanently leased IP address.

Hubs can be used. The hub that connects nodes should create a dedicated segment for the interconnect, which has no other systems connected to it.

Once the nodes are interconnected, the clustering software can be installed. The communications between cluster nodes are known as *heartbeats* and primarily involve keeping track of node states. If an irregular heartbeat is detected from a cluster partner, the process of failover begins.

REQUIRED DOMAIN ACCOUNTS

Computer accounts must be established for each node before installation of Cluster Services, and they must be in the same domain. An account should become a member of the local Administrators group; if the nodes are configured as domain controllers, however, it becomes a member of the Domain Administrators group. The **Change password on next logon** property should also be disabled.

POSSIBLE POINTS OF FAILURE

Clustering assumes reliability of hardware and interconnectivity, so the system administrator has a responsibility to reduce the number of possible failure points. As discussed in Chapter 14, "Disk Management," Windows Server 2003 supports both disk mirrors and RAID-5 striping with parity. It is strongly recommended that nodes be built with multiple network interfaces in case an adapter fails and that disk redundancy be implemented. A UPS system is also highly recommended.

Cluster Administration

Clusters are managed with a number of tools and utilities. The Application Configuration Wizard manages cluster-serviced software. The Cluster Administrator tool, automatically installed on all nodes with Cluster Services, views cluster configurations and manages failover activities. The cluster.exe utility provides command-line support.

THE APPLICATION CONFIGURATION WIZARD

The Application Configuration Wizard configures software for clusters. It helps to define dependencies and sets failover/failback policies, and it creates a virtual server to run the applications. The virtual server must have an IP address in order to run applications. You should reserve the IP address before running the Applications Configuration Wizard.

UNDERSTANDING DEFAULT GROUPS

The Cluster Administrator tool is used to view cluster and disk groups, which contain default settings and resources for generic clusters and failover. The cluster group attributes contain the information necessary for network connectivity. This information—a name and IP address that apply to the entire cluster—is entered during Cluster Services setup. The cluster group should never be deleted, renamed, or modified. If changes must be made, do it through the disk group.

Each shared storage disk has its resources identified through the disk group. Also part of this group is the physical disk resource data. It is possible to add IP address resources and the network name resource. The latter can then be renamed to distinguish its function.

FAILOVER ADMINISTRATION

Failover occurs when either the entire node or a node resource fails. In this case, the Cluster Administrator tool is notified. Resource failures do not always bring down the entire node and may cause only group failovers. Unfortunately, group failures are more difficult to detect. The Cluster Administrator should be employed to periodically check group ownerships to determine if a failover has occurred; even minor failovers can cause performance degradation and decrease resource availability. It should also be used regularly to review cluster states and make appropriate corrections.

USING THE CLUSTER.EXE COMMAND-LINE UTILITY

Many administrative tasks can be accomplished using the cluster.exe utility from the **command prompt** or **Start** menu → **Run**. The syntax is shown here, with the cluster name as an optional component:

```
cluster [cluster name] /option
```

These are the cluster.exe command options:

- */rename: new name* renames the client.
- */version* displays the version number for Cluster Services.
- */quorumresource: resource name [/path:path] [maxlogsize:maximum size in kilobytes]* changes the name of the quorum resource and its location and log size.
- */list: domain name* lists the cluster in the named domain.
- */?* provides more cluster.exe syntax information.

The following are the cluster.exec functions that can be used for administration:

- *Cluster [name] Node [name] /option* locates the option information for the specified node. Options include status, pause, resume, evict (or remove node), listinterfaces, privproperties (private properties), properties, and help.
- *Cluster [name] Group [name] /option* permits viewing and managing of cluster groups. The options include status, create, delete, rename, moveto, online, offline, properties, privproperties, listowners, setowners, and help.
- *Cluster [name] Network [name] /option* permits the management of cluster networks. Options include status, properties, privproperties, rename, and listinterfaces.
- *Cluster [name] Netinterfaces [name] /option* supports the management of the network interfaces. The options include status, properties, and privproperties.
- *Cluster [name] Resources [name] /option* administers cluster resources. The options include status, create, delete, rename, addowner, removeowner, listowner, moveto, properties, privproperties, online, fail, offline, listdependencies, removedependencies, and help.

Setting Cluster Properties

Cluster configuration can be changed by altering the settings in the selected cluster's **File** menu → **Properties** dialog box.

Group properties are viewed and modified from the **State** option, which also allows the node that currently owns the group to be viewed. The **State** option is used to change the **Name, Description**, and **Preferred** owner properties.

Failover policy and **failback policy** are set by selecting their respective tabs and making appropriate changes. The number of times a group can failover during a given period is established by the **Failover** tab. If a group failover occurs more often than the amount set in the policy, Cluster Services takes the resource offline until it can be fixed. The default policy is not to have this function occur automatically. However, in some cases it may be appropriate to have an automatic failback after a specific number of hours.

The **Properties** dialog box is used to check and modify other settings, including

- *Resource dependencies*. A great number of dependencies affect clusters. For example, DHCP, File share, ISS Server Instance, Message Queuing Services, WINS Services, and Print spoolers all depend on the availability of the physical disk or storage device. Many also depend on network name and IP address availability.
- *Network settings*. This option is used to view and change the network name, description, state, IP address, and address mask, as well as to enable or disable the network cluster. If enabled, the communication types can be set as client-to-cluster and/or node-to-node.
- *Advanced settings*. This option is used to determine whether the resource is to be restarted or allowed to fail. If the latter, the **Affect the group** box must be checked. Then a **Threshold**—the number of times a restart is attempted within a defined **Period** of time—must be defined. When that threshold is exceeded during that period, failover occurs. It will not occur if the **Affect the group** option is not checked.

Clustering Features New to Windows Server 2003

Windows Server 2003 introduces new or significantly enhanced features to its server clustering technology. The following highlights some of the most relevant enhancements for administrators:

- *Active Directory support for virtual servers.* A computer object in Active Directory supports cluster-aware and Active Directory–aware applications. The new object in Active Directory permits the association of related configuration information. IT administrators use this feature to find virtual server computer objects. On the downside, viewing of cluster topology information or the association between virtual servers and clusters is not supported.

- *Cluster password changes without reboot.* A requirement to reboot a clustered system obviously defeats the purpose of a failover; fortunately, Windows Server 2003 reduces this requirement. It allows the cluster account to be updated while the cluster service remains online. For example, administrators can now change passwords on a node without rebooting the server. This is accomplished through the **cluster.exe** command.
- *Cluster availability metrics for individual groups.* An individual group in a cluster can now be reviewed. It logs group success and failure of events either online or offline in the system's event log. Internode clock skew events are written to the system's event log. Administrators can review the event log streams from all the cluster nodes to examine the times between offline and online events. A calculation of the amount of time a group is online versus offline can then be determined. This will provide information on the availability of a cluster resource group.
- *Network load virtual clusters balancing.* Windows Server 2003 provides for the setting of port rules. This means that the administrator can set rules for every hosted application, Web site, or Virtual Internet Protocol (IP) address in a Network Load Balance (NLB) cluster. Virtual clusters can thereby be managed independently.
- *Quorum of nodes.* Windows Server 2003 introduces a quorum device that is accessible to all nodes in a cluster. Since this disk is used in the event of communication failures to centrally store highly available configuration data, administrators can use the Quorum of Nodes feature to support multiple sites. This is practically helpful in a geographically dispersed cluster because it lessens the need for shared storage technology to span the sites.
- *SAN support.* Storage Area Network (SAN) technology is designed to allow all the disks in a cluster to be included on the same storage fabric through a single host bus adapter (HBA). All server storage can be centralized into a SAN. This includes boot, page file, and system disks using a single or multiple redundant HBAs. All disks, except the boot disk, the system disk, and disks that contain page files, can be configured as shared disks regardless of the storage bus technology. Since SAN technology is a method of data consolidation and eased management, administrators of clustered services should delve beyond the scope of this book for additional information on the use of Windows Server 2003 expanded facilities.
- *Virtual name Kerberos authentication.* This feature permits Kerberos authentication when clients access a cluster via a cluster virtual name. When enabled, Active Directory creates a virtual computer object.

NOTE A convenience notation on printer driver enhancements is appropriate to round out this section. Windows 2000 painfully required the manual installation of each printer driver on every node of the cluster. A new feature provides a method to install a printer driver on the virtual cluster. The installation will propagate to all nodes of the cluster. This feature is available via **Start → Control Panel → Printers and Other Hardware**.

Postscript on Cluster Technology

This section provides a conceptual and administrative overview of Windows Server 2003 clustering technology, with shared disk clustering at its center. Much information needs to be gathered before deploying a cluster. Moreover, the technology is shifting. Thus, it is highly recommended that a system administrator download the latest Microsoft white papers on clusters prior to installing and deploying Cluster Services.

INDEXING SERVICE

Windows Server 2003 Indexing Service builds an index catalog from local and remote disk drives that contain information about document contents and properties. Like a regular index, this catalog includes all words that will help a user locate data. Typically, 15 to 30 percent of the contents of a document are cataloged. The rest are held in an exception list and include common nouns, verbs, articles, prepositions, and other words deemed not appropriate to finding data.

Document properties cataloged include creation date, author name, and size in number of characters. Each document type treats properties differently, requiring that some be generated automatically and others entered manually. This is the case with products like Microsoft Office. Meta tags found in html files must be stored in the property cache in order for html properties to be indexed.

The indexing process involves scanning documents, on either a full or an incremental basis. The first time indexing is run, all documents in the selected directory or directories are scanned for the catalog. A new full scan can be created at any time using the Indexing Services snap-in, selecting **Directories**, right-clicking the desired directory, selecting **All Tasks**, and choosing **Full Scan** (Figure 17.3). Manual incremental scans are initiated in the same manner except, of course, for the final selection. Automatic incremental scans are conducted each time Indexing Services is started, and when a document is modified, Indexing Services is

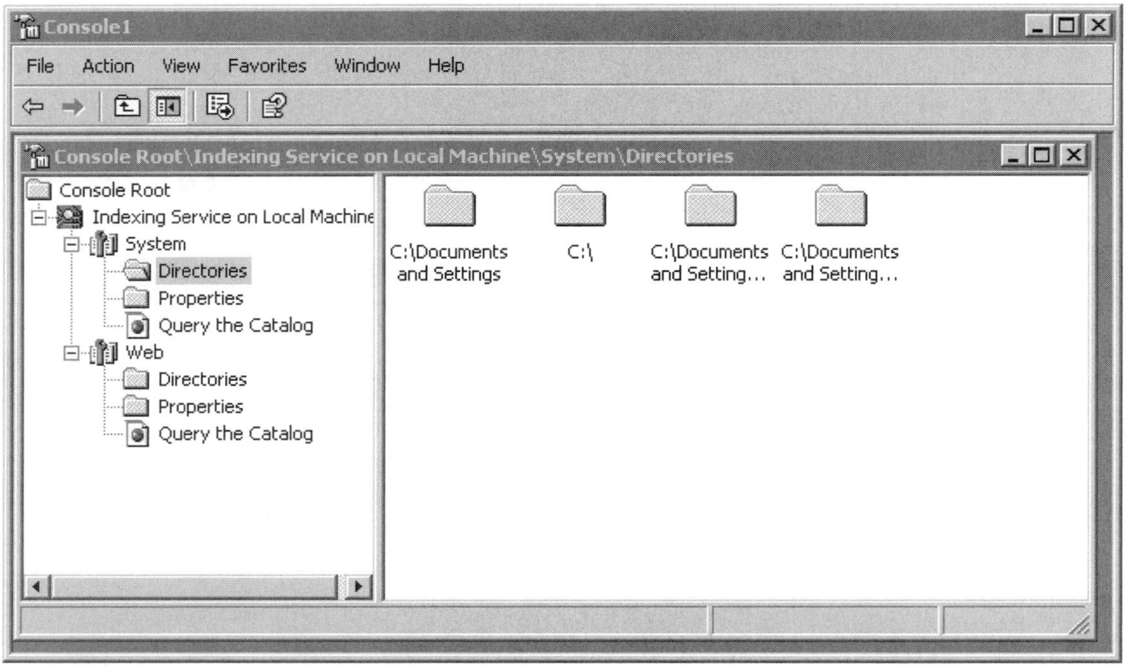

FIGURE 17.3 The MMC Indexing Service Snap-in Full Scan Option

notified that it requires rescanning. Incremental scans index only new or modified documents.

The full process invoked by Indexing Services has a number of steps. First, it identifies the type of file involved and then loads the appropriate document filter. A filter merely reflects the document's structure. Word processors from different vendors, for example, have different structures, and the filters strip encoded structural information from the content. They also determine the international language in which the document is written and parse the information into words. At that point the exception list of verbs, common nouns, articles, and prepositions for the international language is applied, and those words are dropped from the process. Every international language supported by Windows Server 2003 has an exception list. All words that remain are placed in the index. Properties are also collected and stored in the properties cache.

NOTE In terms of security, users will be able to view only those files for which they have permission on NTFS partitions. Catalogs saved on a FAT system will be visible to all users. Encrypted documents are never indexed.

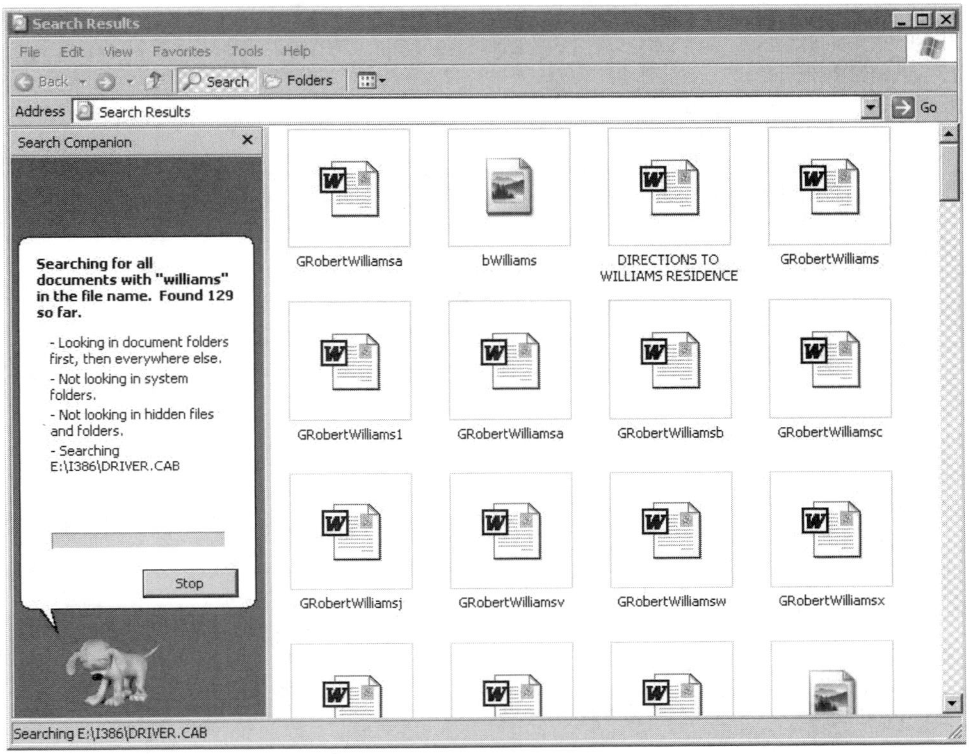

FIGURE 17.4 Content Location from the Search Dialog

Using Indexing Service to Find Data

Indexed information can be found in one of two ways. The one best known by users is **Start** menu → **Search** function, discussed in Chapter 4. Any of the found items can be opened by selecting the targeted item and double-clicking it.

The second method of locating content is the Indexing Service query form, which locates content and data output according to several criteria. Figure 17.4 shows a simple query and its results. Note that the query provides direct hot links to each found item. To open one of the files, simply double-click its icon (see Figure 17.5).

Indexing Service Sizing

As with any other Windows Server 2003 service, indexing large numbers of documents increases the pressure on the host server. The complexity and rapidity of

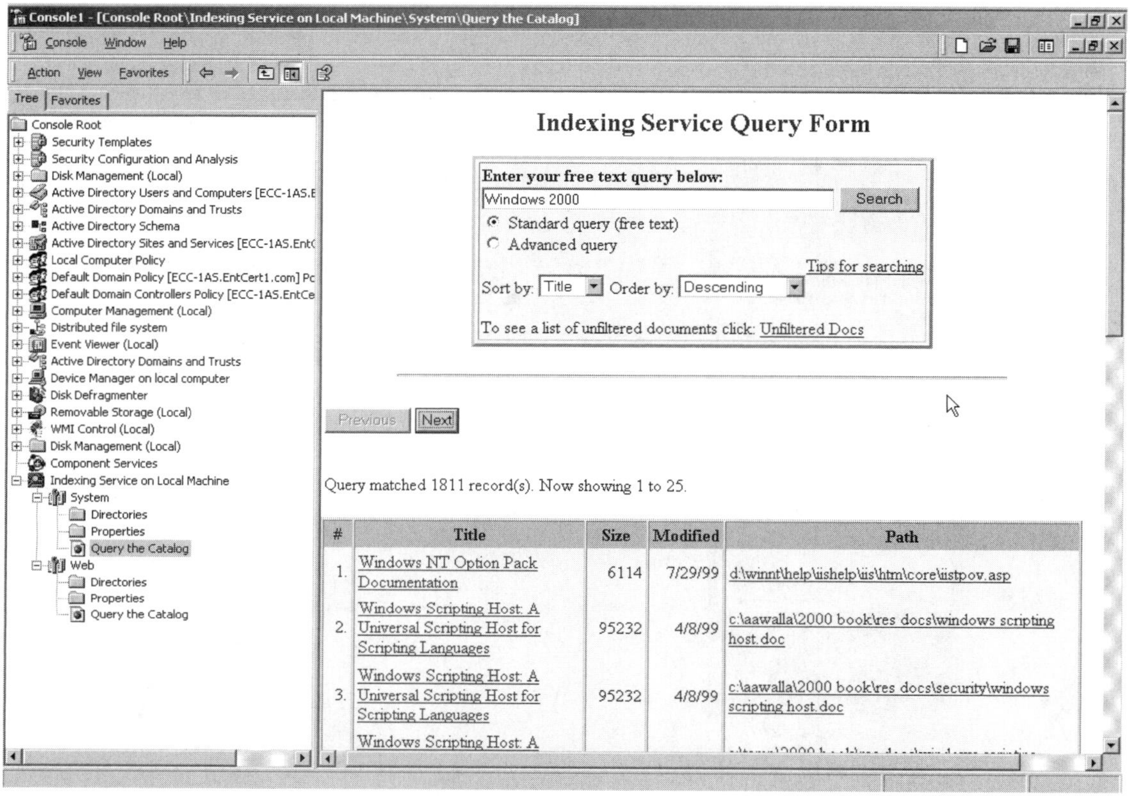

FIGURE 17.5 The Indexing Service Query Form and Output

queries also dictate system requirements. For fewer than 100,000 documents, 64 MB to 128 MB of storage memory should be sufficient. However, for 500,000 documents, the memory demands can easily exceed 256 MB. The system administrator should monitor memory demands and routinely add memory as the number and complexity of queries shift upward. CPU speed also impacts indexing efficiency, as does disk space. As a general rule, allocate an additional 30 percent for disk storage for all documents saved on a FAT system. Catalogs on NTFS require about 15 percent of the disk space used by the indexed documents.

Indexing Service Query Language

A query is simply a structure string of data that narrows the scope of a search. Its syntax is precise and generally takes the form

```
[Mode] [property name] [query_text] [attribute=value] query_text [/mode]
```

The mode is optional and defines the type of query, including free text, phrase, relational, and regular expressions (regex). Free text is the default if mode is not used. Short-form inquiries use @ for phrase mode, # for regular expressions, and $ for free text. Long-form queries use curly braces to define the type. For example, the long form for a query about a title is {prop name=title}; the short form is #name #title.

Indexing Service recognizes more than 40 property types that can be queried. These include creation time, time last accessed, physical path, number of characters, and document author. Refer to the Windows Server 2003 Help menu for a full list of query properties.

RULES AND OPERATORS

Indexing Service requires adherence to several query rules, within which standard query operators can be applied. The following rules are applicable to all Indexing Service queries:

- Queries are not case-sensitive.
- A number of special characters must be enclosed in quotation marks (' '). They are &, @, $, #, ^, ( ), and |. (How these characters can be applied is covered later.)
- Two forms of date and time queries are recognized: yyyy/mm/dd hh:mm:ss and yyyy-mm-dd hh:mm:ss.
- No words in the exception list can be used. Remember, these include verbs, common nouns, articles, and pronouns.
- Numeric values can be hexadecimals or decimals.

Available Operators

Standard industry operators can be applied to queries. The following describes them and how they are applied. This is not a comprehensive treatment; the Help menu provides additional information.

- *Contains and Equals*. The contains operator is employed to find specific words or phrases. For example, if you want to find the phrase "all basset hounds are cool," use the short form `@DocTitle "all basset hounds are cool"` or the long form `{phrase name=DocTitle} Contains {phrase}all basset hounds are cool{/phrase}{/prop}`. The equals operator specifies an exact equivalent condition. The short form is `@DocTitle = "all basset hounds are cool"`, which finds documents with that exact phrase.
- *Boolean*. Boolean operators use conditions that are strung together by AND (&), OR (|), NOT (&!), and NEAR (~). For example, to find documents that

contain the words "basset hound" and "cool," use "basset hound & cool" or "basset hound and cool." (Don't forget the quotation marks.) The order of precedence for Booleans is NOT, AND or NEAR, and OR.

- *Free text*. Free text is the default operator. The words or phrases are entered without filtering.
- *Phrase*. In a phrase query, the quotation in the short form is basset hounds are cool. In the long form, the {phrase} tag is in the form `{phrase} basset hounds are cool {/phrase}`.
- *Wildcards*. Wildcards are used for very simple pattern matching using the asterisk or question mark. The asterisk with the letters *b, a,* and *s*— bas*— results in findings such as "basset," "basket," "bass," and many others. The short form of the query is `@filename = bas*`.
- *Regular expression pattern matching*. Regular expressions are used commonly in statistical and other forms of analysis. If you are unfamiliar with regular expressions, refer to the Help pages.
- *Alternative word forms*. These forms are often called fuzzy or imprecise queries and are of two types. The first finds all words with common prefixes, and the short form simply uses the wildcard asterisk. The second type involves alternative forms of the word, such as "come" and "came." Here the long form for the inflected operator is `{Generate method=inflect} come {/Generate}`.
- *Relational.* These forms permit you to set parameters that include constraints such as less than (<), less than or equal to (<=), equal to (=), greater than or equal to (>=), greater than (>), and not equal to (|=).
- *Vector space queries*. In the vector space model that is common in information retrieval, the order can be separated by a comma—`basset, hound`—and a ranking can be applied to set the priority of the query match. In this case, ranking `basset [20], hound [4]` places a greater importance on the word "hound."
- *Term weighting queries*. This operator assigns a relative value to each word being queried. The syntax is {weight} word, and a value between 0.0 and 1.0 is assigned. For example, a query on 'basset hounds are cool' might be weighted with this structure: `{weight value = .300}basset AND {weight value=.600} hound AND {weight value=.100}cool`. In this example, "hound" has a much heavier weight than "cool."

Common Indexing Service Administrative Tasks

Indexing Service is one of the simplest Windows Server 2003 applications to administer. In this section, we will review only some of the common administrative tasks; the complete task scope is fairly obvious when exploring the Indexing Services MMC snap-in or via **Computer Management** snap-in → **Server Applications and Services** → **Indexing Service**. Both provide the same set of options and can be used interchangeably, but for the sake of simplicity we will refer to the Indexing Service snap-in the following examples.

Launch Indexing Service by opening the **Indexing Service** snap-in, clicking the **Action** menu, and selecting **Start**. To pause or stop Indexing Service, follow the same steps, but select **Pause** or **Stop** as appropriate.

CREATING A CATALOG

The creation of an Indexing Service catalog requires the following steps:

1. Open the **Indexing Service** snap-in.
2. Select the **Action** menu, click **New**, and select **Catalog**.
3. In the **Add Catalog** dialog box, type the name of catalog and enter the location. Use the **Browse** button to navigate to the desired location (Figure 17.6).
4. Click **OK** to complete the process.

ADDING OR EXCLUDING A DIRECTORY TO THE CATALOG

To add or exclude an Indexing Service directory to the catalog, follow these steps:

1. Open the **Indexing Service** snap-in.
2. Open the **Systems** tree console and click the **Directories** folder.
3. Select the **Action** menu, click **New**, and select **Directory.**
4. In the **Add Directory** dialog box, type the name of the catalog and enter the location. Use the **Browse** button to navigate to the desired location. Enter an alias name for the directory in the **Alias (UNC)** text box (Figure 17.7).
5. If this is a remote directory, add an authorized user name and password in the appropriate text boxes.

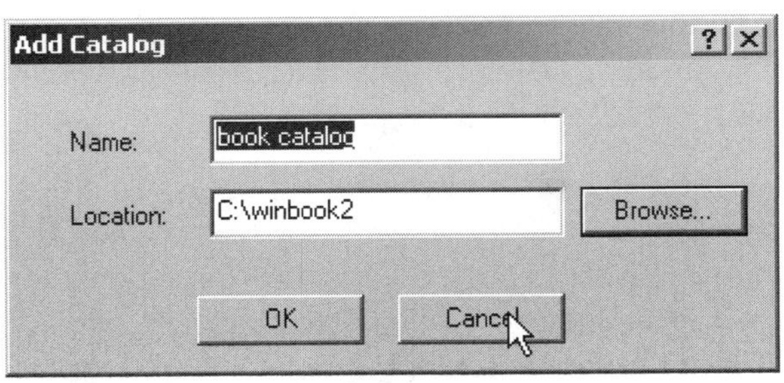

FIGURE 17.6 The Add Catalog Dialog Box

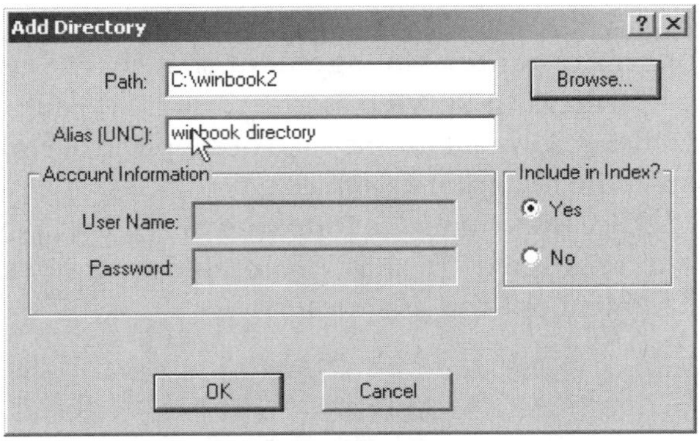

FIGURE 17.7 The Add Directory Dialog Box

6. To include the directory, select **Yes**; to exclude the directory, select **No.**
7. Click **OK** to complete the process.

The removal of a directory from a catalog is accomplished by loading the **Indexing Service** snap-in, double-clicking the targeted catalog, double-clicking the **Directories** folder, selecting the targeted directory, clicking the **Action** menu, and clicking **Delete**.

ADDING, EDITING, AND REMOVING PROPERTIES

In the properties cache, to add, edit, and remove properties, follow these steps:

1. Open the **Indexing Service** snap-in.
2. Double-click the targeted catalog.
3. Click **Properties** from the catalog console tree.
4. In the right-hand details pane, move to the **Property Set** column and select the property **ID** to add to the cache.
5. Click the **Action** menu and select **Properties**.
6. From within the **Properties** dialog box, check the **Cached** option and select the data type appropriate for the property from the Datatype list. Set the size in bytes for the property in the **Size** box.

To remove the properties, follow the preceding process in steps 1 through 5. Then in the **Properties** box, remove the check mark on the **Cached** option. Edit properties by following these steps and making appropriate changes.

The Indexing Service snap-in does not have to be installed for a typical user to find things using the **Start** menu → **Search** function. However, with the service in place, searches can be more detailed, accurate, and efficient. Remember, the primary function of Indexing Service is to catalog document content and properties for fast retrieval.

MESSAGE QUEUING SERVICES

Microsoft Message Queuing (formerly MSMQ) gives system administrators the ability to manage a communications infrastructure. Message Queuing is also of great interest to software developers who want to build message-queuing-aware applications. Such applications go by several industry names, including message queuing, message-oriented middleware (MOM), and store-and-forward software. Unlike e-mail, which passes messages between people, message queuing passes messages between applications.

A *queue* is a temporary storage environment that buffers data transmission until an appointed time or until the recipient is available. This allows communication regardless of the state of the receiving computer and even if the system is offline. Message Queuing communications remain in the queue until the receiving application is available to accept it (unless other parameters are set to discharge the message after a specific number of attempts or period of time).

NOTE The developmental aspect of Message Queuing is outside the scope of Windows Server 2003 administration. Administrators or developers interested in developing message-queuing applications should obtain the MSMQ Software Development Kit.

NOTE Cross-platform connectivity to IBM MQSeries versions 2 and 5 is provided with the optional SMQ-MQSeries Bridge available from the Microsoft SNA Server version 4 Service Pack 2 or later. The Bridge was purchased from Level8 Systems and was commercially known as FalconMQ Bridge.

Concepts

Several concepts must be understood prior to installing and deploying Message Queuing. Messages, queues, network topology, and routing are explored in the following sections.

UNDERSTANDING MESSAGES

Message Queuing messages have two primary parts. The body is either binary or text information readable by the receiving application which can be encrypted. It also contains specific properties, including the message ID and those required by the application. The maximum size of a message is 4 megabytes.

Normal messages are regular communications between applications delivered from public, private, journal, dead letter, or transactions queues. Report messages are generally sent as tests or for route tracking. Response messages are confirmations from the receiving application and are often invoked by the MQPing function. Finally, acknowledgment messages confirm the receipt or failure of a normal message from the receiving application to the sending computer's administrative queue.

Messages are delivered via an express or a recoverable method. Express message delivery takes place in the queues stored in the RAM and is the fastest and most efficient method. However, express messages are lost when Message Queuing service is shut down or, if it is run on a cluster, during a failover. Recoverable messages are written to disk until delivery can be achieved. This method is slower but safer.

UNDERSTANDING QUEUES

The queue is the base structure used by Message Queuing to store and transmit messages. Different queues perform different functions, as follows:

- *Administration* queues are established by the sending application and simply provide acknowledgments from sent messages.
- *Public* queues are available to any computer in an enterprise. Their properties are published by the Active Directory and replicated to domain controllers.
- *Private* queues are used only by Message Queuing applications that have knowledge of the format and path to the queue. They are not known by or published to the Active Directory.
- *Dead-letter* queues hold messages that cannot be delivered or that exceed the time specified for delivery.
- *Response* queues hold response messages sent from the receiving application to the sender.
- *Report* queues simply report the route taken by a message.
- *System* queues combine other queues to conduct system communication and cannot be deleted.
- *Journal* queues copy messages to ensure delivery. Journal messages can be saved to disk on the source or destination computer.

UNDERSTANDING NETWORK TOPOLOGY FOR MESSAGE QUEUING

As the basis for its network topology, Message Queuing uses the Windows Server 2003 site. This site definition is created by the Server's Active Directory, which means that the site topologies for the Active Directory and Message Queuing are identical. (For information about site structure, refer to Chapters 5 and 6.) With specific regard to Message Queuing, it is essential that the intrasite network be permanent and that sufficient bandwidth exist to support the anticipated volume of messages. For intersite messages, multiple Message Queuing servers are commonly configured for redundancy. However, since multiple Message Queuing servers can dramatically increase network traffic, it is recommended that at least one Message Queuing server be installed for each site or subnet.

Routing links are used to communicate messages between sites by Message Queuing services when one or more Message Queuing servers is used. To view and modify Message Queuing data on the Active Directory, the Message Queuing must be installed on a domain controller. Message-queuing services are configured to store and forward messages and provide dynamic routing. Message Queuing can be configured to route messages between sites using either IP-based or IPX-based networks, but the respective Message Queuing server must also be configured for that network routing protocol. Moreover, name resolution is required for Message Queuing configured for IPX, which can be provided by a Novell server. Lacking a Novell server, the Service Advertising Protocol (SAP) agent must be installed.

CAUTION To use IPX with multiple adapters, the computers must be configured with a unique internal network number. This requirement ensures the proper operation of remote procedure calls (RPCs) over IPX. Zero is not an acceptable network number.

Independent Message Queuing clients cannot immediately store and forward message queues. Other than this limitation, they can send and receive messages in a manner similar to the Message Queuing server. The client Message Queuing server generates local messages and sends them when a connection to the receiving computer or application is available. If the system is offline, it will store the messages until connectivity is restored.

The dependent Message Queuing client is similar to the independent client except that it uses synchronous communications, which makes it dependent on its server to perform the Message Queuing functions.

Understanding Message Routing

If a direct connection cannot be established, Message Queuing uses routing to deliver messages and accept acknowledgments. That is, it hops from computer to computer until the destination is found. These hops are measured by Message Queuing to facilitate future communication. Message Queuing attempts to provide the least costly link route, but if the most direct route is not available it will use any available route to complete the delivery.

In large organizations where message volumes are substantial, it is wise to consider creating specialized Message Queuing servers to handle traffic. In-routing servers manage messages within a site; out-routing servers move messages across wide-bandwidth networks and control the message flow. Client servers should be generally configured to employ multiple in-routing and out-routing servers in order to minimize message transmission failure.

Routing is generally predicated on the availability of links and their relative costs. Once multiple links are established, Message Queuing attempts to route to the least costly link based on costs input during the configuration process. These costs are usually derived from throughput divided by the actual cost of the connection, which provides a relative number of megabits or kilobits per second of message transfer per monetary unit. From this calculation, a link value can be calculated and compared to other values.

Routing links use Message Queuing servers to route messages. One or more Message Queuing servers must be assigned to routing links.

When using a firewall with Message Queuing, a PPTP-based secure communication channel should be established. This is usually RCP port 2103 or 2105, although the MQPing uses UDP port 3527. Three basic modes can be set in a firewall environment. First, messages can be sent only through TCP port 1801 for independent client computer access. Second, messages can be sent and Active Directory access allowed using TCP port 1801 and RPC ports 135 and 2101. Third, messages can be sent and read with Active Directory access. Here, in addition to the ports allowed in the second mode, RCP port 2105 can be used to allow remote clients to receive queues from the internal Message Queuing server.

CREATING A ROUTING LINK

The creation of a routing link for Message Queuing is accomplished via these steps:

1. Open the **Active Directory Sites and Services** snap-in.
2. Open the console tree and right-click **MsmqServices**.
3. Select **New**.
4. Select **MSMQ Routing Link**.
5. In the dialog box, select the two sites to be linked by scrolling through the **Site 1** and **Site 2** options list.
6. Assign a relative cost (positive value) for the link in the **MSMQ Link Cost** text box.

CHANGING ROUTING SERVERS FOR A ROUTING LINK

To change the routing server of a routing link for Message Queuing, follow these steps:

1. Open the **Active Directory Sites and Services** snap-in.
2. Open the console tree and right-click **Msmq Services.**
3. Right-click the targeted link and select **Properties**.
4. On the **Site Gates** tab, select **Site Servers** and click **Add**.

To remove a routing server, simply take steps 1 through 3, then in the **Site Gates** gate, click **Remove**.

CREATING A COST FOR A ROUTING LINK

Follow these steps to create a cost for a Message Queuing routing link:

1. Open the **Active Directory Sites and Services** snap-in.
2. Open the console tree and right-click **Msmq Services.**
3. Select **Properties**.
4. On the **General** tab, insert the cost in the **Link Cost** text box.

CHANGING THE ROUTING SERVER FOR INDEPENDENT CLIENTS

To change the routing server for independent Message Queuing clients, perform the following steps:

1. Open the **Active Directory Users and Computers** snap-in.
2. Open the **View** menu and select **Users, Groups, and Computers** as containers.
3. Open the **View** menu and select **Advanced Features**.
4. From the console tree, select **MSMQ**.
5. Right-click **msmq** and select **Properties**.
6. Select the **Routing** tab. From the **In Routing Servers** list, select up to three servers or, to remove in-routing servers, click **None**.

Out-routing servers are changed by the same method: follow steps 1 through 5, then on the **Routing** tab, select **Out Routing Servers**.

TESTING CONNECTIVITY USING MQPING

Test connectivity using MQPing with the following steps:

1. Open the **Active Directory Users and Computers** snap-in.
2. Open the **View** menu and select **Users, Groups, and Computers** as containers.
3. Open the **View** menu and select **Advanced Features**.

4. From the console tree, select **MSMQ**.
5. Right click **msmq** and select **Properties**.
6. Select the **Diagnostics** tab and click **MQPing**.

Installing Message Queuing Services

The installation process begins with an analysis of hardware and network requirements. Once these items are mapped out and available, installation of Message Queuing can begin.

PREINSTALLATION HARDWARE CONSIDERATIONS

One key to efficient message queuing is appropriately sized and configured hardware. Hard disk drives, memory, processors, and network adapters all play important roles.

The number and size of hard drives dedicated to message-queuing servers are important because of the requirement to save to disk-recoverable queues, journals, and logs. With this amount of constant writing to disk, seek times can slow message delivery, so using only a single hard drive is not advised. With two disk drives, the messages should go to one disk and the logs to the other. Microsoft recommends disk configuration of five hard disk drives for storing Message Queuing messages, the message log file, transaction logs, virtual memory paging, and application data files.

NOTE To view the Avg. Disk Queue Length counter: **Start** menu → **Administrative Tools** → **Performance Monitor**. If the queue length exceeds 0.6, adding additional disks are probably warranted.

Sizing a disk is also important. Recoverable messages are allocated 4 KB or 250 messages per megabit. Express messages are stored only if virtual memory is not available and need about one-fourth the amount of storage space that recoverable messages require. If the server runs out of memory, paging will occur and demand additional disk space.

As suggested, system memory should be sufficient to minimize paging, but sizing can be difficult. The receiving server may have enough RAM or disk space to store messages only until the associated application is started. Sending computers have a similar problem with accumulation of messages if the network or receiving system is down. Ideally, systems are configured with sufficient memory to accommodate peak message loads. For example, Microsoft estimates the average message size is 150 bytes and the average header size is 1 kilobyte, for a total of 1,150 bytes. Assuming that the maximum number of messages expected through a message-queuing server is 50,000, that number would be multiplied by 1,150 bytes, meaning that a minimum of 57.5 MB should be added.

The speed of the CPU and of network adapters has obvious impacts on message queuing. Use the fastest economically feasible CPU for message-queuing servers and multiple fast network adapters to enhance message throughput.

INSTALLATION CONSIDERATIONS

Installation of Message Queuing can take several steps. First, the Message Queuing servers must be installed. During this process, it is necessary to determine whether to enable routing support. Then independent and dependent clients are installed. This is automatic for existing message-queuing clients. If appropriate, Message Queuing Exchange connectors are applied. In a domain environment, both Active Directory and RCP must be operational. For each site, Message Queuing must be installed on a domain controller before it is installed on member services or clients within the site.

The actual installation involves these steps: **Start** menu → **Administrative Tools** → **Configure Your Server**. From the dialog box, select **Advanced** → **Message Queuing**. The options afforded by the installation wizard are fairly obvious. For specific questions, refer to the Help menu (see Figure 17.8).

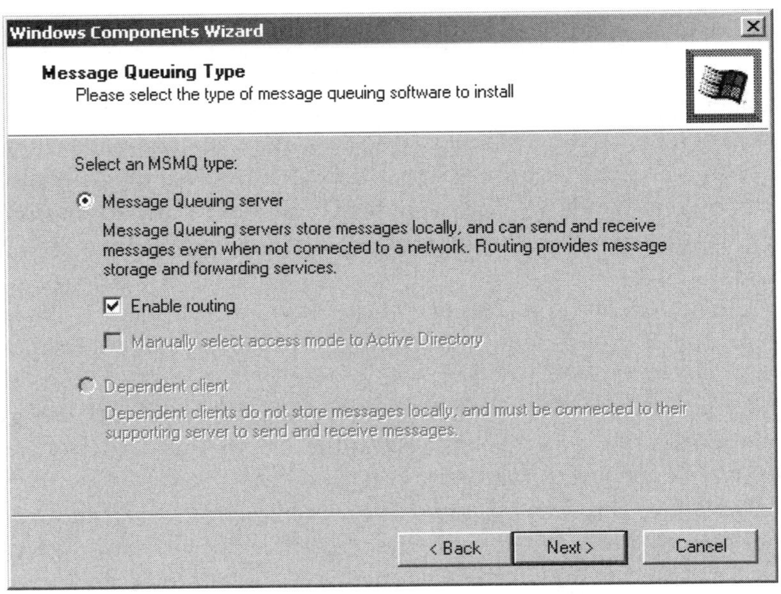

FIGURE 17.8 A Sample Installation Wizard Screen

CAUTION If you are migrating from an existing Windows NT MSMQ server, you must resolve numerous incompatibilities and other issues, many of which can be handled by the Message Queuing Migration Tool wizard. (Previous versions used an MQIS controller server.) The migration tool, which should be run on the MQIS controller and all other MSMQ or Message Queuing client computers, transfers the topology and other information to the Active Directory.

Among the differences that should be noted when upgrading from Windows NT are the following:

- There is no longer an MSMQ-specific database (MQIS) requirement to use the SQL Server to store information such as the network topology.
- There are no MSMQ-specific sites.
- There is no MSMQ-specific enterprise designation.

CAUTION Message-queuing servers can be clustered. If this is desired, group them first and then assign them to a specific node. The major downside to clustering is that messages residing on the node will be lost in a failover.

Administrative Tools for Message Queuing Services

The primary Message Queuing administrative tools are integrated in the Active Directory Users and Computers, Active Directory Sites and Services, and Computer Management snap-ins. The first two tools are used to administer Message Queuing in an enterprise setting, whereas the Computer Management snap-in does this for the local computer or workgroup. These tools replace the standalone MSMQ Explorer used in Windows NT, which is still required for the administration of down-level MSMQ servers that have not been updated to Windows 2000 and Windows Server 2003.

The Active Directory Users and Computers snap-in creates and sets properties of public and private queues, views message properties, and views message-queuing computers with their properties. The properties that can be set and viewed include Admin queue name, format and length, arrived time, authentication, class, delivery mode, encryption options, hash algorithm, message ID, priority, sender ID, sent time, size, and source computer GUID and path.

The Active Directory Sites and Services snap-in views, creates, and sets properties for routing links. It can also create and set foreign computer properties and sites. The Computer Management snap-in views and removes local messages, and views and creates public and private queues and their properties.

FINDING A MESSAGE QUEUING SYSTEM

A message-queuing computer can be located using the following steps:

1. Open the **Active Directory Users and Computers** snap-in.
2. Open the **View** menu and select **Users, Groups, and Computers** as containers.
3. Open the **View** menu and select **Advanced Features**.
4. From the console tree, select the targeted domain and select **Computers**.
5. Sequentially click each computer to see if an MSMQ folder exists.

SETTING A COMPUTER MESSAGE STORAGE SIZE

The message storage size on a computer can be determined as follows:

1. Open the **Active Directory Users and Computers** snap-in.
2. Open the **View** menu and select **Users, Groups, and Computers** as containers.
3. Open the **View** menu and select **Advanced Features**.
4. From the console tree, select **MSMQ.**
5. Right-click **msmq** and select **Properties**.
6. Select the **General** tab. In the **Storage limits** box, check **Limit message storage to (KB)**.
7. Enter the maximum number of kilobytes available for a message.

LIMITING JOURNAL STORAGE SIZE

The journal storage size on a computer can be determined with the following steps:

1. Open the **Active Directory Users and Computers** snap-in.
2. Open the **View** menu and select **Users, Groups, and Computers** as containers.
3. Open the **View** menu and select **Advanced Features**.
4. From the console tree, select **MSMQ**.
5. Right-click **msmq** and select **Properties**.
6. Select the **General** tab. In the **Storage limits** box, check **Limit journal storage to (KB)**.
7. Enter the maximum number of kilobytes available for the journal.

FINDING A QUEUE

To find a queue, take the following steps:

1. Open the **Active Directory Users and Computers** snap-in.
2. Open the **View** menu and select **Users, Groups, and Computers** as containers.
3. Open the **View** menu and select **Advanced Features**.
4. Open the console tree and right-click **Computers or Domain Controllers**. Click **Find**.
5. In the **Find MSMQ Queue** tab, type the appropriate data in the **Label** or **Type ID** text box. Click **Find Now**.

DELETING A QUEUE

Delete a queue this way:

1. Open the **Active Directory Users and Computers** snap-in.
2. Open the **View** menu and select **Users, Groups, and Computers** as containers.
3. Open the **View** menu and select **Advanced Features**.
4. Open the console tree and right-click the targeted queue. Click **Delete**.
5. Click **Yes** to confirm the deletion.

ENABLING OR DISABLING JOURNALS

To enable or disable journaling, take the following steps:

1. Open the **Active Directory Users and Computers** snap-in.
2. Open the **View** menu and select **Users, Groups, and Computers** as containers.
3. Open the **View** menu and select **Advanced Features**.
4. Open the console tree, right-click the targeted queue, and select **Properties**.
5. Select the **General** tab. In the **Journal** section, select the **Enable** check box.

To disable journaling, follow the preceding steps 1 through 4, then on the **General** tab, remove the check mark for **Enable**.

VIEWING MESSAGE PROPERTIES

View message properties according to the following steps:

1. Open the **Active Directory Users and Computers** snap-in.
2. Open the **View** menu and select **Users, Groups, and Computers** as containers.

3. Open the **View** menu and select **Advanced Features**.
4. Open the console tree, right-click **Queue** messages, and right-click the targeted message in the details pane. Select **Properties**.
5. Sequentially review the properties by checking the information configuration in the available tabs.

PURGING ALL MESSAGES

Purge all messages as follows:

1. Open the **Active Directory Users and Computers** snap-in.
2. Open the **View** menu and select **Users, Groups, and Computers** as containers.
3. Open the **View** menu and select **Advanced Features**.
4. Open the console tree. Right-click **Queue** messages, right-click **All** tasks, and select **Purge**.
5. Click **Yes** to confirm the deletion of all messages.

Message Queuing Security Issues and Management

Message Queuing relies on the security features of Windows 2000 and Windows Server 2003, including access control lists (ACLs), encryption, and authentication. Queues, messages, computers, and routing links are all treated by the ACL as objects with associated permissions. The Everyone group is granted Write permission to queues by default. Read permissions allow the user to receive and view messages for a queue. Only the Administrator group has Full Control over all local Message Queuing messages, logs, and queues by default.

The Active Directory Users and Computers snap-in where the MSMQConfiguration object is used to set permissions. First, however, a number of security-related issues must be considered, as follows:

- *Service account*. Message Queuing can be executed through the local system account or a specific user account. For greater security, use a specific user account created for Message Queuing management.
- *Guest account.* The Guest account on Windows Server 2003 is displayed by default. However, it must be enabled to communicate messages between Active Directory domains and the Server's workgroups or Windows NT 4.0 MSMQ. Alternatively, you can create a user account from those systems with Read permission to the Active Directory. This might be preferable to opening the Guest account to anonymous access.
- *Message authentication*. Message authentication is not the default setting. Therefore, ensure that the sender of a message is authenticated with digital

signatures. While this provides a greater level of security, it may slow down the delivery process. Consider this tradeoff before using authentication.

- *MSMQ server authentication*. Message Queuing server certificates are granted to authenticate communication with Message Queuing clients. Although optional, if installed, Server Authentication will be used by both Message Queuing servers and the Internet Information Services for secure HTTP-S Web data exchange.
- *MSMQ encryption*. Message encryption is not used by default. Nevertheless, it is possible to encode and decode messages using the Microsoft Crypto API in conjunction with the Microsoft Base Cryptographic Service Provider, version 2.0 or later. Crypto API must be installed on any Message Queuing system that sends and receives messages. The U.S. version uses 128-bit encryption, whereas international versions do not. The downside of encryption is the reduced speed of message communication because of the requirement to create symmetric keys, encrypt the message with a public key of the receiving system, and use the receiving computer's private key to decrypt the message.
- *Auditing.* The auditing feature permits an administrator to review users who attempt to access the Message Queuing server. Through analysis of the success and failure logs, attempts by unauthorized users are more likely to be detected.

SETTING PERMISSIONS FOR A COMPUTER OR QUEUE

To set the permissions for a computer or queue, do the following:

1. Open the **Active Directory Users and Computers** snap-in.
2. Open the **View** menu and select **Users, Groups, and Computers** as containers.
3. Open the console tree and select the computer or queue.
4. Right-click **msmq** and select **Properties**.
5. Select the **Security** tab and select the desired permissions for the computer or queue.

CHANGING OWNERSHIP OF A COMPUTER OR QUEUE

Change the ownership for a computer or queue as follows:

1. Open the **Active Directory Users and Computers** snap-in.
2. Open the **View** menu and select **Users, Groups, and Computers** as containers.
3. Open the console tree and select the computer or queue.
4. Right-click **msmq** and select **Properties**.

5. Select the **Security** tab and click **Advanced**.
6. Select the **Owner** tab. In the **Change Owner** box, select the new user or group.
7. Click **OK**.

SETTING DEFAULT SECURITY FOR MESSAGE QUEUING STORAGE FILES

Storage of message, log, and transaction files is usually in the WinntSystem32\MSMQ\Storage folder. To set default security for these files, perform the following:

1. Open **Windows Explorer** and navigate to the storage directory.
2. Right-click the storage directory and select **Properties**.
3. Within the **Permissions** option, under **Allow**, select **Full Control**.
4. In the **Name** box, select all users and groups that do not have access to the **MSMQ** directory. Click **Remove**.

SETTING UP COMPUTER OR QUEUE AUDITING

To set the permissions for a computer or queue, take the following steps:

1. Open the **Active Directory Users and Computers** snap-in.
2. Open the **View** menu and select **Users, Groups, or Computers** as containers.
3. Open the console tree and select the computer or queue.
4. Right-click **msmq** and select **Properties**.
5. Select the **Security** tab and click **Advanced**.
6. Select the **Auditing** tab and click **Add**.
7. In the **Select Users, Group, or Computer** dialog box, click the user or group to audit in the **Name** option. Click **OK**.
8. Within the **Auditing Entry** for the **msmq** dialog box, select all objects to audit in the **Apply onto** option. In the **Access** option, select the desired settings.

AUDITING A ROUTING LINK

To audit access to a routing link, do the following:

1. Open the **Active Directory Users and Computers** snap-in.
2. Open the **View** menu and select **Users, Groups, and Computers** as containers.
3. Open the console tree and select the computer or queue.
4. Right-click **msmq**, select the routing link, and select **Properties**.

5. Select the **Security** tab and click **Advanced**.
6. Select the **Auditing** tab. Within the **Access Control Settings** for the **msmq** dialog box, click **Add.**
7. In the **Select Users, Group, or Computer** dialog box, click the user or group to audit in the **Name** option. Click **OK**.
8. From the **Auditing Entry** for the **msmq** dialog box, select all objects to audit in the **Apply onto** option. In the **Access** option, select the desired settings.

Windows Server 2003 Specific Message Queuing Enhancements

While the differences between Windows 2000 and Windows Server 2003 Message Queuing Services are few, the following features deserve mention.

- *Message Queuing deployment.* MSMQ 3.0 clients now use LDAP to directly access Active Directory servers and this eliminates the requirement to deploy MSMQ on domain controllers.
- *Message Queuing Distribution Lists.* Message Queuing permits the sending of messages to Active Directory Distribution Lists (DL) by the "group" class. Usage and format is similar to that of Public Queues: DL=<guid>[@<domain>]. Distribution group object creation and management in the Active Directory is done via the ADSI API or by using the Active Directory MMC snap-in. Only public queues can be elements of DL objects.
- *Message Queuing Alias.* A new Active Directory object is introduced with Windows Server 2003 called Queue Alias. This object acts as a reference to any Message Queuing queue. Private queues can become elements of Message Queuing Distribution List objects.
- *Message Queuing Triggers.* In previous versions, the Triggers feature was delivered by the Software Development Kit (SDK) as an add-on. The Message Queuing Triggers module is now incorporated into the core product. This allows administrators to permit components or executables to be invoked automatically based on message arrival.
- *Message Queuing Internet Messaging.* Message Queuing supports Internet Messaging, a feature that allows the sending of messages to queues on the Internet or an intranet. This is accomplished by introducing a URL-style format name DIRECT=HTTP://*sitename*\msmq*queuename*. Message Queuing Internet/intranet messaging using URL-named queues requires configuration of the Internet Information Services.
- *Message Queuing Real-Time Message Multicasting.* Message Queuing allows message delivery to IP multicast groups using the PGM IP multicast protocol.

Two new operators are introduced: (1) a new queue formatname with syntax: "MULTICAST=<multicast IP address>[:<port address>]"; (2) a new queue property with a multicast address: MSMQQueueInfo.MulticastAddress.

Postscript on Message Queuing

Since Message Queuing and networking, the Active Directory, and other computer management topics are interwoven, we chose not to replicate much of that information here but instead provide a summary view of this application. When installing and deploying Message Queuing, refer to the latest release notes and appropriate sections in this book.

Message Queuing can be used to connect with Exchange Server. Additional information on this feature is available from online Help.

SYSTEM MANAGEMENT SERVER

System Management Server (SMS) 2.0 and 2003 are useful add-on products for system administration. It is one of three primary auxiliary management tools; the others are Application Center 2000 and Microsoft Operations Manager (described in the next section).

SMS is not part of the core Windows Server 2003 operating system, but some of its features can be very valuable in deployment and administration. Since SMS is an optional component, we provide a review of its key features rather than in-depth "how to" instructions. Despite its summary treatment here, however, SMS should be considered seriously for relatively large and complex enterprises.

The five primary SMS features that can be used effectively in the administration of a Windows Server 2003 enterprise are:

- Software and hardware inventory gathering and management
- Software installation and distribution
- Remote tools
- Software metering
- Network diagnostics

System Management Server 2.0 depends on Microsoft SQL Server 6.5 or 7.0 (or later) to store and manage SMS data. SQL Server is available as an independent database. Whether you license SMS independently or as part of the BackOffice suite, you must still calculate the use and cost of installing a local or remote SQL Server.

System Management Server 2.0 supports administrative snap-ins to the Microsoft Management Console (MMC). SMS service pack 2 must be employed.

Software and Hardware Inventory

In Chapter 4 we underscored the importance of inventorying hardware and software as part of Server planning and deployment. SMS can streamline this necessary step by automatically collecting software and hardware data and creating a dynamic inventory database. Moreover, it permits filtering of information so that both global and very granular inventories can be maintained. Through the use of SMS, specific software versions can be obtained, which permits rapid evaluation of enterprise upgrade status. For example, the hardware inventory evaluates a system's components according to processor manufacturer, revision levels, and type.

Software Installation and Distribution

The problems associated with centralized software installation and distribution to a remote computer or groups of computers are greatly reduced by SMS because it automates and schedules installation for minimal impact on the end user. Through the use of SMS's software inventory features, it is possible to create what is known as collector groups. The system administrator should use these to gather systems with the same processor, user group, or existing software, and then, with this information in hand, apply specific software upgrades to define collector groups automatically. In this way, the inventory database is automatically updated.

The SMS installer creates application-specific scripts to support this distribution process. Physical distribution can be direct to the client disk or through the posting of the application to a Web or FTP site.

Remote Administrative Tools

Using SMS, the system administrator can gain access to a remote client system and display the contents locally. By seeing exactly what is displayed on the user's end, the administrator can troubleshoot system problems. Moreover, an interactive chat feature permits the administrator and end user to discuss problems on screen. Client computer commands and applications can be executed with Remote Execute. Remote Boot restarts the client computer.

Software Metering

The software-monitoring feature is used primarily to manage licenses and identify unsupported or unregistered packages. Monitoring concurrent software usage throughout an enterprise makes it easy to determine if too many or too few licenses exist for a given software title. The monitoring tool is set to access and restrict use of applications by the individual user, user group, computer, quota, or license. Mobile users can also use it to check software licenses when not connected to the network.

Network Diagnostics

SMS extends Windows Server 2003 network administrative and monitoring with its network discover and trace functions. These functions provide a framework of the network structure in a dynamic enterprise environment by discovering and tracing network devices. By using SMS, a network topology map can be easily generated.

The Network Monitor is used primarily to troubleshoot a network by capturing packets or frames and "sniffing" them. The information revealed is then displayed and filtered. The system administrator can edit network packets (see Figure 17.9).

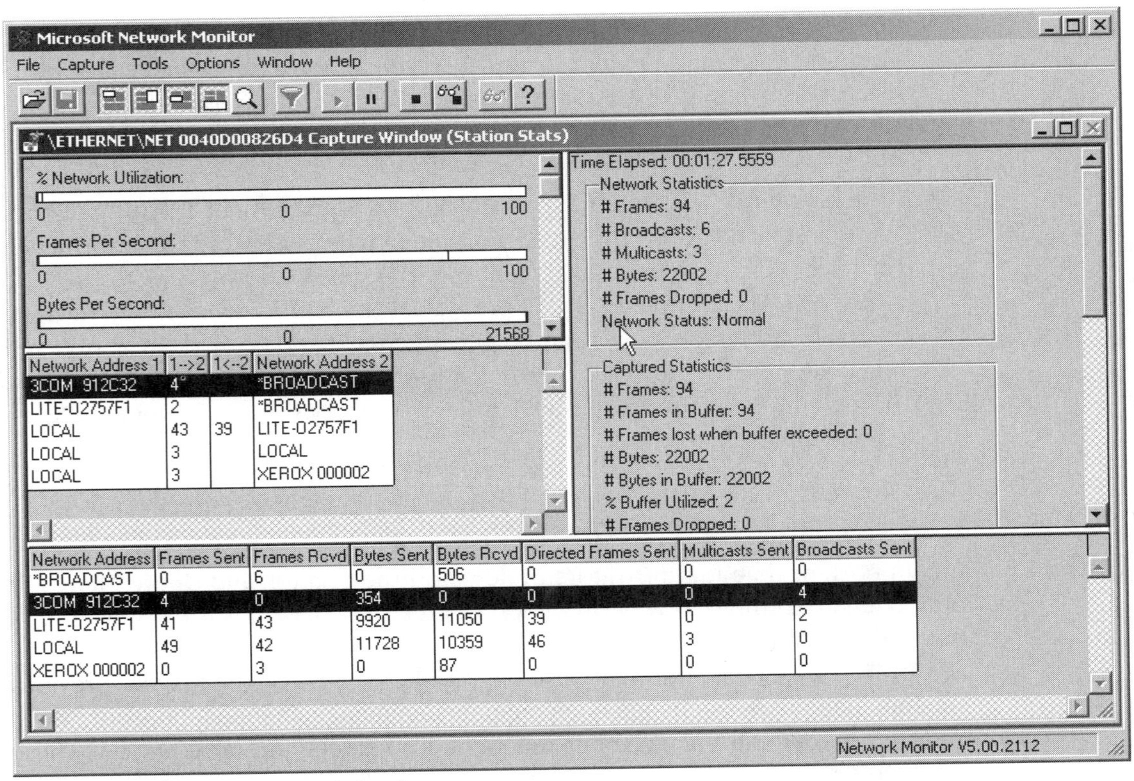

FIGURE 17.9 The SMS Network Monitor

MICROSOFT OPERATIONS MANAGER

Microsoft Operations Manager is the most recent of the optional management suites offered to support Windows 2000 and Windows 2003 servers. The focus of MOM is to provide event and performance monitoring. This product is particularly useful for administrators charged with monitoring Active Directory, Exchange Server, and SQL Server. The relatively open API has also permitted third parties to develop add-ons for cross-platform monitoring from within MOM. The primary architectural features touted by Microsoft include:

- *Enterprise-class scalability.* MOM uses a three-tier architecture designed to handle hundreds of millions of fully redundant and load-balanced events per day.
- *Intelligent agents.* MOM's agents are based on the rule sets defined by the administrators at a central console. The local agents filter, aggregate, and consolidate event streams. They will also trigger local actions.
- *Automated agents and rule deployment.* MOM monitors Active Directory and Windows NT domains to automatically detect and report new servers, applications, and services. MOM loads only appropriate rule sets. Deployment of agents and rule sets can then be set to occur automatically. MOM updates local rule sets as applications are installed and removed.
- *Interoperability.* The integration of Windows Management Instrumentation (WMI) and MOM allows the intake of a wide range of events and performance data from Windows Server 2003, Windows 2000, or Windows NT systems. Additionally, MOM can monitor SNMP event data (traps) for any specified devices. These SNMP trap messages can be generated as part of any defined rule and then delivered to a third-party SNMP management products like HP OpenView. Through the Syslog protocol, MOM can even monitor live events from UNIX systems and many network devices.

NOTE It is important that administrators understand the relationship of the Microsoft optional management tools. Application Center 2000 performs the classic role of managing software applications and licenses. It is targeted at enterprises that manage Web-based and component-based applications. As described in the previous section, SMS provides change and configuration management. By contrast, MOM delivers operational management functions for servers and applications. These products are designed to work in tandem and are generally a good investment for medium to large enterprises.

Microsoft Operations Manager Features

MOM uses the Microsoft Management Console by default to provide a consistent administrative interface. Through the MMC, status and configuration nodes should be snapped in along with other related management tools and applications. This allows administrators to move through the hierarchical tree to access events, rules, reports, and configuration activities. Additionally, MOM's MMC snap-in supports context-sensitive tasks directly from the Alert box or event being viewed. This means that tasks such as Terminal Services sessions or command-line functions can be launched directly from MOM.

DISTRIBUTE EVENT MANAGEMENT

MOM captures system and applications events from Windows-based systems distributed throughout the enterprise and aggregates them into a central event repository. This allows the administrator to consolidate events so that a view of server and service availability can be reviewed easily. In addition to event summaries, a detailed event stream can be obtained for specific troubleshooting activities.

ADMINISTRATIVE DEFINED RULES MANAGEMENT

Once established by the administrator, MOM reacts automatically to incoming message streams. The system can be configured to respond with a predefined action to a specific fault scenario. Alternatively, MOM will consolidate messages so the analysis can be made of broader based events. MOM's rules can be made to react intelligently to anticipated event patterns. These patterns trigger actions including sending alerts to the administrator. Rules may be linked to an event sequence of the Microsoft Knowledge Base articles, thereby providing guidance on probable causes and approved responses to a specific problem.

ALERT MANAGEMENT

Any MOM rule can be configured to generate specific alerts that are associated with severity levels. An alert can represent a single event or multiple events from many sources. One of the nicer features is the ability to trace the history of a given alert. The events can be associated and then used to consult related Knowledge Base articles. Functionally, alerts can trigger e-mail messages, pages, and Simple Network Management Protocol traps. Scripts can even be used to notify administrators of emerging problems.

PERFORMANCE MONITORING

MOM monitors key performance thresholds. Administrators customize and add rules that allow them to monitor trends of system and application performance.

These reports are useful for historical reporting and capacity planning. Local and aggregated thresholds are also used to generate alerts and actions. As system changes occur or application behavior demands intervention, the appropriate alerts are broadcast.

GRAPHICAL REPORTING TOOLS AND WEB REPORTING

MOM provides access to a broad range of preconfigured reports and charts. This allows administrators to review at a glance the status of systems and services on the network. By quickly reviewing clean graphical output, the administrator can plan changes to the infrastructure. Alternatively, MOM can generate HTML-based snapshots of all generated reports. Instead of using MMC, these reports can be exported to a Web server to provide access from Web browsers.

OPTIONAL MANAGEMENT PACKS

To reduce an administrator's burden, Microsoft offers management packs that consist of preconfigured MOM rule sets and Knowledge Base articles. Each pack provides rules for a specific range of applications or services. Developed and refined by experts, the management packs provide an off-the-shelf solution plus a strong foundation for advanced administrators to customize and extend basic MOM functionality.

Most management packs are optional, but several are included with MOM including one that enables management of critical Windows services such as Active Directory service and Internet Information Services. Additional management packs are available from Microsoft and third-party vendors. Among the products and services optionally supported are BackOffice and Windows Server 2003 enterprise applications, plus a wide range of enterprise applications.

WINDOWS SCRIPTING HOST

Windows Scripting Host (WSH 2.0) is a language-independent scripting engine used to automate administrative tasks, such as controlling network connections. WSH supports Windows 2000, Windows NT, and Windows 9x environments. The earlier version of WSH supported only Microsoft languages, such as Visual Basic VBScripts and JScript.

Microsoft and third parties are now providing WSH 2.0 with an augmented list of scripts to support other environments, including Visual Basic, Java, HTML, Perl, and XML. Previously, only Windows native scripts such as the MS-DOS command language were supported.

NOTE An abundance of scripts is available on the Internet and from specialized programming books. We have included only a few scripts here because they tend to be enterprise-specific or task-specific. Instead, we provide an overview of WSH that should give you sufficient information to host your own scripts.

For readers who would like to create scripts, we recommend the Microsoft Windows Scripting Host Programmer's Reference site. A number of sample scripts can be downloaded from *http://www.microsoft.com/scripting*.

Using WSH to Run Scripts

There is both a Windows version and a command-line version of WSH. The Windows version (wscript.exe) provides the standard GUI interface to set properties. The command-line version (cscript.exe) uses switches to do this.

RUNNING WSCRIPT.EXE

Scripts can be launched within the Windows environment in several ways. In Windows Explorer, simply double-click the icon identified as a script, as shown in Figure 17.10. Alternatively, from the **Start** → **Run** command line or the **command**

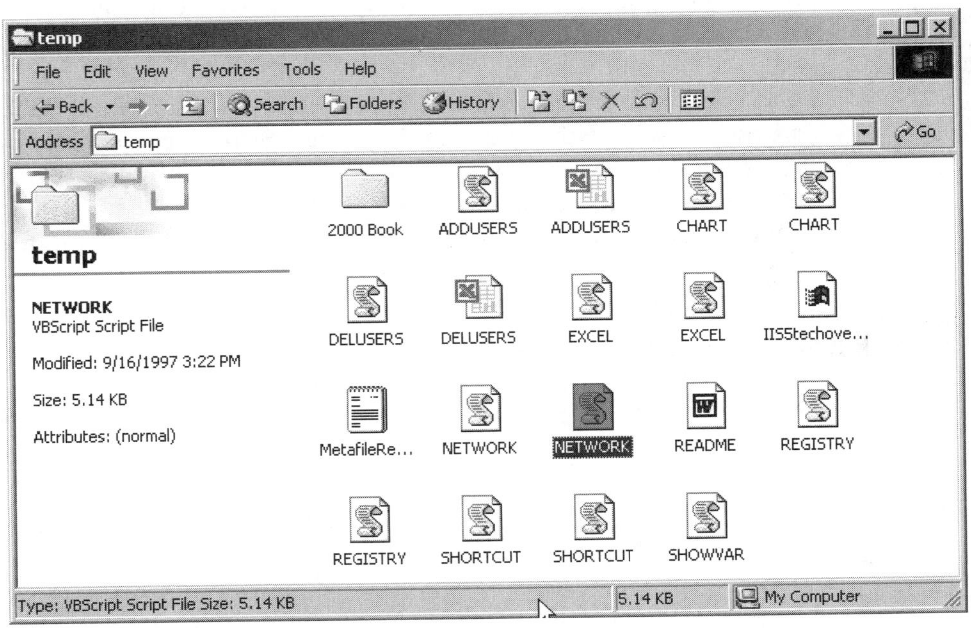

FIGURE 17.10 Launching a Script from Explorer

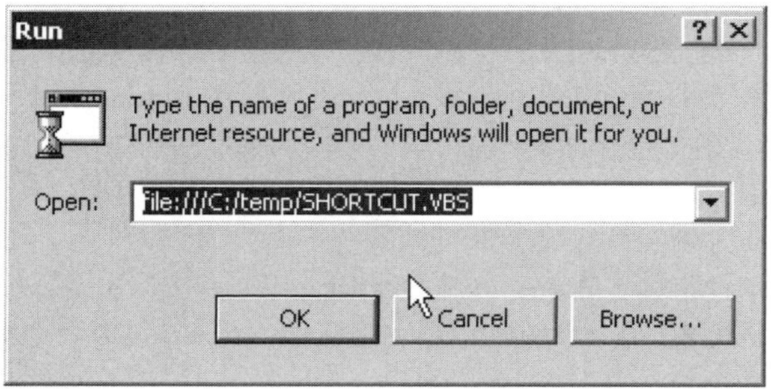

FIGURE 17.11 Launching a Script from the Run Command Line

prompt, enter the name of the script and click **OK** or **Enter**, respectively, as shown in Figure 17.11.

Setting Properties for the Wscript.exe Environment

Two properties can be set for a Wscript.exe-launched script. From **Windows Explorer** → right-click the targeted script and select **Properties,** where you will see two tabs for scripts residing on a FAT/FAT 32 partition and four available for NTFS—common to both are the **General** and **Script** tabs. From the **General** tab, you can set the script to assume a readable or hidden attribute. From the **Script** tab, you can automatically stop the script after the specified (nn) number of seconds, and you can display a logo banner. The two additional **NTFS** partition tabs are **Security** for setting user permissions and **Summary,** as shown in Figure 17.12.

When properties are set on a script, a text file with the .wsh extension on its name is created as a control file for the script's settings. The .wsh file uses the same name as the script and can also be used to launch the script in the manner just described.

Running Cscript.exe

The command-line version of WSH is launched from the command prompt. It uses the following syntax:

```
Cscript [script name] [host options] [script options]
```

The only required item is the script name. The host options enable or disable WSH options. The script options are passed directly to the script and are preceded by a single slash (/).

Table 17.1 lists the functions available for the Cscript.exe tool.

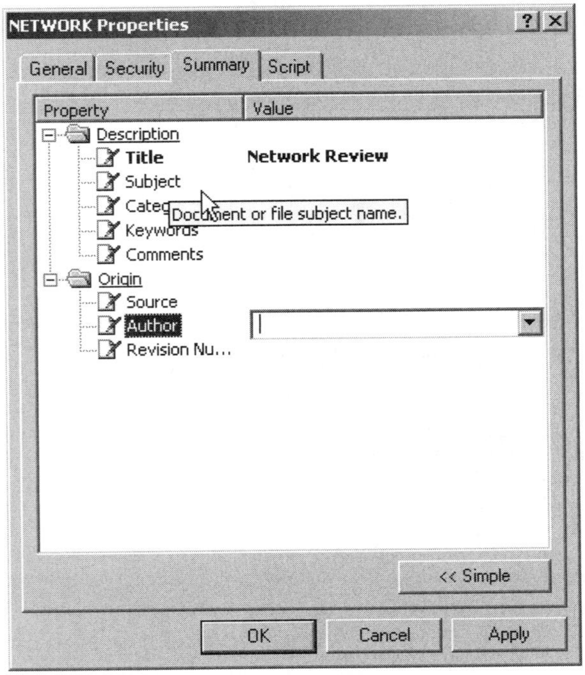

FIGURE 17.12 The NTFS Partition Summary Properties Tab

TABLE 17.1 Cscript.exe Host Parameters

Option	Description
//I	The default setting; permits interactive prompts and the display of errors.
//B	Batch mode; suppresses command displays and user prompts.
//D	Enables the debugger.
//E:engine	Specifies the script language engine.
//Job:xxx	Specifies a batch script to execute.
//T:nn	Enables a time-out on script execution after (nn) seconds.
//logo	The default; displays a logo banner.
//nolog	Suppresses the logo banner.
//H:C script or //H:W script	Registers which version of WSH is the default—C for cscript, W for wscript.
//S	Saves the command-line options.
/?	Displays command usage.

SAMPLE WSH SCRIPTS

Example 1: Programming with the Windows Scripting Host allows direct access to the Active Directory via Active Directory Services Interface (ADSI).

```
  'Display Objects in the Engineering Organizational Unit
Set ou = GetObject ("LDAP://OU=Engineering,DC=Entcert1,DC=Com")
For each obj in ou
  WScript.Echo obj.Name
Next
```

Example 2: Properties relating to the Scripting Engine and executing script are accessible through script and argument properties.

```
'Display Script Properties
wscript.Echo Wscript.Application
wscript.Echo Wscript.Arguments(0)
WScript.Echo Wscript.FullName
WScript.Echo Wscript.Name
WScript.Echo Wscript.Path
WScript.Echo Wscript.ScriptFullName
WScript.Echo Wscript.ScriptName
WScript.Echo Wscript.Version
' Display script argument properties
WScript.Echo Wscript.arguments.Count
WScript.Echo Wscript.arguments.length
WScript.Echo Wscript.arguments.Item
```

Example 3: Environmental parameters from four environments are accessible by setting the environment context.

```
'Create shell object
Set WshShell = Wscript.CreateObject("Wscript.Shell")
' Set variables environmental variable access
' of system, User, Volatile, process
Set SystemEnvironment = WshShell.Environment("System")
Set UserEnvironment = WshShell.Environment("User")
Set VolatileEnvironment = WshShell.Environment("Volatile")
Set ProcessEnvironment = WshShell.Environment("Process")
' Display example parameters from each environment set
wscript.Echo SystemEnvironment("PATH")
wscript.Echo UserEnvironment("PROMPT")
wscript.Echo VolatileEnvironment("OS")
wscript.Echo ProcessEnvironment("PROCESSOR_ARCHITECTURE")
```

Example 4: Advanced dialog window capabilities are available and based on Win32 user interface programming. The Registry may be read and modified through shell methods.

```
' Registry reading and writing
Set WshShell = Wscript.CreateObject("Wscript.Shell")
' Simple Popup window
```

```
WshShell.Popup "Test Popup Window"
' Popup Window with advanced options following Win32 conventions
WshShell.Popup "Test Popup Window",10, "SysAdmin Tool", 4
' Read from the systems registry
str = WshShell.RegRead ("HKCU\Environment\TEMP")
WshShell.Popup str
```

Example 5: The network functions allow drives and printers to be mapped to users and systems throughout the network.

```
' Network methods can be used to add and remove printers and network
drives.
Set WshNetwork = Wscript.CreateObject("Wscript.Network")
' Print out computer name
Wscript.echo WshNetwork.ComputerName
'Add a printer
WshNetwork.AddPrinterConnection"Laser"."\\ecc3s\HP Printer"
'Map a network drive
WshNetwork.MapNetWorkDrive "M:","\\ecc3s\aaECC"
'Display Username and domain
Wscript.echo WshNetwork.Username
Wscript.echo WshNetwork.UserDomain
```

Example 6: Shortcuts can be added to the desktop and assigned properties.

```
' Shortcut properties allow the modification of a shortcut's
arguments, Description
' Hotkey, Iconlocation, TargetPath,WindowStyle and WorkingDirectory.
'
Set WshShell = Wscript.CreateObject("Wscript.WshShell")
strFavoritespath = WshShell.SpecialFolders("My Documents")
Set NewShortcut = WshShell.CreateShortcut(strFavoritespath &
"\short.lnk)
NewShortcut.TargetPath = "path to application here"
NewShortcut.Save
```

POSTSCRIPT

This chapter discusses the concepts and base-level use of five relatively unrelated services. Since, unlike other Windows Server 2003 features, these services will not be applied universally by system administrators, we provide a summary, not a comprehensive review. If you will be employing these technologies, we hope this chapter provides the foundation necessary to do so. Use the release notes and online Help with these products to fill in the necessary details.

Appendix

Windows Server 2003 Commands and Utilities

This appendix is designed as a reference tool for users and system administrators. It defines and discusses a number of procedures and commands with options that are used in the day-to-day operation of a Windows Server 2003 system. The appendix begins with a review of command-line options available for the first time in 2003. The other commands covered in the appendix are common to both Windows 2000 and Windows Server 2003 products. These commands and utilities are listed alphabetically in the index. Here they have been broken down into several categories, as follows:

- Command-line features new to Windows Server 2003
- Backup
- Batch
- Comparison
- Compression
- Display
- File management
- File manipulation
- Miscellaneous
- Networking
- Ownership
- Print
- Search

- System management
- Resource Kit support tools

We distinguish procedures and commands in this way:

- *Procedures* are methods for accomplishing a task using the Windows Server 2003 graphical interface.
- *Commands* are executed within the command prompt, which invokes the Virtual DOS Machine (VDM).

In some cases, we provide both procedures and commands to give the system administrator a broader view of the capabilities of Windows Server 2003.

Within Windows Server 2003 two methods are available to review the file hierarchy: one uses the **My Computer** icon and its accompanying windows and the other uses Windows Explorer. We have chosen to focus primarily on Windows Server 2003 Explorer, which is accessed via **Start** → **Programs** → **Accessories** → **Windows Server 2003 Explorer**. Procedures that can be completed using the My Computer windows will be referenced as appropriate. The command prompt is accessed via **Start** → **Programs** → **Accessories** → **command prompt**. In this mode, Windows Server 2003 is not case-sensitive, so commands and their parameters and options may be entered in either lowercase or uppercase. Here lowercase is used as a matter of style. In addition, Windows Server 2003 has a series of what are referred to as "net commands." These commands assist the system administrator in maintaining the network and are distributed among the other sections where appropriate.

The following syntax conventions are used in the appendix:

- Command names are lowercase.
- *Lowercase italic* represents variables that must be replaced in the command. For example, *filename* must be replaced with the actual file name on which the command will operate.
- [Brackets] surround optional parameters.
- {Braces} surround a list of items, options, or parameters from which one must be chosen.
- The pipe symbol (|) separates options from which one must be chosen. In this case, it works like an "or"; that is, you must choose one or the other.

Navigating the command prompt is very similar to working in a "dumb terminal" environment. Keystrokes are generally interpreted individually. Special shortcuts, known as *doskeys,* facilitate navigation. The following the keys are used most often:

- *UP ARROW* recalls the command used immediately before the command that brought the current screen.

- *DOWN ARROW* recalls the command used immediately after the command that brought the current screen.
- *PAGE UP* recalls the oldest command used in the session.
- *PAGE DOWN* recalls the most recent command used.
- *LEFT ARROW* moves the insertion point back one character.
- *RIGHT ARROW* moves the insertion point forward one character.
- *CTRL-LEFT ARROW* moves the insertion point back one word.
- *CTRL-RIGHT ARROW* moves the insertion point forward one word.
- *HOME* moves the insertion point to the beginning of the line.
- *END* moves the insertion point to the end of the line.
- *ESC* clears the command.
- *F1* copies one character from the same column in the template.
- *F2* searches forward in the template for the next key typed after F2 is pressed.
- *F3* copies the remainder of the template to the command line.
- *F4* deletes characters from the current insertion point position up to the character specified.
- *F5* copies the template into the current command line.
- *F6* places an end-of-file character (CTRL-Z) at the current point.
- *F7* displays all commands for this program stored in memory in a pop-up box.
- *F8* displays all commands in the history buffer that start with the characters in the current command.
- *F9* prompts for a history buffer command number, then displays the command.

For more detail on a particular command or procedure, please refer to Windows Server 2003 Help, which can be accessed from the **Start** menu or from the window in which you are working.

NEW COMMAND-LINE TOOLS WITH WINDOWS SERVER 2003

Windows Server 2003 enhances the command-line functionality for administrators. This section highlights administratively useful command-line functions that are new or significantly changed. This section lists many but certainly not all of the new command-line tools available with Server 2003. Also, look for Microsoft to add command-line tools to subsequent Windows .NET Service Packs.

The following command-line tools are available via **Start** → **More Programs** → **Accessories** → **command prompt** or via **Start** → **Run** → **cmd.exe**.

bootcfg Command

Bootcfg.exe provides the viewing or sets the properties of the boot.ini file on a local or remote server. This tool is not available on 64-bit versions of the operating system.

The following are examples of the **bootfg** command:

```
BOOTCFG /Copy /?
BOOTCFG /Delete /?
BOOTCFG /Query /?
BOOTCFG /Raw /?
BOOTCFG /Timeout /?
BOOTCFG /EMS /?
BOOTCFG /Debug /?
BOOTCFG /Addsw /?
BOOTCFG /Rmsw /?
BOOTCFG /Dbg1394 /?
BOOTCFG /Default /?
BOOTCFG /?
```

TABLE A.1 bootcfg Command Options

Option	Description
/Copy	Makes a copy of an existing boot entry [operating systems] section for which you can add OS options.
/Delete	Deletes an existing boot entry in the [operating systems] section of the Boot.ini file. You must specify the entry # to delete.
/Query	Displays the current boot entries and their settings.
/Raw	Allows the user to specify any switch options to be added for a specified boot entry.
/Timeout	Allows the user to change the timeout value.
/Default	Allows the user to change the default boot entry.
/EMS	Allows the user to configure the /redirect switch for headless support for a boot entry.
/Debug	Allows the user to specify the port and baud rate for remote debugging for a specified boot entry.
/Addsw	Allows the user to add predefined switches for a specific boot entry.
/Rmsw	Allows the user toremove predefined switches for a specific boot entry.
/Dbg1394	Allows the user to configure 1394 port debugging for a specified boot entry.
/?	Displays this help/usage.

bitscli Command

The Bitscli.exe program manages Background Intelligent Transfer Service (BITS) downloads.

choice Command

Choice selects an option from a menu for batch file execution. The **choice** command prompts the user to make a selection in a batch program. It displays a prompt and pauses for the user to choose from among a set of user keys such as **Yes, No,** and **Continue**. The syntax is

```
choice [/c choices] [/n] [/cs] [/t nnnn /d choice] [/m text]
```

clip Command

Clip.exe redirects command-line output to the clipboard from where it can be copied and pasted into graphical user interface (GUI) applications. To copy the list of contents in the c:\Windows folder onto the Clipboard, at the C:\Windows prompt type

```
dir | clip
```

compress Command

Compress.exe compresses one or more files into a cab file. The syntax is

```
compress [-r] [-d] [-zx] [-z] [-zq[n]] Source Destination
compress -r [-d] [-zx] [-z] [-zq[n]] Source [Destination]
```

TABLE A.2 choice Command Options

Option	Description
/**c** *choices*	Defines the user option keys. When displayed, they appear in brackets ([]), and are followed by a question mark. If you do not specify /**c** *choices*, choice.exe displays `[Y, N]` by default.
/**n**	Hides the user option keys.
/**cs**	Specifies case sensitivity. By default, user option keys are not case-sensitive.
/**m** *text*	Specifies the text to be displayed before the prompt.

TABLE A.3 compress Command Options

Option	Description
-r	Rename expanded files.
-d	Update compressed files only if they are not up-to-date.
-zx	Use LZX compression.
-z	Use MS-ZIP compression.
-zq[*n*]	Use quantum compression. Optional level *n* must be in the range 1 to 7. The default is 4.

driverquery Command

DriverQuery.exe provides a view of the currently loaded device drivers and their memory usage. The **driverquery** command displays a list of all installed device drivers and their properties. The syntax is

```
driverquery  [/s computer] [/u domain\user /p password]
[/fo {TABLE|LIST|CSV}] [/nh] [/v] [/si]
```

TABLE A.4 driverquery Command Options

Option	Qualifier	Description
/s	*computer*	Specifies the name or IP address of a remote computer with the local computer the default.
/u	*domain\user*	Runs the command with the account permissions of the user specified by user or domain\user. The default is the permissions of the logged-on user issuing the command.
/p	*password*	Specifies the password of the user account that is specified in the **/u** parameter.
/fo {**TABLE**|**LIST**|**CSV**}		Specifies the format to display the driver information. Valid values are **TABLE**, (the default), **LIST**, and **CSV**.
/nh		Omits the header row from the displayed driver information. Valid when the **/fo** parameter is set to **TABLE** or **CSV**.
/v		Specifies that detailed driver information be displayed.
/si		Displays digital signature information . . . signed and unsigned device drivers.

Directory Services Commands

The Directory Services commands are a suite of tools used to manage the various objects in Active Directory. Theses command-line tools are used to perform queries for information in the directory. The following list briefly describes some commands:

- **dsadd** creates an object instance of a specified type to the Active Directory.
- **dsmod** modifies select attributes of an existing object in the Active Directory.
- **dsrm** removes an object or the complete subtree of an object in the Active Directory.
- **dsmove** moves an object from its current location to a new parent location within the same naming context or to rename an object in the Active Directory.
- **dsquery** finds objects in the Active Directory that match a specified search criteria.
- **dsget** gets or views select properties of an existing object in the Active Directory when the specific location of the object to be viewed is known.

All of the command-line tools can operate on a variety of object types in the directory. The identity of the targeted object is specified following the object type and in the format of a distinguished name such as CN=Jon Smith,OU=Sales, DC=microsoft,DC=com.

EXECUTING COMMANDS ON THE NETWORK

Each tool has parameters that allow you to specify the server, domain, user name, and password to use when executing the command. If parameters are not entered, the tool assumes the local server, domain, user name, and password.

Here is an example of the **dsadd computer** command:

```
dsadd computer ObjectDN
    [-samid SAMName]
    [-desc Description]
    [-loc Location]
    [-memberof Group ...]
    [(-s Server | -d Domain)]
    [-u UserName]
    [-p (Password | *)]
    [-q]
```

COMMAND SYNTAX

The Directory Services commands use strict conventions to document the syntax of the DS command-line tools:

- The option for a targeted object's distinguished name attribute is displayed as *ObjectDN* or, when multiple objects may be specified, *ObjectDN* ....
- A command does not perform any operation without an object type, such as **computer**.
- The targeted object is obtained from standard input if the user does not specify an object at the command prompt.
- The user must type parameters that appear in **bold** exactly as they appear in the syntax.

```
dsmod computer ObjectDN ...
     [-desc Description]
     [-loc Location]
     [-disabled (yes | no)]
     [-reset]
     [(-s Server | -d Domain)]
     [-u UserName]
     [-p {Password | *}]
     [-C]
     [-q]
```

- Parameters in "[" and "]" (square brackets) indicate that they are optional.
- Parameters or options separated by the "|" (pipe) character represent a choice of alternatives.
- All alternatives for a parameter's value are enclosed in "(" and ")" (parentheses).
- If the distinguished names themselves contain spaces, then they should be enclosed with " " (double quotation marks).
- Commas that are not used as separators in distinguished names must be escaped with the backslash ("\") character (for example, "CN=Company\, Inc.,CN=Users,DC=microsoft,DC=com"). Backslashes used in distinguished names must be escaped with a backslash (for example, "CN=Sales\\ Latin America,OU=Distribution Lists,DC=microsoft,DC=com").
- Parameters are not case-sensitive.
- Command-line parameters can be specified with either the "-" (hyphen) or the "/" (forward slash).
- A command-line parameter and any corresponding values for the parameter should be separated by at least one space.
- Space and "newline" characters are treated as argument separators.
- An empty string or null string value can be specified by "" (double quotation marks).

TABLE A.5 eventcreate Command Options

Option	Qualifier	Description
/s	*computer*	Specifies the name or IP address of a remote computer with the local computer default.
/u	*domain\user*	Runs the command with the account permissions of the user specified by *user* or *domain\user*. The default is the permissions of the user on the computer issuing the command.
/p	*password*	Specifies the password of the user account that is specified in the **/u** parameter.
/l {**APPLICATION**|**SYSTEM**}		Specifies the name of the event log where the event will be created. APPLICATION and SYSTEM are valid names of logs.
/so	*SrcName*	Specifies the source to use for the event.
/t {**ERROR**|**WARNING**|**INFORMATION**|**SUCCESSAUDIT**|**FAILUREAUDIT**}		Specifies the type of event to create. The valid types are ERROR, WARNING, INFORMATION, SUCCESSAUDIT, and FAILUREAUDIT.
/id	*EventID*	Specifies the event's ID. A valid ID is any number from 1 through 65535.
/d	*description*	Specifies the description to use for the newly created event.

eventcreate Command

Eventcreate.exe creates a user-defined event and enters it into any of the event logs. The **eventcreate** command enables an administrator to create a customized event in a specified event log. The syntax is

```
eventcreate [/s computer [/u domain\user [/p password]] {[/l
{APPLICATION|SYSTEM}]|[/so SrcName]} /t {ERROR|WARNING|INFORMATION|
SUCCESSAUDIT|FAILUREAUDIT} /id EventID /d description
```

Eventquery.vbs Script

Eventquery.vbs specifies the type of events to extract from the event log; the selected events can be displayed on the screen or saved to a file. The script lists the events and event properties from one or more event logs. The syntax is

```
eventquery[.vbs] [/s computer [/u domain\user [/p password]]] [/fi
FilterName] [/fo {TABLE|LIST|CSV}] [/r EventRange [/nh] [/v] [/l
[APPLICATION] [SYSTEM] [SECURITY] ["DNS server"] [UserDefinedLog]
[DirectoryLogName] [*] ]
```

TABLE A.6 eventquery Command Options

Option	Qualifier	Description
/s	*computer*	Specifies the name or IP address of a remote computer (local computer default).
/u	*domain\user*	Runs the script with the account permissions of the user specified by *user* or *domain\user*. The default is the permissions of the computer issuing the command.
/p	*password*	Specifies the password of the user account that is specified in the **/u** parameter.
/fi	*FilterName*	Specifies the types of events to include in or exclude from the query.
/fo {**TABLE**|**LIST**|**CSV**}		Specifies the format to use for the output. Valid values are **table**, **list**, and **csv**.
/r	*EventRange*	Specifies the range of events to list.
/nh		Suppresses column headers in the output. Valid only for **table** and **csv** formats.
/v		Specifies that verbose event information be displayed in the output.
/l [**APPLICATION**] [**SYSTEM**] [**SECURITY**] [**"DNS server"**]	[*UserDefinedLog*] [*DirectoryLogName*] [*]]	Specifies the log(s) to monitor. Valid values are **Application**, **System**, **Security**, **"DNS server"**, a user-defined log, and Directory log. **"DNS server"** can be used only if the DNS service is running on the computer specified by the **/s** parameter. To specify more than one log to monitor, reuse the **/l** parameter. The wildcard (*) can be used and is the default.

eventtriggers Command

The Eventtriggers.exe program launches a process based on the occurrence of an event written to the event log. The **eventtrigger** command provides the ability create, delete, and query based on triggers.

extract Command

Extract.exe extracts one or more files from a cab file. The syntax is

```
extract cabinet [filename ...] [/a] [{/d | /e}] [/l dir] [/y]
extract source {[newName] | destination /c} [/y]
```

TABLE A.7 extract Command Options

Option	Qualifier	Description
cabinet		Specifies the name of a cabinet file containing two or more files.
filename		Specifies the name of the file to extract from the cabinet. You can use wildcard characters and multiple file names separated by blanks.
/a		Executes all cabinets and follows the cabinet chain starting in the first cabinet mentioned.
/d		Displays the directory of the cabinet file. Use **/d** with the cabinet file name to avoid extracting the files.
/e		Extracts all files from *cabinet*. Use **/e** instead of *.* to extract all files.
/l	*dir*	Extracts files to location *dir*; current directory is the default.
/y		Does not prompt before overwriting an existing file.

forfiles Command

Forfiles.exe operates only on selected file types (such as .bat only or .exe only). The **forfiles** command elects files in a folder or tree for batch processing. You must use **forfiles** within a batch file. The syntax is

```
forfiles [/pPath] [/mSearchMask] [/s] [/cCommand]
[/d{+|/}{mm/dd/yyyy|dd}]
```

freedisk Command

Freedisk.exe allows operation if a specified percentage of disk space is free. The **freedisk** command checks to see if a specified amount of disk space is available when software is being installed. The syntax is

```
freedisk [/s System [/u [Domain\]User [/p [password]]]] [/d Drive] [Value]
```

gettype Command

Gettype.exe determines product type (such as Windows XP Professional, Windows Server 2003, and so on). This establishes the system environment variable ERRORLEVEL to the value associated with the specified **gettype** command-line option. The syntax is

```
gettype [/role | /sp | /ver | /minv | /majv | /type | /build]
```

TABLE A.8 forfiles Command Options

Option	Qualifier	Description
/p	*Path*	Specifies the path on which to start searching. Current folder is the default folder.
/m	*SearchMask*	Searches files according to *SearchMask*. The default *SearchMask* is *.*.
/s		Instructs **forfiles** to recurse into subdirectories.
/c	*Command*	Indicates a command to run on each file. You must wrap command strings with spaces in quotation marks. The default command is **"cmd /c echo @file"**.
/d	{+|–}{*mm/dd/yyyy* |*dd*}	Defines files with a date greater than or equal to (+) or less than or equal to (–) the specified date, where *mm/dd/yyyy* is the specified date in (UTC) format and *dd* is the current date minus *dd* days.
/r		Instructs **forfiles** to select files in subdirectories as well as the current directory.
/v		Runs **forfiles** in verbose mode.

TABLE A.9 freedisk Command Options

Option	Qualifier	Description
/s	*computer*	Defines the name or IP address of a remote computer (local computer is default). This parameter applies to all files and folders specified in the command.
/u	*domain\user*	Runs the script with the permissions of the specified user account. System permissions is the default.
/p	*password*	Defines the password of the user account that is specified in the **/u** parameter.
/d	*Drive*	Defines the drive on which the availability of free space is to be known. Drive name must be specified for a remote computer.

TABLE A.10 gettype Command Options

Option	Qualifier	Description
/role		Defines the role of the operating system.
/sp		Defines the highest service pack installed.
/ver		Defines version information (major and minor).
/minv		Defines only minor version.
/majv		Defines only major version
/type		Defines the type of operating system installed.
/build		Defines the build number of the operating system.

gpresult Command

GPresult.exe launches the Resulting Set of Policies (RSoP) and list of policies that are applied to a computer. The **gpresult** command displays Group Policy settings and the RSOP for a user or a computer. The syntax is

```
gpresult [/s computer [/u domain\user /p password]] [/user
TargetUserName] [/scope {user|computer}] [/v] [/z]
```

TABLE A.11 gpresult Command Options

Option	Qualifier	Description
/s	*computer*	Defines the name or IP address of a remote computer (local computer default.)
/u	*domain\user*	Runs the command with the account permissions of the user that is specified by *user* or *domain\user*. The default is the permissions of the user on the computer that issues the command.
/p	*password*	Defines user account password that is specified in **/u** parameter.
/user	*TargetUserName*	Defines the name of the user whose RSOP data is to be displayed.
/scope	{**user**|**computer**}	Displays either **user** or **computer** results. Valid values for the **/scope** parameter are **user** or **computer**. If you omit the **/scope** parameter, **gpresult** displays both **user** and **computer** settings.
/v		Defines that the output display verbose policy information.
/z		Defines that the output display all available information about Group Policy.

gpupdate

Replaces the **secedit** /refreshpolicy command available to Windows 2000 Servers. Initiates Group Policy refresh for local and Active Directory policy settings. The syntax is

```
gpupdate [/target:{computer|user}] [/force] [/wait:value] [/logoff] [/boot]
```

Option	Qualifier	Description
/target:	{*computer*|*user*}	Limit policy fresh to only the computer settings or user settings. Both settings are updated by default.
/force		Reapplies all settings without optimization.

(continues)

Option	Qualifier	Description
/wait:	*value*	Time, in seconds, to wait for policy refresh; 600 is default, 0 is no wait, and –1 is wait without timeout.
/logoff		Some policies require the user to logoff and logon to obtain new environment settings. If no policies requiring logoff are set, the option has no effect. Folder Redirection and Software Installation are examples of this type of policy.
/boot		Some policies system restart to obtain new environment settings. If no policies requiring restart are set, the option has no effect.
/?		Displays this help/usage

Examples: gpupdate, gpupdate /target:user, gpupdate /force

IIS Scripts

IIS scripts provide command-line tools to configure, provision, and manage Internet Information Services (IIS) servers and Active Server Page (ASP) applications. For example, Ipseccmd.exe permits the user to view and modify the policies and properties of Internet Protocol (IP) security. These scripts are updated regularly by Microsoft. We recommend that you, as an administrator, check the Microsoft site often for updated scripts.

inuse Command

Inuse.exe allows files loaded into memory to be replaced on reboot. The **inuse** command replaces files that the operating system is currently using. You must be a member of the Administrators group to use this tool. The syntax is

```
inuse replacement destination [/y]
```

TABLE A.12 inuse Command Options

Option	Qualifier	Description
replacement		Defines the updated file name. Include the complete physical or UNC path name.
/d	*destination*	Defines the currently locked file that you want to replace on the local drive. Include the complete physical path name.
/y		Suppresses the confirmation prompt to replace the file.

netdom Command

The NetDom.exe permits server renaming. The command can add another name, or alias, for a computer to DNS and Active Directory. Once the new name has successfully replicated in DNS and Active Directory, the old name may then be removed with the NetDom.exe command.

netsh Command

NetSh.exe is a configuration tool that now adds the basic network diagnostic features provided by older NetDiag.exe tool. Netsh is a command-line scripting utility that permits administrators to display or modify the network configuration of a computer that is currently running. Netsh provides a scripting feature that allows you to run a group of commands in batch mode against a specified computer. Netsh can also save a configuration script in a text file for archival purposes or to help you configure other servers. Run the **netsh** command from the **Cmd.exe** prompt and change to the context that contains the command you want to use. The contexts that are available depend on which networking components you have installed.

openfiles Command

Openfiles.exe is used to view the list of connected users and files in use per share on a computer. The **openfiles** command permits the administrator to make queries, and displays or disconnects open files or files opened by network users. This command also enables or disables the system's Maintain Objects List global flag. This can be done on a local, query, and disconnected basis.

pagefileconfig Command

Pagefileconfig.vbs retrieves the current page file's size or sets a new page file size. The **pagefileconfig** command enables an administrator to display and configure a system's paging file Virtual Memory settings. The optional settings permit the administrator to create, change, delete, and query related page file sizes.

powercfg Command

PowerCfg.exe enables power management. The **powercfg** command enables an administrator to control the power settings on a system. The syntax is

```
Powercfg [/list | /query name | /create name | /delete name |
/setactive name | /change settings | /hibernate [on|off] | /export
name [/file file name] | /import name [/file file name] | /?]
```

TABLE A.13 powercfg Command Options

Option	Qualifier	Description
/list or **/l**		Lists the names of existing power schemes.
/query or **/q**		Displays the configuration of the specified power scheme. If no name is specified, the configuration of the currently active power scheme is displayed.
/create or **/c**		Creates the specified power scheme. The new scheme is created with the properties of the currently active scheme.
/delete or **/d**		Deletes the specified power scheme.
/setactive or **/s**		Activates the specified power scheme.
/change or **/x**		Changes settings of the specified power scheme. Additional switches specify the changes as follows: **/monitor-timeout-ac** *minutes* turns the monitor off after the specified number of minutes when the system is operating on AC power. A value of 0 will disable the timeout. **/monitor-timeout-dc** *minutes* turns the monitor off after the specified number of minutes when the system is operating on DC (battery) power. A value of 0 will disable the timeout. **/disk-timeout-ac** *minutes* turns the hard disks off after the specified number of minutes when the system is operating on AC power. A value of 0 will disable the timeout. **/disk-timeout-dc** *minutes* turns the hard disks off after the specified number of minutes when the system is operating on DC (battery) power. A value of 0 will disable the timeout. **/standby-timeout-ac** *minutes* puts the computer in standby mode after the specified number of minutes when the system is operating on AC power. A value of 0 will disable the timeout. **/standby-timeout-dc** *minutes* puts the computer in standby mode after the specified number of minutes when the system is operating on DC (battery) power. A value of 0 will disable the timeout. **/hibernate-timeout-ac** *minutes* saves the contents of the computer's memory to disk and turns off the computer after the specified number of minutes when the system is operating on AC power. A value of 0 will disable the timeout. **/hibernate-timeout-dc** *minutes* saves the contents of the computer's memory to disk and turns off the computer after the specified number of minutes when the system is operating on DC (battery) power. A value of 0 will disable the timeout.

TABLE A.13 Continued

Option	Qualifier	Description
		/processor-throttle-ac [**none** | **constant** | **degrade** | **adaptive**] selects the dynamic throttling policy to be used if your microprocessor supports processor performance state controls when the system is operating on AC power. The desired dynamic throttling policy is selected with one of four additional switches: • **none** causes the microprocessor to operate at the highest performance state at all times. • **constant** causes the microprocessor to operate at the lowest performance state at all times. • **degrade** causes the microprocessor to operate at the lowest performance state, and further reduces performance by applying stop clock throttling as the system battery drains. This option is typically used when the computer is operating on battery power and is therefore seldom used with **/processor-throttle-ac**. • **adaptive** modifies the performance state dynamically based on the demand the system puts on the microprocessor. **/processor-throttle-dc** [**none** | **constant** | **degrade** | **adaptive**] selects the dynamic throttling policy to be used if your microprocessor supports processor performance state controls when the system is operating on DC (battery) power. The desired dynamic throttling policy is selected with one of the four additional switches listed under **/processor-throttle-ac**.
/hibernate or **/h**		Turns the hibernation feature on or off. Hibernation timeout is not supported on all systems that support hibernation.
/export or **/e**		Exports the specified power scheme to a file. If no file name is specified, the default is scheme.pow. This parameter supports the following parameter: **/file** *file name*
/import or **/i**		Imports the power scheme from the specified file. If no file name is specified, the default is scheme.pow. If a scheme with that name already exists, it is replaced with the new one. This parameter supports the following parameter: **/file** *file name*

(Continues)

TABLE A.13 Continued

Option	Qualifier	Description
/numerical or **/n**		Requires you to specify the power scheme using its numeric identifier rather than its name. Use this switch in combination with the **/query**, **/delete**, **/setactive**, **/change**, **/export**, and **/import** commands.
/globalpowerflag or **/g** [**on** | **off**] **/option:** [**batteryicon** | **multibattery** | **resumepassword** | **wakeonring** | **videodim**]		Turns the global power flag features on or off. Use the first switch to indicate whether to turn the feature on or off.
/option:		Is mandatory, and is followed by the name of the feature you are turning on or off. There are five possibilities: **batteryicon** enables or disables the battery meter icon in the notification area. When this flag is cleared, the battery meter icon is not displayed. **multibattery** enables or disables multiple battery display in the system's Power Meter. **resumepassword** enables or disables the requirement that the user supply a password when the system resumes from standby or hibernate. **wakeonring** enables or disables Wake on Ring support. **videodim** enables or disables support for dimming the video display when the system changes from AC power to DC (battery) power.

Print Scripts

Print scripts manages printer services, drivers, and queues. The scripts that are most valuable to administrators include:

- *Prncnfg.vbs* configures or displays configuration information about a printer.
- *Prndrvr.vbs* adds, deletes, and lists printer drivers.
- *Prnjobs.vbs* pauses, resumes, cancels, and lists print jobs.
- *Prnmngr.vbs* adds, deletes, and lists printers or printer connections in addition to setting and displaying the default printer.

- *Prnport.vbs* creates, deletes, and lists standard TCP/IP printer ports in addition to displaying and changing port configuration.
- *Prnqctl.vbs* prints a test page, pauses or resumes a printer, and clears a printer queue.

regfind Command

Regfind.exe searches the registry. The **regfind** command searches the registry for arbitrary data, key names, or value names, and replaces any of these with new values. This is accessible only to members of the Administrators group. The syntax is

```
regfind [{-m \\ComputerName | -h HiveFile HiveRoot | -w
Windows95Directory}] [-i n] [-o OutputWidth] [-p RegistryKeyPath]
[{-z | -t DataType}] [{-b | -B}] [-y] [-n][SearchString [-r
ReplacementString]]
```

sc Command

SC.exe starts and stops and manages Win32 services. The **sc** command communicates with the Service Controller and installed services. SC.exe retrieves and sets control information about services. It is used to test and debug service programs. Administrators can use service properties stored in the registry to set the control for how service applications are started at boot time and run as background processes. Batch files can be used to call various SC.exe commands to automate the startup or shutdown sequence of services. SC.exe provides capabilities similar to Services in the Administrative Tools item in Control Panel. SC.exe options cover *boot, config, continue, create, delete, description, failure, getdisplayname, getkeyname, interrogate, lock, pause, qc, qdescription, qfailure, query, queryex, querylock, sdset, sdshow, start,* and *stop*.

setx Command

Setx.exe allows environment variables to be set with batch files. The **setx** command establishes the environment variables in the local or system environment without requiring programming or scripting. **Setx** also establishes the values of registry keys and writes them to text files. The syntax is

```
setx [/s computer [/u [domain\]user [/p [password]]]] Variable Value
[/m]
setx [/s computer [/u [domain\]user [/p [password]]]] [Variable]
/k Path [/m]
setx [/s computer [/u [domain\]user [/p [password]]]] [Variable]
/f File {/a x,y | /r x,y "String"} [/d Delimiters] [/x] [/m]
```

TABLE A.14 regfind Command Options

Option	Qualifier	Description
-m	*ComputerName*	Defines a remote Windows 2000 computer (machine) whose registry is to be manipulated.
-h	*HiveFile HiveRoot*	Defines a local hive to manipulate.
-w	*Windows95Directory*	Defines the paths to Windows 95 system.dat and user.dat files.
-i	*n*	Defines the display indentation multiple. Default is 4.
-o	*OutputWidth*	Defines how wide the output is to be. By default *OutputWidth* is set to the width of the console window, if standard output (STDOUT) has not been redirected to a file. In the latter case, an *OutputWidth* of 240 is used.
-p	*RegistryKeyPath*	Defines where in the registry to start searching. All entries below this point in the registry hierarchy are also searched. If no path is specified, **regfind** searches the entire registry, which can be time consuming. If the path contains spaces, it must be surrounded by quotation marks: "*Registry Key Path with Spaces*"
-z		Defines to search for REG_SZ and REG_EXPAND_SZ values that are missing a trailing null character and/or have a length that is not a multiple of the size of a Unicode character.
-t	*DataType*	Defines which registry types to search. *DataType* can be REG_SZ, REG_MULTI_SZ, REG_EXPAND_SZ, REG_DWORD, REG_BINARY, or REG_NONE. Default is any of the _SZ types.
-b		Defines that **regfind** should look for occurrences of the *SearchString* inside of REG_BINARY data. Only valid with _SZ searches. Cannot be specified with a *ReplacementString* that is not the same length as the *SearchString*.
-B		Same functionality as **-b**, but also looks for ANSI version of string within REG_BINARY values.
-y		Defines that **regfind** should ignore case when searching. Only valid with _SZ searches.
-n		Defines to include key and value names in the search. You cannot use **-n** with **-t**.
SearchString		Defines the value to search for. If *SearchString* is not specified, **regfind** searches based on type. If *SearchString* contains spaces, you must wrap it in quotation marks (for example, "*Search String With Spaces*").
-r	*ReplacementString*	Defines an optional replacement string to replace any matches.

TABLE A.15 setx Command Options

Option	Qualifier	Description
/s	*computer*	Defines the name or IP address of a remote computer (local computer is default).
/u	*domain\user*	Runs the script with the permissions of the specified user account. The default is system permissions.
/p	*password*	Defines the password of the user account that is specified in the **/u** parameter.

shutdown Command

Shutdown.exe shuts down or restarts a computer and allows a restart explanation to be written to the event log. This allows the administrator to shut down or restart a local or remote computer. The syntax is

```
shutdown [{-i | -l | -s | -r | -a}] [-f] [-m \\ComputerName] [-t xxx]
[-c "comment"] [-d [u] [p]:xx:yy]
```

TABLE A.16 shutdown Command Options

Option	Qualifier	Description
-i		Displays the **Remote Shutdown Dialog** box. Must be the first option.
-l		Logs off the current user. This is also the default. Cannot be used with **-m** *ComputerName*.
-s		Shuts down the computer.
-r		Restarts the computer after shutdown.
-a		Aborts shutdown. Ignores other parameters except for **-l** and *ComputerName*. You can only use **-a** during the timeout period.
-f		Forces running applications to close.
-m	*ComputerName*	Defines the target computer. Cannot be used with **-l**.
-t	*xxx*	Sets the timer for system shutdown in *xxx* seconds. The default is 20 seconds.
-c	"*comment*"	Permits detailed comments about the reason for the shutdown. You can use a maximum of 127 characters. You must enclose the message in quotation marks.

systeminfo Command

Systeminfo.exe views the basic properties of a machine (such as CPU and memory). The **systeminfo** command displays detailed configuration information about a computer and its operating system, including operating system configuration, security information, product ID, and hardware properties, such as RAM, disk space, and network cards. The syntax is

```
systeminfo [/s computer [/u domain\user [/p password]]]
[/fo {TABLE|LIST|CSV}] [/nh]
```

takeown Command

Takeown.exe allows administrators to take ownership of orphaned files. The **takeown** command implements a recovery scheme to allow access to a locked file. The syntax is

```
takeown [/s System [/u [Domain\User [/p [Password]]]] Filename
```

taskkill Command

TaskKill.exe is used to kill or stop a running process. The **taskkill** command ends one or more tasks or processes. Processes can be killed by process ID or image name. The syntax is

```
taskkill [/s computer] [/u domain\user [/p password]]] [/fi
FilterName] [/pid ProcessID]|[/im ImageName] [/f]
```

TABLE A.17 systeminfo Command Options

Option	Qualifier	Description
/s	*computer*	Defines the name or IP address of a remote computer (local computer is default).
/u	*domain\user*	Runs the script with the permissions of the specified user account. The default is system permissions.
/p	*password*	Defines the password of the user account that is specified in the **/u** parameter.

TABLE A.18 taskkill Command Options

Option	Qualifier	Description
/s	*computer*	Defines the name or IP address of a remote computer (local computer is default).
/u	*domain\user*	Runs the command with the account permissions of the user specified by *user* or *domain\user*. The default is the permissions of the user who issues the command.
/p	*password*	Defines the password of the user account that is specified in the **/u** parameter.
/fi	*FilterName*	Defines the types of process(es) to include in or exclude from termination.
/pid	*ProcessID*	Defines the process ID of the process to be terminated.
/im	*ImageName*	Defines the image name of the process to be terminated. Use the wildcard (*) to specify all image names.
/f		Defines that process(es) be forcefully terminated. This parameter is ignored for remote processes; all remote processes are forcefully terminated.

tasklist Command

TaskList.exe is used to view or identify all running processes with PIDs. The **tasklist** command displays a list of applications, services, and the process ID (PID) currently running on either a local or a remote computer. The syntax is

```
tasklist[.exe] [/s computer] [/u domain\user [/p password]]] [/fo
{TABLE|LIST|CSV}] [/nh] [/fi FilterName [/fi FilterName2 [ ... ]]]
[/svc] [/v]
```

timeout Command

Timeout.exe pauses a batch file for a specified number of seconds. The **timeout** command pauses the command processor for the specified number of seconds. Timeout.exe is typically used in batch files. The syntax is

```
timeout /t TimeoutInSeconds [/nobreak]
```

tsecimp Command

Tsecimp.exe imports Telephony Application Programming Interface (TAPI) user account properties and access rights. The **tsecimp** command imports assignment

TABLE A.19 takeown Command Options

Option	Qualifier	Description
/s	*computer*	Defines the name or IP address of a remote computer (local computer is default).
/u	*domain\user*	Runs the script with the permissions of the specified user account. The default is system permissions.
/p	*password*	Defines the password of the user account that is specified in the **/u** parameter.

TABLE A.20 tasklist Command Options

Option	Qualifier	Description
/s	*computer*	Defines the name or IP address of a remote computer (local computer is default).
/u	*domain\user*	Runs the command with the account permissions of the user specified by *user* or *domain\user*. The default is the permissions of the user issuing the command.
/p	*password*	Defines the password of the user account that is specified in the **/u** parameter.
/fo {**TABLE**|**LIST**|**CSV**}		Defines the format to use for the output. Valid values are **TABLE**, **LIST**, and **CSV**. The default format for output is **TABLE**.
/nh		Suppresses column headers in the output. Valid when the **/fo** parameter is set to **TABLE** or **CSV**.
/fi	*FilterName*	Defines the types of process(es) to include in or exclude from the query.
/svc		Outputs all the service information for each process without truncation. Valid when the **/fo** parameter is set to **TABLE**.
/v		Directs that verbose task information be displayed in the output. To see complete verbose output without truncation, use in conjunction with the **/svc** parameter.

TABLE A.21 timeout Command Options

Option	Qualifier	Description
/t	*TimeoutInSeconds*	Defines the decimal number of seconds (between **-1** and **100000**) to wait before continuing processing. The value **-1** causes the computer to wait indefinitely for a keystroke.
/nobreak		Defines to ignore the key press.

TABLE A.22 tsecimp Command Options

Option	Qualifier	Description
-f	*FileName*	Required item that defines the name of the XML file that contains the assignment information that you want to import.
-v		Validates the structure of the XML file without importing the information into the Tsec.ini file.
-u		Checks whether each user is a member of the domain specified in the XML file. The computer on which you use this parameter must be connected to the network. This parameter might significantly slow performance if you are processing a large amount of user assignment information.

information from an Extensible Markup Language (XML) file into the TAPI server security file (Tsec.ini). Administrators can use this command to display the list of TAPI providers and the lines or devices associated with each of them and validate the structure of the XML file without importing the contents. The syntax is

```
tsecimp -f FileName [{-v | -u}]
```

whoami Command

Whoami.exe determines the current logged-on user. The **whoami** command outputs domain or computer name, user name, group names, logon identifier, and privileges for the local computer. The syntax is

```
whoami [/upn | /fqdn | /logonid]
whoami [/user] [/groups] [/priv] [/fo format]
whoami /all [/fo format]
```

TABLE A.23 whoami Command Options

Option	Description
/upn	Outputs the user name in UPN format.
/fqdn	Outputs the user name in FQDN format.
/user	Outputs current user name.
/groups	Outputs group names.
/priv	Outputs privileges.
/logonid	Outputs logon ID.
/all	Outputs the active user name and groups and the security identifiers (SID) and privileges in the current access token.

BACKUP COMMANDS

Chapter 14 examined the recommended backup and restoration methods for Windows 2000 and Windows Server 2003. However, in mixed environments a command-line approach may also be warranted; in this approach, a user can back up data to tape, floppy, and hard disk. Windows NT commands such as **backup** and **restore** are no longer fully supported. The Ntrestore utility can be used either to launch the graphical backup tools or in a command-line mode.

Using Ntbackup on the Command Line

The Ntbackup utility can be used from the command prompt or within a batch file to achieve the same results as with the graphical backup. It has several formats, but the primary syntax is

```
ntbackup backup path [options]
```

The backup parameter must be included except for the other variations of the syntax shown in Table A.24. The path parameter should contain the path or paths of the directories to be copied to the backup tape. Table A.24 identifies the options available for the command. They can be entered in any sequence.

To erase a tape, enter the following command:

```
ntbackup /nopoll
```

No other options are available with the */nopoll* switch. This format requires user input and cannot be used in a batch file.

TABLE A.24 ntbackup Command Options

Option	Qualifier	Description
/b		Backs up the Registry from the local system.
/e		Includes exceptions only in the backup log. The default is to create a full and detailed backup log.
/hc:on		Turns on hardware compression. Not valid if the **/a** option is used.
/hc:off		Turns off hardware compression. Not valid if the **/a** option is used.
/l	"filename"	Creates a log file as file name. The path can be included as part of file name.
/r		Restricts access to the data on the backup tape to members of the Administrators group and the Backup Operators group. Must not be used with the **/a** option.
/t	type	Specifies the backup type, where type can be one of the following values: copy, daily, differential, incremental, normal.
/tape:n		Identifies the number of the tape drive to use, where *n* can be a value from 0 through 9. This option is necessary only if there is more than one tape drive on the system.
systemstate		Specifies that you want to back up the System State data. When you select this option, the backup type will be forced to normal or copy.
@bks file name		Specifies the name of the backup selection file (.bks file) to be used for this backup operation. The at (@) character must precede the name of the backup selection file. A backup selection file contains information on the files and folders you have selected for backup. You have to create the file using the GUI version of Backup.
/J {"*job name*"}		Specifies the job name to be used in the log file. The job name usually describes the files and folders you are backing up in the current backup job as well as the date and time you backed up the files.
/P {"*pool name*"}		Specifies the media pool from which you want to use media. This is usually a subpool. You cannot use the /A, **/G**, **/F**, or **/T** command-line options.
/G {"*guid name*"}		Overwrites or appends to this tape. Do not use this switch in conjunction with **/P**.
/T {"*tape name*"}		Overwrites or appends to this tape. Do not use this switch in conjunction with **/P**.

(Continues)

TABLE A.24 Continued

Option	Qualifier	Description
/N {"*media name*"}		Specifies the new tape name. You must not use **/A** with this switch.
/F {"*file name*"}		Logical disk path and file name used wirh **/P** **/G** **/T**.
/D {"*set description*"}		Specifies a label for each of the backup sets.
/DS {"*server name*"}		Backs up the directory service file for the specified Microsoft Exchange Server.
/IS {"*server name*"}		Backs up the Information Store file for the specified Microsoft Exchange Server.
/A		Performs an append operation. Either **/G** or **/T** must be also used. Do not use this switch in conjunction with **/P**.
/V:{yes|no}		Verifies the data after the backup is complete.
/R:{yes|no}		Restricts access to this tape to the Owner group or the administrator.
/L:{f|s|n}		Specifies the type of log file: f=full, s=summary, n= no log file is created.
/M {*backup type*}		Specifies the backup type as normal, copy, daily, incremental, or differential.
/RS:{yes|no}		Backs up the migrated data files located in Remote Storage. When you back up the %systemroot% folder, Backup automatically backs up the Removable Storage database as well.
/HC:{on|off}		If available on the tape drive, uses hardware compression.
/SNAP:{on|off}		Specifies whether the backup should use a volume shadow copy.
/M {*backup type*}		Specifies the backup type as normal, copy, daily, incremental or differential.
/?		Outputs help at the command prompt.

To eject a tape, the following syntax may be used:

```
ntbackup eject /tape:n
```

The */tape:n* option is necessary only if there is more than one tape drive installed on the system. The variable *n* can be a value from 0 through 9 and designates which tape drive should eject the tape.

EXAMPLE OF NTBACKUP COMMAND

Enter the following command to back up and verify the C drive, including the local Registry. This restricts access to the Administrators and Backup Operators groups with a fully detailed log of the backup in the file C:\winnt\backup.log.

```
ntbackup backup c: /b/r/l "c:\winnt\backup.log"
```

BATCH COMMANDS

Batch commands or programs are also commonly known as batch files. They are essentially simplified scripts that support the execution routine or repetitive tasks. A batch program is written as a text file with one or more command lines that are executed sequentially from top to bottom. They are identified by either a .bat or .cmd extension to their file names.

All Windows Server 2003 commands and many applications can be executed from a batch file. To provide greater flexibility, a number of conditional parameters, shown in Table A.25, can be set.

COMPARISON COMMANDS

In a Windows environment, a user can compare two files visually by displaying each in a separate window. While graphically based file comparisons can be executed with applications that are installed on Windows 2000 or Windows Server 2003, two utilities available within the base system are executed from the command line. Two commands that compare files are **fc** and **comp**.

fc Command

The **fc** command enables a user to compare two files and display the differences, where both are in either an ASCII or a binary format. The syntax is

```
fc [options] file1 file2
```

The file, here shown as file1 and file2, can be just a file name, a path with a file name, or a drive, path, and file name in the format *drive:path\filename*. In addition, they can contain the wildcard characters * and ?. If you use a wildcard character in file1, the **fc** command will compare each file found to file2. In other words, it compares many to one. If you use a wildcard character in file2, the command will compare file1 to a file with a corresponding name in file2's location. Examples using the wildcard characters are given in Table A.26.

TABLE A.25 Batch File Conditional Commands

Option	Description
call	Permits the execution of another batch program without terminating the parent program.
echo	Turns the display of command action on or off as the batch file is executed. Can also be used to output a message to the screen—for example, "One moment please, while searching . . ."
endlocal	Ends the **setlocal** command described below.
for	Executes a specific command for every file in a set of files. Can also be run directly from the command prompt.
goto	Directs Windows Server 2003 to process the line in the batch file that is specified.
if	Processes a command when the specified condition is true; ignored when the condition is not met. The conditions of NOT and ELSE can also be used in combination as part of this option.
pause	Temporarily suspends the batch file until the user takes an action such as pressing a key to confirm an action.
rem	Short for remarks that can be added to the batch file for referencing. These are programming notes that are not executed.
setlocal	Permits the establishment of new localization variables. The localization is retained until the *endlocal* option resets the environment.
Shift **| (pipe)**	Modifies the position of parameters in a batch program and permits the stringing together of multiple commands on one line.
>	Outputs command results to the directed point.
()	Groups commands.
||	Executes either the first or next command.
&&	Executes the first command and, if successful, executes the next one.

FC COMMAND EXAMPLES

To compare two binary files with the names Test.exe and Test1.exe, the command can be entered as

```
fc /b test.exe test1.exe
```

or

```
fc test.exe test1.exe
```

TABLE A.26 fc Command Options

Option	Description
/a	Used only for ASCII comparisons and provides the output display in abbreviated form. Only the first and last lines of each set of differences are displayed.
/b	Does a comparison of binary files. This option is automatically the default for files whose names have one of these extensions: .exe, .com, .sys, .obj, .lib, .bin. The files are compared by byte, and differences are output in the format *xxxxxxxx: yy zz*, where *xxxxxxxx* is the address of the bytes being compared in hexadecimal; *yy* is the contents of the byte from file1; and *zz* is the contents of the byte from file2.
/c	Ignores the distinctions between uppercase and lowercase.
/l	Compares ASCII files. This is considered the default for all files except those mentioned in the **/b** option above. The comparison is executed line by line and the differences are output in the following format: the name of file1, then the lines of file1 that differ from file2, the first line of file1 that occurs in both files, the name of file2, the lines of file2 that differ from file1, the first line of file2 that occurs in both files. After a difference is found, the command tries to resynchronize the two files.
/lbn	Sets the size of the internal line buffer to *n*. The default size is 100 lines. If the number of consecutive differences is greater than *n*, the command terminates.
/n	Displays the line numbers; used only for ASCII files.
/t	Does not treat tabs as spaces. The default is to treat tabs as spaces.
/w	Treats consecutive tabs/spaces as one space. Does not compare tabs/spaces at the beginning and end of a line.
/nnnn	Considers the file to be resynchronized when *nnnn* number of consecutive lines match; otherwise, matching lines are displayed as differences. The default value for *nnnn* is 2.

Both formats are acceptable because a file with an .exe extension is assumed to be binary by default.

To compare the files autoexec.bat, autoold.bat, and autoex3.bat to the file newauto.bat, enter the following:

```
fc auto*.bat newauto.bat
```

Suppose that a system administrator needs to compare some test result .tst files in the C:/test directory with files of the same name in test directory named bob on the D: drive. He enters

```
fc c:/test/*.tst d:/bob/test/*.tst
```

comp Command

Another comparison command available through the command line is **comp**, which compares the content of files by byte. Output consists of error messages of the format

```
Compare error at OFFSET xxxxxxxx = yy = zz
```

where *xxxxxxxx* is the memory address of the differing bytes, *yy* is the content of the bytes in file1, and *zz* is the content of the bytes in file2. The addresses and contents are in hexadecimal format unless an option is specified to display them in decimal or character format.

The syntax of the comp command is

```
comp [file1] [file2] [options]
```

The elements file1 and file2 in this line can be the names of two files, including as necessary the drive designation and the directory path. The wildcard characters * and ? can be used to compare multiple files. Options are listed in Table A.27.

TABLE A.27 comp Options

Option	Description
/a	Displays the differences between the files in character format.
/d	Displays the differences between the files in decimal format instead of hexadecimal.
/l	Displays the line number of the differences instead of the number of the byte offset.
/n=num	Compares the first num lines of both files, particularly when two files are different sizes.
/c	Ignores uppercase and lowercase distinctions.

EXAMPLE OF COMP COMMAND

To compare the first 15 lines of the files newtest.log and oldtest.log, displaying the line numbers where the differences occur, enter the following:

```
comp newtest.log oldtest.log /n=15 /l
```

WINDIFF

Windows Server 2003 Support Tools provides a graphical tool that compares two files, as shown in Figure A.1.

COMPRESSION COMMANDS

Each file in the Windows Server 2003 NTFS file system contains a compression attribute that indicates either that the file should be stored as compressed or is already compressed. Compression is recommended for large files that are used infrequently. When this attribute is selected, files are automatically compressed when they are saved and decompressed when accessed for use. (Remember that this compression technology is not available with the FAT file system.)

The compression attribute can be set from within the My Computer windows or through Windows Server 2003 Explorer. From **Explorer**, select the file you wish to view or set the compression attribute. Next, select from the menu bar **File → Properties**. In the Properties window, select the **General** tab if it is not already displayed. On the **General** tab, select **Advanced**. In the **Attributes** box, check the **Compress Contents to Save Space** box to compress or decompress a file.

As an alternative to the menu bar, you can right-click the file and, from the menu that appears, select **Properties**.

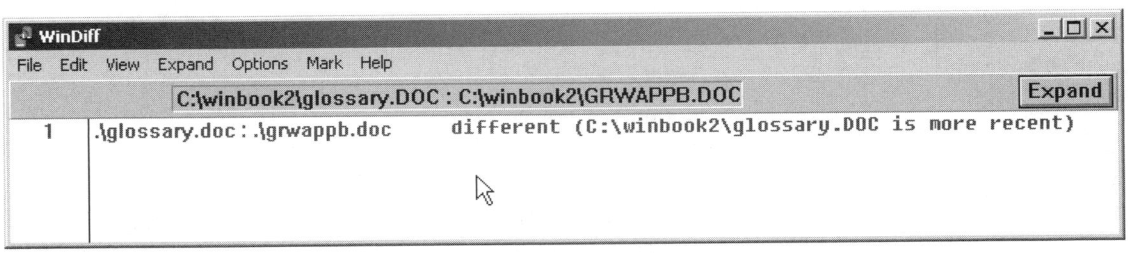

FIGURE A.1 Windows 2000 and Windows Server 2003 Resource Kit WinDiff

compact Command

The **compact** command allows the user to set or display the compression attribute on NTFS files from the command line. Its syntax is

```
compact [options] [filename]
```

The file name parameter can actually be the name of a file or a directory. In a directory, the compression attribute indicates that any new files added to it will automatically have their compression attributes set and they will be compressed. This does not change the compression attribute for files that already exist in the directory. For them, wildcard characters can be used as part of the file parameter.

If no options are used or no file names are entered, the compression attribute for the current directory is displayed. See options list in Table A.28.

To set the compression attribute on the directory \ellen\oldfiles as well as any of its subdirectories, enter the following:

```
compact /c /s c:\ellen\oldfiles
```

To remove the compression attribute from the directory d:\bob\contracts, enter

```
compact /u d:\bob\contracts
```

Remember, the above command will only remove the attribute from the directory and will not affect any of the files and subdirectories currently in the directory \bob\contracts.

TABLE A.28 compact Options

Option	Qualifier	Description
/c		Compresses the named file(s).
/u		Decompresses the named file(s).
/s	*:directory*	Compresses or decompresses all subdirectories for the identified directory. The *:directory* qualifier is optional. The default is the current directory.
/i		Ignores any errors that occur.
/a		Displays hidden or system files. These will be omitted by default.
/f		Forces file name to be compressed or decompressed. The main use for this option occurs when a file was only partially compressed or decompressed and the system administrator needs to complete the task.

TABLE A.29 expand Command Options

Option	Qualifier	Description
-d		Displays a list of files in the source volume.
-f:	*filename*	Specifies a file.
-r		Renames the expanded file.

expand Command

The **expand** command is used to decompress one or more files as well as to retrieve files from a distribution disk. Its syntax is

```
expand [-r] source [destination]
```

Table A.29 lists the options for the **expand** command.

DISPLAY COMMANDS

The display commands display the contents of files, the properties of files, lists of files, and Help files. They also organize displays into a sequence the user desires. This section will describe the procedures and commands available.

Displaying the Contents of Files

Windows Server 2003 primarily uses installed applications for file viewing. The Registry maintains a list of installed applications and attempts to match file extensions to appropriate software so that the file can be viewed in its native format. When you double-click a file name or icon in Explorer, the file opens within the application. If the file type is unknown, the **Open With** window is displayed, allowing you to select the application that should be used to open the file.

The WordPad applications that are part of the base Windows Server 2003 system allow the user to display and create text or ASCII files. These applications are accessed by selecting **Start** → **Programs** → **Accessories** → **WordPad**.

From the command line, two commands are available for displaying files: **more** and **type**. The **more** command displays long files one screen at a time; the **type** command just displays the entire contents of a file and is usually used for short files only.

CLS COMMAND

The **cls** command is used to clear the command prompt screen.

MORE COMMAND

The **more** command displays long text files from within the command prompt window one screen at a time. Its basic syntax is

```
more [options] [file(s)]
```

Options for the more command are listed in Table A.30.

The file(s) parameter is not necessary when data is passed to the **more** command from another command using the pipe symbol (|). If it is used, it can be in the format of one or more file names, including the drive designation and path if necessary.

If the **/e** switch is used, the commands in Table A.31 may be used whenever the "—More—" prompt displays.

TYPE COMMAND

The **type** command simply displays the contents of one or more files and is similar to the UNIX **cat** command. Its syntax is

```
type file(s)
```

The file(s) parameter can consist of just the file names entered with the drive designation and path name if necessary. Multiple files in the file(s) list are separated by spaces. When entering a file name, remember to enclose it in quotes if it contains spaces.

TABLE A.30 more Command Options

Option	Description
/e	Enables the "extended" features that allow the user to control how the file is displayed by entering commands whenever the "—More—" prompt displays. The commands are identified Table A.31.
/p	Expands any form-feed characters.
/s	Consolidates multiple blank lines into one blank line.
/tn	Substitutes *n* spaces for each tab.
+n	Starts displaying the first file in the file(s) list at line *n*.

TABLE A.31 more Commands

Command	Description
Space bar	Displays the next page of text.
ENTER key	Displays the next line of text.
f	Displays the next file in the file(s) list.
pn	Displays the next *n* lines.
sn	Skips *n* lines.
?	Displays the commands that are acceptable at the **"--More—"** prompt. In other words, the Help function.
=	Displays the line number.
q	Quits.

Displaying Attributes and Properties of Files and Folders

Windows Server 2003 provides graphical and command prompt methods of displaying the file and directory hierarchy of a system and its network. The graphical methods are available through the My Computer window, Explorer, and the My Network Places. My Network Places, accessible either from its desktop icon or through Explorer, allows the user to display network files and directories.

This section describes the file and folder views available through Windows Server 2003 Explorer as well as the **dir** command that you can type in at the command crompt.

DISPLAYING FILE PROPERTIES USING WINDOWS SERVER 2003 EXPLORER

In Windows Server 2003 Explorer, the left pane of the Primary window (Figure A.2) shows the top level of the hierarchy for the desktop. Here directories have file folder icons and are referred to as folders. To view the subdirectories, left-click the box that contains a plus sign. When the subdirectories are displayed, the plus sign becomes a minus sign. To display both the files and subdirectories of a particular folder, select the folder by clicking it with the mouse. The folder contents will appear in the right pane.

To view detailed information about each file in the **Contents of** pane, select **View → Details** from the menu bar. This detailed information includes the name of the file, its size in bytes, its type, the date it was last modified, and the attributes associated with it, which can be Archive (A), Read-Only (R), Hidden (H), System (S), or Compressed (C) (Compressed will display only on NTFS file systems).

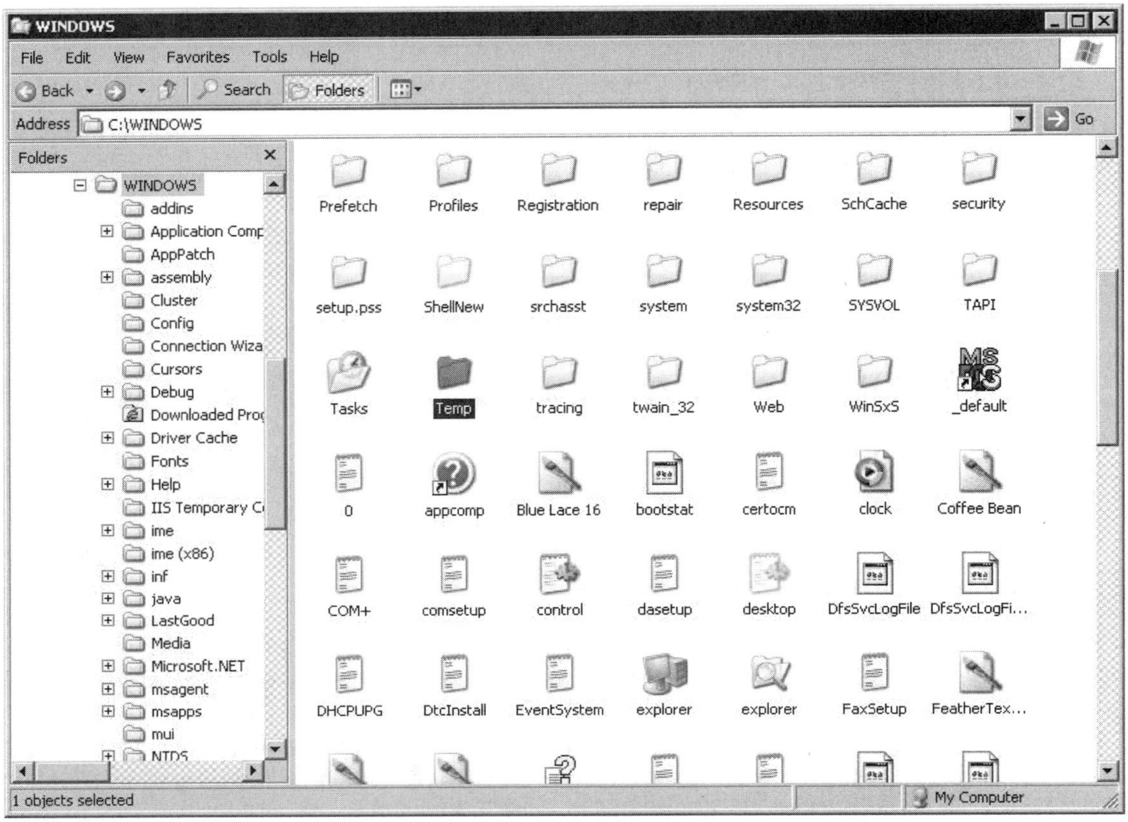

FIGURE A.2 The Windows Server 2003 Explorer Primary Window

Note that by default certain file types are omitted (or hidden) from the Explorer hierarchical display, such as system (.Ssys) and application extension (.dll). To automatically show all files or to view a list of the hidden file types, select **Tools → Folder Options → View**. Then select **Show all files**.

Files in the **Contents of** pane can be sorted for viewing by name, type, size, or date. To change this display sequence, select **View → Arrange Icons** from the menu bar and choose the desired sort order.

There are two ways to view the properties and attributes of a particular folder. After selecting a file or folder in the **Contents of** pane, do the following:

1. Right-click or select **File** from the menu bar.
2. Select **Properties**.
3. In the **Properties** window, select the **General** tab.

Figure A.3 displays the General tab for a file using the FAT file system. If the NTFS file system were used, an Advanced Attributes option would also be displayed.

DIR COMMAND

The **dir** command is available from the command prompt and gives the user the ability to display file and directory properties and attributes via the command line. Its default output display includes the volume label and serial number of the disk, a list of the contents of the current or selected directory, the number of files listed, the total size of the files listed, and the amount of disk space remaining. The listing for each file or directory includes its size in bytes as well as the date and time it was last modified. The file extension, if any, is displayed following the file name.

An example of a portion of the **dir** command output is shown in Figure A.4. Its syntax is

```
dir [file(s)] [options]
```

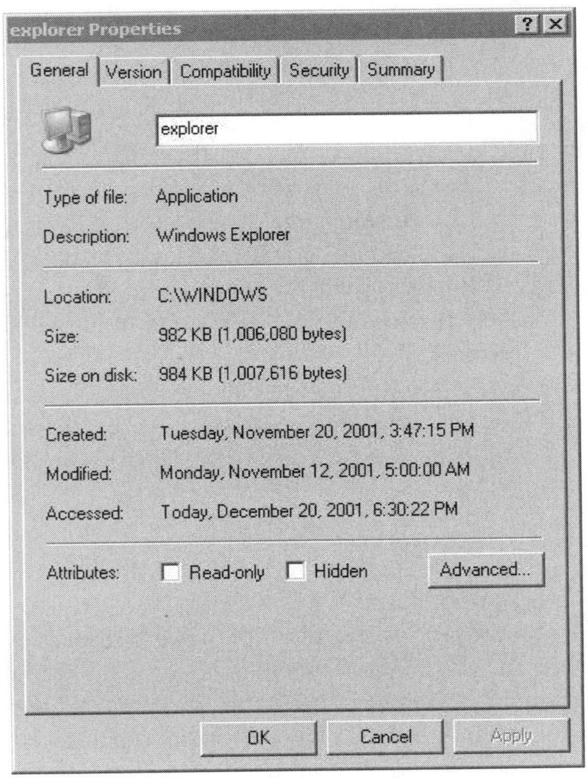

FIGURE A.3 File Properties

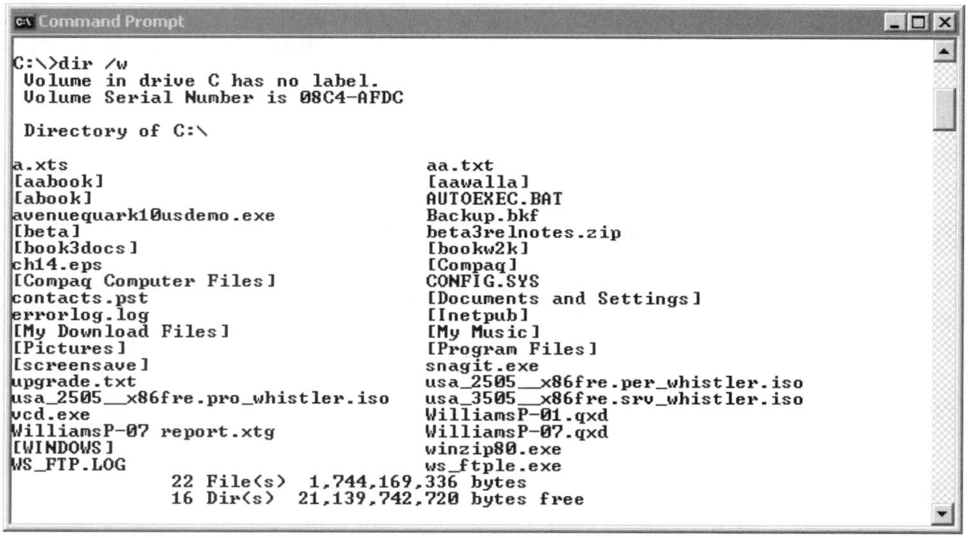

FIGURE A.4 Directory Listing

Neither *file(s)* nor options is required. Without these parameters, the **dir** command will simply display the default information for the current directory. The **file(s)** parameter can be one or more file names or directories. Its format can be just the file or directory name or the drive designation and path as well, using the standard syntax *drive:path\filename*; the wildcard characters * and ? may also be used (unlike early versions of DOS that require *.*). Separate multiple file names with spaces, commas, or semicolons.

Windows Server 2003 allows a user to create his own default results for the **dir** command through the dircmd environment variable. To set the default switches to be automatically executed whenever **dir** is entered at the command line, enter the following:

```
set dircmd=options
```

This action will bring up options available via any of the switches identified in Table A.32, which are considered the default until they are reset or Windows .NET is restarted. To override the default for a single command, enter a minus sign before the switch. For example, if the user enters the command set **dircmd=/n** and wants to see the shorter, wide listing for a directory that contains a large number of files, he enters **dir /-n/w**. Refer to the **set** command for more information regarding setting, overriding, and clearing environment variables.

TABLE A.32 dir Command Options

Option	Qualifier	Description
/a	*:attributes*	Displays only those files that match the attributes listed. The default (which is without the **/a** switch) displays all files except those with the Hidden or System attribute set. The attributes qualifier is optional; when not used, the **dir /a** command will display all files, even hidden and system. The colon (:) is optional as well. Multiple attributes may be entered in any order as long as there are no spaces between them, but only files that match all of the attributes will be displayed. A minus sign in front of the attribute will display all files that do not match that attribute. Acceptable values are **a** (files that have the Archive or Backup attribute set), **-a** (files that do not have the Archive attribute set), **d** (directories only), **-d** (files only, no directories), **h** (hidden files), **-h** (files that are not hidden), **r** (read-only files), **-r** (files that are not read-only), **s** (system files), **-s** (nonsystem files).
/b		Prohibits display of any heading or summary information. Do not use in conjunction with the **/w** option.
/d		Displays the files/directories in columns, sorting by columns.
/l		Displays any unsorted files/directories in lowercase letters.
/n		Displays the following information for each file/directory: date and time last modified, whether the file is a directory, the size of the file, the name of the file or directory. This is the default format for the **dir** command. If the user wants the file names to display on the left, enter this option **as /-n.**
/o	*:order*	Displays the files sorted in the order given. The default (without the **/o** switch) is to display the files/directories in the order stored. Using the **/o** switch without any order specified will display the directories sorted alphabetically, then the files sorted alphabetically. The colon (:) is optional. Values for order may be entered in any order and combination as long as there are no spaces between them, but the sort order will be defined by the order of the values, such that the first order value will be the primary sort key, the next one the secondary sort key, and so on. Acceptable values are **d** (sort in ascending order by date and time, oldest first), **-d** (sort in descending order by date and time, newest first), **e** (sort alphabetically by file extension), **-e** (sort in reverse alphabetical order by file extension), **g** (display with directories grouped before files), **-g** (display with directories grouped after files), **n** (sort alphabetically by file or directory name), **-n** (sort in reverse alphabetical order by name), **s** (sort in ascending order by size, smallest first), **-s** (sort in descending order by size, largest first).

(Continues)

TABLE A.32 Continued

Option	Qualifier	Description
/q		Pauses after each full screen of data.
/p		Displays only one screen at a time. Any key can be pressed to display the next screen.
/s		Displays all occurrences of the file name given in the specified directory as well as its subdirectories. Obviously, this option requires the file(s) parameter.
/t	*:time*	Displays the selected time for each file, where time can be **c** for the creation time, **a** for the time the file was last accessed, or **w** for the time the file was last written. When used in conjunction with the **/od** or **/o-d**, it identifies the time field that is used for sorting.
/w		Displays the directory contents in wide format, which contains up to five columns of file/directory names.
/x		Displays the MS-DOS names for the files before the Windows Server 2003 names. Remember that the Server allows longer file names than the MS-DOS 8/3 character limit. The format of the display is similar to that of the **/n** option.
/4		Displays four-digit years.

dir Command Examples

For recursive listings, enter the following while in the root directory:

```
dir /s/n/o/p
```

This command produces a long alphabetical listing of all files, directories, and subdirectories, pausing at the end of each full screen of information. The directories display first, then the files.

To display files in the current directory that have both the Hidden and System attributes, enter the following:

```
dir /ahs
```

or

```
dir /a:hs
```

To simply display all files with a .doc extension in the current directory and its subdirectories, enter the following:

```
dir *.doc /s
```

TABLE A.33 echo Command Options

Option	Description
On	Turns on the echo feature. In other words, displays (or echos) each command as it is executed.
Off	Turns off the echo feature. Typing **echo off** on the command line removes the prompt from the screen.
Message	Displays the message on the screen. This command is usually used in batch files following an **echo off** command.
. (period)	Displays a blank line. The syntax for this option is **echo.** with no space between the word echo and the period.

ECHO COMMAND

The **echo** command is used primarily in batch files to either enable or disable the command echoing feature or to display a message to the screen. Its syntax is

```
echo [options]
```

Using echo without options will display whether the echo feature is turned on or off. See Table A.33 for options.

Displaying Help

Windows Server 2003 provides both graphical and command-line methods of displaying Help documentation to the user. The graphical version is accessed from the **Start** menu by choosing **Start** → **Help** as shown in Figure A.5.

HELP COMMAND

Through the command line, the **help** command can be used to display Help information about Windows commands except net commands. The syntax is

```
help [command]
```

The parameter command is the name of the command for which you wish information. Omitting the command creates a display of each available command along with a brief description.

As an alternative to typing **help** and then the command name, the user can use the **/?** switch after the command. For example, **dir /?** and **help dir** will both produce the same Help information.

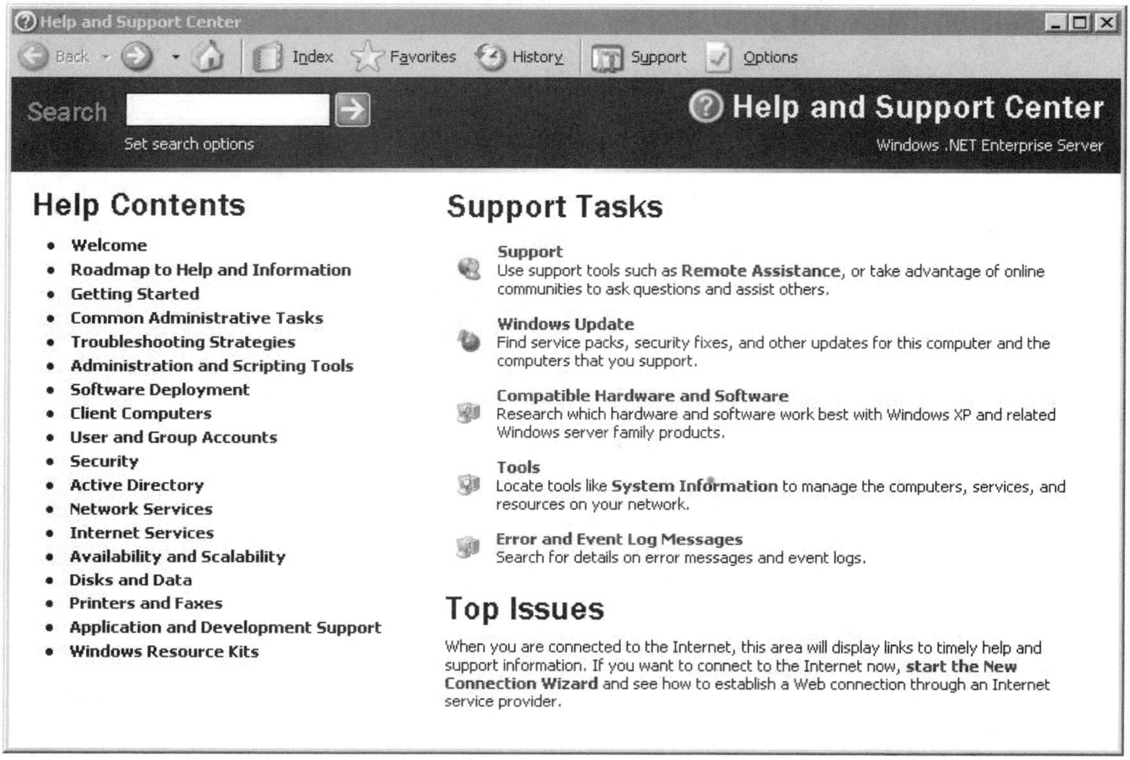

FIGURE A.5 Help Display

NET HELP COMMAND

The **net help** command provides Help information for the Windows Server 2003 net commands. It has two acceptable formats:

```
net help [command]
```

and

```
net command {/help | /?}
```

The command parameter can contain one of three values:

- A net command, such as net account, net start, net user, and so on.
- The word services, which provides a list of network services the user executing the command can start.
- The word syntax, which provides information on interpreting the syntax used within the net Help documentation.

NET HELPMSG COMMAND

The **net helpmsg** command provides the user with more information regarding a net error message. The syntax is

```
net helpmsg number
```

The number parameter is the number of the net error message. Net error messages are displayed in the following way:

```
NET ####: Message
where #### is the number included in the net helpmsg command.
```

FILE-MANAGEMENT COMMANDS

The file-management commands and procedures allow a user to create, remove, copy, move, and rename files and directories. These tasks may be completed using graphical methods in Windows Server 2003 Explorer or My Computer windows. My Network Places windows will permit some of these actions for resources shared across the network, provided that the user has the permission to execute them. Explorer is the application we use for most examples.

Displaying Path Names

While in Windows Server 2003 Explorer, a user can view the full path name of her current location by selecting **View** from the menu bar and then selecting **Options** → **View**. In the **View** tab, select the option **Display the full path in the title bar**, which is the default setting.

If you want to determine the current directory while at the command prompt, type **cd** and press **ENTER**.

Creating and Removing Folders

Windows Server 2003 provides command-line and graphical procedures for creating and removing directories or folders. This section discusses both.

CREATING FOLDERS

New folders can be created through Windows Server 2003 Explorer and My Computer windows using the same procedure. To create a folder (or directory) from Windows Explorer, follow this procedure:

1. Select the folder that will contain the new directory.
2. Select **File** from the menu bar.

3. Select **New**.
4. Select **Folder**.
5. In the **Contents of** pane, the **New Folder** icon will appear at the bottom of the file list. Enter the name of the new folder.

MKDIR COMMAND

The **mkdir** command enables the user to create a directory from the command line. Another name for it is **md**, and its syntax is

```
mkdir directory-name
```

or

```
md directory-name
```

The *directory-name* parameter is the name of the folder (or directory) you wish to create. The drive designation may be included here as well as a path should you wish to create a subdirectory. Suppose, for example, that the current directory is the root directory on the C: drive and you want to create the folder budget in the year2002 directory on the D: drive. To do this without moving from the current location, enter

```
mkdir d:\year2002\budget
```

REMOVING FOLDERS

Windows Server 2003 provides several ways to remove folders through Explorer or My Computer. Removing a folder places it in the **Recycle Bin** where it can still be accessed. Only when the **Recycle Bin** is cleared are folders permanently removed from the system.

The simplest way to remove a folder is to select it and then click **Delete**. A confirmation message similar to the following will display: "Are you sure you want to remove the folder and move all its contents to the Recycle Bin?" to which you must respond by clicking **Yes** or **No**.

Another way to remove a folder using Windows Server 2003 Explorer is:

1. Select the folder.
2. Select **File** from the menu bar.
3. Click **Delete**.

Step 2 is not necessary if you select the folder by right-clicking it. Doing so displays a menu that also contains the **Delete** option.

As an alternative, you can select the folder and then, while holding down the left mouse button, drag the folder to the **Recycle Bin** icon and release the button. If you want the folder to be permanently removed from the system, hold down the SHIFT key while dragging the folder to the **Recycle Bin**.

rmdir Command

The **rmdir** command, also known as **rd**, deletes the given directory (or folder). The syntax is

```
rmdir directory-name [/s]
```

or

```
rd directory-name [/s]
```

The *directory-name* parameter is the name of the directory or folder you wish to delete. It can contain both the drive designation and the path name if necessary.

The **/s** switch is optional and enables any files and subdirectories in the folder to be deleted as well. If it is not used, the directory must be empty before it can be removed.

Moving between Folders

Moving between folders in Windows Server 2003 is as simple as selecting a different folder with the mouse, which you can do in Explorer either in the **All Folders** or the **Contents of** pane. Within My Computer windows, just click the icon that represents the folder or the folder name.

CHDIR COMMAND

The **chdir** command, also known as **cd**, enables the user to display the name of the current directory as well as to change to a different directory. The syntax is

```
chdir [/d] [[drive:]directory-name]
```

or

```
cd [/d] [[drive:]directory-name]
```

The parameters **/d** and *drive:directory-name* are optional. If neither is entered, the **chdir** command will display the name of the current directory, including the drive designation.

The **/d** switch changes the current drive designation. The *drive:directory-name* parameter identifies the new drive and directory. The drive designation is entered only when necessary. Using a double period (..) in place of the directory name will change the directory from the current one to its parent.

Creating and Removing Files

This section provides procedures and commands for creating and removing files within Windows Server 2003.

CREATING FILES

Files are usually created in Windows Server 2003 via an installed application such as Notepad or WordPad. From within Windows Server 2003 Explorer and the My Computer windows, selecting **File → New** will provide a list of the file types you can create based on the applications installed on your system. In addition, the MS-DOS editor, edlin, is accessible from the command prompt.

REMOVING FILES

The procedure for removing files is the same as that for removing folders. The simplest method is to select it and then click **Delete**. To do so using Windows Server 2003 Explorer:

1. Select the file.
2. Select **File** from the menu bar.
3. Click **Delete**.

Step 2 is not necessary if you select the file using the right mouse button. Right-clicking will display a menu that also contains the **Delete** option.

As an alternative, you can select the file and drag it to the **Recycle Bin** icon. If you want the file permanently removed from the system, hold the SHIFT key down while dragging it to the **Recycle Bin** or simultaneously press the SHIFT and DELETE keys.

To select multiple files for deletion, hold down the CRTL key while selecting the files with the mouse and then drag them to the **Recycle Bin**.

DEL AND ERASE COMMANDS

The **del** command deletes or erases files from the system. Another name for this command is **erase**, and its syntax is

```
del file(s) [options]
```

or

```
erase file(s) [options]
```

TABLE A.34 del Command Options

Option	Qualifier	Description
/a	*:attributes*	Deletes files that match the given attributes: r for Read-Only, h for Hidden, s for System, a for Archive. A minus (–) sign may be used in front of any of the above options to identify files that do not match the given attribute.
/f		Forces Read-Only files to be deleted.
/p		Requires the user to confirm whether a file should or should not be deleted by displaying the following prompt: file, Delete (Y/N)? Y will delete the file, N will not. (To abort the delete command altogether, enter a CTRL+C.)
/q		Does not prompt for confirmation. This is the default option.
/s		Deletes the files listed not only from the current directory but also from the subdirectories.

The *file(s)* parameter identifies the files to be removed from the system and can contain the drive designation and the directory path in the format *drive:path\file*. More than one file can be deleted using one **del** command by separating the multiple file names with spaces, commas, or semicolons.

The wildcard characters * and ? can be used when specifying files to be deleted. It is important that these be used with care to reduce the risk of deleting critical files. See Table A.34 for options.

Copying and Moving Files

The copy procedure creates a duplicate of the original file in another location so that more than one copy exists. The move procedure places the original file in another location without making a duplicate of it.

Windows Server 2003 provides both graphical and command-line methods for copying and moving files. The graphical method using the Explorer application provides the user multiple ways to copy and move, such as menus and drag and drop. In addition, it enables a user to copy and move files within and between disks, or across the network.

The following sections discuss both the graphical and command-line procedures for these tasks.

COPYING FILES

To copy a file using the drag-and-drop method in Windows Server 2003 Explorer:

1. Display the file in the **Contents of** pane.
2. Make sure that the destination directory is visible in the **All Folders** pane. (Or start another copy of Explorer and display the destination directory in the **Contents of** pane.)
3. Select the file you wish to copy.
4. Hold down the CTRL key and drag the file to its destination.

For multiple files, in step 3, hold down the CTRL key while selecting.

To use the menu bar in Explorer to copy files:

1. Select the files.
2. Select **Edit** → **Copy** or press **CTRL+C**.
3. Select the destination directory.
4. Select **Edit** → **Paste** or press **CTRL+V**.

Selecting the files with the right mouse button also displays a menu that contains the **copy** command.

Copying an executable file (one that has a .exe or .com extension) may create a shortcut—that is, a link to the executable that gives the user an alternative way of executing the program. Shortcuts are often dragged and dropped to the main screen so that the user can bypass the menus.

COPY COMMAND

The **copy** command copies the source file or files to the indicated destination. It can also be used to combine the contents of files. The syntax is

```
copy [/a|/b] source-file [/a|/b] dest-file [/a|/b] [options]
```

The *sourcefile* is the name of the file to be copied. It can be just the file name, it can include the drive designation and the directory path as necessary, or it can be an actual device.

The *dest-file* is the name of the destination file but can be extended to include the drive designation and the directory path, or it can be a device name such as COM1 or LPT1. If this parameter is omitted, a file with the same name, creation date, and time is created in the current directory and on the current drive. If a file with that name already exists, an error is displayed.

The parameter [**/a**|**/b**] indicates whether the file is ASCII (**/a** switch) or binary (**/b** switch). The default value is binary when copying and ASCII when combining.

TABLE A.35 copy Options

Option	Used after the source-file	Used after the dest-file
/a	Copies all data in the file up to the first end-of-file character. The end-of-file character is not copied. The data is considered to be in ASCII format.	Adds an end-of-file character to the end of the *dest-file* as the last character.
/b	Copies all data in the file including the end-of-file character. The data is considered to be in binary format.	Does not add an end-of-file character to the end of the *dest-file*.

When the [**/a**|**/b**] switch is entered before the name of the source file, all items that follow use that flag until a different [**/a**|**/b**] switch is entered. This new switch applies to the source file that immediately precedes it as well as to any source files that follow it. Placement of the **/a** or **/b** after the source file or the destination file results in different copy procedures, as explained in Table A.35.

When the *dest-file* is a device, the **/b** switch should be used so that special control characters are copied to it as data. If the **/a** switch is used in this instance, the ASCII copy might cause those control characters to be interpreted, providing unpredictable results.

Four additional options are available, indicated in the syntax line as options, and defined in Table A.36.

copy Command Examples

To copy the file Budget.xls, which exists on the C: drive, to the directory d:\financial\year2000, enter the following:

```
copy budget.xls d:\financial\year2000
```

TABLE A.36 copy Command Options

Option	Description
/n	Uses the MS-DOS file name format of *filename.ext* when copying files with longer names.
/v	Verifies each file copied. If an error occurs, a message is displayed. This switch causes the copy command to execute more slowly.
/y	Suppresses the prompt to overwrite an existing file.
/z	Copies networked files so that they are in restart mode.

If you want to copy an ASCII file up to the first end-of-file character and output it to a file with the end-of-file character added, enter

```
copy demo.txt /a newdemo.txt /a
```

COMBINING FILES WITH THE COPY COMMAND. To instruct the **copy** command to combine files, enter multiple source files separated by plus signs. Remember that the default file type is considered ASCII when combining files. For binary files, you must enter the **/b** switch. The syntax for combining files is

```
copy [/a|/b] source-file1 [+ source-file2 [/a|/b] [+ source-file...]]
dest-file [/a|/b] options
```

Wildcard characters can also be used to designate multiple files to be combined.

A special use of the plus sign parameter allows the user to update the date and time of the file to the current date and time without changing the file's contents. The syntax is

```
copy [/a|/b] source-file+ ,,
```

COPY COMMAND EXAMPLES USING THE COMBINING OPTION. Suppose that a department manager wants to combine all of her employees' monthly status reports for April into one file. She enters

```
copy grwapr.rpt + ebgapr.rpt + eegapr.rpt April.rpt
```

If all of the above files were in the same directory, a variation of this command could be entered:

```
copy *apr.rpt April.rpt
```

XCOPY COMMAND

The **xcopy** command is more comprehensive than the **copy** command; it allows the user to copy not only files and directories but also subdirectories. The syntax is

```
xcopy source-file [dest-file]
[options]
```

The *source-file* parameter represents the names of the files to be copied and their locations. It must include either a drive designation or a directory path.

The *dest-file* parameter is the destination of the files to be copied and may include the file name as well as the drive designation and the directory path as necessary. Specifying *the dest-file* is optional, and if it's not included, the source files are copied to the current drive and directory. The destination files automatically have the archive attribute set.

xcopy Command Example

To copy the directory budget and all of its files and subdirectories to the year2000 directory, creating a directory named budget at the same time, enter

```
xcopy \budget \year2000 /i/s/e
```

The **/i** switch will create a directory named budget under this directory, copying both files and subdirectories; the **/e** switch will ensure that empty subdirectories get copied as well. See Table A.37 for options.

MOVING FILES

To move a file using the drag-and-drop method in Windows Server 2003 Explorer:

1. Display the file in the **Contents of** pane.
2. Make sure that the destination directory is visible in the **All Folders** pane. (Or start another copy of Explorer and display the destination directory in the **Contents of** pane.)
3. Select the file you wish to move.
4. Drag the file to its new destination if it is on the same disk as its current location. Otherwise, hold down the SHIFT key while dragging the file to force the move. If the SHIFT key is not held down, the file will be copied, not moved.

Remember, to select multiple files, hold down the CTRL key while selecting. To use the menu bar in Windows Server 2003 Explorer to do this:

1. Select the files.
2. Select **Edit** → **Cut** or press **CTRL+X**.
3. Select the destination directory.
4. Select **Edit** → **Paste** or press **CTRL+V**.

move Command

The **move** command actually moves files from one directory to another so that they no longer exist in their original location. The syntax is

```
move source-file(s) dest-file
```

The *source-file(s)* parameter indicates the files that you wish to move. It can be just the file name or it can include the drive designation and directory as necessary. Wildcard characters can be used to move multiple files.

TABLE A.37 xcopy Command Options

Option	Qualifier	Description
/a		Copies only those source-files with the Archive attribute set. Using this switch does not cause the Archive attribute to change.
/d	*:date*	Copies only those files with a modification date the same as or after the :date qualifier, which is in the format of MM-DD-YY. The :date qualifier is optional; if it is not used, only those files that are more recent than any existing destination files are copied.
/e		Must be used with the /s and /t options and allows empty subdirectories to be copied as well as those containing files.
/exclude	*:filename*	Excludes from copying the files contained in filename. Filename is a file that can contain one pattern per line without the use of wildcard characters. A file is not copied when any portion of the source-file parameter matches a line in filename.
/i		Creates a directory called dest-file, if the source-file contains wildcards or if the source-file is a directory and if dest-file does not exist. Then copies all source-files to the dest-file directory. When not set, the xcopy command prompts the user to identify the dest-file as a file (F) or a directory (D).
/k		Copies the source-files without changing the Read-Only attribute. Automatically removes the Read-Only attribute whenever this option is not used.
/n		Copies files using the short file name format of filename.ext. This is required when copying files to a system that can only handle shorter file names.
/p		Displays a confirmation prompt prior to creating the destination file.
/q		Does not display messages.
/r		Enables the command to copy over read-only files.
/s		Copies both directories and subdirectories, except empty ones. When omitted, subdirectories are not copied.
/t		Does not copy files under subdirectories but only the subdirectories themselves. Must be used with the **/e** switch to copy empty subdirectories.
/u		The update option. When used, it will copy only files that already exist at the destination, thereby updating them.
/v		Verifies each new file.
/w		Displays a message that requires the user to press any key to start the copy process.
/x		Copies file auditing settings.
/y /-y		Suppresses prompting before overwriting a file; **-y** forces the prompt.
/z		Copies files over the network in restartable mode.

The *dest-file* parameter represents the new location. It too can be a new file name or it can include a new drive designation or new directory path as necessary. Wildcard characters can be used here as well, such as when you need to change the extensions on a number of file names.

RENAMING FILES OR FOLDERS

To rename a file using Windows Server 2003 Explorer:

1. Select the file or folder.
2. From the menu bar select **File → Rename**.
3. Enter the new name for the file or folder.

or

1. Select the file or folder by right-clicking to display a menu.
2. Select **Rename**.
3. Enter the new name for the file or folder.

RENAME COMMAND

The **rename**, or **ren**, command permits changing the name of a file or directory without changing its location. In other words, file names cannot be changed across drives or directories with this command. For that, you need the **copy** or **move** command. The syntax for both formats of **rename** is

```
rename oldfile newfile
```

or

```
ren oldfile newfile
```

The *oldfile* parameter is the name of the file you wish to change and may include the drive designation and directory path. The *newfile* parameter is the new name for the file and may not include a drive or path. If a file already exists with the new file name, an error will be displayed. Wildcard characters can be used in names of both old files and new files.

Determining File Type

Windows Server 2003 Explorer will automatically attempt to identify a file type, which is displayed in the **Type** column of the **Contents of** pane as long as a detailed view is selected (**View → Details**). Another method of displaying the file type is to select **File → Properties → General**. You can also select the file with the right mouse button and then select **Properties → General**.

FILE-MANIPULATION COMMANDS

Several commands may be entered at the command prompt that allow the manipulation of files, such as **attrib, copy,** and **sort**. **Attrib** permits the user to change file attributes; **copy** permits the user to combine files; and **sort** sorts data. The **attrib** and **sort** commands are discussed below; **copy** was discussed in the "File-Management Commands" section.

assoc Command

The **assoc** command displays and changes the file name extension that is associated with a file type or application. The syntax it uses is

```
assoc [.ext[=[filetype]]]
```

To view the associated extension of file type .doc

```
Type assoc .doc
```

attrib Command

The **attrib** command allows the user to either display or change a file's attributes—Archive, Hidden, Read-Only, Compressed, and System (Compressed is available only on NTFS file systems and cannot be altered using this command). The syntax is

```
attrib [attributes] filename [/s]
```

Neither the *attributes* parameter nor the **/s** switch is entered to display the attributes associated with a particular file. Instead, the syntax is **`attrib`** *`filename`*. The *filename* parameter is the name of the file with the drive designation and path included where necessary. The **/s** switch is used when setting or changing attributes and instructs the command to change not only the files in the current directory but also those in the subdirectories. As with most commands, the wildcard characters * and ? may be used to designate multiple files to change.

Table A.38 identifies the acceptable values for the *attributes* parameter. More than one attribute can be set within a single command, but if the system or hidden attribute is set, it must be removed before any other attribute can be modified.

ATTRIB COMMAND EXAMPLE

To add the Archive attribute to all the files in the current directory, enter

```
attrib +a *.*
```

TABLE A.38 Attribute Values

Attribute	Description
+a	Adds the Archive attribute.
-a	Removes the Archive attribute.
+h	Adds the Hidden attribute.
-h	Removes the Hidden attribute.
+r	Adds the Read-Only attribute.
-r	Removes the Read-Only attribute.
+s	Adds the System attribute.
-s	Removes the System attribute.

SORT COMMAND

The **sort** command sorts the input data and outputs the result to the screen, a file, or a device. It also accepts input from another command, from a file, or from data entered on the terminal screen. The syntax of sort can be one of the following:

```
sort options < infilename > outfilename
command | sort options > outfilename
```

The *infilename* parameter is the name of the file that contains the data to be sorted. The drive designation and directory path may be entered as necessary. The *outfilename* parameter is the name of the file that contains the sorted data. Once again, the drive designation and directory path may be entered if needed. The *command* parameter is a command whose output will be sorted by **sort**. Two options are available as shown in Table A.39.

If the *command* or *infilename* parameters are omitted, the **sort** command will take input as the user enters it on the screen until a CTRL+Z+ENTER sequence is encountered. If the *outfilename* parameter is omitted, the sorted data will display on the screen.

TABLE A.39 sort Command Options

Option	Description
/+n	Sorts the data based on the character in column *n*. The default sort is based on the character in column 1.
/r	Executes a reverse sort either in reverse alphabetical or reverse numerical order

MISCELLANEOUS COMMANDS

The following commands do not fit neatly into a broader category, so we have placed them in a miscellaneous group simply for editorial convenience.

cacls Command

The CACLS command-line utility displays and modifies a file's access control list (ACL). See Table A.40 for options. The syntax is

```
cacls filename [/option] [permissions]
```

Converting to NTFS

Windows Server 2003 can run on FAT and FAT32 file systems, but using NTFS has advantages. You do not have to reinstall the OS to change a file system to NTFS, but once you do, you cannot change it back.

CONVERT COMMAND

The **convert** command will change an existing FAT or FAT32 file system volume to NTFS. The current active drive cannot be converted during the present session with **convert** but only at the next system reboot. The syntax is

```
convert [drive:] /fs:ntfs [/v]
```

TABLE A.40 cacls Command Options

Option	Qualifier	Description
/e		Edits rather than replaces the ACL.
/c		Makes changes even if errors are found.
/g	*User:perm*	Grants special rights to the specified user.
/t		Changes the ACL in the defined files and all subdirectories.
n		No permission.
r		Read permission.
c		Change or Write permission.
f		Full Control permission.
/r	*User*	Revokes the rights of a specified user.
/p	*User*	Replaces the permissions of specified users with new ones.

Setting and Displaying Date and Time

To display the current date, move the cursor to the time display in the bottom right corner of the taskbar. To modify this date, double-click on the time to bring up the Date/Time Properties window (Figure A.6). On the **Date/Time** tab, you can change the current date as well as view a calendar for the month and year selected. You can also modify the time from this window. An alternative way to display the Date/Time Properties window is by selecting **Start** → **Settings** → **Control Panel** → **Date/Time**.

To change the format of a date or time display, select **Start** → **Settings** → **Control Panel** → **Regional Settings**. Once in the Regional Settings Properties window, select either the **Date** or the **Time** tab as appropriate. Within these tabs, you can, for example, change the time format to a 24-hour clock or change the date to the format yy/mm/dd. Another method of displaying the date and time is by selecting **Start** → **Programs** → **Accessories** → **Clock**.

The command line also offers options to assist in displaying and changing the date and time. These are discussed below.

DATE COMMAND

The **date** command allows the user to either display or change the date. The syntax is

```
date [mm-dd-yy]
```

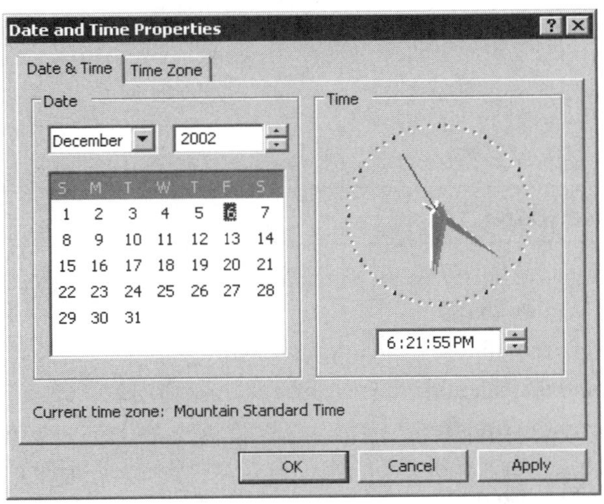

FIGURE A.6 Date/Time Properties Windows

If the *mm-dd-yy* parameter is omitted, the current system date is displayed. If not, the date is set to the value you enter. Acceptable values for the month, or *mm*, parameter are 1 through 12; for the day, or *dd*, parameter, 1 through 31. The year, or *yy*, parameter can be 80 through 99 or 1980 through 2099. If you prefer not to use dashes to separate the month, day, and year, parameters can be replaced with either a period (.) or a slash (/).

TIME COMMAND

The **time** command allows the user to either display or change the system time. The syntax is

```
time [hrs:[min[:sec[.hun]]]][AP]
```

When no parameters are entered, the current system time is displayed, which you can change if necessary. If you do not enter a new time, just press ENTER. If you do, use the syntax identified in Table A.41.

NET TIME COMMAND

The **net time** command allows a user to synchronize the time on her current system and another domain (or computer) across the network. It also allows her to display the time for any system on the network. The syntax is

```
net time [\\computername | /domain[:domainname]] [/set]
```

When no parameters are given, the **net time** command will display the time from the time server system. The **/set** parameter is optional and required only when you want to change the time. If omitted, the time on the system named is displayed; if used, the time on the current system is synchronized with the time on the system named.

TABLE A.41 time Options

Option	Description
hrs	Enters the hour in either regular or 24-hour format. Acceptable values are 0 through 23.
min	Enters the minutes, ranging from 0 through 59.
sec	Enters the seconds, ranging from 0 through 59.
.hun	Enters the hundredths of a second, ranging from 0 through 99.
AP	Enters A for A.M. or P for P.M. This field is not necessary if the 24-hour format is used.

The *computername* or the **/domain**:*domainname* identifies the system for which to display the time or the system with which the current system's time is synchronized. The *domainname* portion of the **/domain**:*domainname* parameter is optional. (Chat is not available from within a Terminal Services session.)

Logging on as Another User

To log on as another user, you must first access the Windows Server 2003 Security window by pressing **CTR+ALT+DEL**. This window displays who you are currently logged on as, the name of the current domain, and the date and time of logon. Select the **Logoff** button to log off as this user.

Chat Mode

The Windows Server 2003 winchat application allows users to converse with each other. It is accessed by typing **winchat** from the command prompt. To initiate a conversation, select **Conversation → Dial** from the menu bar. In the Select Computer window that appears, either enter the name of the computer of the person you want to chat with or select one from the list.

When you receive a chat message, a **Chat** button will display on the taskbar. To respond to the message, click **Chat** and select **Conversation → Answer**.

While researching some problems with this utility, we discovered Microsoft's NetMeeting software, which enables communication over the Internet or an intranet. Windows Server 2003 has the Internet phone feature along with multi-user data conferencing, which allows application sharing, an electronic white board, a text-based chat facility, and binary file transfer.

NET NAME COMMAND

The **net name** command adds, deletes, or displays names that are authorized to receive messages. These names are used only for messaging and must be unique throughout the network. Windows Server 2003 acknowledges three types of names here: computer, user, and messaging. To execute the **net name** command, the Messenger service must be running. The syntax is

```
net name [name [/action]]
```

Executing the **net name** command without parameters will display a list of all names that can accept messages on this computer. The *name* parameter is the unique name authorized to receive messages and can be up to 15 characters. Acceptable values for the */action* parameter are **/add** and **/delete**, which instructs the command to add or delete the messaging name entered. The */action* parameter is optional, with **/add** as the default.

TABLE A.42 net send Options for the destination Parameter

Option	Qualifier	Description
*		Sends the message to all names in the user's group.
/domain	*:domainname*	Sends the message to all names in either the current domain or the domain or workgroup given by the *:domainname* parameter.
name		Enters the user name, the computer name, or the messaging name of the recipient of the message. Names that include space characters should be enclosed in quotes.
/users		Sends the message to all users connected to the server.

NET NAME COMMAND EXAMPLE

To add the messaging name techsupport to the computer, enter one of the following commands:

```
net name techsupport /add
```

or

```
net name techsupport
```

NET SEND COMMAND

The **net send** command works in conjunction with the Messenger service and enables you to send messages on the network to users, computers, and messaging names. Only users connected to the network and running the Messenger service will receive them. The syntax for **net send** is

```
net send destination message
```

The *message* parameter contains the message that will be delivered, which should be in quotes if it contains special characters, such as a slash. A message can hold up to 128 characters.

The values for the *destination* parameter are described in Table A.42. This parameter is required and must contain one of these values.

NETWORKING COMMANDS

In this section, we review some of the networking commands and procedures on Windows 2000 and Windows Server 2003, and we discuss how to connect to a system via modem and determine and set the system's host name.

Each net command is identified here but its detailed description may actually appear in another section. When this is the case, we refer you to that section.

arp Command

The **arp** (Address Resolution Protocol) command displays and changes the IP to an Ethernet (or Token Ring) physical address translation table. The syntax for **arp** is

```
arp -option inet_addr eth_addr [if_addr]
```

The *inet_addr* is the Internet address; the *eth_addr* is the Ethernet address; and the *if_addr* is the address translation table to be modified for the Internet address of the network interface. See Table A.43 for options.

HyperTerminal

The HyperTerminal application is bundled with Windows Server 2003 and enables a user to dial out to another computer via modem. It is accessed by selecting **Start → Programs → Accessories → HyperTerminal**.

Take the following steps to set up and connect to a remote location:

1. In the **Connect Description** window, enter the name of the connection you wish to make, such as "Microsoft BBS."
2. Click **OK** to display the **Connect To** window. Enter the appropriate information in the **Country Code, Area Code, Phone #,** and **Connect Using** text boxes to identify the number you wish to call using which modem installed on the system.

TABLE A.43 arp Options

Option	Description
/-a	Displays all ARP entries in the current protocol data. When the *inet_addr* is specified, the specific IP and physical address are displayed.
/-g	Performs the same function as **–a**.
/-N	Displays the specified *if_addr* network interface.
/-d	Deletes the *inet_addr* host. All hosts can be deleted by using the wildcard with *inet_addr*.
/-s	Associates the Internet address with the physical address (presented as 6 hexadecimal bytes separated by hyphens).

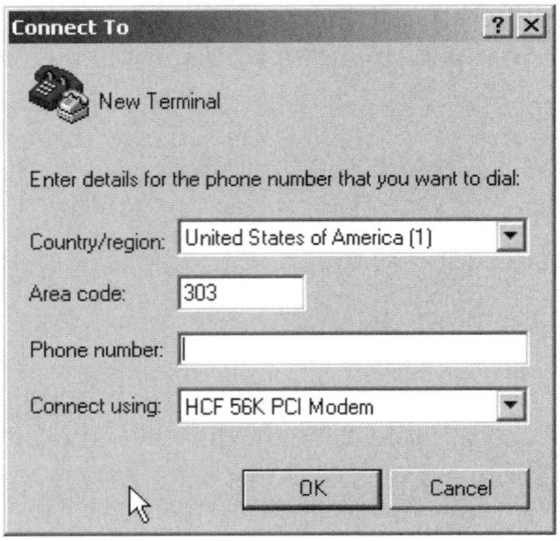

FIGURE A.7 The Connect To Window

3. After entering the phone number and modifying any other field, the **Connect To** window displays (Figure A.7). Change the phone number as well as the configuration of the local modem, including baud rate, data bits, and parity via the **Modify** button.
4. Click **Dialing Properties** to define the location from which to dial; include dialing prefixes to access an outside line or to turn off call waiting.
5. Click **Dial** to display the status of the modem, such as disconnected.
6. Click **Dial Now** to initiate the connection process.

To transfer files between systems, select **Transfer** from the menu bar; then **Send File** to send a file or **Receive File** to receive one. Within each of these options, the transfer protocol can be selected. To terminate a session, select the **Disconnect** icon from the toolbar or select **Call → Disconnect** from the menu bar.

ftp and tftp Commands

The file transfer protocol, **ftp,** command enables a user to transfer files between systems that have ftp installed and running. See Table A.44 for options list. Its syntax is

```
ftp [options] [hostname]
```

The *hostname* is the name or IP address of the remote system. When given, the **ftp** command establishes a connection with that system. Otherwise, it goes into command mode waiting for the user to enter a command. A list of the avail-

TABLE A.44 ftp Command Options

Option	Qualifier	Description
-d		Turns on the debugging option, which displays all ftp commands that are passed between the systems.
-g		Turns off file name "globbing," which means that wildcard characters are not expanded.
-I		Turns off interactive prompting, which means that ftp will automatically execute a given command for all file names entered.
-n		Does not allow auto-logon when the initial connection is made. Instead, the user must log on to the remote system.
-s	*:filename*	The file name qualifier is the name of a file that contains ftp commands that are executed immediately upon connection. Do not include spaces in this parameter.
-v		Does not display responses from the remote system.
-w	*:size*	Changes the size of the transfer buffer to size. The default is 4096.

able ftp commands can be retrieved by entering **help** at this point. Given the number of commands available, we do not discuss them here but recommend that you refer to Windows Server 2003 Help.

The trivial file transfer protocol (tftp) is a nonsecure version of ftp. Its use is generally not recommended, and it should not be enabled.

hostname Command

The host name is the name of a device that is on the network, which can be the computer name. In Windows Server 2003 it can be displayed from the command prompt by entering **hostname**. To identify the computer's full name and domain, click **Control Panel**, select **System Properties**, and select the **Network Identification** tab.

ipconfig Command

TCP/IP network configuration values are displayed by an **ipconfig** diagnostic command. They are the DNS suffix, IP address, subnet mask, and default gateway. When the **/all** option is used, much additional information is output, including the host name, node type, adapter physical address, and more. The syntax used is

```
ipconfig [/all] [/renew] [/release]
```

The **ipconfig** command is of great value when running DHCP because it permits the identification of DHCP-configured TCP/IP values. The ***/renew*** option reaffirms the current DHCP values. The **/release** option disables the related TCP/IP configuration values.

ipxroute Command

The ipBxroute command permits the viewing and modification of routing-table data employed by the IPX protocol, which uses options different from those for source routing. The **ipxroute** syntax for IPX is

```
ipxroute servers [type=x]
ipxroute stats [/show] [/clear]
ipxroute table
```

The syntax for source routing is

```
ipxroute board=n
ipxroute config
nbtstat Command
```

The **nbtstat** command is a diagnostic tool that displays current TCP/IP data and connections using NetBIOS over TCP/IP (NBT). See Table A.45 for an options list. The syntax is

```
nbtstat [- a remotename] [-A IP address] [-c] [-n] [-R] [-r] [-S] [-s]
[interval]
```

TABLE A.45 nbtstat Options

Option	Qualifier	Description
-a	*remotename*	Lists the remote computer's name table.
-A	*IP address*	Lists the remote computer's address.
-c		Lists the NetBIOS cache including the IP addresses.
-n		Lists the NetBIOS registration by type.
-R		Loads the lmhost file after deleting the NetBIOS cache.
-r		Lists WINS name-resolution statistics.
-S		Lists client and server connections. For remote computers, these are listed by IP address.
-s		Lists client and server connections and converts IP addresses to names.

netstat Command

The **netstat** command displays protocol statistics and current TCP/IP connection information. See Table A.46 for an options list. The syntax is

```
netstat [options]
```

Without options, the output includes

- *Proto*—the protocol used by the connection, such as TCP/IP.
- *Local Address*—either the IP address or host name of the local system as well as the connection's port number displayed as *name:port*. An asterisk displays in the port field if it hasn't been established yet.
- *Foreign Address*—displays either the IP address or the host name of the remote system as well as the port number, displayed as *name:port*.
- *State*—the state of the TCP/IP connection. Some examples are CLOSED, ESTABLISHED, and LAST_ACK.

TABLE A.46 netstat Command Options

Option	Qualifier	Description
-a		Displays the status of all connections and listening ports.
-e		Displays Ethernet statistics.
	interval	Displays statistics after each interval, where interval is the number of seconds between capturing statistics. To terminate the display, press CTRL+C. This option should be the last one on the command line.
-n		Displays addresses numerically—for example, the IP address instead of the host name.
-p	*protocol*	Displays the connections for the protocol given. Acceptable values are *tcp* and *udp*. If the **-s** option is also used, *icmp* or *ip* are also acceptable values.
-r		Displays the network routing tables.
-s		Displays protocol statistics for tcp, ucp, icmp, and ip. To reduce the number of protocols displayed, use this in conjunction with the **-p** option.

nslookup Command

The **nslookup** command provides data from the Domain Name System (DNS) server(s) both interactively and noninteractively. It also supports more than a dozen subcommands. With **nslookup,** the IP address of a host can be identified or a reverse lookup performed. The syntax is

```
nlslookup [-subcommand] [IP address]
```

ping Command

The **ping** command is used to test and verify network connections by sending ICMP (Internet Control Message Protocol) data packets to a remote computer and waiting for a reply. By default, four packets are transmitted and validated when received. See Table A.47 for an options list. The syntax of this command is

```
ping [options] hostname(s)
```

The host name(s) is the remote computer whose network connections you wish to test. It may contain either the host name itself or the IP address.

pathping Command

The pathping tool combines ping and tracert plus additional information. The statistics it provides allow network router or link problems to be identified. The **pathping** command forwards packets to routers and then computes the results based on returned packets for each network hop. See Table A.48 for an options list. Its syntax is

```
pathping [-n] [-h maximum_hops] [-g host-list] [-p period]
[-q num_queries] [-w timeout] target_name
```

rcp Command

The **rcp** command copies files between networked machines, including UNIX systems. It must be initiated by Windows Server 2003, and other systems must be running rshd, the remote shell daemon, and have the RCP utility installed. See Table A.49 for a list of options. The syntax for this command is

```
rcp [options] host.user:srcfile(s) host.user:dest-file
```

The *host.user:srcfile(s)* parameter is the name of the file to be copied to another system. It breaks down as follows:

- *host*—the name of the source computer system. It is required only if the source system is different from the system from which the command was executed,

TABLE A.47 ping Command Options

Option	Qualifier	Description
-a		Converts numerical addresses to their corresponding host names.
-f		Includes a flag in the data packet that instructs the gateways not to fragment the data.
-i	*time*	Sets the Time to Live field in the echo request packet to time, where time can be a value from 0 to 255.
-j	*list*	Routes the data packets through up to 9 host names contained in list. This option allows loose source routing, which means that intermediate gateways may separate consecutive hosts. **-j** cannot be used in conjunction with the **-k** option.
-k	*list*	Routes the data packets through up to 9 host names contained in list. This option allows strict source routing, which means that intermediate gateways may not separate consecutive hosts. **-k** cannot be used in conjunction with the **-j** option.
-l	*length*	Sends echo packets containing the amount of data specified by length. The default is 32 bytes; the maximum is 65,527.
-n	*count*	Defines the number of packets (count) transmitted before terminating the **ping** command. Zero is the default, where ping keeps running until receiving an interrupt signal.
-r	*count*	Sends the echo request directly to the host, bypassing routing tables.
-t		Only for multicast addresses, sets the Time-to-Live (TTL) field in the echo request packet (datagram), where TTL is a value from 0 to 255. The Time-to-Live field defines the maximum number of systems through which the packet can be sent. For example, a TTL of 0 limits the datagram to the local system. A TTL of 1 (the default) limits the transmission to systems directly connected to the default interface address (or the address specified by the **-i** option).
-v	*type*	Displays other packets received in addition to the echo request packets.
-w	*time*	Defines the timeout interval in milliseconds.

TABLE A.48 pathping Command Options

Option	Qualifer	Description
-n		Does not resolve host names.
-m	*maximum_hops*	Sets the maximum number of hops.
-g		Lists hosts within the intermediate gateways.
-p	*period*	Specifies the milliseconds to wait between pings; default is 250.
-n	*num_queries*	Specifies the number of queries to each computer; default is 100.
-w	*timeout*	Specifies the milliseconds to wait for a response; the default is 3000 (or 3 seconds).

TABLE A.49 rcp Command Options

Option	Description
-a	Copies files in ASCII mode. This is the default.
-b	Copies files in binary mode.
-h	Copies files that have the Hidden attribute set. By default, these files are not copied even if they are specifically requested.
-r	Copies the contents of a directory and its subdirectories. This is considered a recursive copy. Both the source-file and the dest-file should be directories.

or if a specific user name must be entered. The host can be either the host name or the IP address.

- *user*—the logon name of the user whose files are being copied. It is required when the host is entered as an IP address and when copying files that belong to another user.
- *srcfile*—the name of the file being copied. It may contain the entire path, if necessary, to locate the file if it is not in the current directory or in the user's logon directory when *host.user* is used.

The parameter *host.user:dest-file* is the name of the destination file or directory to which the file is copied. If more that one *srcfile* is listed, *dest-file* must be a directory. The *host.user* portion identifies the remote system as well as the logon name of the destination system. If the *host.user:dest-file* parameter is omitted, the local system is considered the default.

For the **rcp** command to be successful with UNIX systems, the *.rhosts* file must exist in the user's home directory on the remote computer. This file contains the host name of the local system as well as the user's name. It is recommended that the host name of the local system also be included in the remote system's /etc/hosts or /etc/hosts.equiv file.

route Command

The **route** command is used to manage and manipulate network routing tables under TCP/IP environments. See Table A.50 for an options list. Its syntax is

```
route [-f] [-p] [command [destination] [mask subnetmask] [gateway]
[metric costmetric]]
```

The **-f** parameter option clears all gateway routing tables. The **-p** parameter option is employed in conjunction with the **add** command to create a persistent route across boots of the system. (By default, routes are not preserved between system boots.)

Other parameters used with the route command are

- *destination*—determines the computer from which to send command.
- *mask subnetmask*—identifies a subnet mask to be associated with this route entry; the default is 255.255.255.255.
- *gateway*—identifies the gateway.
- *metric costmetric*—specifies an integer cost metric (from 1 to 9999) used in calculating the fastest, most reliable, and/or least expensive routes.

TABLE A.50 route Commands

Command	Description
Add	Adds a route.
Print	Prints a route.
Delete	Deletes a route.
Change	Changes the current route.

TABLE A.51 rsh Command Options

Option	Qualifier	Description
-l	*user*	Logon to the remote computer uses the name represented by user. When not used, logon is the user executing the **rsh** command.
-n		Redirects the input to NULL.

rsh Command

When the Remote Shell Service is running, the **rsh** command permits a user to execute commands on a remote system. See Table A.51 for an options list. The syntax is

```
rsh hostname [options] command
```

The *hostname* parameter is the name of the system on which you wish to run a command. The *command* parameter contains the command to be run on the remote system.

When the RSHutility is run from a Windows Server 2003, the primary domain controller must be available to validate the name of the user currently logged on. Also, to access a remote UNIX system, an .rhosts file should exist in the user's home directory. This file contains both the host names and the logon names of computers and users who have access to this remote system.

Telnet

Using telnet enables a user to connect to and communicate with another system using that system's own protocol. To access telnet within Windows 2000 and Windows Server 2003, select **Start → Programs → Accessories → telnet**. To connect to a remote system:

1. Select **Connect** from the menu bar.
2. Select **Remote System**.
3. In the **Connect** window, select or enter the **Host Name, Port,** and **TermType** (terminal emulation type).
4. Click **Connect**.

From the **Terminal** menu, select **Preferences** to define default preferences such as cursor type, terminal emulation, and fonts.

From the command prompt, simply type **telnet** to launch the telnet window; however, it is important to understand that this is a telnet client only. To accept telnet sessions from other systems, you must install the telnet Server, which is included on the Windows Server 2003 Resource Kit.

Net Commands

Windows Server 2003 provides a series of commands, known as *net commands*, that may be executed from the prompt or within batch files. Many of them can be performed through the graphical interface, but users sometimes prefer to use the command-line interface instead.

All of the net commands are identified here with at least a brief description. When necessary, we have indicated the section where a more detailed definition may be found.

The common options available for all net commands are described in Table A.52.

TABLE A.52 Common net Command Options

Option	Description
/no	Automatically responds to any prompt the net command issues with a "no." An alternative format is **/n**.
/yes	Automatically responds to any prompt the net command issues with a "yes." An alternative format is **/n**.

net accounts Command

The **net accounts** command allows authorized users to update the user accounts database. In addition, it facilitates modifications to the password and logon requirements for all users. For **net accounts** to execute properly, the Net Logon service must be running on the system that contains the accounts you wish to change. See Table A.53 for an options list. The syntax is

```
net accounts [options]
```

When **net accounts** is run without options, the current settings for password, logon limitations, and domain information are displayed.

TABLE A.53 net accounts Command Options

Option	Qualifier	Description
/forcelogoff	*:minutes*	Defines the number of minutes a user has before the system automatically logs him off after the expiration of either the account or logon time. The variable minutes can be numeric or the value "no." The value "no" is the default and does not allow a forced logoff. When a numeric value is entered for minutes, a warning is sent to the user.
/minpwlen	*:length*	Defines the minimum password length for a user account password. Acceptable values are 0 through 14, with 6 being the default.
maxpwage	*:days*	Defines the maximum number of days that a password is valid. Acceptable values for days are 1 through 49, 710, and "unlimited," which means that the password does not expire. The value used here must be greater than that defined for the **/minpwage** option.
/minpwage	*:days*	Defines the minimum number of days that must pass before a user can change his password. Acceptable values are 0 through 49 and 710, with 0 as the default, which means that no limitations are set.
/uniquepw	*:number*	Defines the number of password changes that must occur before a password can be reused. Acceptable values are 0 through 8, with 5 as the default.
/domain		Updates the user accounts database based on the parameters given for the primary domain controller of the current domain. Omitting this parameter updates the database on the current system.
/sync		Can only be used with the **/domain** option. It synchronizes the user account database. When executed from the primary domain controller, all backup domain controllers are synchronized. When executed from a backup domain controller, the backup is synchronized with the primary.

NET ACCOUNTS COMMAND EXAMPLES

To synchronize the user account databases on all member servers, enter

```
net accounts /sync
```

If you are currently using a Windows Server 2003 workstation and want to set the minimum password length to 10 characters for the domain to which the workstation is connected, enter

```
net accounts /minpwlen:10 /domain
```

NET COMPUTER COMMAND

The **net computer** command enables the user to add or delete computers from the domain database. These modifications are automatically forwarded to the primary domain controller. **net computer** can only be executed from a server. Its syntax is

```
net computer \\computername option
```

The *computername* parameter is the name of the computer to add or delete. The option parameter can contain one of two options: **/add** to add the computer name to the domain; and **/del** to delete the computer name from the domain.

net computer Command Example

To delete the computer \\incy from the domain, enter the following:

```
net computer \\incy /del
```

NET CONFIG COMMAND

Executing the **net config** command without parameters displays the services that are both configurable and running. With the appropriate parameters and options, this command enables a system administrator to permanently change the settings for a running service.

Two variations of **net config** are **net config server** and **net config workstation**. A discussion of both follows.

NET CONFIG SERVER COMMAND

The **net config server** command either displays or modifies the settings of the Server service while the service is running. Any changes are permanent. See Table A.54 for an options list. The syntax of this command is

```
net config server [options]
```

Executing the **net config server** command without options will display the current settings for the Server service. An example of the output display follows:

```
Server Name                          \\incy
Server Comment
Software version                     Windows Server 2003
Server is active on                  NetBT_NDISLoop1 (204c4f4f5020)
NetBT_NDISLoop1 (204c4f4f5020)
Server hidden                        No
Maximum Logged On Users              Unlimited
Maximum open files per session       2048
Idle session time (min)              15
The command completed successfully.
```

TABLE A.54 net config server Command Options

Option	Qualifier	Description
/autodisconnect	*:time*	Sets the maximum amount of time that a user's login session can be idle before it is automatically disconnected. Acceptable values are –1 through 65535 minutes, with 15 minutes as the default. Setting time to –1 instructs the service to never disconnect an idle user.
/hidden	*:{yes | no}*	Determines whether the computer name of the server will display on the lists of servers depending on whether yes or no is entered as the qualifier. The default is no.
/srvcomment	*:"text"*	Defines a message that can be displayed in many Windows Server 2003 windows as well as with the net view command. The qualifier text can be 48 characters long. The quotation marks are required.

net config server Command Example

To disconnect users after 30 minutes of idle time, enter the following command:

```
net config server /autodisconnect:30
```

NET CONFIG WORKSTATION COMMAND

The **net config workstation** command either displays or permanently modifies the settings of the Workstation service while the service is running. See Table A.55 for an options list. The command syntax is

```
net config workstation [options]
```

Executing the **net config workstation** command without options will display the current settings for the Workstation service on the local computer. The following is an example of the output display:

```
Computer name                 \\incy
User name                     Administrator
Workstation active on         NetBT_NDISLoop1 (204C4F4F5020)
Software version              Windows Server 2003
Workstation domain            BOOK
Logon domain                  BOOK
COM Open Timeout (sec)        3600
COM Send Count (byte)         16
COM Send Timeout (msec)       250
The command completed successfully.
```

TABLE A.55 net config workstation Command Options

Option	Qualifier	Description
/charcount	*:bytes*	Sets the number of bytes of data to be collected prior to sending them to a communications device. Acceptable values are 0 through 65535, with 16 bytes as the default.
/chartime	*:msec*	Sets the number of milliseconds (msec) for collecting data prior to sending it to a communications device. Acceptable values for msec are 0 through 65,535,000 milliseconds, with 250 milliseconds as the default.
/charwait	*:sec*	Specifies the number of seconds (sec) to wait for a communications device to become available. Acceptable values are 0 through 65535 seconds, with 3600 seconds as the default.

If both the **/charcount:bytes** and **/chartime:msec** options are used, Windows Server 2003 sends data to a communication device based on whichever parameter is fulfilled first.

NET CONTINUE COMMAND

The **net continue** command reactivates a service that has been suspended by the **net pause** command, without canceling a user's connection. The syntax is

```
net continue service
```

Acceptable values for the *service* parameter for standard services follow. Other services may be acceptable depending on what is installed on the system.

- ftp publishing service
- lpdsvc
- Net logon
- Network dde
- network dde dsdm
- lm security support provider
- remoteboot (at the Windows Server 2003 level only)
- remote access server
- Schedule
- Server
- Simple TCP/IP services
- Workstation

TABLE A.56 net file Command Options

Option	Description
id	Enters the identification number of the file, which is found in the first column of the net file list that displays all open files.
/close	Must be used in conjunction with the **id** option. It closes the file represented by the identification number, *id*.

NET FILE COMMAND

The ability to share files among computer systems and users is at the heart of a networked system. These shared files can be periodically left open or locked to prohibit access. The **net file** command enables the user to display both the names of any open shared file and the number of locks on it. In addition, it can close shared files and remove file locks. The syntax for net file is

```
net file [options]
```

When used without options, the command displays a list of all shared open files on the server as well as the number of locks each file has. The two possible options are shown in Table A.56.

NET GROUP COMMAND

The **net group** command permits the addition, display, or modification of global groups on Windows Server 2003 domains and can be run only from these domains. Users who work together or who have the same requirements for system use are usually classified as members of the same group. Table A.57 lists the options available for the **net group** command.

It is important to remember that the **net group** command deals with global groups. In essence, this means that group members can only be from the domain in which the group was created, but they can be assigned privileges anywhere in the network as long as there is a trust relationship among domains.

There are three syntax formats for this command:

```
net group [options]
net group groupname [options]
net group groupname user(s) [options]
```

When the **net group** command is executed without options, the display will include the name of the server as well as the name of each group on it. When the group name is displayed, it is preceded by an asterisk, which assists the user in differentiating group from user names when both are displayed.

TABLE A.57 net group Command Options

Option	Qualifier	Description
groupname	*/comment:"text"* or */action*	Enters the name of the group (*groupname*) to add, modify, or delete. When used without qualifiers (**net group groupname**), users in that group are displayed. When used with just the qualifier */comment:"text"*, the comment, text, is added to the existing group name entered, where text can be 48 characters long and must be enclosed in quotes. The */action* qualifier either adds the group name as new or deletes it. Acceptable values for */action* are */add* and */delete*. When using the */add* qualifier, the */comment:"text"* option can be used as well as in the format: **net group groupname /add** */comment:"text"*.
user(s)	*/action*	Lists the user(s) to be added to or deleted from group name based on the action given. Acceptable values for */action* are */add* and */delete*. If more than one user is entered, separate them with a space character.
/domain		Can be used with any of the syntax formats and is necessary only when executing the command from a workstation that is a member of a Windows Server 2003 domain. The option causes the **net group** command to execute on the primary domain controller of the current domain. The default (without this option) is to execute the command for the local computer.

net group Command Examples

To display all the users in the group sales1, enter

```
net group sales1
```

To add a comment to the record for this group, enter

```
net group sales1 /comment:"Direct Sales Personnel"
```

To add a group called sales2 and include a comment, enter

```
net group sales2 /add /comment:"Indirect Sales Personnel"
```

To delete the user gregh from sales1 and add the user to sales2, enter

```
net group sales1 gregh /delete
net group sales2 gregh /add
```

NET LOCALGROUP COMMAND

The **net localgroup** command enables the addition, deletion, or modification of local groups. Remember that a local group can contain users from the domain in which it was created as well as global users and global groups from other domains that have a trust relationship with that domain. One difference between a local group and a global group is that the former can be assigned privileges only in its own domain, whereas the latter can be assigned privileges in trusted domains. See Table A.58 for an options list.

The three syntax formats for the **net localgroup** command are

```
net localgroup [options]
net localgroup groupname [options]
net localgroup groupname name(s) [options]
```

TABLE A.58 net localgroup Command Options

Option	Qualifier	Description
groupname	*/comment:"text"* or */action*	Enters the name of the local group (*groupname*) to add, modify, or delete. When used without qualifiers (**net localgroup** *groupname*), the users and global groups within the local group *groupname* are displayed. When used with just the qualifier */comment:"text",* the comment, text, is added to the existing group name entered, where text can be 48 characters long and must be enclosed in quotes. The */action* qualifier either adds the group name as new or deletes it. Acceptable values are **/add** and **/delete**. When using the **/add** qualifier, the */comment:"text"* option can be used as well as in the format **net localgroup groupname /add** */comment:"text".*
name(s)	*/action*	Lists the name(s) to be added to or deleted from *groupname* based on the action given. Acceptable values include either local users or users on trusted domains or global groups. If more than one name is entered, separate them with a space. Acceptable values are **/add** and **/delete**.
/domain		Can be used with any of the syntax formats and is necessary only when executing the command from a workstation that is a member of a Windows Server 2003 domain. The option causes the **net localgroup** command to execute on the primary domain controller of the current domain. The default (without this option) is to execute the command for the local computer.

When the **net localgroup** command is executed without options, the display will include the name of the server as well as the name of each local group on it.

net localgroup Command Examples

To display all the users in the group tech1, enter

```
net localgroup tech1
```

To add a comment to the record for tech1, enter

```
net localgroup tech1 /comment:"Primary Tech Support Team"
```

To add a group called tech2 and include a comment, enter

```
net localgroup tech2 /add /comment:"Secondary Tech Support Team"
```

To add the names nancyd and phill from the helpdesk domain and global group sales2, respectively, to the tech2 local group, enter

```
net localgroup tech2 nancyd helpdesk\phill sales2 /add
```

NET HELP COMMAND

The **net help** command provides help for the Server's net commands by listing all of the commands or by providing detailed information on a requested one. This command is discussed in more detail in the "Display Commands" section.

NET HELPMSG COMMAND

The **net helpmsg** command displays an explanation for the requested Windows Server 2003 error message. This command is discussed in more detail in the "Display Commands" section.

NET NAME COMMAND

The **net name** command adds, deletes, or displays names that are authorized to receive messages. These names are used only for messaging and must be unique throughout the network. In Windows Server 2003 three types of names—computer, user, and messaging—are set up by net name. In order to execute this command, the Messenger service must be running. For more information, please refer to the "Miscellaneous Commands" section.

NET PAUSE COMMAND

The **net pause** command is used to suspend a Windows Server 2003 service or resource. Pausing a service instead of stopping it enables current users to continue working while prohibiting new users from gaining access. System administrators sometimes do this in order to warn users and give them an opportunity to finish what they are doing. The **net continue** command reactivates a service that has been paused. Its syntax is

```
net pause service
```

The *service* parameter is required and can be one of the following standard services. Other services may also be available depending on the configuration of your system.

- File server for Macintosh (at the Windows Server 2003 level only)
- ftp publishing service
- lpdsvc
- Net logon
- Network dde
- Network dde dsdm
- lm security support provider
- remoteboot (at the Windows Server 2003 level only)
- Remote access server
- Schedule
- Server
- Simple TCP/IP services
- Workstation

NET PRINT COMMAND

The **net print** command displays information about both printer queues and printer jobs. Print jobs can also be deleted, put on hold, or reactivated. This command is described in more detail in the "Print Commands" section.

NET SEND COMMAND

The **net send** command uses the Messenger service to send messages to users, computers, and messaging names set up on the network. It is described in more detail in the "Miscellaneous Commands" section.

NET SESSION COMMAND

The **net session** command provides a list of the current sessions between the local computer and its clients, and it enables an administrator to disconnect them. A session between the client and the server is established when a user contacts a server from a client computer and successfully logs on.

The syntax for **net session** is

```
net session [\\computername] [/delete]
```

The **net session** command can only be executed from a server. When run without parameters, its display will contain the following information regarding each session on the local computer: computer name, user name, client type, number of open files, and idle time.

The *\\computername* parameter is the name of the computer for which you wish to list sessions. If specified, the user name, computer name, guest logon, client type, session time, idle time, and a list of all the shared resources connected to the user are displayed. The shared resource list includes the share name, the type of resource, and the number of open files.

The */delete* parameter is used to disconnect a session with the *\\computername* given. If the *\\computername* parameter is not used, */delete* will disconnect all sessions associated with the server.

NET SHARE COMMAND

The **net share** command displays, creates, or deletes shared resources. Once created, a shared resource is available immediately and remains shared until it is deleted. See Table A.59 for an options list. There are three syntax formats for this command:

```
net share sharename [options]
net share sharename=drive:path [options]
net share {sharename | drive:path } /delete
```

TABLE A.59 net share Command Options

Option	Description
/delete	Stops sharing the resource identified by either *sharename* or *drive:path*.
/users:number	Sets the maximum number of users that can access a shared resource at the same time. This option cannot be used in conjunction with **/unlimited**.
/unlimited	Allows an unlimited number of users to access a shared resource simultaneously. This option cannot be used in conjunction with **/users:number**.
/remark:"text"	Defines a comment, text, to be associated with the shared resource. Surround the text of the comment with quotes.

When **net share** is executed without options or parameters, it displays the share name, the device name or path, and a comment field for all shared resources on the local system.

The *sharename* parameter contains the name by which the network refers to the shared resource. The command **net share sharename** displays the share name, path, remark, maximum number of users, and users connected to the share.

To establish a directory share, use the parameter *sharename=drive:path*, where *sharename* is the network name for the directory and *drive:path* is the absolute path of the directory being shared. Remember to enclose the *drive:path* in quotes if there is a space in the directory name.

net share Command Examples

To share the directory c:\customers with the name contacts, limit the access to a maximum of 15 users, and include a comment, enter the following:

```
net share contacts:c:\customers /user:15 /remark:"Contact Information"
```

To remove the share when the shared resource is no longer needed, enter

```
net share taskforce /delete
```

NET STATISTICS COMMAND

The **net statistics** command, also known as net stats service, displays network statistics information for either the Workstation or the Server service. The syntax is

```
net statistics [service]
```

Running net statistics without specifying a service will display a list of the services that are running and for which there are statistics. Acceptable values for the *service* parameter are the words "Workstation" and "Server" (not the actual name of the server or workstation).

Running net statistics server displays the following statistics for the local server:

- Number of sessions started, timed-out, or terminated due to an error
- Number of kilobytes sent and received
- Average response time
- Number of system errors and permission and password violations
- Number of files and communication devices accessed
- Number of print jobs spooled
- Number of times the memory buffer was exceeded

Running net statistics workstation displays the following statistics for the local workstation:

- Number of bytes and Server Message Blocks (SMB) received and transmitted
- Number of read and write operations
- Number of failed read and write operations
- Number of network errors
- Number of successful and failed connections to shared resources
- Number of reconnections to shared resources
- Number of sessions started, failed, and disconnected
- Number of failed operations
- Total use count and the total failed use count

NET START COMMAND

The **net start** command either displays services that are currently running or starts a new service. The syntax is

```
net start service
```

Executing net start without the service parameter will provide a list of the services currently running. The service parameter is the name of the service you wish to start. (If that name contains more than one word, be sure to enclose it in quotes.) Table A.60 identifies the Windows .NET services that may be started with this command along with a brief description.

NET STOP COMMAND

The **net stop** command stops the Windows .NET service named. The syntax is

```
net stop service
```

Executing **net stop** without the service parameters will display a list of the valid services. The service parameter can be any of the standard services listed in Table A.60 as well as any other services that were installed on your system.

NET TIME COMMAND

The **net time** command allows the user to synchronize the time across the network between the current system and another domain (or computer). It also allows the user to display the time for any system on the network. This command is described in more detail in the "Miscellaneous Commands" section.

TABLE A.60 Windows .NET Services

Service	Description
Alerter	Enables alert messages to be sent to specific users and users connected to the server. Must be used in conjunction with the Messenger service.
Client Service for NetWare	Available only on Windows 2003 Workstation when Client service for NetWare has been installed. Starts the Client service for NetWare.
ClipBook Server	Enables cutting and pasting over the network.
Computer Browser	Enables computers to be browsed over the network and the computer starting the service to be browsed by other computers on the network. The alternative command is **net start browser**.
DHCP Client	Allows IP addresses to be retrieved from a DHCP server.
Directory Replicator	Ensures that designated files are the same on all requested servers. These files and servers must be set up prior to starting this service. The alternative command is **net start replicator**.
Eventlog	Logs any type of system, security, or application event that requires a notification to be sent to users. This service cannot be stopped or paused and must be running to use the Event Viewer.
File Server for Macintosh	Allows file sharing with Macintosh computers and is available only on Windows Servers.
FTP Publishing Service	Available only if the Internet Information server is installed.
Gateway Service for NetWare	Available only if the Gateway Service for NetWare is installed.
Lpdsvc	Enables UNIX clients to print via a printer connected to a Windows Server 2003 computer, available only if the TCP/IP protocol has been installed.
Messenger	Enables a computer to receive messages.
Microsoft DHCP Server	Provides network clients with IP addresses and is available only on Windows Servers and if both TCP/IP and the DHCP server have been installed. The alternative command is **net start dhcpserver**.
Net Logon	Verifies requests to log on and controls copies of the user accounts database in the domain. This service is started on all servers in a domain that use a copy of the domain's user accounts database. The alternative command is **net start netlogon**.
Network DDE	Starts the Network Dynamic Data Exchange service.
Network DDE DSDM	Starts the Network Dynamic Data Exchange Share Database Manager service.
Network Monitor Agent	Enables remote monitoring of a client machine's network communication.
LM Security Support Provider	Available only if the LM Security Support Provider is installed.

TABLE A.60 Continued

Service	Description
Print Server for Macintosh	Enables printing from Macintosh computers and is available only on Windows Server 2003.
Remoteboot	Permits networked computers to load the operating system from the server and is available only on Windows Server 2003.
Remote Access Connection Manager	Allows remote access to the network through a dial-up connection and is available only if the Remote Access service is installed.
Remote Access ISNSAP Service	Available only if the Remote Access service is installed.
Remote Access Server	Available only if the Remote Access Service is installed.
Remote Procedure Call (RPC) Locator	Allows applications to use the Microsoft RPC name service and manages the RPC name service database.
Remote Procedure Call (RPC) Service	Allows applications to use dynamic endpoints and manages the endpoint map database.
Schedule	Enables use of the **at** command to start programs at a specified time.
Server	Enables a computer to share resources, such as files and printers, on the network, and provides RPC support.
Simple TCP/IP Services	Activates the TCP/IP services of Character Generator, Daytime, Discard, Echo, and Quote of the Day and is available only if TCP/IP and the simple TCP/IP service are installed.
SNMP	Enables a server to report its status to the SNMP management system and is available only if both the TCP/IP and SNMP protocols are installed.
Spooler	Starts the spooler service.
TCP/IP NetBIOS Helper	Enables NetBIOS over the TCP/IP service and is available only if TCP/IP is installed.
UPS	Manages an uninterruptible power supply (UPS) that is connected to the computer.
Windows Internet Name Service	Enables the mapping of computer names to TCP/IP addresses for networked client systems and is available only on Windows Servers.
Workstation	Enables a computer to connect to and communicate with network resources.

NET USE COMMAND

The **net use** command either connects or disconnects a computer and a shared resource and displays shared resources currently connected to a computer. Its syntax has several formats:

```
net use [devicename] [\\computername\sharename[\volume]] [password]
[/user:[domainname\]username] [[/delete] | [persistent:{yes | no}]]
net use devicename [/home[password]] [/delete:{yes | no}]
net use [persistent:{yes | no}]
```

Executing **net use** without options will produce a display of all currently connected shared resources.

Table A.61 defines the options that are valid for use in all syntax formats of the net use command.

Another syntax format of the net use command is net use `persistent{yes | no}`. When *yes* is used, all current connections will be reestablished at subsequent logons. When *no* is entered, no subsequent connections will be saved and therefore will not be reestablished at subsequent logons.

net use Command Examples

To disconnect from the printer designated by LPT2:, enter

```
net use lpt2: /delete
```

To connect to the shared resource g:\Sales\Contacts as the user bosco, enter

```
net use g:\Sales\Contracts * /user:bosco
```

The asterisk forces a password to be entered at a prompt before allowing the connection to occur.

NET USER COMMAND

The **net user** command allows an administrator to perform many of the user management tasks from the command line or command prompt. It adds, modifies, and deletes user accounts, and it displays information about a specific user account or lists all user accounts on the system. Executing this command at a Windows Server 2003 will update the user accounts database on the primary domain controller. That data is then replicated to the backup domain controllers.

There are three syntax formats for this command:

```
net user [username [password]] [options] [/domain]
net user username password /add [options] [/domain]
net user username [/delete] [/domain]
```

TABLE A.61 net use Command Options

Option	Qualifier	Description
devicename		Enters the name of the device to be connected or disconnected. Acceptable values are *D:* through *Z:* for disk drives, *LPT1:* through *LPT3:* for printers, or an asterisk (*) to assign the next available device designation. Executing the command **net use devicename** displays information about the connection made to the shared resource, *devicename*.
\\\\computername sharename	**\volume**	Enters the name of the computer that controls the shared resource for *computername*, which can be no longer than 15 characters, or for the shared resource for *sharename*. The *\volume* qualifier contains the name of a volume on a NetWare server and can only be used if either Client Services for NetWare or Gateway Services for NetWare is installed.
password		Enters the password necessary to access the shared resource. Using an asterisk (*) in place of the password forces a prompt for the password, which is often preferred since the password is not visible on the screen when it is entered in response to the prompt. This option can only be used after the **\\\\computername\sharename** option.
/user:name		Makes the connection using the user, name, instead of the currently logged on user. A domain different from the current one can be specified as part of name (**/user**:*domainname\name*).
/delete		Disconnects the connection to the shared resource and removes it from the list of persistent connections. This option cannot be used in conjunction with **/persistent**.
/persistent:{yes | no}		Identifies whether a connection is persistent or not. Entering yes {*yes* | *no*} saves each connection made as a persistent connection so that it can be reestablished at each login. Entering no {*yes* | *no*} stops saving the current connection and all future connections so that only existing connections will be reestablished at the next logon. The current persistent setting remains the default until it is changed. Once a connection is considered persistent, it can only be removed from the recurring list with the **/delete** option.
/home		Connects the user to his home directory.

Without parameters or options, **net user** will display a list of the user accounts set up for the current system. With only the *username* parameter, it will display information specific to that user account. The display contains such information as the expiration date of the account, password-related information such as expiration dates, the name of the user's logon script and profile, the user's home directory, the date of the last logon, and the name of the account's local and global groups. Tables A.62 and A.63 define the parameters and the options available for net user.

net user Command Examples

The following command sets up a user named emilyg, prompting for a password. This user is permitted to log on Monday through Friday from 8:00 A.M. to 6:00 P.M. from the workstations named incy, sales, techsupp, and mktg.

```
net user bosco * /add /times:M-F,08:00-18:00
/workstations:incy,sales,techsupp,mktg
```

To delete the user bosco from the system, enter

```
net user bosco /delete
```

TABLE A.62 net user Parameters

Option	Description
username	Enters the name of the user account to be added, changed, deleted, or displayed. A user name can contain a maximum of 20 characters.
password	Either sets up a password for a new account or changes the password for an existing account. The password can consist of a maximum of 14 characters and must conform to the password specifications defined by the **net accounts** command. Entering an asterisk (*) instead of the actual password forces a prompt for the password, which in this instance will not be displayed on the screen while it is entered.
/domain	Specifies the command be executed on the primary domain controller of the current system's domain. This parameter should be used only from Windows Server 2003 workstations that are members of a Windows Server 2003 domain.
/add	Adds the user name to the user accounts database. The password parameter is required with this function.
/delete	Deletes the user name from the user accounts database.

TABLE A.63 net user Command Options

Option	Description
/active:{yes | no}	Enters *yes* to activate the user account or *no* to disable it and thus prohibit the user from accessing the server. The default is *yes*.
/comment:"text"	Enters a comment up to a maximum of 48 characters for text.
/countrycode:nnn	Enters the numeric value for the operating system country code for *nnn* in order to display the user's help and error messages in a different language. Zero signifies the default.
/expires:date	Enters the date the account will expire. Acceptable values are *never* (the account will never expire) or a date in the default format defined by the country code. Examples of date formats are *mm/dd/yy*, *dd,mm,yyyy*, *mm,dd,yy*. The month can be either numeric or alphabetic; the year can be 2 or 4 digits. Either slashes or commas can be used to separate the components of the date.
/fullname:"name"	Enters the user's full name for the variable name.
/homedir:path	Enters the path for the user's home directory for the variable path. The path specified must already **exist.**
/homedirreq:{yes | no}	Enters *yes* to specify that a home directory is required or *no* if not.
/passwordchg:{yes | no}	Enters *yes* to identify whether a user can change his password or *no* if not. The default is *yes*.
/passwordreq:{yes | no}	Enters *yes* to require a password for a user or *no* otherwise. The default is *yes*.
/profilepath:path	Enters the pathname for the user's logon profile for path.
/scriptpath:path	Enters the pathname of the user's logon script for path.
/times:time	Enters the times of day that a user can log on to the system. Acceptable values include all (a user can always log on), a space or blank (a user can never log on), and days and times in the format day, hour. Days are the days of the week either spelled out or abbreviated as M, T, W, Th, F, Sa, Su; time can be either in 12- or 24-hour format. When 12-hour format is used, use A.M. or P.M., am, pm, a.m., or p.m. to designate. Days and times are separated with commas. If multiple days and times are listed, they are separated with semicolons. There should be no spaces. For example, **/times:M,8am-5pm ,12pm-8pm;W,13:00-17:00.**
/usercomment:"text"	Enters a comment for the variable text.
/workstations:name(s)	Substitutes for name a list of workstations from which a user can access the network. A maximum of eight workstations can be listed, separated by commas. An asterisk (*) allows the user to log on to the network from any computer.

To deactivate rather than delete user bosco, enter

```
net user bosco /active:no
```

NET VIEW COMMAND

The **net view** command displays the resources being shared on the computer. Depending on the parameters selected, the output is a list of computers in the current domain or a list of all domains in the network. The syntax can be one of the following:

```
net view \\computername
net view /domain:domainname
```

Entering **net view** without parameters will produce a list of all computers on the network. Specifying a computer name for the *\\computername* parameter will produce a listing of all resources that are shared with that computer. Using the */domain:domainname* parameter and specifying a particular domain name will produce a list of all resources shared with the computer in the named domain. Omitting the domain name will produce a list of all domains in the network.

A special format of this command will display all the servers available on a NetWare network:

```
net view /network:nw
```

PRINT COMMANDS

Within Windows Server 2003 a printer can be attached to the local system or to the network. This section outlines the steps necessary to create a printer, send files to print, determine the status of a print job, manage printer operations, and define printer properties.

Creating a Printer

Here creating a printer means installing it so that it is accessible to both users and applications. Windows Server 2003 simplifies this process with the Add Printer Wizard, which can be accessed in three ways:

- From the **My Computer** icon, double-click the **Printers** folder.
- Select **Start** → **Settings** → **Control Panel**, then double-click the **Printers** folder.
- Select **Start** → **Settings** → **Printers**.

Printers can be created as local or as remote. To create a local printer, from the **Add Printer Wizard:**

1. Click **My Computer** and click **Next**.
2. Choose the port the printer is connected to from the **Available Ports** list; then click **Next**.
3. Choose the manufacturer and printer from the lists provided; click **Next.** (Before clicking **Next,** you may click **Have Disk** in order to install the printer driver at this point. If a printer driver is necessary, you will have an opportunity to install it later as well.)
4. Enter a name for the printer that your users will understand and recognize. You may also designate whether this printer will be considered the default for the system. Click **Next**.
5. If the printer is to be shared over the network, select **Shared** and either accept the shared printer name displayed or enter one that you prefer. Remember, if this printer is to be available to MS-DOS and Windows 3.x users, be sure the name is consistent with their file-naming restrictions of eight characters before a period and three characters after (filename.ext).
6. If sharing the printer over the network, select the operating systems that will be accessing it. Click **Next**.
7. Click **Yes** to print a test page; **No** to bypass it.
8. Click **Finish** to complete the installation.
9. At this point, the wizard may request that you insert the media that contains the print drivers for the operating systems that you selected. Just follow the instructions on the screen.

Creating a remote printer is often referred to as "connecting to a network printer." This printer can be new or it may have already been installed elsewhere on the network. To create a remote printer, access the **Add Printer Wizard** and follow these steps .

1. Select **Network Printer Server**; click **Next**.
2. The **Connect to Printer** window displays. From the **Shared Printers** list, choose the network printer to which you wish to connect, then click **OK**.
3. Click **Finish** to complete the installation.

Sending Files to Print

To ensure that a file is printed correctly, we recommend using the print facility provided by the application that created the file. From within a Windows-based application, select the **Printer** icon to send a file to the default printer. To select a specific printer, select **File** → **Print** from the menu bar.

Files recognized by Windows Server 2003 can be dragged and dropped on the icon for the desired printer. To accomplish this, select **Start** → **Settings** → **Printers** to display the printer icons. Then, using either **Explorer** or the **My Computer** windows, select a file and drag it to the appropriate icon in the **Printers** window; release the mouse button to drop it.

IPR COMMAND

The **lpr** command enables a user to print to a computer that is running the LPD server. Thus, a Windows Server user can print to a UNIX printer. The syntax is

```
lpr -Sserver -Pprinter [options] filename
```

Enter for *filename* the name of the file to be printed. All other parameters and options are described in Table A.64.

TABLE A.64 lpr Options

Option	Qualifier	Description
-S	*server*	Enters the name of the computer where the printer is attached for the variable server. This is a required parameter.
-P	*printer*	Enters the name of the printer in place of the variable printer. This is a required parameter.
-C	*class*	Enters the class of the print jobs in order to list the contents of the banner page. This is an optional parameter.
-J	*jobname*	Enters name of this print job in place of the variable *jobname*.
-O	*option*	Describes the type of file to be printed. The default is a text file. A lowercase l is entered to signify a binary file, such as a PostScript file. In this case, the option is **–Ol**.

PRINT COMMAND

The **print** command enables the user to print a text file in the background. The syntax is

```
print [/d:device] filename(s)
```

Executing **print** without options or parameters will display a list of the files currently in the print queue.

The first parameter, */d:device*, is optional and designates the name of the print device. Acceptable values are LPT1, LPT2, and LPT3 for parallel ports; COM1, COM2, COM3, and COM4 for serial ports; and *\\servername\sharename* for a network printer where *servername* is the name of the server and *sharename* is the name of the shared printer resource. The default value for */d:device* is PRN, which is the same as LPT1, the first parallel port.

The *filename(s)* parameter is optional and should include the name of the file or files to be printed. Multiple file names are separated by a space. If necessary, a drive designation and pathname may be entered in the format *drive:path\filename*.

As a note of interest, PostScript files require the **copy**, not the **print**, command. For example, **copy file.ps lpt1:** prints a PostScript file on LPT1.

Print Status

To determine the status of files in the print queue, select **Start** → **Settings** → **Printers** and double-click the appropriate printer. A status window for that printer will display containing the following information for each print job printing or waiting to print:

- *Document name.* At a minimum, the name of the file being printed and possibly the name of the application that created the file.
- *Status*. If nothing displays in this field, the file is waiting to print; otherwise, the status is displayed— printing, spooling, paused, or deleting.
- *Owner* indicates the logon name of the owner of the document.
- *Pages* indicates the number of pages in the document.
- *Size* indicates the size of the document in bytes.
- *Submitted* indicates the date and time the print request was submitted.
- *Port* indicates the port where the printer is connected.

LPQ COMMAND

The **lpq** command displays status information for a print queue on a host computer running the LPD server. The syntax is

```
lpq -Sserver -Pprinter [-l]
```

Table A.65 lists the options for the **lpq** command.

TABLE A.65 lpq Command Options

Option	Qualifier	Description
-S	*server*	Enters the name of the computer with the printer attached for the qualifier server. This is a required parameter.
-P	*printer*	Enters the name of the printer to identify the queue to display status information. This parameter is required.
-l		Included only when a detailed status report is desired.

NET PRINT COMMAND

The **net print** command displays information about printer queues and printer jobs. It also deletes, suspends, or reactivates print jobs. **Net print** has two formats, the first of which is

```
net print \\computername\sharename
```

This format displays, for each print queue, name, number of jobs, and status. For each job in the queue, it displays user name, job number, size, and status. Table A.66 defines the parameters.

The second format is

```
net print [\\computername] job# [options]
```

This format either displays information about a specific job number or enables you to control network print jobs. The *\\computername* parameter is optional and should contain the name of the computer sharing the printer queue. The *job#* parameter is required and should contain the number of the print job in question. This number is part of the print queue listing that can be displayed using the net print **\\computername** command. The options are described in Table A.67.

TABLE A.66 net print Parameters

Option	Description
\\computername	Enters the name of the computer sharing the print queue.
\sharename	Enters the name of the specific print queue. This parameter is optional; when not entered, the net print **\\computername** command displays all print queues on this computer.

TABLE A.67 net print Command Options

Option	Description
/delete	Deletes *job#* from the printer queue.
/hold	Puts a hold on a *job#* that is waiting in the print queue so that it will not print but stays in the print queue until it is released or deleted.
/release	Releases a *job#* that has been put on hold.

net print Command Examples

To display all print jobs in the marketing print queue on the computer incy, enter

```
net print \\incy\marketing
```

To delete print job 12 from that computer, enter

```
net print \\incy 12 /delete
```

Managing Printer Operations

Once a document is in the print queue, several operations can be executed to pause and resume printing, restart documents from the beginning, and cancel documents.

PAUSING AND RESUMING A PRINTER

Pausing a printer stops printing but permits files to be accepted into the print queue. To pause a printer:

1. Select **Start** → **Settings** → **Printers**.
2. Double-click the icon for the desired printer.
3. From the selected printer's window, select **Printer** → **Pause Printing**; the title bar will display "Paused."

To resume printing, select **Printer** → **Pause Printing** from the printer's window.

PAUSING AND RESUMING PRINTING

To suspend printing:

1. Select the desired document from the printer's window.
2. From the menu bar, select **Document** → **Pause**; the status column for the document will display "Paused."

To resume printing

1. Select the paused document from the printer's window.
2. From the menu bar, select **Document → Resume.**

RESTARTING AND CANCELING A DOCUMENT

To restart the printing of a document from the beginning:

1. Select the document to be restarted from the printer's window.
2. From the menu bar, select **Document → Restart**.

To remove a document from the print queue (i.e., cancel it):

1. Select the document to be canceled from the printer's window.
2. From the menu bar, select **Document → Cancel**.

Defining Printer Properties

In order to define or change the default behavior of a printer, the printer properties must be modified. To do this, first select **Start → Settings → Printers** and right-click the desired printer icon. From the menu that displays, select **Properties**. Another way is to double-click the desired printer icon to display the printer's window and then, from the menu bar, select **Printer → Properties**.

The Properties window contains six tabs. A brief description of each follows.

- *General* contains comments and printer location information. It also enables you to configure a separator page or a print processor, or to print a test page.
- *Ports* enables the addition, deletion, and configuration of ports. It can be used to create a printer pool that consists of more than one printer device of the same type connected to the same print server.
- *Scheduling* defines when the printer is available for printing. It also has options to configure the spooler operation, such as whether to start the printing of the document before it is completely spooled.
- *Sharing* defines whether a printer is shared over the network.
- *Security* defines or displays parameters for permissions, auditing, and ownership.
- *Device Settings* displays a hierarchical list of the printer's hardware features and allows them to be changed based on the content of the printer driver.

LPD Service

The LPD Service (lpdsvc), referred to as the TCP/IP Print Service in Windows Server 2003, enables printers to print jobs from remote clients such as UNIX systems. As part of the Resource Kit, it is installed as follows: Select **Start → Settings → Control Panel → Network → Services.** Within the Services window, select **Add**. From the Network Service list, select **Microsoft TCP/IP Printing**, then click **OK**. At this point, follow the instructions on the screen, including inserting the Windows Server 2003 Resource Kit CD-ROM so that additional files may be installed. Once the files have been installed, restart the computer.

To start the LPD Service, select **Start → Settings → Control Panel → Services**. From the list, select **TCP/IP Print Server**, then click **Start**.

SEARCH COMMANDS

Windows Server 2003 provides commands for locating files and folders as well as a specific string of text within files. This section covers some of them.

find Command

The **find** command searches for a specified string of text in one or more files and displays any matches. The syntax is

```
find [options] "string" filename(s)
```

The *"string"* parameter is required and consists of the string of text that you wish to match. As in the above syntax example, the string must be enclosed in quotes and must be found in files in its entirety. It cannot be interrupted with a carriage return.

The *filename(s)* parameter is the name of one or more files to be searched, with the drive designation and path name included if necessary. Multiple file names should be separated by a space, and cannot be designated with wildcard characters. In place of a file name, the **find** command can accept input from the keyboard, from another command via a pipe, or from a file via a redirection command (<).

The options available for the **find** command are defined in Table A.68.

TABLE A.68 find Command Options

Option	Description
/c	Outputs a count of the lines that match the string instead of the lines themselves. This option should not be used in conjunction with the **/n** option.
/i	Ignores differences between uppercase and lowercase when trying to match the string.
/n	Includes the line number of the matched line when displaying it.
/v	Displays the lines that do not match the string. If used in conjunction with the **/c** option, displays the number of lines that did not match the string.

FIND COMMAND EXAMPLES

Enter the following to find all files on a disk that contain the word "auto":

```
dir c:\ /s | find /i "auto"
```

findstr Command

The **findstr** command is a more comprehensive search mechanism than **find**; it will match a string of text exactly or use regular expressions to match a pattern of text. Regular expressions use both metacharacters and actual characters to define the search pattern. Table A.69 describes acceptable metacharacters, which can be used singly or in combination.

The syntax for **findstr** is

```
findstr [options] strings file(s)
```

The strings parameter contains the text the command is searching for in the *file(s)* listed. If there is more than one string of text, they must be separated with

TABLE A.69 Metacharacters

Character	Description
. (period)	Wildcard. Will match any character.
*	Repeat. Will find zero or more occurrences of the previous character or class.
^	Beginning of the line.
$	End of the line.
[class]	Matches any one character (class) enclosed in the brackets. For example, **[abc]** will match one of the characters a, b, or c.
[^class]	Matches any character (class) not enclosed in the brackets. For example, **[^abc]** will match any character except a, b, or c.
[range]	Will match any character within the range, where range is in the format of *x*–**y**. To match any character in the range *m–p*, enter **[m-p].**
\x	Represents the metacharacter, *x*, literally. For example, to match $, enter \\**$**.
\\<xyz	Matches *xyz* at the beginning of a word.
xyz\\>	Matches *xyz* at the end of a word.
\\<xyz\\>	Finds anything containing the letters *xyz*.

.*Matches any string of characters.

TABLE A.70 findstr Command Options

Option	Qualifier	Description
/b		Matches the string pattern if it is at the beginning of a line.
/e		Matches the string pattern if it is at the end of a line.
/l		Interprets the strings literally. In other words, it does not use metacharacters.
/c	:*"string"*	Matches the entire text defined by string literally. Use this option to find a string consisting of two or more words separated by spaces.
/r		Interprets metacharacters in search strings as regular expressions. This option is the default unless the **/l** option is included.
/s		Searches the current directory and its subdirectories for matching files.
/i		Ignores uppercase and lowercase distinctions.
/x		Displays lines that match exactly.
/v		Displays only those lines that do not contain a match.
/n		Displays the line number before each line that matches.
/m		Displays only the file name of the file that contains a match.
/o		Displays the seek offset before each line that contains a match.
/g	*:filename*	*filename* is the name of the file that contains the search strings.
/f	*:filename*	*filename* is the name of the file that contains the file names to be searched.

spaces. If the string itself has spaces, the **/c:string** option must be used as described in Table A.70.

The *file(s)* parameter contains the name of the file(s) that will be searched and can use wildcard characters such as * and ? to designate multiple files. For example, to search all files in a particular directory, enter *.*. If necessary, this parameter can include the drive designation and the path in addition to the file name.

By default **findstr** will display the lines of the file(s) that match the specified string. This display may vary based on the options selected, which are described in Table A.70.

FINDSTR COMMAND EXAMPLES

Suppose a user is looking for a particular email message with the subject "Mary's Retirement Party." To search all of her saved email messages, even those in the subdirectories, and display the file name that contains the message, she enters

```
findstr /s /i /m /c:"Mary's Retirement Party" *.*
```

Now suppose a user wants to display the numbers of the lines that contain the acronym "GOSIP" in the govt.txt file. He enters

```
findstr /n GOSIP govt.txt
```

SYSTEM-MANAGEMENT COMMANDS

System-management commands help the system administrator keep the system running smoothly on a day-to-day basis. They include disk management, process management, password management, user and group management, and service management.

Disk Management

System administrators must keep track of how disks are being used and how they are performing so that they can maintain them and add disks if necessary. Windows Server 2003 provides both graphical and command-line functions that assist in these tasks. The graphical disk management facilities were discussed in Chapter 14, "Disk Management." In the following sections, we describe their command-line counterparts.

CHKDSK COMMAND

The **chkdsk** command can be used by the Administrators group and provides the status of the disk as well as a list of errors. The command's options allow these errors to be corrected. For errors to be displayed and corrected accurately, the drive being checked should be locked; this means that no files are open and in use. If the drive is not locked, **chkdsk** offers the user the option of automatically executing the command at the next reboot. In this instance, any errors are automatically corrected.

The syntax for **chkdsk** is

```
chkdsk [drive:][[path\]filename] [options]
```

Table A.71 lists the options available with the **chkdsk** command.

TABLE A.71 chkdsk Command Options

Option	Description
/f	Fixes the errors found on the disk. The disk must be locked; if not, it will be checked at the next reboot.
/v	Displays the name of each file as it is checked.
/r	Identifies bad sectors, then tries to recover readable information.

Running **chkdsk** without parameters or options displays a status report for the current disk drive. The *drive*: parameter is the letter designation for the drive you want checked. For FAT file system volumes, a *path\filename* parameter can be entered to designate one or more files to be checked for fragmentation. Wildcard characters can be used to specify multiple files.

CHKNTFS COMMAND

The **chkntfs** command determines when or if automatic system checking is to occur on FAT, FAT32, or NTFS volumes when the computer boots. It is launched from the command prompt with the following syntax:

```
chkntfs [/t[:time]] [/d][/x] [/c] volume: [...]
```

Table A.72 lists the options available with the **chkntfs** command.

The following is an example of the **chkntfs** command:

```
chkntfs /d
```

restores the default settings, and

```
chkntfs /x c: d: e:
```

excludes the c, d, and e volumes from checking.

TABLE A.72 chkntfs Parameters

Option	Description
/c	Checks the specified volume at boot time.
/d	Resets the default settings, except the countdown time for checking.
/t	Sets the countdown time for scheduled checking.
/x	Does not check the specified volumes.

TABLE A.73 diskperf Command Options

Option	Qualifier	Description
-y	*e*	Flags the disk-performance counters to start the next time the system is rebooted. These counters continue to collect data until they are turned off using the **-n** option. Use the *e* qualifier only to measure the performance of the drives in a striped disk set. To revert to the standard performance measurements, execute the command again with just the **-y** option.
-n		Stops gathering the disk performance information after the next reboot.
computername		Enters the name of the computer on which to start or stop the disk-performance counters. When the **-y** or **-n** parameters are omitted, this option displays whether the performance counters have been activated for the specified computer.

DISKPERF COMMAND

The **diskperf** command starts and stops the system disk performance counters. It works in conjunction with the **Performance Monitor** (**Start** → **Programs** → **Administrative Tools** → **Performance Monitor**), and its syntax is

```
diskperf [-y[e] | -n] [\\computername]
```

When **diskperf** is executed without parameters, it displays whether the disk performance counters have been activated. The other options are described in Table A.73.

Process Management

Process management governs the running of processes and applications on the local system. It includes such tasks as scheduling programs, terminating applications and processes, displaying active applications and processes, and monitoring the performance of processes and the local system.

AT COMMAND

The **at** command works in conjunction with the Schedule service and enables commands and programs to be executed in the background at a predefined date and time. The user executing **at** should be a member of the Administrators group on the local system. (The Schedule service is started by selecting **Start** → **Settings** → **Control Panel** → **Services**. In the **Services** window, select **Schedule** and click **Start**.)

The two syntax formats for the **at** command are

```
at [\\computername] [[id] [/delete [/yes]]]
at [\\computername] time [/interactive] [/every:date | /next:date]
"command"
```

When **at** is executed without options, it performs two functions. First, it displays a list of the scheduled commands with their status, identification number, and day and time to be executed. Second, it synchronizes the scheduler with the system clock to ensure that the commands will be executed at the proper time, especially after the system clock has been adjusted.

Both required and optional parameters are described in Table A.73.

TABLE A.73 at Parameters

Option	Description
\\computername	Enters the name of the remote system on which to schedule the command. The default (without the parameter) is the local system.
id	Enters the identification number of the scheduled command that is displayed when the **at** command is run without parameters. To display information specific to this particular job number, enter the command **at id**.
/delete	Deletes the scheduled command represented by **id** or deletes all scheduled commands on the computer. Use the */yes* parameter in conjunction with **/delete** to automatically respond "yes" to any prompts that **/delete** provides.
time	Enters the time a command is to run using the format of *hours:minutes*, where acceptable values are 00:00 through 23:59. The hours must be in 24-hour format.
/interactive	Permits the scheduled command to interact with a logged-on user's desktop while the command is running. Use this option only when you know that a user will be logged on. It is not a good idea to use it when scheduling off-hours backups.
/every:date	Executes the scheduled command on every specified day of the week (M, T, W, Th, F, S, Su) or specified days of the month (1 through 31). Separate multiple date entries with commas. The default is the current date.
/next:date	Executes the scheduled command on the next specified day of the week (M, T, W, Th, F, S, Su) or next specified days of the month (1 through 31). Separate multiple date entries with commas. The default is the current date.
"command"	Enters the command to be run at the scheduled day and time, where *command* is a Windows Server 2003 command, a program (files with extensions .exe or .com), or a batch program (files with extensions .bat or .cmd). All types of commands except those with an .exe extension should be preceded by **cmd /c**. Use only absolute path names when path names are required. When specifying remote computers, use the **\\computername\sharename** designation rather than the assigned remote drive letter. Enclose the command in quotes.

Since the **at** command runs in the background, it is a good idea to redirect its results to a file using the redirection symbol (>).

at Command Examples

To display the network statistics for the server every Monday, Wednesday, and Friday at 10:00 a.m., enter the following:

```
at 10:00 /every:M,W,F "net statistics server > srvrstat"
```

The *srvrstat* file will be placed in the system's root directory.

To delete a scheduled job, first determine the ID number by running the **at** command without options. If, say, the ID number is 3, enter the following

```
at 3 /delete
```

TASK MANAGER

The Task Manager enables a user to display and control the processes and applications running on the local system. It also allows the user to monitor the system performance.

To access the Task Manager, right-click in an open area of the taskbar and select this application. The taskbar displays at the bottom of the screen by default and displays the **Start** menu button as well as a list of the open windows on the desktop.

There are three tabs within the Task Manager: Applications, Processes, and Performance. Each of these will be discussed briefly.

Applications

The Applications tab displays the name and status of any applications currently running on the local computer. It offers three functions: ending a task, switching to a task, and starting a new task.

Ending a task is the same as terminating an application. To do it,

1. Select the application you wish to terminate.
2. Click **End Task.**

As an alternative to selecting a task from the taskbar, the Task Manager can switch to another task in this way:

1. Select the application you wish to switch to.
2. Click **Switch To**.

As an alternative to starting a task from the desktop or from the **Start** menu, the Task Manager can start a new program as follows:

1. Press the **New Task** button.
2. Enter the name of the new task or select **Browse** and browse through the available programs to select one.

Processes

The Processes tab offers information about the processes currently running on the local system. The default information for each process includes name, ID number, CPU and CPU time, and memory usage. To display additional or different information, select **View → Select Columns** from the menu bar.

To end, or kill, a process, first select it and then click **End Process** at the bottom of the window. Or right-click the process and select **End Process** from the menu that displays. Also, see the **Process View** and Kill.exe options described in the Resource Kit Support Tool section.

To change the priority for a process, right-click the process. From the menu that displays, select **Set Priority**, and then choose **Realtime, High, Normal,** or **Low**.

Performance

The Performance tab allows the user to monitor the performance of the local computer. Information, displayed numerically or graphically, includes CPU usage and history; memory usage and history; total number of threads, handles, and processes; and physical and kernel memory.

Windows Server 2003 also provides a configurable Performance Monitor that can be accessed by selecting **Start → All Programs → Administrative Tools → Performance**.

Other System Management Tools

This section briefly discusses other system management tools that are of interest to administrators and users.

LOGGING OFF THE SYSTEM

To log off the system, press **CTRL+ALT+DEL** to display the Windows Server 2003 **Security** window. Then select the **Logoff** button. You can log in again as the same or as a different user.

SHUTTING DOWN THE SYSTEM

There are two ways to shut down the system: Select **Start → Shutdown** or select **Shutdown** from the Windows Server 2003 **Security** window, which is accessed via **CTRL+ALT+DEL**.

ENVIRONMENT VARIABLES

There are times when a user or an administrator must define or change system environment variables, such as default paths and temporary directories. To do this, select **Start** → **Settings** → **Control Panel** → **System**, and in the **System Properties** window, select the **Environment** tab. Only administrators may change **System Variables**, but users or administrators may change **User Variables.**

To change a variable, select it and it will display in the **Variable** and **Value** fields at the bottom of the screen. Make whatever changes are necessary, and then click **Set**.

To add a variable, just enter its name and value in the appropriate fields and then click **Set**.

To delete an environment variable, select it and then click **Delete**. In all cases, click **OK** to exit the window. Changes made to system variables are effective the next time the computer is restarted. Changes made to user variables are effective the next time the user logs on to the computer.

RESOURCE KIT SUPPORT TOOLS

The Resource Kit provides a variety of support tools that can aid in system administration activities. Since they are optional, we provide only an overview of each. Please note that their inclusion or exclusion in the Resource Kit is subject to change. Unless otherwise noted, these tools are launched from the *command prompt* or the **Start** → **Run** menu. They are described in alphabetical order.

Acldiag.exe—ACL Diagnostics

This tool troubleshoots issues associated with Active Directory permissions associated with object access control lists. It reads ACL security attributes and outputs the results in either text or tab-delimited format for review with a text editor or spreadsheet. The command syntax is as follows:

```
acldiag "ObjectDN" [/chkdeleg] [/fixdeleg] [/geteffective:{User | Group}]
[/schema] [/skip] [/tdo]
```

ObjectDN refers to the distinguished name of the object and must be included in quote marks. Other Acldiag.exe required and optional parameters are described in Table A.74.

ADSIEDIT.MSC—ADSI EDITOR

The ADSI development tool is described in Chapter 5.

TABLE A.74 acldiag Parameters

Option	Description
/chkdeleg	Checks the security on the object to view delegation templates in use by the Delegation of Control Wizard in the Active Directory Users and Computers snap-in.
/fixdeleg	Fixes any applied delegations by the Delegation of Control Wizard.
/geteffective: **{user | group}**	Outputs effective permissions of the specified user or group in a text-readable format. The wildcard (*) for user or group prints the effective rights of all users and groups in the ACL.
/schema	Verifies if the object's security includes schema defaults.
/skip	Suppresses security descriptions.
/tdo	Outputs in tab-delimited format for use in databases or spreadsheets.

APCOMPAT.EXE—APPLICATION COMPATIBILITY TOOL

The Application Compatibility tool determines if a specified application can be used in a Windows Server 2003 environment. It is described in Chapter 2.

APMSTAT.EXE—ADVANCED POWER MANAGEMENT STATUS

This tool provides the status of Advanced Power Management (APM) features and is primarily intended to support older notebook computers. The Advanced Configuration and Power Interface (ACPI) is the default power management scheme for Windows Server 2003.

The syntax for Apmstat.exe is

```
Admstat [-v]
```

where **-v** is used to output the verbose version.

CLONEPR.DLL—CLONE PRINCIPAL

This tool moves users from Windows NT to Windows Server 2003 and is particularly helpful when incremental movement is desired. It also provides an emergency fallback to the older Windows NT policies if Windows Server 2003 fails during the migration period. Clonepr.dll must be run on the destination Windows Server 2003 domain controller, on which objects are duplicated (not moved) from the Windows NT domain controller. It can only be applied within a domain. While clonepr.dll does not recognize the user's password, it works in connection with the Movetree support tool, which does retain the password.

The following files are required to use the Clone Principal.

- *Clonepr.dll*—A COM object to support Clone Principal operations.
- *Clonegg.vbs*—A sample script to clone global groups in a domain.
- *Cloneggu.vbs*—A sample script to clone all the global groups and users.
- *Clonelg.vbs*—A sample script to clone all the local groups in a domain.
- *Clonepr.vbs*—A sample script to clone a single security principal.
- *Sidhist.vbs*—A sample script to add the SID of a source account to the SID History of a destination account.

For more information on the Clone Principal refer to the ClonePrincipal User Guide (clonepr.doc) shipped with the Resource Kit.

DCDIAG.EXE—DOMAIN CONTROLLER DIAGNOSTIC TOOL

This utility analyzes domain controllers and identifies abnormal behavior in the system. It is used in the review of domain controller problems such as connectivity, replication, topology, logon rights, domain controller locator, intersite state, and trust verification.

The Dcdiag.exe syntax is

```
dcdiag /s:DomainController [/n:NamingContext] [/u:Domain\Username
/p:{* | Password | ""}] [{/a | /e}] [{/q | /v}] [/i] [/f:LogFile]
[/ferr:ErrLog] [/c [/skip:Test]] [/test:Test] [{/h | /?}]
```

Table A.75 lists the options available with **dcdiag** command

DEPEND.EXE—DEPENDENCY WALKER

The Dependency Walker is launched from the command prompt by invoking Depend.exe. It is used to ascertain dependencies for applications and DLLs and is discussed in Chapter 2.

DFSUTIL.EXE—DISTRIBUTED FILE SYSTEM UTILITY

This tool permits the command prompt to query the distributed file system (Dfs). It is used for Dfs root maintenance and troubleshooting, and helps remove metadata left after removal of a domain-level Dfs root.

The syntax for Dfsutil.exe is

```
Dfsutil [option(s)]
```

TABLE A.75 Dcdiag Parameters

Option	Description
/n:NamingContext	Defines the type of naming—NetBIOS, DNS, or Distinguished Name.
/s:DomainController	Uses the home service.
/u:Domain\Username /p:{* | Password | " "}	Employs the Domain\Username credentials and binds with the password, where " " is a null password and * prompts for a password.
/a	Tests all site servers.
/e	Tests all servers enterprise-wide and overrides **/a**.
/q	Prints out messages in quiet mode.
/v	Prints information in verbose or extended mode.
/f:logfile	Redirects the output to a specified log file.
/ferr:Errlog	Redirects only fatal errors to a designated error log.
/c	Runs a comprehensive (all) tests. If the **/skip** option is also used, it will ignore those tests specified.
/skip:test	Skips the specified test.
/test:test	Runs only the test specified. The following tests are valid: *Connectivity*—tests if the domain controller is DNS registered and has connectivity. *Replications*—checks for timely domain controller replication. *Topology*—checks that the topology is connected for all domain controllers. *CutoffServers*—checks for any down replication domain controller. *NetLogons*—checks for appropriate replication logon privileges. *LocatorGetDc*—checks each domain controller promoting its capabilities. *Intersite*—checks for failures that would prevent intersite replication. *RolesHeld*—checks that global role-holders can be located and responding. *RidManager*—checks to see if RID master is accessible with information. *MachineAccount*—checks if the machine account has the proper information. *Services*—checks if appropriate domain controller services are running. *OutboundSecureChannels*—checks that secure channels exist. *ObjectsReplicated*—checks for replication of machine account and DSA objects.
{/h | /?}	Displays the proper syntax options in the command prompt.

TABLE A.76 Dfsutil.exe Parameters

Option	Description
/list:Domain [/dcname:DcName]	Outputs the Dfs in the domains that are fully qualified, with the Active Directory domain name defining a specific domain controller.
/view:\\dfsname\dfsshare [/dcname:DcName] [/level:Level]	Displays the metadata in *\\dfsname\dfsshare* and dumps the Active Directory-based Partition Knowledge Table (PKT) that shows the Dfs tree for each computer directory and site location. The **|more pipe** command can be used. The **/dcname** option defines a specific domain controller and **/level** specifies the level of viewing material, with the highest providing greater detail.
/verify:\\dfsname\dfsshare [/dcname:DcName] [/level:Level]	Verifies metadata in *\\dfnsame\dfshare*. The **/dcname** option defines a specific domain controller and **/level** specifies the level of viewing material, with the highest providing greater detail.
/reinit:ServerName	Reestablishes or refreshes the Dfs server name.
/whatis:ServerName	Displays the type of the specified server.
/dfsalt:UNCPath	Resolves the UNC path for the server.
/clean:ServerName	Removes the Dfs designation within the registry of the defined server.
/dclist:Domain	Lists all the domain controllers in the defined domain.
/trusts:Domain	Lists the trust relationships of the specified domains.
/pktinfo [/dfs] [/level:Level]	Shows the Partition Kit Table for the designated Dfs.
/pktflush[:EntryToFlush]	Removes or flushes Partition Kit Table entries.
/spcinfo [/all]	Outputs the SPC information—the /all switch outputs all the data.
/spcflush[:EntrytoFlush]	Removes or flushes the SPC data.

DNSCMD.EXE—DNS TROUBLESHOOTING TOOL

This administrative tool is used to view and diagnosis DNS settings and properties of DNS servers, zones, and resource records. The syntax is

```
dnscmd ServerName Command [Command Parameters]
```

DSACLS.EXE—DSACLS

This tool is used to manage access control lists. It permits the manipulation of security attributes for Active Directory objects and serves as a command-line alternative to the Active Directory snap-in tools.

TABLE A.77 Dnscmd.exe Parameters

Option	Description
ServerName	Specifies the server to be managed.
IP address	Specifies the IP address.
Command	Defines the command desired from the following options: **/Info**—provides DNS server properties. **/Config**—resets server or zone configuration. **/Statistics**—provides server statistics data. **/ClearCache**—clears the cache for a DNS server. **/WriteBackFile**—writes back all data for the specified zone. **/StartScavenging**—initiates server scavenging. **/ResetListenAddresses**—resets/selects server IP address(es). **/ResetForwarders**—resets/selects and forwards IP address(es). **/EnumZone**—enumerates zones on the DNS server. **/ZoneInfo**—displays zone data. **/ZoneAdd**—creates a new zone. **/ZoneDelete**—deletes a specified zone. **/ZonePause**—pauses the specified zone. **/ZoneResumes**—resumes the specified zone. **/ZoneReload**—reloads the specified zone from its database. **/ZoneWriteBack**—writes back the specified zone to the file. **/ZoneRefresh**—forces a refresh of the secondary zone. **/ZoneUpdateFromDs**—updates the specified DS integrated zone by data from DS. **/ZoneResetType**—changes a type of the specified zone. **/ZoneResetSecondaries**—sets/resets a notify list for the specified zone. **/ZoneResetScavengeServers**—resets scavenging servers for a zone. **/EnumRecords**—enumerates records at a name. **RecordAdd**—creates a record in the specified zone on the DNS server. **/RecordDelete**—deletes a record from the specified zone on the DNS server. **/NodeDelete**—deletes all records at a name from the specified zone, RootHints, or Cache at the specified DNS server. **/Restart**—restarts the DNS server. **/AgeAllRecords**—forces timestamping and aging on a zone.

TABLE A.78 Dsacls.exe Parameters

Option	Description
/a	Outputs permissions, ownership, and auditing data.
/d	Denies permissions for the specified user or group.
/g	Grants permissions for the specific user or group.
/i:{c | o | i | p}	Specifies the inheritance—**p** = propagate inheritable permissions one level only; **s** = subobjects only; **t** = this object and subobjects.
/n	Replaces the object permissions.
/p	Sets the object as protected (y = yes) or not (n = no). Lacking the /p option, the current protection flag is preserved.
/r	Removes the security permissions for specified user or group.
/s	Restores the security permissions for the specified user or group.
/t	Restores the security permissions for the object tree.
/?	Output to syntax options.

The Dsacls.exe command syntax is as follows:

```
dsacls object [/a] [/d {user | group}:permissions [...]] [/g {user |
group}:permissions [...]] [/i:{p | s | t}] [/n] [/p:{y | n}] [/r {user
| group} [...]] [/s [/t]] [/?]
```

DSASTAT.EXE AND DSASTAT COMMAND

This tool compares naming contexts on domain controllers and detects differences. In the case of a Global Catalog, it compares two directory trees within the same or different domains, gathering capacity statistics that include megabytes per server, objects per server, megabytes per object class, and attribute comparisons for replicated objects.

The syntax for Dsastat.exe is

```
dsastat [/?] [-loglevel:option] [-output:option] [-f:filename]
[-s:servername[portnumber][;servername[portnumber];...]] [-t:option]
[-sort:option] [-p:entrynumber] [-b:searchpath] [-filter:ldapfilter]
[-gcattrs:option[;option;...]]
```

DSKPROBE.EXE—DISK PROBE

The Dskprobe.exe command launches the graphical Disk Probe application discussed in Chapter 14.

TABLE A.79 Dsastat.exe Parameters

Option	Description
/?	Displays the syntax options.
-loglevel:option	Establishes the extent of logging performed during execution. The valid option values are INFO (default), TRACE, and DEBUG.
-output:option	Sets where the output of **DsaStat** is displayed. The valid option values are SCREEN (default), FILE, or BOTH.
-f:filename	Sets the name for the initialization file to use for parameters if not user-specified
-s:servername[portnumber] [;servername[portnumber]]	Sets the name of servers to be compared, separated by a semicolon. The server name can include the IP port number. The default port number is the default LDAP port (389).
-t:option	Determines if a full or statistical comparison is to be made. The option TRUE is for statistical; FALSE is for a complete content comparison.
-sort:option	Determines if the GUID is to be used as the sorting basis. The option TRUE will sort by GUID; FALSE will not.
-p:entrynumber	Sets the page size for ldap-search from 1–999, with 54 as the default.
-filter:ldapfilter	Sets the LDAP filter used in the LDAP search operation. The default is "(objectclass=*)".
-b:searchpath	Uses the Distinguished Name as the basis of comparison and allows reviews of all subtrees.
-gcattrs:option[;option;...]	Specifies attributes to be returned for the search.

DUMPCHK.EXE—DUMP CHECK

This is a debugging tool used to review crash and other system dumps. Its syntax is as follows:

```
dumpchk [-v] [-p] [-c] [-x] [-e] [-y] [-?] CrashDumpFile
```

FILEVER.EXE—FILE VERSION VERIFICATION

This is a command-line utility employed to verify the version level of an .exe or .dll file. The syntax is as follows:

```
filever [/s] [/v] [/e] [/x] [/b] [/a] [/d] [[drive:][path][filename]]
```

TABLE A.80 Dumpchk.exe Parameters

Option	Description
-e	Performs a dump examination.
-c	Validates the dump file.
-v	Outputs in verbose mode.
-x	Performs extra dump file examination.
-y	Sets the path to the symbols file.

TABLE A.81 Filever.exe Parameters

Option	Description
/a	Does not display attributes.
/b	Outputs a bare format with directories.
/d	Does not display time and date.
/e	Lists executable components only.
/s	Shows all directories and subdirectories.
/v	Uses verbose mode.
/x	Generates a short name for even non-8.3-based names.

GFLAGS.EXE—GLOBAL FLAGS

The **gflags** command launches a graphical application used by system administrators and developers to edit *NTGlobalFlag*. This command is used to modify the current flags for the kernel or the global Registry.

CAUTION Modifying global flags is not advised except by the most experienced developer or system administrator. Consult with Microsoft Professional Services when doing this because flag changes that are inappropriately applied can damage your system.

The syntax used for **gflags** is

```
gflag [-r [flag [maxdepth]] [-k [flag]] [-i ImageFileName [flag]] [-l
flag commandline...]
```

TABLE A.82 Gflag.exe Parameters

Option	Description
-i	Operates on the specified image.
-I	Launches the command line for a specified flag.
-r	Displays Registry settings.
-k	Operates on the kernel settings.

The global flag abbreviations and their meanings are

- *kst*—create kernel mode stack trace database.
- *ust*—create user mode stack trace database
- *dic*—debug Initial Command.
- *dwl*—debug WINLOGON.
- *dhc*—disable Heap Coalesce on Free.
- *ddp*—disable kernel mode DbgPrint output.
- *dps*—disable paging of kernel stacks.
- *dpd*—disable protected DLL verification.
- *ece*—enable Close Exception.
- *d32*—enable Win32 Subsystem debugging.
- *eel*—enable Exception Logging.
- *hat*—enable Heap API Call Tracing.
- *hfc*—enable heap free checking.
- *hpc*—enable heap parameter checking.
- *htg*—enable heap tagging.
- *htd*—enable Heap Tagging by DLL.
- *htc*—enable heap tail checking.
- *hvc*—enable heap validation on call.
- *ksl*—enable loading of kernel debugger symbols.
- *eot*—enable Object Handle Type Tagging.
- *pfc*—enable pool free checking.
- *ptg*—enable pool tagging.
- *ptc*—enable pool tail checking.
- *otl*—maintain a list of objects for each type.

- *hpa*—place heap allocations at ends of pages.
- *sls*—Show Loader Snaps.
- *soe*—Stop On Exception.
- *shg*—Stop on Hung GUI.
- *idp*—unused.

KILL.EXE—TASK KILLING UTILITY

This command-line utility is employed to terminate one or more processes, using the process identification number (PID) to recognize them. See the Tlist.exe to view the tasks. The syntax for the Kill.exe utility is

```
kill [/f] {process_id | pattern}
```

The **/f** option forces termination.

KSETUP.EXE—KERBEROS CLIENT CONFIGURATION

KSetup is a command-line tool that configures Windows Server 2003 or Professional clients used by an MIT Kerberos server. The Windows .NET client employs a Kerberos realm (instead of a Windows Server 2003 domain), which establishes a single sign-on to the Key Distribution Center (KDC) and a local Windows Server 2003 client account.

The syntax for KSetup.exe is as follows:

```
ksetup [/SetRealm DnsDomainName] [/MapUser Principal Account] [/AddKdc
RealmName KdcName] [/DelKdc RealmName KdcName] [/AddKpasswd Realmname
KpasswdName] [/DelKpasswd Realmname KpasswdName] [/Server Servername]
[/SetComputerPassword Password] [/Domain DomainName] [/ChangePassword
OldPasswd NewPasswd] [/?] [/Help]
```

KTPASS.EXE—KERBEROS TAB KEY SETUP

The command-line tool Ktpass.exe is a configuration utility that creates Kerberos keytab Ktpass files. It generates a mapping of password and account names for UNIX services that use Windows Server 2003 KDCs. Along with the Trustdom.exe utility, they establish Kerberos interoperability by creating a key shared by UNIX and Windows Server 2003 Kerberos services. The syntax for Ktpass.exe is

```
ktpass /out filename /princ username [/mapuser] [/in filename]
[/crpyto type] [/ptype type] [/keyno keynum] [/?]
```

TABLE A.83 KSetup.exe Parameters

Option	Description
/AddKdc Realmname Kdcname	Adds the Kpasswd server address for a realm.
/ChangePassword OldPasswd NewPasswd	Changes a logged-on user's password via Kpassword.
/DelKdc RealmName KdcName	Deletes instance(s) of the KDC address for the realm.
/DelKpasswd Realmname KpasswdName	Deletes the Kpasswd server address for a realm.
/Domain DnsDomainName	Uses the current domain if no domain name is set.
/MapUser KerbName LocalName	Maps the name of a Kerberos principal and an account (* = any/all).
/SetComputerPassword Passwd	Sets the local computer password.
/SetRealm DnsDomainName	Establishes /SetRealm DnsDomainName.
/Server servername	Sets the target Windows Server 2003 that will be changed.

TABLE A.84 Ktpass.exe Parameters

Option	Description
/crypto [DES-CBC-CRC | DES-CBC-MD5]	Establishes the cryptographic type—DES-CBC-CRC is the default.
/DesOnly	Establishes the use of DES only.
/in	The keytab to digest or read.
/kvno	The key version number—the default is 1.
/mapOp	The mapping attribute—*add: add value* (default) or *set: set value*.
/mapuser	Maps the user of the Kerberos principal to a local account; this is done by default.
/out	Sets the name of the Krb5 keytable file. This keytable file is transferred to the UNIX system and then merged with (or replaces) the /etc/krb5/keytab.
/pass	Sets password for the principle. The wildcard * prompts for the password.
/princ	Inputs the principal name in the form *user*@REALM, for example, "example" or "host/unix.com".
/ptype [KRB5_NT_PRINCIPAL | KRB5_NT_SRV_INST | KRB5_NT_SRV_HST]	Specifies the principal type: KRB5_NT_PRINCIPAL for the general type and the name of the principal is recommended; KRB5_NT_SRV_INST for user service instance; or KRB5_NT_SRV_HST for host service instance.

LDP.EXE—LDAP TOOL

The Ldp.exe tool launches a graphical utility for performing LDAP (Lightweight Directory Access Protocol) functions. These functions include connect, bind, search, modify, add, and delete against any LDAP-compatible directory, such as the Active Directory.

MEMSNAP.EXE—MEMORY PROFILING TOOL

The Memsnap.exe utility is used to capture information about the memory used by active processes. This data is dumped to a log. The syntax of Memsnap.exe is as follows:

```
memsnap [-t] [-g] [-?] [logfile]
```

The **-t** option adds tags for Greenwich mean time (GMT), date, and computer name. The **-g** option adds GDI and USER resource counts.

MOVETREE.EXE—MOVETREE OBJECT MANAGER

The command-line MoveTree.exe interfaces with the Active Directory Object Manager (MoveTree) that allows the movement of Active Directory objects such as domains within a tree or organizational units. When organizational units are moved, the linked grouped policies remain intact. Universal groups are moved intact during a MoveTree.exe operation, whereas local and domain global groups are not moved at all with this utility. Other objects that can not be moved with movetree include

- System objects that identified by the objectClass as systemOnly
- Configuration or schema naming contexts objects
- Special container objects in the domain including Builtin, ForeignSecurityPrincipal, System, and LostAndFound
- Domain controllers
- Objects with the same name as an object that exists in the target domain

The syntax for the MoveTree.exe utility is

```
movetree {/start | /startnocheck | /continue | /check} /s SrcDSA
/d DstDSA /sdn SrcDN /ddn DstDN [/u [Domain\]Username /p Password]
[/verbose] [{/? | /help}]
```

MSINFO32.EXE—MS SYSTEM INFORMATION TOOL

The Msinfo32.exe utility gathers system configuration data including hardware, software, and other system components. It is used to rapidly gather data necessary to resolve system conflicts or other problems.

TABLE A.85 MoveTree.exe Parameters

Option	Description
/check	Performs a test of MoveTree before actually moving any objects. The reports provide an opportunity to correct noted errors.
/continue	Continues to the move effort even after it is paused or a network failure occurs.
/d Destination DSA	Sets the fully qualified primary DNS name of the destination server.
/ddn DestinationDN	Sets the full distinguished name for the destination server subtree.
/s SrcDSA	Sets the DNS of the source server.
/sdn SrcDN	Sets the full distinguished name for the source server subtree.
/start	Starts the MoveTree operation with the **/check** option.
/startnocheck	Starts without the **/check** option.
/u [Domain\]Username /p Password	Launches MoveTree with the specified user and password account.
/verbose	Uses the verbose mode.

TABLE A.86 Msinfo32.exe Parameters

Option	Description
/computer computername	Establishes the computer to be analyzed.
/categories +|-categoryname(s)	Sets the category of data to be retrieved for the output report.
/report filename	Saves the report in the specified text file.
/s filename	Saves the report in a System Information file.

The syntax for Msinfo32.exe is as follows:

```
msinfo32 [/?] [/report filename] [/s filename] [/info filename]
[/computer computername] [/categories +|- category name(s)]
```

NETDIAG.EXE—NETWORK CONNECTIVITY TESTER

The Netdiag.exe command-line diagnostic tool identifies network connectivity problems and tests network client connectivity. Its syntax is

```
netdiag [/q] [/v] [/l] [/debug] [/d:DomainName] [/fix]
[/DcAccountEnum] [/test:testname] [/skip:testname]
```

TABLE A.87 Netdiag.exe Parameters

Option	Description
/d:DomainName	Locates the specified domain.
/debug	Places in debug mode and outputs more data that even the verbose mode.
/DcAccountEnum	Enumerates domain controller accounts.
/fix	Fixes any identified minor problems automatically.
/l	Outputs results to the netdiag.log log file.
/q	Uses quiet mode and outputs errors only.
/skip:TestName	Skips the named test among those listed below: • Autonet—Automatic Private IP Addressing (APIPA) address test • Bindings—bindings test • Browser—redirect and browser test • DcList—domain controller list test • DefGw—default gateway test • DNS—DNS test • DsGetDc—domain controller discovery test • IpConfig—IP address configuration test • IpLoopBk—IP address loopback ping test • IPX—IPX test • Kerberos—Kerberos test • Ldap—LDAP test • Modem—modem diagnostics test • NbtNm—NetBT name test • Netstat—netstat information test • Netware—netware test • Route—routing table test • Trust—trust relationship test • WAN—WAN configuration test • WINS—WINS service test • Winsock—Winsock test
/test:TestName	Performs the specified test. The optional tests are the same as those listed in the **/skip** option.
/v	Outputs in verbose mode.

NETDOM.EXE—DOMAIN MANAGER

The Netdom.exe command-line utility manages domains and trust relationships. It can be used to join Windows Server 2003 domains to either a Windows NT or Windows Server 2003 domain and to create one-way explicit trusts. Relationships can be viewed and displayed.

The syntax for the Netdom.exe utility is as follows:

```
netdom command object [/D:domain] [options]
```

NOTE This command should be used only by the most knowledgeable system administrator. We recommend that you use the graphical Active Directory snap-in tools while gaining familiarity with Windows Server 2003 domains. The options available for this utility are expansive. If you use it, refer to the published information supplied for the Netdom Resource Kit Support Tool.

NLTEST.EXE—NETWORK DOMAIN TEST

The Nltest.exe utility identifies domain controllers and trust relationships. It can also be used to force a shutdown and to synchronize Windows NT 4.0 user accounts. The syntax is as follows:

```
nltest [option] ...
```

PMON.EXE—PROCESS MONITOR

The Pmon.exe tool launches the Process Monitor, which examines processes to identify problems like memory leaks. Chapter 2 has more information on process monitoring.

PVIEWER.EXE—PROCESS VIEWER

The Pviewer.exetool launches the Process Viewer. It is used to view processes and identify problems such as memory leaks. See Chapter 2 for more information on process monitoring.

REPADMIN.EXE—REPLICATION DIAGNOSIS TOOL

The Repadmin.exe command-line utility permits the administrator to view the replication topology (also called RepsFrom and RepsTo) from each domain controller and can be used to manually create the replication topology. The syntax is as follows:

```
repadmin command arguments [/u:[domain\]user /pw:{password|*}]
```

TABLE A.88 Nltest.exe Parameters

Option	Description
/SERVER:ServerName	Directs nltest to a specified remote computer.
/QUERY	Verifies the health of the named *Servername* domain controller.
/REPL	Forces a partial replication on the local system or the *Servername*.
/SYNC	Forces a full replication on the local system or the *Servername*.
/SC_QUERY:DomainName	Verifies the secure channel.
/SC_RESET:DomainName	Resets the secure channel between Windows 2003 computers.
/DCLIST:DomainName	Lists all domain controllers—Windows 2000/.NET, PDC, and BDC.
/TRANSPORT_NOTIFY	Notifies of a new transport.
/USER:UserName	Displays user account attributes.
/LOGON_QUERY	Outputs the cumulative number of logon attempts.
/PARENTDOMAIN	Identifies the parent domain.
/BDC_QUERY:DomainName	Identifies all domain BDCs and their current state of replication.
/SHUTDOWN:Reason [Seconds]	Shuts down in the specified time period.
/SHUTDOWN_ABORT	Aborts the shutdown command.

Here *command* represents one of the commands listed in Table A.89, and *arguments* specifies the command's arguments.

REPLMON.EXE—REPLICATION MONITOR

The Replmon.exe utility launches the graphical Replication Monitor snap-in tool, which provides a view of Active Directory replication status and topology. It can also be used to force replication, as discussed in Chapter 6.

RSDIAG.EXE—REMOTE STORAGE DIAGNOSIS TOOL

The Rsdiag.exe command-line utility is used to view diagnostic information about jobs, managed NTFS volumes, removable media, and other remote storage data (see Table A.90). The syntax is

```
rsdiag [/c jobname] [/d filetype fullpath&filename] [/e errorcode]
[/i] [/j [jobname]] [/m] [/r [/f]] [/s] [/t] [/v [driveletter]]
[/x queuedrecall] [/w fullpath&filename]
```

SDCHECK.EXE—SECURITY DESCRIPTOR CHECK UTILITY

The Sdcheck.exe command-line tool outputs the security descriptor for any Active Directory object stored (see Table A.91). This descriptor contains the object's ACL.

TABLE A.89 Repadmin.exe Parameters

Option	Description
/u:[domain\]user	Sets an optional user as the administrator.
/pw:{password | *}	Sets the password for the alternative administrator set with the **/u** option.
/sync name-context DestDC DSA_UUID [/force] [/async] [/full] [/addref] [/allsources]	Starts the replication with following options: **/force**—overrides the normal replication schedule. **/async**—starts the replication but does not wait for the replication event to complete. **/full**—forces a full replication of all objects. **/addref**—Adds a notification entry for this destination if one does not exist. **/allsources**—Syncs the destination with all sources instead of just one.
/showreps [Naming_Context] [DSA [SourceDCUUID]] [/verbose] [/unreplicated] [/nocache]	Outputs the replication partners.
/showmeta Object_DN [DSA] [/nocache]	Shows the metadata for Active Directory objects.
/?	Outputs all optional commands.

The syntax for Sdcheck.exe utility is as follows:

```
sdcheck Server Object [-dumpSD] [-dumpAll] [-debug] [[-domain:
DomainName] - user: UserName -password: Password] [/?]
```

SECEDIT COMMAND

secedit /refreshpolicy has been replaced with **gpupdate** (see page 769).

Analyzes security settings comparing settings in the specified database with the systems current security settings. The results may be viewed in the Security Configuration and Analysis snap-in. The syntax is

```
secedit /analyze /db filename.sdb [/cfg filename] [/overwrite]
[/log filename] [/quiet]
```

Configures local security policy settings by applying the stored database settings. The syntax is

```
secedit /configure /db filename [/cfg filename ] [/overwrite]
[/areas area1 area2...] [/log filename] [/quiet]
```

TABLE A.90 Rsdiag.exe Parameters

Option	Description
/c jobname	Cancels the specified job.
/d filetype fullpath&filename	Converts the database to a text file. The file type identifies the source file type from among the following (*fullpath&filename* must include the full path): e—Engine database f—File System Agent database a—File System Agent collection n—Engine collection s—Subsystem collection
/i	Identifies the version data.
/j [jobname]	Specifies the job to be output. If not specified, all jobs are output.
/m	Displays the volumes that can be managed.
/s	Outputs physical storage information.
/t	Loads the trace files.
/v [driveletter]	Displays extended information about the specified drive.

TABLE A.91 Sdcheck.exe Parameters

Option	Description
-dumpSD	Outputs the security descriptor of the specified object only.
-dumpSD	Outputs the security descriptor of the object and its parents.
-domain: DomainName	Specifies the domain for the object.
-user: UserName	Specifies a user other than the one currently logged on.
-password: Password	Identifies the password for the specified user.

Export security settings stored in the database. The syntax is

```
secedit /export [/DB filename] [/tablename] [/CFG
filename] [/areas area1 area2...]
[/log filename] [/quiet]
```

Import a security template into the named database. The syntax is

```
secedit /import /db filename.sdb /cfg filename.inf [/overwrite]
[/areas area1 area2...]
[/log filename] [/quiet]
```

Validates security temple syntax. Enter

```
secedit /validate filename
```

Creates a rollback template with respect to a configuration template. When applying a configuration template to a computer, you have the option of creating rollback template which, when applied, resets the security settings to the values before the configuration template was applied. The syntax is

```
secedit /GenerateRollback /CFG filename.inf /RBK
SecurityTemplatefilename.inf [/log Rollbackfilename.inf] [/quiet]
```

Option	Qualifier	Description
/db	*filename*	Database used to perform the security configuration.
/overwrite	*Filename*	Database is deleted prior to importing the security template. Without this parameter, security settings are accumulated into the database, giving priority to template settings where conflicts occur.
/areas	*area1 area2 . . .*	Security setting areas to be applied to the system. If not specified, all security settings defined in the database are applied to the system. To configure multiple areas, separate each area by a space. The following areas are supported: SECURTY POLICY, GROUP_MGMT, USER_RIGHTS, REGKEYS, FILESTORE, and SERVICES.
/log	*filename*	File to log the status of the configuration process. The default file isscesrv.log is located in the %windir%\security\logs directory.
/quiet		Configuration takes place without prompting the user.
/CFG	*filename*	Security template name.
/RBK	*filename*	Rollback template name.

SIDWALK.EXE—SID WALK

The Sidwalk.exe command-line utility takes a mapping file as input and scans its ACLs in the Registry, file system, file and print shares, and local group membership. The mapping file can be used for Sidwalk conversion on multiple computers.

The syntax for this utility is as follows:

```
sidwalk profile_file [profile_file …] [/t] [/f [path]] [/r] [/s] [/p]
[/g] [/l file] [/?]
```

TABLE A.92 Sidwalk.exe Parameters

Option	Description
/l file	Creates a converter file as named.
/f [path]	Scans all directories unless the path is set, then only the subtree directories are scanned.
/g	Scans local groups.
/p	Scans shared printers.
/r	Scans the Registry.
/s	Scan all shares.
/t	Performs a test or dry run.

TABLE A.93 Tlist.exe Parameters

Option	Description
-m *pattern*	Lists all processes with associated DLLs.
-p *processname*	Outputs the PID for the specified process.
-s	Outputs the services associated with a process.
-t	Outputs a process tree.

SNMPUTILG.EXE—SNMP UTILITY TOOL

The Snmputilg.exe utility invokes the graphical SNMP Utility Tool and is used in conjunction with the older SNMP Browser Tools (Snmputil.exe.) to manage SNMP network elements.

TLIST.EXE—TASK LIST VIEWER

The Tlist.exe command-line utility lists currently executing processes (tasks) and outputs information such as the process identification number (PID) and process name. Its syntax is

```
tlist [pid] [pattern] [-m pattern] [-p processname] [-s] [-t]
```

POSTSCRIPT

This appendix provides an overview of the most frequently used utilities available under Windows 2000 and Windows Server 2003. Our selection was based on feedback from system administrators who reviewed early versions of the book. A special note of appreciation is made to Ellen Beck Gardner for her help in compiling the command descriptions.

Glossary

Account lockout Based on the lockout security policy, a user will be denied access, or locked out, after a predefined number of failed logon attempts. The duration of the lockout is also set in the lockout security policy.

ACE (access control entry) An entry in the access control list (ACL) that includes a security ID (SID) and an access rights list. When the SID is matched, access rights are granted or denied.

ACL (access control list) An object's owner controls whether access to the object is allowed or disallowed. For this purpose, each object has an ACL that comprises access control entries (ACE). Also known as the discretionary access control list (DACL), the ACL is the portion of the security descriptor that enforces permissions associated with an object. (The other components of the security descriptor are the object's creator [otherwise known as its owner], its group [a POSIX compliance element that relates to the "primary group"], and the system access control list, or SACL, which regulates auditing.)

ACPI (Advanced Configuration and Power Interface) An industry power management specification used by Windows 2000 Plug and Play hardware management.

ACS (Admission Control Service) The part of the Quality of Service (QoS) network management feature that defines who shares shared network resources and how they are used. It also regulates subnet bandwidth.

Active Directory services Microsoft Corporation's advanced directory service that is shipped with Windows 2000 Server versions. See Chapters 5 and 6 for information about directory concepts and Active Directory's capabilities.

Active partition The partition from which the operating system starts; it must be the primary partition on a basic disk. On Windows 2000 systems, the active partition can also be the system volume. If Windows 2000 is dual-booted with earlier Microsoft operating systems, all start-up files for both operating systems must reside on the active partition.

ActiveX An umbrella term for Microsoft technologies that permit applications developers to create Web-interactive content.

Adapter card A printed circuit board or hardware chip set that permits network connections between computers. Also known as a network card.

Address A DNS resource record that maps the domain name to an IP address.

Address classes Three levels of address class exist based on IP numbers: A, B, and C. For additional information, see Chapter 12.

Address pool The group or collection of scoped addresses available for license by a DHCP Server.

Address Resolution Protocol (ARP) As part of the TCP/IP suite, this protocol provides resolution between IP and MAC addresses.

Administrator As defined by Windows 2000, a member of the Administrators group, with full control over a specific computer or domain.

ADSI (Active Directory Service Interface) An API that permits applications on Windows 9x, Windows NT, and Windows 2000 to interface with networked directory services.

Agent A computer or network device that runs SNMP (the Simple Network Management Protocol) and provides information about its location and configuration.

API (Application Programming Interface) A routine that can be called by an application to carry out requests of other applications or the operating system. An example is the display-handling routines available from the Win32 API.

AppleTalk The default network protocol for Apple Macintosh computer systems. Windows 2000 Server provides connectivity to AppleTalk clients.

Asymmetric encryption A system of encryption that uses mathematically related public and private encryption keys. The private key remains confidential; the public key is passed out freely. To encrypt a message, a sender uses the receiver's public key. The receiver can then decrypt the message with the corresponding private key.

Asynchronous communication Transmission of data at irregular intervals. Start and stop bits signal when each character has been received.

ATM (asynchronous transfer mode) A communication protocol that transmits fixed-length 53-byte packets. It is generally viewed as a rapid method of data communication.

Attribute In terms of files, designation of a file as read-only, archival, encrypted, or compressed. In terms of Active Directory schema, definition of the features of the object class.

Auditing A means of tracking the activities of system and user behavior.

Authentication The process of matching a user's logon name and password against Windows 2000 security files. For standalone computers, it is carried out on the local system. For network logon, it is conducted by an Active Directory domain controller.

Authoritative restore A form of object resolution used by the Backup tool in which specified objects are replaced.

Backup media pool Defined by the Backup tool, the hardware devices dedicated to storage.

Backup Operators A predefined user group whose members have authority to perform backup of data regardless of the object's attribute.

Bandwidth In digital communications terms, the bits-per-second (bps) transfer rate. In analog communications, a range between high and low frequencies.

Basic disk The hard drive that contains the primary partition, extended partitions, and logical drives. It can also access MS-DOS.

Basic volume A storage method used by Windows NT 4.0 or earlier systems.

Batch program A form of a text-based (ASCII) script that invokes other applications or batch programs. It uses the extension .cmd or .bat.

BDC (Backup Domain Controller) Used by Windows NT Server 4.0 or earlier as a subordinate domain controller to the Primary Domain Controller, the BDC contains read-only copies of information such as the domain's security account manager (SAM). It is used in a Windows 2000 domain when the domain is configured in mixed mode.

BIND (Berkeley Internet Name Domain) A version of DNS ported to most variants of UNIX.

BIOS (basic input/output system) The system used in personal computers to check hardware, for basic operating system startup, and to initiate data communications. It is stored in Read-Only Memory (ROM).

Bit (binary digit) The smallest unit of information used by personal computers. It is expressed as a 1 or 0 to designate true or false.

Bits per second (bps) A measure of communication speed based on character transfer. A character is defined as 8 bits. In a typical asynchronous environment, an additional start and stop bit is added.

Boot The process of starting or resetting a computer's operating system.

Boot files Files required to initiate a Windows 2000 operating system, for example, Ntldr and Ntdetect.com.

Boot logging A process that occurs automatically with system startup and saves information regarding boot activities. It is stored in the root directory as an ASCII file called Ntldr.txt.

Boot partition The location of Windows 2000 operating system and support files. It has to be located in the same partition used for initial booting that contains Ntldr and Ntdetect.com.

BOOTP (Bootstrap Protocol) Part of the TCP/IP used by diskless workstations or devices like network printers.

Browser An application that interprets HTTP communications and displays HTML output from the Internet or an intranet.

Built-in groups Shipped by default with Windows 2000 to incorporate a standard set of rights, these groups are provided so that rights can be easily applied to user accounts.

CA (certification authority) The issuer of digital certificates or the corporate authority that establishes and verifies public keys. See Chapter 10 for additional information about the public key infrastructure and Microsoft's implementation of CA.

Cache A local store of data commonly used by programs like DNS.

Callback number Defined by the end user or the administrator, the number the server will call to connect with a remote client. It is often used for roaming users who want to limit hotel toll costs while connected to the home office server.

Canonical name An object's distinguished name that is output without LDAP attribute tags such as DC= or CN=.

CDFS (Compact Disk File System) A protected-mode file system used for CD-ROM storage and access.

Certificate A certificate binds an encryption key with encrypted data. Certificates are digitally signed by certificate authorities.

CGI (Common Gateway Interface) A server-based script that initiates services, it is commonly used in association with Web services.

Child domain Part of a domain hierarchical tree. It shares the domain namespace, Global Catalog, and schema with all other domains in the tree. For example, if the child domain is called "sales" in the *EntCert.com* domain, its name is sales.*EntCert.com*.

Child object An object nested within a parent object.

Client Any system connected to or requesting services from another computer. That other computer is known as a server. At any given time, a computer can be a client or a server.

Cluster A group of computers that share a workload and perform redundant fault tolerance. If a member of a cluster fails, another member will assume the workload in a process known as failover.

Cluster Services The software component that manages cluster functions.

Cluster-aware application Applications that conform to the cluster API. Not all applications are designed to work in a cluster environment. For additional information, see Chapter 17.

COM (Component Object Model) The programming model that permits object interoperability and reusability. Theoretically, COM components can be used by different applications and within varied operating system environments. Microsoft's Object Linking & Embedding (OLE) and ActiveX are based on COM. DCOM (Distributed Component Object Model) is the network variant of COM.

Command prompt The character-based window in which supported MS-DOS utilities and certain scripts such as batch files are run.

Common groups The list of groups accessible from the Start menu that are common to all users.

Communication port The port that permits single-bit asynchronous data transmission. Also known as the serial port.

Community name The name used to group SNMP devices.

Compact Disk File System (CDFS) A 32-bit protected-mode file system used for compact disks.

Computer account Created by the domain administrator, the account that identifies a unique computer in the domain.

CPU time The total processor time in seconds used by a process.

CPU usage The percentage of the CPU that is being used. It is shown in the Task Manager.

CRC (cyclical redundancy check) Checks for errors in data transmission. Each transmission includes data and extra (redundant) error-checking values. CRC is used by communications protocols such as XMODEM and Kermit.

Cryptographic Service Provider (CSP) Code that performs authentication, encoding, and encryption services. It creates and destroys keys and their utilization. Windows-based applications gain access through the CryptoAPI.

DACL (discretionary access control list) The part of an object's security descriptor that defines who has permission to use, or is specifically denied access to, an object.

DDE (dynamic data exchange) A Microsoft implementation of Interprocess Communication (IPC) that permits DDE-enabled applications to share data.

Device driver A code that communicates between Windows 2000 and hardware such as a modem, network card, and printer. Without it, a device is not recognized by Windows 2000. The Hardware Compatibility List (HCL) lists device drivers shipped with Windows 2000. Other drivers must be obtained from the hardware manufacturer.

Device Manager Interfacing within the Executive, or kernel, mode of Windows 2000, it is an administrative tool used to control computer devices. It lists device properties and performs updates and further configuration.

Dfs (distributed file system) The system of shared folders located on different servers that are linked into a single namespace, permitting transparent access to shared folders regardless of their location on the network.

Dfs link The link from the Dfs root to shared folders or other Dfs roots.

Dfs root A container for Dfs files and links.

DHCP (Dynamic Host Configuration Protocol) An industry-standard networking protocol that provides TCP/IP-based networks with the ability to dynamically assign Internet Protocol (IP) addresses and eliminate address conflicts for the defined IP number range.

Dial-up connection A connection that permits communication from a computer or network through telephone exchanges. It can be made through a modem, ISDN line, or X.25 network.

Differential backup A backup of all files that have been added or modified since the last scheduled full or incremental backup. It does not set the Archival attribute, thereby marking the files as having been backed up.

Digital signature The security method that binds the identity of a user to a file or object.

Digital Signature Standard (DSS) A cryptographic standard that uses the Digital Signature Algorithm (DSA) to generate and verify signatures and SHA-1 as its message hash algorithm. DSA is a public-key cipher used to create digital signatures. It is not employed for data encryption.

Directory A list of people, places, and things. A phone book is a common example.

Directory partition The Active Directory has three partitions that are really directory subtrees, each of which has a separate replication schedule. The three partitions are the schema, the configuration, and actual objects.

Directory replication The process of copying a database. Active Directory uses a multimaster replication model in which all domain controllers have read/write capacity and communicate changes to their peers through defined policies.

Directory Service The network service that manages elements in the directory and permits users to locate objects based on definitions known as attributes.

Disk mirroring The creation of a duplicate or mirrored version of a disk. Mirrored volumes must reside on different disks. In the event of a disk failure, access is obtained to the mirrored volume.

Distinguished name Defines the domain and related container(s) in which objects reside. See Chapter 5 for a discussion on naming conventions.

DLL (dynamic-link library) The collection of executable routines whose specific functions can be called by applications. As a specific function is needed, the application will locate and execute the required .dll file. DLLs are reusable.

DNS (Domain Name System) An industry-standard service that works with TCP/IP networks, DNS is a hierarchical name service for host computers. It is used as a foundation technology by the Active Directory. DNS lists host names and IP addresses so that a computer can be located in either fashion.

DNS Dynamic Update Protocol An enhanced version of DNS that permits the dynamic registration of hosts.

Domain The Active Directory manages a hierarchical infrastructure of networked computers with the domain as the foundation. A domain comprises computer systems and network resources that share a logical security boundary and can store more than 17 terabytes in the Active Directory's database. Although a domain can cross physical locations, it maintains its own security policies and security relationships with other domains. Domains are sometimes created to define functional boundaries such as an administrative unit (e.g., marketing versus engineering). They are also viewed as groups of resources or servers that use a common domain name known as a namespace.

Domain controller A server that contains a copy of the Active Directory. All domain controllers are peers and maintain replicated versions of the Active Directory for their domains. The domain controller plays an important role in both the logical and the physical structures of the Active Directory. It organizes all the domain's object data in a logical and hierarchical data store. It also authenticates users, provides responses to queries about network objects, and replicates directory services. The physical structure provides the means to transmit this data through well-connected sites.

Domain local group A security or distribution group. It may contain universal groups, global groups, and accounts from any domain in the domain tree or forest.

Domain model The Active Directory model that involves connection of one or more domains into hierarchical trust relationships. Domain trees and forests are created as part of this model. Also included are subadministrative structures known as organizational units.

Domain name and namespace The name used by DNS to identify a computer, host, or network device. It is made up of a preface identifier (like "EntCert" or "Microsoft") and a suffix (like "com," "gov," "net," etc.) separated by a dot. The namespace is the database structure used by DNS for names.

Domain Naming Master One of the several operations masters, this domain controller is responsible for adding and removing domain controllers from the forest.

Domain tree When multiple domains share one schema, security trust relationships, and a Global Catalog, a domain tree is created, defined by a common and contiguous namespace. For example, all domains with the ending namespace of *EntCert.com* belong to the EntCert domain tree. A domain tree is formed through the expansion of child domains like *Sales.EntCert.com* or *Research.EntCert.com*. In this example, the root domain is *EntCert.com*.

EFS (Encrypting File System) An extension to NTFS that permits users to secure files through encryption.

Event Any significant activity or process that requires logging for documentation.

Event Log service A documentation service that organizes a variety of events into lists that describe them and underscores whether they are normal or abnormal.

Explicit permissions Permissions that are automatically set on an object or those that are set by the object's owner.

Extensible Authentication Protocol (EAP) An extension of the Point-to-Point Protocol (PPP) that provides remote user access authentication. Authentication schemes supported by EAP include dial-up using Kerberos V5, one-time passwords, and public key authentication using smart cards and certificates. EAP can be used with dial-up, PPTP, and L2TP clients. It offers security against brute-force or dictionary attacks and greater protection against password guessing than other authentication methods, such as CHAP.

Failback The process of reestablishing cluster node responsibilities when the original failure has been corrected. It is used in clustering environments.

Failover The process of handing over responsibility to another node when a failure occurs. It is used in clustering environments.

FAT32 An extension of FAT introduced with Windows 98. Although FAT32 is supported in Windows 2000, it is still an older file system that limits many operating system features.

Fault tolerance The ability of a system to ensure data integrity in the event of hardware failures. It is most closely associated with clustering.

File Allocation Table (FAT) A file system used in MS-DOS and earlier versions of Windows. Although FAT is supported by Windows 2000, it has many limitations, especially regarding security and storage.

File Transfer Protocol (FTP) A protocol used in TCP/IP networks to transmit files across the network.

Firewall A system used to secure a computer or enterprise from unauthorized external access; usually includes a combination of software and hardware.

Forest Trust relationships can be formed between domain trees with different namespaces, thus creating a domain forest. Forests allow the formation of an enterprise with different domain names such as *EntCert.com* and *unint.com*. All trees in the forest share a number of attributes, including a Global Catalog, configuration, and schema. A forest simply is a reference point between trees and does not have its own name.

Forward lookup The DNS name locator that uses the friendly name (as opposed to the IP address).

Fragmentation As data is stored on a disk, files may be divided and located in a number of physical locations. As files are so distributed, the disk is said to be fragmented. Unless defragmentation programs are run, this can cause system performance loss.

Gateway A device that connects dissimilar networks and transmits the data.

Global Catalog (GC) MA database that is designed for two primary functions. First, it is a domain controller that stores object data and manages queries on locating objects according to their most common attributes. Second, it provides data that permits network logon. In single-domain-controller environments, the Active Directory and the GC reside on the same server.

Global group The group used to organize users within the domain.

Group A collection of users, computers, and other groups. It is the method by which rights and other characteristics can be assigned to multiple users.

Group memberships Users are members of one or more groups and derive rights from group membership.

Group Policy The Group Policy is an administrative mechanism for defining and managing the way objects are used by users and computers.

Group Policy Object (GPO) A collection of Group Policy settings.

Guest account An account for users who do not have a regular user account.

GUID (globally unique identifier) The code that identifies a device or component through the use of a 16-byte value.

HAL (Hardware Abstraction Layer) A layer of code that separates the hardware interface from the kernel and Executive Services.

Hash A one-way mathematical function (hash algorithm) that is applied to data to secure it. Also known as a message digest.

Hive A portion of the Registry that appears as a file on the hard disk. It is edited by the Registry Editor.

Home directory The directory accessible by a user for the storage and manipulation of her files. Every user has a home directory, whose default location can be set by the administrator.

HTML (Hypertext Markup Language) A text-based markup language interpreted by Web browsers to format and output file contents.

HTTP (Hypertext Transfer Protocol) The protocol used to transfer information on the World Wide Web.

IAS (Internet Authentication Service) A method of providing security and authentication for dial-in connections.

IIS (Internet Information Server) Microsoft Corporation's software that maintains and configures Internet services. It includes Web, Network News Transfer Protocol (NNTP), file transfer protocol (FTP), and Simple Mail Transfer Protocol (SMTP) services.

Incremental backup Storage of only those files that are new or that have been modified since the last full backup and marking them as having been backed up.

Indexing Service An advanced search facility that indexes data for more rapid location.

.inf The file extension for device drivers.

Infrastructure Master One of the operations masters, this domain controller manages group-to-user references as changes within group membership occur. This data is then replicated to the other domain controllers.

Inheritance The method of passing permissions or attributes from parent to child.

IP (Internet Protocol) The messenger protocol in the TCP/IP suite. It is responsible for addressing and sending TCP packets.

IP address A unique, logical set of numbers that identifies each host computer or node in a TCP/IP network. It is a 32-bit number divided into four decimal numbers from 0 to 255, with the numbers separated by periods. An example of an IP address is 111.111.111.111.

KCC (Knowledge Consistency Checker) The process used to create and manage site topology for Active Directory replication.

KDC (Key Distribution Center) A distributed network service that supplies session tickets and temporary session keys used by Kerberos.

Kerberos The MIT-developed authentication protocol used by Windows 2000 to verify a user's encrypted password so that he can achieve logon rights.

Kernel Windows Server 2003 uses a nonconfigurable microkernel that provides basic operating system functions. The microkernel dispatches and controls threads serving as the heart of the operating system.

Kernel mode One mode in which an operating system operates. The kernel mode manages such services as security, I/O, device drivers, and HAL—that is, generally those things that are not directly involved with users or the Win32 subsystem. Also known as the Executive mode.

L2TP (Layer 2 Tunneling Protocol) An industry-standard tunneling protocol.

LAN (local area network) A group of computers, printers, and other devices situated in a relatively small area that are linked for communications.

LDAP (Lightweight Directory Access Protocol) A network protocol used by the Active Directory to locate objects within a Windows 2000 domain. As an industry standard, it also permits some directory service interoperability.

Line printer remote (LPR) A service used to support remote printer jobs received from clients.

Local account Accounts created for users who want access only to the local computer. The Active Directory is not aware of local accounts, and network logon cannot occur through a local account.

Local computer A computer that is not part of a domain.

Local group A group used to assign permissions to local users for the specific computer in which the group resides.

Logon The process in which the user provides a name and password that are passed to Windows 2000 for authentication. Logon scripts are read to provide unique user environments.

Master file table (MFT) The first file on an NTFS volume, it contains information about folders and files on that volume.

MBR (Master Boot Record) The booting process starts by initiating the MBR data structure. If this sector is corrupted, booting will not occur.

Member server Any computer that runs Windows 2000 Server or above but is not a domain controller.

Message Queuing A Microsoft feature that allows messages between applications to be queued and distributed across the network, even to systems that may be offline. Message Queuing provides guaranteed message delivery and priority-based messaging.

Microsoft Management Console (MMC) The MMC provides administrative tools with a consistent interface. An administrator can create one or more MMCs and add to it the administrative tools desired. An MMC can also be distributed to other administrators.

Mirror set A fully redundant copy of data. It provides fault tolerance.

Mixed mode An environment that exists when domain-level domain controllers have not be promoted to the Active Directory and still run the Windows 2000 MMC (Microsoft Management Console).

MS-DOS The original Microsoft operating system. Many of its utilities are available on Windows 2000 and are accessible from the command prompt.

Multimaster replication The replication process that replaces the Windows NT replication model in which a Primary Domain Controller (PDC) writes updates to Backup Domain Controllers (BDC). With Windows 2000, all domain controllers have read and write capability so that they all share the same data.

Multiple boot Windows 2000 permits system configuration so that more than one operating system can be booted from the computer. For example, for reasons of legacy application support, it may be necessary to configure a system with both MS-DOS and Windows 2000 boot capability. Multiple boots present some security risks and are not highly recommended.

Named pipe The name for dedicated memory shared by two processes that is used for exchanging data.

Namespace A group of names of objects that occupy one network or system, and defined by conventions such as the Domain Name System (DNS), Fully Qualified Domain Name (FQDN), distinguished names (DN), and User Principle Names (UPN)s used by the Active Directory to locate users, hosts, and objects throughout the domain.

Native mode The mode in which all domain controllers are running Windows 2000 Server and have been converted from mixed mode. Windows NT 4.0 BDCs are no longer allowed to participate in Active Directory replication or to perform administrative functions.

Network adapter A hardware circuit board that interfaces between the computer system and the shared network media. Each network interface card, supporting the TCP/IP protocol suite, must obtain a unique IP address to communicate with other interface cards on the network.

Network card driver A driver that allows the protocol driver to communicate with the network adapter card. A driver is programmed with vendor-specific and model-specific hardware requirements for each type of card. This driver must be found from among the Windows 2000 drivers or retrieved from the network adapter's vendor.

NNTP (Network News Transfer Protocol) A subset of the TCP/IP suite that allows clients to read and post news messages to a news site. It allows readers to follow conversation threads.

Node A member of a server cluster or a device with one or more network interfaces.

Nonauthoritative restore Restoration of Active Directory from a directory backup. The restored directory is not given the same priority as current domain controller information.

Noncontainer object An object that may not contain another object—for example, a leaf object, such as a file.

Nonpaged memory Sections of the computer's RAM that are not paged to disk. Data stored in them is always available for quick read and write operations.

Nontransitive trust Either a one-way or a two-way trust that does not support transitivity. If A trusts B and B trusts C, then A does not trust C.

Normal backup During backup, the archive attribute is set on all files that have been backed up. Incremental backups then back up files that have been updated since the last normal backup.

NS (Name Server) resource record The record that identifies authoritative DNS name servers for a domain.

Nslookup A DNS client command-line tool for testing the DNS lookup functionality.

NTFS The most advanced file system for Windows 2000-supported special file/folder permissions, auditing, file encryption, and large volumes.

NTLM The authentication mechanism for Windows NT and down-level versions of Windows. It is supported in Windows 2000 to authorize these earlier systems.

Object An instantiation of a class definition. Typical objects include files and folders. In the Active Directory, user accounts, computers, and containers are all examples of objects. An object such as a user account has associated attributes like name, telephone, and title.

ODBC Open Database Connectivity is based on the Call Level Interface (CLI) for implementing common Structured Query Language (SQL) statements when access is desired for different database implementations.

Offline A cluster server node is offline when it is inactive or shutdown.

OLE In Object Linking and Embedding technology, portions of documents, spreadsheets, or graphics are either linked to another document or embedded and copied. Linking objects allows changes to an object to be reflected in the link. Embedding or copying the object creates two separate objects, and changes in one object will not be reflected in the other.

On-disk catalog A list of files and folders that have been backed up using the Backup utility on the local drive.

On-media catalog A list of files and folders that have been backed up, using the Backup utility, to a medium other than the local drive.

One-way trust In a one-way trust relationship, one domain trusts another, but the second domain does not trust the first. This type of trust is nontransitive.

Online A Cluster Server node is online when it is active or running.

Operations master A unique role that is performed by a single domain controller, as discussed in Chapter 5.

Operator The symbol or character used to make string matches and comparisons when performing searches.

Organizational unit (OU) A subcategory of a domain used to provide more granular control over the application of Group Policies and the delegation of administrative authority.

Orphan A crashed or failed volume in a RAID-5 configuration.

Orphan file A briefcase file not related to any other file on the system.

Owner A user who may change permissions on an object regardless of its permission settings.

Packet A collection of binary data used to communicate information over networks. The packet definition is limited to the network layer (OSI layer 3) and above. Data link layer information is considered frame information.

Packet header The section of a data packet that appears first. It contains the source, destination, and size of data contained in the packet.

Page fault The interruption that occurs when a process cannot find needed memory from RAM. If it must retrieve memory paged to the disk, a hard page fault occurs. When a process cannot access needed memory from RAM because of resource demands from another process, a soft page fault occurs.

Paged pool The amount of virtual memory allocated to a process.

Paging file A hidden file on the hard disk that stores paged data. Paging file information is accessed when a hard page fault occurs. RAM and paging files make up the virtual memory space.

Parent domain The domain above a given domain in the domain hierarchy.

Parent object An object that contains a given object.

Partition A physical disk may be divided into as many as four partitions that appear to be separate disk drives to the user.

Partition Boot Sector The sector of a computer's hard disk that contains information necessary to read disks and load the operating system during startup.

Password A unique string that may be up to 14 characters long for Windows 2000 user accounts.

Path The route marked by a disk volume, folders, and a file name that are ordered to identify a particular file or folder in the directory's hierarchy. Domain names and host names may also be used to identify objects—for example, \\Entcert.com\Documents*username*\Address Book.

PDC Emulator The domain controller designated in Windows 2000 to function as the operations master that handles PDC responsibilities for down versions of Windows NT and handles all Group Policy modifications and updates.

Peak memory usage The highest amount of memory consumed by a process since it started.

Pel The smallest controllable video screen component. Also known as a pixel.

Per Seat Licensing In this type of licensing, each client is given a license to access a given server, and all licensed clients may access the server at once.

Per Server Licensing This type of licensing dedicates licenses to a given number of clients. Any client may use an available license, but no more then the number of client licenses may access the server at one time.

Permission The ability of a user to access an object. Permissions are assigned to users and security groups and govern access privileges and actions that may be performed on an object.

Ping A command-line utility used to verify IP connectivity to a given IP address.

Pixel The smallest controllable video screen component. Also known as a pel.

Plug and Play A facility that automatically detects hardware components so that the correct driver may be loaded for further communication with the device.

Point of presence (POP) Post Office Protocol.

Point-to-Point Protocol (PPP) The protocol designed to provide serial encapsulation of IP/IPX/AppleTalk protocols over remote access connections.

Point-to-Point Tunneling Protocol (PPTP) A protocol that supports two endpoints of a tunnel, allowing encapsulated data to travel between them. Encryption and authentication supported by the tunneling protocol create a virtual private network (VPN) through the tunnel to give users secure access to corporate networks over the Internet or an intranet.

Pointer (PTR) resource record A record that permits the reverse mapping of an IP address to a host name. PTR records can be found in reverse lookup zones.

Policy Group Policies that determine the look and feel of the desktop environment, user profile locations, application availability, security settings, and logon/logoff scripts.

POP (point of presence) The closest Internet remote access point for a traveling user that permits the use of a local telephone number. Once the user dials in to an ISP's POP, she can establish access to her corporate network without long-distance phone charges.

Port The interface of two hardware devices. It can be a serial (COM) port, a parallel (LPT) port, a Universal Serial Bus (USB) port, and any other communication port on the computer.

Port ID Usually a communication protocol's port number used by the service. For example, HTTP servers usually listen for communication on TCP port 80.

Port rule A rule that determines the action taken when traffic attempts to send or receive on a given port.

POSIX (Portable Operating System Interface for UNIX) A set of standards drafted by the Institute of Electrical and Electronic Engineers (IEEE) that define various aspects of an operating system, including programming interface, security, networking, and graphical interface. Programs that adhere to the POSIX standard can be easily ported from one system to another.

Predefined key The section or category of the Registry accessible through the Registry Editor.

Primary Domain Controller (PDC) The domain controller that contains the writeable version of the user accounts database for Windows NT 4.0 domains and down-level versions. Only a PDC can exist for a Windows NT 4.0 domain. BDCs contain read-only versions of the database.

Primary partition Up to four primary partitions may be created on a disk and act as a reference point for booting the system.

Print job The queued data for printing and associated print format commands.

Print server The computer assigned to handle print jobs for a printer or set of printers.

Print spooler The application on a print server that handles print jobs and distributes them to corresponding printers.

Printer A device that transfers electronic data to paper or film media.

Printer driver The driver that allows the operating system to interface with a particular printer designated by a vendor and printer model.

Printer fonts Text fonts contained in nonvolatile memory on a printer. The printer is capable of printing only these font types.

Printer permissions Access permissions for a particular printer.

Printing pool One or more printers attached to a print server that are assigned print jobs based on current load.

Private key A key owned by one user or computer that is not accessible to any other party. It has a corresponding public key that may be used to decrypt data encrypted by the private key. The public key can also be used to encrypt data that can be decrypted only by the private key.

Process An application or program that has associated dynamic memory, static memory, and program memory space. Threads can also be created in the process's memory space.

Process identifier (PID) A unique number that identifies a process that is easily accessible from the Task Manager.

Protocol A standard for interpreting data transmitted from one process to another. Some protocols, such as the Internet Protocol, allow routing over the Internet, and some, such as the Transfer Control Protocol, guarantee packet delivery via a connection.

Public key A key owned by a user or computer that is accessible to other parties. It has a corresponding private key that may be used to decrypt data encrypted by the public key. It can also be used to encrypt data that can be decrypted only by the private key.

Public key cryptography An asymmetric key technology that uses private and public keys to exchange information.

Public Key Infrastructure (PKI) Methods and strategies for distributing public and private keys for secure communication, authentication, and integrity of data.

Quality of Service (QoS) The attempts to guarantee bandwidth and delivery of IP packets using protocols implemented by Windows 2000.

Query The criteria for a search using Index Services.

Queue A buffer or list of items waiting to be processed.

Quota The amount of disk space a user may consume.

RAID-5 A fault-tolerant strategy implemented by Windows 2000 using three or more dynamic volumes to protect data. Parity information is stored along with protected data across several disks. When one disk fails, the data may be reconstructed from what's left of it and the parity information.

Random-Access Memory (RAM) The volatile memory used by the system's microprocessor; it is lost when the computer loses power or is turned off. It provides the fastest memory accesses (Reads/Writes) available to the system.

Read-Only Memory (ROM) The nonvolatile memory, which is not lost when the system's power is turned off and is not modified frequently or quickly. Most ROM is not modifiable by the system.

Recovery agent A user account that is provided a recovery key for decrypting files using the Encrypted File System (EFS). Usually this is the Administrator account.

Recovery Console The system console that allows basic disk access, format ability, and some repair abilities. It is started from the Windows 2000 recovery disks or directly from the command prompt using the **Winnt32.exe /cmdcons** command.

Recycle Bin A temporary storage for deleted files and folders. Once it has been emptied, data is lost and disk space is freed.

Redundant array of independent disks (RAID) A storage system that categorizes six levels of disk fault tolerance (0–5). Windows 2000 implements striping (0), mirroring (1), and Raid-5 (5). See RAID-5.

Registered file type A file type recognized by the operating system.

Registry The database that contains application and operating system configuration information; it can be viewed and modified using the **regedit.exe** command.

Registry boot The Windows 2000 DNS server has a couple of boot options: registry settings and boots with settings contained in the text file.

Relative distinguished name (RDN) A subset of an object's full distinguished name, usually the CN, or common name, portion.

Relative ID An identification number that relates to a specific domain controller. A domain controller requests relative IDs from the relative ID master. A combination of the domain ID and retrieved relative IDs forms a security ID, which is then assigned to identify users, security groups, and computers in the domain.

Relative ID Master One domain controller, the master, is assigned the responsibility to generate relative IDs for all domain controllers in the domain. See Relative ID.

Relative name The host name portion of the Fully Qualified Domain Name used in DNS naming. For example, in *ahost@domainname.com* the relative name is *ahost*.

Remote access Ability of users outside the intranet to dial in for access or use a network interface attached to the Internet.

Remote Access Server (RAS) A system configured to accept remote access.

Remote administration Administration of system settings without local logon.

Remote Authentication Dial-In User Service (RADIUS) A protocol used by many ISPs to authenticate, authorize, and provide accounting for users who access their corporate intranets using tunneling protocols.

Remote computer A computer that is not available for a local logon.

Remote procedure call (RPC) A message-passing facility that allows a distributed application to call services from other computers in the system.

Replication The process of copying data to provide redundancy and object availability. A multimaster replication screen is used so that all domain controllers have the same information and read/write capability.

Replication topology The configuration of replication, by which information is shared between pairs of domain controllers. The KCC automatically generates the topology of a site. An administrator establishes replication between sites.

Root The highest level of the structure. For example, the first domain created is the root domain.

Router A network server designed to support connectivity and interoperability. It analyzes network addresses in a packet and then passes the packet along. Routers make packet-forwarding decisions.

RR (resource record) Records that associate addresses to other data. They are defined by RFC 1035 and used by DNS.

RSA The default for Microsoft Windows, RSA is a public and private key algorithm utilization.

SACL (system access control list) A partial list of an object's security descriptor. It defines which events are to be audited per user or group.

Safe mode As part of the option menu system accessed by pressing F8 during the initial boot phase of a system, safe mode loads Windows 2000 with minimal services. It provides an environment in which a system that will not normally boot can be corrected and repaired. Safe mode can be launched in its default manner, from the command prompt or with networking services.

SAM (Security Account Manager) A protected subsystem of Windows 2000 and Windows NT that maintains the Security Account Manager database. The Active Directory supplants SAM in domain environments.

Schema A framework of definitions that establishes the type of objects available to the Active Directory. The definitions are divided into object classes and attributes. Attributes are divided into two types: those that must exist and those that may exist. For example, the schema defines a user object class as having the user's name as a required attribute and the user's physical location or job description as an optional attribute. Attributes help distinguish an object from other objects. They are defined to include the Object Name, Object Identifier (OID), Syntax, and optional information.

Schema Master A domain controller that functions as an operations master to manage schema changes and replicate them to other domain controllers.

Scope The range of IP address available for assignment by DHCP.

Script A program that executes a series of instructions. The Windows Scripts Hosting facility permits the launching of a variety of scripts. Batch programs (with .bat or .cmd extensions) are scripts.

Secure Hash Algorithm (SHA-1) A message digest hash that creates a 160-bit hash value.

Secure Multipurpose Internet Mail Extensions (S/MIME) A secure extension to the industry-standard mail protocol.

Secure Sockets Layer (SSL) A protocol for securing network communication using public and private keys.

Security descriptor A set of data attached to an object. It specifies the permissions granted to users and groups and defines the security events to be audited.

Security group Anything that can be listed in the DACL that provides or defines permissions.

Security ID (SID) The unique identifying number of a user or other network object.

Service (SRV) resource record A resource record employed in a zone to register and locate TCP/IP services.

Shared folder Folder that permits other defined users to access files on a remote system.

Simple Mail Transfer Protocol (SMTP) A protocol used on the Internet to transfer mail. It can relay mail across transport service environments.

Simple Network Management Protocol (SNMP) A TCP/IP–based network management protocol that transports information and commands between management programs. The SNMP agent sends status data. SNMP defines the form and meaning of the messages exchanged.

Site In Active Directory, the basic units of the physical network structure. A site comprises one or more IP subnets that are tied together by high-speed, reliable connections. It is the administrator's responsibility to design sites that ensure the greatest network performance.

Smart card A credit-card-size device that contains public/private key information and other data.

Snap-in An application that is added to the Microsoft Management Console and conforms to its standard API.

Socket A bidirectional pipe for incoming and outgoing data between networked computers.

Spanned volume The range of volumes in which data is stored. If one of the disks in the volume fails, all the data is lost.

Special access permissions Customized permissions available under NTFS.

Static routes Permanent routing network tables.

Stripe set A set of disks that permits the storage of identical partitions on different disks.

Stripe set with parity Extension of the basic disk stripe sets to allow for fault tolerance.

Subkey In the Windows 2000 Registry structure, the subkey is simply a child key within a key.

Subnet mask A 32-bit value that distinguishes the TCP/IP network ID portion of the IP address from the host ID portion. TCP/IP hosts use the subnet mask to determine whether a destination host is located on a local or remote network.

System partition The section of the hard drive that contains the configuration files necessary to boot Windows 2000.

System State The portion of the backup that archives the system configuration used for emergency recovery.

SYSVOL A shared directory that stores the server's copy of the public files, which are replicated among all domain controllers.

TAPI (Telephony API) An applications programming interface that allows data/fax/voice calls by programs including HyperTerminal, Dial-up Networking, Phone Dialer, and other communications.

TCP/IP (Transmission Control Protocol/Internet Protocol) One of the most common networking protocols on the Internet. It includes a suite of applications and standards for intercomputer communication and conventions for connecting networks and routing traffic.

Telnet A terminal emulation protocol widely used on the Internet.

Terminal Services An application that supports traditional multiuser environments for Windows 2000. An application run on a server can be displayed and interfaced from a client computer. Microsoft supplies Terminal Services for its Windows products. Terminal Services for other environments like UNIX or Macintosh are available from third-party vendors.

TFTP (Trivial File Transfer Protocol) A nonsecure TCP/IP file transfer protocol. Its use is generally discouraged.

TGS (Ticket-Granting Service) Part of the public key infrastructure, a service that authorizes the granting of certificates.

TGT (Ticket to Get Tickets) The ticket issued to obtain a security certificate.

Thread A type of object within a process that executes the program instructions. Multiple threads permit the running of concurrent operations within a process.

Topology The structure that defines the relationships among domains, sites, and network devices.

Transitive trust A two-way trust relationship established between domain trees and forests. Assuming a user has permission, a transitive trust relationship permits access to objects anywhere in the tree or forest.

Trojan horse A program that appears to perform one function but executes other functions, generally to the detriment of the user or computer system.

Trust relationship Relationship between domains that allows exchange of authentication and permissions. A trust relationship allows users and global groups access to another user account's database. With trust relationships, a user who has only one user account in one domain can potentially access the entire network. All domains in a tree or forest automatically establish two-way trust relationships. In addition, explicit one-way trusts can be established between two single domains.

UNC (Universal Naming Convention) A convention for naming files and other resources that begins with two backslashes (\).

URL (Uniform Resource Locator) An address that uniquely identifies a location on the Internet. A URL for a World Wide Web site is preceded with http:// and can contain more detail, such as the name of a page of hypertext, usually identified by a suffix of .html or .htm.

User account The collection of a user's properties, including a unique name and password, that allows her access to a system.

User mode The portion of the operation system that works to facilitate use and application integrity and interaction.

User profile The file that defines the configuration data for a user, including desktop settings, persistent network connections, and application settings.

User rights Designation of the activities a user is permitted to perform. Many user rights are established through membership in security and distribution groups.

User rights policy Security settings that underscore user rights.

Virtual DOS machine (VDM) The VDM is invoked when MS-DOS commands or utilities are invoked.

Virtual memory Memory used on a temporary basis to execute programs and processes.

Virtual private network (VPN) An extended private network that involves authentication and encryption of data across public networks.

Volume A disk or partition on a disk that operates as if it were a separate physical disk.

WAN (wide area network) A communications network that is spread out geographically.

Windows Internet Name Service (WINS) A Microsoft service that maps computer names to IP addresses. It is used by earlier versions of Windows and is supplanted by Windows 2000/.NET Server use of DNS and DHCP.

Workgroup A collection of Windows 2000 and other computers that are interconnected but do not belong to a domain.

X.500 A set of standards that define a distributed directory service. The standards are developed and supported by the International Standards Organization (ISO).

Zone A subtree of the DNS database. It is administered as a single DNS server. This administrative unit can consist of one domain or more than one child domain.

Index

YOU DO EVERYTHING YOU CAN
TO SATISFY YOUR CLIENTS.

Also from Addison-Wesley

0-321-11357-8

0-201-61621-1

0-672-32125-4

0-201-61576-2

0-201-70046-8

0-201-74203-9

0-201-75283-2

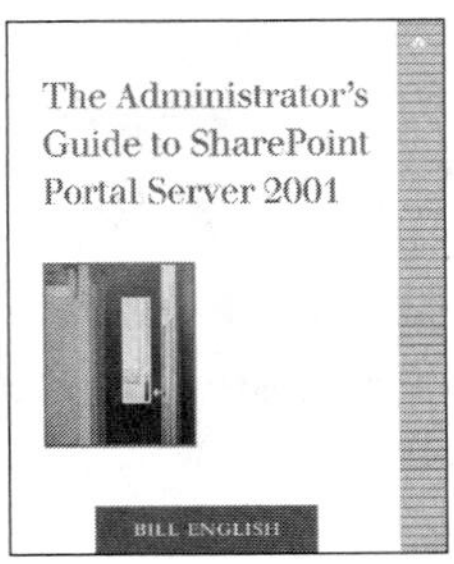

0-201-77574-3

0-201-61613-0

0-7357-1192-5